International Economic Law

VOLUME VI

PUBLIC CONTROLS ON INTERNATIONAL TRADE

SECOND EDITION

ANDREAS F. LOWENFELD

Charles L. Denison Professor of Law
New York University School of Law

1983

MATTHEW
BENDER

235 E. 45TH STREET, NEW YORK, N.Y. 10017
450 SANSOME STREET, SAN FRANCISCO, CALIF. 94111

To My Students

ACKNOWLEDGMENTS

This book, like the others in this series, is essentially that of an outsider. Though I did have the opportunity in the early 1960's to learn some of the material "from the inside" as a member of the economics staff of the Office of Legal Adviser in the State Department, I was eyewitness or participant in only a small portion of the events here described. I believe I did carry away from my government service some feeling for the interlacing tensions that form the central theme of this book—among government, business, and labor; among economic doctrine, political reality, and legal commitment; among unilateral, bilateral, and multiliteral decision-making. If I have succeeded in communicating some of this feeling to the reader, it is in large part due to my colleagues in the State Department a decade and a half ago, and I thank them all.

For the particular contents of this book, I have been fortunate in receiving help from a large number of persons, who took the time to talk, to write, to read portions of the manuscript, and to supply information that one could not find in the library. I express my gratitude to Charles Bloom, Charles Butler, James Collins, William Diebold, Jr., Peter Ehrenhaft, Harry First, Eleanor M. Fox, Thomas R. Graham, Jacques Guevremont, Norman M. Hinerfeld, Thomas Hoya, Richard E. Hull, Julius L. Katz, Tomokatsu Kobayashi, Dominic King, Ella Krugoff, Cynthia Crawford Lichtenstein, Harold P. Luks, Robert H. Mundheim, John B. Rehm, D.W. Romanko, Leonard Santos, Barbara Sloan, Helena Stalson, Philip H. Trezise, William N. Walker, Allan Wm. Wolff, and Matsuo Watanabe.

Diana Vincent-Daviss of the New York University Law Library maintained her high level of enthusiasm and resourcefulness in meeting my rather unusual and sometimes unreasonable requests for source materials.

As in the preceding volumes in this series, several generations of students at New York University Law School contributed to this book by their questions, interests, perceptions, and confusions. I want to extend particular thanks to my student research assistants, Jake Arbes, Roger Meltzer, Robert Romano, and especially Terry V. Thiele for the first edition, and Mary Mycio and Richard D. Sider for the second.

Above all, my thanks go to my secretary, Mrs. Aphrodite Xidas, a true professional.

Whoever has attempted to write a book of this kind will understand my debt not only to research assistants, secretaries and persons who supplied information, though without them this book would not have been possible. I want to acknowledge my debt to the small but admirable group of lawyers and economists who have written about the subjects here covered—Kenneth W. Dam, William Diebold, Jr., Isaiah Frank, Robert E. Hudec, and John H. Jackson. Each of them is quoted several times; their learning, I hope, is reflected throughout this book.

PREFACE TO THE FIRST EDITION

This is the sixth, and for the time being, the last volume in the present series of books on International Economic Law. Like the others, it attempts to combine history, economics, politics, and law in the form of narrative and questions, with generous reference to the Documents Supplement. Even more than in the preceding volumes, I had to make a series of decisions about how current the material should be, and when I should go to press. I had left the subject of public controls on international trade to the last, because I expected that in the late 1970's substantial changes, and a major international negotiation would take place. Perhaps I should have expected that all target dates and deadlines would be pushed forward. So, in fact, were the publication dates, until at the end I was like a writer for a weekly news magazine, wondering whether his Friday essay will be obsolete by the time his journal hits the newstands on Monday. The bulk of the book was written in 1978, based in part on earlier collections of teaching materials. But as the GATT, United States law and the steel industry which forms the centerpiece of the story here told kept undergoing new adventures, a variety of changes seemed in order, until the last sections were deposited with the printer on the Monday after "recommendations" for the implementing legislation for the not quite complete Multilateral Trade Negotiations (1973–79) were agreed to by the relevant committees of the United States Congress. I hope the volume makes up in immediacy and even suspense what it may lack in reflection. I am certain the issues raised will not go away, even if the data base changes before the ink is dry.

This book is in a sense a complement to Volume I of this series, which explored the private techniques of international trade, payments, and dispute settlement, and to Volume III, which explored trade controls for political ends—boycotts, embargoes, sanctions, and trade discrimination. Here we deal with politics too, but in a more subtle way. The main emphasis is on economic principles, and their translation, or non-translation, into legal rules and exceptions. The theme, more than any other, is ambivalence—not (except incidentally) hypocrisy, not (except now and then) simple avarice—but commitments to efficiency, to competition, to the market that can never be quite complete because of other commitments and other values, personal and national, economic and social.

Unlike the international monetary field, of which lawyers in America have only recently become aware, foreign trade has always been a preserve of lawyers in the United States, going back to the days of Hamilton and Calhoun. It has also been, since the beginnings of the Republic, a preserve of lobbyists of all kinds. Since lobbying is in substantial part the work of lawyers—indeed may soon be recognized as a neglected branch of the art of advocacy so fashionable in law schools today—I have thought it appropriate to give some account of the processes of law making, whether by Congress, by courts, or by departments and agencies. Throughout the events described here, it is apparent that this art is not so much one of oratory or flattery as it is of preparation, and of understanding of the possibilities of technical and often arcane rules of law. Plenty of possibilities, plenty of surprising ingenuities, emerge from these materials.

In a sense this is a casebook, though only one appellate decision is reproduced in extenso, and not many judicial decisions are discussed at all. The case—spread out in sections 4 through 6—is a single industry, steel, which in a little over a decade experienced virtually all of the problems of international trade, and attempted to utilize nearly all the remedies available under United States (and somewhat later under European) law, plus a few no one had thought of before. If the steel industry is not in all respects typical of industries in trouble—one could perhaps have focused on textiles, or shoes, or consumer electronics—it nevertheless furnishes a vehicle for illustrating much of the law, domestic and international, of world trade, and all of the dilemmas. I would hope the reader makes use of this version of the case method in two ways: (1) To make the abstract and complex rules understandable by applying them to particular sets of facts; and (2) to put a fairly detailed look at a single industry in the perspective of a world-wide trading system. The aim is to develop the ability to see both the trees and the forest, to dedicate professional skills both to technical matters and to issues of high policy.

Like the preceding volumes in this series, this book is intended in the first instance as a classroom teaching tool for law students. The format remains the same, with sections of roughly 20 pages of narrative, followed by a series of notes and questions around which a class may be built. As in all of these books, there are frequent references to the documents; an ability to handle these documents is an essential goal of the method here employed.

In my own 42-hour course, I have found that with some picking and choosing, I can cover four, but not five volumes. To cover most of the material in this book will take about 12 hours. An instructor may comfortably skip (or assign as background reading) the sections on Japan (§§ 3.3-4), or on the Kennedy Round (§ 3.7), and perhaps even exercise some selectivity in the steel story. While a few years ago I might have thought dumping and subsidies were overly specialized for an introduction to the law of international trade, recent history has shown that these subjects belong to the main events. For an instructor who wishes to emphasize public regulation of the international economy, Volume IV on the International Monetary System and the present volume make a convenient pair, with very little overlap. An instructor more interested in trade could combine Volume I (private trade) and this one, or use those two plus volume III (political trade controls). This volume and Volume II, contrasting trade and investment, also make a suitable combination. The volumes were completed and published essentially with a view toward external events; there is no necessary connection between the sequence of their publication and sequence in the classroom.

Though, as noted, the book is designed primarily as a teaching tool, it need not teach only students or only in the classroom or indeed only lawyers. To experts in the steel industry, it may be interesting how their adventures appear to an observer who had a motive to look carefully but had no client or program to defend. To the growing number of officials in Washington concerned with trade matters, the book may provide some insights that no government desk or agency memorandum can provide. For the lawyers practising in the field, this book will disappoint you if you are looking for a hornbook or treatise, and the book's usefulness for instant research will depend on who is asking what question. I would hope that the stress on history, and on the interplay between technical and political issues attempted throughout the volume would contribute from time to time to argument, whether before administrative agencies, a Congressional committee, or a court. To readers in Europe, Canada, or Japan, I would hope you would come away with a somewhat better understanding of the perplexing laws and institutions of the United States, as well as of the difficulty that an American observer has in trying to understand your laws and institutions.

To all readers, I trust that the series of questions will serve not as irritant but as stimulant, and as a continuing reminder that there are no final answers.

A.F.L.
May 1979

PREFACE TO THE SECOND EDITION

Four years have elapsed since the completion of the first edition of this book—a period characterized by prolonged recession in both developed and developing countries, and by continuing controversy among the major trading nations about the conditions of international trade. When the Contracting Parties of the GATT met for the first time in nearly a decade at ministerial level in November 1982, they could agree on very little, except that "the multilateral trading system . . . is seriously endangered."* But they did agree that the GATT remains the legal foundation of that system, and that responses of governments to the current challenges have tended to undermine the system. To what extent the legal rules are inadequate, and to what extent adequate rules are weakened by faulty procedures or shaky commitments, is one of the themes of this book, and particularly of the material added in this second edition.

The first edition traced the problems of the steel industry in the United States and Europe, and the various devices, some traditional, some novel, to affect the trade in steel products. That story is continued in this volume (§§ 8.5–8.6), through two more rounds of confrontation, primarily between the United States and Europe, and in the European Community itself. Another plot, only dimly visible on the horizon in 1978 (at least seen from America), came to play a central role in the years 1979–82—the fate of the American automobile industry in the face of massive imports, primarily from Japan. That story (§§ 8.1–8.4) is interesting not only because of its importance to the economies of the countries concerned, but because at one level it presents a sharp contrast with steel, in that there were no significant assertions of "unfair trade," while at another level it shows a striking similarity—plant closings, lay-offs, and appeals to government for help.

These two stories—automobiles and steel—make up the bulk of the new material in this volume. In addition, the new edition takes up legislative developments in the United States, notably the Trade Agreements Act of 1979, but also the reorganization of the agencies in Washington dealing with trade (§ 7.61) and of the relevant courts and their jurisdiction over trade matters (§ 7.62). I had hoped, when lengthening the book by inclusion of these new materials, to be able to make corresponding cuts in material included in the earlier edition; alas, all of the material and all of the issues remain pertinent.

---

* See the Ministerial Declaration issued at the close of the meeting in Geneva, November 29, 1982, ¶ 1, Documents Supplement p. DS-647.

Possibly an instructor pressed for time could assign § 4.4 as background reading, covering the subjects of dumping and subsidies only in connection with the Tokyo Round (§§ 7.22, 7.41(a), and 7.52) and with the crises of the 1980's (§§ 8.5–8.6). In that way, the bulk of this volume could be covered in 15–16 hours, rather than the 17–18 hours that coverage of all the material would require.

There is no doubt that the prediction in the preface to the first edition that dumping and subsidies would become bread-and-butter subjects for international trade lawyers has been borne out—perhaps too much so. The hope in this second edition—as in all the volumes in this series—remains that attention can be focused both on the technicalities and on the larger picture. It is ever more evident that the professional in this field needs to understand both the forest (not to say jungle) and the trees.

A.F.L.
July 1983

SUMMARY TABLE OF CONTENTS

Prefaces vii

§ 1 Why People Trade 1

§ 2 An Introduction to the GATT 11

§ 3 The International Trading System: The Principal Actors .. 43

§ 4 Steel 143

§ 5 Voluntary Restraint Agreements 1968–74 195

§ 6 Steel in Crisis: The United States and Europe 253

§ 7 The Multilateral Trade Negotiations 1973–79 303

§ 8 More Doubts about International Trade: Problems Old and New 375

Documents Supplement .... DS- 1

   I.   International Agreements .... DS- 5

   II.   Documents of the European Community DS-105

   III. Japanese Statutory Materials.................... DS-229

   IV. United States Statutory Materials DS-241

   V.   Miscellaneous Documents DS-561

   VI. Selected Documents of the Multilateral Trade Negotiatons DS-660

Tables DS-745

Table of Cases TC-1

Index I-1

TABLE OF CONTENTS

§ 1 WHY PEOPLE TRADE 1
  1.1 Introduction 1
  1.2 Some Motives for International Trade 2
      1.21 Absolute Scarcity 2
      1.22 Specialization and Efficiency 3
      1.23 A First Look at Comparative Advantage 3
  1.3 Preliminary Notes and Questions about Comparative Advantage 5

§ 2 AN INTRODUCTION TO THE GATT 11
  2.1 A Small Dose of History 11
  2.2 The Origins of the GATT—Birth by Caesarean Section 15
  2.3 The GATT—A First Look at the Substantive Standards 21
      2.31 The Growth of the GATT 21
      2.32 The Major Principles 23
      2.33 The Qualifications 24
  2.4 Notes and Questions on the GATT 28

§ 3 THE INTERNATIONAL TRADING SYSTEM: THE PRINCIPAL ACTORS 43
  3.1 The European Economic Community 43
      3.11 Customs Unions and the GATT 43
      3.12 European Integration, Phase I: The Coal and Steel Community 47
      3.13 European Integration, Phase II: The Common Market 52
      3.14 The European Economic Commuity and the GATT 56
      3.15 Expansion of the Community 60
  3.2 Notes and Questions 62
  3.3 Japan, the Improbable Giant 77
      3.31 Japan's Economic Growth 78
      3.32 The Government's Role in Japan's Economic Growth 82
      3.33 Japan and the International Rules 84
  3.4 Notes and Questions 91
  3.5 The United States as a Trading Nation.......... 99
      3.51 Trade Regulation up to 1934 99
      3.52 The Reciprocal Trade Agreements Program 107

        3.53 The Trade Expansion Act of 1962 112

  3.6   Notes and Questions 120

  3.7   The Three Actors Come Together: The Kennedy Round 131

        3.71 The Idea of Linear Reductions 132

        3.72 Sectoral Negotiations 135

        3.73 Results of the Kennedy Round 140

§ 4 STEEL 143

  4.1   The Basic Metal 143

  4.2   The American Steel Industry 145

  4.3   Steel Imports to the United States: The First Crisis . . . 148

  4.4   The Search for a Response: Notes and Questions 154

        4.41 Dumping and Anti-Dumping 155

        4.45 Subsidies and Countervailing Duties 174

        4.48 Other Remedies 192

§ 5 VOLUNTARY RESTRAINT AGREEMENTS 1968–74 195

  5.1   The First Round 195

        5.11 Background of the Agreements 195

        5.12 The First Agreements 202

  5.2   Notes and Questions 206

  5.3   The Second Round 209

        5.31 The VRA's in Operation 209

        5.32 Renewal 212

  5.4   The Legal Challenge 214

        5.41 "Litigation in the Public Interest" 214

        5.42 *Consumers Union of U.S. Inc. v. Kissinger*. 216

  5.5   Notes and Questions 236

        5.56 Specialty Steel and the Escape Clause 243

        5.57 "Unfair Trade Practices" and the European-
             Japanese Agreements 247

§ 6 STEEL IN CRISIS: THE UNITED STATES AND EUROPE 253

  6.1   Challenge in America 253

        6.11 Losses and Layoffs 253

        6.12 The Trigger Price Mechanism 259

  6.2   Notes and Questions on the Trigger Price Mech-
       anism 263

  6.3   Challenge in Europe 275

        6.31 The Beginnings of Dirigisme 276

		6.32 The Simonet-Davignon Plan: Phase I	279
		6.33 The Davignon Plan: Phase II	287
	6.4	Notes and Questions on the Davignon Plan	292

§ 7   THE MULTILATERAL TRADE NEGOTIATIONS (1973–79) 303

	7.1	Toward New Trade Negotiations	303
		7.11 A Changing Mood	303
		7.12 The Agenda	304
	7.2	The Issues	307
		7.21 "Safeguards"	307
		7.22 Subsidies and Countervailing Duties	309
		7.23 Dispute Settlement and Consultations	311
		7.24 Other Matters	313
		7.25 Tariffs	316
	7.3	Notes and Questions	317
	7.4	The MTN: The Closing Stages	331
		7.41 The Package	332
		7.42 Reading the Trade Act Again	337
		7.43 The Unraveling Process	345
		7.44 The Outcome	351
	7.5	Notes and Questions on the Outcome of the MTN	354
	7.6	Implementing the Tokyo Round	364
		7.61 Reorganization in Washington	364
		7.62 Judicial Review Expanded	366
		7.63 Changes in the Trade Law	369

§ 8   MORE DOUBTS ABOUT INTERNATIONAL TRADE: PROBLEMS NEW AND OLD 375

	8.1	The Automobile Invasion	375
		8.11 The Automobile in the American Economy	375
		8.12 Foreign Cars on American Roads 1955–1980	377
		8.13 Auto Imports and the Escape Clause	383
	8.2	Notes and Questions	389
	8.3	The Automobile Story Continued	399
	8.4	Further Notes and Questions about Automobiles	402
	8.5	Back to Steel: Europe and America	420
		8.51 The European Crisis Prolonged	420
		8.52 Ups and Downs of the U.S. Trigger Price Mechanism	423
		8.53 Confrontation: the United States and the European Community (1981–82)	427
	8.6	Notes and Questions	436
	8.7	Final Notes and Questions: Why *Do* People Trade	449

§ 1—Why People Trade

§ 1.1—Introduction

People have been trading with one another since at least the bronze age, and whether the traders were individuals, firms, cities, city-states, or nations, the movement of goods seems to have been a common phenomenon in nearly all of recorded history. By and large trading societies prosper more than those that aim at self-sufficiency, but neither complete autarchy nor complete specialization is possible except at primitive levels, and different countries and generations have had varying goals as to the mix of independence or interdependence that they aim for.

Some regard international trade as a necessary evil, some as an ideal in itself; most traders and most consumers do not ask the question in terms more sophisticated than "Can I make a profit?" or "Is the imported item cheaper?" or "Can we sell more—possibly 'can we achieve greater economies of scale?'—if we establish markets abroad?"[a]

Governments—well before they adopted the kind of internally directed devices such as income taxes, fiscal policies, wage and price controls, regulation of competition, and so on—regulated international trade, both to raise revenue and to keep control of their national wealth. In Venice in the Middle Ages, for instance, the city itself owned the ships (and often the cargoes that were shipped around the world), and a given portion of the profits was dedicated to the construction of cathedrals, palaces and other civic assets.[b] Mazarin and Colbert, in the time

---

[a] There are of course certain costs—such as transport and insurance—and certain risks—such as currency changes, embargoes, credit failures, and the like, that must be taken into account by individual enterprises in answering these questions. Some of these are addressed in other volumes in this series, especially Vol. I, A. Lowenfeld, *International Private Trade*, esp. §§ 1.2–1.3 (1975). Monetary problems are dealt with in Vol. IV, A. Lowenfeld, *The International Monetary System*, esp. § 9 (1977); political controls such as embargoes and boycotts, in Vol. III, A. Lowenfeld, *Trade Controls for Political Ends* (1977), and tax problems in Vol. V, D. Tillinghast, *Tax Aspects of International Transactions* (1978).

[b] Dante, in the XXI Canto of the Inferno, likened hell to the Venetian shipbuilding operations:

As the Venetians in their arsenal boil
The lumps of pitch in winter, stiff as glue,
To caulk the ships whose timbers warp and spoil,
Since sail they cannot then. . .

1

of Louis XIV, sought by trade controls to husband the economic strength of the country they served. Throughout the eighteenth century, governmental regulation of international trade was one of the major devices of both foreign and economic policy—for instance the Molasses and Sugar Acts directed to the American Colonies, and the Corn Laws for the British Isles. With the rise of economics as a serious subject of study in the eighteenth and nineteenth centuries, its leading innovators—David Hume, Adam Smith, John Stuart Mill, and David Ricardo—focused in large measure on international trade in developing their "laws" . . . of supply and demand, of equilibrium prices, of the flow of gold,[c] of marginal factor costs, and so on. While the economists were never able to build a perfect model or to assemble empirical proof, their theories had important impact, especially in England, the premier trading country of the nineteenth century.

§ 1.2—Some Motives for International Trade

In this initial look at why people and countries trade we may distinguish three phenomena—absolute scarcity, relative efficiency, and comparative advantage.

1.21—ABSOLUTE SCARCITY

This motive for trade is by far the easiest to understand. If one lives in a temperate zone and likes to eat bananas or drink coffee, he has to import them or buy them from someone who imports them. Raw materials are not evenly distributed around the globe, and neither are consumers. For some products, there is no alternative to trade other than doing without. Oil, coffee, tin, and minerals in general are only found in certain places, and if one wants them, he has to import them.[a] For other products, absolute scarcity shades into rational resource allocation: many tropical products, for instance, can be produced in temperate zones under hothouse conditions, and temperate products can be grown in arid lands with sufficient irrigation. But it would not make sense to grow cotton in Norway, even if it were technically possible. In common

---

[c] Compare Volume IV of this series, § 1.31.

[a] Of course, trade may be combined with investment, so that the importer buys from itself; still, from a geographic or political point of view, such trade is import (or export) trade just as much as is trade among strangers.

have probably gone to Patria as the cheaper (more efficient) supplier of both products.

§ 1.3—Preliminary Notes and Questions about Comparative Advantage

The doctrine of comparative advantage, announced first in 1817 by David Ricardo in looking at cloth from England and wine from Portugal,[a] has an intriguing appeal—black magic explained by each participant doing his own thing. Indeed it was the theory of comparative advantage, developed further by John Stuart Mill, that eventually prevailed in the decades-long debate in nineteenth century England. In 1846, England—the first mature industrial society—repealed the famous Corn Laws, which in various forms and at varying rates had excluded imports of grain to protect English landholders,[b] and from that time until the first World War, England was essentially a free trade country.

But comparative advantage—for all its elegance—is not free from difficulties. Debates about countries' commercial policies antedated enunciation of the theory of comparative advantage, and were not stilled by its articulation.[c]

In nearly every country, the theory (or law) of comparative advantage has been the focus of those favoring free or freer trade. Opponents of free trade have tried to find flaws in the theory, or to show that their industry or country was a special case, or to argue that there were values

---

[a] D. Ricardo, *Principles of Political Economy and Taxation* Ch. VII (1817).

[b] 9 & 10 Vict. c. 22 (1846). It is fair to add that while Robert Peel, the British Prime Minister and a Conservative, was apparently persuaded by the writings of Ricardo, Smith, Mill, and their followers even to the point of betraying the landholding classes that had elected him, the legislative battle was won only in the context of a potato blight in Ireland; as it became clear that it would be impossible to feed Ireland from England, it was morally impossible to allow the Irish to starve with foreign corn (wheat) waiting to enter. See, e.g., G. M. Trevelyan, *British History in the Nineteenth Century and After,* 262–71 (Pelican 1965).

[c] See, e.g., Alexander Hamilton's famous *Report on Manufactures* of 1791 and the sharp debates thereon that preceded the first United States tariff, adopted in the Revenue Act of 1792, 1 Stat. 259. In a real sense, this first debate between the followers of Hamilton and Jefferson, over protectionism vs. free trade, has never been stilled, though the party labels and associated attitudes concerning the constitution, the conduct of foreign relations, etc. have varied widely.

superior to the maximization of production at lowest cost that seemed to result from trade flows following the doctrine of comparative advantage. Many of these arguments will appear explicitly or implicitly throughout this volume. At this point, note some preliminary hints of issues not addressed in our simple model of lamps and tables:

1.31—When we say that both Patria and Xandia are better off as a result of specialization and trade, that may not be much comfort to the table makers in Patria or the lamp makers in Xandia who have lost their businesses and jobs. The example assumed that the factor inputs were mobile, so that the table-maker in Patria was able to devote himself to making lamps, and the lamp-maker in Xandia was able to devote himself to making tables.[d] The mobility of factor inputs—capital, labor, land, possibly know-how and various other intangible factors—may well be uneven, and the dislocations may be of a longer term character than anticipated.

1.32—The example assumed constant costs and prices of lamps and tables. But as there is greater demand for Patria's lamps and Xandia's tables, the costs may change and not necessarily in parallel; similarly, the prices may change and the increase of lamp prices in Patria may not be at the same rate as the increase of table prices in Xandia. The changes in prices in turn may affect—and not necessarily symmetrically—the demand for lamps and tables in both countries.

1.33—The model, like Ricardo's original example and like the introductory section on trade of every economics text, focused on only two products, two factors and two countries. In fact, of course, there are a myriad of products, countless factors of production, and over a hundred countries. But while quantifying the effect of any given movement or restraint on movement of goods is very difficult, the principle of comparative advantage should work just as well: even if, for instance, there are large discrepancies in wage rates—say between the United States and the countries of South East Asia—and no reciprocities or equalities of demand, the sum of a thousand examples such as the one used here should result in higher total production and lower overall cost.

---

[d] Of course this assumption need not be taken literally. The lamp business in Patria may not have been working up to capacity, for instance, or the now unemployed resources previously devoted to tables may make a third product. At bottom, however, substantial (if not 100 per cent) mobility of factor inputs is essential to the theory.

1.34—The assumption is made in the example that costs for a given product (including profits) are identical within a given country (Patria or Xandia), or at least move in a constant proportion. This assumption is not likely to be true even in perfectly competitive markets, and quite improbable in markets subject to various kinds of manipulation, differences in taste, traditional selling patterns, and so on.

1.35—Finally, of course, transportation costs are not negligible, and may also vary—not only according to distances involved, but according to the amount of the product traded and to its physical characteristics. There is no reason to suppose, for instance, that lamps and tables move at the same freight rate.

1.36—None of these points is fatal to the theory of comparative advantage. They just mean (a) that the equation as set forth in the text is oversimplified, and that the graphs and diagrams favored by economists (and deliberately omitted here) may contain more curves and fewer straight lines than the example suggests; (b) that the quantitative gains from trade as a function of the volume may well be substantially lower than the example suggests; and (c) that precise forecasting becomes very difficult if not impossible. If, to peek ahead, the government of Patria makes it possible for buyers in Patria to import tables from Xandia, it may well not know what it is getting in return when it accepts Xandia's offer to permit greater purchases of lamps from Patria.

1.37—Thus far in looking at comparative advantage we have omitted the role of governments. Before examining the various devices and rules of law by which governments deal with the subject of international trade, consider how governments should view the doctrine of comparative advantage.

(a) Some governments—notably the Soviet Union under Stalin—have rejected it altogether, preferring self-sufficiency and economic planning, and resorting to imports only to overcome absolute scarcity and shortfalls in the Plan, and to exports only to the extent required to pay for imports.[e] Other governments—notably the United States in the period 1930-34—have regarded exports as desirable and imports as un-

---

[e] For more on the attitude of the USSR and other communist countries to foreign trade, and on changes in the post-Stalin era, see Vol. III of this series, A. Lowenfeld, *Trade Controls for Political Ends*, Ch. II § 1.2 (2d ed. 1983).

desirable—also a form of rejection of comparative advantage.[1] Most governments in recent times have recognized the basic truth of specialization and the gains of trade as shown by the theory of comparative advantage. But they have been ambivalent, fearing the short-term losses or local political pressures even as they contemplated the long-term gains, and fearing in some inarticulate way that greater advantages were accruing to their trading partners than to their own countries.

(b) Considering our example of lamps from Patria and tables from Xandia, would you be most concerned, as adviser to Patria, about your table makers? About your lamp makers? About the balance of goods moving in both directions (which might well not, of course, result in 100 per cent displacement of Patria's tables and Xandia's lamps)? About the danger that if you closed the door to tables, you would lose export possibilities to Xandia?

(c) What would you expect to be the effect on prices in Patria of the trade in lamps and tables described here? Could you conclude that trade is anti-inflationary—other things being equal? Or are other things never equal?

(d) Suppose the wood used by the table makers in Xandia comes from Patria? Would you consider prohibiting export of wood to Xandia in order to give advantage to (protect) Patria's table makers? Remember that they are already more efficient than Xandia's table makers (p. 3 supra): only the *relative* efficiency of Xandia's table makers is what stimulated the trade.

(e) If you were persuaded by the essential soundness of comparative advantage and were attempting to resist pressures for trade restraints in Patria, would you feel more confident if you knew Xandia was resisting similar pressures? Reversing the question, if the government of Xandia had imposed restraints on Patria-Xandia trade—say on exports

---

[1] The most famous exponent of this view—before the theory of comparative advantage was articulated—was Jean Baptiste Colbert, financial adviser to Louis XIV of France in the mid-seventeenth century, whose high tariff policies led to tariff wars with the Netherlands and to retaliation by England that almost stopped all trade between France and England for more than 15 years at the close of the century.

See, e.g., C. W. Cole, *Colbert and a Century of French Mercantilism*, Vol. 1, pp. 428 -50 (1939).

from Patria to Xandia, would you feel you should "get even," and impose your own restraints on top of those of Xandia?

The remainder of this volume, in a real sense, is addressed to probing these questions more deeply.

§ 2—An Introduction to the GATT

§ 2.1—A Small Dose of History[a]

In the popular perception, the sixty years between the conversion to free trade by Great Britain and the beginning of World War I were the golden age of trade, when the lessons of Ricardo and Mill, of specialization and exchange, and of multilateral, open, markets governed the world's commerce. The precise facts—as is common with recollections a generation removed—do not fit the image in close detail.[b] But it is true that the leading industrial nation was also the leading trading nation, that England and France concluded a commercial treaty[c] that contained a most-favored-nation clause,[d] and that most European countries tied into that arrangement at one end or the other and among themselves.[e] Currency moved relatively freely, the volume of trade and general prosperity increased (despite some ups and downs), and not coincidentally—or so it was believed—there were no prolonged wars involving the major powers.[f]

The shock of World War I is hard to comprehend for the generations that grew up only in the period of war, turmoil, depression, and war again—some have called it the Twentieth Century's Thirty Years War. One of the United States' principal planners and draftsmen of what became the GATT, Clair Wilcox, put it as follows:

---

[a] A convenient and concise account of the historical antecedents of the GATT, heavily relied on for this note, is G. Curzon, *Multilateral Commercial Diplomacy,* Ch. I (1965).

[b] The United States and Russia, for instance, pursued sharply protectionist policies throughout the period, and as Note e points out, France and Germany were not consistent.

[c] The Cobden-Chevalier Treaty of Jan. 23, 1860, 50 British & Foreign State Papers 13, 121 Consol. Treaty Series (Parry, ed.) 243.

[d] Article XIX. For more on MFN clauses, see § 2.42 *infra.*

[e] After the Franco-Prussian War of 1870-71, first France, the loser, and then Germany, the winner, turned again toward protectionism, in Germany's case to protect the landholding classes against cheaper agricultural exports from the United States. Still, the average rate of import duty in France and Germany at the beginning of the Twentieth Century was less than 10 per cent. See, G. Curzon, N. a *supra* at 19 and sources there cited.

[f] For the role of Great Britain and sterling as the world's entrepôt, see Volume IV of this series, A. Lowenfeld, *The International Monetary System,* § 3.1 (1977).

The foundations of economic liberalism were shaken by the First World War. The economy of Europe was disorganized; productive facilities were destroyed; channels of trade were broken; heavy debts were incurred. Nationalism and protectionism were stimulated by the revision of boundaries and the creation of new states.[g] Economic and political uncertainty weakened devotion to principles that were once unquestioned. . . .[h]

Point 3 of Woodrow Wilson's Fourteen Points called for "[t]he removal, so far as possible, of all economic barriers and the establishment of an equality of trade conditions among all the nations consenting to the peace and associating themselves for its maintenance," and some efforts were made in the 1920's to return to the pre-war legal bases for commercial relationships. A number of conferences, some under the auspices of the League of Nations and some outside the League framework, sought to establish joint commitments to reduce trade barriers.[i] But while these conferences were partly successful in Western Europe, the United States moved in the opposite direction. The Fordney-McCumber Tariff Act of 1922[j] not only reversed the Wilsonian policies of reduced trade barriers, but gave the President authority to adjust tariffs up or down by up to 50 per cent—an authority that was exercised in the following eight years to raise duties 32 times and to lower them only 5 times.[k]

Then came the 1930's—a decade that began with a depression that spread quickly from the United States to Europe and around the world,

---

[g] Whatever one may think of nationalism and linguistic and ethnic self-determination, note that until 1914 trade in Eastern Europe moved within Russia, or within Austria-Hungary, or crossed one boundary between them. After the war, the same territory embodied Austria and Hungary as separate countries, plus Poland, Czechoslovakia, Yugoslavia, Lithuania, Latvia, Estonia, Finland, and the free city of Danzig—each with a customs frontier, a separate currency, claims for "infant industries" or newly established enterprises, and so on.

[h] C. Wilcox, *A Charter for World Trade* 5 (1949, repr. 1972). This paragraph is also quoted at greater length in R. Hudec, *The GATT Legal System and World Trade Diplomacy* 4–5 (1975).

[i] See Hudec, N. h *supra,* at pp. 6–8 for brief summaries of and citations to the various inter-war conferences that attempted to resurrect the pre-war principles, in a world whose political leaders had neither the strength nor the economic resources to put them into practice.

[j] 42 Stat. 941 (Sept. 21, 1922).

[k] See G. Curzon, N. a *supra* at 23. For more on this act as the forerunner of United States trade legislation, see § 3.51 *infra.*

and ended in the most brutal war the world had known. In the interval, to quote Wilcox again,

> The foundations of economic liberalism, badly shaken by the First World War, were all but demolished. . . . The gold standard disappeared; currencies were thrown into chaos; exchanges were subject to national controls. There was a sharp contraction of the world's trade.[1] The attention of governments turned inward; the issue of unemployment dominated domestic politics. . . . Governments assumed still further authority over economic life, controlling prices and output in the interest of domestic stability. Nations no longer permitted production to adjust itself to the requirements of the world economy; where national and international interests came into conflict, internationalism gave way. The world was unprepared to face adversity; each for himself and the devil take the hindmost became the general rule.[m]

In May 1930, the United States adopted the Smoot-Hawley Tariff Act,[n] which raised duties to the highest levels in American history. More than a thousand American economists urged President Hoover to veto the Tariff Act of 1930, on the ground that it would "plainly invite other nations to compete with us in raising another barrier to trade,"[o] and that prediction quickly came to pass, as country after country retaliated against the United States and against one another.[p] First Canada, then France, Mexico, Italy, Spain, Australia, and New Zealand raised their tariffs. In February 1932, Great Britain abandoned free trade and adopted a general tariff.[q] Thereafter, the British Commonwealth countries established a system of "imperial preferences," including raised duties against non-members. As unemployment remained high in nearly all industrial countries, a variety of bilateral trading arrangements grew up whereby particular countries sought to secure themselves against

---

[1] See, e.g., § 3.52 N. f for U.S. trade figures.

[m] C. Wilcox, N. h *supra*, at p. 7.

[n] 46 Stat. 590 (1930).

[o] The petition was drafted by Paul Douglas, then a professor at the University of Chicago and later for many years a member of the United States Senate from Illinois.

[p] See § 3.52 N. f *infra*.

[q] An Act to provide for the imposition of a general ad valorem duty of customs, 22 Geo. 5 c. 8(Feb. 29, 1932).

being cut off from markets closed to the rest of the world. In some cases these arrangements were reciprocal and voluntary; in the case of Nazi Germany, under the leadership for this purpose of Hjalmar Schacht, a network of restrictive and discriminatory trading arrangements was established, whereby the smaller countries (especially in Eastern and Central Europe) were paid for their products in scrip or inconvertible marks, usable only to make purchases from Germany and at prices set by the German government. Everywhere the policy seemed to be "Beggar-my-neighbor"—sometimes vicious, as in the German case, sometimes merely based on the priority given to increasing employment, which was seen by Lord Keynes and his followers as requiring government intervention and therefore (it seemed) insulation of the domestic economy from world market forces.[r]

The only significant effort to liberalize these conditions was the United States Reciprocal Trade Agreements Program, whereby the Roosevelt Administration, in a major reversal of more than a decade of American policy, sought to make agreements with foreign countries to reduce trade barriers on a reciprocal basis, and then to generalize reductions so negotiated on a most-favored-nation basis.[s] In the period from 1934 to the outbreak of the war, the United States concluded 20 such agreements (half with countries in the Western Hemisphere). But while this program and change of attitude was to have important consequences for the post-war world,[t] it came too late to reverse the trend started by the United States itself in 1930. By the outbreak of World War II in 1939, the prevailing pattern was preferences, bilateralism, restrictionism, and economic recovery only in the context of renewed armament industry.

The war made all but the experts forget the details. In a general way,

---

[r] See, e.g., G. Curzon N. a *supra* at p. 28 and the works of Keynes and Joan Robinson there cited. Keynes wrote in 1933 in an article entitled "National Self-Sufficiency," 22 Yale Review 755, 758 (1933) "Let goods be homespun whenever it is reasonably and conveniently possible," and again,

> We do not wish . . . to be at the mercy of world forces working out, or trying to work out, some uniform equilibrium according to the ideal principles. . . . We want to be our own masters, and to be as free as we can make ourselves from the interference of the outside world.

J. M. Keynes, *The General Theory of Employment, Interest, and Money*, 382–83 (1936).

[s] The details of U.S. trade legislation and of MFN are discussed in §§ 3.5 and 2.42 *infra*.

[t] See § 2.2 *infra*.

however, the perception gained currency that trade restraints had fostered retaliation, had failed to produce recovery, and had contributed to the outbreak of the War.[u] In looking to the future, the planners of post-war international economic policies, especially in the United States, were determined not to repeat the errors of the 1920's and 1930's. Whether this meant return to the "good old days" of comparative advantage was unclear. At the least, it meant a commitment to multilateral, as contrasted to bilateral arrangements, and a commitment to reduction of trade barriers on an MFN basis. Also, in the age of optimistic institution-building, it seemed to mean construction of legal rules and an organization to administer them. All these commitments, as we shall see, were hedged about with exceptions, grandfather clauses, and various degrees of ambivalence. Nevertheless, taken together with the general outlook on post-war planning emanating (mainly) from Washington in the mid 1940's, they provided the background for what became the General Agreement on Tariffs and Trade.

§ 2.2—The Origins of the GATT—Birth by Caesarean Section

Planning for a liberal, comprehensive, and multilateral organization devoted to international trade began in the United States and Great Britain about half-way through World War II. Shortly after the United States and Britain began exchanging drafts on a post-war monetary system,[a] officials of the U.S. State Department and the Economic Section of the British War Cabinet began to exchange working-level drafts for rules and institutions to look after the commercial side of international economic exchange. Just why trade and monetary matters were from the beginning separate is not clear: possibly the explanation lies simply in the fact that at governmental as well as at private levels in both countries the Treasury/banking communities were distinct from the Commerce/business/labor communities. The general outlook on the trade issues, however, was similar to the outlook on monetary matters: international

---

[u] How accurate the third point is is hard to tell; it is true, however, that much of the appeal of the Nazis in the early 1930's coincided with unemployment in Germany, attributed by Hitler to betrayal at Versailles but in good measure attributable to trade restraints traceable to the Fordney-McCumber and Smoot-Hawley tariffs and chain reactions thereto.

[a] See the discussion of the exchanges between Harry Dexter White of the United States and Lord Keynes of Great Britain that led to convening of the Bretton Woods Monetary and Financial Conference in July 1944, in Vol. IV of this series, A. Lowenfeld, *The International Monetary System* § 1.4 (1977).

economic activity was to be encouraged; it was to be conducted primarily by private firms;[b] governmental intervention was to be subject to a code of conduct designed to reduce restrictions; and there was to be an overriding rule of non-discrimination.[c] As on the monetary front, the British tended to be more concerned with the question of employment, and the Americans to give more emphasis to the removal of trade barriers; both agreed, however, at least at the general level, that the two aims were complementary.[d]

In the beginning of December 1945, the United States issued a document entitled "Proposals for Considerations by an International Conference on Trade and Employment,"[e] purporting to represent a consensus resulting from the United States-British discussions over the preceding two years. The proposals called for a detailed code of conduct relating to governmental restraints on international trade, and for an International Trade Organization (ITO) to administer the code and to perform other functions designed to promote trade.[f] Two weeks after issuing the proposals looking to long-term trade arrangements, the United States invited 15 countries to enter into negotiations looking to conclusion of a multilateral trade agreement,[g] under the authority of the reciprocal trade legislation which had just been extended by the Congress.[h] Every invited country except the Soviet Union accepted the in-

---

[b] Rules on state trading would be designed to assimilate such activity as much as possible to activity by, and regulation of, private firms.

[c] On this issue, however, American and British views were for a long time at odds, because of the prevalence of "Imperial (later Commonwealth) preferences," which were seen on one side of the Atlantic as holding the Empire or Commonwealth together, and on the other side as discrimination directed in large part against the United States.

[d] For a detailed account of the early British-American discussions on trade issues, the so-called "Seminar on Commercial Collaboration," see R. Gardner, *Sterling-Dollar Diplomacy*, pp. 101–109, 145–161 (2d ed. 1969).

[e] U.S. Dept. of State Publication No. 2411, Comm. Policy Ser. No. 79 (1945).

[f] Among these functions, for instance, might be collection and dissemination of statistics, producing uniform definitions and classifications for customs purposes, issuing guidelines for customs valuation, and resolving trade disputes.

[g] U.S. State Dept. Press Release of Dec. 16, 1945, 13 Dept. State Bull. 970 (1945).

[h] Whether Congress had multilateral negotiations in mind when it extended the Reciprocal Trade Act in 1945, 59 Stat. 410, (eff. July 5, 1945) is doubtful. But there was no prohibition on such action, and negotiations under the reciprocal trade legislation thereafter were nearly all conducted on a multilateral basis. See

vitation to enter into trade negotiations.[i] The proposals for an International Conference on Trade and Employment came before the United Nations Economic and Social Council at its first meeting in Paris in February 1946,[j] and in accordance with a resolution introduced by the United States, that body appointed a Preparatory Committee of 19 countries to draft the document to be considered at such a conference.

Thus as of the summer of 1946 two parallel initiatives were in progress, both launched by the United States. One initiative aimed at an early multi-party trade agreement, setting the trend to lowered duties and to regular multilateral negotiations to that end. The other initiative was more ambitious: it aimed at creating a permanent institution, and it contemplated addressing not only tariffs and quotas but also such subjects as international investment; cartels and other restrictive business practices; commodity agreements; and economic development. But the two initiatives were obviously related. It was hard to draft long-term rules on trade without thinking of the current negotiations, and it was hard to plan for the current negotiations—for the first time on a multilateral basis—without thinking about ground rules and precedents. The countries that participated in the two sets of negotiations were for the most part the same, and so, in many instances, were the negotiators. Inevitably, the two initiatives became intertwined.

The Preparatory Committee to draft an ITO Charter met in London in October-November 1946, again in Geneva from April to August of 1947, and finally at a plenary conference at Havana from November 1947 to March 1948.[k] At its first meeting in London, the Preparatory

---

Jackson. "The General Agreement on Tariffs and Trade in United States Domestic Law." 66 Mich. L. Rev. 249, 256–259 (1967). For a substantive discussion on multilateral vs. bilateral tariff negotiation in the context of most-favored-nation treatment, see § 2.42 (b-c) *infra.*

[i] The Soviet Union, which had participated in the Bretton Woods Monetary Conference but had declined to join the organizations which that conference produced, did not reply at all to the invitation to negotiate reduction of trade barriers. Early in 1983, the Soviet government let it be known that it was taking renewed interest in the GATT, and might apply for observer status. See New York Times, Jan. 25, 1983, p. D1, col. 6.

[j] For the mandate and organization of the U.N. Economic and Social Council, see Art. 61–72 of the U.N. Charter, Documents Supplement p. DS -103. The hope that this body would become a kind of umbrella organization for the many specialized agencies of the United Nations with economic responsibilities was never realized.

[k] For the citations to the various reports and documents issued by these conferences, see J. Jackson, *World Trade and the Law of GATT,* Ch. 2 (1969); R.

Committee divided up into committees corresponding roughly to each of the major subjects on the agenda—employment, commercial policy, restrictive business practices, commodity arrangements, and institutional questions. The committee on commercial policy prepared a report on the procedures that would be followed in a multilateral tariff negotiation. To make certain that tariff concessions—i.e., promises to lower (or not to raise) duties[1]—would be kept and would not be nullified by contrary measures, the committee suggested a General Agreement on Tariffs and Trade, which would also contain "such other provisions as may be appropriate." A "Drafting Committee" meeting was scheduled for Lake Success, New York, in January-February 1947, two months in advance of the next scheduled meeting of the full Preparatory Committee. The Drafting Committee, drawing in large part on the relevant sections of the proposed ITO Charter, prepared the first draft of the General Agreement. The point of departure was that the General Agreement should be able to go into force immediately, in order to give impetus to and preserve the momentum for the forthcoming tariff negotiations, without the lengthy ratification procedures that would be required for the ITO Charter. This meant that the General Agreement should contain no articles depending on the existence of the international organization, which might well be some time off; when the ITO did come into being, the General Agreement would be folded into it and would be administered by the Organization to be created.

The two-track negotiation continued at Geneva throughout the spring and summer of 1947. On one track the work centered on the draft charter for the ITO. On the other track, tariff negotiations were conducted by 23 countries, bargaining in 123 separate country pairs.[m] Work on the charter draft—the semi-final round before submission to the plenary conference scheduled for Havana—was completed in August; tariff bargaining continued until the end of October on a country-by-country, product-by-product basis. When the bargaining was completed, all the concessions were incorporated into a single instrument—the General Agreement on Tariffs and Trade, substantially as it had been

---

Hudec, *The GATT Legal System on World Trade Diplomacy*, Chs. 4–5 (1975). For a book-length account of the negotiations by one of the participants, see C. Wilcox, *A Charter for World Trade* (1949, repr. 1972).

[1] More of this later. See § 2.32 *infra*.

[m] Of the bilateral negotiations, the United States participated in 22, i.e., one with every other country represented. See C. Wilcox N. k *supra* at 46–47.

drafted in New York.[n] The principal effect of this incorporation was that the results of each country pair's negotiations were generalized to every other participant. In addition, the concessions would be subjected to and protected by the substantive provisions of the General Agreement, as soon as that document could enter into force.

Bringing the General Agreement into force, however, was not so easy. The United States executive branch, as already mentioned, had taken the position that what was being signed at Geneva was a "Trade Agreement" within the scope of the authorization contained in the 1945 statute extending the reciprocal trade agreements program.[o] To get around the objection (in other countries as well as in the United States) that substantive rules were being agreed to that might conflict with existing law, the General Agreement was divided into three parts. Part I contained the Most Favored Nation Clause and the Schedule of Concessions; Part III contained the administrative articles, an important provision concerning customs unions, and the territorial scope of the agreement; and the rest of the agreement, including the provisions arguably inconsistent with existing law, were placed in Part II. A Protocol of Provisional Application was drawn up,[p] whereby the signatories would undertake, as soon as the Agreement went into effect, to apply Parts I and III, and to apply Part II "to the fullest extent not inconsistent with existing legislation." The Protocol of Provisional Application said that the General Agreement would enter into force provisionally on January 1, 1948 if eight named countries, including Great Britain, France, Canada, and the United States, had signed by November 14, 1947. The named countries did so, and the General Agreement entered into effect "provisionally" as planned. All but one of the participants at the Geneva Conference signed the Agreement by June 30, 1948 and thereby became "original contracting parties."[q]

---

[a] One interesting difference, brought about by Congressional criticism of the New York draft, was that all reference to an "Interim Trade Committee" was dropped, because of doubts that the United States executive branch had authority to enter into even such a provisional organization without new legislation. See Jackson, N.h *supra* at 270–271.

[o] See N. h *supra*.

[p] Documents Supplement, p. DS-79.

[q] See Protocol of Provisional Application, ¶ 4(b), Documents Supplement p. DS-80. Chile, which did not make the June 30 deadline, signed on February 14, 1949.

The plenary United Nations Conference on Trade and Employment convened in Havana on November 21, 1947 with 56 countries represented. The conference opened amid considerable acrimony, as the less developed countries launched a major concerted attack on the work of the Preparatory Committee. Eventually, however, most of the issues were resolved, compromised, or left for another day, and a Final Act containing the text of the charter of the ITO—the so-called Havana Charter—was signed by 53 countries.

Most participants in the Havana Conference looked to the United States to take the lead in ratification of the Havana Charter. But by the time the conference had finished its work and the various documents had been prepared and published, the United States was about to begin a Presidential campaign; moreover, for those officials whose job it would be to shepherd the Charter through the (Republican-controlled) Congress,[r] the Marshall Plan for the reconstruction of Europe and the need to secure extension of the Reciprocal Trade Act[s] took precedence. When the ITO Charter was submitted to the Congress in the spring of 1949, not only had opposition to it mounted, but support had waned. In part this had to do with specific provisions of the Charter, which were seen as too liberal by protectionists, too riddled with exceptions by free traders, and too much oriented toward governmental controls by the business community.[t] In part, lack of enthusiasm for the ITO may have been related to disenchantment with the United Nations and with the immediate post-war vision of a chain of institutions administering agreed principles in an orderly way. Perhaps too, the existence of the GATT and conduct of trade negotiations under its auspices reduced the pressure for the more permanent, more comprehensive, and more structured agreement. Hearings on the ITO Charter were held by the House Foreign Affairs Committee in April–May 1950,[u] but the Committee did not issue

---

[r] The administration intended the Charter to be adopted in the same way that the IMF and World Bank Agreements had been adopted, i.e., by authorizing and implementing legislation, rather than by the treaty route.

[s] See Trade Agreements Extension Act of 1948, 62 Stat. 1053, which, amid increasing controversy, extended the President's authority for a single year only.

[t] For an interesting essay discussing the grounds for lack of support for the ITO from various groups that might have been expected to favor it, see Diebold, "The End of the I.T.O.," Princeton Essays in International Finance No. 16 (1952). See also, R. Gardner, *Sterling-Dollar Diplomacy*, 348–80 (2d ed. 1969).

[u] *Membership and Participation by the United States in the International Trade Organization*, Hearings on H.J. Res. 236 before the House Comm. on For. Affairs, 81st Cong. 2d Sess. (1950).

a report and the legislation never reached the floor. Eventually, as the country became absorbed in the Korean War, economic mobilization, and strategic controls on exports, the ITO was permitted to fade away. First the State Department issued a press release stating

. . . the interested agencies have recommended, and the President has agreed, that, while the proposed Charter for an International Trade Organization should not be resubmitted to the Congress, Congress be asked to consider legislation which will make American participation in the General Agreement more effective.[v]

A few weeks later the British government noted the American statement and announced it too would not ask for ratification of the ITO.[w] The International Trade Organization was dead.[x] What was left was the General Agreement on Tariffs and Trade—a reasonably adequate statement of trading rules for member states, but an agreement that lacked organizational and institutional provisions, that was supposed to last only three years, and that lacked in many countries the explicit support of the legislature. The fact that the GATT survived at all suggests that, on the whole, its substantive provisions made sense and were associated, in most countries, with the increasing trade and overall prosperity that characterized the years after the Second (in contrast to the First) World War. But the status and charter of the GATT were hard to explain, its authority was always somewhat questionable, and its provisions, as we shall see, were quite difficult even to read.

§ 2.3—The GATT—A First Look at the Substantive Standards

2.31—THE GROWTH OF THE GATT

Despite its strange and incomplete beginnings (or perhaps because of them?)[a] the GATT survived and grew. It never had an official secretariat;

---

[v] State Dept. Press Release Dec. 6, 1950, 23 Dept. State Bull. 977 (1950).

[w] 483 Parl. Deb., H.C. 5th Sess. 232–33 (Written Answers) Feb. 8, 1951.

[x] Buried, as an Italian journal pointed out, in a "second class funeral." See Diebold, N. t supra at p. 2.

[a] In the Trade Agreements Extension Act of 1951, 65 Stat. 72, the U.S. Congress provided:

The enactment of this Act shall not be construed to determine or indicate

it was never accepted definitively (as contrasted with "provisionally"); and it did not formally become a specialized agency of the United Nations. But with the help of a variety of fictions—for instance the contracting parties when acting together become the CONTRACTING PARTIES (see Art. XXV),[b] and the secretariat is technically the staff of the Interim Commission for the ITO [c]—the GATT became the most important worldwide agency devoted to the regulation of international commerce. Over a hundred countries eventually joined the GATT, accounting for about 80 per cent of the trade of the non-communist world.[d] The provisions of the GATT became the governing standards for most of the regulation of trade by member countries, and the procedures of the GATT became the forum for most of the intergovernmental collaboration to reduce barriers to international trade. Attempts to put GATT more fully on the map—for instance by creating a permanent organization to administer it[e]—failed; but so did—as of 1983—attempts to supplant GATT by other organizations or codes, for instance the United Nations Conference on Trade and Development (UNCTAD) and the New International Economic Order.[f] Needless to say, the understanding and application of the General Agreement have changed over the more than three decades of its ex-

---

approval or disapproval by the Congress of the Executive Agreement known as the General Agreement on Tariffs and Trade.

This provision was repeated in the 1953, 1954, 1955 and 1958 extensions of trade agreements authority, but not in the Trade Expansion Act of 1962. It reappeared, in somewhat altered form in § 121(d) of the Trade Act of 1974, Documents Supplement p. DS-305.

[b] Documents Supplement p. DS-48.

[c] See J. Jackson, *World Trade and the Law of GATT*, § 6.1 (1969).

[d] Poland joined the GATT in 1967, Romania joined in 1971, and Hungary in 1973; Czechoslovakia, which was an original member, remained in the organization even after it joined the Communist bloc, though a number of countries, including the United States, suspended the application of GATT obligations to that country. See Jackson N. c *supra*, at 748–50.

[e] This was to have been an "Organization for Trade Cooperation" or OTC. See Jackson, N. c *supra*, at 51–2.

[f] The UN General Assembly adopted a Charter of Economic Rights and Duties of States in December 1974 on the initiative of Mexico and with the support of most of the "Third World," but without the support of most non-communist industrial states. To say the Charter has had no effect on the actual conduct of trade would be an exaggeration, but as of the publication of this volume, at least, the Charter had not taken on any of the GATT's functions as a code of conduct, and had assumed a function in the area of dispute settlement more designed to infuse disputes with political pressures than (like the GATT) to defuse and depoliticize them.

istence. Whether the standards have changed too much, or not enough, and indeed whether the underlying premises are still sound is one of the pervasive themes of this volume. In this first look, the major principles are set forth with a broad brush, followed by a brief discussion of the major exceptions. Both the principles and the exceptions are probed somewhat further in the Notes and Questions at the end of the section.

2.32—THE MAJOR PRINCIPLES

The GATT rests on three essential principles:

(1) *Trade should be conducted on a basis of non-discrimination.* In particular, all contracting parties are obligated by the most-favored-nation (MFN) provision in Article I to apply duties (and similar charges) on importation of goods equally, without regard, as among contracting parties, to the country of origin of the goods.

(2) *Governmental restraints on the movement of goods should be kept to a minimum, and if changed, should be reduced, not increased.* The Protocol of Provisional Application, as we saw, had the effect of permitting continuance of certain arrangements—discriminatory or otherwise—inconsistent with the basic principles of the GATT. But these arrangements were to be changed, if at all, only in the direction of free or freer trade. Moreover, contracting parties are to submit Schedules of Import Restrictions which become part of the General Agreement; they shall not impose "duties in excess of those set forth and provided for therein." (Art. II(1)(b)).

(3) *The conditions of trade, including the level of tariffs and other restrictions, should be discussed and agreed on within a multilateral framework.* Article XXVIII BIS provides for negotiations "from time to time" among the contracting parties looking to reduction of trade barriers.[g] In the first twenty years of the GATT's existence six general nego-

---

[g] The original 1947 version of the GATT did not contain a provision for periodic negotiations, since, as we saw, it was conceived of as the product, not the framework, of the negotiations (Cf. Jackson, N. c *supra* at 220–21), and the continuing institutional arrangements were to be contained in the ITO charter. Present Article XXVIII bis was inserted (hence the peculiar numbering) into the GATT at the General Review Session held at Geneva in 1955.

tiations of this character were held, beginning with Geneva in 1947 and ending with the so-called Kennedy Round in Geneva 1964–67.[h]

In addition to these three fundamental commitments—to MFN, to reduction of trade barriers, and to multilateral negotiations—the GATT contains several further principles:

(4) *No prohibitions or restrictions other than tariffs are to be instituted or maintained by contracting parties* (Art. XI). Specifically, this means that quantitative restrictions or quotas on imports of goods—a favorite device of the inter-war as well as early post-war years—are not permitted. We shall explore the reason for this taboo below and throughout the volume.

(5) *The Agreement limits and disapproves (but does not quite prohibit) subsidies on exports,* on the theory that a subsidy on the export side may have a distorting effect comparable to a tariff on the import side (Art. XVI).

(6) *The Agreement lays down some general rules concerning customs unions and free trade areas,* designed to preserve the overriding principle of nondiscrimination and multilateral trade (Art. XXIV).

2.33—THE QUALIFICATIONS

One might have thought that the drafters of the GATT would stop with declaration of the principles sketched above, and then devote themselves to remedies, enforcement, dispute settlement, and the like. Reading the text of the General Agreement as it emerged from drafting sessions in New York, Geneva, and Havana is likely to create the opposite impression: Almost every principle is hedged by exceptions, grandfather clauses, or special cases. Some of the critics of the ITO Charter (whose chapter on commercial policy was substantially identical with the GATT) made exactly this point—the idealism, vision, and economic theory seemed to be compromised at each step.[i] In fact, as the GATT developed, the exceptions did not eat up the principles, though not all the principles

---

[h] A seventh round, originally known as the Nixon Round and later as the Tokyo Round, was formally initiated in 1973. For discussion of the Tokyo Round, see § 7 *infra*.

[i] See Diebold, § 2.2, N. t *supra*, esp. 10–11.

have withstood the test of time with equal vigor. Only a few points need be mentioned in this first view:

(1) *Existing preferential tariff schemes were permitted to continue* (Article I(2)). This provision, insisted on by Great Britain, preserved the Imperial (or Commonwealth) preference system, as well as preferences granted by the French Union to present and former colonies and by the United States to the Philippines and Cuba.[j] In the long run, of course, as all tariffs were reduced, the significance of preferential arrangements would decline. Meanwhile, the hopes of preserving by economic means some of the ties that were dissolving on the political level had strong enough attraction to permit a substantial undercutting of the most-favored-nation principle. The GATT did say, however, that the margin of preference in any existing permitted arrangement could not be increased from that prevailing on the date the Geneva negotiations started—April 10, 1947.[k]

(2) *The prohibition on quotas was made inapplicable to agricultural products subject to price support schemes in the importing country* (Article XI(2)). Some persons had thought agricultural products should be excluded from the GATT altogether, because nearly everywhere parts of the agricultural sector are subsidized, supported, or otherwise shielded from the "free market," and because the politics and even sociology— e.g. rural vs. urban lifestyles—of farmers are something of a special case. That course was not followed. but Article XI(2) plus the Protocol of Provisional Application protected most American farm support programs from import competition. When in later years the United States stood, generally, for lowering trade barriers and enforcing the GATT principles, the protection accorded American agriculture legally through these exceptions was often cited as an example of American hypocrisy.[l]

(3) *A National Security exception was written into the General Agreement* (Article XXI), with no procedure for judging when it could

---

[j] See GATT Annexes A-D, and Article I(2)(c).

[k] GATT Article I(4)(a) and (b), Documents Supplement p. DS-7. For a definition and some illustrations of this point, see Note Ad Art. I, para. 4, Documents Supplement p. DS-63.

[l] Of course the major United States farm crops—wheat, corn, other feed grains, rice, and soy beans—did not need protection, in that the United States was the low cost supplier on the world market. The comment in the text refers principally to meat and dairy products.

be applied. The United States for years restricted imports of oil under this provision, during the years when Middle East and Venezuelan oil were substantially below the United States price.

(4) *The prohibition on quotas was made inapplicable in the case of serious balance of payments difficulties* (Article XII), subject to some conditions (Article XII(2)(4)), and subject to the requirement that permitted quotas not be applied discriminatorily (Article XIII).[m] At first critics of the GATT/ITO feared that since practically all countries other than the United States were in balance of payments difficulties, this was the biggest loophole of all. In fact, by about 1960 all the major currencies had become convertible, and while balance of payments problems did not cease,[n] Article XII did not destroy all that came before.[o]

(5) *Countries were permitted at stated intervals to withdraw concessions bargained for under the Agreement* (Article XXVIII). Though schedules of tariffs notified under Article II were supposed to be firm—indeed they were referred to generally as "bound tariffs" or "bindings," the framers of the GATT thought countries would be more likely to make significant offers if they did not think the decision to do so was irreversible. Again, this clause, which entitled beneficiaries of withdrawn concessions to make withdrawals of their own, could have, but in fact did not, unravel the whole Agreement.[p]

---

[m] Note that Article XIII is itself subject to exceptions spelled out in Article XIV.

[n] See Volume IV of this series, A. Lowenfeld, *The International Monetary System* passim (2d ed. 1984).

[o] Interestingly enough, as the international monetary system and in particular the system of fixed exchange rates broke down in the late 1960's and early 1970's, several countries did the opposite from what the GATT provided. GATT said 'tariffs only' except in balance of payments crises, and then only quotas as emergency measures: Great Britain in 1964 and the United States in 1971, among others, imposed across-the-board tariff surcharges rather than quotas. For the reaction of the GATT to the Nixon surcharge of August 15, 1971, see Vol. IV, N. n *supra*, § 5.46 and Documents Supplement thereto.

[p] The original version of the General Agreement provided for a single time for withdrawal of concessions at the expiration of the first three-year period of the Agreement—January 1, 1951. The periodic "open season" was introduced in the amendments to the GATT effective on January 1, 1958; at the same time concessions previously given subject to renewal at three-year intervals were made effective without limit of time. See G. Curzon, *Multilateral Commercial Diplomacy*, 114–15 (1965).

(6) *An "Escape Clause" permitted withdrawal of a concession at any time if as a result of "unforeseen developments" and of concessions made under the Agreement any product was being imported into a territory in such increased quantities and under such conditions as to cause or threaten serious injury to domestic producers of like or directly competitive products* (Article XIX). This clause followed comparable provisions in United States bilateral agreements under the Reciprocal Trade Agreements program, and was pressed by the United States as necessary to win approval of the Agreement. Though this too looked like a major loophole, its scope was reduced by the consultation provisions and the general scheme of compensatory action by other countries. How the theory of the escape clause squares with the theory of comparative advantage is another one of the themes we shall follow throughout this volume.

(7) Notwithstanding the principles of multilateralism and MFN, the GATT proved flexible enough to accept as members countries that were not prepared to negotiate with one another. Under Article XXXV,[q] added in 1948 at the request of India, which was boycotting South Africa,[r] a country could announce when it became a member of the GATT that it would not apply the Agreement to another party, or if it was already a member when another country became a party, that it would not apply the Agreement to that other party. Not only South Africa and its growing list of enemies, but Israel and several Arab countries, Portugal (when it was a colonial power) and several African countries, and the United States and Hungary and Rumania have been able to join in the multilateral trade negotiations of the GATT without negotiating with or applying MFN to each other.[s] In addition, when Japan joined the GATT in 1955, 15 countries that had no political reason but were afraid of Japan's economic power applied Article XXXV against that country. Subsequently, the Contracting Parties, pursuant to paragraph 2 of Article XXXV, induced several countries to withdraw their invocation of the Article against Japan,[t] but as of 1983, three countries still had not agreed to apply the Agreement to Japan.

---

[q] Documents Supplement p. DS-57.

[r] See Curzon N. p *supra* at 37.

[s] For the reasons why the United States had to invoke Article XXXV against Rumania until 1975 and against Hungary until 1978, see Volume III of this series, A. Lowenfeld, *Trade Controls for Political Ends,* Ch. I § 1.23, Ch. II § 3.2 (2d ed. 1983).

[t] See J. Jackson, *World Trade and the Law of GATT* § 4.6 (1969); see also § 3.33 *infra.*

§ 2.4—Notes and Questions on the GATT

2.41—(a) Putting to one side the qualifications and "provisional" character of most countries' adherence, is the General Agreement a legislative adoption of the law of comparative advantage, a consensus by the contracting parties that trade benefits everyone—importers as well as exporters?

(b) In fact, tariff negotiations have been conducted under auspices of the GATT on the basis that an actual or potential exporting country (Patria) requests concessions from an actual or potential importing country (Xandia) with respect to stated goods, i.e., Patria seeks a promise from Xandia to lower (or in some cases not to raise) duties on the products in question. In return, of course, Xandia has a list of products which it exports or wants to export to Patria, and on which it seeks concessions from Patria.[a] We shall have occasion later to ask how one should measure these exchanges of benefits and just what should be bound. But why, if comparative advantage is accepted as the overriding rationale, is the subject of the negotiation always spoken of as a "concession," with the importing country as grantor and the exporting country as beneficiary obligated to give something in return? Recalling the example with lamps and tables (§ 1.23 supra), wouldn't it be to Xandia's advantage to remove any impediments to importation of lamps from Patria simply as a rational act, rather than as a concession to be paid for by Patria?

(c) If you are not sure you recognize—or at least do not recognize clearly—the agreement suggested in (a), is the GATT at least a consensus (again putting aside the qualifications) that technical efficiencies (= costs?) should determine prices, and that transnational market forces should, in principle, determine the movement of goods?

2.42—(a) Given an answer to the question of the underlying theory of the GATT somewhere along the spectrum suggested by the preceding question, why should the most-favored-nation principle be so important to the vision of reduced trade barriers? The MFN clause

---

[a] Just by way of reminder, expanded on in § 2.42 and elsewhere in this volume, it is worth repeating that, under the MFN principle, if the negotiation were successful and Xandia gave the concession to Patria, that concession would also apply to the same or like products of Tertia, Quarta, and all other member countries when offered for import to Xandia.

was not new—indeed the concept has been traced as far back as the Italian city-states of the late Middle Ages, and versions of MFN clauses occurred in various agreements at the time of the rise of the nation states at the end of the sixteenth and beginning of the seventeenth centuries.[b] But until the creation of the GATT, MFN clauses had typically been contained in bilateral agreements whereby countries *A* and *B* wanted to be sure that the value of concessions they had exchanged with one another would not be undermined or impaired by a more favorable deal made by either side with *C*.[c] Often, in other words, MFN had in the past been a means of protecting a special deal, not a device for generalizing reduction in trade restrictions. Is it clear that the requirement of generalized most-favored-nation treatment as contained in Article I of the GATT will contribute to lowering of trade barriers?

(b) Would you suppose that Patria and Xandia are more likely or less likely to grant concessions to one another if both are obligated —as they are by Article I of the GATT—to make these concessions freely available to all other member countries? How would you respond to the argument that while Patria and Xandia might well be prepared to lower barriers and increase trade between themselves, both would hesitate if as a result of their agreement Tertia, the most efficient producer, would be permitted to enter into a market (or two markets) previously denied to it? The consequence, the argument continues, would be that Patria and Xandia would make no deal at all, or that they would retain barriers at least high enough to keep out Tertia's producers, and as a result these barriers might then not be sufficiently reduced to stimulate the trade between Patria and Xandia.

(c) The framers of the GATT answered this argument in several ways. For one thing, they said, the example of lamps and tables moving into Patria and Xandia with Tertia getting a "free ride" is too narrow. In a multi-country, multi-product round of negotiations, everyone gains

---

[b] See, e.g., J. Jackson, *World Trade and the Law of GATT* p. 249 and sources cited at footnote 1. (1969).

[c] Two types of MFN clauses were common in bilateral agreements—(1) whereby *A* and *B* promised each other that any concession granted to third countries would automatically be extended to each other—so-called unconditional MFN; and (2) whereby *A* promised *B* (and vice versa) that any concession granted by *A* to third countries would be made available to *B* if *B* was prepared to pay the same price as *C* had paid—so-called conditional MFN. The United States vacillated throughout its history between the two types of treaties, beginning with a conditional MFN agreement with France in 1778.

(i.e., benefits from concessions) about as much as he gives up.[d] Furthermore, they predicted—on the whole correctly—that if in respect both of the volume of trade and of the difference between the duties in question before and after a negotiation, Patria's offer of a concession on tables is not sufficient to induce Xandia to give a meaningful concession on lamps, then bringing Tertia, Quarta, and others into the negotiations—both as grantors and as beneficiaries—will make it easier to achieve substantial equivalence of benefits so as to get the negotiations under way and keep them going. Still further, the architects of GATT pointed out that if Xandia should have thoughts of changing its mind (whether wrongfully or as of right),[e] the pressure not only of Patria but of Tertia, Quarta, and the other beneficiaries is likely to keep Xandia to its original resolve, and thus to preserve the duty reduction in question.

(d) In addition to the above, and perhaps most important, there was, of course, the general spirit at the end of World War II in favor of multilateralism, and a distrust of the opposite—the special deals and bilateralism that, as we saw, had characterized the decade before the outbreak of the war. The pre-war experience had also shown that differential, as contrasted with non-discriminatory tariffs, tended to work to the disadvantage of smaller states.[f] MFN, in contrast, would enable efficient producers without strong "muscle" to enter or remain in important markets, thus promoting the overall goals of efficient resource allocation and increased trade.[g] By the 1960's, as we shall see, the distrust of special deals had waned, and the claims of the develop-

---

[d] For continuing doubts on this point, see, e.g., *Report of the Senate Comm. on Finance on the Trade Reform Act* of 1974, S. Rep. 93–1298, 93d Cong. 2d Sess. at 94 (1974):

> The Committee feels that the "unconditional" most-favored-nation principle has led, in the past, to one-sided agreements. . . . Under this principle, there is an inherent incentive for countries to "get a free ride," since they . . . automatically receive the benefits of any trade agreement [whether or not they have provided reciprocal concessions during the concession]

See Trade Act of 1974, § 126, Documents Supplement p. DS-312 for the translation of this thought into a legislative mandate. We return to this topic at the end of the volume. § 8.7 *infra*.

[e] See § 2.33 ¶ 5, *supra*.

[f] See G. Curzon, *Multilateral Commercial Diplomacy* at p. 60 (1965). All of Chapter III of that book is useful in elaborating the question of the most-favored-nation clause, and has been drawn on in preparing the present discussion.

[g] Compare the following remarks made in 1956 by the Director of Commercial

ing countries for better than MFN were pressed much more intensively than they had been in Geneva and Havana in the late 1940's. Still, non-discrimination—expressed in the language of international trade by the MFN concept[h]—remains the cardinal principle, the "golden rule" of the GATT and of the trade policy of most developed countries. Like other expressions of the concept of non-discrimination, such as "equal protection of the laws," "equal rights," or "equal opportunity," MFN is not always easy to define at the margin.[i] But it remains a standard— some would say *the* standard—against which all governmental regulation of international trade is tested.[j]

(e) Note finally that the principle of non-discrimination recurs throughout the GATT, even with respect to authorized exceptions to other rules.[k] Further, note that Article I applies to *all* customs duties

---

Policy of GATT, who later became the United States Representative to the GATT Council.

> While the most-favored-nation clause in GATT is the direct descendant of the unconditional most-favored-nation clause as enshrined for decades in bilateral agreements, in its multilateral context it has a significance, and perhaps even a purpose, which goes beyond that of bilateral agreements. . . . In its multilateral context . . . the basic idea is that discrimination in any form is likely to lead to more discrimination, and that in the long run all countries will suffer from the inevitable distortion of trade patterns which will arise out of discrimination, even though they may be the temporary beneficiaries.

John W. Evans, Lecture before Bologna Center of Johns Hopkins School for Advanced International Studies, Feb. 20, 1956, quoted in Curzon, N. e *supra*, at pp. 67–68.

[h] Compare the analogous rules of the Articles of Agreement of the International Monetary Fund, discussed in Vol. IV of this series, A. Lowenfeld, *The International Monetary System*, § 1.52 and passim (2d ed. 1984).

[i] A famous instance in the history of dispute settlement under the GATT concerned the question of whether Norwegian sardines were true sardines or rather small herrings for purposes of the "like product" clause of Article I, so that Norway could benefit from a concession concerning sardines granted by Germany to Portugal. For an interesting account of the procedure and outcome of this case, see R. Hudec, *The GATT Legal System and World Trade Diplomacy* 159–64 (1975).

For a series of hypotheticals testing the meaning of the MFN article, see J. Jackson, *Legal Problems of International Economic Relations*, 540–42 (1977).

[j] Compare the long and continuing debate about MFN treatment by the United States to products of Communist countries, set forth in Vol. III of this series, *Trade Controls for Political Ends*, Ch. I, § 1.23, Ch. II, § 3 (2d ed. 1983).

[k] See, e.g., Articles II(1)(a); V(2) and (5); IX(1); XIII(1); XVII(1)(a); XVIII(20); XX(j).

and charges, not just those subject to concessions bound under Article II. Thus even if a country withholds certain products from trade negotiations, which means that it can lawfully raise duties on such products without violating any GATT rule, it cannot do so in a manner that discriminates among member countries.

2.43—(a) So far we have been talking only about tariffs—i.e., taxes imposed by the government of Xandia upon the importation of products into Xandia. Typically, the tariff (also called "customs duty" or just "duty") is based on the value of the imported item—e.g., a 15 per cent tariff *ad valorem* on a $100 item made in Patria will result in a tariff of $15; alternatively, a tariff may be measured by weight, volume, or unit—e.g., $25 per ton—generally known as a *specific tariff*.[1] One could conceive of a uniform tariff rate regardless of product; nearly all countries or other trading units, however, have developed schedules of tariffs based on individual products or categories of products. It is these schedules that are the subject of the typical trade negotiation under GATT, and that, if agreement is reached, are notified and bound under Article II.[m]

(b) Technically, the importer pays the tariff, as a condition of taking the merchandise through customs and introducing it into the stream of commerce in Xandia. But the assumption of international trade policy is that the exporter—and therefore the exporter's country —bears the burden of the tariff: in our example the assumption is that when the tariff is added to the export price (as well as costs of transport, insurance, etc.), Patria's competitive position vis-à-vis similar products made in Xandia will be hurt.

Whether this is what actually happens in any given case depends on a number of factors not usually taken into account in trade negotiations —e.g., the amount of the tariff in relation to the price; the mark-up or profit-margin at both ends; the characteristics of the product and of the patterns of trade applicable to it; the price elasticity of demand for

---

[1] Some products may be subject to *mixed tariffs*—i.e., $20 per ton + 8 per cent of the value. For the principles of valuation as set forth in the GATT, see Article VII, Documents Supplement p. DS-16.

[m] For the Tariff Schedules of the United States, see 19 U.S.C. following § 1202.

the product;[n] and the comparability of the Xandian with the Patrian product. Also, the effect in the particular case will depend on the response of Xandia's industry to the protection afforded by the tariff— e.g., greater volume of output at a price lower than the Patrian product plus tariff, or an increase in prices by Xandia's industry without an attempt to increase its share of the market.[o] Overall, however, there is no doubt that tariffs discourage trade, and that the higher the tariff as a percentage of the product's price, the greater the distortion in the market.

(c) As we saw (p. 24, ¶ 4) tariffs are supposed to be the only device used to control the flow of imports by member governments; other devices—most notably import quotas—are basically forbidden (GATT Article XI(1)), subject to a number of exceptions. What do you suppose accounts for the insistence by the framers of the GATT on tariffs to the exclusion of all other forms of restraint, at the same time that tariffs themselves were declared to be the object of a concerted effort at reduction or elimination?

(d) Consider some suggested answers to question (c):

(i) Tariffs are easy to identify and measure, and hence to bargain about. Quotas, in contrast, are difficult to measure, to compare with one another, and hence to reduce through bargaining.

(ii) Tariffs can be applied in a non-discriminatory manner—i.e., x per cent per item, regardless of country of origin; quotas, in contrast, are likely to lead to (or cover up) discrimination of various kinds, country-by-country, importer-by-importer, season-by-season, even historical "rights" vs. new entrants into a market. Thus, the argument goes, over time quotas are inconsistent with a code founded on non-discrimination.

(iii) Tariffs are rarely completely effective, for the reasons suggested in (b) above; even when they have the desired effect, it takes time, and the dislocations tend to be gradual. Quantitative restrictions on imports, however, leave the excluded exporter in Patria with

---

[n] I.e., the volume of consumption lost for each 1 per cent increase in price, or gained for each 1 per cent decrease in price.

[o] Of course speaking about Xandia's industry as if it were unified on these issues may also be contrary to fact.

no possibility of sale in Xandia, and no remedy in terms of price or other marketing strategy.

(iv) While tariffs on imports into Xandia may raise prices in that country, the height of the tariff and the willingness of exporters in Patria (or Tertia, Quarta, etc.) to lower their prices will serve to limit the amount of the price rise. A quota, in contrast, leaves the domestic producers with no external check on their prices, which will be limited only by internal demand or intra-Xandian competition— or by governmental price controls.

(v) Quotas tend to call for administrative controls through licensing; at best this will involve a substantial increase in governmental interference in market forces; not improbably, it will involve distribution of valuable rights without clear standards, accompanied by lobbying, influence-peddling, and corruption or the appearance of corruption.[p]

(vi) Tariffs had a history, going back many centuries, through good times and bad; quotas and comparable devices[q] were relatively recent in origin, widely practiced at the time the GATT was being negotiated but associated with the bad times of two world wars and the years in-between.

Do you find any or all of these arguments persuasive? Can you think of other arguments not here suggested in favor of banishing quotas from the approved arsenal of trade restraints? How much would you give up to secure the statement in Article XI(1), and to limit or contain the possible exceptions?

(e) In fact, the United States pushed hard for the prohibition on quotas: the principal United States negotiator of the GATT and the ITO Charter, who felt passionately that quotas were an evil that must be contained to the utmost extent possible, wrote in 1949:

---

[p] For a fascinating description of the evolution of the United States Mandatory Oil Import Program from 1959 to 1973 (when foreign oil was cheaper than the domestic product), involving no major scandal but an accumulation of ad hoc decisions, adjustments, and determinations extraneous to the avowed purpose of the program, see Dam, "Implementation of Import Quotas: The Case of Oil," 14 J. Law & Economics 1 (1971).

[q] E.g., tied sales, multiple exchange rates, rationing of foreign exchange by country or product, and the like.

Quantitative restrictions present the major issue of commercial policy. Tariffs are thought to be old-fashioned; exchange controls are governed by the IMF; quota systems are the most effective methods of protection that remains. Nations all over the world are experienced in their use. If uncontrolled, they promise to become universal and permanent. Freedom to employ them is not readily to be surrendered. The proposal that this freedom be limited evoked a debate that went on for many months. The toughest problem in the trade negotiations came to be known by its initials: Q.R. It would not be inaccurate to describe the meetings at London, Geneva, and Havana as the United Nations Conferences on Q.R.[r]

The countries that wanted to preserve the right to impose quotas did not disagree with the United States arguments—roughly along the lines outlined in paragraph (d) above. They wanted to have the use of quotas precisely for the reasons that the United States opposed them—to have a quick and flexible tool, to discriminate (for the most part against the United States during the post-war "dollar shortage"), and to insulate their inefficient industries from world markets.[s] The compromise, spelled out in five articles of the Agreement, wound up with

(i) the general prohibition on the use of quotas (with some exceptions, especially directed to agriculture)—Article XI;

(ii) Exceptions to the general prohibition for balance of payments reasons—Article XII;

(iii) Rules for application of the exceptions contained in Article XII—generally in the direction of preserving MFN as much as possible—Article XIII;

(iv) Exceptions to the rules for application of the exceptions as set forth in Article XIII—Article XIV;

(v) Mandatory reference to and consultation with the International Monetary Fund on balance of payments questions.[t]

---

[r] C. Wilcox, *A Charter for World Trade*, p. 82 (1949, repr. 1972).

[s] See K. Dam, *The GATT, Law and International Economic Organization*, p. 148–49 (1970).

[t] For a detailed explanation of these articles, see J. Jackson, *World Trade and the Law of GATT*, Ch. 13 and 26 (1969).

2.44—If the elimination of quotas was the central issue in the negotiations of the GATT,[a] the preference of the post-war drafters for tariffs over all other barriers to international trade, and the effort to preserve the reciprocal and binding effect of tariff negotiations had to be expressed also in provisions—not to say prohibitions—on a variety of other protectionist or potentially protectionist techniques. Some of these provisions are mentioned here briefly, just to develop the vocabulary of international trade regulation and to illustrate the attendant tensions. Many of the devices touched on lightly here will be subjected to more thorough analysis later in the volume, both under the GATT and under changing national legislation.

(a) Dumping and Anti-Dumping

(1) The popular definition of the term "dumping" embraces any sales by a producer at low prices to get rid of surplus—if possible after the costs of production of the entire line have been recovered. In international trade language, the definition of dumping is more limited and technical. Article VI of the GATT, modeled roughly but not precisely on U.S. legislation,[b] defines dumping as an export of goods by a producer or seller in Patria to importers in Xandia at "less than the normal value"—i.e., (i) at less than the price at which the products are sold in Patria, or, if there are no such sales; (ii) at less than the price at which the Patrian products are sold in Tertia or Quarta; or (iii) at less than the cost of production plus reasonable mark-up for cost of sales and profit.

As so defined, dumping "is to be condemned." We shall return to the technical questions related to this concept later, in connection with a close look at the steel industry.[c] For the moment it is pertinent to note only that dumping is conceived of as unfair trade—comparable to price discrimination or predatory pricing inside a country—practiced by private exporters, rather than by governments.[d]

---

[a] Compare Wilcox, § 2.43 N. r *supra* at 41.

[b] The Antidumping Act of 1921, 42 Stat. 11, Documents Supplement p. DS-417. The Act is discussed in detail at § 4.41–.44 *infra*. The GATT's attempt to refine the definitions of Article VI and impose stricter procedural requirements in an International Antidumping Code, are discussed at § 4.44 *infra*.

[c] See § 4.41–.44 *infra*.

[d] But as Prof. Dam points out, if the problem were really discrimination, Xandia would act against Patrian exporters if they sold to Xandia at *higher* than domestic

(2) Anti-dumping duties are duties imposed by governments to offset alleged dumping. Typically they are directed to particular producers or exporters, not necessarily to all exporters from a country, and usually not to all imports of a product regardless of country of origin, as would be required by MFN. But suppose Patrian producers lowered their export prices to meet competition from Tertia for the Xandian market. Is that an unfair trade practice? Or suppose the Xandian industry is not in fact injured by Patrian competition—say because its own costs and prices are lower than those in Patria, or because the producer in Patria, not faced with competition in its home market, was maintaining higher than world market prices for home consumption? Can the government of Xandia nonetheless impose anti-dumping duties? Again saving the technical questions for later,[e] it is useful at this stage to note that the framers of the GATT were concerned both to avoid dumping and to avoid protectionism in the guise of anti-dumping duties. Their solution was to authorize anti-dumping duties only if the practice of the foreign producer "causes or threatens material injury to an established industry" in the importing state.

(b) *Subsidies*

Direct governmental aid to industry or agriculture[f] can work as trade distortions in at least two ways. (1) *Export subsidies* by Patria can give a price advantage to Patrian, as compared to Xandian, products not justified by actual efficiencies; (2) *production subsidies* in Xandia may make Xandian products cheaper than comparable products imported from Patria, even though the Xandian producers had higher costs (lower efficiencies) than their foreign competitors.[g]

---

prices. In fact it is *downward* price discrimination that brings forth anti-dumping measures. See K. Dam, *The GATT: Law and International Economic Organization* at 168 (1970). For a brief discussion of the dumping problem where the exporter is a state trader, see Vol. III of this series, A. Lowenfeld, *Trade Controls for Political Ends* Ch. II §§ 1.45(b), 2.35, both concerned with a United States-Soviet trade agreement (2d ed. 1983).

[e] § 4.43 *infra.*

[f] I.e., we exclude, by international consensus, the variety of indirect supports, from aid to education to construction of transport facilities to military purchases to investment credits that may aid a country's industry, including its exports.

[g] A third distortion would be that Patria's subsidies enhance Patrian exporters' share of the Xandian market as compared to unsubsidized producers in Tertia.

The GATT recognizes both of these points in Article XVI,[h] but requires only notification and consultation. As to export subsidies, GATT distinguishes between primary products in which the restraint is only to avoid securing "more than an equitable share" of the world export trade in the product in question,[i] and other—i.e., manufactured or semi-manufactured—products, in which no new subsidies are permitted which lower the export price below the domestic price.[j]

(c) *Countervailing Duties*

The way Xandia as importing country could offset export subsidies by Patria would be to impose a so-called countervailing duty. The effect of a countervailing duty would be the same as the effect of an anti-dumping duty, and in fact the two devices are treated together in Article VI of the GATT. But whereas anti-dumping duties are directed against individual (and typically private) exporters, Xandia's countervailing duty would be directed specifically against measures of the Patrian government. Also, the essential element in the dumping concept—export sales at lower prices than home market sales—may or may not be present in the case of a duty designed to countervail a subsidy.[k] Article VI(3) of the GATT limits the amount of a countervailing duty to the amount of the foreign subsidy—interestingly enough regardless of whether the subsidy was legal or not under Article XVI. However, the requirement that industry in Xandia be injured or threatened with injury is applicable to countervailing as well as to anti-dumping duties.[l]

---

[h] Documents Supplement p. DS-30.

[i] Article XVI(3).

[j] Article XVI(4). This provision, contained in a "declaration" opened for signature in 1957 and ultimately an amendment effective in 1962, is binding only on 17 countries, including, however, all the major developed countries in the GATT. For a detailed account of the negotiation of and adherence to this commitment, see Jackson, § 2.43 N. t *supra*, § 15.3.

[k] Various illustrations of this point can be adduced. The simplest would be a production subsidy in Patria that reduced both the internal and the export price. Looked at from Xandia, a countervailing duty would still be justified.

[l] GATT Article VI(6). Whereas the injury requirement in respect to anti-dumping was taken from the U.S. Antidumping Act of 1921, the United States countervailing duty statute, § 303 of the Tariff Act of 1930, 19 U.S.C. § 1303, contained no injury requirement. Technically this meant that by virtue of the Protocol of Provisional Application, the U.S. countervailing duty statute prevailed against a conflict with the GATT. However, failure to conform its law to the

(d) *National Treatment*

(1) *Taxes.* It is obvious that the same effect as a tariff could be achieved by an excise tax, imposed not upon entry but upon sale (whether wholesale or retail), if the excise discriminates between imported and domestic products. Article III of the GATT outlaws such devices. If the imported and domestic products are not exactly the same but compete for the same market, some interesting problems may arise. What about a tax on oleomargarine, for instance, but not on butter,

(i) if all oleo is imported and all butter is domestically produced;

(ii) if the tax is designed to protect domestic butter against both domestic and imported oleo;

(iii) if both butter and oleo are produced at home and abroad, and the tax on oleo supplements protection against foreign butter afforded by a tariff or quota not applicable to oleo?[m]

(2) *Health and Safety Regulations.* Governments have always imposed some standards on the basis of public health and safety: since the 1960's, world concern with the environment as well as increased attention to the causes and consequences of accidents have given rise to a plethora of regulations, which may have uneven impact on foreign

---

international standard was one of the criticisms raised against the United States by other countries, especially when they were criticized or accused by the United States. For more on countervailing duties under U.S. law, see §§ 4.45–.46, 7.63(b), 8.53, 8.6,*infra*.

[m] The example is taken from Dam, N. d *supra* at 118–19, referring particularly to a Swedish inquiry of the GATT. A controversy between the United States and Great Britain and Ireland that dragged on for more than a decade involved the so-called "water in the whiskey" problem, which arose from the United States practice of imposing a "revenue tax" on whiskey measured by the alcohol content. The effect of the tax was to favor domestic bottlers who paid the tax on 100 proof alcohol in bulk before diluting and bottling it to standard 86 proof, as against producers of Scotch and Irish whiskey, who generally sent their products to the United States already bottled for retail consumption.

The U.S. Court of Customs and Patent Appeals twice upheld the tax against challenge by importers, once under the GATT, *Bercut-Vandervoort & Co. v. United States*, 46 C.C.P.A. 28, (1958), cert. denied, 359 U.S. 953 (1959), a second time under the national treatment clause of the U.S.-Ireland Treaty of Friendship, Commerce and Navigation of 1950, applicable also to Britain under the MFN Clause of the U.S.-British Convention to Regulate Commerce of 1815, *Schieffelin & Co. and Beitzell & Co. Inc., v. United States*, 424 F.2d 1396 (C.C.P.A. 1970). For criticism of the *Bercut* case under Article III of GATT, see Dam, pp. 219–30.

and domestic products. Often—notably in regard to automobiles—the regulations grew out of negotiations between the government and the domestic, but rarely the foreign industry. If a headlight or bumper or glass standard imposed by the United States Highway Transportation Administration is consistent with existing practices of General Motors and Ford, but not Toyota or Volkswagen, has there been a GATT violation?

A famous instance where a safety standard worked as a non-tariff barrier involved compressed gas cylinders. There is no question that such cylinders, used in fire extinguishers, valves, and a variety of construction industries, are dangerous products if defectively made.[n] The U.S. government has therefore issued detailed regulations concerning the interstate transport of such cylinders, including a requirement that the cylinders be inspected in the course of manufacture.[o] But testing is conducted only in the United States, thus effectively excluding foreign compressed gas cylinders, including those made in Great Britain and Japan. Consider

(i) how you might suggest solving this problem if you represented Japanese manufacturers of compressed gas cylinders;

(ii) how you might use the safety argument for protectionist purposes on behalf of United States domestic manufacturers;

(iii) how the GATT should address this problem in the context of the national treatment requirement of Article III.

2.45—Note that in this introduction to the GATT code of conduct, nothing has been said about what happens (i) when Xandia violates a GATT prohibition; (ii) when Patria thinks Xandia has violated the Agreement and Xandia denies it; or (iii) when Tertia seeks release from an obligation. In fact these questions are quite difficult to answer, partly because, as we saw, the GATT was not originally conceived as an integrated institution, partly because the relation between right and

---

[n] On October 31, 1963, for instance, 70 persons were killed and over 400 were injured when a tank of liquid petroleum gas (LPG) exploded at the Indianapolis State Fairground Coliseum. See New York Times Nov. 1, 1963, p. 1, col. 5; Nov. 2, p. 11, col. 3.

[o] 49 C.F.R. § 178.36, esp. § 178.36–3, .36–4. For a discussion of the more numerous barriers of this kind in Japan, see Abegglen and Hout, "Facing Up to the Trade Gap with Japan," 57 Foreign Affairs 146, 158–99 (Fall 1978).

remedy has been an indistinct and changing one, not easily or obviously characterized even as a legal system.[p] We shall return to this topic later.

*   *   *

2.46—One more provision of the GATT, briefly mentioned earlier, forms the focus of the next section—the exemption from the MFN requirement for customs unions (Art. XXIV). One customs union, the European Common Market, was to change not only the economic and political map of the world, but—in a way that is hard to articulate or prove but nonetheless true—was to change the perceptions, the attitudes, and the consensus of the members of the GATT, both about that institution and about the code of conduct they had accepted, however tentatively, in the 1940's.

---

[p] This is the theme of R. Hudec. *The GATT Legal System and World Trade Diplomacy* (1975). which spells out both the assumptions and the ebb and flows of the GATT through focus on the disputes that have come before it.

§ 3—The International Trading System: The Principal Actors

Every nation, of course, conducts some trade, and there are well over 100 nations as of the last quarter of the Twentieth Century. But if East-West and North-South issues—which are in large part different from those discussed here—are put aside, it turns out that there are three dominant forces, both in terms of volume and in terms of their influence on the rules and practices of the international trading system. Each is discussed separately in this section, and each will return to a leading role in the succeeding sections, focusing on trade in steel.[a]

§ 3.1—The European Economic Community

3.11—CUSTOMS UNIONS AND THE GATT

A customs union is an arrangement by states, otherwise independent and sovereign, whereby for trade purposes they draw a single border around themselves and eliminate the borders between or among themselves. Thus (leaving aside transitional periods or exceptions) (i) in trade among the members of a customs union, there are no duties or other governmental trade barriers; and (ii) in trade with the outside world, duties and other barriers are identical and set in common.[b] Inevitably in a world measured by nation states, a customs union results in discrimination against non-members. If Xandia and Patria enter into a customs union, Tertia's products are discriminated against in Xandia in favor of Patria's products, and in Patria in favor of Xandia's products.

The framers of the post-war trading system were well aware of the contradiction between customs unions and a generalized regime based on MFN. Indeed throughout the nineteenth century, arguments and diplomatic disputes raged among the states and principalities of Europe about whether entry into a customs union was or was not compatible

---

[a] The classification here is somewhat arbitrary, in that Great Britain did not join the European Community until 1973, and that from the United States' point of view, Canada should certainly be included if only volume of trade were at issue. But in an examination from a lawyer's standpoint of the trading system of the non-communist world, it makes sense to focus on the EEC, the United States and Japan.

[b] A third common element is that the revenues from customs duties are shared or put into a common fund.

with a most-favored-nation commercial treaty, and whether the outsider was or was not entitled to the benefits of a customs union.[c] But not to have included any provision on customs unions in the GATT would have meant that countries too small to be viable trading units—Luxembourg, for example, and perhaps all of the Low Countries—would have had to choose between natural commercial ties and the General Agreement.[d] Moreover, while thoughts about the future organization of Europe were not yet worked out in detail, even in the early post-war years some sort of link between France and Germany was envisaged—probably in a wider regional context based on trade. Finally, though the economic theory of customs unions had not been fully developed[e]—perhaps even because of this gap—the framers of the GATT had a rationale for permitting and even encouraging customs unions, provided they were organized under appropriate safeguards. The chief United States delegate to the conferences that developed the GATT wrote:

> Preferences have been opposed and customs unions favored, in principle, by the United States. This position may obviously be criticized as lacking in logical consistency. In preferential arrangements, discrimination against the outer world is partial; in customs unions, it is complete. But the distinction is nonetheless defensible. A customs union creates a wider trading area, removes obstacles to competition, makes possible a more economic allocation of resources, and thus operates to increase production and raise planes of living. A preferential system, on the other hand, obstructs economy in production, and restrains the growth of income and demand. It is set up for the purpose of conferring a privilege on producers within the system and imposing a handicap on external competitors. A customs union is conducive to the expansion of trade on the basis of multi-lateralism and non-discrimination; a preferential system is not.[f]

Whether this statement is accurate—in theory or history—is still a

---

[c] The most famous of the nineteenth century customs unions was the Zollverein organized by Prussia, but a variety of other unions came and went among the states of the Italian peninsula, Austria, and the Balkan states. See J. Viner, *The Customs Union Issue* 5-12 (1950) and sources there cited.

[d] In fact, Belgium, Luxembourg, and the Netherlands, acting through their governments in exile in London, had agreed as early as 1944 that they would form a customs union—later known as BENELUX.

[e] That came, surprisingly, only in 1950, in the book by Viner cited at N. c *supra*.

[f] Clair Wilcox, *A Charter for World Trade*, 70–71 (1949, repr. 1972).

matter of considerable debate, which we shall follow as one of the threads of this volume. The framers were quite conscious of the risks. The passage quoted above continues:

> In the formation of a customs union, established interests may be threatened and substantial readjustments required. It is therefore desirable that the transition to such an arrangement be gradual. . . . While this process is going on, however, preferences will be established. An exception to the general rule of non-discrimination will be required. But such an exception may be dangerous. Progress toward the complete elimination of internal barriers may stop short of its appointed goal. And, if this happens, a preferential system will survive. If this outcome is to be avoided, the exception must be so framed as to insure its proper use.[g]

The original "Proposals" put forward by the United States in December 1945 contained only a brief provision on customs unions.[h] By the time of the Havana Conference of 1947-48, the provision had been expanded into a complex article with 10 paragraphs, dealing not only with customs unions but also with free trade areas—i.e., groupings of countries that have eliminated trade barriers inter se, but have not adopted a common posture vis-à-vis non-participants.[i]

Essentially, Article XXIV followed the United States drafts,[j] in line with the consensus expressed above. (i) Customs unions must not serve as a cover for special deals and preferential arrangements; therefore a customs union could not be limited to particular industries or sectors, but must apply to all trade between the members. (ii) Customs unions must not be used to increase international trade barriers; therefore

---

[g] Wilcox, N. g *supra* at 71.

[h] U.S. Dept. of State Pub. No. 2411, p. 16 *supra* at 18, 13 Dept. of State Bull. p. 918, 924 (1945).

[i] Compare the definitions in Article XXIV(8)(a) (customs union) and (b) (free trade area). It is interesting that the addition of provisions regarding free trade areas came at the insistence of Lebanon and Syria (both formerly French mandates), which wanted to eliminate restraints between themselves and France, without agreeing to a common foreign economic policy.

[j] The original GATT of October 30, 1947 contained some but not all of the provisions here discussed; the remainder were agreed on at the Havana Conference and incorporated into the GATT by a Special Protocol Relating to Article XXIV concluded in 1948. See J. Jackson, *World Trade and the Law of GATT,* § 24.1 for a detailed account of the various drafts.

tariffs and other barriers to the outside world in a customs union may not "on the whole" be higher than the average of the tariffs of the components before formation of the union. But as it emerged from several years of negotiations, Article XXIV of the GATT contained several ambiguities, reflecting on this issue too some of the ambivalence that characterized the entire Agreement. The definition of a customs union in paragraph (8) speaks of *"substantially* all the trade" among members of the union without making clear what this means; there are provisions for interim arrangements leading to the function of customs unions (as well as free trade areas) according to a plan and schedule "within a reasonable length of time" (para. 5) but no criteria are given for that term; and there is provision for notification to the CONTRACTING PARTIES of any proposal to form a customs union, but the consequences of submitting a non-conforming plan—for instance without a final date when the interim is over—are only rather loosely indicated (para. 7).

Much debate in later years turned on the question of whether paragraphs 5 to 9 were the operative provisions of Article XXIV, with paragraph 4 merely a hortatory purpose clause; or whether, on the contrary, paragraph 4 was the critical provision, so that if it were satisfied—i.e., trade were facilitated among the members and not restrained with non-members—all the rest would be assumed.[k]

Apart from the technical questions of how a customs union would work in relation to the MFN principle, the question of customs unions was, of course, also a political one, raising some of the same issues of universalism vs. regionalism that had been raised when the United Nations had been organized in 1945. Whether the link between increasing freedom of trade and closer integration of the economies of members of customs unions recited in Article XXIV(4) would in fact come to exist was, of course, not known in 1947-8. But the possibility of momentum, initiative, and negotiating balance through such integration might well be a complement—or even an alternative—to the global vision of the GATT, whose success could also not be predicted with confidence in the early post-war years.

---

[k] See, e.g., Dam, "Regional Arrangements and the GATT: The Legacy of a Misconception," 30 U. Chi. L. Rev. 615, 663 (1963); Dam, *Law and International Economic Organization* 276 (1970); J. Jackson, *World Trade and the Law of GATT* 599–603 (1969).

3.12—EUROPEAN INTEGRATION, PHASE I: THE COAL AND STEEL COMMUNITY

As Europe endeavored to recover from the ravages—physical and moral—of six years of total war, several goals competed in the minds of the new generation of leaders. Nations must be rebuilt, in terms of institutions, physical plant, employment, and sense of purpose; on the other hand the nationalism that had brought on two long Europe-centered wars in three decades must somehow be restrained. More particularly, Germany must not be permitted to again menace the world as it had the last time—first after too vengeful peace terms and then after too careless a response to violation of those terms; on the other hand, the idea of Germany as a nation of shepherds, though briefly entertained in the United States and elswhere, made no sense.

At the most general level, the idea of European integration was to permit Germany to be rebuilt without threat to France, and to permit the smaller European countries to join with the larger ones as a counterpoise to the victorious giants—the United States and the Soviet Union. By the late 1940's, as it turned out, Germany was split in two—apparently irreversibly—with a western part that became the Federal Republic and an eastern part that would remain in the Soviet orbit. The split was replicated in Berlin, the pre-war capital, and the siege status of that city (as well as the 11-month blockade of 1948-49) became continuing symbols of the "iron curtain," the cold war, and the threat of Soviet-led communism. In the view of its proponents—importantly including the United States—integration of Western Europe would not only avoid recurrence of the nightmare of World War II but would provide a bulwark—democratic and prosperous—against the new nightmare in the East.

In a speech in Zurich in September 1946, Winston Churchill, then out of office but recognized as the hero of the Allied war effort, proposed creation of a Council of Europe as a central policy-making institution for a unified and democratic "Greater Europe." A treaty creating a Council of Europe was actually signed three years later, but the Council became a forum for discussion—most notably of human rights —rather than an operative political/legal institution. In 1947, the United States launched a program for European recovery through the Marshall Plan, and at the same time promoted cooperation among the states that would be receiving aid, through an Organization for European

Economic Cooperation.[a] That organization undertook, along with its role in the allocation of Marshall Plan aid, to promote "the maximum possible interchange of goods and services," and accordingly to "cooperate in relaxing restrictions on trade and payments between one another." Further, the members undertook "to continue the study of Customs Unions or analogous arrangements," and reduction of tariffs and other barriers to the expansion of trade.[b]

The program of trade liberalization under the auspices of the OEEC worked to some extent in eliminating quotas for intra-European trade;[c] in respect to tariffs (whose importance was increased as quotas were being removed), the regional efforts ran up against resistance from Britain and others, which preferred the global (i.e., MFN) efforts being undertaken in the GATT. At the close of the decade, a variety of proposals was being debated in the OEEC, the Council of Europe, and the GATT, to speed up reduction of tariff barriers. Some of the proposals concentrated on regional arrangements, some on categories measured by the rates of duty, and some by categories of products or industrial sectors.[d]

The first breakthrough came in May of 1950, when the Foreign Minister of France, Robert Schuman, proposed that France and West Germany should put their coal and steel industries under control of a joint High Authority of supranational character. Such a plan, he argued, could remove one of the major sources of Franco-German conflict,[e] create conditions "which will in themselves insure the most effective rationalization of production on the basis of the highest level of productivity;" and "lay the first concrete foundation for a European federation."[f] The new government of the Federal Republic of Germany

[a] See Convention for European Economic Cooperation signed at Paris, April 16, 1948, reproduced conveniently in *Documents on American Foreign Relations* Vol. X, 1948, pp. 244–50 (1950).

[b] See *id.* Articles 4, 5, and 6.

[c] As contrasted with the quotas maintained against dollar imports under GATT Article XII and IMF Article XIV.

[d] For a discussion of these proposals, see I. Frank, *The European Common Market,* pp. 12–25 (1961) and sources there cited.

[e] Including the question of the Saar, Germany's richest coal-producing area, then under control of France, and the question of the Ruhr, Germany's steel center, then under U.S.-British occupation but emerging from the tight controls on production imposed just after the war's end.

[f] The text of the proposal, made at a press conference on May 9, 1950, is

accepted the proposal, and so did the Low Countries and Italy. Great Britain was invited to participate but declined.[g] In less than a year the Schuman Plan was translated into the Treaty of Paris of 1952, creating the European Coal and Steel Community (ECSC in its English abbreviation).[h]

We shall have occasion to examine the specifics of the Treaty of Paris later in this volume, in the context of examining world production and trade in steel. For the moment, only two points need be stressed. First, unlike prior efforts at trans-national integration, which had involved consultation, coordination, or agreement on policy among member states, the Treaty of Paris created a High Authority—in effect the executive of the Coal and Steel Community—and delegated to it the power to make policy binding on governments and firms directly, without implementing legislation or specific concurrence by individual member governments.[i] This feature of the European Coal and Steel Community was regarded by many supporters of European integration—including the United States and the GATT Secretariat—as so pioneering and so important as to justify major departures from the principles of commercial policy so arduously negotiated just a few years earlier.[j]

---

reproduced in the Preface to P. Reuter, *La Communautée Européenne du Charbon et de l'Acier*, pp. 1–5 (1953).

[g] The reasons for Britain's position, which kept recurring in different contexts throughout the following decades, related in part to the desire to maintain its ties—including preferential trade arrangements—with the Commonwealth; and in part to reluctance to yield as much sovereignty as the Schuman Plan contemplated, particularly in view of the possibility that considerations other than full employment might be given priority.

[h] 261 U.N.T.S. 140. For the economic provisions of the Treaty of Paris (in contrast to the institutional provisions which have been in large part superseded), see Documents Supplement pp. DS-105–133.

[i] Of course the High Authority—and even more its successor the Commission of the European Communities, had to act within the scope of its authority; it was not, in other words, a federal government. The relation between the High Authority and Commission and the member governments represented in the Council of Ministers has been a continual subject of discussion and even litigation within the European Communities, the details of which are beyond the scope of this volume.

[j] See, among the many works dealing with this subject, E. Stein, P. Hay, M. Waelbroeck, *European Community Law and Institutions in Perspective*, esp. Ch. I (1976); Mathijsen, *Guide to European Community Law* (1975); Kepsteyn and Verloren van Themat, *Introduction to the Law of the European Communities* (1973).

Second, the European Coal and Steel Community was designed to eliminate over time all trade barriers in coal and steel (and their ingredients) among the member countries. But member countries would retain the right to set their own commercial policy, including tariffs and quotas, vis-à-vis outsiders, subject to some initially vague criteria about "harmonization." In GATT terms the ECSC would be a free trade area, not a customs union. But it would not come within the requirements of GATT Article XXIV(5) and (8), in that it was limited to two industries, far from "substantially all the trade." Whether it would satisfy the condition of Article XXIV(4) was also not clear at the outset. Not only was the ECSC clearly inconsistent with Article I of the GATT—the golden rule of MFN; it was also inconsistent with Article XXIV, an exception to MFN that, as we saw, had been constructed on the pillar of across-the-board elimination of internal trade barriers, as distinguished from preferential arrangements confined to particular sectors.

The creation of the Coal and Steel Community thus presented the GATT with one of the first of many occasions when the ideals and rules of the General Agreement clashed with other objectives of the same parties—or many of them—developed in different context. Given the support for European integration on the part of the United States, and the importance in the GATT of the members of the Coal and Steel Community, it was highly unlikely that the GATT would be an obstacle to implementation of the Treaty of Paris. But the GATT itself was still in its formative stage,[k] and too easy a relaxation of its rules the first time they were tested by major participants could have undermined both the organization and the code of conduct for which it stood. The parties to the ECSC were encouraged, therefore, to adhere to GATT principles as much as possible: At least, for example, they should provide for completely free internal trade in the products covered—even if this meant a risk for relatively inefficient Belgian coal and Italian steel.[l] The Treaty of Paris also was written to provide (in Article 71) that the powers granted to the Community concerning commercial policy toward third countries shall not exceed the powers which the member states were free to exercise under international agreements to which they were

---

[k] See, e.g., text at § 2.33 N. p *supra*.

[l] The Belgian coal and Italian steel industries were, accordingly, provided for in the "Convention Containing the Transitional Provisions," section 26 (Belgium) and section 30 (Italy).

parties; in a transitional convention the members agreed to act jointly to seek a waiver of Article I of the GATT.[m]

The GATT did grant a waiver,[n] but only after long negotiations and subject to carefully drawn conditions. Some members of the GATT were concerned about their sources of supply of coal or steel, others were concerned about their markets in the Community, and both insisted on assurances that their interests would be protected. Accordingly, the waiver contained a commitment by the members of the ECSC to harmonize their customs duties and other trade regulations applicable to coal and steel products of third parties "upon a basis which shall be lower and less restrictive than the general incidence of the duties and regulations of commerce now applicable;" and also a commitment to avoid placing "unreasonable barriers upon exports to third countries, including, specifically, unreasonable duties and unreasonable quantitative restrictions."[o] Perhaps equally important, the members of the Coal and Steel Community undertook as a condition of the waiver, to submit annual reports to the GATT during the five-year transitional period.[p] These reports provided the focus for complaints and discussions, which in turn exerted a kind of pressure in the direction of liberal and expansionist behavior by the Community.[q]

As the European Community and the GATT developed together, the role of the latter as a quasi-legal, quasi-diplomatic forum began to emerge. The rules of the GATT influenced, to a considerable extent, but did not really restrain, formation of the ECSC. Even the MFN principle, it turned out, was malleable, in the overall interest of increasing trade and subject to safeguarding perceived interests of third states. If injury could be avoided, in other words, specific rules could be manipulated. But to quote from an important American study of the European Common Market and its antecedent, the GATT stood as a constant counter-pressure

to the natural tendency of a regional economic grouping to resolve

---

[m] Convention Containing the Transitional Provisions, section 20.

[n] Documents Supplement p. DS-561.

[o] Sixth and seventh preambular clauses, Documents Supplement pp. DS-561–62.

[p] *Id.* ¶ 7, Documents Supplement p. DS-565.

[q] See Frank, N. d *supra* at 29.

internal differences by shifting the burdens of adjustment to outsiders. It forced a way of looking at the [coal and steel] Community in terms of its place in the world economy instead of only in the more usual manner, as a new kind of integration in which internal relations are the sole focus.[r]

3.13—EUROPEAN INTEGRATION, PHASE II: THE COMMON MARKET

European integration suffered a severe setback shortly after the Coal and Steel Community got under way. As the cold war grew sharper in Europe while a hot war raged in Korea, Western defense planners led by the United States concluded that it was necessary to re-arm the portion of Germany not under Soviet control. France and the Low Countries, however, viewed such a suggestion with alarm, only a few years after the end of World War II and with the memory of the mistakes of the inter-war years still fresh in mind. The proposed solution, also put forward originally by France, was a European Defense Community, to consist of the same six countries that had joined in the Coal and Steel Community, making use of some of the same institutions, and calling for an integrated military budget, a "European" ministry of defense, and a unified command structure. A treaty to this effect was drafted in 1953, but it was rejected by the French National Assembly in the following year, and thereafter the EDC project was abandoned. It was too soon for military—and political—integration.

But the "Europeans," led by another Frenchman, Jean Monnet, were determined not to give up their efforts.[a] Several plans were discussed in the mid-1950's to keep the "European" momentum going. Some supported further sectoral integration, along the lines of the Coal and Steel Community, possibly in energy, transportation or both; others favored some kind of coordination of monetary policies. When the foreign ministers of the "Six" met at Messina, Sicily in June 1955, they decided both on a common market covering all aspects of exchange of goods, and on common policies concerning transport and energy.

---

[r] *Id.* at p. 35, in part quoting from W. Diebold, Jr., *The Schuman Plan* at p. 530 (1959).

[a] Monnet stepped down from the presidency of the ECSC to devote all his energies to an Action Committee that he organized to further the integration movement.

A commission headed by Belgium's Foreign Minister, Paul-Henri Spaak, was appointed to come up with detailed proposals.

The Spaak Report, as it was called, was prepared in less than a year, and in May of 1956 the Report was approved by the ministers of the Six. On the basis of that report, two treaties were prepared, one to establish the European Economic Community, the other to establish a European Atomic Energy Community (known as EURATOM). Both treaties were signed in Rome on March 25, 1957, and both were quickly approved by the respective parliaments. (Britain was again invited to join, and again declined.) On January 1, 1958, the European Economic Community (as well as EURATOM) came into being.

This time the Six did create a customs union (or at least an interim agreement leading to a customs union), within the definition of Article XXIV of the GATT. (1) The member states undertook to eliminate all duties on intra-Community trade—not all at once but according to a fixed schedule in three stages (Rome Treaty, Article 14(3)(a));[b] and (2) the member states agreed to adjust their external tariffs with a view to achieving a Common External Tariff within 12 or at most 15 years from January 1, 1958 (Article 23).[c] While there was some flexibility on the timing of the two aspects of economic integration, it was clear that the process was considered irreversible. In fact both aspects of formation of a customs union went faster than scheduled in the Treaty. By July 1, 1962, intra-Community tariffs on individual products had been reduced by 50 per cent rather than by the 30 per cent called for in the original schedule, and zero duties for intra-Community trade in industrial goods were achieved by July 1, 1968, 18 months ahead of the schedule set forth in the Treaty. As to the Common External Tariff, the move from stage 1 to stage 2 (see Article 23) was made effective on July 1, 1963 rather than December 31, 1965.[d] Leaving aside agricultural goods—a subject that was to create major conflicts within the Community and with the outside world, the Common External Tariff was complete at the same time as the total elimination of internal duties, July 1, 1968. The Treaty of Rome repeated (in Article 234)[e] the provision contained in the Treaty of Paris that rights and obligations resulting from agreements concluded before the Treaty shall

---

[b] Documents Supplement p. DS-139.

[c] Rome Treaty, Article 23, Documents Supplement p. DS-144.

[d] The stages referred to in both Article 14 and Article 23 are defined in Article 8 of the Rome Treaty.

[e] Documents Supplement, p. DS-224.

not be affected, and that in so far as such agreements are not compatible with the Treaty, the member states concerned "shall take all appropriate steps to eliminate any incompatibility found to exist." Looked at from the outside, this meant that the Rome Treaty realized the continuing obligation of member states under the GATT, and that to the extent these obligations would be impaired—for instance by increases in bound tariffs for some products in the process of establishing the Common External Tariff, the Community stood ready to negotiate under Article XXIV(6) of the GATT.

An in depth examination of the European Common Market is well beyond the scope of this volume. For present purposes, it is sufficient to note that some institutions—for instance the Court of Justice—were shared with the European Coal and Steel Community: others, for instance the Commission, were created on the ECSC model, but (as the change in name from "High Authority" suggests) perhaps somewhat reduced in power. The institution of Council of Ministers—i.e., the focus of the members' national interests—was also modeled on the corresponding body in the ECSC—but, it seems, gradually assumed relatively stronger powers.[f] The still evolving institutions and philosophies of the European Communities have stimulated an enormous body of writing; English and American writers have tended to focus on the novel place of the Community in international law: on the relation of the rulings of the Court of Justice to national law: and on the introduction of antitrust law, European style, designed (with expectable ambivalence) to see to it that elimination of governmental trade barriers would in fact result in increased flow of trade and not be thwarted by cartels or other anti-competitive practices.[g] We focus here on the so-called commercial policy aspect of the EEC, i.e., the posture of this new, powerful trading unit vis-à-vis the outside world.

---

[f] For the formal description of the institutions of the EEC, see Articles 4, 137–88; some of the authorities were modified by Articles 1–18 of the Merger Treaty, § 3.24(a) infra.

[g] For English language works by and for lawyers, see, e.g., E. Stein, P. Hay, and M. Waelbroeck, European Community Law and Institutions in Perspective (1976); H. Smit and P. Herzog, ed., The Law of the European Economic Community, A Commentary on the EEC Treaty (6 vols. 1976 and Supp.); and on competition law, H. M. Blake and J. A. Rahl, Business Regulation in the Common Market Nations, (4 vols. 1969). Each of these works, in turn has an extensive bibliography.

U.S. TRADE WITH THE EUROPEAN COMMUNITY[1]

[In billions of U.S. dollars]

	Exports	Imports	Balance
1958	3.9	2.6	1.3
1959	4.1	3.7	.4
1960	5.7	3.4	2.3
1961	5.6	3.3	2.3
1962	5.9	3.6	2.3
1963	6.4	3.8	2.6
1964	7.2	4.1	3.1
1965	7.2	4.9	2.3
1966	7.6	6.2	1.4
1967	8.0	6.5	1.5
1968	8.7	8.3	.4
1969	9.7	8.3	1.4
1970	11.3	9.2	2.1
1971	11.1	10.4	.7
1972	11.9	12.5	—.6
1973	16.7	15.6	1.1
1974[2]	21.8	18.9	2.9

[1] Exports are f.a.s. and imports are customs values, generally the market value in the foreign country.
[2] January-September at seasonally adjusted annual rates.
Source: U.S. Department of Commerce.

The chapter on commercial policy in the Treaty of Rome opens with a statement of intent "to contribute . . . to the harmonious development of world trade, the progressive abolition of restrictions on international trade, and the lowering of customs barriers."[h] To this end the Commission is authorized to negotiate with third countries[i] upon approval by the Council of Ministers of a mandate submitted by the

[h] Article 110, Documents Supplement p. DS-183.

[i] Article 113.

Commission itself. Since the Dillon Round of 1960–61, the EEC commission has in fact been in charge of all trade negotiations for member countries, both within the GATT and under other auspices, except in respect to East-West trade and arrangements concerning oil supplies, where politics has been considered too intimately involved for delegation to a supra-national and professional body.[1]

3.14—THE EUROPEAN ECONOMIC COMMUNITY AND THE GATT

As we have seen, the European Common Market qualifies generally under the definition of customs unions contained in Article XXIV(8) of the GATT. When the Rome Treaty was notified to the GATT by the member states in accordance with Article XXIV(7), the Six took the position that the treaty was in compliance with the General Agreement, and that in any event the numerous compromises reflected in the Treaty of Rome—e.g., between agricultural and industrial interests, between the colonial and non-colonial countries, and between low and high tariff nations—were not open to change in response to "judgment" by the GATT.[a] The Contracting Parties of the GATT, however, had numerous questions, not only with regard to Article XXIV but with regard to various other provisions of the General Agreement. How, for instance, would the Common External Tariff be constituted? Would there be merely an arithmetic average, as the Community proposed; or would there be a weighted average; or would there be an opportunity for examination of actual trade effects? Even harder, what about quotas? Would members in balance of payments difficulties be entitled to impose quantitative restrictions against outsiders, but not against other

---

[1] According to Article 114, the Council must conclude agreements negotiated by the Commission under authority of Article 111, acting unanimously in the first two stages, by a qualified majority thereafter. In practice, a representative of the Council is present, along with the delegates of the Commission, at important negotiations, and sometimes member states also send "silent representatives" to advise the Commission delegation. Agreements are initialled by a representative of the Commission, then formally signed by the President of the Council of Ministers, following approval by that body. Since a compromise in 1966 following a seven-month walkout by the French from all Community bodies, significant measures in the field of commercial policy have been adopted by unanimous vote. For a brief account of the 1965–66 crisis and the so-called Luxembourg Compromise, see Stein, Hay, and Waelbroeck, N. g supra, at 63–66.

[a] See generally, I. Frank, *The European Common Market*, Ch. IV, p. 160–201 (1961).

members of the Community? Still harder, would the Common Agricultural Policy, so vaguely sketched in Articles 38–47 of the Rome Treaty, set support prices at levels required to keep the least efficient producers in business, thereby diverting trade away from more efficient producers such as the United States and Canada? Finally, what about the EEC's proposals to deal with overseas and former overseas territories—essentially through free trade arrangements that could work to the disadvantage of non-members?

The substantive issues were genuine, and the answers by an Interim Committee of the EEC to a series of questions by the GATT not wholly satisfactory.[b] But as Professor Hudec has put it, the conformity of the Common Market with the GATT was an "oversized legal issue."[c] Forced to choose between the GATT and the Community, the member countries would probably have chosen the Community, and even for outsiders such as the United States, the success of the EEC was as important an element in overall foreign policy as was the success of the GATT. Thus a series of legal determinations under the GATT would have been ultimately counterproductive, if not disastrous. The Community asserted that its aims were consistent with those of the GATT; discrepancies should be discussed in terms of discouraging possible adverse effects on GATT members, not in terms of "legality" of the EEC or its measures.

If it was unrealistic to expect the Six to renegotiate the Treaty of Rome to conform with the details of GATT, perhaps GATT could have been renegotiated to conform to the realities of the 1960's, rather than to the quite incomplete understanding and experience that went into the draft of Article XXIV in 1947. But a renegotiation of the GATT—given its fragility and ambiguous acceptance in the United States and elsewhere—would have been very risky indeed.

What happened was a kind of de facto renegotiation, not of the General Agreement itself, but of the meaning given to the Agreement. "Pragmatic solutions"—i.e., diplomatic compromises—took the place of legal determinations.

---

[b] The discussions between the EEC and the GATT are summarized in GATT, *Basic Instruments and Selected Documents* (BISD) 6th Supp. 68–112 (1958).

[c] R. Hudec, *The GATT Legal System and World Trade Diplomacy*, p. 195 (1975).

Over time these pragmatic solutions spread to other areas. The Community, for instance, began to make "association agreements"[d] not only with present or former colonies, but with a series of the nations that had or wanted to have a special trading relationship with Western Europe. Greece was the first country to make application for association with the EEC. It argued that its principal export, tobacco, would be disadvantaged by the new Common External Tariff of 30 per cent, coupled with preferential arrangements granted by the Community to African countries formerly in the French colonial empire; while Greece had little to offer to the Community by way of reciprocal economic benefits, it could point to Eastern Europe as its principal alternative market, with at least an implied effect on Greece's role in the North Atlantic Treaty. Possibly for this reason the United States, which in general sought to preserve the principle of MFN and which also had tobacco exporters of its own to consider, did not oppose the Association Agreement between the Community and Greece.[e] The Treaty of Athens, (effective Nov. 1, 1962)[f] provided for a free trade area between Greece and the EEC, to be achieved over a ten-year period: That might pass muster under GATT, though whether a country could be a member both of a customs union and a free trade area under Article XXIV (or indeed a customs union itself could be a member of a free trade area) was, to say the least, unsettled. But looked at closely, the Association Agreement with Greece appears rather different: for one thing, Greece was entitled immediately to "intra-Community treatment" (i.e., duty free entry by 1968) for its products; for another, Greece could stretch out its commitments to accord duty-free treatment to products of the Community to 22 years for about 40 per cent of its imports from the Six; further, there was a series of protocols whereby the state tobacco monopolies in France and Italy undertook to make specific purchases from Greece, Greece could impose tariff quotas on certain imports from Commmunity countries, and the Community could adopt special "remedial action" if imports of citrus, grapes, or peaches rose above a certain level, deemed dangerous to Italy. . . . and so on. In short, the Association Agreement with Greece recognized that some countries could be hurt by formation of the Community unless they

---

[d] See Article 238 of the Rome Treaty, Documents Supplement p. DS-225.

[e] For a detailed description of the negotiations leading to the Association Agreement between Greece and the EEC, including this explanation of the United States attitude, see S. Henig, *External Relations of the European Community, Associations and Trade Agreements,* 72–91 (London 1971).

[f] 1963 O. J. 293 (Feb. 18, 1963).

were given special treatment; but it ignored—one could almost say defied—the principles of MFN and opposition to special deals.[g]

Following the agreement with Greece, the Community was faced with the demands for a similar agreement by Turkey, not only a political rival of Greece, but also an exporter of tobacco and citrus fruits to the Community. In 1963 the Community signed an agreement with Turkey, and thereafter Morocco and Tunisia, Malta and Cyprus, and Spain, Israel, Egypt and Lebanon all negotiated agreements with the EEC.[h] In each case at least some of the justification was that the applicant's position as a supplier to the Community had been impaired by the preceding agreement.[i] Each of the agreements was somewhat different in coverage, duration, and exceptions. The distinctions between "association" and bilateral trade agreements became blurred. As for the GATT, it investigated, but not very hard, while the EEC maintained that the essential principles were being maintained. Occasionally arguments were heard within the EEC about whether this or that feature in a proposed agreement was consistent with the GATT, especially in the more and more theoretical context of the difference between association (which the Community regarded as within Article XXIV) and preferential arrangements which might require a waiver under Article XXV. But no waivers were sought, and the degree of restraint exercised by the GATT rules—on these issues—became less and less apparent. By the end of the 1960's the European Economic Community had developed into a trading bloc made up of an inner group of six contiguous and essentially homogeneous industrial states, plus a widening group of weaker outside states that benefited from preferential (though not unrestricted) access to the Common Market, and in some instances from financial aid as well, in return for limited reciprocity but support for the Community in the GATT and other trading forums.

---

[g] The Agreement between Greece and the EEC was suspended in 1967 after the overthrow of the King and parliamentary democracy by the "colonels' regime"; it was reinstated when the colonels fell from power and democracy was restored in the context of the Cyprus crisis in the summer of 1974. On January 1, 1981 Greece became a full member of the Community.

[h] For a convenient citation to these agreements, see H. Smit and P. Herzog, ed., *The Law of the European Economic Community*, Vol. VI, pp. 6-344–6-348.4 (1981 ed.).

[i] Outside the Mediterranean area, Nigeria and the (no longer functioning) East African Community (Kenya, Tanzania, Uganda) also signed association agreements with the EEC.

3.15—EXPANSION OF THE COMMUNITY

Great Britain, as we saw, was from the first ambivalent about the movement toward European integration, or at least about its participation in that movement. Britain declined the invitation to join the Coal and Steel Community, and it declined the opportunity to join in the organization of the EEC in the mid-1950's. Typically the British public, and whichever party was out of power, preferred to emphasize the insular, as well as global traditions in Britain and the Commonwealth, while successive governments saw that Britain, (in contrast to the United States) was not likely to be strong enough in the long run to survive as an outsider the shifts in trading patterns taking place on the continent.

From the point of view of Western Europe, the smaller countries and Germany generally favored a wider free trade zone—either with Great Britain as a member of the EEC or in the context of a larger trading area that would include all the members of the OEEC.[a] When the negotiations for a large free trade area broke down, Great Britain organized a smaller European Free Trade Area (EFTA) of the so-called "outer seven" (Sweden, Denmark, Norway, Austria, Switzerland and Portugal, plus Great Britain), which would eliminate trade barriers *inter se* except for agricultural products, but would not attempt to build any kind of integrated institutions or harmonize other aspects of commercial policy.[b]

From the beginning, Europe "at sixes and sevens," as the British press referred to it, seemed to be a makeshift operation; some thought the British government was trying to undermine the Common Market, others that it was trying to prepare its own people for joining the European Community. In July of 1961, Britain (followed by Ireland, Norway, and Denmark) applied for membership in the EEC, and for 15 months serious negotiations took place on the conditions of entry— especially about such matters as Commonwealth preferences, association of former British colonies, import of dairy products, and the structure of the Common Agricultural Policy. The United States, in an effort to help, provided in the Trade Expansion Act of 1962 (§ 3.53 infra) a drastic expansion of the President's power to reduce tariffs

---

[a] I.e., all of Western Europe except Spain, plus Canada and the United States.

[b] For the GATT's response to this effort under Article XXIV(8), see GATT BISD 9th Supp. p. 70 (1961).

effective if, but only if, Britain joined the European Community.[c] In January, 1963, however, President de Gaulle announced his view that Britain was not ready for integration into Western Europe, because it was "too insular and maritime," and (at least by inference) too close to the United States.

The shock of this French veto was greater in Europe than in Britain, for it represented a unilateral, surprise stroke against a consensus—a triumph, as many thought, of nationalism over the spirit of integration on which the Community had been founded.[d] No doubt the veto did change the character of the Community as a political movement.[e] Britain renewed its application for membership in 1967, but the application was again vetoed by President de Gaulle just after the devaluation of the British pound.[f] Following de Gaulle's fall from power in 1969, the EEC agreed to revive efforts to enlarge the Community, and from July 1970 to January 1972 serious negotiations were again carried on over terms of accession of the same countries that had been rejected earlier. On January 1, 1973, Great Britain, Ireland, and Denmark became members of the European Communities; the government of Norway did not ratify the Treaty of Accession after the proposal failed to win a majority in a popular referendum. From 1973 on the Six became the Nine.[g] The remaining members of EFTA (the original members plus Finland and Iceland) all signed free trade agreements with the enlarged Community.

---

[c] Trade Expansion Act § 211, Documents Supplement p. DS-252. The section is discussed in § 3.53 at Ns. 1–o, and § 3.64.

[d] Germany's Minister of Economy (and later Chancellor) Ludwig Erhard, said "This is a black day for Europe. The Common Market is now only a mechanism and no longer a living thing."

[e] Indeed an even more serious crisis occurred in 1965, also brought on by President de Gaulle, when France's representatives were withdrawn from all participation in the Community's institutions for seven months in protest over financing the Common Agricultural Policy, and more generally over the excessive role, as France saw it, of the Commission. See § 3.13 N. j supra.

[f] See Volume IV of this series, A. Lowenfeld, The International Monetary System, § 3 (2d ed. 1984).

[g] Britain's successful negotiations for entry into the EEC had been conducted by the Conservative government of Prime Minister Heath; when Labour returned to power in 1974, the government demanded renegotiation of some of the terms of entry, with a view to submitting continued membership to a popular referendum in the summer of 1975. The renegotiations were held, were pronounced a success by Prime Minister Wilson, and a referendum approved British membership in the Community by almost exactly a two-thirds majority.

"It's Not THAT Common!"

Ray Osrin. *The Plain Dealer* (Cleveland), 1967.

§ 3.2—Notes and Questions

3.21—The place of customs unions in the postwar regime of international trade, as we have seen, cannot be explained solely in terms of economics. Considerations of history, politics, and the ambiguous and incomplete acceptance of the GATT itself are at least as important in explaining the origin and evolution of Article XXIV as is economic theory. But in considering the legal aspects of the rise of the European Common Market, as well as the European Community's attitude toward the GATT, some economic theory is highly instructive. The critical element, as we saw, is whether the customs union (or free trade area) leads to more trade—and therefore to more efficient allocation of resources—or simply diverts trade from more efficient producers outside to less efficient producers inside the customs union.

(a) Suppose Xandia and Patria agree to form a Common Market. If they now exchange goods that were not subject to trade before elimination of the trade barriers between them, Patria and Xandia will both—as we saw in the example of lamps and tables (pp. 3–5)—be better off, raising the level of economic activity, output, and demand. The combined increase in prosperity will, in turn, stimulate both exports from and imports to the Xan-Pat Union. So reads the prediction (requirement?) of Article XXIV(4).

(b) But suppose a different outcome. Suppose that before formation of the common market, Patria had a tariff on typewriters of 10 per cent. Tertian producers offered typewriters at $100 landed cost, and Xandian producers offered comparable typewriters at $106. So long as both products were subject to the same tariff, Patria's imports of typewriters would come predominantly from Tertia, and would sell in Patria at $110 (plus distributors' mark-up). But once Xandia joins the Xan-Pan Union, its producers' typewriters can come into Patria at $106, while Tertia's will continue to come in at $110 including the tariff. Thus Patria's imports will be diverted from the most efficient supplier in Tertia to a less efficient supplier in Xandia. The consumer in Patria may have made a small saving (that is if the elimination of the tariff is passed on and not retained by the distributor); from the point of view of efficient allocation of resources, however, the effect is negative.[a]

(c) To continue the example in (b), if Patria's duty on typewriters had been bound under the GATT, the value of that binding to Tertia, (which directly or indirectly had paid for it) will have been impaired, even if the rate of duty has not been changed. It is not clear that the GATT provides a remedy for Tertia, other than the general momentum and inducement to negotiate toward reduction of tariff barriers.

(d) Finally, since Xandia and Patria are supposed to average their duties,[b] it may well be that Patria's duty on typewriters will go up—say

---

[a] This example, which seems easy to understand once it is explained, was introduced into economic literature by Prof. Viner only after the GATT was negotiated. J. Viner, *The Customs Union Issue*, 41–56. (1950). The analysis of when the example is (b) and when the assumption of (a) is more likely to occur was carried further by J. Meade, *The Theory of Customs Unions* (1955) and B. Belassa, *The Theory of Economic Integration* (1961). For more detailed discussion in the context of a law review article, see Dam, "Regional Economic Arrangements and the GATT: The Legacy of a Misconception," 30 U. Chi. L. Rev. 615, esp. 622–35 (1963).

[b] See GATT Article XXIV(5)(a), Documents Supplement p. DS-46.

to 12.5 per cent.[c] This result may—or may not—be cured by reductions negotiated under Article XXIV(6); even so, as we saw in (b) and (c), the effect on Tertia may still be adverse.[d]

3.22—(a) The GATT, as pointed out first by Professor Viner, made no attempt to distinguish between the two prospects—trade creation and trade diversion—here discussed. When one moves away from concentrating on any given product such as typewriters and views the whole range of traded items, would you expect that removal of some restraints (inside the union) and a promise not to raise others (the customs union's external tariffs) will result in more efficient allocation of the world's resources?

(b) Note that an affirmative answer to question (a) is essential to the conclusion urged by Wilcox (p. 44 *supra*) that preferential arrangements are bad, because they are partial, while customs unions (though equally discriminatory) are not bad, because they cover "all the trade" and hence permit the trade creating to outweigh the trade diverting effects, to the overall gain of comparative advantage.

(c) How might a non-member—Tertia, the United States, or the GATT secretariat—encourage the expansive and discourage the restrictive tendency?

3.23—(a) Article XXIV (5), as we saw, requires that the common external tariffs of a customs union "shall not on the whole be higher or more restrictive" than the pre-existing duties of the member states.[e] How should Patria and Xandia—or the European Common Market—go about meeting this obligation? Should they (i) go item by item and average the duties of each of the constituents on each product? (ii) If so, should the average be weighted in some way? Note that if tariffs were weighted in proportion to the amount of trade moving over the tariff, the more successful a tariff were in restricting imports, the less it would weigh in the averaging process. If the tariffs were weighted in proportion to consumption of the item in question in the importing

---

[c] This is not unlikely in the stylized example here developed, where apparently Xandia, but not Patria, is a major producer of typewriters.

[d] For a brief account of the so-called Article XXIV (6) negotiations between the EEC and the other GATT members, see § 3.52 at N. r *infra*.

[e] Note that this obligation applies not only to bound duties, but to all previously unbound duties as well.

country, the larger the country the more its tariffs would count in the balance.

(b) Look at Article 19 of the Treaty of Rome[f] in the light of the above questions. Note that Article 19 adopts the approach of unweighted averaging—but then introduces a series of qualifications. Weighting seems to have been rejected in part because agreement could not be reached on any given technique, in part because each of the formulas suggested implied a future pattern of trade for the customs union similar to that of the past—an assumption contrary to the very purpose of formation of the union.[g]

(c) When the Treaty of Rome was being negotiated, BENELUX and German tariffs were, in general, relatively low, French and Italian tariffs relatively high. But apart from this generalization, the trade interests of the states that were about to embark on economic integration occasionally diverged to a substantial extent. One can get an idea once more of the ambivalence—and sheer complication—of trade negotiations in seeing how Article 19 was drafted.[h] On the one hand, some of the countries —and industries within the countries—were convinced that the level of protection to which they had become accustomed would be destroyed. Not only would an industry in Italy that had prospered behind a protective wall now be faced with competition from within the Common Market; it might also be faced with increased imports from outside—say Great Britain or the United States. On the other hand, some industries— particularly in the Netherlands—that relied on imports for their raw materials, might now be faced with increased costs, without greater protection for their finished product. In part, of course, the phasing over a 12-year period was designed to ameliorate such problems. But since France and Italy would be making the greatest "concessions", they received a kind of compensation by substituting somewhat higher figures in the averaging process for the duties actually applicable. (This was the purpose of List A). The other lists, each of which provided for a ceiling on tariff rates, were designed to afford assurance to importing countries (especially BENELUX) that certain products would not be subjected to

---

[f] Documents Supplement p. DS-142.

[g] See I. Frank, *The European Common Market,* 102–105 (1961).

[h] This note is based on the more detailed discussion in I. Frank, N. g *supra* at 102–110 (1961).

tariffs in excess of the amounts stated.[i] For certain very sensitive products averaging was not used at all, but the duties were set by negotiation and recorded in the treaty itself. This list included commodities of particular interest to overseas territories of member countries, such as coffee, bananas, sugar, and cotton, which would, of course also be of great importance to non-member countries, especially among the less developed countries.[j] On some 70 products, no agreement could be reached at all, and these were left by Article 20 to future negotiations. An interesting illustration of the conflict of interests among the six reflected in Article 20 was aluminum.[k] BENELUX had no production of primary aluminum, and zero duty; France, Germany, and Italy all protected aluminum, with duties of 20, 12, and 25 per cent respectively. Since Belgium and the Netherlands used aluminum but did not produce it, they had no interest in agreeing to pay a duty designed to protect domestic industries in the other member countries. Eventually the EEC did set a tariff on aluminum at 9 per cent, with year to year permission to Belgium and Germany to import aluminum at 5 per cent.

(d) Note finally the relation between the level of duties and the timing of moves toward the common external tariff established by Article 23 of the Treaty of Rome. Where the disparity between the common rate and individual rates was less than 15 per cent up or down, the common tariff was to be implemented by the end of the first stage; where the disparity was greater, it was to be reduced by 30 per cent at the end of the first stage, by another 30 per cent at the end of the second stage, and to be entirely eliminated at the end of the third stage.[l]

(e) Would you regard the techniques adopted under Articles 19 and 20 of the Treaty of Rome, taken together, (i) as sensible; (ii) as consistent with the GATT?

---

[i] List B included 80 commodities, mostly raw materials, that would not be subjected to tariffs in excess of 3 percent; List C included 142 semi-finished products, not to be subjected to tariffs in excess of 10 per cent; List D was made up of inorganic chemicals and List E of organic chemicals, subject to duty ceilings of 15 and 25 per cent respectively.

[j] The negotiated duty on sugar was fixed at 80 per cent; the duty on petroleum, on the other hand, was set at 0.

[k] See Frank, N. g supra at 106–7 and the GATT Working Party Report there cited.

[l] For a detailed account of the problems of construction of the common tariff, see Menneus, "The Common Customs Tariff of the European Economic Community," 1 J. World Trade Law 73 (1967).

3.24—(a) For the first decade of its existence, the European Economic Community existed side by side with the European Coal and Steel Community, (as well as with EURATOM), sharing some institutions—notably the Court of Justice and the Parliamentary Assembly—but with separate executives (i.e. the Commission and the High Authority), separate Councils of Ministers, and separate staffs for these two bodies.[m] The reason for existence of the separate institutions seems to have been that, after the defeat of the treaty that would have created the European Defense Community, the founders of the European integration movement did not want to increase the risks which any given treaty ran before the parliaments of member states by linking it to any of the others.[n] But as the European Economic Community gained in strength and confidence, it made sense to merge the three communities into a single European Community. In part, this step was accomplished through the so-called Merger Treaty effective on July 1, 1967,[o] which established a single Commission and a single Council of the European Communities.[p] However, the treaties (as contrasted with the institutions of the three Communities) were not merged, so that in principle the single Commission, Council, and Court of Justice administer different treaties, depending on whether they are concerned with coal and steel, atomic matters, or the rest. In practice, of course, many issues—for instance energy, financial policy, and foreign trade policy—cut across the subject matter of all three treaties, as do such matters as industrial property, competition policy, and company law. The dominant models clearly were the Rome Treaty and the organs of the EEC; however, on certain issues, including regulation of price and production, the Treaty of Paris creating the Coal and Steel Community gave greater powers to the Community organizations than did the Rome Treaty, and greater power to

---

[m] In fact the Council of Ministers under the Rome Treaty and the Special Council under the Paris Treaty were usually made up of the same persons; but the staffs were distinct, and coal and steel questions were discussed separately from matters coming under the EEC and EURATOM treaties.

[n] See E. Stein, P. Hay, and M. Waelbroeck, *European Community Law and Institutions in Perspective*, pp. 30–31 (1976).

[o] Treaty Establishing a Single Council and a Single Commission of the European Communities, signed at Brussels April 8, 1965, 1967 O. J. No. 152, reproduced in Stein, Hay, and Waelbroeck N. n *supra*, Documentary Annex p. 245.

[p] For details of the changes this entailed in such matters as the number of members of these commissions, the duration of their term of office, the term of office of the President of the Council, the consequence of abstention for a vote requiring unanimity, and other similar issues, see, e.g., Weil, "The Merger of the Institutions of the European Community," 61 Am. J. Int'l. L. 57 (1967).

the Commission (High Authority) to act without express approval of the Council of Ministers.[q] The Commission did in fact exercise the power to set prices and production quotas in the late 1960's, and early 1970's with respect to steel (and earlier with respect to coal) as market conditions began to reflect long term world-wide surplus.[r]

(b) Apart from the creation itself of a supra-national economic regulatory body having direct impact on enterprises, the most remarkable aspect of the Treaty of Paris was the scope of the powers conferred on the High Authority (later the Commission) over competition policy. In fact, as was frequently pointed out, the member states delegated powers to the Community that they did not, for the most part, possess themselves—on the one hand to break up and punish efforts at market division, price fixing and other anticompetitive aspects of the cartelized coal and steel industries, on the other hand to encourage "rationalization," including mergers and in some instances joint operations.[s] The overriding criterion was that elimination of governmental trade barriers inside the Six (later Nine) should not be counteracted by private trade barriers such as cartels, monopolies, or abuse of dominant position. But arguments of efficiency through scale, of equalizing competition within the Community among the major units, and strengthening the Community vis-à-vis the United States and Japan, seemed to become more persuasive with the High Authority and Commission than similar arguments in the United States—especially in the late 1960's and thereafter.[t]

(c) The High Authority (and later the Commission) took an interesting middle ground between a regulatory and a planning agency. It collected a great mass of information from firms in the coal and steel industries, as well as from external market reports and general economic data. On the basis of this information, it made semi-annual estimates of capacity and demand, broken down by areas and product lines. The High

---

[q] See e.g. Paris Treaty Articles 57–58, 60–61, Documents Supplement pp. DS-116–17, 119–21.

[r] See §§ 6.3–.4 infra.

[s] See Articles 85 and 86 for authority directly applicable to firms and Article 87 for authority applicable to actions by member states.

[t] For a detailed account of the Community's thinking in this area, compared with similar questions in the United States, see Mueller, "The Policy of the European Coal and Steel Community towards Mergers and Agreements of Steel Companies," 14 Antitrust Bull. 413 (1969).

Authority (Commission) not only gave advice on proposed investments, but if it approved a contemplated investment, it was prepared to give financial assistance in the form of loans or guarantees of credit. If the project did not meet with the High Authority's approval, it would be discouraged and not supported, though usually not prohibited.[u] At the same time, the ECSC seems to have followed a policy of equalization and integration among the members, so that in the first decade Germany and Italy, the defeated and (at the outset) least advanced countries from the point of view of coal and steel, were enabled to catch up and modernize. The ECSC also helped to finance industries not directly under its jurisdiction but related to the purposes of the treaty, such as construction of workers' apartments to support new coal or steel projects.

Part of the ECSC's funds came from levies on the production of coal and steel (Articles 49–50); the major sources of funds used to make loans and support construction and modernization, however, came from loans. In the early years the ECSC borrowed primarily in the United States, both from the Export-Import Bank of the United States and through bonds sold on the New York market.

(d) Trade in coal and steel within the Community increased enormously in the early years of the ECSC, as national barriers came down. Prices and wages, while not quite identical, moved close to a Community-wide level, subject to the fluctuations in exchange rates among members of the Six, which despite determined efforts could not be maintained within a fixed range.[v] As we saw, the Treaty of Paris did not, like the Rome Treaty, require a common external tariff; it provided, however, that the Council could, by unanimous decision on a proposal from the High Authority, set a minimum/maximum range within which national tariffs had to be set (Article 72). In practice, the ECSC negotiated as a unit with the United States as early as 1956, and the Six adopted a common negotiating tariff for purposes of negotiating in the Kennedy Round in the mid 1960's. (§ 3.7 infra).

(e) We shall have further occasion to look at the Coal and Steel Community as we examine the world crisis in steel in succeeding sections of this volume. Consider, on the basis of the above, whether the waiver

---

[u] But see the later developments § 6.3 infra.

[v] For the experience with the European "snake," see Vol. IV of this series, A. Lowenfeld, The International Monetary System, § 7.2 at N. j and § 7.42 (2d ed. 1984).

given to the ECSC in 1952 (i) was proper, (ii) was lived up to; (iii) should be revised. Does the fact that the European Coal and Steel Community blended into the Common Market make the case for the waiver stronger or weaker?

3.25—Putting aside the various side arrangements, association agreements and the like with Mediterranean nations, former colonies, and other developing countries,[a] the European Economic Community on the whole kept the promise that overall trade would be increased and that trade creation would outweigh trade diversion.[b] An important exception was agriculture.

(a) When the Common Market was in the planning stage, there was a good deal of discussion about whether agriculture should be included at all. But the requirements of Article XXIV of the GATT, the importance of agriculture in the total economy of the members of the Community, and the fact that France, which feared competition in industrial products from Germany and the Low Countries, stood to gain from greater exchange of agricultural products, all led to the decision to include agriculture in the Treaty of Rome, but under separate and substantially different provisions (Articles 38–47).[c] Industrial trade could by and large be left to the pull of market forces, with the task of the Community organs largely defined as seeing to it that those forces were not improperly distorted.[d] In contrast, agricultural production in all of the members of the Community (as well as in most other countries of the world) had traditionally been strongly affected by government purchases, price supports, production controls, loan programs, marketing quotas, and the like, covering of necessity both domestic and international trade.[e] The framers of the Rome Treaty saw their task with respect

---

[a] See pp. 58–59 *supra*.

[b] See Table II-2, p. DS-758.

[c] Documents Supplement pp. DS-150–57.

[d] See e.g., Articles 85–86 on which the rules of competition of the Community are based.

[e] For a brief survey of the regulation of agriculture in Western Europe before the Treaty of Rome, see the Preliminary Observations on Articles 38–47 in H. Smit and P. Herzog, *The Law of the European Economic Community, A Commentary on the EEC Treaty*, Vol I. pp. 2-186–92 (1976). The entire commentary on the Title on Agriculture in that volume, prepared by Prof. S. Riesenfeld, is highly instructive and is heavily drawn on in this note. For an earlier discussion of the Common Agricultural Policy by the same author, see Riesenfeld, "Common

to agriculture not as providing for elimination of government intervention, but as making possible a common governmental policy (as contrasted with separate policies of the member states), designed to increase productivity, and to safeguard farmers' incomes, consumers' supplies of food, and relative stability in the price levels of essential commodities. (See Rome Treaty, Article 39). When the Rome Treaty went into effect on January 1, 1958—and indeed even four years later—the many problems of the Common Agricultural Policy had not been worked out. But by about 1962—63, the outlines of the policy had emerged, subject to continuing variations and complications.[f]

(b) The central focus of the Common Agricultural Policy is grains— wheat, rye, barley and corn. Other products, such as meat and poultry, are treated to a large extent as grain in semi-processed form. Each year the Council of Ministers establishes a *target price* for each product. This price is subject to serious controversy and heated negotiations among the members, because, in general, a higher price is favorable to relatively inefficient (typically German) producers and a lower price is favorable to relatively efficient (typically French) producers. Once the price is fixed, however, it is uniform throughout the Community for the harvest year in question.[g] In order to attain the target price, the Council also sets an *intervention price*, 5–10 per cent below the target price, at which government intervention agencies (using Community funds) stand ready to purchase any domestic grain offered.[h] To protect the target price from foreign, lower-priced competition, a *threshold price* is fixed by the Council on the basis of the target price minus transport and handling costs between Duisburg, Germany, the principal deficit area, and Rotterdam, the principal port of entry. The difference between

---

Market for Agricultural Products and Common Agricultural Policy in the European Economic Community" in W. LaFave and P. Hay, eds., *International Trade, Investment, and Organization* p. 262 (1967).

[f] According to Prof. Riesenfeld, more than 90 per cent of all acts of the Community institutions have been concerned with various aspects of the Common Agricultural Policy. 1 Smit and Herzog, N. e *supra* ¶ 40.02.

[g] In its earlier versions, there were separate target prices for the different countries within a range set by the Council. The entry of Great Britain, Ireland and Denmark has again created problems of variation and transition. For present purposes only the basic and stereotypical plan is set forth in the text.

[h] To be precise, a basic intervention price is fixed with reference to Duisburg, in the German Ruhr, and derived intervention prices are fixed at other market centers within the Community, typically somewhat lower than the basic intervention price.

the most favorable offered price c.i.f. Rotterdam (i.e., the world market price) and the threshold price is made up by a *variable levy* paid to the Community. Thus world market price + variable levy + handling and transport costs to Duisburg = target price. If the world market price goes down, the variable levy goes up, in order to maintain the target price.[i] If oversupply results as a consequence of a high target price (as happened from time to time) "refunds" are available to exporters from the Community, in principle based on the difference between the Community price and the world market price.

(c) No provision of the GATT expressly prohibits the variable levy system, apparently because no one had thought about a system that worked just the way the Common Agricultural Policy does. The variable levy has aspects of a quota system, in that the outsider becomes the residual supplier, but no quantitative restrictions are directly imposed (compare GATT Article XI); it has aspects of a tariff, but the amount of the duty is inversely, and not directly, proportional to the price of the product to be imported (compare GATT Article VII), and there seems to be no possibility of binding the duty (compare Article II).[j] More generally, the target price/variable levy system is designed to insulate inefficient producers from the outside world in order to achieve (or approach) autarchy for the Community, precisely the opposite of an international trading system based on comparative advantage.

Should (i) the GATT, or (ii) the principal agricultural exporters, led by the United States, have launched a major campaign against the Common Agricultural Policy?

(d) There were major interests in the United States who believed

---

[i] To put some numbers on the statement in the text, suppose the target price for ordinary wheat in a given marketing year is $125 per metric ton; the intervention price will be, say, 8 per cent lower or $115; and the threshold price will be somewhere in between, say $120. If wheat from North America arrives at $100 c.i.f. Rotterdam, a levy (like a tariff) of $20/ton will have to be paid to bring the cargo into the stream of commerce; if the shipment is to be consumed in or near Duisburg, the transport and handling charges will bring the price of the imported wheat to $125 or a little above. If the North American exporter lowers his price to $95, the levy will increase to $25, but the importer and consumer will pay the same as before. In contrast, a French or German producer may find it advantageous to cut his price somewhat in order to attain a larger share of the market.

[j] Note also Article X of GATT, requiring advance notice and publication of all regulations.

that a strong initiative should be launched against the Common Agricultural Policy in 1962–63 before it became too entrenched. Others, however, eventually including President Kennedy, sought to avoid a major confrontation with the European Community, primarily because such a confrontation might jeopardize the Kennedy Round of trade negotiations in which the United States and the EEC would be the principal protagonists. Also, the United States had its own record of agricultural price supports and quotas, especially on meat and dairy products. To be sure, some of the United States programs had come in under the Protocol of Provisional Application[k] and some under the carefully drafted (by the United States) exception in Article XI(2)(c).[l] While the United States was complying with the letter of the GATT, including a very broad waiver granted in 1955 without limit of time,[m] it was not in the best of positions to assert comparative advantage in respect to grains, but prior rights and waivers in respect to butter and cheese.

(e) As the Community had predicted, the actual sales of most grains and other agricultural products from North America to the EEC countries rose in the 1960's, due to the rise in living standards and purchasing power in Western Europe, though almost certainly not as much as they would have risen in the absence of the Common Agricultural Policy.[n] However, on one commodity, frozen broiler chickens, the United States share of the market dropped sharply after imposition of the Common Poultry Policy, a derivative of the policy on grains. The United States, whose share of the Market had risen sharply in the period 1958–61 as

---

[k] § 2.12 at N. p *supra.*

[l] Documents Supplement p. DS-21. Eric Wyndham White, who was for many years the Executive Secretary and guiding spirit of the GATT, commented that although Article XI was "largely tailor-made to United States requirements . . ., the tailor cut the cloth too fine." Address at Europe House, London, May 1960, quoted in K. Dam, *The GATT, Law and International Economic Organization,* at 260 (1970).

[m] See Waiver Granted to the United States in connection with Import Restrictions Imposed under Section 22 of the United States Agricultural Adjustment Act (of 1933) as amended, March 5, 1955 GATT, *Basic Instruments and Selected Documents* (BISD) 3rd Supp. pp. 32, 141 (1955). For an account of earlier disputes involving United States restrictions on imports of dairy products, see R. Hudec, *The GATT Legal System and World Trade Diplomacy,* Ch. 16 (1975).

[n] Between 1962 and 1972, U.S. agricultural exports to the EC-6 rose 12 per cent in items subject to the variable levy, and 134 per cent in items not subject to the variable levy. For this and other comparisons, see *The Common Agricultural Policy of the European Community,* Exec. Branch GATT Study No. 12. Sen. Comm. on Finance, Subcomm. on Int'l Trade, 93rd Cong., 1st Sess. (1973).

American producers came up with a low-price, mass produced product, launched a sharp protest, threatened retaliation, and eventually participated in a kind of arbitration before a GATT panel,—the so-called "Chicken War."[o] While the United States was permitted to withdraw some concessions that it had previously negotiated in favor of European countries,[p] no basic judgment was rendered, or indeed sought, as to the compatibility of the Common Agricultural Policy with the GATT.[q] The EEC's regulation on poultry, and the Common Agricultural Policy itself, remained in place.[r]

3.26—(a) The Common Agricultural Policy was the subject in the early 1970's of an interesting litigation before the Court of Justice of the European Communities, testing the standing of the GATT as an international obligation of the Community,[a] and the view of the Community's Court of Justice of the character of the obligations under the GATT.[b] In implementation of a regulation first issued in 1962 concerning the Progressive Establishment of a Common Organization of the Market in Fruits and Vegetables,[c] the Council of Ministers adopted a regulation in December 1969 on coordination and standardization of imports of fruits and vegetables from outside the Community. The regulation, in principle, prohibited quantitative restrictions on imports, but authorized "appropriate measures" if one of the covered products—in this case eating apples—suffered, or was threatened with, serious disturbance capable of jeopardizing the objectives of the CAP. On the basis of a finding of a "crisis situation" with respect to apples in four of the countries of the

---

[o] For a detailed account of the Chicken War, see A. Chayes, T. Ehrlich, A. Lowenfeld, *International Legal Process*, Vol. I, Ch. IV (1968).

[p] It chose brandy and light panel trucks.

[q] Uruguay did ask the Contracting Parties for a legal ruling in 1961 and 1962 on whether the variable levy violated the obligations of the General Agreement, but the Contracting Parties declined to rule. See GATT, BISD 11th Supp. 95 at 100 (1963); see also Hudec, N. m *supra*, pp. 220–222.

[r] Agriculture was discussed in the Kennedy Round, but none of the problems connected with the legality of the Common Agricultural Policy were solved. The United States avoided formally recognizing the CAP, and the European Economic Community got by without any declaration critical of the CAP on legal grounds.

[a] See Rome Treaty, Article 234 and Text § 3.13 at N. e *supra*.

[b] *International Fruit Company N.V. et al v. Produktschap voor Groenten en Fruit*, cases 21–24/72, [1972] E.C.R. 1219 (12 Dec. 1972).

[c] Regulation No. 23 of 4 April 1962, O.J. English Special Ed. 1959–1962, p. 97.

EEC and a "difficult situation" in the two others,[d] the Commission in March of 1970 issued a regulation requiring that apples could be brought into the territory of the Community only by holders of import certificates, and that these would be issued week by week on the basis of the situation at the time. Importers were to receive certificates in any given month up to a maximum of 80 per cent of their imports of apples in the corresponding month of the previous year.

Plaintiffs, four fruit importing companies from Rotterdam, applied to the relevant agency in the Netherlands for import certificates for apples; their applications were rejected, apparently because they had not met the deadline for filing. Plaintiffs challenged the action on several grounds, among them on the ground that the regulation was contrary to Article XI of GATT.[e] The Netherlands Appeal Court in Economic Matters referred the question to the Court of Justice of the European Communities, and that court held—for the first time—that it did have jurisdiction under Article 177 of the Rome Treaty[f] to determine whether the regulation or action in question was consistent with international law.

(b) The Court of Justice held that the GATT was binding on the Community, because the members of the EEC could not, by concluding a treaty among themselves, withdraw from their obligations to third countries; moreover, this view was confirmed by the text and objectives of the Rome Treaty itself (Articles 110, 111, 113, and 234) as well as the declarations made by the Member States when they presented the Rome Treaty to the CONTRACTING PARTIES of the GATT in accordance with the obligations of GATT Article XXIV.

---

[d] Evidently, production had increased over a long period of time and prices had dropped below a specific threshold. This and other facts not given in the Court's opinion are taken from the opinion of the Advocate General in [1972] E.C.R. at 1230.

[e] The other grounds, not here relevant but interesting to students of administrative law, were (i) that the Regulation was inconsistent with Articles 40(3) and 113 of the Rome Treaty; and (ii) that the licensing function had been improperly delegated to a domestic producers' group. (Compare a similar challenge to a tomato marketing order in the United States—*Walter Holm Company v. Hardin*, 449 F.2d 1009 (D.C. Cir. 1971). The first point was rejected by the EC Court of Justice [1971] E.C.R. 411 (13 May 1971); the second was originally brought before a Netherlands court and referred by it to the EC Court of Justice, which sustained the delegation as one to be decided by each member state under its own laws. [1971] E.C.R. 1107 (15 Dec. 1971).

[f] Documents Supplement p. DS-203.

That brought the Court of Justice to the question whether the GATT, and particularly Article XI, conferred rights on citizens of the Community.

For this purpose, the spirit, the general scheme and the terms of the General Agreement must be considered . . . .

This agreement which, according to its preamble, is based on the principle of negotiations undertaken on the basis of "reciprocal and mutually advantageous arrangements" is characterized by the great flexibility of its provisions, in particular those conferring the possibility of derogation, the measures to be taken when confronted with exceptional difficulties and the settlement of conflicts between the contracting parties.[g]

The Court pointed to the consultation provisions of Articles XXII of the GATT, the waiver provisions of Article XXV,[h] and the dispute settlement provisions of Article XXIII.

Those measures include, for the settlement of conflicts, written recommendations or proposals which are to be "given sympathetic consideration," investigations possibly followed by recommendations, consultations between or decisions of the CONTRACTING PARTIES, including that of authorizing certain contracting parties to suspend the application to any others of any obligations or concessions under the General Agreement and, finally, in the event of such suspension, the power of the party concerned to withdraw from that agreement.

Finally, where by reason of an obligation assumed under the General Agreement or of a concession relating to a benefit, some producers suffer or are threatened with serious damage, Article XIX gives a contracting party power unilaterally to suspend the obligation and to withdraw or modify the concession, either after consulting the contracting parties jointly and failing agreement between the contracting parties concerned, or even, if the matter is urgent and on a temporary basis, without prior consultation.

---

[g] [1972] E.C.R. at 1227.

[h] Indeed, the Advocate General (a kind of permanent friend of the Court) had called attention in his presentation to the waiver granted to the United States in 1955 § [3.25 N. m *supra*], "covering the greater part of its agricultural policy." [1972] E.C.R. at 1239.

Those factors are sufficient to show that, when examined in such a context, Article XI of the General Agreement is not capable of conferring on citizens of the Community rights which they can invoke before the courts.[i]

Accordingly, the Court of Justice, having given a small boost to the GATT, rejected the action of the plaintiffs not because the import licensing scheme with respect to apples was consistent with the General Agreement, but because the Court could not tell whether it was or was not, and whether some other form of settlement—waiver, compensation, or perhaps simply disregard—might have been applied had the issue been raised by a state in the GATT itself.[j]

*   *   *

Putting together the unwillingness of the members of the GATT to confront the Common Agricultural Policy directly, the unwillingness of the EEC to be guided by the GATT in developing its rules of trade in agricultural products, and the unwillingness of the Court of Justice of the European Communities to step in where others feared to tread,[k] Professor Jackson was clearly right: with respect to agriculture, at least, the law had not kept pace with the technology of trade protection.[l]

§ 3.3—Japan, the Improbable Giant[a]

When the economic arrangements for the post-war world were being formulated, Japan was not only not a participant, but was a defeated

---

[i] [1972] E.C.R. at 1228.

[j] For a strong criticism of this decision, primarily in terms of EEC law, see Waelbroeck, "Effect of GATT within the Legal Order of the EEC," 8 J. World Trade Law 614 (1974).

[k] Note that an American jurist might have characterized the issue before the court in *International Fruit* as a political question.

[l] J. Jackson, *World Trade and the Law of GATT* 521 (1969).

[a] Much of the material in this note is drawn from H. Patrick and H. Rosovsky, ed., *Asia's New Giant: How the Japanese Economy Works* (Brookings 1976), a 900-page compendium of studies by American and Japanese scholars covering nearly all aspects of post-war Japan's economic development. Another, somewhat earlier, compendium of essays on Japan useful in preparation of this note was I. Frank, ed., *The Japanese Economy in International Perspective* (Committee for Econ. Development 1975).

country with its industrial base in ruins and its resource base largely cut off. A quarter century later, Japan, a nation of 100 million people crowded on four islands with an area less than that of California, had become the world's third largest industrial country,[b] a leading power in international commerce, and possessor of one of the strongest (and fastest growing) economies. In the five years between 1965 and 1970, Japan actually doubled its industrial capital stock, a feat never before accomplished by an advanced industrial nation.[c] Starting as an exporter chiefly of low-price, labor-intensive products such as toys, textiles, and pottery, Japan became in the 1960's the world's largest exporter of capital- and technology-intensive products such as steel, ships (especially super tankers and bulk carriers), optical equipment, and consumer electronics, and a major competitor in heavy machinery and sophisticated business machines. On the import side, Japan had by the end of the 1960's become the world's largest national market for raw materials— nearly $8 billion in 1969, as compared with $6.2 billion for the United States, $5.4 for West Germany, and just under $5 billion for Great Britain. In contrast, Japan imported less in manufactured goods than Belgium, the Netherlands, or Italy.[d]

The rest of the world did not quite know how to react to the Japanese "miracle." Were the Japanese doing something right that others could emulate? Were they violating the international code of commercial conduct? Or were they demonstrating practices that were not forbidden but perhaps should be? These questions came to a head in the monetary field in the early 1970's;[e] they came to a head in the area of trade in the mid- and late 1970's in textiles, electronic appliances, and most critically in steel.

3.31—JAPAN'S ECONOMIC GROWTH

By any measure, Japan's growth rate in the quarter century following

---

[b] Behind the United States and the Soviet Union, ahead of West Germany, France, and all other countries. In per capita gross national product, Japan at $3,700 still ranked behind West Germany and France, but ahead of Great Britain and Italy, and roughly three-fifths of that of the United States.

[c] Patrick and Rosovsky, N. a *supra* at vii. By capital stock is meant plant and equipment and other industrial factors of production.

[d] *Japan's Economic Expansion and Foreign Trade, 1955 to 1970*, p. 40, (GATT Studies in International Trade No. 2, 1971).

[e] See, e.g., Vol. IV of this series, A. Lowenfeld, *The International Monetary System*, §§ 5.3–5.4 (2d ed. 1984).

the end of the American occupation was extraordinary. Prime Minister Ikeda announced in 1961 that Japan would double its national income in a decade, which would have required an annual growth rate of 7.2 per cent. In fact from 1959 to the early 1970's, the Japanese economy grew at an annual average rate of 10.8 per cent, while other industrial countries were growing at rates of from 7.2 per cent per annum (West Germany) to 3.8 per cent (United States), to 2.3 per cent (Great Britain).[f]

Precise measurements and comparisons are difficult, since there are no laboratories or control groups.[g] Some interesting facts, however, emerge from detailed inquiry, each to some extent cause, to some extent consequence, of the others. For instance, while total employment increased in the United States and Japan at roughly the same rate in the decade of the sixties (in both cases considerably less than in West Germany), Japanese worked during the early 1960's about 12 hours more per week than (non-agricultural) workers in the United States. Education of the Japanese labor force was roughly comparable to that of the United States, Canada, and Northwestern Europe, but well ahead of that for economies at the level of Japan's economy in the 1950's. During the two decades of Japan's economic "miracle," the educational level of the Japanese work force rose substantially, partly as older employees retired and younger, better educated persons took their place, partly as the public school system introduced during the occupation caught hold and its graduates joined the labor force.

Perhaps the most striking ingredient in Japan's economic growth has been the rate of saving and investment. From an average of 17.2 per cent of gross national product in 1952–54, gross private investment rose to 30.5 per cent of a much larger GNP in 1970–71; of this investment, roughly two-thirds was made by corporations, one-third by private busi-

---

[f] See Patrick and Rosovsky pp. 12, 96. The years from which the averages are derived are not precisely the same and the measurements—GNP, GDP, or Total National Income—not precisely comparable. It is also true, of course, that a rate of growth is more impressive as the starting base is smaller. For purposes of showing the order of magnitude and relative achievement of Japan's economic growth, however, the comparative figures in the text are roughly accurate.

[g] For a detailed analysis, including discussion of methodology in measuring the Japanese economy and drawing comparisons with other industrialized countries, see Denison and Chung, "Economic Growth and its Sources," in Patrick and Rosovsky at pp. 63–151. Other data are given in *Japan's Economic Expansion and Foreign Trade, 1955 to 1970*, (GATT Studies in International Trade No. 2, 1971).

nesses and individuals. The comparable figure for the United States throughout the post-war period has been around 16 per cent, roughly the same as Japan's before that country took off. Expressing the same basic fact somewhat differently, net corporate saving in Japan after taxes in the period 1967–71 averaged around 85 per cent (leaving 15 per cent for dividends), and net personal saving averaged nearly 20 per cent of disposable personal income. More than a third of Japan's national income was thus plowed back into investment, rather than being spent on items of consumption.

Of course the rate of economic growth and the savings/investment rate fueled each other: the booming economy created strong demand for capital; the economy was booming in part because of a strong demand for end-products; and the demand for end-products was fueled by the increase in income, which was in turn a result of the continuing increase in production. Along with the favorable factors previously mentioned, plus a sympathetic government, moderate and stable tax system, relatively stable price structure, and relatively low interest rates, a savings/investment/production spiral kept going in Japan for a full quarter century, with the interruption only of the period just after oil prices quadrupled in 1974.

A related, and to foreigners surprising, aspect of the high savings/investment rate is that most major businesses in Japan are highly leveraged—i.e., a relatively small portion of their resources is represented by equity capital and the major portion is contributed through borrowing. In contrast to the United States, for example, in which share capital accounts for 55–60 per cent of the capital of manufacturing enterprises,[h] only about 15 per cent of total capital of manufacturing enterprises in Japan is contributed by share capital, the rest being made up of long- and short-term borrowing.[i] In hard times, of course, such a high debt/equity ratio means high risk for the investors and for the enterprise itself; in the good times that Japan has known in the post-war period, it has meant that the costs of modernization and expansion by Japanese firms have been less than for comparable firms in the West.

---

[h] See, e.g., J. F. Weston and E. F. Brigham, *Essentials of Managerial Finance,* p. 5 (1974, 1977).

[i] See, e.g., Wallich and Wallich, "Banking and Finance," in Patrick and Rosovsky, N. a *supra* p. 249 at 267–72; Yamamura, "Structure is Behavior" in Frank, N. a *supra* p. 67 at 71.

Interestingly enough—and by conscious decision of the government, direct foreign investment (in contrast to licensing of technology) played virtually no role in Japan's economic miracle. Of course export sales, as discussed below, were important (though probably not as important as is popularly believed). Since Japan imports nearly all its industrial raw materials,[j] exports are necessary to maintain the economy; as domestic demand for imports grows, so must exports, and the government deliberately encouraged both expansion and upgrading of export industries. Whether this policy, as carried out by the government or by particular industries, went beyond promotion to subsidization in order to sustain employment or in order to stimulate economic growth, is a problem both of analysis and of legislation that we return to in later chapters of this volume.[k] Overall, the volume of exports expanded only slightly more rapidly than total production; in the particular boom periods in Japan, 1955–61 and 1965–69, production increased faster than exports.[l] But if one focuses on particular sectors, the picture looks somewhat different. Manufacturing, which accounts for about 31 per cent of Japan's GNP, accounts for more than 90 per cent of its exports. As the table shows, iron and steel exports at the turn of the decade stood at more than 25 per cent of total production, not counting indirect steel exports in ships and automobiles. Shipbuilding was over 60 per cent export-oriented.[m]

---

[j] E.g., 99.7 per cent of its crude oil, 58.4 per cent of its coal, 99.3 per cent of its iron ore, 94 per cent of its copper ore, and 100 per cent of lead ore, bauxite, cotton and wool. These statistics, for calendar year 1970, are taken from Krause and Sekiguchi, "Japan and the World Economy," in Patrick and Rosovsky, N. a supra, pp. 383–458. The figures represent imports as a per cent of domestic consumption.

[k] §§ 4.41–.47 infra.

[l] See GATT, Japan's Economic Expansion and Foreign Trade 1955-1970, N. d supra at p. 23; for a more intricate analysis of the basic data, including use of price deflators and exchange rate developments, see Krause and Sekiguchi, N. j supra, at pp. 398–402.

[m] The figures in the text, as well as the tables, are drawn from Hollerman, "Foreign Trade in Japan's Economic Transition" in I. Frank, ed., The Japanese Economy in International Perspective, N. a supra p. 168 at 177.

Ratio of Exports to Total Production in Key Industries,
Selected Years, 1969 to 1971

Industry	Export Ratio (percent)		
	1969	1970	1971
Iron and steel	25.4	26.5	—
Motor vehicles	18.3	—	32.7
Color television sets	20.7	—	23.0
Machine tools	9.1	7.6	—
Ships	60.4	60.7	—
Petrochemical products			
Polyethylene	23.6	28.6	—
Polypropylene	18.7	23.8	—
Synthetic rubber	24.8	29.6	—
Fertilizer	21.7	22.3	—
Textiles	32.8	—	34.0
Synthetic fiber	38.5	—	47.0
Industrial machinery	15.2	—	18.4

Source, L. Hollerman, "Foreign Trade in Japan's Economic Transition" in I. Frank, ed. *The Japanese Economy in International Perspective* (1975).

3.32—THE GOVERNMENT'S ROLE IN JAPAN'S ECONOMIC GROWTH

As early as 1949—three years before the formal end of the American occupation—the Japanese government organized a Ministry of International Trade and Industry, soon known world-wide by its English initials as MITI. In the same year, the government, with the concurrence of General MacArthur's financial adviser, set an exchange rate of 360Y = U.S. $1 which was maintained throughout Japan's two decades of growth, well after the purchasing power of the yen in comparison to the currencies of other countries had substantially increased.[a] When Japan gained full independence in 1952, its government embarked on two interrelated policies: It would promote and rationalize the country's industry, particularly certain target industries such as steel, shipbuilding, heavy machinery, and automobiles; and it would manage its foreign trade through schemes designed to discourage import of consumer goods, to encourage import of raw materials at an unprocessed stage (e.g., ores

[a] Japan joined the International Monetary Fund in 1952 with the 360Y = $1 par value and a quota of $250 million, about 2.75 per cent of the total quota. By 1971, Japan's quota had been increased to $1,200 million, 4.21 per cent of the total.

rather than refined metals or alloys), and to give priority to capital equipment and technology useful in the preferred industries. Notwithstanding an overall commitment to private enterprise capitalism, the government of Japan and MITI in particular engaged in elaborate planning: goals were set for reduction of costs in particular industries, and for achievement of stated levels of output; the government gave financial aid in the form of low-interest loans to firms working toward the targets, and it gave tax incentives for investment in preferred industries. Typically, the plans and targets were developed through advisory councils that brought business, government, and outside experts together on a regular basis—not, as was sometimes alleged, in a gigantic Japan, Inc., but in relationships quite different from the formal and often adversary government-business relationships typical in the United States.

Government controls on imports were often used as incentives to export, sometimes without any relation between the items in question.[b] MITI also encouraged Japanese firms to buy or secure licenses to use foreign technology; since foreign firms could not invest in Japan and in many cases were restricted or discouraged from exporting to Japan, the only way to enter the world's fastest growing market was to grant licenses to Japanese firms in return for royalties. License agreements were subject to approval by MITI, and approval was often withheld until the price was reduced to what the ministry regarded as fair.[c] Many of Japan's leading exports in the 1960's and 70's were products that either did not exist at all a decade earlier—such as color television and electronic calculators—or had not previously been produced in Japan on a world-competitive basis—power generators, for instance, office machinery, and optical equipment. It is worth adding that the Japanese government also encouraged domestic research and development, that Japan had a serious research capacity, and that omitting defense-related R & D, Japan by 1970 was comparable, if not quite equal to the United States, West Germany, France, and Great Britain in commitment of resources to research.[d] But Japan's strengths, encouraged by government

[b] For instance, permits to import sugar, on which high domestic mark-ups were possible, were given to shipbuilders until 1955 in order to subsidize export of ships. See Krause and Sekiguchi, § 3.31 N. j *supra* at pp. 413–14.

[c] Screening of technology transfer agreements is increasingly common in developing countries and countries with serious balance of payments difficulties, such as Brazil and Mexico. Japan seems to have been the only member of the OECD—that is the developed countries of Western Europe and North America (and since 1963 Japan)—to maintain such controls into the late 1960's. See Peck and Tamura, "Technology" in Patrick and Rosovsky, § 3.31 N. a *supra*, 525 at 544.

[d] See Peck and Tamura at 933. Comparable in this context refers to the ratio

measures though evidently inherent in the country itself, were quality control, improvement in design, and aggressive selling at home and abroad, rather than innovation or discovery.

3.33—JAPAN AND THE INTERNATIONAL RULES

When Japan entered the GATT in 1955, no less than 14 of the 33 member countries at the time, including France and Great Britain (as well as their dependent territories), announced that they would invoke Article XXXV in order not to have to apply the General Agreement to Japan.[e] That article, as we saw (§ 2.33(7)), had been designed to permit countries politically at odds with each other, such as India and South Africa or Egypt and Israel to participate in the same multilateral organization without having to negotiate with (and extend MFN to) each other. Resort to Article XXXV in respect to Japan, however, had nothing to do with political animosities; the Western European countries, and also many countries in South East Asia and the Pacific, were afraid of the competition of Japanese products if protectionist measures could no longer be applied against them.

Not all of the countries invoking Article XXXV actually denied MFN to Japanese products. Some preferred to embody MFN in bilateral agreements, subject to exceptions for "sensitive products"; others maintained quotas on selected commodities, which they were prepared to negotiate about product-by-product; still others did not want to make any commit-

---

of R & D expenditure to GNP; by 1971 the percentage stood at 1.6 for Japan, 1.5 for France, 1.7 for Great Britain, and 1.9 for the United States and West Germany. Military R & D expenditures would add most to the U.S. figure, least to that of Japan.

[e] Among the other countries that applied Article XXXV to Japan were Australia and New Zealand, Belgium and the Netherlands, Cuba and Brazil, Austria, India, and South Africa. Altogether the countries declining to extend full GATT benefits to Japan accounted at the time for about 40 per cent of the trade of the contracting parties of the GATT. As French and British dependencies gained independence, many of them also invoked Article XXXV, in some cases after the former mother country had terminated its resort to that article. At one time or another over 40 countries invoked Article XXXV against Japan, and many developing countries continued to apply the Article until the late 1970's, when Japan declared that it would not extend its generalized system of preferences to any country that applied Article XXXV to it. As of summer 1978 only 3 countries were left in this group.

For a detailed account of Japan's efforts to join the GATT and the responses thereto, see G. Patterson, *Discrimination in International Trade: The Policy Issues* pp. 283–300 (1965).

ment with regard to products of Japan.[f] Seen from Tokyo, the welcome
—or rather the rest of the world's commitment to comparative advantage—must have seemed very far from complete. Nevertheless in the
first five years of Japan's membership in GATT, coinciding with the first
phase of Japan's economic recovery, nearly all countries' imports from
Japan increased—absolutely and as a percentage of their total imports
—including most of the countries that had invoked Article XXXV.
A GATT Working Party that reviewed the question in 1961 observed that
many countries had feared that some Japanese goods might be imported
"under such conditions as to result in serious damage or threat of serious
damage to domestic industries."[g] Some—but not all—members of the
Working Party thought that invocation of Article XXXV "was dispro-
portionate to the problems which had in practice arisen."[h] Other countries, however, wanted assurance that their products would in practice
have access to the Japanese market before they disinvoked Article
XXXV. Japan, for its part, was reluctant to dismantle its import restrictions as called for by GATT, so long as there was widespread resort
to Article XXXV.

Japan maintained a variety of protectionist devices—some overt and
visible such as tariffs, quotas, and import licensing, others more subtle,
such as industrial standards,[i] restraints on establishment of foreign-
owned firms in Japan, and state trading in agricultural commodities.[j]
When Japan joined the GATT in 1955, only 16 per cent of the products
imported by Japan were free of quotas or similar quantitative restraints,
and by 1959 the figure stood at only 22 per cent.[k] In part the import

---

[f] Note that under Article XXXV(1)(b), Documents Supplement p. DS-57, the decision
not to participate in negotiations with another member can be made only once, at the time
the new member becomes a contracting party.

[g] *Report on Review of Application of Article XXXV to Japan* adopted 7 Dec.
1971, GATT, Basic Documents and Related Instruments, 10th Supp. p. 69 at
71 (1962).

[h] *Ibid.*

[i] Compare the compressed gas cylinders regulations in the United States,
discussed at p. 40 *supra.*

[j] For a detailed account, including English translation of the principal statutes
and the Master Plan for Liberalization of Foreign Trade and Exchange approved
by the Japanese Cabinet in June 1960, see R. Ozaki, *The Control of Imports and
Foreign Capital in Japan* (1972). For a brief law review treatment, see Henderson,
"U.S./Japanese Trade: Its Scope and Legal Framework," 42 Wash. L. Rev.
333 (1967).

[k] See Ohara, "Legal Aspects of Japan's Foreign Trade," 1 J. World Trade 1

controls were designed to ration and conserve Japan's foreign exchange, which was scarce in the early years of Japan's recovery, and in part they were designed to protect domestic industries until they could modernize and achieve the economies of scale sufficient to become world competitive.[1] But while Japan neither observed nor benefited fully from the GATT rules, the GATT did serve as a continuing forum for pressure on Japan to liberalize its trade.

In 1959, as the GATT Contracting Parties met (for the first time) in Tokyo, the government of Japan complained about the number of countries still invoking Article XXXV against it; the United States and the other Western countries criticized Japan for its lack of trade liberalization. In response to the pressures in GATT, as well as to pressures within Japan looking to freer trade, the government developed a Master Plan for Liberalization of Foreign Trade and Exchange.[m] Under the plan Japan's imports were classified into four categories—those that could be liberalized immediately, those that would be liberalized within three years; those that should be liberalized "as soon as possible," and those whose liberalization was deemed difficult for a long time. According to the Plan, 80 per cent of commodity categories would be liberalized (i.e., quotas but not necessarily tariffs would be removed) within a three-year period from mid-1960. A Cabinet Council was created to oversee liberalization of foreign trade and exchange, and by 1962 most of the plan had been carried out, partly by Japan on its own, partly in bargains with other countries. In November 1962, for instance, following seven years of negotiations, Great Britain gave major concessions to Japan—including disinvocation of Article XXXV—in return for opening of Japan to imports of eight items, including woolen yarn, synthetic fabrics, and razor blades.[n] France and Hong Kong disinvoked Article XXXV in return for similar bargains in 1963, Australia and BENELUX in 1964.

---

at 6 (1967). Note that these figures refer not to value or volume, but to the number of categories of goods.

[1] In addition, as mentioned previously, agriculture and certain cottage industries were protected, without any expectation that they would become internationally competitive.

[m] Reproduced in Ozaki, N. j *supra* at 187–201.

[n] See N. u *infra*.

U.S. TRADE WITH JAPAN[1]

[In billions of U.S. dollars]

	Exports	Imports	Balance
1958	1.0	0.7	0.3
1959	1.1	1.0	.1
1960	1.5	1.1	.4
1961	1.8	1.1	.7
1962	1.6	1.4	.2
1963	1.8	1.5	.3
1964	2.0	1.8	.2
1965	2.1	2.4	—.3
1966	2.4	3.0	—.6
1967	2.7	3.0	—.3
1968	3.0	4.1	—1.1
1969	3.5	4.9	—1.1
1970	4.7	5.9	—1.2
1971	4.1	7.3	—3.2
1972	4.9	9.1	—4.2
1973	8.3	9.7	—1.4
1974[2]	10.5	11.8	—1.3

[1] Exports are f.a.s. and imports are customs values, generally the market value in the foreign country.
[2] January–September at seasonally adjusted annual rates.
Source: U.S. Department of Commerce.

In February 1963, the International Monetary Fund decided that Japan's foreign exchange reserves had reached the point where (i) import quotas for balance of payments purposes were no longer justified under Article XII of the GATT; and (ii) Japan was no longer justified in avoiding the obligations of Article VIII of the IMF Articles of Agreement, i.e., the obligation not to impose exchange controls on current transactions.° Japan thereupon announced that it no longer relied on

---

° See Vol. IV of this series, A. Lowenfeld, *The International Monetary System*, §§ 1.52, 1.63 (2d ed. 1984).

Article XII of the GATT as justification for its remaining quotas;[p] in 1964 Japan moved from Article XIV to Article VIII status in the IMF,[q] a step that required elimination of the foreign exchange budget system.

The removal of most import quotas still left tariffs, as well as various forms of administrative guidance, as restraints on imports into Japan; in addition some 120-30 items[r] remained subject to quotas, until the United States put strong pressure on Japan in the context of the massive bilateral trade imbalance in the period 1969–71. Altogether, the slow and grudging pace of Japan's trade liberalization left the impression that Japan was the most protectionist of all developed countries; in fact, considering the various grandfather clauses used by the United States and the novel devices of the EEC, that impression is probably unfair; by the standards of Japanese decision-making through consensus, the change in Japan from insulation to integration into the world economy proceeded relatively fast.[s]

In addition to restraining imports and investment, the government of Japan waged an aggressive campaign to promote exports. Not only were export-oriented industries encouraged through credits and preferences in approval of licenses for imports of goods and technology; export transactions themselves received favorable credit terms backed by the Bank of Japan, and benefited from research and trade promotion by the Japan Export Trade Organization (JETRO).

From 1953 to 1964 Japan had in effect an Export Income Deduction System, whereby a substantial portion of net income (or of gross sales) from exports was excluded from taxable income. In 1957 this scheme was amended to give an additional deduction for increases in exports over the prior year.[t] When Great Britain and Japan signed their treaty

---

[p] It claimed, however, that some 40 items were not subject to Article XI by virtue of the national security and public health exemptions of Articles XX and XXI.

[q] See IMF *15th Annual Report on Exchange Restrictions* pp. 275, 282 (1964).

[r] The difference in figures used in various sources seems to stem from differences in classification of categories, as well as differences concerning announced vs. effective dates of quota removal.

[s] Several commentators have made this point. See esp. P. Trezise, "U.S.-Japan Economic Relations," in *Papers Submitted to the Commission on International Trade and Investment Policy* (the Williams Commission) Vol. II, p. 183 at 187 (1971).

[t] For details of this and other tax schemes, see, Okita, "Japan's Fiscal In-

of Commerce and Navigation in November 1962[u] and Britain disinvoked Article XXXV, Japan agreed to adhere to Article XVI(4) of the GATT, and abandoned this particular device. Instead of outright deductions, the tax benefits were converted into various forms of deferral, for example by authorizing accelerated depreciation of assets used in production of exported items, on the basis of formulas that reward increases in exports over a base period, or on the basis of formulas that reward increases in exports as a share of total sales from the base to the current period. Like many governments, Japan imposed a variety of excise taxes on domestic sales of consumer items such as automobiles, television sets and air conditioners; these taxes were not collected, or were remitted, in respect of exported items. Whether this practice constituted an improper subsidy became the subject of a major litigation in the United States in the 1970's.[v]

VALTMAN - ROTHCO CARTOONS

centives for Exports" in I. Frank, ed., *The Japanese Economy in International Perspective*, § 3.3 N. a *supra*, pp. 207–230.

[u] Treaty of Commerce, Establishment and Navigation between Great Britain and Japan, signed at London, Nov. 14, 1962, 53 T. S. 1963, Cmnd. 2085, 478 U.N.T.S. 29, 86.

[v] See discussion of the *Zenith case* § 4.47(c) *infra*.

At the same time that it was encouraging exports by the techniques described (and others), the government of Japan was aware that other countries were disturbed by the penetration of their markets by Japanese industry. Both the United States and the European Community, as we shall see, had mixed feelings about the increase in trade, and particular domestic industries such as textiles and rubber-soled footwear exerted strong pressure on their governments to restrict imports, especially from Japan, as well as from Korea, Hong Kong, and Taiwan. Japan's response, typically, was to undertake "voluntary" export restraints, in return for the importing country's agreement not to impose import restrictions. Export cartels, originally authorized to limit "excessive competition" and encourage cooperation in development of export markets under the supervision of MITI,[w] would receive "administrative guidance" from MITI concerning the levels of permissible exports of particular products to stated countries. Such guidance was known as "orderly marketing," and when the trade in question was in the hands of a few exporters, it was usually not necessary to establish formal prohibitions.[x] When outsiders tried to take advantage of restraint by the majors, the government had the authority under the Foreign Exchange and Foreign Trade Control Law to impose mandatory export limits. The government was also prepared in principle to enter into "orderly marketing agreements," as it did with the United States government (and later with other countries) in respect of cotton textiles in the early 1960's.[y]

---

[w] And, not incidentally, exempt from the Anti-Monopoly Law applicable domestically in Japan.

[x] MITI defined "orderly marketing" as follows:

What Japan means by orderly marketing . . . is not merely a policy of export restraint, but a planned systematic development of international trade on the basis of free and fair competition and the spirit of international division of labor. It certainly does not mean an arbitrary curtailment of the growth rate of individual Japanese export items. The definition of what is a truly healthy expansion of trade must be determined by taking into account a great many factors, such as the present state of trade between Japan and any other country, and the specific situation of industries and markets in all nations concerned.

MITI Statement Concerning Orderly Marketing of April 1972, quoted in Hollerman, § 3.31 N. m *supra* at 182–83.

[y] For a brief account of voluntary export restraints by Japan and other countries, see U.S. Tariff Commission, *Trade Barriers,* a Report to the U.S. Senate, T.C. Pub. No. 665, Part 2, pp. 241–68 (1974). According to that report, Japan had in force export restraints on 28 categories of products in addi-

As is shown in succeeding sections of this book, an orderly marketing agreement was one of the solutions proposed—and for a while implemented—in respect of the crisis in steel in the late 1960's and thereafter.

§ 3.4—Notes and Questions

3.41—(a) Summarizing the necessarily general overview presented in the preceding section, it seems fair to say that Japan did not begin its miracle growth with the same degree of commitment to the international rules of economic behavior as that of the other developed non-communist nations. Gradually, a combination of international persuasion, external pressures, and the embarrassment of riches moved Japan much closer to the post-war consensus, even as that consensus was being subjected to increasing doubts in the West. Does the Japanese story reinforce, or undermine, your confidence in the GATT and related principles?

(b) A former U.S. Assistant Secretary of State for Economic Affairs with substantial experience in Japan testified as follows to the Williams Commission established by President Nixon to examine the principal problems in the field of United States foreign trade and investment:

. . . In the early postwar years, most experts doubted that Japan could become a viable economy. A chain of rocky islands only one-fifth usable, subject to typhoons and earthquakes, with no iron ore, no oil, little coking coal, little in the way of mineral resources for industry, and with a food and population problem of staggering dimensions, Japan was precariously dependent on the U.S. for support. Its trade was chronically unbalanced; the World Bank considered Japan's capacity to service external loans as limited to a few hundred million dollars. Few saw much chance that Japan would cease to be anything more than a client state of the U.S. for as long into the future as anyone cared to look. . . . As late as 1960, we still had an aid program in Japan designed to improve its industrial productivity.[a]

---

tion to textiles and steel, some only with respect to particular destinations, some with respect to all destinations.

[a] P. Trezise, "U.S.-Japan Economic Relations" in *Papers Submitted to the Commission on International Trade and Investment Policy,* Vol. II pp. 183–84 (1971).

What, would you think, accounts for the outcome so vastly different from these expectations? Does the result suggest that—at least in combination with an ambitious, energetic, and talented people—protection is justified? That the infant industry argument is correct? That planning, not in the Soviet but in the Japanese style, pays off?

(c) The same writer went on to warn against another, opposite prediction:

> . . . Now "Things Japanese" are enveloped in another myth. The Japanese are seven feet tall; their economy a juggernaut spewing out goods at an ever faster rate; their traders singlemindedly engage in ruthless, not to say unfair, competition; their penetration of foreign markets a threat to the West . . ."[b]

His answer to such a prediction was to urge that Japanese markets be opened up further, and that Japanese exports be subject to the same criteria as the exports of other developed countries. What should these criteria be?

(d) One factor not so far emphasized was that the Japanese yen had by the early 1970's become a vastly under-valued currency. There was no way that an exchange rate established in 1949 in the middle of the American occupation could accurately reflect the relative productivity, purchasing power, and asset value of the Japanese economy two decades later. Indeed, the disparity of the dollar and the yen, more than any other single cause, brought down the American dollar—and with it the Bretton Woods monetary system—in the early 1970's.[c] But if an undervalued yen was, as President Nixon and others said, a hidden protectionism, the yen's rise in the mid- and late 1970's—to about Y200 = 1 U.S. $ in summer 1978 should have cured any trade imbalance. In fact wage costs did, roughly speaking, reach parity with those in the United States and the EEC. Japan's export surplus, however, continued.

---

[b] *Id.* at 184.

[c] See Volume IV of this series, A. Lowenfeld, *The International Monetary System,* §§ 5 *et seq.* (2d ed. 1984).

Reprinted by permission of United Feature Syndicate, Inc.

3.42—(a) Another aspect of Japan's international commerce is worth noting, if only briefly. Japan, alone among major industrial countries, conducts much of its import-export business through so-called "general trading companies." Originally these companies were the vehicle that led Japan out of two and a half centuries of isolation into an aggressive effort to enter modern industrial society following restoration of the Meiji dynasty in 1868. Whereas most Japanese had little knowledge of foreign languages and foreign markets—and vice versa—the trading companies built up foreign contacts, international lines of credit, and broad lines of merchandise moving into and out of Japan and sometimes between foreign countries. The trading companies, operating on the basis of high volume, rapid turnover, and low profit margins, maintain world-wide economic intelligence, purchasing missions (especially for primary commodities) and sales forces, typically not tied to particular products. They also can secure transportation, warehousing and insurance, and they can assume (and cover) foreign exchange risks. They enable small and medium sized enterprises that would not on their own be able to organize an export campaign to participate actively in the international economy. And through the trading companies, Japanese industry is able to maintain a continuing relationship with the government, especially with MITI.

(b) Six giant trading companies[d] dominate the field, accounting for about 40 per cent of Japan's exports and 50 per cent of its imports; four medium-sized trading companies add about 10–15 per cent to each of these totals.[e] Several of the big six trading companies are descendants of the so-called *Zaibatsu*—the family-controlled holding companies through which much of pre-war Japan's wealth was held and managed— which were broken up by the American occupation. While the interconnections between manufacturing, banking, insurance and trading companies are not as close as they were before the War and the family holdings are gone, it seems likely that comparable organizations in the United States—or even in the European Economic Community—would not be acceptable under the antitrust laws. Indeed even Japan's Fair Trade Commission wrote of the big trading companies in 1974 that while "their activities are highly assessed in the field of distribution in the national economy . . . there is the danger that their acts will not be in the interest of the policy of competition . . . By taking advantage of their position, they are apt to engage in unjust trade methods, such as placing unjust restrictions on the opposite party or imposing disadvantageous conditions. . . ."[f] Could, or should, United States antitrust laws be applied to Japanese trading companies engaged in business with the United States? Or would that be an improper attempt to transport American values to where they may not belong?

(c) Quite apart from antitrust considerations, there is substantial indication that the trading companies form a kind of unique non-tariff barrier, even as they form an international commercial bridge between Japan and the outside world. Whether they open or close more doors, keep prices up or down, and implement or countervail government policy

---

[d] Mitsubishi, Mitsui, Sumitomo, C. Itoh, Marubeni, and Nissho Iwai. The first three named are affiliated with banking and manufacturing complexes as well, and bear names going back to the great industrial empires of the Meiji restoration.

[e] See *Report of Japan's Fair Trade Commission on the Investigation of General Trading Companies,* January 1974, reproduced in English in 20 Antitrust Bull. 171–86 (1975).

[f] JFTC Report N. e *supra* at 185–86.

has not been conclusively demonstrated. The existence and importance of the trading companies suggests, however, that discussion of tariffs, quotas, licensing and the like may well not cover the whole story of the movement of goods into and out of Japan.

3.43—(a) Turning now to the more technical/legal aspects of Japan's international commercial policies, a substantial body of criticism in the United States and Europe asserted that Japan was unfairly subsidizing its exports. Subsidy, in international as in domestic economic activity, however, is difficult to define and isolate. The government did not pay exporters a fixed sum of money for every ton or unit of export, as the United States, for example, did for many years with wheat and other crops.[g] Consider what kinds of government activities are—or should be—deemed improper subsidies:

(i) Easy or easier credit provided by government agencies

(1) for export-related industries;

(2) for particular export transactions;

(ii) Exemption from environmental regulations for export-related industries;

(iii) Reservation of tidewater sites for import/export related industries, such as plants that import iron ore and export steel;

(iv) Accelerated depreciation for investment in capital goods; would it matter whether this advantage is available for all investment of a certain type (e.g., heavy machinery) or only for the proportion dedicated or allocated to exports?

(v) Assistance by a government agency in attending trade fairs, searching out potential markets, and market research;

(vi) Governmental establishment and policing of industrial standards and quality controls.

(b) The GATT provision on subsidies, Article XVI[h] is, as we saw,

---

[g] See, e.g., the description of the United States' wheat export subsidy program, in the context of the massive grain sales to the Soviet Union, in Volume III of this series, A. Lowenfeld, *Trade Controls for Political Ends*, Ch. II, § 2.12 (2d ed. 1983).

[h] Documents Supplement p. DS-30.

rather vague. As adviser to the government of Japan, would you recommend that any of the devices mentioned here be reported under paragraph 1 of Article XVI?

(c) As adviser to the United States government, would you complain about any of the devices listed? How could the requirement of paragraph 4 be demonstrated?

(d) Some of the practices listed were carried out by other countries as well as by Japan, though perhaps not with equal fervor. The Export-Import Bank of the United States, for instance, also gives favorable credits for export transactions, but recently has been more interested in assisting developing countries in acquiring American goods than in pushing American goods to other developed countries. The DISC (Domestic International Sales Corporation) is a device adopted by Congress in 1971 to reduce taxes on American corporations in respect of export transactions.[i] Does the fact that a practice is widespread among nations take it out of the disapproval (not to say prohibition) of Article XVI? Would you regard the converse true as well?[j]

(e) Under pressure from Great Britain and others, Japan abolished, as we saw, its Export Income Deduction System, but preserved the accelerated depreciation allowances, measured in part by increases in exports, or in the ratio of exports to total sales, over a base period. A Japanese economist writing in a volume cited several times here, says:

> There is no legal conflict between the [accelerated depreciation] tax schemes outlined here and Article XVI of GATT. The article prohibits subsidies on exports, but because the depreciation schemes

---

[i] Pub. L. 92–178 § 501–507; See, e.g., Note, "Domestic International Sales Corporations, A New Concept for American Trade Policy," 4 N.Y.U. J. Int'l L. & Pol. 92 (1971). For a discussion of how the international community addressed the DISC, see Jackson, "The Jurisprudence of International Trade: The DISC Case in GATT," 72 Am. J. Int'l L. 747 (1978); 16 J. World Trade Law 361 (1982).

[j] Assistant Secretary Trezise, whose testimony is quoted in § 3.41 (b) and (c), wrote:

> While it is not surprising that Western businessmen are concerned about their Japanese competitors, I believe that most of the charges of unfair competition are founded more on myth than on fact. The system is not inherently unfair, merely different.

Trezise, N. a *supra* at 190.

amount only to deferment (rather than reduction) of taxation, there is no contravention of Article XVI.[k]

Do you agree? If so, is this a loophole in the GATT that should be plugged? Or does the answer depend on whether the effect of the special depreciation is simply to commit more resources to export industries, or, on the other hand, to permit exporters to lower prices?

(f) Do the Japanese examples cited suggest that Article XVI(5) of GATT needs to be implemented, and more precise attention needs to be given to the subject of subsidies? Or would you conclude this was likely to be a blind alley in international trade law, removed from the real factors that affect exchange of goods and services?

3.44—(a) Probably the most important factor in the export success of Japanese manufacturing industry was the decline in relative prices between Japanese goods and those of other industrial countries.[1] In part this was attributable to increases in labor productivity in Japan as the result of the rationalization programs sponsored by MITI and the major enterprises; in part, to the decline in some world commodity prices in the 1960's. But export prices of many Japanese industries—including, for example, steel—declined more than domestic prices in Japan for the same products in the first half of the 1960's, and increased more slowly than domestic prices in the second half of the decade. Are these facts evidence of unfair competition by Japanese industry? Of dumping? Of the success of the program of subsidies?

(b) Suppose, as seems to have been true at least from 1965 on, that the inflation rate in the United States was steeper than in Japan, so that (i) Japanese products seemed more attractive to American importers; and (ii) Japanese products could be sold in third countries for less than comparable American products. If nearly every country tries to combat inflation, and one does it more successfully than others, are the foreign trade effects just reward for a job well done? Or are they somehow improper?

---

[k] Okita, "Japan's Fiscal Incentives for Exports," in I. Frank, ed., *The Japanese Economy in International Perspective.* p. 207 at 216 (1975).

[1] See Krause and Sekiguchi, "Japan and the World Economy," in H. Patrick and H. Rosovsky, ed., *Asia's New Giant,* p. 382 at 419–20 for statistics demonstrating this point.

(c) As we saw, the typical Japanese firm has a very high debt/equity ratio—i.e., a larger element of fixed cost for a given size of operation than does the typical American or European firm. In addition, under the Japanese employment system, employees are virtually guaranteed lifetime jobs, and are very rarely laid off even in periods of slack demand. Thus industrial labor in Japan is essentially a fixed cost, whereas in the United States and other Western nations labor is in substantial part a variable cost. The combination of high fixed interest and fixed wage costs means that, in periods of slack demand (of which Japan has had several), the pressure is strong to keep the mill or factory working, and to export the surplus.[m] From the point of view of the producer, the export price to a new market need only be high enough to cover the variable costs, even if the profit measured by overall costs or return on capital is unsatisfactory. From the point of view of the importing country, is such a sale unfair competition? Export of one country's recession to another? More technically, how should fair value be measured in the case where an exporter continues his production level in the face of lower domestic sales, and exports the surplus at a reduced profit margin? Should a "normal" profit be built into the calculation of the cost? We shall return to this question later.

3.45—(a) Consider finally the concept of "orderly marketing," developed by Japan in response to the campaign in Europe and the United States to impose import quotas or higher tariffs, on the ground that the safeguard clause of the GATT, Article XIX, was inadequate to meet sudden market penetration. Would you think that an orderly marketing agreement—indeed the very phrase—sounds like division of markets, cartels, and the antithesis of free trade? Or is it a recognition that free trade and comparative advantage have implied quantitative limits attached to them?

(b) Should the United States government permit—or participate in —orderly marketing agreements?

This question, too, will return.

---

[m] Note that even where there was no previously established export connection, the trading companies are in position to be able to find a potential market on relatively short notice.

§ 3.5—The United States as a Trading Nation

3.51—TRADE REGULATION UP TO 1934

Governmental measures concerning international trade have played a critical part in the development of the United States since its earliest history. Such pre-revolutionary sources of conflict as the Navigation Acts (1660–73) and the Molasses Act (1733), and later the Townshend Duty Acts (1769) and the Boston Tea Party (1773), as well as the continuing controversy about "taxation without representation," all centered on the international trade of the colonies and on their desire to make their own decisions free from the often conflicting commercial interests of the mother country. Among the "repeated Injuries and Usurpations" laid to King George III in the Declaration of Independence were "Acts of pretended Legislation . . . for cutting off trade with all parts of the World," and among the consequences declared to follow from severance of Allegiance to the British Crown, was the "full Power to . . . establish Commerce, and to do all other Acts and Things which independent States may of right do."

When the Constitution was being drafted, there was general agreement not to repeat the experience under the Articles of Confederation, when the Congress had several times failed to secure from the states the authority to levy taxes of any sort, including a tariff on imports from abroad. Hamilton and Madison, who disagreed on many issues (including foreign trade policies), agreed that creation of a "more perfect union" would, among other benefits, end the confusing and contradictory array of import duties that had been imposed by the several states, and would result in one national tariff. The first of the enumerated powers listed in the Constitution was the "Power to lay and collect Taxes, Duties, Imposts, and Excises . . . but all Duties, Imposts and Excises shall be uniform throughout the United States."[a] At the same time—in contrast to the practices of many other countries—taxes on exports were forbidden.[b]

Throughout the history of the United States, regulation of foreign

---

[a] Article I, Section 8, cl. 1. Correspondingly, Article I, Section 10, cl. 2 provides that "No State shall, without the consent of Congress, lay any Imposts, or Duties on Imports or Exports. . . "

[b] U.S. Constitution Article I, section 9, cl. 5.

trade has been a major element of debate in election campaigns and in the Congress. Indeed, until World War I, tariffs were the principal national revenue measure and one of the few national measures of economic regulation. Since the rise of individual and corporate income taxes and a wide range of economic regulatory programs, the tariff has lost its central place as a political issue dividing American parties and regions. Foreign trade policy has continued, however, to be an important issue, as the questions raised in § 1 of this volume have come up in a variety of political, judicial, and regulatory contexts.

The second statute passed after ratification of the Constitution was the Tariff Act of 1789,[c] like many of its successors a compromise between southern, predominantly agricultural interests that favored free trade and northern, predominantly manufacturing interests that favored protection. At the same time the tariff was seen as an important—indeed the most important—source of revenue for the new nation.[d] Most imported goods were subjected to a 5 per cent ad valorem duty, but a number of items were subjected to specific duties regardless of their value (e.g., boots, 50 cents a pair); the overall average was about 8½ per cent ad valorem.[e]

Alexander Hamilton, who became the first Secretary of the Treasury, was not satisfied with the Tariff Act of 1789, and published his famous *Report on Manufactures*[f] in 1791 in the hope of persuading the Congress to adopt a more protectionist policy. The Tariff Act of 1792[g] raised duties to an average of 13½ per cent—not as much as Hamilton had

---

[c] 1 Stat. 24 (July 4, 1789). The first statute had established the oaths of office for members of Congress and other officers of the United States.

[d] For the role of tariffs as a source of revenue in United States history, see chart p. 104 *infra*.

[e] I.e., the average is computed by conversion of specific duties to a percentage of the estimated value of the imported items. The figures, as well as much of the material in this and the following paragraphs, are taken from J. Dobson, *Two Centuries of Tariffs, The Background and Emergence of the U. S. International Trade Commission* (Government Printing Office, 1976). See also *History of the Committee on Finance*, S. Doc. 91–57, pp. 49–61, 1st Cong., 2d Sess. (1970).

[f] A. Hamilton, *Report on Manufactures* (1791), repr. e.g., in *American State Papers, Finances* Vol. I (1832); F.W. Taussig, *State Papers and Speeches on the Tariff* (1895, repr. 1968).

[g] 1 Stat. 259 (1792).

urged. During the Napoleonic Wars, while the United States was both the victim and the author of trade embargoes (and ultimately wound up on the wrong side in the War of 1812), American manufactures increased significantly. When the wars ended and international commerce revived, severe pressures for protection arose in the United States. The Tariff Act of 1816[h] fixed the average rate of duty at about 20 per cent and provided special protection for the newly established cotton textile industry in New England.[i] By the Tariff Act of 1824[j] the average rate was raised to 33½ per cent ad valorem, and by the so-called Tariff of Abominations of 1828,[k] the average rate of duties exceeded 60 per cent of the value of dutiable imports.[l] In 1832, duties were reduced roughly to the 1824 level;[m] nonetheless the rates remained too high for the South, and it was over the Tariff Act of 1832 that John C. Calhoun's nullification doctrine was put to the test by the South Carolina legislature.[n] Just after Britain repealed the Corn Laws in 1846, the administration of President Polk pushed through the so-called Walker Tariff of

---

[h] 3 Stat. 310 (April 27, 1816).

[i] Manipulation of duty rates goes back a long way: the protection for more expensive cotton goods was fixed in the Tariff of 1816 at 25 per cent ad valorem; grades costing less than 25¢ per yard were assessed a minimum duty of 6¼ ¢ yard, i.e., the duty was set as if the goods in fact had a value of 25¢ per yard. Tariff Act of 1816, § fourth, 3 Stat. 310–11. Minimum value provisions were used throughout the nineteenth century as an effective barrier against "cheap foreign goods."

[j] 4 Stat. 25 (May 22, 1824).

[k] 4 Stat. 270 (May 19, 1828).

[l] The Tariff Act of 1828 was said by John Randolph of Virginia to be related "to manufactures of no sort or kind but the manufacture of a President of the United States." Andrew Jackson, who had secured the most popular votes in 1824 but had been defeated in the House of Representatives by John Quincy Adams after deadlock in the Electoral College, sought the presidency again in 1828; his followers sponsored a set of tariffs so high as to win over protectionist allies of Adams, in the expectation that in the end the bill would fail. The strategy misfired, however, (at least from the point of view of tariff legislation) and the bill was enacted. Jackson thereafter campaigned against the tariff and was elected, but the Tariff Act of 1828 remained in effect until 1832.

For a detailed account of the economics and politics of the Tariff Act of 1828, see F.W. Taussig, *The Tariff History of the United States* 68–108 (8th ed. 1931, repr. 1967).

[m] Tariff Act of 1832, 4 Stat. 583 (July 14, 1832).

[n] Following Calhoun's resignation as Vice President, President Jackson rein-

1846,[o] which eliminated all specific duties, created a substantial free list, and reduced the level of duties to an average of about 30 per cent. This was still protectionist, but not excessively so, and increased trade over the reduced tariffs led to increased federal revenue, useful to pay off the debts from the Mexican War of 1846.

When the Republican Party was organized in the late 1850's, a high tariff policy was one of its principal doctrines. Secession of the Southern states after Lincoln's election enabled the Republicans to enact a high tariff even before the inauguration of Lincoln.[p]

During the Civil War five major tariff bills were enacted, primarily with a view to raising revenue for conduct of the war. After the War, with the Republicans in firm control of Congress, tariffs remained high even though the need for governmental revenues had declined. Not until the late 1880's— forty years after Great Britain had moved to free trade—was tariff reduction again a subject of public controversy in the United States. President Grover Cleveland, having lost his fight with Congress to reduce tariffs, made free trade a major campaign issue in 1888—and lost. With this signal from the voters, the Republican Congress and the President passed the McKinley Tariff Act of 1890,[q] a frankly protectionist measure.[r] Cleveland won the election of 1892—with tariffs again a major issue—but his effort to secure reduction in duties foundered; the Wilson Tariff Act of 1894,[s] portions of which re-

---

forced the garrison in Charleston Harbor and secured authority from Congress to use force to collect the duties if necessary. The Tariff Act of 1833 defused the first great crisis of the Republic: federal duties would be gradually lowered to the 1824 level, and South Carolina repealed the Nullification Ordinance.

[o] 9 Stat. 42 (July 30, 1846).

[p] Morrill Tariff Act of 1861, 12 Stat. 178 (March 2, 1861).

[q] 26 Stat. 567 (Oct. 1, 1890).

[r] It is worth remarking that this was the same year in which the Sherman Antitrust Act was adopted by the Congress. The idea that the two acts might be inconsistent seems not to have occurred to anyone, or at least not to the (Republican) sponsors of the two measures. See H. Thorelli, *The Federal Antitrust Policy*, 166–68 (1955). It is also interesting that the McKinley Tariff Act contained a reciprocity clause, under which bilateral tariff agreements were negotiated with a number of Latin American countries.

[s] 28 Stat. 509 (August 27, 1894).

mained in effect in the 1980's, became law without the President's signature.[t]

TRYING TO KICK IT OVER

The Republican Party was the champion of tariff protection when this cartoon was published in 1904. It shows the GOP elephant, labeled "protection," preventing the "free trade" donkey from upsetting turn-of-the-century U.S. prosperity symbolized by the "full dinner pail." It was widely believed that protective tariffs had contributed to this prosperity.

Source: Library of Congress, Washington, D.C.

---

[t] An interesting subplot in the period 1865–1900 was the changing United States duty arrangements concerning sugar: (1) High United States tariffs made it impossible for the Kingdom of Hawaii to export sugar profitably to the United States; (2) in 1875 Hawaii negotiated a reciprocal trade agreement allowing Hawaiian sugar to enter the United States duty free. Thereafter, American planters purchased huge tracts of land in Hawaii and imported Oriental laborers to cultivate the sugar fields; (3) The McKinley Tariff Act of 1890 eliminated the duty on sugar, thus destroying Hawaii's advantage over other tropical regions. The ensuing crisis in Hawaii led to the overthrow of the monarchy and establishment of a Republic of Hawaii, which sought annexation by the United States. Meanwhile (4) Cuba boomed after elimination of the U.S. duty on sugar in 1890; (5) When the U.S. sugar duty was restored in 1894, Cuba's economy suffered; and Cuban revolutionaries resumed their struggle for independence which culminated in the Spanish-American War, Cuban independence, and emergence of the United States as a colonial power.

Over the next forty years, Democrats typically favored lower and Republicans higher tariffs. The Tariff Act of 1913, adopted by a special session of Congress called by President Wilson just after his election, achieved the lowest tariff rates since 1857. The effect on trade, however, was less dramatic than expected—evidently because the previous tariffs had been set well above the level needed to create a barrier to imports. The result was less revenue for the Treasury from the tariff; in the same year, however, the Sixteenth Amendment entered into force, and from that time on income taxes replaced tariffs as the principal source of governmental revenues.

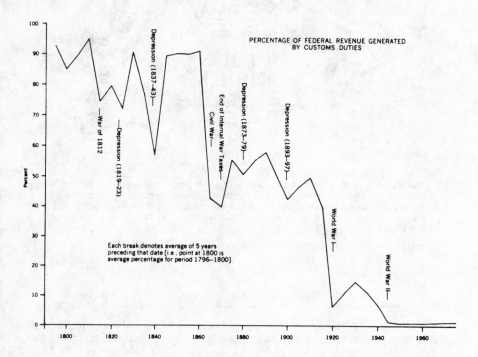

Source: John M. Dobson, *Two Centuries of Tariffs*, p. 31 (1976).

Until World War I, tariffs had all been set by Congress, item by item, without any systematic factual background or economic analysis. Several attempts to establish scientific or expert commissions to recommend a rational tariff structure had been defeated, essentially because of the fear that their recommendations would lead to lessened protection for domestic industries.[u] A first Tariff Board to investigate differences in costs of production at home and abroad was appointed by President Taft in 1909, but the members were all Republicans and protectionists; even when Taft added two Democratic members, the Democrats were not satisfied, and Congress refused to appropriate funds for the Board. In the following years a variety of groups—business, labor, and academic, urged creation of a non-partisan tariff commission. President Wilson was at first cool to the idea, because he distrusted regulatory agencies of the kind favored by Theodore Roosevelt. By 1916, however, he was persuaded that the country wanted a Tariff Commission, and he sent to Congress a proposal for a commission

> . . . as much as possible free from any strong prepossession in favor of any political policy and capable of looking at the whole economic situation of the country with a dispassionate and distinterested scrutiny.[v]

The proposal became law as part of the Revenue Act of 1916.[w] The non-partisan character of the Commission was supposed to be assured by a provision—still the law in the early 1980's[x]—that the Commission have six members, no more than three from each party.[y] The Tariff Commission was not to have policy-making functions, but it was to be a fact-finding body, in response to requests from both the Executive Branch and the Congress. A Harvard economics professor and expert in the tariff policies of the United States, Frank W. Taussig, became the first Chairman,[z] and under his

---

[u] This paragraph is drawn largely from Dobson, N. e *supra*, pp. 83–105.

[v] Letter from Pres. Wilson to Rep. Kitchin, 53 Cong. Record 10529 (July 6, 1916).

[w] 39 Stat. 756, 795 (Sept. 8, 1916).

[x] For the current version of the law, see Trade Act of 1974, §§ 171–75, Documents Supplement, pp. DS-335-37.

[y] Note that in nearly all other regulatory commissions created by Congress, such as the CAB, FCC, NLRB, etc.. there is an odd number of members, with not more than a simple majority permitted from either party.

[z] It is interesting that Taussig accompanied President Wilson to the Versailles Peace Conference as an adviser on economic matters. Subsequent chairmen of the Tariff Commission have not had comparable roles, either as confidants of Presidents or as advisers on matters outside their direct jurisdiction.

leadership a series of Tariff Information Surveys were prepared on a commodity-by-commodity basis concerning methods and costs of production, geographical distribution, and the impact of existing duties, American and foreign. Notwithstanding these Surveys and the emergence of the United States from World War I as a creditor and no longer a debtor nation, the next permanent tariff legislation (after an Emergency Tariff Act of 1921)[a], was a high tariff measure designed to protect American manufacturers from depreciated European currencies. The Fordney-McCumber Tariff Act of 1922[b] was 50 per cent higher on average than the 1913 Act. Protectionism continued to be the prevailing sentiment in the Congress, and largely in the White House and in the Tariff Commission as reconstituted by Presidents Harding and Coolidge as well.[c] Contrary to popular belief, the House (Hawley) version of what became the Smoot-Hawley Tariff Act of 1930 had been passed in May of 1929—five months before the great stock market crash; when that crash came, however, it stengthened protectionist views in the United States and convinced those who, like President Hoover, had been in doubt that high tariffs were the answer for a country whose employment rolls were every day shrinking.[d] Despite the public objections of over 1000 economists led by Professor (later Senator) Paul Douglas, as well as protests from 34 foreign countries, the Smoot-Hawley Tariff Act became law on June 17, 1930—the highest tariff act in United States history.

The Tariff Act of 1930 is still the basic tariff law of the United States, in the sense that succeeding acts until 1962 were in form amendments to the 1930 Act, and that reductions in duties pursuant to the Reciprocal Trade Agreements Program (§ 3.52) have been reductions from the

---

[a] 41 Stat. 9 (May 27, 1921).

[b] 42 Stat. 858 (Sept. 21, 1922).

[c] The Fordney-McCumber Act introduced the concept of a flexible tariff, i.e., a tariff that could be changed by the Commission to equalize the differences in costs of production in the United States and the principal competing foreign country. This device was used only rarely in the 1920's, and mostly to raise duties; in somewhat changed version, it became the principal tool of the reciprocal trade agreements program a decade later. See § 3.52 *infra*.

[d] "Nothing," President Hoover said, as he signed the bill with six gold pens, "would contribute to retard business recovery more than continued agitation [over the tariff]." *Public Papers of the Presidents, Herbert Hoover 1930*, p. 230 at 235 (1976). See also A. M. Schlesinger, Jr., *The Crisis of the Old Order*, p. 164 (1957).

"statutory rates" adopted in 1930.[e] Some of the ambivalence concerning trade matters that we saw reflected in development of the GATT also can be attributed to the statutory framework of Smoot-Hawley. The overall approach to trade legislation, however, made a 180° turn between 1930 and 1934, when the first trade legislation of the Roosevelt Administration was adopted.

3.52—THE RECIPROCAL TRADE AGREEMENTS PROGRAM

The Smoot-Hawley Tariff Act produced not only anger, but a series of retaliatory measures on the part of the United States' trading partners. As is often the case, cause and effect as among decline in international trade, decline in domestic demand, massive unemployment, stock market collapse in the United States and Europe, and major bankruptcies were hard to disentangle. There could be no doubt, however, that the rise in tariff barriers initiated by the United States and emulated by other countries contributed in large measure to the worldwide depression of the early 1930's. What Paul Douglas and his 1000 economists predicted had come to pass.

By 1933, United States imports stood at 33 per cent of their 1929 value, exports at 32 percent.[f] Some economists, and for a while Secretary of State Hull as well, had urged a unilateral tariff reduction by the United States, on the theory that only an increase in imports would lead to an increase in America's exports. But the political consensus for such a move was not there, and the decision was made by the Roosevelt Ad-

---

[e] The non-MFN duties, such as those applicable since 1951 to products of Communist countries set forth in Column 2 of the Tariff Schedules of the United States, are (with minor exceptions) the duties enacted in 1930. For discussion of withdrawal of MFN from Communist countries and the effort to reverse that move, see Vol. III of this series, *Trade Controls for Political Ends,* Ch. I, § 1.23, Ch. II, §§ 1.4, 2.2, 3 (2d ed. 1983).

[f] Merchandise trade of the United States for the years compared (in millions of dollars) was as follows:

	1929	1933
Exports	$5,241	$1,675
Imports	4,399	1,450
Total	$9,640	$3,125

See *Historical Statistics of the United States,* vol. 2, Table Ser. U 187–200 (Bicentennial Ed. 1975).

ministration to seek authority from Congress to modify duties on the basis of bilateral agreements in which the United States would secure reductions in other countries' duties in return for reductions of its own duties.

The result was the Reciprocal Trade Agreements Act of 1934[g], enacting section 350 of the Tariff Act of 1930. By this Act, the President was authorized to enter into trade agreements with foreign countries in accordance with stated criteria, and pursuant to such agreements to reduce duties from the 1930 levels set by Congress. The main criterion was reciprocity—U.S. duties would be reduced in return for an undertaking by the other country to grant "equivalent concessions" in duties of interest to the United States. But the principle of unconditional most-favored-nation treatment was built into the statute, so that bilateral negotiations with individual countries had a generalized effect on the level of United States duties.

The authority of the President to enter into agreements was limited to three years, but it was extended in 1937, 1940, and 1943, so that the Reciprocal Trade Agreements Program was in effect for the entire period of the Roosevelt Administration from June 1934 on. Over that period, the United States concluded bilateral trade agreements with 27 countries, involving tariff reductions on approximately 64 percent of dutiable imports. Rates on these articles were reduced on the average by about 44 per cent of their 1930 level.[h] If the United States at the close of World War II was still a relatively high tariff country, it had at least come down from the levels—and attitudes—of 1930.

After the War, as we have seen, the United States abandoned the pattern of bilateral negotiations. Though the Trade Agreements Extension Act of 1945[i] did not explicitly refer to the possibility of multilateral negotiations or agreements, it was understood that that statute was part of the post-war foreign economic policy of the United States, including the International Monetary Fund and the World Bank as well as other international (i.e., multilateral) economic organizations.[j]

---

[g] 48 Stat. 943 (June 12, 1934), Documents Supplement, p. DS-241.

[h] U.S. Tariff Commission, *Operation of the Trade Agreements Program, June 1934–April 1948* pt. II, pp. 10–14.

[i] 59 Stat. 410 (July 5, 1945).

[j] For a discussion of the authority for a multilateral approach to trade negotia-

The authority to enter into trade agreements was extended for three years; moreover, the President was authorized to reduce any duty (by agreement) by up to 50 per cent of the duty existing on January 1, 1945. Since the duties on about 40 percent of dutiable imports had already been reduced by 50 per cent in bilateral agreements since 1934, this meant that on those items tariffs could be reduced to a level as low as 25 per cent of the 1930 Smoot-Hawley rates. On other items the full 50 per cent authority had not been used up prior to 1945, and so the potential floor would be a higher percentage of the 1930 rate. Still, the pattern was set for reduction from present, rather than from the "statutory" rates, and the United States negotiators came to Geneva in 1947 with substantial room to bargain.

In the Geneva negotiations—actually a series of contemporaneous bilateral bargains among the 23 participating countries—about 54 per cent of the United States' dutiable imports were affected by tariff reductions. Tariffs on U.S. dutiable imports as a whole were reduced by an average of 18.9 per cent from their 1945 levels.[k]

Over the next 15 years, the trade agreements legislation was extended regularly, though with variations as to the amount of the negotiating authority and the period of the extension.[1] The same ambivalence that we saw reflected in the drafting of the GATT and in the preparation and then abandonment of the ITO (§ 2.2 supra) came out in the extensions and modifications of trade legislation. Until 1951, the President's authority to reduce duties remained at 50 per cent of the rates prevailing in 1945, so that to the extent that authority was used up in the first GATT Round (Geneva 1947), it could not be used in succeeding rounds. The 1955 Act authorized the President to reduce the tariff on any product by 15 per cent of the January 1955 rate or to 50 per cent ad valorem; the 1958 Act authorized 20 per cent reduction in tariffs from their level in January 1958.

---

tions, including citation to the relevant Congressional debates, see Jackson, "The General Agreement on Tariffs and Trade in United States Domestic Law," 66 Mich. L. Rev. 250, 257–59 (1967).

[k] See J. Evans, *The Kennedy Round in American Trade Policy*, 10–11 (1971), summarizing U.S. Tariff Commission, *Operation of the Trade Agreements Program*, June 1934–April 1948 (1949).

[1] Trade Agreements Extension Acts of 1948, 62 Stat. 1053; 1949, 63 Stat. 697; 1951, 65 Stat. 72; 1953, 67 Stat. 472; 1954, 68 Stat. 360; 1955, 69 Stat. 162; 1958, 72 Stat. 673.

Over time, a number of so-called "safeguards" were added to the authorizing legislation. One safeguard provision was the "escape clause" procedure, under which the Tariff Commission could, on request of the President, on request of either House of Congress (or the relevant committee), on petition of a domestic industry, or on its own motion, recommend tariff or quota relief if it found that the industry had been injured or was threatened with injury as a consequence of an increase in imports of articles that had been the subject of trade agreements concessions. The President could accept or reject the Tariff Commission's recommendations in whole or in part. If he disagreed with the recommendation, he had to report his decision and the reasons to the Congress. In 1958, the law was amended to provide that the Congress could by two-thirds vote of each house override the President's decision to disapprove the Commission's recommendation and thereby put it into effect.[m]

Another "safeguard" introduced into the trade agreements legislation was designed to take effect before, rather than after, an article had been made subject to a trade negotiation. Under the so-called "peril-point" procedure,[n] a list was made up by the executive branch of articles considered for possible modification of duties; thereafter, the Tariff Commission was supposed to investigate and report to the President as to the limit to which each such modification could be extended "without causing or threatening serious injury to the domestic industry producing like or competitive articles." The President was not prohibited from going below these "peril-points," but if he did he was required to report that fact and the reasons therefor to the Congress.[o]

---

[m] The first use of an "escape clause" by the United States came in a Reciprocal Trade Agreement with Mexico (Art. XI), 57 Stat. 833, E.A.S. No. 311 (eff. Jan. 30, 1943). President Roosevelt and later President Truman promised the Congress that an escape clause would be included in every trade agreement, and President Truman issued an executive order to this effect between the GATT preparatory sessions. Ex. O. No. 9832 of Feb. 27, 1947, 3 C.F.R. § 624 (1947). The United States drafts of the GATT contained an escape clause—Article XIX in the final version, but Congress insisted on including such a clause in the Trade Agreements Extension Act of 1951. The description in the text refers to §§ 6 and 7 of that Act, as amended through 1958, Documents Supplement p. DS-245. For more on the issues involved in escape clause procedures, see § 3.53 at Ns. r-v, *infra*, as well as § 8.13.

[n] The peril-point procedure was enacted in the 1948 Trade Agreements Extension Act, repealed in the 1949 Act, and restored in the 1951 Act. For the version described in the text, see sections 3 and 4 of the latter act as amended through 1958, Documents Supplement pp. DS-243–45.

[o] Peril-points on products involving some $76 million in U.S. imports from

Both the escape clause and the peril-point devices were in some sense inconsistent with the theory of comparative advantage that underlay the Reciprocal Trade Agreements Program, but both were felt to be compromises necessary to secure renewal of the basic negotiating authority from successive Congresses. But in combination with the time and percentage limits on the negotiating authority of the United States Presidents, the peril point and escape clauses significantly restricted the bargaining possibilities of the United States in trade agreement conferences.[p]

As the table shows, each of the major renewals of the United States' reciprocal trade agreement legislation gave the impetus to—and also set the limits on—a tariff negotiating session under Article XXVIII bis of the GATT.

United States duty reductions in GATT negotiations

GATT Conference	Imports of items on which tariff was reduced as a percentage of total dutiable imports	Average reduction of tariffs that were reduced (percent)	Weighted average reduction of all duties
First Round, Geneva, 1947	54	35	18.9
Second Round, Annecy, 1949	5.6	35.1	1.9
Third Round, Torquay, 1950-1951	11.7	26	3.0
Fourth Round, Geneva, 1955-1956	16	15	2.4
Fifth Round, Geneva, 1961-1962	20	20	4.0

Source: J.W. Evans, *The Kennedy Round in American Trade Policy*, p. 12 (1971). (Footnotes omitted.)

the EEC were breached in one instance late in 1961 by decision of President Kennedy, in order to save the Dillon Round. See *Message from the President to the Congress Transmitting Copies of Trade Agreements with the European Economic Community, the United Kingdom, Norway, and Sweden . . . and Reporting Actions Taken With Respect to Peril Points*, March 7, 1962, H. Doc. No. 358, pp. 1–5, 87th Cong., 2d Sess. (1962).

[p] For a more detailed account of the escape clause and peril-point provisions

As the table also shows, the results of Rounds II-V, measured by the amount of trade liberalization on the part of the United States, were much less substantial than the results of the first round shortly after the War.[q] The last of these rounds—the so-called Dillon Round[r]—was actually two negotiations, a regular tariff-cutting session under Article XXVIII bis and the session called for by Article XXIV(6) of the GATT[s] to work out "compensatory adjustment" in respect of bound duties that were unbound by establishment of the European Economic Community and its Common External Tariff. On the whole the Community and the United States (as well as Great Britain and the lesser participants) came to agreement on the Article XXIV(6) issues, with the important exception of agriculture.[t] But overall, as the table also shows, by the beginning of the 1960's, the momentum seemed to have gone out of periodic, item-by-item tariff negotiations, just as the European Economic Community was taking its place as an international economic entity comparable in strength to the United States.

3.53—THE TRADE EXPANSION ACT OF 1962

In his State of the Union message of January 1962, President Kennedy said "We need a new law—a wholly new approach—a bold new instru-

---

and their administration, see Leddy and Norwood, "The Escape Clause and Peril Points under the Trade Agreements Program," in W. B. Kelly, Jr. ed. *Studies in United States Commercial Policy* 124–173 (1963). An appendix to this article contains a summary of all of the escape clause actions undertaken by the U.S. Tariff Commission in the period 1947–1962. Of the 134 investigations begun, 33 resulted in recommendations to the President to take restrictive action, and 8 were submitted to the President by an evenly divided Commission—i.e., without a recommendation but with a report on which he could act. President Truman acted 3 times under the escape clause authority, President Eisenhower 10 times, and President Kennedy twice.

[q] It is pertinent to mention that preceding the fourth round in 1955, Japan negotiated with most of the members of the GATT, including the United States, as a prerequisite for entering the General Agreement.

[r] Named after Douglas Dillon, Under Secretary of State for Economic Affairs in the Eisenhower Administration when the session was launched, and later Secretary of the Treasury under Presidents Kennedy and Johnson.

[s] Documents Supplement pp. DS-46, DS-53.

[t] The Community argued that in 1960–61 it was not in a position to make long-term commitments on agriculture, since its own Common Agricultural Policy had not yet been formulated. The United States, as a leading agricultural exporter, was concerned that the CAP might become excessively protectionist, but was able only to secure a Joint Declaration and Standstill Agreement reserving the right to negotiate on the consequences of the formation of the EEC in the future.

ment of American trade policy."[a] A few days later, Kennedy followed up this call with a detailed message and the draft of a proposed Trade Expansion Act, designed, as he said, to meet the new challenges and opportunities of the 1960's, and to provide "a new and modern instrument of trade negotiations."[b] Recalling the landmark initiative of President Roosevelt in 1934, Kennedy's message asserted that new developments since that time had made our traditional trade policy obsolete.[c] The principal new development, of course, was the establishment of the European Common Market.[d] On the one hand, the discriminatory effects of the common market (§ 3.21–22 *supra*) would be reduced by a general reduction in tariffs; on the other hand the prospect of a negotiation between market units of roughly equal strength called for a new kind of tariff-cutting authority, ample in scope as well as duration, and not limited to item-by-item negotiation.

Many of the arguments for freer trade were familiar, though sold to Kennedy and by him to the Congress and the public in the context also of the struggle against communism, the effort to support developing countries, and the challenge of Japan.[e] One new and interesting argument was that with the EEC's economy growing roughly twice as fast as that of the United States, American manufacturers would be further tempted to locate new plants in Europe in order to get inside the Community's common tariff wall: if this wall could be lowered, the inference

---

[a] *Public Papers of the Presidents, John F. Kennedy, 1962*, p. 5 at 14 (1963).

[b] *Id.* at 68; the message, draft bill, and an executive branch summary of the bill appear also in *Trade Expansion Act of 1962*, Hearings before the House Comm. on Ways and Means on H.R. 9900, pt. 1 at pp. 1–53 (87th Cong., 2d Sess., 1962), [hereafter *House Hearings*].

[c] The question of whether to seek a simple extension of the Trade Agreements Act or to introduce comprehensive new trade legislation had in fact divided President Kennedy's advisers throughout most of his first year in office, until it was resolved by the President himself in November 1961. For an account of the issues in this debate, see, e.g., E. H. Preeg, *Traders and Diplomats*, pp. 44–47 (1970). See also T. Sorensen, *Kennedy*, pp. 410–12 (1965).

[d] The President's message listed the others as (2) the growing pressures on our balance of payments position; (3) the need to accelerate our own economic growth; (4) the communist aid and trade offensive; and (5) the need for new markets for Japan and the developing countries.

[e] See N. a *supra*. For a description of President Kennedy's approach to the Congress on the Trade Expansion Act, see Sorensen, N. c *supra* at 410–12, Preeg, N. c *supra* at 49–51; see also A. M. Schlesinger, *A Thousand Days*, 842–48 (1965).

was, American manufacturers could still gain the business, but the jobs and the capital would remain in the United States.

As it turned out, the "bold new program" was not as different from prior United States trade legislation as the President's message had proclaimed. The basic concept was still tariff-cutting by negotiation, and negotiation was to be based (at least vis-à-vis the developed countries) on mutual exchange of benefits, i.e., on reciprocity. The authority to enter into trade agreements was retained essentially as in the 1934 Act,[f] but for a five-year period from July 1, 1962 (§ 201).[g] The authority to reduce duties was to be up to 50 per cent of any rate existing on that date,[h] except that if the rate was 5 per cent ad valorem or less, the duty could be reduced by more than 50 per cent or eliminated altogether. (§ 202).[i] Like earlier post-war trade legislation,[j] the Trade Expansion Act provided that duty reductions be implemented in stages (§ 253).[k]

The innovative aspect of the Trade Expansion Act, as introduced and essentially as passed, was contained in a grant of authority to the President to reduce duties below 50 per cent of their existing rate or to eliminate them entirely pursuant to an agreement with the European Economic Community with respect to any article in a category of goods in which the EEC and the United States together accounted for 80 per cent of world trade. (§ 211)[l] The economic rationale for this formula was that if 80 per cent of the exports of any given category of products came from the two large trading units, both should be sufficiently competitive so as not to require tariff protection.[m] The political rationale was

---

[f] Documents Supplement p. DS-241.

[g] The full text of the Trade Expansion Act appears in the Documents Supplement at pp. DS-250–96. § 201 is at p. DS-251.

[h] § 201(b)(1).

[i] This point, not immediately obvious from reading the statute, is true because § 201(a) but not § 201(b)(1) is applicable in the circumstances described in § 202.

[j] See § 350(a)(3)(B) of the Tariff Act of 1930, as amended by § 3(a) of the Trade Agreements Act of 1955, 69 Stat. 162, 164 (June 21, 1955), 19 U.S.C. § 1351(a)(3)(B) (1958).

[k] Documents Supplement DS-262.

[l] For this purpose intra-EEC trade, and trade to and from communist countries were to be excluded. (§ 211(c)(2)(i) and (ii)).

[m] This may, however, be a non sequitur, since the statute does not refer to net

that the authority would be significant for all but a very few products only if Great Britain joined the Common Market.[n] By proposing and insisting on the bill in this form, the Kennedy Administration was throwing its weight behind that move, both in urging an ambivalent Britain to press forward with its application and in urging a doubtful Six to accept it. When President de Gaulle vetoed Britain's entry into the Community in January 1963 (p. 61 supra), section 211 became, for practical purposes, a dead letter.[o] The negotiations to be conducted under GATT auspices in response to the Trade Expansion Act went forward, but the political energy, the Grand Design for an Atlantic partnership based on free trade, seemed to die down, to be replaced by hard bargaining among countries that within an overall set of shared values were prepared to confront each other as economic rivals, and occasionally as adversaries.

The Trade Expansion Act made certain changes in the so-called "safeguard" provisions of United States trade law. We shall examine these provisions in detail in the following chapter, in the context of exploring the "remedies" available to the troubled steel industry in the mid 1960's, and to the pressures for further legislative changes in the early 1970's.[p] Brief mention here, however, is useful in illustrating the ebb and flow of America's outlook on international trade.

The *peril point* procedure that had been introduced by Congress in the 1950's[q] was eliminated, and replaced by a procedure for advice by the Tariff Commission in advance of negotiations as to the probable

---

exports, and several of the potential categories were quite unbalanced as between the EEC (as it might be enlarged) and the United States. This point is made in J. Evans, *The Kennedy Round in American Trade Policy*, pp. 143–44 (1971). See also § 3.64 *infra*.

[n] On the basis of 1960 figures, Secretary of Commerce Hodges introduced a list of 26 categories that would come under the 80 per cent authority if the EEC were enlarged by admission of Great Britain, including motor vehicles, glass, non-alcoholic beverages, power generating machinery, industrial machinery and coal, *House Hearings* pt. I at 97. For a somewhat different presentation of the same information, see Hawkins and Norwood, "The Legislative Basis of United States Commercial Policy," in William B. Kelly, ed. *Studies in United States Commercial Policy* 69 at 116–17 (1963).

[o] Only aircraft, in which the United States had 80 per cent of the world market (as defined) by itself, would have come under the formula without Britain in the Community.

[p] § 4.4 *infra*.

[q] § 3.52 at Ns. 1–m *supra*.

economic effect of modifications of duties, but without specification as to a particular minimum level of duty, as in prior law. (§ 221). The *escape clause* was retained, but made somewhat harder to invoke.[r] Under the new version, labeled "tariff adjustment" (§ 301–302), the Tariff Commission could still find injury from imports and recommend that the President take remedial measures, including increased tariffs or quotas. But the law was modified (i) to require a finding that imports had increased ". . . as a result *in major part*" of concessions granted under trade agreements, in place of the earlier version ". . . as a result, in *whole or in part*" of trade agreement concessions;[s] (ii) to eliminate the provision in the prior version that the increase in imports which would trigger the escape clause procedure may be "either actual or relative"[t]; (iii) to require a finding that increased imports meeting the first two criteria *"have been the major factor* in causing or threatening to cause" serious injury to the domestic industry concerned, in contrast to the prior wording calling for a finding that increased imports ". . . *have contributed substantially* towards causing or threatening serious injury . . ."[u]; (iv) to require that any import restrictions imposed by the President on recommendation of the Tariff Commission would terminate not later than four years after their imposition unless the President made a new determination, on the advice of the Commission and of the Secretaries of Commerce and Labor, that an extension was in the national interest.[v]

An interesting new device, which had been talked about for a decade or more, won the Administration's support in 1962 and became part of United States trade law. The concept of *adjustment assistance,* first promoted by the president of the United Steelworkers of America in

---

[r] The findings required for escape clause action were set forth in § 301; the action that would follow an affirmative recommendation of the Tariff Commission was described in §§ 302, 351, and 352.

[s] Compare Trade Expansion Act § 301(b)(1), Documents Supplement p. DS-268 with Trade Agreements Extension Act §§ 6(a), 7(a) Documents Supplement p. DS-245.

[t] Trade Agreements Extension Act §§ 6(a), 7(a).

[u] Compare Trade Expansion Act § 301(b)(3) with Trade Agreements Extension Act § 7(b).

[v] Trade Expansion Act § 351(c)(2): For a discussion of these as well as some other changes in the escape clause in the 1962 act, see Metzger, "The Trade Expansion Act of 1962," 51 Georgetown L.J. 425, 442–48 (1963).

the early 1950's,[w] was that if governmental measures, such as reductions in tariffs, led to loss of jobs or business profits, then the government should assume some of the costs of adjustment to these consequences, such as retraining and relocation of laid-off workers and financing new lines of endeavor for firms no longer able to compete. In that way, the argument went, consumers would not be forced to pay higher prices or buy inferior products, and uncompetitive resources would not continue to be inefficiently employed. Moreover, while escape clause proceedings leading to tariff increases or quotas could be employed only if a significant portion of the industry were affected, adjustment assistance might be available for particular firms and its employees heavily hit by imports. In addition, adjustment assistance might be a way of insuring the support of labor and some business interests for the trade bill—the centerpiece, as Sorensen described it,[x] of President Kennedy's legislative program for 1962.[y]

One other provision must be mentioned to round out the picture of relief available to domestic industries affected by increased imports. In addition to the escape clause and the provisions for adjustment assistance, Congress bestowed on the President a power he had not sought—the power to enter into "orderly marketing agreements."[z] Orderly marketing, as we saw, was a concept developed originally in Japan, partly as a way of avoiding unilateral restraints by importing countries.[a] Under section 204 of the Agricultural Act of 1956,[b] the President had been granted authority to enter into orderly marketing agreements for agricultural commodities and products thereof and textiles, and in fact numerous bilateral and multilateral cotton textile agreements were con-

(Text continued on page 119)

---

[w] See Leddy and Norwood, "The Escape Clause and Peril Points under the Trade Agreements Program," in W. Kelly, *Studies in United States Commercial Policy* 124, 162-65 and sources there cited, including the documents of the Randall Commission on Foreign Economic Policy of 1953–54.

[x] T. Sorensen, N. c *supra* at 410.

[y] The statutory basis for adjustment assistance appeared in §§ 311–20 with regard to aid to business, and §§ 322–38 with regard to labor.

[z] The authority was not in the administration bill or in the bill as passed by the House. Section 352 was added by the Senate Finance Committee at the urging of Senator Muskie on behalf of the domestic shoe industry. See *Trade Expansion Act of 1962*, Hearings before Sen. Comm. on Finance on H.R. 11970, pt. 2, pp. 856, 863 (87th Cong. 2d. Sess. 1962).

[a] See § 3.33 at p. 90 *supra*.

[b] 70 Stat. 200, 7 U.S.C. § 1854 (1976).

TRENDS IN TRADE AND TARIFFS, 1928-1978

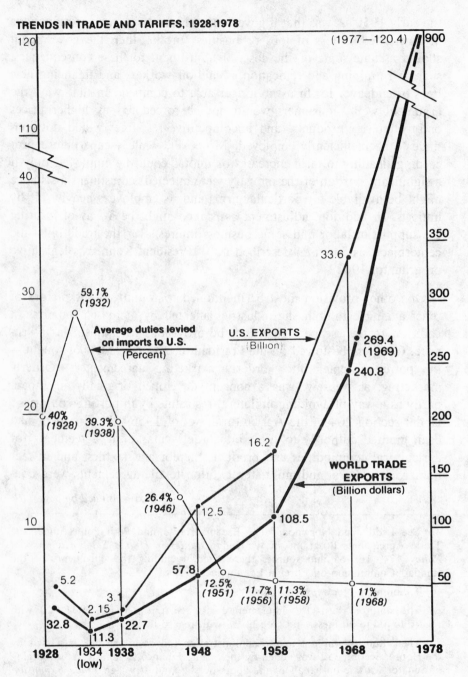

Note.—U.S. Export totals include military grant-aid and foreign merchandise.

Source.—U.S. Dept. of State, THE TRADE DEBATE, publication 8942 (May, 1978).

cluded under authority of section 204.[c] Under the generalized provision included in the Trade Expansion Act (§ 352),[d] if the Tariff Commission had, with respect to any product, made the finding of injury as a result of increased imports required for implementation of the escape clause or of adjustment assistance,[e] the President was authorized to enter into an agreement with one or more foreign countries whereby the foreign countries would agree to limit their exports of the product to the United States to stated amounts. If such an agreement were in effect on a multilateral basis including a significant portion of world trade in the product in question, the President was authorized to restrain imports of the product from non-participating countries.

*   *   *

In all, once the special authority for agreements with the European Community had become unusable, the Trade Expansion Act constituted a rather modest change in United States trade law. But the commitment to further tariff reduction was there—backed by surprisingly large votes in both houses of Congress.[f] With a $5 billion annual surplus in the balance of trade,[g] the United States would continue to take the posture of promoting international trade. If the ambivalence still showed, the forces of protectionism had once more been beaten back, and the stage had been set for the sixth round of multilateral trade negotiations, soon to be named the Kennedy Round.[h]

---

[c] Most notably the so-called Long-Term Arrangement Regarding International Trade in Cotton Textiles negotiated in 1961, 13 U.S.T. 2672, T.I.A.S. No. 5240, 471 U.N.T.S. 296, and amendments and revisions thereof in 1967 and 1973. See § 3.72 N. s *infra.*

[d] Documents Supplement p. DS-292.

[e] I.e., the finding called for by § 301(b), discussed at Ns. r–v *supra.*

[f] 298–125 in the House, 78–8 in the Senate.

[g] I.e., exports minus imports of goods and services; note that the overall balance of payments of the United States was in deficit from 1959 on and throughout the decade of the 1960's. See Volume IV of this series, A. Lowenfeld, *The International Monetary System,* esp. § 4 (2d ed. 1984).

[h] The name seems to have originated in Europe, and not to have pleased President Kennedy, who didn't know how the negotiations would come out. Kennedy wondered why the negotiations could not be named after Chancellor Adenauer or President de Gaulle. See Sorensen, N. c p. 113 *supra* at 412, Preeg, *ibid.* at 59.

§ 3.6—Notes and Questions

3.61—(a) From the time of the first Trade Agreements Act of 1934 through the Trade Expansion Act of 1962 and beyond, United States trade legislation has rested on the concept of reciprocity. At the simplest level, you gave only as much as you got; giving meant lowering your own import barriers, getting meant that others' import barriers would be lowered on items you exported or could export. Thus unilateral tariff-cutting, such as the British had undertaken in 1846 was, by common consent, excluded.[a] But beyond the primitive consensus against something for nothing, how should reciprocity be understood?

(b) Suppose in the base year Patria imported $10 million worth of tables from Xandia, and Xandia imported $20 million worth of lamps from Patria. If each country's applicable tariff is 20 per cent, would a reduction by Xandia of its duty on lamps to 15 per cent be reciprocated by Patria's reduction of the duty on tables to 15 per cent? to 10 per cent? Or would you want to know something about the ratio of imports to domestic consumption and about the price elasticity of supply and of demand before giving a meaningful reply?

(c) If, as was true throughout the post-war period, trade negotiations were not between Xandia and Patria, but (with a few exceptions) among a large number of nations assembled in the GATT, would measurement of reciprocity for the United States require adding up all the potential advantages to be gained by foreign exporters to the United States and comparing them with the potential advantages to American exporters abroad?[b]

(d) Suppose, as was the general hope after the limited success of the Dillon Round, that tariff negotiations could be conducted on an across-the-board or "linear" basis, i.e., not Xandia cutting its duties

---

[a] The statement in the text does not necessarily apply to imports from developing countries, as was made clear by the adoption in 1964 of part IV of the GATT, Documents Supplement p. DS-80-87. However, the concept of preferences—as contrasted with a mere "free ride"—was not generally accepted in the United States until the late 1960's, and did not become part of U.S. law until the Trade Act of 1974. (Title V, Documents Supplement pp. DS-402-10.

[b] In fact the U.S. government published the results of the Dillon and Kennedy Rounds to show comparisons of this kind. Except in a very general way, however, it is not clear that the negotiations were conducted as would be suggested by an affirmative answer to the question in the text.

on lamps in return for Patria cutting its duties on tables, or all countries cutting their duties on chairs, but every country cutting all of its duties by a stated percentage. Would reciprocity require that each country's duties be cut by the same percentage? By the same number of percentage points? To the same level? By a fraction inversely proportional to the size of its imports? Something else?

(e) Note that neither the GATT nor the Trade Expansion Act[c] gives any clues to this fundamental question.[d] The Trade Expansion Act spoke of reciprocity only in the Statement of Purposes (§ 102), and there only of "trade agreements affording mutual trade benefits,"[e] but this was construed as a legal limitation by the U.S. government negotiators operating under the Act.[f]

3.62—(a) The Trade Expansion Act provided (in § 251) that any duty proclaimed in carrying out a trade agreement shall apply to products of all foreign countries, whether or not they were members of the GATT, were parties to a trade agreement with the United States, or accorded most-favored-nation treatment to products of the United States.[g] For reasons that we explored in our first look at the GATT (§ 2.42 supra), MFN has been one of the fundamentals of United States trade law since at least 1934,[h] along with reciprocity. Are reciprocity and MFN consistent with each other?

(b) The Congress seems to have asked this question too, but in the

---

[c] Nor for that matter the Trade Act of 1974.

[d] For an interesting discussion of reciprocity and how to measure it, see Preeg, "Reciprocity and the U.S. Trade Agreements Program," in *United States International Economic Policy in an Interdependent World,* Papers submitted to the Commission on International Trade and Investment Policy (the Williams Commission) Vol. II. p. 475 (1971).

[e] Compare the somewhat fuller formulation in § 2 of the Trade Act of 1974, Documents Supplement p. DS-296.

[f] See, e.g., Rehm, "The Kennedy Round of Trade Negotiations," 62 Am. J. Int'l L. 403, 407–8, 412–13 (1968). The author was the General Counsel of STR, and as such the lawyer to the United States negotiators in the Kennedy Round.

[g] Products of communist countries not then receiving MFN treatment were excluded, however, by § 231 of the Trade Expansion Act, See § 3.51 N. e *supra.*

[h] Trade Agreements Act of 1934 § 350(a)(2), Documents Supplement p. DS-241. The comparable provision in the Trade Act of 1974 is § 126(a), Documents Supplement p. DS-312.

context of distinguishing between fair and unfair competition. Section 252 of the Trade Expansion Act,[i] one of the few sections substantially written by the Congress (i.e., by the House Ways and Means Committee) rather than by the executive branch, points (in paragraph (a)) to unjustifiable foreign import restrictions, directs the President to take "all appropriate and feasible steps within his power" to eliminate them, but prohibits him from negotiating for the reduction or elimination of any United States import restriction in order to obtain the reduction or elimination of the foreign "unjustifiable" import restriction. If the United States was concerned, as was surely true, about Japanese restrictions on import of agricultural and other products, does the prohibition in section 252(a) tie the President's hands? Would you expect fruitful results from section 252(a)(3), which seems to require reciprocity on the part of the United States in the sense of an eye for an eye (at least as to restraints on U.S. agricultural products), notwithstanding the provisions of any trade agreement?[j]

(c) Section 252 seems to authorize further departures from MFN in situations calling for retaliation for non-tariff restrictions "including variable import fees" or "discriminatory" or other unjustifiable actions (paragraph (b)), or for "unreasonable import restrictions" (paragraph (c)) restricting United States commerce. But note that both paragraphs (b) and (c) are subject to the requirement that the action taken be consistent with the purposes of section 102,[k] and that in acting under section 252(c) the President must have "due regard for the international obligations of the United States." Presumably, the President could breach an international obligation of the United States, such as the GATT requirement of MFN, but only if he did it deliberately and recited the fact that he had considered the issue and decided to proceed nonetheless.

(d) The issue of conformity of the retaliation clauses of United States law to the GATT came up in connection with the "Chicken War" between the United States and the European Economic Community mentioned previously (§ 3.25(e) supra). In fashioning its response to the Poultry Policy of the EEC, the United States had opted to proceed under Article XXVIII rather than

---

[i] Documents Supplement p. DS-261.

[j] Note, however, the phrase in § 252(c)(3) ". . . to the extent [the President] deems necessary and appropriate. . . ."

[k] Documents Supplement p. DS-250.

XXIII of the GATT; the point of this decision was to forego the contentious (not to say accusatory) procedure of Article XXIII, in favor of the approach that the Community had withdrawn a concession (Article XXVIII (1)) and that it was open to the United States—consultations having failed—to withdraw substantially equivalent concessions under Article XXVIII (3).[1] Once a GATT panel had determined the value of the concession withdrawn by the EEC (omitting any determination of whether the EEC had been justified or whether the United States had been a principal supplier[m]), the United States withdrew concessions on four products of important export interest to members of the Community.[n] But in accordance with Article XXVIII of the GATT, it did so on the basis of MFN, so that for each of the products selected, the duty was raised from the trade agreements rate all the way to the 1930 Smoot-Hawley rate, regardless of the origin of any particular product. One of the products selected was brandy valued over $9.00 per gallon. Star Industries, an importer of Spanish brandy, took the position that Spain had not been accused of any unfair or unreasonable import restriction, and that section 252(c) authorized suspension or withdrawal of concessions with respect "to products *of such country* or instrumentality," i.e., to products of the EEC but not of Spain. The importer, met with the 1930 duty ($5 instead of $1.25 per proof gallon), brought suit in the U.S. Customs Court. How should this case be decided?

(e) The Customs Court decided in favor of the importer.[o] It read GATT Article XXVIII (3) as not *requiring* suspension of trade agreement concessions on an MFN basis, but as authorizing reciprocal action following breakdown in negotiations. As to section 252 of the Trade Expansion Act, the Customs Court found authority only to withdraw concessions of the country or instrumentality that was maintaining un-

---

[1] Documents Supplement p. DS-51. The situation was more complicated, because of a so-called Standstill Agreement between the United States and the EEC reserving certain agricultural products, including poultry, from the settlement under the Dillon Round. For the full background and documentation of this aspect of the dispute, see A. Chayes, T. Ehrlich, A. Lowenfeld, *International Legal Process* Vol. I, ch. IV (1968).

[m] See *id*. at 289–301.

[n] Proclamation Increasing Rates of Duty on Specified Articles, Procl. No. 3564 of Dec. 4, 1963. 28 Fed. Reg. 13,247 (1963).

[o] *Star Industries, Inc. v. United States,* 65 Cust. Ct. 662, 320 F. Supp. 1018, C.D. 4155 (1970).

reasonable import restrictions against products of the United States. On the basis of its interpretation of Article XXVIII of GATT, the court did not need to interpret the "due regard" clause of section 252(c): The President exceeded the authority granted to him in that section, and so the Proclamation and duties proclaimed under the Proclamation were invalid and void.[p]

(f) On appeal by the U.S. government, the decision of the Customs Court was reversed.[q] The Court of Customs and Patent Appeals construed Article XXVIII(3) in context with the rest of the GATT, and concluded that departures from the principle of MFN were expressly enumerated and limited, and that no inference of derogation from that principle could be drawn from the provisions for compensatory withdrawal of concessions set forth in Article XXVIII. The Appeals Court then turned to the clause requiring the President to have "due regard" for the international obligations of the United States. Not only, said the court, was that clause a limitation on the powers of the President; the intent of section 252(c) was precisely satisfied because the retaliatory measures were "sharply focused" on the EEC, whose members supplied the dominant share of the U.S. imports of the products in question. "Thus," said the court, "the legislative intent to take strong measures against those who maintain unreasonable import restrictions was upheld, and at the same time we did not breach our international obligations."[r]

3.63—Apart from the rather tricky issue of the meshing between U.S. statutory law and the GATT, the *Star Industries* case and the Chicken War raise two related important issues of commercial policy.

(a) Should retaliation be undertaken on an MFN basis, on the theory that "innocent" third parties, such as Spain in the brandy case, may put pressure on the "offender" to reform its ways? Or, on the contrary, should retaliation be discriminatory, on the ground that punishment should be directed only at the "guilty" and at no one else? Note that to the extent that exporters in different foreign countries compete with one another and not merely with domestic producers, discriminatory appli-

---

[p] 320 F. Supp. at 1024.

[q] *United States v. Star Industries, Inc.*, 462 F.2d 577, 65 C.C.P.A. (Cust.) 662, C.A.D. 1060 (C.C.P.A. 1972), *cert. denied* 409 U.S. 1076 (1972).

[r] 462 F.2d at 564. For a more detailed account of this case and the surrounding facts, see Lowenfeld, " 'Doing Unto Others . . .'—The Chicken War Ten Years After," 4 J. Mar. L. &. Comm. 599 (1973).

cation of a trade barrier such as an increased tariff hurts the target country more than a trade barrier applied across-the-board.

(b) What is the purpose of retaliation anyway? Is it deterrence of similar conduct in the future? Is it punishment/revenge? Or is it an attempt to redress on a macro-economic, balance-of-trade level, a grievance that cannot be settled directly? In the aftermath of the Chicken War, for example, Volkswagen panel trucks and French cognac for a time came into the United States in decreased quantities.[s] But the exporters of these items seem to have made no effort—and certainly had no success—at inducing the Community to change its policy on poultry.[t]

(c) This point, too, will return, in a somewhat different cast, in our exploration into what to do about excessive imports of steel.

3.64—The special provisions concerning the European Community are, as we saw, among the great might-have-beens of recent economic history. Not only was Britain's application for membership in the Community vetoed in the early 1960's:[u] by the time Britain (as well as Ireland and Denmark) did join the Community in the mid-1970's, the perceptions on regulation of international trade had changed in a number of ways. Still, sections 211–13 of the Trade Expansion Act[v] are worth exploring, to see whether the underlying idea has, or had, merit apart from the immediate political motivation.

(a) The basic concept was that if the EEC and the United States together accounted for 80 per cent of world exports of a category of products (not counting intra-Community or East-West trade) there was no reason for protective tariffs, and so they could be reduced on the basis of reciprocity without limit—i.e., all the way to zero. Is it sound

---

[s] See Lowenfeld, N. r *supra* at 613–14. For an ironic twist with respect to cognac, reflecting a difference in invoicing by French exporters in order to come under the minimum price level for the higher duty, see Lowenfeld, "The Chicken War: A Postscript," 5 J. Mar. L. &. Comm. 317 (1974).

[t] For the sequel on the European poultry front, see E. Preeg, *Traders and Diplomats at* 76 (1970).

[u] In fact twice, once in 1963 and again in 1967, both times by France under de Gaulle.

[v] Documents Supplement pp. DS-252–54.

to say that dominant suppliers do not require protection, because by definition they are world-competitive?

(b) Note that the statute did not require that both the United States and the EEC be net exporters, though in most of the categories this was the case. The assumption seems to have been that if in a given category (e.g., aircraft) the EEC was not a net exporter, its imports would come from the United States—and vice versa. By granting each other concessions on these categories, the advantages of trade would be kept "in the family," even though the actual duties would be generalized on an MFN basis.[w] Is there something in this scheme contrary to the spirit—if not the letter—of the GATT? How for instance should Japan (whose continuing growth seems to have been underestimated by the drafters of section 211) have reacted to this plan? What about the developing countries?

(c) Section 212, requiring an advance determination by the President that a trade agreement with the Community would tend to assure the maintenance or expansion of United States exports of the (agricultural) products in question, proved unworkable, and was probably out of phase in any event with the Common Agricultural Policy. Section 213, however, was interesting in that it represented an offer by the United States to reduce its duties on products of developing countries on an MFN basis if the EEC would do the same. The effort by the United States was to weigh in in favor of the Latin American countries, which were not enjoying association or other forms of preferred access to the Common Market, as were the African and a few Asian countries. The idea behind this section was consistent with MFN; however, most tropical products already entered the United States free of duty[x]; even for those few products for which a tariff cut would improve ease of entry into the United States, the statute hardly gave leverage to the United States for negotiations with the Community. In the event, section 213 did not succeed in weening African countries away from their special arrangements with the Community, in the hope of gaining increased access to markets in the United States.

---

[w] For a discussion of these points, see J. Evans, *The Kennedy Round in American Trade Policy* pp. 143–44 (1971).

[x] Sugar was a notable exception, but it could not in any event qualify under § 213(a)(2), because about half the American consumption was produced in the United States.

(d) One of the liveliest debates in the course of the hearings on the Trade Expansion Act concerned the suggestion by Senator Douglas that section 211 be amended so as to count not only the United States and the EEC in measuring whether the dominant supplier provision would be applicable, but also the members of the European Free Trade Area. Senator Douglas made the proposal in late summer, as signals from the continent began to cast doubt whether Britain would be accepted into the European Community. The Administration—in particular Under Secretary of State Ball—opposed the amendment, on the ground that it would be seen either as relaxing the pressure on Britain to join the Community or as intervening in the negotiations. Moreover, Ball argued, the dominant supplier authority would not work if it were used with several, as contrasted to a single negotiating partner.[y] The Douglas amendment was adopted by the Senate, but without Administration support it failed in the Senate-House conference. Whether the Community would have been prepared to negotiate on the basis of section 211 as it would have been amended by Senator Douglas' proposal may be doubted.[z] If negotiations along the lines envisioned by Senator Douglas had gone forward, do you think the objections raised in paragraph (b) above would have been more or less compelling than in the actual version?

3.65—Coming back to the Trade Expansion Act as passed, the major innovation, apart from the provisions dealing with the EEC, had to do with adjustment assistance.

(a) Would you regard the idea as a major improvement over the negative approach of peril points and escape clauses—protecting where protection is justified, without impairing the bargaining power of American negotiators or depriving consumers of the benefits of efficiency?

(b) Or would you, on the contrary, regard adjustment assistance as intrusion into the fields of employment, training, and credit that had traditionally not been subject to federal bureaucracy? Or, as the President of Du Pont put it, "an undesirable cushion for unskilled negotiators?"[a] More basically, if *A Company* in Massachusetts lays off work-

---

[y] See *Senate Hearings* pt. 4, pp. 2259–62.

[z] The Community had rejected a suggestion in 1958 that a free trade area be formed among the six members of the Common Market and the other European members of the OEEC.

[a] *Senate Hearings* pt. 3, p. 1273.

ers or closes a plant because of competition from a new firm in South Carolina, are *A* and its employees less deserving of aid than *B Company,* whose business is impaired by competition from abroad?

(c) The supporters of adjustment assistance answered this argument partly in psychological terms: "The average man accepts more readily the capture of a local market by another American than he does when the culprit is a foreigner."[b] Some went further and said that if other aspects of assistance for adjustment to changing market conditions are inadequate—e.g., programs of unemployment compensation, manpower training, aid to depressed areas, etc.—then these should be strengthened as well. Meanwhile adjustment assistance limited to dislocations caused by foreign trade could be a significant first step forward.

(d) Note that the criteria for invoking adjustment assistance under the Trade Expansion Act were the same as those for invoking relief under the escape clause. The Tariff Commission must find "serious injury" or threat thereof, caused "in major part" by increased imports as a result of concessions granted under trade agreements.[c] In fact, in the first seven years of the Act, the Tariff Commission did not make a single affirmative finding in an adjustment assistance case. In November 1969 the Tariff Commission approved three worker petitions; between that date and June 1971, the Tariff Commission found injury in 10 worker petitions out of 79 filed, no injury in 41, and divided evenly in 28; of 14 petitions filed by firms, the Commission found injury in one case, no injury in 5, and divided evenly in 7.[d] Consider what the criteria for adjustment assistance should be (assuming the concept as a whole is retained).

(e) As between adjustment assistance and escape clause relief, which should be more difficult to obtain? How might the criteria be meaningfully separated, bearing in mind the concerns expressed in paragraph (b) above? Should the Tariff Commission be excluded from

---

[b] Metzger, "The Trade Expansion Act of 1962," 57 Geo. L.J. 425, 448 (1963).

[c] See Trade Expansion Act § 302(a)(2), Documents Supplement p. DS-270, referring back to an affirmative finding under § 301(b). The statement in the text is a reminder, rather than a paraphrase of the statute. Compare the fuller discussion in the context of the escape clause at p. 116 *supra*.

[d] *United States International Economic Policy in an Interdependent World,* Report to the President by the Commission on International Trade and Investment Policy (the Williams Commission) p. 50 (1971).

the process of determining eligibility for adjustment assistance?[e] Does the fact that the escape clause procedure leading to withdrawal of concessions is subject to GATT scrutiny under Article XIX and compensatory action by other countries,[f] while adjustment assistance is purely domestic, affect the answer? Which way?

3.66—(a) Note briefly one other aspect of United States trade legislation not previously mentioned. Under section 232(b),[g] the President was authorized, on advice from the Director of the Office of Emergency Planning[h] that an article is being imported in such quantities or under such circumstances as to threaten to impair the national security:

> to take such action, for such time as he deems necessary, to adjust the imports of such article and its derivatives so that such imports will not threaten the national security.

This section, first made part of the United States trade law in 1958, had been designed to authorize the Mandatory Oil Import Program, a system of import quotas and allocations imposed by President Eisenhower in 1959 and extended with many variations by succeeding presidents throughout the period when Middle East oil was available at a fraction of the cost of domestic oil.[i] The program had been heavily criticized

---

[e] Compare the changed provisions, both as to causality and as to who makes the determination, in the Trade Act of 1974, §§ 222 (workers) and 251 (firms). Documents Supplement pp. DS-348 and DS-363.

[f] For example, as Congress was beginning to consider the Trade Expansion Act in March 1962, President Kennedy issued escape clause proclamations (under the prior law) on Wilton carpets and flat glass, Procl. No. 3454, 3455 of March 19, 1962, 27 Fed. Reg. 2789, 2791 (1962). Both of these articles were imported primarily from Belgium, and that country reacted vigorously, demanding consultations, a GATT inquiry, and retaliatory measures. President Kennedy delayed the effectiveness of the action by 60 days (Procl. 3458 of March 27, 1962, 27 Fed. Reg. 3101 (1962), and consultations were held under GATT auspices. After these failed, the EEC suspended application to the United States of concessions on five products.

[g] Documents Supplement p. DS-351.

[h] An office that for the most part is concerned with such matters as civil defense, rehabilitation in the event of enemy attack, and assistance to states struck by natural disasters such as floods and hurricanes. In the revised version of this statute adopted in the Trade Act of 1974 (§ 127(d)), the functions of the Director of OEP are assigned to the Secretary of the Treasury and those functions were reassigned to the Secretary of Commerce pursuant to President Carter's Reorganization Plan No. 3, described in § 7.61 *infra*.

[i] For a fascinating account of what happens with such a program, essentially

in the United States,[i] but not in the GATT, partly because most of the oil producers (notably Venezuela, Iran, and Saudi Arabia) were not members of GATT,[k] partly because Article XXI, though not clearly applicable, seemed to be a self-judging provision that no one wanted to challenge directly.

(b) Look at the criteria for application of the national security provision set forth in section 232(c), and especially the clauses concerning ". . . the close relation of the economic welfare of the Nation to our national security" and "the impact of foreign competition on the economic welfare of individual domestic industries." Are these appropriate criteria for application of the apparently unlimited authority conferred on the President by section 232(b)? Could they be applied to products other than oil?[l]

3.67—Finally, one institutional provision not in the Administration's bill but added by the Congress is of interest. The feeling in the Congress was that entrusting trade negotiations to the State Department might lead to sacrificing American economic interests to broader considerations of foreign policy; assigning the task to the Departments of Commerce or Labor, however, might (i) short change the international relations aspects of trade negotiations; and (ii) be excessively subject to domestic (presumably protectionist) pressures. Accordingly the House Ways and Means Committee suggested (and President Kennedy accepted) establishment of a new office, the Special Representative for Trade Negotiations, known in the Washington alphabet game as STR (§ 241). State, Commerce, and Labor, as well as Treasury, Agriculture, and Interior, would continue to participate in the formulation of trade policy and of negotiating positions, but an independent agency would preside over interdepartmental committees and make the final decisions or recommendations to the President.

---

free from both domestic and international legislation, see Dam, "Implementation of Import Quotas: The Case of Oil," 14 J. Law & Econ. 1 (1971). See also C. Fulda and W. Schwartz, *Regulation of International Trade and Investment*, pp. 306–63 (1970) and materials there cited.

[j] In addition to the sources cited in N. i, see especially *The Oil Import Question*, A Report on the Relationship of Oil Imports to the National Security by the Cabinet Task Force on Oil Import Control, (Feb. 1970).

[k] Canada, which was also an important supplier and is an active member of GATT, was given an "overland exemption" which, with complications not here relevant, largely excluded it from the restrictive effects of the U.S. import quota.

[l] For a decision upholding an oil import fee on oil imposed by the President under § 232, see *Federal Energy Administration v. Algonquin SNG, Inc.*, 426 U.S. 548 (1976).

President Kennedy nominated as Special Representative Christian A. Herter, a former Republican governor of Massachusetts and Secretary of State in the last years of the Eisenhower Administration. Though not all holders of the post have had equal national and international standing, the office of STR did become a major new office in the United States executive branch, and, on the whole, a focus for internationalism within the government.[m]

§ 3.7—The Three Actors Come Together: The Kennedy Round[a]

Officially, 46 countries participated in the Kennedy Round, the sixth general tariff negotiation carried out under the auspices of the GATT. But the "big four," brought together in various working groups and in frequent moments of crisis, were the United States, the EEC, Great Britain and Japan, and the really tough negotiations were conducted between the United States and the European Community. Japan, as in other international negotiations,[b] defended its interests firmly, but did not take leadership positions commensurate with its economic strength. Britain, after 1964 under a Labour government, was not sure whether it would (or should) end up inside or outside the European Community. The EEC's own position was complicated by a variety of internal tensions—between France and the other Five, between the Commission and the Council, among high- and low-cost agricultural producers, and between industrial and agricultural interests. The United States had, perhaps, the strongest position of leadership (though not in comparison with earlier rounds), but was most subject to statutory constraints. The negotiations themselves took nearly five years, from the tentative decision of the GATT Contracting Parties in November 1962 to hold a new round of trade

---

[m] It is interesting that President Carter named as his Special Trade Representative Robert S. Strauss, a former chairman of the Democratic National Committee, whose career and reputation had been made chiefly in domestic politics, not in international affairs or economics. Equally interesting, Mr. Strauss was also given the assignment of being the Carter Administration's Special Counselor on Inflation.

[a] Two fine full-length accounts of the Kennedy Round by participants are heavily drawn on in this section: J. Evans, *The Kennedy Round in American Trade Policy*, (1971); E. Preeg, *Traders and Diplomats*, (1970). For lawyers' analyses, see Rehm, "The Kennedy Round of Trade Negotiations," 62 Am. J. Int'l. L. 403 (1968); K. Dam, The GATT, *Law and International Economic Organization*, pp. 68–78 (1970).

[b] For instance in the negotiations concerning revision of the Articles of Agreement of the IMF and the international monetary system in the years 1971–76, see Vol. IV of the series, A. Lowenfeld, *The International Monetary System*, §§ 5–8 (2d ed. 1984).

negotiations to a frantic series of round-the-clock sessions right up to the deadline established in the Trade Expansion Act—June 30, 1967.

3.71—THE IDEA OF LINEAR REDUCTIONS

The Kennedy Round was conceived by the United States and the other major participants as putting an end to item-by-item negotiations which, as we saw, had proved disappointing in the Dillon Round.[c] The way to overcome the problems of measuring reciprocal advantage, weighing thousands of items in terms of actual trade, potential trade, principal suppliers, third party suppliers, etc. would be to agree to an overall tariff cut across the board—in principle of 50 per cent of prevailing duties. Furthermore, it was expected that this approach would avoid the problem of meshing a series of bilateral negotiations into a single multilateral agreement, as had been done in prior rounds with increasing difficulties.

The United States Congress had accepted what became known as the linear approach, but with a significant exception. Under section 225 of the Trade Expansion Act,[d] the authority to negotiate tariff reductions did not extend to products on which actions had been taken under the escape clause or national security provisions; nor did the authority extend to products for which the Tariff Commission had recommended but the President had declined to take escape clause action and for which, according to the Tariff Commission, conditions had not changed. Thus by the time the Ministers gathered in Geneva in May

---

[c] Note that Article XXVIII bis of the GATT provides (in para. 2(a)) for negotiations "on a selective product-by-product basis or by the application of such multilateral procedures as may be accepted by the contracting parties concerned." United States law prior to the Trade Expansion Act did not expressly exclude across-the-board negotiations, but the legislative history and the statutory procedures for negotiating advice by industries and by the Tariff Commission implied that the delegation of authority was for negotiations on an article by article basis. See Jackson, *World Trade and the Law of GATT*, p. 223 (1969). Section 201 (a)(2) of the Trade Expansion Act does not contain the words "of any article" contained in § 350(a)(2) of the 1934 Act, and the legislative history of the 1962 Act is clear that across-the-board or "linear" negotiations were contemplated and authorized. See, e.g., Report of Sen. Finance Comm. on the Trade Expansion Act, S. Rep. No. 2059, 87th Cong. 2d Sess. p. 13 (1962); Rehm, N. a *supra* at p. 410.

[d] Documents Supplement p. DS-256.

1963 to organize the Kennedy Round, about 12 per cent of United States imports had been reserved from negotiations.[e] Other countries, guarding the reciprocity principle, wanted to be sure they could submit their own lists of exceptions, either at the start or when they saw how offers of their trading partners would affect them. The EEC, which had used linear tariff-cutting in negotiations with the EFTA countries and which had proposed across-the-board cuts in the Dillon Round, now also had products it wanted to hold back from "automatic" tariff-cutting, and it was not prepared to include agriculture in any automatic formula, if indeed it would be included in the Kennedy Round at all.

Another problem, known as the "disparities issue," interfered from the outset with the linear approach to tariff-cutting. The EEC pointed out that its tariffs on industrial products—the result of averaging member countries' tariffs in the formation of the common external tariff—were nearly all in the medium range of 10–20 per cent ad valorem, whereas the tariffs of the United States and Britain were widely dispersed, with many quite low duties but a good number in the 30–50 per cent range. The EEC argued that a 50 per cent cut would leave most of its tariffs at relatively low levels, whereas British and American (as well as Japanese and other) duties would continue to offer substantial protection. The EEC proposed, therefore, that instead of cuts by equal percentages, in which a 30 per cent tariff would go to 15 per cent and a 15 per cent tariff to 7.5 per cent, a formula should be adopted whereby tariffs would be reduced in the direction of (say half way to) equal targets, for instance 10 per cent for manufactures, 5 per cent for semi-manufactures, and zero for raw materials. From the United States point of view, a formula of this kind would not only be a major departure from reciprocity, but would subject the most sensitive commodities—i.e., the ones enjoying the highest levels of protection—to the most severe cuts.[f]

In the first meeting of the participants at the ministerial level in May 1963, the issues of reciprocity, exceptions, and disparities almost led to collapse at the outset. But after several post-midnight meetings—

---

[e] GATT Document L/1982, (14 March 1963) p. 5, quoted in Dam, N. a *supra* at 68. This figure, which seems high, included petroleum and its products, which, as previously mentioned, have not been subject of negotiations in the GATT.

[f] See Evans, N. a *supra*, Ch. 9, Preeg, N. a *supra* Ch. 4 for more detailed discussion of this issue in its several formulations.

a custom of the EEC Council that was picked up by the Kennedy Round —a compromise Ministerial Declaration was worked out:

> . . . in view of the limited results obtained in recent years from item-by-item negotiations, the tariff negotiations . . . shall be based upon a plan of substantial linear tariff reductions with a bare minimum of exceptions which shall be subject to confrontation and justification. The linear reductions shall be equal. In the cases where there are significant disparities in tariff levels, the tariff reductions will be based upon special rules of general and automatic application.[g]

Thus there would be exceptions, but "a bare minimum" (whatever that meant), and they would be subject to confrontation and justification (i.e., not just to preserve reciprocity?); moreover there would have to be inquiries into whether tariff disparities were significant—apparently meaning tariffs of major participants within particular industries.[h] On both counts, the assumption of comparative advantage that underlay the linear principle gave way to comparisons of conditions—tariffs, employment, competition, technology—in particular industries in the participating countries. Item-by-item negotiation did not return in quite the way it had been conducted before, but negotiating about exceptions, about reciprocal advantages, and about disparities within given industries made of the Kennedy Round an event rather different from what was envisioned at the outset. Indeed the bargaining about the negotiating rules—from November 1962, when the working party was organized, to the formal opening of the negotiations in May 1964—took as much time as any prior negotiating round.[i]

The course of the negotiations from May 1964 to June 1967 need not be traced here.[j] In brief, most of the major participants (but not

---

[g] GATT Ministerial Meeting May 16–21, 1963, Resolution on Arrangements for the Reduction or Elimination of Tariffs and Other Barriers to Trade, and Related Matters ¶ A(4), GATT, Basic Instruments and Selected Documents, 12th Supp. p. 47 (1964), reproduced also in 48 Dept. of State Bull. 995 (1963) and Preeg, N. a *supra,* at pp. 296–8.

[h] According to a negotiated interpretation attributed to the Chairman (the Swiss Minister), "significant" was defined as "meaningful in trade terms." See 48 Dept. of State Bull. 995 (1963).

[i] Evans, N. a *supra* p. 184.

[j] But for those who like contemporary history and politics, combining high drama with petty details and complex economic questions, the story is fascinating, and either the Preeg or the Evans book, N. a *supra,* is highly recommended.

Canada or Australia) accepted the principle of linear tariff cuts for industrial products. They spent from May to November 1964 preparing their exceptions lists, and then two and a half more years bargaining about each others' lists, about reciprocity, about the links (if any) between industrial and agricultural concessions, and about a variety of so-called non-tariff barriers. At the risk of taking one element out of context, however, it is worth looking at the so-called sectoral negotiations, both for the way they reflect departures from the initial assumptions of the Kennedy Round and as background for the problems of steel discussed in succeeding sections of this book.

3.72—SECTORAL NEGOTIATIONS

Once the exceptions lists of the major participants had been analyzed, discussions began on five major industries—pulp and paper, aluminum, iron and steel, cotton textiles, and chemicals.[a] The latter two were the most difficult; the negotiations on steel, however, were perhaps the most interesting, and are summarized here for the light they shed both on the Kennedy Round and on the problems of the 1970's.

Steel, as we will see in more detail in the next section, was beginning to be in oversupply worldwide in the mid-1960's. Steel plants had been constructed in many parts of the world, including developing countries— once the export preserve of the United States and Western Europe; some uses of steel had been taken over by plastics and aluminum, and patterns of trade had shifted substantially from those of the 1950's. The United States, once a leading exporter of steel, had become a net importer in 1959, and by 1966 imported about 11 per cent of its consumption. In the EEC (ECSC), production was running at about 80 per cent of capacity. Japan had been increasing its production from about 20 million tons before 1960 to over 50 million tons by the middle of the decade. Exports from Japan had increased fastest to the United States, but Great Britain and the Community were also worried. The Big Four, plus Sweden and Austria, made up the steel sector group.

---

[a] There were also, by common consent, separate and highly controversial negotiations on agriculture, based not on linear reductions or departures therefrom, but on the basis of "acceptable conditions of access to world markets for agricultural products." Ministerial Declaration of May 21, 1963, N. g *supra* ¶ A(7). These negotiations were further broken down into a Grains Group and a Meat and Dairy Products Group, but ultimately resolved in a "package deal" that left everyone rather unsatisfied.

The United States, which had relatively low tariffs on steel (about 7–9 per cent)[b] was anxious to have steel included in the linear tariff reductions, because neither the members of the European Community nor Great Britain had bound their duties on steel under Article II of the GATT. Thus, though Britain's duties on steel averaged about 11 per cent and the duties of the Community countries averaged about 9 per cent, these duties could be raised without fear of retaliation, and with possible diversion of exports to the United States, whereas if the United States should want to raise its duties, it would be liable to pay heavy compensation to its suppliers.[c] The Community was prepared to consider linear cuts of up to 50 per cent, but took the position that as there was not yet a common external tariff on steel,[d] the "legal rates" of the member states—averaging about 14 per cent—should be used as a base from which to compute the percentage reduction. In fact the ECSC countries had achieved substantial reduction and harmonization of tariffs on steel, as called for by the GATT waiver when the Coal and Steel Community had been formed.[e] BENELUX and German duties had gone up from 4 to 6 per cent in 1958, and French and Italian duties down from 7 and 11 per cent respectively, resulting in a weighted average of just under 7 per cent. Britain had agreed in 1957 to reduce its tariffs on steel in return for the Community's promise not to raise its members' steel tariffs. Britain did not want to pay for a reduction it had already paid for, and the United States did not want to cut its actual tariffs in return for cuts by the Community from a hypothetical rate to a rate equal to the actual pre-Kennedy Round rate. In other kinds of tariff negotiations, an offer by the United States on steel might have been matched by an offer from the Community on machines or radios or whatever. By virtue of the sectoral negotiating format, reductions in steel duties by one participant required matching cuts by the others.

By spring of 1965, discussion of steel on the basis of linear cuts was

---

[b] The numbers here are estimates, because numerous tariffs on distinct products—plate, rods, alloys, etc.—are involved, and in some cases the duties were imposed on a specific (i.e., per ton) rather than an ad valorem basis. The estimates here used, as well as much of the narrative, are taken from Preeg, § 3.7 N. a *supra*, pp. 103–06.

[c] In fact the ECSC had raised duties on steel of member countries in February 1964—i.e., in contemplation of the Kennedy Round—from an average of 7 to 9 per cent.

[d] See § 3.12 *supra*.

[e] § 3.12 at ns. n–q *supra* and Documents Supplement p. DS-561.

completely deadlocked, and another approach, favored by the EEC for various other products, was tried on steel—"harmonization." A long and tedious examination began in which all the individual tariffs and tariff classifications would be matched, with a view to achieving a target that all of the Big Four could approach in stages. But no clear target emerged, no norm around which the others were dispersed symmetrically. During the year of discussions, United States imports rose rapidly, partly as the result of a strike threat, partly as the result of a costly wage settlement and price rise.[f] Britain was absorbed in the debate over nationalization of the steel industry—a major plank of the Labour Party, which had returned to power in the fall of 1964 after 13 years of opposition. Japan, for its part, was meeting increasing resistance in Europe as in North America against its textile exports and might make substantial withdrawals in its linear offers if it did not see prospects of reductions in steel duties. Moreover, Japan took the view that it was not concerned so much with United States tariffs as with its burdensome anti-dumping procedures.[g]

To break the two-year long stalemate, the idea of harmonization was reintroduced early in 1967. Without having to agree on the proper base (and therefore without having to determine the size of a cut for purposes of measuring reciprocity), the ECSC countries would establish a common external tariff on steel at an average of about 5.7 per cent ad valorem, roughly 1 per cent below the average of the duties actually applied before the Kennedy Round began[h]; the United States would cut its rates just enough to match ("harmonize with") the Community's rates— roughly from 7.5 per cent to 6 per cent.[i] Britain would cut its duties on steel by about 20 per cent, and Japan, which started at about 15 per cent (but of course was a heavy exporter of steel) cut its duties by a flat 50 per cent. Austria and Sweden also aligned their duties, so that all the major steel countries ended up with duties of about 6–7 per cent ad valorem—all bound in the GATT. Britain was the most reluctant. having made the largest cut of any of the importing countries, but it finally said

---

[f] See § 4.2 *infra.*

[g] See § 4.41–.44 *infra.*

[h] Compare N. c *supra.*

[i] The discrepancy between the ECSC and the U.S. rates—just one of the many controversial details—is explained by the fact that while most of the world, including the Community, computes duties on the basis of c.i.f. prices—i.e., landed cost, customs valuation in the United States is based on f.o.b. prices—i.e., not including insurance and freight. For the U.S. method of valuation for customs purposes, see 19 U.S.C. § 1401a.

yes in the last days of the Kennedy Round, as everything was coming down to a package deal or bust.[j]

Comparable negotiations were held with regard to each of the other sectors, with mixed results. Each sector had its own problems, and a somewhat different group of participants. In paper and pulp, for instance, the Community would not make concessions with regard to paper without assurance by the Nordic countries of access to pulp; a special deal between the Nordics and the Community, however, would be objectionable to Canada and the United States. On aluminum, the interests were as much those of several multinational enterprises as they were of participating countries.[k] One might expect this would lead to a desire for maximum tariff cuts; but the Western countries did not want to reduce their duties on aluminum if Japan did not. Japan was reluctant because it was bound to grant MFN to the Soviet Union, and the EEC, as we saw, had conflicting interests among the Six[l] which it sought to resolve by distinguishing between ingot and fabricated aluminum.

On chemicals, the United States was on the defensive, because of a system of customs valuation known as American Selling Price. ASP had been enacted as part of the Fordney-McCumber Tariff in 1922[m] as protection for portions of the domestic chemicals industry against renewed competition from Germany. ASP duties protected less than 10 per cent of the American chemical industry (principally coal tar derivatives), and only 5 per cent of imports; but because ASP duties were applied on the domestic wholesale price as set by domestic producers rather than on export value as set by foreign producers, the protective wall could be very high indeed.[n] The United States negotiators acknowledged this,

---

[j] For some detailed estimates from the point of view of U.S. Imports, see Office of Special Representative for Trade Negotiations, *1964–67 Trade Conference: Report on United States Negotiations,* vol. I, pp. 178–80 (1968).

[k] Not only did most of the majors have overseas bauxite and unwrought aluminum subsidiaries, but they also had fabricating subsidiaries and affiliates in other producing countries. For instance, Alcoa had a fabricating affiliate in Japan; Reynolds in Germany, the Netherlands, Belgium, Italy and Japan; Pechiney (French) in Belgium and USA; Kaiser in Germany, Italy and Japan. See Evans, § 3.7 N. a *supra* at 232–33.

[l] See § 3.23(c) *supra.*

[m] § 315 of the Tariff Act of 1922, 42 Stat. 941, 19 U.S.C. § 1401a(e) and 1402(g).

[n] Converted to normal valuation, some ASP duties came to more than 100

and made no attempt to defend ASP on the merits[o]; they concluded, however, that ASP could not be eliminated except by Act of Congress.[p] Britain and the EEC, which had made a major issue of ASP in the chemical sector talks, proposed that all reductions in tariffs on chemicals be made contingent on elimination of ASP by the United States; the United States negotiators, however, did not want to confront Congress with a fait accompli or to risk unraveling of the entire agreement in the important chemical sector if Congress failed to act. Eventually, as part of the last-minute settlements of May 1967, a package (or rather two-package) deal was worked out: In the first package the United States would reduce its duties on chemicals by an average of 43 per cent (not counting products covered by ASP), the EEC would reduce its duties by a weighted average of 20 per cent, Britain by 25 per cent, and Japan by 44 per cent; in the second package, to be implemented if Congress repealed ASP by January 1, 1969, the United States would convert ASP duties to equivalent duties calculated in the usual way, and then cut them in half; the EEC would reduce its duties so as to come close to a full cut of 50 per cent from the pre-Kennedy round rates; Britain, whose duties on chemicals had been lower, would align its rates with those of the Community, and Switzerland, Britain, and several EEC countries would eliminate certain practices (notably a road tax that discourages purchases of large automobiles) that had discriminated against United States products.[q]

In the end, the two-package deal—along with several other last minute packages—prevented the Kennedy Round from failing. The second package, however, was never delivered. Congress debated ASP for several years, but no legislation was adopted. Following a number of extensions, the ASP agreement was allowed to lapse in 1972.[r]

---

per cent ad valorem, the arithmetic average was 52 per cent, and the highest (known as Mont Blanc during the Kennedy Round) reached 172 per cent.

[o] While ASP would have contravened Article VII and perhaps other articles of the GATT, is was technically not a violation by virtue of the grandfather clause (§ 2.2 at N. p. *supra*) in the Protocol of Provisional Application.

[p] For analysis of this point, as well as a more detailed account of the ASP controversy in general, see Rehm, § 3.7 N. a *supra,* at pp. 414–20.

[q] For a more detailed summary, see *Report on United States Negotiations* N. j *supra* vol. I, pp. 173–76.

[r] The Trade Act of 1974 did address ASP, as one of the non-tariff barriers for whose removal the President was authorized to negotiate, but subject to express approval by the Congress. See § 102(b), (d), (e) and (g), Documents Supplement p. DS-298–300.

* * *

And so it went. A Grains Agreement was concluded that did not guarantee access to European markets, but attempted to cut the developing (and presumably hungry) countries in on some of the surpluses generated by Community price supports. The Long Term Arrangement in Cotton Textiles—essentially an import quota agreement built around GATT Article XIX—was extended, as a condition for tariff cuts by the developed countries.[s]

In short, the sensitive issues were somehow resolved, compromised, or postponed, so that in the end none of them led to a breakdown of the Conference. But reciprocity, as perceived by the participants, stood in the way of across-the-board liberalization, and to a significant extent defeated the hope of eliminating the prior practice of product-by-product (and bilateral) haggling.

3.73—RESULTS OF THE KENNEDY ROUND

In a sense, emphasizing the sectoral negotiations in this brief account of the Kennedy Round is unfair, in that the sectors picked out for special consideration were precisely the most difficult, the most sensitive, the most challenging to the assumptions of comparative advantage. On the other hand, these issues were the ones that caused the Conference to go on for nearly five years, and to dilute—though not to destroy—the bold vision of President Kennedy. One can point out, as Professor Dam does,[t] that 30 per cent of the dutiable imports of the major participants were left untouched by tariff reductions; or one can stress, as Eric Wyndham White, the GATT's Director General, did at the close of the Conference, that the industrialized countries participating in the Kennedy Round made duty reductions on 70 per cent of their dutiable imports—and that two thirds of these cuts amounted to 50 per cent or more.[u] One can point to the generalized acceptance—at least by the

---

[s] As must be obvious by now and will be even clearer from the succeeding chapters of this book, each industry and each agreement has its own special characteristics, its own reasons—not to say justifications—for departure from the GATT principles. For relatively brief but analytical accounts of the Long Term Arrangements in Cotton Textiles, see Dam, § 3.7 N. a *supra* at pp. 296–315; G. Patterson, *Discrimination in International Trade, the Policy Issues, 1945–1965* pp. 307–17 (1966).

[t] Dam, § 3.7 N. a *supra* at 77.

[u] Statement at the meeting of the Trade Negotiations Committee by the Director

developed countries—of the concept of linear duty reductions, or one can seek to inquire why some products or sectors seem not to lend themselves—in the real world—to this approach.

Overall, the average level of tariffs on dutiable non-agricultural products for the big four participants in the Kennedy Round was reduced from 12.8–16.6 per cent ad valorem to 8.1–10.6 per cent after the staging requirements of the Kennedy Round were completed in 1972.[v] The amount of these reductions—roughly 36–39 per cent of previous levels of duties—suggests at least a rough balance of concessions, and a substantial step along the way to the goal of 50 per cent reductions.[w] Moreover, the danger that the European Common Market would become inward-directed and produce massive trade diversion (§ 3.21 supra) seems to

---

General of the GATT, June 30, 1967, reproduced in full in Preeg, § 3.7 N. a *supra* at 299, 300.

[v] See Preeg, § 3.7 N. a *supra* p. 264. For a detailed breakdown of this summary statement in a variety of ways by countries, products, high and low level duties, etc. see *id.* pp. 204–48. The aggregate figures given in the text may be broken down by countries as follows:

Reductions in Duties on Non-Agricultural
Products other than Mineral Fuels

	A Pre-K-R Duties (ad valorem on dutiable imports)	B Post K-R Duties (ad valorem on dutiable imports)	C Percentage Cut (A minus B)* A
USA	13.5%	9.6%	36%
EEC	12.8	8.1	37
UK	16.6	10.6	39
Japan	15.5	9.5	39

* trade weighted

These figures were computed on the assumption that the ASP agreement would go through; accordingly, the figures in column B for the United States, EEC and Britain should be raised somewhat, and those in column C lowered.

Source: Preeg, op. cit. tables 13.1–13.4.

[w] The official United States report says the United States granted tariff concessions on $8.5 billion of its imports, of which $7.9 billion came from participants; other participants made concessions affecting about $30 billion, including $7.6 billion from the United States. *Report on United States Negotiations*, N. j *supra* pp. iii-v. This formulation, as the Report recognizes, does not identify the depth of tariff cuts, and indeed includes binding of duty-free treatment or binding previously unbound duties without modification, which may be valuable concessions but will not change the pattern of trade.

have been largely overcome—always excepting agriculture. Trade effects of these cuts were hard to foresee, and are equally hard to measure a decade and a half later, because the international monetary crisis, followed by the oil crisis, shifted statistical measurements, as well as patterns of trade, beyond hope of retrieval for accurate comparison. But all those concerned with international trade—whether to promote it or to defend against it—began to widen their horizons after the Kennedy Round. From now on, not only tariffs, but subsidies, dumping, internal taxes, and a variety of old and new forms of quantitative restrictions, would require the attention of business, labor, and government.

§ 4—Steel

§ 4.1—The Basic Metal

Steel has always been a symbol of strength. It was the product par excellence of the industrial revolution, and for most of the nineteenth century Great Britain was the world's leading producer of steel. When the United States became the world's largest steel producer at the turn of the century, that fact, more than any other, demonstrated its arrival as the predominant industrial state. Germany became Europe's leading industrial power before World War I by reaching a level of steel production nearly double that of Britain and four times that of France. When the Soviet Union embarked on its campaign of industrialization, and later on its campaign to surpass the United States, steel was the main focus.[a] Japan's post-war recovery, as we saw, focused in major part on steel, and on the materials to make and carry it. The European integration movement focused first on steel and on the coal needed to produce it. Developing countries—notably Brazil and India, but also Mexico, Argentina, South Korea, and others—have measured their advance in terms of their steel production, even when neither close-by resources nor the size of the market made such production economical. In 1950 32 countries produced steel; in 1976 the number had reached 71. Still, the United States, the Soviet Union, the European Community (including Great Britain), and Japan together produce about three fourths of the world's steel.

Steel, and its principal component, iron, have been civilization's most useful metals. Indeed, the Iron Age, when man learned to shape iron through repeated heating and pounding, is considered for many purposes the beginning of modern civilization—about 1,000 B.C. in Greece, somewhat earlier in Egypt.[b] Blast furnaces for making iron from ores date back to the 14th century, and they crossed the Atlantic with the earliest colonial settlers. In fact, many of the men who chose the new

---

[a] And of course the Soviet Union's leader for 30 years took a name meaning Man of Steel, which he lived up to in more ways than one. The Soviet Union did surpass the United States in steel production in 1971, and has continued as the world's largest single producer of steel. By various other measures, such as Gross National Product, per capita income, etc., the Soviet Union continues to be well back of the United States, and of the EEC considered as a unit.

[b] The Bronze Age, dependent on various alloys of copper and tin, preceded the Iron Age by about 1,000 years.

143

world in preference to prisons in England or Scotland worked off their sentences in colonial iron mines. Later, one of the many sources of conflict between the colonies and the mother country was the latter's effort to prevent iron or steel works from being built in North America.[c] While steel—iron tempered and hardened with carbon—was known throughout much of recorded history, witness the famous Damascus and Toledo swords, the major industrial metal until the middle of the nineteenth century remained iron. The steam engine, the spinning jenny and power loom, even early railways and steamships, all began in the age of iron.

The modern era—the age of steel—began in 1856, when Sir Henry Bessemer, an Englishman, perfected a method for making steel from pig iron in a pneumatic converter by blowing air at high temperature and pressure through molten iron. Not only was Bessemer's product stronger and harder than prior iron and steel products, but it could be made in great volume, high speed, and (comparatively) low cost. As railroads were built all over Europe and North America, the technological revolutions in metallurgy, transportation, machinery, and (somewhat later) electric power generation all fueled each other in the second half of the nineteenth century, in the greatest technical advance society had known up to that time.

Today the Bessemer process is no longer used in the United States, Japan, or the Soviet Union, and to a declining degree in Europe. Most steel is made in open hearth, electric, or basic oxygen furnaces. But all of these techniques are variations of the method inaugurated by Bessemer. First coal is converted to coke for use as fuel and reductant for smelting iron ore. Next, the ore plus scrap iron, coke, and limestone are combined in a blast furnace to produce molten iron. Third, the molten iron is transported to a furnace (open hearth, basic oxygen or electric) where it is converted to steel by addition of heat, air (or oxygen) and carbon plus other alloying materials such as manganese, chromium, tungsten, or nickel. Nearly all steel mills are vertically integrated from the ore (or scrap) stage through production of steel in the form of slabs, billets, or blooms and on to one of the basic crude steel

---

[c] See e.g., "An Act to Encourage the Importation of Pig and Bar Iron from His Majesty's Colonies in America; and to Prevent the Erection of Any Mill or other Engine for Slitting or Rolling of Iron or any Plateing Forge to Work with a Tilt Hammer or any Furnace for Making Steel in any Part of the said Colonies," 23 Geo. 2 c. 29 (1750).

products—sheets, plates, rods, tube rounds, structural shapes or rails. The tonnages used here and elsewhere to measure production, imports, consumption, etc. are usually in terms of one of these products. Many steel operations carry the process further and produce pipe, wire, nails, galvanized sheets, tin plate, etc. in various standard or made-up versions, often with chemical and metallurgical properties designed for particular uses.

A basic steel operation requires substantial technical knowledge, capital and organization. Among major industrial countries, however, steel is not today considered a high technology or dynamic industry. There are always small improvements, but in comparison with other industries, research and development is relatively low and is directed largely to cost reduction rather than to discovery of new products or markets. All the major enterprises in Europe, North America and Japan—some 20–30 firms[d]—seem to command about the same levels of technology and to produce a roughly homogeneous line of products. This means, of course, that trade is in very large measure affected by price—and by trade barriers or their removal.

§ 4.2—The American Steel Industry[a]

At about the time Bessemer was revolutionizing the production of steel in Great Britain, an American named William Kelly was also perfecting a system of making steel; indeed in litigation after the Civil War, it was determined that Kelly's patents antedated Bessemer's. Another American engineer, Alexander L. Holley, combined the best elements of Bessemer's and Kelly's inventions, and under the leadership of Andrew Carnegie, a Scottish immigrant and master builder, the steel industry in the United States grew at an enormous pace, passing Britain in the 1890's, and by the close of World War I accounting for nearly 60 per cent of the world's production.[b] The United States possessed low cost,

---

[d] The number varies as a result of various mergers in all the principal countries.

[a] See generally W. Adams, ed. *The Structure of American Industry*, ch. 3, "The Steel Industry" (1977).

[b] See Table III–1, DS-761.

Between 1893 and 1913, as British production increased by 136 per cent and Germany's by 522 per cent, the United States' production increased by 715 per cent. See *Steel Imports*, Staff Study of Sen. Comm. on Finance, S. Doc. No. 107, 90th Cong., 2d Sess. p. 1 (1968). (Hereafter *Senate Staff Study*.)

high quality iron ore deposits in the Mesabi range near Lake Superior, the world's best coking coal deposits near Pittsburgh, and in the Great Lakes an inexpensive means to bring the iron to the coal. In addition, the United States had a continent-size market free from trade barriers, and a social climate hospitable to dynamic entrepeneurs such as Carnegie and Rockefeller. In many instances growing steel plants attracted central European immigrants seeking jobs, as is still reflected in the ethnic composition of major steel producing centers—Pittsburgh, Youngstown, Gary—several generations later. Steel, with its best customer, automobiles, became the backbone of the American economy. Even as other materials—notably aluminum—grew in importance, steel in the mid-1960's still accounted for about 95 per cent (by tonnage) of the metals used in the United States.[c]

The steel industry in the United States was in a number of respects different from other American industries. For one thing, the largest firm controlled a declining, not increasing share of domestic production. When the United States Steel Corporation was formed in 1901 by J.P. Morgan in a "combination of combinations" that directly or indirectly brought about 180 independent concerns under a single control with the Carnegie Steel Corporation as its centerpiece,[d] "Big Steel" accounted for about 65 per cent of the nation's steel capacity. After the first War, the U.S. Supreme Court rejected (4–3) the government's attempt to break up U.S. Steel as it had broken up American Tobacco and Standard Oil,[e] but Judge Gary and his successors at the head of U.S. Steel seem

---

[c] See Senate Staff Study, N. b *supra* pp. 1–2 for much of the information in this paragraph.

[d] See *United States v. United States Steel Corporation*, 251 U.S. 417, 439 (1920). For a brief, interesting account of the maneuvering to put U.S. Steel together, involving not only Morgan and Carnegie, but Charles Schwab, "Bet-a-Million" Gates, Judge Elbert Gary, and other legendary figures from the business history of the United States, see F. L. Allen, *The Great Pierpont Morgan,* ch. IX "Billion-dollar Adventure," (1949). A little known fact related to this enterprise is that shortly after U.S. Steel was organized, Morgan purchased for it from John D. Rockefeller the Lake Superior Consolidated Iron Mines, which controlled the largest deposits of ore in the Mesabi Range in Minnesota. Thus in one operation, Morgan completed both horizontal and vertical integration of the American steel industry.

[e] *United States v. United States Steel Corporation,* 251 U.S. 417 (1920). The suit was originally filed in 1911, the year the Standard Oil and Tobacco cases were decided, but various delays, including America's entry into World War I, stretched the case out till 1920. Justices McReynolds and Brandeis did not participate in the case.

to have taken the hint that excessive size could make the company
vulnerable, and to have endeavored to keep the company's capacity at
or below fifty per cent of the nation's capacity. By the late thirties U.S.
Steel controlled about a third of United States steel production, and by
the mid-1960's, its share was down to about 25 per cent.

The four largest companies—U.S. Steel, Bethlehem, National, and
Republic, control about 50 per cent of United States capacity, and the
eight largest—the first four plus Armco, Jones & Laughlin, Inland, and
Youngstown—control close to 75 per cent of U.S. capacity. Moreover,
all of the top eight and most of the top twenty companies are vertically
integrated, i.e., they operate coke ovens, blast furnaces, steelmaking furnaces, and rolling and finishing facilities; many firms also are integrated
further back, with coal and iron, and forward, with facilities for fabricating finished products.[f]

There has been competition among steel companies in the United
States—essentially for market shares and for particular customers and
product lines. But the competition did not take the form of differential
pricing. From the time Judge Gary gave a famous series of dinners
to which his competitors were invited (1907–11),[g] prices in the steel
industry have tended to move together, nearly always with U.S. Steel
in the lead. From 1920 to 1948, steel prices in the United States were
quoted according to the "basing point" system, whereby steel delivered
at any point in the country was priced as if it had been produced and
shipped from the nearest basing point (Pittsburgh, Chicago, Birming-
ham, etc.) regardless of the actual point of shipment or the freight
paid. Even when basing point pricing was abandoned in the steel industry in 1948 after the cement industry lost a basing point case in
the Supreme Court,[h] price leadership persisted, not only in meeting
competitors' reductions, but, typically in matching Big Steel's price increases.[i]

[f] See Federal Trade Commission, *Staff Report on the United States Steel Industry and Its International Rivals,* esp. pp. 83–90 (1977).

[g] See e.g., *United States v. U.S. Steel Corp.,* 251 U.S. at 440, 445; for a fuller
account, see *Hearings before the House Comm. on Investigation of the U.S. Steel
Corporation,* 62d Cong., 2d Sess. (1911).

[h] *Federal Trade Commission v. Cement Institute,* 333 U.S. 683 (1948). See
also an almost contemporaneous case involving steel pipe, *Triangle Conduit &
Cable Co.* v. *Federal Trade Commission,* 168 F.2d 175 (7th Cir. 1948).

[i] For a record of price changes in the steel industry by leaders and followers

The effect of price leadership has been much more stability than in other industries—slower increases in periods of strong demand, slower (or no) reductions in periods of slack demand. On the firmly held assumption that the demand for steel was not price-elastic but moved in parallel with general economic conditions, the United States producers made their adjustments in output, not in price. Whether another effect of price stability was lack of pressure for technological innovation has been the subject of sharp dispute.[1] At all events, when the press of imports came upon the American steel industry in the 1960's, it found itself in the position of a high price, and rather price-rigid, producer, searching for means other than price competition to preserve its market position.

§ 4.3—Steel Imports to the United States: The First Crisis

For nearly all of the twentieth century until 1959, the United States was a net exporter of steel. At the end of the decade of the 1950's, three events came together to change that pattern. The United States industry went through a 116-day strike, during which many users turned to foreign steel and found it satisfactory in terms of quality and reliability, and advantageous in terms of price. The St. Lawrence Seaway was opened, making the industrial heartland of the United States accessible to seaborne shipments from abroad. And Japan's steel production began to outstrip its steel consumption, even as both increased at a rapid rate.

Between 1957 and 1959, the United States position as a steel trader slipped from that of a net exporter of over 4 million tons to that of a net importer of 2.7 million tons. By 1966 the net import figure had climbed to about 9 million tons, nearly 10 per cent of consumption. The Senate Finance Committee, which as we saw had gone along with President Kennedy in supporting the Trade Expansion Act, but which shared with

---

over a six year period beginning with the celebrated confrontation between President Kennedy and the steel industry in April of 1962, see *Foreign Trade and Tariff Proposals*, Hearings before House Comm. on Ways and Means, pt. 4, pp. 1460–68, 90th Cong., 2d Sess. (1968).

[1] For a well-known debate on this issue, focusing on the delay in introducing the basic oxygen furnace into American steelmaking, see Adams and Dirlam, "Big Steel, Invention, and Innovation," 80 Q. J. Econ. 167 (1966); McAdams, "Big Steel, Invention, and Innovation Reconsidered," 81 Q. J. Econ. 457 (1967).

much of the country mixed feelings both about trade and about steel, commissioned a major study of the steel import problem. The findings of the 523-page study were summarized as follows:[a]

SUMMARY OF FACTUAL FINDINGS

(1) U.S. steel production has fallen from 61 percent of world output in 1945 to 26 percent in 1966, and will probably drop to 21 percent in 1975. Between 1947 and 1966 Japan's share of world steel output has increased tenfold, Italy's tripled, the U.S.S.R.'s doubled, and Red China produced more steel in 1966 than any country had in 1947, with the exception of the United States and the U.S.S.R.

(2) Annual growth rates of steel production since 1900 have progressively declined in the United States and increased in the rest of the world, as shown below:

[In percent]

Year	United States	Rest of world
1900–18	7.4	4.4
1920–45	3.2	3.7
1950–66	1.4	8.3

(3) World steel capacity on January 1, 1966, has been estimated as 590 to 600 million tons (MT) compared to world output in 1966 of 520 MT, leaving a surplus capacity of 70–80 MT. An official estimate of the ECSC published in June 1967 projects annual increases of 33 MT in world capacity to 1970. This study estimates increases in world demand of only 20–25 MT, indicating a progressive aggravation of the world steel surplus problem.

(4) Because the U.S. steel industry promptly adjusts output to orders and in the Communist countries output and capacity are about equal, the rest of the free world has a surplus capacity of some 45–55 MT.

(5) The Kennedy round will result in a five-stage reduction of U.S. steel tariffs, from a weighted average of 7.44 percent in 1966 to 6.5 percent in 1972. Other major countries reduced their tariffs on steel generally by more than the United States, with the result that steel tariffs are now more closely harmonized among major countries. This does not, however, take into account the very high and rising nontariff barriers, which foreign countries use to their advantage.

(6) In 1966, the balance of trade in steel was:

	Million tons	In billions of dollars
Imports	10.8	1.313
Exports	1.7	.635
Net imports	9.1	.678

[a] *Steel Imports*, Staff Study of Sen. Comm. on Finance, S. Doc. No. 107, Dec. 19, 1967, pp. XXV–XXIX, 90th Cong., 2d Sess. (1968).

Imports were 12 percent of domestic shipments (90 MT) and 10.7 percent of domestic consumption (104.4 MT).

Excluding AID financed exports, the deficit was $899 million. When end-use products (machinery, trucks, etc.) are included, the deficit was reduced to $496 million. Adjusted further to include net trade in steel-making raw materials (iron ore, coal, scrap) the deficit was $499 million.

(7) Overvaluation of the dollar cannot be considered a cause of increasing steel imports. The general price level between 1957 and 1965 rose faster abroad than in this country.

(8) On the basis of research and development (R. & D.) as a percentage of sales, the steel industry ranked among the lowest of 19 major U.S. industries. The largest export industries, in relation to sales, were shown by those with the highest ratios of R. & D. to sales.

(9) Steel imports are not yet a dominating factor in the regional growth of domestic steel production. Regional population shifts and relative growth rates of steel-consuming industries are more relevant factors at present.

(10) Between 1947 and 1966, the steel industry has decreased somewhat its relative standing among major industries in sales, profits, Federal income taxes, cash dividends, total assets, total employment, and total payroll, but has increased in capital expenditure and value added.

(11) Steel demand actually declined in this country between 1957 and 1963 due to these factors:

(a) A shift in GNP from durables to services.

(b) Long-term downward trend of certain steel-consuming industries such as railroads and oil-well drilling.

(c) Stronger, lighter gage steels and a trend toward lighter functional designs.

(d) Corrosion resistant steels increase life expectancy of products made from steel.

(e) Increase of competition from substitutes (plastics, aluminum, and other light weight nonferrous metals, etc.).

(12) Steel prices rose between 1946 and 1957 by 132.5 percent compared to 60.8 percent for all industrial commodities. This was caused by managerial decisions to obtain funds internally rather than through the capital markets in order to increase capacity and to find new sources of iron ore. Unfortunately, these higher prices resulted in greater competition from imports and substitutes thus thwarting the objective for which they were imposed. From 1957 to 1966, steel prices rose by 7.7 percent while prices of all industrial commodities rose by an average of 5.5 percent. However, steels were of improved quality by 1966 and the yield of finished steel products from raw steel had declined from 75 (1959) to 67 percent, accounting in part for the steel price increases.

(13) In 1966, the steel industry ranked in 39th place out of 41 major industries in the ratio of net profit after taxes to net worth. As a result, steel equities sold at 81 percent of book value compared to 196 percent for all industries, and at only 9.5 times earnings compared to 15.2 for all industries.

(14) For the years 1956–66, capital expenditures exceeded cash flow (depreciation, depletion, amortization, and retained earnings) by $1.2 billion. As a result, long-term debt as a percentage of net worth and debt rose from 15 to 24 percent. Interest costs as a percentage of sales rose from 0.4 to 1 percent. Working capital was still satisfactory at 225 percent of current liabilities, but the liquidity of working capital as measured by the percentage of cash and securities had fallen from 72 to 49 percent.

(15) An analysis of the financial statements of U.S. and foreign steel producers shows the following salient facts:

(a) *Current ratio.*—Standard U.S. managerial practice requires that current assets should be, at least, double current liabilities. With the exception of the British and Dutch companies, none of the West European or Japanese industries approach this standard. For Japan, current assets are only 117 percent of current liabilities, and for Italy, only 77 percent.

(b) *Profits after taxes as a percentage of total assets.*—U.S. profits ranked 39th out of 41 major U.S. industries in 1966, but they were 5.7 percent compared to 0.5 percent for Belgium, 1.5 percent for Germany, 0.3 percent for France, 1 percent for Italy, and 2 percent for Japan.

(c) *Total debt as a percentage of total assets.*—For the United States, debt as a percent of total assets was, in 1965, 34 percent as compared to 60 percent for Germany, 65 percent for France, 73 percent for Italy, and 69 percent for Japan. The German steel industry reported that for most producers long-term debt is about 180 percent of equity, which means that creditors own about two-thirds of the German steel producers.

(16) The decline in European profit margins and future profit expectations is clearly reflected in the nearly 50-percent reduction in investment between 1963 and 1965, while the United States showed almost a 50-percent increase. Data for 1966 would show a continuation of these diverse trends.

Annual capital investment per annual tonnage of raw steel output

Year	United States	Japan	ECSC	United Kingdom
1965	$15.2	$12.3	$10.9	$5.1
1964	13.9	11.6	15.9	5.9
1963	10.5	14.6	20.1	9.4

(17) By investing at an annual rate of $2 to $2.5 billion for the next 5 years, the industry expects to lower its cost of making carbon steel by about $5 a ton, assuming other costs remain constant. Even if we assume annual plant and equipment outlays of only $2 billion, depreciation charges alone in 5 years would be higher by $0.4 billion or by about $4 a ton. Unless output increases by at least 2 to 2.5 million tons annually and at prices fully compensating for all cost increases, the industry cannot expect to improve its stance in competition with foreign imports.

(18) The price differential for domestic buyers between domestic steel and imported steel appears to be in a range of $20 to $25.

(19) To gauge the present competitive position of U.S. steel products in the home market, an attempt was made to compare domestic prices and average costs with average costs of Japanese and Western European steel producers. Because costs vary greatly between Western European countries, and in each country between companies and even individual plants of the same companies, and because they depend on accounting practices, it cannot be emphasized too strongly that the data given below are merely for bench-mark purposes.

Average cost at mill and delivered to U.S. customer for a ton of carbon steel products

	United States	Japan	Western Europe
Average production costs at mill	$133	$100	$116
Average cost delivered to U.S. customer	163	127	143
Differential between U.S. and foreign delivered costs		36	20

On the basis of the producer's average cost of carbon steel products delivered to U.S. customers and a price differential of $20 to $25, the Europeans appear to sell here at cost or below, while the Japanese steel industry would still make a profit of from $16 to $20 a ton if it sold at a differential of $20 to $25 a ton.

These profit margins still have to be qualified in two ways:

(*a*) While Japanese mill costs are below Western European mill costs, and while cost of entry (transport from mill to port, ocean freight, tariff, and U.S. freight from port of entry to U.S. customer) are roughly equal, the average prices f.o.b. foreign ports in 1966 actually were as follows:

ECSC . . . . $ 99
Japan 112
United Kingdom 114

The reason is found in the much higher grade product mix (cold-rolled sheet and strip) of Japanese and United Kingdom imports than of ECSC imports. Profit margins, however, would still be determined basically by cost at the mill.

(*b*) Indicated profit margins would exist only insofar as foreign steel mills were to sell directly to U.S. customers. If mills sell through Japanese trading companies, which may charge as high as 30 percent commission, their profit margins would be decreased in proportion. If Western European mills sell through domestic importers, their margins of profit or loss would be changed in proportion to the importers' commission.

(20) Charts (and tables published in the statistical appendix) show imports of

foreign steel have been stimulated by the periodical fear of steel shortages resulting from expected or actual steel strikes.

(21) For the years 1947–66 the average annual rate of increase in unit labor costs for all manufacturing industries compared with the steel industry were:

[In percent]

	All manu-facturing industries	Steel industry
Output..	3.6	1.7
Total compensation per man-hour	5.0	5.7
Output per man-hour...........................	2.9	1.7
Unit labor cost.................................	2.0	3.9

(22) The capital-output ratio measures the dollar amount of capital needed to produce a dollar of value added, and thereby indicates the productivity of the invested capital. When this ratio and the unit labor cost ratio discussed above rise, profits are squeezed; when they fall, profits improve. For the domestic steel industry gross (undepreciated) plant and equipment per dollar of value added had doubled between 1947 and 1966 from $1.26 to $2.52, which compares with a decline from $0.95 to $0.86 for all manufacturing industries (1947–65; 1966 data not yet available). This evidence is probably unexpected because the new technology, such as the basic oxygen furnace (BOF) and continuous casting, greatly reduces investment per ton of output. Competition on a quality basis, however, has forced the domestic steel industry to invest even more in new, costlier finishing facilities than in cost-saving BOF's.

(23) Hourly steel labor costs in 1966 were $4.63 in this country compared with $1.87 in West Germany, $1.76 in Italy, $1.53 in France, and $1.10 in Japan. It is quite true that between 1960 and 1964 these hourly labor costs had increased by 61.2 percent in Italy, 41.9 percent in Japan, 40 percent in France, and 32.2 percent in West Germany as compared to only by 14.1 percent in the United States. But even if one were to assume that hourly labor costs here and abroad were to rise from 1964 at the same rates as shown above for 1960–64, it would still take the following number of years for foreign wages to catch up with U.S. rates:

	Years		Years
Italy	11	Japan	26
France	21	United Kingdom	39
Western Germany	25	Luxembourg	54

It is true that output per man-hour abroad today is still below ours, but it has been rising faster abroad. According to an official but unpublished British calculation, output per man-hour in the United States increased by 15 percent for all employees and by 20 percent for production workers between 1955 and 1965, while in Japan (for all employees) it increased 250 percent.

(24) Seven domestic steel facilities have been dismantled or idled as a result of rising imports. The impact on employment is difficult to gauge, however, because during the years 1964–66 the United States experienced increased domestic production of steel despite sharply rising imports.

(25) Despite higher prices, Federal income taxes paid by steel companies in years 1958–66 average less than 70 percent of those paid in 1951 and 1955–57, due primarily to lower profits.

(26) Steel imports during the first half of 1967 approached 13 percent of domestic shipments and were over 40 percent for certain specific products.

(27) The adverse effects of a reduction in output by 7 percent on costs per ton, caused in part by heavy fixed costs (depreciation, maintenance, interest, and property taxes), were again shown in the first half of 1967 when, compared to the first half of 1966, profits declined by 28 percent. During the comparable periods, imports had risen from 4.6 million tons to 5.2 million tons.

§ 4.4—The Search for a Response: Notes and Questions

The situation summarized in the preceding section was plainly one calling for some hard decisions of public policy. All the issues raised throughout this volume—of the advantages vs. the perils of trade, of efficiency vs. self-sufficiency, of economics vs. national security, of discrimination vs. MFN, of precedents vs. ad hoc solutions—would be involved in the U.S. government's response or lack of response to what

"And to think I set him up in business!"

Gib Crockett. *Washington Star*, 1971.

came to be known as the crisis in steel imports. In addition, because of the great importance of steel as an ingredient in other products and the great number of workers employed in the steel industry, the consistency of the commitment of the administration to (i) stable prices, but (ii) full employment might soon be challenged. In the first instance, however, the problem was for the parties most immediately affected—the major American steel producers and their allies (for this purpose), the United Steelworkers of America.

The notes and questions in this section explore the remedies open to the American steel companies under the law as it existed in the late 1960's and early 1970's. Succeeding sections of this volume take the search further, into avenues not contemplated when the basic domestic and international trade legislation was being developed.

4.41—DUMPING AND ANTI-DUMPING

(a) One remedy for an industry concerned over excess imports is to assert that the foreign competitors are engaged in dumping. Dumping, it will be recalled (§ 2.44(a) supra) is a species of international unfair competition, in which the seller improperly reduces its prices in a foreign market in order to obtain a share of the market that it would not obtain if it priced its export product on the same basis as it priced the product sold for home consumption. If dumping has occurred, the remedy is an anti-dumping duty, applied on top of the normal duty on imports from the country concerned, and in some cases only on products of specified exporters. Thus anti-dumping duties are one form of deviation from MFN expressly permitted both by domestic law and by the GATT, and they may be imposed, if the conditions are met, regardless of the fact that the resulting duty is in excess of a duty bound in the GATT.[a] The amount of the additional duty is not supposed to be punitive, but is supposed to be equivalent to the "margin of dumping." As explained further below, the determination that relief shall be granted against dumping involves two elements: (1) price discrimination, usually referred to as sales of foreign merchandise at less than fair value; and (2) injury to an industry by reason of importation of such merchandise. From 1921 to 1954, the Secretary of the Treasury (or his delegate) made both determinations; since then the second function has been assigned to the Tariff Commission, evidently because it was felt that the

---

[a] See, e.g., J. Jackson, *World Trade and the Law of GATT* p. 421 (1969). See also Article 8(b) of the 1967 Antidumping Code (§ 4.44 *infra*), Documents Supplement p. DS-96.

Commission, which regularly made inquiries into the question of injury in escape clause and peril point cases,[b] would have the requisite staff and expertise to do so in dumping cases as well.[c] Thus in order to secure relief through the anti-dumping route, a complainant must satisfy two substantive tests in two separate proceedings.[d]

(b) Consider what must be shown to establish sales at less than fair value. The law could hardly require precise equivalence between home and foreign prices. There may be credit charges, taxes, shipping charges, quantity discounts, warranty and service obligations, all different (higher or lower) in domestic trade from those applicable in international trade. Foreign merchandise sold in the United States may bear special packing costs, transportation charges (if the sale is on a c.i.f. or c. & f. basis), discounts for quantity, allowance for import duties payable, and possibly costs of—or allowances for—selling, advertising, and so on. One or both prices may vary in the period examined. And of course the home market prices will be quoted in marks, pounds, yen, etc., whereas the price of the imported item will usually be quoted in dollars. Assuming all relevant facts are known or can be ascertained, and assuming you accept the basic proposition that a seller must not sell in the United States for less than he sells at home, how would you evaluate (add, subtract, or disregard) the factors mentioned? What other factors should be taken into account?[e]

(c)(i) For many products an exporter will have no significant home market. In such cases the Act provides that the exporter risks antidumping duties if he sells for less to the United States than to Xandia

---

[b] See § 3.52 at Ns. k–n *supra*.

[c] See Ehrenhaft, "Protection against International Price Discrimination: United States Countervailing and Antidumping Duties," 58 Colum. L. Rev. 47, 67 (1958). It seems that under the prior law the Treasury might duck some of the difficult problems of pricing discussed in Paragraph (b) when it thought the injury question was easier. The separation of functions precludes this. See Hendrick, "The United States Antidumping Act," 58 Am. J. Int'l. L. 914, 919–920 (1964).

[d] In 1980 the functions of the Treasury here described were transferred to the Department of Commerce. See § 7.61 *infra*.

[e] See Antidumping Act § 205, Documents Supplement p. DS-421, for the statutory standard of determining the foreign market price, as it read until 1975.

or Patria. (§ 205) Is that sensible? Suppose, for instance, a particular Japanese firm is the principal or the only supplier of a line of steel products to the Philippines, and it charges what the market will bear in the absence of meaningful competition. Why is it improper if in a crowded American market the same producer charges less?

(ii) If the exporter has neither home market nor third country sales —say a Korean manufacturer of baseball gloves or a Hong Kong maker of souvenir Empire State Buildings—the Act calls on the Treasury to construct the fair value on the basis of the cost of materials and fabrication, plus a minimum of 10 per cent of costs for overhead, and a minimum of 8 per cent of costs plus overhead for profit. Is this sensible? Suppose, for example, a producer is prepared in a time of slack demand to reduce his profit to 4 per cent, rather than abandon an export market or lay off employees. Is this in some sense unfair?

(iii) Coming back to the principal test—sale in the United States at less than the price for which the product is sold in the home market—why (absent a predatory intent)[f] is this unfair competition? If a producer or a group of producers cover their costs plus a small profit on sales to the United States, while they charge higher prices in their protected home market, is that a proper concern of United States law?[g]

The answer to this question, which may well be relevant to the case of steel, runs something like this: Excessive mark-ups at home may be averaged with low prices abroad to cover the producer's costs plus profit, and so the home market is "subsidizing" the export market. Is this argument persuasive?[h]

---

[f] I.e., a deliberate lowering of price with the intention of driving out a competitor, so that the price can thereafter be raised higher than before. For a discussion of cases raising this issue, see Baier, "Substantive Interpretations Under the Antidumping Act and the Foreign Trade Policy of the United States," 17 Stan. L. Rev. 409, 417-19 (1965).

[g] For example, in dumping proceedings involving *Television Sets from Japan*, 36 Fed. Reg. 4576 (1971), it was disclosed that color television sets selling in the United States for around $500 were selling in Japan for $1200-1600. When this news got out, Japanese consumer groups organized boycotts and forced the prices down; moreover, the government of Japan launched an investigation against the producers for (domestic) price fixing and monopolization. This information, and a more detailed discussion of the case, may be found in Fisher, "The Antidumping Law of the United States: A Legal and Economic Analysis," 5 Law & Pol'y Int'l Bus. 85, 118-23 (1973).

[h] Professor Dam, for one, answers no to this question. K. Dam, *The GATT, Law and International Economic Organization*, pp. 169-72 (1970).

(d) Moving closer to the problem of steel, we saw (§ 3.44(c)) that in certain respects the Japanese economy is differently organized than American industry. Fixed costs tend to be a greater proportion of total costs, both because employees are not ordinarily laid off in slack periods and because the ratio of debt to equity is much higher in Japanese than in American firms. Thus the pressure is strong to keep the mills running and revenue coming in, even if demand is down and profits are reduced. (i) Is refusal to reduce production in the face of reduced demand in some sense unfair? (ii) If a Japanese producer (or every Japanese producer) reduced both its home and its export price, rather than only the latter, would the problem be cured from the point of view of the American firm?

4.42—In one sense, the questions in § 4.41 concerning the theoretical basis for the concepts of dumping and fair value are beside the point in a proceeding before the Bureau of Customs under a statutory mandate. But the questions raised in § 4.41(b), at least, suggest that there is sufficient play in the joints so that both the advocate's persuasiveness in putting a case in context (whether on behalf of the importer or the domestic complainant) and the decision-makers' attitude towards trade, the industry in question, and the country concerned play a part in the determinations reached.[i]

Beyond this, however, the United States statute, as well as the GATT, seek to moderate the restraint against "sales at less than fair value," as defined, by calling for a finding of injury before an anti-dumping duty may be imposed.[j] How should "injury" be interpreted?

(a) Would you start with the assumption that sale at less than fair value is a wrong, and that "no injury" is a defense to be proven by the

---

[i] An interesting illustration of this point is the change made by the Treasury on its own, after much debate, with regard to assurances by an exporter in the course of an investigation that he would eliminate the dumping margin, either by raising the export price or by lowering the home price. Until 1970, Treasury normally accepted such assurances and closed its investigations because there was no longer a problem. On reflection, Treasury changed its mind, on the ground that the prior practice had given the exporter a risk-free opportunity to dump and gain a foothold until he was caught. See 35 Fed. Reg. 8275 (May 27, 1970). The issue is discussed at some length in Department of the Treasury, "Antidumping Duties," *Papers Submitted to the Commission on International Trade and Investment Policy* (The Williams Commission), Vol. 1, p. 395 at 403–07 (1971).

[j] It is interesting that Canada, alone among major trading nations, did not have an injury criterion for application of anti-dumping duties. Under international pressure in connection with the International Antidumping Code negotiated as part of the Kennedy Round (§ 4.44(b) *infra*), Canada agreed to change its statute to conform to international consensus. Canada, Anti-dumping Act, § 3, 17 Eliz. II c. 10, Dec. 19, 1968, Rev. Stat. of Canada c. A–15 (1970).

exporter or importer? Or is it the effect on domestic competition that gives to the transactions discussed in § 4.41 their unfair character?

(b) Would you expect that motive is relevant to the question of injury? If so, how can one distinguish between the foreign producer's declaration that he wants to gain a share of the American market—presumably what every exporter to the United States seeks—and an intent to gain improper advantage?[k]

(c) Injury in dumping cases must, under the statute, be to "an industry in the United States." Would you think that whatever test of injury is used must be applied on a nationwide basis? For example, if a steel plant in the Pacific Northwest closes down because of competition from Japan, but that plant had only 3 per cent of the national market of a given product—say wire rods—and wire rods constitute, say, 2 per cent of total steel production, should the Commission decline to find injury? Compare the different wording of section 7 of the Clayton Antitrust Act,[l] which prohibits corporate mergers or acquisitions that may substantially lessen competition or tend to create a monopoly "in any line of commerce in any section of the country." Could (should?) the Tariff Commission interpret the Antidumping Act as if it read like the Clayton Act? Should the Antidumping Act be amended to conform to the Clayton Act in this respect? or are the considerations different?[m]

(d) Assume agreement is reached in a particular case on the definition of industry, in terms both of geography and of product:

(i) If the domestic industry expanded in absolute terms in the period in question, should that fact defeat the claim for relief under the Antidumping Act?

(ii) Conversely, if the domestic industry decreased its sales or profits

---

[k] A partial answer to the question of intent may be seen by the contrast with so-called accidental dumping. For instance, a Canadian seller of cement who had been counting on moving his product by water was obliged to ship by rail instead. Since the delivered price to the purchaser had been fixed by contract, the Canadian exporter had to absorb the higher transport cost, which left the part of the purchase price attributable to the cement below his home market price. The Commission declined to find injury. *Portland Cement from Canada*, 25 Fed. Reg. 2191 (1960).

[l] 15 U.S.C. § 18.

[m] For a summary of cases in which the Tariff Commission has addressed the issue of defining the industry claiming injury, see Fisher, N. f *supra* 104–07; Hendrick, N. c *supra* 927–28; Baier, N. e *supra* 426–28. The inconsistency of the Commission's approach to this (and other) questions is criticized in Note: "Innovation and Confusion in Recent Determinations of the Tariff Commission Under the Antidumping Act," 4 N.Y.U. J. Int'l. L. & Pol. 212, 216–24 (1971).

in the period of the sales from abroad at less than fair value, is that strong evidence of injury? Or would you, as a Commissioner, require further proof of cause and effect?

(iii) Suppose the domestic industry increased its prices in the period when the allegedly dumped products were introduced into the United States. Should the complainant be required to justify its price increases as a condition for an affirmative injury finding?

(e) Suppose the foreign producer offers the merchandise at the market price prevailing in the United States. He may well run afoul of the "sale at less than fair value" test, because his home market price is higher, or because he has had to absorb transport and sales expenses to compete in the United States. So long as he does not undersell domestic producers, must he be absolved of the charge of dumping?

(f) Note that the statute calls for a determination whether an industry "is being *or is likely to be injured.*" In at least one case, the Commission observed that the foreign producer's export price, though below his domestic price, was not below his cost and made a "positive contribution to net return"; that the United States market was "a continuing and attractive lure" for management; and that therefore it was likely that the practice would be continued and that injury would occur.[n] Would you agree with this reasoning?

(g) Making due allowance for differences in the text of the respective statutes, should the standard for a finding of injury be the same, harder, or easier in dumping cases, as compared with escape clause or adjustment assistance cases?[o]

(h) Finally, what about a Xandian producer who asserts, with supporting evidence, that he set his export price to meet the price at which Patrian products were sold in the United States. Assuming different home prices, is it permissible or appropriate to impose anti-dumping duties against the Xandian but not against the Patrian producer?

4.43—The points raised in the preceding sets of questions are recurring

---

[n] *Portland Cement from the Dominican Republic*, 28 Fed. Reg. 4047 (1963). The Commission followed the same line a year later in *Steel Reinforcing Bars from Canada*, 29 Fed. Reg. 3840 (1964). In both cases, the Chairman dissented strongly, on the ground that the same standard of proof should apply to likelihood of injury as to actual injury.

[o] See § 3.53 *supra* at Ns. r–v and w.

ones, and give an idea of the issues on which anti-dumping cases turn. Answers to the questions have not, however, become clear. The Tariff Commission, rather like the Civil Aeronautics Board, the Interstate Commerce Commission and other regulatory agencies, does not regard itself bound by its own prior decisions, and its responses to the questions here raised have—at least at the margin—tended to reflect the shifting predilections of the Commissioners as much as any fixed rule of law.[p] In fact, in the decade up to the time the steel problem first became urgent in the United States, the Tariff Commission had considered about 40 cases out of some 300 filed with the Treasury, and had made affirmative dumping findings in 8.[q] In the mid-1960's, the American steel industry decided to see whether the Antidumping Act could provide it with relief.[r]

The Wire Rod Cases

(a) DEPARTMENT OF THE TREASURY
Office of the Secretary
STEEL WIRE RODS FROM JAPAN
Fair Value Determination[s]

MAY 6, 1963

A complaint was received that hot-rolled carbon steel wire rods from Japan were being sold in the United States at less than fair value within the meaning of the Antidumping Act of 1921.

---

[p] But note that the Commission's decisions are essentially not subject to judicial review. See *Ellis K. Orlowitz v. United States*, 200 F. Supp. 302 (Cust. Ct. 1961), *aff'd* 50 C.C.P.A. (Customs) 36 (1963); *City Lumber Co. v. United States*, 290 F. Supp. 385 (Cust.Ct. 1968), *aff'd* 311 F. Supp. 340 (Cust.Ct. 1970), *aff'd* 457 F. 2d 991 (C.C.P.A. 1972). Determinations of sales at less than fair value by the Treasury were subject to judicial review both at the behest of the foreign producer or importer and (expressly since 1974) at the behest of United States manufacturers and wholesalers. Trade Act of 1974 § 321(g). For revisions in judicial review pursuant to the Trade Agreements Act of 1979, see § 7.62 *infra*.

[q] See Hendrick, N. c *supra*, pp 932–33. As the author points out, in 62 cases filed with the Treasury but not referred to the Tariff Commission, the complainant got satisfaction, in that the foreign producer ended the price discrimination either by raising the export price or by lowering the home price. See also Coudert, "The Application of the United States Antidumping Law in the Light of a Liberal Trade Policy," 65 Colum. L. Rev. 189, 216–19 (1965).

[r] In fact, according to the Federal Register, in the period 1963-1967, various members of the American steel industry brought a total of 27 complaints in respect of 14 different products imported from 12 different countries. The countries involved included all of the original members of the European Community except the Netherlands, plus Great Britain, Sweden, Norway, Canada, Australia, and Japan. The cases reproduced in the text, collectively known as the *Wire Rod Cases*, are the most interesting and were the ones most widely discussed.

[s] 28 Fed. Reg. 4636 (May 8, 1963).

I hereby determine that hot-rolled carbon steel wire rods from Japan are not being, nor likely to be, sold at less than fair value within the meaning of section 201(a) of the Antidumping Act 1921, as amended (19 U.S.C. 160(a)).

Statement of reasons. Based on the information available, it was determined that the appropriate comparison for fair value purposes should be between purchase price and adjusted home market price.

Purchase price was calculated by deducting cost of inland freight and insurance from the f.o.b. Japan prices for the merchandise. Adjusted home market price was calculated by deducting commission differential, differences in credit terms, and inland freight and insurance from the weighted-average price in the home market. The difference between the higher cost of export packing and the lower cost of home market packing was added. Purchase price was not less than adjusted home market price in the period under consideration.

This determination and the statement of reasons therefor are published pursuant to section 201(c) of the Antidumping Act, 1921, as amended (19 U.S.C. 160(c)).

[SEAL]   JAMES A. REED,
                                  Assistant Secretary of the Treasury.

(b) DEPARTMENT OF THE TREASURY
Office of the Secretary
STEEL WIRE RODS FROM FRANCE
Determination of Sales at Less Than Fair Value[1]

MAY 27, 1963.

A complaint was received that hot-rolled carbon steel wire rods from France were being sold in the United States at less than fair value within the meaning of the Antidumping Act of 1921.

I hereby determine that hot-rolled carbon steel wire rods from France, except as to importations from the firm of Societé Metallurgique de Norman-

---

[1] 28 Fed. Reg. 5392 (May 30, 1963).

die, are being, or are likely to be, sold at less than fair value within the meaning of section 201(a) of the Antidumping Act, 1921, as amended (19 U.S.C. 160(a)).

The United States Tariff Commission is being advised of this determination.

Statement of reasons. The available information established that the appropriate fair value comparison is between purchase price and adjusted third country price as to all except one firm. The appropriate comparison as to that firm is between purchase price and adjusted home market price.

Purchase price was calculated by deducting the included ocean freight, insurance, and inland freight in France, as applicable, in the case of the importations from the firms with respect to which adjusted third country price represented fair value. In the case of the firm as to which the adjusted home market price represented the fair value of the merchandise exported by it to the United States, purchase price was calculated on the basis of the f.o.b. shipping port price from which was deducted the inland freight in France.

The adjusted third country price was computed on the basis of the weighted-average, net, ex-mill price, after deducting cash discounts, as applicable. Deductions were made where applicable for the difference in credit terms and in processing costs. Commissions paid on sales for exportation to third countries were offset by approximately equal commissions paid on sales of exportation to the United States. There were no packing cost differentials involved.

The adjusted home market price was computed on the basis of the manufacturer's list prices for home consumption. Consideration was given to the alignment of prices on the competing prices of other manufacturers in accordance with the rules of the European Coal and Steel Community. From such prices were deducted inland freight and credit terms differentials. There were no packing cost differentials involved.

Purchase price was found to be lower than adjusted third country price and lower than adjusted home market price, as applicable, except as to the firm of Societé Metallurgique de Normandie.

This determination and the statement of reasons therefor are published pursuant to section 201(c) of the Antidumping Act, 1921, as amended (19 U.S.C. 160(c)).

[SEAL]   JAMES A. REED,
                                        Assistant Secretary of the Treasury.

(c) TARIFF COMMISSION
HOT-ROLLED CARBON STEEL WIRE RODS FROM FRANCE
Determination of No Injury or Likelihood Thereof[u]

JULY 15, 1963.

On May 29, 1963, the Tariff Commission received advice from the Treasury Department that "hot-rolled carbon steel wire rods from France, except as to importations from the firm of Societé Metallurgique de Normandie, are being, or are likely to be, sold in the United States at less than fair value as that term is used in the Antidumping Act." Accordingly, the Commission on the same date, instituted an investigation under section 201 (a) of the Antidumping Act, 1921, as amended, to determine whether an industry in the United States is being or is likely to be injured, or is prevented from being established, by reason of the importation of such merchandise into the United States.

. . . . .

No request for a hearing was made by any interested party, but written statements were received. These statements were given due consideration by the Commission, together with all other information available to the Commission on this subject, in arriving at a determination in this case.

On the basis of the investigation, the Commission has unanimously determined that an industry in the United States is not being, and is not likely to be injured, or prevented from being established, by reason of the importation of hot-rolled carbon steel wire rods from France, sold at less than fair value, within the meaning of the Antidumping Act, 1921, as amended.

Statement of reasons. The wire rods here considered are semifinished articles made by passing heated billets through a series of reducing rolls. Most wire rods range between 7/32 and 47/64 inch in diameter and are generally marketed in coils. The characteristics of wire and wire products made from such rods depend not only upon the drawing and other operations employed but also upon the kind of steel from which the rods are made.

The bulk of the steel produced in the United States for use in making wire rods is made by the basic open-hearth process, but some is made by other

---

[u] 28 Fed. Reg. 7368 (July 18, 1963). For companion decisions by the Tariff Commission involving steel wire rods from other West European countries, see 28 Fed. Reg. 6474 (Belgium), 6476 (Luxembourg), and 6606 (West Germany). The corresponding determinations of Sales at Less Than Fair Value by the Treasury Department appear at 28 Fed. Reg. 2747 (Belgium), 2927 (Luxembourg), and 3364 (West Germany).

processes. Steel for wire rods is produced by the same processes abroad, but some such steel, particularly in European countries, is made by the Thomas, or basic Bessemer, process. The Thomas process has never been used commercially in the United States.

Thomas wire rods are not as suitable as open-hearth wire rods for conversion into the finer gages of wire or for conversion into wire used for certain purposes. For this reason, as well as for others, prices of Thomas wire rods generally are significantly lower than those of open-hearth rods. It is estimated that in the period 1960–62 Thomas rods accounted for about 17 percent of steel wire rods imported from all countries, for 65 to 75 percent of those imported from France, and for 35 to 45 percent of those imported from Belgium, Luxembourg, West Germany, and France combined.[2]

"Average unit value" price comparisons between imported and domestic wire rods must be interpreted with caution because, inter alia, (1) imports from the aforementioned four countries consist mostly of industrial quality rods, principally of the open-hearth variety but in considerable proportion of Thomas rods; (2) imports from Japan consist solely of open-hearth rods, including industrial and extra-quality grades; and (3) domestic rods consist principally of open-hearth rods having a wide range of qualities.

In assessing the impact on domestic industry of imports of French hot-rolled carbon steel wire rods sold at less than fair value (LTFV), the Commission took into account the following factors:

1. The ratio of the combined LTFV imports from Belgium, Luxembourg, West Germany, and France to total U.S. imports;

2. The ratio of aggregate imports from those four countries to imports from all countries (including imports not sold at less than fair value from such countries);

3. The share of total LTFV imports supplied by France;

---

[2] The Treasury Department found sales of hot-rolled carbon steel wire rods at less than fair value not only from France but also from Belgium (notice received Mar. 19, 1963), from Luxembourg (Mar. 21, 1963), and from West Germany (Apr. 2, 1963). The Treasury concluded its investigation of imports of wire rods from Japan on May 6, 1963, after having found no evidence of sales from that source at less than fair value. There are no other wire rod cases pending before the Treasury Department at this time.

4. The "margins of difference"[3] applicable to the LTFV imports from France;

5. The U.S. market prices of the rods imported from France at less than fair value in relation to the corresponding prices of comparable rods imported from Japan and all other suppliers of imported wire rods entered at not less than fair value;

6. The comparative volume of sales of the above-mentioned rods from France, from Japan, and from other foreign countries;

7. The existing and prospective capacity of rod mills in France;

8. Domestic producers' prices of steel wire rods sold in the open market during the past several years;

9. The volume of aggregate sales of domestic steel wire rods during the same period; and

10. The trend in recent years of U.S. production of wire rods, including that used by captive mills.

The Commission recognizes that the large quantities of imported wire rods marketed in the United States at prices substantially below those for domestic rods have disturbed the integrated domestic producers of wire rods, wire, and wire products. Such disturbance cannot properly be taken into account under the Antidumping Act unless attributable in significant part to imports of wire rods sold at less than fair value. LTFV imports, however, have not been a significant factor in the situation. The significant factor has been the large volume of imports of wire rods from countries that have not been found to be selling at less than fair value, particularly those from Japan, which Treasury specifically found were not being sold at less than fair value.

Whether importers of rods from Japan or other countries, including France, initiated price reductions at any particular time or place in the United States is immaterial in view of the dominant proportion of the total imports that were sold at fair value and at prices little, if any, different from those that were sold at less than fair value.

---

[3] A "margin of difference" is the difference between the foreign market value of an article and the price at which that article is sold for export to the United States. The margins found by the Treasury Department to exist in the present case are not public information.

The Commission's finding that injury to the domestic industry could not be assigned to LTFV imports of wire rods from France is applicable whether the domestic industry is conceived of in narrow terms or in broad terms. Therefore the Commission does not feel called upon to delineate the precise scope of the industry. The Commission deems it appropriate, however, to comment on certain concepts advanced by complainants[1] concerning the scope of the domestic industry that they claim is being, or is likely to be, injured by the LTFV imports of rods from France.[5]

The complainants contend that this industry is coextensive with the production of wire rods for sale in the market, i.e., they exclude the portion used by the manufacturers in their own integrated mills. Further, they contend that each of four geographic areas of the United States that they describe (the boundaries of which vary seasonally) constitute a separate "industry" within the meaning of the Antidumping Act.

With regard to "captive" production, the Commission observes that no domestic producer of wire rods is without facilities for using rods in a captive wire mill. Some 70 to 75 percent of the total domestic production of such rods is in fact used in captive mills, with the result that only 25 to 30 percent of the domestic production is sold to "arms-length" customers. Moreover, the determination of the quantity of rods to be produced and the proportion thereof to be used in captive mills, as well as the pricing policies relating to market sales, are almost fully within the managerial discretion of the domestic producers. The Commission consequently finds no merit in the complainants' contention that the output of an article by integrated producers does not embrace the totality of such output but merely the share sold in the market.

With regard to the "regional industry" claim, the Commission recognizes the propensity of users to buy from the lowest priced suppliers. It recognizes also that domestic producers of such articles as wire rods can generally

---

[4] Bethlehem Steel Co., Colorado Fuel and Iron Corp., Detroit Steel Corp., Armco Steel Corp., Jones and Laughlin Steel Corp., Republic Steel Corp. Youngstown Sheet and Tube Co. joined in the complaint on Nov. 14, 1962, and the Pittsburgh Steel Co., on Feb. 8, 1963. These eight concerns accounted for less than half of of the domestic production and also less than half of the total shipments (open market sales) of hot-rolled carbon steel wire rods in 1962. At least nine other domestic producers, including the largest single domestic producer, did not join in the complaint.

[5] The concepts concerning scope of industry referred to here were advanced by the complainants in connection with the investigations recently concluded involving wire rods from Belgium, from Luxembourg, and from West Germany. Complainants have not advised the Commission that their concepts regarding the scope of the industry are different for the purposes of this investigation.

supply nearby users at lower costs than can the more distant domestic producers. Nevertheless, virtually all such domestic producers, in greater or lesser degree, regularly penetrate one another's "natural" markets. Moreover, both the buyers and sellers in each of such markets take vigilant note of the happenings in each of the other of such markets. Accordingly, in the case of wire rods, the Commission finds no merit in the "regional industry" concept.

The foregoing observations on industry concepts advanced by the complainants should not be construed as Commission subscription to those advanced by the importers.

The Commission's determination and statement of reasons are published pursuant to section 201(c) of the Antidumping Act, 1921, as amended.

By the Commission.

[SEAL]　　　　　　　　　　　　　　　　　　DONN N. BENT,
　　　　　　　　　　　　　　　　　　　　　　　 Secretary.

(d)(i)　Do these cases answer the question put at § 4.42(h)? Do they answer it correctly? (ii) Do they shed any light on question 4.42(d)? (iii) What about question 4.41(c)(i)? Is the comparison between the United States and the third country market correctly handled, so far as one can tell from the reports?

(e)　Following the frustration experienced in the *Wire Rod Cases* (as well as in nearly all the other cases brought in this period),ᵛ the American steel industry decided to sponsor an amendment to the Antidumping Act.ʷ On the question of injury, section 201(a) would be amended to read

　　. . . The Commission shall then determine . . . whether in any line of commerce in any section of the Country an industry or labor in the United States has been, is being, or is likely to be more than insignificantly injured (or prevented from being established), in whole or in part, by reason of the importation of such merchandise into the United States from the country or countries with respect to which the Secretary has made [an] affirmative determination [of sales at less

---

ᵛ See N. r *supra.* Two exceptions, in which antidumping complaints were successful, both involved sales from Canada to a particular region—the Pacific Northwest. *Steel Reinforcing Bars from Canada,* 28 Fed. Reg. 14245 (Dec. 24, 1963), 29 Fed. Reg. 3840 (March 27, 1964); *Carbon Steel Bars and Shapes from Canada,* 29 Fed. Reg. 7294 (May 28, 1964), 29 Fed. Reg. 12599 (Sept. 4, 1964).

ʷ H.R.10832, 88th Cong., 2d Sess. (1964), H.R. 979, 89th Cong. 1st Sess. (1965). The quoted paragraph together with analysis appears in Baier, N. f *supra* at 457-62.

than fair value], whether or not such merchandise is sold with predatory intent or at prices equivalent to or higher than prices of such or
similar merchandise imported from other countries.

It seems clear that such a bill, had it been passed, would have changed
the result in the *Wire Rod Cases,* and probably in some of the cases dismissed by the Commission on grounds of insufficient impact on the
domestic industry. Would the Antidumping Act, as so amended, continue to maintain the distinction between fair and unfair competition?

4.44—(a) One more important fact must be mentioned to give an accurate
picture of the United States Antidumping Act as it read until 1979. When
a complaint with supporting data was brought to the Treasury Department,
the Customs Service made a preliminary review within 30 days to decide
whether a full-scale investigation was justified. If the decision was to go ahead
with an investigation, requests for information were sent to the complainant,
to foreign manufacturers, and to the Treasury's own investigators in the United
States and abroad. Under the practice prevailing when the *Wire Rod Cases*
were brought, the Commissioner of Customs could issue an order at any time
during this stage of the investigation that "appraisement be withheld" on the
merchandise in question, if there was "reason to believe or suspect" that
sales were being made at less than fair value.[a] This order did not mean that
the goods could not come in, but it meant that the assessment of the applicable
duty was postponed until completion of the antidumping proceeding, and that
if the importer wanted to bring in the goods in the meantime, he had to give
a bond against which the final duty—including an antidumping duty if one
were imposed—could be collected.

Though no finding—even tentative—regarding injury was involved,
a withholding of appraisement order was likely to have a chilling effect
on imports of the products covered by the order.[b] As there was no limit
on the time within which the Treasury could conduct its investigation,[c]
the order to withhold appraisement could impose a substantial barrier
to imports, even if in the end the requirements for an antidumping duty

---

[a] See Antidumping Act § 201(b), Documents Supplement p. DS-418.

[b] If the foreign exporter undertook to reimburse an American importer for outstanding
duties for which he might become liable, the amount of promised reimbursement would be
deducted from the calculation of the purchase price, in effect increasing the amount of the
duty payable by the amount of the reimbursement.

[c] In contrast to the three months given in § 201(a) to the Tariff Commission
for the completion of its functions.

were not met. In the *Wire Rod Cases,* for example, the complaints were filed late in September 1962, orders to withhold appraisement were issued on December 14, 1962,[d] and these orders remained in effect until the Tariff Commission issued its findings of no injury in June and July 1963. Overall, about half of all antidumping investigations led to withholding of appraisement, though as we saw less than 10 per cent of the cases led to an affirmative finding by both Treasury and the Tariff Commission.[e]

(b) In the course of the Kennedy Round, a special Group on Antidumping Policies was established within the general framework of examination of non-tariff barriers. Though the United States had the most explicit law and the most open procedures on dumping, it was criticized for its procedures and especially for the practice of withholding appraisement and, as the critics charged, retroactive application of antidumping duties. For its part, the United States agreed that Article VI of the GATT left a good deal to be desired, and it was prepared to negotiate an understanding that might spell out some of the Article's opaque phrases. Moreover, the United States saw the chance to get Canada to include an injury standard in its antidumping statute, and to get the European Economic Community to spell out its own antidumping practices for the first time.[f] But just as on American Selling Price,[g] the United States delegation did not want to go back to Congress while the Kennedy Round was in progress, and was reluctant to negotiate an agreement that would have to be submitted to Congress afterwards.[h]

After two years of negotiations—in fact as the first real accord to come out of the many working groups in the Kennedy Round—agreement was reached on an International Antidumping Code—a middle

---

[d] 27 Fed. Reg. 12651 (Dec. 19, 1962). The orders were directed against imports from Belgium, France, Luxembourg, and West Germany, but not against imports from Japan.

[e] See Prosterman, "Withholding of Appraisement Under the United States Antidumping Act: Protectionism or Unfair Competition Law?," 41 Wash. L. Rev. 315 (1966).

[f] Canada's antidumping law, as well as the laws of several other countries, were exempted from Article VI by virtue of the Protocol of Provisional Application (§ 2.2 at N. p *supra*).

[g] § 3.72 at Ns. m–p *supra.*

[h] See Rehm, "The Kennedy Round of Trade Negotiations," 62 Am. J. Int'l L. 403, 427–434 (1968).

course between a restatement of the vague phrases of Article VI and a document that would require amendment of United States law.[i] Canada, and also Great Britain, changed their antidumping laws, and the European Economic Community issued a regulation on the subject for the first time.[j] As for the United States, the executive branch took the position that adherence to the Antidumping Code had taken place neither pursuant to existing legislation (e.g., the Trade Expansion Act) nor subject to implementation by legislation. The Code, it argued, had been signed by the United States pursuant to the inherent powers of the President to conduct foreign affairs; furthermore, nothing in the Code conflicted with the Antidumping Act of 1921 as amended: to the extent prior administrative practices were inconsistent with the Code—in particular with respect to withholding of appraisement for extended periods and prior to any inquiry as to injury—the practices would be changed by modification of the Regulations.[k]

(c) Would you agree that harmonization of the United States practices with the Code could be done by regulation, without change in the statute?

(1) Compare, for example, Article 3 of the Code concerning determination of injury, with section 201 of the Act.[l] (i) Do the words "that the imports are demonstrably the principal cause of material injury . . ." in Article 3(a) curb the discretion of the Tariff Commission? Or do they simply give some policy guidance to the questions put in § 4.42 above? (ii) What about the list in Article 3(c) of the "other factors" to be taken into account in determining the causal relation between dumping and injury?

(2) Are the definitions of industry in Article 4, including the limited scope for segmentation, a curb on the judgment of the Com-

---

[i] The Code, technically known as the Agreement in Implementation of Article VI of the General Agreement on Tariffs and Trade, 19 U.S.T. 4348, T.I.A.S. 6431 appears in the Documents Supplement at p. DS-89.

[j] For citation to these enactments as well as to commentary on them, see Barcelo, "Antidumping Laws as Buttress to Trade—The United States and the International Antidumping Code," 57 Cornell L. Rev. 491, 530–32 (1972).

[k] See *Hearings on the International Antidumping Code* before Sen. Comm. on Finance, Testimony of Ambassador Roth, pp. 11, 13–18; Exec Branch Analysis, pp. 279–315, 90th Cong., 2d Sess. (1968).

[l] Documents Supplement p. DS-417.

mission—interference by international executive agreement with an independent regulatory agency? Or, again, do they give guidance where it is needed in an area that inevitably involves more than one nation?

(3) As to antidumping procedures, could the U.S. Treasury under the Antidumping Act inquire into both sale at less than fair value and injury, as seems to be required by Article 5 of the Code? Or get the Tariff Commission to make a preliminary inquiry into the injury question before the Treasury embarks on a full-scale investigation of price discrimination?

(4) Could the United States obligate itself to restrict provisional measures, such as withholding of appraisement, to a period of three months (six with consent of the parties) as called for by Article 10(d)?

(5) Do you find other problems?[m]

(d) The steel and cement industries, which were the principal complainants in the antidumping actions throughout the 1960's, strongly opposed the Code. The President of the American Iron and Steel Institute testified that the "principal cause" provision of the Code would place "a tremendous additional burden" on the domestic industry. The steel industry had prevailed in only two of the approximately 15 dumping cases it had brought since steel imports had become a major factor. "I think we can say here," he told the Senate Committee, "that on those two cases where we did prevail, that under the Code we are convinced we would not have prevailed . . . We would just despair of ever prevailing in any antidumping proceeding if the Code were adopted."[n]

(e) The Congress (by 1968 impatient with the President on a variety of executive-legislative issues, from the Tonkin Gulf on) was not prepared to accept the executive branch's arguments.[o] The Senate tacked

---

[m] The Tariff Commission split 3–2 in its report to the Senate Finance Committee on the Antidumping Code, with the majority taking the position that the Code was in conflict with the Act. See *Hearings*, N. k *supra*, pp. 317–388.

[n] Hearings, N. k *supra* at pp. 138, 142, 148.

[o] See Barcelo, N. j *supra* at pp. 534–36; Pintos and Murphy, "Congress Dumps the International Antidumping Code," 18 Cath. U. L. Rev. 180 (1968). For

an amendment to an unrelated bill in 1968 that would have simply prohibited both the Treasury and the Tariff Commission from implementing the International Anti-Dumping Code, but the House of Representatives refused to go along with this amendment. In a compromise worked out by the Senate-House conference, Congress provided that nothing in the Code "shall be construed to restrict the discretion of the . . . Tariff Commission," and that both the Commission and the Treasury shall resolve any conflict between the Code and the Act "in favor of the Act as applied by the agency administering the Act"; with these provisos, the two agencies were to take the Code into account in performing their functions under the Act.[p]

(f) In fact the Treasury did change its procedures to comply with the requirements of the Code. Withholding of appraisement was now ordered (unless the parties agreed otherwise) at the same time that a finding of sales at less than fair value was issued, so that the three - month period provided for in the Code was coterminous with the three months for decision by the Tariff Commission called for by the Act.[q] Also, the Treasury now required some evidence of injury as well as of sales below fair value before initiating an investigation, and in case of doubt, referred the question to the Commission for a preliminary investigation, to be completed within 30 days.[r] It is not clear that the Tariff Commission changed its definitions of industry or injury to coincide with the Code. In some cases, for example, the Commission did apply the test of injury to a segmented market as it had declined to do in the *Wire Rod Cases*,[s] and it did not always consider the "other fac-

---

detailed argument against the Code by the Chairman of the Senate Finance Committee, see Long, "United States Law and the International Anti-Dumping Code," 3 Int'l Lawyer 464 (1969).

[p] Section 201 of the Renegotiation Act Amendments of 1968, Pub. L. 90–634 (1968). The complete text of Section 201 appears in the Documents Supplement at p. DS-426.

[q] In fact most exporters and importers asked for the extension provided for in the Code. in order to have some opportunity to persuade the Treasury to change its tentative determination, either as to the fact of dumping or as to the margin of dumping. See E. Rossides, *U.S. Customs, Tariff, and Trade* p. 442 (1977).

[r] 19 C.F.R. § 153.29(b) (1978).

[s] For instance, in another of its many steel cases, *Steel Bars and Shapes from Australia*, 35 Fed. Reg. 4161 (1970), the Commission (by a vote of 4–2) defined the injured industry as producers in Washington and Oregon, though one of the complainants was a national firm and one of the two regional firms did not join in the complaint. Imports at less than fair value amounted to 5.5

tors'' called for by Article 3 of the Code. Whether an argument based on the Code was likely to be effective before the Commission depended on the outlook of the Commissioners.[t]

4.45—SUBSIDIES AND COUNTERVAILING DUTIES

(a) As the Antidumping Act was designed as a remedy against price discrimination practiced by firms exporting to the United States, so the countervailing duty statute[a] was designed as a remedy against subsidies paid by governments in respect of exports to the United States. The idea, as we saw in the discussion of subsidies and the GATT (§ 2.44(b) *supra*), was that international competition based on relative efficiency is distorted by government subsidies,[b] and that the distortion could be offset by an extra duty equal to the subsidy. Interestingly enough, however, the United States statute, enacted in the McKinley Tariff Act of 1890[c] with respect to sugar and generalized in the Tariff Act of 1897,[d] applied

---

per cent of consumption of steel products in Washington and Oregon; on a nationwide basis the figure would have been 0.5 per cent. "Injury to a part of national industry," the majority said, "is an injury to the whole industry." (at 4162) Neither the majority nor the dissent referred to the Code.

[t] Compare the following comment by an official of the Canadian Department of Finance:

> [A] clearly highly protectionist interpretation by the Canadian Anti-Dumping Tribunal would be an important argumentation in front of the United States Tariff Commission when Canadian exporters are accused of dumping in the United States . . . or in the United Kingdom, for example. And in a certain sense, jurisprudence will become internationalized because we are operating under the same Code.

Remarks of Mr. R.Y. Grey to the Finance Committee of the Canadian House of Commons, 1968, quoted in Barcelo, N. j *supra* at p. 530, note 171.

[a] Section 303 of the Tariff Act of 1930. Documents Supplement p. DS-439. The statute was amended by § 331 of the Trade Act of 1974; and the amended version appears in the Documents Supplement at pp. DS-440–43 and again by the Trade Agreements Act of 1979. Documents Supplement pp. DS-478-92, 508-530. See § 4.47(b) and 7.62 *infra*.

[b] Compare Adam Smith, *The Wealth of Nations* (1776):

> The effect of bounties, like that of all the other expedients of the mercantile system, can only be to force the trade of a country into a channel much less advantageous than that in which it would naturally run of its own accord.

Book IV, ch. 5 (Modern Library Ed. p. 473 (1937)).

[c] See § 3.51 *supra* at N. q.

[d] 30 Stat. 151, 205 (July 24, 1897).

only to dutiable products. The purpose of the statute, it seems, was not really to establish international price competition free from distortions, but to defend the integrity of the (then high) United States tariff. If the U.S. tariff protected American producers of a given product from Patrian competition and the government of Patria wanted its producers to stay in the American (or world) market sufficiently to subsidize them, the United States would defend itself by raising the tariff—vis-à-vis Patrian products only—in an amount equal to the subsidy. Accordingly, there was no need to write an injury standard into the statute, as was done later with the Antidumping Act. If a product was not subject to duty in the United States, presumably it did not need protection; more likely it was not produced in the United States at all. In that case, if a subsidy by the government of Patria gave its exporters an edge over exporters from Xandia, that was no concern of the United States. But "whenever any country . . . shall pay . . . any bounty or grant upon the export . . . of any article . . . and such article . . . is dutiable . . . ," the statute provided that "there shall be levied and paid an additional duty equal to the net amount of such bounty or grant. . . ." In 1922, the statute was amended to include subsidies on manufacture or production as well as on export of dutiable articles. Administration of the statute was assigned to the Secretary of the Treasury, with no role for the Tariff Commission. The countervailing duty statute was reenacted with a slight change as section 303 of the Tariff Act of 1930, and was not changed in any of the Reciprocal Trade Agreements acts, including the Trade Expansion Act of 1962.[e]

(b) No discretion, or so it seemed, was built into the countervailing duty statute: if there was a bounty or grant, the Secretary of the Treasury was to ascertain (or if necessary estimate) the amount, announce it, and impose a corresponding additional duty. The Supreme Court, in a case arising out of a British allowance on the export of spirits, said "there can be . . . but one inquiry: Was something—bounty or grant— paid or bestowed upon the exportation of spirits?"[f] But the question was not that simple. Some countries did pay direct subsidies on exports on

---

[e] For a more complete history and analysis of the countervailing duty statute, see Feller "Mutiny Against the Bounty: An Examination of Subsidies, Border Tax Adjustments, and the Resurgence of the Countervailing Duty Law," 1 Law & Pol'y Int'l Bus. 17, 19–23 (1969).

[f] *G. S. Nicholas Co. & Co.* v. *United States*, 249 U.S. 34, 39 (1919).

a per unit basis—typically on agricultural products.[g] For instance, in 1959 the government of Spain paid 8 pesetas (about 13 cents) per kilo on exports of almonds, and the U.S. Treasury imposed a corresponding duty until the subsidy came off.[h] In its crisis of May–June 1968 following massive student and worker riots,[i] the government of France was compelled to grant an across-the-board 10 per cent rise in wages plus various fringe benefits; in order to remain competitive on world markets, the government announced a payment to exporters of 6 per cent of labor costs. Even as the U.S. government was taking the lead in arranging a $1.3 billion stand-by credit for France, the Bureau of Customs announced that it was considering a countervailing duty,[j] and a few weeks later a uniform surcharge of 2½ per cent ad valorem was imposed on all goods covered by the French subsidy.[k] But the typical governmental aid to industry was more subtle or indirect; moreover, every country with a private economic sector aids business in a variety of ways, from education to highway or port construction to export promotion to credits of various kinds. Characterizing all such activity as subsidy, though correct in some economic sense, would plainly run counter to the way the whole world operated.[l]

(c) Consider how (without the benefit of an injury standard) you might distinguish between acceptable—i.e., non-countervailable—and non-acceptable subsidies on the production or export of merchandise

---

[g] Indeed, the United States paid export subsidies on cotton and wheat for many years, as an adjunct to domestic price support programs, so that American farmers could compete on the world market at the same time as they were obtaining higher prices in the United States related to the "parity" formula. For a description of the wheat subsidy program in the context of the massive sales of grain to the Soviet Union in the 1970's, see Vol. III of this series, A. Lowenfeld, *Trade Controls for Political Ends*, Ch. II, §§ 2.12, 2.31–33, 4.22 (2d 1983).

[h] T.D. 54,792, 24 Fed. Reg. 1177 (Feb 17, 1959), revoked T.D. 55,184; 25 Fed. Reg. 7099 (July 27, 1960).

[i] See Volume IV of this series, A. Lowenfeld, *The International Monetary System* § 5.1 (2d ed. 1984).

[j] 33 Fed. Reg. 9834 (July 9, 1968).

[k] T.D. 68–192, 33 Fed. Reg. 11543 (August 10, 1968), republished with translation of French decree 33 Fed. Reg. 11661 (Aug. 16, 1968). The decision was modified in October to reduce the duty surcharge to 1.25 per cent, T.D. 68–270, 33 Fed. Reg. 16056 (Nov. 1, 1968), and was revoked as of February 1, 1969, T.D. 69–41, 34 Fed. Reg. 1377 (Jan. 29, 1969).

[l] See to the same effect, the majority opinion in the *Hammond Lead* case discussed in paragraph (e) below. 440 F. 2d at 1030.

destined for the United States. In particular, turn back to the discussion of the Japanese economy at § 3.32. Are any of the practices there described subsidies within the meaning of section 303? As legal adviser to the American Iron and Steel Institute or one of its member companies, would you petition the Treasury for a countervailing duty proceeding in respect of

(i) an undervalued yen;

(ii) expansion loans to the steel industry backed by government guarantees;

(iii) governmental support for a merger between two of the largest steel companies in Japan;

(iv) accelerated depreciation allowances for investments in new plant and equipment;

(v) any of the other elements listed in § 3.43(a)?

(d) (i) If some of these governmental aids to business—to avoid the technical terms for the moment—enabled a firm or any industry to improve its competitive position world-wide, but were not measurable in x dollars per ton or y yen per kilo, would that fact take the measures out of the reach of the countervailing duty statute?

(ii) What about the defense that—whether on steel or on some other products—the United States had adopted similar practices as the ones objected to—export credit guarantees, for instance, investment tax credits, or accelerated depreciation?

(e) Since the United States countervailing duty statute was in effect in 1947, it was exempt from strict compliance with the GATT by virtue of the Protocol of Provisional Application.[m] Accordingly, the United States was free, legally, to continue to administer its statute without reference to injury to domestic industries. But should the criteria for subsidies set forth in Article XVI be considered binding—or at least persuasive—on the Secretary of the Treasury in countervailing duty cases? For instance, one of the hardest questions in this area is the exemption from (or refund of) various "indirect" taxes such as excise and sales taxes said to be borne by the product—i.e., by the consumer,

---

[m] § 2.2. at N. p *supra.*

not by the nominal taxpayer—the producer/exporter. Postponing for the moment the substance of this issue,[n] should the General Counsel of the Treasury advise the Commissioner of Customs or the Secretary of the Treasury to conform his interpretations as much as possible to Article VI(4) of the GATT? If the issue came before a United States court, would you expect the court to (i) defer to the Treasury's interpretation of the GATT? (ii) interpret the GATT on its own? or (iii) address the statute as it would address other statutes—first the text itself, then the legislative history, and (if pertinent) prior judicial decisions—without reference to the international agreement?[o]

(f) Hard as the preceding question is—whether looked at from the point of view of attempting to understand other countries' tax systems or of understanding the relation between international executive agreements and statutes,[p] it was compounded in difficulty—for the

---

[n] See § 4.46-.47 *infra*.

[o] Recall in this connection (1) the peculiar legal origins of the GATT. § 2.2 *supra;* (2) the experience with the retaliation statute following the Chicken War, § 3.62; and (3) the experience with the Antidumping Code, § 4.44, *supra.*

An opinion letter by a major law firm to a group of steel fabricators concerned with alleged rebates of taxes by the government of Italy advised that while the Treasury had taken the position that it would follow the GATT in excluding refunds of indirect taxes from the definition of subsidies subject to countervailing duties, if the matter reaches the Customs Court, "we would no longer be faced with the problem of reconciling the imposition of the desired countervailing duty with the standards set forth in Article VI of the GATT." See *Foreign Trade and Tariff Proposals,* Hearings before the House Comm. on Ways and Means, pt. 5, pp. 2219, 2222, 2225, 90th Cong. 2d Sess. (1968). The case to which that opinion was addressed is discussed in § 4.46(b) and (c) *infra.*

[p] For guidance of a sort on this question, the reader may look to the American Law Institute's *Restatement of the Foreign Relations Law of the United States* (Revised) (Tent. Draft No. 1, 1980):

§ 144.   Effect on Domestic Law of Executive Agreement Pursuant to President's Constitutional Authority

(1) An executive agreement, made by the United States without reference to a treaty or act of Congress, conforming to the constitutional limitations stated in § 121, and manifesting an intention that it shall become effective as domestic law of the United States at the time it becomes binding on the United States

(a) supersedes inconsistent provisions of the law of the several states, but

Treasury, for importers, and for domestic manufacturers—by the curious procedure that prevailed with respect to countervailing duties until 1975. A domestic producer could bring a potential countervailing duty case to the attention of the Treasury, and both the domestic producer and the importer could make informal submissions to the Department orally or in writing. (No provision was made for a hearing.)[q] If a countervailing duty was imposed by the Department, the importer could challenge the duty in the Customs Court, in the same way any importer could challenge the imposition of any duty.[r] But if the Secretary declined to impose a countervailing duty, there was substantial doubt that judicial review was available. The technical reason was that the statute permitting review of American manufacturers' protests[s] referred to valuation, to classification (e.g., is an automobile headlamp an auto part or a lamp?) and to the rate of duty applicable; the argument was that determination by the Secretary of whether the measure of the foreign government under challenge was or was not a "bounty or grant" did not fit in any of these categories.[t] Beyond this, there was a feeling that judging another country's economic and fiscal measures was a delicate matter involving foreign policy, the possibility of retaliation, and other considerations not suitable for placing on the record for decision by courts. In 1971, a divided Court of Customs and Patent Appeals (reversing the Customs Court) apparently resolved the doubts against review of a negative decision by the Secretary of the Treasury, in a case which on the merits involved a very close question:[u]

The true Congressional intent . . . we believe contemplates some moderate degree of executive discretion in defining what sort of

---

        (b) does not supersede inconsistent provisions of earlier acts of Congress.

(§ 121 refers to the powers of the President to enter into executive agreements pursuant to the independent powers of the President).

[q] See Feller, N. e *supra* at pp. 28–29; E. Rossides, *U.S. Customs, Tariffs, and Trade,* p. 465 (1977).

[r] Tariff Act of 1930, § 514, Documents Supplement p. DS-444. The leading cases were *Downs v. United States*, 187 U.S. 496 (1903) and *G.S. Nicholas v. United States*, 249 U.S. 34 (1919).

[s] Tariff Act of 1930 § 516, Documents Supplement p. DS-445.

[t] For a discussion of these doubts as of 1969 by an official of the Treasury, see Feller, N. e *supra* at 31–32.

[u] *United States v. Hammond Lead Products Inc.*, 440 F. 2d 1024 (C.C.P.A. 1971), cert. denied, 404 U.S. 1005 (1971).

foreign governmental actions constitute indirect bounties or grants. An alleged indirect bounty or grant reasonably not seen as such by the executive is a case outside the contemplation of Congress [when it created jurisdiction to hear manufacturers' protests.][v]

The effect seemed to be that affirmative findings by the Treasury were subject to judicial review, negative ones apparently not.[w] Where significant issues of trade policy—or indeed of foreign policy—were involved and the substantive issue was not so clear, it seems likely that the pressures on the Secretary would be in the direction of not imposing a countervailing duty.[x]

4.46—(a) The steel industry—and indeed all industry in the United States—was slow to resort to the countervailing duty law. Between 1897 and 1968, only 68 countervailing duty orders were issued, nearly all in response to the kind of direct subsidy discussed in § 4.45(b) above.[a] From 1959 to 1967, an average of less than three complaints were filed per year, and none resulted in an affirmative determination of a bounty or a grant.[b] In 1967, however, the situation changed when the Treasury Department held that a bounty or grant was being paid or bestowed by the government of Italy on electric transmission towers, a

---

[v] *Id*. at 1031.

[w] The word "apparently" is used because in 1974 the U.S. District Court for the District of Columbia held that if there were no jurisdiction in the Customs Court to review negative determinations in countervailing duty cases, then the exclusive grant of jurisdiction over customs duty cases was inoperative, and the district courts had jurisdiction under 28 U.S.C. § 1340. *National Mills Producers Federation v. Shultz*, 372 F. Supp. 745 (D.D.C. 1974). Before appeal could be taken from this decision, the Trade Act of 1974 was adopted, which inter alia amended § 516 to make clear that judicial review was possible from both affirmative and negative determination by the Secretary. See Documents Supplement p. DS-450. It was under the amended law that the *Zenith* case (§ 4.47(c) *infra*), originally brought in 1970, was taken all the way to the Supreme Court.

[x] For the issue of discretion concerning countervailing duties in a different context, that of responding to a complicated duty rebate scheme introduced by Canada in 1963 in regard to automotive exports, see A. Chayes, T. Ehrlich, A. Lowenfeld, *International Legal Process*, Vol. I, Ch. V, esp. pp. 320–22 (1968).

[a] See Feller, N. e *supra* at pp. 30–31. The available statistics do not record the petitions filed prior to 1934, and until 1970 negative determinations were not published.

[b] See submission by the U.S. Department of the Treasury on Countervailing Duties in *Papers Submitted to the Commission on International Trade and Investment* (The Williams Commission) Vol. I, p. 409 at 413 (1971).

product consisting essentially of steel made up by small, typically non-integrated, firms for sale to electric power utilities.[c] In the period 1967–70 seven countervailing duty determinations were issued, and numerous others were applied for, including a major complaint brought by U.S. Steel against all six member countries of the European Community.[d]

(b) The transmission-tower case that gave the new impetus to countervailing duty proceedings involved nearly all the issues suggested in § 4.45. The chairman of the Ad Hoc Committee of Galvanized Transmission Tower Fabricators told his story to the House Ways and Means Committee as follows:[e]

> Our company first became aware of the serious situation that we faced in the importation of transmission towers from Italy in 1964 when we lost a rather sizeable contract to an Italian fabricator. The amount of the contract was in the neighborhood of one and a quarter million dollars.

> We lost this contract by something like $70,000. At that time I visited with members of the TVA. I visited with our representatives in the House and Senate and we made a rather intense study in an effort to convince the Tennessee Valley Authority that it was in our interest and the interest of this country to purchase these towers locally but the contract was eventually awarded to the Italians.

> Imports of galvanized transmission towers have been increasing at an alarming rate since 1964.

> In the year 1965, 25 percent of the total domestic market was furnished by foreign concerns.

> We are a small company and, realizing that we were facing increased competition from foreign sources selling at prices significantly below what we at Flint could meet, we enlisted the help of other

---

[c] T.D. 67–102, 32 Fed. Reg. 6274 (April 21, 1967).

[d] *Williams Commission* papers at 413; for description of the U.S. Steel complaint, see § 4.46(d) *infra*.

[e] *Foreign Trade and Tariff Proposals,* Hearings before House Comm. on Ways and Means, pt. 9, pp. 2212–3, 91st Cong., 1st Sess. (1969).

domestic producers and formed an ad hoc committee in early 1966, the purpose being to determine what was happening to our industry as a result of these imports.

Our investigation revealed that the Italian producers of electrical transmission towers shipping into this country were being subsidized in one way or another by the Italian Government under Italian law No. 639 of July 5, 1964, and in the amount of approximately $25 per ton and also they were being subsidized in the amount of 7.8 percent of the export price under Italian law No. 570 of July 31, 1954, and as implemented by law number 1162 of November 15, 1964.

It is our estimate that the total subsidies paid under these two Italian laws amounts to somewhere between $38 and $45 per ton.

Our further investigation revealed that our Treasury Department was not imposing countervailing duties against the Italian producers as required under section 303 of the Tariff Act of 1930 and the law plainly states that subsidies shall be countervailed.

Mr. Chairman, the above-mentioned conditions were pointed out in our submission to Director of Customs and the Treasury Department on June 21, 1966.

Since our filing and to date on all electrical tower contracts on which foreign competition was invited to bid an estimated 191,000 tons or 88 percent went to foreign producers and 26,500 or a mere 12 percent went to our domestic producers.

I might add that all governmental agencies invite foreign bids. This does not happen to be the case with private power companies. We do not, as a company, bid on a great many of these large governmental contracts, the reason being that we are not competitive, we have not been competitive for the last several years with the Italians and cannot go to the expense of preparing a bid that would be obviously lost.

After 10 months of investigation, the Treasury Department issued an order effective May 22, 1967, that provided for the countervailing duty assessment of $20 per net ton against the refund [on] galvanized electrical transmission towers under Italian law 639.[f]

---

[f] See N. c *supra*. Note that thirty days after an affirmative countervailing duty determination was issued, "liquidation of duties" would be suspended, and entry of the goods would be precluded unless the extra duty were paid.

I highly commend the Treasury for the action taken.

However, according to judicial interpretation of a grant or bounty under our countervailing law I believe the Treasury Department should have countervailed in the full amount of our request.

Now, after another 14 months we still have not received a decision from the Treasury Department on the remission of taxes under Italian law No. 570, and strongly feel that Treasury should countervail in the full amount of the subsidy granted under this law.

(c) Having gotten partial relief, the fabricators were not sure whether they could, or should appeal; but as they half-hoped, the importer appealed. Thus the facts of the case were spread on the judicial record.[g] There was no *direct* bounty or grant, all agreed, upon manufacture or export of transmission towers. The case turned on remission by the government of two sets of taxes ordinarily collected from Italian manufacturers of the category of merchandise to which the transmission towers belonged. (1) Italy, like many West European countries, used as a major source of revenue a transaction or turnover tax, which is collected at each stage of transfer of a product from raw material supplier to processor to wholesaler to distributor to end-user.[h] By law No. 570, this tax was refunded on export. The American complainants thought the refund constituted a bounty or grant; the Treasury, following, it said, an interpretation consistent with Article VI(4) of the GATT, did not agree. The taxes remitted by Law 570 were taxes on the product that would have been borne by the end-user in a domestic sale; since in the cases before it, the end-user was not in Italy, a refund was appropriate.

---

[g] *American Express Company v. United States,* 332 F. Supp. 191 (Cust. Ct. 1971), *aff'd* 472 F. 2d 1050 (C.C.P.A. 1973).

[h] With variations not here relevant, this is the so-called "cascade tax." Since harmonization of the tax system in the EEC in the late 1960's, the cascade or turnover system has been replaced by the so-called Value Added Tax; the principal difference between the two systems is that the VAT focuses not on the number of transfers of title, but on the increment in value of a product, by giving credit at each stage for taxes paid at prior stages. Apart from simpler accounting, the VAT is thought to be more equitable as between integrated firms that engage in several stages of manufacture and independent firms that come in at only one stage of manufacture or distribution. See E. Schiff, *Value Added Taxation in Europe* (1973).

In addition, (2) Italy imposed taxes on a variety of transactions which the manufacturer of transmission towers had to pay, and which therefore affected its costs, but which were not directly related to the towers: registration taxes, several kinds of stamp taxes, insurance and mortgage taxes, taxes on advertising, vehicle registration, and various permits and licenses required by the government. Law No. 639 provided for refund of a portion of these taxes on exports of certain products, including transmission towers. There was no allegation that the allocation between domestic and export activity for purposes of the refund was improper. But the Minister of Finance in introducing Law No. 639 had argued that the refunds were necessary to compensate for disadvantages in international trade for Italian products caused by differences in systems of internal taxation.[i] That kind of "equalization," the Treasury held, was not a case coming under Article VI(4) of GATT, in that it was a refund not of a tax on a product but of items of general expense, comparable to rebate of an income or payroll tax.[j] Thus a countervailing duty was imposed to offset the $20 per ton paid under Law 639, but not the $18-25 per ton paid under Law 570. Is the distinction between the two types of tax refunds persuasive?[k]

---

[i] See Hearings, N. e *supra* at 2217.

[j] Both the Customs Court and the Court of Customs and Patent Appeals affirmed the Treasury's imposition of countervailing duty on the remission of the taxes on overhead expenses; the issue under Law 570 did not come before the courts, since it was the importer who, as we saw, brought the appeal. The Customs Court held that the importer's argument under Article VI(4) of the GATT, even assuming it were correct, would have to give way to section 303: "GATT is a trade agreement, which if in conflict with a law of Congress, must yield to the latter." 332 F. Supp. at 200–01. The Court of Customs and Patent Appeals seemed to agree, 472 F. 2d at 1059, note 14. Recall the discussion of this point in § 4.45(e) *supra*.

[k] It is interesting that before Italian Law No. 639 came before the U.S. Treasury, it was challenged by the Commission of the European Economic Community as in contravention with Article 96 of the Rome Treaty. After negotiations between the Commission and the Italian government broke down, the Commission brought the matter before the Court of Justice, which upheld the Commission. Case 45/64 *Commission of the EEC* v. *Italian Republic,* [1965] E.C.R. 857 (1 Dec. 1965).

The countervailing duty remained in effect through 1981. When an injury standard was added to the U.S. countervailing duty law in 1979, § 7.63 *infra*, the International Trade Commission (formerly the Tariff Commission) was requested to conduct an investigation, pursuant to § 104(b) of the Trade Agreements Act of 1979, Documents Supplement p. DS-528, to determine whether the domestic industry would be materially injured if the countervailing duty order were revoked. The Commission determined (4–1) that little, if any, increase in imports could be foreseen from removal of the duty, and that there would therefore be no

(d) Once the countervailing duty statute is construed to go beyond simple cash payments and to include indirect economic aid to exports, unexpected consequences can follow. One instance, which put considerable strain on relations between the United States and Canada, involved imports of steel-belted radial tires manufactured in Canada by a subsidiary of the Michelin Tire Company of France.[1] In response to a variety of provincial and national inducements to invest in depressed areas, Michelin established two plants in Nova Scotia, one to make steel cord and the other to make tires. Under the Area Development Incentives Act of 1965[m] and the Regional Development Incentives Act of 1969,[n] investors received grants and concessional loans for approved projects in areas with substantial unemployment or economic stagnation; also, the investments were eligible for a variety of tax exemptions and deferrals, including for instance a 20 per cent depreciation rate for buildings (instead of the usual 5 per cent) and 50 per cent depreciation rate for machinery (instead of the usual 20 per cent). Local authorities gave exemptions from property taxes for stated periods, and in some instances—including the Michelin project—donated the land where the plant was to be erected. The benefits, in part determined by statute, in part by negotiation, were linked to the amount of capital invested and the number of jobs created in the designated regions; they were not linked to production for export as contrasted with domestic consumption.[o] Michelin conceded, however, that the size of the investment would not have been justified by the Canadian market alone: a major share of the output of the plants was to be exported to the United States, and indeed the plants were designed as a base from which to penetrate the United States market.

---

injury. *Galvanized Fabricated Structural Steel Units for the Erection of Electrical Transmission Towers from Italy*, Investigation No. 104–TAA–4, USITC Publ. 1204, Dec. 1981, 46 Fed. Reg. 62966 (Dec. 29, 1981).

[1] *X-Radial Steel Belted Tires from Canada*, T.D. 73–10, 38 Fed. Reg. 1018 (Jan. 8, 1973). For a full discussion of the facts and arguments in this case, drawn on for the present note, see Guido and Morrone, "The Michelin Decision: A Possible New Direction for U.S. Countervailing Duty Law," 6 Law & Pol'y Int'l Bus. 237 (1974).

[m] 14 Eliz. II c. 12 (1965).

[n] 17–18 Eliz. II c. 56 (1969); Canada Rev. Stat. R-3. This Act is reproduced in Vol. II of this series, A. Lowenfeld, *International Private Investment*, Documents Supplement pp. DS-39–49. (2d ed. 1982).

[o] The arrangements were thus quite similar to the arrangements for the forestry and pulp project established in Northeastern Quebec by ITT/Rayonier at about the same time, described in Chapter I of Volume II of this series, N. n *supra*.

Exports from the Nova Scotia plants started in late 1971; by the spring of 1972, the U.S. Rubber Manufacturers Association, whose members until then had largely had the American market to themselves, brought a petition under the countervailing duty statute.

1) How would you argue in favor of the petition?

2) How would you argue against the petition

    i) on behalf of Michelin;

    ii) on behalf of the government of Canada?

3) In fact the tires subject of the complaint were higher priced than most American tires, but, said Michelin, safer and better, in that they would be the first steel-belted radial tires introduced into American commerce in significant volume. Does this fact, stressed by Michelin, affect the outcome?

4) Suppose the Secretary of the Treasury tells you he has no choice but to impose a countervailing duty. How should the amount of the duty be computed?[p]

4.47—(a) In September 1968, U.S. Steel filed six complaints with the U.S. Treasury, alleging subsidies on steel exports by France, West Germany, Italy, the Netherlands, Belgium/Luxembourg, and also by Great Britain.[a] The complaints tied the alleged subsidies directly to "whopping increases" in exports of steel products from the named countries to the United States, "detrimental to our business and to this nation's balance of payments." In

---

[p] In the actual case, a countervailing duty was imposed, initially set at 6.6 per cent of the f.o.b. value of each tire. The rate of the duty was revised downward several times, from 4.195 per cent during 1974 to 2.513 per cent during 1975 to 2.28 per cent during 1976 to 1.98 per cent (estimated) for 1978. See 41 Fed. Reg. 30325 (July 23, 1976), 43 Fed. Reg. 1790 (Jan. 12, 1978). The *Michelin* case led to protracted litigation, first about the scope of review of administrative determinations by the Treasury (held, the importer was entitled to a de novo trial in the Customs Court), *Michelin Tire Corporation v. United States*, 469 F. Supp. 270 (Cust. Ct. 1979), appeal dismissed 603 F. 2d 192 (C.C.P.A. 1979); and eventually a decision on the merits, sustaining the Treasury in its finding of a subsidy, but ordering certain changes in the calculation of the margin of subsidy. *Michelin Tire Corp. v. United States*, 1 CIT 81–94, 3 ITRD (BNA) 1177 (U.S. Ct. Int'l Trade Oct. 26, 1981).

[a] This account is based on copies of the complaints and other papers furnished by the Law Department of U.S. Steel. For contemporary accounts of the action, see e.g., New York Times, Oct. 1, 1968, p. 1, col. 1; "Steel's New Weapon for Import Battle," Iron Age, Oct. 17, 1968, p. 52.

part, the subsidies attacked were such items as special freight rates for steel moving within the Community; favorable rates on export credits or guarantees of credit; accelerated depreciation allowances on modernization of plants; and, in the case of Italy, the workings of laws 570 and 639. The main thrust of the petition, however, was directed at remission of the Value Added Tax, which had been in effect in France since the mid-1950's and was being adopted (with some variations) in all the member countries of the EEC.

In brief, the VAT (or TVA) has some attributes of an excise tax, in that it is included in the purchase price of merchandise, whether at wholesale or retail; and some attributes of an income tax, in that it is designed as a major source of governmental revenue from commercial activity, and is applied to nearly all products and services, without distinction as to their origin or social utility. Each entity dealing with the product in question pays a tax based on the selling price, less a credit it receives for the tax paid by the previous entity that dealt with the product or its components. Thus the net tax is a fraction—e.g., 11 per cent in Germany—of the rise in price attributable to the taxpayer's own effort, whether as manufacturer, processor, or distributor. For imports, the tax is assessed at the border, with no credits for taxes paid elsewhere; for exports, taxes paid in the course of manufacture are refunded to the last taxpayer (i.e., the exporter) and no tax is imposed on the export sale.

The Europeans took the position that since the VAT is borne ultimately by the consumer at the place of sale, if the final sale is not within the country imposing the tax, it should be forgiven or refunded. This position seemed to be consistent with Article VI(4) and Note Ad Article XVI of the GATT.[b] U.S. Steel contended, however, that the effect of the rebate or exemption of the VAT for export sales (i) made it possible to sell abroad (i.e., in the United States) for less than at home, with the same profit margin; and (ii) represented a direct subsidy—ergo a "bounty or grant"—on exports. It argued that the distinction reflected in the GATT (as well as in prior attitudes of the U. S. Treasury) between direct taxes borne by the producer (e.g., income or payroll taxes), and indirect taxes borne by the consumer (e.g., turnover or value-added taxes) was unsound. Neither was it clear that corporate income (i.e., direct) taxes were wholly absorbed by producers without effect on price, nor, more directly to the point, was it

---

[b] Documents Supplement pp. DS-14 and DS-69.

clear that the VAT in domestic sales was paid entirely by consumers. Putting the point another way, U.S. Steel's argument was that domestic sales price in the EEC was determined by demand and market conditions, and that these did not always, or even generally, permit complete shifting forward of the VAT. If a particular product in Germany sold for DM 1000, for instance, was the producer's price really DM 900.90 plus a tax of DM 99.10 (11 per cent of 900.90) paid by buyer? If so, a refund of any VAT paid by the producer and a sale for export at DM 900.90 would be trade neutral. But if not—for instance if the product would have sold for DM 1000 even without the VAT—then the producer absorbed some or all of the VAT in the domestic sale, and (so the argument went) the tax should not be forgiven upon export, and if it was forgiven, a countervailing duty should be imposed.

On behalf of the U. S. Treasury, how would you evaluate this argument? If you do not reject it outright, would you wish to make some factual inquiries? How would you go about establishing the relevant facts? If the facts are difficult to determine, does that suggest that the argument, whatever its merits in economic theory, is deficient as a legal matter under section 303?

(b) The Treasury Department seems to have wondered about the preceding questions as well. For more than six years it did not take any action on U.S. Steel's complaint. At the urging of U.S. Steel and others, Congress amended section 303 in the Trade Act of 1974 to require all petitions for countervailing duties to be determined by the Secretary of the Treasury within 12 months from the filing of the petition.[c] The Senate Committee Report made clear that this time limit was to apply to pending cases as if they had been filed on the day after the Trade Act became law.[d] Nonetheless U.S. Steel filed a new petition in September 1975,

---

[c] § 303(a)(4) of the Tariff Act of 1930, as amended by § 331 of the Trade Act of 1974. Documents Supplement p. DS-441. It is interesting to note in passing that the same amendment also authorized, for the first time, imposition of countervailing duties on duty-free, as well as dutiable products; since this was a substantive change not covered by the Protocol of Provisional Application of the GATT (§ 2.2 at N. p supra), an injury requirement was inserted for the non-dutiable products only, in order to be consistent with Article VI(6)(a) of the GATT. As in the Antidumping Act, the injury determination was committed to the Tariff Commission, renamed International Trade Commission. (Revised § 303(a)(1), (a)(2), and (b)).

[d] Trade Reform Act of 1974, Report of Sen. Comm. on Finance, S. Rep. No. 93-1298, 93rd Cong., 2d Sess. 191 (1974).

bringing up to date both the descriptions of the (now enlarged) European Community, and the statistical and economic analyses in support of the arguments made in the earlier petitions. This time the Treasury responded within a month: it advised U.S. Steel by letter that its petition had been rejected, on the ground that

> the Treasury, for many years, has treated the rebate or remission of indirect taxes, directly related to the exported product or its components, as not being bounties or grants within the meaning of the countervailing duty law. Since the value-added taxes are viewed by the Department as being indirect taxes directly related to the products upon which they are imposed, the rebate or remission of such taxes upon exportation does not constitute a bounty or grant.[e]

U.S. Steel thereupon brought suit in the Customs Court[f] under the newly amended provisions of section 516(d).[g] For twenty months, government counsel engaged U.S. Steel in discovery procedures. Meanwhile another petition for countervailing duties, brought in 1970 by the Zenith Radio Corporation but also decided by Treasury only after passage of the Trade Act of 1974, was making its way through the courts on an agreed statement of facts. U.S. Steel's case was held in abeyance pending determination of the Zenith case.

(c) The Zenith case concerned not the European value added tax but a Commodity Tax imposed by the government of Japan on a variety of consumer goods, including television receivers, radio receivers, phono-

---

[e] Letter to U.S. Steel dated Oct. 20, 1975. See also Press Briefing by Asst. Secy of the Treasury David R. MacDonald of Oct. 20, 1975, reproduced at p. 78 of the Joint Appendix submitted to the U.S. Supreme Court in *Zenith Radio Corporation v. United States*, discussed at paragraph (c) below. Mr. MacDonald said in the briefing which announced the decision of the Treasury:

> The fact that we have not found the remission of value-added taxes to be a bounty or grant within the meaning of our law does not mean that the United States Government is wild about other taxes of this sort. In fact, if there was one thing that was quite persuasive in the petition filed by U.S. Steel, it was their economic argument that, *in fact,* there should be no distinction between direct and indirect taxes.

(*Id.* at 80).

[f] United States Customs Court, Case No. 76-2-00456, Feb/18/76 Reserve File.

[g] See § 4.45(e) N. w *supra*.

graphs, and the like. The tax applied both on products manufactured in Japan and on imports. For products made in Japan, the tax was levied upon shipment from the factory; if the product was shipped for export it was exempt from the tax, and if a tax had been paid on a product that was subsequently exported, the tax was refunded.

Zenith, a major American producer of television sets, asserted that in remitting the commodity tax on exports to the United States, the government of Japan had bestowed a "bounty or grant." Following an investigation, the Bureau of Customs issued a negative determination, essentially on the same grounds as those in the steel case.[h] Zenith brought suit in the Customs Court, and on motions by both sides for summary judgment, that court ruled in favor of Zenith. The Customs Court conceded that the Treasury had decided the petition consistently with its own precedents, but held that those precedents could not stand in light of the Supreme Court's decision in 1903 in *Downs v. United States*,[i] in which the Supreme Court had held a Russian tax remission scheme in respect of sugar exports to constitute a bounty or grant. Accordingly the Customs Court ordered the Secretary to assess countervailing duties on all Japanese consumer electronic products named in Zenith's complaint.[j]

The Court of Customs and Patent Appeals reversed (3–2),[k] but Zenith applied for certiorari (supported by a brief as amicus curiae filed by U.S. Steel), and the Supreme Court accepted the case.[l] The

---

[h] 41 Fed. Reg. 1298 (Jan. 7, 1976). Preliminary determinations relating to the same application, which suggested that a "bounty or grant" was being bestowed by Japan by virtue of preferential interest rates on loans from the Japan Development Bank, promotional assistance from JETRO (§ 3.33 *supra*) and by virtue of certain tax deferrals, appear at 40 Fed. Reg. 5375 (Feb. 5, 1975) and 40 Fed. Reg. 19853 (May 7, 1975). By the time of the final determination, the offending programs had either been terminated or were declared *de minimis* per dollar value of the exported product, so that what was left was the tax remission described in the text.

[i] 187 U.S. 496 (1903).

[j] *Zenith Radio Corporation v. United States*, 430 F. Supp. 242 (Cust. Ct. 1977).

[k] *United States v. Zenith Radio Corporation*, 562 F. 2d 1209 (C.C.P.A. 1977).

[l] Other amicus briefs in support of Zenith's position were filed by a Committee to Preserve American Color Television and by Bethlehem Steel. The Ford Motor Company, concerned both about imports in competition with its American production and with its own ability to import automobiles and components from abroad, filed an amicus brief urging remand with a view to careful examination

U.S. government, fearing a major chain reaction not only in Japan but in Europe if it were ordered to impose countervailing duties, made a major effort to sustain its position.[m] The Supreme Court responded with a unanimous ruling in favor of the Treasury.[n] The opinion by Justice Marshall elaborately traced the legislative history of the countervailing duty statute from 1890 on, and carefully distinguished the *Downs* case, on the ground that the tax remission in *Downs* had been greater than the amount of the domestic excise tax.[o] The Court sidestepped the economic argument that indirect taxes such as the Japanese Commodity tax may not really be shifted forward in their entirety in domestic sales, and that therefore rebate of such taxes in full constitutes a subsidy:

> Aside from the contention . . . that the Department's construction is inconsistent with this Court's decisions, petitioner's sole argument is that the Department's position is premised on false economic assumptions that should be rejected by the courts. In particular, petitioner points to "modern" economic theory suggesting that remission of indirect taxes may create an incentive to export in some circumstances, and to recent criticism of the GATT rules as favoring producers in countries that rely more heavily on indirect than on direct taxes. But, even assuming that these arguments are at all relevant in view of the legislative history of the 1897 provision and the long-standing administrative construction of the statute, they do not demonstrate the unreasonableness of the Secretary's current position. Even "modern" economists do not agree on the ultimate economic effect of remitting indirect taxes, and—given the present state of economic

---

into the economic effects of tax remissions, rather than a broad holding that remission of all indirect taxes constitutes a "bounty or grant," or that no remission of an indirect tax may constitute a bounty or grant, as seemed to be argued by Zenith and the U.S. government respectively. A coalition of importers of electronic products from Japan sought to file in opposition to Zenith's position, arguing that they were the real parties in interest because they would be paying any countervailing duty that might be imposed, but that under § 516(d), they were not permitted to be heard. The Union of Industries of the EEC and the American Importers Association also filed briefs in support of affirmance, i.e., against the imposition of countervailing duties.

[m] Solicitor General McCree personally argued the case, and he told a reporter that he considered the case second in importance for the 1977–78 term only to the *Bakke* case involving reverse discrimination in admission to professional schools.

[n] *Zenith Radio Corporation v. United States*, 437 U.S. 443 (1978).

[o] 437 U.S. at 459–629.

knowledge—it may be difficult, if not impossible, to measure the precise effect in any particular case. . . . More fundamentally, as the Senate Committee with responsibility in this area recently stated, "the issues involved in applying the countervailing duty law are complex, and . . . internationally, there is [a] lack of any satisfactory agreement on what constitutes a fair, as opposed to an 'unfair,' subsidy." S. Rep. No. 93–1298, p. 183 (1974). In this situation, it is not the task of the judiciary to substitute its views as to fairness and economic effect for those of the Secretary.[p]

(d) When the *Zenith* case was decided by the Supreme Court, U.S. Steel's action was still pending before the Customs Court.

(i) Can you think of a persuasive argument for distinguishing remission of the European value-added taxes from remission of the Japanese Commodity Tax?

(ii) If you think U.S. Steel may be right in economic terms[q] but is precluded by the Supreme Court's decision in *Zenith*, would you advise the industry to launch a major campaign to amend the U.S. countervailing duty statute? Try to draft a reasonable amendment meeting the point.

(iii) What other suggestions might you have?[r]

4.48—OTHER REMEDIES

Apart from the remedies for unfair competition discussed in the preceding sections, the steel industry could look to remedies for fair but disruptive competition.

(a) One of these might have been the escape clause.[s] But while the operative conditions for escape clause action could probably have been shown—imports into the United States "in such increased quantities as to cause, or threaten to cause, serious injury to the domestic industry . . ."—

---

[p] 437 U.S. at 458–59.

[q] Compare Asst. Secy. MacDonald's remarks quoted at N. e *supra*.

[r] See e.g. § 303(d) as amended by the Trade Act of 1974, Documents Supplement p. DS-442.

[s] See §§ 3.52 at N. k, 3.53 at Ns. r-v *supra*.

the other necessary condition—". . . as a result in major part of concessions granted under trade agreements"—would have been very hard to prove.[t] Whatever it was that caused the changes in steel trade in the period 1958–68—whether it was higher wage settlements in the United States, increased investment and productivity in Japan, greater economic activity in the countries now joined in the European Common Market, elimination of earlier technology gaps, inflation in the United States induced by the war in Vietnam, or all of these in some measure— it would be hard to attribute the plight of the American steel industry to trade agreements concessions. While some reductions in United States duties on steel products had been effected pursuant to the Dillon Round of 1960–61— roughly from 9–11 per cent to 7–9 per cent ad valorem, the major reductions from the 25–30 per cent Smoot-Hawley rates had taken place long before the surge in imports to the United States.[u]

(b) Another possibility might have been the national security clause —section 232(b) of the Trade Expansion Act[v]—and apparently some thought was given within the United States government to action under this authority. After all, it would be hard to question the proposition that steel was vital to national defense, and, as we saw, the statute expressly recognized "the close relation of the economic welfare of the Nation to our national security" and called on the President to "take into consideration the impact of foreign competition on the economic welfare of individual domestic industries."[w] But as mentioned previously, the national security provision had never been used for any product except oil; it would have been hard to persuade the United States government to take unilateral action to restrict imports on a major industrial product—either as the Kennedy Round was coming to a close or just

---

[t] See Trade Expansion Act of 1962 § 301(b)(1). Documents Supplement p. DS-268. Note that the link between injury and trade agreement for escape clause action was eliminated in the Trade Act of 1974. See § 201(b)(1), Documents Supplement p. DS-338.

[u] Under section 253 of the Trade Expansion Act, concurred in by the other participants in the Kennedy Round, duty reductions agreed on at Geneva were to come into effect in five annual stages. Since all the agreements, as we saw, came into effect only on June 30, 1967, the reductions, small as they were, were spread out over the period 1968–72, well after the increase in steel imports described in § 4.3.

[v] See § 3.66 *supra*.

[w] Trade Expansion Act § 232(c). Documents Supplement p. DS-258.

after, especially considering the important role that the steel negotiations had played in Geneva.[x]

(c) Still another possibility might have been the so-called "orderly marketing" provision of the Trade Expansion Act, which as we saw had been adopted by the Congress primarily at the behest of the foot-wear industry.[y] Section 352 authorized the President to negotiate agreements of the kind in effect for cotton textiles (and later for man-made textiles as well), whereby under threat of unilateral import restraints foreign countries would agree to limit their exports of specified products to stated amounts—typically the average of the three (or five years preceding the agreement—plus an annual increment to take account of the growth of the economy. But from the point of view of the American steel industry, section 352 had the same flaw as the escape clause: The authority was available only upon an affirmative finding after investigation by the Tariff Commission under section 301(b), that is a finding not only of increased imports and injury (or threat of injury) but of a causal link to concessions granted under trade agreements.

The idea of an orderly marketing agreement, however, had a certain appeal. If the sellers of steel to the United States—primarily in the European Community and Japan—could be induced to limit their exports to the United States, the United States could not be accused of unilateral action, or of renunciation of the policies of free trade that it had espoused for over three decades. Further, if somehow the foreign companies, rather than the governments, could be induced to promise to limit their exports to acceptable levels, then Washington could also avoid formal participation in the arrangements, and thus avoid the criticism on both ideological and procedural grounds that would flow from an agreement entered into on a government-to-government basis.

The search thus turned to a relative newcomer to the international trade scene—the voluntary restraint agreement.

---

[x] See § 3.72 *supra*.

[y] See § 3.53 at Ns. z-e *supra*.

§ 5—Voluntary Restraint Agreements 1968–74

§ 5.1—The First Round

5.11—BACKGROUND OF THE AGREEMENTS[a]

In the course of 1967, a number of bills were introduced in Congress that would have authorized or directed the imposition of import quotas on various products. In particular, Senator Hartke of Indiana introduced a bill, with 35 co-sponsors, that would have contained a Congressional finding "that increased imports of pig iron and steel mill products have adversely affected the United States balance of payments, contributed substantially to reduced employment opportunities for United States workers in the domestic iron and steel industry, and captured such an increased share of the market . . . as to threaten the soundness of the domestic iron and steel industry and therefore the national security."[b] The bill would have authorized the President to negotiate multilateral or bilateral agreements establishing annual quantitative limits on imports of steel products into the United States, based on the ratio of imports to consumption for the preceding three years—overall, by product categories, and by country of origin.[c] If within six months after passage of the bill an agreement had not been reached with any given nation, the President would have been required to proclaim a quota applicable to imports from countries that had not entered into bilateral agreements.[d] The quotas would remain in effect for five years, after which the Secretary of Commerce would be required to hold hearings and issue a report, together with recommendations on whether the quotas should be continued.[e]

Other bills focused on other products—textiles, meat, dairy products,

---

[a] This account draws on Comment: "Executive Authority and Antitrust Considerations in 'Voluntary' Limits on Steel Imports," 118 U. Pa. L. Rev. 105 (1969); W. Hogan, *The 1970's: Critical Years for Steel* ch. 3 (1972); and the papers submitted in connection with the litigation described in § 5.3 *infra*.

[b] S. 2537, Oct. 16, 1967, § 2, 90th Cong., 1st Sess. (1967). The complete text of the bill appears in the Documents Supplement at p. DS-567.

[c] *Id.* § 4. The statement in the text is simplified somewhat, in that the reference years varied, and in that the product and country limits, in contrast to the overall limits, were based on shares of total imports, rather than of consumption.

[d] *Id.* § 5.

[e] *Id.* § 9(3).

lead and zinc, and glass—or on imports in general which exceeded a stated percentage of domestic consumption or production, or which had expanded faster than a specified annual rate.[f]

The administration took the bills, which seemed to command substantial support in the Congress, quite seriously. Secretary of State Rusk testified:

> Let us suppose that all or most of the restrictions on imports currently being considered were put into effect. What would other countries do? Would they issue protests, make nasty speeches and criticize us? They would do a great deal more than that. They would undoubtedly strike back. Nor would this be an unfriendly act on their part. Indeed, a number of our leading trading partners, with all of whom we have the closest political ties, have already submitted formal diplomatic notes to the Department of State expressing their very great concern about the possible impairment of trade concessions negotiated with us if the bills under consideration were to become law. Australia, for example, drew our attention to its estimate that 60 percent of Australia's exports to the United States would be affected if these restrictive measures were applied.

> Retaliation would simply be what is permitted by the rules of the game as that game is now practiced by some seventy countries accounting for about 85 percent of world trade. I refer, of course, to the General Agreement on Tariffs and Trade—the GATT.

> . . . . .

> We have the sovereign right, of course, to impose restrictions to protect particular sectors of our economy, but we have no control over who will pay the costs. Thus a congressional decision to isolate our steel industry from foreign competition might be paid for not just by higher prices for steel in this country but by reduced foreign sales opportunities for our farmers, our producers of machine tools, computers, canned fruit, automobiles, and who knows what else. And reduced sales opportunities for our export industries mean reduced production, employment, and profit in these industries.

---

[f] For instance S. 1446, introduced by Senator Muskie with 20 co-sponsors including Senators Ervin, Kennedy, Morse, and Scott, would have required imposition of quotas on any article produced in the United States if the ratio of imports to domestic production was at least 15 per cent and had increased by 50 per cent over the preceding 5 years.

We cannot act in isolation in trade policy, any more than we can in political and military policies.

. . . . .

We are currently confronted with an array of protectionist appeals which, if the Congress were to succumb, would constitute not an exception to, but a reversal of, policy. It would be beyond the bounds of plausibility for us to argue internationally that U.S. trade restrictions affecting $5 or $6 billion or more of our imports were just an exception. That is the immense volume we think might be involved if we were to further restrict all forms of textiles, steel, petroleum, watches, meat, dairy products, and lead and zinc. All of our trading partners—and virtually all of them would be affected—would interpret such a move, correctly I believe, as a fundamental shift in American trade policy.

The particular form of protection being sought by most of the special interest groups is that of quotas. Quotas are illegal under the GATT except under certain carefully prescribed circumstances, which do not cover the kind of sweeping protection currently pending in the Congress. The general GATT prohibition against quotas was adopted largely at American insistence—it has always been regarded as one of the GATT's greatest achievements. This is because the absolute limitations imposed by quotas are a far more drastic interference with market forces than even high tariffs which can be overcome by increasing efficiency, reducing costs, or offering a product with special design, quality or other features. However, no amount of efficiency or ingenuity can overcome a quota, and the resulting monopoly position of domestic producers reduces the incentive for cost reduction and product improvement. In addition to these disadvantages, quotas are difficult and costly to administer.

. . . . .

A reversion to a protectionist policy would nullify 20 years of our efforts in Western Europe to build up a healthy partner able to defend itself and join us in meeting the vast needs in other parts of the world. A massive outbreak of trade restrictions in the United States would turn Western Europe inward and against us because they would have no realistic alternative. This would have incalculable consequences for our political and military positions. Economically, it would destroy the great initiative of John F. Kennedy embodied in the Trade Expansion Act of 1962 and the multilateral achievement which bears his name: the Kennedy round.[g]

Ambassador Roth, the Special Representative for Trade Negotiations, fresh from completion of the Kennedy Round, added:

> I do not think it is possible to exaggerate the gravity of the decisions that this committee has been asked to make by the authors of the quota bills that are the subject of these hearings. If they were to be enacted not only would these most recent gains from the trade agreement program be sacrificed but all the progress made by the United States since 1934 toward establishing fair and orderly international trade relations would be put in serious jeopardy.
>
> These bills, if enacted, would run contrary to international commitments undertaken under authority expressly conferred by the Congress. U.S. imports of the products covered by bills to impose new quotas or make existing ones more restrictive amounted last year to over $6 billion. If the general quota bill that has been described in the press were to be added to these specific product bills, the figure would not be $6 billion but more than $12 billion, or nearly 50 percent of our total imports in 1966.
>
> . . . . .
>
> I do not say, Mr. Chairman, that particular firms or groups of workers, or possibly even specific industries, are not experiencing difficulty because of imports. I do say that if they are being adversely affected by imports, they should seek relief through the procedures provided under existing legislation, rather than attempting to bypass them.
>
> . . . . .
>
> The basic question here is what kind of an economy we want—one cosseted by quotas and immunized from competition, or one vigorous enough to compete effectively in the world market.
>
> To give quotas to one industry, experience shows, merely sparks demands for them by others. The national interest is much more than the mere totality of sectional interests. The national interest, as

---

[g] *Import Quotas Legislation,* Hearings before Sen. Comm. on Finance, 90th Cong., 1st Sess. pt. 1 p. 8, at 10, 11, 12, 13 (Oct. 18, 1967).

Presidents and Congresses of both parties have determined it for the past third of a century, lies in the expansion of world trade, not its contraction, and in free competition, not protectionism.[h]

But as an election year approached and the nation was becoming increasingly disillusioned with international commitments of all kinds, the possibility that one or another of the quota bills might be adopted remained real.[i] In Europe and Japan, persons interested in the American market were getting nervous. So, in an election year, were the officials of the United States government concerned with foreign trade policy.[j]

In March of 1968, Yoshihiro Inayama, the chairman of the Japan Iron and Steel Exporters' Association, came to Washington for talks with the State Department about steel imports and the quota legislation pending in Congress. It is not clear who made the first suggestion, but discussion turned to the possibility that the Japanese steel industry might limit its exports to the United States if the quota legislation could be set aside. Mr. Inayama indicated his country's steel producers might be interested in such an arrangement, but only if the European producers also undertook to limit their sales to the United States. He went to Europe to discuss the proposal with producers in the Community, and they also indicated interest. By July 1968, discussions had turned to negotiations, with numbers attached to the offers of restraint.

It seems to have been agreed early in the talks that the shares of the American market for the ECSC and for Japan should be equal. But that left for decision how large imports into the United States should be; what should be the estimate for imports from non-participants—primarily Canada and Great Britain but also some fifteen other countries;[k]

---

[h] *Id.* p. 34 at 35, 36, 37.

[i] Altogether 22 bills providing for quotas were considered by the Senate Finance Committee in the Hearings cited at N. g *supra.*

[j] Note that this was the same period when President Johnson's balance of payments program had been introduced, essentially without benefit of legislation. See Vol. IV of this series, A. Lowenfeld, *The International Monetary System* § 4.2 (2d ed. 1984).

[k] The largest in terms of tonnage were Argentina, Brazil, Poland, Mexico and Australia, all between 150.000 and 180,000 in 1968. By 1971 Mexico had more than doubled its steel exports to the United States, to become the leader of the smaller countries in this category.

and, most difficult, what rate of growth should be built into the restraint formula. The first Japanese proposal seems to have been a limit of 5 million tons, plus 10 per cent annual growth.[1] In July, the offer was modified and made more definite—a limit of 5.5 million tons for 1969, with annual increases of 7 per cent.[m] The American Iron and Steel Institute, though pleased with the idea of export limitations, immediately termed the offer unrealistic, especially the proposed rate of growth.[n] But almost simultaneously, Senator Long, the Chairman of the Senate Finance Committee, announced that consideration of the steel quota bills pending before his committee would be postponed indefinitely, in order to provide time for the negotiations on voluntary limitations.[o] And

" AH SO... TO AVOID YOUR NEED FOR PROTECTION, I PLAN TO GO A LITTLE EASIER "

Reprinted by permission of United Feature Syndicate, Inc.

---

[1] See Wall Street Journal, Oct. 30, 1968, p. 3, col. 2.

[m] New York Times, July 11, 1968, p. 53, col. 6; Wall Street Journal, July 11, 1968, p. 6, col. 2.

[n] Wall Street Journal, July 12, 1968, p. 5, col. 2.

[o] Wall Street Journal, July 10, 1968, p. 32, col. 2; New York Times, July 10, 1968, p. 49, col. 2.

the negotiations did continue, among the U.S. Congress, the Japanese industry, the European industry, and the American industry, with the U.S. State Department a kind of middleman—the only party (if that is the right word) free to talk to each of the others.[p] The Japanese and European governments, including the High Authority of the Coal and Steel Community, were doubtless kept informed, but were apparently not participants in the negotiations.[q]

As 1968 drew to a close, agreement was reached not very far from the offer communicated by Mr. Inayama in July. Total exports from Japan—from the majors as well as from smaller producers—would be limited to 5.75 million tons in 1969, with a maximum annual increase of 5 per cent for 1970 and 1971. An identical commitment was made by the steel producers of the European Community—both on the assumption that total imports into the United States would not exceed 14 million tons in 1969, thus leaving roughly 18 per cent for third countries. But how should the agreement be concluded? The foreign producers, now taking counsel, wanted assurance that the United States Department of Justice had cleared the arrangement; after all, its very purpose was a restraint of trade and sharing of markets. Justice seems to have taken the position—possibly with some "guidance" from on high—that so long as the United States government was involved, the agreements would not be regarded as violating the antitrust laws, but it was reluctant to give a formal clearance. The American Iron and Steel Institute notified the State Department it accepted the arrangement, but its members did not want to become parties. For its part, the State Department had been careful not to engage in government-to-government talks, or to make promises that it might not be in position to keep. Eventually the arrangements were announced by the chairmen of the Congressional Committees charged with trade legislation, who released a letter from the Secretary of State attaching letters to him from the foreign steel producers' associations:

---

[p] On July 30, 1968, as imports were increasing at an annual rate of about 50 per cent, the major steel companies and the United Steelworkers of America reached a wage settlement calling for a 6 per cent increase in wages and benefits over a three-year period, thus averting a strike. See Wall Street Journal, July 31, 1968, p. 3, col. 1.

[q] According to the Wall Street Journal, the Japanese Ministry of International Trade and Industry at first opposed the negotiations, on the ground that they might set precedents for other American industries; later, however, MITI concurred, because of the apparent strength of the protectionist drive in the Congress. Wall Street Journal, July 11, 1968, p. 6, col. 3.

5.12—THE FIRST AGREEMENTS

FOR IMMEDIATE RELEASE. . . . . . .
TUESDAY, JANUARY 14, 1969

JOINT RELEASE
COMMITTEE ON
WAYS AND MEANS,
HOUSE OF REPRESENTATIVES:
SENATE FINANCE COMMITTEE,
UNITED STATES SENATE

CHAIRMAN OF HOUSE COMMITTEE ON WAYS AND MEANS
AND SENATE COMMITTEE ON FINANCE RELEASE LETTER
FROM SECRETARY RUSK ANNOUNCING VOLUNTARY
RESTRAINTS BY JAPANESE AND EUROPEAN
STEEL INDUSTRIES

The Chairmen of the Committee on Ways and Means and the Committee on Finance, the Honorable Wilbur D. Mills and the Honorable Russell E. Long. jointly announced today the receipt of a letter from the Secretary of State transmitting communications from Japanese and certain European steel industries in which those industries express their intention to limit their exports of steel mill products in 1969, 1970 and 1971. The Japanese and European industries, which together account for about 82 percent of our imports, intend to limit their exports to the United States during 1969 to 5.75 million net tons each. Growth in these exports will be limited to 5 percent in the two following years. As a result of the export limitation by our two major suppliers, imports are estimated to total about 14 million tons in 1969, 14.7 million tons in 1970, and 15.4 million tons in 1971. Imports of steel mill products in 1968 are estimated to have totalled 17.5 million tons.

The Chairmen have noted the special character of the trend of steel imports in recent years in this critical industry. Periods of uncertainty about the outcome of labor negotiations and possible strike anticipation have led to large jumps in imports. Thus in 1968, imports increased by about 6 million tons to an estimated level of 17.5 million tons. Typically, once such increases have been recorded, they constitute a new plateau of imports, irrespective of the level of domestic production.

In the circumstances, the Chairmen regard the action of the Japanese and European steel industries as a welcome and realistic step.

The text of the Secretary of State's letter, together with the communications from the Japanese and European industries follows:

DEPARTMENT OF STATE
Washington, D. C. 20520

January 14, 1969

The Honorable
  Wilbur D. Mills
    Ways and Means Committee
    House of Representatives.

Dear Mr. Chairman:

The President has asked me to transmit to you communications received from the steel industry of Japan and the steel industries of the European Coal and Steel Community (ECSC) expressing the intentions of these industries to limit their exports of steel mill products to the United States in the years 1969 through 1971.

We estimate that as a result of the export limitation of the Japanese and ECSC producers, which together provide about 82 percent of our steel imports, total imports will amount to about 14 million net tons in 1969, about 14.7 million net tons in 1970 and about 15.4 million net tons in 1971. Other major foreign producers have not formally offered to cooperate in the voluntary export limitations but, as a practical matter, are expected to maintain their exports at levels which yield the estimates stated above.

Sincerely yours,

Enclosures   /s/   Dean Rusk

MEMORANDUM   December 23, 1968

TO:
The Honorable Secretary of State,
Washington 25, D.C., U.S.A.

FROM:
Yoshihiro Inayama, Chairman,
Japan Iron & Steel Exporters' Association

SUBJECT: Statement of the Intention of the Japanese Steel Industry

*Statement of the Intention of
the Japanese Steel Industry*

1. With the desire to assist in the maintenance of an orderly market for steel in the United States, the nine leading steel companies of Japan,

namely, Yawata Iron & Steel Co., Ltd., Fuji Iron & Steel Co., Ltd., Nippon Kokan Kabushiki Kaisha, Kawasaki Steel Corporation, Sumitomo Metal Industries, Ltd., Kobe Steel Works, Ltd., Nisshin Steel Co., Ltd., Osaka Iron & Steel Co., Ltd., and Nakayama Steel Works, Ltd. gave assurances in their statement of July 5, 1968 that their steel mill product shipments from Japan to the United States would not exceed 5.5 million metric tons during Japanese fiscal year 1968. These nine companies account for approximately 85 percent of all Japanese steel mill products shipped to the United States. In the light of subsequent events and as a result of discussions concerning this matter with the representatives of the Government of the United States of America, they now want to make a new statement to the following effect.

2. With greater understanding of market conditions for steel in the United States, and with the cooperation of the medium and small steelmakers of Japan which account for the remaining 15 percent of shipments to the United States, the same nine leading steel companies wish to state their intention, subject to measures permitted by the laws and regulations of Japan, to limit the Japanese shipments of steel mill products to the United States to a total of 5,750,000 net tons during calendar year 1969.

3. During the subsequent two calendar years (through 1971), it is also their intention to confine the Japaneses shipments within limits which would represent, at most, a 5 percent increase over 5,750,000 net tons in 1970 and over 6,037,500 net tons in 1971, depending upon demand in the United States market and the necessity to maintain orderly marketing therein. During this period the Japanese steel companies will try not to change greatly the product mix and pattern of distribution of trade as compared with the present.

4. This statement is made upon the assumptions: i) that the total shipments of steel mill products from all the steel exporting nations to the United States will not exceed approximately 14,000,000 net tons during 1969, 105 percent of 14,000,000 net tons in 1970, and 105 percent of 14,700,000 net tons in 1971, ii) that the United States will take no action, including increase of import duties, to restrict Japanese steel mill product exports to the United States, and iii) that the above action by the Japanese steel companies does not infringe upon any laws of the United States of America and that it conforms to international laws.

s/Yoshihiro Inayama
Chairman
Japan Iron & Steel Exporters' Association

December 23, 1968

The Honorable
Secretary of State
New State Building
Washington 25, D. C.
U.S.A.

Sir,

The associations of the steel producers of the ECSC united in the "Club des Siderurgistes", to wit:

—Associazione Industrie Siderurgiche Italiane ASSIDER, Milan, represented by Prof. Dr. Ernesto Manuelli

—Chambre Syndicale de la Siderurgie Francaise, Paris, represented by the President, Mr. Jacques Ferry

—Groupement des Hauts Fourneaux et Acieries Belges, Brussels, represented by the President, Mr. Pierre van der Rest

—Groupement des Industries Siderurgiques Luxembourgeoises, represented by the President, Mr. Rene Schmit/Luxembourg

—Vereniging de Nederlandse Ijzer-en Staalproducerende Industrie, represented by Mr. Evert van Veelen/Ijmuiden

—Wirtschaftsvereinigung Eisen- und Stahlindustrie, Dusseldorf, represented by the President, Bergassessor Dr. Hans-Gunther Sohl

referring to the repeated talks they have had in this matter with representatives of the Government of the United States in behalf of the sustenance of liberal international trade in steel and to assist in the maintenance of an orderly market for steel in the United States declare the following:

1.) It is their intention to limit the total ECSC deliveries of steel mill products, i.e. finished rolled steel products, semis, hot rolled strip, tubes, and drawn wire products, to the United States to 5.750.000 net tons during the calendar year 1969.

2.) It is also their intention in the calendar years 1970 and 1971 to confine their deliveries within limits which would at the utmost represent for the year 1970 a five percent increase over 5.750.000 net tons and for the year 1971 a five percent increase over 6.037.500 net tons.

During the named periods the ECSC producers will try to maintain approximately the same product mix and pattern of distribution as at present.

This statement is based on the assumption

A) that the total shipments of steel mill products (finished rolled steel products, semis, hot rolled strip, tubes, and drawn wire products) from all the steel exporting nations to the USA will not exceed approximately 14 million net tons during 1969, and five percent over 14 million net tons in 1970, and five percent over 14.7 million net tons in 1971, and

B) that the United States will take no action to restrict ECSC steel mill product exports to the USA like

a) quota systems

b) increase of import duties

c) other restrictions on the import of steel mill products to the USA.

This proposal of the ECSC steel producers is made provided that it does not infringe on any laws of the United States and that it conforms to international laws.

/s/ – Ernesto Manuelli –   /s/ – Jacques Ferry –
/s/ – Pierre van der Rest –   /s/ – Rene Schmit –
/s/ – Evert van Veelen –   /s/ – Hans-Gunther Sohl –

§ 5.2—Notes and Questions

5.21—Look back at the discussion of quotas in section 2.43 supra, and especially at the excerpt from the chief American negotiator of what became the General Agreement on Tariffs and Trade.[a] In their testimony before the Senate Finance Committee, Secretary Rusk and Ambassador Roth made essentially the same arguments against quotas, that they tend to be inefficient, self-perpetuating, and distorting of rational allocation of resources. In addition, of course, the Secretary of State and the Special Representative for Trade Negotiations pointed to two decades of successful commercial policy, in which the United States view of quotas had for the most part prevailed among industrial countries. Do the Voluntary Restraint Agreements overcome the objections to import quotas?

---

[a] p. 35.

5.22—As a legal matter, are the Voluntary Restraint Agreements a resourceful solution to the problems described in section 4.4? Or are they an illegitimate attempt to circumvent the controls of trade legislation, antitrust laws, international obligations, and diplomatic practice?

(a) Is it proper, for instance, for the State Department to throw a cloak of antitrust immunity around a deal whereby European, Japanese, and American firms divide up the market for steel mill products in the United States?

(b) Is it proper for the United States steel industry to bargain its support for quota legislation (for steel as well as other products) for support from the executive branch for restraints on steel imports that it can live with? Is the bargain proper for the executive branch? For the Committee Chairmen in the Congress?

(c) What about the interested parties in the United States that were not consulted—steel importers, fabricators of steel products who had used foreign steel to compete with the integrated majors, and the public in general?

(d) Do you think the preceding questions represent meaningful concern for established rules of international trade and domestic government? Or are they academic questions, reflecting a misunderstanding of the 'real world' coping pragmatically with situations unforeseen when the rules were written?

(e) (i) Consider how the legal concerns might be brought before a court in the United States. Who would be a proper plaintiff? Who would be the defendants?

(ii) If a court were persuaded by one or more of the legal objections to the VRA's suggested above, what kind of relief might it grant? Could it undo a major action in the nation's foreign economic policy?

5.23—(a) Coming back to the VRA's as written, Secretary Rusk argued that import quotas are difficult and costly to administer. Presumably these difficulties and costs will not be incurred under the VRA's, at least for the United States. But how will the agreements be enforced?

(b) What should a customs collector in San Francisco do if he thinks unusually large shipments of steel are entering the United States in his port? What should the United States government do if it receives and verifies such reports? Is the sanction of non-renewal of the agreements and support for quota legislation sufficient to discourage "cheating" by exporters in Europe or Japan? Do the foreign governments—or the ECSC—have an enforcement responsibility?

(c) What about the problem of allocation of exports among individual producers in Europe and Japan? Is that "their problem," and no concern of the United States? Or should United States authorities cooperate with the foreign exporters' associations? Are they authorized to do so?

(d) Note that the two letters of intent state that during the period of their effectiveness the exporters "will try not to change greatly the product mix and pattern of distribution of trade as compared with the present." Is that a satisfactory assurance that exports will not tend to move to "top of the line" products, as had been the experience with the textile export restraints? Should the documents have said something about price, as well as tonnage?

5.24—(a) Note that the VRA's covered only three years—1969, 1970, and 1971. Would you expect them to really be temporary, or do they contain the seeds of their own renewal?

(b) On the assumption that the American majors favored the VRA's, should some conditions have been exacted from the domestic industry?

For instance (i) a commitment to a program of plant modernization, installation of basic oxygen furnaces, or continuous casting at a stated schedule;

Or (ii) a commitment to restrained wage settlements? Or moderation in price increases?

How might suggestions along these lines have been carried out, in the context of an agreement that formally was simply two letters of intent from foreign producers' associations to the Secretary of State?

§ 5.3—The Second Round

5.31—THE VRA's IN OPERATION

Steel imports into the United States fell from nearly 18 million tons in 1968 to about 14 million tons in 1969, or from 16.7 to 13.7 per cent of consumption.[a] Imports from Japan exceeded the quota by about half a million tons, chiefly because of heavy purchases in December 1968 which arrived in the United States in January 1969. But European shipments fell substantially below the agreed level, so that overall the goals of the VRA's were almost exactly achieved in their first year. Imports in 1970 fell still further, to about 13.4 million tons, apparently because a substantial boom in the European Community countries absorbed much of the output of the European steel industry in the first half of the year.[b] But while steel imports measured by tonnage fell some 25 per cent from 1968 to 1970, the dollar value remained just about the same—$1,976 million in 1968, $1,967 million in 1970. In part this was because of a steady price rise, as the quotas limited price competition, in part because the product mix had changed from mostly ordinary carbon steel to an increasing proportion of so-called specialty steels.[c]

In 1971, the final year of the first VRA's, 18.3 million tons came in, approximately 2.7 million tons above the agreed level and more than the pre-restraint level of 1968, both in tonnage and in market share. Some of the increase came from non-participating countries—notably Mexico, Spain, South Korea, and the Philippines; but over 1.5 million tons in excess of the agreed level came from countries whose exporters had agreed to restraint. Shipments from Japan increased 16 per cent between 1970 and 1971, from West Germany by 43 per cent; from Belgium/Luxembourg by 60 per cent; and from Italy, which had started small, by 250 per cent, from 143,000 to 505,000 tons. Clearly the 1968 agreements were dead.

---

[a] See Table pp. 210–11.

[b] See Hogan § 5.11 N. a *supra* p. 59.

[c] Specialty steels are low volume, high price, and often custom-ordered alloys. At a time when ordinary carbon steels were selling in the $120–200 range, depending on the product, stainless steel was selling for over $1,000 a ton and certain tool steels sold for more than $7,000 a ton. For more on specialty steels, see § 5.56 *infra*.

Growth Trends in Production, Shipments, Imports and Exports of Steel Mill Products: 1950–76

Year	Raw steel production	Net industry shipments	Imports	Exports	Apparent consumption	Imports relative to apparent consumption	Exports relative to net industry shipments
	(Thousands of short tons)					Percent	
1976	128,000	89,447	14,285	2,654	101,078	14.1	3.0
1975	116,642	79,957	12,012	2,953	89,016	13.5	3.7
1974	145,720	109,472	15,970	5,833	119,609	13.4	5.3
1973	150,799	111,430	15,150	4,052	122,528	12.4	3.6
1972	133,241	91,805	17,681	2,873	106,613	16.6	3.1
1971	120,443	87,038	18,304	2,827	102,515	17.9	3.2
1970	131,514	90,798	13,364	7,062	97,100	13.8	7.8
1969	141,262	93,887	14,034	5,229	102,682	13.7	5.6
1968	131,462	91,856	17,960	2,170	107,646	16.7	2.4
1967	127,213	83,897	11,455	1,685	93,667	12.2	2.0
1966	134,101	89,995	10,753	1,724	99,024	10.9	1.9
1965	131,462	92,666	10,383	2,496	100,553	10.3	2.7
1964	127,076	84,945	6,440	3,442	87,943	7.3	4.1
1963	109,261	75,555	5,452	2,180	78,827	6.9	2.9
1962	98,328	70,552	4,100	2,013	72,639	5.6	2.9

Year							
1961	98,014	66,126	3,163	1,990	67,299	4.7	3.0
1960	99,282	71,149	3,359	2,977	71,531	4.7	4.2
1959	93,446	69,377	4,396	1,677	72,096	6.1	2.4
1958	85,255	59,914	1,707	2,823	58,798	2.9	4.7
1957	112,715	79,895	1,155	5,348	75,702	1.5	6.7
1956	115,216	83,251	1,341	4,348	80,244	1.7	5.2
1955	117,036	84,717	973	4,061	81,629	1.2	4.8
1954	88,312	63,153	788	2,659	61,282	1.3	4.2
1953	111,610	80,152	1,674	2,907	78,919	2.1	3.6
1952	93,168	68,004	1,186	3,918	65,272	1.8	5.8
1951	105,200	78,929	2,178	3,051	78,056	2.8	3.9
1950	96,836	72,232	1,016	2,639	70,609	1.4	3.7

Note: Apparent consumption equals domestic shipments plus imports less exports. It differs from actual consumption to the extent that inventories are built up and drawn down by steel users.

Source: Federal Trade Commission, *Staff Report on the United States Steel Industry and Its International Rivals*, p. 70 (from AISI Reports) (Nov. 1977).

Comparison of U.S. Imports of Steel Mill Products
with Voluntary Restraint Agreement Ceilings

	Actual Imports (thousand net tons)				Imports Relative to VRA Ceilings (percentage)	
Year	Japan	European Community	Other Nations	Total	Japan	European Community
1969	6,253	5,199	2,582	14,034	109	90
1970	5,935	4,573	2,856	13,364	98	72
1971	6,908	7,174	4,242	18,324	109	113
1972*	6,440	7,779	3,462	17,681	99	97
1973	5,637	6,510	3,003	15,150	85	80
1974	6,159	6,424	3,387	15,970	90	77

* Data for the European Community include the United Kingdom beginning
with 1972, the year in which the producers of the UK joined the VRA.

Source: Federal Trade Commission, *Staff Report* p. 76.

5.32—RENEWAL

In its Report on the proposed Trade Act of 1970[d]—a bill that would
have authorized or required a variety of protectionist devices, including
quotas on textiles and footwear (but not steel)—the House Ways and
Means Committee said of the VRA's, "it is the sentiment of the committee
that the administration should endeavor to have these voluntary undertakings extended and improved . . . ."[e] The American steel industry
favored renewal, and after an inter-agency review within the Administration, President Nixon in December 1970 directed the State Department
to seek extension of the arrangements. As before, the State Department
negotiated directly with the foreign producers' associations, while consulting with the domestic industry and the relevant committees of the
Congress. But the objectives were more detailed, in particular the de-

---

[d] H.R. 18970, 91st Cong. 2d Sess. (1970). The proposed legislation was approved by the House of Representatives but blocked in the Senate. For an
analysis and sharp attack, see Metzger, "The Mills Bill," 5 J. World Trade Law
235 (1971).

[e] *Trade Act of 1970*, Report of House Comm. on Ways and Means, H.R. Rep.
No. 91–1435, 91st Cong., 2d Sess. p. 92 (1970).

sire to meet some of the concerns raised in § 5.2, and actual negotiations took more than a year, from May 1971 to May 1972.[f]

Basically, the format was the same as before, with letters to the Secretary of State setting forth the intentions of the signatories. But specialty steels were made subject to specific restraints within the overall restraint level, at a figure lower than actual shipments for 1971; made-up products, such as bridges and transmission towers, though not included in the overall restraints because they were not "steel mill products," were assigned a target for growth not to exceed 2½ per cent; and a provision for consultation on request of either side was included.

Great Britain, which had declined to participate in 1968 but was now finally about to enter the European Common Market (see § 3.15 supra), joined the second round of VRA's, with both the large nationalized British Steel Corporation and the independent producers' association as signatories. This meant, of course, that the parity between the European Community and Japan could no longer be maintained. Japan's level for 1972 was set about 7 per cent below the agreed level for 1971, 15 per cent below the actual shipments for that year. The Community's target was set just above the agreed level for 1971 plus actual shipments from Britain in that year. In line with the slower estimated growth in the American market as compared with the expectations of 1968, the rate of growth was set at 2.5 per cent per year, except that in 1973 the Community was supposed to restrain its shipments to the United States to only 1 per cent over 1972. As before, the agreements were to run for three years.[g] President Nixon, in announcing the agreements, said

> I am especially pleased that this undertaking was reached on a voluntary basis. Such statesman-like cooperation is vital to our mutual efforts to build a more equitable and a more progressive system of international trading arrangements.[h]

---

[f] In the interval, of course, the Bretton Woods system of fixed exchange rates broke down, the yen increased more than 16 per cent against the dollar; European currencies were realigned; the United States imposed for four months a ten per cent ad valorem surcharge on most products, including those covered by the VRA's; and all international trade and payments were for a time in turmoil. See e.g., Vol. IV of this series, A. Lowenfeld, *The International Monetary System,* §§ 5–6 (2d ed. 1984).

[g] The full text of the 1972 Voluntary Restraint Agreements appears in the Documents Supplement at pp. DS-571–77.

[h] 8 Weekly Comp. Pres. Docs. 823, 824 (May 8, 1972).

§ 5.4—The Legal Challenge

5.41—"LITIGATION IN THE PUBLIC INTEREST"

Less than three weeks after the second round of VRA's was announced, a major legal challenge was launched against the arrangements—not by the steel importers, not by the fabricators, but by Consumers Union, the non-profit membership organization that tests and rates consumer products and recently has assumed a litigation role similar to that of the Sierra Club, the Environmental Defense Fund, some of the Ralph Nader projects and comparable groups. Consumers Union was represented by the Center for Law and Social Policy, and it is not clear whether CU found the Center as its counsel, or the Center found CU as its client. At all events CU and the Center initiated two major law suits against government-sponsored import control programs, one against the Mandatory Oil Import Program,[a] the other against the Voluntary Restraint Agreements applicable to steel.

CU's general attack, as spokesman for the public interest, was directed at quantitative restrictions that enable prices to be raised, taking, as it said, money out of the pockets of consumers. In its press release and its monthly magazine, CU asserted that the restrictions on steel imports had cost consumers about $1 billion per year in price increases attributable directly or indirectly to the quotas. It claimed also that steel prices increased 5 times as much in the three years of the first VRA's as they had during the preceding eight years, despite substantial unused capacity.[b] In its complaint, CU charged (1) an agreement in restraint of trade under section 1 of the Sherman Antitrust Act;[c] and (2) unlawful action by officials of the State Department, in that they had negotiated restrictions on international commerce without going through the procedures and requirements of the Trade Expansion Act, in particular the provisions for investigation and findings by the Tariff Commission (§ 301) and the provisions for orderly marketing agreements (§ 352).

---

[a] See § 3.66 *supra*. The action, *New England Governors Conference v. Morton, Secretary of the Interior*, (D. Me. Civ. Action No. 13–59) was eventually dismissed as moot.

[b] See Consumers Union/Consumer Reports News Release, "Law Suit Challenges Steel Import Quotas," May 24, 1972; "The Case Against Oil and Steel Import Quotas," 37 Consumer Reports 528 (August 1972).

[c] 15 U.S.C. § 1.

The complaint named the Secretary of State, the Deputy Assistant Secretary of State who had been in charge of the negotiations, U.S. Steel, the American Iron and Steel Institute, the Japan Iron and Steel Exporters Association, and those foreign steel companies that did business and could be conveniently served with process in the United States.[d] Defendants took the position, essentially, that the procedures set forth in the Trade Expansion Act were not exclusive, and that the President had acted pursuant to his inherent constitutional powers over foreign affairs. Further, if the executive branch had acted lawfully, the private parties, American and foreign, could not be held liable under the antitrust laws for agreeing to do what the United States government had urged them to do.[e]

As the litigation progressed, Consumers Union and the Center for Law and Social Policy found that they did not have the resources for a major antitrust litigation.[f] In an amended complaint, CU stipulated to a withdrawal of the antitrust count, relying solely on the allegation that the government officials had acted ultra vires.[g] The District Court sustained the defendants, on the ground that

> While the legislative pattern is indeed comprehensive and the President's authority has been narrowed [by the Trade Expansion Act and the Sherman Act], these acts cannot be read as a Congressional direction to the President prohibiting him from negotiating

[d] *Consumers Union of United States, Inc., v. Rogers et al.,* Civil Action No. 1029–72 (D.D.C. filed May 24, 1972). The named foreign defendants were Nippon Steel Corporation, Fried. Krupp Hüttenwerke, and British Steel Corporation; the complaint alleged that other American, European and Japanese steel producers, producer-associations, and their representatives; and other officials of the United States government—but not the European Coal and Steel Community—had acted in concert with the named defendants and other co-conspirators in the conspiracy alleged.

[e] Antitrust experts will recognize this argument as the *Parker v. Brown* defense, though here applied to action by the federal government, as contrasted to the state marketing program involved in *Parker v. Brown* itself, 317 U.S. 341 (1943).

[f] The Center, a small, low-budget group of lawyers only a few of whom were engaged in the international side of its watchdog activities, found itself arrayed not only against the Department of Justice's Civil Division and the Department of State's Office of Legal Adviser, but against nine of the country's major law firms, including Shearman & Sterling; Milbank, Tweed; Davis, Polk; White & Case; Arnold & Porter; and Wilmer, Cutler & Pickering.

[g] The other parties, however, were not dismissed from the action, which sought declaratory and injunctive relief.

in any manner with private foreign companies as to commercial matters.[h]

As to the assumption that participation by the United States government immunized the participants from the antitrust laws, Judge Gesell said:

> The Court declares that the Executive has no authority under the Constitution or acts of Congress to exempt the Voluntary Restraint Arrangements on Steel from the antitrust laws and that such arrangements are not exempt. . . .

> Because of the Amended Complaint, the question of whether or not a violation of the Sherman Act is present is not before the Court to decide. However, it is apparent on this limited record that very serious questions can and should be raised as to the legality of the arrangements under the Act, and that the undertakings of the foreign steel companies were made on a mistaken assumption which at least was encouraged, albeit in good faith, by the Secretary.[i]

The State Department and the producers appealed from the declarations by Judge Gesell about the Sherman Act; Consumers Union appealed from the refusal of the District Court to declare that the agreements had been negotiated without authority.

5.42—CONSUMERS UNION OF U.S., INC., v. KISSINGER

United States Court of Appeals
District of Columbia Circuit

506 F.2d 136 (1974), *cert. denied* 421 U.S. 1004 (1975)

McGOWAN, Circuit Judge:

These consolidated cross-appeals are directed respectively to two declarations made by the District Court in a suit challenging efforts by the Executive Branch of the United States Government to bring about reductions in steel imports by means of self-imposed limitations on foreign producers. Arrayed against each other are a complaining consumers organization, on the one side,

---

[h] *Consumers Union of U.S. Inc. v. Rogers*, 352 F. Supp. 1319, 1323 (D.D.C. 1973).

[i] 352 F. Supp. at 1323–24.

and, on the other, the State Department, and foreign and domestic steel producers, individually and in association. In the form eventually taken by the litigation in the District Court, we consider that the only question before us is whether the actions of the Executive were a regulation of foreign commerce foreclosed to it generally by Article I, Section 8, Clause 3 of the Constitution, and in particular by the Trade Expansion Act of 1962, 19 U.S.C. § 1801 et seq. To the extent that the District Court declared no such conflict to exist, we affirm its decision.

[Part I of the opinion reviews the background of the Voluntary Restraint Agreements, and Part II reviews the course of the litigation before the District Court.][1]

III

A substantial portion of the briefs and argument before us has been devoted to the Sherman Act. The defendant-appellants are, not surprisingly, perturbed by some of the comments made by the District Court with respect to possible Sherman Act liability. Although the court stated in terms that, by reason of the stipulation of dismissal, "the question of whether or not a violation of the Sherman Act is present is not before the Court to decide," it did not leave the matter at that. One of its declarations is that the Executive has no authority to exempt from the antitrust laws the arrangements here involved, and "that such arrangements are not exempt."

Since there is nothing in the record that shows the Executive as purporting to grant such an exemption,[7] this observation by the court does not have the stature of a declaratory disposition of an actual controversy. The court's other comments in this connection are not couched in adjudicatory form, as indeed, so the court recognized, they could not be in the light of the abandonment by the plaintiff of its antitrust claim. With the declaration vacated, as we shall direct in our judgment, these expressions of the court's opinion are without judicial force or effect and are not appropriate for pursuit upon appeal.

---

[1] The District Court heard the matter on cross-motions for summary judgment, and the facts are not in dispute. This section of the opinion draws mainly upon the affidavit of Julius L. Katz, one of the State Department defendants and Deputy Assistant Secretary of State for International Resources and Food Policy, filed in support of the motion for summary judgment.

[7] In a post-argument communication to the District Court, the Department of Justice represented that no assurances of immunity from the antitrust laws had been given to anyone. It went on to say that "the Executive Branch did not and it would not request any party to enter any arrangement it believed to be unlawful."

We think that the Sherman Act issue, for all practical purposes, disappeared from this case when the plaintiff, for reason best known to itself, stipulated its dismissal with prejudice. It is apparent from the face of the original complaint that the Sherman Act claim was originally conceived by the plaintiff as a vital aspect of its lawsuit. Its resolution would almost certainly have required the exploration by adversarial trial of a number of complex questions of fact and law, and the making of legal rulings in an area not distinguished for its simplicity. When the plaintiff, confronted by that formidable prospect, elected to abandon its antitrust claim, the Sherman Act could no longer play a significant part in this controversy, and we have no occasion to concern ourselves with the discussions by the parties of the precise reach of that statute.[8]

IV

We turn, then, to the District Court's declaration that, in respect of the the actions of the Executive culminating in the undertakings stated in the letters of intent, "the Executive is not preempted . . . and that there is no requirement that all such undertakings be first processed under the Trade Expansion Act of 1962." That statute, as its name suggests, had as its principal purpose the stimulation of the economic growth of the United States and the maintenance and enlargement of foreign markets for its products.[9]

---

[8] As might be expected in light of the stipulation, the amended complaint nowhere refers expressly to the Sherman Act. Under the caption "VIOLATION OF LAW ALLEGED," it charges that the actions of the State Department defendants constitute a prohibited regulation of foreign commerce "within the meaning of the laws of the United States relating to the regulation of foreign trade as set forth in Title 19 of the United States Code, including Sections 301 and 352 of the Trade Expansion Act of 1962, 19 U.S.C. Sections 1901, 1982." Having asserted these actions to be unlawful for this reason, the complaint does go on to say that the State Department defendants, by securing the limitation arrangements in a manner not authorized by Congress (i. e., by not using the provisions of Title 19), acted in conflict with the power of Congress "to determine the antitrust policy of the United States by enacting the antitrust laws and to determine the circumstances under which exceptions to those laws shall be permitted." To the extent that this seems to say that there was an antitrust violation because the State Department officials did not employ the provisions of Title 19, the point fails in the light of our holding hereinafter that the Executive did not engage in conduct implicating those provisions.

We note that the third and last paragraph under this caption in the amended complaint alleges that the foreign defendants acted in violation only of provisions of Title 19, which, of course, does not contain the Sherman Act. The domestic steel producers, in our reading of the amended complaint, are not alleged to have acted in violation of any law.

[9] The other stated purposes were "to strengthen economic relations with foreign

This was to be achieved through trade agreements reached by the President with foreign countries. Title II of the Act provided that, for a period of five years (1962–67), the President was authorized to enter such agreements whenever he determined that any existing tariff duties or other import restrictions of either the United States or any foreign country were unduly burdening and restricting the foreign trade of the United States. Upon reaching any such trade agreement, the President was delegated the unmistakably legislative power to modify or continue existing tariffs or other import restrictions, to continue existing duty-free or excise treatment, or to impose additional import restrictions, as he determined to be necessary or appropriate to the carrying out of the agreement. 19 U.S.C. § 1821.[a] In connection with the first two of these powers, the Tariff Commission was given an advisory function, which included public hearings; and public hearings were also directed to be held, by an agency designated by the President, in connection with any proposed trade agreement. 19 U.S.C. §§ 1841, 1943.[b]

Title III of the Trade Expansion Act of 1962, recognizing that domestic interests of various kinds may be adversely affected by concessions granted under trade agreements, authorizes the making of compensating adjustments of various kinds. Section 301 (19 U.S.C. § 1901) provides that the Tariff Commission shall undertake investigations of injuries allegedly being done to domestic businesses or workers by such things as increased imports flowing from a trade agreement. After holding public hearings, the Tariff Commission shall make a report to the President. If it affirmatively finds injury to domestic industry, the President may under Section 351 increase or impose tariff duties or other import restrictions, 19 U.S.C. § 1981, or alternatively he may under Section 352 negotiate agreements with foreign governments limiting the export from such countries to the United States of the article causing the injury. 19 U.S.C. § 1982. If this latter option is taken, the Acts provides that the President is authorized to issue regulations governing the entry or withdrawal from warehouse of the article covered by the agreement.

The foregoing description of the Trade Expansion Act of 1962 covers, among others, Sections 301 and 352. They are the only provisions expressly identified in the amended complaint as constituting the allegedly preemptive exercise by Congress of its constitutional power to regulate foreign commerce that, so it is said, forecloses the actions of the Executive challenged in this case. The description extends also to Sections 302 and 351, which are referred to in plaintiff-appellant Consumers Union's brief, as is also Section 232, 19

---

countries through the development of open and nondiscriminatory trading in the free world"; and "to prevent Communist economic penetration." 19 U.S.C § 1801.

[a] Trade Expansion Act § 201, Documents Supplement p. DS-251.

[b] *Id.* §§ 221, 223.

U.S.C. § 1862. This last is the so-called national security clause which provides that the President shall not decrease or eliminate tariffs or other import restrictions if to do so would impair the national security. The Director of the Office of Emergency Planning is directed to investigate any situation where imports threaten to impair the national security; and if he finds such threat, and the President concurs, action shall be taken "to adjust the imports" of the article in question, which means that the article may by regulation be excluded from entry or withdrawal from warehouse.[10]

What is clear from the foregoing is a purpose on the part of Congress to delegate legislative power to the President for use by him in certain defined circumstances and in furtherance of certain stated purposes. Without such a delegation, the President could not increase or decrease tariffs, issue commands to the customs service to refuse or delay entry of goods into the country, or impose mandatory import quotas.[11] To make use of such delegated power, the President would of course be required to proceed strictly in accordance with the procedures specified in the statutes conferring the delegation. Where, as here, he does not pretend to the possession of such power, no such conformity is required.

The steel import restraints do not purport to be enforceable, either as contracts or as governmental actions with the force of law; and the Executive has no sanctions to invoke in order to compel observance by the foreign producers of their self-denying representations. They are a statement of in-

---

[10] The Katz affidavit asserts that consideration was given to the utilization of both Section 352 and Section 232. The former "could not seriously be considered" because it was in terms made available by Congress only for the purpose of softening injuries to domestic commerce caused in major part by prior concessions in trade agreements; and this was not a major cause in this instance. As to Section 232, national security was only one of the factors contributing to the problem, and the attempt to solve it by a method which armed the President with legislative power to stop foreign imports at the water's edge would have had an unfortunate impact on foreign trade policy and international relationships.

[11] The United States Customs Court has quite recently invalidated the imposition by Presidential proclamation of a 10% supplemental tariff increase on imported merchandise. *Yoshida International, Inc. v. United States*, 378 F. Supp. 1155 (Cust. Ct. 1974). This action was held by the court to be an exercise of legislative power by the Executive in the regulation of foreign commerce, for which no delegated authority could be discerned in the statutes relating to tariffs. We mention the case not with reference to the rightness or wrongness of the decision but only because of the contrast between the action taken by the Executive in that case, *i.e.*, goods from abroad were excluded by force of asserted law unless the supplemental duties were paid, with what was done here, *i.e.*, no legal power to exclude foreign steel imports was either claimed or exercised by the Executive. [Ed.: The *Yoshida* case was reversed shortly after the *Consumers Union* decision, 526 F.2d 560 (C.C.P.A. 1975). The case is discussed in Volume IV of this series, A. Lowenfeld, *The International Monetary System* at § 5.47 (2d ed. 1984).]

tent on the part of the foreign producer associations. The signatories' expectations, not unreasonably in light of the reception given their undertakings by the Executive, are that the Executive will consult with them over mutual concerns about the steel import situation, and that it will not have sudden recourse to the unilateral steps available to it under the Trade Expansion Act to impose legal restrictions on importation. The President is not bound in any way to refrain from taking such steps if he later deems them to be in the national interest, or if consultation proves unavailing to meet unforseen difficulties; and certainly the Congress is not inhibited from enacting any legislation it desires to regulate by law the importation of steel.

The formality and specificity with which the undertakings are expressed does not alter their essentially precatory nature insofar as the Executive Branch is concerned. In effect the President has said that he will not initiate steps to limit steel imports by law if the volume of such imports remains within tolerable bounds. Communicating, through the Secretary of State, what levels he considers tolerable merely enables the foreign producers to conform their actions accordingly, and to avoid the risk of guessing at what is acceptable. Regardless of whether the producers run afoul of the antitrust laws in the manner of their response, nothing in the process leading up to the voluntary undertakings or the process of consultation under them differentiates what the Executive has done here from what all Presidents, and to a lesser extent all high executive officers, do when they admonish an industry with the express or implicit warning that action, within either their existing powers or enlarged powers to be sought, will be taken if a desired course is not followed voluntarily.

The question of congressional preemption is simply not pertinent to executive action of this sort. Congress acts by making laws binding, if valid, on their objects and the President, whose duty it is faithfully to execute the laws. From the comprehensive pattern of its legislation regulating trade and governing the circumstances under and procedures by which the President is authorized to act to limit imports, it appears quite likely that Congress has by statute occupied the field of *enforceable* import restrictions, if it did not, indeed, have exclusive possession thereof by the terms of Article I of the Constitution. There is no potential for conflict, however, between exclusive congressional regulation of foreign commerce—regulation enforced ultimately by halting violative importations at the border—and assurances of voluntary restraint given to the Executive. Nor is there any warrant for creating such a conflict by straining to endow the voluntary undertakings with legally binding effect, contrary to the manifest understanding of all concerned and, indeed, to the manner in which departures from them have been treated.[12]

---

[12] In 1969 the Japanese, and in 1972 all foreign producers, exported to the

In holding, as we do, that the District Court did not err in declining to characterize the conduct of the Executive here under attack as in conflict with the Trade Expansion Act of 1962, we are not to be understood as intimating any views as to the relationship of the Sherman Act to the events in issue here. The Sherman Act is not, as noted above, one of the regulatory statutes charged as preempting the field, and the question of its possible substantive applicability vanished from this case with the original complaint.

The declaration in the District Court's order with respect to antitrust exemption is vacated, and the declaratory aspect of that order is confined to the proposition that the State Department defendants were not precluded from following the course they did by anything in the Constitution or Title 19 of the U.S. Code. As so confined, the order appealed from is affirmed.

It is so ordered.

DANAHER, Senior Circuit Judge (concurring):

Assuredly I join in Judge McGowan's excellent opinion. Pragmatic in the sense that it represents the view of a jurist skilled in law and state affairs, Judge McGowan's treatment does not ignore the background of the problem here posed nor does it fail to take account of the allegations of Consumers' amended complaint with its appended exhibits and the agreed statement of facts submitted in the District Court. I feel impelled to voice additional comment only in view of the approach offered in dissent by our respected colleague.

. . . . .

I.

Our dissenting colleague regards the arrangements with the foreign private concerns as "solemn negotiated bilateral understandings". The record shows that the private producers themselves limited their own exports. Our colleague sees the Executive in position to call upon nonjudicial exercises of power if the foreign producers violate the arrangements. He suggests, e.g., that there could be "possibly a call to reduce assistance programs" to the *country* of a foreign producer. He ventures "Suppose the President directed customs officials to deny entry to United States ports of commodities violating the undertaking." None of these things happened.

United States more steel or particular types of steel product than their undertakings contemplated. In no case were the "excess" goods denied entry into the United States. Rather, consultations were sought and the next year's voluntary quota reduced by the amount of the excess.

Rather, the record shows, that during the years 1957 through 1968 there developed an unprecedented increase in steel imports, particularly from producers in Japan and European countries. Import tonnages of steel mill products in 1957 totaled 1,155,000 net tons which by 1968 had become 17,960,000 net tons. Bills were introduced in Congress directed toward the imposition of restraints and controls of steel imports, with the result that worriment overtook our own officials as well as representatives of foreign producers. A Japanese economic mission sent its chairman in March 1968 to discuss problems of the steel trade with the particular objective of avoidance of congressionally imposed limitations upon the entry of Japanese steel.

It is not to be doubted that importantly placed officials in our Executive departments were fully aware of our tariff laws and regulations and of the legislative restrictions upon Presidential action.

By May 1968 Department of State officials and European steel industry representatives had joined in discussions which went forward through June and July 1968. Perhaps it is not too much to "suppose" (our colleague's word) that President Johnson said "Why don't you get those people in here and see if you can reason together with them?"—or words to that effect.

Before the undertakings by and among the foreign steel producing companies were activated, the Department of State sought and obtained the views of members of Congress, representatives of domestic steel producing interests, unions involved in the steel industry and others.

II.

So successful were the original three-year programs, so happily without incident, that an extension for an additional three years went forward only to be challenged in this action.

In this great nation with its complex economy and its varying conflicts requiring judicious accommodation, flexibility in achieving desirable results is a constant imperative. Fairly we may say that here there had been no Presidential action, legislative in character, undercutting the congressional prerogatives deemed by the dissent to be "plenary". If it be a penchant of our press to coin applicable expressions, "jawboning" could here be taken as apt and that is what happened, nothing else.[1]

---

[1] *Cf.* United States v. Guy W. Capps, Inc., 348 U.S. 296, at 297, 75 S. Ct. 326, 99 L.Ed. 329 (1955) refusing to pass upon the ruling by the court of appeals (204 F.2d at 658) that an international agreement to limit Canadian exports was void "as not authorized by Congress and as contravening the provision for pro-

Collaterally and obviously not here controlling, we might well today applaud exhortations by our officials to companies producing oil in the Middle East to reduce their charges and to increase their exports of oil to our power starved economy. We might take it to be desirable that coffee producing companies in nations such as Brazil and Colombia be induced by our officials not to exploit our dependence upon their product by the imposition of unreasonable and exorbitant charges for their coffee exports. Surely no formal trade agreement should be required to persuade companies to export to us the bauxite so essential to the continued maintenance of our aluminum industry.

Judge McGowan, it is submitted, succinctly and authoritatively has concluded that "the State Department defendants were not precluded from following the course they did by anything in the Constitution or Title 19 of the U.S. Code".

LEVENTHAL, Circuit Judge (dissenting):

With all respect, I must record my disagreement with the ruling of the majority that the President had the authority to negotiate detailed arrangements with foreign steel producers to limit their shipments of products to the United States.

In my view, this case is controlled by Congress's exercise of its plenary authority over the regulation of foreign commerce through passage, over the past forty years, of legislation establishing a comprehensive scheme occupying the field of import restraints. While there is room for a role based on inherent authority of the executive, in this case the actions taken by the President are inconsistent, by fair implication, with the scheme Congress has provided. My point is not that the President has taken the kind of action that Congress had forbidden to the Executive. On the contrary, the statutes passed by Congress established a broad executive discretion, and with a subject like steel imports and the kind of expansive scope of the "national security" provision (which emerged in the 1950's and now appears in § 232 of the Trade Expansion Act of 1962) that permits a restriction of imports which threaten to impair the national security by weakening the internal economy, there is a likelihood that the President would have been able to make the findings required by that law. But Congress has made the exercise of executive authority over import restraints dependent on public ventilation of the issues and has prescribed a procedure with safeguards and right of comment by affected interests. The President has concededly not followed that procedure, and this course cannot stand consistently with the statutory pattern.

---

cedure through the Tariff Commission", *id.* 348 U.S. at 301, 75 S. Ct. at 329. *See* Appendix, *id.* 305, 75 S. Ct. 326.

Recent events, notably those affecting currency exchange rates and prices and supplies of fuels, have dramatically changed the economic climate that sparked these trade arrangements. While the particular issue may be less pressing, there has been no dilution of the principle that the Executive cannot circumvent procedures delineated by Congress. That principle is paramount even though it may sometimes lead judges to particular results that are dubious pragmatically. *Compare* Wilderness Society v. Morton, 156 U.S.App. D.C. 121, 479 F.2d 842 (1973); Natural Resources Defense Council, Inc. v. Morton, 148 U.S.App.D.C. 5, 458 F.2d 827 (1972).

I am not persuaded by the majority's pronouncement that the statutes are not pertinent to the present case because the arrangements, incorporated in letters from foreign steel producers which describe themselves as "voluntary restraint undertakings," did not contemplate the mandate of judicial enforceability. These undertakings by the President and foreign steel producers were carefully structured in considerable detail, obviously after detailed consultation with American steel interests, without exposure to the kind of input by purchasers that would have been provided if the Congressional procedures had been followed. These undertakings are bilateral and establish obligations. Their bite persists notwithstanding the majority's effort to coat them bland vanilla. The majority tolerates executive detours around the limits staked by Congress in the field it has occupied. Its concept that a different route is available for executive arrangements discerned as not intended for judicial enforcement is, in my view, unsound.

I. THE 1972 LETTERS

The subject of this litigation is, specifically, the arrangements made in 1972 between the Executive and foreign steel producers. In early 1970, various steel industry and labor union representatives, still concerned about the effect of dramatically increased steel imports on domestic industry, urged the State Department to seek an extension of commitments that had been made for the years 1968 to 1971. Following a study by a special committee, the President, in December 1970, directed the Department of State to seek new pledges from the foreign producers. The State Department, according to the affidavit of a cognizant official, "met with various domestic interests," and "received information and advice from diverse elements of the steel industry." The affidavit goes on to say: "The arrangements 'were entirely the result of negotiations between the foreign producer representatives and State Department officials who . . . spoke for and represented the policy judgments of the United States Government alone."[1]

---

[1] Affidavit dated August 25, 1972, of Julius L. Katz, Deputy Assistant Secretary of State for International Resources and Food Policy, Bureau of Economic Affairs, paragraph 14.

The 1972 arrangements were embodied in separate letters to the Secretary of State—from the Japan Iron and Steel Exporters' Association, and from the steel producers of the European Economic Community, including the United Kingdom. The letters were released by the White House on May 6, 1972, along with a Statement by the President and a Fact Sheet. President Nixon characterized this "welcome development" as the product of more than a year's effort by Deputy Under Secretary of State for Economic Affairs Nathaniel Samuels. The President's Statement announced that under the 1972 arrangements the foreign steel producers "pledge a three-year restraint" on steel exports to the United States, and further stated that this undertaking "represents a substantial improvement" over prior arrangements.

The arrangements set limitations on total amounts of steel mill products to be shipped to the United States in 1972—6.498 million short tons from Japan, and 8,013,794 short tons from the United Kingdom and European Community; and a limit of 2.5% of growth increase in each of the following two years. There were also more specific and detailed arrangements, summarized as follows in the White House Fact Sheet:

"The provisions of the renewed undertakings also include a firmer understanding on product mix and geographic distribution, with specific tonnage limitations on each of the three categories of specialty steel—stainless, tool and other alloys."

Thus the limit on shipments of stainless steel mill products in 1972 was set at 16,873 metric tons for the steel producers of U.K. and EEC, and at 72,463 metric tons for the steel producers of Japan.

Each of the letters contained a paragraph on "Consultations"—which recorded the understanding that the producer associations "hold themselves ready to consult with representatives of the United States Government . . . [and] expect that, similarly, the United States Government would be prepared to consult with their representatives on any problem or question that may arise with respect to this voluntary restraint undertaking."[2]

---

[2] Paragraph 5 of the May 2, 1972, letter of the associations of the steel producers of the U.K. and the EEC, provides:

    Consultations—The above-mentioned producer associations, through their authorized representatives, hold themselves ready to consult with representatives of the United States Government on any problem or question that may arise with respect to this voluntary restraint undertaking. They expect that, similarly, the United States Government would be prepared to consult with their representatives on any problem or question that may arise with respect to this voluntary restraint undertaking. They reserve the right to request consultation in the event that they consider they have been placed in a disadvantageous position with respect to other exporters of steel to the United States by developments in the international steel market taking place sub-

Each letter stated that its "voluntary restraint undertaking is based upon the following assumptions"—(a) that the disadvantages imposed by the arrangements should be equalized for importing producers, (b) that the United States Government will take no unilateral action to restrict the quantity of steel imports, or to raise tariffs, or to impose supplemental duties on import of steel, and (c) that the undertaking is not in violation of "any law of the United States or international rule."

It is undisputed that the President, in negotiating these steel import limitations, did not act pursuant to any authority delegated by Congress. The State Department affidavit tendered by the defendants sets forth that Executive action under existing statutory authority was pondered and rejected.[3] Presidential imposition of import quotas is authorized under the "escape clause" provisions of Title III of the Trade Expansion Act of 1962, 19 U.S.C. § 1901, but only on a finding of injury caused in major part by "concessions" granted under trade agreements; and the difficulties of the domestic steel industry were ascribed to excess capacity, superior technology, and a cheaper supply of labor available to foreign producers, rather than to concessions.

Under § 232 of the Trade Expansion Act of 1962, 19 U.S.C. § 1862, the President has authority to limit imports to protect the national security, but this authority was also eschewed, for the reason that national security was only one of several factors pointing toward import restrictions.

II. THESE ARRANGEMENTS ARE IN SUBSTANCE
INTERNATIONAL AGREEMENTS NEGOTIATED BY THE
PRESIDENT THAT EMBODY OBLIGATIONS AND MUST
COMPLY WITH THE PROCEDURAL SAFEGUARDS PRE-
SCRIBED BY CONGRESS AS A CONDITION OF
EXECUTIVE RESTRAINTS ON IMPORTS

The contention, accepted by the majority, that the President's action is valid, notwithstanding its lack of statutory authorization, is based on two

---

sequent to entering this undertaking, or if developments in the international steel market should take place which could substantially impair the carrying out of this undertaking. Similarly, they recognize that the United States Government may request consultation if it considers that developments in the international steel market have taken place during the term of this undertaking which substantially affect any of the provisions of this arrangement.

The above-mentioned producer associations reserve the right to request consultation with respect to the exclusion in particular situations from the export limitation quantity in paragraph 1 above of shipments of large-diameter line pipe.

The May 4, 1972 letter of the Japanese steel producers contains a virtually identical paragraph.

[3] Affidavit of Mr. Katz, ¶ 7. JA 115a–117a, referring to 1968 consideration "by senior officials of the responsible agencies of the Government."

propositions: (1) the action is within the President's independent "foreign affairs" power; and (2) the import restraint achieved as a result of the President's action is not pre-empted by the Congressional regulatory structure.

Though there is no specific Constitutional clause granting the President power to conduct foreign affairs, that power has long been recognized. *See* United States v. Curtiss-Wright Export Corp., 299 U.S. 304, 320, 57 S.Ct. 216, 81 L.Ed.2d 255 (1936). The President's role in shaping foreign policy is rooted in and enhanced by his ability to communicate with foreign governments in the conduct of diplomacy. *See* L. Henkin, Foreign Affairs and the Constitution 47 (1972). Presumably, diplomacy ordinarily comprehends negotiation with officials of foreign governments, rather than direct negotiations with foreign firms as here, but I hesitate to suggest that this constitutes an absolute limitation on the President's authority. What has been called the "foreign relations 'apparatus,' " Henkin, *supra,* at 46, gathers a variety of commercial information in foreign countries, and this function inevitably involves contact with foreign firms, whether or not their governments are a conduit for communication.

However, to say that executive communications with a foreign national are within the President's foreign affairs role only opens the door to analysis. Here the purpose of the communication was to manage commerce between the United States and the foreign producers involved—a matter over which Congress has plenary power conferred by Article I, § 8. While it would be too narrow a view of the executive function to say that foreign commercial relations are not a proper subject of executive communications with foreign entities, the executive cannot, through its communications, manage foreign commerce in a manner lying outside a comprehensive, regulatory scheme Congress has enacted pursuant to its Article I, § 8 power. As Mr. Justice Jackson said in speaking of shared Congressional and executive powers:

> When the President takes measures incompatible with the expressed or implied will of Congress, his power is at its lowest ebb, for then he can rely only upon his own constitutional powers minus any constitutional powers of Congress over the matter.

Youngstown Sheet & Tube Company v. Sawyer, 343 U.S. 579, 637, 72 S.Ct. 863, 871, 96 L.Ed. 1153 (1952) (concurring opinion).

The proper inquiry, then, is whether the executive action in obtaining the agreements for steel import restrictions comports with the Congressional program for foreign trade, or whether Congress, by occupation of the field of foreign import restraints, has precluded the President's taking action on an

independent basis without complying with the standards and procedures provided by Congress as a condition of executive effectuation of import restraints.

The majority says that the steel import restraints are in harmony with the
statutory program because they are not enforceable in courts of law; they are
said to be mere precatory expressions which Congress never intended to cir-
cumscribe by the procedural requirements applicable to mandatory import
controls.

This response presents an issue that focuses on the nature and effect of
the undertakings before us. Turning first to effect, Presidents may engage
in many activities that have a perceivable economic impact upon the volume
of commodities imported. The effects vary in terms of their stability, their
specificity, and their duration. At one pole would lie general Presidential
exhortations—say, to consumers to "Buy American"—or general alarms,
announcing that protective legislation will be sought if imports are not contained. Such appeals are valid even though they may have the effect of in-
hibiting some market behavior, and no one would view them as prohibited
by even the strongest Congressional "free trade" legislation. At the other
extreme is a Presidential proclamation that foreign-trade commodities will
not be allowed to enter, which plainly cannot be reconciled with the existing
statutory structure, or legitimated by reference to some aura of "inherent"
Presidential authority. In between is a continuum of restrictions. In my view,
the comprehensive statutory program constrains some but not all of the activities in this continuum. Here, the undertakings have an economic effect
that parallels that of import quotas proclaimed by the President.

Turning to its nature, the Presidential action here goes far beyond a speech
or announcement—even one preceded by "feelers" to foreign governments to
ascertain how much they will tolerate. Far from being mere expressions of
desire and intent, these are solemn negotiated bilateral understandings.

The arrangements are not unilateral announcements but the culmination of
bilateral discussions that were not only participated in, but initiated by State
Department officials. Although the final letters that embody the specific
limitations are astutely couched in a litany of a "voluntary restraint undertaking" on the part of the foreign steel producers, the circumstances are instinct with bilateral undertaking.

Obviously, foreign firms that have vigorously marketed their products in
the United States do not voluntarily withhold production without some reciprocal aspect indicating that forbearance is to their advantage. Here, the undertakings of the foreign producers rest on Government assurances that
disadvantages would be equalized among producers; that the United States
Government—or at least the not uninfluential Executive Branch—would

not take or start other measures to limit steel imports or increase duties; and the transaction would not violate any law of the United States.[4]

The specificity of the limitations imposed by the undertakings also indicates that they were the result of bilateral bargaining and agreement.

Significantly, by the terms of the arrangements, the parties contemplate continuing consultations. The foreign steel producers "hold themselves ready to consult" on any question that may arise on the interpretation of their "undertaking." Does one accompany a unilateral declaration of intent with an offer to "consult" about what he has declared? When the foreign producers go on to say that their undertakings are based on their expectation that the United States Government will consult with them on questions that arise, and the White House releases these letters, along with a detailed Fact Sheet, as a "welcome development" that is the product of Executive negotiation, can it be meaningfully denied that there is a reciprocal undertaking by the United States Government to engage in consultations with the producers?

The inference of bilateral undertaking is strengthened when the arrangement is placed in the context of historical practice. Export forbearance by foreign producers has historically been obtained by diplomatic exchange of notes between the United States and foreign governments. The diplomatic notes themselves have referred to an "agreement" or "gentlemen's agreement" to limit shipments.[5]

International agreements are not limited to those embodied in formal documents, authenticated with ceremony, but include, as here, the specifying of an arrangement, together with mutual assurances and understandings as to how all parties will behave in response. To cast the steel restraints as unilateral undertakings rather than as agreements is to exalt form over substance.

The majority asserts that, unlike agreements negotiated pursuant to statute, which may be enforced by executive regulations and ultimately by judicial sanctions, the steel arrangements are unenforceable. But it is by no means clear that the Executive is without sanctions if the producers fail to abide by the arrangements. The very specificity of the limitations described by the letters makes violations easy to detect and the arrangements easy to enforce.

---

[4] Letters of the European Economic Community and United Kingdom associations of steel producers and of the Japan Iron and Steel Exporters' Association, ¶ 6, [Documents Supplement pp. DS-574, 577].

[5] See the 1935 limitation on imports of Japanese cotton goods and the 1936 limitation on imports of Japanese cotton rugs, both described in the Appendix.

That the threat of sanctions may carry considerable weight is indicated by the cooperation of the Japanese producers in making compensatory adjustments when they exceeded the quota for 1969 established by the original agreement. The remedy was a reduction of the 1970 quota by the amount of the overshipment. *See* Fifteenth Annual Report of the President of the United States on the Trade Agreements Program 28 (1970). Similarly, when the Japanese producers exceeded their aggregate quotas for 1972, "consultations" resulted in an agreement by the Japanese producers to charge the 1972 overshipments against 1973 quotas. *See* Seventeenth Annual Report of the President of the United States on the Trade Agreement Program 44 (1972).

If, as the Government argues, the President has inherent power to negotiate these and similar restraints, I fail to see why the courts would or should refrain from enforcement if sought. Products shipped to the United States in excess of the restraints might be denied entry, or domestic firms might be enjoined from handling them.

The common law of international agreements respects voluntary undertakings even in the absence of the "consideration" that is required under historic Anglo-American common law for domestic agreements to be enforceable in most state courts. If there must be a diplomatic peppercorn, there is consideration in the fact that the undertakings by the producers were plainly not meant to be revocable at will, and were based on a United States Government undertaking for consultation in the event problems arose and for avoidance of unilateral action against imports and tariffs. As I earlier indicated, this undertaking was binding on the Government which released and thus acknowledged this aspect of the letter arrangements. Further, principles of promissory estoppel may bind the foreign parties, even in the absence of a finding of initial consideration, once the Executive has relied on their representation that they intend to abandon any right they may have had to exceed the stated limitations on imports—as it has relied here by failing to take other steps to limit imports. . . . Even if judicial enforcement was not contemplated by the parties, the arrangements still embody a restraint. Trade agreements between foreign nations, and indeed many international agreements, may be "enforceable" only in the sense that they depend for enforcement on "good faith" performance by the parties. That does not make them any the less solemn agreements, that are both intended to affect the conduct of the parties and likely to have that result.

Moreover, the Executive may call on non-judicial resources if foreign producers violate the arrangements. Actions that would ordinarily be resisted as inconsistent with amicable relations, possibly a call to reduce assistance programs to the country in question, could hardly be assailed in the face of foreign producer bad faith.

A deliberate breach may well have an outcome intermediate between direct judicial enforcement and complete non-involvement on the part of the judiciary. Suppose the President directed customs officials to deny entry to United States ports of commodities violating the undertaking, and suppose such actions were sought to be enjoined. It seems to me entirely likely that the parties might have contemplated both this executive action, and the judicial consequence—on the assumption that the negotiations were valid—that the courts had no basis for holding the executive action invalid.[7]

What is the significance of the reiteration that these undertakings were "voluntary" on the part of the foreign producers? It is commonplace for a businessman to decide "voluntarily" that he will enter into an agreement, although the agreement, once entered into, has binding effect. The mandate may issue from a court of law or arbitration. But the obligations enforced in a court of commercial good faith and good will are as rigorous and insistent as a black-robed judgment. Congress has expressly authorized negotiated limitations in the orderly marketing agreement provision, § 352 of the Trade Expansion Act of 1962. And the national security provision authorizes restrictions imposed by Presidential proclamation, which embraces the authority to arrange restraints to which foreign producers consent.

In my view, the steel quotas before us present an import restraint having a composite characteristic, in terms of effect and nature, as to be subject to the procedures and requirements set forth in the Trade Expansion Act of 1962.

This is the critical question in the case—where to draw the line. There is a continuum of restraints, as noted above. In my view, the critical distinction is between executive actions that rest wholly in the domain of appeals and exhortations, and executive actions that culminate in obligations. A good faith agreement with the kind of specificity present here puts an obligation on the foreign producer, in any realistic assessment. Accordingly, I think the executive negotiation and acceptance of these undertakings are activity in a field that has been preempted by Congress, and can only be engaged in by following the procedures set forth in the Congressional enactments.

. . . . .

There is only local color, no legal significance, in the fact that in this case the Chairmen of key House and Senate Committees concerned with regulation of international trade voiced their approval on the occasion of the White House announcement of the undertakings. The Government does not contend, and I do not see how it could rightfully contend, that such participation by particular Congressmen can invest the President with executive authority not otherwise possessed, or constitute a legally decisive definition of the

---

[7] This assumes the court would pass on the merits. A court might well dismiss an action on another ground, like lack of clean hands.

demarcation between the zone that belongs to Congress as a whole and that which belong solely to the President.

III. COMPREHENSIVE ENACTMENTS OCCUPYING THE FIELD OF PRESIDENTIAL ACTIONS RESULTING IN OBLIGATORY IMPORTS RESTRAINTS

The ascertainment of pertinent legislative intent depends not only on express wording of the Trade Expansion Act of 1962, and specific notations in its immediate legislative history, but on its character as a culmination of comprehensive enactments on the subject of executive actions resulting in obligatory foreign trade restraints, including agreements by the executive regarding imports. The Congressional pattern makes clear that such executive action is tolerated only if it is accompanied and safeguarded by procedural protections that ensure a right of comment by those whose interests may be affected. This not only avoids the vice of complete secrecy within the Government, it also avoids the vice of cozy confidentiality, in which the public is informed only when the matter is a fait accompli.

[The judge summarizes the Tariff Act of 1930, the Trade Agreements Act of 1934, and the Trade Expansion Act of 1962, as well as certain special legislation affecting imports, such as the Sugar Act of 1948 and § 204 of the Agricultural Adjustment Act of 1956. In particular, he describes the powers granted and the procedures required under §§ 232, 301, 351, and 352 of the Trade Expansion Act.]

. . . . .

b. *Orderly marketing agreements.*

Of particular pertinence is the alternative provision in § 352 of the Trade Expansion Act. It provides that the President—after receiving the Tariff Commission's affirmative finding under § 301(b), and in lieu of issuing a proclamation imposing duty or other import restriction under § 351—may "negotiate international agreements with foreign countries limiting the export from such countries and the import into the United States of the articles causing or threatening to cause serious injury to [a domestic] industry, whenever he determines that such action would be more appropriate to prevent or remedy serious injury to such industry than action under" § 351(a)(1). Here again there is indication of Congressional authorization as underpinning for Executive power to negotiate trade agreements, including those restricting imports.

c. *National security provision.*

Another provision for import restrictions, applicable to any commodity, is the "national security provision," which originated in the 1950's and was transposed into § 232 of the Trade Expansion Act of 1962, 19 U.S.C. § 1862.

. . . . .

The President may adjust imports under this provision, but only after the Director of the Office of Emergency Planning conducts an investigation and reports that continued importation of a commodity is a threat to national security. Section 232(d), 19 U.S.C. § 1862(d), requires publication of a report of each investigation made by the Director and requires the Director to "publish procedural regulations to give effect to the authority conferred on him by subsection (b)." These regulations were intended to provide for public hearings except where it would be impracticable or injurious to the national security to do so.

Existing regulations of the Office of Emergency Planning provide that public notice of an investigation shall appear in the Federal Register unless "contrary to the interests of national defense," and that interested parties shall have an opportunity to make written presentations, to inspect the presentations filed by other parties, and to submit rebuttal presentations. The Director also must "seek information or advice from appropriate Government departments and agencies" and may, "when he deems it appropriate," hold public hearings.

The national security clause represents another Congressional action to authorize Executive adjustment of imports in times of domestic crisis, but, once again, the Executive is not permitted to act in secrecy, without regard to interests that might be adversely affected.

.   .   .   .

Whatever may be the President's prerogative when Congress has not spoken, it is untenable, in my view, to assert a continuing inherent Executive authority to negotiate import restraints outside and in disregard of a consistent and comprehensive Congressional pattern for protective procedures.

IV. PRIOR EXECUTIVE PRACTICE

The Government and the foreign steel producers urge on the court that Presidents have long negotiated restraints similar to the steel quotas without specific statutory authority, and that this tradition validates the President's action here. An appeal to past executive practice is not without relevance, but it is not decisive and often raises as many questions as it purports to answer.

So far as this case is concerned, it suffices to say that while defendants cite examples of import restraints, described more fully in the Appendix,[c] they fail to present a history of import restraints consistently negotiated by the President without regard for the procedures established by Congress and so represented to the Congress.

In the seventeen Annual Reports on the Trade Agreements Program that

---

[c] The Appendix, 506 F.2d 158–65, is not reproduced here.

the President has submitted to Congress every year since 1957, there is no indication that import limitations on foreign products were sought by the President of the United States acting outside statutory authority. The only exception is that of the steel import quotas involved in the case at bar, described in the reports of 1968 through 1971. Congress cannot fairly be said to have acquiesced in an executive practice perceivable only dimly if at all.

Some of the examples that the Government cites describe executive action colored with statutory authority. This characterization fairly describes the voluntary oil import program of 1957, the 1936 limitation on export of Canadian red cedar shingles, and six of the ten commodity limitations cited in Congressional testimony of Secretary of State Dulles.[31] Taken as a whole, the examples do not show that the President has consistently asserted an extra-statutory authority to regulate imports by agreements with foreign governments or firms.

Finally, all the import restraints cited by the defendants were obtained before the enactment of the Trade Expansion Act of 1962. When it enacted the Trade Expansion Act of 1962, Congress had an opportunity to review all of the President's power to regulate imports. In my view, the Act has scope as a Congressional preemption which "occupies the field" of import restrictions. This approach is heightened by the fact the 1962 Act included authority under § 201 that was expressly limited to run to June 30, 1967. Congress deliberately contracted Presidential latitude by permitting the expiration of that authority, as of July 1, 1967, notwithstanding Executive requests for extension.

V. DISPOSITION

This case must be decided as if the complaint had never contained a claim under the antitrust laws. However, in considering whether this is a claim on which relief may be given, I would take into account that relief in adjudicating invalidity may be wrought so as not to engender injustice in any future claim under the antitrust laws based on the conduct of the foreign producers. Any defense foreign producers might raise in future actions of reliance upon authoritative representations by government officials that an executive participation in the arrangement insulated them from antitrust liability would be undercut by a conclusion that executive participation is not authorized.

When a court is asked for a declaratory judgment—here that executive action restricting steel imports is invalid—it may act on the basis of equitable principles, and may respond to broad public interest concerns beyond those articulated by the parties. . . . In this extraordinary situation, the steel producers

---

[31] Hearings on Renewal of Trade Agreements Act Before the House Committee on Ways and Means, 85th Cong., 2d Sess. 399 (1958).

have since 1969 engaged in actions designed to further an arrangement that all assumed was lawfully entered into. The need to protect the reliance interests of these parties is highlighted by the complexity and the closeness of the issue of the validity of executive action. *Compare* Blair v. Freeman, 125 U.S. App. D.C. 207, 217, 370 F.2d 229, 239 (1966). Accordingly, in my view, a declaration that executive participation in the agreements is invalid should be given prospective effect only. This would permit courts to rule, should the question arise, that liabilities of the parties for acts prior to the effective date of the judgment be determined as if executive participation in the agreements were valid.

It remains to consider the prospective effect that I would give a holding that the action here was outside Executive authority. It is likely that the Executive would have had authority to invoke the national security clause—if minded to do so after following its hearing procedures and appraising the comments of all affected interests. Here the Executive has failed to follow the procedures mandated by Congress. . . . I would withhold the court's mandate for a period of 90 days. This would permit the President, if he should conclude that it is now desirable to limit steel imports and that either escape clause or the national security provision is applicable, to invoke their procedures.

Alternatively, the President may wish to seek legislation authorizing him to negotiate the kind of voluntary import restraints at issue here, or perhaps broader import control authority. The terms and history of any such legislation might support a ruling of a ratification of the authority of the President to achieve the steel arrangements before us. I would consider it appropriate to entertain an application by the Government for this court to stay its mandate so as to provide a reasonable opportunity to consider validating legislation.

Although I would decide this case against the executive, I am sensitive to the delicacy of the issue of preemption. Where, as here, the power of Congress to regulate a matter committed expressly to it by the Constitution is at stake, a close case should be decided so as to protect Congressional power. But it is likewise appropriate, in a matter so laced with delicate international relationships, for the court to shun a Procrustean rigidity in deference to possible clarification or correction by the President and Congress together.

§ 5.5—Notes and Questions

5.51—(a) It is easy to understand why the American steel industry —companies and union—would favor the Voluntary Restraint Arrangements. It is at least comprehensible why the United States government— Congress as well as the Administration, President Johnson as well as President Nixon—would favor the VRA's. They offered a unique way out of a tight political problem, a way to achieve protection for a single industry while advocating free trade in general, a special case for quotas while preaching elimination of non-tariff barriers. But why would the producers in Europe and Japan go along?

(b) One answer has already been suggested, a kind of bird-in-hand approach that negotiated, and not tightly controlled, restraints were better than the situation that might result if the Hartke bill or similar legislation had been adopted. Even if Japan, or the European Community, or both had retaliated against quotas imposed unilaterally by the United States, such retaliation would probably not have helped the steel industries. Consider some other factors, however:

1) Western Europe was itself facing overcapacity and relative inefficiency in steel; the VRA's preserved the European producers' share of the American market in competition with Japan; and they might serve as a precedent for the time—which did in fact arrive[a]—when the ECSC might want to negotiate a restraint agreement with Japanese producers about exports to the Community.

2) By limiting the amount of steel that could be exported from Japan to the United States, the Voluntary Restraint Agreements reduced competition among Japanese steel producers, strengthened the steel exporters' cartel, and led to higher export prices. Before the VRA's, Japanese steel was selling in the United States at 20–25 per cent below domestic steel, providing, as we saw, a variety of allegations about dumping or subsidies; with the VRA's, the price differential narrowed to about 10 per cent—just enough, under a steel user's rule of thumb, to enable foreign producers to make their sales.[b]

(c) Consumers Union, as we saw, estimated $1 billion per year in higher prices paid by American consumers as a result of the VRA's, counting both the content of steel in automobiles, appliances, etc. and

---

[a] See § 5.57(a) *infra*.

[b] See U.S. General Accounting Office, *Economic and Foreign Policy Effects of Voluntary Restraint Agreements in Textiles and Steel*, p. 25 (Report B-179342, March 21, 1974). The rule of thumb in the United States seems to be that with less than a 10 per cent price differential, users prefer to buy domestic, for the sake of easier accessibility of the product free from transport delays, lesser need to keep inventories, and reduction of other risks of international trade. Of course, as imports increased in volume, especially from Japan, these risks tended to diminish.

the indirect effects of steel price increases. The General Accounting Office was unable to make a comparable estimate, partly because there was no way of assuming what alternative measures, if any, might have been taken if there had been no VRA's.[c] But precision aside, the effect of the VRA's on price is clear. Domestic producers can raise prices, knowing the share of the market reserved to them;[d] and foreign producers have every incentive to follow the domestic prices up (as long as they keep their margin), since lower prices will not yield greater volume.

5.52—(a) As in challenges to political action by the executive branch in the international arena,[e] the courts in the United States have been most reluctant to overturn major executive actions in the economic field. In each of the principal judicial challenges to action by the executive—*Star Industries* (retaliation against the EEC);[f] *Yoshida* (across-the-board import duty surcharge in the monetary crisis);[g] *Federal Energy Administration* v. *Algonquin SNG, Inc.*[h](use of the national security clause to impose an import fee on oil); and *Consumers Union* (the voluntary restraint agreements), the legal authority of the government was questionable but was ultimately upheld.[i] Is

---

[c] See GAO, Report on Voluntary Restraint Agreements, N. b *supra* at p. 25.

[d] Recall the discussion of price leadership within the domestic steel industry, § 4.2 *supra*.

[e] See e.g., the Southeast Asia cases, *Velvel v. Nixon*, 415 F.2d 236 (10th Cir. 1969), *cert. denied*, 396 U.S. 1042 (1970); *Massachusetts v. Laird*, 400 U.S. 886 (1972); *Orlando v. Laird*, 443 F.2d 1039 (2d Cir. 1971); *Luftig v. McNamara*, 373 F.2d 664 (D.C. Cir. 1967), *cert. denied* 387 U.S. 945 (1967); *Mitchell v. Laird*, 488 F.2d 611 (1973); *Holtzman v. Schlesinger*, 414 U.S. 1304; 414 U.S. 1316; *Schlesinger v. Holtzman*, 414 U.S. 1321 (1973).

[f] *United States v. Star Industries, Inc.* 462 F.2d 557 (C.C.P.A. 1972), *cert. denied* 409 U.S. 1076 (1972), discussed at § 3.62 (d)-(f) *supra*.

[g] *United States v. Yoshida Int'l Inc.*, 526 F.2d 560 (C.C.P.A. 1975), see p. 220, N. 11 *supra*.

[h] 426 U.S. 548 (1976), reversing *Algonquin SNG, Inc. v. Federal Energy Administration*, 518 F.2d 1051 (D.C. Cir. 1975).

[i] See also *Zenith Radio Corporation v. United States*, 447 U.S. 443 (1978), discussed at § 4.47(c) *supra*, in which administrative interpretation of a statute was sustained against assertion by the petitioner of a duty to act against foreign imports; and *Consumers Union of United States, Inc. v. Committee for the Implementation of Textile Agreements*, 561 F.2d 872 (D.C. Cir. 1977), in which CU's standing was doubted and the District Court was held not to have jurisdiction.

there something special about action in the international economic area that should make courts resolve doubts in favor of the government?[j]

(b) Was the trouble with the VRA's from a domestic legal point of view that the government's action was taken without express authority, or that there was an authorized way for the government to do what it did, but that the prescribed procedures were not followed?

(c) If you are inclined to say yes to the second alternative in (b), does that suggest that *Consumers Union* was wrongly decided? Or was it the *Steel Seizure Case*,[k] which arose in the middle of the Korean War, that was insufficiently alert to the national security aspect of executive action?[l]

(d) Quite apart from the requirements of the Trade Expansion Act, it seems peculiar for the United States government to be negotiating with foreign business enterprises or trade associations. Normally government agencies, and especially the State Department, deal with other nations through their governments, and via diplomatic channels. As Legal Adviser to the State Department in 1968, would you have given an opinion that negotiation with the Japanese and European exporters was sounder,

---

[j] For the extreme statement of the affirmative response to this question, in the context of an international air route award, see *Chicago & Southern Air Lines, Inc. v. Waterman Steamship Corp.*, 333 U.S. 103 (1948). Compare also the three principal cases on delegation of powers to the executive branch, all decided by the Supreme Court at roughly the same time. In *Schechter Poultry Corp. v. United States*, 295 U.S. 495 (1935) and *Panama Refining Co. v. Ryan*, 293 U.S. 388 (1935), broad delegations of domestic power were struck down, while in *United States v. Curtiss-Wright Export Co.*, 299 U.S. 304 (1936), an equally broad grant of authority over foreign trade (the power to restrict arms exports) was upheld.

[k] *Youngstown Sheet & Tube Company v. Sawyer*, 343 U.S. 579 (1952).

[l] Compare Justice Jackson's famous concurrence in *Youngstown*, quoted by Judge Leventhal at p. 228, with the following excerpt from Chief Justice Vinson's dissent:

The broad executive power granted in Article II [of the Constitution] to an officer on duty 365 days a year cannot, it is said, be invoked to avert disaster. Instead, the President must confine himself to sending a message to Congress recommending action. Under this messenger-boy concept of the Office, the President cannot even act to preserve legislative programs from destruction so that Congress will have something left to act upon. . . . No basis for claims of arbitrary action, unlimited powers or dictatorial usurpation of Congressional power appears from the facts of this case. On the contrary, judicial, legislative and executive precedents throughout our history demonstrate that in this case the President acted in full conformity with his duties under the Constitution. 343 U.S. at 708–10.

or less vulnerable to legal attack, than negotiation with the government of Japan or the Commission (High Authority) of the European Coal and Steel Community?

5.53—(a) As we saw, Consumers Union and the Center for Law and Social Policy concluded shortly after filing suit that they could not sustain a massive antitrust action. Moreover, they were anxious for a decision by summary judgment within a time frame that would be meaningful for agreements of three years' duration. Accordingly, they agreed to drop the count under the Sherman Act while maintaining their allegation that the government's participation in the VRA's was unlawful. Judge Gesell in effect enabled plaintiff to have its cake and eat it too, by stating that even if there were no complaint under the Sherman Act on which he could give judgment, that Act could not be read out of the case and remained as a standard against which to measure the lawfulness of the government's action. Had Judge Gesell's opinion been sustained, presumably other plaintiffs—importers, fabricators, and other users of steel—could have brought suit against the steel producers and secured either an injunction or treble damage awards. Even if such remedies had been considered too harsh with respect to conduct prior to the judgment in view of the government's blessing of the arrangements,[m] a declaratory judgment would have effectively thwarted the VRA's. Should the executive branch—assuming State and Justice are together—ever be able to waive the antitrust laws? What, if anything, do you make of footnote 7 to Judge McGowan's opinion?[n]

(b) "Ever" is a strong word, and of course there are numerous instances in which the regulatory agencies—ICC, CAB, FMC, SEC, and so on—grant immunity from antitrust laws for agreements or other conduct subject to agency regulation. Typically such clearance or exemption reflects a conclusion by the Congress and the regulatory agency that the advantages of competition are outweighed by the needs for service to the public.[o] Can such a case be made for steel? If so, should the steel industry's rate of investment, rate of return on investment, prices charged, wages and salaries paid, and similar matters now be subjected to government scrutiny?

---

[m] Compare Judge Leventhal's proposal for disposition of the case at pp. 235–36.

[n] P. 217. *supra.*

[o] See, e.g., B. Fox and E. Fox, *Corporate Acquisitions and Mergers*, ch. 19 (1968 and later revisions).

(c) Judge McGowan criticizes Judge Gesell rather sharply, stating (at p. 219) that the district court's comments "are not coucned in adjudicatory form," and are "without judicial force or effect." Further, Judge McGowan says the Sherman Act issue, for all practical purposes, disappeared from the case when the plaintiff stipulated dismissal of the antitrust count with prejudice. Is this the appropriate way to dispose of a troublesome issue in an area that, as the judge says, is not distinguished for its simplicity? Does Judge Leventhal meet the point adequately in his proposed disposition of the case?

(d) Do these questions all "smell of the scholar's lamp?" Is Judge Danaher right in praising Judge McGowan's opinion as "pragmatic in the sense that it represents the view of a jurist skilled in law and state affairs"?

5.54—(a) Judge McGowan asserts in defense of the VRA's that they do not purport to be enforceable. Indeed, as we saw (table p. 212), the VRA's were only partly observed, though seen as a whole an overrun in one year tended to be followed by undershipment in the next. What follows from Judge McGowan's point? If the Customers Collector can only report, but not prevent, excess shipments (compare question 5.23(b) supra), does that make the executive branch's conclusion of the agreement a non-act? . . . and therefore invulnerable to judicial challenge?

(b) Judge McGowan seeks to escape from this position by turning the argument to the field of preemption. "It appears quite likely," he says, "that Congress has by statute occupied the field of enforceable import restrictions," but not, apparently, the field of voluntary undertakings and reciprocal assurances.

(c) Judge Leventhal, in dissent, takes up Judge McGowan on this issue, arguing (p. 225) that the VRA's bite persists, notwithstanding the majority's effort to coat them bland vanilla. He suggests that the President is not, in fact, without sanctions against overshipments: he could order withholding foreign assistance [sic], or indeed order the Customs Collector to deny entry to excess shipments and wait for the exporter or importer to sue. How should a suit by Nippon Steel against the United States for denying entry to steel in excess of the "voluntary quota" come out? Alternatively, how should a suit come out in which the United States seeks to enjoin a domestic firm from handling shipments in excess of the quota?

(d) Judge Leventhal describes the President's acts in the field of foreign economic affairs in terms of a spectrum (p. 229). At one pole would lie general Presidential exhortations, at the other a Presidential Proclamation that foreign-trade commodities will not be allowed to enter. He agrees with the majority that the comprehensive statutory program constrains some but not all of the activities in this continuum. But the VRA's, he concludes, are within the field occupied by Congress—particularly since Congress has regulated agreements and the VRA's are "instinct with bilateral undertaking." Moreover, the specificity of the arrangements in terms of numbers of tons, categories of products, provisions for consultations, and applicable dates distinguish the VRA's, in his view, from, say, communiques at summit conferences or State of the Union messages. The approval of the chairmen of the Congressional committees, he adds (p. 232) provides only local color, not legal significance.

(e) Putting the merits of the VRA's aside temporarily, who do you think has the better of the argument on the issue of distribution of powers?

5.55—(a) The judicial challenge to the Voluntary Restraint Agreements under United States law was, as we have seen, troublesome. But perhaps the most troublesome legal issue, precisely because no court was around to consider it, was the relationship between the VRA's and the GATT. Does it turn out from the experience with steel that the GATT is not really a code of conduct founded on shared perceptions of the theory of comparative advantage, but rather a series of promises which are open at any time for release (or is it accord and satisfaction?)?

(b) When the VRA's expire, do the exporting countries—i.e., the beneficiaries of GATT concessions from the United States—still have a binding, enforceable under the rules of the GATT? If so, then the VRA's, as among the participants, are a kind of "time-out," with the tacit acquiescence of the countries whose enterprises and trade associations signed the letters. What about outsiders, who may argue that they were obliged to absorb extra imports because the United States market was restricted?

(c) Should the Director General of the GATT close his eyes and ears to phenomena such as the VRA's on steel, pretending along with the parties that (i) governments are not involved and (ii) nobody is hurt? Or should he campaign against "voluntary" trade restrictions of all kinds on the ground that they run counter to the fundamental tenets of the post-war economic understandings?

(d) Might another lesson from the experience of the VRA's be that a long-range effort to revise the GATT—for instance by rewriting Article XIX on market disruption—is called for? Or that other devices of trade control—neither permitted nor prohibited in the GATT—might be explored? Consider whether an effort along the lines suggested should look to procedural reform—i.e., deals such as the VRA's could be subject to international scrutiny and evaluation, or whether substantive criteria for excessive market penetration are (i) possible or (ii) desirable.

We shall return to this question at the end of the volume.

* * *

Before turning to the next round of major developments in the continuing conflict between trade and protection in steel, two other episodes deserve mention, each showing one more provision of United States law sought to be applied to the problems of steel.

5.56—SPECIALTY STEEL AND THE ESCAPE CLAUSE

(a) In the first Voluntary Restraint Agreement, as we saw, no distinction was made between ordinary carbon steel and specialty steel.[p] The second VRA established a specific ceiling for specialty steels within the overall restraints. When the VRA expired, imports of specialty steel rose dramatically. In the first nine months of 1975, as overall consumption of specialty steels in the United States fell by close to 40 per cent, imports made up 19.1 per cent of American consumption of stainless steel, compared to 9.2 per cent over the same period in 1974; as to alloy steel, imports rose from 17.7 to 27.5 per cent of consumption. Put another way, the combination of sharp drop in domestic demand and sharp rise in imports meant that domestic shipments in the first three quarters of 1975 were barely over half of what they had been in the comparable period of 1974, while imports had increased by more than 20 per cent. In terms of tonnage, specialty steel accounted for only about one per cent of total American steel imports. Still, if specialty steel could be deemed to be a separate industry, 25 per cent of its work force of 30,000 was laid off in 1975, and less than half of its productive capacity was being utilized.

---

[p] See § 5.31 *supra* at N. c.

(b) In July 1975, the Tool and Stainless Steel Industry Committee for Import Relief and the United Steelworkers of America filed a petition for import relief under section 201 of the Trade Act of 1974, the revised escape clause provision. As discussed in earlier portions of the book,[q] the escape clause had had a zig-zag history in United States trade law, both with respect to the relief available and with respect to the required link between increased imports (and their cause) and injury to the domestic industry. Under the Trade Act of 1974 it was no longer necessary to establish a connection between increased imports and trade agreements concessions; moreover, the requirement that increased imports were "the major factor" in the injury to the domestic industry, added in the Trade Expansion Act of 1962, had been replaced by the requirement only of a "substantial cause" of serious injury.[r] Both of these changes were essential to the petition, since it was not duty reductions but price differentials that had caused increased imports, and since the drop in domestic demand for specialty steel had been the single greatest factor in injury to the domestic industry. But in considering this first petition under the amended escape clause, the International Trade Commission (the new name of the Tariff Commission[s]) determined by a majority vote that all but one of the products covered by the petition "are being imported into the United States in such increased quantities as to be a substantial cause of serious injury or threat thereof."

(c) In its Report to the President of January 16, 1976,[u] the Commission recommended relief in the form of import quotas for each of the categories—fixed amounts for 1976 and a percentage of apparent United States consumption in the immediately preceding year for each of the years 1977 through 1980. For 1976, the total would have been 146,000 tons, about 15 per cent below the 1974 totals; for the succeeding years there would be an alternate method of computing the level of permitted imports, based on the average of imports in each

---

[q] See § 3.25 at N. k, § 3.53 at Ns. r–v.

[r] Compare Trade Expansion Act § 301(b) 3, Documents Supplement p. DS-269, with Trade Act of 1974 § 201(b)(1), Documents Supplement p. DS-338.

[s] See Trade Act of 1974, § 171, Documents Supplement p. DS-335.

[t] *Stainless Steel and Alloy Tool Steel,* **Report to President on Investigation No. TA–201–5, USITC Publ. 756** (January 1976). Three Commissioners supported the decision fully, one as to all products except stainless steel plates and sheets and strips. One Commissioner dissented, and one abstained.

[u] N. t *supra.*

category for the five years 1970–74. The Commission recommended that the import quotas be allocated for each country among supplying countries on the basis of their historical market shares during the period 1972–74.[v]

(d) President Ford, who under the statute had the last word (subject to being overriden by a vote of both Houses of Congress),[w] announced in March that he accepted the need for import relief to the specialty steel industry, but he put off imposition of the quota system recommended by the Commission. Instead, he directed the Special Representative for Trade Negotiations to attempt to negotiate "orderly marketing agreements"[x] with the principal supplying countries of the products covered by the Commission's affirmative finding of injury—Japan, Sweden, Canada, France, Great Britain, Austria and West Germany. If orderly marketing agreements could not be negotiated, the President said, he would impose quotas at levels comparable to those recommended by the Commission, but for three rather than for five years.[y]

(e) The Japanese, as usual, were prepared to negotiate, and on June 11, 1976, the President announced that an orderly marketing agreement had been negotiated with the government of Japan.[z] For imports of specialty steel from the other countries, a three-year quota

---

[v] *Id.* at pp. 4–6. The Report consisted of a six-page memorandum to the President, 47 pages of views of individual Commissioners (including the dissenter); and 94 pages of information gathered in the investigation plus 69 pages of tables and charts. It is interesting that while the justification of the affirmative finding under § 201 is detailed and voluminous, there is no discussion at all of the basis for the recommendation of quota rather than some other form of relief, (see § 203(a)) nor of the figures used in designing the quota.

[w] Trade Act of 1974, §§ 202(a), 203(b), 203(c), Documents Supplement pp. DS-341, 343, 344. The statement in parentheses was in doubt as this volume went to press, following the decision of the Supreme Court in an immigration case holding legislative vetoes unconstitutional. *Immigration and Naturalization Service v. Chadha,* 103 S.Ct. 2764 (1983).

[x] Compare § 3.53 *supra* at Ns. z–c. The statutory authority for orderly marketing agreements, § 203(a)(4) of the Trade Act of 1974, is substantially the same as the prior authority contained in § 352 of the Trade Expansion Act.

[y] See Office of Special Representative for Trade Negotiations, Press Release No. 220, March 16, 1976.

[z] Agreement between the United States and Japan concerning Specialty Steel Imports, T.I.A.S. 8442, 27 U.S.T. 4145, signed at Washington June 11, 1976. The text of the Agreement, (without all of the annexes and clarifications) appears in the Documents at pp. DS-578-84.

was proclaimed, equal to the average annual quantity or volume of imports over the period 1971–1975, allocated among the European Community, Canada, Sweden and "other."[a] Total imports under the combination of OMA and quota would be limited to 147,000 tons for the first year, compared to 151,000 actual imports in 1974, 153,000 in 1975, and an annual rate of 169,000 for the first four months of 1976. President Ford announced that he was acting "under the authority vested in me by the Constitution and the statutes of the United States . . . and in accordance with Article XIX of the General Agreement on Tariffs and Trade."[b] The European Community issued a statement reaffirming its position that the difficulties experienced by the American specialty steel industry were mainly attributable to a falling off in internal demand, rooted in the worldwide recession from which the United States was already recovering:

> Community steel exports have not caused or threatened material injury to the U.S. industry.

> The Community, therefore, keenly regrets that the President of the United States has thought it necessary to impose quotas on Community exports. The Community has reserved its rights to take countermeasures under Article XIX of the General Agreement on Tariffs and Trade. It will follow closely the development of trade in this sector and will keep the implementation of the restrictions under constant review in order to determine how far the Community's trade suffers or is likely to suffer harmful effects.[c]

(f) One product category (bearing steel) was eliminated from the quota program in June 1977, following a finding by the International Trade Commission that the effect of such action would be negligible, because imports of bearing steel were coming in at less than half of the

---

[a] Proclamation 4445 of June 11, 1976, *Temporary Quantitative Limitation on the Importation into the United States of Certain Articles of Stainless Steel or Alloy Tool Steel*, 12 Weekly Comp. Pres. Docs. 1047, 41 Fed. Reg. 24101, (June 15, 1976), corrected in 41 Fed. Reg. 29089 (July 15, 1976). The European Community, apparently, did not agree to an OMA because the Nine could not agree among themselves how the quota would be allocated. By letting the United States set the quota, the Community passes the burden of allocation to U.S. Customs, which acts on a 'first come first served' basis twice a year. Spain succeeded in getting a separate allocation, thereby avoiding the race to the docks with purchasers in the Community.

[b] Proclamation 4445, first operative clause.

[c] European Community Press Release No. 10/1976, Washington, June 11, 1976.

levels permitted.[d] But following a general review of the quotas on specialty steel initiated in May 1977, President Carter decided at the beginning of 1978 to retain the quota system on the five other product categories, substantially as it had been proclaimed by President Ford.[e]

5.57—"UNFAIR TRADE PRACTICES" AND THE EUROPEAN-JAPANESE AGREEMENTS

(a) From the mid-1960's on, representatives of the European Coal and Steel Community and the Japanese Ministry of International Trade and Industry met regularly to discuss trade in steel. From 1972 (and perhaps earlier) through 1974 an agreement seems to have been in effect limiting shipments of steel from Japan to the Community, with a ceiling of 1.2 million metric tons in the final year. The agreement was in some ways similar to the VRA's covering exports to the United States, except that these agreements were not made public. Since actual shipments in late 1974 (the time of world-wide shortage) did not come up to the ceiling, MITI and the ECSC agreed to terminate the restraints. As it turned out, however, the end of the restraints coincided with a fall in the demand for steel, and Japanese mills began to solicit orders in the Common Market with considerable success. In the first quarter of 1975 Japanese steel accounted for about 2.5 per cent of the Community's consumption, and in the first seven months of 1975 imports of Japanese steel exceeded the total shipments into the Community for each of the three preceding years.

In response to urgent requests by the Community, MITI "advised" the Japanese steel industry to devise a program for restraining exports to the Common Market. The industry agreed to cut its exports to the Community in half, and to allocate to each of the Big Six Japanese producers a share of the reduced total. Subsequently MITI wanted the arrangement to be more permanent, and the producers applied for and were given permission to form an export cartel,[f] to voluntarily re-

---

[d] Proclamation 4509 of June 15, 1977, 13 Weekly Comp. Pres. Docs 887, 42 Fed. Reg. 30829 (June 17, 1977). For subsequent developments concerning specialty steel, see § 8.66 N. y. *infra.*

[e] See Office of Special Representative for Trade Negotiations, Press Release No. 260, January 18, 1978. The President thus upheld the recommendation of the International Trade Commission, which had voted 3–1 that removal of the quotas would have a serious adverse economic effect on the domestic industry.

[f] See § 3.33 *supra* at N. w.

strict and divide up exports of steel to the Community. After a series of meetings, some at governmental and some at industry level,[g] the Japanese exporters agreed to a limit of 1.2 million tons for 1975 and 1.3 million tons for 1976, subject to consultations about how much would be shipped in each quarter.[h]

(b) One might think that these events, while interesting from the point of view of overall trade policy, would be of no concern—no legal concern, at any rate—to the United States. The American Iron and Steel Institute, however, thought otherwise. AISI contended, with some support from the statistics, that as Japanese mills reduced their sales to the Common Market, they did not cut back their production or sell more at home: instead, AISI said, the Japanese producers diverted their output to the United States. The amount of the diversion was figured at somewhere between 1.5 and 2.5 million tons per year, depending on estimates of what Japanese producers would have sold in Europe with a totally free market or a market guided by MITI and the ECSC but not subject to specific restraints. Furthermore, AISI took the position that this diversion and the agreements between the Community and Japan that caused it constituted "unjustifiable or unreasonable . . . import restrictions which impair the value of trade commitments made to the United States" within the meaning of section 301 of the Trade Act of 1974.[i]

Assuming the facts are as stated by AISI, does the argument persuade you? If there is a violation of some kind against which remedial action or retaliation is justified, is it by the European Community, by Japan, or by both?

(c) Section 301 of the Trade Act of 1974 is a somewhat amplified

---

[g] The sequence of meetings was Tokyo, June 1975 (ECSC-MITI); Toronto, September 1975 (industry representatives); Brussels October 1975 (ECSC-MITI); Mexico City, October 1975 (industry representatives); Rome, January 1976, (industry representatives); Tokyo, June 1976 (ECSC-MITI); Brussels, November 1976 (ECSC-MITI plus foreign afairs officials from both the Japanese Government and the European Commission).

[h] The statement of facts in this note is drawn from the papers submitted in support of the petition discussed in the succeeding paragraphs and from testimony given by representatives of the American Iron and Steel Institute. The essential facts, as contrasted with the causal relationships alleged, seem to be substantially undisputed, though many of the details came to public knowledge in the United States only as a result of the petition.

[i] Documents Supplement p. DS-379.

version of section 252 of the Trade Expansion Act of 1962, discussed previously in connection with American response to the Common Agricultural Policy of the EEC.[j] In particular, the scope of retaliatory authority given to the President in section 301 was substantially broader than in section 252 of the Trade Expansion Act,[k] and a procedure was provided for formal presentation of complaints to the Special Representative for Trade Negotiations.[l] The American Iron and Steel Institute filed a complaint under section 301 in accordance with the procedures established pursuant to the statute.[m] It asked for "such relief as will (a) eliminate the burden, restriction, and discrimination caused by the Agreement, and (b) provide compensation for the burden, restriction, and discrimination already sustained." AISI did not make any more specific request for relief; its counsel said:

> We hardly need presume to tell the President how to exercise his powers to obtain abrogation of the discriminatory arrangement between Japan and Europe. We know the Chief Executive will be skillful and imaginative enough to bring a prompt termination to this arrangement that has deflected Japanese steel to this country. We believe the international influence of our President should assure his success in bringing these cartel arrangements to an end. He may, if need be, suspend all privileges awarded to Japan and the EEC under the GATT or any other trade agreements extant between the U.S., Japan, and the EEC. . .[n]

Assuming the soundness of the argument that the ECSC-MITI Agreement comes within the terms of section 301, (i.e. assuming an affirmative answer to the questions put in (b) above), what kind of remedy do

---

[j] See § 3.62 *supra*. For a detailed discussion of § 301, with emphasis on the relation between the statute and GATT procedures, see Hudec, "Retaliation against 'Unreasonable' Foreign Trade Practices: The New Section 301 and GATT Nullification and Impairment," 59 Minn. L. Rev. 461 (1975).

[k] Both the problems that arose in the *Star Industries* case (§ 3.62(d)–(f) *supra*) —whether or not retaliation could be on an MFN basis and whether a concession could be suspended as well as withdrawn—were resolved in the 1974 Act. See § 301(a)(A), (a)(B), and (b).

[l] § 301(d) and (e). Congress' role in the procedure is set forth in § 302.

[m] The Complaint is reproduced in 41 Fed. Reg. 45628 (October 15, 1976).

[n] Statement of Dominic King, Ass't. General Counsel, U.S. Steel Corporation, before the Interagency 301 Committee, Office of Special Representative for Trade Negotiations, Dec. 9, 1976, at p. 1.

you think might be appropriate? Why do you suppose AISI was not more specific in its request for relief?

(d) At the hearing called under section 301, the Vice Chairman of U.S. Steel testified:

It has been suggested that the U.S. industry does not come into these hearings with clean hands because of its participation in the Voluntary Restraint Agreements of nearly a decade ago. I point out that we in the industry did not participate in fashioning those arrangements. They were instigated by and brought about by our government, not by the producers in the steel industry. It would not have been our choice of solution. But it was what our government was willing to do at the time. And, it had very little influence on steel trade.[o]

(e) Apart from attempting to prove diversion and demonstrating the surreptitious character of some of the European-Japanese arrangements, AISI had one more string to its bow. The MITI-ECSC agreements, it said, violate Articles XI and XIII of the GATT. Do you agree?

(i) Is it open to a non-exporter to claim violation of the GATT prohibition against quotas?

(ii) Is it open to the United States in domestic proceedings (1) to interpret, and (2) to enforce the provisions of the GATT?[p]

(f) After holding a hearing in December 1976, the Office of the Special Representative for Trade Negotiations sat on the section 301 case for over a year. On January 18, 1978—the same day (and in fact in the same press release) as the announcement that specialty steel quotas would be continued, STR announced that "The President has . . . decided . . . to discontinue a review of the complaint filed by the AISI under section 301 of the Trade Act."[q] In the Press Release, Ambassador Strauss said that "while it was

---

[o] Statement of R. Heath Larry before the Interagency 301 Committee, Office of Special Representative for Trade Negotiations, December 9, 1976 at pp. 4–5.

[p] Compare on this point the response of the Court of Justice of the European Communities in the suit brought by the Dutch apple importers, § 3.26 *supra.*

[q] Office of Special Representative for Trade Negotiations, Press Release No. 260, January 18, 1978.

clear that a bilateral understanding had been reached between Japan and EC on steel, the evidence presented was insufficient to substantiate any significant diversion of Japanese steel to the U.S. market.'" Thus there was no need to face the legal questions raised here. In a formal announcement of discontinuance of the proceeding a few days later, STR said:

> The following major factors were significant in the determination to discontinue the section 301 complaint:
>
> (1) During the period covered by the understanding, exports to the EC by the six largest Japanese steel companies, operating as a government approved cartel, were limited to 1.22 million metric tons per year. However, actual exports by these companies were substantially less in both 1976 and 1977, suggesting that depressed market conditions in the EC were a more effective restraint than the understanding.
>
> (2) The pattern of Japanese exports to the United States of steel products covered by the cartel has been generally consistent with domestic market conditions here. The major growth in export volume in 1976 was in product categories where U.S. demand grew substantially (e.g., sheets).
>
> (3) The surge in Japanese steel exports in 1976 and 1977 was widespread and the increases in shipments to the U.S. market were not more pronounced than increases to many other markets. The U.S. share of one-fifth of total Japanese steel exports has remained relatively stable. The surge appears to be principally the result of the depressed domestic demand in Japan and low rates of steel capacity utilization which created pressure on Japanese firms to increase exports.
>
> On the basis of these considerations, there is not sufficient justification to claim that the EC/Japanese understanding created any unfair burden on the United States.[s]

---

[r] *Ibid.*

[s] 43 Fed. Reg. 3962 (January 30, 1978).

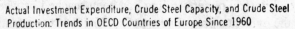

Actual Investment Expenditure, Crude Steel Capacity, and Crude Steel
Production: Trends in OECD Countries of Europe Since 1960

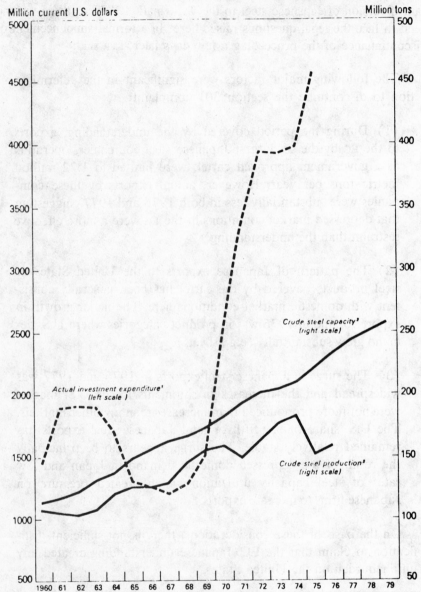

Source: OECD, *The Iron and Steel Industry in 1975* (Paris, 1977), p. 45.
[1] Excluding Norway from 1964 to 1967, excluding Turkey in 1964 and 1965, and including Finland since 1968.
[2] Including Finland since 1968.

§ 6—Steel in Crisis: The United States and Europe

§ 6.1—Challenge in America

6.11—LOSSES AND LAYOFFS

As the second round of Voluntary Restraint Agreements was coming to an end in 1974, there was a world-wide boom in demand for steel. Neither the EEC nor Japan filled its quota in the final year of the VRA, as demand exceeded supply in Europe and foreign prices were as much as 30 per cent higher than prices in the United States. Looked at from the United States, foreign suppliers supplemented, rather than replaced, the output of American mills in 1974. Quite apart from the legal infirmities of the VRA's as shown in the *Consumers Union* litigation,[a] there was no economic pressure for renewal of the arrangements at the close of the second round.

It did not take long, however, for the situation to change again. All over the industrial world the year 1975 was a year of recession, following the rapid OPEC-generated inflation of 1974. Among the 24 countries that make up the Organization for Economic Cooperation and Development,[b] industrial production fell 7.7 per cent in 1975 and gross national product fell by 1.2 per cent. The demand for steel, typically a reflection of economic activity generally, declined sharply.

---

[a] At the request of the State Department, the Senate Finance Committee included, and the Congress ultimately adopted a provision in the Trade Act of 1974 that relieved all persons who had participated in the VRA's of any liability under the antitrust laws. Trade Act 1974, § 607, Documents Supplement p. DS-413. However, the grant of immunity was limited to arrangements undertaken before adoption of the Act, and the Committee Report expressly stated:

> This section is not intended to modify the application of the aforementioned laws except to the extent that they may have applicability to the voluntary arrangement described. This section of the Committee's bill is deliberately limited in scope and purpose, and is not intended to be a precedent for the future.

Trade Reform Act of 1974, Report of Sen. Comm. on Finance on H.R. 10710, S. Rep. No. 93–1298, 93d Cong., 2d Sess. 232 (1974).

[b] Originally the OECD included the countries of Western Europe plus Canada and the United States that had collaborated in the reconstruction of Western Europe. By the mid-1970's, the organization included also Japan, Australia, and New Zealand, as well as Greece and Turkey. The OECD served as a frequent forum for economic discussions among the developed non-communist countries, as well as a collection and publication point for a great mass of economic statistics.

Domestic shipments in the United States fell by 30 million tons, and imports by nearly 4 million tons. (See table p. 210). For the first four months of 1975, foreign producers attempted to maintain their prices at the prevailing United States level; when they cut prices in May, business did not improve.

In 1976, as demand picked up both in the United States and in Europe, the share of the American market filled by imports increased from 13.5 to 14.1 per cent. Imports of steel from Japan (whose domestic demand continued to decline) increased by 36.5 per cent to 8 million tons, even as imports from the Community were declining by 22.7 per cent to just 3.2 million tons. Thus in the two years following the end of the vRA's the rough equality between the Japanese and European share of the United States market had changed into a ratio of more than 2.5:1 in favor of Japan. In part, the reason for the change seems to have been lower costs in Japan; in part also, the explanation lies in the fact that domestic demand in Japan continued to decline, while production rose.

In 1977 the European steel producers, faced with continued slack demand within the Community, launched a major export expansion program directed at the American market. In the first nine months of 1977, imports from the EEC totaled 4.4 million tons, over a third more than the full year's total in 1976. By September 1977, European and Japanese shipments of steel seemed to be running neck and neck again, and total imports into the United States from all sources[c] had reached 13.5 million tons—about 20 per cent of total consumption as compared with an average of 13 per cent in the period 1973–76. Putting the same point another way, as America led the world out of recession, 84 per cent of the increase in its demand for steel was being filled by imports.[d]

The reasons for the increased penetration of foreign steel were hard to sort out. Numerous major studies were made in this period comparing costs and efficiencies of American and foreign steel plants, with similar, but not identical, conclusions.[e] Japan, which had produced 5.3 million

---

[c] I.e., including Canada, Mexico, South Korea, etc.

[d] See table p. 257.

[e] Council on Wage and Price Stability, *Report to the President on Prices and Costs in the United States Steel Industry* (October 1977); Federal Trade Commission, *Staff Report on the United States Steel Industry and Its International*

tons of steel in 1950 when the United States was producing close to 100 million tons, clearly had the most recent and most modern steel making capacity, and (even after realignment of the yen) the lowest costs. But when transport and handling costs were added (about $55-60 a ton), the cost differential was small—possibly (depending on which set of calculations one followed) smaller than the differential in price. Costs within the European Community were somewhat below costs in the United States, but when transport costs (about $50 a ton) were added, the price of European steel in the United States should have been higher than domestic steel. Of course, even when the data base was secure (which was not always the case), all of these calculations were to some extent arbitrary—in regard to depreciation rates, allocation of overhead, averaging of different products, intra-company transactions,[f] and allowance for profit. But, given these estimates, the dumping issue once more took on major significance. Indeed in the period following the end of the VRA's, 19 separate antidumping proceedings were initiated by the American steel industry.

Thus far, the story of the mid-1970's was not so different from that of the mid-1960's. In the summer of 1977, however, the public, the press, and the politicians were engaged by a phenomenon much more direct, much more apparent, than debates about relative costs, efficiency, technology, or the relation between inflation, environmental controls, and trade. In September, 1977, Youngstown Sheet and Tube announced that it was permanently laying off 5,000 of its 22,000 workers in Youngstown, Ohio. Bethlehem Steel said it would lay off 3,500 workers at its Lackawanna, New York, plant, and would not resume full operations in Johnstown, Pennsylvania, which had been interrupted by a disastrous flood. U.S. Steel and Inland Steel laid off 4,000 workers in the Chicago area. Alan Wood, a relatively small producer that had operated near Philadelphia since 1826, went into bankruptcy, and had to sell off

---

Rivals (November 1977); Merrill Lynch, Pierce, Fenner & Smith, The Japanese Steel Industry. A Comparison with Its United States Counterpart (June 1977); Putnam, Hayes and Bartlett, Inc., Economics of International Steel Trade (May 1977); OECD Council, The Situation in the Iron and Steel Industry (June 1977); U.S. Central Intelligence Agency, World Steel Market, Continued Trouble Ahead (May 1977). See also World Steel Trade: Current Trends and Structural Problems, Hearing before Subcomm. on Trade of House Comm. on Ways and Means, 95th Cong., 1st Sess. (Sept. 20, 1977); W.T. Hogan, Steel in Crisis (Steel Communities Coalition, Nov. 21, 1977).

[f] Especially where, as was common in the United States, steel companies owned iron or coal mines or both.

its plant piece by piece as no one could be found to buy the whole facility. Jones and Laughlin announced reductions not only in its plant, but also among its engineering and research staffs. By the end of September, 1977, some 18,000 employees, including white collar and technical personnel as well as production workers, had lost their jobs, and "steel towns" such as Gary, Lackawanna, Johnstown, and Youngstown, were in real distress.[g]

In Washington, a "steel caucus" was quickly formed in Congress, with 120 Representatives and 20 Senators from both parties and nearly every region of the country. Representatives of the domestic steel industry and the United Steelworkers fanned out all over the city, advising the steel caucus on Capitol Hill, negotiating relaxation of environmental regulations, discussing costs and prices with the Council on Wage and Price Stability, and urging the Justice Department to clear joint research or production arrangements.

The Administration was uncertain as to how to proceed. The Labor Department speeded up Adjustment Assistance proceedings for workers in the Youngstown area. The State Department advised the European Community that it would not tolerate assistance to European steel producers that resulted in increased or lower-priced exports to the United States. The OECD called an urgent meeting of its Ad Hoc Steel Group with a view to establishing a world-wide body to monitor trade in steel. The Japanese industry began to talk again of voluntary restraints if U.S. Steel and other American firms would drop the legal proceedings pending before the Treasury.[h] A few weeks later the European producers made a similar offer, and suggested also negotiating an international market sharing agreement.[i] At his press conference on September 29, 1977, President Carter said the steel question was "highly complex," and announced that he had had an interdepartmental task force working on it for several weeks.[j]

On October 3, 1977, the Treasury Department issued a tentative

(Text continued on page 258)

---

[g] Unlike some of the earlier events here recounted, the layoffs and plant-closings were widely reported in the press and on television newscasts. See, e.g., New York Times, Sept. 20, 1977, p. 1, col. 1; Sept. 25, 1977, § 3, p. 1; Oct. 1, 1977, p. 1, col. 4.

[h] See New York Times, Sept. 25, 1977, § 3, p. 1, col. 5.

[i] See New York Times, Oct. 11, 1977, p. 51, col. 6.

[j] See New York Times, Sept. 30, 1977, p. A18, col. 4.

STEEL IMPORT DATA: STEEL MILL PRODUCTS, TOTAL ALL GRADES, BY COUNTRY OF ORIGIN

	January to December 1977			January to December 1976			Quantity total year 1976			Average value per ton		
	Quantity (net tons)	Percent of total	Value (thousands)	Quantity (net tons)	Percent of total	Value (thousands)	Percent change 1977/76	Quantity (net tons)	Percent of total	Year to date 1977	Year to date 1976	Total year 1976
Japan	7,820,480	40.5	$2,438,609	7,984,094	55.9	$2,206,235	—2.0	7,984,094	55.9	$311.82	$276.33	$276.33
European Economic Community/United Kingdom, total	6,828,200	35.4	1,762,929	3,176,862	22.2	893,924	+114.9	3,178,862	22.2	758.18	281.39	281.39
West Germany	2,006,645	10.4	528,948	758,718	5.3	228,257	+164.5	758,718	5.3	263.60	300.85	300.85
Belgium-Luxembourg ..	1,146,670	5.9	290,297	462,600	3.2	136,756	+147.9	462,600	3.2	253.17	295.62	295.62
France	1,586,171	8.2	397,707	730,358	5.1	204,441	+117.2	730,358	5.1	250.73	279.97	279.92
Italy	662,710	3.4	165,337	303,391	2.1	70,721	+118.4	303,391	2.1	249.49	233.10	233.10
Netherlands	607,827	3.1	143,662	388,722	2.7	93,393	+ 56.4	388,722	2.7	236.35	240.26	240.26
United Kingdom	818,176	4.2	236,979	533,072	3.7	160,357	+ 53.5	533,072	3.7	289.64	300.82	300.82
Canada	1,892,017	9.8	595,063	1,303,676	9.1	422,862	+ 45.1	1,303,676	9.1	314.51	324.36	324.36
Austria	21,327	.1	10,406	17,797	.1	9,693	+ 19.8	17,797	.1	487.93	544.64	544.64
Sweden	175,980	.7	108,540	106,515	.7	101,324	+ 18.3	106,515	.7	861.57	951.27	951.27
All others	2,618,765	13.6	615,896	1,695,649	11.9	391,204	+ 54.4	1,695,649	11.9	235.19	230.71	230.71
Total	19,306,768	100.0	5,531,443	14,284,593	100.0	4,025,242	+ 35.2	14,284,593	100.0	286.50	281.79	281.79

Source: Subcomm. on Trade of House Comm. on Ways and Means, *Background Data on the American Steel Industry and International Steel Trade*, 95th Cong., 2d Sess. (Comm. Print May 16, 1978).

finding that the five largest Japanese mills had been selling carbon steel plate to purchasers in the United States at less than fair value, with a margin of dumping of 32 per cent.[k] This finding was later modified,[l] and in fact imports of carbon steel plate constituted only about ·8 per cent of steel imports from Japan. But the Treasury's finding in this case was the first affirmative finding ever of sales at less than fair value by Japanese steel producers, and as appraisement was ordered withheld[m] on all carbon steel plate from Japan, all new trade in that product effectively stopped. All sides wondered whether the carbon steel plate case was an indication of how the other 18 pending steel dumping cases would turn out.

On October 7, 1977, the Council on Wage and Price Stability issued a report characterizing the steel industry as a "source of serious inflationary pressures" on the American economy, and in fairly clear terms opposing any kind of import quota, whether voluntary or mandatory.[n] Three days later, the President of FIAT, Giovanni Agnelli, proposed to the International Iron and Steel Institute a world-wide agreement to "organize" steel markets in what he called "a new international division of labor."[o] On October 13, President Carter met for four hours in the White House with leaders of the American steel industry—

---

[k] *Carbon Steel Plate from Japan,* Antidumping, Withholding of Appraisement Notice, 42 Fed. Reg. 54489, (Oct. 6, 1977). The margin of dumping means, in the Treasury Department's definition, the percentage of the United States weighted average prices in the period under review—in this case, Oct. 1, 1976–March 31, 1977—by which the imported prices are less than the "fair value" of the merchandise. Thus if fair value of a product is $100, and the weighted average U.S. price of the imported product is $85, the margin of dumping is 15/85 or 17.6 per cent.

[l] The final determination, on January 8, 1978, fixed the margin of dumping of the five firms concerned at 5.4 to 13.9 percent. U.S. Treasury, *Carbon Steel Plate from Japan.* Determination of Sales at Less than Fair Value, 43 Fed. Reg. 2032 (Jan. 13, 1978), amended 43 Fed. Reg. 12780 (March 27, 1978). On April 18, 1978, the U.S. International Trade Commission determined (unanimously) that the carbon steel plate industry in the United States was being injured by reason of imports of carbon steel plate from Japan. Int'l Trade Comm., *Carbon Steel Plate from Japan,* 43 Fed. Reg. 17410 (April 24, 1978). Antidumping duties were imposed by final Treasury action on May 23, 1978. 43 Fed. Reg. 22937 (May 30, 1978).

[m] See § 4.44(a) *supra.*

[n] Council on Wage and Price Stability, *Prices and Costs in the United States Steel Industry,* p. 1, also pp. xviii, 99; see also New York Times, October 8, 1977, p. 29, col. 4.

[o] New York Times, October 12, 1977, p. D1, col. 5.

management and labor—as well as members of the Congressional steel caucus. The Special Representative for Trade Negotiations, Ambassador Strauss, told reporters later that the meeting had produced a "very, very vigorous, open and candid dialogue." The head of the United Steelworkers of America and many of the industry executives urged mandatory import quotas. The President said only:

> Within the next month or interim period, there will be actions taken to insure that the present concern about the steel industry is alleviated, not by words or promises but by actions and decisions.[p]

6.12—THE TRIGGER PRICE MECHANISM

By the middle of November, 1977, the President's task force, headed by Under Secretary of the Treasury Anthony M. Solomon, had agreed on the outlines of a plan, at least for purposes of testing it informally with members of Congress, the press, and the steel industry, as well as interested parties abroad.[q] When no one protested too loud, and indications were received that U.S. Steel and other American producers might drop their antidumping complaints if the plan were put into effect, the Solomon report was put in final form and published.

One of the amendments to the Antidumping Act of 1921 made by the Trade Act of 1974 was to play a major part in the search by the task force for a device that would preserve the advantages of international commerce while distinguishing between fair and unfair trade. As we saw (§ 4.41, *supra*), the determination of whether there had been sales at less than fair value was supposed to be based on a comparison between the purchase price paid by the importer and the foreign market value—i.e., the price at which the product in question was being sold for home consumption in the country where it was produced.[r] If no significant sales were being made in the home market, the Act provided for use of "constructed value" based on costs as an alternative basis for comparison with purchase price in the United States. What if, however, the product was being sold in substantial quantity in the home market, but at a price that did not cover fully-allocated costs? Under the law as it stood through 1974, no finding of sales at less than fair value could

---

[p] New York Times, Oct. 14, 1977, p. D2, col. 6.

[q] See, e.g., New York Times, Nov. 19, 1977, p. 27, col. 4.

[r] Antidumping Act of 1921. § 205, Documents Supplement p. DS-433.

be made in these circumstances, since there was no price discrimination (after all the allowances for taxes, transportation, etc.) between domestic (e.g., Japanese) and export (e.g., American) prices. In the Trade Act of 1974, Congress added a new subsection (b) to section 205 of the Antidumping Act addressed to this situation.[s] The Secretary of the Treasury was directed, when he has "reasonable grounds to believe or suspect" that home market sales are being made at less than the cost of producing the merchandise in question, to make an inquiry into these costs: if his belief or suspicion was borne out and the practice was continued over an extended period of time in substantial quantities, the Secretary was to disregard home market sales in making the required comparison with the United States import price, and instead to look to constructed value—i.e., cost of production + 10 per cent for overhead + 8 per cent of the preceding total for profit.[t]

It was under this provision that the inquiry in the *Carbon Steel Plate* case[u] had been conducted, and it was this provision—or at least the concept underlying the provision—that now inspired the Solomon Task force:[v]

REPORT TO THE PRESIDENT
BY THE INTERAGENCY STEEL TASK FORCE,

(December 1977)

. . . . .

We recommend that the Department of the Treasury, in administering the Antidumping Act, set up a system of trigger prices, based on the full costs of production including appropriate capital charges of steel mill products by the most efficient foreign steel producers (currently the Japanese steel industry), which would be used as a basis for monitoring imports of steel into the United States and for initiating accelerated antidumping investigations with respect to imports priced below the trigger prices.

The trigger price mechanism is intended to provide the Secretary of the Treasury with a basis for initiating antidumping investigations without any

---

[s] Documents Supplement, p. DS-433.

[t] Antidumping Act §§ 205(b), 206(a), discussed at § 4.41(c) *supra.*

[u] § 6.61 at Ns. k–l *supra.*

[v] *A Comprehensive Program for the Steel Industry,* Report to the President by the Interagency Task Force, Anthony Solomon, Chairman, pp. 13–16 (Dec. 6, 1977).

prior industry complaint. Such authority exists under the Antidumping Act although it has not been used in recent years. As such it does not detract from any of the legal rights that foreign producers or the domestic industry presently enjoy under the Act. The trigger price is also a device for applying the resources of the Treasury Department to a constant monitoring of imports affecting a particularly sensitive industry viewed as a whole, instead of focusing on the investigation of individual complaints with respect to specified products—and then taking expedited action under the law. It thus meets the principal criticisms of present practices under the Act.

1. *Determining the Trigger Price*

The trigger price will be determined by the Treasury as follows:

— The unit cost of producing carbon and alloy steel in the most efficient exporting country—currently Japan—will be estimated at current prices and exchange rates from the best evidence available. Such evidence will consist of financial statements routinely prepared by the largest producers of carbon steel in Japan, data on the cost of labor, materials, and capital equipment used in the production of Japanese steel, as well as cost data which the companies have agreed to make available in aggregate form to the Treasury. The "costs of production" as calculated are intended to cover the traditional costs of labor, materials and directly related overhead, as well as general administrative expenses and a capital charge.

— Discrete product groups will be established pursuant to internationally recognized classifications for steel mill products. For each product a trigger price will be determined either directly from the financial statements and cost of production information supplied by the steel companies, or will be derived through procedures based upon the best available information on Japanese input costs and production experience.

— It is contemplated that trigger prices will be adjusted quarterly to reflect intervening changes in costs of production components and in currency values.

— At the time of each quarterly adjustment, the trigger price for each product will be set within five percent of that product's full cost of production. The flexibility in either direction will permit smoothing out sharp fluctuations of the components of the costs of production that may only be temporary. Taking immediate account of all such fluctuations would be unnecessarily disruptive to both domestic and international patterns of trade.

— The trigger price will be identical for all imports regardless of source and constructed on a "CIF" basis. Transportation from Japan to each major importing region of the country and insurance costs for each product class will be added to the production cost to arrive at the higher price.

— Stainless steel will be excluded from the trigger price system because a quota system is in effect with respect to such products. On the other hand, alloy products will be included.

— Onlv steel mill products as conventionally defined in the United States will be included in the system.

2. *Operation of Trigger Price Mechanism*

The Customs Service will organize a special task force to administer the trigger price system. Regulations will be published shortly for public comment which would obligate importers to present at entry of all steel imports a new "Special Customs Steel Invoice," and to certify on the invoice or otherwise that no rebates, drawbacks or unrelated incentives have been or will be paid or granted in connection with the transaction reflected in the invoice. The Special Customs Steel Invoice would be modeled upon the Special Customs Invoice presently in use and would provide space for the recording of product definitions, the base price and significant extras used in calculating the transaction price for the imported product. The total price shown on the Special Customs Steel Invoice would be compared to the trigger price data at the port of entry. Imports priced below the trigger price would be promptly identified and the information immediately forwarded to the Treasury in Washington for further investigation. If warranted, a formal antidumping investigation could be initiated within a matter of weeks.

Once the trigger price mechanism has been set in place, it is contemplated that information will be currently obtained both in the United States and abroad concerning steel prices and costs of steel production and the condition of the domestic industry. Therefore, if a formal antidumping investigation should appear warranted, it could not only be opened quickly but it could be concluded within a time period substantially shorter than is presently the case. In general, except where a case is unusually complex, we expect that action could be taken under this procedure within 60 to 90 days, as opposed to the 7 months-plus period required under the normal procedures, although in more intricate cases it may take longer. In the event the investigation indicates such action is warranted, existing statutory powers to impose a retroactive withholding of appraisement could be ordered at the time the tentative determination is published. Following completion of the Treasury's "fast track" investigation, the case would be referred to the U.S. International

Trade Commission for the required injury determination, which could similarly be expedited.[w]

§ 6.2—Notes and Questions on the Trigger Price Mechanism

6.21—Before looking in detail at the legal and economic ramifications of the Trigger Price Mechanism, it is worth attempting a brief overview of how the plan was supposed to work.

(a) The idea, as stated in the Solomon Report, was derived from the Antidumping Act. The U.S. Government says to the domestic steel industry, "if, as you keep asserting, you are competitive in terms of cost and price against fair foreign competition (including transportation), here is your chance to prove it. But you will not get the guaranteed share of the market or free ride to raise prices that an import quota would provide. What we have done is to remove the procedural obstacles to preparing and proving antidumping complaints, by setting forth some presumptions of our own about fair value with respect to steel mill products. Further, there is an (unstated) presumption that whoever sells below fair value as we have defined it is quite unlikely to escape a finding of injury by the International Trade Commission." There was every expectation, therefore, that the trigger price would act as a floor price for the vast majority of steel imports.[a]

(b) Consider the Trigger Price Mechanism in relation to the European Coal and Steel Community. In the past, as we saw, European producers had usually been permitted to match Japanese delivered prices, regardless of their own home market prices, on the ground that the domestic industry could not be said to be injured by the European imports so long as the Japanese were permitted to sell at the same price.[b] The same concept seemed to underlie the Trigger Price Mechanism. If a producer from the ECSC sold at the Trigger Price on the basis of a profit of, say, 3 per cent above cost, it is clear that

---

[w] The announcement by the U.S. Treasury of Implementation of the Trigger Price Mechanism appears in the Documents Supplement at p. DS-585.

[a] In fact, a few Canadian producers were able to show that their home market prices and delivered costs were less than the corresponding trigger price for particular products, and were permitted through a pre-clearance procedure to bring in their products at fair value calculated on the basis of their own prices and costs.

[b] See, e.g., the opinion of the Tariff Commission in the *Wire Rod Cases*, § 4.43(c) *supra*.

the Treasury would not undertake an antidumping investigation. While it could not, under the statute, prevent a private party from bringing an antidumping complaint in these circumstances, the Treasury discouraged such complaints, on the ground that conducting the necessary investigations and hearings within the tight time deadlines set in the 1974 amendments would divert its limited resources from the task of administering the Trigger Price Mechanism.[c]

6.22—(a) Assuming the Trigger Price Mechanism worked as planned, the U.S. Treasury would announce a set of reference prices for steel products every few months, and if there were any foreign offerings below these prices, an antidumping investigation would be launched, with a view to bringing the offered prices up to the fair market value of that product.[d] Can you distinguish this arrangement from the system of variable import levies used by the European Community in support of its Common Agricultural Policy (§ 3.25 *supra*)?

(b) Proponents of the Trigger Price Mechanism in the United States would quickly respond that there is a fundamental difference, in that the threshold price in the Common Agricultural Policy is set on the basis of a target price designed to balance the interests of domestic producers (farmers) and consumers, whereas the trigger price for steel is set on the basis of calculations of foreign costs of production without reference to domestic costs or prices. Is this on principle—i.e., without reference to the method of computation used—a persuasive distinction? Or would you conclude, rather, that some of the same constraints of politics and public opinion that went into the European system of agricultural controls are relevant (appropriate?) to the production of steel in the United States in the late 1970's? Recall that while both the United States and the GATT secretariat grumbled from time to time about the Community's Common Agricultural Policy, neither was prepared to challenge it directly.

---

[c] See, e.g., the exchange of letters between the chairman of ARMCO and the General Counsel of the Treasury concerning withdrawal of an antidumping complaint filed in December 1977 against steel products from Great Britain, 43 Fed. Reg. 47041-42, (Oct. 12, 1978).

[d] The summary in the text telescopes the several steps that would take place if an importer insisted on going through the procedure: (i) a notice of antidumping proceeding; (ii) withholding of appraisement and permission of the goods to enter only against a bond equal to the estimated antidumping duty; (iii) a final, though expedited, determination by the Treasury of sales at less than fair value; (iv) a determination of injury by the International Trade Commission; and (v) imposition of the antidumping duty as of the date of withholding of appraisement. Of course the plan was designed so that these steps would not, in fact, have to be followed.

(c) Putting the same point another way (or is it a different point?), we have thus far distinguished between ordinary tariffs and even quotas designed to moderate the effects of *fair* competition, and antidumping or countervailing duties designed to defend against *unfair* competition. On which side of the line is the trigger price mechanism?

(d) As we saw, the price discrimination aspect of the concept of dumping is not relevant to the Trigger Price Mechanism, which relies solely on comparison of sales prices with the cost of production. It seems clear that over time an entire industry is unlikely to sell below cost of production. But it may not be so unlikely that an industry would sell at prices that do not yield the rate of profit that the United States government arbitrarily adds to its calculation of cost of production.[e] How does this consideration affect your answer to the preceeding question?

6.23—(a) Assuming, as the Solomon Report states, that cost of production of the low-cost producer is the critical element in setting the trigger price, how should that cost be computed? If a large portion of the costs of valuing steel consists of fixed costs (and we saw, a larger portion for Japan than for the United States or Europe), then the cost per ton will depend in substantial measure on the utilization of available capacity. As Table III-3 in the Documents Supplement shows, the capacity utilization in Japan dropped sharply in 1975 and 1976 from the pattern of preceding years, and the figure for 1977 was approximately the same as for 1976. Yet the Treasury Department initially used a figure of 85 per cent capacity utilization as the basis of its calculation of unit costs, on the ground that this represented the average rate through Japan's business cycles since 1956.[f] The higher the figure used for capacity utilization, the lower will be the cost per unit,[g] and therefore the lower

---

[e] Note that the 8 percent figure used by the Treasury was not a rate of return figure, but an amount (like overhead) added to the sum of costs of materials, labor, depreciation, and other expenses. Recall that in Japan, equity capital typically makes up a much smaller portion of total capital dedicated to an industry than is the case in the United States. See §§ 3.31 at N. i, 3.44(c), 4.41(c)(ii). The U.S. Treasury tried to take account of this fact by counting interest payments, along with dividends, as return on capital, rather than as production costs.

[f] See the announcement of implementation of the Trigger Price Mechanism, paragraph 4(b), Documents Supplement p. DS-590.

[g] A simple example will illustrate this point. Suppose it costs $1,000 to keep a facility operating for one hour, and that at full capacity it can produce 100 units. Then if it operates at full capacity, the cost is $\frac{\$1,000}{100}$ or $10 per unit. If the plant

the trigger price based on that cost. In its mid-year review of the Trigger Price Mechanism announced in July 1978,[h] the Treasury reduced the period of measurement of capacity utilization to five years, with the result that the average rate of utilization was reduced from 85 to 83.29 per cent. In combination with changes in other assumptions—for instance the relation of fixed to variable costs of labor, interest, and depreciation—the cost of production used to calculate the trigger price was increased by $18 per ton.[i] Why shouldn't cost at any given time reflect actual capacity utilization, rather than a historical average, however computed? Does the U.S. Treasury's method suggest an obligation on the foreign producer to cover historical costs?

(b) The General Counsel of the Treasury answered this question as follows:

MR. STEIGER:[j] . . . In view of the fact that the trigger mechanism was to address current problems and that you are going to revise the trigger price quarterly for that very reason, why didn't you use the latest available data of Japanese production utilization instead of using this 85 per cent 20-year average?

MR. MUNDHEIM:[k] . . . In part we are constructing the trigger price on the definition in the Trade Act of the cost of production. Section 205 (b) of the Trade Act[l] talks about whether or not the prices charged would permit the recovery [of] costs over a reasonable period of time.

---

operates at 85 per cent capacity it will produce 85 units and the cost of each will be $\frac{\$1,000}{85}$ or $11.76. If it operates at 70 per cent capacity, the unit cost will be $\frac{\$1,000}{70}$ or $14.29. Of course in the steel industry the calculation would be much more complex, because the difference in units of steel produced could involve not only the plant itself but also differences in raw material and other costs that would vary with plant utilization.

[h] 43 Fed. Reg. 32710 (July 27, 1978).

[i] See *id.* at Paragraph A. Offsetting this, however, were increases in the credit for greater yield from crude steel to finished product, in particular for the amount of recoverable scrap. See *id.* at Paragraph B.

[j] Representative from Wisconsin.

[k] General Counsel of the Treasury.

[l] Documents Supplement p. DS-433.

The question is what is a reasonable period of time. We thought that a reasonable period of time in the intent of the statute was a business cycle because that is the way people plan their activities. Another construction would not make a great deal of sense.[m]

Is this persuasive?

(c) Robert Crandall, the principal author of the study on *Prices and Costs in the United States Steel Industry* prepared by the Council on Wage and Price Stability,[n] and the person who was coopted by the Treasury to make the cost calculations on which the original trigger prices were based, published an article a few months later (no longer as a government official) in which (among other points) he addressed the question of considering fair pricing in terms of historical average costs.[o] Assuming that the Treasury correctly interpreted section 205 (b) of the Antidumping Act, as amended, along the lines of Mr. Mundheim's testimony, Mr. Crandall wrote:

> As currently written, the U.S. Antidumping Law prohibits marginal cost pricing during a recession. In a competitive market, excess capacity would lead firms to reduce their prices to the level of the additional costs required to produce another unit of output. With large fixed costs, these prices would be substantially below average or unit costs. Because these fixed costs would be allocated across a smaller output, this statute might actually require exporters to raise their prices during a recession in order to meet the cost-of-production test. If other countries were to follow our lead, recessions would be exacerbated by declining export demand and reduced exploitation of comparative advantage. Therefore, the 1974 Trade Act amendments to the antidumping law are potentially a source of macroeconomic instability in the world.[p]

In light of this argument, could you develop a different legal interpretation of section 205(b)? If not, should the statute be changed, or is

---

[m] *Administration's Comprehensive Program for the Steel Industry,* Hearings before the Subcomm. on Trade of the House Comm. on Ways and Means, 95th Cong., 2nd Sess. 234–35 (Jan. 25–26, 1978).

[n] § 6.11 N. e *supra.*

[o] Crandall, "Competition and 'Dumping' in the U. S. Steel Market" Challenge, Vol. 21, No. 3, p. 13 (July–August 1978).

[p] *Id.* at p. 18.

marginal cost pricing precisely the evil against which a realistic anti-dumping statute should be directed?[q]

(d) If you were acting for the Japan Iron and Steel Exporters Association, would you argue for or against the Treasury's interpretation on this point? What about the American Iron and Steel Institute? Or Consumers Union?

6.24—(a) Speaking of the statute, consider the legal authority for the Trigger Price. No one contended that the plan had been discussed with or contemplated by the Congress. Indeed, as we have seen, the plan was developed only by the crisis task force appointed by President Carter in the fall of 1977. But the executive branch took the position that what the plan did was to create a "fast track" for administering an existing statute, that is the Antidumping Act of 1921 as amended. No attempt was made to secure legislative authorization, either before or after introduction of the Trigger Price Mechanism.

(b) As legal adviser to the President's Task Force, would you have given an opinion that the TPM was lawful? Would you have cleared the following statement in the Solomon Report?

The trigger price mechanism is intended only to provide the Secretary with a basis for self-initiating antidumping investigations; they are not a "minimum price" system. Thus, none of its terms are keyed to statutory definitions of, for example, "foreign market value" or "constructed value." But they are fully consistent with existing statutory law and with the international obligations of the United States under the General Agreement on Tariffs and Trade and the International Antidumping Code.[r]

(c) In its hearing on the Trigger Price Mechanism in January 1978, the Subcommittee on Trade of the House Ways and Means Committee touched only briefly on the question of legal authority for the plan:[s]

---

[q] $\text{Average cost} = \frac{\text{Fixed Cost} + \text{Variable Cost}}{\text{No. of Units Produced}}$. *Marginal cost* does not take the fixed cost into account at all, but describes the incremental variable cost of the nth unit produced.

[r] *A Comprehensive Program for the Steel Industry,* § 6.12 N.u. *supra* at p. 17.

[s] *Hearings,* N. m *supra* at pp. 243-44.

MR. VANIK:[1] . . . Why couldn't the United States simply strictly enforce the existing antidumping law, as first mentioned by the President?

MR. MUNDHEIM: First of all, as Indicated when I was beginning, Mr. Chairman, I do think the trigger-price system is a way of making our laws, really—our laws here are your laws—effective . . .

The trigger-price mechanism represents the effort to find a more comprehensive solution [to the dumping problem] and a quickly implemented program to remedy injury by eliminating unfair trade practices, which is precisely what the statute is aimed at . . . . That's what the trigger-price mechanism does but it does it within the context of the Antidumping Act. It doesn't remove any remedies at all or any rights under that act.

It simply takes advantage of the fact that under the statute we do have a right to self-initiate and it provides us with a standard so that we can pick these cases which are appropriate for self-initiation under an objective standard that everyone can see . . . .

MR. VANIK: Well, I don't recall anything in the Antidumping Act that refers at all to the most efficient producer.

It refers to the product and to the country. So what is there in the statute that leads us to that concept?

MR. MUNDHEIM: That concept is a way that we can signal—

MR. VANIK: I am talking about what is the statutory basis. I know what the objective is, but what is the statutory basis for that concept?

MR. MUNDHEIM: You see, when we ultimately investigate a complaint, we have to investigate it in terms of the statute.

MR. VANIK: I understand.

---

[1] Representative from Ohio and Chairman of the Subcommittee on Trade.

MR. MUNDHEIM: What we are talking about—you are right, there is nothing in the statute that says trigger-price mechanism or average cost of the most efficient producer.

MR. VANIK: The fundamental question is where is the law being written in the executive branch or is it being written here?

We are very sensitive to that.

[Laughter] . . .

MR. VANIK: I don't want to prolong the discussion, but you did say there was no basis in the statute that you could find, no language, no legislative history that dealt with the "most efficient producer" concept.

That is what you have evolved as a means to carry out what you consider to be the legislative mandate?

MR. MUNDHEIM: Anything could be attacked but I don't think it could be attacked successfully . . . .

6.25—(a) One lawsuit was filed, shortly after publication of the regulations implementing the Trigger Price Mechanism.[u] Plaintiff was an independent manufacturer of wire and wire products, for which the principal raw material is wire rods. Plaintiff imported wire rods from foreign manufacturers, and then sold its finished products in competition with the integrated majors. Since the Trigger Price Mechanism applied to wire rods but not to finished wire products, plaintiff feared that it would be squeezed at both ends: its raw material costs would rise, but competition both within the United States and from foreign manufacturers would prevent it from passing its higher costs on to consumers. With this economic background, consider how you might fashion a legal challenge to the program.

(b) In fact, counsel for plaintiff made three charges:

(i) that the TPM circumvents the procedures prescribed in the Antidumping Act by establishing a minimum price system that will

---

[u] *Davis Walker Corporation v. Blumenthal et al*, Civ. Action 78–0421 (D.D.C. 1978).

deter imports of steel with products at prices below the published prices, without regard to the fair value of such imports or whether such imports are likely to injure an American industry;

(ii) that the TPM is a substantive rule subject to the rulemaking requirements of the Administrative Procedure Act,[v] and is invalid for failure to comply with those requirements;

(iii) that as to plaintiff the TPM is arbitrary and capricious, because wire rods were, and wire products were not, included.

Plaintiff applied for declaratory relief and an injunction.

(c) The court did grant a preliminary injunction limited to steel wire rods, and it required the Treasury to undergo extensive discovery and to make a specific finding on the effect of inclusion of wire rods in the TPM on domestic wire manufacturers. After the Secretary made such a finding and the depositions of relevant officials were taken and submitted to the court, Judge Gasch of the District Court for the District of Columbia granted the government's motion for summary judgment on all counts.[w] The judge concluded that:

the adoption of the TPM is within the Treasury's authority to administer the Antidumping Act. . . . The TPM itself does not establish any restrictions upon the affected industry; rather its serves to aid the Treasury in the administration of the Antidumping Act. The implementation of the TPM does not *by its terms* set trigger prices as minimum import prices or preclude the importation of goods at less than trigger prices. . . ."[x]

The court rejected the argument that implementation of the TPM had caused foreign manufacturers to raise prices to the trigger price level: "The decision by foreign manufacturers to increase prices to the trigger price level," the Judge said, "is not the legal equivalent of the imposition of dumping duties with respect to all such goods imported

---

[v] 5 U.S.C. § 553.

[w] *Davis Walker Corporation v. Blumenthal,* 460 F. Supp. 283 (D.D.C. May 25, 1978).

[x] 460 F. Supp. at 291, 292.

at the trigger price level."[y] Even if plaintiffs' allegations concerning the factual effects of the TPM (i.e., foreign manufacturers' refusal to sell steel wire rods at less than trigger prices) were true, the TPM would not be contrary to the Antidumping Act.

Having ascertained that the TPM is a guide to aid the Secretary in determining whether to self-initiate an investigation, the court concluded that nothing in the statute restricts the means by which the Secretary obtains information or launches an investigation.[z]

So far as is known, no other legal challenge to the TPM was brought.[a]

6.26—(a) One unforeseen development in the early months of the TPM was the rapid fall of the dollar in relation to other major currencies, especially the yen. Since the trigger price was stated in dollars, each time (or rather each quarter) that the yen appreciated in comparison to the dollar, an upward adjustment was made in the trigger price, equal (other factors aside) to 60 per cent of the change in the exchange rate.[b] Since American steel prices tended to move in parallel with imported prices, the link of the trigger price to the yen/dollar rate had the effect, throughout most of 1978, of reflecting the lowered value of the dollar in higher domestic steel prices. Whether recovery of the dollar—spontaneous or through governmental intervention— would have the reverse effect, remained to be seen.[c]

---

[y] 460 F. Supp. at 292.

[z] 460 F. Supp. at 293. As to the argument under the Administrative Procedure Act, the Court concluded that the TPM was a "policy statement" within the meaning of § 553 7(b)(A) of the APA, rather than a rule, and was therefore exempt from the notice and comment procedures. The analogy, in the Court's view, was to adoption of merger guidelines by the Department of Justice—which like the TPM definitely affect behavior in the business community, but were held to be notice to the public as to how the executive branch would carry out its discretionary authority.

On the "arbitrary and capricious" point, the court granted extensive discovery to plaintiff, but ruled that the information obtained had failed to demonstrate that the decision to limit the TPM to the 32 products covered was irrational. Furthermore, the court was satisfied that the calculations made by the Treasury, though they involved a series of adjustments from raw data and some extrapolation from incomplete evidence, were carefully made and reasonable.

[a] Plaintiff in *Davis Walker* first filed an appeal, then moved that the appeal be dismissed.

[b] See e.g., 43 Fed. Reg. 20070 (May 10, 1978); 43 Fed. Reg. 32713 (July 27, 1978). The reason for the 60 percent figure was that as labor and capital costs in Japan rose in dollar terms, costs denominated in dollars for coal, iron and other raw materials fell for the Japanese producers.

[c] For the reverse effect, when the dollar rose in relation to European currencies in 1981, see § 8.52 *infra*.

(b) The prediction that the trigger price would be the effective floor price for imports generally held up, at least in the first two years of the TPM. While there was a good deal of negotiation about particular products, about dates of contracting or shipment, and about costs of transportation,[d] by and large the predictions of widespread cheating, intolerable bottlenecks and bureaucratic nightmares did not develop. To the Japanese producers, the TPM had something of the same effect as the VRA's, in that it led to higher export prices and increased profits, and legitimization of continuing large sales in the United States without threat for the time being of quotas or duty surcharges, or indeed of protracted antidumping proceedings. With some reluctance, MITI collaborated with the U.S. Treasury in supplying sufficient data to make calculation of trigger prices possible with reasonable accuracy. As with the VRA's, European producers increased their sales—and their share of the market—while Japanese purchasers were cutting back.

(c) Just after the Solomon Report was published, the president of United States Steel called for a trigger price averaging $360 per ton delivered.[e] When the trigger prices were announced by the Treasury Department in January 1978, the cost of production was estimated at $297.80, plus transport costs. The resulting delivered prices varied by region, but averaged about $330 per ton on the East Coast of the United States—about $20 per ton or 5.7 per cent below the prices at which comparable products were being sold by domestic purchasers. Two increases in the course of 1978 brought the trigger prices up by about 11 per cent for the fourth quarter of 1978, to $329.42.[f] In the mean time, price charged by American steel producers had increased by about 9.5 per cent.

(d) In late October 1978, President Carter announced a major drive against inflation, based on voluntary restraints according to government "guidelines."[g] Among the guidelines was a limitation on price increases

---

[d] See, e.g., Tables 2 and 3, Documents Supplement pp. DS-588, 589. Note that what is referred to in the text as costs of transportation includes not only freight, but insurance, interest and wharfage or handling charges. For a more detailed explanation of these charges, see Paragraph 3 of the initial notice by the Secretary of the Treasury, Documents Supplement p. DS-587.

[e] New York Times, December 9, 1977 p. A26, col. 1. The figure used was not broken down by region, though transport costs varied by more than $20 per ton between the Pacific Coast and the Great Lakes area.

[f] See 43 Fed. Reg. 32710 (July 27, 1978); 43 Fed. Reg. 33993 (Aug. 2, 1978).

[g] 14 Weekly Comp. Pres. Docs. 1839–48 (Oct. 30, 1978).

to one half percentage point below the average of price increases in 1976 and 1977. Under Secretary Solomon told a press conference called to announce a 7 percent increase in the trigger price effective January 1, 1979 that the American steel industry had been the first industry to make a commitment to abide by the guidelines.[h]

6.27—(a) Consider how, if the Trigger Price Mechanism proved successful, the technique might fit into the overall trade policy of the United States. Would it be possible to apply trigger prices or reference prices to other industries as well? The Administration took the view that steel was a special case, and that the TPM was not suitable, say, for textiles or shoes, or motorcycles, or other industries affected by competition from abroad. What facts should another industry be required to establish in order to make out a case for an import reference price?

(b) Given that something like dumping appears to be necessary—albeit with some elasticity of definition in respect to foreign production costs—could you, for example, make a persuasive argument on behalf of the United States color television industry, still smarting from defeat in the *Zenith* case?[i] Or would you think that even if a showing sufficient for individual dumping complaints might be made, TV sets could not match steel in terms of capital invested, number of persons employed (and unemployed) and impact on the overall economy? Consider also how you might cope with the problem of monitoring the prices of imports of TV sets, given the large variety of differentiations in terms of size, special features, models, brands, etc.

(e) The representatives of the AFL-CIO argued as follows to the House Sub-committee looking into the TPM:

There is overcapacity in many different types of products in different countries. There is a tendency to try to export unemployment, to dump goods in another country in order to maintain employment at home.

---

[h] See New York Times, Nov. 10, 1978 p. D14, col. 1. Prior to this episode, the Council on Wage and Price Stability had apparently used the threat of eliminating the TPM in an effort to keep American steel prices in line. See Meadows, "The Jawboners' Earnest Exercise in Futility," Fortune June 19, 1978 p. 48 at 50.

[i] See § 4.47(c) *supra*.

This is an unfair [labor] practice and we need to have adequate defenses to meet it. . . .

[We] believe the U.S. Treasury Department should investigate whenever imports increase by more than 10 per cent or there is reason to believe that dumping is taking place. We think this could be more effective than Government trying to establish a fair price possibly for every product imported into the United States.[j]

Do you think something like the approach suggested is the inarticulate premise behind the Trigger Price Mechanism for steel? Or behind the redefinition of dumping in terms of foreign production costs as constructed by the importing country?

(d) Would you think the GATT Committee on Antidumping Practices should investigate the Trigger Price Mechanism? If so, in the direction of bringing Article VI of the General Agreement, as well as the International Antidumping Code, in line with current realities? Or in the direction of bringing American practice into line with the international rules?[k]

We shall return to this question in the next chapter. First, however, it is time for another look at the European Community and its reactions to the steel crisis.

§ 6.3—Challenge in Europe

The year 1975—a year of mild economic downturn in the United States— was a year of major economic retreat in Western Europe. For a variety of reasons that all seemed to converge in 1975, steel was hurt more than any other industry in the Community, and it was hurt more than the steel industry in any other major producing area. Between 1974 and 1975 capacity utilization dropped from 85 to 65 per cent; the total value of production dropped by 20 per cent, reaching just about the level attained in 1969; and steel prices within the Community fell by about 35 per cent. The European Community

---

[j] Testimony of Dr. Rudolph Oswald, Director, Dept. of Research, AFL-CIO at *Hearings on Administration's Comprehensive Program for the Steel Industry*, § 6.23 N. m *supra* at p. 144.

[k] In fact the Committee on Antidumping Practice did take up the TPM at its April 1978 meeting. The results of the discussions begun at that meeting were incorporated in the Subsidies/Countervailing Duties Code that emerged from the Multilateral Trade Negotiations, discussed in § 7.41(a) *infra*.

reported that for some companies prices no longer even covered variable costs. Employment did not fall correspondingly, as companies, under pressure from unions and governments, resorted to short work weeks, maintenance in lieu of production, and redundant labor forces rather than massive lay-offs. Nearly all steel companies in Western Europe lost money in 1975, some as much as 10 per cent of their paid-in capital per month. Investment capital for even essential new plants and equipment became impossible to obtain, and nearly all the European companies resorted to heavy borrowing. In numerous companies, senior executives were replaced or took early retirement.

6.31—THE BEGINNINGS OF DIRIGISME

As early as March 1975, the President of the French Steel Federation, Jacques Ferry, requested that the ECSC formally recognize a "manifest crisis" under Articles 58 and 61 of the Treaty of Paris[a] and impose production quotas, minimum prices, import quotas, or some combination of these or comparable measures.[b] The Commission, however, was not yet ready for such measures, which would be contrary to the overall philosophy of the Common Market (putting aside agriculture) as well as of the broader agreements to which the Community and its members were parties.

The first response of the Commission was a series of "forward programmes" as provided for in Article 46(2) of the Treaty of Paris,—i.e. published economic forecasts designed to induce all enterprises to make their investment and production decisions on the basis of the same, sophisticated forecasts of supply, demand, inventories and economic activity. The difficulty with the forward programmes, of course, was that the "self-discipline" they called for was not universally observed. Moreover, so long as imports were not controlled, reduced production might not result in higher prices at all, but rather in increased imports. Some industry representatives, especially from France, Belgium and Luxembourg, wanted the Commission to go further, and make provision for minimum prices (see Article 61); but this suggestion inevitably raised the further question whether producers within the Community should or should not be permitted to align their prices against offers from third countries. Some spokesmen for the impacted domestic steel industries argued that if alignment were permitted, the effect would be to undercut the scheme of minimum prices, and therefore should be prohibited.

---

[a] Documents Supplement pp. DS-116, 120.

[b] See Article 61 of the Treaty of Paris for the options available to High Authority (Commission) in a situation of manifest crisis.

But that argument inevitably led to the suggestion of import quotas, and neither the Commission nor a majority of the member countries was prepared in 1975–76 to move in that direction. Not only would such a step be contrary to the professed (and on the whole practiced) commercial policy of the European Community; since the real cause of Western Europe's steel crisis was the sharp drop in demand and not the increase in imports, any scheme of quotas would run directly counter to Article XI of the GATT, and not be defensible under Article XIX.[c]

At the end of 1975, the Commission, by a majority vote, decided not to fix minimum prices for steel, and not to impose any restraints on imports.[d] For the time being, the Commission would intensify the monitoring and dissemination of data—on production, employment, imports, exports, orders, and inventories. Meanwhile the advisability of fixing minimum prices would be subjected to consultation with the Council and the Consultative Committee of the Coal and Steel Community.[e]

In the summer of 1976, as voluntary production cutbacks in line with the forward programme seemed not to be working, the European Commission issued a document sponsored by its Commissioner of Industry, Henri Simonet of Belgium, proposing permanent monitoring of the steel market and construction of an advanced econometric model.[f] The document proposed a clearance procedure for investments, on the basis of guidance by the Commission to the members of the industry, so that "redundant investments" would be avoided to the maximum possible extent:

> The Commission can, should the need arise, extend its influence by adopting less noncommittal positions on investment projects . . .

---

[c] Documents Supplement pp. 22, 41. Note that import quotas designed to sustain a domestic price support or production control scheme were contemplated in Article XI of the GATT, but for agricultural and fisheries products only. (Article XI (2)(c)).

[d] *Commission Decision of 10 December 1975 establishing Community surveillance in respect of the importation of certain products covered by the ECSC Treaty,* O.J. Jan. 14, 1976 No. L 7/15.

[e] The Consultative Committee consists of 30–51 members, made up of an equal number of producers, workers, consumers and dealers, serving two years terms without, according to the Treaty, any instructions from the organizations which proposed them. (Treaty of Paris Article 18).

[f] The European Commission, *Problems in the Steel Industry.* July 21, 1976.

where excess capacity can be foreseen. In particular, the annual survey on investments could provide an opportunity for closer contacts with the steel industry, and for discussions on the foreseeable development of capacities, with a view to better coordination of investment intentions. The regional and social implications of projected investments would also be borne in mind.[g]

These procedures would be based on consent, though coupled, it was understood, with the bestowal or withholding of benefits by the Commission, particularly with respect to credits.[h] In addition the Commission proposed adoption of a stand-by program, to be implemented by the Commission in the event another crisis arose. The term "crisis" could be defined in advance by reference to certain key economic forecasts, related to production, capacity utilization, orders, changes in inventory, and revenues by steel enterprises as compared to anticipated costs. In the event a crisis was determined to exist or to be imminent, "there should be a greater degree of compulsion in the Forward Programmes," possibly production quotas under Article 58 of the Treaty of Paris or minimum prices under Article 61. Furthermore, "a prolonged drop in prices on the international market could be taken to show the need for contacts with producers in non-member countries."[i] The Commission said that the crisis measures would be subject to a strict time limit and could be cancelled by a Commission decision. "The Commission would then make sure that the usual rules of competition would once again apply."[j]

In October, 1976, the Simonet Plan for a Steel Policy was further refined with a view to alerting the Commission as far in advance as possible of any possible crisis.[k] A reporting system was introduced combining not only information from all branches of the steel industry, but also macroeconomic indicators on a biweekly basis. "An alarm will automatically be triggered when a threshold [of reduced economic activity] yet to be established is reached."[l] Under the proposal, the Commission could introduce mandatory

---

[g] *Problems in the Steel Industry*, N. f *supra*, ¶ C2.

[h] Compare § 3.24(c) *supra*.

[i] *Problems in the Steel Industry* N. f *supra* ¶ D.

[j] *Id.* ¶ D1.

[k] *Community Steel Policy*, Commission of the European Communities, Press Release P–80, October 1976.

[l] *Id.* Explanatory Annex ¶ A.

notification by enterprises of shipments of stated steel products, with authority in the Commission to order reductions. As a precursor to actually fixing prices, the Commission would publish minimum reference prices, "with the extreme caution required, bearing in mind the difficulties involved . . ."[m]

6.32—THE SIMONET-DAVIGNON PLAN: PHASE I

In December 1976, the Simonet Plan was officially adopted, effective January 1, 1977.[n] In addition to the various reporting requirements, the Commission said that if a new crisis breaks out it expects that enterprises "will display solidarity," and tailor their production or deliveries to indicative tonnages published in the Forward Programmes.[o]

Soon after Viscount Davignon, also of Belgium, had succeeded Simonet as Commissioner in charge of Industry Affairs early in 1977, the crisis plans began to be implemented in earnest. On May 5, 1977, the Commission published a series of decisions that became known as the Davignon Plan. First, the Commission, acting under Article 61 of the Treaty of Paris, issued a mandatory minimum price schedule for concrete reinforcing bars, a product used in housing construction that accounted for about 8.8 per cent of the total iron and steel production of the Community. Reinforcing bars were a particular problem, because mini-mills recently built near the Italian city of Brescia were turning them out at prices well below those charged by the integrated producers, forcing down the prices charged by the established firms. The Commission set the minimum price at about 20 per cent above the average then prevailing on the Continent; contrary to prior practices, producers in the Community were prohibited from aligning their prices with lower-priced offers from non-member countries.[p]

---

[m] *Id.* Explanatory Annex ¶ C.

[n] *Common Steel Policy*, O.J. Dec. 23, 1976 No. C 303/3; Commission Decision No. 3017/76/ECSC of 8 Dec. 1976, O.J. Dec. 14, 1976 No. L 344/24.

[o] *Id.* ¶ 1.

[p] *Commission Decision No. 962/77/ECSC of 4 May 1977, fixing minimum prices for certain concrete reinforcement bars*, O.J. May 5, 1977 No. L 114/1. The decision was also made applicable to transactions in those countries of the European Free Trade Association (§ 3.15 *supra*) with which the Community had concluded free trade agreements for ECSC products—i.e., Austria, Finland, Norway, Sweden and Portugal. Mr. Simonet, having finished his term on the European Commission, joined the Belgian cabinet as Foreign Minister.

Second, six other steel products were made subject to guide or reference prices. The Commission said in its decision that it "is asking steel undertakings to raise their prices [in accordance with the published schedule] where appropriate, and to respect these guidance prices when aligning on the delivered prices of other Community undertakings or undertakings of third countries."[q] However, compliance with the published prices for these products was not made compulsory.

Third, the Commission had to address the international aspects of the Davignon Plan. It was clear that minimum prices—whether compulsory or merely recommended from on high, and whether or not accompanied by controls on production—could not have their desired effect if imports were permitted to come in without restraint. But the international aspects of the Davignon Plan were not yet fully worked out, and indeed a fully developed plan would have added more controversy than the already innovative proposals of Simonet and Davignon might have been able to stand. Moreover, as we saw,[r] the signatories of the Treaty of Paris that created the European Coal and Steel Community had not granted to the High Authority (now the Commission[s]) powers over external commercial policies comparable to those later granted to the Commission under the Treaty of Rome. Thus whereas the Commission functioning under the Treaty of Paris had a high degree of authority over all aspects of the coal and steel industries within the Community—more, indeed, than it had over other industries when it was functioning under the Treaty of Rome—it could only make recommendations to member states with respect to external trade. Accordingly the Commission adopted three "Recommendations" to member states concerning imports of steel:

1. Member states were requested, in reliance on Article 74(3) of the Treaty of Paris,[t] to implement a prospective (in contrast to the previous retrospective) system of monitoring for 16 categories of steel products. To accomplish this, all imports of the products listed were to be made subject to a licensing requirement. The licenses were to be

---

[q] *Communication from the Commission of the ECSC concerning the publication of guidance prices for certain steel products.* O.J. May 5, 1977 No. L 114/18.

[r] See § 3.12 at Ns. j–o *supra.*

[s] See § 3.24(a) *supra.*

[t] Documents Supplement, p. DS-132.

issued by the member states within six days of application, free of charge, and for any quantity requested. But each time a license was requested, information would be gathered by the governments of member states for transmission to the Commission, concerning the product to be imported, the price, the importer, the country of origin, the date of the import contract, and the date and place of importation.[u]

2. Member countries were requested to notify the Commission of any danger resulting from trends in imports which appeared to call for safeguard measures.[v] The Commission would arrange for consultation among the member states within eight working days after receipt of any such notification, with a view to taking action under Article 74(3) of the Paris Treaty—i.e. with a view to imposing import quotas.[w] If the consultations did not result in agreed action on a Community-wide basis, member states would be free to take national measures, subject to consultation with the Commission and other member states.

3. The Commission recommended that member states adopt a uniform set of rules for protection against dumping and export subsidies.[x] The rules were substantially similar to the regulations already in force in the European Economic Community (i.e., for transactions covered by the Rome Treaty and not the Paris Treaty).[y] Thus in conformity to the International Antidumping Code adopted in the Kennedy Round (§ 4.44(b) *supra*), duties could

---

[u] *Commission Recommendation of 15 April 1977 to the Governments of the Members States of the Community establishing Community surveillance in respect of the importation in the community of certain iron and steel products covered by the Treaty establishing the ECSC, originating in third countries*, O.J. 5 May 1977, No. L 114/15.

[v] *Commission Recommendation of 15 April 1977 relating to protection against imports which constitute or threaten to constitute a serious danger to production in the common market of similar or directly competitive products*, O.J. 5 May, 1977, No. L 114/4.

[w] This follows because the final Paragraph of Article 74 limits action under Paragraph 3 to the conditions set forth in Article 58, which is by its terms applicable only in a period of "manifest crisis." The effect of the Commission's Recommendation, it appears, was to lay the foundation, on a contingency basis, of the exercise of the powers granted in Article 58.

[x] *Commission recommendation of 15 April 1977 on protection against dumping or the granting of bounties or subsidies by countries which are not members of the European Coal and Steel Community*, O.J. 5 May, 1977, No. L. 114/6.

[y] EEC Regulation No. 459/68 of April 5, 1968, O.J. 17 April 1968 No. L 93/1, as amended by Regulation No. 2011/73 of July 24, 1973, O.J. 17 July, 1973 No. L 206/3.

be imposed only upon findings both of sales at less than normal value and of injury; dumping was defined (with the usual alternatives[z]) as sales for export at less than home market prices; evaluation of injury must be based on "all factors having a bearing on the state of the industry in question," and there must be a link between the dumping and the injury, as contrasted with "all other factors which individually or in combination may be adversely affecting the community industry," including competition between Community producers themselves, contraction in demand due to substitution of other products, or to changes in consumer tastes. No provision was included at this time comparable to the 1974 amendment to the United States Antidumping Act,[a] whereby cost of production of the imported product could be substituted for home market sales as the basis for comparison with the price at which the product was imported. But the antidumping and countervailing duty rules put forward as part of the Davignon Plan would for the first time bring Community-wide procedures and decision-making by the Commission to bear on imports of coal and steel.

The combination of price fixing—mandatory and voluntary—increased surveillance of imports, and coordinated responses to potential dumping and market disruption were not universally popular within the Community, and indeed there were dissents in all three bodies that passed on the measures—the Consultative Committee, the Commission, and the Council of Ministers. In general, the industries and government representatives of France, Belgium and Luxembourg supported the Davignon Plan fully; the Germans were nervous about price fixing, even on one product line, although German steel factories at that time were operating with the most idle capacity; Italian producers (especially the "Bresciani")[b] thought that the prices for reinforcing bars had been set too high, and would deprive them of their competitive edge in southern France; and the British thought the prices set by the Commission were too low, and would tend to drive down their own internal prices.[c] Im-

---

[z] § 4.41(c) *supra.*

[a] § 205(b) of the Trade Act of 1974, Documents Supplement p. DS-433, discussed in § 6.12 *supra* at N. s.

[b] See § 6.44 *infra.*

[c] Viscount Davignon, it was reported, replied to the British objection that if account were taken of the various discounts and rebates offered by British Steel, the differences between its prices and the new minimum and target prices would disappear. Moreover he pointed out that the English Channel still offered a margin of protection for Britain's steel industry, as sea transport added about £25 per ton to the cost of steel. *European Report* p. X, May 5, 1977.

porters of steel were not reassured that the system of import licenses would long remain "for information only," and they feared that today's reference prices would be tomorrow's mandatory minimum prices. But all of the relevant institutions of the Community approved the Plan, and the member states promised their cooperation. Viscount Davignon summarized his purpose to the European Parliament as follows:

The Commission's action is guided by three principles:

1. The problem of the steel industry is in the first instance one that concerns the job of one in seven of the 700,000 workers in the industry. This social problem by its very magnitude constitutes a political problem. It is all the more political because it is precisely the old established industrialized regions in the heart of the Community which are affected this time. There can therefore be no acceptable plan for the steel industry which does not embody a solution to the problem of employment.

2. The steel industry is a key factor in our independence; Europe cannot therefore allow responsibility for its steel supplies to pass outside the Community for the sake of the international division of labour.

However, there are two things which the EEC cannot do:

(a) Isolate its market by protectionist measures; if one depends on outside sources for 75% of one's supplies of raw materials and energy, one must be able to export finished products, which means that an outward-looking attitude must be reciprocal.

Moreover, the problem of steel imports is not a quantitative one (10%). It is a problem of prices and . . . . this is the area in which the Commission's plan will take effect.

(b) Ensure that the steel industry remains competitive by means of public subsidies, for which none of the Member States has the resources and which the EEC does not want because they would jeopardize the unity of the market.

Protectionism on the one hand and the artificial maintenance of the steel industry by public subsidies on the other hand would create difficulties for industries further on in the processing chain, whose raw materials would be too dear, and would impose unacceptable financial burdens on all our economies. Consequentiy, we must undertake a structural reorganization of the sector in order to guarantee its ability to compete effectively. As there is no question of increasing what are already excessive production capacities, this means that plant modernization must of necessity be accompanied by a reduction in employment in the steel industry, which is only socially and politically acceptable if alternative jobs outside the steel industry are at the same time created in the regions affected by structural reorganization.

Hence: a proper programme of modernization keyed into regional redeployment and retraining of workers.

3. Structural reorganization is the keynote of the policy to be pursued. It is only conceivable within a Community framework which will guarantee its cohesion, and hence minimize its cost, while at the same time safeguarding the essential unity of the market.

Structural reorganization implies and justifies public aid which would not otherwise be acceptable. This aid will come mainly from contributions by the Member States, but the Community, initially by way of funds drawn from the ECSC levy and subsequently by way of its own resources as a whole, will be able and willing to provide a considerable degree of financial support. But public subsidies are not all that is needed.

The market must also make its contribution. This is the purpose of the short term measures which the Commission has decided to take and which can only be justified to the extent that they serve the objectives of structural reorganization and a return to the rule of the market. . . .[d]

Even as the European Commission, under the leadership for this purpose of Viscount Davignon, was attempting to organize, induce and support long-term restructuring of Western Europe's steel industry, current problems continued to absorb the Commission. Demand within the Community seemed to be growing at only 1 per cent per year,

---

[d] "Steel Policy," Summary of Address of Commissioner Davignon to the European Parliament, Strasbourg April 21, 1977, as released by the Community Press Office, IP(77) 105, Brussels 22 April, 1977.

and exports to developing countries and to Europe outside the Community kept declining. Only the United States offered prospects of increased sales by producers in the Community, and there Japanese competition was as strong as ever. Davignon attempted to address both problems simultaneously: The Community steel industry must modernize, to regain its world-competitive position (both abroad and at home); and it must raise current earnings, if necessary by raising prices and restraining imports. At the same time the Commission appreciated (though with differing fervor among the different Commissioners) that increased steel prices meant increased prices for most other goods in the economy.

In its first review of the Davignon Plan in action, the Commission concluded that almost all producers of concrete reinforcing bars had "corrected" their price lists to incorporate the minimum basic prices; as for the indicative or reference prices, the Commission found that after an initial period of adjustment, companies accounting for 90 per cent of total production had undertaken to adhere to the published prices. The Commission decided therefore to continue the program of reference prices, but to increase the price levels by amounts varying between 2.5 and 14.5 per cent, and to add two more products "with technical and commercial links" to items already subject to the crisis plan.[f]

The Commission said:

> The new indicative prices have been set at a level that will help to restore profitability while ensuring that prices within the Community remain below the prices for the domestic market published by the large representative steel companies in Japan and the United States, so that industries farther down the production line can remain competitive.[g]

At the same time the ECSC went forward with its program of modernization loans. The Commission announced in mid-July 1977 that it

---

[e] *How the Crisis Plan for the Steel Industry is Working,* Commission of the European Communities, Press Release IP(77)163, June 28, 1977.

[f] *Communication from the Commission of the ECSC concerning the publication of guidance prices for certain steel products, O.J.* July 22, 1977, No. C. 174/2.

[g] *How the Crisis Plan . . . is Working,* N. e *supra.*

was prepared to provide interest subsidies and rebates in accordance with Article 54 and 56 of the Treaty of Paris for investment projects that were "in line with the general objectives defined for the steel industry. . ." The overriding condition, however, was that the planned investments "do not entail any overall increase in production capacities and help to achieve the aim of improving competitiveness." The Commission announced that the maximum amount of a rebated loan was 20,000 European Units of Account (about $24,000) per job created in new activities, up to 40 per cent of fixed investment.[h] For approved loans, 3 percentage points of interest would be rebated for the first five years. Firms benefiting from the loans must give priority to former ECSC workers.[i]

In the fall of 1977, even as President Carter's task force was seeking to develop a plan to meet the crisis in the United States steel industry, Commissioner Davignon traveled to Washington to talk with Ambassador Strauss and Under Secretary Solomon. The community was concerned about the many antidumping complaints filed by United States firms (p. 255 *supra*) and it was also anxious that any minimum prices for imports that might be set by the United States not be so high as to exclude imports from Europe. Both American and European officials were concerned that their unilateral measures not be misinterpreted as a departure from the principles of the GATT, at the same time as each side was thinking about borrowing ideas and devices from the other. Industry leaders in the Community spoke more and more of an international three-way orderly marketing agreement. Davignon, however, cautioned a press conference in Washington against a "three of us against them" strategy.

As 1977 drew to a close the Simonet-Davignon plan was working, in the sense that (except for the Bresciani and reinforcing bars) voluntary target prices and production ceilings were being generally observed.[j] But overall production of steel within the Community was running 20 per cent below forecasts, with the result, as the Commission found that sales even at the higher target prices were no longer sufficient to ensure profits to the producers.

---

[h] Compare the quite similar criteria under Canada's Regional Development Incentives Act, discussed in Vol. II of this series, A. Lowenfeld, *International Private Investment*, Ch. I § 3.6 (2d ed. 1982).

[i] *Community Financial Aid for the Steel Industry,* Commission of the European Communities Press Release IP(77)176, July 14, 1977.

[j] That, at least, was the official version; there was continuous talk within the industry of unreported discounts, rebates, allowances, and the like.

Moreover imports, at prices well below those prevailing (under "guidance") within the Community, were increasing, not from Japan, whose industry, as we saw, had entered into a Voluntary Restraint Agreement, but from Spain and Eastern Europe. In response, the Commission proposed, and after Council assent, implemented another crisis plan, known generally as Davignon II.

6.33—THE DAVIGNON PLAN: PHASE II

The principal new feature of the second crisis plan was that it directly faced the problem of international trade. Though the Community was still a net exporter of steel, it now proposed to curb imports of steel mill products, through a technique similar to that being introduced at just about the same time by the United States. The Commission published a list of minimum or "basic prices" for some 140 products. Imports at prices below those basic prices would be deemed to be dumped, and antidumping measures would be immediately invoked, without any prior inquiry into the question of injury.[k] The basic prices would be derived "by reference to the lowest normal costs in the supplying country or countries where there are normal conditions of competition" (i.e., excluding the state trading countries of Eastern Europe.)[1] In fact, at least at the outset, the "basic prices" were based on calculations of Japanese production costs made by the United States Treasury, adjusted for differentials in transport costs and exchange rates. Making allowance for variation among the many products involved, the "basic prices" averaged about 6-7 per cent below the current minimum and guide prices set by the Commission under Davignon I.

Mr. Davignon said he did not envision permanent import levies for steel such as those applicable to agricultural products.[m] The automatic antidumping duties would be implemented only for such time as it would take—up to three months according to the original forecast—

---

[k] Thus the period between importation and imposition of duties would be made as short as possible, something like the American withholding of appraisement to which the Eurpoeans had earlier objected. The Plan did not exclude subsequent administrative or even judicial challenges.

[1] *Commission Statement concerning basic prices of certain iron and steel products,* O.J. Dec. 31, 1977, No. L 353/1. All of the decisions adopted in December in implementation of the Davignon Plan II appear in O.J. Dec. 31, 1977 No. L 352. The provisions concerning "basic prices" for imports appear in Commission Decision No. 3004/77 ECSC of Dec. 28, 1977, O.J. Dec. 31, 1977 No. L 352/13.

[m] See § 3.25(b) *supra.*

to negotiate a series of bilateral agreements with countries that exported steel to the Community. The idea was that the exporting countries would agree, as a condition for a lifting (or non-imposition) of the antidumping duties to adapt their sales to the undertakings given by producers within the Community, both with respect to tonnage and with respect to price.[n] The inducement to the foreign producing countries would be permission to bring in steel at a "penetration margin" of 7 per cent below the ECSC guide prices. Since the producers within the Community would be prohibited from aligning their prices with those of imports coming in under such agreements, producers from countries signing on would be getting, in effect, a guaranteed outlet for their steel products. For its part, the Community would be getting a guarantee that the exporting countries' producers would not ship more than the agreed amount into the Community, and (at least by inference) that these countries would not bring or support a complaint in the GATT.

With this program of partial insulation from external forces, the ECSC proposed to raise the internal guide prices by 15 per cent in three installments. Moreover, the mandatory minimum prices, previously applicable only to concrete reinforcing bars were made applicable also to merchant bars and hot rolled coils, bringing the total of products subject to mandatory price control up to about 30 per cent of total steel production in the Community.[o] Enforcement measures were strengthened at various levels, both by requiring dealers, as well as manufacturers, to report all their transactions, and by a reinforced customs service for each of the member countries.

Davignon II was soon put into effect. Even as bilateral negotiations with countries exporting steel to the Community were being launched, the Commission imposed countervailing and temporary antidumping duties under its accelerated procedures against six categories of steel products. The duties were imposed against three East European coun-

---

[n] The countries in question were Japan, whose producers already were parties to a voluntary restraint agreement, South Korea, South Africa, Brazil and Spain; Romania, Poland, Hungary, Bulgaria, and Czechoslovakia; and Sweden, Norway, Finland, Ireland, Portugal, Austria and Switzerland—that is the surviving members of the European Free Trade Association.

[o] *Commission Decision No. 3000/77/ECSC of 28 Dec. 1977 fixing minimum prices for hot-rolled wire strips, merchant bars and concrete reinforcing bars*, O.J. Dec. 31, 1977 No. L 352/1.

tries, against Spain, Canada and South Korea, and against Japan.[p] Only members of the European Free Trade Association were left out. While there were complaints about lower priced imports from those countries also, all the EFTA countries except Switzerland[q] had previously agreed to apply the same steel reference prices as those in effect within the ECSC, as part of the continuing free trade arrangements between the Community and EFTA. If the EFTA countries were now to be hit with ''fast-track'' special duties, chances for cooperation—in steel and other sectors—between EFTA and the European Community would quickly erode.[r]

In fact, agreement with the EFTA countries was soon reached. Member countries would limit their exports to the Community to "traditional levels"—i.e. they would promise not to increase the level of their exports to the Community or their share of the market. In return, EFTA steel was to enjoy a 3 per cent ''margin of competitivity'' in comparison with the prices promulgated by the Commission for internal producers.[s] The margin, so the argument went, was sufficient to keep foreign steel competitive with the domestic (Community) products.[t] For the time being, the new antidumping procedures would not be applied.

Negotiations with Japan took somewhat longer, but by early March 1978 a deal was made with that country as well. Japanese and European producers, as we saw, had concluded a voluntary restraint arrangement in 1976 for a 1.25 million ton import ceiling.[u] Now the Community and the Japanese government signed an agreement whereby

---

[p] See e.g., *Commission Recommendation No. 161/78/ECSC of Jan. 27, 1978 imposing a provisional antidumping duty on certain sheets and plates of iron or steel, originating in Japan*. O.J. Jan. 28, 1978 No. L. 23/35.

[q] I.e., Austria, Finland, Norway, Portugal and Sweden.

[r] Reports from Brussels indicated that Viscount Davignon, the Commissioner of Industry Affairs, wanted to impose antidumping duties against imports from Sweden, but that the Foreign Affairs and Legal Departments vetoed the proposal. See *Europe* Jan. 25, 1978, p. 8.

[s] Commission of the European Communities, Press Release IP(78)64, March 20, 1978.

[t] Compare the similar rule of thumb (but with a wider margin) thought to apply between United States and overseas steel, p. 239, N. b *supra*.

[u] See § 5.57(a) *supra*.

Japanese products could come in at 6 per cent below the basic prices set by the Community (4 per cent for specialty steels), but at a volume 9 per cent below 1976 shipments.[v] A similar agreement was negotiated in April with the Republic of South Africa—again with a 6 and 4 per cent penetration margin on price and a volume ceiling 9 per cent below deliveries in 1976.

By the end of April the Commission stated that the special anti-dumping measures announced in December had been suspended for imports from all countries with which bilateral agreements had been signed—the EFTA countries, South Africa, Japan, and Czecho-slovakia.[w] For imports from countries which had not yet concluded bilateral agreements but with which negotiations were in progress—notably Spain, the provisional antidumping duties were to be extended for a further three months.[x] For products of countries with which no agreement was in prospect, the provisional antidumping duties were to be made definitive, on the basis of the differential between the import price and the basic prices published by the Commission.[y] Spain quickly got the message and signed on.[z] So, within a few weeks, did Hungary, and nearly all the remaining hold-outs. By the beginning of May 1978, only Australia among non-Communist steel exporters to the Community had not been brought into line,[a] a fact that led Mr. Davignon to express his astonishment, and the Commission to formally

---

[v] See O.J. April 8, 1978, No. L 94/21; O.J. July 22, 1978, No. L 198/1.

[w] The suspension applied to all pending cases. Where antidumping duties had already been imposed (notably for sheet and plate products from Japan), the Commission said the duties would be continued for three more months, and then lifted.

[x] European Commission Press Release IP(78)89, April 21, 1978; *Commission Recommendation No. 843/78 ECSC of April 25, 1978, Extending the Provisional Antidumping Measures Established in Relation to Imports of Steel Products Originating in Spain,* O.J. April 27, 1978, No. L 115/37.

[y] *Commission Recommendation No. 811/78/ ECSC of April 21, 1978, imposing a definitive antidumping duty on certain sheets and plates of iron and steel originating in Bulgaria, the German Democratic Republic, and Rumania.* O.J. April 22, 1978, No. L 108/26.

[z] See *Commission Recommendation No. 931/78, ECSC of April 28, 1978, providing for suspension of antidumping duties established in relation to imports of steel products originating in Spain,* O.J. May 5, 1978 No. L 120/21. See also O.J. May 11, 1978, No. C, 110/8–10; O.J. July 27, 1978, No. L 203/28.

[a] Accordingly the provisional antidumping measures established in relation to imports of steel products from Australia were extended, Commission Recommendation No. 971/78/ECSC of May 11, 1978, O.J. May 13, 1978, No. L 125/20.

express its disappointment in a letter to the Australian government.[b] But Australia eventually came around as well, as did Romania.[c]

Throughout the year 1978, the Commission was busy revising production targets, "basic," "guidance," and minimum price levels, and future forecasts. Enforcement, both of price and of production limits, became more complicated and more stringent; five firms, including the giant French firm of USINOR, were fined a total of over $200,000 for violations of various aspects of the Davignon Plan.[d] Putting aside variations in different products, the Community's efforts to raise prices seemed to have worked.[e] But while foreign competition could be curbed and domestic production limited, it was not possible to create demand. By autumn 1978, the steel industry of the ECSC was still operating at less that 65 per cent of capacity, compared with 85–90 per cent for the United States. Layoffs continued, and so did losses. In October the French government, having survived a major electoral challenge from the left, carried out a massive "restructuring" of France's steel industry, the effect of which was to put the government (as owner of the major banks) in control of management.[f] In November, Belgium announced that its two largest steel

---

[b] See *Europe*, May 4, 1978, p. 7.

[c] See O.J. July 22, 1978, No. L 198/4; O.J. Aug. 2, 1978, No. C 184/2.; O.J. June 9, 1978, No. L 153/19.

[d] Commission Decision of May 30, 1978, O.J. June 7, 1978, No. C 133/4. The Commission also approved a system of mandatory deposits of cash by firms pending conclusion of investigations by the Commission of possible violation of the Common Steel Policy; if a fine were found to be payable, it would be collected from the funds deposited and the rest returned to the company. See Commission Decision No. 1525/78/ECSC of 30 June, 1978, O.J. July 1, 1978, No. L 178/90, amended and extended for two months by Commission Decision No. 2292/78/ECSC of 29 Sept. 1978, O.J. Sept. 30, 1978, No. L 275/90. The deposit scheme was not renewed after November 1978.

[e] Mr. Davignon reported to the Council of Ministers in November 1978 that minimum prices had been increased by 12 per cent since they were first imposed in December 1977; actual prices obtained in the market had increased by 20–22 per cent over the same period. The Commission did not, therefore, implement in the fall of 1978 the final 5 per cent of its projected increase in the minimum price for reinforcing bars, leaving open the possibility of doing so early in 1979.

[f] The details of this program go beyond the scope of this volume but they are interesting. In brief, debt was converted into equity, with the result that the banks became the principal shareholders of the big three steel companies and appointed new management. The government declared that the restructuring did not amount to nationalization (as in England a decade earlier), because the original equity holders would be protected, and no compensation would be due or paid to them.

enterprises would be nationalized. Thus by year end, steel in Britain, France, Italy and Belgium, accounting for about half of the Community's total production, was in one way or another under direct government control. The Commission voiced its concern that countries might be pulling in separate directions (i.e., seeking to keep their own labor employed rather than cutting back production in accordance with the plan.) As the original time table for the crisis plan (one year) was coming to an end, Mr. Davignon told the Community that enforcement would be stricter in 1979, and that greater attention would be paid to restructuring, that is to closing down obsolete plants and erecting new ones. Davignon requested renewal of all the authorities given to the Commission in 1977 (plus a doubling of the ECSC's operating budget).[g] The Council did not accede to the Commission's budget request, and debated all aspects of the Community Steel Policy at two lengthy sessions, one in November, the other in December. But after more than twenty hours of debate, the Council agreed to extend the Davignon Plan, at least for another year.[h]

§ 6.4—Notes and Questions on the Davignon Plan

6.41—(a) Compare the Davignon Plan to the American Trigger Price Mechanism. In some ways, as we saw, the two plans are alike, in that both make use of minimum prices and that imports below those prices subject the goods to antidumping measures on a fast track procedure. But the TPM was the principal feature of the United States government's program to aid the American steel industry, which was otherwise largely left alone. In the Coal and Steel Community, by contrast, the list of "basic prices" for imports was an

---

For the allegation that those measures amounted to subsidization of exports entitling U.S. domestic producers to seek countervailing duties, see § 8.63(e) *infra*.

[g] Apart from an acrimonious dispute about the amount of the ECSC budget— 32 versus 64 million European Units of Account (roughly 40 versus 80 million dollars) the debate over the budget revealed an interesting dispute about how to meet the budget. The Commission and most member states favored an assessment based on the members' GNP in 1976; France, which imported relatively little steel, insisted on an assessment based on customs collection in the steel sector. At year-end, this dispute had not been resolved.

[h] *Commission Decision No. 3139/78/ECSC of Dec. 29, 1978, fixing minimum prices for hot-rolled wide strip, merchant bars, and concrete reinforcing bars*, O.J. Dec. 30, 1978, No. C 370/79.

adjunct of a much more comprehensive plan, including minimum prices (mandatory and voluntary), production restraints, and investment targets. Viewed from the vantage point of international trade policy and law, does this make one plan more attractive (or less unattractive) than the other?

(b) The ECSC attempted throughout 1977-78 to raise the prices received by its steel producers, as a way to make up for declining demand. The United States government, on the other hand, attempted to discourage domestic price increases, in part to preserve the domestic share of the market, in part because steel prices were an important ingredient of the overall movement of prices in an inflationary period. As we saw, there was at least a hint of a link between domestic price discipline and the level at which the TPM was set. Again looking at the two plans from a world perspective, is an attempt to raise prices different from an attempt to hold prices down? Or do both plans stand or fall by the same criteria?

(c) The United States government made no attempt to negotiate government-to-government agreements, as it had done with respect to footwear, textiles, television receivers, and other products in the past. In contrast, the European Community used the "basic import prices" and antidumping proceedings linked to these prices to secure bilateral restraint agreements, so that by mid-1978 the external aspect of the Davignon Plan looked less like the American TPM and more like a hub-and-spoke market sharing arrangement.

6.42—Assuming you accept the principle of reference prices for steel made and sold locally (i.e., within the Community), how should the prices be set?

(a) Given the wide variation in location, age, efficiency and profitability of the steel mills in the Community, is the aim to set prices at a level that will enable the least efficient to survive, the most efficient to prosper? Or should prices be set so as to eliminate the weak, thereby strengthening the survivors?

(b) Should there be a target rate of return? Allocation of markets? Differentiation between "old steel" and "new steel?"[a]

---

[a] Compare the many similar problems faced in the United States in the late 1970's with respect to oil.

6.43—(a) While the European Commission was attempting to align prices, demand, and production through "forward programmes," reference prices, and the like, the manufacturers themselves were establishing a producers association known formally as the European Confederation of Iron and Steel Industries and colloquially as "Euro-fer." Eurofer took the place of an informal "steel club" that had been functioning for some time as a forum for the major firms to talk with one another and to develop positions vis-à-vis the Commission. The Commissioners for Industry Affairs, first Simonet and then Davignon, regarded Eurofer as a useful ally, both in the formulation of internal Community policies and in dealing with outsiders, particularly the Japanese. The Commissioners in charge of competition policy were not so sure. Would you expect that once the Commission begins to interfere with the market to the extent undertaken in the Simonet and Davignon plans, antitrust considerations are inevitably subordinated?

(b) Would you have the same concerns about what happens to basic principles of international trade?

(c) Though Messrs. Simonet and Davignon seem not to have been plagued by doubts as they developed their plans for steel in 1976-78, the Common Market as a whole was indeed troubled by questions such as those suggested in the preceding paragraphs. The West German Minister of the Economy, Count Lambsdorff, for example, submitted a memorandum to the Council of Ministers in May 1978 sharply critical of the "activist," "dirigiste" attitude of the Commission:

> Discussion of specifically sectoral solutions for individual industries is on the increase in the face of only slow economic growth and major employment problems. The German government has not been opposed to such solutions in justified exceptional cases such as steel and textiles. But any cumulation of sectoral interventions of this type would seriously alter the whole economy's effectiveness. Consequently such intervention should not be extended beyond a strict minimum, particularly as many sectoral problems are not of a structural by a cyclical nature. . . .

> The most important stimulus for adjustment of outdated structures is competition in the market. Without it the impetus for technical progress would be reduced and this would jeopardise the Community's competitivity. . . .

Competition should not be restricted by marketing agreements. On the contrary it should be strengthened by the addition of new firms. Experience has also shown in many cases that because of the rationalisation effect they aim to achieve, mergers often increase rather than reduce the employment risk in the medium and long term. Moreover small and medium-size businesses adapt more readily to change structures than large ones.

On the Community level there is the additional central task of guaranteeing free movement of goods and the elimination of the barriers which still exist between Member States. . . .

In the international framework the degree of liberalisation in international trade must be maintained and expanded. A successful outcome to the trade negotiations in GATT will strengthen confidence in the workability of the free international economic system and thus become an important stimulus for growth. But for this to be achieved it is essential that the comprehensive solutions on tariff and non-tariff measures which are being sought should effectively lead to an improvement in the conditions of international trade. In particular the additional flexibility in application of the safeguard clause by making it more selective must be offset by stricter conditions on intervention and tighter international supervision. . . .

Should it however become necessary in the light of the slow economic growth and the considerable employment problems facing us at present to slow the market-oriented adjustment process for regional or social policy reasons in limited exceptional cases, then specific transitional solutions may be allowed if they provide firms with the help to help themselves and do not prevent the necessary adjustment to different market conditions.

On no account however should one sector after the other be brought into the ambit and regulated. Regulation in the steel sector should not become a model for intervention in other sectors. The Community and the Member States must avoid the whole economy's effectiveness becoming hampered by a cumulation of intervention.[b]

---

[b] Memorandum on EEC Structural Policy submitted by the Government of the Federal Republic of Germany to the Council of Ministers, May 1, 1978, as translated in European Report May 4, 1978, pp. 4–8.

(d) Messrs. Simonet and Davignon, supported generally by the French, Belgian, and British governments, responded that their positions were more pragmatic, less dogmatic than the position exemplified in the Lambsdorff memorandum. They too believed in competition inside and free trade outside, but they recognized the demands of "special situations" and did not regard "laissez faire" as the complete solution to current problems. In a detailed reply to Count Lambsdorff, Viscount Davignon said:

> Although there are those who complain that we do not pursue any coherent industrial policy; those who claim that we have no right to pursue an industrial policy; those who fear that we are surreptitiously, or negligently slipping into a protectionist and interventionist industrial policy; nevertheless our ultimate aim remains to create a prosperous market economy in an increasingly prosperous and freely trading world.

> Although our model might be said to be the large and successful US market, Europe could never be quite like the USA. Many Member States had large colonial responsibilities. These reinforce our general desire to help the poorer countries develop. But these moral impulses apart, Europe has a much greater need than the USA for world development. Their exports, large though they may seem, are marginal. Moreover, in spite of their growing oil imports, the U.S. remains substantially self-sufficient. But Europe is vitally dependent on imported raw materials. It is, therefore, vitally dependent on its substantial exports. It would be the first to suffer from barriers to world trade.

> One of our tactical aims must be to persuade our overseas trading partners to accept the need for some temporary slowing down in their rate of penetration of our markets, to give our economy time to adapt, and to prevent far worse and purely protective reactions by the Member States. Another aim must be to ensure that our economy does adapt in the breathing space that we secure. . . .

> But we must not simply react to our present crises, and let new ones creep up on us. . . . We must create an early warning system. . . . More important, we should not neglect, rather we should concentrate on sectors or sources of growth. There are some sectors, e.g. electronics, that are in clear growth. But there are

also thriving subsectors or even firms throughout industry, even in our crisis sectors. We can do this best, like a gardener, by providing the environment in which those industrial plants that can best thrive in our European climate may best do so.[c]

Is this a long way round back to comparative advantage?

6.44—(a) The effects of price fixing on both internal and external trade can be illustrated by the case of the "Bresciani," small, non-integrated, privately owned producers with "mini-mills" near the city of Brescia, between Milan and Venice in Northern Italy. The Bresciani, as we saw, were unhappy with minimum prices for reinforcing rods, which, they said, deprived them of their competitive advantage and made it impossible for them to recover their investments made in 1974.[d] The Bresciani had lower costs, because they relied principally on scrap for their raw materials, and scrap was down in the late 1970's in Europe as elsewhere. Their electric furnaces, they argued, had higher productivity than blast or basic oxygen furnaces operated by the integrated firms for whose benefit the minimum prices had been set. How should the European Commission respond to this argument?

(b) The Commission could not ignore the Bresciani, as it might have liked to do, because while concrete reinforcing bars accounted for only 8.8 per cent of the Community's steel production, they made up over 20 per cent of Italy's steel output. Apart from being a constant reminder of the inefficiency of older plants, for example in Belgium, Luxembourg and Lorraine (as well as in Italy), the Bresciani proved to be a major enforcement problem, and once even provoked a closure of the customs frontier between France and Italy.

(c) Viscount Davignon's solution was to insist on maintaining the Community price levels, but to offer the Commission's assistance to the Bresciani in disposing of their products outside of the Community. Is this fair?

---

[c] Commissioner Etienne Davignon, Notes for a Speech on "Industrial Policy," The Hague, June 8, 1978 (EC Release June 9, 1978).

[d] The Bresciani contended that 3.5–4 hours of labor in their plants had an output equal to 6 hours in West Germany and as much as 8 hours in the older French plants.

(d) The proposal of Mr. Davignon did not satisfy the Bresciani, who had prospered by remaining outside of the centralized Italian steel enterprise (ITALSIDER) and were not about to play dead in favor of the authorities in Brussels. The Commission kept threatening major penalties under Article 64 of the Treaty of Paris for violating the minimum price schedule, and in the course of 1978 did actually bring a series of enforcement proceedings resulting in substantial penalties. The companies appealed to the European Court of Justice, asking annulment not only of the individual decisions of the Commission imposing fines, but of the basic decision to impose minimum prices on reinforcing bars.[e]

The Bresciani asserted: (i) that they operated modern, integrated mini-steelmills concentrated on a single product and managed by individual families, and thus were able to achieve efficiencies not achieved by the over-aged, mammoth steel works in the Community; (ii) that the Community policy of encouraging inefficient oligopolies and preventing competition would, in the long run (citing Samuelson), prevent the only way of pruning excess and obsolete capacity; (iii) that in setting prices at a level designed to permit un-profitable enterprises to continue in existence, rather than at a level designed to encourage efficient production, the Commission had acted inconsistently with the Treaty of Paris, especially Article 3(c);[f] (iv) that the Commission's decision was inconsistent with Article 3 (f), in that it did not promote the growth of international trade and promoted protectionism by preventing align-ment on non-member prices; and (v) that the decision was inconsistent with statements of Commissioner Davignon concerning the need to close obsolete and unprofitable production units and encourage the free market in steel.

The Commission answered, in essence: (i) that it was necessary to make compromises among the various objectives stated in Article 3 of the Treaty of Paris; (ii) that no rule of the Treaty imposes an obligation to encourage competition at all costs; and (iii) that while it did not intend to harm the Bres-ciani in its decision, the Commission, acting under Article 61 in conditions of manifest crisis, had to take account of all elements of the steel industry in the Community.

Thus the challenge of the Bresciani was in a sense a challenge to the whole Davignon Plan, as well as a test of the authority and willingness of the Court of Justice to review major economic policy decisions of the Community.[g]

---

[e] Commission Decision No. 962/777 of 4 May, 1977, § 6.32 at N. p, *supra*.

[f] Documents Supplement p. DS-107.

[g] Joined Cases 154, 205, 206, 226 to 228, 263 and 264/78 39, 83 85/79, *S.p.A. Ferriera Valsabbia and Others v. Commission of the European Communities* ("Concrete Reinforce-

Putting aside the special constraints on and traditions of the European Court of Justice, how would you think the case should be decided?

(e) The Court of Justice, in a fifty-page decision, held:

(i) the actions challenging the decision of the Commission were admissible, notwithstanding the provision in Article 33 of Paris that "the Court may not review the High Authority's evaluation of the situation based on economic facts and circumstances . . . except where the High Authority is alleged to have abused its powers or to have clearly misinterpreted the . . . Treaty;"

(ii) the formal requirements of consultation and notice in Article 61 were complied with, even though the Bresciani were not represented in the Consultative Committee;

(iii) The Commission was entitled under Article 61 to recognize the existence of a manifest crisis and to take measures in the common interest, even to the detriment of certain individual interests;

(iv) the level of prices fixed by the Commission was not inconsistent with either Article 3(c) or the penultimate paragraph of Article 61; and

(v) Challenges under other provisions of the Treaty of Paris are not relevant to exceptional measures taken under Article 61, which refers only to Article 3.

Thus the challenge to the basic decision failed, as did nearly all the defenses raised by individual defendants to imposition of fines—including "legitimate self-protection," "force majeure," and "necessity."

(f) Suppose reinforcing bars produced by one or more of the Bresciani arrive in the United States at a price below that of the minimum price in the Community. Should the U.S. Treasury automatically find dumping? Or would a showing by the exporter that (i) it wasn't always adhering to the Community price; or (ii) that it was adhering to the reference price only under coercion from the Commission and EUROFER be a good defense? Would a showing that the export price was in excess of the cost of production help the exporter in these circumstances?

6.45—(a) The example of the Bresciani is a special case of a more basic problem, increasingly stressed by the American steel industry. The steel prices set by the Community from 1977 on—whether mandatory or for

---

ment Bars''), [1980] E.C.R. 907 (March 18, 1980). The summary of the arguments in the text (as well as of the decision) omits various points not directly relevant to the discussion here. Overall the report of the arguments, decision of the Court, and opinion of the Advocate General takes up 176 pages in the official report.

"guidance"—were approximately 20 per cent above the prices at which steel was moving in international trade. But at the same time as the ECSC was trying to limit imports and raise internal prices, it was exporting substantial quantities of steel to the rest of the world, notably to the United States. If European steel came in to the United States at or above the American trigger price, the U.S. Treasury took the position that it would not self-initiate antidumping procedures, and would discourage the American steel industry from doing so. The United States industry, for the most part, acquiesced in the Treasury's reliance on the TPM, though it contended (i) that imports from Europe were coming in at less than home market sales prices; and (ii) that since (as a matter of fact and by definition) the triggger price reflected the costs of the low-cost producers in Japan, European sales at the trigger price must be below their average costs of production. Moreover, the American steel industry said, (iii) it was precisely the artificially high prices within the Community that enabled the European steel industry to engage in a long-term program of sales below cost in the United States.[h]   How should the United States government respond?

(b) Is it true that Trigger Price Mechanism combined with the Davignon Plan gives European producers "a license to dump?"[i] That the effect is a misallocation of resources and a greater penetration of the U.S. market than sales by the most efficient producer (i.e., Japan) would by themselves achieve?[j] Should the United States reply by introducing a two-tier trigger price, one for imports from Japan, the other, presumably higher, for imports from Europe?

(c) The United States Treasury did not take this step, and maintained the position that it could not both administer the TPM and process individual dumping complaints brought by the steel industry. But as imports of steel from Europe to the United States increased by more than 20 per cent in 1978 over 1977, even as imports from Japan were declining by 17 per cent—from 40 per cent to 32 per cent of total imports and from 7.2 to 5.7 per cent of total American consumption, both industry and government wondered how long the two plans could be continued on separate tracks.[k]

---

[h] These arguments were presented in various forms, public and private. The data base was collected in a study prepared for the American Iron and Steel Institute, Putnam, Hayes & Bartlett, *The Economic Implications of Foreign Steel Pricing Practices in the U.S. Market,* esp. pp. iii, 21–25 (August 1978).

[i] See *id.* at p. v.

[j] *Id.* at p. 41.

[k] For the continuation of this plot, see § 8.52 *infra.*

6.46—In traditional GATT terms, which provided for restraints on import restrictions and claims by exporting countries, the United States was not directly affected by the Davignon Plan (more precisely by Davignon II), in that American steel producers were not typically exporting in volume to the Community. More generally, however (and in addition to the point made in § 6.45), one might suggest that the United States had an interest—a legal interest—in an open, multilateral trading system. Has the United States given up its right to object to the Davignon Plan by imposing its own TPM?

(b) Should the objective of the United States government be to seek to integrate the European and American interventions in the steel industry? Without Japan such an effort would be doomed to failure. But there were indications all along that Japan was prepared to negotiate something like a division of market agreement, provided the numbers were acceptable. Could any such agreement be squared with (i) the theory of comparative advantage; (ii) the trade law and policy of the United States; (iii) the trade law and policy of the European Common Market; (iv) the General Agreement on Tariffs and Trade?

(c) It is interesting to note, in passing, how Canada reacted to all the new developments in steel. Canada is essentially self-sufficient in steel, and its three principal steel mills, all in Ontario, were operating at close to full capacity in 1977–78. These mills are modern, efficient, and as we saw, were from time to time able to demonstrate to the U.S. Treasury that their costs were below the trigger prices established with reference to Japanese production. Nevertheless, Canada established its own benchmark price system shortly after introduction of the American and European plans.[1] The idea was to forestall any diversion of low-price steel from markets in the United States or the European Community to Canada. Customs officers were directed to report all steel imports to a special steel task force in Ottawa; if increased imports at prices below the benchmarks were disclosed, an accelerated antidumping proceeding would be undertaken, looking to provisional antidumping duties within a three month period, and in some instances, retroactive application of such duties. The benchmark prices were derived from the American trigger price and the European basic price, adjusted for transport and exchange rate variations.

6.47—(a) As early as May 1977, the Council of the Organization for Economic Cooperation and Development—that is, the organization of the

---

[1] See Revenue Canada, Customs and Exercise, Communique of Feb. 20, 1978.

industrialized non-communist countries—discussed possible arrangements for consultation on the problems of steel. The OECD's secretariat prepared a substantial statistical and analytical study in June 1977,[m] and in September an Ad Hoc Steel Group was created, consisting of government officials at the "export level." This group, like the OECD generally, had no regulatory powers, but the government representatives could exchange and standardize information, analyses, and issue statements, at least for the record, that "efforts to shift the burden of adjustment from one producing nation to another must be avoided in both the short and longer terms."[n]

By November 1978, even as the Multilateral Trade Negotiations were reaching their climax (§ 7 *infra*), the major steel producers decided to turn the Ad Hoc Committee into something more than a forum for exchange of information. Acting by formal Council decision, the member countries of the OECD established a standing Steel Committee, complete with a kind of charter and a mandate to seek both short and long term solutions.[o]

(b) As this volume went to press, it was too early to tell whether the OECD could be used as a regulatory forum—which would be a new departure for the organization, or as a negotiating forum—which had worked on and off in the monetary field. But evidently creation of the Steel Committee was a signal that whatever the countries might eventually decide with respect to steel, they wanted to be free from the constraints of the GATT; conversely, perhaps equally important, they wanted to be able to address the steel problem without the concern that their every move would be seen to set a precedent applicable to every other sort of product. If this was indeed the motivation behind the creation of the Steel Committee in the OECD, is it justified? Can steel, for this purpose, be equated to agriculture, or fishing, or nuclear energy, or other commodities that by gradual consensus have been exempted from normal GATT rules?[p]

---

[m] OBCD Council, *The Situation in the Iron and Steel Industry* OBCD Doc. No. C(77) 104 (7 June 1977).

[n] Conclusions adopted by the Ad Hoc Steel Group Dec. 1, 1977, quoted in Bulletin of the European Communities December 1977, ¶ 2.2.46.

[o] Documents Supplement p. DS-617. Mr. Alan Wolff, the Deputy Special Representative for Trade Negotiations of the United States, was elected the first chairman of the OECD *Committee*.

[p] Another motive for moving steel to the OECD might be thought to be the possibility of addressing the steel question without the participation of the developing countries. If that motive was present, however, it was well disguised. See e.g., Article 2(a)(iii), Documents Supplement p. DS-618.

§ 7—The Multilateral Trade Negotiations (1973–79)

§ 7.1—Toward New Trade Negotiations[a]

7.11—A CHANGING MOOD

By the mid-1970's, as the preceding chapters on the steel industry illustrate, the perceptions and the realities of international trade had changed substantially from those of the mid-1960's. The most obvious changes, of course, had been the collapse of the Bretton Woods arrangements for the international monetary system (1971–73), and the rise to dominant power of the OPEC oil cartel (1973–74). Both of these events were in some measure caused by the decline in the preeminent role of the United States in the world economy; in even greater measure they emphasized and accelerated that decline. The United States was still the biggest producer, the biggest market, even the major law-giver. In the trade field, international negotiations still depended on the negotiating authority granted to the executive branch by the United States Congress. But the agenda was more crowded, the objectives more complex, and the negotiating partners more evenly matched than ever. Not only had the European Community survived its internal crises and external expansion, but Japan seemed finally ready to take its place at the negotiating table, as it already had in the marketplaces of the world.

One may also observe, at least in retrospect, a certain lessening of optimism, and recurring anxiety among the populations of the major industrial powers, more concern with job security and equity in distribution, less with efficiency and economic growth.[b] These concerns seemed to grow after the shock waves of the oil crisis of 1973–74, the recession of 1974–75, and the inflation of the late 1970's, which (contrary to earlier doctrine) did not seem

---

[a] In contrast to the discussion of the Kennedy Round (§ 3.7 *supra*), which benefited from two full-length books by participants, a variety of articles, and a decade to reflect on what was and what was not important, most of this section was written before the negotiations had even been concluded. Among the writings drawn on, mention may be made of S. Golt, *The GATT Negotiations, 1973–75: A Guide to the Issues,* (British North American Committee 1974); S. Golt, *The GATT Negotiations 1973–79: The Closing Stage* (British North American Committee 1978); Alan Wm. Wolff, "The U.S. Mandate for Trade Negotiations," 16 Va. J. Int'l L. 505 (1976); Thomas B. Graham, "Reforming the International Trading System: The Tokyo Round Trade Negotiations in the Final Stage," 12 Cornell Int'l L. J. 1 (1979); and the *Twenty-Second Annual Report of the United States in the Trade Agreements Program*—1977, pp. 15–26 (1978).

[b] For development of these themes, see M. vN. Whitman, "A Year of Travail: The United States and the International Economy." 57 Foreign Affairs 527, 545–47 (1979).

to abate even as unemployment spread. Perhaps the emphasis on security and distribution, as contrasted with growth, was strongest in England; it was prevalent throughout the industrial world, however, especially among persons associated with particular industries, such as textiles, footwear, shipbuilding, steel, and later automobiles, in which reduced demand and increased foreign trade seemed to come hand in hand. It wasn't that there was a major move to renounce the doctrine of comparative advantage; but somehow resistance seemed to stiffen throughout Europe and North America to the adjustment that is at the heart of the doctrine—Patrian table-makers learning to make lamps, in our original example.[c]

7.12—THE AGENDA

After the reductions negotiated in the Kennedy Round had been fully carried through in 1972, tariffs (except on particular products) were no longer perceived as the major impediment to trade that they had once been. A variety of other impediments, lumped together under the name of non-tariff barriers (NTB'S) drew the attention of trade negotiators and their respective constituencies. Some of these NTB's were based on formal statutory constraints, such as "buy national" laws for government procurement;[d] some were less visible governmental practices such as subsidies of various kinds; some had grown up as health or safety standards, but with no attempt at harmonization; some were not reflected in law at all but were nevertheless real, such as market resistance to imports, inspired or condoned by governments.[e] By the early 1970's, it was realized in the international trade community that if the gains of the Kennedy Round were not to be dissipated, some consensus on definition and reduction of NTB's would have to be reached in the next round of trade negotiations. Agreement to hold such negotiations was reached—at least in general terms—at a Joint Declaration between the EEC and the United States of February 1972.[f]

---

[c] See pp. 3–5 *supra*.

[d] See, e.g. the Buy American Act, 41 U.S.C. § 10a– 10d; Exec. Order No. 10,582 of Dec. 17, 1954, 3 C.F.R. 230 (1954–58). For a brief survey of comparable laws or practice by members of the EEC, EFTA, Canada and Japan, see Exec. Branch GATT Study No. 5, "Discriminatory Government Policies" Sen. Comm. on Finance, 93rd Cong., 1st Sess. (Comm. Print 1973).

[e] This charge, as we saw (§ 3.33 *supra*), was frequently leveled at Japan.

[f] U.S.-European Community Declaration to the Director General of GATT, signed at Brussels, Feb. 11, 1972, 66 Dep't State Bull. 515 (1972).

The United States Congress (on this point accepting almost verbatim the Administration's draft) had written into the Trade Act of 1974 the finding "that barriers to (and other distortions of) international trade are reducing the growth of foreign markets for the products of [the] United States . . . , diminishing the intended mutual benefits of reciprocal trade concessions, and preventing the development of open and non-discriminatory trade among nations," and had urged the President to "take all appropriate and feasible steps within his power . . . to harmonize, reduce, or eliminate such barriers to (and other distortions of) international trade."[g] The Council of the European Communities had adopted an "Overall Approach" to the forthcoming negotiations in the summer of 1973 in which a whole chapter was devoted to NTB's, looking to "broad spread of solutions . . . to make up a worthwhile and well-balanced package."[h] The expectation then, was that the new round of trade talks would be different from prior rounds, in that there would be more attention to rules, codes, possibly to means for dispute settlement, and that tariffs were only one among several subjects before the negotiators. Just how these "new" subjects would be addressed, how in particular reciprocity could be achieved (or fairly dispensed with) was far from clear.

It had originally been hoped that the U.S. Congress would adopt the new and expanded trade legislation in the same year that it was submitted, 1973. With this in mind, the Ministers of the GATT Contracting Parties met in Tokyo in September 1973 to lay the groundwork for the next round of trade negotiations. In the Declaration issued at the close of the Tokyo Conference,[i] the Ministers said that "they intend that the trade negotiations be concluded in 1975."[j] But the United States legislation did not get enacted until the last days of 1974, largely for reasons unrelated to the GATT negotiations.[k]

---

[g] Trade Act of 1974 § 102(a).

[h] Overall Approach to Trade of the European Community, Bull. of European Communities 6–1973 No. 2437 (June 1973); CCH Common Market Reptr. 1973–75 Transfer Binder ¶ 9588.

[i] Documents Supplement p. DS-660.

[j] Id. paragraph 11.

[k] The principal hurdle was the Administration's proposal to grant MFN treatment to the U.S.S.R., in implementation of the Trade Agreement between the United States and the Soviet Union of October 1972. Congress sought to link MFN to liberalization of the policies of the Soviet Union, especially with respect to emigration. For the arguments and outcome of that controversy, see Volume III of this series, A. Lowenfeld, *Trade Controls for Political Ends*, Chapter II, § 3 (2d ed. 1983).

Equally serious, the years 1973–75 were the years when the European Community was attempting to work out the details of entry by Great Britain, Ireland and Denmark, which proved harder (especially with respect to agriculture) than anticipated, and thus the Community was not in position to work out a meaningful mandate for the Multilateral Trade Negotiations. These two restraints, plus the oil crisis, the effort at monetary reform, and the serious world-wide recession of 1974–75, and not least the Watergate crisis in the United States, combined to delay the effective start of the MTN by two years. Even 1975, by which time the Community had a negotiating mandate and the United States a statute, saw little progress. The next year was an election year in the United States, and while there was some discussion in the campaign of trade issues (including apparently various commitments to industries and unions), everyone agreed it would be a bad time for serious negotiations.

The GATT secretariat did its best to prevent the Tokyo Round from "languishing into irrelevance," as its Director General put it,[1] by establishing six groups at the technical level—on tariffs, non-tariff measures, agriculture, safeguards, sectoral talks, and tropical products. These working groups, plus a seventh one created late in 1976 on the "framework" of the agreement (meaning for the most part how to accommodate the interests of the developing countries), produced important staff work —the intellectual underpinning of an increasingly complex endeavor. Negotiations, however, did not really begin until after the Carter Administration was installed early in 1977, and Robert Strauss, the former chairman of the Democratic National Committee and a consummate negotiator, was appointed Special Representative for Trade Negotiations. In July 1977 Strauss proposed, and the others accepted, a timetable for the negotiations looking to December 15, 1977 as the target for agreement on a series of codes of conduct and on a "working hypothesis" of a gen-

---

The Nixon Administration, knowing that the East-West trade questions would be controversial, thought it could piggy-back them on the less controversial proposals for trade among non-communist countries. The judgment was half-right: the legislation concerning trade other than with communist countries—though controversial in many details—encountered less resistance than did the East-West trade provisions; but instead of the traditional trade bill carrying along the sections dealing with Communist countries, the latter dragged down and delayed the former.

In addition, of course, the period of consideration of the Trade Bill by the U.S. Congress—April 1973–December 1974—was the period of the Watergate crisis, the resignation of the President, and the effort of President Ford to rebuild the executive branch.

[1] See Olivier Long, "International Trade under Threat: a Constructive Response," 1 The World Economy 251 (1978).

eral formula for tariff-cutting:[m] by January 15, 1978 the major participants were to make their offers of tariff reductions based on that formula as well as proposals regarding agriculture; the whole negotiation
was to be concluded not later than July 15, 1978. Though this schedule,
too, proved to be unattainable, it constituted a definition of the task
(as well as a reminder of the expiration of the United States' negotiating
authority in January 1980) that thereafter governed the progress of the
MTN.

§ 7.2—The Issues

7.21—"SAFEGUARDS"

By 1977, if not by 1973, the most important issue, it seemed, was "market
disruption," the sudden and massive surge in the levels of imports of particular products. When the General Agreement had been written in the 1940's,
this topic had been included in Article XIX, which makes provision for escape
clause actions. That article, it will be recalled (§ 2.33(6)), permitted countries to suspend an obligation or withdraw a concession if "as a result of
unforeseen developments" imports of a product caused or threatened serious
injury to domestic producers of a like product. Article XIX permitted unilateral
action if necessary, but subject to a requirement of prior notification and of
consultation with affected states. Consultation could result in agreement on
compensation by the state taking the escape clause action or in withdrawal
of an equivalent concession by the country affected. In fact, however, this
scenario rarely took place, though both the phenomenon of market disruption (postponing for the moment the definition of that term) and governmental responses thereto were becoming fairly common.

When countries took unilateral action to restrain imports, they increasingly preferred not to notify and consult under Article XIX but
simply to act and wait for initiation of a complaint under Article XXIII—
which often did not come and would in any event take a long time to run
its course. Orderly marketing agreements, voluntary restraint arrangements, and the like were being construed by the parties concerned as not
subject to the GATT at all, because (i) they were voluntary; or (ii) they
contained an express release of GATT obligations; or (iii) they were

---

[m] For an explanation of the formula, see § 7.41(e) N. i *infra*.

focused on exports, not imports.[a] As we saw, none of the various steel arrangements entered into by the United States, the European Community and Japan became subject of GATT proceedings, nor did similar arrangements with regard to footwear or television receivers. The GATT did, as an organization, embrace restraints on textile trade, but only to prevent discrimination and too obvious departure from the code, not to apply the body of rules drafted in the 1940's. Meanwhile the crises in steel, as well as in textiles, shipbuilding, footwear, consumer electronics, and (especially in England) automobiles, persisted, as did Japan's export surplus and apprehension about "new Japans" (South Korea, Hong Kong, Singapore, perhaps also Brazil).

By the late 1970's there was, on the one hand, widespread doubt about the continued viability of the traditional GATT system; and on the other hand, growing fear of unilateral, unsupervised protectionism.[b] Moreover, the huge and unplanned-for expenditures for imports of oil led everywhere to export drives and, as we saw, to a variety of charges of unfair trade practices and new and old types of defensive measures. The Director General of the GATT spoke of "international trade under threat," estimating that at the beginning of 1978 some $100 billion in world trade, roughly ten per cent of the total, was under restrictions imposed in the preceding three years, at least philosophically (and often technically as well) in contravention to the principles of the GATT.[c] And this figure did not count earlier but continuing restrictions, affecting roughly another ten per cent of world trade, including trade in temperate agricultural products which had never fully come under the rules of the GATT.

How to distinguish market disruption—exceptional and temporary—from longer term shifts in the elements of comparative advantage was,

---

[a] Professor Hudec, in his book on the breakdown of the GATT legal system, said of the United States defense of VRA's: "The cynical defense was taken for what it was—a declaration of independence from GATT in these matters." R. Hudec, *The GATT Legal System and World Trade Diplomacy*, p. 213 (1975).

[b] For evidence of the latter among the major international economic organizations, see, e.g. Blackhurst, Marian, and Tumlir, *Trade Liberalization, Protectionism and Interdependence* (GATT Studies in International Trade No. 5, 1977); Nowzad, *The Rise in Protectionism* (IMF Pamphlet Series, No. 24, 1978).

[c] Long, § 7.12 N. 1 *supra* at 252. About half of the $100 billion total was in trade in textiles, which was subject to the Multifibre Arrangement of 1974, renewed in 1978, a multilateral orderly marketing agreement within the institutional framework (though not the doctrine) of the GATT. For a brief discussion of the Long Term Cotton Textile Agreement, the predecessor of the Multifibre Arrangement, see references cited at § 3.72 at N. s *supra*.

of course, not self-evident. The Tokyo Declaration spoke of "an examination of the adequacy of the multilateral safeguard system, considering particularly the modalities of application of Article XIX, with a view to furthering trade liberalization and preserving its results."[d] The U.S. Congress, less diplomatically, directed the President to seek "the revision of Article XIX of the GATT into a truly international safeguard procedure which takes into account all forms of import restraints countries use in response to injurious competition or threat of such competition."[e] In addressing this task, the proponents of the MTN sought, by setting forth clearly the ground rules for emergency action—so called "safeguards"— to inspire confidence that the rest of the trading system could absorb the increased trade expected from reduction of other tariff and non-tariff trade barriers. The goal was to develop a safeguards code that would permit emergency action but under agreed standards, international surveillance, and on a non-discriminatory basis.

7.22—SUBSIDIES AND COUNTERVAILING DUTIES

For years it had been clear that the international trading rules, though unsympathetic to subsidies, did not do much about them.[f] Article XVI, as we saw, recognized subsidies as a distortion of the free flow of goods and services, and paragraph (4) of that article[g] contained a commitment to "cease to grant either directly or indirectly any form of subsidy" on the export of a non-primary product that reduces the price of the exported product below its domestic price. But that commitment—a so-called "standstill" to which the major industrial countries but not the majority of GATT members subscribed[h]—had not been honored even

---

[d] Tokyo Declaration of GATT Ministers of September 14, 1973, paragraph 3(d), Documents Supplement p. DS-661.

[e] Trade Act of 1974 § 121(a)(2). It is worth remarking that section 121, containing various suggestions for reforming and strengthening the GATT, was not in the Administration bill, but was added in the House Ways and Means Committee.

[f] For an account of the origins of the GATT provisions on subsidies in U.S.– British wartime negotiations, as well as some proposals for the MTN on this subject, see O'Cleireacain, "Toward a Code on Subsidies and Countervailing Duties," 1 The World Economy 437 (Oct. 1978).

[g] Documents Supplement p. DS-31.

[h] GATT Basic Instruments and Selected Documents [BISD] 9th Supp. p. 32 (1961). For the Report of the Working Party that prepared the declaration, see id. at p. 185.

within its terms. The criterion of lower export than home market price was not essentially persuasive, especially if the same subsidy applied both to domestic and to export sales; the exclusion of primary products was a very big exclusion; and the most critical question, how to define subsidy in the context of international trading rules, had not been touched at all. The notification requirement of Article XVI(i) had rarely been observed, and there was no complaint procedure by which *A* could allege that some measure of *B*'s was an improper subsidy. As for the response to subsidies, the countervailing duty, though permitted by Article VI, often seemed an inappropriate approach, and there was no international mechanism for determining either the character or the monetary value of the alleged subsidy.[i] Thus there was general agreement that the subsidy field called for new rules; most participants in the MTN, whatever their views on the merits, considered that the multilateral, multitopical Tokyo Round would be the right place to attempt to write such rules.

The United States was primarily concerned about the effect of remissions of various "indirect" taxes, which as we saw (and as the Supreme Court had confirmed in the *Zenith* Case[j]) were not prohibited by the GATT, and about the system of "border tax adjustments" whereby European and other countries collected value-added taxes on imports and remitted them on exports.[k] Indeed Congress had written a specific mandate into the Trade Act of 1974, directing the President to seek "the revision of GATT articles with respect to the treatment of border adjustments for internal taxes to redress the disadvantage to countries relying primarily on direct rather than indirect taxes for revenue needs."[l] Developing countries sought assurances that in certain circumstances subsidies—whether on production or on exports—would be considered an acceptable tool in the development process. In particular, they sought a specific link between the rules concerning imposition of countervailing duties and Article XXXVII(3)(c) which obligates developed countries to have "special regard to the trade interests of less developed con-

---

[i] Compare, for example, the response by the United States to the investment inducements given by Canada to the Michigan Tire Company, discussed at § 4.46(d) *supra*.

[j] See § 4.47(c).

[k] See e.g., the discussion of the Italian steel towers case at § 4.46(a)–(c), as well as of U.S. Steel's complaints against European countries at § 4.47(a), (b) and (d) *supra*.

[l] § 121(a)5 of the Trade Act of 1974.

tracting parties when considering the application of . . . measures permitted under [GATT]."[m]

Nearly every country sought to bring the United States into line with the rest of the world in requiring a finding of injury to domestic industry before imposing countervailing duties.

7.23—DISPUTE SETTLEMENT AND CONSULTATIONS

The GATT, as many observers have pointed out,[n] contained only rudimentary procedures for dispute settlement, and these had been gradually going into disuse. This fact should not be exaggerated, for in large part the GATT did influence (if not always control) the foreign trade policies of member states.[o] The exceptions were precisely in the areas discussed in this section—escape clause actions and subsidies, orderly marketing agreements, and agriculture. But many of those issues, plus dumping and the various devices that we saw in looking at steel, were complicated and controversial, in fact as in law. Though self-policing and even self-judging had their value, many cases would benefit by being addressed internationally, and not just by working groups whose reports had tended, after long delay, to recite everyone's position without coming to any operative conclusion.[p]

---

[m] Article XXXVII was adopted in 1966 as part of Part IV of the General Agreement—the GATT's answer to the organization of UNCTAD (The United Nations Conference on Trade and Development). The complete text of Article XXXVII appears in the Documents Supplement at p. DS-82.

[n] See e.g., R. Hudec, *The GATT Legal System and World Trade Diplomacy* (1975); R. Hudec, *Adjudication of International Trade Disputes* (Thames Essay No. 16), Trade Policy Research Centre, London (1978); Jackson, "The Crumbling Institutions of International Trade," 12 J. World Trade Law 93 (1978); Jackson, Governmental Disputes in International Trade Relations: A Proposal in the Context of GATT," 13 J. World Trade Law 1 (1979).

[o] In his Thames Essay cited at N. n *supra,* Professor Hudec put this point well:

> The real problem [of the relation between rules and adjudication in the GATT] is a tendency [on the part of countries' trade officials] to think that GATT rules can be burned at both ends, so to. speak—that the rules can be asserted vigorously and rigorously at home and then, once a trade dispute enters the GATT, the same rules may be put aside so that diplomats can fashion better answers based on their expert sensitivity to 'realities.' *Id.* at p. 40.

[p] For an interesting account of such a procedure, which took 3½ years from initiation to issuance of reports by panels to the contracting parties, see Jackson,

If every issue became a political issue, then *A*'s transgression might well be forgiven by the group of *B, C,* and *D,* each of which would expect *A*'s vote when next it was the subject of a working party or other investigation. From an original reluctance to become involved with lawyers, the GATT seemed to have gradually moved out of the business of resolving (as contrasted with composing) disputes. By the late 1970's, however, the lesson that rules, conduct, and enforcement were interrelated was gaining hold within the international trade community. Whether there should be a GATT court, or panels of arbitrators, or distinct dispute settlement procedures for the different codes being developed, was not clear.[q]

At the same time as the search for quasi-judicial procedures was going on, the MTN looked to create standing procedures for consultations. In its thirty-year history, the GATT had become a forum (with mixed results, as we have seen) for settlement or adjustment of disputes, turning on dumping by *A* and retaliation by *B;* or withdrawal of a concession by *C* and *D*'s intention of withdrawing an equivalent one; or a claim by *E* that an internal tax in *F* was really meant to impair *E*'s rights, and so forth. The idea now was that the GATT might talk about trade problems in their earlier stages, and also consider related social problems (for instance how to deal with unemployed steel workers) without waiting for a formal dispute to arise.[r]

As it turned out, both dispute settlement and standing consultations were assigned to a group on the "Framework for International Trade" created in 1976 on the initiative of Brazil to consider "improvements in the international framework for the conduct of world trade, particularly with respect to trade between developed and developing countries and differential and more favorable treatment to be adopted in such

---

"The Jurisprudence of International Trade: The DISC Case in GATT," 72 Am. J. Int'l L. 747 (1978).

[q] For a discussion of these issues by a panel of international lawyers and economists under the chairmanship of Anthony M. Solomon (§ 6.12 *supra*), see *Remaking the System of World Trade, A Proposal for Institutional Reform,* A Report of the Panel on International Trade Policy and Institutions of the American Society of International Law (1976).

[r] Recall that a lack of such a forum in the GATT had been one of the reasons for creation of the Steel Committee in the OECD in the fall of 1978, § 6.47 *supra*.

trade."[s] Thus the developing nations, which had always felt themselves to be outsiders in the GATT, sought to link their demands with the drive, especially on the part of the United States, for institutional reform. This linkage, in the words of the official American report, represented a "potentially useful mix of negotiating possibilities."[t] Like so much else in the MTN, it also meant that one failure to agree could bring down several other efforts, and perhaps the whole negotiation.

7.24—OTHER MATTERS

Once the scope of the negotiations had been enlarged to go beyond the traditional bargaining about tariff cuts, negotiating formulas, and exceptions lists, a variety of other issues not previously made the subject GATT negotiations found their way on to the agenda.

(a) *Government procurement* had usually been handled outside of normal GATT rules, on the assumption that each country preferred its own suppliers for the needs of the government, just as its civil servants traveled, when possible, on the national airline.[a] But with governments running railroads, telephone systems, national oil companies, and as we saw, even steel industries, the impact on international trade of such national preferences was becoming substantial.[b] The United States, with fewer state enterprises (apart from the military) than most of the other participants in the MTN, pressed hard for a code on government procurement practices, which would cover such subjects as publicity for government purchases, elimination of margins of preference for home-made products, definitions of permissible exemptions for national se-

---

[s] Compare paragraph 9 of the Tokyo Declaration of September 1973, Documents Supplement p. DS-662.

[t] *Twenty-Second Annual Report of the President of the United States in the Trade Agreements Program—1977* p. 26 (1978).

[a] See GATT Article III (8)(a), which exempts government purchasing from the requirements of national treatment. See also Article XVII.

[b] The particular topic most often brought up by American negotiators concerned the procurement practices of the Nippon Telephone and Telegraph Company (NTT), the Japan National Railways, and the Japan Monopoly Corporation (cigarettes and tobacco). These three companies plus more than a hundred comparable "special legal entities" were said to have annual budgets equal to half of the official state budget, but their purchases were limited almost entirely to Japanese sources. See e.g. Abegglen and Hout, "Facing Up to the Trade Gap with Japan," 57 Foreign Affairs 146, 157–58 (Fall 1978). See also the GAO Report cited at N. c *infra*, pp. 49–53.

curity, and the size and scope of procurement that would be covered by a new code.[c]

(b) The question of *technical standards* was becoming more important to international trade, as concern with pollution and with product safety was increasing in nearly all countries. How to distinguish genuine health or safety regulations from protectionism (recall the example of gas-fired cylinders § 2.44(d)(2) supra) was seen as another task of a revived and revitalized GATT.

(c) For 30 years countries had been negotiating in the GATT about binding or reducing rates of duty, without ever being concerned about how the value of the products to which the duties applied was measured. Article VII(2) of the GATT[d] provided that value for customs purposes should be based on "the actual value of the imported merchandise," but no particular method of valuation was prescribed.[e] It now appeared that some countries, even while agreeing on the rate of duty—i.e., the numerator—were leaving to discretion (negotiation or worse) the denominator of the fraction that determined the duty payable. One of the goals of the MTN was to establish a uniform *system of customs valuation*, eliminating the opportunity for artificial inflation or manipulation of customs values and promoting the predictability of duty assessments. For the United States, that would mean elimination of American Selling Price[f] as well as some other complicated features of a complicated statutory system;[g] for other countries (notably including Canada), it might mean similar revisions or indeed a requirement to set forth the scheme of customs valuation for the first time, on the basis of a uniform—or at least harmonized—set of rules. The hope was that by reaching agreement on a customs valuation code, the participants in the MTN might give added importance to the tariff negotiations of this as well as prior rounds.

---

[c] For example, the tendency might be to exempt all purchases by the army; but perhaps a distinction could be drawn between purchases of artillery pieces and purchases of blankets. For a survey of practices by states, see General Accounting Office, *Governmental Buy-National Practices of the United States and Other Countries—An Assessment,* Rept. No. ID-76-67, September 30, 1976.

[d] Documents Supplement p. DS-16.

[e] For a discussion of the origins and compromises in Article VII, see J. Jackson, *World Trade and the Law of GATT,* pp. 446-54 (1969).

[f] See § 3.72 at Ns. m-r *supra.*

[g] Tariff Act of 1930, §§ 402 and 402a, 19 U.S.C. §§ 1401a and 1402.

(d) *Agriculture,* it was by now realized, did not really fit the GATT pattern, because nearly everywhere social and political considerations were perceived as outweighing considerations of comparative advantage and a liberal trading system.[h] Still, practices of various states seemed to go beyond the bounds of rational allocation of resources, on the one hand producing surpluses, on the other hand not reacting to conditions of famine in many parts of the world. Another attempt at an international agreement on grains—or perhaps only on wheat—was made a part of the MTN agenda.

(e) After adoption of Part IV of the GATT in 1966, the *Developing Countries* had essentially been freed from the obligation of reciprocity.[i] But they still felt left out of the major decision-making, and they saw the commitment to preferential treatment in tariff matters[j] (uneven as it was[k]) eroding as tariffs in general were being reduced. The suggestion was made, but eventually rejected, that margins of preference for developing countries be bound in the GATT. For their part, some of the developed countries, led by the United States, wanted to secure from the developing countries at least a commitment to MFN treatment of developed country exports. Also, there was general agreement on the need (but not on the formula) for making distinctions between countries that really required charity—such as Bangladesh, and those, such as Mexico and Brazil, that, as we saw with regard to steel, were in fact competitors in the international market.[l]

---

[h] Perhaps the extreme example of this feeling, shared in varying degrees by almost all countries, is Japan. Eleven per cent of total employed Japanese are engaged in agriculture, compared with 3 per cent in the United States and 6 per cent in West Germany. The price of rice in Japan, protected from international competition, is more than three times the world price. A leading Japanese official observed that if Japan removed all restraints on imports of rice, its trade surplus might disappear overnight. But so would the stability of Japanese society, as well as survival of the Liberal-Democratic Party which has been governing the country since the time of the American occupation.

[i] See GATT Article XXXVI(8), Documents Supplement p. DS-82.

[j] See e.g. Title V of the Trade Act of 1974, Documents Supplement pp. DS-402-10 for authorization of the United States' version of a Generalized System of Preferences.

[k] See e.g. § 503 of the Trade Act of 1974, excluding textiles, watches, transistors, steel, shoes, glass and other articles that the President might designate. See also § 504(c) limiting preferences to $25,000,000 (as adjusted) or 50 per cent of total imports per country per year.

[l] It is worth remarking, at least in a footnote, that nothing on the agenda concerned the European Community's ever-widening network of preferential arrange-

7.25—TARIFFS

Tariffs, this time, were perhaps the easiest issue. There was general agreement among the developed countries that there should be further reductions in duties on industrial products, and that the reductions should be on an across-the-board, not an item-by-item basis.[m] There was in fact agreement, as there had not been a decade earlier, on "harmonization," that is on the principle that the highest duties should be reduced more than medium or low tariffs, and that at the end of a staging process the tariff profile of the industrialized countries should look as much alike as possible.

Following the so-called Downing Street Summit Conference in London in May of 1977, the major sticking point was removed, when it was agreed that whatever harmonization formula would emerge need not be applied to agriculture, but that agricultural products would be included (on an item-by-item basis) in the negotiations. By November 1977 agreement had been reached on a tariff writing formula, and by January 1978 the United States and several other countries had put forward their comprehensive offers, including the list of products they would include or exclude from the general formula.

Again, the exceptions to the general formula could beget exceptions by others, and until the end there was no assurance that the package deal might not unravel. But it seemed that safeguards and subsidies, institutional reform and special problems, rather than the traditional haggling over tariffs, would make or break the Tokyo Round.

*
*   *

Apart from this large collection of issues—some new, some old—it was clear that the GATT secretariat and the international trade community (public and private) in all the major trading countries used the pendency of the Multilateral Trade Negotiations as a defense against the rising protectionism referred to at the beginning of this chapter.[n] Should the MTN fail, these

---

ments with Mediterranean and developing countries, though as we saw (§ 3.14 *supra*) there was substantial doubt about the compatibility of these arrangements with the MFN principle.

[m] Recall the discussion of this point in connection with the Kennedy Round, § 3.71 *supra*.

[n] § 7.11 *supra*.

dammed up forces might well burst forth with renewed vigor and impetus. As with the Kennedy Round a decade earlier, but perhaps more so, the fate of the Tokyo Round took on a life of its own, over and above any specific issues in the package. So long as governments shared a fear of sheltered inefficiency, rising costs, and smaller markets, so long, in other words, as there was a general commitment to relatively freer trade, there was a commitment to the formal success of the MTN. Whether that commitment would prevail over disagreement on the large number of specific issues on the agenda remained, until the end, a matter of high tension.

§ 7.3—Notes and Questions

7.31—"SAFEGUARDS"

(a) As we saw in looking at the various measures taken by the United States and the European Community with respect to steel imports, the concept of "market disruption" seems to straddle the line between fair and unfair competition.[a] An industry of an exporting country—say Japan or South Korea—may not be selling for less abroad than it is at home; and the export aids from which it benefits may not come under the category of forbidden subsidies. Yet there seems to be a feeling that if the growth in exports of a particular product to a particular market is too swift, or the market share is too great in comparison with some former time, "something needs to be done" either by the exporting or by the importing country. On the other hand, the importing country should not be permitted to shelter an inefficient or unimaginative industry or an overpaid labor force. Competition, after all, is what international trade, the doctrine of comparative advantage, and the GATT itself are all about. How might this most fundamental of dilemmas be resolved?

(b) Lawyers, and perhaps economists and diplomats as well, might be inclined to suggest a procedural solution if a substantive one eludes

---

[a] The term "market disruption" does not appear in the General Agreement, though recently Article XIX has sometimes been referred to as the market disruption article. The term appears to have come into use in the GATT environment in 1959–1960, in the context of the cotton textile problem. In November 1960, a working party of the GATT proposed a definition of market disruption and recommended establishment of a standing committee to deal with the subject, and both recommendations were adopted. See GATT BISD 9th Supp. pp. 26, 106 (1961). The committee gradually went out of existence, as the textile problem was "handled" with a long-term agreement, but the term market disruption gained general currency. See J. Jackson, *World Trade and the Law of GATT*, pp. 567–73 (1969).

crisp definition. Could you develop a procedure whereby if imports of a particular product into Patria have increased by more than x percent,

(i) Patria would be entitled to initiate a market disruption proceeding before an international panel;

(ii) Patria would lay its proposals for remedial action before the panel;

(iii) The exporting country or countries would be given the opportunity to be heard; and

(iv) The panel would give an opinion, including recommendations to both parties?

(c) If you like this suggestion, what inducements could you suggest that would make Patria submit its complaint to the Panel?

(d) Should there be a symmetrical procedure whereby Xandia, the exporting country, would be entitled to initiate a complaint proceeding before the same body if Patria acted without following the procedures called for in paragraph (b)?

(e) Should there be a "fast track" or temporary restraint procedure, building on the last sentence of Article XIX(2)?

(f) Consider how the body that would make the decision or recommendation under the procedure suggested above should be constituted. The alternatives—standing vs. ad hoc body, lawyers vs. economists or GATT professionals, public vs. closed-door proceedings, binding vs. recommendatory decisions, etc.—are explored (in this and other contexts) in question 7.37. For the moment, notice only that the more the procedural solution, the "common law" approach, is a way out of the difficulty in fashioning a precise substantive standard, the more important are the composition, the fairness, and the skill of the body to which the problem is to be referred.

7.32—(a) Even harder than the issues in the preceding question is the issue of whether Patria should be entitled to apply "escape clause" or similar protective measures against particular countries—say Xandia only—or whether the most-favored-nation principle must prevail in application of safeguard measures. Consider what position on this question, known in the MTN as the "selectivity question", should be taken by

(i) The developing countries,

(ii) Japan,

(iii) The European Community,

(iv) The United States,

(v) The GATT secretariat.

(b) Traditionally, the United States had stood firm for MFN, even where the target country could be said to have done wrong, and certainly in all other situations.[b] The Trade Act of 1974 had begun to authorize inroads into the doctrine of most-favored nation treatment in the context of perceived wrongdoing.[c] The EEC, of course, was not as firmly committed to MFN,[d] but it had usually found some justification for departure from non-discrimination in its preferential arrangements—whether on the basis of Article XXIV or on the basis of special help for developing countries, or whatever.

Article XIX of the GATT did not expressly address the point, but given the pervasive application of the MFN principle throughout the General Agreement and specific mention whenever MFN is not required,[e]

---

[b] Recall the discussion of MFN in the section of the GATT's fundamental principles. §§ 2.41–.42, and especially the quotation from Mr. Evans at § 2.42, N. g *supra*. Recall also the discussion of how the United States should go about retaliating against the European Community in the aftermath of the Chicken War of 1962–63, §§ 3.62–.63.

[c] See e.g., § 126(b) and (c), calling for discriminatory treatment of countries that fail to observe reciprocity in their dealings with the United States; § 122, authorizing import restrictions for balance of payments purposes, according to MFN on principle ((d)(1)), but in special circumstances (apparently with Japan in mind) on a discriminatory basis ((d)(2)); and § 301(b) giving an option in response to unfair trade practices of foreign governments. See also § 203(k)(1), providing that actions by the President under the escape clause procedure may be taken without regard to the statutory MFN requirement, "but only after consideration of the relation of such actions to the international obligations of the United States."

[d] See e.g., the association agreements between the Community and a variety of Mediterranean countries, discussed briefly in § 3.14 *supra*.

[e] See e.g., Article I (2–4) (historical preferences), Article XIV (certain balance

the presumption had always been that escape clause or market disruption actions must be taken on an MFN basis.[f] Should that presumption now be changed?

(c) Suppose Patria, Xandia and Tertia all export a particular product—say carbon steel or television receivers—to the United States. In the base year, 90 per cent of consumption is produced domestically, and the rest comes from the three countries concerned in roughly equal shares. In the next year imports account for 20 per cent of consumption, with Patria accounting for 14 per cent, Xandia and Tertia remaining at about 3 per cent each.[g] Assume that the conditions for market disruption have been found, as discussed in § 7.31. Should the United States (assuming it has decided to take an escape clause action) be obligated to:

> (i) raise duties or impose quantitative restrictions against all three countries, thus "punishing" Xandia and Tertia for Patria's excesses; or,

> (ii) restrain imports from Patria only, leaving producers in Xandia and Tertia free to compete with American producers for the U.S. market on substantially equal terms?

Should the choice between (i) and (ii) depend on whether Patria had joined with the United States in a Safeguards Code?

(d) Many commentators said that the pattern of the 1970's would have shown neither (i) nor (ii), but an orderly marketing agreement between Patria and the United States (or even more likely, in similar circumstances, with the European Community.)[h] Is it correct to characterize OMA's as a fundamental breach of MFN? As selectivity with the consent of the selectee?

---

of payments measures), Article XX and XXI (security exceptions), Article XXIII (nullification and impairment), and Article XXIV (customs unions).

[f] See J. Jackson, *World Trade and the Law of GATT*, at pp. 564–65 (1969).

[g] Put another way, this means Patria accounts for 70 per cent of all imports of the product in question.

[h] Recall the description of the OMA between the United States and Japan on Specialty Steel, § 5.56, and the comparable agreements covering all types of steel between Japan and the European Coal and Steel Community, § 5.57, *supra*.

If you favor MFN in regard to safeguards,—as the United States on the whole did in the Tokyo Round—does that suggest a renunciation of OMA's? Submission of OMA's to international scrutiny?[i] Or would you expect (to paraphrase de la Rochefoucault) that OMA's will continue to be the homage that selectivity pays to non-discrimination?

(e) Consider finally how the two issues discussed here under safeguards are related. Is selectivity more acceptable if coupled with a requirement of (prior?) international scrutiny? Or, on the other hand, would you expect the issues of discriminatory application of safeguard measures to add so much weight to the problems before an international panel or committee that the essential function of determining market disruption could not be carried through?

7.33—SUSIDIES AND COUNTERVAILING DUTIES

(a) One of the recurring tensions between the United States and the rest of the world in the MTN was the fact that for three decades the United States had maintained a statutory scheme with respect to subsidies that was in two important respects at variance with the GATT standard[j]: (1) Under American law, countervailing duties were directed

---

[i] The Atlantic Council of the United States, an organization designed to provide public support for the North Atlantic Treaty but which recently has paid attention to economic as well as politico-military issues, proposed in 1975 that the industrial nations agree among themselves to a "Code in Furtherance of GATT Objectives," containing obligations that it thought unlikely to win approval among the developing countries. In its section on Safeguards, the proposed code said:

> 1. No member shall enter into or facilitate an intergovernmental or other international voluntary or other arrangement for the application of trade measures which limits import competition, whether by export restraints or otherwise, with its domestic producers unless such arrangements shall have been approved by the Trade Council [to be created pursuant to other provisions of the proposal].

> 2. The Trade Council shall, not later than two years after entry into force of the Code, review . . . arrangements existing on the date of entry into force of the Code. If the Council disapproves such an existing arrangement, the arrangement shall be terminated forthwith.

Atlantic Council of the United States, *GATT Plus—A Proposal for Trade Reform*, pp. 43–44 (1976).

[j] The United States was not, of course. in formal violation, by virtue of the Protocol of Provisional Application, discussed in § 2.2 at N. p, *supra.*

both to export and to production subsidies, whereas the GATT seemed to prohibit only export subsidies (Article (XVI)(4));[k] and (2) according to the GATT, countervailing duties were to be imposed only upon a finding of injury (or threat of injury) to an established domestic industry (Article VI(6)(a)),[l] whereas for dutiable products the United States countervailing duty statute contained no requirement of a finding of injury or threat of injury. To the extent resentment against the United States on this score stemmed from failure to bring its domestic law into line, there was no real defense. But what about the merits?

(b)(1) If subsidies are inherently bad, why shouldn't there be a *per se* rule, as for instance in regard to price-fixing under the antitrust laws, so that proof of damages or injury is irrelevant?[m] Is the real objection to the United States law that it calls for unilateral decision-making, in theory not subject to negotiation?[n] Or are subsidies not inherently bad?

(2) If subsidies distort the market by using public funds to make up for competitive disparities, is there any real difference from the point of view of the importing country between a subsidy focused on exports and one directed to all production of a given product?

(c) Professor Barcelo, in urging the negotiators of the Tokyo Round to look more to economic efficiencies and free trade theory in addressing the question of subsidies, wrote:

> There seems little reason, when dealing with export subsidies, to support the present GATT provision predicating the right to impose countervailing duties on the existence of injury to a domestic injury . . . It is not producer injury in the importing country which makes bounty-fed exports objectionable. . . . The escape clause provisions . . . would be adequate to protect against such general import-caused injury. . . . The objectionable nature of export subsidies lies in their distorting effect on global efficiency, hence countervailing

---

[k] Documents Supplement p. DS-31.

[l] Documents Supplement p. DS-15.

[m] See e.g. *United States v. Trenton Potteries Co.*, 273 U.S. 392 (1927).

[n] But recall the *Hammond Lead* case, § 4.45 at N. u *supra,* in which the Court of Customs and Patent Appeals declined to authorize judicial review of a negative finding by the Treasury, on the basis that executive discretion, apparently including some room for international negotiation, was built into the statutory scheme.

action should be designed to discourage their use altogether and not to protect injured importer country producers.[o]

Professor Dam, writing some years earlier, looked at the issue rather differently:

> Since tariffs are considered lawful for protective purposes, should not subsidies . . . also be considered lawful? One might go even further and argue that production subsidies are better than tariffs and should be encouraged, at least where the alternative is the imposition of a new tariff or the preservation of an existing tariff.[p]

Which of these arguments do you find more persuasive? Is it possible to reconcile the two approaches by retaining the distinction in the GATT between export and production subsidies?

(d) The preceding quotations, reflecting doubts about the whole subject for many years, may explain some of the ambivalence in the GATT provisions regarding subsidies.[q] But why do you suppose Article XVI(4), embodying the stand-still declaration of the major industrial nations,[r] contains a price discrimination test? Is this an unfortunate confusion of dumping (private action) with subsidies (public action)? Or are the two subjects essentially alike, so that the task of the negotiators should be to assimilate the rules, procedures, and remedies in these two areas as much as possible?

7.34—(a) Should the negotiators try to devise a mechanism for bargaining about subsidies in the way countries have bargained for years about tariffs—i.e. Patria will reduce its subsidy on apples if Xandia will reduce its subsidy on pears? Or would you expect that the problems of definition and measurement make such a suggestion impossible to carry out in practice?

---

[o] Barcelo, "Subsidies and Countervailing Duties—Analysis and a Proposal," 9 Law & Pol'y Int'l Bus. 779, 801 (1977).

[p] K. Dam, *The GATT, Law and International Economic Organization*, 135 (1970).

[q] Compare the discussion at § 2.44(b) *supra*.

[r] See § 7.22 at N. h *supra*.

(b) As the negotiations in the MTN progressed, it seemed that the Europeans were most concerned about establishment of an injury standard in the United States countervailing duty law, and the United States was most concerned about securing stricter definitions of what constitutes a prohibited subsidy. Would you think these rival positions contain the elements of a trade-off?

(c) Assuming that the United States agreed to introduce an injury standard—whether on the basis of the trade-off suggested above or as part of some other "package deal"—how should the injury standard be defined?

(i) Is it the same standard as the one used in dumping cases?

(ii) Is it the same as the standard used for escape clause cases?

(iii) Or should there be still a third standard?

(d) Can you think of any way of solving the problem that arises if Xandia complains about loss of export markets in Tertia as a result of Patria's export subsidies?

(e) Given the problems alluded to here as well as numerous others, would the best solution be a procedural one, say a court or committee that could hear complaints and issue opinions that over time might result in a common law of subsidies and countervailing duties? What enforcement powers, if any, should the Contracting Parties bestow on such a body?[8]

7.35—DISPUTE SETTLEMENT

Exploration of the questions of safeguards and subsidies, as well as of numerous other actual and potential trade issues, again and again leads back to the question of procedures for settlement of trade disputes. The GATT had been reluctant throughout its history to formalize its dispute settlement procedures. Complaints had been entertained, under

---

[8] Just by way of reminder, nothing in this discussion has dealt with the vexing problem of agricultural commodities (GATT Article XVI (3)). Discussion of that question was on the whole avoided in the context of a subsidies code, because it was too enmeshed both with the North-South dialogue and with the continuing disarray with respect to agriculture.

Article XXIII as well as under other articles;[a] but the distinctions between consultations, settlement negotiations, fact-finding and arbitration were often blurred, and the issue of sanctions for wrong-doing was nearly always avoided. A pervasive question before the MTN was whether the international trading community, no longer the "club" it had been in the 1940's, could afford to maintain this tradition, or should move toward more formal, more precise and more institutionalized modes of dispute settlement.

(a) A panel of the American Society of International Law, contemplating the adoption of several codes—on safeguards, subsidies, government procurement, technical standards, etc.—suggested that a single uniform procedure be established, along the following lines:[b]

(i) Consultation between parties to a dispute would be required as an initial obligation for all members;

(ii) conciliation and mediation services would be available if consultation under (i) were not successful;[c]

(iii) if steps (i) and (ii) had not resolved the dispute, an impartial tribunal would be convened, made up of experts who would determine the facts (if these were in dispute) and issue a ruling on the relation of the facts found to the GATT or to the applicable code.

(iv) The tribunal would be authorized, but not required, to recommend appropriate remedies to the parties—for example phasing

---

[a] See, e.g., the discussion of the Chicken War § 3.25(e) *supra* in which a GATT panel was appointed to determine the amount of trade damage inflicted by the European Community in respect of which the United States would be justified under Article XXVIII in withdrawing equivalent concessions. The panel was not asked and did not decide whether either the action by the EEC or the proposed counter-action by the United States was lawful.

[b] *Re-Making the System of World Trade: A Proposal for Institutional Reform*, a Report of the Panel on International Trade Policy and Institutions of the American Society of International Law, at pp. 33–35 (1976).

[c] In both conciliation and mediation a neutral person or group of persons attempts to guide the parties towards agreement. The difference between the two terms—often blurred in practice—is that a mediator goes back and forth between the parties transmitting each side's proposals to the other side, while a conciliator is free to offer proposals of his own. Both conciliation and mediation are different from arbitration in that they cannot result in an imposed settlement, while arbitration (like adjudication) can do so.

out of an objectionable subsidy or import restraint or withdrawal by the injured party of a concession, or conceivably even payment of monetary damages.

(v) A supervising body—perhaps the GATT Council or a committee comprising all the signatories of the particular code in question —would receive the report (award?) of the tribunal, and would have the responsibility of recommending action, whether or not the tribunal had done so. If the code in question contained a provision on sanctions—for instance provision for cease and desist orders—the supervising body would administer the sanctions.[d]

Would you favor a dispute settlement mechanism along these lines?

(b) Consider how a procedure along the above lines might have dealt with the various episodes concerning steel in the period 1968–78:

(i) "Market disruption" in the United States in the late 1960's;

(ii) The voluntary restraint agreements between the United States, Japan and the EEC;

(iii) The alleged effect on the United States of Japan-Europe restraint agreements;

(iv) "Market disruption" in the United States and the European Community in the late 1970's;

(v) Complaints about dumping by Japanese producers;

(vi) Complaints about anti-dumping measures by the United States;

(vii) The American trigger price mechanism;

(viii) The European Simonet-Davignon Plans;

---

[d] Actually the Panel's report contemplated a series of agreements with varying membership and purposes, all within an umbrella organization which would have statistical, public affairs, and rulemaking functions as well as the role in dispute settlement described in the text. The suggestions in regard to dispute settlement, however, do not depend on the existence of such an umbrella organization.

(ix) American complaints about European and Japanese tax rebates;

(x) European complaints about American countervailing duties.

In general, how should the proposed dispute settlement procedures—the ones suggested in (a) or others—relate to domestic law and domestic procedures?

(c) So far the discussion has proceeded on the assumption that all sides participate in the resolution of a dispute in which they are involved. Should there be some kind of provision for ex parte determination or even for a "default judgment"? If that seems too strong medicine, could you think of an alternative way to handle the problem of the reluctant participant? Does the proposed progression from consultation to conciliation to adjudication serve the purpose?

(d) Professor Hudec writes that the most important contribution of adjudication procedures lies in their impact on the object government's willingness to cooperate:

When consultations are the terminal event, the only real incentive to cooperate is the object government's concern for maintaining good relations with the complainant, the same concern which activates all diplomatic activity. When, on the other hand, failure of a consultation proceeding will expose the object government to the risk of an embarrassing law-suit, the incentive to cooperate is tangibly increased. Paradoxically the more credible the risk of that law-suit, the better the consultation machinery will work, and the less the adjudication procedure itself will appear to be needed.[e]

7.36—If, as previously suggested, procedural solutions are a way to postpone substantive differences until they arise in specific cases, the details of the procedures bear looking at with some care.

(a) Consider the pros and cons of establishing time limits for each of the steps outlined in § 7.35(a).

---

[e] R. Hudec, *Adjudication of International Trade Lisputes*, p. 28 (Thames Essay No. 16, 1978).

(b) What about attempting to seek in the MTN a declaration setting forth each party's obligation to furnish information expeditiously at the request (i) of the other party in a consultation; or (ii) of the mediator, conciliator, or tribunal?

(c) One of the recommendations of the panel whose suggestion was described in § 7.35(a) was that the decisions of the tribunal be published, both as soon as they were issued and in an annual volume of reports, with a view to establishing a body of trade law precedents. Would you favor this suggestion? Or would you expect it might weaken support for the proposal? Do you think the prospect of publication might inhibit the tribunal in finding that Patria had violated its obligations to Xandia under one of the codes? Or would you, rather, expect that the combination of publicity and permanence would strengthen respect for law all around? Compare with the dispute settlement here contemplated the different models in the private sector (both domestic and international) of *adjudication*, nearly always public and usually published with precedental effect, and *arbitration*, generally conducted behind closed doors, rarely published, and in most instances (labor relations excepted) conducted by tribunals assembled for the particular dispute.

7.37—If some kind of mechanism is to be created for establishing tribunals of experts to aid in resolution of trade disputes, how should the tribunals be constituted?

(a) Should the experts be lawyers, government officials, businessmen active in the industry involved, or full-time "GATT judges"?

(b) Would you look, as the GATT did in the past, to GATT "insiders," the veterans of the organization who usually made things work without precise reference to the rules? Or is this just the model that is to become obsolete in the new era of the Tokyo Round?

(c) Presumably the classification of members of the tribunals as "experts" would imply that they should not take instructions from their governments. But how might you encourage panel members to develop their loyalty to the institution rather than to their origins?[f]

---

[f] The members of the United States Supreme Court, for instance, do not by and large think of themselves as Minnesotans or Ohioans or Arizonians; to a les-

(d) Should government parties to disputes be entitled to select the members (or at least one of the members) from a list maintained by the secretariat? Should they be able to block nominations by the secretariat?

(e) Would you want at least one member of any panel to come from each country (or group of countries) involved in the dispute? Alternatively, would you want at least one developed and one developing country-member to hear a North-South dispute, and an American and a European to hear a U.S.-EEC dispute? Or do all of these questions suggest a departure from the model of a court in the direction of a jury or a political conference?

7.38—(a) Are the points raised in §§ 7.36–37 matters of detail on which compromises can be made to secure acceptance of the basic decisions on the questions raised in § 7.35? Or would you want firm answers on the composition and procedures of the tribunal before you committed your country (or gave your endorsement in Congress) to the concept set forth in § 7.35(a) and to the possible inroads on national sovereignty suggested in § 7.35(b)?

(b) Would you think the responses to the preceding questions should be uniform for each of the substantive matters that might underlie an international trade dispute? Or may different solutions be appropriate for different substantive issues? For example, are dumping and subsidies different for this purpose from market disruption and escape clause actions? What about an assertion of unfair government procurement practices, or the charge that a technical standard is being used as a protectionist device?

(c) If the mechanisms can be different, could a major issue—say safeguards—be safely left without a disputes procedure that is available for agreements on subsidies? Or would that be a polite indication that the parties didn't take their settlement on that issue seriously?

---

ser extent the same is true of the members of the European Court of Justice and of the Commission of the European Communities. It is less true of, say, members of the U.S. Congress, and much less true of delegates to a national convention or an international conference. In the early years of GATT dispute settlement, the "insiders" were plainly members of the "club" first, and not Englishmen, Swedes, or whatever. The question is whether a golden mean can be found between clubbiness and politicization, permitting a rule of law to develop.

(d) All of the preceding questions have been presented as if to some kind of Olympian architect. Do the answers change if one puts the questions to representatives of, say, the United States, the European Community, Japan, the successful developing countries, or the least developed countries? What about the GATT Director General, anxious to build up his organization against threats from protectionism, rival institutions, and indifference?

*

*   *

7.39—Taking the issues of safeguards, subsidies, and disputes settlement together, plus the other issues mentioned briefly in § 7.24 (technical standards, government procurement, customs valuation, possibly agriculture), one further over-arching issue emerges: The GATT was originally signed by 23 countries and negotiated by even fewer. Other countries (many not even in existence in the 1940's as independent sovereigns) adhered to the original articles without any negotiation except as to their own conditions of entry. By 1979, close to 100 countries were parties to the GATT and almost that many were participants in the MTN.[g] Now a series of new or revised rules was being proposed in various codes or similar arrangements, which might command agreement in different proportions and combinations of states.

Should there be a single standard for entry into effect of each of these codes—e.g. an absolute majority of the membership—with the understanding that if the required majority is attained the code in question is binding on everyone?

(b) Or could each of the codes go into effect as among the members who subscribed, provided a minimum number (for instance 25 countries or countries accounting for 50 per cent of the world's trade) had given their assent?

(c) If you prefer the suggestion in (b), how do you propose treating the non-subscribers, parties to the GATT but not, say, to the agreement on subsidies? Is the tendency of all the preceding discussion toward a

---

[g] Some non-members of the GATT participated in the MTN and some members did not participate. The official list of participants put the figure at 98, of which three had provisionally acceeded to the GATT and 26, including Mexico, Iran and Algeria, were non-members. GATT membership as of June 1978 stood at about 110, depending on how the various types of membership—permanent, provisional, and de facto—were counted. See Press Release–GATT/1215, June 1978.

return to some kind of conditional MFN, as contrasted with the unconditional MFN treatment on which the GATT was constructed in the 1940's?[h]

§ 7.4—The MTN: The Closing Stages

Most of the questions raised in the preceding sections were in fact faced by the negotiators of the Tokyo Round, both while the countries (and especially the European Community) were establishing their own positions, and across the table at Geneva. The parties did not quite keep to the deadlines set for them by Ambassador Strauss after the summit conference of May 1977. But by July 1978, just before another summit conference in Bonn, they hammered out a Framework of Understanding on the Tokyo Round, setting forth "the elements which, taken together, should lead to a successful conclusion of the negotiations based on an overall reciprocal balance."[a] The Framework of Understanding, signed by the developed countries only, renewed the delegates' commitment to complete the detailed negotiations on the remaining issues (including safeguards, subsidies, and agriculture) by December 15, 1978. That deadline, too, was missed, but not by much—or so it appeared. On December 22, 1978, the delegates of the European Community and the United States issued a joint communiqué that "noted with satisfaction the significant progress made both multilaterally and bilaterally across the full range of subjects under discussion."[b] On December 27, Ambassador Strauss notified his Advisory Committee[c] that "in conformance

---

[h] In making its proposals for trade reform, the Atlantic Council adopted the title "GATT Plus," the thought being that the undertaking there put forward would constitute a higher level of obligations. Looked at from the point of view of MFN, however, "GATT Minus" might be a better characterization. Note that the Trade Act of 1974, in § 102(f), left the option to the President to answer this question in favor of conditional or unconditional MFN or even in some variation thereof if that was consistent with the particular agreement.

[a] *Statement by Several Delegations on Current Status of Tokyo Round Negotiations*, Geneva, July 13, 1978. The full text is reproduced, e.g., in *Multilateral Trade Negotiations*, Hearing Before Subcomm. on Trade of House Ways and Means Committee, 95th Cong., 2nd Sess. pp. 7–12 (1978).

[b] *Joint Statement by the Delegations of the European Communities and the United States on the Tokyo Round of Multilateral Trade Negotiations*, Geneva, Dec. 22, 1978, as reproduced in Office of Special Representative for Trade Negotiations, Press Release #291, Dec. 22, 1978.

[c] See Trade Act of 1974 § 135.

with the agreement of the Heads of State at the Bonn summit last July, we have substantially completed the Tokyo Round of multilateral trade negotiations."[d] Thereafter President Carter gave the formal 90-day notice of intention to conclude a trade agreement called for by section 102(e) of the Trade Act of 1974.[e]

7.41—THE PACKAGE

It was a big package that President Carter notified to the Congress, bigger than any that had ever come out of a multilateral trade negotiation.[f] The package consisted of thirteen documents, some fully completed agreements, some with blanks in the texts, some "outlines of arrangements for a likely agreement," some (such as the undertaking on steel)[g] simply procedural devices to remove a contentious item from the agenda.

(a) *Subsidies*.[h] The agreement basically incorporated the trade-off suggested in section 7.22, i.e., a stricter prohibition of subsidies by international consensus in return for commitment by the United States to an injury standard as a condition precedent for imposition of countervailing duties. But it contemplated a "two track" approach to the problem of subsidies. In addition to the traditional remedy of countervailing duties imposed by importing countries (Article 1–6), the agreement provided that any country affected by a subsidy (i.e. a rival exporting as well as an importing country) may request consultations with the country alleged to be subsidizing. From consultations, there was a graduated progression to conciliation and a kind of arbitration by a panel

---

[d] Memorandum from Ambassador Strauss to Advisory Committee Members of Dec. 27, 1978.

[e] Documents Supplement p. DS-299.

[f] The formal notification, including "executive summaries" but not the actual texts of the agreement, was published as a separate pamphlet by the Federal Register, 44 Fed. Reg. 1933–54 (Jan. 8, 1979).

[g] The same agreement mentioned in § 6.47 *supra* and reproduced in the Documents Supplement at p. DS-617.

[h] Documents Supplement pp. DS-663–690. Except as noted, the differences between the December 1978 version and the final text were stylistic only.

which could result in approval of counter-measures by the aggrieved party—the whole procedure to be completed within 180–210 days (Articles 12, 13, 17, and 18). The prohibition of export subsidies followed GATT Article XVI(4) in exempting primary products, but minerals were for the first time excluded from this exemption (Article 9).[i] Subsidies other than upon exportation were not prohibited, but a declaration was included that all signatories are to weigh the possible adverse effect on international trade of any production subsidies (Article 11(2)). The Code included in this category not only subsidies on production but also provision of credits, tax relief, supply of services, research and development, and, interestingly, government provision of equity capital (Article 11(3)).[j]

(b) *Safeguards*.[k] The "outline of an arrangement" provided that safeguard measures as defined could be taken only in case of *serious* injury (or threat of serious injury) to domestic producers, to be determined "on the basis of positive findings of fact and not on mere conjecture" (Ch. 1(1)). The draft left open for further negotiation whether imports must be "the cause," or "the principal cause" of serious injury (Ch. 1(3)),[l] and it left open whether the injury must be to "domestic producers" or to a "major part of all producers" (Ch. 1(1) or 1(4)); further, it left open whether an illustrative list of other relevant factors would be included, which individually or in combination might be deemed to contradict a finding that imports were the [principal] cause of injury to domestic producers. (I(3)). There was a provision for a time limit to safeguard measures (Ch. 3(b)) but the initial time was left blank and the overall time permitted for a safeguard measure had 3 and 8 years as alternatives. Various other restraints on safeguard measures— with regard to frequency of application, phasing out, and minimum permitted imports—were included (Ch. 3(c)–(e)), but all within brackets or with the numbers left blank. Altogether this code looked far from complete when it was made public.

---

[i] The draft of December 1978 contained a definition of subsidy as "any charge on the public account . . . which is conveyed directly or indirectly upon an exported product and which results in differential treatment, including price, covering products sold for export over like or directly competitive products sold domestically." (Part II(c)(2) of the draft). The final version omitted the definition.

[j] See also Article 14, exempting developing countries from the prohibition against export subsidies, but acknowledging that such subsidies may result in adverse effects on other signatories.

[k] Documents Supplement p. DS-691.

[l] Recall the changes in United States law on this point, discussed at §§ 3.53 and 5.56(b) *supra*.

But the most contentious issue in the Safeguards Code—left blank in the version circulated by Ambassador Strauss[m]—concerned selectivity. Great Britain and France (and therefore the Community as a whole) insisted on a statement of the right to adopt safeguard measures against individual countries; the developing countries were afraid that they would be targets; and the United States seemed to be in the middle, even as the Trade Act itself was.[n] That might well mean that if the United States did not strongly support one side in this controversy, the whole code could come apart.[o]

(c) *Dispute Settlement.* Many of the proposed codes, including the ones on subsidies and on safeguards, contained provisions for "committees" to supervise adherence to the rules and to organize dispute settlement procedures were necessary.[p] In addition, the proposed Framework Agreement contained an agreed text on dispute settlement, which turned out to be a "reaffirmation" of adherence to Articles XXII and XXIII of the GATT, including the statement that use of Articles XXIII "should not be intended or considered as contentious acts."[q] The agreement contemplated establishment of panels or working parties, with a mixture of settlement and adjudication functions— "in accordance with standing practice." An annex contained a description of that practice, on the whole reflecting the actual state of affairs with respect to dispute settlement in the GATT.[r] Given the inadequacies and dissatisfaction with existing practice,[s] one could fairly wonder whether the agreement represented a step forward.

(d) *Other Matters.* The most specific agreement covered *customs valuation.* As of 1981, all signatories (other than developing countries,

---

[m] See Chapter 4, Documents Supplement p. DS-695.

[n] See § 7.32(b) *supra,* and the sections of the Trade Act cited in N. c thereto.

[o] Note also that Chapter 4 bis, the proposal that was to deal with voluntary restraint agreements and similar restraints on exports, was left blank.

[p] See e.g., Articles 12, 13, 17 and 18 of the Subsidies Code, Documents Supplement pp. DS-678, 679, 683.

[q] Documents Supplement pp. DS-703-718.

[r] One interesting difference, doubtless reflecting dissatisfaction with the United States' conduct in the DISC case (§ 7.23 at N. p. *supra*), was the statement that "complaints and counter-complaints in regard to distinct matters should not be linked." See Documents Supplement p. DS-710.

[s] See § 7.23 *supra.*

which could obtain a three-year extension and technical assistance) would be obligated to use the same techniques for computing the dutiable value of imported goods. The basic method would be "transaction value," i.e. the price actually paid by the importer, with adjustments for specified items such as packing costs, sales commissions, royalties, and the like. If the transaction value is not appropriate—for instance in case of sales between affiliated entities—the Code provides a hierarchy of alternative methods, looking first to sales of identical goods to the same market, then to sales of similar goods to the same market, then to resale of the same or similar goods in the importing country, and so on.[a]

The *Standards Code*, bringing together not only issues of protection vs. free trade, but also differing emphases on health and safety (as well as problems of federalism, regionalism, and government/industry relations) was looser. Except for dispute settlement, only future and not existing technical standards and certification systems were to be made subject to the Code. The principal provisions stated that covered technical standards and certification systems shall not be prepared with a view to creating obstacles to international trade.[b] Enforcement of this principle was to be through advance publicity and notification; opportunity for foreign as well as domestic interests to comment on proposed regulations; increased responsibility on the part of central governments for regulations promulgated by subordinate units;[c] and a dispute settlement procedure based on the consultation/committee/panel model but with provision also for advice from technical experts.

The proposed *Government Procurement Code stated* clearly that the basic GATT principles of national and most favored nation treatment would apply to purchases by governments coming under the Code.

---

[a] The last method, to be used only with consent of the producer, provides for determination of the cost of production plus overhead and profit, similar to the alternate value used in dumping cases and in the Trigger Price Mechanism. See § 6.12 at Ns. s–t.

[b] Agreement on Technical Barriers to Trade, §§ 2.1 and 7.1, Documents Supplement pp. DS-719, 720.

[c] The obligation is stated in terms of "such reasonable measures" as may be available to [the central governments] to ensure that local government bodies and non-governmental bodies comply with the [basic] provisions." Draft Agreement, Articles 4.1 and 8.1 A provision making this obligation applicable also to standards set by industry associations was dropped between the December 1978 and the March 1979 versions.

Enforcement was to be through publicity, opportunity for a foreign potential bidder to consult with the procuring agency, and ultimately a governmental dispute settlement procedure along the familiar pattern. But the big dispute all along had been over the exclusions from the basic rule. The Code put the minimum or threshold figure of a covered procurement at SDR 150,000—roughly $195,000—subject to further negotiation of the amount; the entities to be covered—e.g. national telephone monopolies,[d] or states in a federal union—were to be set forth in an annex which was left blank in the published version.

In addition, there were proposed arrangements on *commercial counterfeiting;*[e] various non-tariff measures peculiar to particular countries; a proposal to reduce duties and NTB's on *aircraft;*[f] and an agreement on *import licensing.*[g] And there was a fat, though perhaps shaky package on agriculture, including a proposed Wheat Trade Convention, a Coarse Grains Trade Convention (both involving the United States as exporter, the European Community as importer); an International Dairy Agreement (with the roles reversed); a Bovine Meat Arrangement; and an understanding to establish within the GATT an International Agricultural Consultative Council to monitor the agreements that came out of the MTN and to consult on the international effects of the parties' domestic farm policies.

(e) *Tariffs.* Tariffs, as mentioned earlier, had been much less contentious in the Tokyo Round than in the Kennedy Round, in part because they were already fairly low, in part because it was agreed early on that any reductions would be phased in over eight years (with a review after five years), in part because some areas—including textiles, agriculture, and steel—had been treated separately almost from the start. The so-called disparities issue, which had so absorbed the Kennedy Round,[h] was compromised this time without great controversy, accord-

---

[d] Recall the United States' concern about Japan's NTT, § 7.24 N. b *supra.*

[e] To prevent, for example, the sale of "Levis" not made by or under license from Levi, Strauss of San Francisco.

[f] This was a late American initiative, reflecting the fact that a five-nation consortium producing the "Airbus" had finally cracked the near-monopoly in airliner production maintained by Boeing, McDonnell-Douglas, and Lockheed until the late 1970's.

[g] This was not a code on administration of quotas, but on red tape. Recall the use of even automatic import licensing as a semi-protectionist measure in connection with the first phase of the Simonet-Davignon Plan, p. 280 *supra.*

[h] See § 3.71 *supra.*

ing to a formula proposed by Switzerland whereby the higher the initial tariff, the higher the percentage by which it would be reduced.[i] The final negotiations over the items to be included or excluded, were to take place over the coming weeks, between the United States and Japan, the EEC and Japan, the United States and Canada, and so on.

7.42—READING THE TRADE ACT AGAIN

(a) *A New Legislative Formula*. The Trade Act of 1974 was in a number of respects pioneering legislation for the United States. Unlike the Trade Agreements Acts from 1934 through 1958[a] and the Trade Expansion Act of 1962,[b] which focused on tariff-cutting authority, the Trade Act of 1974 authorized and directed the President to seek agreement on a series of reforms of the international trading system, with special emphasis on so-called non-tariff barriers. This mandate, as we have seen, had given the primary impetus to the Tokyo Round that was now coming to a close. But Congress had not been willing in this relatively uncharted area to give an unrestricted delegation to the executive branch to negotiate binding agreements. Indeed, if the negotiations were successful, specific legislation would probably be required for the United States to comply with new rules on such matters as dumping, subsidies, countervailing duties, government procurement, and technical standards. On the other hand, the experience in the Kennedy Round with respect to elimination of American Selling Price[c] and to implementation by the United States of the International Anti-Dumping Code[d] suggested that simply authorizing negotiations ad referendum was a bad idea.

---

[i] The formula, agreed to as early as November 1977, provided that if the initial duty was $x\%$, the final duty would be $\dfrac{14x}{14+x}$ %. For example, a 30 per cent duty would be reduced in stages so that it would come to rest at $\dfrac{14(30)}{44} = 9.5\%$; a 15 per cent duty would be reduced to $\dfrac{14(15)}{29} = 7.24\%$. In terms of percentage of reductions, the first was a 68.2% reduction, the second a 51.7% reduction. Since the authority to reduce duties under § 101(b)(1) of the Trade Act of 1974 was limited for most duties to a reduction of 60 per cent from the existing duty, the United States entered a reservation limiting its reductions pursuant to the formula to that amount.

[a] See § 3.52 *supra*.

[b] See § 3.53 *supra*.

[c] See § 3.72 at Ns. m–r *supra*.

[d] See § 4.44 *supra*.

The United States executive branch might get itself in the position of making commitments it could not keep, and the foreign governments (especially the European Community) might well be reluctant to make forthcoming offers to reach agreements that could be delayed or rebuffed by the American Congress.

In facing this dilemma in 1973, the Nixon Administration came forward with a novel compromise. Congress would be given a chance to scrutinize any non-tariff agreement before it became effective, but only within a brief, finite period; furthermore, if there were a package deal, Congress would have to approve or reject it in toto, without picking and choosing and without amendment. In the administration's version of this compromise, the President would have been required to give 90 days' notice in advance of concluding any agreement, in order to give time for consultation with the appropriate committees of Congress; after an agreement was signed, the President would submit the agreement and his proposed implementing orders to the Congress, subject to rejection by a vote of an absolute majority of the members of either the House or the Senate.[e] The House Ways and Means Committee essentially agreed with this approach, but in order to forestall proponents of an agreement (i.e. administration supporters) from using filibuster or other delaying tactics to prevent a resolution of disapproval from coming to a vote within the 90 days allowed, the Committee added and the House passed provisions for expedited and privileged consideration of resolutions of disapproval, both within the Committees and on the floor of the House and Senate.[f]

The Senate Finance Committee also agreed with the need for a middle way between excessive delegation to the executive branch and unlimited possibility for consideration by the Congress after international negotiations had been completed. But it insisted that if domestic statutes were to be changed in order to conform to international agreement, the Congress should take affirmative action to do so. But recognizing the perils

---

[e] H.R. 6767, as introduced by request of the President April 10, 1973, § 103(d) and (e), 93rd Cong., 1st Sess. (1973). For a list of precedents for such a scheme, which is not free from constitutional doubts on several grounds, see Wolff, "The U.S. Mandate for Trade Negotiations," 16 Va. J. Int'l L. 505, 514 note 45 (1976).

[f] H.R. 10710 § 151, as passed by the House of Representatives on Dec. 11, 1973. For a more detailed explanation, see *Trade Reform Act of 1973*, Report of House Ways and Means Comm., H. Rept. No. 93–571 at pp. 108–110, 93rd Cong., 1st Sess. (1973).

of amendment and delay if the agreements were simply submitted subject to the ordinary legislative process, the Finance Committee proposed a complicated process for expedited action by the Congress on the package that would come out of the Multilateral Trade Negotiations.[g] The Senate as a whole, and ultimately the Senate-House conference, adopted the Committee's proposals, which became law as sections 102(f) and 151 of the Trade Act of 1974.[h] Section 151 provides for submission by the President of an implementing bill (subsection (b)(i)), which is not subject to amendment (subsection (d)); the bill must be reported out by each committee to which it is referred within 45 legislative days and thereafter each House has 15 legislative days to vote on the bill (subsection (e)(i)).

A further complication arose because a portion of the implementing legislation might affect duties, and might therefore fall within Article I § 7 of the Constitution, which provides that all revenue bills must originate in the House of Representatives. For "implementing revenue bills," an extra 15 days was added for consideration by Senate Committees after passage by the House, and then 15 more days for consideration by the full Senate (§ 151(e)(2)). Thus the full procedure must be completed within 90 days.[i] Motions for recommital or postponement were not permitted, and a time limit for debate was written right into the bill (subsections (f) and (g)).

When the Trade Act was going through Congress, everyone seemed satisfied with this procedure,[j] though not quite sure how it would work out in practice. When the procedure was put to the test in the early months of 1979, the answer came out. Since the legislation could not be amended once introduced, the waiting period following President Carter's notice of intention to enter into a trade agreement was used for intensive negotiations between the Congressional committees and the executive branch over the details of the bill. But since the bill had not been intro-

(Text continued on page 341)

---

[g] For a somewhat more detailed account of the negotiation between the executive branch and the Senate Finance Committee on this point, see Marks and Malgrem, Negotiating Nontariff Distortions to Trade," 7 Law & Pol'y Int'l Bus. 327, 338–41 (1975).

[h] Documents Supplement pp. DS-299, 323.

[i] The "days" in this calculation, as is made clear by § 151(e)(3), are days when the House in question is in session.

[j] See e.g. Wolff N. e *supra* at 518; Marks and Malmgren, N. g *supra* at 341.

Behind closed doors, Robert Strauss (left) and Russell Long (right) are horse trading on the trade bill and lobbyists want in. Huenergarth, *The New York Times*, March 25, 1979.

duced, there could be no public hearings, and as one observer put it, decisions were taken "in small rooms late at night." With the United States executive branch, foreign governments, members of Congress, and lobbyists of all interests and persuasions[k] trying to follow (and of course to influence) the action, the chairmen of the Finance Committee of the Senate and the Trade Subcommittee of the House took to issuing press releases recording agreements on particular aspects of the legislation that, officially, did not even have a bill number. If the process worked out, by the time the bill was introduced, its passage though the Congress would have been assured. The scope of maneuver was, of course, not very wide, because the legislation had to be in implementation of the MTN agreements.[l] But if, say, the steel caucus[m] as a condition for its support of the bill, could gain a few extra points on such technical matters as whether or not provisional antidumping duties could be bonded or how to define injury in a subsidy case, a deal made in this fashion could be opposed only by opposing the entire six-year 98-country MTN.[n]

(b) *Countervailing Duty Waivers.* As we saw in examining the steel industry's applications for countervailing duties (§ 4.45–.47 supra), there had been a good deal of dissatisfaction both among particular industries and among many members of Congress with the administration of the countervailing duty law. Congress made sure in the Trade Act of 1974 that the Treasury would act on countervailing duty petitions within 12 months from their filing,[a] and that negative determinations by

---

[k] The executive branch itself mobilized some of the most prestigious lawyers and lobbyists in Washington in a committee to drum up support and lubricate the deals necessary to "clear" the implementing legislation.

[l] But even here, some changes were still possible. For example, in response to pressure from small business and minority groups, Ambassador Strauss agreed to modify the government procurement code so as to permit preservation of preferences for minority business and small businesses in the United States, to the exclusion of potential foreign bidders. In return, the United States would have to yield on some of its insistence on inclusion of previously reserved items of government procurement in the national treatment obligation.

[m] Recall § 6.11 *supra.*

[n] Ambassador Strauss, who oversaw this strange negotiation, was seen by both his admirers and his detractors as a master wheeler-dealer, in the Texas tradition of Lyndon Johnson and John Connally. To the question of whether in these last hectic days in Washington he was "giving away the store," one of his supporters replied "Better the store than the whole shopping center." For a fascinating account of Ambassador Strauss in operation, see Elizabeth Drew, "Profiles (Robert S. Strauss)," The New Yorker, May 7, 1979, pp. 50–129.

[a] Section 303(a)(4) of the Tariff Act of 1930, as amended, Documents Supplement p. DS-441.

the Treasury would be subject to judicial review.[b] But Congress also realized that the whole subject of subsidies and countervailing duties called for international negotiations,[c] and it was sensitive to the danger that if the Treasury were now forced to act in a twelve-month period on all the cases which it had been gentling along plus new ones that were sure to be filed, the possibilities of negotiating an international subsidies code might well be impaired. Accordingly, the Secretary of the Treasury was authorized to waive the imposition of countervailing duties if he found (A) that adequate steps had been taken to reduce the adverse effects of a bounty or grant; (B) that there was reasonable prospect of a successful negotiation of an agreement to reduce NTB's; and (C) that imposition of a countervailing duty would be likely to jeopardize negotiations of such an agreement.[d] But this waiver authority was made effective for a four-year period from the passage of the Trade Act, i.e. one year less than the period of the negotiating authorities on which the MTN would be based.[e] The House Report on the bill said that the shorter time limit was provided "to facilitate the international negotiations."[f]

In the following four years, the Treasury granted 19 waivers, of which 15 were in effect at the close of 1978, concerning about $600 million worth of imports. All of these waivers would have to terminate on January 2, 1979, four years after the effective date of the Trade Act. Several of the major participants in the MTN, led by the European Community, took the position that they could not negotiate a new subsidies code under the threat of imposition by the United States of countervailing duties for practices that might be deemed lawful under a new code or (more likely) under procedures that would be declared unlawful (because no determination of injury had been made). The United States

---

[b] Section 515 and 516 of the Tariff Act of 1930, as amended, Documents Supplement p. DS-444-47.

[c] Trade Act of 1974, § 121(a)4, Tariff Act of 1930 as amended § 303(d)(1).

[d] Tariff Act of 1930 as amended, § 303(d)2. Note, as an example of lobbying pressure, the clause in that section excluding non-rubber footwear from the waiver authority.

[e] The Senate bill would have given only a two-year waiver authority, while the House bill did not contain the requirement for finding (A), (B), and (C) as a condition for exercising the waiver authority. In the House-Senate Conference, the Senate accepted the four-year period and the House accepted the conditions plus the one-House veto that became § 303(e)(2).

[f] *Trade Reform Act of 1973*, Report of House Ways and Means Comm., H. Rept. No. 93-57 at pp. 76, 93rd Cong., 1st Sess. (1973).

government, on the other hand, was reluctant to go to Congress with a request for extension of the waiver authority without a subsidies code in hand. After the Framework of Understanding had been negotiated in July 1978, the administration was ready to seek an extension. But rather than introducing a bill to do so as separate legislation, the administration agreed to its introduction as an amendment to the Sugar Stabilization Bill,[g] in a deal whereby proponents of the sugar bill (which would have established higher support prices than the President wanted) hoped to forestall a veto by linking it to the countervailing duty bill, and proponents of countervailing duty waivers sought to get their bill through by tying it to the sugar bill which the Chairman of the Senate Finance Committee wanted. The strategy worked in the Senate, but the House balked. A countervailing duty waiver extension amendment was then added to the Trade Adjustment Assistance Bill,[h] which was also passed by the Senate and sent to the House. The House made changes in respect to adjustment assistance[i] (but not to the duty waiver extension) and sent the bill back to the Senate. Amid a rush of non-germane amendments[j] in the closing days of the session, the Senate failed to take final action before adjournment. Thus the Senate had twice voted in favor of duty waiver extension and the House once, but no legislation emerged and the waiver authority expired.

Ambassador Strauss, trying to keep both the European Community and the Congress in line, issued a statement affirming his belief "that conditions will exist for [the next session] of Congress . . . to act immediately to resolve this potentially serious problem in trade relations."[k] The EC Council of Ministers said it was prepared to continue the trade talks, but "unless the uncertainty over the imposition of countervailing duties from 3 January can be resolved, the common assumption of shared responsibility on which we have based the Tokyo Round would no longer exist. . . ."[l]

---

[g] H.R. 7108 in its Senate version, 95th Cong., 2d Sess. (1978).

[h] H.R. 11711, Senate version, 95th Cong., 2d Sess. (1978).

[i] Recall § 3.53 at Ns. w–y *supra*.

[j] Dealing with such subjects as family assistance and welfare.

[k] Office of Special Representative for Trade Negotiations, Press Release #280, Oct. 16, 1978.

[l] Statement of the Council of Ministers of the European Community, October 16, 1978, as released by European Communities Information Service, Washing-

When Congress reconvened in January 1979, a bill was immediately introduced to extend the waiver authority through October 1979 or passage of legislation implementing the MTN, whichever came first. This bill was not, of course, governed by any special procedures, and the fear was that protectionist or other special interests would use it as a "Christmas tree" on which to hang various amendments connected to the trade talks or otherwise. The textile, sugar, and steel industries focused on this bill as they did on the major implementing legislation, and for a time in the period February–April 1979 negotiations on both bills were in progress simultaneously, especially with the chairman of the Senate Finance Committee. Meanwhile the Treasury suspended liquidation on imports of the products that had been found to be subsidized (on which the waiver had now expired), but it permitted importers to furnish bonds or irrevocable letters of credit to cover the additional duties rather than actually paying the duties.

Once Ambassador Strauss made his peace with the textile industry, the waiver bill went through the Ways and Means Committee and the full House without difficulty. In the Senate the sticking point was sugar, but once that industry had been pacified through a promise of higher domestic support prices, the Finance Committee also passed the waiver authority without amendments.[m] The bill had smooth sailing in both Houses, and on April 3, 1979, the duty waiver extension was signed by the President.[n] The signal to

---

ton, EC News No. 19/1978, October 16, 1978. The Community's insistence on the countervailing duty waivers, as often in such matters, appears to have been led by the French, although no French goods were involved in the countervailing duty waivers. The actual products at issue for the Community were canned beans and dairy products, plus butter cookies, all from Denmark. Other products included various cheeses from Finland, Austria, Norway and Switzerland, plus leather goods from several South American countries, textiles from Brazil, and fish from Canada. A subsidy (actually a freight rate rebate) on exports of steel plate from Mexico, calculated at $0.76 per ton was withdrawn in October, 1978, and accordingly the waiver of a countervailing duty on Mexican steel plate was revoked. See 43 Fed. Reg. 50170 (Oct. 27, 1978).

[m] According to Elizabeth Drew, § 7.42(c) N. n *supra* at 51–52, Ambassador Strauss told Chairman Long that if an amendment to extend child support and day-care programs were permitted to be attached to the bill as already passed by the House he would resign, because the delay that would be required by a Senate-House Conference would not permit him to keep his promise to the European Community that the bill would be passed before the April meeting of the Council of Ministers: "If that amendment goes through," Strauss said, "I'm getting out of the government tomorrow, because that will louse it all up."

[n] Pub. L. 96–6, April 3, 1979. In the House, the waiver bill was adopted by voice vote; in the Senate the vote was 82–15.

Geneva, Brussels and Tokyo was clear. The United States was ready to sign the Tokyo Round Agreements.

7.43—THE UNRAVELING PROCESS

Between December 1978 and April 1979 several sets of negotiations went on simultaneously. One set, as we saw, involved American industry/labor groups, the two committees of Congress, and the Special Representative for Trade Negotiations. In another set of negotiations, Ambassador Strauss and his staff attempted to coordinate the bargaining in Washington with the final stage of bargaining in Geneva. In a third set of negotiations, bilateral bargaining was continuing, on tariff offers and exceptions to the general formula, on government procurement, and on a variety of additional trade issues that concerned some but not all of the participants in the Tokyo Round. Finally, GATT's version of the North-South dialogue was continuing, focused particularly on the Safeguards Code but more generally on the perception by the developing countries that the promise of special and differential treatment[a] (known in Geneva as the "s & D issue") had not been fulfilled.

The first casualty of these processes was the *Safeguards Code*. The European Community, as we saw, wanted to reserve the right to impose escape clause or other emergency measures against particular countries;[b] the Developing Countries threatened to walk out of the Conference and sign no agreement at all if a provision authorizing selective safeguards were included in the code. Japan, though quiet on the issue, had reason to suspect that it too might be the target of selectivity,[c] and in general, stood to gain little from a safeguards code. The United States was officially neutral in this controversy, though it had been the main proponent of a safeguards code. But as we saw, United States law already authorized selective application of escape clause action in certain circumstances,[d] and to the

---

[a] See paragraph 2 of the Tokyo Declaration of GATT Ministers, Documents Supplement p. DS-660.

[b] Like much of the MTN as well as other negotiations concerning the international economy, the position of the European Community represented the results of a negotiation within a negotiation. West Germany, it seems, was for MFN and against selectivity, but was not prepared to engage on a major confrontation over the issue with France and Great Britain.

[c] Recall the experience of the 1950's, when many countries invoked Article XXXV of the GATT in order to deny the benefits of MFN to Japan. See § 3.33 *supra.*

[d] See § 7.32(b) at N. c *supra.*

extent a safeguards code would subject voluntary restraint agreements to international scrutiny (Chapter 4 bis of the proposed safeguards code, left blank in the version published in December 1978[e]) the United States may have been, to put it politely, ambivalent. By mid-March, if not before, the Safeguards Code was dead.

The *Government Procurement Code*, as published in December 1978, had left for further negotiations the list of entities of each participating government whose purchases would come under the Code. Early in the legislative process described in § 7.42, the American textile industry had secured a commitment from the Carter administration to continue support for the so-called Berry Amendment,[f] which reserved to domestic sources virtually all defense procurement, not only guns, tanks and aircraft, but also textiles, shoes, food, and all items subject to escape clause or other restraint arrangements.[g] The Administration originally planned to do away with so-called "set-asides" in United States procurement for small business and minority business.[h] Ambassador Strauss argued that small and minority business stood to lose some $400 million per year in U.S. government purchases, but would gain much more in access to foreign markets. Representatives of these interests (including various Congressional subcommittees), however, contended that the losses would be theirs and the gains from foreign procurement would go to the big multinationals; moreover, they were reluctant to see any curtailment of "affirmative action" by the U.S. government. The Administration had to back down, and the United States reduced its offers under the Procurement Code accordingly.

More serious, less than two weeks before the scheduled signing of the MTN agreements, the United States broke off its negotiations on government procurement with Japan, on the ground, as Ambassador Strauss said, that Japan's proposals were "wholly inadequate."[i] Since

---

[e] Documents Supplement p. DS-696.

[f] Department of Defense Appropriation Act, 1976, Pub. L. 94–212, § 723, 90 Stat. 172 (1976), renewed in DoD Appropriation Act, 1979, Pub. L. 95–457, § 824, 92 Stat. 1248 (1978).

[g] For instance specialty steels, see § 5.56 *supra*.

[h] See Department of Defense Appropriation Act 1976, Pub. L. 94–212 § 709, 90 Stat. 169 (1976), renewed in DoD Defense Appropriation Act, 1979, Pub. L. 95–457 § 810, 92 Stat. 1245 (1978). See also Public Works Employment Act of 1977 § 103(f)(2), 42 U.S.C. § 6705(f)(2), upheld in *Fullilove v. Kreps,* 584 F.2d 600 (2d Cir. 1978), cert. granted May 21, 1979, aff'd *sub nom.*, Fullilove v. Klutznick, 448 U.S. 448 (1980).

[i] Office of the Special Representative for Trade Negotiations, Press Release #303, March 29, 1979. Japan's list of covered entities did include the Japan

the Code (both in its provisional and its final version) had a mini-Article XXXV,[j] the United States could lawfully sign the agreement but give notice that it did not consent to its application as between the United States and Japan.[k]

As other countries made and withdrew offers (i.e., included or excluded purchasing entities), the vision of open international procurement gradually receded. For the United States, for instance, not only the bulk of purchases by the Defense Department, but also those by the Departments of Transportation and Energy, the Army Corps of Engineers, the TVA, as well as Amtrak, Conrail, and the Postal Service, were excluded, and so were all state and local purchases, even those based on federal grants.[l] Altogether, adding the effect of exclusions plus the threshold, Ambassador Strauss estimated that approximately 15 per cent of United States procurement would be covered by the Code; a fair assumption was that no more (and probably less) of other countries' public procurement would now be internationalized. The estimate of STR was that the market that was opening up amounted to about $20 billion per year, on which a reasonable share for American bidders would be between 7 and 12 per cent.

Discussion of the *Subsidies Code* among industry, STR, and Congress did not look to textual changes in the Code. The December version, like the final text, provided that once the procedural requirements have been

---

National Railways and NTT (§ 7.24(a) N. b *supra*), but both subject to footnotes that excluded substantial purchases.

[j] Government Procurement Code Part IX, para. 9.

[k] Following the announcement of March 29, 1979, there were further negotiations on the government procurement issue, in anticipation of the visit to Washington of Japan's Prime Minister Masayoshi Ohira. As of the end of April, however, there was no agreement. The chairman of NTT, hoping to develop his firm's own computer technology, was reported to have offered to open procurement to the United States for buckets, rags, mops, office supplies, and steel telephone poles, but not for high technology products. See, e.g. New York Times, April 26, 1979, p. D4, col. 4; Newsweek, May 7, 1979, p. 61, col. 2–3. "Now how many steel telephone poles do you think we'll sell in Japan, with their steel business," Ambassador Strauss asked. "What the hell good does that do us?" Quoted in Elizabeth Drew, § 7.42(a) N. n *supra* at 62.

[l] But the American Battle Monuments Commission, the Federal Deposit Insurance Corporation, the Smithsonian Institution, and the Office of Personnel Management were included; the United Kingdom included the British Museum and the National Galleries of Scotland, the Royal Commission on Gardening, and the Boundary Commission for Northern Ireland, but not British Railways, or the telecommunications services of the Post Office. France also excluded its railways, but included hundreds of schools, institutes, and museums.

met, "the decision whether or not to impose a countervailing duty," and if so for how much, "are decisions to be made by the authorities of the importing country."[m] That being so, the focus turned to the implementing legislation.

The lead, as might be expected, was taken by the American Iron and Steel Institute. In January 1979, U.S. Steel finally withdrew the countervailing duty petition left over from the *Zenith* case,[n] which had argued that remission of value-added or turnover taxes gave an incentive to produce for export rather than for domestic sale.[o] But faced with the introduction of a requirement for an injury determination as a condition precedent to imposition of a countervailing duty, the steel industry sought to make that requirement as easy to satisfy as possible.[p] The Subsidies Code, precisely following for this purpose the International Anti-Dumping Code of 1967, states that "the term injury shall, unless otherwise specified, be taken to mean *material* injury to a domestic industry, threat of material injury . . . or material retardation of the establishment of such an industry. . . ."[q] (emphasis added). The steel industry, which as we saw had been unsympathetic to the Anti-Dumping Code[r] was anxious not to see repeated in the subsidy field the kind of experience it had had before 1975 in its antidumping complaints (for example in the *Wire Rod Cases*), where injury had not been found because the prices of country *A's* products matched those of Country *B*, and Country *B's* exports to the United States were not found to be dumped or subsidized. The steel industry sought a definition of material injury as "any injury more than inconsequential or

---

[m] For the final version, see Subsidies Code Article 4(1), Documents Supplement p. DS-668.

[n] See § 4.47(d) *supra.*

[o] Note that among the prohibited practices listed in the illustrative Annex to the Subsidies Code is exemption or remission of indirect taxes *in excess* of those levied in respect of products sold for domestic consumption. The footnote to the Annex (Documents Supplement p. DS-689) distinguishes between direct and indirect taxes in the traditional way, i.e. rejecting the arguments and doubts suggested by U.S. Steel and Zenith (§ 4.47 *supra*).

[p] Compare § 7.34(c) *supra.*

[q] Subsidies Code, Article 2(1) note 6 (as renumbered).

[r] Recall the struggle in the United States over the Anti-Dumping Code in the 1960's, § 4.44 *supra.*

[s] § 4.43 *supra.*

immaterial." This proposed definition was not accepted by the Senate Committee, which voted to omit the word "material" altogether. Under pressure from the EEC, which insisted that the word "injury" be modified by the word "material" as a condition for its adherence to the Subsidies Code, the three-way House-Senate-STR negotiations finally agreed to include the term "material injury", to be defined as "harm which is not inconsequential, immaterial, or unimportant.'" Moreover, the Code required "a causal link between the subsidized imports and the alleged injury.'" The Congressional Committees wanted to be sure that this requirement did not impose a burden on the complainant to prove that its injury was not the result of other factors.'

Still another important issue, focused on by steel and similarly situated interests, was that the Subsidies Code prohibited only *export* subsidies (Article 9(1)),ʷ some of which were set forth in an illustrative Annex. Other types of subsidies were discouraged if they caused injury, serious prejudice, or impairment to the interests of another signatory (Article 8(3)), but on the other hand the Code stated that they are "widely

---

ᵗ Joint Press Release, Sen. Comm. on Finance, House Comm. on Ways and Means, May 24, 1979, p. 1. Apparently the EEC was mollified by use of the word "unimportant", which differentiated the new text from the language of the Senate Finance Committee's discussion of § 201(a) of the Anti-dumping Act, as it had been amended in the Trade Act of 1974. That Report read:

> The term "injury," which is unqualified by adjectives such as "material" or "serious," has been consistently interpreted by the [Tariff] Commission as being that degree of injury which the law will recognize and take into account. Obviously, the law will not recognize trifling, immaterial, insignificant or inconsequential injury. Immaterial injury connotes spiritual injury, which may exist inside of persons not industries. Injury must be a harm which is more than frivolous, inconsequential, insignificant, or immaterial.

Report of Sen. Finance Comm. S. Rep't No. 93–1298, 93d Cong., 2d Sess. at p. 180 (1974).

ᵘ Subsidies Code, Article 2(c); see also Article b(2)–(4).

ᵛ The Senate Report cited at N. t *supra* continues:

> . . . the law does not contemplate that injury from less-than-fair-value imports be weighed against other factors which may be contributing to injury to an industry. The words "by reason of" express a causation link but do not mean . . . a (or the) principal cause, a (or the) major cause, or a (or the) substantial cause of injury caused by all factors contributing to overall injury to an industry.

> In short, the Committee does not view injury caused by unfair competition, such as dumping, to require as strong a causation link to imports as would be required for determining the existence of injury under fair trade conditions.

ʷ Note that developing countries were exempt from this prohibition. See Article 14(2).

used as important instruments for the promotion of social and economic policy objectives. . . ." (Article 11). The U.S. Congress, spurred on by the negotiating process described in § 7.42, decided that the term subsidy should be defined to include (i) the traditional concept of "bounty or grant" that had been part of U.S. law since the 1890's;[x] (ii) any export subsidy listed in the Annex to the Subsidies Code; and (iii) a series of domestic subsidies including provision of capital on non-commercial terms (recall the reorganization of the French steel industry, described briefly in § 6.33); the provision of goods or services at preferential rates; the grant of funds or forgiveness of debts; and the assumption of any costs of manufacturing, production or distribution.[y]

Finally, the Code, though it accepted countervailing duties, preferred at all stages a negotiated resolution of a controversy over subsidies, and it provided expressly for undertakings by exporters to revise their prices "so that the investigating authorities are satisfied that the *injurious effect* of the subsidy is eliminated" (Article 4(5)(a)). The American steel industry and its allies persuaded the Congress to write a provision in the implementing legislation authorizing suspension of an investigation if the exporting country agrees to eliminate the subsidy or the exporter agrees to revise its price, but only if such agreement *completely offsets the net amount of the subsidy,* and subject to the right of the competing domestic manufacturer, union, or trade association to appeal suspension of the investigation to the International Trade Commission.[z]

How long this process could go on was not clear. The chief spokesman for the European Community issued a statement—rather unusual in diplomatic practice—saying that:

"the Council of Ministers will be closely scrutinising the implementing legislation of this part of the Agreement, and we hope that the injury test and related procedures, which are complicated but important, will be faithfully carried into American domestic law.'"[a]

---

[x] See § 4.45(a) *supra.*

[y] Subcomm. on Trade, House Comm. on Ways and Means, *Summary of Recommendations for Legislation implementing the MTN.,* pp. 4–5, Comm. Print WMCP 96–21, 96th Cong., 1st Sess. (1979); Sen. Comm. on Finance Press Release #116 p. 3, May 8, 1979. For the final version of these Provisions, see Trade Agreements Act of 1979, § 771(5) and (7) and § 704(b), Documents Supplement pp. DS-483, 511–12.

[z] Ibid (House) p. 6, (Senate) p. 14.

[a] Statement of Sir Roy Denman, Director General for External Relations of

The Senate Finance Committee, for its part, circulated a draft bill including a statement that:

> "no provision of any trade agreement [submitted to and approved by the Congress] nor the application of any such provision to any person or circumstances, which is in conflict with any statute of the United States, shall be given effect under the laws of the United States."[b]

7.44—THE OUTCOME

While all of these events were in progress—in Washington, Brussels, Tokyo, and Geneva—the deadline for concluding the Multilateral Trade Negotiations was fast approaching. If the ninety-day period from President Carter's notice of intention to conclude an agreement[a] had been fully utilized, an agreed bill would have emerged for up or down consideration by the Congress at just about the time scheduled for signing of the agreements. But that 90-day period (in contrast to the later period for legislative consideration) was only a minimum. Drafting of United States legislation could continue even after the agreements were signed, though it was clear that no country would implement the agreements until the United States did. The Council of Ministers of the European Community did not formally accept the agreements until April 3, 1979, the same day that President Carter signed the countervailing duty waiver extension bill.[b] But now it was time to move quickly, before the unraveling process went further, and before nearly all the countries (and many of the delegates) that had participated in the Tokyo Round would direct their attention to the fifth general conference of UNCTAD, scheduled to begin early in May in Manila.

On April 12, 1979, the countries signed. To be precise, 23 countries signed—the 9 members of the European Community, most of the mem-

---

the European Commission, April 12, 1979, as released in Washington by the Embassy of France. Thereafter, the Community hired its own monitor/lobbyist, to look out for the Community's interests in the legislative process.

[b] Senate Discussion Draft Bill, as revised through April 19, 1979, § 3. The final version of this provision appears as § 3(a) of the Trade Agreements Act of 1979, Documents Supplement pp. DS-475.

[a] § 7.4 N. e *supra*.

[b] § 7.42(b) *supra*.

bers of EFTA,[c] two East European countries,[d] Canada, Australia and New Zealand, and the United States and Japan, plus Argentina, the only developing country in the group.[e] Whether the last-minute boycott by the developing countries would remain permanent was not clear. The hope among the proponents of the MTN was that after UNCTAD was out of the way and the benefits of the various codes became clear—e.g. the requirement of an injury determination as a condition of countervailing duties against subsidies on exports—the developing countries, or at least a substantial number of them, would come along. Not only would that result be important as a political matter in the North-South dialogue and for the continued viability of the GATT; the more developing countries accepted the results of the bargain six years in the making, the less acute would be the problems of conditional MFN and possible discrepancy between the General Agreement itself and the new rules adopted in explication and implementation of the General Agreement.

For the time being, however, the results had to be assessed in terms of those countries that did sign and those documents that were put on the table. Twelve agreements were submitted for signature, not counting tariff offers from all of the developed country participants. The Safeguards Code, as we saw, had been withdrawn, though the parties said in the document of signature that work on the subject should be continued "as a matter of urgency," with a target date of July 15, 1979.[f]

---

[c] Sweden, Finland, Norway, Austria, and Switzerland.

[d] Hungary and Bulgaria.

[e] To be precise, the countries signed a *"Procès Verbal"* prepared by the Director General of GATT, by which they indicated

> "their intention to submit the relevant texts or legal instruments to be formulated on the basis of the said texts for the consideration of their respective authorities with a view to seeking approval of, or other decisions on the relevant texts or other instruments in accordance with appropriate procedures in their respective countries."

Procès Verbal of 11 April, 1979, GATT DOC. MTN/28. The representatives were invited to indicate whether their signature related to all, or only to certain of the texts before them. Argentina "reserved" with respect to the Subsidies and Government Procurement Codes.

It is interesting that Ambassador Strauss, who more than any other person had made completion of the MTN possible, was too busy in Washington to attend, and sent Ambassador McDonald, one of his two deputies, to the ceremony.

[f] Procès Verbal N. e *supra,* para. 6.

Wheat and Coarse Grains, only marginally part of the GATT negotiations, had also fallen by the wayside since December 1978, and the agreement on commercial counterfeiting (a late starter in the Tokyo Round) did not make it by the due date. That left the Subsidies/Countervailing Duties Code, substantially as in the December package; an agreement to bring the Anti-Dumping Code negotiated in the Kennedy Round[g] into line with the Subsidies Code; the Government Procurement Code, subject, as we saw, to notifications by each participant of its covered entities and of the countries entitled to benefit from its adherence to the Code; and the Agreement on Customs Valuation. Further, there were a Standards Code; and Agreement on Import Licensing, two agreements on agriculture (a price agreement on dairy products and a consultation agreement on bovine meat[h]); and an agreement signed by the Big Three plus Canada to eliminate all duties on civil aircraft and aircraft parts. Finally, the developed countries signed the so-called Framework Agreement, designed to formalize through an "enabling clause" the special and differential treatment for developing countries, and also, as we saw, to establish a general disputes settlement mechanism for matters not covered by one of the specialized codes.[i]

Altogether, it was an impressive accomplishment in international legislation. Olivier Long, completing a decade as Director-General of the GATT, could honestly say at the end of the signing ceremony that he was very happy to announce the agreements reached:

> Never before have there been trade negotiations so ambitious in aim, so complex in structure and subject matter, or, perhaps so long drawn-out over time. But the enormous effort invested in them has paid off.[j]

---

[g] § 4.44 *supra.*

[h] I.e. beef, veal, and live cattle.

[i] For a convenient source of the texts of the agreements as submitted by President Carter to Congress on June 19, 1979, see *Agreements Reached in the Tokyo Round of the Multilateral Trade Negotiations,* H.R. Doc. No. 96-153, 96th Cong., 1st Sess. (1979). Some, but not all of the agreements had been published in the U.S. Treaties series as of 1983. See 31 U.S.T. 405 (Standards); 513 (Subsidies); 619 (Civil Aircraft); 679 (Dairy Products); 4919 (Anti-Dumping). Except as indicated, the final version of the agreements was, for purposes here relevant, substantially similar to drafts described in § 7.41 *supra.*

[j] Press Release containing Statement by GATT Director-General at the close of the meeting of the Trade Negotiations Committee and Publication Agreements, April 12, 1979, p. 1, Doc. No. GATT/1234.

If he was concerned about the failure to reach agreement on a safe-guards code, upset about the failure—at least for the time being—of the developing countries to join in, and nervous about implementation of the agreements in Washington, Mr. Long could still be pleased with the outcome, considering the pressures that were pulling the other way:

> All negotiation demands compromise, and no negotiator ever obtains all that he asks for at the beginning. I have no doubt that many—indeed perhaps all—participants will not fail to remind us that the results of the Tokyo Round fall short of their declared initial expectations. Nonetheless, the results achieved represent, when taken together, a very substantial achievement.[k]

§ 7.5—Notes and Questions on the Outcome of the MTN

7.51—(a) In addition to its many other functions as a legislative and policy-setting conference, the Tokyo Round continued the tradition of periodic tariff-cutting sessions in accordance with Article XXVII bis of the General Agreement. As part of the agreement signed on April 12, 1979, the 14 developed countries (i.e., the nine members of the Community acting together plus the other signatories except Argentina) deposited with the GATT their negotiated tariff offers, subject to submission of schedules in final form under Article II of the GATT by June 30, 1979. The preliminary analysis by the GATT secretariat indicated that all industrial tariffs taken together would be reduced by about one third—slightly less in terms of percentage than the duty reductions in the Kennedy Round. The reductions would be staged over an eight-year period (longer than ever before) beginning on January 1, 1980, subject to a joint review after five years.

(b) The slow phase-in of duty reductions in a world of volatile movements in currency exchange rates explains why the tariff aspect of the Tokyo Round received less attention from all sides than was the case in prior rounds. Still, the amount of trade affected by the reductions was estimated at about $110 billion as of 1976, substantially more for later years.[a] The most important

---

[k] *Id.* p. 4.

[a] These estimates are drawn from the detailed Press Release issued by the GATT

cuts were concentrated in non-electrical machinery, wood products, chemicals, and transport equipment; textiles and leather goods were reduced less than the average, and as we saw, steel was excluded.[b] Agricultural products, though not governed by the harmonization formula,[c] were also made subject to exchanges of tariff concessions, and indeed the United States fought hard for and received reductions in duties on soybeans (America's leading export commodity) as well as tobacco, citrus fruit, and other products.[d] In all, the GATT secretariat estimated that about $12 billion worth of trade (out of a total of $48 billion trade in agricultural products) was affected by the tariff concessions negotiated in the Tokyo Round.[e]

(c) The developing countries complained that items of interest to them, such as tropical products and low-technology, labor-intensive goods were cut the least. This perception, indeed, may have been the main reason why, at the last minute, the Group of 77 countries declined to sign the agreements of the MTN.[f] Of course the more all duties are reduced, the less value there is in preferential duty arrangements for developing countries, and the less scope for "special and differential treatment" for developing countries. Beyond that, the pattern of the steel industry (as well as, earlier, for textiles) suggests that at least for what

---

on April 12, 1979, GATT/1234. Estimates by officials of the U.S. government were similar.

[b] So, for the United States, were items subject to import relief measures, such as television receivers, specialty steel and shoes.

[c] § 7.41(e) supra.

[d] In return, the United States had to open the door a bit wider to imports of cheese, pursuant to a Protocol on Certain Cheeses annexed to the International Dairy Agreement, and to promise to finally resolve the "water in the whiskey" or wine-gallon problem, § 2.44(d), N. m supra.

[e] The United States government estimated that the overall tariff disparity on dutiable trade with Japan would be changed from 4.3 points (U.S. 6.8%, Japan 11.5%) to 0.6 points the other way (U.S. 4.6%, Japan 4.0%). If duty-free as well as dutiable trade were counted, Japan would at the end of the staging process have a 2.4% lower average tariff than the United States (U.S. 4.6%, Japan 2.2%). From U.S. Dept. of State, MTN Multilateral Trade Negotiations, Current Policy 56 (Revised April 1979).

[f] The GATT secretariat, while acknowledging the perception, contended that if one looked at potential, and not just actual exports of the developing countries, the average cuts for items of interest to them were roughly the same as for all industrial countries. See GATT Press Release on the Tokyo Round Agreements p. 6, GATT/1234, 12 April 1979.

became known as the NIC's (newly industrializing countries),[g] the hospitality of the industrial world to new entrants has its limits.

(d) Perhaps the most perplexing question raised by the MTN was whether the developing countries would in the long run view their interests as better served inside or outside the club; if a substantial number of developing countries chose not to adhere to the Tokyo Round results, after participating in its evolution for half a decade, what would become of the most favored nation principle, and in the long run, of the GATT itself?

7.52—(a) The most ambitious intellectual effort, as we have seen, concerned the problem of subsidies. The breakthrough, if it can be called that, was creation of the two-track approach. An *importing country* complaining of subsidies by an exporting country has two routes available under the Code. It may resort to the traditional remedy of countervailing duty, subject to rules previously discussed concerning the required determination of the amount of the subsidy and the amount of injury. Alternatively, (or perhaps cumulatively) the importing country can call for consultations with the exporting country, followed by conciliation, fact-finding and recommendation by a panel, and decision by the Committee of Signatories.

An *exporting country*, which had no effective remedy previously,[h] does not have a choice of remedies under the Code, but for the first time it does have a specific remedy, exercisable, it seems in one of three situations:

(1) Xandia may initiate the consulation/panel/committee procedure on the basis of a complaint that it is losing export markets in Tertia, as a result of export subsidies by Patria;

(2) Patria may initiate the procedure against Tertia on the ground that Tertia is imposing countervailing duties against its products inconsistently with the Code; and

---

[g] Brazil, Mexico, Taiwan, South Korea, and Singapore were usually included in this category. For certain purposes, Venezuela, Colombia, Argentina, and India have sometimes been added to this group, which thus far has not attempted a political coalition on its own.

[h] In theory, the text of Articles XVI(1) and (2) of the GATT might have been used to fashion a right, combined with a remedy under Article XXIII; in practice, this did not happen.

(3) Xandia and Patria may both complain that Tertia is impairing their export opportunities by giving subsidies to domestic producers.

(b) For all four of these situations the Code provides quite rapid disputes settlement, 150 days following 30 days for consultations in the case of an export subsidy, and following 60 days for consultations in the case of complaint about any other kind of subsidy.[i] But consider the substantive aspect of the dispute-settlement scheme:

(i) Presumably if the subsidy is a prohibited one—e.g. a direct payment on exports of manufactured products by a developed country—the facts can be found with reasonable dispatch, and either a phasing out of the subsidy, or withdrawal of an equivalent concession, or an "appropriate countermeasure" can be recommended by the Panel or Committee. (Note that under this track there is no requirement of injury in a case coming under Articles 9(1) and 12(1); note further that the provision in GATT Article XVI(4) concerning a lower export than home market price is not carried over into the Code.)

(ii) But what if some or all of these easily identified elements are absent? Suppose, for example, Xandia requests consultations with Patria concerning a subsidy that is not an export subsidy, but that Xandia contends causes injury to its domestic industry within the meaning of Article 12(3). Patria replies that the practice in question is used by its government to promote important objectives of social and economic policy as recognized in Article 8(1), for instance the economic revival of a depressed region. Would you suppose that the conciliation/fact finding/recommendation/decision procedures set forth in the Code could resolve the dispute? Note that Article 12(3), the complainant's article, speaks of causing "injury," "nullification or impairment," or "serious prejudice." But Article 8(3), which sets forth the obligations under the Code, does not say "Patria *may not cause* . . .", only "Patria *shall seek to avoid causing* injury, nullification or impairment, or serious prejudice . . . ."

(iii) What about the provisions on primary products? Note that paragraph 1 of Article 10 follows GATT Article XVI(3) (though not pre-

---

[i] See Article 13, Documents Supplement p. DS-679. The Code does not prescribe any fixed period for consultations in the case of any other dispute, for example about countervailing duties, but paragraph 3 of Article 13 seems to indicate that the panel/committee procedure is available following consultations.

ciselyʲ), then paragraph 2 attempts an elaboration of the concept of equitable market share, and paragraph 3 introduces the criterion of effect on price in a particular market.

(c) Would you expect that over time a common law would develop giving content to these phrases, as on the whole did not happen under Articles VI and XVI of the General Agreement? Or would you expect, rather, that the institutional pressures will tend toward ad hoc compromises? Should the GATT secretariat attempt, through appointment of and instructions to panels, to develop legal precedents? Or would you, rather, move toward inarticulate compromises that all parties accept?

7.53—Consider briefly how the Code would work with respect to developing countries, assuming they became signatories.

(a) Suppose that the United States and Trinidad both export citrus fruit to Europe, but Trinidad gives an export subsidy to its growers in order to gain a larger share of the European market. Suppose that the United States brings a complaint under Article 12(3) of the Code, and demonstrates "serious prejudice" to its citrus industry. After consultations fail to resolve the controversy, Trinidad contends to the conciliation or fact-finding panel that its subsidies are not prohibited, because it is exempt under Article 14(2) from the prohibition of export subsidies contained in Article 9, and because it is acting in accordance with the principle set forth in Article 14(1).ᵏ The United States could then attempt to invoke paragraph 5 of Article 14, though if a commitment were given under that paragraph, paragraph 8 says that it would not be subject to review. If no commitment under paragraph 5 were forthcoming, the United States could attempt to invoke paragraphs 6, 7, and 8 but the provisos, double negative and exceptions suggest the prospects for success would not be great. Do you conclude that the Code is useful only as among developed countries? Or does such a conclusion take too lightly the educational (as contrasted with legally binding) value of the Code vis-a-vis the developing countries?

(b) One of the developing countries that has worked out its scheme of subsidies most elaborately in recent years is Brazil. In support of its efforts to industrialize, to reduce its dependence on coffee, to earn foreign exchange, and also to support depressed areas, Brazil has developed a series of pro-

ʲ Minerals, for example, are excluded by the footnote.

ᵏ Trinidad was a participant in the MTN; for purposes of the question, the assumption is that Trinidad has become a signatory to the Subsidies Code.

grams including tax exemptions and rebates, preferential allocations of foreign exchange, and in some instances cash grants either directly for exports or for "export-related" industries. In several countries, including the United States and Canada, these programs have led to countervailing duty investigations and negotiations at governmental level. Leaving aside the politics of the Group of 77 and concentrating only on the substance, would you advise the Government of Brazil to sign the Subsidies Code or not?[l]

7.54—(a) When the negotiators of the Subsidies Code reached agreement in December, 1978, they published their draft with a footnote indicating their intention to amend the International Anti-Dumping Code negotiated twelve years earlier[m] so as to conform it as much as possible to the new Subsidies Code. The United States government, without committing itself to any particular changes, said "there is no conceptual problem" in making the relevant changes.[n] Do you agree?

(b) By April, a new version of the revised Anti-Dumping Code was ready, including a clause stating that signature of the new version carried with it denunciation of the original version of the Code. An appreciation of the MTN's approach both to subsidies and to dumping can be gained by examining some of the changes made in the Anti-Dumping Code.[o]

(i) The provision in Article 3 of the 1967 Anti-Dumping Code that states "A determination of injury shall be made only when . . . the dumped imports are demonstrably the *principal* cause of *material* injury . . ." is eliminated, and replaced by a provision paralleling Article 6(1) of the new Subsidies Code.[p]

---

[l] § 4.44 *supra.*

[m] After some hesitation, Brazil did accept the Subsidies Code, as well as the revised Anti-Dumping Code and the Customs Valuation Code. As of Dec. 31, 1982, Chile, India, Korea, Pakistan, and Uruguay had accepted the Subsidies Code, but no other developing countries had done so. All developed country members of the GATT (and the EEC for its members) had accepted the Subsidies Code.

[n] This position was expressed in several contemporaneous discussions of the status of the MTN. See, e.g. the memorandum attached to President Carter's formal notice of intention to enter into trade agreements transmitted to Congress on January 4, 1979, 44 Fed. Reg. 1933, 1936 (Jan. 8, 1979).

[o] The 1967 version of the International Anti-Dumping Code appears in the Documents Supplement at p. DS-89. The new version appears at p. DS-727.

[p] But the footnote to Article 3 of the 1967 Anti-Dumping Code, reproduced in the footnote to Article 2(1) of the Subsidies Code, is retained in the new Anti-Dumping Code as well, so that all three documents contain, in a footnote, the statement that injury, unless otherwise specified, should be taken to mean material injury to a domestic industry.

(ii) the provision in Article 7(a) of the 1967 Code concerning price undertakings is modified to replace reference to elimination of the *margin of dumping* by reference to elimination of the injurious *effect* on the dumping, paralleling Article 4(5)a of the Subsidies Code;

(iv) a new provision is added to the Anti-Dumping Code calling for "special regard" to the interests of developing countries,[q]

(v) A Committee on Anti-Dumping Practices is established, together with a procedure for consultations, conciliation, and creation of a panel similar to that created by Articles 12 and 13 of the Subsidies Code.[r]

Though both the American Trigger Price Mechanism, and the Europen Community's Davignon Plan seemed to look to cost of production by the most efficient producer rather than to home market price for comparison with the export price, no change was made in the basic definitions of dumping contained in Article 2 of the Anti-Dumping Code.

(c) Given these (and a few other) conforming changes, is it now fair to say that actions designed to distort fair trade have been subjected to uniform tests and application of uniform penalties?[s]

(d) If dumping and subsidies have been substantially assimilated, should market disruption be brought under the same roof as well? Or is there still a significant distinction, made more meaningful by the progress in the MTN, between fair and unfair trade? We shall return to this question, for one last time, at the very end of the volume.[t]

---

[q] Article 13 of the new version.

[r] New Article 14 of the Anti-Dumping Code.

[s] The text is a slight paraphrase from Ambassador Strauss' statement to the U.S. Chamber of Commerce, given before the revision of the Anti-Dumping Code had been completed. See Chamber of Commerce of the United States, *Results of the Tokyo Round*, Proceedings of a Conference on the MTN, January 25-26, 1979, p. 14.

[t] See § 8.73 *infra*. One additional suggestion emerged in the discussion of revision of the Anti-Dumping Code. Some of the developing countries, not content with new Article 13 (N. p *supra*), proposed that for products imported by developed countries from developing countries, the comparison to establish fair or normal value should not be between the export and the home market price but between the export price to the complaining country and to a third (presumably developed) country.

7.55—Speaking of market disruption, we saw that agreement on the Safeguards Code[a] broke down over the selectivity issue. But the final package did contain a series of texts developed by the Framework Group,[b] including a Draft Understanding on Notification, Consultation, Dispute Settlement and Surveillance in GATT[c]. Could this "Understanding" fulfill some of the goals set for the Safeguards Code?

(a) Suppose the European Community proposes to apply an emergency measure on imports of television receivers. In fact, television receivers have been coming into the Community in increased volume from Japan, South Korea, and Xandia. The Community, following the pattern in steel,[d] offers voluntary restraint agreements to all three countries, but Xandia, dissatisfied with the level of exports permitted to its producers, refuses to sign. Thereupon an import quota is imposed, applicable to Xandia only. Doesn't Xandia have a valid complaint under Article XXIII of the GATT?[e]

(b) In the past, as we have seen, complaints under Article XXIII have tended to be unsatisfactory in providing relief. Moreover, the Community (as well as other importing countries) have typically called in the ambassador of Xandia in these circumstances, and with a combination of carrot and stick have sought to dissuade his country from going through with the complaint. Does the new Framework Agreement do anything for Xandia in these circumstances? See Point 3, and especially the statement that requests under Article XXIII(2) should not be intended or considered as contentious acts.[f]

(c) Take the same facts as in (a) but with the United States as the importing country. Assume in both cases that the elements of dumping or subsidies could not be shown, but the requirements for action under sections 201-203 of the Trade Act of 1974[g] could be made out. Should the United States im-

---

[a] See §§ 7.21, 7.31–.32, 7.41(b), 7.43 *supra*.

[b] § 7.23 *supra*.

[c] Documents Supplement p. DS-708.

[d] See § 6.33 *supra*.

[e] Documents Supplement p. DS-44.

[f] For a thorough exploration of these and other questions concerning the GATT as a forum following conclusion of the MTN, see Hudec, "GATT Dispute Settlement after the Tokyo Round: An Unfinished Business," 13 Cornell Int'l. L.J. 145 (1980). See also Teese, "A View from the Dress Circle in the Theater of Trade Disputes," 5 The World Economy 43 (March 1982), relating the GATT disputes mechanism before and after the MTN to Australia's frustrations in complaining against sugar subsidies by the EEC.

[g] Documents Supplement pp. DS-338–47.

pose a quota on imports from Xandia only? How would you argue (i) for Xandia, (ii) for Patria, which is thinking of exporting television sets to the United States but has not thus far done so; for Zenith (§ 4.47 (c) *supra*), the complaining domestic manufacturer; for STR, trying to keep the package deal of the MTN together? How, on behalf of any of these interested parties, would you construe section 203 (k) (l) of the Trade Act, which authorized departures from MTN, "but only after consideration of the relation of such actions to the international obligations of the United States"?

(d)(i) Under either of the preceding scenarios, could the Director General of GATT take some action on his own, such as asking for a report and assessment from a working group?

(ii) If you conclude that the step suggested is neither directly authorized nor prohibited, the answer may well depend on the person and prestige of the Director General. Assuming, as was expected, that the incumbent Director General, Mr. Long, would step down shortly after completion of the Tokyo Round, would you want a strong, aggressive person for the job—a Dag Hammarskjold of trade, or would you prefer a less enterprising, more political and deferential person, à la Kurt Waldheim?[h]

(iii) Which interests should take what position on this question?

7.56—One more question may serve to shed light on the package deal that permitted the Tokyo Round to be completed. Each of the previous trade negotiating conferences, and particularly the Dillon and Kennedy rounds in the 1960's, carried within itself the seeds for the next round. If tariffs are now in large measure harmonized and reduced in importance, if most of the other trade issues are subject to a regime of consultation/conciliation/dispute settlement, and if the really difficult sectors—steel, textiles and apparel, grains, meat and dairy products, perhaps others to come[i]—are dealt with in special committees, would you expect the Tokyo Round to be the last of the series, to be replaced by a more or less continuous consultation/dispute settlement process? Consider whether such a prognosis bodes good or ill for the rule of law in international trade.

7.57—For more than a month after the MTN signing ceremony in Geneva, the process of negotiating, compromising, and drafting described in § 7.42 continued in Washington. On May 8, 1979, the Senate Finance Committee

---

[i] For instance ships, consumer electronics, or automobiles.

[h] On April 28, 1980, the GATT Contracting Parties chose Arthur Dunkel of Switzerland to succeed Mr. Long as Director-General. Dunkel, like his predecessor, was an able Swiss diplomat, but not an international household name. He assumed office on October 1, 1980.

issued a press release summarizing the conclusions of its "consultations with the Administration" over the implementation of the MTN.[j] In the following week the Trade Subcommittee of the House Ways and Means Subcommittee also completed its list of "recommendations," and in the week of May 21, the two Committees held a "non-Conference Conference," ironing out and trading off some fifty differences concerning the proposed legislation.[k] Instead of now submitting an agreed text of the proposed statute to the two Houses of Congress, however, the recommendations and draft (not made public) went back to the Administration for review, prior to being introduced in both Houses pursuant to section 151 of the Trade Act of 1974.

On June 19, 1979 President Carter submitted to Congress the final package—i.e., the agreements as signed in Geneva and the completed draft of the statute.[l] By July 3, the House Ways and Means Committee was ready with its Report of several hundred pages,[m] and two weeks later the Senate Finance Committee submitted its Report, similar in length and content, but not identical.[n] The bill went through both Houses with little debate and no difficulty,[o] and there was, of course, no need to have a Senate-House Conference.

President Carter signed the Trade Agreements Act of 1979 into law on July 26, 1979.[p] He said it was "perhaps the most important and far-reaching piece of trade legislation in the history of the United States.[q]

---

[j] U.S. Senate, Committee on Finance, Press Release #116, May 8, 1979.

[k] The results of the non-Conference Conference were made public in a joint press release dated May 24, 1979.

[l] See § 7.44 N. i *supra.*

[m] *Trade Agreements Act of 1979,* Report of House Comm. on Ways and Means to Accompany H.R. 4537, H.R. Rept. No. 96-317, 96th Cong., 1st Sess. (July 3, 1979).

[n] *Trade Agreements Act of 1979,* Report of Sen. Comm. on Finance on H.R. 4537, S. Rept. No. 96-249, 96th Cong. 1st Sess. (July 17, 1979).

[o] 395-7 in the House, 90-4 in the Senate.

[p] The complete Table of Contents of the Act, the introductory sections, plus titles I, IX and XI of the Act are reproduced in the Documents Supplement and title X is reflected in the integrated version of §§ 1514–1516A at pp. DS–453–61. In addition, a summary of the Act prepared by the Office of the U.S. Trade Representative is reproduced in the Documents Supplement at pp. DS–462–68. The full statute takes up 174 pages of the Statutes at Large, of which 22 are devoted to distilled spirits (§§ 801–856).

[q] 15 Weekly Comp. Pres. Docs. 1311 (July 26, 1979). The determinations called for by the Trade Agreements Act were (with some exceptions) made by President Carter by Proclamation No. 4707 of December 11, 1979, 44 Fed. Reg. 72348 (Dec. 13, 1979), set out in special pamphlet to Title 19 of the U.S.C.A. Thereafter, the agreements were formally

§ 7.6—Implementing the Tokyo Round

7.61—REORGANIZATION IN WASHINGTON

One of the conditions exacted from the Carter administration in the negotiations over acceptance of the Multilateral Trade Negotiations was that administration of the rules—old and new—be improved. Many persons in and out of Congress thought the time had come for the United States to have one Department of International Trade and Industry, a DITI modeled on Japan's MITI.[a] But too many departments and agencies, too many constituencies, too many vested interests would have to be shaken up to accomplish such a shift. Not only State, Treasury and Commerce, but Departments as diverse as Defense and Labor, Energy and Agriculture, and Transportation, would have to cede expertise and influence, not to speak of such independent agencies as the International Trade Commission and executive agencies such as the Office of the Special Representative for Trade Negotiations. Moreover, creating a DITI would have raised the basic question of whether to attempt to develop an industrial policy, a concept in favor of Japan and (in part) in the European Economic Community, but one for which the United States was probably not ready.[b] Congress settled for a requirement that the President submit a proposal to restructure the international trade functions in the executive branch, even before passage of the Act.[c]

President Carter accepted the condition, and supplied an initial proposal on July 19—nine days after the deadline set by the Senate and House Committees marking up the legislation.[d] On September 24, 1979, he submitted a fully elaborated Reorganization Plan, entitled Reorganization of Functions Relating to International Trade.[e] In accordance with the Reorganization Act of 1977,[f] the plan could be put into effect if not disapproved within 60

---

signed and accepted by the Deputy U.S. Trade Representative in Geneva on December 17, 1979, the opening day of the three-year signing period. The Customs Valuation Code and Government Procurement Code entered into force for the United States on July 1, 1980 and January 1, 1981, respectively.

[a] See Trade Agreements Act of 1979, § 1109, Documents Supplement p. DS–545.

[b] See, generally, W. Diebold, Jr., *Industrial Policy as an International Policy* (1980).

[c] See Trade Act of 1979 § 1109(a), first sentence. The proposal was released as a Fact Sheet, issued by the White House News Secretary.

[d] See New York Times, July 20, 1979, p. D1, col. 6.

[e] Documents Supplement p. DS–549.

[f] Pub. L. 95-17, 91 Stat. 29 (1977) revising 5 U.S.C. § 901-912.

days,[g] and President Carter issued an executive order on January 4, 1980 formally promulgating the reorganization.[h]

Congress was particularly concerned that administration of measures against dumping and subsidies—the "unfair trade" measures so much emphasized during the Tokyo Round—be taken away from the Department of the Treasury.[i] Critics of the Treasury, especially in the Senate Committee on Finance, believed that the Department had been too quick to accept assurances from foreign producers, not quick enough to find violations, and generally too concerned with international relations and not enough with protecting American industry.[j] Under the Reorganization Plan, accordingly, the antidumping and countervailing duty functions committed to the executive branch were transferred to the Department of Commerce, which was expected to be more responsive to the interests of domestic producers.[k] At the same time other operational responsibilities, including supervision of U.S. commercial attachés in foreign embassies and consulates, were transferred to the Commerce Department,[l] which would get a new Under Secretary for International Trade as well as two new assistant secretaries, one for Trade Ad-

---

[g] See 5 U.S.C. § 906(a). Under this section, a presidential reorgranization plan goes into effect within 60 days unless either House of Congress adopts a resolution of disapproval.

[h] Executive Order 12188 of Jan. 2, 1980, 16 Weekly Comp. Pres. Docs. 7 (Jan. 21, 1980), 45 Fed. Reg. 989 (Jan. 4, 1980). Resolutions of disapproval were introduced in both Houses, but failed to clear the respective committees.

[i] Note that §§ 701–07 with regard to countervailing duties and §§ 731–39 with regard to antidumping duties speak of the functions of the "administering authority," defined in § 771(1) as the Secretary of the Treasury or any other officer to whom the functions there spelled out might be delegated.

[j] See, e.g., the testimony of Charles R. Carlisle, spokesman for a group of domestic manufacturers, unions, and lawyers known as the Ad Hoc Subsidies Coalition, summarized in 125 Cong. Rec. H2308 (Daily ed. April 24, 1979). See also Feller, "Observations on the New Countervailing Duty Law," 11 Law & Pol'y Int'l Bus. 1439, 1443–1444; Palmeter and Kossl, "Restructuring Executive Branch Trade Responsibilities: A Half-Step Forward," 12 Law and Pol'y Int'l Bus. 611, 627–28 and sources there cited. For a defense of the Treasury practices, by one who had substantial responsibility for its role in the trade field, see Ehrenhaft, "What the Antidumping and Countervailing Duty Provisions of the Trade Agreements Act [Can] [Will] [Should] Mean for U.S. Trade Policy," 11 Law and Pol'l Int'l Bus. 1361, 1369–77. Essentially, Ehrenhaft's point is that major issues of economic policy have tended to come up in cases quite trivial to the economy. Steel, of course, was the exception.

[k] See Reorganization Plan No. 3, §§ 2(a) and 5(a). Ordinary duty determinations remained under the Customs Service, which, as a tax collection agency, stayed within the Treasury Department. Also, collection of antidumping and countervailing duties, as well as acceptance of bonds or other security for admission of merchandise pending determination of dumping and subsidies cases, remained a function of the Customs Service.

[l] Reorganization Plan § 5(b).

ministration, the other for Trade Policy and Programs. Of course while the
department heads and their principal deputies were different, most of the staffs
that had worked in other departments on trade matters were simply transferred to new offices.

As to policy matters, President Carter chose the Office of the Special
Representative for Trade Negotiations (STR) to have primary responsibility,
with a revised title as United States Trade Representative (USTR). Not only
negotiations under GATT, but commodity agreements, and representation in
the OECD and the U.N. Conference on Trade and Development (UNCTAD),
were to be centered in USTR.[m] In submitting his plan to the Congress, President Carter wrote:

> It is indeed appropriate that this proposal follows so soon after the
> overwhelming approval by the Congress of the Trade Agreements Act
> of 1979, for it will sharpen and unify trade policy direction, improve
> the efficiency of trade law enforcement, and enable us to negotiate
> abroad from a position of strength.[n]

Whether that prediction was achieved was not proven as of the time this volume
went to press, three years after the reorganization took effect.[o]

7.62—JUDICIAL REVIEW EXPANDED

More significant, probably, than the shift of functions within the executive
branch were the changes in judicial review of antidumping and countervailing duty determinations. Until 1974, as we saw,[a] affirmative determinations
by the Treasury leading to imposition of antidumping or countervailing duties
were subject to review in the Customs Court like any other determination
to impose duties, but negative determinations were apparently not subject

---

[m] But international trade in agriculture was, in general, excepted from the reorganization,
and remained under the U.S. Department of Agriculture. Note also § 7 of the Reorganization
Plan, stating that nothing in the Plan was intended to derogate from the responsibility of the
Secretary of State for advising the President on foreign policy matters, including international trade. When George P. Shultz, an expert on international economics, became Secretary
of State in the summer of 1982, the State Department's role in foreign trade matters seems
to have again expanded.

[n] Message of the President to Congress transmitting Reorganization Plan No. 3, 15 Weekly
Comp. Pres. Docs. 1729 at 1734 (Sept. 25, 1979).

[o] For a detailed, and skeptical, analysis of the reorganization of trade functions, written
after the plan was fully implemented but before experience could be gathered with its operation, see Palmeter and Kossl, N. j *supra*.

[a] § 4.45(f) *supra*.

to judicial review, at least with respect to countervailing duties.[b] The Trade Act of 1974 made clear that unsuccessful petitioners both for antidumping and for countervailing duties had the right to judicial review in the Customs Court,[c] subject thereafter to appeal by either side to the Court of Customs and Patent Appeals. Whether negative injury determinations by the International Trade Commission, (which at the time were applicable only to antidumping, and not to countervailing duty determinations) were subject to judicial review was in doubt.[d] In the 1979 Act, when the focus on injury in general became sharper[e] and when a finding of injury would be required (for exports from signatories of the Subsidies Code) for countervailing as well as for antidumping duties,[f] determinations by the Commission concerning injury were expressly made subject to judicial review, whether the finding was affirmative or negative.[g] Also, a variety of interlocutory orders by the Secretary or the Commission could not be challenged in the Customs Court, and in certain circumstances, injunctive relief appeared to be authorized at the behest of the petitioner.[h] However, contrary to the decision of the Customs Court in the late 1970's that the complaining party in a countervailing duty or antidumping case could get a trial de novo,[i] the standard for

---

[b] See § 4.45(f) N. w *supra.*

[c] See § 516(d) of the Tariff Act of 1930, as amended by the Trade Act of 1974, Documents Supplement p. DS-451.

[d] See *SCM Corp. v. United States International Trade Commission*, 404 F.Supp. 124 (D.D.C. 1979), reversed and remanded in 549 F.2d 812 (D.C. Cir. 1977); *SCM Corp. v. United States,* 450 F. Supp. 1178 (Cust. Ct. 1978). For a discussion of this and related cases, the effect of which seemed to be to exclude jurisdiction by the district court but recognize jurisdiction in the Customs Court, see Vance, "Judicial Review of Antidumping Orders in the United States and the European Community," 26 New York L.S. L. Rev. 577, 582–87 (1981).

[e] See § 7.63 at Ns. g–h *infra.*

[f] See § 7.41(a) *supra.*

[g] Section 516A(a)(1) and (a)(2) of the Tariff Act of 1930, as adopted by § 1001 of the Trade Agreements Act of 1979, Documents Supplement p. DS-455. Note that judicial review was made available not only to American manufacturers and wholesalers but, if it had participated in earlier phases of the proceedings, to "any interested party," including, for example, employees of a domestic producer or their union. See § 516A(a)(1), (a)(2), and (d).

[h] Thus the only adjudicatory function of the International Trade Commission that was not subject to some form of judicial review was the proceeding under the escape clause, in which both the President and the Congress could become involved. See § 5.56 *supra.*

[i] *Michelin Tire Corporation v. United States*, 81 Cust. Ct. 157 (Cust. Ct. 1978); 469 F. Supp. 270 (Cust. Ct. 1979), appeal dismissed 603 F.2d 192 (C.C.P.A. 1979). See § 4.46 N. p *supra* (importer entitled to de novo trial after imposition of countervailing duty); *ASG*

judicial review under the 1979 Act is like that normally applicable to review of decisions of administrative agencies—as to interlocutory orders whether they are arbitrary, capricious or an abuse of discretion,[j] and as to final orders whether they are supported by substantial evidence on the record.[k]

Following these amendments to the trade laws, Congress adopted the Customs Courts Act of 1980,[l] changing the name of the Customs Court to the Court of International Trade "with all the powers in law and equity of . . . a district court of the United States,"[m] including, in particular, the power to grant injunctions and interlocutory orders.[n] The court would remain a court of national jurisdiction, with its headquarters in New York City but with authority to hold hearings in any U.S. courthouse, and even in foreign countries.[o] To resolve the controversy about the jurisdiction of the court as compared to jurisdiction of district courts generally,[p] the new legislation provided that for all actions over which the Court of International Trade had jurisdiction, that jurisdiction was to be exclusive.[q]

Until 1982, appeals from the Customs Court/Court of International Trade were heard by the Court of Customs and Patent Appeals. In 1982, in legislation not particularly growing out of international trade controversies, the law concerning judicial review was again changed. In the Federal Courts Improvement Act of 1982,[r] the Court of Claims and the Court of Customs and Patent Appeals were merged to create a new U.S. Court of Appeals for the

---

Industries v. United States, 610 F.2d 770 (C.C.P.A. 1979) (domestic manufacturer entitled to de novo trial of refusal to find subsidy).

[j] § 516A (b) (1)(A).

[k] § 516A(b)(1)(B).

[l] Pub. L. No. 96–417, 94 Stat. 1727 (1980).

[m] 28 U.S.C. § 1585, as amended.

[n] The Customs Court, originally created as an Article I court in 1926, had been declared to be an Article III court in 1956, but with only limited jurisdiction to review decisions of the Customs Service. See, generally, Symposium on International Trade Law, 26 New York L.S. L. Rev. 431 (1980), esp. articles by Re, Rodino, Cohen, and Vance.

[o] 28 U.S.C. § 256. Hearings in foreign countries are permitted only with consent of the foreign state.

[p] See N. d *supra*; also § 4.45, N. w *supra*.

[q] 28 U.S.C. §§ 1581–83. § 1584 provided for transfer if an action was erroneously commenced in a district court of the United States. That section is now incorporated in the general transfer section, 28 U.S.C. § 1631, adopted pursuant to § 301 of the Federal Courts Improvement Act, N. r *infra*.

[r] Pub. L. No. 97–164, 96 Stat 25 (1982).

Federal Circuit, to hear appeals in specified classes of cases, including decisions of the Court of International Trade.[s]

The changes in the name and jurisdiction of the Customs Court reflected recognition of the fact that ordinary tariffs were now lower and less important, so that controversies concerning valuation and classification for customs purposes were of less concern than they had been in earlier days, whereas controversies concerning dumping, subsidies, and perhaps other issues growing out of the Tokyo Round agreements, were increasing in volume and importance. Taken together, the reforms in the specialized courts concerned with trade reflected the same sentiment as that which had led to transfer of trade functions in the executive branch discussed in § 7.61. In contrast to the practice in Europe and (to a lesser extent) to the practice in the United States in earlier years, unfair trade issues would be more difficult to handle by negotiation and compromise, and would be more committed to mandatory determinations on the record, subject to judicial review. Whether major controversies, such as the renewed challenges by the U.S. steel industry to imports from the European Community, would lend themselves to "legal" solutions remained to be seen.[t]

7.63—CHANGES IN THE TRADE LAW

(a) *Accepting the Agreements.* The basic trade legislation of the United States remained the Trade Act of 1974, though of course the negotiating authority contained in that Act was about to expire.[a] Section 2 of the 1979 Act completed the assignment begun in accordance with section 102 of the 1974 Act, in that it accepted and approved all of the agreements signed in Geneva. Section 3(a) made clear that the agreements were not self-executing and that in the event of a conflict between a U.S. statute and one of the

---

[s] Among the claims for which the Federal Circuit Court would have appellate jurisdiction were those related to patents, copyrights, trademarks, and unfair competition. The new Court was also given authority, previously exercised by the C.C.P.A., to review decisions of the International Trade Commission under § 337 of the Tariff Act of 1930, 19 U.S.C. 1337. That section, rarely resorted to and not separately discussed in this volume, is concerned with certain unfair methods of competition in international trade, including violations of antitrust and patent laws. When the International Trade Commission finds such violation, it is authorized to issue a cease and desist order, as well as (since 1979) civil penalties. See Trade Agreements Act of 1979, § 1105, Documents Supplement p. DS-540. For thorough discussion of that section before the 1979 amendments, see Symposium on Section 337 of the Trade Act of 1974, 8 Ga. J. Int'l & Comp. L. 27 (1978).

[t] See § 8.53 *infra*.

[a] See Trade Act of 1974, § 101(a)(1), Documents Supplement p. DS-297. In addition to the 1974 Act, of course, portions of the Tariff Act of 1930 and the Trade Expansion Act remained in effect.

agreements, the statute would apply, regardless of whether it had been enacted before or after the Agreement.[b]

(b) *Tailoring Domestic Law to the Agreements*. The basic effort, of course, was to adopt legislation that would be in compliance with the Agreements, and Titles I through VIII follow the respective Agreements reached in Geneva.[c] As we saw,[d] however, some pulling and hauling was still possible. For instance, in the basic provision concerning countervailing duties, (§ 701),[e] the requirement of an injury finding was added as a conditon precedent for imposition of countervailing duties, with respect to exports from countries that had accepted the Subsidies Code;[f] moreover, in accordance with the footnote to Article 2 of the Code,[g] "injury" was preceded by "material." In the definitions section, however, "material injury" was defined to mean "harm which is not inconsequential, immaterial, or unimportant."[h] Also, though the prohibition in the Code runs only to export subsidies (Articles 8(2) and 9)[i] and the illustrative list contained in the Annex to the Code excludes other kinds of subsidies, the Act followed the prior version of the countervailing duty statute ". . . a subsidy with respect to the *manufacture, production, or exportation* of . . . merchandise imported into the United States."[j] As to the issue of causation, which had proved critical in injury determinations under antidumping and escape clause cases in the past, the Act followed the Code (Article 6) as well as the prior text of the Antidump-

---

[b] See Documents Supplement p. DS–475. Thus the Act changes the usual rule that as between an international agreement and a statute, a conflict, if not avoidable by fair construction, is resolved in favor of whichever document is adopted later in time. See Restatement of Foreign Relations Law (Revised) § 135 (Tent. Draft No. 1, 1980).

[c] See the Table of Contents of the Trade Agreements Act of 1979 and the summary of the various titles at pp. DS–468–73, 462–68.

[d] See §§ 7.42–.43 *supra*.

[e] Documents Supplement p. DS–479.

[f] See § 7.41(a) *supra*.

[g] Documents Supplement p. DS–665.

[h] § 771(7) Documents Supplement p. DS–512. Compare the earlier discussion of this point, § 4.43(e) *supra*.

[i] Documents Supplement pp. DS–674–75. See also Article 11.

[j] Compare § 303 of the legislation as it existed prior to 1979, Documents Supplement p. DS–440, with § 701(a)(1) of the new Act. See also new § 771(5), Documents Supplement p. DS–511, which incorporates the Annex to the Code into the definition of subsidy, but adds four other kinds of domestic subsidies.

ing Act of 1921,[k] in stating the issue to be determined by the Commission to be injury to an industry "by reason of imports of [like] merchandise. . . ." The House Report stated that "[t]he law does not, however, contemplate that injury from such imports be weighted against other factors . . . which may be contributing to overall injury to an industry."[l] That explanation might, or might not turn out to be consistent with Article 6(2) and (4) of the Code.

(c) *MFN and the Multilateral Codes.* Congress and the executive branch were agreed that those changes in U.S. domestic law that were required to assure compliance with the results of the Tokyo Round—notably the addition of an injury requirement to the countervailing duty statute—would be made applicable only to trade with signatories to the codes. In part this decision reflected a desire to induce states that might be wavering to sign up; in part the United States did not wish, in so far as the codes conferred benefits on other states, to give non-signatories a "free ride."[a] Accordingly the countervailing duty statute was split into two parts, one to apply to imports from states that had signed the Subsidies Code (§ 701(a) of the new Act), the other, (old § 303)[b] to imports from countries that had not.

The question of how to treat MFN obligations to states that were parties to GATT or to other agreements providing for MFN treatment[c] was handled in a quite straightforward way.[d] GATT members that did not sign the Code (or a comparable agreement) were excluded from the new injury provisions of the countervailing duty statute, whether or not they were parties to a Treaty of Friendship, Commerce and Navigation with the United States that contained a general MFN clause; non-GATT members that were parties to treaties assuring unconditional reciprocal most-favored-nation treatment were included in the new statute, but only if the FCN (or other) treaty did not permit actions required or permitted by the GATT.[e] This provision[f] seemed to apply to

---

[k] See § 201(a) of the 1975 version of the Anti-Dumping Act, Documents Supplement p. DS–427.

[l] *House Report* p. 47. Compare the different standard applicable to proceedings under the escape clause, § 8.13 *infra*.

[a] Compare the discussion at § 2.42 *supra*.

[b] Documents Supplement p. DS–440.

[c] See § 7.39 *supra*.

[d] Trade Agreements Act, § 701(b), Documents Supplement p. DS–479.

[e] The Standard Treaty of Friendship, Commerce and Navigation concluded by the United States after World War II contained a clause stating:

seven states—Honduras, Venezuela, Nepal, North Yemen, El Salvador, Paraguay, and Liberia.[g] As for members of GATT that did not sign the Code, the United States took the position that they were not entitled to the benefits of the Code because the prior inconsistent U.S. law was subject to the Protocol of Provisional Application[h] and thus the entitlement to an injury determination was not covered by Article I of the GATT. Benefits of other codes, notably the Agreement on Government Procurement, were dealt with along the same lines.[i] With respect to the legislative results of the MTN (as contrasted with tariff concessions), the United States had clearly moved to a policy of conditional MFN.[j]

(d) *Procedure for Subsidies and Dumping Cases.* Both the Subsidies and the Antidumping Code contained fairly elaborate provisions about procedures,[k] in particular a requirement that a preliminary investigation concerning injury or threat of injury be initiated at the same time that the investigation of alleged subsidization or dumping is undertaken. The object, of course, was to prevent unnecessary costs and delays to the importer, possibly with chilling effect on trade, if at the end of the day no injury was likely to be found. The Trade Agreements Act implemented that obligation, and at the same time responded to the criticism that antidumping and countervailing duty cases had in the past been nursed along or buried by the executive branch, rather than being decided with dispatch.

The provisions of the present Treaty relating to the treatment of goods shall not preclude action by either Party which is required or specifically permitted under the General Agreement on Tariffs and Trade during such time as such Party is a contracting party to the General Agreement. Similarly, the most-favored-nation provisions of the present Treaty shall not apply to special advantages accorded by virtue of the aforesaid Agreement.

See, e.g., Article XXII(4) of the Treaty of Friendship, Commerce and Navigation between The Netherlands and the United States, signed March 27, 1956, 8 U.S.T. 2043; T.I.A.S. 3942; 285 U.N.T.S. 231.

[f] § 701(b)(3).

[g] See *House Report* p. 50, *Senate Report* p.45.

[h] See § 2.2 at ns. p–q; § 4.45(e) *supra.*

[i] See Trade Agreements Act of 1979 § 301(b), 19 U.S.C. § 2511(b) (not here reproduced). The argument there was that government procurement was in any event excluded from the GATT. See Article III(8)(a) and Note 1 ad Article I, Documents Supplement pp. DS–11, 62. For a discussion of this issue, see Hufbauer, Erb, and Starr, N. j *infra* at 88–90.

[j] For a thoughtful article on this subject which concludes after some doubt that the U.S. policy is sound and defensible, see Hufbauer, Erb, and Starr, "The GATT Codes and the Unconditional Most-Favored-Nation Principle," 12 Law & Pol'y Int'l Bus. 59 (1980.)

[k] See Subsidies Code, Article 2, Documents Supplement p. DS–664; Anti-Dumping Code, Article 5, Documents Supplement p. DS–731.

The following table is a simplified version of sections 702-05 of the Act, which sets out deadlines for the various stages of countervailing duties case. Numbers in brackets represent alternative dates for "extraordinarily complicated cases," (§ 703(c)); asterisks denote stages at which review may be sought in the Court of International Trade:[1]

Schedule in Countervailing Duty Cases

(i) *Day 1*   Petition filed with Department of Commerce, copy to ITC.

(ii) *Day 20* Decision by Department whether to initiate investigation. (If yes, ITC is informed. If no, case is terminated.*)

(iii) *Day 45* Preliminary Determination by ITC whether there is reasonable indication of material injury. (If no, case is terminated.*)

(iv) *Day 85* [*150*]   Preliminary Determination by Department of existence of subsidy. (If yes, liquidation is suspended. If no, case can continue, but no security is required of importer.*)

(v) *Day 160* [*225*]   Final Determination by Department of existence of subsidy. (If no, case is terminated.* If yes and preliminary determination (step (iv)) was negative, liquidation is suspended.*)

(vi) *Day 205* [*270*]   Final Determination of injury by ITC.[m]* (If yes, Department issues a countervailing duty assessment within 7 days. If no, case is terminated.)

For antidumping cases, the timetable is similar,[n] except that step (iv) is not normally taken until Day 160 (except if verification of information developed during the first 60 days by the Department is waived by all parties, in which case step (iv) can be taken by Day 110); or the petitioner requests or all parties agree on an extension, in which step (iv) can be taken up to Day 210, with the subsequent steps adjusted accordingly.[o]

---

[1] For a somewhat more elaborate table, from which the present table is adapted, see Ehrenhaft, § 7.61 N. j *supra* at 1370–72.

[m] An extra 30 days could be added to this step if step (iv) resulted in a negative decision but step (v) resulted in a positive determination.

[n] Trade Act of 1979 §§ 732–36; Documents Supplement pp. DS–493–506.

[o] For further possibilities for departures from the normal schedule, see, e.g., § 735(b)(3).

Thus the normal subsidy/countervailing duty case was supposed to take no more than 205 days from start to finish, with the most complicated cases to be conducted in 300 days.[p] The normal dumping case was supposed to take no more than 280 days, with the most complicated case to be completed at the latest by Day 420. Judicial review could, of course, extend the controversy, but not the date for imposition of duties. Also, in something of an innovation, the statute made various provisions (in § 777) for information and disclosure, including establishment of a kind of public library of foreign subsidy practices, and provision for disclosure, properly shielded, even of confidential information.

Altogether, the unfair trade aspects of international trade law were addressed with considerable skill and attention to detail. Whether the various amendments could provide a mechanism suitable to the big case—for example, to the crisis in steel that was almost sure to recur—might well be doubted. For lawyers, on the other hand, the legislative implementation of the Tokyo Round by the United States was sure to be a boon.

---

[p] See N. m *supra* for the explanation why the outside figure is 300, and not 270 as shown on the table.

§ 8—More Doubts about International Trade: Problems New and Old

§ 8.1—The Automobile Invasion

8.11—THE AUTOMOBILE IN THE AMERICAN ECONOMY

As steel was the symbol of the industrial revolution in the 19th century, so automobiles symbolized the spread of the products of that revolution throughout the population in developed countries. Standard of living in different countries was measured by the number of automobiles per population, and in the number (and quality) of roads. The automobile transformed whole societies—none more than the United States: Railroads declined; central cities became places for work but not for living; suburban supermarkets and shopping centers and drive-in theaters replaced the traditional urban clusters of commercial and residential facilities.

Mass production of automobiles in the United States began in 1913, and the huge expansion of automobile sales and ownership took place throughout the 1920's. Indeed, that decade took its name from the automobile—the "Roaring Twenties." By 1930, 23 million passenger vehicles were registered in the United States, one car for every 5.3 persons. In the depression of the 1930's, the sale and use of motor vehicles declined somewhat relative to population, but in the last full year before the United States entered World War II, 27 million automobiles were in circulation, or one car for every 4.8 persons. During the War, passenger car production was halted as the giant motor companies turned to production of tanks, trucks, and other military equipment, but the pent-up demand for automobiles led the post-war expansion of the American economy, so that in 1950 there were 40 million passenger cars in circulation, and 6.6 million new cars were sold. Of the new car sales, 17.6 percent were sold by Chrysler, 24 percent by Ford, and 45 percent by General Motors; other American manufacturers, now virtually forgotten,[a] accounted for another 12.75 percent of sales. Imports totalled 16,336 vehicles, barely one quarter of one percent of the market.

Apart from Canada, which in many ways was integrated into the United States industry,[b] the American automobile manufacturers exported relatively little, in part because of protected markets in most industrial countries, and also because nearly every country other than Canada imposed excise taxes

---

[a] Kaiser-Frazer, Hudson, Nash, Packard, Studebaker, Willys, and Crosley.

[b] See § 8.23 *infra*.

Table 1

The Passenger Car in the United States
1900–1975

	Passenger Cars Sold (000's)	Passenger Cars Registered (000's)
1900	4	8
1910	181	458
1920	1,906	8,132
1930	2,787	23,035
1940	3,717	27,466
1945	70	25,793
1950	6,666	40,334
1955	7,920	52,136
1960	6,675	61,724
1965	9,306	75,300
1970	6,547*	89,200
1975	6,713	106,700

* The reduction in 1970 reflects a two months strike of General Motors.

based on the output and displacement of the engine, with the result that large American cars, typically with eight-cyclinder, high-horsepower motors, were unattractive in foreign markets.[c] But General Motors, Chrysler, and Ford all had manufacturing plants around the world, and automobile and truck manufacture were among the first of the multinational businesses.

Two more facets of the automobile industry as seen from the United States became acutely relevant in the late 1970's. First, American owners seemed to like large cars, to cover the great distances on ever-improving highways. Gasoline was cheap—until 1973 between 30 and 40¢ per gallon, as compared to $1–$2 in Europe, and horsepower, acceleration, glamor, and gadgets rather than economy or maneuverability were the big selling points. From the point of view of the automobile producers, extras—automatic transmission, power brakes and power steering, air conditioning, showy fenders and decorations—were the road to profit, and "bare bones" cars were not in favor.

Second, automobiles were marketed like women's fashions, with new styles,

---

[c] How much of the foreign countries' tax policy was designed to protect domestic manufacturers and how much to conserve fuel is hard to tell. Gasoline in Europe was generally priced at four times the U.S. price, in the days before 1959 when the United States was a low-cost producer, and net exporter, of petroleum and petroleum products.

new designs, and planned obsolescence. Later, there was much controversy about whether the American cars were actually built to last only three years or whether they could last longer but would be out of fashion. There was no question, however, that the American dream—a shiny new automobile— was supposed to be repeated every few years. The permanent design, such as the Volkswagen Beetle that remained almost unchanged for nearly 30 years, was quite alien to the American view of the automobile industry.

8.12—FOREIGN CARS ON AMERICAN ROADS 1955–1980

Until the mid-1950's, the domestic industry had the American automobile market to itself, and the concerns of the public were with the survival of the independents,[d] not with competition from abroad. In 1955, the first big wave of imports began, accounting for 58,000 cars—about 0.75 percent of the market. By 1958, a depressed year for Detroit, 379,000 foreign passenger cars were sold, accounting for just over 8 percent of the market. In 1959, imports reached 609,000, just over 10 percent of the market. As American cars were growing larger—the standard Chevrolet expanded from a 115-inch wheel base and 195-inch overall length in 1955 to a 117.5-inch wheel base and 209-inch overall length in 1958—imports began to attract a significant share of the market. The leading import was the Volkswagen Beetle, with a wheel base of 94.5 inches, overall length of about 163 inches, and a list price of about $1,600, roughly $400 below the cheapest American-made car.[e]

The major American manufacturers had had small cars on their drawing boards for many years, and these projects were now revived, but with less than full enthusiasm. What the majors feared, it seems, was that small American cars would draw customers away from their own larger, more pro- fitable models.[f] As a temporary expedient, the Big Three imported smaller cars made by their subsidiaries and affiliates abroad—Opel (German) and Vauxhall (British) for General Motors, English and German Fords, and French Simcas for Chrysler. When "compact" American-made cars were brought out in the early 1960's—the Chevrolet Corvair, Ford Falcon, and Plymouth Valiant/Dodge Dart—they recaptured some of the market that had been taken

---

[d] See N. a *supra*.

[e] The last figure may be somewhat misleading, as discounts and trade-in allowances pro- bably reduced the effective price of domestic cars below published figures. At all events, the VW as a market entrant did come in as the lowest-price car, both to buy and to operate.

[f] See, e.g., L. White, *The Automobile Industry Since 1945*, ch. 11, "The Small Car Story," (1971).

by the imports, so that for 1962 imports fell back to 339,000 units, just under 5 percent of total sales. But the American majors' plans to introduce still smaller "subcompact" cars in the fall of 1962 were cancelled, and in fact the compacts gradually grew larger and more expensive.

"YOU BETTER MAKE IT LONGER, LOWER AND WIDER . . . If we're going into the small car field we want it to be the GIANT of the small car field!" a 1959 cartoon by Lichty of the *Chicago Sun-Times* syndicate

Possibly the majors thought they had turned back the threat of the imports. In fact, from the 1962 low, imports of passenger cars increased nearly every year, passing the 1 million mark in 1968, the 1½ million mark in 1971, and the 2 million mark in 1978.

Until 1972, the principal source of imports of cars was West Germany, led, as noted, by Volkswagen.[g] In 1972, the Japanese manufacturers caught up to imports from West Germany, and from 1975 on, imports from Japan far outstripped imports from all other countries. Toyota, Datsun, and Honda became household words, first on the West Coast but soon throughout the United States.

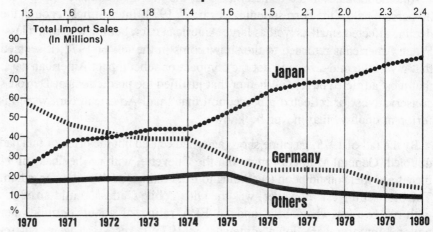

Shares of Import Sales in U.S.

WARD'S AUTOMOTIVE YEARBOOK 1981

The reaction of the American majors, as in the earlier period, was relatively slow. A second generation of small cars was not introduced until 1970, when Ford came out with the Pinto and GM with the Vega—both styled "subcompacts," and both clearly influenced by the Volkswagen Beetle. By that time, however, imports had secured a major share of the American market, and a nationwide network of dealers and service stations had been established, so that the reluctance to buy foreign cars because of difficulty in servicing them had been largely overcome. If Vega and Pinto sold well, as they did for a number of years, it seemed that they were cutting into the market shares of their own big brothers, rather than of the imports.

In the winter of 1973–74 came the world-wide energy crisis. It started with the Yom Kippur war between Egypt and Israel; the United States came to the support of Israel, and the Arab members of the Organization of Petroleum Exporting States answered with an oil embargo of the United States and The

---

[g] For example, in 1968, of 1.119 million cars imported into the United States (other than from Canada), 708,000 or 63 percent, came from West Germany, 170,000 or 15 percent came from Japan, and 242,000 or 22 percent came from all other countries.

Netherlands. Iran did not join the embargo, but announced that it would sell crude oil to all comers at $10–$12 a barrel, about four times the previous price in the Middle East. In the United States as in Europe, there were panic buying, shortages, long lines at gasoline stations, and for a time Sunday closings, odd- and even-day purchasing, limits on "topping off," and a variety of reminders that petroleum was a scarce resource in large part derived from undependable sources of supply.

Automobile sales in the United States for the first six months of 1974 were 30 percent below the corresponding period in 1973. Interestingly enough the decline affected small as well as large American cars, but imports much less. When Americans returned to the showrooms in the fall of 1974, it seemed that it was the mid-size, and not the compact or subcompact American cars, that most attracted buyers. Whether that justified the predictions of Detroit's conservatives, or reflected a perception that small American cars were inferior in quality, may never be known.

By the fall of 1975, gasoline shortgages had ceased but the price of fuel had doubled. General Motors brought out the Chevette, with a wheelbase of 94 inches and fuel consumption (according to EPA ratings) of 40 miles per gallon. The best-selling car, however, was the Oldsmobile Cutlass, a mid-sized car with a 116-inch wheel base and an EPA rating of about 22 miles per gallon.[h] Imports were down somewhat in 1975, a recession year, but retained their market share.

In retrospect, 1976 may have been the critical year for the United States automobile industry. On the basis of the public's reaction to the oil crisis of 1973–74, the companies had prepared to concentrate on small and mid-size cars; but as gasoline prices stabilized (i.e., fell in real terms in an inflationary period), full-size cars seemed to return to favor. For a time in the fall of 1976, Detroit could not keep up with the demand for the "good old stand-bys," as the small American-made cars gathered dust in the showrooms.[i]

The same trend continued in 1977. Though most American models were

---

[h] The ratings of the Environmental Protection Agency were universally conceded to be too high except in very controlled conditions (i.e., the average driver consumed more fuel per mile than the EPA chart indicated), but the indications of relative fuel economy were roughly accurate.

[i] For most of the year 100 days' supply of small cars remained in unsold inventory, as compared with 20–30 days' supply inventory for the large cars. Normal inventory is considered 60 days' supply. American Motors reduced the price of its subcompact Gremlin by $225, and began to offer various discounts and rebates as well. General Motors also offered discounts on Vegas and Chevettes.

reduced in size and weight,[j] large cars accounted for 32.2 percent of their sales, mid-size cars for 39.3 percent, compacts for 19.8 percent, and sub-compacts for only 8.5 percent. That still left room, however, for 1.9 million imports, nearly all compacts and subcompacts. Putting the same point another way, about 40 percent of American consumers purchased compact or sub-compact cars, divided roughly half and half between imports and domestics. But nearly three quarters of the American majors' sales and a substantially larger proportion of their revenues were in mid-size or full-size cars. Once again, as for decades before 1973, the full-size Chevrolet was the industry's best-selling car. In 1978, though imports continued to gain in market share,the U.S. automobile industry sold over 9 million cars, a level that had not been reached since 1973. The oil shortage of 1973–74 seemed, if not quite forgotten, to recede in the memory of car makers and car buyers.[k]

Two events shocked the American auto industry, and indeed the country as a whole, in 1979. First Iran, which had been providing about 12 percent of the oil supply of the non-communist world, underwent a bloody and con-fused revolution in the winter of 1978–79.[l] As the Shah was forced to flee and the Ayatollah Khomeini returned from exile to establish the Islamic Revolution in Iran, exports of oil from that country ceased almost com-pletely. OPEC responded with a series of price increases, and as panic buy-ing broke out in Europe and Japan, contract prices rose from $12 per barrel at the end of 1978 to over $30, and spot prices in Rotterdam climbed as high as $40/barrel. In the United States, though the effect was less than in most other parts of the world, it looked like 1974 all over again—long lines at service stations, restricted buying, and sharply higher prices at the pump. Between January 1979 and June 1980, gasoline prices in the United States doubled, from roughly 65¢ to about $1.30 per gallon.

Second, the Chrysler Corporation, one of America's great companies but long the weakest of the Big Three automakers, announced that it had lost

---

[j] In part in response to federal fuel economy regulations, issued pursuant to the Energy Policy and Conservation Act of 1975, Pub. L. 94–163, 89 Stat. 871, requiring the motor companies to meet fleet-wide fuel economy standards over a stated period.

[k] Volkswagen, which had fallen to third place in imports, announced in 1977 that it would go forward with plans to assemble cars in a plant in Pennsylvania. The first U.S.-made VW Rabbits came off the assembly line in April 1978, using foreign parts equal to approximately 30 percent of value added. VW's produced in the United States are included as domestic, not imported products in the statistics of the ITC used here.

[l] For a brief account of the Iranian revolution, in the context of the hostage crisis which began in November 1979, see Volume III of this series, *Trade Controls for Political Ends*, Ch. V, § 1.2 (2d ed. 1983).

over $700 million in the first nine months of 1979—the largest corporate deficit in U.S. history up to that time. Chrysler said its losses for the whole year might exceed $1 billion, that it could no longer draw on private bank credit, and that it might have to go out of business before the end of the year if it did not receive massive government assistance. The questions that this request raised for the United States government in general—for the perception of competitive enterprise, the capitalist system, and relation of government to business, the need (or not) to preserve a decaying inner city with large numbers of minority employees, as well as the mistakes of Chrysler's management—are well beyond the scope of this note.[m] For present purposes, the significance of the Chrysler crisis was that it brought the problems of the U.S. auto industry to national attention and prominence. As the arguments in Chrysler's request were carried on in the press, on television, and in Congress, what the experts had long known now became common currency. The automobile industry involved not only the Detroit area, but communities all across the country, and not only major banks but pension funds, large and small investors, and if the proposal for government aid were accepted, all taxpayers.[n] Also, in contrast to the steel industry, which, as we saw, had been seeking import relief of one kind or another since the early 1960's, the auto industry had been essentially profitable and internationalist, and had not looked to government for relief against imports. As 1979 drew to a close, both management and labor, and particularly the latter, thought the time had come to attempt to restrain competition from abroad.

---

[m] A combination of bad moves and bad luck seems to have hit Chrysler in a brief period. Its new subcompact, Horizon/Omni, was reviewed by Consumer Reports as "unacceptable" because of unpredictable (i.e., unsafe) steering, 43 Consumer Reports 381 (July 1978). That judgment was later revised, apparently because of an adjustment by the manufacturer, see 44 Consumers Reports 216 (April 1979), but the damage was done as sales were well below expectations. At the same time, Chrysler discontinued its full-size Plymouth Gran Fury and Dodge Royal Monaco, just as demand for full-size cars was reviving. Also, in contrast to GM and Ford, Chrysler built cars in the factory in advance of orders from dealers; thus when the reduction in purchases took place in 1979, Chrysler had relatively far larger inventories than its competitors, and was forced to launch a massive rebate campaign that eventually moved the cars, but did not bring in profits. For the 1979 market year, Chrysler's share of domestic sales dropped to 12 percent, compared to 26.4 percent for Ford, 1.7 percent for American Motors, and 59.9 percent for GM.

[n] Eventually, Congress did adopt the Chrysler Corporation Loan Guarantee Act of 1979, Pub. L. 96–185, 93 Stat. 1324, 15 U.S.C. § 1861–75 (1979) authorizing loan guarantees of up to $1.5 billion over a ten-year period, provided Chrysler could secure $2.1 billion in concessions from workers, executives, suppliers, dealers, and creditors, as well as sale of certain assets not directly concerned with automobile production. It is interesting to note that one of the arguments against aid to Chrysler was that if that company went under, its facilities, workers, and sales would be picked up by GM and Ford, or perhaps a new entrant; against that argument, the contention was advanced that the gap left by Chrysler would be filled not by other American firms but by imports.

8.13—AUTO IMPORTS AND THE ESCAPE CLAUSE

Total domestic automobile production, having peaked at 9.1 million units in 1978, fell to 8.4 million in calendar year 1979, and was falling further in the first few months of 1980, eventually reaching just over 3 million units for the first half year 1980, compared with 4.3 million units in the corresponding period of 1979. Each week brought news of temporary lay-offs at automobile plants, and suggestions that some of the employees might never be recalled. By early June 1980, 238,600 auto workers were idle, including 155,000 at General Motors alone.[a] But while much of this downturn was attributable to economic conditions in the United States—a weak economy coupled with inflation, rising unemployment, and high interest rates—these conditions seemed not to hurt sales of imported cars. Some members of the auto industry looked to the administration to ''do something,'' as had been done for steel a few years earlier;[b] others looked to Congress. The United Auto Workers decided to submit a petition for import relief to the International Trade Commission,[c] pursuant to section 201 of the Trade Act of 1974.[d]

Section 201, as we saw,[e] requires a finding that an article is being imported into the United States ''in such increased quantities as to be a *substantial cause* (or threat) of *serious injury*'' to the domestic article in question.[f] If the finding were affirmative, the Commission could recommend, and the President could act to raise tariffs, impose quotas, negotiate an orderly marketing agreement or apply some combination of these measures, without any requirement of a finding of wrongdoing or unfair trade by the exporter.[g] The UAW, in its petition, sought an increase in tariffs on passenger vehicles fom the current rate of 2.9 percent ad valorem to 20 percent, and quotas limiting annual imports for a five-year period to the average quantity imported in 1975 and 1976.[h] Thus the quota would permit approximately 1.5 million cars to enter, as compared to the 2.3 million cars that came in

---

[a] See New York Times, June 13, 1980, p. D1, col. 1.

[b] See § 6.1 *supra*.

[c] The UAW's petition was filed with the ITⁿ on June 12, 1980, and on June 30, 1980 the Commission formally initiated an investigation, as required by § 201(b)(1) of the Trade Act of 1974, 45 Fed. Reg. 45731 (July 7, 1980).

[d] Documents Supplement p. DS—338.

[e] See §§ 3.52 at N. m, 3.53 at Ns. r-v, and 5.56(b) *supra*.

[f] Section 201(b)(1).

[g] Trade Act of 1974, § 203.

[h] See New York Times, June 13, 1980, p. D9 col. 1.

in 1979 and the even greater number that seemed to be coming in as the petition was filed.

Table 2

New Passenger Automobiles Sold in United States
1964–1980
(000's)

	Domestic Factory Sales	Imports other than from Canada	Imports as a Share of Apparent Consumption*
1964	7,752	527	6.5%
1965	9,305	530	5.5
1966	8,598	747	8.1
1967	7,437	697	8.5
1968	8,822	1,119	11.0
1969	8,224	1,155	11.9
1970	6,546**	1,321	15.9
1971	8,584	1,785	16.6
1972	8,823	1,643	15.1
1973	9,657	1,565	13.5
1974	7,311	1,755	18.9
1975	6,713	1,341	16.5
1976	8,497	1,711	16.5
1977	9,199	1,940	17.2
1978	9,165	2,167	18.8
1979	8,419	2,328	21.8
1980	6,400	2,522	28.3

* Apparent Consumption = Domestic Factory Sales + Imports from Canada (not listed in table) + Imports from other sources, (Col. 2) − exports (not listed on table).

Source: Derived from tables in U.S. Int'l Trade Commission, Automotive Trade Statistics 1964–1980, USITC Publ. 1171 (Aug. 1981).

** The sharp reduction in 1970 reflects a two-month strike of General Motors.

There was, of course, no doubt that the domestic auto industry was in trouble, and there was no doubt that imports of automobiles were increasing. But whether the industry's troubles were caused by a shift in consumer tastes stemming from the second energy crisis, by high interest rates, by general economic conditions, or by imports, was not so clear. Nor, despite some guidance in the statute itself,[i] was it clear what proportion of these causes,

---

[i] See § 201(b)(2), (3) and (4).

assuming some of each could be found relevant, was required to bring the escape clause into play. On August 4, 1980, the Ford Motor Company filed its own petition for relief under section 201,[j] and the two petitions were consolidated for investigation and hearing.[k] It was the biggest case ever to come before the Commission, and as Commissioner Stern wrote, virtually every possible question of legal and economic analysis was at issue.[l]

In accordance with Commission practice, a staff investigation was undertaken, pulling together a variety of statistics and other economic analysis for submission to the Commissioners. Originally the Commission had planned a two-stage proceeding, the first to determine whether relief was called for and a second stage, if necessary, to determine what relief would be recommended to the President. When President Carter wrote to the Commission asking that the Commission accelerate its investigation in view of the large number of businesses, workers, and consumers for whom an investigation taking the full six months permitted by the statute "could cause major uncertainties," the Commission decided to speed up the proceedings and hold a consolidated single-stage hearing.[m] The staff investigation was finished by September 11, 1980, and on October 8-11, 1980, the Commission held a hearing on the petitions. On November 10, 1980 (the Monday after the Presidential election), the Commission announced its decision.[n]

The Commission did its work very systematically.[o] First, it concluded, without dissent, that while passenger cars, light trucks, and medium and heavy trucks were separate industries for purposes of section 201, a passenger car was a passenger car, without meaningful distinction for its purposes between

---

[j] Washington Post, August 5, 1980, p. D7, col. 4–7.

[k] 45 Fed. Reg. 55873 (Aug. 21, 1980).

[l] *Certain Motor Vehicles*, N. o *infra* at 93.

[m] See 45 Fed. Reg. 48996 (July 22, 1980).

[n] See New York Times, Nov. 11, 1980, p. 1, col. 3. The formal Report of the Commission, containing the opinions of the commissioners and the results of the staff investigation, was released on Dec. 3, 1980. That Report, N. o *infra*, is the basis of the discussion that follows.

[o] *Certain Motor Vehicles and Certain Chassis and Bodies Therefor*, Report to the President on Investigation TA-201-44 under Section 201 of the Trade Act of 1974, USITC Publ. 1110, December 1980, 45 Fed. Reg. 85194 (Dec. 24, 1980). In the text that follows, as in the prior portions of this section, only the portions directed to passenger automobiles are discussed. Citations in the following pages are to USITC report which sets out all the views of the Commissioners, as well as the Staff Investigation and various statistical appendices. For a law review summary of the decision, see Note: "Car Wars: Auto Imports and the Escape Clause," 13 Law & Pol'y Int'l Bus. 591 (1981).

subcompact, compact, medium and full-size cars or between four-cylinder, six-cylinder, and eight-cylinder, fuel-efficient and fuel-extravagant, low-price and high-price vehicles. All passenger cars performed essentially the same function, and were in competition with one another for the same market.[p]

Second, what about increased imports? There was little doubt that imports of passenger cars had increased significantly.[q]

Third, was there serious injury? Chairman Alberger wrote:

> . . . [T]he facts and testimony before us overwhelmingly demonstrate that the [American] passenger automobile industry in the aggregate is in serious difficulty. . . . [T]he declines in production, employment, profitability and sales [in the first six months of 1980] are devastating.[r]

Not only were sales and production down (see table, p. 384), but capacity utilization had dropped from 86.2 percent in 1978 to 79.5 percent in 1979 and to 66.5 percent in the first half of 1980. Profits by the U.S. manufacturers on automotive operations went from $5.6 billion in 1978 to $1.3 billion in 1979, and to a loss of $2.9 billion in the first six months of 1980.[s] Employment had fallen from just over 1 million in 1978[t] to 971,000 in 1979 and to about 750,000 in the first half of 1980. "There is no doubt," the Chairman concluded, "that both the passenger automobile and light truck industries are seriously injured."[u]

Thus far, the Commission's findings were useful to a system of decision-making that depends on a formal record, but hardly startling. The critical issue, of course, was whether increased imports could be linked to serious

---

[p] See *Certain Motor Vehicles* pp. 4–11 (Chairman Alberger); 53–64 (Vice Chairman Calhoun);95–103 (Member Stern), 168–69 (Members Moore and Bedell). Chairman Alberger added (pp. 10–11) that since the domestic manufacturers all produce a full line of automobiles, an effort to measure injury in regard to a portion of its production only would involve "nightmarish problems in attempting to allocate profits, production costs and employment data."

[q] The Commission included imports from Canada in its calculations, and accordingly came up with different figures from those given in the table on page 384. The trend, of course, was the same, including a rise of 13.6 percent in imports of passenger cars from the first six months of 1979 to the first six months of 1980.

[r] *Certain Motor Vehicles* at 17.

[s] *Id*. at 18–19. See also Staff Investigation, *id*. at A–32–33.

[t] Only Volkswagen of America showed a profit in the first half year of 1980.

[u] *Certain Motor Vehicles* at 20.

injury through what the statute called "substantial cause," i.e., "a cause which is important and not less than any other cause."[v]

Three members of the International Trade Commission said "No." What really happened, they said, was a severe decline in overall demand, which, as it turned out, fell unevenly on Detroit. In 1976–78, good years for U.S. manufacturers, imports were going up faster than in the later period. In 1979, when all sales had declined, so had imports, though their share of the market had increased. If the decline in demand could be laid to general economic conditions and the sharp rise in oil prices, then imports could not be found to be a cause "not less than any other cause."

To measure the relative importance of various possible causes, the majority of the Commission constructed a hypothetical comparison:

Assuming that total consumption of cars in 1979 had equalled the actual reported figure, suppose the share of that figure accounted for by imports from all sources had remained the same as in 1978, roughly 26.2 percent, as compared with the 27.1 percent of apparent consumption actually reported.[w] That would have resulted in a decrease in imports of 94,500 units, and correspondingly an increase in that amount for domestically produced cars. But domestic shipments were down by 738,700 units, so only 94.5/738.7 or 12.8 percent of the decline in domestic sales could be attributed to imports, not enough to meet the statutory standard.[x]

The petitioners argued that the trouble with the majority's approach was that it lumped "all other" factors together and then compared that lump with imports. If one broke down "general economic conditions" into inflation, unemployment, high interest rates, and rise in fuel costs, perhaps no given factor would appear more significant than imports. Moreover, the UAW argued, the recession was not really so much a cause of the decline in demand for cars as an effect of increased imports. Chairman Alberger regarded inflation, unemployment, and high interest rates as "part and parcel of a generalized recession," not attributable in sufficient measure to auto imports to draw the calculation about reduced demand into question.

---

[v] Trade Act of 1974, § 201(b)(4), Documents Supplement p. DS—339.

[w] These figures are different from the ones in table 2, because they include imports from Canada, which are excluded in the table in the book. For the difference that change makes in the calculation, see § 8.23(d) *infra*.

[x] *Certain Motor Vehicles* pp. 21–26 (Chairman Alberger); 85–87 (Chairman Calhoun). Commissioner Stern rejected the mathematical model, but came up with much the same conclusion. *Id*. at 146.

Cyclical downturns in the economy are to be expected, and must not force a reliance on unnecessary import remedies. The problem which auto producers confront is one which confronts many sectors of the economy (the building industry, for example) and it cannot be solved by import relief.[y]

Vice Chairman Calhoun made the same point somewhat differently:

While one could make very good arguments supporting the need for an industrial policy which would provide assistance to worthy industries suffering generalized difficulty unassociated with imports, section 201 cannot be so construed. It is plainly and simply an import relief provision and, therefore, our fundamental task on the face of it and from the legislative history is to determine that *imports* are an important cause of the injury and to determine that no other cause is more important than imports. . . .[z]

The dissenters had no real disagreement with the majority's economic analysis, but they interpreted the legal requirement differently:

We reject the notion that the statute permits the Commission to aggregate a number of economic factors which in combination are to be weighed against increased imports to find the substantial cause of serious injury. . . . We do not believe that Congress envisioned that the Commission would consider an economic downturn per se to be a single economic factor in determining injury in section 201 investigations. Instead, we believe that Congress intended the Commission to examine imports and their impact on the domestic industry over the course of the business cycle—during both good and bad years—in order to ascertain whether import penetration is increasing and, if so, whether the increasing penetration is seriously injuring the domestic industry.[aa]

To the dissenters, the situation of the American automobile industry in 1980 was the "classic case" for an affirmative determination under section 201:

We believe that import restrictions in the form of reasonable quotas on imports of passenger automobiles would not have caused disruptions in international trade, but would have provided the domestic passenger car industry with a much needed opportunity to adjust to the new competitive conditions in the marketplace which are the result of economic factors beyond its control.[bb]

---

[y] *Certain Motor Vehicles* at 28.

[z] *Id*. at 72.

[aa] Dissenting Opinion of Commissioners Moore and Bedell, *id*. at 173–74.

[bb] *Id*. at 176–77.

§ 8.2—Notes and Questions

8.21—(a) Since injury is found and fault on the part of foreign suppliers (in contrast to the various steel cases) is not an issue, the automobile case turns almost entirely on the question of cause, or rather "substantial cause." Do you suspect that for all its efforts to apply a statutory standard to a set of facts presented in an elaborate staff investigation and record of hearing, what is really going on is a judgment on the conduct of the domestic automobile industry?

(b) Suppose there is truth to this suspicion: The domestic industry, never happy with "Smallsville,"[a] has made a blunder in not bringing out high-quality small cars in sufficient time and quantity. The blunder reflects the industry's misjudgment of the consumer shift in the American consumer's taste, in part resulting from the unforeseen jump in gasoline prices. Does this render the industry undeserving of import relief? Note that the principal petitioner was the United Automobile Workers of America, which surely was not to blame for decisions made by management.[b]

(c) Given that the Commission—properly—is concerned not to become an instrument of protectionism, one way to approach the preceding question is to look at the petition from the point of view of the foreign suppliers. If the vote of the Commission had been affirmative, would Japan have had a legitimate complaint under the GATT? Or is Article XIX designed just for the kind of situation that did occur in the American auto industry in 1979–80? Note that Article XIX speaks of unforeseen, not unforeseeable developments.

(d) Speaking of Article XIX, note that it also says "as a result . . . of the effect of the obligations incurred by a contracting party under this Agreement." No one claimed that tariffs had anything to do with the problems

---

[a] Compare Rukeyeser, "Detroit's Reluctant Ride into Smallsville," Fortune, March 1969, p. 111.

[b] Chairman Alberger, while acknowledging this argument, said he rejected it:

. . . [T]here may be some implication from the record . . . that we should give greater weight to the shift in demand as a cause because the industry brought injury upon itself by refusing to recognize in a timely manner the long-term change in consumer preference away from "gas guzzlers." This "self-inflicted injury" theory has superficial appeal. . . . However it ignores the fact that large car sales were exceedingly healthy in the period 1976–78. Events such as the revolution in Iran . . . are what disturbed the pattern. The auto producers now see the inevitability of the future and are adjusting to meet it, but I cannot find their own management misjudgments or lack of planning to be superseding causes of injury.

Certain Motor Vehicles at 33.

of the U.S. auto industry, which had stood at 3 percent ad valorem since the final stage of the Kennedy Round reductions went into effect on January 1, 1972.[c] What obligations do you think might meet that criterion?[d]

(e) Coming back to the American industry, note that only the union and Ford filed for relief. Chrysler, as we saw,[e] was getting help from another part of the U.S. government; General Motors, with close to 60 percent of domestic production of passenger cars and about 46 percent of the market counting imports, must have felt it would be poor taste (as well as poor long-term strategy) to apply for import relief, even if it did sustain a loss for the year of $762 million—the first loss for the company since 1921. How, if at all, do these considerations affect your judgment of the Commission's rejection of the petition?

8.22—Prices of Japanese cars in the United States were increasing substantially faster than were prices of U.S.-made cars,[f] and in the period 1979–80 price differences between foreign and domestic small cars seem not to have been a significant factor in consumers' choices. In that sense, the auto industry at the end of the decade was different from steel or most consumer electronics. But quality differences, or perception of quality differences, may well have been a significant cause of consumer preference for imports. The Commissioners were not sure how to deal with that issue.

(a) It is hard to define quality in an automobile, but there is no doubt that the impression was growing in the United States that foreign-made cars (especially from Japan and Germany) were the product of more careful

---

[c] A further reduction of 0.5 percent was negotiated in the Tokyo Round to be implemented in 5 stages, so that as of January 1, 1980 the duty on passenger vehicles stood at 2.9 percent ad valorem.

[d] Professor Jackson suggests that the obligation may simply be the promise not to impose quotas, and the unforeseen developments may be the increased imports themselves. J. Jackson, *World Trade and the Law of GATT*, 559–60 (1969).

[e] § 8.12 N. n *supra*.

[f] See *Certain Motor Vehicles*, Staff Investigation, pp. A–56–61. By way of illustration, the median price of the Toyota Corolla increased 87.5 percent in the period 1976–1980, and the Datsun 210 48.6 percent, the Chevrolet Chevette rose 42.9 percent in the same period, and the Ford Pinto rose 27 percent. By the first half of 1980, the Toyota Corolla's median sales price was $6,000, the Datsun 210 $5,500, the Chevette $5,000, and the Pinto $4,700. Chrysler's entry into the subcompact market, Dodge Omni/Plymouth Horizon, came out in 1979 at $5,000–$5,100, and sold in 1980 for $6,100–$6,200.

Of course all these figures are not wholly comparable, since they include or exclude items that are standard on some models, optional on others.

workmanship than cars made in Detroit. The impression went not so much to the major components of the automobile—engines, transmissions, brakes[g]—as to what is known in the industry as "fits and finishes"— whether paint came off, doors and windows rattled, and things like windshield wipers, seat adjusters, or turn signals performed without trouble. The frequency of repair reports prepared by Consumers Union based on readers' replies to questionnaires regularly rated Japanese (and West German) cars as better or far better than average, while no American-made car received such a rating.[h] When several hundred domestic automotive engineers were asked in 1979 by Ward's Auto World, "As of today, the best quality cars are produced in what country?", 47 percent said Japan, 23 percent said Germany, 3 percent France, and only 27 percent pointed to their own country.[i] Moreover, what seems to have happened in 1979–80 is that American buyers began to care. Not only did fuel economy become an important consideration with car buyers, but as such considerations as brand loyalty and custom styling receded in car buyers' priorities, quality of workmanship became an important consideration in their choice of automobile, and increasingly pointed to imports.[j]

How should these facts affect the decision on import relief by the International Trade Commission?

(b) The staff report submitted to the Commission had a section on comparative quality, citing various studies of consumers' perception of the quality of small cars, American and foreign, including the studies referred to in the

---

[g] Indeed, American power-trains were considered the best in the world—so much so that Rolls Royce used GM transmissions.

[h] See, e.g., 45 Consumer Reports No. 4, pp. 263–72 (April 1980); 46 Id. No. 4, pp. 225–35 (April 1981); 47 Id. No. 4, pp. 198–207 (April 1982). Typically these reports reflect responses from about 250,000 readers and auto users.

[i] See Subcomm. on Trade of House Comm. on Ways and Means, Auto Situation: 1980 at 47, 96th Cong., 2d Sess. (Committee Print 1980). Also, none of the four largest Japanese automobile producers had a recall rate higher than one-third the lowest rate shown by a U.S. producer.

[j] The Chrysler Corporation did a survey comparing consumer values in 1975 and 1979. In that period "previous experience with make" (i.e. brand loyalty) went from first in importance to sixteenth; "styling" from second to ninth; "manufacturer's reputation" from fifth to fifteenth. On the other hand, "quality of workmanship" went from sixteenth to second place, and "value" from eighth to first. Purchase price and fuel economy, rated third and fourth in 1975, just reversed places in 1979. See "'Quality', A Special Report," in Car and Driver, March 1981, p. 43.

preceding paragraph.[k] Commissioner Stern considered quality as an explanation of how imports may have contributed to the injury of the domestic industry, "because they function in the same manner as a price advantage."[l] In other words, relatively higher quality was a cause of injury attributable to imports, but not as great (alone or in combination) as the overall decline in demand. Commissioner Calhoun said he regarded the events of 1979–80 as an aberration due not primarily to imports, but to domestic supply and quality problems.[m] The inference seemed to be that if Detroit improved the quality of the product, it could get a larger share of the market, and restraining imports would be the wrong way to stimulate such a development. Is this attitude (not wholly explicit in the Commissioners' views)[n] consistent with the objective of an open global market system and the benefits of competition? With the function of the escape clause?

(c) Douglas Fraser, the President of the United Auto Workers, had his answer to that question:

> I think we've made some mistakes in the past. I think in 1977, 1978, where you could sell every single car that went out the door, the whole orientation was toward quantity. . . . But I think there is a new awareness and sensitivity out there. We haven't built the kind of cars that we're capable of building. I would suggest to anyone that they go into the plants now and they will see a marked difference between the attitude now and what it was two and three years ago.[o]

The implication, of course, was that import relief, limited in time and scope, would permit the American auto industry to recover not only from management errors, but from laxity with regard to quality and absenteeism on the assembly line.[p] It was hard to put this argument and the argument sug-

---

[k] *Certain Motor Vehicles*, pp. A–63–66.

[l] *Id*. at 145.

[m] *Id*. at 75.

[n] Chairman Alberger did not allude to quality at all in his opinion.

[o] Comments of Douglas A. Fraser, NBC Meet the Press, March 22, 1981 at 6. Mr. Fraser testified to the same effect at the ITC hearing, as well as in hearings before various Congressional committees looking into the situation of the American automobile industry.

[p] Mr. Fraser said, in the same interview excerpted above:

> The auto workers are being maligned, I think unfairly and terribly . . . and to those writers and cartoonists who depict the auto workers as lazy and unattentive and careless, the only way I could educate them is put them on that assembly line for about 30 days.

gested in paragraph (b) together, particularly in the context of a legal proceeding. Ultimately, however, neither argument seemed controlling, as the Commission concentrated on identifying the most important cause of injury to the industry—the shift in demand.

8.23—One issue that turned out to be very important in the decision of the ITC has not been discussed so far—the issue of how to treat imports from Canada. To understand that issue, a brief historical digression is in order:

(a) *The U.S.-Canada Automotive Agreement.*[a] From the 1920's on, all of the major U.S. auto producers had plants in Canada, 100 percent owned by the parent companies, and producing (with minor variations) the same models as in the United States. As in the United States, Canadian automobile plants were clustered around the Great Lakes, with several in Windsor, Ontario, just across the river from Detroit. The same labor union organized the plants on both sides of the border, but negotiations were separate, and wages, as of the early 1960's, were somewhat lower in Canada. There was no indigenous Canadian automobile industry.

For Canada, the presence of the American automotive giants—General Motors, Ford, and Chrysler (as well as American Motors)—was a prominent, perhaps the most prominent—illustration of the domination of its economy by foreign investors.[b] In addition, while Fords, Plymouths, Chevrolets, etc. were assembled in Canada, much of the sourcing, as well as nearly all research and development, was done in the United States. In the period 1960-64, the balance of trade between the United States and Canada in automotive products, including vehicles and parts, ran about $400 million per year adverse to Canada. In the early 1960's, as Canada's nationalism was being revived, a prominent target was the ''branch plant'' aspect of the Canadian motor vehicle industry.

Until 1962, Canada had relied primarily on two devices to protect its

---

For a picture of life in an automobile plant, both the dehumanizing aspect of the assembly line and the don't-give-a-damn attitude of the workers on the line, see A. Hailey, *Wheels*, esp. Ch. 14 (1971), a best seller both in hard cover and in paper back for many months, later made into a movie.

[a] Portions of this note are adapted from A. Chayes, T. Ehrlich, A. Lowenfeld, *International Legal Process*, Ch. V (1968).

[b] For a more detailed discussion of this problem, leading in 1973 to passage of Canada's Foreign Investment Review Act, see Volume II of this series, A. Lowenfeld, *International Private Investment*, Ch. I, esp. §§ 1.12, 4.1 (2d ed. 1982).

automobile industry: relatively high tariffs,[c] and a "Commonwealth content" requirement under which no vehicle or part could be sold in Canada unless a stated percentage of its value—on most items 60 percent—represented Commonwealth (in practice Canadian) labor, parts, and other inputs. The result of these restrictions was to compel the major companies to maintain a certain volume of production in Canada in order to be able to sell in Canada at all. The combination of high duties and relatively small production runs, however, resulted generally in auto prices for Canadian consumers significantly higher than prices for comparable models in the United States. There were virtually no exports of automotive products from Canada to the United States.

In the fall of 1963, the newly elected Liberal Government of Prime Minister Lester Pearson introduced a Rebate Plan, under which duties on imports of automotive products into Canada were forgiven or rebated to the extent that exports by vehicle producers (i.e., the Canadian subsidiaries of the U.S. companies) exceeded in a given year their exports (measured in Canadian content) in the base year.[d] Canada's exports of automobile parts immediately increased, to the detriment not of the majors, but of independent American suppliers to them. One such supplier brought a countervailing duty proceeding under § 303 of the Tariff Act of 1930,[e] asserting that the Rebate Plan was a form of subsidy on exports.[f] The U.S. Treasury delayed decision on the petition, but essentially agreed with the petitioner that a "bounty or grant" was involved in the Rebate Plan which required imposition of a countervailing duty. However, the Canadian government was fully and politically committed to the Rebate Plan, and imposition of countervailing duties by the United States would certainly have required some counter-countervailing move by Canada, possibly raising the content requirement even higher or even taking over the auto companies.

Cooler heads prevailed on both sides, and a trade war between the two

---

[c] Tariffs on finished vehicles stood at 17.5 percent, tariffs on parts between 20 and 25 percent ad valorem, compared with U.S. duties at the time (pre-Kennedy round) of 6.5 percent on vehicles and 8.5 percent on parts.

[d] Order in Council Establishing Rebate Plan, P.C. 1963-1/1544, Oct. 22, 1963. The text of the Order in Council, as well as a detailed analysis of the plan, appear in Chayes, Ehrlich, and Lowenfeld, N. a *supra* at 312–15.

[e] See § 4.45 *supra*.

[f] *Modine Manufacturing Company*, Petition before the Commissioner of Customs for Issuance of a Countervailing Duty Order with Respect to Motor Vehicle Radiators Exported from Canada with Benefit of a Bounty or Grant, filed April 15, 1964.

nations that shared a continent and were each other's largest trading partners was averted. Instead, negotiations were begun, and after several months successfully concluded, to eliminate all duties on trade in motor vehicles and parts between Canada and the United States in either direction.[g] The Automotive Products Agreement was in a sense a Free Trade Area limited to one industry;[h] in order to make sure that the major producers would remain in Canada in strength, however, each of them was required to submit a Letter of Intent to the Canadian government committing it (1) to preserve at least the proportion of Canadian content in its products that prevailed before the Agreement (but by producer, not by individual product); and (2) to invest a stated (and negotiated) sum in Canadian plant over the next four years.

When the Agreement became effective, all duties on transborder trade in motor vehicles—American and Canadian—were eliminated, and all the manufacturers proceeded to rationalize and integrate their production, so that certain parts were made and models assembled only in Canada, others only in the United States. Car prices fell in Canada relative to the United States, wage levels became roughly equal, and transborder trade in auto products rose dramatically.[i] By 1978, 833,000 passenger automobiles were imported into the United States from Canada, and 523,000 were exported to Canada from the United States.[j]

(b) Coming back to 1980 and the escape clause action, the question now arose how to treat transborder (and essentially intra-company) trade, both for purposes of defining the industry,[k] and for purposes of measuring the

---

[g] Agreement between United States of America and Canada concerning Automotive Products signed at Johnson City, Texas, Jan. 16, 1965, 17 U.S.T. 1372, T.I.A.S. No. 6093. The Agreement was implemented in the United States pursuant to the Automotive Products Trade Act of 1965, Pub. L. 89-283, 79 Stat. 1016, 19 U.S.C. § 2001-2033.

[h] The Agreement was thus plainly inconsistent with Article XXIV of the GATT, as discussed in § 3.11 *supra*. The United States sought, and with some misgivings, secured a waiver from the GATT Contracting Parties under Article XXV, GATT Docs. L/2409, 25 March 1965, L/2528, 20 December 1965, BISD 14th Supp. 37–44, 181–190 (1966). Canada took the position that it did not need a waiver, because it abolished its duties on an MFN basis. The GATT documents cited are reproduced and discussed in Chayes, Ehrlich, and Lowenfeld, N. a *supra* at 372–76, and also in J. Jackson, *Legal Problems of International Economic Relations* at 554–56 (1977).

[i] See, e.g., Welch, "U.S.-Canada Automotive Trade Agreement" in Commission on International Trade and Investment Policy (The Williams Commission), *United States International Economic Policy in an Interdependent World*, Vol. 2, p. 239 (1971).

[j] International Trade Commission, *Automotive Trade Statistics 1964–1980*, Table 1D, USITC Publ. 1171 (August 1981).

[k] See § 201(b)(3) of the Trade Act of 1974, Documents Supplement p. DS-339.

movement in imports. (i) Should imports from Canada simply be excluded from the calculations, as they have been from the table at p. 384? (ii) Should the industry be treated as one North American industry and market, so that production, consumption, and imports would be measured for the USA and Canada? or (iii) Should all imports into the United States be treated the same, regardless of origin, so that a decline in imports from Canada would offset an increase in imports from Japan?

(c) The UAW took the position that imports from Canada should be excluded from any remedy recommended by the Commission, because such imports were not injurious. Ford went further and argued that vehicles produced in Canada and shipped to the United States should not be considered "imports" at all. The Commission said it might have accepted the union's suggestion concerning remedy had it recommended relief. But as to the basic question, it held that since nothing in the U.S.-Canada Agreement or the implementing legislation[l] exempted products of Canada from application of section 201, the Commission could not exclude the products of Canada from the scope of the case. In fact the Senate Committee report on the implementing legislation, quoted by the Commission,[m] had been careful to state that escape clause and antidumping actions were not precluded by the Agreement, but of course that statement related to fear by the Congress that excessive (or unfairly priced) imports might be coming from Canada to the United States. That was not the situation when the International Trade Commission was considering the petition of Ford and the UAW. In fact imports from Canada had declined from 834,000 units in 1978 to 678,000 units in 1979, as demand for all American-type cars fell, and to 313,000 for the first six months of 1980.[n] It may be that this decision turned out to be the critical element in the case.

(d) Consider how the formula used by the Commission to measure the importance of imports to injury (p. 387 *supra*) would have come out had imports from Canada not been counted:

Assuming total consumption of 10.315 million units (as actually reported

---

[l] See N. g *supra*.

[m] See *Certain Motor Vehicles*, Opinion of Chairman Alberger at 14, quoting from *Automotive Products Trade Act of 1965*, Report of Sen. Comm. on Finance at 7, S. Rept. No. 782, 89th Cong., 1st Sess. (1965).

[n] The full year statistics for calendar year 1980 show 594,770 units imported, as against 507,413 units exported from the United States to Canada.

in 1979)[o] and imports (other than for Canada) at the 1978 rate of 18.8 percent, then 1.939 million units would have been imported from Europe and Japan, in contrast to the 2.328 million actually reported. Thus the difference between hypothetical and actual imports was 389,000 or 52 percent of the decline in U.S. shipments.

The reason for the discrepancy, of course, is that imports from Canada declined by 160,000 units between 1978 and 1979, and this amount, seen in the Commission's calculations as an offset to increased imports from Japan and Europe, masked the actual increase from those areas. Thus the Commission's calculations show a rise in imports as a percent of consumption of 0.9 percentage points, whereas the table at p. 384 shows a rise in imports (other than from Canada) as a percent of consumption of 3.0 percentage points.

(e) Is the inclusion of imports from Canada the fatal flaw in the decision? Or do you think the decision was right, even if the formula was unpersuasive? Or, finally, was the Commission correct in applying its formula as it did, so that the suggestion in paragraph (d) would have been error? The dissenters did not address the issue of imports from Canada at all.

8.24—(a) A final point that needs to be addressed is whether the kinds of questions raised by the auto industry escape clause proceeding belong before an independent regulatory agency at all. Note that under sections 201–203 of the Trade Act of 1974, if the Commission recommends relief, the final decision is up to the President, subject to being overridden by majority vote of both Houses of Congress.[p] But a negative decision by the Commission, as in *Certain Motor Vehicles,* leaves the President without authority to implement whatever remedy he might choose to apply to what was clearly a serious problem for the nation.

(b) The argument for committing the decision to an independent agency, of course, is to take the decision out of politics—politics likely to take a short-run view and tend to protectionism and against free trade.[q] When the issue involves mushrooms or clothespins or machine needles (to take three recent cases before the Commission), this argument is certainly persuasive. When it involves a basic industry such as steel or automobiles, the question is at

---

[o] Note that this figure does include imports from Canada as part of total consumption; see note to table at pp. 384.

[p] See § 203(c). But see § 5.56 N. w *supra* concerning the consitutionality of the provision for Congressional veto.

[q] Recall the origin of the Tariff Comission, as it was then called, during the administration of Woodrow Wilson, § 3.51 *supra* at Ns. u–z.

the least different, though perhaps the argument for insulating the decision from political pressure is equally (more?) compelling.

(c) It seems, though one cannot prove it with precision from the statute,[r] that the injury causation tests that are committed to the Commission are harder for the petitioner to satisfy in a case such as *Certain Motor Vehicles*, where no unfair practice by the foreign producers or their countries is alleged, than in a case in which dumping or subsidies have been found by the Treasury or Commerce Department.[s] Put another way, with no finding in the executive branch of unfair trade attributable to the foreign producers, the critical question for the Commission is what level of causation and injury justifies interfering with free and *fair* trade. Do you think the unemployed auto worker in Detroit can explain that distinction to his brother-in-law in Gary? Does the auto industry case suggest that prior cases and the law in general have been too concerned with the exporting, and not enough with the importing country? We return to this question in the last section of this volume.[t]

(d) The executive branch is entitled to appear in proceedings before the International Trade Commission, but though *Certain Motor Vehicles* was the biggest case ever to come before the Commission, the Carter administration saw fit not to do so. The only U.S. government party represented before the Commission (other than the Commission staff itself) was another independent regulatory agency, the Federal Trade Commission, which strongly opposed relief, as it had opposed quotas on steel imports in 1977.[u] What inference do you draw from the absence of representation on behalf of the administration?

---

[r] Compare § 201(b)(2) of the Trade Act of 1974, Documents Supplement DS-338, with § 771(7) of the Tariff Act of 1930, as amended by the Trade Agreements Act of 1979, Documents Supplement p. DS-512.

[s] Compare, e.g., *Carbon Steel Plate from Japan*, § 6.1, Ns. k-1 *supra*; see also the *Steel Subsidy Cases* § 8.53 *infra*. The statement in the text is supported by the House Report on the Trade Agreements Act of 1979, which states, in commenting on amendments to the Antidumping Act, that

The Committee does not view overall injury caused by unfair competition, such as dumping, to require as strong a causation link to unfairly competitive imports as would be required for determining the existence of injury under fair trade conditions.

Trade Agreements Act of 1979, Report of House Comm. on Ways and Means to accompany H.R. 4537 at 47, 96th Cong., 1st Sess. (1979).

[t] For a brief discussion of this question by the present author in the context of a symposium about the Tokyo Round, see Lowenfeld, "Fair or Unfair Trade: Does It Matter?" 13 Cornell Int'l L.J. 205 (1980).

[u] See § 6.1 N. e *supra*.

(e) In light of the experience with steel a few years earlier, how would you expect the story of auto imports to continue? How would you advise

(i) the United Automobile Workers, AFL-CIO;

(ii) General Motors, Ford, or Chrysler;

(iii) the incoming administration of President Reagan;

(iv) the Japan Automobile Manufacturers Association?

§ 8.3—The Automobile Story Continued

Immediately after the outcome of the proceeding before the ITC was announced, the proponents of restraints against auto imports began to look for other means to achieve their objectives.[a] The chairman of Ford, Philip Caldwell, said, "This is now a matter for the President and Congress to determine. . . .This country cannot afford the continuing exploitation of our auto market by the Japanese."[b] Douglas Fraser, the president of the United Auto Workers, said, "We will take up the battle with Congress.... This is just one of the battles in a long struggle."[c] Reubin Askew, the former governor of Florida who had succeeded Robert Strauss as U.S. Trade Representative, said, "We remain concerned about the health of the domestic industry and will continue exploring ways in which the Government may be of assistance in this difficult period of transition."[d] But while some persons thought a President and Congress no longer concerned about re-election were in good position to take on the automobile situation, eventually all sides wanted to see how the incoming administration would balance its devotion to laissez-faire with candidate Reagan's statement during the campaign that "this is something where I think the government has a responsibility that it's shirked so far." Japan's Minister of International Trade and Industry wrote to Washington that his government fully recognized that the sound development of the American industry "is indispensable to the American economy," and promised that the Japanese government would urge its car makers to exercise "prudence" in selling to the United States.[e]

Soon after President Reagan and the new Congress took office in 1981, legislative proposals of various kinds were introduced to curb auto imports,

---

[a] New York Times, November 11, 1980, p. 1, col. 3, p. D6, col. 1.

[b] New York Times, November 11, 1980, p. D6, col. 5.

[c] Ibid.

[d] New York Times, November 19, 1980, p. D5, col. 4.

[e] New York Times, November 18, 1980, p. Dl, col. 3–6.

most founded on some kind of quota. The most prominent of the bills, sponsored by Senator John C. Danforth of Missouri, proposed a three-year quota, limited to imports from Japan, at 1.6 million units per year, compared with the 1.9 million units actually imported in 1980.[f] The administration, however, was reluctant to support such legislation, at least until it had worked out its overall foreign economic policy, as well as its anti-inflation program.[g] Press reports indicated that the President's cabinet was split about evenly on the issue of restraints on auto imports.[h] The Secretary of State, the Secretary of the Treasury, and the Trade Representative warned against weakening the international trading system, and the Chairman of the Council of Economic Advisers and the Director of the Office of Management and Budget were concerned about the inflationary impact of import restraints. On the other side, the Transportation, Commerce, and Labor Departments favored temporary quotas, to give the domestic industry a chance to adapt itself to current market conditions. In the early months of the new administration, agreement could be reached on deferral of new environmental and safety requirements for the auto industry, but not on trade restraints.

When the Japanese foreign minister, Masayoshi Ito, came to Washington late in March, 1981, auto imports were high on the agenda, but apparently no specific requests for cutbacks were submitted by the United States. President Reagan evidently hoped that the way to resolve the sharp controversy within his administration (as well as the country as a whole) was to have the Japanese take action on their own, without a direct proposal from the United States.[i] Thus, it was hoped, restraints might come about without any protectionist stance by the administration, which might be cited on a variety of other fronts. The target date was the proposed visit of Japan's prime minister, Zenko Suzuki, early in May.

On March 30, 1981, President Reagan was shot, and though he recovered with surprising speed, the task of producing a unified policy from a divided government was pushed back by a month. Early in April, a middle level

---

[f] S.396, 97th Cong., 1st Sess. (Feb. 5, 1981).

[g] See, e.g., *Issues Relating to the Domestic Auto Industry*, Hearing before Subcomm. on International Trade of Sen. Comm. on Finance, Part 2, pp. 39–80 (testimony of Secretary of Commerce Malcolm Baldrige, Secretary of Transportation Andrew L. Lewis, Jr., and U.S. Trade Representative William E. Brock, III, 97th Cong., 1st Sess. (March 9, 1981).

[h] See, e.g., New York Times, March 5, 1981, p. Dl, col. 6; March 6, 1981, p. D2, col. l; March 13, 1982, p. l, col. 4–6; March 16, 1981, p. D2, col. 3; March 18, 1981, p. Dl, col. 5; March 20, 1981, p. Dl, col. 6. See also, "The Administration's Split on Auto Imports," Fortune, May 4, 1981, p. 156.

[i] Thus the word in Washington was that there would be "talks," but not "negotiations" with Japanese leaders about automobiles. See New York Times, March 26, 1982, p. Dl, col. 1.

delegation from the United States government briefed the Japanese government on the condition of the American auto industry, but made no demands or proposals. By the middle of April, though there were no negotiations, figures began to appear in public discussion. Reports from Tokyo indicated that MITI might recommend a 1.7 million unit ceiling to the Japanese automobile manufacturers for exports to the United States.[j] Meanwhile, Senator Danforth suggested that he might revise his bill to impose a quota of 1.4 instead of 1.6 million cars per year.[k] Secretary of Commerce Baldrige said the President had not yet decided whether he would veto an automobile quota bill if one were passed by Congress, and Chairman Dole of the Senate Finance Committee scheduled action by his committee on the Danforth bill for May 12.[l]

At the end of April, another U.S. delegation flew to Tokyo, this one headed by Bill Brock, the former Chairman of the Republican National Committee who became President Reagan's Trade Representative. On May 1, an agreement was announced, in the form of a press statement issued by MITI:[m]

> The Government of Japan will take the following measures during the period of April 1981-March 1984, based on the understanding that the next three years are crucial for the recovery of the U.S. automobile industry.
>
> (1) For the three year period through March 1984, a new oversight system on passenger car exports to the United States will be implemented, under authority of the Foreign Exchange and Foreign Trade Control Law,[n] pursuant to which each manufacturer will be required to submit monthly reports on its exports of passenger cars to the United States.
>
> (2) During the first year (April 1981-March 1982), MITI will limit the export of passenger cars to the United States by issuing directives to individual companies. The total volume of permitted exports will be 1.68 million units.

---

[j] New York Times, April 20, 1981, p. D1, col. 3.

[k] New York Times, April 17, 1981, p. D1, col. 3.

[l] Wall Street Journal, April 20, 1981, p. 14, col. 3.

[m] *Measures on Passenger Car Exports to the United States: Statement by the Ministry of International Trade and Industry*, Tokyo, May 1, 1981. No official text in English was released. For an unofficial translation of the full communiqué, see Documents Supplement p. DS-624.

[n] Documents Supplement p. DS-231.

(3) During the second year (April 1982-March 1983), exports will be limited in the same manner. The total volume of permitted exports will be the export ceiling for the first year plus an amount equal to 16.5 percent of the estimated increase in the U.S. passenger car market for that year.

(5) During the third year (April 1983-March 1984) MITI will monitor the trend of passenger car exports to the United Stastes through the system described in paragraph (1), and will consider whether to continue the restraints in the light of trends in the U.S. car market at that time.

(6) In any event, these measures will expire not later than March 1984.

In Washington, Senator Danforth said he would not expect to proceed at this time with his bill for import quotas, and Chairman Dole canceled his committee's meeting to mark up the quota legislation. Douglas Fraser said the Japanese restraint was "a modest, but positive step that we hope will improve the job prospects of American workers in the months ahead." He would have preferred a lower figure of imports and a longer period. In Tokyo, the former ambassador to Washington, Nobuhiko Ushiba, was critical. "The proposal for voluntary restraint ended up in a game without ground rules." The president of the Toyota Motor Co., Eiji Toyoda, said, "American consumers will bear heavier burdens and the Japanese economy will suffer a serious blow."[o]

Mr. Brock, on his return to Washington, said, "I think it was very forthcoming and I think a positive step. . . . The action offers us the prospect of good recovery of the domestic automobile industry and the maintenance of a very healthy free trade and expanding trade between our two countries."[p]

§ 8.4—Further Notes and Questions on Automobiles

8.41—(a) The Japanese Measures of Restraint on Automobile Exports were in many ways like the Voluntary Restraint Agreements of 1969-1974 with respect to steel.[a] What looked like a unilateral act was in fact negotiated, and what came out was a quota on imports, administered by the exporting

---

[o] Quotations assembled in BNA, Import-Export Reporter, May 6, 1981, pp. A2–A4.

[p] Press Conference of Ambassador William E. Brock, Washington, May 2, 1981, as released by Office of U.S. Trade Representative, p. 1.

[a] § 5.1 *supra*.

country. As in 1968 with steel, the pressure from the American side was the picture of losses and layoffs, accompanied by various legislative proposals far more protectionist—and far more ominous as precedent—than unilaterally imposed restraint on exploiting a weak market. Again as in 1968, the pressure from Congress was felt not only by the foreign exporters, but at least equally by an Administration (regardless of party) that did not want a trade war, and did not want legislation that might be used as a model in a dozen markets in which American exporters competed successfully with local foreign producers. The principal difference between 1968 and 1981 (apart from the product) was that this time only Japan was involved, and not the European countries. Does it look as if the "voluntary" restraint agreement is an institution that is here to stay, the ultimate "safeguard" because no one has standing to object?

(b) Ambassador Brock was asked at his press conference what the Japanese got out of the Measures of Restraint, other than relief from legislative action. He answered:

> Well, I think they got two or three things. First of all the Japanese have as their priority interest the maintenance of free and expanding access to this market. I think their actions will ensure that further opportunity. Secondly, there was a legitimate expression of concern on the part of the Japanese manufacturer that had the legislation passed with an absolute cap of anywhere from 1.2 million to 1.6 million units for three years, that if our projections of economic recovery did in fact come true they would have no chance at all to participate in an improved sales climate. What we have achieved, I think, is the best of both worlds—that is some predictability in the level of shipments so that our manufacturers can borrow the funds necessary to retool but at the same time we were able to give to their manufacturers an increasing amount of sales. In other words, if sales improve by a million units next year over this, they could have another 165,000 units that the Japanese Government would allow them to sell. So they continue to share in the growth of the market if, in fact, we can restore our domestic economic health. And I think that simply says that we tried very carefully to be sure that all parties would benefit by the decision of the Japanese Government.[b]

Is Mr. Brock persuasive? Is this a good deal for everybody? What if, as in fact happened in the first two years, there is no substantial recovery in the American demand for cars?

---

[b] Press Conference of Ambassador Brock, Washington, May 2, 1981, pp. 4–5.

8.42—(a) Ambassasdor Brock seemed anxious to deny that he "negotiated" the Auto Restraints:

> You have got to understand what my position was. I was under instructions from the President to say two things. First that . . . whatever their action, we would oppose any legislation in the Congress, period. Regardless of the action taken by them, or non-action, we would make a commitment to the maintenance of free trade. Secondly, I was under instructions not to negotiate because we were not trying to reach an agreement. It was my purpose . . . to be available to advise them on how the Congress might react to a particular proposal.[c]

If there is a difference between negotiation and what Mr. Brock was doing, why is it important to stress it? Doesn't this effort undermine the credibility of his more significant points?

(b) Would you guess this statement is made on advice of counsel, recalling the problems of the VRA's on steel? Would you think Consumers' Union, or someone with comparable interests, could mount a successful challenge to the Measures of Restraint in a U.S. court?[d]

(c) The architects of the Measures of Restraint (or their lawyers) seem to have felt they had protected themselves against the kind of challenge that nearly succeeded on *Consumers Union v. Kissinger.*[e] They were more concerned by the prospect of an antitrust action, not so much by the U.S. government, which had after all, sought the restraints, as by some person injured by the restraints, for example, a U.S. Toyota dealer whose allocation of cars had been reduced. Would you think the Measures of Restraint imposed by Japan could give rise to a violation of U.S. antitrust law?[f]

---

[c] *Id.* at 12.

[d] Consumers Union had not, as of summer 1983, brought suit. Its magazine did, however, run an editorial, entitled "Auto Import Quotas: The Sneaky Tax," concluding that,

While the [Measures of Restraint] will lead to higher prices, they'll do little to encourage Detroit to build automobiles whose quality matches that of the Japanese imports.

46 Consumer Reports 374 (July 1981).

[e] §§ 5.42, 5.51-.54, *supra.*

[f] In a letter to Ambassador Brock of February 18, 1981, just as the administration was beginning to develop its strategy, Attorney General Smith wrote:

If United States negotiators urge only mandatory foreign governmental action, we believe that they would run no substantial risk of antitrust liability, even if the foreign government fails to implement a government-to-government agreement by mandatory, legally binding

(d)   Japanese officials and the U.S. Department of Justice negotiated an exchange of letters, prepared before Ambassador Brock traveled to Tokyo, but signed only after the Measures of Restraint were announced in Tokyo:

AMBASSADOR OKAWARA TO ATTORNEY GENERAL SMITH:

. . . .

The Government of Japan considers the orderly export of Japanese products to be one of its basic trade policies so as not to create disruption in the national economies of other countries. On May 1, 1981, the Cabinet members concerned met, considered the attached scheme, and approved it.

. . . .

The above-mentioned measures concerning Japanese car exports to the U.S. will be put into practice through written directives setting the maximum number of exportable units of passenger cars to the U.S. for each Japanese automobile company, to be given by MITI in accordance with its authority for bringing into action trade policies set forth in Article Three (3) of the establishment law of MITI, as well as Article Forty-eight (48) of The Foreign Exchange and Foreign Trade Control Law (Law No. 228 of 1949).[g]

. . . .

If on the basis of the above reports it becomes clear that any company threatens to exceed the limits set forth by MITI, the Government of Japan will promptly make car exports to the U.S. subject to export licensing, by amending the Export Trade Control Order (Cabinet Order No. 378 of 1949) in accordance with Article Forty-eight (48) of the Foreign Ex-

---

measures. Nevertheless, it should be noted that any private antitrust suit challenging import restraints in such circumstances might involve United States government negotiators in depositions in which the circumstances of the agreement would be examined.

.   .   .

In order to minimize the likelihood of [allegations of liability on the part of government negotiators], we believe that any negotiations seeking import restraints should be kept on a government-to-government level, and direct dealings with foreign manufacturers . . .avoided. Similarly . . . United States negotiators are best advised to avoid contacts that could be characterized as facilitating or serving as a conduit for a private arrangement between American firms and their foreign counterparts.

.   .   .

In summary . . . if the foreign government does not provide adequate protection by mandating the restraints in a legally binding manner, private antitrust suits could jeopardize the effective implementation of any agreements that are negotiated.

[g] Documents Supplement p. DS–237.

change and Foreign Trade Control Law. MITI would then enforce the export maximums it had established for each company by refusing to license exports in excess of those maximums. The Government of Japan has the authority under Japanese law to impose this requirement. It would be a violation of Japanese law to export cars without an export license in that situation, and any company engaging in such violation would be proceeded against for imposition of fines, penalties or other sanctions as provided by Article Seventy (70) of the Foreign Exchange and Foreign Trade Control Law.

. . . .

The Government of Japan considers that implementation of such an export restraint by the Government of Japan, including the division of the maximum number of exportable units among the companies by MITI, and compliance with the restraints by Japanese automobile companies, would not give rise to violations of American antitrust laws. However, the Government of Japan requests that the Department of Justice, as the authority chiefly responsible for administering the U.S. laws, support the views of the Government of Japan.

. . . .

ATTORNEY GENERAL SMITH TO AMBASSADOR OKAWARA:

. . . .

This letter is in response to the request of the Government of Japan for the views of the Department of Justice on antitrust questions regarding measures now being considered by the Government of Japan to unilaterally restrain the export of passenger cars to the U.S. so as to cooperate with the U.S. Government's domestic automobile industry recovery program.

. . . .

In these circumstances, we believe that the Japanese automobile companies' compliance with export limitations directed by MITI would properly be viewed as having been compelled by the Japanese government, acting within its sovereign powers. The Department of Justice is of the view that implementation of such an export restraint by the Government of Japan, including the division of the maximum exportable number of units among the companies by MITI, and compliance with the program by Japanese automobile companies, would not give rise to violations of United States antitrust laws. We believe that United States courts interpreting the antitrust laws in such a situation would likely so hold.[h]

---

[h] Exchange of letters between Ambassador Yoshio Okawara of Japan and Attorney General

(e) Whatever this exchange leaves to be desired from the point of view of iron-clad assurance, or from the point of view of antitrust theory, isn't it clear that if the President and the Congress want this "agreement" (though they have not formally negotiated it and may not have authority to do so), the antitrust laws should not stand in the way? Or would you, as a district judge hearing a complaint filed by a private party against the members of the Japan Automobile Manufacturers' Association, be prepared to disregard the letters and call for discovery on how compelled the restraints were and by whom?

8.43—(a) It appears that the administration made no demands on the U.S. auto industry in return for persuading the Japanese government to impose restraints on exports, other than a promise to hold off for a while on the drive for protectionist legislation. Given the experiences with protection of various kinds for the steel industry, should the administration have been tougher on the American auto industry?

(b) If you believe the answer is yes, what would you suggest? For instance, a guarantee from each of the companies that prices would not be increased more rapidly than the rise in the Consumer Price Index?

(c) How about a requirement of a plan (whether for the industry as a whole or for each company separately) covering plant closings, automation, executive compensation, wage policy, etc.?

(d) If your answer to (b) or (c) is affirmative, how could the suggestions be implemented? Would you favor introducing, whether by statute or by custom, the practice of "administrative guidance" that seems to work well in Japan?

(e) Note that the Measures of Restraint are firm for only two years, contingent on future events for Year III. Could the administration adopt some performance criteria by which the United States would judge whether to seek extension of the Restraints for a third year?[i]

8.44—(a) Lee A. Iacocca, the chairman of the board of the Chrysler Corporation, wrote shortly before the announcement of the Measures of Restraint:

Everybody these days is an expert on automobile imports. We welcome

---

William French Smith of May 7, 1981. The complete exchange is reproduced in Bureau of National Affairs, U.S. Import Weekly, May 13, 1981, pp. M–1–M–2.

[i] The Government of Japan announced on February 15, 1983 that the Measures of Restraint would be extended for the third year, 1983–84, at the same level as for the first two years, 1.68 million units. The provisions for growth in the American market remained unused, as the market expanded. See New York Times, Feb. 16, 1983, p. D19, col. 3.

the debate, but some of the ivory-tower stuff I've been reading lately needs an answer. I read that if our government does anything at all to reduce the flood of Japanese cars into this country, it will stand as a violation of the sacred principles of free trade, and will take away the basic right of all Americans to buy anything they want, no matter where it's produced.

The fact is that they don't have that right now, nor does any nation on earth grant it to its people—especially when it devastates a basic domestic industry and puts hundreds of thousands out of work.[j]

(b) Mr. Iacocca did not advocate drawing an iron curtain around the U.S. automobile market. What he sought was very much along the lines of what came out of the "non-negotiations," except that Mr. Iacocca would have imposed the restraint at 1977-78 levels—approximately 1.4 million cars "for two or three years."

After that, take the gloves off. Free enterprise forever. We can compete. Yankee ingenuity is still alive and well. But we do need time to get up off the canvas and catch our breath.

Is that a reasonable position, given the variety of problems Detroit had in the preceding years? Or would you expect that when the first three years are up, the same arguments will be made again?[k]

8.45—(a) No one event ever is the sole determinant of an economic phenomenon, as indeed the U.S. automobile industry discovered the hard way in the escape clause proceeding before the International Trade Commission. Nevertheless, a few early returns may be worth mentioning:

(i) The Japanese automobile industry appears to have had remarkable control of its operations. In the period April 1, 1981-March 31, 1982, precisely 1,679,999 passenger cars were exported from Japan to the United States.[l]

(ii) Though volume of exports measured in terms of cars declined by precisely 7.7 percent over the prior year's figure, dollar volume increased by about an equal amount, slightly over 7 percent. The reason,

---

[j] Iacocca, "Give Us a Chance to Compete," Newsweek, April 20, 1981, p. 15.

[k] As this volume was going to press, there were indications that Japan was willing to extend the Restraints for a fourth year, at a level of 2.2 million units. See Wall St. Journal Oct. 10, 1983, p. 3, col. 1.

[l] New York Times, November 1, 1982, p. 2, col. 1. This figure does not include sales to Puerto Rico, which were excluded from the Measures of Restraint. With exports to Puerto Rico added in, the figure was 1,833,313, compared with 2,011,822 in the preceding 12 month period. See USITC, The U.S. Automobile Industry, Monthly Report on Selected Economic Indicators, May 1982, Table 2.

of course, was that the price of imported cars rose—in fact much faster than the price of domestic cars.[m] This was so despite a fall in the yen against the dollar in 1981 of almost 12 percent and of the German mark of about 10 percent. With volume fixed, discounting and generous trade-in allowances ceased for imported cars, and top-of-the-line Toyota Cressidas and Datsun Maximas replaced Corollas and Sentras in dealers' showrooms.

(iii) U.S. producers tried to raise prices as well, but their increases did not stick, and they were forced again to offer incentive programs to move the 1982 models.

(iv) Overall, and most ominous, the demand for automobiles in the United States kept declining.[n]

Sales of New Cars—Calendar Years 1980–81
(In thousands of Units)

	1980	1981	1982
U.S. and Canadian-built cars	6,578	6,205	5,757
Imports	2,394	2,321	2,215
TOTAL	8,972	8,526	7,972

Source: U.S. ITC: The U.S. Automobile Industry, Monthly Report, Jan. 1982, Jan. 1983, Table 6.

The ratio of imports to total sales rose from 26.7 to 27.2 percent; imports from Japan alone were over 80 percent of imports, and 21.8 percent of total sales.[o] As compared to the last good year, 1978, sales of U.S.-made new cars in 1981 were off by 32 percent.

(b) On the basis of these figures, and indications that the trend was con-

---

[m] See, e.g., U.S. Department of Commerce, *Status Report on United States Automobile Industry* (December 1, 1981) pp. 5–6.

[n] For some attempts at explanation of this phenomenon, going beyond high interest rates and recession to such causes as a decline of the "new car population" (16–24 year–olds), longer period of use of vehicles, and shift in passions from cars to sound systems and video equipment, see "How Far Will Car Sales Rebound?" Fortune, Nov. 15, 1982, p. 69. The subtitle reads "Not as far as Detroit hopes." In the summer of 1983, the trend seemed to reverse, as both sales and profits rose for the U.S. auto makers, though the market share for imports remained at about 27 percent. Fortune came out with another article, entitled "Will Success Spoil General Motors?", August 22, 1983, p. 94.

[o] In California, almost 50 percent of new car sales and 70 percent of small car sales were made up of imports, predominantly from Japan. See "Ford to Close Last West Coast Plant," New York Times, November 19, 1982, p. Dl, col. 3–5.

tinuing in 1982, do you judge that the Measures of Restraint were not strict enough and should be tightened? Or that they were irrelevant? How would you respond to the following letter, written by Honda to Senator Danforth, the Chairman of the Senate Finance Committee's Subcommittee on International Trade, who had withdrawn his quota bill in May 1981 when the Measures of Restraint were announced:

> . . . After the voluntary restraint was in place, U.S. car sales showed no improvement, proving that the voluntary restraint did not provide the relief necessary to turn the U.S. automobile industry around. This justified the ITC's conclusion that there had been no causation between the U.S. industry's current problems and Japanese car sales in the U.S., nor was there any threat of injury. The restraint has resulted in an increase in car prices which has a negative impact on U.S. consumers.[p]

(c) Senator Danforth's answer was to look for more effective restraints, while at the same time pressing Japan to open its markets to American products, including parts for Japanese cars:

> You will remember that last winter I introduced a bill which would have restricted the imports of Japanese automobiles, stating at the time that I did so reluctantly, that I had always considered myself to be a free trader, not a protectionist, but that I was not willing to just stand by and see a major American industry go down the drain. . . .

> I did not press that bill when the Japanese agreed to restrict their exports to this country, but I stated at the time that I wanted to see how the management would work out in practice.

> It would appear . . . that overall it really has not worked out very well: the agreement itself has been complied with but the parts arrangement has not worked out;[q] the total trade imbalance with Japan has gotten worse, not better; and our auto industry continues do be in a very bad slump.[r]

What remedy would you suggest to Senator Danforth?

8.46—(a) Several remedies were suggested and introduced in the Congress.

---

[p] Letter from the Washington representative of American Honda Motor Co., Inc., Dec. 8, 1981, reproduced in *Issues Relating to the Domestic Auto Industry III*, Hearing before Subcomm. on Int'l Trade of Sen. Comm. on Finance, 97th Cong., 1st Sess. at 235 (Dec. 1981).

[q] This refers to a so-called "automobile package" of May 1980 in which Japan abolished "in principle" all customs duties on imports of automobile parts and encouraged joint ventures between U.S. and Japanese manufacturers.

[r] *Issues Relating to the Domestic Auto Industry III*, N. p *supra*, at 77.

One would be a renewal of the *quota legislation* proposed and then put aside in 1981. But to revive this proposal now would seem to be going back on the assurances given to the Japanese in the spring of 1981. Moreover, quotas had never been popular in the United States, and indeed had once been anathema to the shapers of American foreign trade policy.[s] Another idea was to legislate *reciprocity*, i.e., a requirement that the President determine with respect to each of the United States' major trading partners whether it was denying trade or investment opportunities to the United States; if a lack of reciprocity were found, the President would be required to propose corrective actions, in accordance with section 301 of the Trade Act of 1974 as amended in 1979, including various kinds of retaliation.[t] But while such a proposal, if it worked, might open up the Japanese market somewhat and possibly lead to a partial redress of the United States' massive trade deficit with Japan, it would not do much for the domestic auto industry. Still another proposal—so-called "*content legislation*"—seemed to be in favor in the latter part of 1982. The idea, in general terms, was similar to laws in many developing countries, and as we saw also in Canada with respect to automobiles.[u] If cars were going to be sold in the United States, they (or a specified portion) should be made in the United States. And if the American public preferred Datsuns to Buicks, let Americans make Datsuns. While this would not help the shareholders of Chrysler or Ford, it would help the United Auto Workers—at least if the U.S. production were made in union shops, and it would help parts and component makers in the United States. The UAW ran newspaper advertisements showing what looked like a Japanese car but bore a "made in U.S.A." tag, with the legend "Why not a Datsun made in Detroit? a Toyota from Texas?" Do you regard this, in principle as a sound concept?

(b) The most discussed bill along these lines was the proposed "Fair Practices in Automotive Products Act."[v] The bill defined "domestic content ratio" to mean the added domestic value—i.e., labor and domestically produced parts—as a percentage of the wholesale price of an automotive pro-

---

[s] See § 2.43 *supra*, esp. paragraph (e); see also the statements by Secretary Rusk and Ambassador Roth, § 5.11 *supra*.

[t] See, e.g., S. 2094, 97th Cong., 2d Sess. (1982).

[u] See § 8.23(a) *supra*. Australia and Spain, among developed countries, maintained content requirements on automobiles—85 percent local value added for Australia, 55 percent for Spain.

[v] H.R. 5133, S. 2300, 97th Cong., 1st and 2d Sess. (1981–1982), Documents Supplement p. DS–626. Note that the table in the text reflects the bill as introduced; the version reproduced in the Documents Supplement is the one considered by the full House after nearly a full year of debate, and has a somewhat different formula, directed to the years 1984–1986.

duct, and then prescribed the following schedule applicable to each manufacturer:

No. of Vehicles Sold in the U.S.	Required Minimum Percentage U.S. Content Requirement		
	1983	1984	1985
Fewer than 100,000	0	0	0
100,000 to 149,999	8.3	16.7	25.0
150,000 to 199,999	16.7	33.3	50.0
200,000 to 499,999	25.0	50.0	75.0
500,000 or more	30.0	60.0	90.0

Violation by a manufacturer of the schedule would be unlawful, and a knowing violation (determined after hearing) would be punished by limiting the number of vehicles of that manufacturer that could be imported to 75 percent of the actual number of vehicles imported in the year in which the violation occurred.

What do you think? Would you agree with the New York Times that the plan, if adopted, "would rock the foundations of world trade"?[w] Would the answer be the same if the numbers were substantially reduced—say to a maximum requirement of 30 instead of 75-90 percent?[x]

(c) The idea of assembling, or indeed manufacturing products in the country where they are to be marketed has, of course, been a very popular one, accounting for most of the world-wide expansion of multinational corporations in industrial countries.[y] Vokswagen had come into the United States in the mid-1970's, with indifferent results, at first assembling largely imported parts

---

[w] Editorial "The Made in America Trap," New York Times, August 2, 1982, p. 14, col. 1-2.

[x] In September 1982, the bill made it through the House Committee on Energy and Commerce, 24–17. Ambassador Brock, the U.S. Trade Representative wrote: "It is probably the worst piece of economic legislation to have a chance of passage in 50 years." Brock, "What Is Needed from the GATT Talks?" New York Times, Nov. 21, 1982, § 3 p. 2. The bill passed the full House of Representatives in December 1982 by a vote of 215–188, but with an amendment that nothing in the bill should be deemed to supersede the terms or conditions of any treaty, international convention, or agreement on tariffs and trade to which the United States was a party on the effective date of the Act. See 128 Cong. Rec. 9856, 9898–99, 9909 (Daily Ed., Dec. 15, 1982). The bill did not come to a vote in the Senate. The bill was reintroduced (with the dates pushed forward) in 1983, but had not again come to a vote as this volume went to press.

[y] See Volume II of this series, International Private Investment, esp. pp. 1–9 and the sections on Canada, §§ 1.12 and 4.1 (2d ed. 1982).

and gradually increasing the domestic content of its Rabbit. Honda, which had in 1979 opened a motorcycle plant in Marysville, a small town in Ohio, inaugurated assembly of the Accord automobile at Marysville late in 1982.[z]

(d) In February 1983 a bombshell of sorts struck the international automobile industry, when the biggest American manufacturer, General Motors, and the biggest Japanese manufacturer, Toyota, announced an agreement to jointly produce in the United States a new small front-wheel-drive car, designed by Toyota to replace the rear-drive Corolla.[a] Production would center on a mothballed GM factory in Fremont, California, near San Jose; each company would supply half the components, and each would have half the seats on the board of directors of the joint enterprise. Each company would contribute half the capital to the venture, estimated at $300 million, but Toyota would name the chief executive officer and, it was understood, would apply its production techniques. Where that left the United Automobile Workers (including some 6,000 laid off from the Fremont plant) was not clear as this volume went to press. The new car, unnamed as of summer 1983, would be marketed through General Motors' Chevrolet dealers, probably in place of the Chevette, with an estimated production run of 200,000 cars per year. What do you think?

(e) Traditionally, a joint venture between two very large competitors— one a potential entrant into manufacturing in the USA, the other a holder of 50 percent of the U.S. market and a potential entrant (or re-entrant) into manufacture of a subcompact car—would seem to raise substantial questions under American antitrust law.[b] But as a way to transfer technology—the management skills to produce a high-quality small car at reasonable cost— the "Toyvrolet" seemed an attractive proposition. Moreover, it provided a way to induce Toyota to invest in manufacture in the United States at relatively low risk, at the same time deflecting renewed pressure for a "domestic content" bill and possibly other import relief bills. With Toyota providing engines, transmissions, and other power train components (as well as the

---

[z] It is interesting that Honda sent some of its Ohio production workers to Japan to learn the company's techniques, to be passed on to their fellow workers on their return. As of close of 1982, the Honda plant was not unionized. See New York Times, November 2, 1982, p. D4, col. 1–4. A plant was being built by Nissan in Smyrna, Tennessee to assemble light trucks, also in the hope that the workers—called "production technicians"—would remain non-union and willing to adapt to Japanese-style cooperation with management. See, e.g., Newsweek, Feb. 21, 1983, p. 64.

[a] See Wall St. Journal, Feb. 15, 1983, p. 3, col. 1; New York Times, Feb. 15, p. 1, col. 3.

[b] See, generally, Pitofsky, "Joint Ventures Under the Antitrust Laws: Some Reflections on the Significance of Penn–Olin," 82 Harv. L. Rev. 1007 (1969); Brodley, "Joint Ventures and Antitrust Policy," 95 Harv. L. Rev. 1521 (1982).

design), General Motors providing the bodies, seats, and interior trim (as well as the plant), comparative advantage and division of labor, 1980's style, might actually receive a current demonstration.

(i) Is this a case where considerations of international trade should outweigh antitrust doctrines more suited to an earlier day?

(ii) Should the United States insist that some of the product of the Fremont plant be exported to Japan? . . . to third countries?

(iii) How should an independent American Toyota dealer react to the plan to distribute the new car through GM dealers?

8.47—No sooner had Japan agreed to restrain its exports to the United States than the Europeans began to worry. In fact Western Europe had been worrying about automobile imports from Japan for several years, and several of the markets inside the Community had already been restricted. But following the Measures of Restraint of May 1, 1981, West Germany, the last major hold-out for the cause of free trade in automobiles within the European Community, changed its policy, and sent its Economics Minister to Tokyo to negotiate a "voluntary restraint agreement" on cars bound for the Federal Republic. The concern seems to have been—as in steel and other products—that when Japanese manufacturers (or their government) agreed to limit exports to a given market, they did not always make a corresponding reduction in their production for export. Before coming back to the European response to Japanese cars, a brief backward look is necessary into development of the European automobile industry.

(a)[c] In the years following World War I when the automobile became a mass consumer product, important automobile production grew up in France, Great Britain, Germany, and Italy, and each of these countries protected their auto producers. Great Britain introduced a 33⅓ percent duty on cars in 1915 and subsequently added a horsepower tax. France introduced a duty on cars of 45 percent in 1922, and raised it to 90 percent in 1931. Germany used a combination of tariffs, exchange controls, and local content requirements to protect its local industry, and Italy did likewise. Ford and General Motors established (or acquired) numerous facilities in the major European countries and were active participants in the European markets even though they exported very few finished products from their home bases in the United

---

[c] Portions of this note are based on *The Competitive Status of the U.S. Auto Industry*, § 8.48 N. t *infra*, Ch. 4.

States.[d] By the beginning of the Second World War, international trade in automobiles was insignificant.

(b) In the first decade after the end of World War II, the pattern continued of local manufacture and little international trade in motor vehicles. As late as 1955 no major European country imported more than 5 percent of its automobiles, and in France, Italy, and Great Britain, the ratio of imports to total sales stood at about 2 percent.

(c) Following the creation of the Common Market, automobiles became one of the largest items of intra-Community trade, with Volkswagens a common sight in Italy, Fiats in Germany, and so on. By 1970, West Germany and Italy each imported over 20 percent of its passenger cars, and France about 14 percent, nearly all from each other. Japanese cars, which had begun to establish a market in America,[e] had a negligible share of Europe's automobile market.

(d) By 1978, Japanese cars (by now dominant among imports into the United States) had begun to penetrate the European market, reaching about 6.3 percent of the Community's market, including 18 percent of imports and 9 percent of total sales in Great Britain;[f] and 21 percent of imports and 4.5 percent of the total market in West Germany.[g] In 1979, 600,000 Japanese cars were sold in the European Community, equal to about 6.9 percent of the total market, including more than 10 percent of the market in West Germany. As in the United States, Japanese cars were considered high quality, high value products, about 20 percent cheaper than comparable German vehicles. At the rate of growth for Japan's auto sales in the late 1970's, European economists calculated that the Community would become a net importer of cars by 1983.[h]

---

[d] In addition to the trade barriers, of course, the North American automobile was substantially different from the European product, even the product of Ford/Europe and GM/Europe; cars sold in the United States and Canada were larger, cheaper, less fuel-efficient, and for the most part less designed for high performance than for mass marketing.

[e] See Chart p. 379, *supra*.

[f] Note that in the interval Great Britain had joined the European Community, and by 1978 over half of all sales of cars in Great Britain came from imports.

[g] Japan's shares of the market of the non-EEC countries of non-Communist Europe—Spain, Portugal, Norway, Finland, Switzerland, Austria, and Sweden—was roughly the same.

[h] The calculation was not solely based on imports from Japan. Imports were also growing from Eastern Europe, the "world cars" of the American majors would take some share of the market, and exports to developing countries were being replaced by increased production in Brazil, Mexico, South Korea, and elsewhere.

Japanese penetration

% of car sales in 1980 by Japanese models

Denmark	31.3
Ireland	30.5
Holland	26.6
Belgium and Luxembourg	25.2
Britain	12.3
West Germany	10.3
France	2.9
Italy	0.1
United States	21.3

The Economist, May 23, 1981, p.81.

(e) In 1980, as the world-wide recession had led to a decline of about 20 percent in European (as in American) automobile production, Europe's automobile industry began to strike back, though interestingly enough not through the Community, but each concerned member country on its own. France announced that Japanese auto manufacturers would be restricted to 3 percent of the French market until the Japanese market was opened to French auto exports.[i] In Great Britain an informal auto restraint agreement was negotiated, limiting Japanese cars to 11 percent of the market.[j] Italy imposed the most stringent quota—just 2,200 Japanese cars per year. Only West Germany, among the major producing countries, refrained from imposing restraints, in part as a matter of principle, in part because it was still a net exporter not only of cars but of all industrial products. Of course so long as the Federal Republic remained firm in this position, the European Community could not adopt a common automobile policy, comparable to its policies on steel in the late 1970's.[k]

---

[i] New York Times, October 4, 1980, p. 30, col. 5.

[j] This agreement was widely reported in the trade and financial press, but no precise data or document seems to be attached to it. It appears to have been negotiated in the offices of the British Ministry of Trade, between members of the industry of both countries, without the presence of government officials. The statistics make clear that whether or not there was an international agreement in the legal sense, restraint on imports was in effect at least from 1980 on.

[k] See §§ 6.3–6.4 supra.

Market Shares in the World Automotive Industry
(percentage of)

Producer	1965	1975	1979
General Motors	30.9	19.0	21.8
Ford	19.6	12.4	12.4
Chrysler	9.6	7.8	3.4
Volkswagen	7.3	4.5	5.3
Renault	3.0	5.3	4.6
Peugeot	1.4	3.0	8.3
Fiat	5.3	4.6	4.2
Toyota	2.5	7.3	7.4
Nissan	1.3	6.7	5.7

SOURCE: *World Motor Vehicle Data*, Motor Vehicle Manufacturers Association, 1980.

(f) Early in 1981 the Community began to stir. On February 27, 1981, the Commission of the European Communities announced a monitoring system on Japanese automobiles, television sets, and computer-controlled machine tools.[1] The clear implication was that if imports increased, formal Community-wide restraints might be next.[m] Before such a step could be taken, however, the Federal Republic sent its mission to Tokyo, as mentioned above, just before Prime Minister Suzuki was to make a state visit to Bonn. Japan did not quite accept the suggestion to make an agreement with the Community analogous to the one it had made with the United States, but it agreed to hold the increase in exports of cars to West Germany to 10 percent per year, as compared to the increase of 39.4 percent in 1980 over 1979, and a 60 percent rise in the first 4 months of 1981. Practically, that meant a slight decrease compared to the 1980 pace for the rest of 1981.[n] When Count Otto Lambsdorff, West Germany's outspoken proponent of free trade,[o] was asked whether the agreement on automobiles (which he

---

[1] *Commission Regulation (EEC) No. 535/81 of 27 Feb. 1981 introducing Community surveillance of imports of motor vehicles originating in Japan.* O.S.C 54/61 Feb. 28, 1981; also Regulations 536/81 (Machine Tools); 537/81 (Television receivers and components, O.S.C 54/62–63).

[m] Recall a similar step at the beginning of the Community's program on steel, § 6.31 *supra*.

[n] Japan also agreed to reduce its sales to Belgium by 7 percent over the prior year. Belgium had no indigenous auto maker, but General Motors and Ford, as well as Renault, and formerly British Leyland and Citroen, maintained automobile plants in Belgium.

[o] Recall his criticism of the Davignon plan on steel in 1978, § 6.43(c) *supra*.

had negotiated) did not contravene Bonn's strong stance against protectionism, he admitted "it did go over the line a little."[p]

(g) With West Germany, as well as Belgium,[q] now parties to voluntary restraint agreements, the "agreement" with Britain apparently holding, and France and Italy maintaining their own restraints, there was now pressure for a Community-wide restraint, which might have satisfied Article 113 of the Treaty of Rome, if not the GATT.[r] The London Economist wrote: "The main loser was free trade—and European consumers."[s]

8.48—Coming back to the United States, as more and more persons, in the business community, in the labor movement, and in Congress and the administration became concerned with the problems of the automobile industry in America, a committee drawn from the National Academy of Engineering and the National Research Council, under the chairmanship of a professor at the Harvard Business School, prepared a study on the competitive status of the U.S. auto industry.[t] The Committee suggested three alternative diagnoses:

(i) *Transient Economic Misfortune*—caused in part by the energy crisis, in part by management error with regard to small-car capacity. Presumably with time and money, the problems could be cured. Essentially this theory is consistent with the plea of Lee Iacocca (§ 8.44 *supra*), and in general with temporary measures such as voluntary export restraints or orderly marketing agreements.

(ii) *Natural Consequence of Maturity*—the idea that for most of the century the automobile industry in the United States and Europe had prospered as a result of technological innovation, but that by the late 1970's technology had run its course, as in textiles, shoes, television receivers, and similar products, so that competitive advantage no longer depended on product development but principally on relative factor prices, notably labor costs. In this

---

[p] International Herald Tribune, June 11, 1981, p. 9, col. 5–8.

[q] N. n *supra*.

[r] Denmark, Ireland, and Greece had no domestic automobile production, and thus no incentive to push for import restraints. The Netherlands did have some domestic car production, but it seemed not to regard import restraints on cars as a matter of priority.

[s] The Economist, June 13, 1981, p. 66–67.

[t] Automobile Panel, Committee on Technology and International Economic and Trade Issues, *The Competitive Status of the U.S. Auto Industry: A Study of the Influences of Technology in Determining International Industrial Competitive Advantage* (Nat'l. Academy Press, 1982).

view, the timing and the surge of imports in the United States (and Europe) was perhaps unexpected, but in the long run the shift was inevitable—barring (an assumption not made in the study) effective legal restraints. Consider what (if any) kinds of restraints—within or without the GATT/Trade Act framework—are appropriate if one is convinced by this interpretation.

(iii) *Fundamental Structural Change*—in which technological innovation will once more dominate competition, with radically different power plants, drive trains, body structure and control systems. The auto industry, in this vision, is at the threshold of a new period of industrial "de-maturity" in which the standardization and technological commonality of the period 1945-78 will be replaced, by a process already started, by a "greening of the automobile industry," with more firms less fully integrated, increasing product differentiation,[u] more global sourcing, and reward for invention.[v] Consider what legal regime would best suit this scenario.

---

[u] For instance electric cars for commuters, engines using new fuels, and new uses of synthetic materials in place of steel.

[v] The suggestion made in the book is that this scenario tends to favor the United States and Europe, whose forte is innovation, rather than Japan, whose strength lies in refining an established technology and maintaining quality control and cost-effective production. *Id.* at 159. It would follow that Japanese firms would retain their lead in standard 1970's vehicles, but that these vehicles would form a declining share of the total market.

§ 8.5—Back to Steel: Europe and America

8.51—THE EUROPEAN CRISIS PROLONGED: DAVIGNON PHASE III

As the critics of the Davignon Plan had predicted, the temporary measures of crisis proved to be difficult to terminate. With demand for steel falling and plants becoming obsolescent even before the outset of the world-wide recession in 1979, the circumstances recited in the early phases of the European Steel Policy—reduced sales, unremunerative prices, and above all increased unemployment, continued to prevail, particularly in France, Belgium, Great Britain and Italy. One might have taken the position that a situation that had gone on with little sign of improvement for five years was not a "crisis" calling for emergency measures, but rather reflected a long-term problem calling for basic industrial restructuring.[a] But while that view was generally appreciated in terms of economic analysis, in terms of day-to-day (or even year-to-year) decision-making no one was up to drawing the social or political consequences.[b] Nor did anyone attempt to derive from the text of the Treaty of Paris[c] any limitation on the duration of a crisis, so long as the current Plan was regularly submitted to the Council of Ministers for approval.[d]

The measures described in §§ 6.31–.33 were renewed at the end of 1978,[e] and again (with some modifications) at the end of 1979.[f] Early in 1980 the

---

[a] For an expression of this view by a Belgian law professor, see Joliet, "Cartelization, Dirigism, and Crisis in the European Community," 3 The World Economy 403 (Jan. 1981).

[b] To some extent the British government of Mrs. Thatcher did draw the consequences, hiring a retired American executive, Ian MacGregor, formerly head of AMAX, to stop the huge losses and separate efficient from inefficient facilities of the nationalized British Steel Corporation. See, e.g., Lubar, "An American Leads British Steel Back From the Brink," Fortune, Sept. 21, 1981, p. 88. But even Mrs. Thatcher was not able to push through the massive plant closings and lay-offs required to turn BSC around—"open-hearth surgery," in the phrase of The Economist—and at year end 1982 BSC was still losing 300 million pounds a year, not counting huge costs of "redundancies," i.e., severance pay, early retirement, and write-down of assets. In two and a half years of MacGregor's stewardship, BSC's work force had been reduced from 166,000 to 92,000 as of October 1982. See the Economist, Dec. 4, 1982, p. 40.

[c] See Articles 58, 61, Documents Supplement pp. DS–116, 120.

[d] One German observer said, "The industry has suffered along for seven years now. When it drags on that long, you no longer talk of crisis. It's become normality." New York Times, November 10, 1982, p. D1, col. 3.

[e] See § 6.33 N. h.

[f] *Commission Decision No. 3060/79/ECSC of Dec. 27, 1979 fixing minimum prices for hot*

Commission attempted to go an important step further, in that it would take control of —not abolish but manage—the various programs of assistance by member states to their respective steel industries.[g] Whether adherence by the Community and its members to the Subsidies Code negotiated in the MTN had anything to do with this decision is not apparent;[h] but obviously it would be hard to achieve a common and rational policy designed to limit supply to demand for steel in the Community if each of the member states was attempting by means of subsidies to maintain employment and production, while output could move freely within the Common Market. Member states were to notify the Commission of all measures of state aid for investment, for plant closing, for continued operation, and for emergency relief to prevent a firm from collapsing. Such measures, the Commission said, could be implemented, but only with approval of and under conditions laid down by the Commission.

The effect of coordinating subsidy programs, of course, was to identify the Community directly with the various measures of subsidy for steel springing up throughout Western Europe. Thus when the American steel industry decided to launch a wholesale attack on these national subsidies early in 1982, the Community found itself identified with those subsidies, and inevitably locked in a major struggle with the United States.[i]

Before that confrontation took place, however, the Davignon Plan took another major step toward dirigisme. In October 1980, faced with a 20 percent decline in demand for the third quarter of 1980 compared with the same period in 1979, and a 13 percent drop in prices, the Council of Ministers and Commission decided to apply Article 58 of the Treaty of Paris and to introduce a system of production quotas.[j] For the final quarter of 1980 and the

---

rolled wide strip, and imposing certain requirements on undertakings and dealers in the iron and steel industry, O.J. L 344/7, Dec. 31, 1979; also Communication from the Commission concerning publication of guidance prices for certain steel products, O.J. L 344/13, Dec. 31, 1979; Communication from the Commission amending the basic prices for certain iron and steel products, O.J. L 344/15, Dec. 31, 1979; and Recommendation No. 2907/79/ECSC of Dec. 21, 1979 to the Member States extending the Community system of monitoring imports into the Community of certain iron and steel products . . . . , O.J. L 326/27, Dec. 22, 1979.

[g] Commission Decision No. 257/80 of Feb. 1, 1980 establishing Community rules for specific aids to the steel industry,O.J. L 29/5, Feb. 6, 1980.

[h] Recall that the Code entered into force for its members on Jan. 1, 1980.

[i] See § 8.53 infra.

[j] Commission Decision No. 2794/80/ECSC of 31 October 1980, establishing a system of steel production quotas for undertakings in the iron and steel industry, O.J. L 291/1, Oct. 31, 1980. See also accompanying Decision No. 2795/80/ECSC O.J. L 291/30.

first two quarters of 1981, all steel producers were assigned maximum output levels of crude steel and four basic steel products for delivery within the Community. The quotas were based on the highest level of production of each product by each firm in any month in the given quarter in the preceding three years (July 1977-1980), reduced by a formula published for each quarter by the Commission. The reductions, designed to keep total supply equal to estimated consumption less imports, averaged 13-18% below the calculated level; any firm that exceeded its quota was subject to a fine of EUA 100 for every ton of excess.[k] Bonuses in the form of extra quotas were available for installation of modern facilities, and also for elimination of obsolete plant.[l]

The system of production quotas was not universally popular, and in fact Germany, whose steel mills were the most efficient in the Community, had opposed (but not vetoed) introduction of the system. But when the first nine-month period of the production quotas expired in mid-1981, all quotas were renewed, this time for a full year.[m] When the second period expired in mid-1982, the system was again renewed for a full year, until June 30, 1983.[n] Likewise, the programs of minimum prices within the Community,[o] of "basic" import prices,[p] and of monitoring imports [q] were all renewed at the end of 1981, and so were the various "voluntary restraint agreements" concerning exports of steel to the Community negotiated in the spring and summer of 1978.[r]

---

[k] The EUA or European Unit of Account, was roughly equal to a U.S. dollar during 1981-82.

[l] Decision 2794/80, Article 4(4) and 4(5), discussed in connection with the *Krupp* case, § 8.64 N. g *infra.*

[m] *Commission Decision No. 1831/81/ECSC of June 24, 1981 establishing for undertakings in the iron and steel industry a monitoring system and a new system of production quotas in respect of certain products,* O.J. L. 180/1, July 1, 1981, amended by *Commission Decision No. 1832/81/ECSC of July 3, 1981,* O.J. L 184/1, July 4, 1981.

[n] *Commission Decision No. 1696/82/ECSC of June 30, 1982 on the extension of the system of monitoring and production quotas for certain products of undertakings in the steel industry,* O.J. L 191/1, July 1, 1982. For the further extension of Davignon III, see § 8.62, N. c *infra.*

[o] *Communication from the Commission concerning the objectives of the steel price policy,* O.J. L 294/3, Nov. 14, 1981.

[p] *Communication from the Commission amending the basic prices for certain iron and steel products of Dec. 29, 1981,* O.J. L 372/1, Dec. 29, 1981.

[q] *Commission Decision No. 3753/81/ECSC of Dec. 22, 1981 on retrospective Community surveillance in respect of the importation and exportation of certain iron and steel products . . .originating in certain non-member countries,* O.J. L 374/16, Dec. 30, 1981.

[r] See 14 Bull. of European Communities No. 12, 1981, ¶ 2, 2, 12 (December 1981). The

As of the close of 1981, virtually all aspects of steel production in the Community were (at least on paper) subject to management by the European Commission, except one—exports to non-member countries.

8.52—UPS AND DOWNS OF THE U.S. TRIGGER PRICE MECHANISM

In 1979, imports of all steel products to the United States came to 17.5 million tons, compared to 21.16 million tons in 1978. More than 2 million tons of that decline was attributable to a decline in imports from the European Community, and another 1.4 million reflected decline in imports from the developing countries. Imports from Japan (as well as from Canada) remained approximately the same. While the first three quarters of 1979 were passable for the American steel industry, the last quarter was disastrous, reflecting not only the generally slack economy but in particular the decline in production of automobiles in the United States.[a] U.S. Steel, still the biggest American steel producer with about 23 percent of U.S. production, reported a loss of $561.7 million in the fourth quarter of 1979, and a loss for the year as a whole of $293 million, on sales of $12.9 billion.[b] In what the New York Times called "the greatest shrinking act in the history of the industry,"[c] U.S. Steel decided to close permanently 13 steelmaking and fabricating plants (including Youngstown, Ohio) eliminating some 12,400 jobs from its payroll of 160,000.

Whether the trigger price mechanism[d] was working well was a matter of opinion.[e] The American Iron and Steel Institute, while urging that the TPM be continued, argued that the trigger price (or rather the prices of the several products included in the program) should be set higher, and also criticized the government for not enforcing the program strictly enough.[f] A more par-

---

negotiating mandate was to reduce the import quantities by 9.5 percent from the 1980 levels, subject also to closer monitoring of observance of the price rules.

[a] See § 8.12 *supra*.

[b] See New York Times, January 30, 1980, p. Dl, col. 3, p. Dl6, col. 1.

[c] New York Times, Dec. 2, 1979, p. 1F, col. 5.

[d] § 6.12 *supra*.

[e] For a generally skeptical judgment, pointing out that the TPM raised prices and did not contribute to nationalization of the domestic industry, see General Accounting Office, "New Strategy Required for Aiding Distressed Steel Industry," EMD 81-29 (Jan. 8, 1981).

[f] See American Iron and Steel Institute, *Steel at the Crossroads: The American Steel Industry in the 1980's*, 56 (Jan. 1980).

ticular complaint was that if European costs of production were higher than Japanese costs, as was implicit in basing the TPM on Japanese costs, and if European internal prices were substantially higher than the U.S. trigger prices, as was certainly true if the price guidelines under the Davignon Plan could be believed, then every ton of steel coming in from Europe was being dumped, but getting a "free ride" through the truce embodied in the TPM.

On March 21, 1980 just after the Commerce Department announced that the TPM would not be raised in the following quarter, the truce ended.[g] United States Steel filed antidumping actions against 16 producers of five principal types of carbon steel products[h] from all the steel producing countries of the European Community, accounting for some 75 percent of all shipments of steel to the United States. The Carter administration had previously warned Big Steel that if it went ahead with its threat to file the massive antidumping complaint, the trigger price mechanism would be suspended. It turned out that the administration meant what it said: on the same day that U.S. Steel's petitions were received, the Commerce Department suspended the trigger price mechanism, effective immediately.[i] Even as the United States was trying, with indifferent success, to rally its European allies against the Soviet Union because of the invasion of Afghanistan and against Iran because of continued detention of U.S. hostages,[j] dark words came from the European capitals suggesting retaliation against American exports to the Community. Viscount Davignon said that he regarded U.S. Steel's suit as not impressive, but that the anti-crisis measures under the Davignon Plan might have to be strengthened.[k]

The U.S. Steel action, contained in 1700 pages of pleadings, briefs, and exhibits delivered in 70 boxes, and naming 16 European manufacturers in seven countries, put the new streamlined procedures for antidumping cases[l] to the test. In 20 days, the Department of Commerce had to determine whether

---

[g] Since the Trigger Price Mechanism was formally a device for enforcing the antidumping law, when administration of that law was shifted to the Commerce Department at the beginning of 1980, § 7.61 *supra,* responsibility for the TPM was shifted as well.

[h] Cold rolled sheet, galvanized sheet, hot rolled sheet, steel plate, and structural shapes. Pipe and tube products, in high demand as oil exploration in the United States resumed following deregulation of oil prices in the United States, were not included in the complaint.

[i] 45 Fed. Reg. 20150 (March 24, 1980).

[j] See Vol. III of this series, A. Lowenfeld, *Trade Controls for Political Ends*, Ch. II, § 5.45, ch. V, § 2.22 (2d ed. 1983).

[k] Financial Times, London, March 28, 1980, p. 44, col. 5.

[l] § 7.63 *supra.*

to conduct an investigation, and on April 10, 1980 the Department announced it would do so.[m] The International Trade Commission had 45 days from March 21 to make a preliminary determination, and on May 1, the Commission found there was "reasonable indication of material injury."[n] In announcing its investigation, the Commerce Department had said it regarded the cases as normal ones so that its preliminary determination of dumping would be due 160 days after filing, or August 28, 1980; as that time approached, and as negotiations of various kinds were under way, the Department announced that the cases had been determined to be "extraordinarily complicated" within the meaning of section 733(c)(1)(B), so that the deadline for preliminary determination of dumping (and suspension of liquidation)[o] would be postponed to day 210, or October 17, 1980. The extension gave the various parties—Big Steel, the U.S. government, the foreign producers, and the Commission (High Authority) of the European Community—an opportunity to settle.

One suggestion for a settlement, made as early as 1978 and repeated from time to time thereafter, was to establish a two-tier TPM, one for steel from Japan and other low-cost producers (e.g., in South Korea), the other for steel from Western Europe, based on real costs in the Community.[p] Alternatively, a new TPM would be based entirely on European costs, or simply on some figure designed to give an adequate market share to the U.S. industry, possibly coupled with assurance from the foreign suppliers that they would not try to establish entitlement to bring steel products in below the trigger price.

The Carter Administration, working under the deadline of the antidumping suits as well as under pressure from the steel caucus in the heat of a Presidential election, chose not to wait for agreement from Brussels, but to come out with its own "Program for the American Steel Industry, Its Workers and Communities," pursuant to a report of the Steel Tripartite Advisory Committee.[q] President Carter personally announced the program on national

---

[m] The determination was announced in five separate notices for the five classes of products, 45 Fed. Reg. 26109, 26110, 26111, 26112, and 26114.

[n] As in prior cases, the decision of the Commission came out in a public meeting and vote. The formal opinion was released on May 6. *Certain Carbon Steel Products from Belgium, the Federal Republic of Germany, France, Italy, Luxembourg, the Netherlands, and the United Kingdom*, Investigations Nos. 731–TA–18–24 (Preliminary), USITC Pub. 1064 (May 1980), 45 Fed. Reg. 31814 (May 14, 1980).

[o] See § 733(d)(1) and (2), Documents Supplement p. DS–495.

[p] See § 6.45(b) *supra*.

[q] 16 Weekly Comp. Pres. Docs. 1959, 1960 (Sept. 30, 1980).

television, flanked by the chairmen of four of the major American steel companies and the President of the United Steelworkers of America. In essence, the package provided for reinstitution of the trigger price mechanism with a 12 percent increase in the price plus a special anti-surge mechanism, in return for withdrawal of the antidumping actions. In addition, the administration undertook to seek delays for mandatory compliance with clean air and clean water standards, accelerated depreciation, and increased tax credits for investment in distressed areas.[r] The new anti-surge mechanism began to move toward articulation of what had only been implied in the past:

> Whenever steel mill product imports rise over 13.7% of apparent domestic consumption, the United States industry is operating below 87% capability utilization, and there appears to be a surge in imports of one or more specific products from one or more specific countries, Commerce will review the situation . . . . Whenever aggregate imports exceed 15.2% of apparent consumption, the U.S. industry is operating below 87% capability utilization, and there appears to be a surge in imports . . ., Commerce will examine the situation to ascertain whether the imports are apparently (1) being dumped on a cost or price basis, (2) the result of government subsidization, or (3) the result of fair competition . . . . During [the 90-day period of review] the U.S. Trade Representative will discuss the issue with the government concerned . . . .[s]

If the review disclosed unfair competition (i.e. dumping or subsidization) and no agreement was reached with the foreign government, the Department said it would either initiate antidumping or countervailing suits itself or make its information available to the domestic industry for use in an antidumping or countervailing duty action that would not lead to suspension of the TPM.[t] In other cases of antidumping or countervailing duty petitions, the TPM might again be withdrawn.[u] According to the announcement of the plan, the re-

---

[r] Since investment tax credits would not be directly useful to firms without net taxable income, the tax law was amended to permit so-called "safe harbor leasing" under 26 U.S.C. § 168(f)(8), as enacted by § 201 of the Economic Recovery Tax Act of 1981, Pub. L. 97–34, 95 Stat. 214. The advantages of safe harbor leasing—a kind of negative income tax for eligible corporations—to companies such as the steel producers were largely eliminated by §§ 208–09 of the Tax Equity and Fiscal Responsibility Act of 1982, Pub. L. 97–248, 96 Stat. 435, principally because of negative publicity as some major companies were able to reduce their tax liability dramatically.

[s] Department of Commerce, Announcement of Oct. 1, 1980 on Reinstatement of the Steel Trigger Price Mechanism, 45 Fed. Reg. 66833 (Oct. 8, 1980), ¶ 11.

[t] *Ibid.*

[u] *Id.* ¶ 14.

vised TPM would be in effect for five years, subject to a mid-term review of the progress of the industry's modernization program.[v]

8.53—CONFRONTATION: THE UNITED STATES AND THE EUROPEAN COMMUNITY (1981–82)

For a short time the new trigger price mechanism worked reasonably well, as the domestic industry tended to keep its prices just above the TPM prices adjusted for transport costs. When demand for steel fell sharply late in 1980, the domestic industry dropped its price below the TPM, which meant that foreign producers could not stay within the TPM system and still sell in quantity in the U.S. market. In the first quarter of 1981, shipments from the European Community to the United States declined 17 percent compared to the corresponding period in 1980. As world-wide demand remained soft, Japanese steel mills (themselves injured by competition from South Korea), cut back even more on their sales to the United States except for pipe and tube.[a] In the second quarter of 1981, however, another element entered the continuing controversy over steel prices. A combination of high interest rates in the United States, reaction to election of a socialist government in France, and general economic stagnation in Western Europe led to a sharp rise in the value of the U.S. dollar in terms of all the West European currencies. As the exchange rate for francs, guilders, marks and pounds fell by as much as 25–30 percent in 1981 compared to early 1980, some European manufacturers who had found their market shares reduced by the TPM believed they could sell below the trigger price and still defeat charges of dumping. This would be true to the extent home market price, converted to dollars at the new exchange rates, were lower than previously, and thus not above the prices at which the products were offered to the United States.[b] Of course, to the extent subsidies, expressed in francs, pounds, etc. remained in effect, the movement in the exchange rate would not affect the basic question of fair/unfair competition, only the amounts at issue.

In August 1981, as imports for the prior month were reported at about 20 percent of apparent consumption, the Commerce Department invoked the

---

[v] Id. ¶ 12.

[a] According to the London Economist, Jan. 24, 1981, p. 88, the framers of Japan's trade and industrial policy decided not to jeopardize export sales of higher value products such as automobiles, ships, and consumer electronics by threatening more of the West's steel industry.

[b] For example, it was reported that German steel selling at $528/ton in the summer of 1980 was now selling, in dollars, at $384. See New York Times, August 2, 1981, § 3, p. 1.

surge mechanism of the revised TPM, and began a 90-day "review."[c] When the August figures came out, the import total reached a record high of 25 percent of consumption, and overall imports for the first nine months of 1981 reached 14.5 million tons, equal to a market share of 20.5 percent. The Commerce Department announced it would itself initiate a countervailing duty proceeding,[d] and on November 12, 1981, it actually did so, invoking for the first time in a major case the Subsidies Code negotiated during the Tokyo Round. The Department did not take on the full range of products, but limited itself to *Carbon Steel Plate from Belgium*[e] and *Hot Rolled Carbon Steel Sheet* from France.[f] The Department contended that imports of hot rolled sheet from France had increased by 10.7 percent in the first eight months of 1981, while imports excluding France had declined 20.3 percent. Further, the Department contended that the Rescue Plans adopted by the French government for its steel industry had amounted to substantial subsidization derived from low-interest (or interest free) loans, estimated at $38.15 per ton. The Department suggested that during the proceeding it was initiating other benefits would be calculated, adding to the amount of the countervailing duty to be imposed if the Commission found injury. For the time being, since this case was initiated by the Department itself, the TPM would remain in place. Also, the Secretary of Commerce, Malcolm Baldrige, traveled again to Europe to try to negotiate—whether an agreement to refrain from shipments below the trigger prices, or an agreement to limit shipments to a given amount, along the lines of the automobile restraints negotiated earlier with Japan.

By coincidence, the American delegation was in Western Europe in December 1981 to negotiate about steel exports just before President Reagan imposed sanctions against the Soviet Union for imposition of martial law against Poland.[h] In Washington, the two events were considered unrelated;

---

[c] 46 Fed. Reg. 42323 (Aug. 20, 1981). The conclusions of the Department's review, in some instances resulting in self-initiated antidumping or countervailing duty investigations, were published in November, 46 Fed. Reg. 57584 (Nov. 24, 1981).

[d] New York Times, Nov. 6, 1981, p. 1, col. 1.

[e] 46 Fed. Reg. 56635 (Nov. 18, 1981). Companion proceedings concerning steel plate were initiated against products from Brazil, 46 Fed. Reg. 56636, and Romania, 46 Fed. Reg. 56637 and South Africa, 46 Fed. Reg. 56638.

[f] *Hot Rolled Carbon Steel Sheet from France, Initiation of Countervailing Duty Investigation*, 46 Fed. Reg. 56639 (Nov. 18, 1981).

[g] § 8.3 *supra*. It appears that the U.S. industry, as well as the Community, was looking for a quota agreement, but the Administration was not then prepared to consider that solution.

[h] See Volume III of this series, A. Lowenfeld, *Trade Controls for Political Ends*, Ch. II,

seen from Paris, Brussels, London, and Bonn, however, sanctions against the Soviet Union and Poland designed to slow down construction of a proposed natural gas pipeline between the Siberian Arctic and Western Europe would have direct impact on Western Europe's steel mills and fabricating plants, precisely the same industry that was attempting to preserve or expand its share of the American market for steel, even as demand in the Community was shrinking and unemployment was growing. At all events, it proved impossible to negotiate a settlement, and these cases proceeded.

On December 22, 1981, the ITC voted without dissent that there was reasonable indication of material injury to the U.S. industry.[i] Not content, however, with the Government's action, on January 11, 1982 the major steel companies filed their own cases with the Department—naming five of the six major product groups, the seven steel-producing countries of the Community (plus Spain, Romania, Brazil and South Africa) and alleging (in separate, simultaneously filed actions) both subsidization and dumping. At this point the Department again suspended the Trigger Price Mechanism, apparently for good.[j] The Industry Ministers of the European Community, meeting in Brussels, immediately issued a statement expressing concern at the numerous suits filed by American steel companies, and declaring that the difficulties of the American steel industry "are in no way due to Community exports . . . [but] are attributable to the deterioration in the economic situation in the United States." Further,

> In the interests of European steel producers, the Community will make sure that the relevant international agreements are being correctly applied, in particular the GATT code on subsidies and countervailing duties, and will take all appropriate steps to defend its producers' rights.[k]

Since the issues raised were the same as in the Department's own proceeding, but the number of products and countries involved was greater, the

---

§ 5.4 (2d ed. 1983) for details of these sanctions and the surrounding circumstances. While the December 1981 restraints were not expressly extraterritorial, as were the amended sanctions imposed in June 1982, the effect was to prevent shipments from U.S. producers of components used by European contractors in connection with construction of the pipeline.

[i] *Hot Rolled Carbon Steel Sheet from France*, Investigation No. 701–TA–85 (Preliminary), USITC Pub. 1206 (Jan. 1982), 47 Fed. Reg. 1054 (Jan. 8, 1982); *Hot Rolled Carbon Steel Plate from Belgium, Brazil, and Romania*, Investigations Nos. 701–TA–83 and 84 and 731–TA–51 (Preliminary) USITC Pub. 1207 (Jan. 1982), 47 Fed Reg. 1050 (Jan. 8, 1982).

[j] 47 Fed. Reg. 2392 (Jan. 15, 1982).

[k] Statement of the Industry Ministers of the Ten, Jan. 13, 1982, 15 Bull. of European Communities No. 1 § 2.2.24 (Jan. 1982).

companies' petitions overtook the earlier cases, which were terminated.[l] As the Department initiated investigations on the companies' petitions,[m] the Commission again found reasonable indication of injury (though in only 38 of the 92 investigations).[n] Since the Department determined that the investigations were "extraordinarily complicated,"[o] the preliminary countervailing duty determinations fell due on June 10, and the antidumping cases on August 9, 1982.[p] At the same time negotiations continued at various levels. But agreement could not be reached—not yet, in any case.[q]

On June 10, 1982, the first shoe dropped. The Department of Commerce issued its preliminary determinations in the countervailing duty cases.[r] In 28 cases,[s] involving 3.9 million tons of steel according to 1981 figures, subsidies were found, including over 40 percent ad valorem for some products of British Steel, 20-30 percent for products from France, and about 21 per-

---

[l] 47 Fed. Reg. 5754 (Feb. 8, 1982).

[m] 47 Fed. Reg. 5739–53 (Feb. 8, 1982).

[n] 47 Fed. Reg. 9087 (March 3, 1982). In fact, the petitions originally covered 132 cases, including 38 antidumping and 94 countervailing duty cases, but 7 had been dismissed by the Department and 16 had been withdrawn by petitioners prior to the Commission's determination. The Department also declined to launch a separate investigation into allegations of subsidization by the European Community itself, on the ground that the Community's subsidies would be covered in the investigations of products from the respective countries. One of the petitioners appealed from this negative determination under § 516A(a)(1)A(i), Documents Supplement p. DS–458, and in July the Department's decision concerning the Community was reversed by the Court of International Trade. *Republic Steel Corp. v. United States*, 544 F. Supp. 901 (Ct. Int'l Tr. July 22, 1982). By that time the remaining case and negotiations had gone so far that the petition against the Community was not restarted.

[o] 47 Fed Reg. 11738 (March 18, 1982).

[p] Recall the extra time given in the statute for antidumping cases, as compared with countervailing duty cases, § 7.63(d) *supra*.

[q] The indication of injury, of course, related to the U.S. industry's strongest cases, which in fact concerned the largest volume of imports. The negotiations, however, concerned the other products as well.

[r] Dept. of Commerce, *Preliminary Affirmative Countervailing Duty Determinations; Certain Steel Products from Belgium, Brazil, France, Federal Republic of Germany, Italy, Luxembourg, Netherlands, South Africa, and United Kingdom, 47 Fed. Reg. 26300–26348, (June 17, 1982).*

[s] Including 20 countervailing duty cases as to which the ITC had made preliminary injury determinations plus 8 cases concerning steel from South Africa, which had not gone to the Commission because no injury finding was required, since South Africa had not signed the Subsidies Code.

cent for products from Belgium.[t] In all, 20 percent of U.S. steel imports from all sources, and 4 percent of apparent U.S. consumption, were affected by the determinations. Though the cases were not yet final, liquidation was ordered suspended in all cases of affirmative findings, requiring bonds equal to the estimated subsidy. According to Secretary Baldrige, the products affected accounted for about 3 percent of the European Community's steel output. The Secretary said:

> I will remain open to approaches from foreign producers and governments on ideas for reaching an accommodation short of completing our investigations, as provided for in our law.[u]

Viscount Davignon, in Brussels, said, "It's a very bad business. . . ."[v]

Negotiations continued throughout the summer between the U.S. government and representatives of the European Commission. But the further along the cases proceeded to formal determinations, the harder it became to reach a settlement, because the complaining companies now had, if not yet a vested right to countervailing duties, at least a growing say about the circumstances in which they would agree to dismiss these petitions.[w] At the beginning of August it seemed that the negotiations at government level had succeeded, with an agreement by the Community to reduce shipments of eleven products by about 10 percent from 1981 levels, to take no more than 5.8 per cent of the U.S. market for three years, subject to withdrawal of the pending countervailing duty and antidumping suits. But the American industry immediately rejected the proposal. David Roderick, the chairman of U.S. Steel, said the tentative agreement "falls far short of what was expected, and is neither fair nor equitable."[a]

On August 9, the antidumping cases, brought by U.S. Steel et al. at the

---

[t] West German and Dutch producers were, in effect, acquitted, as for most of them the amount of subsidy was found to be less than 1 percent.

[u] Statement of Secretary Baldrige, June 11, 1982.

[v] New York Times, June 12, 1982, p. 45, col. 1.

[w] Note that under § 704(c) of the Trade Agreements Act of 1979, Documents Supplement p. DS–484, the U.S. government and the European Community could have reached an "out-of-court" settlement at any time up to the final determination by the Department of Commerce. Under § 704(g) the industry would have the right to require the investigation to be reopened, but not, apparently, to prevent an agreement made under § 704(c) from going into effect. Politically, of course, the idea of an agreement to which the industry was strongly opposed would have been impossible.

[a] BNA, U.S. Import Weekly, Aug. 11, 1982, p. 577.

same time as the countervailing duty cases, came up for preliminary determination, once more the determination was affirmative, in respect of products from Belgium, West Germany, France, Italy and Great Britain (as well as Romania).[b] Whether the antidumping duties, if made final, would be added to the countervailing duties previously determined preliminarily, or whether one would be credited against the other was not clear.[c] But a new element was introduced into some of the cases, derived from an amendment to the antidumping law in the 1979 Act not previously discussed: Under § 733(e),[d] consistent with Article 11(1)(ii) of the revised antidumping Code,[e] if (i) there is a history of dumping of the product in question and (ii) there has been a massive surge of imports of the product in the period of the investigation, then the Department may make a finding of "critical circumstances," which means that not only may liquidation be suspended (and security required) for goods entered on or after the date of the preliminary finding, but the suspension of liquidation (and ultimate commencement of any duty imposed) may be made retroactive for 90 days from the date of the finding.[f] In several of the antidumping cases from France and Belgium,[g] the Department now invoked the "critical circumstances" provision, on the basis of finding of a massive increase in imports in the period March-June 1982.[h]

On August 24, the time came for final decision in the Commerce Department in the countervailing duty cases, and to no one's surprise, the deter-

---

[b] *Preliminary Determinations of Sales at Less Than Fair Value: Certain Steel Products from Belgium, Federal Republic of Germany, France, Italy, the Netherlands, United Kingdom; Carbon Steel Shapes from Luxembourg and Carbon Steel Plate from Romania*, 47 Fed. Reg. 35646 (Aug. 16, 1982). Note that the products of the Netherlands and Luxembourg were determined not to be dumped, as the margin of difference between the home and export price was *de minimis*. 47 Fed. Reg. at 35663, 35664.

[c] See § 8.65(b) *infra*.

[d] Documents Supplement p. DS–496; the corresponding provision applicable to preliminary countervailing duty determination is § 703(e), Documents Supplement p. DS–483.

[e] Documents Supplement DS–737. The corresponding provision in the Subsidies Code is Article 5(9), Documents Supplement p. DS–671.

[f] Note that under the Trade Agreements Act of 1979, "suspension of liquidation" is used for both dumping and countervailing duty cases, rather than the term "withholding of appraisment" for dumping cases, as before. No legal consequence flowed from this change in terminology.

[g] But not with respect to imports from West Germany, Italy, the United Kingdom, or Romania.

[h] 47 Fed. Reg. at 35648 (Belgium), 35659 (France). For imports from other countries subject to investigation, the determination on this issue was negative or moot.

minations were affirmative with respect to imports from France, Belgium, Great Britain, and Italy, though in most instances the final determination of the amount of subsidy was substantially lower than the amount estimated in June.[i] The reasons for the big difference between preliminary and final findings could be explained in part because the Department decided to allocate government grants to producers so as to cover losses only in the year conferred, rather than over a fifteen year period, and in part because, having seen the severe tentative findings of the Department on the basis of incomplete information, some of the foreign companies furnished cost data they had previously withheld.[j] Secretary Baldrige kept trying for an "out of court" settlement. In his statement announcing the subsidy findings, he said:

> Earlier this month I joined with the Commission of the European Communities in recommending an EC export restraint program to U.S. steel producers as an alternative. . . . To date, several U.S. producers have indicated a preference to see the cases to conclusion. While I disagree with their assessment, it is up to the producers themselves to evaluate what method of relief from unfair trade is in their best interest before the International Trade Commission's final injury determinations in October.[k]

The U.S. producers not only were not in the mood to settle, they announced they would appeal to the Court of International Trade, on the ground that the reduced findings of subsidization "reflect the pressures that are undoubtedly being brought to bear on the Administration from E.C. countries."[l]

The last round, if it went to the end, would take place in the International Trade Commission, which now had until Friday, October 8 (Day 270) to make the final injury determination.[m] If there was to be a settlement, there

---

[i] *Final Affirmative Countervailing Duty Determinations, Certain Steel Products from Belgium, France, Federal Republic of Germany, Italy, Luxembourg, Netherlands, South Africa, and United Kingdom,* 47 Fed. Reg. 39302–39395 (Sept. 7, 1982). The difference between the preliminary and final determinations may be illustrated by the following figures for SACILOR, one of the two major French steel enterprises: The estimated subsidy on structurals, hot-rolled sheet, and cold-rolled sheet was 30.029%; the final determination was 14.223%, 21.416%, and 19.494% for the three products, respectively. For British Steel, the June estimated subsidy was 40.362%; the final determination was 20.33% subsidy.

[j] Also, on the issue of loans to "uncreditworthy" enterprises, the critical date was moved forward, from 1975 to 1978. See § 8.62(c) *infra*.

[k] Statement of Secretary of Commerce Malcolm Baldrige, Aug. 25, 1982.

[l] BNA, U.S. Import Weekly, Sept. 1, 1982, p. 663.

[m] There was some doubt about the deadline under § 705(b)(2) of the Act, depending on

wasn't much time. For the administration, still embroiled in the controversy with Western Europe about the natural gas pipeline from the Soviet Union, any settlement acceptable in Pittsburgh would look good; for the U.S. industry, the issue was primarily one of the numbers—i.e., how much steel could be sold over the various tariffs likely to be imposesd; for the Community there was an additional consideration—the countervailing and antidumping duties would come out very unevenly as among the various producers and companies under the calculations made by the Commerce Department, falling most heavily on Belgium, Britain and France, least on Germany; in a negotiated settlement, the Community could probably sort out—within the framework of its own steel policy—how much of the export market would be assigned to which producer, region, or country. The irony—if it can be called that—was that a settlement almost certainly would mean quotas, while no settlement would mean tariffs, albeit not the kind the framers of the GATT had in mind in the 1940's. The reduced findings of subsidy as compared to the preliminary determinations, if they did not reduce the leverage of the U.S. companies, certainly made them recalculate the relative advantage of settlement in contrast to "victory."

In early September, Viscount Davignon succeeded in securing a revised party line from the European steel industry on a settlement with the United States: those "acquitted"—i.e., Dutch and German producers—agreed to share the burdens of export restraints with the producers found to be heavily subsidized—British, Belgian, French, and Italian. Davignon flew once more to Washington, and the Commerce Department sought an extension of two weeks before the ITC would make its final determination. The Commission voted (3-1) to comply with the request, but not past the week of October 10. By now the administration, as well as the American industry, were willing to accept the idea of an export restraint in place of the various remedies provided for in the Act; but the domestic producers wanted lower levels of permitted imports than had been set in the failed August agreement, and they wanted coverage not only of the five groups of products subject to the antidumping and countervailing duty cases, but also of alloy and pipe and tube products. For two weeks, as cables and delegates criss-crossed between Washington and Brussels (as well as between the negotiators and their constituencies), it was not clear whether these two demands could be compromised. On October 15, the International Trade Commission, in a public session, voted to issue final injury determinations in 14 of the 16 remaining

---

whether the time was computed from the day the Department made its determination, or when it gave "formal notice," which in this instance came only through publication in the Federal Register, two weeks after the actual determination. See N. i *supra*.

countervailing duty cases.[n] That seemed to mean that duties would have to be assessed not later than October 21,[o] and if that happened, a settlement might become impossible. In Brussels, the Community announced it had found a way to limit exports on pipe and tube products without subjecting them to the same regime as the other products. Only in Bonn, where a new government had taken office less than two weeks previously,[p] was there still resistance to the deal. But even as the spokesman of the American Iron and Steel Institute said, "No pipes, no deal,"[q] the deal was made, sweetened for the European industry by a decision to reduce by more than 10 percent the permitted imports of steel into the Community from the developing and East European countries. The Community would establish an export licensing system for each of the ten products involved in the proceedings for a three-year period beginning November 1, 1982, with ceilings varying product-by-product but averaging about 5.12 percent of apparent U.S. consumption, compared with a (rising) market share of about 7.5 percent in the first quarter of 1982. In return, all of the countervailing duty and antidumping cases would be dropped, and the petitioners would undertake not to bring any new proceedings under any of the import relief provisions of U.S. law.[r] President Reagan, traveling in the Middle West to campaign for Republican candidates in the Congressional election, made the announcement at 10:37 a.m. from the Iowa Room of the Red Lion Hotel, Omaha, Nebraska:

---

[n] See New York Times, Oct. 16, 1982. For reasons which will become clear in the following paragraphs, the vote was not followed, as is normal, by publication of the decision and accompanying report. However, the public session revealed that of the four members of the Commission (there being now two vacancies) the vote had been 2–2 in the two cases in which the Commission declined to find injury.

[o] See Trade Agreements Act of 1979, § 706(a), Documents Supplement p. DS–491.

[p] This was the government of Chancellor Helmut Kohl, the leader of the Christian Democratic Party, who took office after Chancellor Helmut Schmidt, who had held office since 1974, lost a vote of confidence. Count Lambsdorff, the Economic Minister and advocate of free trade who was a member of the small Free Democratic party whose split with the Social Democrats had led to the fall of Schmidt, remained in office in the new coalition organized by Kohl.

[q] New York Times, Oct. 21, 1982, p. D1, col. 5; Oct. 22, 1982, p. D2, col. 9.

[r] The text of the agreement and some of the supporting documents appear in the Documents Supplement at pp. DS–633–46. The promise not to bring renewed proceedings is in Article 2(b), Documents Supplement p. DS–634. The individual product ceilings appear in Article 4(a). Note also the statement in one of the accompanying exchanges of letters between Viscount Davignon and Secretary Baldrige that the Community does not admit to having bestowed subsidies or that such subsidies caused injury. Documents Supplement p. DS–640.

And I have another announcement, if you don't mind, that I'd like to make this morning also that I think is encouraging news and I'm pleased to announce, one that I think is a piece of good news for the American steel industry and the many thousands of American workers and their families who depend on the steel industry for their livelihood and good news for the economy.

Commerce Secretary Baldrige and Vice President Haferkamp and Davignon at the Commission of the European Communities have successfuly ended negotiations for an agreement, an arrangement that will restrain European steel exports to the United States for the next three years. These revisions to the Steel Trade Agreement, concluded last August 5th, covered 90 percent of steel imports from Europe and will relieve our domestic steel industry from the unfair competition of subsidized foreign products. And that, in turn, will mean more and lasting jobs in the steel industry, which will translate into good news on the employment front.

In return for the agreement on imports, the American steel industry will drop its countervailing duty and dumping suits against over 40 European companies. Reaching this agreement was a long and arduous process, and I want to commend both Secretary Baldrige and his European counterparts for their outstanding efforts. They have resulted in a mutual understanding that is reassuring evidence that America and her allies and trading partners can work together for the amicable settlement of differences in an atmosphere of cooperation and understanding. It's also one more small but important step toward the last inflation-proof job-creating economic recovery we've all been working so hard to achieve for our people.[s]

§ 8.6—Notes and Questions

8.61—The struggle over exports of steel from the European Community to the United States can be viewed on several levels.

(a) At one level, the *Steel Subsidy Cases* suggest that while the detailed rules and procedures concerning determination of subsidies and assessment of countervailing duties may work for butter cookies or canned mushrooms, they can only affect but not in the end govern commerce in a major product between major trading partners. The attempt by Congress in successive trade acts to take the discretionary or political element out of international trade

---

[s] 18 Weekly Comp. Pres. Docs. 1367 (Oct. 21, 1982). A few days later the International Trade Commission published a brief notice, *Termination of Countervailing Duty Investigations Concerning Certain Carbon Steel Products*, 47 Fed. Reg. 49104 (Oct. 29, 1982).

administration, in other words, can succeed only up to a point, and far from completely.

(b) At another level, one may ask, what happened to the crowning achievement of the Tokyo Round, the Subsidies and Countervailing Duties Code? While the change in United States law is apparent and clearly relevant—i.e., introduction of a finding of injury as a condition for imposition of countervailing duties, the express prohibition of export subsidies on non-primary products seems to be irrelevant. Not one of the many items of alleged subsidization investigated by the Department of Commerce was an export subsidy within the meaning of Article 9 of the Subsidies Code and the illustrative list in Annex A.[a] The *Steel Subsidy Cases*, then, may be viewed as a test of the compromise reflected in Articles 8 and 11 of the Subsidies Code between the American position that all kinds of subsidies should be subjected to GATT restraint (not to say prohibition) and the Community's position that domestic subsidies should not be considered countervailable.[b] Keep this compromise in mind in considering some of the items of aid to the steel industry—national and Community-wide—against which the United States proposed to impose countervailing duties.

8.62—Consider the outcome of the confrontation over steel from the point of view of the several interested parties.

(a) The American steel industry winds up with no guaranteed increase in the price of steel from Western Europe, but with assurance that imports from the Community will not exceed roughly 5 percent of consumption. From the point of view of U.S. Steel and its co-petitioners, isn't that better than seeing the countervailing and antidumping duty cases through to the end? Haven't they, in effect, traded in tariff relief for a quota?

(b) As for the European Coal and Steel Community and its member states, the system of subsidies and other forms of government intervention can remain in place, subject of course to internal reconsideration but not to any rulings from America. The Community loses some market penetration, but may be able to raise its export prices somewhat with guaranteed (or almost guaranteed) access. Moreover, the intra-Community disputes about the steel

---

[a] Documents Supplement pp. DS–676 and 687–89.

[b] For a discussion of the respective positions on this point, including reproduction of several negotiating documents, by two of the American negotiators of the Code, see Rivers and Greenwald, "The Negotiation of a Code on Subsidies and Countervailing Measures: Bridging Fundamental Policy Differences," 11 Law & Pol'y Int'l Bus. 1447, esp. 1465–75 (1979).

program are composed, at least for a while, as West Germany agrees (reluctantly) to assume a share of the reduction in exports, despite the finding that its firms were not benefiting from subsidies.[c]

(c) What about the international economy as a whole? On the one hand a trade war between the two biggest trading units is averted. On the other hand, one trade distortion—an export quota—is piled on another—subsidized European production. The agreement does little to promote efficiency in steel production in either the Community or the United States.

(d) As for the GATT, except for a disclaimer in the exchange of letters,[d] it is once more left out, once more a silent witness to managed trade.

8.63—The Commerce Department's analysis of the 57 varieties of subsidies alleged in the petitions by the American steel industry took up almost 50 triple-column pages in the Federal Register in the preliminary determinations in June,[e] and nearly 100 pages (including discussion of the parties' comments on the preliminary determinations) in the final determinations in August.[f] An idea of the involvement of government in Europe's steel industry on the one hand, and of the United States' view of that involvement on the other, can be gained from a look at the Department's treatment of steel products from France, in particular from the two major combines SACILOR and USINOR[g].

---

[c] In the spring of 1983, as the renewed authority for Davignon III was coming to an end, § 851 N. n, the Commission sought approval from the Council of Ministers for an extension of two and a half years, with the addition of two more categories of steel products. The Council, though sharing the Commission's opinion on continuance of the state of manifest crisis, was willing to extend the quota system for only one month, from June 30 to July 30, pending negotiation of the permitted production quotas. At 3 a.m. on July 26, the member states reached agreement on production quotas, with increases from the Commission's proposal particularly for French and British firms. Thereupon the Council approved extension of the Plan, but only to January 31, 1984, instead of to December 31, 1985, as the Commission had proposed. *Commission Decision No. 2177/83/ECSC of July 28, 1983 on the extension of the system for monitoring and production quotas for certain products of undertakings in the steel industry,* O.J. L/208, July 31, 1983. Evidently, Italy urged the short leash on the Commission in order to prevent future production cuts that might be directed against its producers, and Britain, Denmark, Greece, and France, each for its own reasons, were not prepared to override an Italian veto, as they could have done under Treaty of Paris.

[d] Documents Supplement p. DS–641.

[e] Dept. of Commerce, *Preliminary Affirmative Countervailing Duty Determinations, Certain Steel Products,* 47 Fed. Reg. 26299–26348 (June 17, 1982).

[f] Dept. of Commerce, *Final Affirmative Countervailing Duty Determinations, Certain Steel Products,* 47 Fed. Reg. 39303–39395 (Sept. 7, 1982).

[g] Societe des Acieries et Laminoirs de Lorraine; Union Siderurgique du Nord et de l'Est de la France.

(a) *Export Credit Insurance.* USINOR (but not SACILOR) had taken out export insurance from COFACE,[h] a state-owned agency. In its preliminary determination, the Department of Commerce held that in 1980, as well as in prior years, COFACE's insurance activity operated at a deficit, which was made up by proceeds from investments. The difference between a premium rate that would cover, over time, all of COFACE's risks plus administrative expenses, and the premium rate actually charged was deemed to be an export subsidy and countervailable. Prior to the final determination, USINOR was able to show that it had bought only commercial, and not political risk insurance for its sales to the United States, and that COFACE's losses had been attributable only to the political risk coverage. Accordingly the finding of subsidy—0.078% ad valorem—was dropped from the final determination. But suppose USINOR had not had this defense—either because it had taken out political risk insurance or because all of COFACE's coverages had been operating at a loss—is this the kind of activity that you would regard as countervailable?

(b) *Preferential Loans.* France had since 1955 maintained an organization known as FDES,[i] something like the Reconstruction Finance Corporation that operated in the United States from the early 1930's to the end of World War II. FDES lent funds to individual enterprises for development or relocation, usually taking back a mortgage or pledge on the borrower's assets. The funds for FDES came from the national treasury, but were replenished as loans were repaid. Generally FDES loans were at lower rates than commercial rates; they were not limited, however, to the steel industry. Similarly, France has a semi-public credit institution, Credit National (CN), which makes loans to business, and a Caisse des Dépôts et Consignations (CDC), which invests funds deposited in French savings banks, pension funds, and the like. The Department asserted that CN and CDC loans were made to USINOR and SACILOR at government direction and at preferential rates. Since it was not satisfied by the information furnished by the respondents or the French government on this point,[j] it assumed the initial assertion was correct, and regarded the difference between the actual and a constructed commercial rate as an equity infusion,[k] and therefore countervailable. Would you agree?

(c) *Loans to Uncreditworthy Enterprises.* More important, in terms of the sums involved, the Department took the position in June that as of the end

---

[h] Compagnie Francaise d'Assurance pour le Commerce Exterieur.

[i] Fonds de Développement Economique et Social.

[j] See Trade Agreements Act of 1979, § 776, Documents Supplement p. DS–522; Subsidies Code, Article 2(9), Documents Supplement p. DS–666.

[k] Paragraph (c) below.

of 1975 SACILOR and USINOR were uncreditworthy, and therefore that all loans and loan guarantees made by public bodies, whether by the French financial organs, by the European Investment Bank, or by the European Coal and Steel Community, were equivalent to "equity infusions." In its final order, the Department revised its finding as to the dates the companies slipped into uncreditworthiness (as contrasted with unprofitability) from 1975 to 1978. From that time on and so long as any principal was outstanding, the Department deemed the loans to be capital contributions, measured for each year by the difference between the company's return on equity (which might well be zero) and the average return on equity for the country as a whole, stated to be 18 percent in 1981.[1] Once the amount of this subsidy was determined per borrower, the result would be divided by the amount of steel produced by the firm in question to arrive at an amount (or percentage) of subsidy per ton.

Is this persuasive?

(d) *Grants.* In one sense grants—whether from the national government or from the ECSC—were the easiest for the Commerce Department. The U.S. countervailing duty statute had spoken of "bounty or grant" since 1897,[m] and given the American position that domestic as well as export subsidies were subject to countervailing, it was hard to contest the proposition that a grant could be met with a countervailing duty, provided that duty did not exceed the amount of the subsidy found to exist.[n] But how should a grant to be used for long-term capital improvement be translated into a subsidy over a given period of time or a given quantity of steel? The Senate Report on section 771(6) of the Trade Agreements Act of 1979[o] had recognized the problem of "nonrecurring subsidy grants . . . which aid an enterprise in acquiring capital equipment," and had called for "[r]easonable methods of allocating the value of such subsidies over the production or exportation of the products benefiting from the subsidy."[p] In prior cases, the Department had taken the capital sum, divided it by half the useful life of the equipment associated with the grant, and then assigned the quotient as

---

[1] Any interest received on the loan would be subtracted when received; for each year the amount of outstanding principal would be subject to a comparable calculation. If the formula yielded a higher rate than treating the face amount of the loan as a grant (see paragraph (d) below) then the so-called "grant cap" would be used as a measure of the subsidy.

[m] See § 4.45(a) *supra.*

[n] See GATT Article VI(3), Documents Supplement p. DS–14. Subsidies Code Article 4(2), Documents Supplement p. DS–668.

[o] Documents Supplement p. DS–512.

[p] *Senate Report* § 7.57 N. n *supra* p. 85.

a subsidy for each of the years in question. Thus a grant of $100,000 to purchase a machine with a 20-year life would have been treated as a subsidy of $10,000 per year ($100,000 ÷ 20/2) for ten years.

In the *Steel Subsidy Cases*, however, the Department changed its technique, in response to criticism that its prior method ignored the true value of money.[q] The Department pointed out that $100,000 today is worth much more than $10,000 per year over the next 10 years. A concern operating solely in the market would, presumably, have borrowed the $100,000 (or made use of a reserve or retained earnings, with similar accounting effect), and amortized that amount over the useful life of the machine. The Department assumed that interest and principal would have been paid in equal instalments over a 15-year period (the average life of capital assets in the steel industry), with an interest rate determined for each country by the secondary market for long-term government debt.[r] Thus the Department treated a grant used for capital purchases as if the beneficiary had taken out a mortgage, with each year's hypothetical payment of principal and interest the measure of the subsidy in that year, so that the $100,000 grant for a machine in our example, with an interest rate of 12 percent over 15 years, would be deemed to benefit from a yearly subsidy of $14,453.18.[s] As with respesct to the other subsidy programs, the amount so determined would be divided by the enterprise's output to determine the subsidy per ton.

The French (and other) steel companies regarded this method as contrary both to the legislative intent (in section 771(5) and (6)),[t] and to commercial reality.[u] The Department changed its method of calculating the interest rate between the preliminary and final determination,[v] but stuck to its

---

[q] The Department's methodology was set out in Appendices to the determinations—preliminary and final—concerning *Steel Products from Belgium*, but incorporated by reference in all cases. See 47 Fed. Reg. 26306–26310 (June 17, 1982) (preliminary determinations); 47 Fed. Reg. 39315–39331 (Sept. 17, 1982) (final determinations).

[r] This method was chosen to focus only on the true cost of money, removing all elements of interest that reflect risk.

[s] Based on standard mortgage amortization schedule of a 15-year mortgage with level quarterly payments at interest of 12 percent per year. The calculation differed from that used for normal real estate mortgages in that the first annual installment was deemed to be received on the day of the grant (year zero), rather than on the first anniversary, as would be the practice with typical mortgages.

[t] Documents Supplement pp. DS–511–12.

[u] See, e.g., *In the Matter of Steel Countervailing Duty Investigations*, Brief on behalf of USINOR, pp. 12–18 (July 26, 1982).

[v] The preliminary finding had used an estimate of each company's weighted cost of capital

methodology. Does it seem sound to you? Consistent with the statute? With the Subsidies Code?

(e) *Restructure of Loans.* Under the Rescue Plan for the French steel industry, as we saw,[w] debt that had been accumulating between 1965 and 1978 was restructured in several ways. About F.Fr. 12.8 billion was converted into Loans of Special Characteristics known by their French initials as "PACS."[x] PACS were nominally subordinated loans bearing an interest rate of 0.1 percent for the first five years and 1.0 percent thereafter, but since principal was to be repaid only when the companies returned to profitability, they had some of the characteristics of preferred stock.[y] The companies argued that PACS represented no infusion of capital, simply a reorganization of an insolvent company's accounts, as an alternative to bankruptcy which (quite apart from social and political consequences) would not have benefited the creditors. The Department treated PACS as if they were loans to uncreditworthy enterprises, as described in paragraph (c) above, amounting to 6.45-10.816 percent ad valorem for SACILOR and 4.041-9.732 percent ad valorem for USINOR.[z]

Who has the better of this argument? Is any arrangement to keep an insolvent enterprise functioning a subsidy for purposes of countervailing duties? Does the answer depend on whether the enterprise returns to profitability?

(f) *Government purchase of stock.* If the government purchased stock of a company at market prices, there would be no subsidy. The nationalization by the French government, for example, of five major industrial groups in 1981 raised questions of fair compensation to shareholders, but not of subsidization, even though the price paid exceeded the book value or the share price on the Paris stock exchange.[a] But when the government paid substantially more than the market price for shares issued by the companies, or exchanged debt for equity, or contributed capital to companies already

---

at the time of grant receipt; the final method, designed to eliminate the risk factor as a cost of capital, was as described at N. t *supra*.

[w] § 6.33 N. f *supra*.

[x] Prêts a Caracteristiques Speciales.

[y] PACS were carried on a special line on the companies' balance sheet between equity and debt. To the extent the prior debt was held by private persons, arrangements were made that they would be paid in full through organizations making use of government funds and guarantees.

[z] The numbers vary depending on the products.

[a] See Volume II of this series, A. Lowenfeld, *International Private Investment*, Epilogue § 2.57 (2d ed. 1982).

government-owned, the purchase or contribution was deemed to be a subsidy, measured for each year by the "rate of return shortfall," i.e., the difference between, say, USINOR's rate of return on equity and the average rate of return on equity in France as a whole for that year, multiplied by the amount of the purchase or contribution. If treating the subsidy as if it were a grant amortized as described in paragraph (d) would result in a lower figure, the latter was used.[b]

(g) *Other state aids.* The list of aids alleged by the U.S. steel companies to be countervailable went on and on.[c] Just one more category is worth mention here, apart from the European Community aids discussed below. The most surprising idea had to do with laid-off workers. Under French labor law, companies releasing workers after stated periods of employment are required to make payments to unemployment or retirement funds. When the government, as part of the "rationalization" of 1978, urged closing down various facilities, it reimbursed the companies for the amounts paid on account of discharge of the employees, which had been funded in part by payroll deductions and employer contributions during the years of employment. The Department said this constituted a subsidy. In the preliminary determination, the Department also proposed countervailing against loans received to construct workers' housing, arguing that these, too, relieved the companies of an obligation they would otherwise have, or enabled them to pay lower wages than would have to be paid without the subsidized housing. The determinations regarding housing were dropped in the final determination in the absence of any showing of effect on wages.

8.64—Thus far we have examined only aids provided by the government of France. The Department, of course, examined comparable programs for each of the countries whose steel products were under investigation.[d] In addition to the programs mentioned, of course, all of the steel enterprises in

---

[b] This item, equal in the final determination to 4.5 percent for USINOR and 4.8 percent for SACILOR, was the major item in the finding in respect of British Steel Corporation, in which so-called "public dividend capital" plus "new capital" was determined to be equal to about 16 percent ad valorem. For a full-length article devoted to this item, see Barshefsky, Mattice, and Martin, "Government Equity Participation in State-Owned Enterprises: An Analysis of the Carbon Steel Countervailing Duty Cases;" 14 Law & Pol'y Int'l Bus. 1101 (1983).

[c] It included, for example, a research and development institute of the French steel industry, to which the government contributed 3 percent (held countervailable) and the ECSC contributed 10 percent (held not countervailable because the results were made publicly available by the Community).

[d] All the members of the European Community except Ireland and Denmark, plus Spain, Brazil and South Africa.

the European Community had participated in the Davignon Plan. The Department looked particularly at programs under Article 54 of the Treaty of Paris,[e] which authorizes the European Coal and Steel Community to make or guarantee loans to enterprises engaged in the production of steel or coal.

(a) The Department took the position that the Community enjoyed a high credit rating because ot its quasi-governmental character, making it able to borrow at far lower rates than could almost any private company, let alone the troubled steel companies. When the Community re-lent these funds to the steel companies without markup in the interest rate, the Department said it was bestowing a benefit to the companies equal to the difference between the ECSC loan rate and the loan rate at which the companies could borrow on the market. Similarly, when commercial loans were made with an ECSC guarantee, the differential between the interest rate without and with a guarantee was deemed to be a subsidy.[f]

(b) When the ECSC gave "reconversion loans," i.e., funds to promote investment by the steel companies in non-steel ventures, that would not seem to be a subsidy to steel production; in its final determination, however, the Department of Commerce concluded that some industrial reconversion loans had gone for new steel-making facilities, and thus were countervailable.

(c) The Department was not sure what to do about items financed out of the ECSC budget, since that budget seemed to be funded by assessments on the coal and steel producers. In its final determination, however, the Department concluded that in the years 1978-81 some 16-20 percent of the ECSC budget had come from member state contributions. Accordingly, the Department proposed to treat ECSC grants pro tanto as countervailable. This finding applied to a variety of ECSC programs, including interest rebates, industrial reconversion, and labor retraining within the steel industry.

(d) The most interesting point made by the respondents with regard to the ECSC was the contention that all of the Community's programs concerning steel were designed to reduce steel-making capacity and steel production in the Community. How then could the effects of the Davignon Plan be regarded as subsidizing steel production? Granted that this characterization of the

---

[e] Documents Supplement p. DS-113.

[f] The same reasoning was applied to loans made, presumably for purposes of regional development, by the European Investment Bank, established pursuant to Articles 129–130 of the Treaty of Rome. See Documents Supplement p. DS-191.

Davignon programs is something of an oversimplification,[g] is the argument persuasive?

(e) The Department said that the motive of a program of subsidization is not relevant for purposes of the U.S. countervailing duty law. The fact that a subsidy or group of subsidies is consistent with the objectives recited in Article 11(1) of the Subsidies Code[h] does not mean it is not countervailable in accordance with Part I of the Code—that indeed was the compromise on which the Code was based. "Further," the Department said, "while restructuring aids may be devoted in part to reducing production capacity, such aids, by making the recipient steel companies more efficient and relieving them of significant financial burden, are of unquestioned benefit to the continuing production of steel, and, as such, confer subsidies."[i]

Would you accept this position? How far should it be carried?

Suppose a given plant produces 100,000 tons of steel in high-cost and inefficient facilities; the Community or the national government prescribes a program of laying off 20 percent of the work force and replacing an obsolete open-hearth furnace with a modern electric furnace, so that when the program is complete the plant will produce 60,000 tons with a smaller payroll, reduced fuel costs, and a world-competitive selling price. If some of the plant's output is sold to the United States, one might consider that a concessional loan used to purchase the new furnace might give rise to a countervailing duty, the amount of the concession being allocated over, say, 15 years. But should the severance pay to the workers be countervailed? The unpaid portion of the loan with which the now obsolete equipment was purchased?

---

[g] For example, grants were available also to support acquisition of modern facilities. See, e.g., *Krupp Stahl A. G. v. Commission of the European Communities, cases 275/80 and 24/81*, [1981] ECR 2489, involving the question of whether a steel producer receiving a subsidy for closing an inefficient plant can also receive a subsidy for putting a more efficient plant into operation.

[h] Documents Supplement p. DS–664.

[i] *Steel Subsidy Cases*, Appendix 3, Comment 13 and reply thereto. 47 Fed. Reg. 39326–27. In response to a charge by the Community that it was making unilateral interpretations of various provisions of the Code, the Department said:

> The fact that the Code is silent with respect to whether a specific practice consitutes a subsidy does not mean that no signatory may make a determination with respect to that practice in the course of a proceeding. The fact that the signatories have not agreed on a methodology for the calculation of the amount of a subsidy does not mean that no signatory may adopt a methodology in the absence of such agreements, since the inability to calculate the amount of the subsidy found to exist would clearly frustrate the intent of the Code and the GATT.

Id. Appendix 4, Response to Comment 9, 47 Fed. Reg. at 39330.

8.65 (a)—Throughout this book, as in U.S. law prior to 1979 and in the GATT, the effort has been made to distinguish between dumping, carried on by firms, and subsidization, carried on by governments. The steel complaints against imports from Europe in 1980 and 1982 make the distinction harder than ever to maintain. Not only were many of the firms nationalized, especially in Great Britain and France (as well as Italy); the allegations were that export sales were *both* benefiting from subsidies *and* were being made at lower than home market prices. Given the way the Davignon Plan was supposed to work, there was good reason to believe that, at least for some products, the allegation was correct. Would you think antidumping and countervailing duties are alternative remedies, or can they be cumulated?

(b) Suppose a ton of hot-rolled carbon steel plate is determined to cost $400 to produce (not counting any government aids); it sells for $380 at home, and $360 in the United States (after deduction of freight and handling charges). If there is a $25/ton subsidy, should the United States assess

(i) a countervailing duty of $25/ton;

(ii) a countervailing duty of $25 plus an antidumping duty of $20;

(iii) an antidumping duty of $40, on the ground the home market sales below cost are to be disregarded in measuring foreign market value?[j]

(c) As we saw, the Department of Commerce considered the dumping complaints after the subsidy complaints, because the timetable was somewhat slower.[k] In its preliminary findings on the dumping cases,[l] the Department chose none of the alternatives proposed in paragraph (b). It said (substituting the numbers in the example for the actual numbers) that the amount of subsidy would be subtracted from its calculation of costs, so that constructed value would stand at $375, less than home market value. Accordingly, an antidumping duty would be assessed for $20;[m] presumably a separate countervailing duty could be assessed for $25, but that issue was not before the Department in an antidumping case. If the numbers in the example were changed so that, say, the home market price were $370 and constructed value were used to compute the antidumping duty, that figure would be $375 and the antidumping duty would be set at $15/ton.[n]

---

[j] See Trade Agreements Act of 1979, § 773(b) and (e), Documents Supplement pp. DS–518–21.

[k] See § 7.63(d) *supra*.

[l] § 8.53 at N. e *supra*.

[m] Dept. of Commerce, *Preliminary Determinations of Sales at Less than Fair Value, Certain Steel Products*, 47 Fed. Reg. 35645–35671 (August 17, 1982).

[n] See, e.g., *Preliminary Determinations of Sales at Less than Fair Value: Certain Steel Products from France*, 47 Fed. Reg. 35656 at 35657.

(d) The Department was not certain that its approach was correct, and invited comments from interested parties prior to its final determination.[o] Does it seem correct to you? Could you develop a rule that on the one hand does not double-count subsidies and dumping, but on the other hand does not let objectionable practices slip between two proceedings?[p]

(e) The antidumping phase of the controversy between the United States and the European Community over trade in steel raised another issue that we explored earlier[q] but that may look different in light of the crisis in steel. For many products it was necessary to compute a constructed value since the home market sales were alleged to have been below the cost of production.[r] The Trade Agreements Act of 1979 carried forward, in section 773(e)[s] the formula previously found in section 206(a) of the Antidumping Act of 1921[t] whereby constructed value comprised a cost of materials and labor; b general expenses, deemed to be at least 10 percent of a; and c profit, deemed to be at least 8 percent of $(a+b)$. Information supplied by the companies might raise b above 10 percent,[u] but it could not lower either b or c below the statutory figures, though the Department knew perfectly well from its countervailing duty investigation that there were no profits at all. Is the statute nevertheless correct, in tolerating exports to the United States only at a hypothetical profit margin, attained in times of recession neither by the European nor by the American producers? Note that Article 2(4) of the Anti-Dumping Code negotiated in the Tokyo Round[v] (unchanged in this respect from the 1967 Code) says that "as a general rule" the addition for profit shall not exceed the profit realized for corresponding products in the domestic market of the country of origin—i.e., France, Belgium, etc. If there have

---

[o] That determination, as we saw, was not made, because the target date fell after the settlement.

[p] In the preliminary determination quoted at N. n, as well as in comparable determinations with respect to products from Belgium, Great Britain, Italy, etc., the Department said its approach seemed consistent with a decision of the Court of International Trade in *Connors Steel Co. v. United States*, 527 F. Supp. 350 (Ct. Int'l Trade 1981). That decision seems to support the view that subsidization reduces the cost of production for purposes of the antidumping law, but could not be said to so hold.

[q] See §§ 4.41(c)(ii), 6.22(d), *supra*.

[r] I.e., the allegation was that the second variation in the hypothetical case put in paragraph (c) was the operative one.

[s] Documents Supplement, p. DS–520.

[t] Documents Supplement p. DS–435.

[u] This was the case, for instance, for Nuova Italsider, S.p.A., the Italian state-owned steel enterprise.

[v] Documents Supplement p. DS–728.

been no profits, as we know, since 1975, is the U.S. formula inconsistent with the Code?

8.66 (a)—Altogether, the Subsidies Code looks different after a detailed examination of the steel cases than what emerged at the congratulatory stage of the Tokyo Round in April 1979. Would you now want to renegotiate the Code, possibly prohibiting some kinds of domestic subsidies, and excluding others from countervailability? Who might stand to gain from such an amendment?

(b) Given that none of the legal/mathematical determinations made by the Commerce Department in the *Steel Subsidy Cases* and the *Steel Dumping Cases* were implemented, would you nevertheless regard them as precedents for future, less massive and political cases? Consider how you might advise (i) a foreign government; (ii) a U.S. industry; or (iii) the Assistant Secretary of Commerce for Trade Administration on this issue.[w]

(c) Having worked all the way through the *Steel Cases*, consider the following warning, written late in 1979 by one of the most experienced Washington lawyers in matters of subsidies and dumping:

> [T]he draftsmen of the Trade Agreements Act of 1979. . . have made of a matter of trade policy a legal program questionably suited to the task. But it *is* questionable. No prudent person dares state what the Trade Agreements Act *will* mean. It *could* have meant and still *may* mean that we have devised a procedure that realistically deals with real problems. Alas, it may be no less true that we have erected a stately court upon the beach that is no more effective against the tides of change than was the seat of King Canute.[x]

Three years later, do you think the author's apprehensions were justified?

---

[w] Some of the Department's reasoning, though for smaller stakes, was implemented in the proceeding against Spain, which was of course not covered by the agreement with the European Community. See *Certain Steel Products from Spain*, Final Affirmative Countervailing Duty Determination 47 Fed. Reg. 51438 (Nov. 15, 1982), Countervailing Duty Orders, 48 Fed. Reg. 51 (Jan. 3, 1983). The proceeding against Brazil was settled, 47 Fed. Reg. 39394 (Sept. 7, 1982), and the proceeding against South Africa (a non-signatory to the GATT Subsidies Code), though it involved countervailing against some export subsidies, did not involve the domestic subsidies at issue in the cases concerning steel from the Community. See *Certain Steel Products from South Africa*, Final Affirmative Countervailing Duty Determinations and Countervailing Duty Orders, 47 Fed. Reg. 39379 (Sept. 7, 1982).

[x] Ehrenhaft, "What the Antidumping and Countervailing Duty Provisions of the Trade Agreements Act [Can] [Will] [Should] Mean for U.S. Trade Policy," 11 Law & Pol'y Int'l Bus. 1361 at 1402. Mr. Ehrenhaft was Deputy Assistant Secretary of the Treasury and Special Counsel in 1977–79, with responsibility for administering the Trigger Price Mechanism for steel described in §§ 6.1–6.2, *supra*.

Is the tide—of lawyers, deadlines, determinations, confrontations—irreversible like that of Canute? Or would you expect that as the industrial world recovers from recession, trade disputes will shrink until they again fit into the legal framework devised to contain them?[y]

8.7—Final Notes and Questions: Why *Do* People Trade?

8.71 (a)—This book, like the international trade chapters of virtually all textbooks on economics, started with a discussion of comparative advantage, i.e., with the ratio of U.S. costs of steel (or auto) production relative to U.S. costs of other goods, compared with similar ratios for other countries. Looking back after detailed examination of the three great trading entities, the trade experience of two major industries, the principal rule-making institution for international trade, and two long conferences bringing all these elements together, does the doctrine of comparative advantage seem beside the point?

Is the real concern of nations, their businessmen, workers, political leaders and planners with something else? Or do you judge that comparative advantage—the doctrine of the worldwide market place—is still the fundamental principle, all the rest annoying compromises with political and social pressures?

(b) Consider the concepts with which we have been wrestling throughout the volume: most-favored-nation treatment, discrimination, and preferences; reciprocity and retaliation; market disruption and injury; dumping and subsidies. In every case, as we attempted to attach legal content—obligation and remedy—to these concepts, the comparison was between producers of the same (or like) product in an exporting and in an importing country. We asked not about the ratio of steel to soybeans in Japan vs. the ratio of steel to soybeans in the United States, but about the ratio—in cost, or price, or productivity—between steel in Japan and steel in the United States.

Is the inarticulate major premise that in a perfect market price movements even in a given product will reflect comparative advantage? If so, then the

---

[y] Not all conflicts with the Community over steel were settled. The specialty steel industry, § 5.56 *supra*, filed for relief shortly after the Ford-Carter relief program expired, under § 301 of the Trade Act, alleging unfair trade practices by producers in six countries. President Reagan, however, treated the case as an escape clause action, and the International Trade Commission ruled in favor of the petitioners. After sitting on the ITC's recommendations for two months, the President imposed a mixture of increased tariffs and import quotas. *Specialty Steel Import Relief Determination*, 48 Fed. Reg. 31177 (July 7, 1983), 19 Weekly Comp. Pres. Docs. 978, 979 (July 5, 1983). The European Community demanded compensation under GATT Article XIX(3), in the form of concessions on items of trade interest to it, including textiles, chemicals, machine tools, steel, and spirit beverages. The United States indicated that it was prepared to discuss compensation and preliminary consultations were held in Geneva, but as this volume went to press no agreement had been reached on the amount of compensation due.

task is to remove distortions to a perfect market, such as tariffs, quotas and "unfair" trade practices. Or does it turn out that the major premise is not acceptable, and therefore false, because people and countries are not prepared to tolerate the shifts in factors of production (labor, capital and physical resources) necessary to make the premise true?

(c) If, to take an easy case, neither the United States nor Japan would be prepared to accept a regime under which Japan produced all the steel and automobiles, and the United States produced all the food, then perhaps the comparison is a different one—the degree to which each country is prepared to accept (or the international community is prepared to require each country to accept) mobility of factors of production. Is this what, at bottom, is meant by reciprocity?

8.72—People, evidently, are less mobile, less able to adjust, than capital; labor-intensive industries, therefore, tend to be the "sensitive" ones—textiles for example, many agricultural products, shoes. But consider whether the experience with steel and automobiles suggests a somewhat different picture— toleration of foreign competition up to a point, to some percentage of domestic consumption, but not beyond. In the deals with foreign suppliers under Davignon II,[a] the European Community spelled the thought of a penetration margin out rather directly; so, not much more subtly, did the American Voluntary Restraint Agreements. The Trigger Price Mechanism was not framed in terms of a share of consumption or a margin of penetration; but looking at the circumstances in which the President's Task Force was mobilized, one might well conclude that a similar criterion lay behind the TPM. The automobile "settlements," both in the United States and Europe, as well as the accord on steel between the United States and the Community in October 1982, may also support this hypothesis.

8.73—Consider how the preceding thought might be reflected in legal rules, domestic and international.

(a) Looking first at domestic law for the United States, one proposal would be to repeal all of the various statutory remedies that we have explored in this volume concerning dumping, subsidies, unjustifiable trade practices, unfair import practices, escape clause relief etc.,[b] and replace them by a single

---

[a] See § 6.33 *supra*.

[b] "Unfair import practices" refers to § 337 of the Tariff Act of 1930, as amended, Documents Supplement p. DS-385. That section, not separately discussed in this volume, has been used primarily for complaints analogous to antitrust complaints, but was also utilized in at least one instance by the steel industry. For a discussion of this section, see Symposium: "Section 337 of the Trade Act of 1974," 8 Ga. J. Int'l. & Comp. L. 27 (1978). See also Note on International Trade Commission Activities 1977–78, § 337 of Tariff Act of 1930, 11 Law & Pol'y Int'l Bus. 1–10 (1979).

statute to provide relief from excessive imports. If the steel industry is in trouble and needs (deserves?) help, the argument would run, why go through all the various remedies with their differing procedures, cumbersome and internationally painful fact-finding, most of which pretend in some way to focus on the exporter, when the real concern is the displaced domestic manufacturer? Instead, under this proposal, an industry (or perhaps part of an industry) could apply for import relief upon a showing

(i) that it was being or was likely to be injured; and

(ii) that the cause of the injury was excessive imports.

Of course such a statute would still require elaboration—how is "industry" to be defined; how is injury measured; and what degree of causation would be sufficient to justify the relief.[c] One might for instance, build into such a statute some presumptions, e.g., if

(1) prices in the domestic industry were rising in the relevant time period, or

(2) the volume of sales by the domestic industry had risen in the relevant time period,

there could be no finding of injury, even if there had been a loss of market share. Alternatively, the presumption might be phrased so that it operated only if both (1) and (2) could be shown.[d]

Injury might be defined along the lines of section 201(b)(2) of the Trade Act of 1974,[e] i.e. with a mandate to examine utilization of productive facilities, employment and profits; causation might be defined so as to avoid attributing to imports domestic failure resulting from domestic causes, such as strikes, inadequate maintenance, perhaps wage settlements out of line with some norm. Indeed, one might build into such a statute a comparative cause standard, so that, for instance, if a slump in the domestic industry were attributable 40 per cent to increased imports and 60 per cent to reduced domestic demand, a proposed 12 per cent tariff surcharge could be set at 4.8 per cent.[f]

---

[c] Also, who would be making the decisions, and if it were some kind of board or commission, what if any role there would be for the President.

[d] Compare the similar questions raised under the Antidumping Act, § 4.42(d) *supra*.

[e] Documents Supplement p. DS–338.

[f] An interesting decision of the International Trade Commission illustrates how one might take different views of causation with or without fault by the exporter. *Perchloroethylene from Belgium, France, and Italy*, U.S.I.T.C. Pub. 969. April, 1979, 44 Fed. Reg. 22217 (May 4, 1979). Perchloroethylene, a liquid chemical used principally for dry cleaning, was produced by seven firms in the United States, five of which joined in bringing an antidump-

The New York Times, Sunday, March 6, 1983, p. E3

"Cheer up — we're still the highest paid unemployed workers
in the world."

But however the terms were defined, this "no fault" concept of import relief would focus on the injured party or industry, not on scrutiny of the exporting country or enterprise.

---

ing complaint. The Treasury Department found that imports from the three countries named had been coming in at less than home market prices, and forwarded the case to the Commission for determination of injury. The three-member majority derived a finding of injury attributable to the imports in question from the fact that the share of these imports had increased from 2 to 6.3 per cent of domestic consumption, at the same time as there was close to 10 per cent drop in domestic consumption and an overall price decline. The two dissenters pointed out that exports from the United States had more than doubled in the same period, and they explained the fall in prices by reference to inventory built up by a single firm that had made a major miscalculation of its customer's needs, and to entry by a new domestic producer.

Comparing this case with the automobile escape clause case, § 8.12, it seems unlikely that import relief would have been available on the basis of an injury standard only. The question raised by the proposal made in the text is whether the fact of sales at less than home market price (though not less than cost) should tip the scale toward protection and away from trade.

(b) Would you think in the long run a suggestion along these lines makes more sense than the grab-bag of standards and procedures now available in the United States, as in many other countries? Or would such a proposal be a negation of five years of struggle in the Tokyo Round, all looking to the development of "fair" trading rules?

(c) In considering suggestions along the above lines, would it be possible to distinguish among different industries or classes of industry?

(i) For example, both the United States and the European Community quite clearly want to maintain a steel industry, an automobile industry, and probably also a chemical industry. But perhaps they do not need to produce golf carts or perchloroethylene, and increased market share or even dominance for foreign producers of these items might not be matters of national concern.

(ii) Again, imports threatening a highly competitive, multi-unit industry may look rather different from imports threatening a tightly controlled monopoly or oligopoly.

Would you think introducing these additional factors makes the suggestion more attractive? Or would the necessary decision-making be beyond anyone's competence?

8.74 (a)—A recurring question throughout these materials, as throughout much recent discussion of import relief measures in advanced industrial countries, has been whether an industry granted special protection should be required to give something in return—a promise not to raise prices or wages, a promise to modernize, a plan to cure the inefficiences that required protection in the first place. None of the events described in this volume show such quid pro quo,[g] though of course a good deal of adjustment, modernization, and cost-cutting was undertaken by the steel and automobile industries in the United States and Europe. Should import relief be conditioned on express commitments to shape up, and express prohibitions on renewal?[h]

(b) Harald Malmgren, a prominent consultant on international trade and former Deputy U.S. Special Trade Representative, put the suggestion as follows:

If I'm the U.S. government and guys come in here and want protection for a period, I'm not going to say, "No way, no how." But I'll ask "If we give you three to five years, what are you going to do? Will

---

[g] The only exception is the government assistance to the Chrysler Corporation, § 8.12 at Ns. m-n *supra*, not an import relief measure.

[h] For a suggestion along these lines, linked to a national industrial policy, see Note: "Protecting Steel: Time for a New Approach," 96 Harv. L. Rev. 866 (1983).

you use that time to get back to speed? If not, why the hell do we want to penalize American consumers and users of your product?"

If the applicant says "Yes, with a little time, we'll do it," Malmgren would ask "Where are you going to raise the capital? What technology will you use?"

> Then I ask bankers and analysts, "Do you think they can do it, do they have good management?"[i]

Would you agree with this approach?

(c) Malmgren himself thinks his approach would work only if required by law. Would you favor amending section 201 of the Trade Act of 1974,[j] or perhaps section 202 or 203, to require review of the kind Malmgren suggests by the International Trade Commission, or the President, as a condition for import relief? Should such review be applicable to countervailing and antidumping duty cases as well? To measures that don't quite fit, such as Measures of Restraint, Trigger Price Mechanisms, or Arrangements like the 1982 deal on steel?

8.75—(a) It seems unlikely that any country would want to adopt proposals such as were outlined in § 8.73 or 8.74 on a unilateral basis. But to suggest that the proposal be made multilateral is to highlight where the Tokyo Round succeeded and where it failed. Unfair practices of importing states—using technical standards for protectionist purposes, manipulating customs valuation, red tape as a trade deterrent—were identified and (one may hope) reduced. Unfair practices of exporting states and enterprises—subsidies and dumping—were also identified and, as we saw, addressed in terms both of substance and of remedies. But fair trade—on the level at which it becomes intolerable and what may be done about it—was to have been addressed in the so-called Safeguards Code, precisely where the negotiations broke down.

Putting aside the question of selectivity (the stated reason for inability to come to agreement) the Code that didn't make it would have subjected all "safeguards" to international criteria, and perhaps to international scrutiny. Among the criteria were not only questions of serious injury and causality such as those discussed above, but statements

> Recognizing that safeguard measures should not be used as a substitute for structural adjustments to [changed conditions of fair competition]; [shifts in comparative advantage]

---

[i] See Guzzardi, "How to Foil Protectionism," Fortune, March 21, 1983, p. 76, at 80.

[j] Documents Supplement p. DS–338.

and

> Desiring that safeguard measures should not constitute an unjustifiable impediment to world trade.[k]

Whether the words mean (or meant) something like the proposal set forth in § 8.73 is hard to tell. Certainly they express the continuing tension between the perceived values and the perceived dangers inherent in international trade.

(b) In November 1982, shortly after the end of the confrontation over steel between the United States and the European Community, a GATT Ministerial Conference was held in Geneva, the first such conference since the Tokyo Conference of 1973.[l] By most accounts the conference was a failure, as the United States and the Community engaged in a public exchange of insults about agricultural subsidies.[m] The *Economist* described the meeting as a "mixture of French pettiness, American aggressiveness and Japanese passivity."[n] Still, in the end the ministers understood that they could not afford to break up in disagreement. Though they were not prepared to commit their countries to a standstill on further trade barriers, they did adopt, by consensus, a long Declaration,[o] pledging their countries

> to make determined efforts to ensure that trade policies and measures are consistent with GATT principles and rules and to resist protectionist pressures in the formulation and implementation of national trade policy and in proposing legislation. . . .[p]

How this pledge would be translated into action in the 1980's remained to be seen as this volume went to press. One illustration given in the Declaration itself was a renewed effort to develop an understanding on Safeguards.[q]

8.76—(a) In focusing on steel or automobiles or perchloroethylene[r] we

---

[k] See Preamble, Documents Supplement p. DS-691. The brackets appear in the published version.

[l] See § 7.12 at N. i.

[m] See, e.g., New York Times, Nov. 28, 1982, p. 1, col. 6; Nov. 29, p. 1, col. 6; Nov. 30, p. D1, col. 4.

[n] "Making Sense of the Mad GATTers Tea Party," *The Economist*, Dec. 4, 1982, p. 67.

[o] Documents Supplement p. DS-647.

[p] Ministerial Declaration of November 19, 1982, ¶ 7(i), Documents Supplement p. DS-648.

[q] *Id*. pp. DS-649-50. Note that the word "Code" is not used; note also that the issue of selectivity is not mentioned.

[r] N. f *supra*.

have still been looking at a single product or industry. But what if overall trade does not balance for a country over a sustained period? In the Hume/Smith/Ricardo/Mill model,[s] this was not supposed to happen, because as Xandia purchased more of Patria's products than vice versa, Patria's currency would rise and Xandia's would fall in value, until equilibrium in trade between the two countries was reestablished. In the more complicated world of the late Twentieth Century, we know things are not so simple and elegant, even with floating (or semi-floating) exchange rates. Japan, for example, has run massive export surpluses—worldwide and with the United States—since the late 1960's, under fixed exchange rates with an undervalued yen, under fixed rates with a revalued yen, and under floating rates.[t]

Is there—or ought there to be—some constraint on countries not to export, over time, more than they import? Should there be some right of countries to impose restraints so that over time they do not import more than they export? Is there, to put the question in the context of the preceding discussion, a standard of injury that goes beyond specific products and industries, beyond data on firms, employment, profits, and market share, and looks to countries as a whole? Should there be? Or is that the function of exchange rates, and out of bounds for those concerned with trade law?[u]

(b) A major premise of the GATT, as well as of the interpretations, practices, and supplementary codes, is that governments negotiate about the rules of international trade, leaving the outcome to market forces. Do the events recounted in the preceding pages suggest that this premise, too, is misleading or obsolescent, and that in fact governments do negotiate about outcomes?[v] If so, do we need quite different rules of the game? Or is it different strategies—"industrial policies" or economic infrastructures—that are needed, not more lawyers' work?[w]

---

[s] See § 1.3 *supra*, as well as Volume IV of this series, A. Lowenfeld, *The International Monetary System* § 1.3 (2d ed. 1984).

[t] See Table 3, Documents Supplement p. DS–760

[u] In the period 1981–82, the dollar rose in value against nearly all currencies—over 30 percent against the German mark and about 23 percent against the yen, for the most part because of high interest rates in the United States. The result of lower-cost imports and high interest rates was to sharply curb inflation in the United States, from 13.5 percent increase in the Consumer Price Index in 1980 to 10.4 percent in 1981 and 4.6 percent in 1982, while increasing the United States merchandise trade deficit to $42.7 billion for 1982.

[v] For an affirmative answer to this question, see Zysman and Cohen, "Double or Nothing: Open Trade and Competitive Industry", 61 Foreign Affairs 1113, 1116 (Summer 1983).

[w] The authors of the preceding article would argue for the latter view—hence the title "double or nothing"—i.e. promote competitiveness actively or an open trading system creating computer activity.

(c) Behold Governor John Connally, former Secretary of the Treasury and one-time aspirant to the American presidency, on how he would negotiate trade matters with the Japanese:

> I would simply say to them, "If you can't take our goods and services, you'd better be prepared to sit on the docks of Yokohama in your Toyotas and watch your own television sets and eat your own oranges, because they're not coming into this country."[x]

What response would you make, as citizen, economist, statesman, or lawyer?

---

[x] As broadcast on CBS Evening News, May 19, 1979.

DOCUMENTS SUPPLEMENT

Page

I. INTERNATIONAL AGREEMENTS

   1. The General Agreement on Tariffs and Trade (amended) .. DS-5

   2. The International Anti-Dumping Code (1967) DS-89

   3. The United Nations Charter (excerpts) DS-101

II. DOCUMENTS OF THE EUROPEAN COMMUNITY

   1. Treaty of Paris Establishing the European Coal and Steel Community (1951) (excerpts) DS-105

   2. Treaty of Rome Establishing the European Economic Community (1957) DS-133

III. JAPANESE STATUTORY MATERIALS

   1. Law Concerning Foreign Investment (1950) DS-229

   2. Foreign Exchange and Foreign Trade Control Law of 1949 (as amended through 1982) (excerpts) DS-231

IV. UNITED STATES STATUTORY MATERIALS

   1. Trade Agreements Act of 1934 .... DS-241

   2. Trade Agreements Extension Act of 1951, as amended through 1958 (excerpts) DS-243

   3. Trade Expansion Act of 1962 .... DS-250

   4. Trade Act of 1974 .... DS-296

   5. Antidumping Act of 1921, as amended through 1970 ...... DS-417

   6. Congressional Response to International Antidumping Code DS-426

   7. Antidumping Act of 1921 (1975–1979) DS-427

   8. U.S. Countervailing Duties Statute
      (a) 1930 version DS-439
      (b) (1975–1979) DS-440

   9. Provisions Concerning Judicial Review of Customs Decisions
      (a) 1930 version DS-444

Page

(b) (1975–1979)................................... DS-447

(c) As amended through 1982 .... DS-453

10. Trade Agreements Act of 1979 (excerpts)

(a) Brief Summary of Act DS-462

(b) Table of Contents DS-468

(c) Introductory Sections DS-473

(d) Title I—Countervailing and Antidumping Duties DS-477

(e) Title IX—Enforcement of United States Rights DS-530

(f) Title XI—Miscellaneous Provisions.............. DS-536

11. Reorganization of U.S. Trade Functions

(a) President Carter's Message to Congress (Sept. 25, 1979) DS-549

(b) Reorganization Plan No. 3 of 1979 .... DS-555

V. MISCELLANEOUS DOCUMENTS

1. GATT: Waiver Concerning European Coal and Steel Community (1952).. DS-561

2. Steel Import Quota Bill (1967) DS-567

3. Voluntary Restraint Agreements of 1972 .... DS-571

4. United States-Japan Orderly Marketing Agreement of Specialty Steel (June 1976) DS-578

5. Implementation of Trigger Price Mechanism by U.S. Treasury (January 9, 1978) DS-585

6. U.S. Treasury Revisions of Trigger Price Mechanism (July, 1978) DS-593

7. U.S. Treasury Determination of Sales at Less than Fair Value Carbon Steel Plate from Japan (January, 1978)......... DS-607

8. Joint Statement by Minister Ushiba and Ambassador Strauss (January 13, 1978) DS-614

9. Decision of OECD Council Establishing a Steel Committee DS-618

10. Japan: Measures of Restraint on Automobile Exports (May, 1981) DS-624

11. Proposed Legislation to Establish Domestic Content Requirement for Motor Vehicles Sold in the United States...... DS-626

12. U.S. ECSC Steel Arrangements 1982................... DS-633

(a) Arrangement Concerning Trade in Certain Steel Products DS-633

Page

(b) Agreed Minute on August-October 1982 Shipments.. DS-640

(c) Exchange of Letters—Davignon-Baldrige
Confirming Basic Arrangements DS-640

(d) Exchange of Letters—Davignon-Baldrige DS-642
Concerning Arrangement on Pipes and Tubes

(e) Letter sent to Chief Executive Officers of Major
American Steel Companies DS-644

(f) Letter—Baldrige to Davignon Concerning Authority to
Require Presentation of Special Export Certificate.. DS-645

13. GATT Ministerial Declaration (Nov. 29, 1982) DS-647

VI. SELECTED DOCUMENTS OF THE MULTILATERAL
TRADE NEGOTIATIONS

1. The Tokyo Declaration (Sept. 14, 1973) DS-660

2. Agreement on Subsidies and Countervailing Duties DS-663

3. Draft Agreement on Safeguards DS-691

4. Agreement on Reform of the GATT (Framework) DS-703

5. Agreements on Technical Barriers to Trade (Standards)
(excerpts) DS-719

6. Revised Antidumping Code DS-727

7. Legal Status of Tokyo Round Agreements DS-743

TABLES

I. WORLD TRADE AND ECONOMIC GROWTH

1. Shares of World Trade DS-745

2. World Trade: Exports and Imports 1965–82 .... DS-746

3. Trade Balances of Selected Areas and Countries. 1965–82 . DS-748

4. Changes in World Trade 1963–1982 .... DS-750

5. Growth Rates in Real Gross National Product, 1960–82 ... DS-752

II. THE THREE PRINCIPAL ACTORS

1. International Comparisons of Economic Performance, Japan and
Major Western Industrialized Countries DS-754

2. European Economic Community Impact on International Trade DS-756

3. Share of World Exports DS-757

4. Value and Share of Industrial Countries' Manufactured Exports DS-758

Page

III. SOME FIGURES ON STEEL

1. World Production of Crude Steel: 1870–1959 .... DS-759

2. World Crude Steel Production: 1967–1981 .... DS-760

3. Steel Production, Capacity, and Capacity Utilization: Japan, ECSC, and United States DS-764

4. United States Imports of Steel Mill Products, 1960–1982 .. DS-766

5. Weight and Percentage of Steel in U.S.-Built New Cars. 1975–85 .... DS-767

6. Steel Mill Products Subject to U.S.-E.C. Arrangement: Shipments, Imports and Consumption 1981–April 1983.. DS-768

7. Prices for Steel Products Subject to U.S.-E.C. Arrangement: October 1982–May 1983 .... DS-770

IV. SOME FIGURES ON AUTOMOBILES

1. The Automobile Industry 1970–80 .... DS-771

2. Estimated Hourly Compensation of Production Workers in Major Producing Countries 1975–80 .... DS-772

3. Geographical Breakdown of Japanese Exports of Passenger Cars 1970–80 .... DS-773

4. U.S. Imports of Passenger Automobiles 1980–82 .... DS-774

5. Sales of New Passenger Automobiles: Domestic and Imported 1980–82 .... DS-775

I. INTERNATIONAL AGREEMENTS

1. The General Agreement on Tariffs and Trade[1] (amended)

Concluded at Geneva, Switzerland, October 30, 1947; entered into force for the United States, January 1, 1948

The Governments of the COMMONWEALTH OF AUSTRALIA, the KINGDOM OF BELGIUM, the UNITED STATES OF BRAZIL, BURMA, CANADA, CEYLON, the REPUBLIC OF CHILE, the REPUBLIC OF CHINA, the REPUBLIC OF CUBA, the CZECHOSLOVAK REPUBLIC, the FRENCH REPUBLIC, INDIA, LEBANON, the GRAND-DUCHY OF LUXEMBURG, the KINGDOM OF THE NETHERLANDS, NEW ZEALAND, the KINGDOM OF NORWAY, PAKISTAN, SOUTHERN RHODESIA, SYRIA, the UNION OF SOUTH AFRICA, the UNITED KINGDOM OF GREAT BRITAIN AND NORTHERN IRELAND, and the UNITED STATES OF AMERICA:

Recognizing that their relations in the field of trade and economic endeavour should be conducted with a view to raising standards of living, ensuring full employment and a large and steadily growing volume of real income and effective demand, developing the full use of the resources of the world and expanding the production and exchange of goods.

Being desirous of contributing to these objectives by entering into reciprocal and mutually advantageous arrangements directed to the substantial reduction of tariffs and other barriers to trade and to the elimination of discriminatory treatment in international commerce,

Have through their Representatives agreed as follows:

---

[1] 61 Stat. part (5) and (6); TIAS 1700; 4 Bevans 639; 55–61 UNTS. The abbreviation "G.A.T.T." is used in the footnotes in referring to the General Agreement on Tariffs and Trade. The General Agreement is reproduced here as amended by various protocols, including those parts of the Protocol Amending the Preamble and Parts II and III and the Proces-Verbal of Rectification concerning that Protocol which became effective for two-thirds of the contracting parties, including the United States, on Oct. 7, 1957, and Feb. 15, 1961 (Article XIV).

Part IV became effective on June 17, 1969, 17 U.S.T. 1977, T.I.A.S. 6139; 572 UNTS 320. For a list of parties as of December 31, 1982, see p. DS-88 *infra*.

PART I

ARTICLE I

GENERAL MOST-FAVOURED-NATION TREATMENT

1. With respect to customs duties and charges of any kind imposed on or in connection with importation or exportation or imposed on the international transfer of payments for imports or exports, and with respect to the method of levying such duties and charges, and with respect to all rules and formalities in connection with importation and exportation, and with respect to all matters referred to in paragraphs 2 and 4 of Article III, any advantage, favour, privilege or immunity granted by any contracting party to any product originating in or destined for any other country shall be accorded immediately and unconditionally to the like product originating in or destined for the territories of all contracting parties.

2. The provisions of paragraph 1 of this Article shall not require the elimination of any preferences in respect of import duties or charges which do not exceed the levels provided for in paragraph 4 of this Article and which fall within the following descriptions:

(a) preferences in force exclusively between two or more of the territories listed in Annex A, subject to the conditions set forth therein;

(b) preferences in force exclusively between two or more territories which on July 1, 1939, were connected by common sovereignty or relations of protection or suzerainty and which are listed in Annexes B, C and D, subject to the conditions set forth therein;

(c) preferences in force exclusively between the United States of America and the Republic of Cuba;

(d) preferences in force exclusively between neighbouring countries listed in Annexes E and F.

3.[4] The provisions of paragraph 1 shall not apply to preferences between the countries formerly a part of the Ottoman Empire and detached from it on July 24, 1923, provided such preferences are approved under paragraph 5 of Article XXV,[5] which shall be applied in this respect in the light of paragraph 1 of Article XXIX.

---

[4] Added by Part A of Protocol Modifying Part I and Article XXIX of the G.A.T.T. (3 U.S.T. 5356).

[5] Pending the entry into force of the Protocol Amending Part I and Articles

4. The margin of preference on any product in respect of which a preference is permitted under paragraph 2 of this Article but is not specifically set forth as a maximum margin of preference in the appropriate Schedule annexed to this Agreement shall not exceed:

(a) in respect of duties or charges on any product described in such Schedule, the difference between the most-favoured-nation and preferential rates provided for therein; if no preferential rate is provided for, the preferential rate shall for the purposes of this paragraph be taken to be that in force on April 10, 1947, and, if no most-favoured-nation rate is provided for, the margin shall not exceed the difference between the most-favoured-nation and preferential rates existing on April 10, 1947;

(b) in respect of duties or charges on any product not described in the appropriate Schedule, the difference between the most-favoured-nation and preferential rates existing on April 10, 1947.

In the case of the contracting parties named in Annex G, the date of April 10, 1947, referred to in sub-paragraphs (a) and (b) of this paragraph shall be replaced by the respective dates set forth in that Annex.

ARTICLE II

Schedules of Concessions

1. (a) Each contracting party shall accord to the commerce of the other contracting parties treatment no less favourable than that provided for in the appropriate Part of the appropriate Schedule annexed to this Agreement.

(b) The products described in Part I of the Schedule relating to any contracting party, which are the products of territories of other contracting parties, shall, on their importation into the territory to which the Schedule relates, and subject to the terms, conditions or qualifications set forth in that Schedule, be exempt from ordinary customs duties in excess of those set forth and provided for therein. Such products shall also be exempt from all other duties or charges of any kind imposed on or in connection with importation in excess of those imposed on the date of this Agreement or those directly and mandatorily required to be imposed thereafter by legislation in force in the importing territory on that date.

XXIX and XXX, this reference to Article XXV actually reads "sub-paragraph 5(a) of Article XXV," although paragraph 5 is no longer divided into sub-paragraphs (a), (b), etc., as was formerly the case. The present text of paragraph 5 was formerly sub-paragraph 5(a) of Article XXV.

(c) The products described in Part II of the Schedule relating to any contracting party which are the products of territories entitled under Article I to receive preferential treatment upon importation into the territory to which the Schedule relates shall, on their importation into such territory, and subject to the terms, conditions or qualifications set forth in that Schedule, be exempt from ordinary customs duties in excess of those set forth and provided for in Part II of that Schedule. Such products shall also be exempt from all other duties or charges of any kind imposed on or in connection with importation in excess of those imposed on the date of this Agreement or those directly and mandatorily required to be imposed thereafter by legislation in force in the importing territory on that date. Nothing in this Article shall prevent any contracting party from maintaining its requirements existing on the date of this Agreement as to the eligibility of goods for entry at preferential rates of duty.

2. Nothing in this Article shall prevent any contracting party from imposing at any time on the importation of any product;

(a) a charge equivalent to an internal tax imposed consistently with the provisions of paragraph 2 of Article III in respect of the like domestic product or in respect of an article from which the imported product has been manufactured or produced in whole or in part;

(b) any anti-dumping or countervailing duty applied consistently with the provisions of Article VI;

(c) fees or other charges commensurate with the cost of services rendered.

3. No contracting party shall alter its method of determining dutiable value or of converting currencies so as to impair the value of any of the concessions provided for in the appropriate Schedule annexed to this Agreement.

4. If any contracting party establishes, maintains or authorizes, formally or in effect, a monopoly of the importation of any product described in the appropriate Schedule annexed to this Agreement, such monopoly shall not, except as provided for in that Schedule or as otherwise agreed between the parties which initially negotiated the concession, operate so as to afford protection on the average in excess of the amount of protection provided for in that Schedule. The provisions of this paragraph shall not limit the use by contracting parties of any form of assistance to domestic producers permitted by other provisions of this Agreement.

5. If any contracting party considers that a product is not receiving from

another contracting party the treatment which the first contracting party believes to have been contemplated by a concession provided for in the appropriate Schedule annexed to this Agreement, it shall bring the matter directly to the attention of the other contracting party. If the latter agrees that the treatment contemplated was that claimed by the first contracting party, but declares that such treatment cannot be accorded because a court or other proper authority has ruled to the effect that the product involved cannot be classified under the tariff laws of such contracting party so as to permit the treatment contemplated in this Agreement, the two contracting parties, together with any other contracting parties substantially interested, shall enter promptly into further negotiations with a view to a compensatory adjustment of the matter.

6. (a) The specific duties and charges included in the Schedules relating to the contracting parties members of the International Monetary Fund, and margins of preference in specific duties and charges maintained by such contracting parties, are expressed in the appropriate currency at the par value accepted or provisionally recognized by the Fund at the date of this Agreement. Accordingly, in case this par value is reduced consistently with the Articles of Agreement of the International Monetary Fund by more than twenty per centum, such specific duties and charges and margins of preference may be adjusted to take account of such reduction; *Provided*, That the contracting parties (i.e., the contracting parties acting jointly as provided for in Article XXV) concur that such adjustments will not impair the value of the concessions provided for in the appropriate Schedule or elsewhere in this Agreement, due account being taken of all factors which may influence the need for, or urgency of, such adjustments.

(b) Similar provisions shall apply to any contracting party not a member of the Fund, as from the date on which such contracting party becomes a member of the Fund or enters into a special exchange agreement in pursuance of Article XV.

7. The Schedules annexed to this Agreement are hereby made an integral part of Part I of this Agreement.

PART II

ARTICLE III

NATIONAL TREATMENT ON INTERNAL TAXATION AND REGULATION [6]

1. The contracting parties recognize that internal taxes and other internal

---

[6] As amended and restated by the Protocol Modifying Part II and Article XXVI of G.A.T.T. (62 Stat. 3679).

charges, and laws, regulations and requirements affecting the internal sale, offering for sale, purchase, transportation, distribution or use of products, and internal quantitative regulations requiring the mixture, processing or use of products in specified amounts or proportions, should not be applied to imported or domestic products so as to afford protection to domestic production.

2. The products of the territory of any contracting party imported into the territory of any other contracting party shall not be subject, directly or indirectly, to internal taxes or other internal charges of any kind in excess of those applied, directly or indirectly, to like domestic products. Moreover, no contracting party shall otherwise apply internal taxes or other internal charges to imported or domestic products in a manner contrary to the principles set forth in paragraph 1.

3. With respect to any existing tax which is inconsistent with the provisions of paragraph 2, but which is specifically authorized under a trade agreement, in force on April 10, 1947, in which the import duty on the taxed product is bound against increase, the contracting party imposing the tax shall be free to postpone the application of the provisions of paragraph 2 to such tax until such time as it can obtain release from the obligations of such trade agreement in order to permit the increase of such duty to the extent necessary to compensate for the elimination of the protective element of the tax.

4. The products of the territory of any contracting party imported into the territory of any other contracting party shall be accorded treatment no less favourable than that accorded to like products of national origin in respect of all laws, regulations and requirements affecting their internal sale, offering for sale, purchase, transportation, distribution or use. The provisions of this paragraph shall not prevent the application of differential internal transportation charges which are based exclusively on the economic operation of the means of transport and not on the nationality of the product.

5. No contracting party shall establish or maintain any internal quantitative regulation relating to the mixture, processing or use of products in specified amounts or proportions which requires, directly or indirectly, that any specified amount or proportion of any product which is the subject of the regulation must be supplied from domestic sources. Moreover, no contracting party shall otherwise apply internal quantitative regulations in a manner contrary to the principles set forth in paragraph 1.

6. The provisions of paragraph 5 shall not apply to any internal quantitative regulation in force in the territory of any contracting party on July 1,

1939, April 10, 1947, or March 24, 1948, at the option of that contracting party; *Provided*, That any such regulation which is contrary to the provisions of paragraph 5 shall not be modified to the detriment of imports and shall be treated as a customs duty for the purpose of negotiation.

7. No internal quantitative regulation relating to the mixture, processing or use of products in specified amounts or proportions shall be applied in such a manner as to allocate any such amount or proportion among external sources of supply.

8. (a) The provisions of this Article shall not apply to laws, regulations or requirements governing the procurement by governmental agencies of products purchased for governmental purposes and not with a view to commercial resale or with a view to use in the production of goods for commercial sale.

(b) The provisions of this Article shall not prevent the payment of subsidies exclusively to domestic producers, including payments to domestic producers derived from the proceeds of internal taxes or charges applied consistently with the provisions of this Article and subsidies effected through governmental purchases of domestic products.

9. The contracting parties recognize that internal maximum price control measures, even though conforming to the other provisions of this Article, can have effects prejudicial to the interests of contracting parties supplying imported products. Accordingly, contracting parties applying such measures shall take account of the interests of exporting contracting parties with a view to avoiding to the fullest practicable extent such prejudicial effects.

10. The provisions of this Article shall not prevent any contracting party from establishing or maintaining internal quantitative regulations relating to exposed cinematograph films and meeting the requirements of Article IV.

ARTICLE IV

SPECIAL PROVISIONS RELATING TO CINEMATOGRAPH FILMS

If any contracting party establishes or maintains internal quantitative regulations relating to exposed cinematograph films, such regulations shall take the form of screen quotas which shall conform to the following requirements:

(a) Screen quotas may require the exhibition of cinematograph films of national origin during a specified minimum proportion of the total screen time actually utilized, over a specified period of not less than one year, in the commercial exhibition of all films of whatever origin, and shall be computed on the basis of screen time per theatre per year or the equivalent thereof;

(b) With the exception of screen time reserved for films of national origin under a screen quota, screen time including that released by administrative action from screen time reserved for films of national origin, shall not be allocated formally or in effect among sources of supply;

(c) Notwithstanding the provisions of sub-paragraph (b) of this Article, any contracting party may maintain screen quotas conforming to the requirements of sub-paragraph (a) of this Article which reserve a minimum proportion of screen time for films of a specified origin other than that of the contracting party imposing such screen quotas; *Provided*, That no such minimum proportion of screen time shall be increased above the level in effect on April 10, 1947;

(d) Screen quotas shall be subject to negotiation for their limitation, liberalization or elimination.

ARTICLE V

FREEDOM OF TRANSIT

1. Goods (including baggage), and also vessels and other means of transport, shall be deemed to be in transit across the territory of a contracting party when the passage across such territory, with or without transshipment, warehousing, breaking bulk, or change in the mode of transport, is only a portion of a complete journey beginning and terminating beyond the frontier of the contracting party across whose territory the traffic passes. Traffic of this nature is termed in this Article "traffic in transit".

2. There shall be freedom of transit through the territory of each contracting party, via the routes most convenient for international transit, for traffic in transit to or from the territory of other contracting parties. No distinction shall be made which is based on the flag of vessels, the place of origin, departure, entry, exit or destination, or on any circumstances relating to the ownership of goods, of vessels or of other means of transport.

3. Any contracting party may require that traffic in transit through its territory be entered at the proper custom house, but, except in cases of failure to comply with applicable customs laws and regulations, such traffic coming from or going to the territory of other contracting parties shall not be subject to any unnecessary delays or restrictions and shall be exempt from

customs duties and from all transit duties or other charges imposed in respect of transit, except charges for transportation or those commensurate with administrative expenses entailed by transit or with the cost of services rendered.

4. All charges and regulations imposed by contracting parties on traffic in transit to or from the territories of other contracting parties shall be reasonable, having regard to the conditions of the traffic.

5. With respect to all charges, regulations and formalities in connection with transit, each contracting party shall accord to traffic in transit to or from the territory of any other contracting party treatment no less favourable than the treatment accorded to traffic in transit to or from any third country.

6. Each contracting party shall accord to products which have been in transit through the territory of any other contracting party treatment no less favourable than that which would have been accorded to such products had they been transported from their place of origin to their destination without going through the territory of such other contracting party. Any contracting party shall, however, be free to maintain its requirements of direct consignment existing on the date of this Agreement, in respect of any goods in regard to which such direct consignment is a requisite condition of eligibility for entry of the goods at preferential rates of duty or has relation to the contracting party's prescribed method of valuation for duty purposes.

7. The provisions of this Article shall not apply to the operation of aircraft in transit, but shall apply to air transit of goods (including baggage).

ARTICLE VI

ANTI-DUMPING AND COUNTERVAILING DUTIES [7]

1. The contracting parties recognize that dumping, by which products of one country are introduced into the commerce of another country at less than the normal value of the products, is to be condemned if it causes or threatens material injury to an established industry in the territory of a contracting party or materially retards the establishment of a domestic industry. For the purposes of this Article, a product is to be considered as being introduced into the commerce of an importing country at less than its normal value, if the price of the product exported from one country to another.

---

[7] As amended and restated by Protocol Modifying Part III and Article XXVI of the G.A.T.T. (62 Stat. 3679).

(a) is less than the comparable price, in the ordinary course of trade, for the like product when destined for consumption in the exporting country, or,

(b) in the absence of such domestic price, is less than either

(i) the highest comparable price for the like product for export to any third country in the ordinary course of trade, or

(ii) the cost of production of the product in the country of origin plus a reasonable addition for selling cost and profit.

Due allowance shall be made in each case for differences in conditions and terms of sale, for differences in taxation, and for other differences affecting price comparability.

2. In order to offset or prevent dumping, a contracting party may levy on any dumped product an anti-dumping duty not greater in amount than the margin of dumping in respect of such product. For the purposes of this Article, the margin of dumping is the price difference determined in accordance with the provisions of paragraph 1.

3. No countervailing duty shall be levied on any product of the territory of any contracting party imported into the territory of another contracting party in excess of an amount equal to the estimated bounty or subsidy determined to have been granted, directly or indirectly, on the manufacture, production or export of such product in the country of origin or exportation, including any special subsidy to the transportation of a particular product. The term "countervailing duty" shall be understood to mean a special duty levied for the purpose of offsetting any bounty or subsidy bestowed, directly or indirectly, upon the manufacture, production or export of any merchandise.

4. No product of the territory or any contracting party imported into the territory of any other contracting party shall be subject to anti-dumping or countervailing duty by reason of the exemption of such product from duties or taxes borne by the like product when destined for consumption in the country of origin or exportation, or by reason of the refund of such duties or taxes.

5. No product of the territory of any contracting party imported into the territory of any other contracting party shall be subject to both anti-dumping and countervailing duties to compensate for the same situation of dumping or export subsidization.

6.[8] (a) No contracting party shall levy any anti-dumping or countervailing duty on the importation of any product of the territory of another contracting party unless it determines that the effect of the dumping or subsidization, as the case may be, in such as to cause or threaten material injury to an established domestic industry, or is such as to retard materially the establishment of a domestic industry.

(b) The contracting parties may waive the requirement of sub-paragraph (a) of this paragraph so as to permit a contracting party to levy an anti-dumping or countervailing duty on the importation of any product for the purpose of offsetting dumping or subsidization which causes or threatens material injury to an industry in the territory of another contracting party exporting the product concerned to the territory of the importing contracting party. The contracting parties shall waive the requirements of sub-paragraph (a) of this paragraph, so as to permit the levying of a countervailing duty, in cases in which they find that a subsidy is causing or threatening material injury to an industry in the territory of another contracting party exporting the product concerned to the territory of the importing contracting party.

(c) In exceptional circumstances, however, where delay might cause damage which would be difficult to repair, a contracting party may levy a countervailing duty for the purpose referred to in subparagraph (b) of this paragraph without the prior approval of the contracting parties; *Provided*, That such action shall be reported immediately to the contracting parties and that the countervailing duty shall be withdrawn promptly if the contracting parties disapprove.

7. A system for the stabilization of the domestic price or of the return to domestic producers of a primary commodity, independently of the movements of export prices, which results at times in the sale of the commodity for export at a price lower than the comparable price charged for the like commodity to buyers in the domestic market, shall be presumed not to result in material injury within the meaning of paragraph 6 if it is determined by consultation among the contracting parties substantially interested in the commodity concerned that:

(a) the system has also resulted in the sale of the commodity for export at a price higher than the comparable price charged for the like commodity to buyers in the domestic market, and

(b) the system is so operated, either because of the effective regulation of production, or otherwise, as not to stimulate exports unduly or otherwise seriously prejudice the interests of other contracting parties.

---

[8] As amended and restated by Part D of the Protocol Amending the Preamble and Parts II and III of the G.A.T.T. (8 UST 1769).

ARTICLE VII

VALUATION FOR CUSTOMS PURPOSES [9]

1. The contracting parties recognize the validity of the general principles of valuation set forth in the following paragraphs of this Article, and they undertake to give effect to such principles, in respect of all products subject to duties or other charges or restrictions on importation and exportation based upon or regulated in any manner by value. Moreover, they shall, upon a request by another contracting party review the operation of any of their laws or regulations relating to value for customs purposes in the light of these principles. The contracting parties may request from contracting parties reports on steps taken by them in pursuance of the provisions of this Article.

2. (a) The value for customs purposes of imported merchandise should be based on the actual value of the imported merchandise on which duty is assessed, or of like merchandise, and should not be based on the value of merchandise of national origin or on arbitrary or fictitious values.

(b) "Actual value" should be the price at which, at a time and place determined by the legislation of the country of importation, such or like merchandise is sold or offered for sale in the ordinary course of trade under fully competitive conditions. To the extent to which the price of such or like merchandise is governed by the quantity in a particular transaction, the price to be considered should uniformly be related to either (i) comparable quantities, or (ii) quantities not less favourable to importers than those in which the greater volume of the merchandise is sold in the trade between the countries of exportation and importation.

(c) When the actual value is not ascertainable in accordance with sub-paragraph (b) of this paragraph, the value for customs purposes should be based on the nearest ascertainable equivalent of such value.

3. The value for customs purposes of any imported product should not include the amount of any internal tax, applicable within the country of origin or export, from which the imported product has been exempted or has been or will be relieved by means of refund.

4. (a) Except as otherwise provided for in this paragraph, where it is necessary for the purposes of paragraph 2 of this Article for a contracting party to convert into its own currency a price expressed in the currency of

---

[9] Paragraphs 1 and 2 as amended and restated by Part I of the Protocol Amending the Preamble and Parts I and II of the G.A.T.T. (8 UST 1770).

another country, the conversion rate of exchange to be used shall be based for each currency involved, on the par value as established pursuant to the Articles of Agreement of the International Monetary Fund or on the rate of exchange recognized by the Fund, or on the par value established in accordance with a special exchange agreement entered into pursuant to Article XV of this Agreement.

(b) Where no such established par value and no such recognized rate of exchange exist, the conversion rate shall reflect effectively the current value of such currency in commercial transactions.

(c) The contracting parties, in agreement with the International Monetary Fund, shall formulate rules governing the conversion by contracting parties of any foreign currency in respect of which multiple rates of exchange are maintained consistently with the Articles of Agreement of the International Monetary Fund. Any contracting party may apply such rules in respect of such foreign currencies for the purposes of paragraph 2 of this Article as an alternative to the use of par values. Until such rules are adopted by the contracting parties, any contracting party may employ, in respect of any such foreign currency, rules of conversion for the purposes of paragraph 2 of this Article which are designed to reflect effectively the value of such foreign currency in commercial transactions.

(d) Nothing in this paragraph shall be construed to require any contracting party to alter the method of converting currencies for customs purposes which is applicable in its territory on the date of this Agreement, if such alteration would have the effect of increasing generally the amounts of duty payable.

5. The bases and methods for determining the value of products subject to duties or other charges or restrictions based upon or regulated in any manner by value should be stable and should be given sufficient publicity to enable traders to estimate, with a reasonable degree of certainty, the value for customs purposes.

ARTICLE VIII

FEES AND FORMALITIES CONNECTED WITH IMPORTATION AND EXPORTATION [10]

1. (a) All fees and charges of whatever character (other than import and export duties and other than taxes within the purview of Article III) imposed

---

[10] Paragraphs 1 and 2 as amended by Part F of the Protocol Amending the Preamble and Parts II and III of the G.A.T.T. (8 UST 1770).

by contracting parties on or in connection with importation or exportation shall be limited in amount to the approximate cost of services rendered and shall not represent an indirect protection to domestic products or a taxation of imports or exports for fiscal purposes.

(b) The contracting parties recognize the need for reducing the number and diversity of fees and charges referred to in sub-paragraph (a).

(c) The contracting parties also recognize the need for minimizing the incidence and complexity of import and export formalities and for decreasing and simplifying import and export documentation requirements.

2. A contracting party shall, upon request by another contracting party or by the contracting parties, review the operation of its laws and regulations in the light of the provisions of this Article.

3. No contracting party shall impose substantial penalties for minor breaches of customs regulations or procedural requirements. In particular, no penalty in respect of any omission or mistake in customs documentation which is easily rectifiable and obviously made without fraudulent intent or gross negligence shall be greater than necessary to serve merely as a warning.

4. The provisions of this Article shall extend to fees, charges, formalities and requirements imposed by governmental authorities in connection with importation and exportation, including those relating to:

(a) consular transactions, such as consular invoices and certificates;

(b) quantitative restrictions;

(c) licensing;

(d) exchange control;

(e) statistical services;

(f) documents, documentation and certification;

(g) analysis and inspection; and

(h) quarantine, sanitation and fumigation.

ARTICLE IX

MARKS OF ORIGIN

1. Each contracting party shall accord to the products of the territories of other contracting parties treatment with regard to marking requirements

no less favourable than the treatment accorded to like products of any third country.

2.[11] The contracting parties recognize that, in adopting and enforcing laws and regulations relating to marks of origin, the difficulties and inconveniences which such measures may cause to the commerce and industry of exporting countries should be reduced to a minimum, due regard being had to the necessity of protecting consumers against fraudulent or misleading indications.

3. Whenever it is administratively practicable to do so, contracting parties should permit required marks of origin to be affixed at the time of importation.

4. The laws and regulations of contracting parties relating to the marking of imported products shall be such as to permit compliance without seriously damaging the products, or materially reducing their value, or unreasonably increasing their cost.

5. As a general rule, no special duty or penalty should be imposed by any contracting party for failure to comply with marking requirements prior to importation unless corrective marking is unreasonably delayed or deceptive marks have been affixed or the required marking has been intentionally omitted.

6. The contracting parties shall co-operate with each other with a view to preventing the use of trade names in such manner as to misrepresent the true origin of a product, to the detriment of such distinctive regional or geographical names of products of the territory of a contracting party as are protected by its legislation. Each contracting party shall accord full and sympathetic consideration to such requests or representations as may be made by any other contracting party regarding the application of the undertaking set forth in the preceding sentence to names of products which have been communicated to it by the other contracting party.

ARTICLE X

PUBLICATION AND ADMINISTRATION OF TRADE REGULATIONS

1. Laws, regulations, judicial decisions and administrative rulings of general application, made effective by any contracting party, pertaining to the classification or the valuation of products for customs purposes, or to rates of duty, taxes or other charges, or to requirements, restrictions or prohibitions on imports or exports or on the transfer of payments therefor, or affecting

---

[11] Paragraph 2 inserted by Part G of the Protocol Amending the Preamble and Parts II and III of the G.A.T.T. (8 UST 1771).

their sale, distribution, transportation, insurance, warehousing, inspection, exhibition processing, mixing or other use, shall be published promptly in such a manner as to enable governments and traders to become acquainted with them. Agreements affecting international trade policy which are in force between the government or a governmental agency of any contracting party and the government or governmental agency of any other contracting party shall also be published. The provisions of this paragraph shall not require any contracting party to disclose confidential information which would impede law enforcement or otherwise be contrary to the public interest or would prejudice the legitimate commercial interests of particular enterprises, public or private.

2. No measure of general application taken by any contracting party effecting an advance in a rate of duty or other charge on imports under an established and uniform practice, or imposing a new or more burdensome requirement, restriction or prohibition on imports, or on the transfer of payments therefor, shall be enforced before such measure has been officially published.

3. (a) Each contracting party shall administer in a uniform, impartial and reasonable manner all its laws, regulations, decisions and rulings of the kind described in paragraph 1 of this Article.

(b) Each contracting party shall maintain, or institute as soon as practicable, judicial, arbitral or administrative tribunals or procedures for the purpose, *inter alia*, of the prompt review and correction of administrative action relating to customs matters. Such tribunals or procedures shall be independent of the agencies entrusted with administrative enforcement and their decisions shall be implemented by, and shall govern the practice of, such agencies unless an appeal is lodged with a court or tribunal of superior jurisdiction within the time prescribed for appeals to be lodged by importers; *Provided*, That the central administration of such agency may take steps to obtain a review of the matter in another proceeding if there is good cause to believe that the decision is inconsistent with established principles of law or the actual facts.

(c) The provisions of sub-paragraph (b) of this paragraph, shall not require the elimination or substitution of procedures in force in the territory of a contracting party on the date of this Agreement which in fact provide for an objective and impartial review of administrative action even though such procedures are not fully or formally independent of the agencies entrusted with administrative enforcement. Any contracting party employing such procedures shall, upon request, furnish the contracting parties with full information thereon in order that they may determine whether such procedures conform to the requirements of this sub-paragraph.

ARTICLE XI

GENERAL ELIMINATION OF QUANTITATIVE RESTRICTIONS

1. No prohibitions or restrictions other than duties, taxes or other charges, whether made effective through quotas, import or export licenses or other measures, shall be instituted or maintained by any contracting party on the importation of any product of the territory of any other contracting party or on the exportation or sale for export of any product destined for the territory of any other contracting party.

2. The provisions of paragraph 1 of this Article shall not extend to the following:

(a) Export prohibitions or restrictions temporarily applied to prevent or relieve critical shortages of foodstuffs or other products essential to the exporting contracting party;

(b) Import and export prohibitions or restrictions necessary to the application of standards or regulations for the classification, grading or marketing of commodities in international trade;

(c) Import restrictions on any agricultural or fisheries product, imported in any form, necessary to the enforcement of governmental measures which operate:

(i) to restrict the quantities of the like domestic product permitted to be marketed or produced, or, if there is no substantial domestic production of the like product, of a domestic product for which the imported product can be directly substituted; or

(ii) to remove a temporary surplus of the like domestic product, or, if there is no substantial domestic production of the like product, of a domestic product for which the imported product can be directly substituted, by making the surplus available to certain groups of domestic consumers free of charge or at prices below the current market level; or

(iii) to restrict the quantities permitted to be produced of any animal product the production of which is directly dependent, wholly or mainly, on the imported commodity, if the domestic production of that commodity is relatively negligible.

Any contracting party applying restrictions on the importation of any product pursuant to sub-paragraph (c) of this paragraph shall give public notice of the total quantity or value of the product permitted to be imported during a specified future period and of any change in such quantity or value. Moreover, any restrictions applied under (i) above shall not be such as will reduce the total of imports relative to the total of domestic production, as compared with the proportion which might reasonably be expected to rule between the two in the absence of restrictions. In determining this proportion, the contracting party shall pay due regard to the proportion prevailing during a previous representative period and to any special factors which may have affected or may be affecting the trade in the product concerned.

ARTICLE XII

RESTRICTIONS TO SAFEGUARD THE BALANCE OF PAYMENTS[12]

1. Notwithstanding the provisions of paragraph 1 of Article XI, any contracting party, in order to safeguard its external financial position and its balance of payments, may restrict the quantity or value of merchandise permitted to be imported, subject to the provisions of the following paragraphs of this Article.

2. (a) Import restrictions instituted, maintained or intensified by a contracting party under this Article shall not exceed those necessary:

(i) to forestall the imminent threat of, or to stop, a serious decline in its monetary reserves, or

(ii) in the case of a contracting party with very low monetary reserves, to achieve a reasonable rate of increase in its reserves.

Due regard shall be paid in either case to any special factors which may be affecting the reserves of such contracting party or its need for reserves, including, where special external credits or other resources are available to it, the need to provide for the appropriate use of such credits or resources.

(b) Contracting parties applying restrictions under sub-paragraph (a) of this paragraph shall progressively relax them as such conditions improve, maintaining them only to the extent that the conditions specified in that sub-paragraph still justify their application. They shall eliminate the restrictions when conditions would no longer justify their institution or maintenance under that sub-paragraph.

---

[12] As amended and restated by Part I of the Protocol Amending the Preamble and Parts II and III of the G.A.T.T. (8 UST 1771).

3. (a) Contracting parties undertake, in carrying out their domestic policies, to pay due regard to the need for maintaining or restoring equilibrium in their balance of payments on a sound and lasting basis and to the desirability of avoiding an uneconomic employment of productive resources. They recognize that in order to achieve these ends, it is desirable so far as possible to adopt measures which expand rather than contract international trade.

(b) Contracting parties applying restrictions under this Article may determine the incidence of the restrictions on imports of different products or classes of products in such a way as to give priority to the importation of those products which are more essential.

(c) Contracting parties applying restrictions under this Article undertake:

(i) to avoid unnecessary damage to the commercial or economic interests of any other contracting party;

(ii) not to apply restrictions so as to prevent unreasonably the importation of any description of goods in minimum commercial quantities the exclusion of which would impair regular channels of trade; and

(iii) not to apply restrictions which would prevent the importation of commercial samples or prevent compliance with patent, trade mark, copyright, or similar procedures.

(d) The contracting parties recognize that, as a result of domestic policies directed towards the achievement and maintenance of full and productive employment or towards the development of economic resources, a contracting party may experience a high level of demand for imports involving a threat to its monetary reserves of the sort referred to in paragraph 2(a) of this Article. Accordingly, a contracting party otherwise complying with the provisions of this Article shall not be required to withdraw or modify restrictions on the ground that a change in those policies would render unnecessary restrictions which it is applying under this Article.

4. (a) Any contracting party applying new restrictions or raising the general level of its existing restrictions by a substantial intensification of the measures applied under this Article shall immediately after instituting or intensifying such restrictions (or, in circumstances in which prior consultation is practicable, before doing so) consult with the contracting parties as to the nature of its balance of payments difficulties, alternative corrective measures which may be available, and the possible effect of the restrictions on the economies of other contracting parties.

(b) On a date to be determined by them, the contracting parties shall review all restrictions still applied under this Article on that date. Beginning one year after that date, contracting parties applying import restrictions under this Article shall enter into consultations of the type provided for in sub-paragraph (a) of this paragraph with the contracting parties annually.

(c)(i) If, in the course of consultations with a contracting party under sub-paragraph (a) or (b) above, the contracting parties find that the restrictions are not consistent with the provisions of this Article or with those of Article XIII (subject to the provisions of Article XIV), they shall indicate the nature of the inconsistency and may advise that the restrictions be suitably modified.

(ii) If, however, as a result of the consultations, the contracting parties determine that the restrictions are being applied in a manner involving an inconsistency of a serious nature with the provisions of this Article or with those of Article XIII (subject to the provisions of Article XIV) and that damage to the trade of any contracting party is caused or threatened thereby, they shall so inform the contracting party applying the restrictions and shall make appropriate recommendations for securing conformity with such provisions within a specified period of time. If such contracting party does not comply with these recommendations within the specified period, the contracting parties may release any contracting party the trade of which is adversely affected by the restrictions from such obligations under this Agreement towards the contracting party applying the restrictions as they determine to be appropriate in the circumstances.

(d) The contracting parties shall invite any contracting party which is applying restrictions under this Article to enter into consultations with them at the request of any contracting party which can establish a *prima facie* case that the restrictions are inconsistent with the provisions of this Article or with those of Article XIII (subject to the provisions of Article XIV) and that its trade is adversely affected thereby. However, no such invitation shall be issued unless the contracting parties have ascertained that direct discussions between the contracting parties concerned have not been successful. If, as a result of the consultations with the contracting parties, no agreement is reached and they determine that the restrictions are being applied inconsistently with such provisions, and that damage to the trade of the contracting party initiating the procedure is caused or threatened thereby, they shall recommend the withdrawal or modification of the restrictions. If the restrictions are not withdrawn or modified within such time as the contracting parties may prescribe, they may release the contracting party initiating the procedure from such obligations under this Agreement towards the contracting party applying the restrictions as they determine to be appropriate in the circumstances.

(e) In proceeding under this paragraph, the contracting parties shall have due regard to any special external factors adversely affecting the export trade of the contracting party applying restrictions.

(f) Determinations under this paragraph shall be rendered expeditiously and, if possible, within sixty days of the initiation of the consultations.

5. If there is a persistent and widespread application of import restrictions under this Article, indicating the existence of a general disequilibrium which is restricting international trade, the contracting parties shall initiate discussions to consider whether other measures might be taken, either by those contracting parties the balances of payments of which are under pressure or by those the balances of payments of which are tending to be exceptionally favourable, or by any appropriate intergovernmental organization, to remove the underlying causes of the disequilibrium. On the invitation of the contracting parties, contracting parties shall participate in such discussions.

ARTICLE XIII

NON-DISCRIMINATORY ADMINISTRATION OF QUANTITATIVE RESTRICTIONS

1. No prohibition or restriction shall be applied by any contracting party on the importation of any product of the territory of any other contracting party or on the exportation of any product destined for the territory of any other contracting party, unless the importation of the like product of all third countries or the exportation of the like product to all third countries is similarly prohibited or restricted.

2. In applying import restrictions to any product, contracting parties shall aim at a distribution of trade in such product approaching as closely as possible the shares which the various contracting parties might be expected to obtain in the absence of such restrictions, and to this end shall observe the following provisions:

(a) Wherever practicable, quotas representing the total amount of permitted imports (whether allocated among supplying countries or not) shall be fixed, and notice given of their amount in accordance with paragraph 3(b) of this Article;

(b) In cases in which quotas are not practicable, the restrictions may be applied by means of import licences or permits without a quota;

(c) Contracting parties shall not, except for purposes of operating quotas allocated in accordance with subparagraph (d) of this paragraph, require that import licences or permits be utilized for the importation of the product concerned from a particular country or source;

(d) In cases in which a quota is allocated among supplying countries, the contracting party applying the restrictions may seek agreement with respect to the allocation of shares in the quota with all other contracting parties having a substantial interest in supplying the product concerned. In cases in which this method is not reasonably practicable, the contracting party concerned shall allot to contracting parties having a substantial interest in supplying the product shares based upon the proportions, supplied by such contracting parties during a previous representative period, of the total quantity or value of imports of the product, due account being taken of any special factors which may have affected or may be affecting the trade in the product. No conditions or formalities shall be imposed which would prevent any contracting party from utilizing fully the share of any such total quantity or value which has been allotted to it, subject to importation being made within any prescribed period to which the quota may relate.

3. (a) In cases in which import licenses are issued in connection with import restrictions, the contracting party applying the restrictions shall provide, upon the request of any contracting party having an interest in the trade in the product concerned, all relevant information concerning the administration of the restrictions, the import licences granted over a recent period and the distribution of such licences among supplying countries; *Provided,* That there shall be no obligation to supply information as to the names of importing or supplying enterprises.

(b) In the case of import restrictions involving the fixing of quotas, the contracting party applying the restrictions shall give public notice of the total quantity or value of the product or products which will be permitted to be imported during a specified future period and of any change in such quantity or value. Any supplies of the product in question which were *en route* at the time at which public notice was given shall not be excluded from entry: *Provided,* That they may be counted so far as practicable, against the quantity permitted to be imported in the period in question, and also, where necessary, against the quantities permitted to be imported in the next following period or periods; and *Provided further,* That if any contracting party customarily exempts from such restrictions products entered for consumption or withdrawn from warehouse for consumption during a period of thirty days after the day of such public notice, such practice shall be considered full compliance with this sub-paragraph.

(c) In the case of quotas allocated among supplying countries, the contracting party applying the restrictions shall promptly inform all other contracting parties having an interest in supplying the product concerned of the shares in the quota currently allocated, by quantity or value, to the various supplying countries and shall give public notice thereof.

4. With regard to restrictions applied in accordance with paragraph 2(d) of this Article or under paragraph 2(c) of Article XI the selection of a representative period for any product and the appraisal of any special factors affecting the trade in the product shall be made initially by the contracting party applying the restriction; *Provided,* That such contracting party shall, upon the request of any other contracting party having a substantial interest in supplying that product or upon the request of the contracting parties, consult promptly with the other contracting party or the contracting parties regarding the need for an adjustment of the proportion determined or of the base period selected, or for the reappraisal of the special factors involved, or for the elimination of conditions, formalities or any other provisions established unilaterally relating to the allocation of an adequate quota or its unrestricted utilization.

5. The provisions of this Article shall apply to any tariff quota instituted or maintained by any contracting party, and, in so far as applicable, the principles of this Article shall also extend to export restrictions.

ARTICLE XIV

EXCEPTIONS TO THE RULE OF NON-DISCRIMINATION[13]

1. A contracting party which applies restrictions under Article XII or under Section B of Article XVIII may, in the application of such restrictions, deviate from the provisions of Article XIII in a manner having equivalent effect to restrictions on payments and transfers for current international transactions which that contracting party may at that time apply under Article VIII or XIV of the Articles of Agreement of the International Monetary Fund, or under analogous provisions of a special exchange agreement entered into pursuant to paragraph 6 of Article XV.

2. A contracting party which is applying import restrictions under Article XII or under Section B of Article XVIII may, with the consent of the contracting parties, temporarily deviate from the provisions of Article XIII in respect of a small part of its external trade where the benefits to the con-

---

[13] Text as amended February 15, 1961, on which date Annex J was deleted. Originally amended and restated by Special Protocol Modifying Article XIV of the G.A.T.T. (62 Stat. 2006). Further amended and restated by Part J of the Protocol Amending the Preamble and Parts II and III of the G.A.T.T. (8 UST 1775).

tracting party or contracting parties concerned substantially outweigh any injury which may result to the trade of other contracting parties.

3. The provisions of Article XIII shall not preclude a group of territories having a common quota in the International Monetary Fund from applying against imports from other countries, but not among themselves, restrictions in accordance with the provisions of Article XII or of Section B of Article XVIII on condition that such restrictions are in all other respects consistent with the provisions of Article XIII.

4. A contracting party applying import restrictions under Article XII or under Section B of Article XVIII shall not be precluded by Articles XI to XV or Section B of Article XVIII of this Agreement from applying measures to direct its exports in such a manner as to increase its earnings of currencies which it can use without deviation from the provisions of Article XIII.

5. A contracting party shall not be precluded by Articles XI to XV, inclusive, or by Section B of Article XVIII, of this Agreement from applying quantitative restrictions:

(a) having equivalent effect to exchange restrictions authorized under Section 3(b) of Article VII of the Articles of Agreement of the International Monetary Fund, or

(b) under the preferential arrangements provided for in Annex A of this Agreement, pending the outcome of the negotiations referred to therein.

ARTICLE XV

EXCHANGE ARRANGEMENTS

1. The contracting parties shall seek co-operation with the International Monetary Fund to the end that the contracting parties and the Fund may pursue a coordinated policy with regard to exchange questions within the jurisdiction of the Fund and questions of quantitative restrictions and other trade measures within the jurisdiction of the contracting parties.

2. In all cases in which the contracting parties are called upon to consider or deal with problems concerning monetary reserves, balances of payments or foreign exchange arrangements, they shall consult fully with the International Monetary Fund. In such consultations, the contracting parties shall accept all findings of statistical and other facts presented by the Fund relating to foreign exchange, monetary reserves and balances of payments, and shall accept the determination of the Fund as to whether action by a contracting

party in exchange matters is in accordance with the Articles of Agreement of the International Monetary Fund, or with the terms of a special exchange agreement between that contracting party and the contracting parties. The contracting parties, in reaching their final decision in cases involving the criteria set forth in paragraph 2(a) of Article XII or in paragraph 9[14] of Article XVIII, shall accept the determination of the Fund as to what constitutes a serious decline in the contracting party's monetary reserves, a very low level of its monetary reserves or a reasonable rate of increase in its monetary reserves, and as to the financial aspects of other matters covered in consultation in such cases.

3. The contracting parties shall seek agreement with the Fund regarding procedures for consultation under paragraph 2 of this Article.

4. Contracting parties shall not, by exchange action, frustrate the intent of the provisions of this Agreement, nor, by trade action, the intent of the provisions of the Articles of Agreement of the International Monetary Fund.

5. If the contracting parties consider, at any time, that exchange restrictions on payments and transfers in connection with imports are being applied by a contracting party in a manner inconsistent with the exceptions provided for in this Agreement for quantitative restrictions, they shall report thereon to the Fund.

6. Any contracting party which is not a member of the Fund shall, within a time to be determined by the contracting parties after consultation with the Fund, become a member of the Fund, or, failing that, enter into a special exchange agreement with the contracting parties. A contracting party which ceases to be a member of the Fund shall forthwith enter into a special exchange agreement with the contracting parties. Any special exchange agreement entered into by a contracting party under this paragraph shall thereupon become part of its obligations under this Agreement.

7. (a) A special exchange agreement between a contracting party and the contracting parties under paragraph 6 of this Article shall provide to the satisfaction of the contracting parties that the objectives of this Agreement will not be frustrated as a result of action in exchange matters by the contracting party in question.

(b) The terms of any such agreement shall not impose obligations on the contracting party in exchange matters generally more restrictive than those imposed by the Articles of Agreement of the International Monetary Fund on members of the Fund.

---

[14] References to paragraph 9 added by paragraph K of the Protocol Amending the Preamble and Parts II and III of the G.A.T.T. (8 UST 1776).

8. A contracting party which is not a member of the Fund shall furnish such information within the general scope of section 5 of Article VIII of the Articles of Agreement of the International Monetary Fund as the contracting parties may require in order to carry out their functions under this Agreement.

9. Nothing in this Agreement shall preclude:[15]

(a) the use by a contracting party of exchange controls or exchange restrictions in accordance with the Articles of Agreement of the International Monetary Fund or with that contracting party's special exchange agreement with the contracting parties, or

(b) the use by a contracting party of restrictions or controls on imports or exports, the sole effect of which, additional to the effects permitted under Articles XI, XII, XIII and XIV, is to make effective such exchange controls or exchange restrictions.

ARTICLE XVI

SUBSIDIES

Section A *Subsidies in General*

1. If any contracting party grants or maintains any subsidy, including any form of income or price support, which operates directly or indirectly to increase exports of any product from, or to reduce imports of any product into, its territory, it shall notify the contracting parties in writing of the extent and nature of the subsidization, of the estimated effect of the subsidization on the quantity of the affected product or products imported into or exported from its territory and of the circumstances making the subsidization necessary. In any case in which it is determined that serious prejudice to the interests of any other contracting party is caused or threatened by any such subsidization, the contracting party granting the subsidy shall, upon request, discuss with the other contracting party or parties concerned, or with the contracting parties, the possibility of limiting the subsidization.

Section B *Additional Provisions on Export Subsidies*[16]

2. The contracting parties recognize that the granting by a contracting

---

[15] This clause as amended and restated by Part D of the Protocol Modifying Part II and Article XXVI of the G.A.T.T. (62 Stat. 3683).

[16] This section added by Part L of the Protocol Amending the Preamble and Parts II and III of the G.A.T.T. (8 UST 1776).

party of a subsidy on the export of any product may have harmful effects for other contracting parties, both importing and exporting, may cause undue disturbance to their normal commercial interests, and may hinder the achievement of the objectives of this Agreement.

3. Accordingly, contracting parties should seek to avoid the use of subsidies on the export of primary products. If, however, a contracting party grants directly or indirectly any form of subsidy which operates to increase the export of any primary product from its territory, such subsidy shall not be applied in a manner which results in that contracting party having more than an equitable share of world export trade in that product, account being taken of the shares of the contracting parties in such trade in the product during a previous representative period, and any special factors which may have affected or may be affecting such trade in the product.

4. Further, as from 1 January 1958 or the earliest practicable date thereafter, contracting parties shall cease to grant either directly or indirectly any form of subsidy on the export of any product other than a primary product which subsidy results in the sale of such product for export at a price lower than the comparable price charged for the like product to buyers in the domestic market. Until 31 December 1957 no contracting party shall extend the scope of any such subsidization beyond that existing on 1 January 1955 by the introduction of new, or the extension of existing, subsidies.

5. The contracting parties shall review the operation of the provisions of this Article from time to time with a view to examining its effectiveness, in the light of actual experience, in promoting the objectives of this Agreement and avoiding subsidization seriously prejudicial to the trade or interests of contracting parties.

ARTICLE XVII

STATE TRADING ENTERPRISES[17]

1. (a) Each contracting party undertakes that if it establishes or maintains a State enterprise, wherever located, or grants to any enterprise, formally or in effect, exclusive or special privileges, such enterprise shall, in its purchases or sales involving either imports or exports, act in a manner consistent with the general principles of nondiscriminatory treatment prescribed in this Agreement for governmental measures affecting imports or exports by private traders.

(b) The provision of sub-paragraph (a) of this paragraph shall be understood to require that such enterprises shall, having due regard to the other provisions of this Agreement, make any such purchases or sales solely ir accordance with commercial considerations, including price, quality, availability, marketability, transportation and other conditions of purchase or sale, and shall afford the enterprises of the other contracting parties adequate opportunity, in accordance with customary business practice, to compete for participation in such purchases or sales.

(c) No contracting party shall prevent any enterprise (whether or not an enterprise described in sub-paragraph (a) of this paragraph) under its jurisdiction from acting in accordance with the principles of sub-paragraphs (a) and (b) of this paragraph.

2. The provisions of paragraph 1 of this Article shall not apply to imports of products for immediate or ultimate consumption in governmental use and not otherwise for resale or use in the production of goods for sale. With respect to such imports, each contracting party shall accord to the trade of the other contracting parties fair and equitable treatment.

3.[17] The contracting parties recognize that enterprises of the kind described in paragraph 1(a) of this Article might be operated so as to create serious obstacles to trade; thus negotiations on a reciprocal and mutually advantageous basis designed to limit or reduce such obstacles are of importance to the expansion of international trade.

4.[17] (a) Contracting parties shall notify the contracting parties of the products which are imported into or exported from their territories by enterprises of the kind described in paragraph 1(a) of this Article.

(b) A contracting party establishing, maintaining or authorizing an import monopoly of a product, which is not the subject of a concession under Article II, shall, on the request of another contracting party having a substantial trade in the product concerned, inform the contracting parties of the import markup on the product during a recent representative period, or, when it is not possible to do so, of the price charged on the resale of the product.

(c) The contracting parties may, at the request of a contracting party which has reason to believe that its interests under this Agreement are being adversely affected by the operations of an enterprise of the kind described in paragraph 1(a), request the contracting party establishing, maintaining or authorizing such enterprise to supply information about its operations related to the carrying out of the provisions of this Agreement.

(d) The provisions of this paragraph shall not require any contracting

---

[17] Sections 3 and 4 and the title to Article XVII added by Part M of the Protocol Amending the Preamble and Parts II and III of the G.A.T.T. (8 UST 1777).

party to disclose confidential information which would impede law enforcement or otherwise be contrary to the public interest or would prejudice the legitimate commercial interests of particular enterprises.

ARTICLE XVIII

Governmental Assistance to Economic Development[18]

1. The contracting parties recognize that the attainment of the objectives of this Agreement will be facilitated by the progressive development of their economies, particularly of those contracting parties the economies of which can only support low standards of living and are in the early stages of development.

2. The contracting parties recognize further that it may be necessary for those contracting parties, in order to implement programmes and policies of economic development designed to raise the general standard of living of their people, to take protective or other measures affecting imports, and that such measures are justified in so far as they facilitate the attainment of the objectives of this Agreement. They agree, therefore, that those contracting parties should enjoy additional facilities to enable them (a) to maintain sufficient flexibility in their tariff structure to be able to grant the tariff protection required for the establishment of a particular industry and (b) to apply quantitative restrictions for balance of payments purposes in a manner which takes full account of the continued high level of demand for imports likely to be generated by their programmes of economic development.

3. The contracting parties recognize finally that with those additional facilities which are provided for in Sections A and B of this Article, the provisions of this Agreement would normally be sufficient to enable contracting parties to meet the requirements of their economic development. They agree, however, that there may be circumstances where no measure consistent with those provisions is practicable to permit a contracting party in the process of economic development to grant the governmental assistance required to promote the establishment of particular industries with a view to raising the general standard of living of its people. Special procedures are laid down in Sections C and D of this Article to deal with those cases.

4. (a) Consequently, a contracting party the economy of which can only support low standards of living and is in the early stages of development shall be free to deviate temporarily from the provisions of the other Articles of this Agreement, as provided in Sections A, B and C of this Article.

---

[18] As amended and restated by Part E of the Protocol Modifying Part II and Article XXVI of the G.A.T.T. (62 Stat. 3684).

(b) A contracting party the economy of which is in the process of development but which does not come within the scope of sub-paragraph (a) above, may submit applications to the contracting parties under Section D of this Article.

5. The contracting parties recognize that the export earnings of contracting parties the economies of which are of the type described in paragraph 4(a) and (b) above, and which depend on exports of a small number of primary commodities may be seriously reduced by a decline in the sale of such commodities. Accordingly, when the exports of primary commodities by such a contracting party are seriously affected by measures taken by another contracting party, it may have resort to the consultation provisions of Article XXII of this Agreement.

6. The contracting parties shall review annually all measures applied pursuant to the provisions of Sections C and D of this Article.

Section A

7. (a) If a contracting party coming within the scope of paragraph 4(a) of this Article considers it desirable, in order to promote the establishment of a particular industry with a view to raising the general standard of living of its people, to modify or withdraw a concession included in the appropriate Schedule annexed to this Agreement, it shall notify the contracting parties to this effect and enter into negotiations with any contracting party with which such concession was initially negotiated, and with any other contracting party determined by the contracting parties to have a substantial interest therein. If agreement is reached between such contracting parties concerned, they shall be free to modify or withdraw concessions under the appropriate Schedules to this Agreement in order to give effect to such agreement, including any compensatory adjustments involved.

(b) If agreement is not reached within sixty days after the notification provided for in sub-paragraph (a) above, the contracting party which proposes to modify or withdraw the concession may refer the matter to the contracting parties, which shall promptly examine it. If they find that the contracting party which proposes to modify or withdraw the concession has made every effort to reach an agreement and that the compensatory adjustment offered by it is adequate, that contracting party shall be free to modify or withdraw the concession if at the same time, it gives effect to the compensatory adjustment. If the contracting parties do not find that the compensation offered by a contracting party proposing to modify or withdraw the concession is adequate, but find that it has made every reasonable effort to offer adequate compensation, that contracting party shall be free to proceed with such modification or withdrawal. If such action is taken, any other contracting party referred to in subparagraph (a) above shall be free to modify or withdraw substantially equivalent concessions initially negotiated with the contracting party which has taken the action.

Section B

8. The contracting parties recognize that contracting parties coming within the scope of paragraph 4(a) of this Article tend, when they are in rapid process of development, to experience balance of payments difficulties arising mainly from efforts to expand their internal markets as well as from the instability in their terms of trade.

9. In order to safeguard its external financial position and to ensure a level of reserves adequate for the implementation of its programme of economic development, a contracting party coming within the scope of paragraph 4(a) of this Article may, subject to the provisions of paragraphs 10 to 12, control the general level of its imports by restricting the quantity or value of merchandise permitted to be imported; *Provided* that the import restrictions instituted, maintained or intensified shall not exceed those necessary.

    (a) to forestall the threat of, or to stop, a serious decline in its monetary reserves, or

    (b) in the case of a contracting party with inadequate monetary reserves, to achieve a reasonable rate of increase in its reserves.

Due regard shall be paid in either case to any special factors which may be affecting the reserves of the contracting party or its need for reserves, including, where special external credits or other resources are available to it, the need to provide for the appropriate use of such credits or resources.

10. In applying these restrictions, the contracting party may determine their incidence on imports of different products or classes of products in such a way as to give priority to the importation of those products which are more essential in the light of its policy of economic development: *Provided* that the restrictions are so applied as to avoid unnecessary damage to the commercial or economic interests of any other contracting party and not to prevent unreasonably the importation of any description of goods in minimum commercial quantities the exclusion of which would impair regular channels of trade; and *Provided further* that the restrictions are not so applied as to prevent the importation of commercial samples or to prevent compliance with patent, trademark, copyright or similar procedures.

11. In carrying out its domestic policies, the contracting party concerned shall pay due regard to the need for restoring equilibrium in its balance of

payments on a sound and lasting basis and to the desirability of assuring an economic employment of productive resources. It shall progressively relax any restrictions applied under this Section as conditions improve, maintaining them only to the extent necessary under the terms of paragraph 9 of this Article and shall eliminate them when conditions no longer justify such maintenance; *Provided* that no contracting party shall be required to withdraw or modify restrictions on the ground that a change in its development policy would render unnecessary the restrictions which it is applying under this Section.

12. (a) Any contracting party applying new restrictions or raising the general level of its existing restrictions by a substantial intensification of the measures applied under this Section, shall immediately after instituting or intensifying such restrictions (or, in circumstances in which prior consultation is practicable, before doing so) consult with the contracting parties as to the nature of its balance of payments difficulties, alternative corrective measures which may be available, and the possible effect of the restrictions on the economies of other contracting parties.

(b) On a date to be determined by them, the contracting parties shall review all restrictions still applied under this Section on that date. Beginning two years after that date, contracting parties applying restrictions under this Section shall enter into consultations of the type provided for in sub-paragraph (a) above with the contracting parties at intervals of approximately, but not less than, two years according to a programme to be drawn up each year by the contracting parties; *Provided* that no consultation under this sub-paragraph shall take place within two years after the conclusion of a consultation of a general nature under any other provision of this paragraph.

(c)(i) If, in the course of consultations with a contracting party under sub-paragraph (a) or (b) of this paragraph, the contracting parties find that the restrictions are not consistent with the provisions of this Section or with those of Article XIII (subject to the provisions of Aricle XIV), they shall indicate the nature of the inconsistency and may advise that the restrictions be suitably modified.

(ii) If, however, as a result of the consultations, the contracting parties determine that the restrictions are being applied in a manner involving an inconsistency of a serious nature with the provisions of this Section or with those of Article XIII (subject to the provisions of Article XIV) and that damage to the trade of any contracting party is caused or threatened thereby, they shall so inform the contracting party applying the restrictions and shall make appropriate recommendations for securing conformity with such provisions within a specified period. If such contracting party does not comply with these recommendations within the specified period, the contracting parties may release any contracting party the trade of which is adversely affected by the restrictions from such obligations under this Agreement towards the contracting parties applying the restrictions as they determine to be appropriate in the circumstances.

(d) The contracting parties shall invite any contracting party which is applying restrictions under this Section to enter into consultations with them at the request of any contracting party which can establish a *prima facie* case that the restrictions are inconsistent with the provisions of this Section or with those of Article XIII (subject to the provisions of Article XIV) and that its trade is adversely affected thereby. However, no such invitation shall be issued unless the contracting parties have ascertained that direct discussions between the contracting parties concerned have not been successful. If, as a result of the consultations with the contracting parties no agreement is reached and they determine that the restrictions are being applied inconsistently with such provisions, and that damage to the trade of the contracting party initiating the procedure is caused or threatened thereby, they shall recommend the withdrawal or modification of the restrictions. If the restrictions are not withdrawn or modified within such time as the contracting parties may prescribe, they may release the contracting party initiating the procedure from such obligations under this Agreement towards the contracting party applying the restrictions as they determine to be appropriate in the circumstances.

(e) If a contracting party against which action has been taken in accordance with the last sentence of sub-paragraph (c)(ii) or (d) of this paragraph, finds that the release of obligations authorized by the contracting parties adversely affects the operation of its programme and policy of economic development, it shall be free, not later than sixty days after such action is taken, to give written notice to the Executive Secretary to the contracting parties of its intention to withdraw from this Agreement and such withdrawal shall take effect on the sixtieth day following the day on which the notice is received by him.

(f) In proceeding under this paragraph, the contracting parties shall have due regard to the factors referred to in paragraph 2 of this Article. Determinations under this paragraph shall be rendered expeditiously and, if possible, within sixty days of the initiation of the consultations.

Section C

13. If a contracting party coming within the scope of paragraph 4(a) of this Article finds that governmental assistance is required to promote the establishment of a particular industry with a view to raising the general standard of living of its people, but that no measure consistent with the other

provisions of this Agreement is practicable to achieve that objective, it may have recourse to the provisions and procedures set out in this Section.

14. The contracting party concerned shall notify the contracting parties of the special difficulties which it meets in the achievement of the objective outlined in paragraph 13 of this Article and shall indicate the specific measure affecting imports which it proposes to introduce in order to remedy these difficulties. It shall not introduce that measure before the expiration of the time-limit laid down in paragraph 15 or 17, as the case may be, or if the measure affects imports of a product which is the subject of a concession included in the appropriate Schedule annexed to this Agreement, unless it has secured the concurrence of the contracting parties in accordance with the provisions of paragraph 18; *Provided* that, if the industry receiving assistance has already started production, the contracting party may, after informing the contracting parties, take such measures as may be necessary to prevent, during that period, imports of the product or products concerned from increasing substantially above a normal level.

15. If, within thirty days of the notification of the measure, the contracting parties do not request the contracting party concerned to consult with them, that contracting party shall be free to deviate from the relevant provisions of the other Articles of this Agreement to the extent necessary to apply the proposed measure.

16. If it is requested by the contracting parties to do so, the contracting party concerned shall consult with them as to the purpose of the proposed measure, as to alternative measures which may be available under this Agreement, and as to the possible effect of the measure proposed on the commercial and economic interests of other contracting parties. If, as a result of such consultation, the contracting parties agree that there is no measure consistent with the other provisions of this Agreement which is practicable in order to achieve the objective outlined in paragraph 13 of this Article, and concur in the proposed measure, the contracting party concerned shall be released from its obligations under the relevant provisions of the other Articles of this Agreement to the extent necessary to apply that measure.

17. If, within ninety days after the date of the notification of the proposed measure under paragraph 14 of this Article, the contracting parties have not concurred in such measure, the contracting party concerned may introduce the measure proposed after informing the contracting parties.

concession included in the appropriate Schedule annexed to this Agreement,

18. If the proposed measure affects a product which is the subject of a the contracting party concerned shall enter into consultations with any other contracting party with which the concession was initially negotiated, and with

any other contracting party determined by the contracting parties to have a substantial interest therein. The contracting parties shall concur in the measure if they agree that there is no measure consistent with the other provisions of this Agreement which is practicable in order to achieve the objective set forth in paragraph 13 of this Article, and if they are satisfied:

(a) that agreement has been reached with such other contracting parties as a result of the consultations referred to above, or

(b) if no such agreement has been reached within sixty days after the notification provided for in paragraph 14 has been received by the contracting parties, that the contracting party having recourse to this Section has made all reasonable efforts to reach an agreement and the interests of other contracting parties are adequately safeguarded.

The contracting party having recourse to this Section shall thereupon be released from its obligations under the relevant provisions of the other Articles of this Agreement to the extent necessary to permit it to apply the measure.

19. If a proposed measure of the type described in paragraph 13 of this Article concerns an industry the establishment of which has in the initial period been facilitated by incidental protection afforded by restrictions imposed by the contracting party concerned for balance of payments purposes under the relevant provisions of this Agreement, that contracting party may resort to the provisions and procedures of this Section; *Provided* that it shall not apply the proposed measure without the concurrence of the contracting parties.

20. Nothing in the preceding paragraphs of this Section shall authorize any deviation from the provisions of Articles I, II and XIII of this Agreement. The provisos to paragraph 10 of this Article shall also be applicable to any restriction under this Section.

21. At any time while a measure is being applied under paragraph 17 of this Article any contracting party substantially affected by it may suspend the application to the trade of the contracting party having recourse to this Section of such substantially equivalent concessions or other obligations under this Agreement the suspension of which the contracting parties do not disapprove; *Provided* that sixty days' notice of such suspension is given to the contracting parties not later than six months after the measure has been introduced or changed substantially to the detriment of the contracting party affected. Any such contracting party shall afford adequate opportunity for consultation in accordance with the provisions of Article XXII of this Agreement.

Section D

22. A contracting party coming within the scope of subparagraph 4(b) of this Article desiring, in the interest of the development of its economy, to introduce a measure of the type described in paragraph 13 of this Article in respect of the establishment of a particular industry may apply to the contracting parties for approval of such measure. The contracting parties shall promptly consult with such contracting party and shall, in making their decision, be guided by the considerations set out in paragraph 16. If the contracting parties concur in the proposed measure the contracting party concerned shall be released from its obligations under the relevant provisions of the other Articles of this agreement to the extent necessary to permit it to apply the measure. If the proposed measure affects a product which is the subject of a concession included in the appropriate Schedule annexed to this Agreement, the provisions of paragraph 18 shall apply.

23. Any measure applied under this Section shall comply with the provisions of paragraph 20 of this Article.

ARTICLE XIX

EMERGENCY ACTION ON IMPORTS OF PARTICULAR PRODUCTS

1. (a) If, as a result of unforeseen developments and of the effect of the obligations incurred by a contracting party under this Agreement, including tariff concessions, any product is being imported into the territory of that contracting party in such increased quantities and under such conditions as to cause or threaten serious injury to domestic producers in that territory of like or directly competitive products, the contracting party shall be free, in respect of such product, and to the extent and for such time as may be necessary to prevent or remedy such injury, to suspend the obligation in whole or in part or to withdraw or modify the concession.

(b) If any product, which is the subject of a concession with respect to a preference, is being imported into the territory of a contracting party in the circumstances set forth in sub-paragraph (a) of this paragraph, so as to cause or threaten serious injury to domestic producers of like or directly competitive products in the territory of a contracting party which receives or received such preference, the importing contracting party shall be free, if that other contracting party so requests, to supend the relevant obligation in whole or in part or to withdraw or modify the concession in respect of the product, to the extent and for such time as may be necessary to prevent or remedy such injury.

2. Before any contracting party shall take action pursuant to the provisions

of paragraph 1 of this Article, it shall give notice in writing to the contracting parties as far in advance as may be practicable and shall afford the contracting parties and those contracting parties having a substantial interest as exporters of the product concerned an opportunity to consult with it in respect of the proposed action. When such notice is given in relation to a concession with respect to a preference, the notice shall name the contracting party which has requested the action. In critical circumstances, where delay would cause damage which it would be difficult to repair, action under paragraph 1 of this Article may be taken provisionally without prior consultation, on the condition that consultation shall be effected immediately after taking such action.

3. (a) If agreement among the interested contracting parties with respect to the action is not reached, the contracting party which proposes to take or continue the action shall, nevertheless, be free to do so, and if such action is taken or continued, the affected contracting parties shall then be free, not later than ninety days after such action is taken, to suspend, upon the expiration of thirty days from the day on which written notice of such suspension is received by the contracting parties, the application to the trade of the contracting party taking such action, or, in the case envisaged in paragraph 1(b) of this Article, to the trade of the contracting party requesting such action, of such substantially equivalent concessions or other obligations[19] under this Agreement the suspension of which the contracting parties do not disapprove.

(b) Notwithstanding the provisions of sub-paragraph (a) of this paragraph, where action is taken under paragraph 2 of this Article without prior consultation and causes or threatens serious injury in the territory of a contracting party to the domestic producers of products affected by the action, that contracting party shall, where delay would cause damage difficult to repair, be free to suspend, upon the taking of the action and throughout the period of consultation, such concessions or other obligations as may be necessary to prevent or remedy the injury.

ARTICLE XX

GENERAL EXCEPTIONS

Subject to the requirement that such measures are not applied in a manner which would constitute a means of arbitrary or unjustifiable discrimination between countries where the same conditions prevail, or a disguised restric-

---

[19] The words "concessions or other obligations" were substituted for "obligations or concessions" by Part O of the Protocol Amending the Preamble and Parts II and III of the G.A.T.T. (8 UST 1786).

tion on international trade, nothing in this Agreement shall be construed to prevent the adoption or enforcement by any contracting party of measures;

(a) necessary to protect public morals;

(b) necessary to protect human, animal or plant life or health;

(c) relating to the importation or exportation of gold or silver;

(d) necessary to secure compliance with laws or regulations which are not inconsistent with the provisions of this Agreement, including those relating to customs enforcement, the enforcement of monopolies operated under paragraph 4 of Article II and Article XVII, the protection of patents, trademarks and copyrights, and the prevention of deceptive practices;

(e) relating to products of prison labour;

(f) imposed for the protection of national treasures of artistic, historic or archaeological value;

(g) relating to the conservation of exhaustible natural resources if such measures are made effective in conjunction with restrictions on domestic production or consumption;

(h)[20] undertaken in pursuance of obligations under any intergovernmental commodity agreement which conforms to criteria submitted to the contracting parties and not disapproved by them or which is itself so submitted and not so disapproved;

(i) involving restrictions on exports of domestic materials necessary to assure essential quantities of such materials to a domestic processing industry during periods when the domestic price of such materials is held below the world price as part of a governmental stabilization plan; *Provided* that such restrictions shall not operate to increase the exports of or the protection afforded to such domestic industry, and shall not depart from the provisions of this Agreement relating to non-discrimination;

(j)[20] essential to the acquisition or distribution of products in general or local short supply; *Provided* that any such measures shall be consistent with the principle that all contracting parties are entitled to an

---

[20] Sections (h) and (j) as amended and restated by Part P of the Protocol Amending the Preamble and Parts II and III of the G.A.T.T. (8 UST 1786).

equitable share of the international supply of such products, and that any such measures, which are inconsistent with the other provision of this Agreement shall be discontinued as soon as the conditions giving rise to them have ceased to exist. The contracting parties shall review the need for this sub-paragraph not later than 30 June 1960.

ARTICLE XXI

SECURITY EXCEPTIONS

Nothing in this Agreement shall be construed

(a) to require any contracting party to furnish any information the disclosure of which it considers contrary to its essential security interests; or

(b) to prevent any contracting party from taking any action which it considers necessary for the protection of its essential security interests

(i) relating to fissionable materials or the materials from which they are derived;

(ii) relating to the traffic in arms, ammunition and implements of war and to such traffic in other goods and materials as is carried on directly or indirectly for the purpose of supplying a military establishment;

(iii) taken in time of war or other emergency in international relations; or

(c) to prevent any contracting party from taking any action in pursuance of its obligations under the United Nations Charter for the maintenance of international peace and security.

ARTICLE XXII

CONSULTATION [21]

1. Each contracting party shall accord sympathetic consideration to, and shall afford adequate opportunity for consultation regarding, such representations as may be made by another contracting party with respect to any matter affecting the operation of this Agreement.

2. The contracting parties may, at the request of a contracting party,

---

[21] As amended and restated by Part Q of the Protocol Amending the Preamble and Parts II and III of the G.A.T.T. (8 UST 1787).

consult with any contracting party or parties in respect of any matter for which it has not been possible to find a satisfactory solution through consultation under paragraph 1.

ARTICLE XXIII

NULLIFICATION OR IMPAIRMENT

1. If any contracting party should consider that any benefit accruing to it directly or indirectly under this Agreement is being nullified or impaired or that the attainment of any objective of the Agreement is being impeded as the result of (a) the failure of another contracting party to carry out its obligations under this Agreement, or (b) the application by another contracting party of any measure, whether or not it conflicts with the provisions of this Agreement, or (c) the existence of any other situation, the contracting party may, with a view to the satisfactory adjustment of the matter, make written representations or proposals to the other contracting party or parties which it considers to be concerned. Any contracting party thus approached shall give sympathetic consideration to the representations or proposals made to it.

2. If no satisfactory adjustment is effected between the contracting parties concerned within a reasonable time, or if the difficulty is of the type described in paragraph 1(c) of this Article, the matter may be referred to the contracting parties. The contracting parties shall promptly investigate any matter so referred to them and shall make appropriate recommendations to the contracting parties which they consider to be concerned, or give a ruling on the matter, as appropriate. The contracting parties may consult with contracting parties, with the Economic and Social Council of the United Nations and with any appropriate inter-governmental organization in cases where they consider such consultation necessary.

If the contracting parties consider that the circumstances are serious enough to justify such action, they may authorize a contracting party or parties to suspend the application to any other contracting party or parties of such concessions or other obligations under this Agreement as they determine to be appropriate in the circumstances. If the application to any contracting party of any concession or other obligation is in fact suspended, that contracting party shall then be free, not later than sixty days after such action is taken to give written notice to the Executive Secretary to the contracting parties of its intention to withdraw from this Agreement and such withdrawal shall take effect upon the sixtieth day following the day on which such notice is received by him.[22]

---

[22] Paragraph added by the Protocol Amending the Preamble and Parts II and III of the G.A.T.T. (8 UST 1787).

PART III

ARTICLE XXIV

TERRITORIAL APPLICATION—FRONTIER TRAFFIC—CUSTOMS UNIONS
AND FREE-TRADE AREAS [23]

1. The provisions of this Agreement shall apply to the metropolitan customs territories of the contracting parties and to any other customs territories in respect of which this Agreement has been accepted under Article XXVI or is being applied under Article XXXIII or pursuant to the Protocol of Provisional Application. Each such customs territory shall, exclusively for the purposes of the territorial application of this Agreement, be treated as though it were a contracting party; *Provided* that the provisions of this paragraph shall not be construed to create any rights or obligations as between two or more customs territories in respect of which this Agreement has been accepted under Article XXVI or is being applied under Article XXXIII or pursuant to the Protocol of Provisional Application by a single contracting party.

2. For the purposes of this Agreement customs territory shall be understood to mean any territory with respect to which separate tariffs or other regulations of commerce are maintained for a substantial part of the trade of such territory with other territories.

3. The provisions of this Agreement shall not be construed to prevent:

(a) advantages accorded by any contracting party to adjacent countries in order to facilitate frontier traffic;

(b) advantages accorded to the trade with the Free Territory of Trieste by countries contiguous to that territory, provided that such advantages are not in conflict with the Treaties of Peace arising out of the Second World War.

4.[24] The contracting parties recognize the desirability of increasing freedom of trade by the development, through voluntary agreements, of closer integration between the economies of the countries parties to such agreements. They also recognize that the purpose of a customs union or of a free-trade area should be to facilitate trade between the constituent territories and

---

[23] As amended and restated by the Special Protocol Relating to Article XXIV of the G.A.T.T. (62 Stat. 2013).

[24] As amended and restated by Part S of the Protocol Amending the Preamble and Parts II and III of the G.A.T.T. (8 UST 1788).

not to raise barriers to the trade of other contracting parties with such territories.

5. Accordingly, the provisions of this Agreement shall not prevent, as between the territories of contracting parties, the formation of a customs union or of a free-trade area or the adoption of an interim agreement necessary for the formation of a customs union or of a free-trade area; *Provided* that:

(a) with respect to a customs union, or an interim agreement leading to the formation of a customs union, the duties and other regulations of commerce imposed at the institution of any such union or interim agreement in respect of trade with contracting parties not parties to such union or agreement shall not on the whole be higher or more restrictive than the general incidence of the duties and regulations of commerce applicable in the constituent territories prior to the formation of such union or the adoption of such interim agreement, as the case may be;

(b) with respect to a free-trade area, or an interim agreement leading to the formation of a free-trade area, the duties and other regulations of commerce maintained in each of the constituent territories and applicable at the formation of such free-trade area or the adoption of such interim agreement to the trade of contracting parties not included in such area or not parties to such agreement shall not be higher or more restrictive than the corresponding duties and other regulations of commerce existing in the same constituent territories prior to the formation of the free-trade area, or interim agreement, as the case may be; and

(c) any interim agreement referred to in sub-paragraphs (a) and (b) shall include a plan and schedule for the formation of such a customs union or of such a free-trade area within a reasonable length of time.

6. If, in fulfilling the requirements of sub-paragraph 5(a), a contracting party proposes to increase any rate of duty inconsistently with the provisions of Article II, the procedure set forth in Article XXVIII shall apply. In providing for compensatory adjustment, due account shall be taken of the compensation already afforded by the reductions brought about in the corresponding duty of the other constituents of the union.

7. (a) Any contracting party deciding to enter into a customs union or free-trade area, or an interim agreement leading to the formation of such a union or area, shall promptly notify the contracting parties and shall make available to them such information regarding the proposed union or area as will enable them to make such reports and recommendations to contracting parties as they may deem appropriate.

(b) If, after having studied the plan and schedule included in an interim agreement referred to in paragraph 5 in consultation with the parties to that agreement and taking due account of the information made available in accordance with the provisions of sub-paragraph (a), the contracting parties find that such agreement is not likely to result in the formation of a customs union or of a free-trade area within the period contemplated by the parties to the agreement or that such period is not a reasonable one, the contracting parties shall make recommendations to the parties to the agreement. The parties shall not maintain or put into force, as the case may be, such agreement if they are not prepared to modify it in accordance with these recommendations.

(c) Any substantial change in the plan or schedule referred to in paragraph 5(c) shall be communicated to the contracting parties, which may request the contracting parties concerned to consult with them if the change seems likely to jeopardize or delay unduly the formation of the customs union or of the free-trade area.

8. For the purposes of this Agreement:

(a) A customs union shall be understood to mean the substitution of a single customs territory for two or more customs territories, so that

(i) duties and other restrictive regulations of commerce (except, where necessary, those permitted under Article XI, XII, XIII, XIV, XV and XX) are eliminated with respect to substantially all the trade between the constituent territories of the union or at least with respect to substantially all the trade in products originating in such territories, and,

(ii) subject to the provisions of paragraph 9, substantially the same duties and other regulations of commerce are applied by each of the members of the union to the trade of territories not included in the union;

(b) A free-trade area shall be understood to mean a group of two or more customs territories in which the duties and other restrictive regulations of commerce (except, where necessary, those permitted under Articles XI, XII, XIII, XIV, XV and XX) are eliminated on substantially all the trade between the constituent territories in products originating in such territories.

9. The preferences referred to in paragraph 2 of Article I shall not be affected by the formation of a customs union or of a free-trade area but may

be eliminated or adjusted by means of negotiations with contracting parties affected. This procedure of negotiations with affected contracting parties shall, in particular, apply to the elimination of preferences required to conform with the provisions of paragraph 8(a)(i) and paragraph 8(b).

10. The contracting parties may by a two-thirds majority approve proposals which do not fully comply with the requirements of paragraphs 5 to 9 inclusive, provided that such proposals lead to the formation of a customs union or a free-trade area in the sense of this Article.

11. Taking into account the exceptional circumstances arising out of the establishment of India and Pakistan as independent States and recognizing the fact that they have long constituted an economic unit, the contracting parties agree that the provisions of this Agreement shall not prevent the two countries from entering into special arrangements with respect to the trade between them, pending the establishment of their mutual trade relations on a definitive basis.

12. Each contracting party shall take such reasonable measures as may be available to it to ensure observance of the provisions of this Agreement by the regional and local governments and authorities within its territory.

ARTICLE XXV

JOINT ACTION BY THE CONTRACTING PARTIES

1. Representatives of the contracting parties shall meet from time to time for the purpose of giving effect to those provisions of this Agreement which involve joint action and, generally, with a view to facilitating the operation and furthering the objectives of this Agreement. Wherever reference is made in this Agreement to the contracting parties acting jointly they are designated as the contracting parties.

2. The Secretary-General of the United Nations is requested to convene the first meeting of the contracting parties, which shall take place not later than March 1, 1948.

3. Each contracting party shall be entitled to have one vote at all meetings of the contracting parties.

4. Except as otherwise provided for in this Agreement, decisions of the contracting parties shall be taken by a majority of the votes cast.

5.[25] In exceptional circumstances not elsewhere provided for in this Agreement, the contracting parties may waive an obligation imposed upon a contracting party by this Agreement; *Provided* that any such decision shall be approved by a two-thirds majority of the votes cast and that such majority shall comprise more than half of the contracting parties. The contracting parties may also by such a vote

(i) define certain categories of exceptional circumstances to which other voting requirements shall apply for the waiver of obligations, and

(ii) prescribe such criteria as may be necessary for the application of this paragraph.

ARTICLE XXVI

ACCEPTANCE, ENTRY INTO FORCE AND REGISTRATION [26]

1. The date of this Agreement shall be 30 October 1947.

2. This Agreement shall be open for acceptance by any contracting party which, on 1 March 1955, was a contracting party or was negotiating with a view to accession to this Agreement.

3. This Agreement, done in a single English original and in a single French original, both texts authentic, shall be deposited with the Secretary-General of the United Nations, who shall furnish certified copies thereof to all interested governments.

4.[27] Each government accepting this Agreement shall deposit an instrument of acceptance with the Executive Secretary of the contracting parties who will inform all interested governments of the date of deposit of each instrument of acceptance and of the day on which this Agreement enters into force under paragraph 6 of this Article.

---

[25] As amended and restated by the Protocol Modifying Certain Provisions of the G.A.T.T. (62 Stat. 1992). Subparagraphs (b) (c) and (d) deleted by the Protocol Amending the Preamble and Parts II and III of the G.A.T.T. (8 UST 1788).

The word "paragraph" has been substituted for the word "sub-paragraph," since paragraph 5 is no longer divided into sub-paragraphs (a), (b), etc., as was formerly the case. The text of the present paragraph 5 was formerly sub-paragraph 5(a).

[26] As amended and restated by Part U of the Protocol Amending the Preamble and Parts II and III of the G.A.T.T. (8 UST 1788).

[27] The last sentence was added by Part V of the Protocol Amending the Preamble and Parts II and III of the G.A.T.T. (8 UST 1789).

5. (a) Each government accepting this Agreement does so in respect of its metropolitan territory and of the other territories for which it has international responsibility, except such separate customs territories as it shall notify to the Executive Secretary to the contracting parties at the time of its own acceptance.

(b) Any government, which has so notified the Executive Secretary under the exceptions in sub-paragraph (a) of this paragraph, may at any time give notice to the Executive Secretary that its acceptance shall be effective in respect of any separate customs territory or territories so excepted and such notice shall take effect on the thirtieth day following the day on which it is received by the Executive Secretary.

(c) If any of the customs territories, in respect of which a contracting party has accepted this Agreement, possesses or acquires full autonomy in the conduct of its external commercial relations and of the other matters provided for in this Agreement, such territory shall, upon sponsorship through a declaration by the responsible contracting party establishing the above-mentioned fact, be deemed to be a contracting party.

6. This Agreement shall enter into force, as among the governments which have accepted it, on the thirtieth day following the day on which instruments of acceptance have been deposited with the Executive Secretary to the contracting parties on behalf of governments named in Annex H, the territories of which account for 85 per centum of the total external trade of the territories of such governments, computed in accordance with the applicable column of percentages set forth therein. The instrument of acceptance of each other government shall take effect on the thirtieth day following the day on which such instrument has been deposited.

7. The United Nations is authorized to effect registration of this Agreement as soon as it enters into force.

ARTICLE XXVII

WITHHOLDING OR WITHDRAWAL OF CONCESSIONS

Any contracting party shall at any time be free to withhold or to withdraw in whole or in part any concession, provided for in the appropriate Schedule annexed to this Agreement, in respect of which such contracting party determines that it was initially negotiated with a government which has not become, or has ceased to be, a contracting party. A contracting party taking such action shall notify the contracting parties and, upon request, consult with contracting parties which have a substantial interest in the product concerned.[28]

ARTICLE XXVIII

MODIFICATION OF SCHEDULES [29]

1. On the first day of each three-year period, the first period beginning on 1 January 1958 (or on the first day of any other period that may be specified by the contracting parties by two-thirds of the votes cast) a contracting party (hereafter in this Article referred to as the "applicant contracting party") may, by negotiation and agreement with any contracting party with which such concession was initially negotiated and with any other contracting party determined by the contracting parties to have a principal supplying interest (which two preceding categories of contracting parties, together with the applicant contracting party, are in this Article hereinafter referred to as the "contracting parties primarily concerned"), and subject to consultation with any other contracting party determined by the contracting parties to have a substantial interest in such concession, modify or withdraw a concession included in the appropriate Schedule annexed to this Agreement.

2. In such negotiations and agreement, which may include provision for compensatory adjustment with respect to other products, the contracting parties concerned shall endeavour to maintain a general level of reciprocal and mutually advantageous concessions not less favourable to trade than that provided for in this Agreement prior to such negotiations.

3. (a) If agreement between the contracting parties primarily concerned cannot be reached before 1 January 1958 or before the expiration of a period envisaged in paragraph 1 of this Article, the contracting party which proposes to modify or withdraw the concession shall, nevertheless, be free to do so and if such action is taken any contracting party with which such concession was initially negotiated, any contracting party determined under paragraph 1 to have a principal supplying interest and any contracting party determined under paragraph 1 to have a substantial interest shall then be free not later than six months after such action is taken, to withdraw, upon the expiration of thirty days from the day on which written notice of such withdrawal is received by the contracting parties, substantially equivalent concessions initially negotiated with the applicant contracting party.

---

[28] As amended and restated by the Protocol Modifying Article XXVI of the Agreement of October 30, 1947 (2 UST 1583).

[29] As amended and restated by Part W of the Protocol Amending the Preamble and Parts II and III of the G.A.T.T. (18 UST 1788).

(b) If agreement between the contracting parties primarily concerned is reached but any other contracting party determined under paragraph 1 of this Article to have a substantial interest is not satisfied, such other contracting party shall be free, not later than six months after action such agreement is taken, to withdraw, upon the expiration of thirty days from the day on which written notice of such withdrawal is received by the contracting parties, substantially equivalent concessions initially negotiated with the applicant contracting party.

4. The contracting parties may, at any time, in special circumstances, authorize a contracting party to enter into negotiations for modification or withdrawal of a concession included in the appropriate Schedule annexed to this Agreement subject to the following procedures and conditions:

(a) Such negotiations and any related consultations shall be conducted in accordance with the provisions of paragraphs 1 and 2 of this Article.

(b) If agreement between the contracting parties primarily concerned is reached in the negotiations, the provisions of paragraph 3(b) of this Article shall apply.

(c) If agreement between the contracting parties primarily concerned is not reached within a period of sixty days after negotiations have been authorized, or within such longer period as the contracting parties may have prescribed the applicant contracting party may refer the matter to the contracting parties.

(d) Upon such reference, the contracting parties shall promptly examine the matter and submit their views to the contracting parties primarily concerned with the aim of achieving a settlement. If a settlement is reached, the provisions of paragraph 3(b) shall apply as if agreement between the contracting parties primarily concerned had been reached. If no settlement is reached between the contracting parties primarily concerned, the applicant contracting party shall be free to modify or withdraw the concession, unless the contracting parties determine that the applicant contracting party has unreasonably failed to offer adequate compensation. If such action is taken, any contracting party with which the concession was initially negotiated, any contracting party determined under paragraph 4(a) to have a principal supplying interest and any contracting party determined under paragraph 4(a) to have a substantial interest, shall be free, not later than six months after such action is taken, to modify or withdraw, upon the expiration of thirty days from the day on which written notice of such withdrawal is received by the contracting parties, substantially equivalent concessions initially negotiated with the applicant contracting party.

5. Before 1 January 1958 and before the end of any period envisaged in

paragraph 1 a contracting party may elect by notifying the contracting parties to reserve the right, for the duration of the next period, to modify the appropriate Schedule in accordance with the procedures of paragraphs 1 to 3. If a contracting party so elects, other contracting parties shall have the right, during the same period, to modify or withdraw, in accordance with the same procedures, concessions initially negotiated with that contracting party.

ARTICLE XXVIII BIS

TARIFF NEGOTIATIONS [30]

1. The contracting parties recognize that customs duties often constitute serious obstacles to trade; thus negotiations on a reciprocal and mutually advantageous basis, directed to the substantial reduction of the general level of tariffs and other charges on imports and exports and in particular to the reduction of such high tariffs as discourage the importation even of minimum quantities, and conducted with due regard to the objectives of this Agreement and the varying needs of individual contracting parties, are of great importance to the expansion of international trade. The contracting parties may therefore sponsor such negotiations from time to time.

2. (a) Negotiations under this Article may be carried out on a selective product-by-product basis or by the application of such multilateral procedures as may be accepted by the contracting parties concerned. Such negotiations may be directed towards the reduction of duties, the binding of duties at then existing levels or undertakings that individual duties or the average duties on specified categories of products shall not exceed specified levels. The binding against increase of low duties or of duty-free treatment shall, in principle, be recognized as a concession equivalent in value to the reduction of high duties.

(b) The contracting parties recognize that in general the success of multilateral negotiations would depend on the participation of all contracting parties which conduct a substantial proportion of their external trade with one another.

3. Negotiations shall be conducted on a basis which affords adequate opportunity to take into account:

    (a) the needs of individual contracting parties and individual industries;

---

[30] Added by Part X(i) of the Protocol Amending the Preamble and Parts II and III of the G.A.T.T. (8 UST 1792).

(b) the needs of less-developed countries for a more flexible use of tariff protection to assist their economic development and the special needs of these countries to maintain tariffs for revenue purposes; and

(c) all other relevant circumstances, including the fiscal, developmental, strategic and other needs of the contracting parties concerned.

ARTICLE XXIX

THE RELATION OF THIS AGREEMENT TO THE HAVANA CHARTER [31]

1. The contracting parties undertake to observe to the fullest extent of their executive authority the general principles of Chapters I to VI inclusive and of Chapter IX of the Havana Charter pending their acceptance of it in accordance with their constitutional procedures.

2. Part II of this Agreement shall be suspended on the day on which the Havana Charter enters into force.

3. If by September 30, 1949, the Havana Charter has not entered into force, the contracting parties shall meet before December 31, 1949, to agree whether this Agreement shall be amended, supplemented or maintained.

4. If at any time the Havana Charter should cease to be in force, the contracting parties shall meet as soon as practicable thereafter to agree whether this Agreement shall be supplemented, amended or maintained. Pending such agreement, Part II of this Agreement shall again enter into force; *Provided* that the provisions of Part II other than Article XXIII shall be replaced, *mutatis mutandis,* in the form in which they then appeared in the Havana Charter; and *Provided further* that no contracting party shall be bound by any provisions which did not bind it at the time when the Havana Charter ceased to be in force.

5. If any contracting party has not accepted the Havana Charter by the date upon which it enters into force, the contracting parties shall confer to agree whether, and if so in what way, this Agreement in so far as it affects relations between such contracting party and other contracting parties, shall be supplemented or amended. Pending such agreement the provisions of Part II of this Agreement shall, notwithstanding the provisions of paragraph 2 of this Article, continue to apply as between such contracting party and other contracting parties.

---

[31] As amended and restated by Part C of the Protocol Modifying Part I and Article XXIX of the G.A.T.T. (3 UST 5357).

6. Contracting parties which are Members of the International Trade Organization shall not invoke the provisions of this Agreement so as to prevent the operation of any provision of the Havana Charter. The application of the principle underlying this paragraph to any contracting party which is not a Member of the International Trade Organization shall be the subject of an agreement pursuant to paragraph 5 of this Article.

ARTICLE XXX

AMENDMENTS

1. Except where provision for modification is made elsewhere in this Agreement, amendments to the provisions of Part I of this Agreement or to the provisions of Article XXIX or of this Article shall become effective upon acceptance by all the contracting parties, and other amendments to this Agreement shall become effective, in respect of those contracting parties which accept them, upon acceptance by two-thirds of the contracting parties and thereafter for each other contracting party upon acceptance by it.

2. Any contracting party accepting an amendment to this Agreement shall deposit an instrument of acceptance with the Secretary-General of the United Nations within such period as the contracting parties may specify. The contracting parties may decide that any amendment made effective under this Article is of such a nature that any contracting party which has not accepted it within a period specified by the contracting parties shall be free to withdraw from this Agreement, or to remain a contracting party with the consent of the contracting parties.

ARTICLE XXXI

WITHDRAWAL [32]

Without prejudice to the provisions of paragraph 12 of Article XVIII or of Article XXIII or of paragraph 2 of Article XXX, any contracting party may withdraw from this Agreement, or may separately withdraw on behalf of any of the separate customs territories for which it has international responsibility and which at the time possesses full autonomy in the conduct of its external commercial relations and of the other matters provided for in this Agreement. The withdrawal shall take effect upon the expiration of six months from the

---

[32] As amended by Part Y of the Protocol Amending the Preamble and Parts II and III of the G.A.T.T. (8 UST 1793).

day on which written notice of withdrawal is received by the Secretary-General of the United Nations.

ARTICLE XXXII

CONTRACTING PARTIES [33]

1. The contracting parties to this Agreement shall be understood to mean those governments which are applying the provisions of this Agreement under Articles XXVI or XXXIII or pursuant to the Protocol of Provisional Application.

2. At any time after the entry into force of this Agreement pursuant to paragraph 6 of Article XXVI, those contracting parties which have accepted this Agreement pursuant to paragraph 4 of Article XXVI may decide that any contracting party which has not so accepted it shall cease to be a contracting party.

ARTICLE XXXIII

ACCESSION [34]

A government not party to this Agreement, or a government acting on behalf of a separate customs territory possessing full autonomy in the conduct of its external commercial relations and of the other matters provided for in this Agreement, may accede to this Agreement, on its own behalf or on behalf of that territory, on terms to be agreed between such government and the contracting parties. Decisions of the contracting parties under this paragraph shall be taken by a two-thirds majority.

ARTICLE XXXIV

ANNEXES

The annexes to this Agreement are hereby made an integral part of this Agreement.

---

[33] As amended by the Protocol Modifying Certain Provisions of the G.A.T.T. (62 Stat. 1992).

[34] As amended and restated by the Protocol Modifying Certain Provisions of the G.A.T.T. (62 Stat. 1992).

ARTICLE XXXV

Non-application of the Agreement Between
Particular Contracting Parties [35]

1. This Agreement, or alternatively Article II of this Agreement shall not apply as between any contracting party and any other contracting party if:

(a) the two contracting parties have not entered into tariff negotiations with each other, and

(b) either of the contracting parties, at the time either becomes a contracting party, does not consent to such application.

2. The contracting parties may review the operation of this Article in particular cases at the request of any contracting party and make appropriate recommendations.

Annex A

List of Territories Referred to in Paragraph 2(A) of Article I

United Kingdom of Great Britain and Northern Ireland

Dependent territories of the United Kingdom of Great Britain and Northern Ireland

Canada

Commonwealth of Australia

Dependent territories of the Commonwealth of Australia

New Zealand

Dependent territories of New Zealand

Union of South Africa including South West Africa

Ireland

India (as on April 10, 1947)

Newfoundland

Southern Rhodesia

---

[35] Added by the Protocol Modifying Certain Provisions of the G.A.T.T. (62 Stat. 1992). As amended and restated by Part Z of the Protocol Amending the Preamble and Parts II and III of the G.A.T.T. (8 UST 1793).

Burma

Ceylon

Certain of the territories listed above have two or more preferential rates in force for certain products. Any such territory may, by agreement with the other contracting parties which are principal suppliers of such products at the most-favoured-nation rate, substitute for such preferential rates a single preferential rate which shall not on the whole be less favourable to suppliers at the most-favoured-nation rate than the preferences in force prior to such substitution.

The imposition of an equivalent margin of tariff preference to replace a margin of preference in an internal tax existing on April 10, 1947, exclusively between two or more of the territories listed in this Annex or to replace the preferential quantitative arrangements described in the following paragraph, shall not be deemed to constitute an increase in a margin of tariff preference.

The preferential arrangements referred to in paragraph 5(b) of Article XIV are those existing in the United Kingdom on April 10, 1947, under contractual agreements with the Governments of Canada, Australia and New Zealand, in respect to chilled and frozen beef and veal, frozen mutton and lamb, chilled and frozen pork, and bacon. It is the intention, without prejudice to any action taken under part I(h) of Article XX, that these arrangements shall be eliminated or replaced by tariff preferences, and that negotiations to this end shall take place as soon as practicable among the countries substantially concerned or involved.

The film hire tax in force in New Zealand on April 10, 1947, shall, for the purposes of this Agreement, be treated as a customs duty under Article I. The renters' film quota in force in New Zealand on April 10, 1947, shall, for the purposes of this Agreement, be treated as a screen quota under Article IV.

The Dominions of India and Pakistan have not been mentioned separately in the above list since they had not come into existence as such on the base date of April 10, 1947.

ANNEX B

List of Territories of the French Union Referred to in Paragraph 2(b) of Article I

France

French Equatorial Africa (Treaty Basin of the Congo [36] and other territories)

French West Africa

Cameroons under French Mandate [36]

French Somali Coast and Dependencies

French Establishments in India [36]

French Establishments in Oceania

French Establishments in the Condominium of the New Herbrides [36]

Guadeloupe and Dependencies

French Guiana

Indo-China

Madagascar and Dependencies

Morocco (French zone) [36]

Martinique

New Caledonia and Dependencies

Réunion

Saint-Pierre and Miquelon

Togo under French Mandate [36]

Tunisia

ANNEX C

List of Territories of the Customs Union of Belgium, Luxemburg and the
Netherlands Referred to in Paragraph 2(b) of Article I

The Economic Union of Belgium and Luxemburg

Belgian Congo

Ruanda Urundi

Netherlands

New Guinea

Surinam

Netherlands Antilles

Republic of Indonesia

For imports into the metropolitan territories constituting the Customs Union.

---

[36] For imports into Metropolitan France and Territories of the French Union.

ANNEX D

List of Territories Referred to in Paragraph 2(b) of Article I as Respects the United States of America

United States of America (customs territory)

Dependent territories of the United States of America

Republic of the Philippines

The imposition of an equivalent margin of tariff preference to replace a margin of preference in an internal tax existing on April 10, 1947, exclusively between two or more of the territories listed in this Annex shall not be deemed to constitute an increase in a margin of tariff presence.

———

ANNEX E

List of Territories Covered by Preferential Arrangements Between Chile and Neighbouring Countries Referred to in Paragraph 2(d) of Article I

Preferences in force exclusively between Chile on the one hand, and

1. Argentina
2. Bolivia
3. Peru

on the other hand.

———

ANNEX F

List of Territories Covered by Preferential Arrangements Between Lebanon and Syria and Neighbouring Countries Referred to in Paragraph 2(d) of

Article I

Preferences in force exclusively between the Lebano-Syrian Customs Union, on the one hand, and

1. Palestine

2. Transjordan

on the other hand.

———

ANNEX G

Dates Establishing Maximum Margins of Preference Referred to in Paragraph 4 [37] of Article I

Australia	October 15, 1946.
Canada	July 1, 1939.
France	January 1, 1939.
Lebano-Syrian Customs Union	November 30, 1938.
Union of South Africa	July 1, 1938.
Southern Rhodesia	May 1, 1941.

———

ANNEX H

Percentage Shares of Total External Trade to be Used for the Purpose of Making the Determination Referred to in Article XXVI [37]

(Based on the average of 1949–1953)

If, prior to the accession of the Government to Japan to the General Agreement, the present Agreement has been accepted by contracting parties the external trade of which under column I accounts for the percentage of such trade specified in paragraph 6 of Article XXVI, column I shall be applicable for the purposes of that paragraph. If the present Agreement has not been so accepted prior to the accession of the Government of Japan, column II shall be applicable for the purposes of that paragraph.

———

[37] As amended and restated by Part AA of the Protocol Amending the Preamble and Parts II and III of the G.A.T.T. (8 UST 1794). The number "4" has been substituted for the number "3" in the heading of Annex G. The reference to Article I was intended to be a reference to the last paragraph of Article I which originally consisted of only three numbered paragraphs.

	Contracting parties on—			Contracting parties on—	
	Mar. 1, 1955 (1)	Mar. 1, 1955 & Japan (2)		Mar. 1, 1955 (1)	Mar. 1, 1955 & Japan (2)
Australia	3.1	3.0	Indonesia	1.3	1.3
Austria	.9	.8	Italy	2.9	2.8
Belgium-Luxemburg	4.3	4.2	Netherlands, Kingdom of the..	4.7	4.6
Brazil	2.5	2.4	New Zealand	1.0	1.0
Burma	.3	.3	Nicaragua	.1	.1
Canada	6.7	6.5	Norway	1.1	1.1
Ceylon	.5	.5	Pakistan	.9	.8
Chile	.6	.6	Peru	.4	.4
Cuba	1.1	1.1	Rhodesia and Nyasaland	.6	.6
Czechoslovakia	1.4	1.4	Sweden	2.5	2.4
Denmark	1.4	1.4	Turkey	.6	.6
Dominican Republic	.1	.1	Union of South Africa	1.8	1.8
Finland	1.0	1.0	United Kingdom ..	20.3	19.8
France	8.7	8.5	United States of America	20.6	20.1
Germany, Federal Republic of	5.3	5.2	Uruguay	.4	.4
Greece	.4	.4	Japan		2.3
Haiti	.1	.1	Total	100.0	100.0
India	2.4	2.4			

Note: These percentages have been computed taking into account the trade of all territories in respect of which the General Agreement on Tariffs and Trade is applied.

ANNEX I

Notes and Supplementary Provisions [38]

Ad Article I

Paragraph 1.

The obligations incorporated in paragraph 1 of Article I by reference to paragraphs 2 and 4 of Article III and those incorporated in paragraph 2(b) of Article II by reference to Article VI shall be considered as falling within Part II for the purposes of the Protocol of Provisional Application.

---

[38] As amended to indicate additions and alterations.

The cross-references, in the paragraph immediately above and in paragraph 1 of Article I, to paragraphs 2 and 4 of Article III shall only apply after Article III has been modified by the entry into force of the amendment provided for in the Protocol Modifying Part II and Article XXVI of the General Agreement on Tariffs and Trade, dated September 14, 1948.

Paragraph 4.

The term "margin of preference" means the absolute difference between the most-favoured-nation rate of duty and the preferential rate of duty for the like product, and not the proportionate relation between those rates. As examples:

1) If the most-favoured-nation rate were 36 per cent *ad valorem* and the preferential rate were 24 per cent *ad valorem*, the margin of preference would be 12 per cent *ad valorem*, and not one-third of the most-favoured-nation rate;

(2) If the most-favoured-nation rate were 36 per cent *ad valorem* and the preferential rate were expressed as two-thirds of the most-favoured-nation rate, the margin of preference would be 12 per cent *ad valorem;*

(3) If the most-favoured-nation rate were 2 francs per kilogramme and the preferential rate were 1.50 francs per kilogramme, the margin of preference would be 0.50 francs per kilogramme.

The following kinds of customs action, taken in accordance with established uniform procedures, would not be contrary to a general binding of margins of preference:

(i) The re-application to an imported product of a tariff classification or rate of duty, properly applicable to such product, in cases in which the application of such classification or rate to such product was temporarily suspended or inoperative on April 10, 1947; and

(ii) The classification of a particular product under a tariff item other than that under which importations of that product were classified on April 10, 1947, in cases in which the tariff law clearly contemplates that such product may be classified under more than one tariff item.

Ad Article II

Paragraph 2(a).

The cross-reference, in paragraph 2(a) of Article II, to paragraph 2 of

Article III shall only apply after Article III has been modified by the entry into force of the amendment provided for in the Protocol Modifying Part II and Article XXVI of the General Agreement on Tariffs and Trade, dated September 14, 1948.

Paragraph 2(b).

See the note relating to paragraph 1 of Article I.

Paragraph 4.

Except where otherwise specifically agreed between the contracting parties which initially negotiated the concession, the provisions of this paragraph will be applied in the light of the provisions of Article 31 of the Havana Charter.

Ad Article III

Any internal tax or other internal charge, or any law, regulation or requirement of the kind referred to in paragraph 1 which applies to an imported product and to the like domestic product and is collected or enforced in the case of the imported product at the time or point of importation, is nevertheless to be regarded as an internal tax or other internal charge, or a law, regulation or requirement of the kind referred to in paragraph 1, and is accordingly subject to the provisions of Article III.

Paragraph 1.

The application of paragraph 1 to internal taxes imposed by local governments and authorities within the territory of a contracting party is subject to the provisions of the final paragraph of Article XXIV. The term "reasonable measures" in the last-mentioned paragraph would not require, for example, the repeal of existing national legislation authorizing local governments to impose internal taxes which, although technically inconsistent with the letter of Article III, are not in fact inconsistent with its spirit, if such repeal would result in a serious financial hardship for the local governments or authorities concerned. With regard to taxation by local governments or authorities which is inconsistent with both the letter and spirit of Article III, the term "reasonable measures" would permit a contracting party to eliminate the inconsistent taxation gradually over a transition period, if abrupt action would create serious administrative and financial difficulties.

Paragraph 2.

A tax conforming to the requirements of the first sentence of paragraph 2 would be considered to be inconsistent with the provisions of the second sentence only in cases where competition was involved between, on the one hand, the taxed product and, on the other hand, a directly competitive or substitutable product which was not similarly taxed.

Paragraph 5.

Regulations consistent with the provisions of the first sentence of paragraph 5 shall not be considered to be contrary to the provisions of the second sentence in any case in which all of the products subject to the regulations are produced domestically in substantial quantities. A regulation cannot be justified as being consistent with the provisions of the second sentence on the ground that the proportion or amount allocated to each of the products which are the subject of the regulation constitutes an equitable relationship between imported and domestic products.

Ad Article V

Paragraph 5.

With regard to transportation charges, the principle laid down in paragraph 5 refers to like products being transported on the same route under like conditions.

Ad Article VI

Paragraph 1.

1. Hidden dumping by associated houses (that is, the sale by an importer at a price below that corresponding to the price invoiced by an exporter with whom the importer is associated, and also below the price in the exporting country) constitutes a form of price dumping with respect to which the margin of dumping may be calculated on the basis of the price at which the goods are resold by the importer.

2. It is recognized that, in the case of imports from a country which has a complete or substantially complete monopoly of its trade and where all domestic prices are fixed by the State, special difficulties may exist in determining price comparability for the purposes of paragraph 1, and in such cases importing contracting parties may find it necessary to take into account the possibility that a strict comparison with domestic prices in such a country may not always be appropriate.

Paragraphs 2 and 3.

Note 1.—As in many other cases in customs administration, a contracting party may require reasonable security (bond or cash deposit) for the payment of anti-dumping or countervailing duty pending final determination of the facts in any case of suspected dumping or subsidization.

Note 2.—Multiple currency practices can in certain circumstances constitute a subsidy to exports which may be met by countervailing duties under paragraph 3 or can constitute a form of dumping by means of a partial depreciation of a country's currency which may be met by action under paragraph 2. By "multiple currency practices" is meant practices by governments or sanctioned by governments.

Paragraph 6(b).

Waivers under the provisions of this sub-paragraph shall be granted only on application by the contracting party proposing to levy an anti-dumping or countervailing duty, as the case may be.

Ad Article VII

Paragraph 1.

The expression "or other charges" is not to be regarded as including internal taxes or equivalent charges imposed on or in connexion with imported products.

Paragraph 2.

1. It would be in conformity with Article VII to presume that "actual value" may be represented by the invoice price, plus any non-included charges for legitimate costs which are proper elements of "actual value" and plus any abnormal discount or other reduction from the ordinary competitive price.

2. It would be in conformity with Article VII, paragraph 2(b), for a contracting party to construe the phrase "in the ordinary course of trade . . . under fully competitive conditions", as excluding any transaction wherein the buyer and seller are not independent of each other and price is not the sole consideration.

3. The standard of "fully competitive conditions" permits a contracting party to exclude from consideration prices involving special discounts limited to exclusive agents.

4. The wording of sub-paragraphs (a) and (b) permits a contracting party to determine the value for customs purposes, uniformly either (1) on the basis of a particular exporter's prices of the imported merchandise, or (2) on the basis of the general price level of like merchandise.

Ad Article VIII

1. While Article VIII does not cover the use of multiple rates of exchange as such, paragraphs 1 and 4 condemn the use of exchange taxes or fees as a device for implementing multiple currency practices; if, however, a contracting party is using multiple currency exchange fees for balance of payments reasons with the approval of the International Monetary Fund, the provisions of paragraph 9(a) of Article XV fully safeguard its position.

2. It would be consistent with paragraph 1 if on the importation of products from the territory of a contracting party into the territory of another contracting party, the production of certificates of origin should only be required to the extent that is strictly indispensable.

Ad Articles XI, XII, XIII, XIV and XVIII

Throughout Articles XI, XII, XIII, XIV and XVIII the terms "import restrictions" or "export restrictions" include restrictions made effective through state-trading operations.

Ad Article XI

Paragraph 2(c).

The term "in any form" in this paragraph covers the same products when in an early stage of processing and still perishable, which compete directly with the fresh product and if freely imported would tend to make the restriction on the fresh product ineffective.

Paragraph 2, last sub-paragraph.

The term "special factors" includes changes in relative productive efficiency as between domestic and foreign producers, or as between different foreign producers, but not changes artificially brought about by means not permitted under the Agreement.

Ad Article XII

The contracting parties shall make provision for the utmost secrecy in the conduct of any consultation under the provisions of this Article.

Paragraph 3(c)(i).

Contracting parties applying restrictions shall endeavour to avoid causing serious prejudice to exports of a commodity on which the economy of a contracting party is largely dependent.

Paragraph 4(b).

It is agreed that the date shall be within ninety days after the entry into force of the amendments of this Article effected by the Protocol Amending the Preamble and Parts II and III of this Agreement. However, should the contracting parties find that conditions were not suitable for the application of the provisions of this sub-paragraph at the time envisaged, they may determine a later date; *Provided* that such date is not more than thirty days after such time as the obligations of Article VIII, Sections 2, 3, and 4 of the Articles of Agreement of the International Monetary Fund become applicable to contracting parties, members of the Fund, the combined foreign trade of which constitutes at least fifty per centum of the aggregate foreign trade of all contracting parties.

Paragraph 4(e).

It is agreed that paragraph 4(e) does not add any new criteria for the imposition or maintenance of quantitative restrictions for balance of payments reasons. It is solely intended to ensure that all external factors such as changes in the terms of trade, quantitative restrictions, excessive tariffs and subsidies, which may be contributing to the balance of payments difficulties of the contracting party applying restrictions will be fully taken into account.

Ad Article XIII

Paragraph 2(d).

No mention was made of "commercial considerations" as a rule for the allocation of quotas because it was considered that its application by governmental authorities might not always be practicable. Moreover, in cases where it is practicable, a contracting party could apply these considerations in the process of seeking agreement, consistently with the general rule laid down in the opening sentence of paragraph 2.

Paragraph 4.

See note relating to "special factors" in connection with the last sub-paragraph of paragraph 2 of Article XI.

Ad Article XIV

Paragraph 1.

The provisions of this paragraph shall not be so construed as to preclude full consideration by the contracting parties, in the consultations provided for in paragraph 4 of Article XII and in paragraph 12 of Article XVIII, of the nature, effects and reasons for discrimination in the field of import restrictions.[39]

Paragraph 2.

One of the situations contemplated in paragraph 2 is that of a contracting party holding balances acquired as a result of current transactions which it finds itself unable to use without a measure of discrimination.

Ad Article XV

Paragraph 4.

The word "frustrate" is intended to indicate, for example, that infringements of the letter of any Article of this Agreement by exchange action shall not be regarded as a violation of that Article if, in practice, there is no appreciable departure from the intent of the Article. Thus, a contracting party which, as part of its exchange control operated in accordance with the Articles of Agreement of the International Monetary Fund, requires payment to be received for its exports in its own currency or in the currency of one or more members of the International Monetary Fund will not thereby be deemed to contravene Article XI or Article XIII. Another example would be that of a contracting party which specifies on an import license the country from which the goods may be imported, for the purpose not of introducing any additional element of discrimination in its import licensing system but of enforcing permissible exchange controls.

Ad Article XVI

The exemption of an exported product from duties or taxes borne by the like product when destined for domestic consumption, or the remission of such duties or taxes in amounts not in excess of those which have accrued, shall not be deemed to be a subsidy.

Section B

1. Nothing in Section B shall preclude the use by a contracting party of multiple rates of exchange in accordance with the Articles of Agreement of the International Monetary Fund.

2. For the purposes of Section B, a "primary product" is understood to be any product of farm, forest or fishery, or any mineral, in its natural form or

---

[39] Text as amended Feb. 15, 1961.

which has undergone such processing as is customarily required to prepare it for marketing in substantial volume in international trade.

Paragraph 3.

1. The fact that a contracting party has not exported the product in question during the previous representative period would not in itself preclude that contracting party from establishing its right to obtain a share of the trade in the product concerned.

2. A system for the stabilization of the domestic price or of the return to domestic producers of a primary product independently of the movements of export prices, which results at times in the sale of the product for export at a price lower than the comparable price charged for the like product to buyers in the domestic market, shall be considered not to involve a subsidy on exports within the meaning of paragraph 3 if the contracting parties determine that:

(a) the system has also resulted, or is so designed as to result, in the sale of the product for export at a price higher than the comparable price charged for the like product to buyers in the domestic market; and

(b) the system is so operated, or is designed so to operate, either because of the effective regulation of production or otherwise, as not to stimulate exports unduly or otherwise seriously to prejudice the interests of other contracting parties.

Notwithstanding such determination by the contracting parties, operations under such a system shall be subject to the provisions of paragraph 3 where they are wholly or partly financed out of government funds in addition to the funds collected from producers in respect of the product concerned.

Paragraph 4.

The intention of paragraph 4 is that the contracting parties should seek before the end of 1957 to reach agreement to abolish all remaining subsidies as from 1 January 1958; or, failing this, to reach agreement to extend the application of the standstill until the earliest date thereafter by which they can expect to reach such agreement.

Ad Article XVII

Paragraph 1.

The operations of Marketing Boards, which are established by contracting parties and are engaged in purchasing or selling, are subject to the provisions of sub-paragraphs (a) and (b).

The activities of Marketing Boards which are established by contracting parties and which do not purchase or sell but lay down regulations covering private trade are governed by the relevant Articles of this Agreement.

The charging by a state enterprise of different prices for its sales of a product in different markets is not precluded by the provisions of this Article, provided that such different prices are charged for commercial reasons, to meet conditions of supply and demand in export markets.

Paragraph 1(a).

Governmental measures imposed to ensure standards of quality and efficiency in the operation of external trade, or privileges granted for the exploitation of national natural resources but which do not empower the government to exercise control over the trading activities of the enterprise in question, do not constitute "exclusive or special privileges".

Paragraph 1(b).

A country receiving a "tied loan" is free to take this loan into account as a "commercial consideration" when purchasing requirements abroad.

Paragraph 2.

The term "goods" is limited to products as understood in commercial practice, and is not intended to include the purchase or sale of services.

Paragraph 3.

Negotiations which contracting parties agree to conduct under this paragraph may be directed towards the reduction of duties and other charges on imports and exports or towards the conclusion of any other mutually satisfactory arrangement consistent with the provisions of this Agreement. (See paragraph 4 of Article II and the note to that paragraph.)

Paragraph 4(b).

The term "import mark-up" in this paragraph shall represent the margin by which the price charged by the import monopoly for the imported product (exclusive of internal taxes within the purview of Article III, transportation, distribution, and other expenses incident to the purchase, sale or further processing, and a reasonable margin of profit) exceeds the landed cost.

Ad Article XVIII

The contracting parties and the contracting parties concerned shall preserve the utmost secrecy in respect of matters arising under this Article.

Paragraphs 1 and 4.

1. When they consider whether the economy of a contracting party "can only support low standards of living", the contracting parties shall take into consideration the normal position of that economy and shall not base their determination on exceptional circumstances such as those which may result from the temporary existence of exceptionally favourable conditions for the staple export product or products of such contracting party.

2. The phrase "in the early stages of development" is not meant to apply only to contracting parties which have just started their economic development, but also to contracting parties the economies of which are undergoing a process of industrialization to correct an excessive dependence on primary production.

Paragraphs 2, 3, 7, 13 and 22.

The reference to the establishment of particular industries shall apply not only to the establishment of a new industry, but also to the establishment of a new branch of production in an existing industry and to the substantial transformation of an existing industry, and to the substantial expansion of an existing industry supplying a relatively small proportion of the domestic demand. It shall also cover the reconstruction of an industry destroyed or substantially damaged as a result of hostilities or natural disasters.

Paragraph 7(b).

A modification or withdrawal, pursuant to paragraph 7(b), by a contracting party, other than the applicant contracting party, referred to in paragraph 7(a), shall be made within six months of the day on which the action is taken by the applicant contracting party, and shall become effective on the thirtieth day following the day on which such modification or withdrawal has been notified to the contracting parties.

Paragraph 11.

The second sentence in paragraph 11 shall not be interpreted to mean that a contracting party is required to relax or remove restrictions if such relaxation or removal would thereupon produce conditions, justifying the intensification or institution, respectively, of restrictions under paragraph 9 of Article XVIII.

Paragraph 12(b).

The date referred to in paragraph 12(b) shall be the date determined by the contracting parties in accordance with the provisions of paragraph 4(b) of Article XII of this Agreement.

Paragraphs 13 and 14.

It is recognized that, before deciding on the introduction of a measure and notifying the contracting parties in accordance with paragraph 14, a contracting party may need a reasonable period of time to assess the competitive position of the industry concerned.

Paragraphs 15 and 16.

It is understood that the contracting parties shall invite a contracting party proposing to apply a measure under Section C to consult with them pursuant to paragraph 16 if they are requested to do so by a contracting party the trade of which would be appreciably affected by the measure in question.

Paragraphs 16, 18, 19 and 22.

1. It is understood that the contracting parties may concur in a proposed measure subject to specific conditions or limitations. If the measure as applied does not conform to the terms of the concurrence it will to that extent be deemed a measure in which the contracting parties have not concurred. In cases in which the contracting parties have concurred in a measure for a specified period, the contracting party concerned, if it finds that the maintenance of the measure for a further period of time is required to achieve the objective for which the measure was originally taken, may apply to the contracting parties for an extension of that period in accordance with the provisions and procedures of Section C or D, as the case may be.

2. It is expected that the contracting parties will, as a rule, refrain from concurring in a measure which is likely to cause serious prejudice to exports of a commodity on which the economy of a contracting party is largely dependent.

Paragraphs 18 and 22.

The phrase "that the interests of other contracting parties are adequately safeguarded" is meant to provide latitude sufficient to permit consideration in each case of the most appropriate method of safeguarding those interests. The appropriate method may, for instance, take the form of an additional concession to be applied by the contracting party having recourse to Section

C or D during such time as the deviation from the other Articles of the Agreement would remain in force or of the temporary suspension by any other contracting party referred to in paragraph 18 of a concession substantially equivalent to the impairment due to the introduction of the measure in question. Such contracting party would have the right to safeguard its interests through such a temporary suspension of a concession; *Provided* that this right will not be exercised when, in the case of a measure imposed by a contracting party coming within the scope of paragraph 4(a), the contracting parties have determined that the extent of the compensatory concession proposed was adequate.

Paragraph 19.

The provisions of paragraph 19 are intended to cover the cases where an industry has been in existence beyond the "reasonable period of time" referred to in the note to paragraphs 13 and 14, and should not be so construed as to deprive a contracting party coming within the scope of paragraph 4(a) of Article XVIII, of its right to resort to the other provisions of Section C, including paragraph 17, with regard to a newly established industry even though it has benefited from incidental protection afforded by balance of payments import restrictions.

Paragraph 21.

Any measure taken pursuant to the provisions of paragraph 21 shall be withdrawn forthwith if the action taken in accordance with paragraph 17 is withdrawn or if the contracting parties concur in the measure proposed after the expiration of the ninety-day time limit specified in paragraph 17.

Ad Article XX

Sub-paragraph (h)

The exception provided for in this sub-paragraph extends to any commodity agreement which conforms to the principles approved by the Economic and Social Council in its Resolution 30 (IV) of 28 March 1947.

Ad Article XXIV

Paragraph 9.

It is understood that the provisions of Article I would require that, when a product which has been imported into the territory of a member of a customs union or free-trade area at a preferential rate of duty is re-exported to the territory of another member of such union or area, the latter member should collect a duty equal to the difference between the duty already paid and any higher duty that would be payable if the product were being imported directly into its territory.

Paragraph 11.

Measures adopted by India and Pakistan in order to carry out definitive trade arrangements between them, once they have been agreed upon, might depart from particular provisions of this Agreement, but these measures would in general be consistent with the objectives of the Agreement.

Ad Article XXVIII

The contracting parties and each contracting party concerned should arrange to conduct the negotiations and consultations with the greatest possible secrecy in order to avoid premature disclosure of details of prospective tariff changes. The contracting parties shall be informed immediately of all changes in national tariffs resulting from recourse to this Article.

Paragraph 1.

1. If the contracting parties specify a period other than a three-year period, a contracting party may act pursuant to paragraph 1 or paragraph 3 of Article XXVIII on the first day following the expiration of such other period and, unless the contracting parties have again specified another period, subsequent periods will be three-year periods following the expiration of such specified period.

2. The provision that on 1 January 1958, and on other days determined pursuant to paragraph 1, a contracting party "may . . . modify or withdraw a concession" means that on such day, and on the first day after the end of each period, the legal obligation of such contracting party under Article II is altered; it does not mean that the changes in its customs tariff should necessarily be made effective on the day. If a tariff change resulting from negotiations undertaken pursuant to this Article is delayed, the entry into force of any compensatory concessions may be similarly delayed.

3. Not earlier than six months, nor later than three months, prior to 1 January 1958, or to the termination date of any subsequent period, a contracting party wishing to modify or withdraw any concession embodied in the appropriate Schedule, should notify the contracting parties to this effect. The contracting parties shall then determine the contracting party or contracting parties with which the negotiations or consultations referred to in paragraph 1 shall take place. Any contracting party so determined shall participate in such negotiations or consultations with the applicant contract-

ing party with the aim of reaching agreement before the end of the period. Any extension of the assured life of the Schedules shall relate to the Schedules as modified after such negotiations, in accordance with paragraphs 1, 2, and 3 of Article XXVIII. If the contracting parties are arranging for multilateral tariff negotiations to take place within the period of six months before 1 January 1958, or before any other day determined pursuant to paragraph 1, they shall include in the arrangements for such negotiations suitable procedures for carrying out the negotiations referred to in this paragraph.

4. The object of providing for the participation in the negotiations of any contracting party with a principal supplying interest, in addition to any contracting party with which the concession was initially negotiated, is to ensure that a contracting party with a larger share in trade affected by the concession than a contracting party with which the concession was initially negotiated shall have an effective opportunity to protect the contractual right which it enjoys under this Agreement. On the other hand, it is not intended that the scope of the negotiations should be such as to make negotiations and agreement under Article XXVIII unduly difficult nor to create complications in the application of this Article in the future to concessions which result from negotiations thereunder. Accordingly, the contracting parties should only determine that a contracting party has a principal supplying interest if that contracting party has had, over a reasonable period of time prior to the negotiations, a larger share in the market of the applicant contracting party than a contracting party with which the concession was initially negotiated or would, in the judgment of the contracting parties, have had such a share in the absence of discriminatory quantitative restrictions maintained by the applicant contracting party. It would therefore not be appropriate for the contracting parties to determine that more than one contracting party, or in those exceptional cases where there is near equality more than two contracting parties, had a principal supplying interest.

5. Notwithstanding the definition of a principal supplying interest in note 4 to paragraph 1, the contracting parties may exceptionally determine that a contracting party has a principal supplying interest if the concession in question affects trade which constitutes a major part of the total exports of such contracting party.

6. It is not intended that provision for participation in the negotiations of any contracting party with a principal supplying interest, and for consultation with any contracting party having a substantial interest in the concession which the applicant contracting party is seeking to modify or withdraw, should have the effect that it should have to pay compensation or suffer retaliat·on greater than the withdrawal or modification sought, judged in the light of the conditions of trade at the time of the proposed withdrawal or modification, making allowance for any discriminatory quantitative restrictions maintained by the applicant contracting party.

7. The expression "substantial interest" is not capable of a precise definition and accordingly may present difficulties for the contracting parties. It is, however, intended to be construed to cover only those contracting parties which have, or in the absence of discriminatory quantitative restrictions affecting their exports could reasonably be expected to have, a significant share in the market of the contracting party seeking to modify or withdraw the concession.

Paragraph 4.

1. Any request for authorization to enter into negotiations shall be accompanied by all relevant statistical and other data. A decision on such request shall be made within thirty days of its submission.

2. It is recognized that to permit certain contracting parties, depending in large measure on a relatively small number of primary commodities and relying on the tariff as an important aid for furthering diversification of their economies or as an important source of revenue, normally to negotiate for the modification or withdrawal of concessions only under paragraph 1 of Article XXVIII, might cause them at such a time to make modifications or withdrawals which in the long run would prove unnecessary. To avoid such a situation the contracting parties shall authorize any such contracting party, under paragraph 4, to enter into negotiations unless they consider this would result in, or contribute substantially towards, such an increase in tariff levels as to threaten the stability of the Schedules to this Agreement or lead to undue disturbance of international trade.

3. It is expected that negotiations authorized under paragraph 4 for modification or withdrawal of a single item, or a very small group of items, could normally be brought to a conclusion in sixty days. It is recognized, however, that such a period will be inadequate for cases involving negotiations for the modification or withdrawal of a larger number of items and in such cases, therefore, it would be appropriate for the contracting parties to prescribe a longer period.

4. The determination referred to in paragraph 4(d) shall be made by the contracting parties within thirty days of the submission of the matter to them, unless the applicant contracting party agrees to a longer period.

5. In determining under paragraph 4(d) whether an applicant contracting party has unreasonably failed to offer adequate compensation, it is understood that the contracting parties will take due account of the special position of a contracting party which has bound a high proportion of its tariffs at very low rates of duty and to this extent has less scope than other contracting parties to make compensatory adjustment.

Ad Article XXVIII BIS

Paragraph 3.

It is understood that the reference to fiscal needs would include the revenue aspect of duties and particularly duties imposed primarily for revenue purposes or duties imposed on products which can be substituted for products subject to revenue duties to prevent the avoidance of such duties.

Ad Article XXIX

Paragraph 1.

Chapters VII and VIII of the Havana Charter have been excluded from paragraph 1 because they generally deal with the organization, functions and procedures of the International Trade Organization.

PROTOCOL OF PROVISIONAL APPLICATION OF THE GENERAL AGREEMENT ON TARIFFS AND TRADE[40]

1. The Governments of the COMMONWEALTH of AUSTRALIA, the KINGDOM OF BELGIUM (in respect of its metropolitan territory), CANADA, the FRENCH REPUBLIC (in respect of its metropolitan territory), CANADA, the FRENCH REPUBLIC (in respect of its metropolitan territory), the GRAND-DUCHY OF LUXEMBURG, the KINGDOM OF THE NETHERLANDS (in respect of its metropolitan territory), the UNITED KINGDOM OF GREAT BRITAIN AND NORTHERN IRELAND (in respect of its metropolitan territory), and the UNITED STATES OF AMERICA, undertake, provided that this Protocol shall have been signed on behalf of all the foregoing Governments not later than November 15, 1947, to apply provisionally on and after January 1, 1948:

(a) Parts I and III of the General Agreement on Tariffs and Trade, and

(b) Part II of that Agreement to the fullest extent not inconsistent with existing legislation.

2. The foregoing Governments shall make effective such provisional application of the General Agreement, in respect of any of their territories other than their metropolitan territories, on or after January 1, 1948, upon

---

[40] 61 Stat., part (6), page A2051.

the expiration of thirty days from the day on which notice of such application is received by the Secretary-General of the United Nations.

3. Any other Government signatory to this Protocol shall make effective such provisional application of the General Agreement, on or after January 1, 1948, upon the expiration of thirty days from the day of signature of this Protocol on behalf of such Government.

4. This Protocol shall remain open for signature at the Headquarters of the United Nations, (a) until November 15, 1947, on behalf of any Government named in paragraph 1 of this Protocol which has not signed it on this day, and (b) until June 30, 1948, on behalf of any other Government signatory to the Final Act adopted at the conclusion of the Second Session of the Preparatory Committee of the United Nations Conference on Trade and Employment which has not signed it on this day.

5. Any Government applying this Protocol shall be free to withdraw such application, and such withdrawal shall take effect upon the expiration of sixty days from the day on which written notice of such withdrawal is received by the Secretary-General of the United Nations.

6. The original of this Protocol shall be deposited with the Secretary-General of the United Nations, who will furnish certified copies thereof to all interested Governments.

IN WITNESS WHEREOF the respective Representatives, after having communicated their full powers, found to be in good and due form, have signed this Protocol.

DONE at Geneva, in a single copy, in the English and French languages, both texts authentic, this thirtieth day of October, one thousand nine hundred and forty-seven.

PROTOCOL AMENDING THE GENERAL AGREEMENT ON TARIFFS AND TRADE TO INTRODUCE A PART IV ON TRADE AND DEVELOPMENT[1]

Done at Geneva February 8, 1965; signed on behalf of the United States of America February 8, 1965; entered into force June 27, 1966

The Governments which are contracting parties to the General Agreement on Tariffs and Trade[1] (hereinafter referred to as "the contracting parties" and "the General Agreement" respectively),

DESIRING to effect amendments to the General Agreement pursuant to the provisions of Article XXX thereof,

HEREBY AGREE as follows:

1. A Part IV comprising three new Articles shall be inserted and the provisions of Annex I shall be amended as follows:

A

The following heading and Articles shall be inserted after Articles XXXV:

"PART IV—TRADE AND DEVELOPMENT

"ARTICLE XXXVI—PRINCIPLES AND OBJECTIVES

"1. The contracting parties,

(a) recalling that the basic objectives of this Agreement include the raising of standards of living and the progressive development of the economies of all contracting parties, and considering that the attainment of these objectives is particularly urgent for less-developed contracting parties;

(b) considering that export earnings of the less-developed contracting parties can play a vital part in their economic development and that the extent of this contribution depends on the prices paid by the less-developed contracting parties for essential imports, the volume of their exports, and the prices received for these exports;

(c) noting, that there is a wide gap between standards of living in less-developed countries and in other countries;

(d) recognizing that individual and joint action is essential to further the development of the economies of less-developed contracting parties and to bring about a rapid advance in the standards of living in these countries;

---

[1] 17 UST 1977; TIAS 6139: 572 UNTS 320.

(e) recognizing that international trade as means of achieving economic and social advancement should be governed by such rules and procedures—and measures in conformity with such rules and procedures—as are consistent with the objectives set forth in this Article;

(f) noting that the contracting parties may enable less-developed contracting parties to use special measures to promote their trade and development;

agree as follows:

"2. There is need for a rapid and sustained expansion of the export earnings of the less-developed contracting parties.

"3. There is need for positive efforts designed to ensure that less-developed contracting parties secure a share in the growth in international trade commensurate with the needs of their economic development.

"4. Given the continued dependence of many less-developed contracting parties on the exportation of a limited range of primary products, there is need to provide in the largest possible measure more favourable and acceptable conditions of access to world markets for these products, and wherever appropriate to devise measures designed to stabilize and improve conditions of world markets in these products, including in particular measures designed to attain stable, equitable and remunerative prices, thus permitting an expansion of world trade and demand and a dynamic and steady growth of the real export earnings of these countries so as to provide them with expanding resources for their economic development.

"5. The rapid expansion of the economies of the less-developed contracting parties will be facilitated by a diversification of the structure of their economies and the avoidance of an excessive dependence on the export of primary products. These is, therefore, need for increased access in the largest possible measure to markets under favourable conditions for processed and manufactured products currently or potentially of particular export interest to less-developed contracting parties.

"6. Because of the chronic deficiency in the export proceeds and other foreign exchange earnings of less-developed contracting parties, there are important inter-relationships between trade and financial assistance to development. There is, therefore, need for close and continuing collaboration between the contracting parties and the international lending agencies so that they can contribute most effectively to alleviating the burdens these less-developed contracting parties assume in the interest of their economic development.

"7. There is need for appropriate collaboration between the contracting parties, other intergovernmental bodies and the organs and agencies of the United Nations system, whose activities relate to the trade and economic development of less-developed countries.

"8. The developed contracting parties do not expect reciprocity for commitments made by them in trade negotiations to reduce or remove tariffs and other barriers to the trade of less-developed contracting parties.

"9. The adoption of measures to give effect to these principles and objectives shall be a matter of conscious and purposeful effort on the part of the contracting parties both individually and jointly.

"ARTICLE XXXVII—COMMITMENTS

"1. The developed contracting parties shall to the fullest extent possible—that is, except when compelling reasons, which may include legal reasons, make it impossible—give effect to the following provisions:

(a) accord high priority to the reduction and elimination of barriers to products currently or potentially of particular export interest to less-developed contracting parties, including customs duties and other restrictions which differentiate unreasonably between such products in their primary and in their processed forms;

(b) refrain from introducing, or increasing the incidence of, customs duties or non-tariff import barriers on products currently or potentially of particular export interest to less-developed contracting parties; and

(c) (i) refrain from imposing new fiscal measures, and

(ii) in any adjustments of fiscal policy accord high priority to the reduction and elimination of fiscal measures,

which would hamper, or which hamper, significantly the growth of consumption of primary products, in raw or processed form, wholly or mainly produced in the territories of less-developed contracting parties, and which are applied specifically to those products.

"2. (a) Whenever it is considered that effect is not being given to any of the provisions of sub-paragraph (a), (b) or (c) of paragraph 1, the matter shall be reported to the contracting parties either by the contracting party not so giving effect to the relevant provisions or by any other interested contracting party.

(b)(i) The contracting parties shall, if requested so to do by any interested contracting party, and without prejudice to any bilateral consultations that may be undertaken, consult with the contracting party concerned and all interested contracting parties with respect to the matter with a view to reaching solutions satisfactory to all contracting parties concerned in order to further the objectives set forth in Article XXXVI. In the course of these consultations, the reasons given in cases where effect was not being given to the provisions of sub-paragraph (a), (b) or (c) of paragraph 1 shall be examined.

(ii) As the implementation of the provisions of sub-paragraph (a), (b) or (c) of paragraph 1 by individual contracting parties may in some cases be more readily achieved where action is taken jointly with other developed contracting parties, such consultation might, where appropriate, be directed towards this end.

(iii) The consultations by the contracting parties might also, in appropriate cases, be directed towards agreement on joint action designed to further the objectives of this Agreement as envisaged in paragraph 1 of Article XXV.

"3. The developed contracting parties shall:

(a) make every effort, in cases where a government directly or indirectly determines the resale price of products wholly or mainly produced in the territories of less-developed contracting parties, to maintain trade margins at equitable levels;

(b) give active consideration to the adoption of other measures designed to provide greater scope for the development of imports from less-developed contracting parties and collaborate in appropriate international action to this end;

(c) have special regard to the trade interests of less-developed contracting parties when considering the application of other measures permitted under this Agreement to meet particular problems and explore all possibilities of constructive remedies before applying such measures where they would affect essential interests of those contracting parties.

"4. Less-developed contracting parties agree to take appropriate action in implementation of the provisions of Part IV for the benefit of the trade of other less-developed contracting parties, insofar as such action is consistent with their individual present and future development, financial and trade needs taking into account past trade developments as well as the trade interests of less-developed contracting parties as a whole.

"5. In the implementation of the commitments set forth in paragraphs 1 to 4 each contracting party shall afford to any other interested contracting party or contracting parties full and prompt opportunity for consultations under the normal procedures of this Agreement with respect to any matter or difficulty which may arise.

"ARTICLE XXXVIII—JOINT ACTION

"1. The contracting parties shall collaborate jointly, within the framework of this Agreement and elsewhere, as appropriate, to further the objectives set forth in Article XXXVI.

"2. In particular, the contracting parties shall:

(a) where appropriate, take action, including action through international arrangements, to provide improved and acceptable conditions of access to world markets for primary products of particular interest to less-developed contracting parties and to devise measures designed to stabilize and improve conditions of world markets in these products including measures designed to attain stable, equitable and remunerative prices for exports of such products;

(b) seek appropriate collaboration in matters of trade and development policy with the United Nations and its organs and agencies, including any institutions that may be created on the basis of recommendations by the United Nations Conference on Trade and Development;

(c) collaborate in analyzing the development plans and policies of individual less-developed contracting parties and in examining trade and aid relationships with a view to devising concrete measures to promote the development of export potential and to facilitate access to export markets for the products of the industries thus developed and, in this connexion seek appropriate collaboration with governments and international organizations, and in particular with organizations having competence in relation to financial assistance for economic development, in systematic studies of trade and aid relationships in individual less-developed contracting parties aimed at obtaining a clear analysis of export potential, market prospects and any further action that may be required;

(d) keep under continuous review the development of world trade with special reference to the rate of growth of the trade of less-developed contracting parties and make such recommendations to contracting parties as may, in the circumstances, be deemed appropriate;

(e) collaborate in seeking feasible methods to expand trade for the purpose of economic development, through international harmonization and adjustment of national policies and regulations, through technical and commercial standards affecting production, transportation and marketing, and through export promotion by the establishment of facilities for the increased flow of trade information and the development of market research; and

(f) establish such institutional arrangements as may be necessary to further the objectives set forth in Article XXXVI and to give effect to provisions of this Part."

B

To Annex I (which, pursuant to Section BB(i) of the Protocol amending the Preamble and Parts II and III,[2] is to become Annex H) the following notes shall be added:

"Ad Part IV

The words 'developed contracting parties' and the words 'less-developed contracting parties' as used in Part IV are to be understood to refer to developed and less-developed countries which are parties to the General Agreement on Tariffs and Trade.

"Ad Article XXXVI

"Paragraph 1

This Article is based upon the objectives set forth in Article I as it will be amended by Section A of paragraph 1 of the Protocol Amending Part I and Articles XXIX and XXX when that Protocol enters into force.

"Paragraph 4

The term 'primary products' includes agricultural products, *vide* paragraph 2 of the note Ad Article XVI, Section B.

---

[2] TIAS 3930; 8 UST 1795.

"Paragraph 5

A diversification programme would generally include the intensification of activities for the processing of primary products and the development of manufacturing industries, taking into account the situation of the particular contracting party and the world outlook for production and consumption of different commodities.

"Paragraph 8

It is understood that the phrase 'do not expect reciprocity' means, in accordance with the objectives set forth in this Article, that the less-developed contracting parties should not be expected, in the course of trade negotiations, to make contributions which are inconsistent with their individual development, financial and trade needs, taking into consideration past trade developments.

This paragraph would apply in the event of action under Section A of Article XVIII, Article XXVIII, Article XXVIII BIS (Article XXIX after the amendment set forth in Section A of paragraph 1 of the Protocol Amending Part I and Articles XXIX and XXX shall have become effective), Article XXXIII, or any other procedure under this Agreement.

"Ad Article XXXVII

"Paragraph 1(a)

This paragraph would apply in the event of negotiations for reduction or elimination of tariffs or other restrictive regulations of commerce under Articles XXVIII, XXVIII BIS (XXIX after the amendment set forth in Section A of paragraph 1 of the Protocol Amending Part I and Articles XXIX and XXX shall have become effective), and Article XXXIII, as well as in connexion with other action to effect such reduction or elimination which contracting parties may be able to undertake.

"Paragraph 3(b)

The other measures referred to in this paragraph might include steps to promote domestic structural changes, to encourage the consumption of particular products, or to introduce measures of trade promotion."

2. This Protocol shall be deposited with the Executive Secretary to the contracting parties to the General Agreement. It shall be open for acceptance, by signature or otherwise, by the contracting parties to the General Agreement and by the governments which have acceded provisionally to the Gen-

eral Agreement, until 31 December 1965; *provided,* That the period during which this Protocol may be accepted in respect of a contracting party or such government may, by a decision of the contracting parties, be extended beyond that date.[3]

3. Acceptance of this Protocol in accordance with the provisions of paragraph 2 shall be deemed to constitute an acceptance of the amendments set forth in paragraph 1 in accordance with the provisions of Article XXX of the General Agreement.

4. The amendments set forth in paragraph 1 shall become effective in accordance with the provisions of Article XXX of the General Agreement following acceptance of the Protocol by two thirds of the governments which are then contracting parties.

5. The amendments set forth in paragraph 1 shall become effective between a government which has acceded provisionally to the General Agreement and a government which is a contracting party, and between two governments which have acceded provisionally when such amendments shall have been accepted by both such governments; *provided,* That the amendments shall not become so effective before an instrument of provisional accession shall have become effective between the two governments nor before the amendments shall have become effective in accordance with the provisions of paragraph 4.

6. Acceptance of this Protocol by a contracting party, to the extent that it shall not have already taken final action to become a party to the following instruments and except as it may otherwise notify the Executive Secretary in writing at the time of such acceptance, shall constitute final action to become a party to each of the following instruments.

---

[3] Extended until the close of the twenty-fourth session of the contracting parties (Decision of Jan. 17, 1966: not printed).

MEMBERSHIP IN GATT AS OF DECEMBER 31, 1982

Argentina
Australia
Austria
Bangladesh
Barbados
Belgium
Benin
Brazil
Burma
Burundi
Cameroon
Canada
Central African
  Republic
Chad
Chile
Columbia
Congo
Cuba
Cyprus
Czechoslovakia
Denmark
Dominican Republic
Egypt
Finland
France
Gabon
Gambia
Germany, Fed. Rep. of
Ghana
Greece

Guyana
Haiti
Hungary
Iceland
India
Indonesia
Ireland
Israel
Italy
Ivory Coast
Jamaica
Japan
Kenya
Korea, Rep. of
Kuwait
Luxembourg
Madagascar
Malawi
Malaysia
Malta
Mauritania
Mauritius
Netherlands
New Zealand
Nicaragua
Niger
Nigeria
Norway
Pakistan
Peru

Philippines
Poland
Portugal
Romania
Rwanda
Senegal
Sierra Leone
Singapore
South Africa
Spain
Sri Lanka
Suriname
Sweden
Switzerland
Tanzania
Thailand
Togo
Trinidad and
  Tobago
Turkey
Uganda
United Kingdom
United States of
  America
Upper Volta
Uruguay
Yugoslavia
Zaire
Zambia
Zimbabwe

Acceded Provisionally (1)

Tunisia

2. International Anti-Dumping Code[1] (1967)

Agreement on Implementation of Article VI of the General Agreement on Tariffs and Trade; Done at Geneva, June 30, 1967; entered into force for the United States, July 1, 1968

The parties to this Agreement,

Considering, That Ministers on 21 May 1963 agreed that a significant liberalization of world trade was desirable and that the comprehensive trade negotiations, the 1964 Trade Negotiations, should deal not only with tariffs but also with non-tariff barriers;

Recognizing, That anti-dumping practices should not constitute an unjustifiable impediment to international trade and that anti-dumping duties may be applied against dumping only if such dumping causes or threatens material injury to an established industry or materially retards the establishment of an industry;

Considering, That it is desirable to provide for equitable and open procedures as the basis for a full examination of dumping cases; and

Desiring, To interpret the provisions of Article VI of the General Agreement and to elaborate rules for their application in order to provide greater uniformity and certainty in their implementation:

Hereby agree, As follows:

PART I—ANTI-DUMPING CODE

Article 1

The imposition of an anti-dumping duty is a measure to be taken only under the circumstances provided for in Article VI of the General Agreement. The following provisions govern the application of this Article, in so far as action is taken under anti-dumping legislation or regulations.

A. DETERMINATION OF DUMPING

Article 2

(a) For the purpose of this Code a product is to be considered as being dumped, i.e. introduced into the commerce of another country at less than its normal value, if the export price of the product exported from one country to another is less than the comparable price, in the ordinary course of trade, for the like product when destined for consumption in the exporting country.

(b) Throughout this Code the term "like product" ("produit similaire") shall be interpreted to mean a product which is identical, i.e. alike in all

---

[1] 19 UST 4348: TIAS 6431.

respects to the product under consideration, or in the absence of such a product, another product which, although not alike in all respects, has characteristics closely resembling those of the product under consideration.

(c) In the case where products are not imported directly from the country of origin but are exported [to the country] of importation from an intermediate country, the price at which the products are sold from the country of export to the country of importation shall normally be compared with the comparable price in the country of export. However, comparison may be made with the price in the country of origin, if, for example, the products are merely trans-shipped through the country of export, or such products are not produced in the country of export, or there is no comparable price for them in the country of export.

(d) Where there are no sales of the like product in the ordinary course of trade in the domestic market of the exporting country or when, because of the particular market situation, such sales do not permit a proper comparison, the margin of dumping shall be determined by comparison with a comparable price of the like product when exported to any third country which may be the highest such export price but should be a representative price, or with the cost of production in the country of origin plus a reasonable amount for administrative, selling and any other costs and for profits. As a general rule, the addition for profit shall not exceed the profit normally realized on sales of products of the same general category in the domestic market of the country of origin.

(e) In cases where there is no export price or where it appears to the authorities[2] concerned that the export price is unreliable because of association or a compensatory arrangement between the exporter and the importer or a third party, the export price may be constructed on the basis of the price at which the imported products are first resold to an independent buyer, or if the products are not resold to an independent buyer, or not resold in the condition as imported, on such reasonable basis as the authorities may determine.

(f) In order to effect a fair comparison between the export price and the domestic price in the exporting country (or the country of origin) or, if applicable, the price established pursuant to the provisions of Article VI:1(b) of the General Agreement, the two prices shall be compared at the same level of trade, normally at the ex factory level, and in respect of sales made at as nearly as possible the same time. Due allowance shall be made in each case, on its merits, for the differences in conditions and terms of sale, for the differences in taxation, and for the other differences affecting price comparab lity. In the case referred to in Article 2(e) allowance for costs, including duties and taxes, incurred between importation and resale, and for profits accruing, should also be made.

---

[2] When in this Code the term "authorities" is used, it shall be interpreted as meaning authorities at an appropriate, senior level.

(g) This Article is without prejudice to the second Supplementary Provision to paragraph 1 of Article VI in Annex I of the General Agreement.

B. DETERMINATION OF MATERIAL INJURY, THREAT OF MATERIAL INJURY AND MATERIAL RETARDATION

Article 3

Determination of Injury[3]

(a) A determination of injury shall be made only when the authorities concerned are satisfied that the dumped imports are demonstrably the principal cause of material injury or of threat of material injury to a domestic industry or the principal cause of material retardation of the establishment of such an industry. In reaching their decision the authorities shall weigh, on one hand, the effect of the dumping and, on the other hand, all other factors taken together which may be adversely affecting the industry. The determination shall in all cases be based on positive findings and not on mere allegations or hypothetical possibilities. In the case of retarding the establishment of a new industry in the country of importation, convincing evidence of the forthcoming establishment of an industry must be shown, for example that the plans for a new industry have reached a fairly advanced stage, a factory is being constructed or machinery has been ordered.

(b) The valuation of injury—that is the evaluation of the effects of the dumped imports on the industry in question—shall be based on examination of all factors having a bearing on the state of the industry in question, such as: development and prospects with regard to turnover, market share, profits, prices (including the extent to which the delivered, duty-paid price is lower or higher than the comparable price for the like product prevailing in the course of normal commercial transactions in the importing country), export performance, employment, volume of dumped and other imports, utilization of capacity of domestic industry, and productivity; and restrictive trade practices. No one or several of these factors can necessarily give decisive guidance.

(c) In order to establish whether dumped imports have caused injury, all other factors which, individually or in combination, may be adversely affecting the industry shall be examined, for example: the volume and prices of undumped imports of the product in question, competition between the do-

---

[3] When in this Code the term "injury" is used, it shall, unless otherwise specified, be interpreted as covering cause of material injury to a domestic industry, threat of material injury to a domestic industry or material retardation of the establishment of such an industry.

mestic producers themselves, contraction in demand due to substitution of other products or to changes in consumer tastes.

(d) The effect of the dumped imports shall be assessed in relation to the domestic production of the like product when available data permit the separate identification of production in terms of such criteria as: the production process, the producers' realizations, profits. When the domestic production of the like product has no separate identity in these terms the effect of the dumped imports shall be assessed by the examination of the production of the narrowest group or range of products, which includes the like product, for which the necessary information can be provided.

(e) A determination of threat of material injury shall be based on facts and not merely on allegation, conjecture or remote possibility. The change in circumstances which would create a situation in which the dumping would cause material injury must be clearly foreseen and imminent.[4]

(f) With respect to cases where material injury is threatened by dumped imports, the application of anti-dumping measures shall be studied and decided with special care.

Article 4

Definition of Industry

(a) In determining injury the term "domestic industry" shall be interpreted as referring to the domestic producers as a whole of the like products or to those of them whose collective output of the products constitutes a major proportion of the total domestic production of those products except that

(i) when producers are importers of the allegedly dumped product the industry may be interpreted as referring to the rest of the producers;

(ii) in exceptional circumstances a country may, for the production in question, be divided into two or more competitive markets and the producers within each market regarded as a separate industry, if, because of transport costs, all the producers within such a market sell all or almost all of their production of the product in question in that market, and none, or almost none, of the product in question produced elsewhere in the country is sold in that market or if there exist special

---

[4] One example, though not an exclusive one, is that there is convincing reason to believe that there will be, in the immediate future, substantially increased importations of the product at dumped prices.

regional marketing conditions (for example, traditional patterns of distribution or consumer tastes) which result in an equal degree of isolation of the producers in such a market from the rest of the industry, provided, however, that injury may be found in such circumstances only if there is injury to all or almost all of the total production of the product in the market as defined.

(b) Where two or more countries have reached such a level of integration that they have the characteristics of a single, unified market, the industry in the entire area of integration shall be taken to be the industry referred to in Article 4(a).

(c) The provisions of Article 3(d) shall be applicable to this Article.

C. INVESTIGATION AND ADMINISTRATION PROCEDURES

Article 5

Initiation and Subsequent Investigation

(a) Investigations shall normally be initiated upon a request on behalf of the industry[5] affected, supported by evidence both of dumping and of injury resulting therefrom for this industry. If in special circumstances the authorities concerned decide to initiate an investigation without having received such a request, they shall proceed only if they have evidence both on dumping and on injury resulting therefrom.

(b) Upon initiation of an investigation and thereafter, the evidence of both dumping and injury should be considered simultaneously. In any event the evidence of both dumping and injury shall be considered simultaneously in the decision whether or not to initiate an investigation, and thereafter, during the course of the investigation, starting on a date not later than the earliest date on which provisional measures may be applied, except in the cases provided for in Article 10(d) in which the authorities accept the request of the exporter and the importer.

(c) An application shall be rejected and an investigation shall be terminated promptly as soon as the authorities concerned are satisfied that there is not sufficient evidence of either dumping or of injury to justify proceeding with the case. There should be immediate termination in cases where the margin of dumping or the volume of dumped imports, actual or potential, or the injury is negligible.

---

[5] As defined in Article 4.

(d) An anti-dumping proceeding shall not hinder the procedures of customs clearance.

Article 6

Evidence

(a) The foreign suppliers and all other interested parties shall be given ample opportunity to present in writing all evidence that they consider useful in respect to the anti-dumping investigation in question. They shall also have the right, on justification, to present evidence orally.

(b) The authorities concerned shall provide opportunities for the complainant and the importers and exporters known to be concerned and the governments of the exporting countries, to see all information that is relevant to the presentation of their cases, that is not confidential as defined in paragraph (c) below, and that is used by the authorities in an anti-dumping investigation, and to prepare presentations on the basis of this information.

(c) All information which is by nature confidential (for example, because its disclosure would be of significant competitive advantage to a competitor or because its disclosure would have a significantly adverse effect upon a person supplying the information or upon a person from whom he acquired the information) or which is provided on a confidential basis by parties to an anti-dumping investigation shall be treated as strictly confidential by the authorities concerned who shall not reveal it, without specific permission of the party submitting such information.

(d) However, if the authorities concerned find that a request for confidentiality is not warranted and if the supplier is either unwilling to make the information public or to authorize its disclosure in generalized or summary form, the authorities would be free to disregard such information unless it can be demonstrated to their satisfaction from appropriate sources that the information is correct.

(e) In order to verify information provided or to obtain further details the authorities may carry out investigations in other countries as required, provided they obtain the agreement of the firms concerned and provided they notify the representatives of the government of the country in question and unless the latter object to the investigation.

(f) Once the competent authorities are satisfied that there is sufficient evidence to justify initiating an anti-dumping investigation pursuant to Article 5 representatives of the exporting country and the exporters and importers known to be concerned shall be notified and a public notice may be published.

(g) Throughout the anti-dumping investigation all parties shall have a full opportunity for the defense of their interests. To this end, the authorities concerned shall, on request, provide opportunities for all directly interested parties to meet those parties with adverse interests, so that opposing views may be presented and rebuttal arguments offered. Provision of such opportunities must take account of the need to preserve confidentiality and of the convenience to the parties. There shall be no obligation on any party to attend a meeting and failure to do so shall not be prejudicial to that party's case.

(h) The authorities concerned shall notify representatives of the exporting country and the directly interested parties of their decisions regarding imposition or non-imposition of anti-dumping duties, indicating the reasons for such decisions and the criteria applied, and shall, unless there are special reasons against doing so, make public the decisions.

(i) The provisions of this Article shall not preclude the authorities from reaching preliminary determinations, affirmative or negative, or from applying provisional measures expeditiously. In cases in which any interested party withholds the necessary information, a final finding, affirmative or negative, may be made on the basis of the facts available.

Article 7

Price Undertakings

(a) Anti-dumping proceedings may be terminated without imposition of anti-dumping duties or provisional measures upon receipt of a voluntary undertaking by the exporters to revise their prices so that the margin of dumping is eliminated or to cease to export to the area in question at dumped prices if the authorities concerned consider this practicable, e.g., if the number of exporters or potential exporters of the product in question is not too great and/or if the trading practices are suitable.

(b) If the exporters concerned undertake during the examination of a case, to revise prices or to cease to export the product in question, and the authorities concerned accept the undertaking, the investigation of injury shall nevertheless be completed if the exporters so desire or the authorities concerned so decide. If a determination of no injury is made, the undertaking given by the exporters shall automatically lapse unless the exporters state that it shall not lapse. The fact that exporters do not offer to give such undertakings during the period of investigation, or do not accept an invitation made by the investigating authorities to do so, shall in no way be prejudicial to the consideration of the case. However, the authorities are of course free to determine that a threat of injury is more likely to be realized if the dumped imports continue.

D. ANTI-DUMPING DUTIES AND PROVISIONAL MEASURES

Article 8

Imposition and Collection of Anti-Dumping Duties

(a) The decision whether or not to impose an anti-dumping duty in cases where all requirements for the imposition have been fulfilled and the decision whether the amount of the anti-dumping duty to be imposed shall be the full margin of dumping or less, are decisions to be made by the authorities of the importing country or customs territory. It is desirable that the imposition be permissive in all countries or customs territories parties to this Agreement, and that the duty be less than the margin, if such lesser duty would be adequate to remove the injury to the domestic industry.

(b) When an anti-dumping duty is imposed in respect of any product, such anti-dumping duty shall be levied, in the appropriate amounts in each case, on a non-discriminatory basis on imports of such product from all sources found to be dumped and causing injury. The authorities shall name the supplier or suppliers of the product concerned. If, however, several suppliers from the same country are involved, and it is impracticable to name all these suppliers, the authorities may name the supplying country concerned. If several suppliers from more than one country are involved, the authorities may name either all the suppliers involved, or, if this is impracticable, all the supplying countries involved.

(c) The amount of the anti-dumping duty must not exceed the margin of dumping as established under Article 2. Therefore, if subsequent to the application of the anti-dumping duty it is found that the duty so collected exceeds the actual dumping margin, the amount in excess of the margin shall be reimbursed as quickly as possible.

(d) Within a basic price system the following rules shall apply provided that their application is consistent with the other provisions of this Code:

If several suppliers from one or more countries are involved, anti-dumping duties may be imposed on imports of the product in question found to have been dumped and to be causing injury from the country or countries concerned, the duty being equivalent to the amount by which the export price is less than the basic price established for this purpose, not exceeding the lowest normal price in the supplying country or countries where normal conditions of competition are prevailing. It is understood that for products which are sold below this already established basic price a new anti-dumping investigation shall be carried out in each particular case, when so demanded by the interested parties and the demand is supported by relevant evidence. In cases where no dumping is found, anti-dumping duties collected shall be reimbursed as quickly as possible. Furthermore, if it can be found that the duty so collected exceeds the actual dumping margin, the amount in excess of the margin shall be reimbursed as quickly as possible.

(e) When the industry has been interpreted as referring to the producers in a certain area, i.e., a market as defined in Article 4(a)(ii), anti-dumping duties shall only be definitively collected on the products in question consigned for final consumption to that area, except in cases where the exporter shall, prior to the imposition of anti-dumping duties, be given an opportunity to cease dumping in the area concerned. In such cases, if an adequate assurance to this effect is promptly given, anti-dumping duties shall not be imposed, provided, however, that if the assurance is not given or is not fulfilled, the duties may be imposed without limitation to an area.

Article 9

Duration of Anti-Dumping Duties

(a) An anti-dumping duty shall remain in force only as long as it is necessary in order to counteract dumping which is causing injury.

(b) The authorities concerned shall review the need for the continued imposition of the duty, where warranted, on their own initiative or if interested suppliers or importers of the product so request and submit information substantiating the need for review.

Article 10

Provisional Measures

(a) Provisional measures may be taken only when a preliminary decision has been taken that there is dumping and when there is sufficient evidence of injury.

(b) Provisional measures may take the form of a provisional duty or, preferably, a security—by deposit or bond—equal to the amount of the anti-dumping duty provisionally estimated, being not greater than the provisionally estimated margin of dumping. Withholding of appraisement is an appropriate provisional measure provided that the normal duty and the estimated amount of the anti-dumping duty be indicated and as long as the withholding of appraisement is subject to the same conditions as other provisional measures

(c) The authorities concerned shall inform representatives of the exporting country and the directly interested parties of their decisions regarding imposition of provisional measures indicating the reasons for such decisions and the criteria applied, and shall, unless there are special reasons against doing so, make public such decisions.

(d) The imposition of provisional measures shall be limited to as short a period as possible. More specifically, provisional measures shall not be imposed for a period longer than three months or, on decision of the authorities concerned upon request by the exporter and the importer, six months.

(e) The relevant provisions of Article 8 shall be followed in the application of provisional measures.

Article 11

Retroactivity

Anti-dumping duties and provisional measures shall only be applied to products which enter for consumption after the time when the decision taken under Articles 8(a) and 10(a), respectively, enters into force, except that in cases:

(i) Where a determination of material injury (but not of a threat of material injury, or of a material retardation of the establishment of an industry) is made or where the provisional measures consist of provisional duties and the dumped imports carried out during the period of their application would, in the absence of these provisional measures, have caused material injury, anti-dumping duties may be levied retroactively for the period for which provisional measures, if any, have been applied.

If the anti-dumping duty fixed in the final decision is higher than the provisionally paid duty, the difference shall not be collected. If the duty fixed in the final decision is lower than the provisionally paid duty or the amount estimated for the purpose of the security, the difference shall be reimbursed or the duty recalculated, as the case may be.

(ii) Where appraisement is suspended for the product in question for reasons which arose before the initiation of the dumping case and which are unrelated to the question of dumping, retroactive assessment of anti-dumping duties may extend back to a period not more than 120 days before the submission of the complaint.

(iii) Where for the dumped product in question the authorities determine

(a) either that there is a history of dumping which caused material injury or that the importer was, or should have been, aware that the exporter practices dumping and that such dumping would cause material injury, and

(b) that the material injury is caused by sporadic dumping (massive dumped imports of a product in a relatively short period) to such an extent that, in order to preclude it recurring, it appears necessary to assess an anti-dumping duty retroactively on those imports,

the duty may be assessed on products which were entered for consumption not more than 90 days prior to the date of application of provisional measures.

E. ANTI-DUMPING ACTION ON BEHALF OF A THIRD COUNTRY

Article 12

(a) An application for anti-dumping action on behalf of a third country shall be made by the authorities of the third country requesting action.

(b) Such an application shall be supported by price information to show that the imports are being dumped and by detailed information to show that the alleged dumping is causing injury to the domestic industry concerned in the third country. The government of the third country shall afford all assistance to the authorities of the importing country to obtain any further information which the latter may require.

(c) The authorities of the importing country in considering such an application shall consider the effects of the alleged dumping on the industry concerned as a whole in the third country; that is to say the injury shall not be assessed in relation only to the effect of the alleged dumping on the industry's exports to the importing country or even on the industry's total exports.

(d) The decision whether or not to proceed with a case shall rest with the importing country. If the importing country decides that it is prepared to take action, the initiation of the approach to the contracting parties seeking their approval for such action shall rest with the importing country.

PART II—FINAL PROVISIONS

Article 13

This Agreement shall be open for acceptance, by signature or otherwise, by contracting parties to the General Agreement and by the European Economic Community. The Agreement shall enter into force on 1 July 1968 for each party which has accepted it by that date. For each party accepting the Agreement after that date, it shall enter into force upon acceptance.

Article 14

Each party to this Agreement shall take all necessary steps, of a general or particicular character, to ensure, not later than the date of the entry into force of the Agreement for it, the conformity of its laws, regulations and administrative procedures with the provisions of the Anti-Dumping Code.

Article 15

Each party to this Agreement shall inform the contracting parties to the General Agreement of any changes in its anti-dumping laws and regulations and in the administration of such laws and regulations.

Article 16

Each party to this Agreement shall report to the contracting parties annually on the administration of its anti-dumping laws and regulations, giving summaries of the cases in which anti-dumping duties have been assessed definitively.

Article 17

The parties to this Agreement shall request the contracting parties to establish a Committee on Anti-Dumping Practices composed of representatives of the parties to this Agreement. The Committee shall normally meet once each year for the purpose of affording parties to this Agreement the opportunity of consulting on matters relating to the administration of anti-dumping systems in any participating country or customs territory as it might affect the operation of the Anti-Dumping Code or the furtherance of its objectives. Such consultations shall be without prejudice to Article XXII and XXIII of the General Agreement.

This Agreement shall be deposited with the Director-General to the contracting parties who shall promptly furnish a certified copy thereof and a notification of each acceptance thereof to each contracting party to the General Agreement and to the European Economic Community.

This Agreement shall be registered in accordance with the provisions of Article 102 of the Charter of the United Nations.

DONE at Geneva this thirtieth day of June, one thousand nine hundred and sixty-seven, in a single copy, in the English and French languages, both texts being authentic.

3. United Nations Charter

(Excerpts)

CHAPTER X—THE ECONOMIC AND SOCIAL COUNCIL

Composition

ARTICLE 61

1. The Economic and Social Council shall consist of fifty-four Members of the United Nations elected by the General Assembly.

2. Subject to the provisions of paragraph 3, eighteen members of the Economic and Social Council shall be elected each year for a term of three years. A retiring member shall be eligible for immediate re-election.

3. At the first election after the increase in the membership of the Economic and Social Council from twenty-seven to fifty-four members, in addition to the members elected in place of the nine members whose term of office expires at the end of that year, twenty-seven additional members shall be elected. Of these twenty-seven additional members, the term of office of nine members so elected shall expire at the end of one year, and of nine other members at the end of two years, in accordance with arrangements made by the General Assembly.

4. Each member of the Economic and Social Council shall have one representative.

Functions and Powers

ARTICLE 62

1. The Economic and Social Council may make or initiate studies and reports with respect to international economic, social, cultural, educational, health, and related matters and may make recommendations with respect to any such matters to the General Assembly, to the Members of the United Nations, and to the specialized agencies concerned.

2. It may make recommendations for the purpose of promoting respect for, and observance of, human rights and fundamental freedoms for all.

3. It may prepare draft conventions for submission to the General Assembly, with respect to matters falling within its competence.

4. It may call, in accordance with the rules prescribed by the United Nations, international conferences on matters falling within its competence.

ARTICLE 63

1. The Economic and Social Council may enter into agreements with any of the agencies referred to in Article 57, defining the terms on which the agency concerned shall be brought into relationship with the United Nations. Such agreements shall be subject to approval by the General Assembly.

2. It may coordinate the activities of the specialized agencies through consultation with and recommendations to such agencies and through recommendations to the General Assembly and to the Members of the United Nations.

ARTICLE 64

1. The Economic and Social Council may take appropriate steps to obtain regular reports from the specialized agencies. It may make arrangements with the Members of the United Nations and with the specialized agencies to obtain reports on the steps taken to give effect to its own recommendations and to recommendations on matters falling within its competence made by the General Assembly.

2. It may communicate its observations on these reports to the General Assembly.

ARTICLE 65

The Economic and Social Council may furnish information to the Security Council and shall assist the Secuurity Council upon its request.

ARTICLE 66

1. The Economic and Social Council shall perform such functions as fall within its competence in connection with the carrying out of the recommendations of the General Assembly.

2. It may, with the approval of the General Assembly, perform services at the request of Members of the United Nations and at the request of specialized agencies.

3. It shall perform such other functions as are specified elsewhere in the present Charter or as may be assigned to it by the General Assembly.

Voting

ARTICLE 67

1. Each member of the Economic and Social Council shall have one vote.

2. Decisions of the Economic and Social Council shall be made by a majority of the members present and voting.

Procedure

ARTICLE 68

The Economic and Social Council shall set up commissions in economic and social fields and for the promotion of human rights, and such other commissions as may be required for the performance of its functions.

ARTICLE 69

The Economic and Social Council shall invite any Member of the United Nations to participate, without vote, in its deliberations on any matters of particular concern to that Member.

ARTICLE 70

The Economic and Social Council may make arrangements for representatives of the specialized agencies to participate, without vote, in its deliberations and in those of the commissions established by it, and for its representatives to participate in the deliberations of the specialized agencies.

ARTICLE 71

The Economic and Social Council may make suitable arrangements for consultation with non-governmental organizations which are concerned with matters within its competence. Such arrangements may be made with international organizations and, where appropriate, with national organizations after consultation with the Member of the United Nations concerned.

ARTICLE 72

1. The Economic and Social Council shall adopt its own rules of procedure, including the method of selecting its President.

2. The Economic and Social Council shall meet as required in accordance with its rules, which shall include provision for the convening of meetings on the request of a majority of its members.

II. DOCUMENTS OF THE EUROPEAN COMMUNITY

1. Treaty of Paris Establishing the European Coal and Steel Community (excerpts)

THE PRESIDENT OF THE FEDERAL REPUBLIC OF GERMANY, HIS ROYAL HIGHNESS THE PRINCE ROYAL OF BELGIUM, THE PRESIDENT OF THE FRENCH REPUBLIC, THE PRESIDENT OF THE ITALIAN REPUBLIC, HER ROYAL HIGHNESS THE GRAND DUCHESS OF LUXEMBOURG, HER MAJESTY THE QUEEN OF THE NETHERLANDS,

CONSIDERING that world peace can be safeguarded only by creative efforts commensurate with the dangers that threaten it,

CONVINCED that the contribution which an organised and vital Europe can make to civilisation is indispensible to the maintenance of peaceful relations,

RECOGNISING that Europe can be built only through practical achievements which will first of all create real solidarity, and through the establishment of common bases for economic development,

ANXIOUS to help, by expanding their basic production, to raise the standard of living and further the works of peace,

RESOLVED to substitute for age-old rivalries the merging of their essential interests; to create, by establishing an economic community, the basis for a broader and deeper community among peoples long divided by bloody conflicts; and to lay the foundations for institutions which will give direction to a destiny henceforward shared,

HAVE DECIDED to create a European Coal and Steel Community and to this end have designated as their plenipotentiaries:

. . . . .

WHO, having exchanged their Full Powers, found in good and due form,

HAVE AGREED as follows:

TITLE ONE

ARTICLE 1

By this Treaty, the HIGH CONTRACTING PARTIES establish among themselves a EUROPEAN COAL AND STEEL COMMUNITY, founded upon a common market, common objectives and common institutions.

ARTICLE 2

The European Coal and Steel Community shall have as it task to contribute, in harmony with the general economy of the Member States and through the establishment of a common market as provided in Article 4, to economic expansion, growth of employment and a rising standard of living in the Member States.

The Community shall progressively bring about conditions which will of themselves ensure the most rational distribution of production at the highest possible level of productivity, while safeguarding continuity of employment and taking care not to provoke fundamental and persistent disturbances in the economies of Member States.

ARTICLE 3

The institutions of the Community shall, within the limits of their respective powers, in the common interest:

(a) ensure an orderly supply to the common market, taking into account the needs of third countries;

(b) ensure that all comparably placed consumers in the common market have equal access to the sources of production;

(c) ensure the establishment of the lowest prices under such conditions that these prices do not result in higher prices charged by the same undertakings in other transactions or in a higher general price level at another time, while allowing necessary amortization and normal return on invested capital;

(d) ensure the maintenance of conditions which will encourage undertakings to expand and improve their production potential and to promote a policy of using natural resources rationally and avoiding their unconsidered exhaustion;

(e) promote improved working conditions and an improved standard of living for the workers in each of the industries for which it is responsible, so as to make possible their harmonisation while the improvement is being maintained;

(f) promote the growth of international trade and ensure that equitable limits are observed in export pricing;

(g) promote the orderly expansion and modernisation of production, and the improvement of quality, with no protection against competing industries that is not justified by improper action on their part or in their favour.

ARTICLE 4

The following are recognised as incompatible with the common market for coal and steel and shall accordingly be abolished and prohibited within the Community, as provided in this Treaty:

(a) import and export duties, or charges having equivalent effect, and quantitative restrictions on the movement of products;

(b) measures or practices which discriminate between producers, between purchasers or between consumers, especially in prices and delivery terms or transport rates and conditions, and measures or practices which interfere with the purchaser's free choice of supplier;

(c) subsidies or aids granted by States, or special charges imposed by States, in any form whatsoever;

(d) restrictive practices which tend towards the sharing or exploiting of markets.

ARTICLE 5

The Community shall carry out its task in accordance with this Treaty, with a limited measure of intervention.

To this end the Community shall:

— provide guidance and assistance for the parties concerned, by obtaining information, organising consultations and laying down general objectives;

— place financial resources at the disposal of undertakings for their investment and bear part of the cost of readaptation;

— ensure the establishment, maintenance and observance of normal competitive conditions and exert direct influence upon production or upon the market only when circumstances so require;

— publish the reasons for its actions and take the necessary measures to ensure the observance of the rules laid down in this Treaty.

The institutions of the Community shall carry out these activities with a minimum of administrative machinery and in close cooperation with the parties concerned.

ARTICLE 6

The Community shall have legal personality.

In international relations, the Community shall enjoy the legal capacity it requires to perform its functions and attain its objectives.

In each of the Member States, the Community shall enjoy the most extensive legal capacity accorded to legal persons constituted in that State; it may, in particular, acquire or dispose of movable and immovable property and may be a party to legal proceedings.

The Community shall be represented by its institutions, each within the limits of its powers.

TITLE TWO

The Institutions of the Community

ARTICLE 7

The institutions of the Community shall be:

— a HIGH AUTHORITY, assisted by a *Consultative Committee;*

— a COMMON ASSEMBLY (hereinafter called the "Assembly");

— a SPECIAL COUNCIL OF MINISTERS (hereinafter called the "Council");

— a COURT OF JUSTICE (hereinafter called the "Court").

* * * * *

TITLE THREE

Economic and Social Provisions

CHAPTER I

General Provisions

ARTICLE 46

The High Authority may at any time consult Governments, the various parties concerned (undertakings, workers, consumers and dealers) and their associations, and any experts.

Undertakings, workers, consumers and dealers, and their associations, shall be entitled to present any suggestions or comments to the High Authority on questions affecting them.

To provide guidance, in line with the tasks assigned to the Community, on the course of action to be followed by all concerned, and to determine its own course of action, in accordance with the provisions of this Treaty, the High Authority shall, in consultation as provided above:

1. conduct a continuous study of market and price trends;

2. periodically draw up programmes indicating foreseeable developments in production, consumption, exports and imports;

3. periodically lay down general objectives for modernisation, long-term planning of manufacture and expansion of productive capacity;

4. take part, at the request of the Governments concerned, in studying the possibilities for re-employing, in existing industries or through the creation of new activities, workers made redundant by market developments or technical changes;

5. obtain the information it requires to assess the possibilities for improving working conditions and living standards for workers in the industries within its province, and the threats to those standards.

The High Authority shall publish the general objectives and the programmes after submitting them to the Consultative Committee.

It may publish the studies and information mentioned above.

ARTICLE 47

The High Authority may obtain the information it requires to carry out its tasks. It may have any necessary checks made.

The High Authority must not disclose information of the kind covered by the obligation of professional secrecy, in particular information about undertakings, their business relations or their cost components. Subject to this reservation, it shall publish such data as could be useful to Governments or to any other parties concerned.

The High Authority may impose fines or periodic penalty payments on undertakings which evade their obligations under decisions taken in pursuance of this Article or which knowingly furnish false information. The maximum amount of such fines shall be 1 per cent of the annual turnover, and the maximum amount of such penalty payments shall be 5 per cent of the average daily turnover for each day's delay.

Any breach of professional secrecy by the High Authority which has caused damage to an undertaking may be the subject of an action for compensation before the Court, as provided in Article 40.

ARTICLE 48

The right of undertakings to form associations shall not be affected by this Treaty. Membership of such associations must be voluntary. Associations may engage in any activity which is not contrary to the provisions of this Treaty or to the decisions or recommendations of the High Authority.

Where this Treaty requires the Consultative Committee to be consulted, any association shall have the right to submit to the High Authority, within such time as the latter may set, the comments of its members on the proposed course of action.

To obtain information which it requires, or to facilitate the performance of the tasks entrusted to it, the High Authority shall normally call upon producers' associations on condition either that they provide for accredited representatives of workers and consumers to sit on their governing bodies or on advisory committees attached to them, or that they make satisfactory provision in some other way in their organisation for the interests of workers and consumers to be voiced.

The associations referred to in the preceding paragraphs shall furnish the High Authority with such information on their activities as it may consider necessary. The comments referred to in the second paragraph of this Article and the information furnished in pursuance of this paragraph shall also be forwarded by those associations to the Government concerned.

CHAPTER II

Financial Provisions

ARTICLE 49

The High Authority is empowered to procure the funds it requires to carry out its tasks:

— by imposing levies on the production of coal and steel;

— by contracting loans.

It may receive gifts.

ARTICLE 50

1. The levies are intended to cover:

— the administrative expenditure provided for in Article 78;

— the non-repayable aid towards readaptation provided for in Article 56;

— in the case of the financing arrangements provided for in Articles 54 and 56, and after recourse to the reserve fund, any portion of the amounts required for servicing loans raised by the High Authority which may not be covered by receipts from the servicing of loans granted by it, and any payments to be made under guarantees granted by the High Authority on loans contracted directly by undertakings;

— expenditure on the promotion of technical and economic research as provided for in Article 55(2).

2. The levies shall be assessed annually on the various products according to their average value; the rate thereof shall not, however, exceed 1 per cent unless previously authorised by the Council, acting by a two-thirds majority. The mode of assessment and collection shall be determined by a general decision of the High Authority taken after consulting the Council; cumulative imposition shall be avoided as far as possible.

3. The High Authority may impose upon undertakings which do not comply with decisions taken by it under this Article surcharges of not more than 5 per cent for each quarter's delay.

ARTICLE 51

1. The High Authority may not use the funds obtained by borrowing except to grant loans.

The issue of loans by the High Authority on the markets of Member States shall be subject to the rules and regulations in force on these markets.

If the High Authority considers the guarantee of Member States necessary in order to contract certain loans, it shall approach the Government or Governments concerned after consulting the Council; no State shall be obliged to give its guarantee.

2. The High Authority may, as provided in Article 54, guarantee loans granted direct to undertakings by third parties.

3. The High Authority may so determine its conditions for loans or guarantees as to enable a reserve fund to be built up for the sole purpose of reducing whatever amounts may have to be paid out of the levies in accordance with the third subparagraph of Article 50(1); the sums thus accumulated must not, however, be used for any form of lending to undertakings.

4. The High Authority shall not itself engage in the banking operations which its financial tasks entail.

ARTICLE 52

Member States shall make all appropriate arrangements to enable transfers of funds derived from the levies, from pecuniary sanctions and periodic penalty payments and from the reserve fund to be effected within the territories referred to in the first paragraph of Article 79 in accordance with the procedure for commercial payments, to the extent necessary to make it possible for them to be used for the purposes intended by this Treaty.

The procedure for effecting transfers, both between Member States and to third countries, arising out of other financial operations carried out or guaranteed by the High Authority, shall be determined by agreement between the High Authority and the Member States concerned or the appropriate agencies; there shall, however, be no obligation upon any Member State which applies exchange controls to permit transfers where it has not expressly undertaken to do so.

ARTICLE 53

Without prejudice to the provisions of Article 58 or of Chapter V of Title III, the High Authority may:

(a) after consulting the Consultative Committee and the Council, authorise the making, on conditions which it shall determine and under its supervision, of any financial arrangements common to several undertakings which it recognises to be necessary for the performance of the tasks set out in Article 3 and compatible with this Treaty, and in particular with Article 65;

(b) with the unanimous assent of the Council, itself make any financial arrangements serving the same purposes.

Similar arrangements made or maintained by Member States shall be notified to the High Authority, which, after consulting the Consultative Committee and the Council, shall make the necessary recommendations to the States concerned where such arrangements are inconsistent, in whole or in part, with the application of this Treaty.

CHAPTER III

Investment and Financial Aid

ARTICLE 54

The High Authority may facilitate the carrying out of investment programmes by granting loans to undertakings or by guaranteeing other loans which they may contract.

With the unanimous assent of the Council, the High Authority may by the same means assist the financing of works and installations which contribute directly and primarily to increasing the production, reducing the production costs or facilitating the marketing of products within its jurisdiction.

In order to encourage coordinated development of investment, the High Authority may, in accordance with Article 47, require undertakings to inform it of individual programmes in advance, either by a special request addressed to the undertaking concerned or by a decision stating what kind and scale of programme must be communicated.

The High Authority may, after giving the parties concerned full opportunity to submit their comments, deliver a reasoned opinion on such programmes within the framework of the general objectives provided for in

Article 46. If application is made by the undertaking concerned, the High Authority must deliver a reasoned opinion. The High Authority shall notify the opinion to the undertaking concerned and shall bring the opinion to the attention of its Government. Lists of such opinions shall be published.

If the High Authority finds that the financing of a programme or the operation of the installations therein planned would involve subsidies, aids, protection or discrimination contrary to this Treaty, the adverse opinion delivered by it on these grounds shall have the force of a decision within the meaning of Article 14 and the effect of prohibiting the undertaking concerned from drawing on resources other than its own funds to carry out the programme.

The High Authority may impose on undertakings which disregard the prohibition referred to in the preceding paragraph fines not exceeding the amounts improperly devoted to carrying out the programme in question.

ARTICLE 55

1. The High Authority shall promote technical and economic research relating to the production and increased use of coal and steel and to occupational safety in the coal and steel industries. To this end it shall organise all appropriate contracts among existing research bodies.

2. After consulting the Consultative Committee, the High Authority may initiate and facilitate such research:

(a) by inducing joint financing by the undertakings concerned; or

(b) by allotting for that purpose any funds received as gifts; or

(c) with the assent of the Council, by allotting for that purpose funds derived from the levies provided for in Article 50; the limit laid down in paragraph 2 of that Article must not, however, be exceeded.

The results of research financed as provided in subparagraphs (b) and (c) shall be made available to all concerned in the Community.

3. The High Authority shall deliver any opinions which serve to make technical improvements more widely known, particularly with regard to the exchange of patents and the granting of licenses for using them.

ARTICLE 56

1. If the introduction, within the framework of the general objectives of

the High Authority, of new technical processes or equipment should lead to an exceptionally large reduction in labour requirements in the coal or the steel industry, making it particularly difficult in one or more areas to re-employ redundant workers, the High Authority, on application by the Governments concerned:

(a) shall obtain the opinion of the Consultative Committee;

(b) may facilitate, in the manner laid down in Article 54, either in the industries within its jurisdiction or, with the assent of the Council, in any other industry, the financing of such programmes as it may approve for the creation of new and economically sound activities capable of reabsorbing the redundant workers into productive employment;

(c) shall provide non-repayable aid towards:

— the payment of tideover allowances to workers;

— the payment of resettlement allowances to workers;

— the financing of vocational retraining for workers having to change their employment.

The High Authority shall make the provision of non-repayable aid conditional upon payment by the State concerned of a special contribution of not less than the amount of that aid, unless an exception is authorised by the Council, acting by a two-thirds majority.

2. *If fundamental changes, not directly connected with the establishment of the common market, in market conditions for the coal or the steel industry should compel some undertakings permanently to discontinue, curtail or change their activities, the High Authority, on application by the Governments concerned:

(a) may facilitate, in the manner laid down in Article 54, either in the industries within its jurisdiction or, with the assent of the Council, in any other industry, the financing of such programmes as it may approve for the creation of new and economically sound activities or for the conversion of existing undertakings capable of reabsorbing the redundant workers into productive employment;

(b) may provide non-repayable aid towards:

— the payment of tideover allowances to workers;

— the payment of allowances to undertakings to enable them to con-

---

* Paragraph (2) added in accordance with the procedure under the third and fourth paragraph of Art. 95 of this Treaty (Official Journal of the European Communities No. 33, 16 May 1960, p. 781).

tinue paying such of their workers as may have to be temporarily laid off as a result of the undertakings' change of activity;

— the payment of resettlement allowances to workers;

— the financing of vocational retraining for workers having to change their employment.

The High Authority shall make the provision of non-repayable aid conditional upon payment by the State concerned of a special contribution of not less than the amount of that aid, unless an exception is authorised by the Council, acting by a two-thirds majority.

CHAPTER IV

Production

ARTICLE 57

In the sphere of production, the High Authority shall give preference to the indirect means of action at its disposal, such as:

— cooperation with Governments to regularise or influence general consumption, particularly that of the public services;

— intervention in regard to prices and commercial policy as provided for in this Treaty.

ARTICLE 58

1. In the event of a decline in demand, if the High Authority considers that the Community is confronted with a period of manifest crisis and that the means of action provided for in Article 57 are not sufficient to deal with this, it shall, after consulting the Consultative Committee and with the assent of the Council, establish a system of production quotas, accompanied to the necessary extent by the measures provided for in Article 74.

If the High Authority fails to act, a Member State may bring the matter before the Council, which may, acting unanimously, require the High Authority to establish a system of quotas.

2. The High Authority shall, on the basis of studies made jointly with undertakings and associations of undertakings, determine the quotas on an equitable basis, taking account of the principles set out in Articles 2, 3 and 4.

It may in particular regulate the level of activity of undertakings by appropriate levies on tonnages exceeding a reference level set by a general decision.

The funds thus obtained shall be used to support undertakings whose rate of production has fallen below that envisaged, in order, in particular, to maintain employment in these undertakings as far as possible.

3. The system of quotas shall be ended on a proposal made to the Council by the High Authority after consulting the Consultative Committee, or by the Government of a Member State, unless the Council decides otherwise, acting unanimously if the proposal emanates from the High Authority or by a simple majority if the proposal emanates from a Government. An announcement on the ending of the quota system shall be made by the High Authority.

4. The High Authority may impose upon undertakings which do not comply with decisions taken by it under this Article fines not exceeding the value of the tonnages produced in disregard thereof.

ARTICLE 59

1. If, after consulting the Consultative Committee, the High Authority finds that the Community is confronted with a serious shortage of any or all of the products within its jurisdiction, and that means of action provided for in Article 57 are not sufficient to deal with this, it shall bring the situation to the attention of the Council and shall, unless the Council, acting unanimously, decides otherwise, propose to it the necessary measures.

If the High Authority fails to act, a Member State may bring the matter before the Council, which may, acting unanimously, recognize that the situation in question does in fact exist.

2. The Council shall, acting unanimously on a proposal from and in consultation with the High Authority, establish consumption priorities and determine the allocation of the coal and steel resources of the Community to the industries within its jurisdiction, to export and to other sectors of consumption.

On the basis of the consumption priorities thus established, the High Authority shall, after consulting the undertakings concerned, draw up the production programmes with which the undertakings shall be required to comply.

3. If the Council does not reach a unanimous decision on the measures referred to in paragraph 2, the High Authority shall itself allocate the

resources of the Community among the Member States on the basis of consumption and exports, irrespective of the place of production.

Within each of the Member States allocation of the resources assigned by the High Authority shall be carried out on the responsibility of the Government, provided that the deliveries scheduled to be supplied to other Member States are not affected and that the High Authority is consulted concerning the portions to be allotted to export and to the operation of the coal and steel industries.

If the portion allotted by a Government to export is less than the amount taken as the basis for calculating the total tonnage to be assigned to the Member State concerned, the High Authority shall, to the necessary extent, at the next allocation, redivide among the Member States the resources thus made available for consumption.

If the portion allotted by a Government to the operation of the coal and steel industries is similarly less and the result is a decrease in Community production of one of these, the tonnage assigned to the Member State concerned shall, at the next allocation, be reduced by the amount of the decrease in production so caused.

4. In all cases, the High Authority shall be responsible for allocating equitably among undertakings the quantities assigned to the industries within its jurisdiction, on the basis of studies made jointly with undertakings and associations of undertakings.

5. Should the situation provided for in paragraph 1 of this Article arise, the High Authority may, in accordance with Article 57, after consulting the Consultative Committee and with the assent of the Council, decide that restrictions on exports to third countries shall be imposed in all the Member States, or, if the High Authority fails to act, the Council may, acting unanimously, so decide on a proposal from a Government.

6. The High Authority may end the arrangements made under this Article after consulting the Consultative Committee and the Council. It shall not do so if the Council unanimously dissents.

If the High Authority fails to act, the Council may, acting unanimously, itself end the arrangements.

7. The High Authority may impose upon undertakings which do not comply with decisions taken under this Article fines not exceeding twice the value of prescribed production or deliveries either not effected or diverted from their proper use.

CHAPTER V

Prices

ARTICLE 60

1. Pricing practices contrary to Articles 2, 3 and 4 shall be prohibited, in particular:

— unfair competitive practices, especially purely temporary or purely local price reductions tending towards the acquisition of a monopoly position within the common market;

— discriminatory practices involving, within the common market, the application by a seller of dissimilar conditions to comparable transactions, especially on grounds of the nationality of the buyer.

The High Authority may define the practices covered by this prohibition by decisions taken after consulting the Consultative Committee and the Council.

2. For these purposes:

(a) the price lists and conditions of sale applied by undertakings within the common market must be made public to the extent and in the manner prescribed by the High Authority after consulting the Consultative Committee. If the High Authority finds that an undertaking's choice of point on which it bases its price lists is abnormal and in particular makes it possible to evade the provisions of subparagraph (b), it shall make appropriate recommendations to that undertaking;

(b) the methods of quotation used must not have the effect that prices charged by an undertaking in the common market, when reduced to their equivalent at the point chosen for its price lists, result in:

— increases over the price shown in the price list in question for a comparable transaction; or

— reductions below that price the amount of which exceeds either:

— the extent enabling the quotation to be aligned on the price list, based on another point which secures the buyer the most advantageous delivered terms; or

— the limits fixed, by decision of the High Authority after the Consultative Committee has delivered its opinion, for each category of product, with due regard, where appropriate, for the origin and destination of products.

Such decisions shall be taken when found necessary to avoid disturbances in the whole or any part of the common market or disequilibria resulting from a difference between the methods of quotation used for a product and for materials involved in making it. Such decisions shall not preclude undertakings from aligning their quotations on those of undertakings outside the Community, on condition that the transactions are notified to the High Authority, which may, in the event of abuse, restrict or abrogate the right of the undertakings concerned to take advantage of this exception.

ARTICLE 61

On the basis of studies made jointly with undertakings and associations of undertakings, in accordance with the first paragraph of Article 46 and the third paragraph of Article 48, and after consulting the Consultative Committee and the Council as to the advisability of so doing and the price level to be so determined, the High Authority may, for one or more of the products within its jurisdiction:

(a) fix maximum prices within the common market, if it finds that such a decision is necessary to attain the objectives set out in Article 3, and particularly in paragraph (c) thereof;

(b) fix minimum prices within the common market, if it finds that a manifest crisis exists or is imminent and that such a decision is necessary to attain the objectives set out in Article 3;

(c) after consulting the associations to which the undertakings concerned belong, or the undertakings themselves, fix, by methods appropriate to the nature of the export markets, minimum or maximum export prices, if such an arrangement can be effectively supervised and is necessary both in view of the dangers to the undertakings resulting from the state of the market and in order to secure the acceptance in international economic relations of the objective set out in Article 3(f); any fixing of minimum prices shall be without prejudice to the measures provided for in the last subparagraph of Article 60(2).

In fixing prices, the High Authority shall take into account the need to ensure that the coal and steel industries and the consumer industries remain competitive, in accordance with the principles laid down in Article 3(c).

If in these circumstances the High Authority fails to act, the Government of a Member State may bring the matter before the Council, which may, acting unanimously, call upon the High Authority to fix such maximum or minimum prices.

ARTICLE 62

If the High Authority considers this the most appropriate way of preventing coal from being priced at the level of the production costs of the mines which have the highest costs but which it is recognised should be temporarily maintained in service in order that the tasks laid down in Article 3 may be performed, it may, after consulting the Consultative Committee, authorise equalisation payments:

— between undertakings in the same coalfield to which the same price lists apply;

— after consulting the Council, between undertakings in different coalfields.

These equalisation payments may, moreover, be instituted as provided in Article 53.

ARTICLE 63

1. If the High Authority finds that discrimination is being systematically practised by purchasers, in particular under provisions governing contracts entered into by bodies dependent on a public authority, it shall make appropriate recommendations to the Governments concerned.

2. Where the High Authority considers it necessary, it may decide that:

(a) undertakings must frame their conditions of sale in such a way that their customers and commission agents acting on their behalf shall be under an obligation to comply with the rules made by the High Authority in application of this Chapter;

(b) undertakings shall be held responsible for infringements of this obligation by their direct agents or by commission agents acting on their behalf.

In the event of an infringement of this obligation by a purchaser, the High Authority may restrict or, should the infringement be repeated, temporarily prohibit dealings with that purchaser by Community undertakings. If this is done, the purchaser shall have the right, without prejudice to Article 33, to bring an action before the Court.

3. In addition, the High Authority is empowered to make to the Member States concerned any appropriate recommendations to ensure that the rules laid down for the application of Article 60(1) are duly observed by all distributive undertakings and agencies in the coal and steel sectors.

ARTICLE 64

The High Authority may impose upon undertakings which infringe the provisions of this Chapter or decisions taken thereunder fines not exceeding twice the value of the sales effected in disregard thereof. If the infringement is repeated, this maximum shall be doubled.

CHAPTER VI

Agreements and Concentrations

ARTICLE 65

1. All agreements between undertakings, decisions by associations of undertakings and concerted practices tending directly or indirectly to prevent, restrict or distort normal competition within the common market shall be prohibited, and in particular those tending:

(a) to fix or determine prices;

(b) to restrict or control production, technical development or investment;

(c) to share markets, products, customers or sources of supply.

2. However, the High Authority shall authorise specialisation agreements or joint-buying or joint-selling agreements in respect of particular products, if it finds that:

(a) such specialisation or such joint-buying or -selling will make for a substantial improvement in the production or distribution of those products;

(b) the agreement in question is essential in order to achieve these results and is not more restrictive than is necessary for that purpose; and

(c) the agreement is not liable to give the undertakings concerned the power to determine the prices, or to control or restrict the production or marketing, of a substantial part of the products in question within the common market, or to shield them against effective competition from other undertakings within the common market.

If the High Authority finds that certain agreements are strictly analogous in nature and effect to those referred to above, having particular regard to the fact that this paragraph applies to distributive undertakings, it shall authorise them also when satisfied that they meet the same requirements.

Authorisations may be granted subject to specified conditions and for limited periods. In such cases the High Authority shall renew an authorisation once or several times if it finds that the requirements of subparagraphs (a) to (c) are still met at the time of renewal.

The High Authority shall revoke or amend an authorisation if it finds that as a result of a change in circumstances the agreement no longer meets these requirements, or that the actual results of the agreement or of the application thereof are contrary to the requirements for its authorisation.

Decisions granting, renewing, amending, refusing or revoking an authorisation shall be published together with the reasons therefor; the restrictions imposed by the second paragraph of Article 47 shall not apply thereto.

3. The High Authority may, as provided in Article 47, obtain any information needed for the application of this Article, either by making a special request to the parties concerned or by means of regulations stating the kinds of agreement, decision or practice which must be communicated to it.

4. Any agreement or decision prohibited by paragraph 1 of this Article shall be automatically void and may not be relied upon before any court or tribunal in the Member States.

The High Authority shall have sole jurisdiction, subject to the right to bring actions before the Court, to rule whether any such agreement or decision is compatible with this Article.

5. On any undertaking which has entered into an agreement which is automatically void, or has enforced or attempted to enforce, by arbitration, penalty, boycott or any other means, an agreement or decision which is automatically void or an agreement for which authorisation has been refused or revoked, or has obtained an authorisation by means of information which it knew to be false or misleading, or has engaged in practices prohibited by paragraph 1 of this Article, the High Authority may impose fines or periodic penalty payments not exceeding twice the turnover on the products which were the subject of the agreement, decision or practice prohibited by this Article; if, however, the purpose of the agreement, decision or practice is to restrict production, technical development or investment, this maximum may be raised to 10 per cent of the annual turnover of the undertakings in question in the case of fines, and 20 per cent of the daily turnover in the case of periodic penalty payments.

ARTICLE 66

1. Any transaction shall require the prior authorisation of the High Authority, subject to the provisions of paragraph 3 of this Article, if it has in itself the direct or indirect effect of bringing about within the territories referred to in the first paragraph of Article 79, as a result of action by any person or undertaking or group of persons or undertakings, a concentration between undertakings at least one of which is covered by Article 80, whether the transaction concerns a single product or a number of different products, and whether it is effected by merger, acquisition of shares or parts of the undertaking or assets, loan, contract or any other means of control. For the purpose of applying these provisions, the High Authority shall, by regulations made after consulting the Council, define what constitutes control of an undertaking.

2. The High Authority shall grant the authorisation referred to in the preceding paragraph if it finds that the proposed transaction will not give to the persons or undertakings concerned the power, in respect of the product or products within its jurisdiction:

— to determine prices, to control or restrict production or distribution or to hinder effective competition in a substantial part of the market for those products; or

— to evade the rules of competition instituted under this Treaty, in particular by establishing an artificially privileged position involving a substantial advantage in access to supplies or markets.

In assessing whether this is so, the High Authority shall, in accordance with the principle of non-discrimination laid down in Article 4(b), take account of the size of like undertakings in the Community, to the extent it considers justified in order to avoid or correct disadvantages resulting from unequal competitive conditions.

The High Authority may make its authorisation subject to any conditions which it considers appropriate for the purposes of this paragraph.

Before ruling on a transaction concerning undertakings at least one of which is not subject to Article 80, the High Authority shall obtain the comments of the Governments concerned.

3. The High Authority shall exempt from the requirement of prior authorisation such classes of transactions as it finds should, in view of the size of the assets or undertakings concerned, taken in conjunction with the kind of concentration to be effected, be deemed to meet the requirements of

paragraph 2. Regulations made to this effect, with the assent of the Council, shall also lay down the conditions governing such exemption.

4. Without prejudice to the application of Article 47 to undertakings within its jurisdiction, the High Authority may, either by regulations made after consultation with the Council stating the kind of transaction to be communicated to it or by a special request under these regulations to the parties concerned, obtain from the natural or legal persons who have acquired or regrouped or are intending to acquire or regroup the rights or assets in question any information needed for the application of this Article concerning transactions liable to produce the effect referred to in paragraph 1.

5. If a concentration should occur which the High Authority finds has been effected contrary to the provisions of paragraph 1 but which nevertheless meets the requirements of paragraph 2, the High Authority shall make its approval of that concentration subject to payment by the persons who have acquired or regrouped the rights or assets in question of the fine provided for in the second subparagraph of paragraph 6; the amount of the fine shall not be less than half of the maximum determined in that subparagraph should it be clear that authorisation ought to have been applied for. If the fine is not paid, the High Authority shall take the steps hereinafter provided for in respect of concentrations found to be unlawful.

If a concentration should occur which the High Authority finds cannot fulfil the general or specific conditions to which an authorisation under paragraph 2 would be subject, the High Authority shall, by means of a reasoned decision, declare the concentration unlawful and, after giving the parties concerned the opportunity to submit their comments, shall order separation of the undertakings or assets improperly concentrated or cessation of joint control, and any other measures which it considers appropriate to return the undertakings or assets in question to independent operation and restore normal conditions of competition. Any person directly concerned may institute proceedings against such decisions, as provided in Article 33. By way of derogation from Article 33, the Court shall have unlimited jurisdiction to assess whether the transaction effected is a concentration within the meaning of paragraph 1 and of regulations made in application thereof. The institution of proceedings shall have suspensory effect. Proceedings may not be instituted until the measures provided for above have been ordered, unless the High Authority agrees to the institution of separate proceedings against the decision declaring the transaction unlawful.

The High Authority may at any time, unless the third paragraph of Article 39 is applied, take or cause to be taken such interim measures of protection as it may consider necessary to safeguard the interests of competing undertakings and of third parties, and to forestall any step which might hinder the implementation of its decisions. Unless the Court decides otherwise, proceedings shall not have suspensory effect in respect of such interim measures.

The High Authority shall allow the parties concerned a reasonable period in which to comply with its decisions, on expiration of which it may impose daily penalty payments not exceeding one tenth of one per cent of the value of the rights or assets in question.

Furthermore, if the parties concerned do not fulfil their obligations, the High Authority shall itself take steps to implement its decision; it may in particular suspend the exercise, in undertakings within its jurisdiction, of the rights attached to the assets acquired irregularly, obtain the appointment by the judicial authorities of a receiver of such assets, organise the forced sale of such assets subject to the protection of the legitimate interests of their owners, and annul with respect to natural or legal persons who have acquired the rights or assets in question through the unlawful transaction, the acts, decisions, resolutions or proceedings of the supervisory and managing bodies or undertakings over which control has been obtained irregularly.

The High Authority is also empowered to make such recommendations to the Member States concerned as may be necessary to ensure that the measures provided for in the preceding subparagraphs are implemented under their own law.

In the exercise of its powers, the High Authority shall take account of the rights of third parties which have been acquired in good faith.

6. The High Authority may impose fines not exceeding:

— 3 per cent of the value of the assets acquired or regrouped or to be acquired or regrouped, on natural or legal persons who have evaded the obligations laid down in paragraph 4;

— 10 per cent of the value of the assets acquired or regrouped, on natural or legal persons who have evaded the obligations laid down in paragraph 1; this maximum shall be increased by one twenty-fourth for each month which elapses after the end of the twelfth month following completion of the transaction until the High Authority establishes that there has been an infringement;

— 10 per cent of the value of the assets acquired or regrouped or to be acquired or regrouped, on natural or legal persons who have obtained or attempted to obtain authorisation under paragraph 2 by means of false or misleading information;

— 15 per cent of the value of the assets acquired or regrouped, on undertakings within its jurisdiction which have engaged in or been party to transactions contrary to the provisions of this Article.

Persons fined under this paragraph may appeal to the Court as provided in Article 36.

7. If the High Authority finds that public or private undertakings which, in law or in fact, hold or acquire in the market for one of the products within its jurisdiction a dominant position shielding them against effective competition in a substantial part of the common market are using that position for purposes contrary to the objectives of this Treaty, it shall make to them such recommendations as may be appropriate to prevent the position from being so used. If these recommendations are not implemented satisfactorily within a reasonable time, the High Authority shall, by decisions taken in consultation with the Government concerned, determine the prices and conditions of sale to be applied by the undertaking in question or draw up production or delivery programmes with which it must comply, subject to liability to the penalties provided for in Articles 58, 59 and 64.

CHAPTER VII

Interference with Conditions of Competition

ARTICLE 67

1. Any action by a Member State which is liable to have appreciable repercussions on conditions of competition in the coal or the steel industry shall be brought to the knowledge of the High Authority by the Government concerned.

2. If the action is liable, by substantially increasing differences in production costs otherwise than through changes in productivity, to provoke a serious disequilibrium, the High Authority, after consulting the Consultative Committee and the Council, may take the following steps:

If the action taken by that State is having harmful effects on the coal or steel undertakings within the jurisdiction of that State, the High Authority may authorise it to grant aid to these undertakings, the amount, conditions and duration of which shall be determined in agreement with the High Authority. The same shall apply in the case of any change in wages and working conditions which would have the same effects, even if not resulting from any action by that State.

If the action taken by that State is having harmful effects on the coal or steel undertakings within the jurisdiction of other Member States, the High

Authority shall make a recommendation to that State with a view to remedying these effects by such measures as that State may consider most compatible with its own economic equilibrium.

3. If the action taken by that State reduces differences in production costs by allowing special benefits to or imposing special charges on the coal or steel undertakings within its jurisdiction in comparison with the other industries in the same country, the High Authority is empowered to make the necessary recommendations to that State after consulting the Consultative Committee and the Council.

CHAPTER VIII

Wages and Movement of Workers

ARTICLE 68

1. The methods used for fixing wages and welfare benefits in the several Member States shall not, in the case of the coal and steel industries, be affected by this Treaty, subject to the following provisions.

2. If the High Authority finds that one or more undertakings are charging abnormally low prices because they are paying abnormally low wages compared with the wage level in the same area, it shall, after consulting the Consultative Committee, make appropriate recommendations to them. If the abnormally low wages are the result of governmental decisions, the High Authority shall confer with the Government concerned, and failing agreement it may, after consulting the Consultative Committee, make a recommendation to that Government.

3. If the High Authority finds that wage reduction entails a lowering of the standard of living of workers and at the same time is being used as a means for the permanent economic adjustment of undertakings or as a means of competition between them, it shall, after consulting the Consultative Committee, make a recommendation to the undertaking or Government concerned with a view to securing, at the expense of the undertakings, benefits for the workers in order to compensate for the reductions.

This provision shall not apply to:

(a) overall measures taken by a Member State to restore its external equilibrium, without prejudice in such case to any action under Article 67;

(b) wage reductions resulting from the application of a sliding scale established by law or by contract;

(c) wage reductions resulting from a fall in the cost of living;

(d) wage reductions to correct abnormal increases that occurred previously in exceptional circumstances which no longer obtain.

4. Save in the cases referred to in paragraph 3 (a) and (b), any wage reduction affecting all or a substantial number of the workers in an undertaking shall be notified to the High Authority.

5. The recommendations provided for in the preceding paragraphs may be made by the High Authority only after consulting the Council, unless they are addressed to undertakings smaller than a minimum size to be defined by the High Authority in agreement with the Council.

If in one of the Member States a change in the arrangements for the financing of social security or for dealing with unemployment and its effects, or a change in wages, produces the effects referred to in Article 67(2) or (3), the High Authority is empowered to take the steps provided for in that Article.

6. The High Authority may impose upon undertakings which do not comply with recommendations made to them under this Article fines and periodic penalty payments not exceeding twice the amount of the saving in labour costs improperly effected.

ARTICLE 69

1. Member States undertake to remove any restriction based on nationality upon the employment in the coal and steel industries of workers who are nationals on Member States and have recognised qualifications in a coalmining or steelmaking occupation, subject to the limitations imposed by the basic requirements of health and public policy.

2. For the purpose of applying this provision, Member States shall draw up common definitions of skilled trades and qualifications therefor, shall determine by common accord the limitations provided for in paragraph 1, and shall endeavour to work out arrangements on a Community-wide basis for bringing offers of employment into touch with applications for employment.

3. In addition, with regard to workers not covered by paragraph 2, they shall, should growth of coal or steel production be hampered by a shortage of suitable labour, adjust their immigration rules to the extent needed to remedy this state of affairs; in particular, they shall facilitate the re-employment workers from the coal and steel industries of other Member States.

4. They shall prohibit any discrimination in remuneration and working conditions between nationals and migrant workers, without prejudice to special measures concerning frontier workers; in particular, they shall endeavour to settle among themselves any matters remaining to be dealt with in order to ensure that social security arrangements do not inhibit labour mobility.

5. The High Authority shall guide and facilitate action by Member States in applying this Article.

6. This Article shall not affect the international obligations of Member States.

CHAPTER IX

Transport

ARTICLE 70

It is recognised that the establishment of the common market necessitates the application of such rates and conditions for the carriage of coal and steel as will afford comparable price conditions to comparably placed consumers.

Any discrimination in rates and conditions of carriage of every kind which is based on the country of origin or destination of products shall be prohibited in traffic between Member States. For the purpose of eliminating such discrimination it shall in particular be obligatory to apply to the carriage of coal and steel to or from another country of the Community the scales, rates and all other tariff rules of every kind which are applicable to the internal carriage of the same goods on the same route.

The scales, rates and all other tariff rules of every kind applied to the carriage of coal and steel within each Member State and between Member States shall be published or brought to the knowledge of the High Authority.

The application of special internal rates and conditions in the interest of one or more coal- or steel-producing undertakings shall require the prior agreement of the High Authority, which shall verify that they are in accordance with the principles of this Treaty; it may make its agreement temporary or conditional.

Subject to the provisions of this Article, and to the other provisions of this Treaty, transport policy, including the fixing and altering of rates and conditions of carriage of every kind and the making of rates on a basis calculated to secure for the transport undertakings concerned a properly balanced financial position, shall continue to be governed by the laws or regulations of the individual Member States, as shall measures relating to coordination or competition between different modes of transport or different routes.

CHAPTER X

Commercial Policy

ARTICLE 71

The powers of the Governments of Member States in matters of commercial policy shall not be affected by this Treaty, save as otherwise provided therein.

The powers conferred on the Community by this Treaty in matters of commercial policy towards third countries may not exceed those accorded to Member States under international agreements to which they are parties, subject to the provisions of Article 75.

The Governments of Member States shall afford each other such mutual assistance as is necessary to implement measures recognised by the High Authority as being in accordance with this Treaty and with existing international agreements. The High Authority is empowered to propose to the Member States concerned the methods by which this mutual assistance may be provided.

ARTICLE 72

Minimum rates below which Member States undertake not to lower their customs duties on coal and steel as against third countries, and maximum rates above which they undertake not to raise them, may be fixed by decision of the Council, acting unanimously on a proposal from the High Authority made on the latter's own initiative or at the request of a Member State.

Within the limits so fixed, each Government shall determine its tariffs according to its own national procedure. The High Authority may, on its own initiative or at the request of a Member State, deliver an opinion suggesting amendment of the tariffs of that State.

ARTICLE 73

The administration of import and export licenses for trade with third countries shall be a matter for the Government in whose territory the place of destination for imports or the place of origin for exports is situated.

The High Authority is empowered to supervise the administration and verification of these licences with respect to coal and steel. Where necessary it shall, after consulting the Council, make recommendations to Member States to ensure that the arrangements in this connection are not more restrictive than the circumstances governing their adoption or retention require, and to secure the coordination of measures taken under the third paragraph of Article 71 or under Article 74.

ARTICLE 74

In the cases set out below, the High Authority is empowered to take any measure which is in accordance with this Treaty, and in particular with the objectives set out in Article 3, and to make to Governments any recommendation which is in accordance with the second paragraph of Article 71:

(1) if it is found that countries not members of the Community or undertakings situated in such countries are engaging in dumping or other practices condemned by the Havana Charter;

(2) if a difference between quotations by undertakings outside and by undertakings within the jurisdiction of the Community is due solely to the fact that those of the former are based on conditions of competition contrary to this Treaty;

(3) if one of the products referred to in Article 81 of this Treaty is imported into the territory of one or more Member States in relatively increased quantities and under such conditions that these imports cause or threaten to cause serious injury to production within the common market of like or directly competing products.

However, recommendations for the introduction of quantitative restrictions under subparagraph 2 may be made only with the assent of the Council, and under subparagraph 3 only under the conditions laid down in Article 58.

ARTICLE 75

The Member States undertake to keep the High Authority informed of proposed commercial agreements or arrangements having similar effect where these relate to coal and steel or to the importation of other raw materials and specialised equipment needed for the production of coal and steel in Member States.

If a proposed agreement or arrangement contains clauses which would hinder the implementation of this Treaty, the High Authority shall make the necessary recommendations to the State concerned within ten days of receiving notification of the communication addressed to it; in any other case it may deliver opinions.

2. Treaty of Rome Establishing the European Economic Community

(1957)

His Majesty the King of the Belgians, the President of the Federal Republic of Germany, the President of the French Republic, the President of the Italian Republic, Her Royal Highness the Grand Duchess of Luxembourg, Her Majesty the Queen of the Netherlands,

Determined to lay the foundations of an ever closer union among the peoples of Europe,

Resolved to ensure the economic and social progress of their countries by common action to eliminate the barriers which divide Europe,

Affirming as the essential objective of their efforts the constant improvement of the living and working conditions of their peoples,

Recognising that the removal of existing obstacles calls for concerted action in order to guarantee steady expansion, balanced trade and fair competition,

Anxious to strengthen the unity of their economies and to ensure their harmonious development by reducing the differences existing between the various regions and the backwardness of the less favoured regions,

Desiring to contribute, by means of a common commercial policy, to the progressive abolition of restrictions on international trade,

Intending to confirm the solidarity which binds Europe and the overseas countries and desiring to ensure the development of their prosperity, in accordance with the principles of the Charter of the United Nations,

Resolved by thus pooling their resources to preserve and strengthen peace and liberty, and calling upon the other peoples of Europe who share their ideal to join in their efforts,

HAVE DECIDED to create a European Economic Community and to this end have designated as their Plenipotentiaries:

. . . .

WHO, having exchanged their Full Powers, found in good and due form, HAVE AGREED as follows:

PART ONE

Principles

ARTICLE 1

By this Treaty, the HIGH CONTRACTING PARTIES establish among themselves a EUROPEAN ECONOMIC COMMUNITY.

ARTICLE 2

The Community shall have as its task, by establishing a common market and progressively approximating the economic policies of Member States, to promote throughout the Community a harmonious development of economic activities, a continuous and balanced expansion, an increase in stability, an accelerated raising of the standard of living and closer relations between the States belonging to it.

ARTICLE 3

For the purposes set out in Article 2, the activities of the Community shall include, as provided in this Treaty and in accordance with the timetable set out therein.

(a) the elimination, as between Member States, of customs duties and of quantitative restrictions on the import and export of goods, and of all other measures having equivalent effect;

(b) the establishment of a common customs tariff and of a common commercial policy towards third countries;

(c) the abolition, as between Member States, of obstacles to freedom of movement for persons, services and capital;

(d) the adoption of a common policy in the sphere of agriculture;

(e) the adoption of a common policy in the sphere of transport;

(f) the institution of a system ensuring that competition in the common market is not distorted;

(g) the application of procedures by which the economic policies of Member States can be coordinated and disequilibria in their balances of payments remedied;

(h) the approximation of the laws of Member States to the extent required for the proper functioning of the common market;

(i) the creation of a European Social Fund in order to improve employment opportunities for workers and to contribute to the raising of their standard of living;

(j) the establishment of a European Investment Bank to facilitate the economic expansion of the Community by opening up fresh resources;

(k) the association of the overseas countries and territories in order to increase trade and to promote jointly economic and social development.

ARTICLE 4

1. The tasks entrusted to the Community shall be carried out by the following institutions:

an ASSEMBLY,

a COUNCIL,

a COMMISSION,

a COURT OF JUSTICE.

Each institution shall act within the limits of the powers conferred upon it by this Treaty.

2. The Council and the Commission shall be assisted by an Economic and Social Committee acting in an advisory capacity.

ARTICLE 5

Member States shall take all appropriate measures, whether general or particular, to ensure fulfilment of the obligations arising out of this Treaty or resulting from action taken by the institutions of the Community. They shall facilitate the achievement of the Community's tasks.

They shall abstain from any measure which could jeopardise the attainment of the objectives of this Treaty.

ARTICLE 6

1. Member States shall, in close cooperation with the institutions of the Community, coordinate their respective economic policies to the extent necessary to attain the objectives of this Treaty.

2. The institutions of the Community shall take care not to prejudice the internal and external financial stability of the Member States.

ARTICLE 7

Within the scope of application of this Treaty, and without prejudice to any special provisions contained therein, any discrimination on grounds of nationality shall be prohibited.

The Council may, on a proposal from the Commission and after consulting the Assembly, adopt, by a qualified majority, rules designed to prohibit such discrimination.

ARTICLE 8

1. The common market shall be progressively established during a transitional period of twelve years.

This transitional period shall be divided into three stages of four years each; the length of each stage may be altered in accordance with the provisions set out below.

2. To each stage there shall be assigned a set of actions to be initiated and carried through concurrently.

3. Transition from the first to the second stage shall be conditional upon a finding that the objectives specifically laid down in this Treaty for the first stage have in fact been attained in substance and that, subject to the

exceptions and procedures provided for in this Treaty, the obligations have been fulfilled.

This finding shall be made at the end of the fourth year by the Council, acting unanimously on a report from the Commission. A Member State may not, however, prevent unanimity by relying upon the non-fulfilment of its own obligations. Failing unanimity, the first stage shall automatically be extended for one year.

At the end of the fifth year, the Council shall make its finding under the same conditions. Failing unanimity, the first stage shall automatically be extended for a further year.

At the end of the sixth year, the Council shall make its finding, acting by a qualified majority on a report from the Commission.

4. Within one month of the last-mentioned vote any Member State which voted with the minority or, if the required majority was not obtained, any Member State shall be entitled to call upon the Council to appoint an arbitration board whose decision shall be binding upon all Member States and upon the institutions of the Community. The arbitration board shall consist of three members appointed by the Council acting unanimously on a proposal from the Commission.

If the Council has not appointed the members of the arbitration board within one month of being called upon to do so, they shall be appointed by the Court of Justice within a further period of one month.

The arbitration board shall elect its own Chairman.

The board shall make its award within six months of the date of the Council vote referred to in the last subparagraph of paragraph 3.

5. The second and third stages may not be extended or curtailed except by a decision of the Council, acting unanimously on a proposal from the Commission.

6. Nothing in the preceding paragraphs shall cause the transitional period to last more than fifteen years after the entry into force of this Treaty.

7. Save for the exceptions or derogations provided for in this Treaty, the expiry of the transitional period shall constitute the latest date by which all the rules laid down must enter into force and all the measures required for establishing the common market must be implemented.

PART TWO

Foundations of the Community

TITLE I

Free Movement of Goods

ARTICLE 9

1. The Community shall be based upon a customs union which shall cover all trade in goods and which shall involve the prohibition between Member States of customs duties on imports and exports and of all charges having equivalent effect, and the adoption of a common customs tariff in their relations with third countries.

2. The provisions of Chapter 1, Section 1, and of Chapter 2 of this Title shall apply to products originating in Member States and to products coming from third countries which are in free circulation in Member States.

ARTICLE 10

1. Products coming from a third country shall be considered to be in free circulation in a Member State if the import formalities have been complied with and any customs duties or charges having equivalent effect which are payable have been levied in that Member State, and if they have not benefited from a total or partial drawback of such duties or charges.

2. The Commission shall, before the end of the first year after the entry into force of this Treaty, determine the methods of administrative cooperation to be adopted for the purpose of applying Article 9(2), taking into account the need to reduce as much as possible formalities imposed on trade.

Before the end of the first year after the entry into force of this Treaty, the Commission shall lay down the provisions applicable, as regards trade between Member States, to goods originating in another Member State in whose manufacture products have been used on which the exporting Member State has not levied the appropriate customs duties or charges having equivalent effect, or which have benefited from a total or partial drawback of such duties or charges.

In adopting these provisions, the Commission shall take into account the rules for the elimination of customs duties within the Community and for the progressive application of the common customs tariff.

ARTICLE 11

Member States shall take all appropriate measures to enable Governments to carry out, within the periods of time laid down, the obligations with regard to customs duties which devolve upon them pursuant to this Treaty.

CHAPTER 1

The Customs Union

Section 1

Elimination of customs duties between Member States

ARTICLE 12

Member States shall refrain from introducing between themselves any new customs duties on imports or exports or any charges having equivalent effect, and from increasing those which they already apply in their trade with each other.

ARTICLE 13

1. Customs duties on imports in force between Member States shall be progressively abolished by them during the transitional period in accordance with Articles 14 and 15.

2. Charges having an effect equivalent to customs duties on imports, in force between Member States, shall be progressively abolished by them during the transitional period. The Commission shall determine by means of directives the timetable for such abolition. It shall be guided by the rules contained in Article 14(2) and (3) and by the directives issued by the Council pursuant to Article 14(2).

ARTICLE 14

1. For each product, the basic duty to which the successive reductions shall be applied shall be the duty applied on 1 January 1957.

2. The timetable for the reductions shall be determined as follows:

(a) during the first stage, the first reduction shall be made one year after the date when this Treaty enters into force; the second reduction, eighteen months later; the third reduction, at the end of the fourth year after the date when this Treaty enters into force;

(b) during the second stage, a reduction shall be made eighteen months after that stage begins; a second reduction, eighteen months after the preceding one; a third reduction, one year later;

(c) any remaining reductions shall be made during the third stage; the Council shall, acting by a qualified majority on a proposal from the Commission, determine the timetable therefor by means of directives.

3. At the time of the first reduction, Member States shall introduce between themselves a duty on each product equal to the basic duty minus 10%.

At the time of each subsequent reduction, each Member State shall reduce its customs duties as a whole in such manner as to lower by 10% its total customs receipts as defined in paragraph 4 and to reduce the duty on each product by at least 5% of the basic duty.

In the case, however, of products on which the duty is still in excess of 30%, each reduction must be at least 10% of the basic duty.

4. The total customs receipts of each Member State, as referred to in paragraph 3, shall be calculated by multiplying the value of its imports from other Member States during 1956 by the basic duties.

5. Any special problems raised in applying paragraphs 1 to 4 shall be settled by directives issued by the Council acting by a qualified majority on a proposal from the Commission.

6. Member States shall report to the Commission on the manner in which effect has been given to the preceding rules for the reduction of duties. They shall endeavour to ensure that the reduction made in the duties on each product shall amount:

— at the end of the first stage, to at least 25% of the basic duty;

— at the end of the second stage, to at least 50% of the basic duty.

If the Commission finds that there is a risk that the objectives laid down in Article 13, and the percentages laid down in this paragraph, cannot be attained, it shall make all appropriate recommendations to Member States.

7. The provisions of this Article may be amended by the Council, acting

unanimously on a proposal from the Commission and after consulting the Assembly.

ARTICLE 15

1. Irrespective of the provisions of Article 14, any Member State may, in the course of the transitional period, suspend in whole or in part the collection of duties applied by it to products imported from other Member States. It shall inform the other Member States and the Commission thereof.

2. The Member States declare their readiness to reduce customs duties against the other Member States more rapidly than is provided for in Article 14 if their general economic situation and the situation of the economic sector concerned so permit.

To this end, the Commission shall make recommendations to the Member States concerned.

ARTICLE 16

Member States shall abolish between themselves customs duties on exports and charges having equivalent effect by the end of the first stage at the latest.

ARTICLE 17

1. The provisions of Articles 9 to 15(1) shall also apply to customs duties of a fiscal nature. Such duties shall not, however, be taken into consideration for the purpose of calculating either total customs receipts or the reduction of customs duties as a whole as referred to in Article 14(3) and (4).

Such duties shall, at each reduction, be lowered by not less than 10% of the basic duty. Member States may reduce such duties more rapidly than is provided for in Article 14.

2. Member States shall, before the end of the first year after the entry into force of this Treaty, inform the Commission of their customs duties of a fiscal nature.

3. Member States shall retain the right to substitute for these duties an internal tax which complies with the provisions of Article 95.

4. If the Commission finds that substitution for any customs duty of a fiscal nature meets with serious difficulties in a Member State, it shall authorise that State to retain the duty on condition that it shall abolish it not

later than six years after the entry into force of this Treaty. Such authorisation must be applied for before the end of the first year after the entry into force of this Treaty.

Section 2

Setting up of the common customs tariff

ARTICLE 18

The Member States declare their readiness to contribute to the development of international trade and the lowering of barriers to trade by entering into agreements designed, on a basis of reciprocity and mutual advantage, to reduce customs duties below the general level of which they could avail themselves as a result of the establishment of a customs union between them.

ARTICLE 19

1. Subject to the conditions and within the limits provided for hereinafter, duties in the common customs tariff shall be at the level of the arithmetical average of the duties applied in the four customs territories comprised in the Community.

2. The duties taken as the basis for calculating this average shall be those applied by Member States on 1 January 1957.

In the case of the Italian tariff, however, the duty applied shall be that without the temporary 10% reduction. Furthermore, with respect to items on which the Italian tariff contains a conventional duty, this duty shall be substituted for the duty applied as defined above, provided that it does not exceed the latter by more than 10%. Where the conventional duty exceeds the duty applied as defined above by more than 10%, the latter duty plus 10% shall be taken as the basis for calculating the arithmetical average.

With regard to the tariff headings in List A, the duties shown in that List shall, for the purpose of calculating the arithmetical average, be substituted for the duties applied.

3. The duties in the common customs tariff shall not exceed:

(a) 3% for products within the tariff headings in List B;

(b) 10% for products within the tariff headings in List C;

(c) 15% for products within the tariff headings in List D;

(d) 25% for products within the tariff headings in List E; where in respect of such products, the tariff of the Benelux countries contains a duty not exceeding 3%, such duty shall, for the purpose of calculating the arithmetical average, be raised to 12%.

4. List F prescribes the duties applicable to the products listed therein.

5. The Lists of tariff headings referred to in this Article and in Article 20 are set out in Annex I to this Treaty.

ARTICLE 20

The duties applicable to the products in List G shall be determined by negotiation between the Member States. Each Member State may add further products to this List to a value not exceeding 2% of the total value of its imports from third countries in the course of the year 1956.

The Commission shall take all appropriate steps to ensure that such negotiations shall be undertaken before the end of the second year after the entry into force of this Treaty and be concluded before the end of the first stage.

If, for certain products, no agreement can be reached within these periods, the Council shall, on a proposal from the Commission, acting unanimously until the end of the second stage and by a qualified majority thereafter, determine the duties in the common customs tariff.

ARTICLE 21

1. Technical difficulties which may arise in applying Articles 19 and 20 shall be resolved, within two years of the entry into force of this Treaty, by directives issued by the Council acting by a qualified majority on a proposal from the Commission.

2. Before the end of the first stage, or at latest when the duties are determined, the Council shall, acting by a qualified majority on a proposal from the Commission, decide on any adjustments required in the interests of the internal consistency of the common customs tariff as a result of applying the rules set out in Articles 19 and 20, taking account in particular of the degree of processing undergone by the various goods to which the common tariff applies.

ARTICLE 22

The Commission shall, within two years of the entry into force of this Treaty, determine the extent to which the customs duties of a fiscal nature referred to in Article 17(2) shall be taken into account in calculating the arithmetical average provided for in Article 19(1). The Commission shall take account of any protective character which such duties may have.

Within six months of such determination, any Member State may request that the procedure provided for in Article 20 should be applied to the product in question, but in this event the percentage limit provided in that Article shall not be applicable to that State.

ARTICLE 23

1. For the purpose of the progressive introduction of the common customs tariff, Member States shall amend their tariffs applicable to third countries as follows:

(a) in the case of tariff headings on which the duties applied in practice on 1 January 1957 do not differ by more than 15% in either direction from the duties in the common customs tariff, the latter duties shall be applied at the end of the fourth year after the entry into force of this Treaty;

(b) in any other case, each Member State shall, as from the same date, apply a duty reducing by 30% the difference between the duty applied in practice on 1 January 1957 and the duty in the common customs tariff;

(c) at the end of the second stage this difference shall again be reduced by 30%;

(d) in the case of tariff headings for which the duties in the common customs tariff are not yet available at the end of the first stage, each Member State shall, within six months of the Council's action in accordance with Article 20, apply such duties as would result from application of the rules contained in this paragraph.

2. Where a Member State has been granted an authorisation under Article 17(4), it need not, for as long as that authorisation remains valid, apply the preceding provisions to the tariff headings to which the authorisation applies. When such authorisation expires, the Member State concerned shall apply such duty as would have resulted from application of the rules contained in paragraph 1.

3. The common customs tariff shall be applied in its entirety by the end of the transitional period at the latest.

ARTICLE 24

Member States shall remain free to change their duties more rapidly than is provided for in Article 23 in order to bring them into line with the common customs tariff.

ARTICLE 25

1. If the Commission finds that the production in Member States of particular products contained in Lists B, C and D is insufficient to supply the demands of one of the Member States, and that such supply traditionally depends to a considerable extent on imports from third countries, the Council shall, acting by a qualified majority on a proposal from the Commission, grant the Member State concerned tariff quotas at a reduced rate of duty or duty free.

Such quotas may not exceed the limits beyond which the risk might arise of activities being transferred to the detriment of other Member States.

2. In the case of the products in List E, and of those in List G for which the rates of duty have been determined in accordance with the procedure provided for in the third paragraph of Article 20, the Commission shall, where a change in sources of supply or shortage of supplies within the Community is such as to entail harmful consequences for the processing industries of a Member State, at the request of that Member State, grant it tariff quotas at a reduced rate of duty or duty free.

Such quotas may not exceed the limits beyond which the risk might arise of activities being transferred to the detriment of other Member States.

3. In the case of the products listed in Annex II to this Treaty, the Commission may authorise any Member State to suspend, in whole or in part, collection of the duties applicable or may grant such Member State tariff quotas at a reduced rate of duty or duty free, provided that no serious disturbance of the market of the products concerned results therefrom.

4. The Commission shall periodically examine tariff quotas granted pursuant to this Article.

ARTICLE 26

The Commission may authorise any Member State encountering special difficulties to postpone the lowering or raising of duties provided for in Article 23 in respect of particular headings in its tariff.

Such authorisation may only be granted for a limited period and in respect of tariff headings which, taken together, represent for such State not more than 5% of the value of its imports from third countries in the course of the latest year for which statistical data are available.

ARTICLE 27

Before the end of the first stage, Member States shall, in so far as may be necessary, take steps to approximate their provisions laid down by law, regulation or administrative action in respect of customs matters. To this end, the Commission shall make all appropriate recommendations to Member States.

ARTICLE 28

Any autonomous alteration or suspension of duties in the common customs tariff shall be decided unanimously by the Council. After the transitional period has ended, however, the Council may, acting by a qualified majority on a proposal from the Commission, decide on alterations or suspensions which shall not exceed 20% of the rate in the case of any one duty for a maximum period of six months. Such alterations or suspensions may only be extended, under the same conditions, for one further period of six months.

ARTICLE 29

In carrying out the tasks entrusted to it under this Section the Commission shall be guided by:

(a) the need to promote trade between Member States and third countries;

(b) developments in conditions of competition within the Community in so far as they lead to an improvement in the competitive capacity of undertakings;

(c) the requirements of the Community as regards the supply of raw materials and semi-finished goods; in this connection the Commission shall take care to avoid distorting conditions of competition between Member States in respect of finished goods;

(d) the need to avoid serious disturbances in the economies of Member States and to ensure rational development of production and an expansion of consumption within the Community.

CHAPTER 2

Elimination of Quantitative Restrictions Between Member States

ARTICLE 30

Quantitative restrictions on imports and all measures having equivalent effect shall, without prejudice to the following provisions, be prohibited between Member States.

ARTICLE 31

Member States shall refrain from introducing between themselves any new quantitative restrictions or measures having equivalent effect.

This obligation shall, however, relate only to the degree of liberalisation attained in pursuance of the decisions of the Council of the Organisation for European Economic Cooperation of 14 January 1955. Member States shall supply the Commission, not later than six months after the entry into force of this Treaty, with lists of the products liberalised by them in pursuance of these decisions. These lists shall be consolidated between Member States.

ARTICLE 32

In their trade with one another Member States shall refrain from making more restrictive the quotas and measures having equivalent effect existing at the date of the entry into force of this Treaty.

These quotas shall be abolished by the end of the transitional period at the latest. During that period, they shall be progressively abolished in accordance with the following provisions.

ARTICLE 33

1. One year after the entry into force of this Treaty, each Member State shall convert any bilateral quotas open to any other Member States into global quotas open without discrimination to all other Member States.

On the same date, Member States shall increase aggregate of the global quotas so established in such a manner as to bring about an increase of not less than 20% in their total value as compared with the preceding year. The global quota for each product, however, shall be increased by not less than 10%.

The quotas shall be increased annually in accordance with the same rules and in the same proportions in relation to the preceding year.

The fourth increase shall take place at the end of the fourth year after the entry into force of this Treaty; the fifth, one year after the beginning of the second stage.

2. Where, in the case of a product which has not been liberalised, the global quota does not amount to 3% of the national production of the State concerned, a quota equal to not less than 3% of such national production shall be introduced not later than one year after the entry into force of this Treaty. This quota shall be raised to 4% at the end of the second year, and to 5% at the end of the third. Thereafter, the Member State concerned shall increase the quota by not less than 15% annually.

Where there is no such national production, the Commission shall take a decision establishing an appropriate quota.

3. At the end of the tenth year, each quota shall be equal to not less than 20% of the national production.

4. If the Commission finds by means of a decision that during two successive years the imports of any product have been below the level of the quota opened, this global quota shall not be taken into account in calculating the total value of the global quotas. In such case, the Member State shall abolish quota restrictions on the product concerned.

5. In the case of quotas representing more than 20% of the national production of the product concerned, the Council may, acting by a qualified majority on a proposal from the Commission, reduce the minimum percentage of 10% laid down in paragraph 1. This alteration shall not, however, affect the obligation to increase the total value of global quotas by 20% annually.

6. Member States which have exceeded their obligations as regards the degree of liberalisation attained in pursuance of the decisions of the Council of the Organisation for European Economic Cooperation of 14 January 1955 shall be entitled, when calculating the annual total increase of 20% provided for in paragraph 1, to take into account the amount of imports liberalised by autonomous action. Such calculation shall be submitted to the Commission for its prior approval.

7. The Commission shall issue directives establishing the procedure and timetable in accordance with which Member States shall abolish, as between themselves, any measures in existence when this Treaty enters into force which have an effect equivalent to quotas.

8. If the Commission finds that the application of the provisions of this Article, and in particular of the provisions concerning percentages, makes it impossible to ensure that the abolition of quotas provided for in the second paragraph of Article 32 is carried out progressively, the Council may, on a proposal from the Commission, acting unanimously during the first stage and by a qualified majority thereafter, amend the procedure laid down in this Article and may, in particular, increase the percentages fixed.

ARTICLE 34

1. Quantitative restrictions on exports, and all measures having equivalent effect, shall be prohibited between Member States.

2. Member States shall, by the end of the first stage at the latest, abolish all quantitative restrictions on exports and any measures having equivalent effect which are in existence when this Treaty enters into force.

ARTICLE 35

The Member States declare their readiness to abolish quantitative restrictions on imports from and exports to other Member States more rapidly than is provided for in the preceding Articles, if their general economic situation and the situation of the economic sector concerned so permit.

To this end, the Commission shall make recommendations to the States concerned.

ARTICLE 36

The provisions of Article 30 to 34 shall not preclude prohibitions or restrictions on imports, exports or goods in transit justified on grounds of public morality, public policy or public security; the protection of health and life of humans, animals or plants; the protection of national treasures possessing artistic, historic or archaeological value; or the protection of industrial and commercial property. Such prohibitions or restrictions shall not, however, constitute a means of arbitrary discrimination or a disguised restriction on trade between Member States.

ARTICLE 37

1. Member States shall progressively adjust any State monopolies of a commercial character so as to ensure that when the transitional period has

ended no discrimination regarding the conditions under which goods are procured and marketed exists between nationals of Member States.

The provisions of this Article shall apply to any body through which a Member State, in law or in fact, either directly or indirectly supervises, determines or appreciably influences imports or exports between Member States. These provisions shall likewise apply to monopolies delegated by the State to others.

2. Member States shall refrain from introducing any new measure which is contrary to the principles laid down in paragraph 1 or which restricts the scope of the Articles dealing with the abolition of customs duties and quantitative restrictions between Member States.

3. The timetable for the measures referred to in paragraph 1 shall be harmonised with the abolition of quantitative restrictions on the same products provided for in Articles 30 to 34.

If a product is subject to a State monopoly of a commercial character in only one or some Member States, the Commission may authorise the other Member States to apply protective measures until the adjustment provided for in paragraph 1 has been effected; the Commission shall determine the conditions and details of such measures.

4. If a State monopoly of a commercial character has rules which are designed to make it easier to dispose of agricultural products or obtain for them the best return, steps should be taken in applying the rules contained in this Article to ensure equivalent safeguards for the employment and standard of living of the producers concerned, account being taken of the adjustments that will be possible and the specialisation that will be needed with the passage of time.

5. The obligations on Member States shall be binding only in so far as they are compatible with existing international agreements.

6. With effect from the first stage the Commission shall make recommendations as to the manner in which and the timetable according to which the adjustment provided for in this Article shall be carried out.

TITLE II

Agriculture

ARTICLE 38

1. The common market shall extend to agriculture and trade in agricultural

products. "Agricultural products" means the products of the soil, of stock-farming and of fisheries and products of first-stage processing directly related to these products.

2. Save as otherwise provided in Articles 39 to 46, the rules laid down for the establishment of the common market shall apply to agricultural products.

3. The products subject to the provisions of Articles 39 to 46 are listed in Annex II to this Treaty. Within two years of the entry into force of this Treaty, however, the Council shall, acting by a qualified majority on a proposal from the Commission, decide what products are to be added to this list.

4. The operation and development of the common market for agricultural products must be accompanied by the establishment of a common agricultural policy among the Member States.

ARTICLE 39

1. The objectives of the common agricultural policy shall be:

(a) to increase agricultural productivity by promoting technical progress and by ensuring the rational development of agricultural production and the optimum utilisation of the factors of production, in particular labour;

(b) thus to ensure a fair standard of living for the agricultural community, in particular by increasing the individual earnings of persons engaged in agriculture;

(c) to stabilise markets;

(d) to assure the availability of supplies;

(e) to ensure that supplies reach consumers at reasonable prices.

2. In working out the common agricultural policy and the special methods for its application, account shall be taken of:

(a) the particular nature of agricultural activity, which results from the social structure of agriculture and from structural and natural disparities between the various agricultural regions;

(b) the need to effect the appropriate adjustments by degrees;

(c) the fact that in the Member States agriculture constitutes a sector closely linked with the economy as a whole.

ARTICLE 40

1. Member States shall develop the common agricultural policy by degrees during the transitional period and shall bring it into force by the end of that period at the latest.

2. In order to attain the objectives set out in Article 39 a common organisation of agricultural markets shall be established.

This organisation shall take one of the following forms, depending on the product concerned:

(a) common rules on competition;

(b) compulsory coordination of the various national market organisations;

(c) a European market organisation.

3. The common organisation established in accordance with paragraph 2 may include all measures required to attain the objectives set out in Article 39, in particular regulation of prices, aids for the production and marketing of the various products, storage and carryover arrangements and common machinery for stabilising imports or exports.

The common organisation shall be limited to pursuit of the objectives set out in Article 39 and shall exclude any discrimination between producers or consumers within the Community.

Any common price policy shall be based on common criteria and uniform methods of calculation.

4. In order to enable the common organisation referred to in paragraph 2 to attain its objectives, one or more agricultural guidance and guarantee funds may be set up.

ARTICLE 41

To enable the objectives set out in Article 39 to be attained, provision may be made within the framework of the common agricultural policy for measures such as:

(a) an effective coordination of efforts in the spheres of vocational training, of research and of the dissemination of agricultural knowledge; this may include joint financing of projects or institutions;

(b) joint measures to promote consumption of certain products.

ARTICLE 42

The provisions of the Chapter relating to rules on competition shall apply to production of and trade in agricultural products only to the extent determined by the Council within the framework of Article 43(2) and (3) and in accordance with the procedure laid down therein, account being taken of the objectives set out in Article 39.

The Council may, in particular, authorise the granting of aid:

(a) for the protection of enterprises handicapped by structural or natural conditions;

(b) within the framework of economic development programmes.

ARTICLE 43

1. In order to evolve the broad lines of a common agricultural policy, the Commission shall, immediately this Treaty enters into force, convene a conference of the Member States with a view to making a comparison of their agricultural policies, in particular by producing a statement of their resources and needs.

2. Having taken into account the work of the conference provided for in paragraph 1, after consulting the Economic and Social Committee and within two years of the entry into force of this Treaty, the Commission shall submit proposals for working out and implementing the common agricultural policy, including the replacement of the national organisations by one of the forms of common organisation provided for in Article 40(2), and for implementing the measures specified in this Title.

These proposals shall take account of the interdependence of the agricultural matters mentioned in this Title.

The Council shall, on a proposal from the Commission and after consulting the Assembly, acting unanimously during the first two stages and by a qualified majority thereafter, make regulations, issue directives, or take decisions, without prejudice to any recommendations it may also make.

3. The Council may, acting by a qualified majority and in accordance with paragraph 2, replace the national market organisations by the common organisation provided for in Article 40(2) if:

(a) the common organisation offers Member States which are opposed to this measure and which have an organisation of their own for the production in question equivalent safeguards for the employment and standard of living of the producers concerned, account being taken of the adjustments that will be possible and the specialisation that will be needed with the passage of time;

(b) such an organisation ensures conditions for trade within the Community similar to those existing in a national market.

4. If a common organisation for certain raw materials is established before a common organisation exists for the corresponding processed products, such raw materials as are used for processed products intended for export to third countries may be imported from outside the Community.

ARTICLE 44

1. In so far as progressive abolition of customs duties and quantitative restrictions between Member States may result in prices likely to jeopardise the attainment of the objectives set out in Article 39, each Member State shall, during the transitional period, be entitled to apply to particular products, in a non-discriminatory manner and in substitution for quotas and to such an extent as shall not impede the expansion of the volume of trade provided for in Article 45(2), a system of minimum prices below which imports may be either:

— temporarily suspended or reduced; or

— allowed, but subjected to the condition that they are made at a price higher than the minimum price for the product concerned.

In the latter case the minimum prices shall not include customs duties.

2. Minimum prices shall neither cause a reduction of the trade existing between Member States when this Treaty enters into force nor form an obstacle to progressive expansion of this trade. Minimum prices shall not be applied so as to form an obstacle to the development of a natural preference between Member States.

3. As soon as this Treaty enters into force the Council shall, on a pro-

posal from the Commission, determine objective criteria for the establishment of minimum price systems and for the fixing of such prices.

These criteria shall in particular take account of the average national production costs in the Member State applying the minimum price, of the position of the various undertakings concerned in relation to such average production costs, and of the need to promote both the progressive improvement of agricultural practice and the adjustments and specialisation needed within the common market.

The Commission shall further propose a procedure for revising these criteria in order to allow for and speed up technical progress and to approximate prices progressively within the common market.

These criteria and the procedure for revising them shall be determined by the Council acting unanimously within three years of the entry into force of this Treaty.

4. Until the decision of the Council takes effect, Member States may fix minimum prices on condition that these are communicated beforehand to the Commission and to the other Member States so that they may submit their comments.

Once the Council has taken its decision, Member States shall fix minimum prices on the basis of the criteria determined as above.

The Council may, acting by a qualified majority on a proposal from the Commission, rectify any decisions taken by Member States which do not conform to the criteria defined above.

5. If it does not prove possible to determine the said objective criteria for certain products by the beginning of the third stage, the Council may, acting by a qualified majority on a proposal from the Commission, vary the minimum prices applied to these products.

6. At the end of the transitional period, a table of minimum prices still in force shall be drawn up. The Council shall, acting on a proposal from the Commission and by a majority of nine votes in accordance with the weighting laid down in the first subparagraph of Article 148(2), determine the system to be applied within the framework of the common agricultural policy.

ARTICLE 45

1. Until national market organisations have been replaced by one of the

forms of common organisations referred to in Article 40(2), trade in products in respect of which certain Member States:

— have arrangements designed to guarantee national producers a market for their products; and

— are in need of imports,

shall be developed by the conclusion of long-term agreements or contracts between importing and exporting Member States.

These agreements or contracts shall be directed toward the progressive abolition of any discrimination in the application of these arrangements to the various producers within the Community.

Such agreements or contracts shall be concluded during the first stage; account shall be taken of the principle of reciprocity.

2. As regards quantities, these agreements or contracts shall be based on the average volume of trade between Member States in the products concerned during the three years before the entry into force of this Treaty and shall provide for an increase in the volume of trade within the limits of existing requirements, account being taken of traditional patterns of trade.

As regards prices, these agreements or contracts shall enable producers to dispose of the agreed quantities at prices which shall be progressively approximated to those paid to national producers on the domestic market of the purchasing country.

This approximation shall proceed as steadily as possible and shall be completed by the end of the transitional period at the latest.

Prices shall be negotiated between the parties concerned within the framework of directives issued by the Commission for the purpose of implementing the two preceding subparagraphs.

If the first stage is extended, these agreements or contracts shall continue to be carried out in accordance with the conditions applicable at the end of the fourth year after the entry into force of this Treaty, the obligation to increase quantities and to approximate prices being suspended until the transition to the second stage.

Member States shall avail themselves of any opportunity open to them under their legislation, particularly in respect of import policy, to ensure the conclusion and carrying out of these agreements or contracts.

3. To the extent that Member States require raw materials for the manufacture of products to be exported outside the Community in competition with products of third countries, the above agreements or contracts shall not form an obstacle to the importation of raw materials for this purpose from third countries. This provision shall not, however, apply if the Council unanimously decides to make provision for payments required to compensate for the higher price paid on goods imported for this purpose on the basis of these agreements or contracts in relation to the delivered price of the same goods purchased on the world market.

ARTICLE 46

Where in a Member State a product is subject to a national market organisation or to internal rules having equivalent effect which affect the competitive position of similar production in another Member State, a countervailing charge shall be applied by Member States to imports of this product coming from the Member State where such organization or rules exist, unless that State applies a countervailing charge on export.

The Commission shall fix the amount of these charges at the level required to redress the balance; it may also authorise other measures, the conditions and details of which it shall determine.

ARTICLE 47

As to the functions to be performed by the Economic and Social Committee in pursuance of this Title, its agricultural section shall hold itself at the disposal of the Commission to prepare, in accordance with the provisions of Articles 197 and 198, the deliberations of the Committee.

TITLE III

Free Movement of Persons, Services and Capital

CHAPTER 1

Workers

ARTICLE 48

1. Freedom of movement for workers shall be secured within the Community by the end of the transitional period at the latest.

2. Such freedom of movement shall entail the abolition of any discrimina-

tion based on nationality between workers of the Member States as regards employment, remuneration and other conditions of work and employment.

3. It shall entail the right, subject to limitations justified on grounds of public policy, public security or public health:

(a) to accept offers of employment actually made;

(b) to move freely within the territory of Member States for this purpose;

(c) to stay in a Member State for the purpose of employment in accordance with the provisions governing the employment of nationals of that State laid down by law, regulation or administrative action;

(d) to remain in the territory of a Member State after having been employed in that State, subject to conditions which shall be embodied in implementing regulations to be drawn up by the Commission.

4. The provisions of this Article shall not apply to employment in the public service.

ARTICLE 49

As soon as this Treaty enters into force, the Council shall, acting on a proposal from the Commission and after consulting the Economic and Social Committee, issue directives or make regulations setting out the measures required to bring about, by progressive stages, freedom of movement for workers, as defined in Article 48, in particular:

(a) by ensuring close cooperation between national employment services;

(b) by systematically and progressively abolishing those administrative procedures and practices and those qualifying periods in respect of eligibility for available employment, whether resulting from national legislation or from agreements previously concluded between Member States, the maintenance of which would form an obstacle to liberalisation of the movement of workers;

(c) by systematically and progressively abolishing all such qualifying periods and other restrictions provided for either under national legislation or under agreements previously concluded between Member States as imposed on workers of other Member States conditions regarding the free choice of employment other than those imposed on workers of the State concerned;

(d) by setting up appropriate machinery to bring offers of employment into touch with applications for employment and to facilitate the achievement of a balance between supply and demand in the employment market in such a way as to avoid serious threats to the standard of living and level of employment in the various regions and industries.

ARTICLE 50

Member States shall, within the framework of a joint programme, encourage the exchange of young workers.

ARTICLE 51

The Council shall, acting unanimously on a proposal from the Commission, adopt such measures in the field of social security as are necessary to provide freedom of movement for workers; to this end, it shall make arrangements to secure for migrant workers and their dependents:

(a) aggregation, for the purpose of acquiring and retaining the right to benefit and of calculating the amount of benefit, of all periods taken into account under the laws of the several countries;

(b) payment of benefits to persons resident in the territories of Member States.

CHAPTER 2

Right of Establishment

ARTICLE 52

Within the framework of the provisions set out below, restrictions on the freedom of establishment of nationals of a Member State in the territory of another Member State shall be abolished by progressive stages in the course of the transitional period. Such progressive abolition shall also apply to restrictions on the setting up of agencies, branches or subsidiaries by nationals of any Member State established in the territory of any Member State.

Freedom of establishment shall include the right to take up and pursue activities as self-employed persons and to set up and manage undertakings, in particular companies or firms within the meaning of the second paragraph of Article 58, under the conditions laid down for its own nationals by the law of the country where such establishment is effected, subject to the provisions of the Chapter relating to capital.

ARTICLE 53

Member States shall not introduce any new restrictions on the right of establishment in their territories of nationals of other Member States, save as otherwise provided in this Treaty.

ARTICLE 54

1. Before the end of the first stage, the Council shall, acting unanimously on a proposal from the Commission and after consulting the Economic and Social Committee and the Assembly, draw up a general programme for the abolition of existing restrictions on freedom of establishment within the Community. The Commission shall submit its proposal to the Council during the first two years of the first stage.

The programme shall set out the general conditions under which freedom of establishment is to be attained in the case of each type of activity and in particular the stages by which it is to be attained.

2. In order to implement this general programme or, in the absence of such programme, in order to achieve a stage in attaining freedom of establishment as regards a particular activity, the Council shall, on a proposal from the Commission and after consulting the Economic and Social Committee and the Assembly, issue directives, acting unanimously until the end of the first stage and by a qualified majority thereafter.

3. The Council and the Commission shall carry out the duties devolving upon them under the preceding provisions, in particular:

(a) by according, as a general rule, priority treatment to activities where freedom of establishment makes a particularly valuable contribution to the development of production and trade;

(b) by ensuring close cooperation between the competent authorities in the Member States in order to ascertain the particular situation within the Community of the various activities concerned;

(c) by abolishing those administrative procedures and practices, whether resulting from national legislation or from agreements previously concluded between Member States, the maintenance of which would form an obstacle to freedom of establishment;

(d) by ensuring that workers of one Member State employed in the territory of another Member State may remain in that territory for the purpose of taking up activities therein as self-employed persons, where they satisfy the conditions which they would be required to satisfy if they were entering that State at the time when they intended to take up such activities;

(e) by enabling a national of one Member State to acquire and use land and buildings situated in the territory of another Member State, in so far as this does not conflict with the principles laid down in Article 39(2);

(f) by effecting the progressive abolition of restrictions on freedom of establishment in every branch of activity under consideration, both as regards the conditions for setting up agencies, branches or subsidiaries in the territory of a Member State and as regards the conditions governing the entry of personnel belonging to the main establishment into managerial or supervisory posts in such agencies, branches or subsidiaries;

(g) by coordinating to the necessary extent the safeguards which, for the protection of the interests of members and others, are required by Member States of companies or firms within the meaning of the second paragraph of Article 58 with a view to making such safeguards equivalent throughout the Community;

(h) by satisfying themselves that the conditions of establishment are not distorted by aids granted by Member States.

ARTICLE 55

The provisions of this Chapter shall not apply, so far as any given Member State is concerned, to activities which in that State are connected, even occasionally, with the exercise of official authority.

The Council may, acting by a qualified majority on a proposal from the Commission, rule that the provisions of this Chapter shall not apply to certain activities.

ARTICLE 56

1. The provisions of this Chapter and measures taken in pursuance thereof shall not prejudice the applicability of provisions laid down by law, regulation or administrative action providing for special treatment for foreign nationals on grounds of public policy, public security or public health.

2. Before the end of the transitional period, the Council shall, acting

unanimously on a proposal from the Commission and after consulting the Assembly, issue directives for the coordination of the aforementioned provisions laid down by law, regulation or administrative action. After the end of the second stage, however, the Council shall, acting by a qualified majority on a proposal from the Commission, issue directives for the coordination of such provisions as, in each Member State, are a matter for regulation or administrative action.

ARTICLE 57

1. In order to make it easier for persons to take up and pursue activities as self-employed persons, the Council shall, on a proposal from the Commission and after consulting the Assembly, acting unanimously during the first stage and by a qualified majority thereafter, issue directives for the mutual recognition of diplomas, certificates and other evidence of formal qualifications.

2. For the same purpose, the Council shall, before the end of the transitional period, acting on a proposal from the Commission and after consulting the Assembly, issue directives for the coordination of the provisions laid down by law, regulation or administrative action in Member States concerning the taking up and pursuit of activities as self-employed persons. Unanimity shall be required on matters which are the subject of legislation in at least one Member State and measures concerned with the protection of savings, in particular the granting of credit and the exercise of the banking profession, and with the conditions governing the exercise of the medical and allied, and pharmaceutical professions in the various Member States. In other cases, the Council shall act unanimously during the first stage and by a qualified majority thereafter.

3. In the case of the medical and allied and pharmaceutical professions, the progressive abolition of restrictions shall be dependent upon coordination of the conditions for their exercise in the various Member States.

ARTICLE 58

Companies or firms formed in accordance with the law of a Member State and having their registered office, central administration or principal place of business within the Community shall, for the purposes of this Chapter, be treated in the same way as natural persons who are nationals of Member States.

"Companies or firms" means companies or firms constituted under civil or commercial law, including cooperative societies, and other legal persons governed by public or private law, save for those which are non-profit-making.

CHAPTER 3

Services

ARTICLE 59

Within the framework of the provisions set out below, restrictions on freedom to provide services within the Community shall be progressively abolished during the transitional period in respect of nationals of Member States who are established in a State of the Community other than that of the person for whom the services are intended.

The Council may, acting unanimously on a proposal from the Commission, extend the provisions of this Chapter to nationals of a third country who provide services and who are established within the Community.

ARTICLE 60

Services shall be considered to be "services" within the meaning of this Treaty where they are normally provided for remuneration, in so far as they are not governed by the provisions relating to freedoom of movement for goods, capital and persons.

"Services" shall in particular include:

(a) activities of an industrial character;

(b) activities of a commercial character;

(c) activities of craftsmen;

(d) activities of the professions.

Without prejudice to the provisions of the Chapter relating to the right of establishment, the person providing a service may, in order to do so, temporarily pursue his activity in the State where the service is provided, under the same conditions as are imposed by that State on its own nationals.

ARTICLE 61

1. Freedom to provide services in the field of transport shall be governed by the provisions of the Title relating to transport.

2. The liberalisation of banking and insurance services connected with

movements of capital shall be effected in step with the progressive liberalisation of movement of capital.

ARTICLE 62

Save as otherwise provided in this Treaty, Member States shall not introduce any new restrictions on the freedom to provide services which has in fact been attained at the date of the entry into force of this Treaty.

ARTICLE 63

1. Before the end of the first stage, the Council shall, acting unanimously on a proposal from the Commission and after counsulting the Economic and Social Committee and the Assembly, draw up a general programme for the abolition of existing restrictions on freedom to provide services within the Community. The Commission shall submit its proposal to the Council during the first two years of the first stage.

The programme shall set out the general conditions under which and the stages by which each type of service is to be liberalised.

2. In order to implement this general programme or, in the absence of such programme, in order to achieve a stage in the liberalisation of a specific service, the Council shall, on a proposal from the Commission and after consulting the Economic and Social Committee and the Assembly, issue directives acting unanimously until the end of the first stage and by a qualified majority thereafter.

3. As regards the proposals and decisions referred to in paragraphs 1 and 2, priority shall as a general rule be given to those services which directly affect production costs or the liberalisation of which helps to promote trade in goods.

ARTICLE 64

The Member States declare their readiness to undertake the liberal'sat'on of services beyond the extent required by the directives issued pursuant to Article 63(2), if their general economic situation and the situation of the economic sector concerned so permit.

To this end, the Commission shall make recommendations to the Member States concerned.

ARTICLE 65

As long as restrictions on freedom to provide services have not been abolished, each Member State shall apply such restrictions without distinction on grounds of nationality or residence to all persons providing services within the meaning of the first paragraph of Article 59.

ARTICLE 66

The provisions of Article 55 to 58 shall apply to the matters covered by this Chapter.

CHAPTER 4

Capital

ARTICLE 67

1. During the transitional period and to the extent necessary to ensure the proper functioning of the common market, Member States shall progressively abolish between themselves all restrictions on the movement of capital belonging to persons resident in Member States and any discrimination based on the nationality or on the place of residence of the parties or on the place where such capital is invested.

2. Current payments connected with the movement of capital between Member States shall be freed all restrictions by the end of the first stage at the latest.

ARTICLE 68

1. Member States shall, as regards the matters dealt with in this Chapter, be as liberal as possible in granting such exchange authorisations as are still necessary after the entry into force of this Treaty.

2. Where a Member State applies to the movements of capital liberalised in accordance with the provisions of this Chapter the domestic rules governing the capital market and the credit system, it shall do so in a non-discriminatory manner.

3. Loans for the direct or indirect financing of a Member State or its regional or local authorities shall not be issued or placed in other Member States unless the States concerned have reached agreement thereon. This provision

shall not preclude the application of Article 22 of the Protocol on the Statute of the European Investment Bank.

ARTICLE 69

The Council shall, on a proposal from the Commission, which for this purpose shall consult the Monetary Committee provided for in Article 105, issue the necessary directives for the progressive implementation of the provisions of Article 67, acting unanimously during the first two stages and by a qualified majority thereafter.

ARTICLE 70

1. The Commission shall propose to the Council measures for the progressive coordination of the exchange policies of Member States in respect of the movement of capital between those States and third countries. For this purpose the Council shall issue directives, acting unanimously. It shall endeavour to attain the highest possible degree of liberalisation.

2. Where the measures taken in accordance with paragraph 1 do not permit the elimination of differences between the exchange rules of Member States and where such differences could lead persons resident in one of the Member States to use the freer transfer facilities within the Community which are provided for in Article 67 in order to evade the rules of one of the Member States concerning the movement of capital to or from third countries, that State may, after consulting the other Member States and the Commission, take appropriate measures to overcome these difficulties.

Should the Council find that these measures are restricting the free movement of capital within the Community to a greater extent than is required for the purpose of overcoming the difficulties, it may, acting by a qualified majority on a proposal from the Commission, decide that the State concerned shall amend or abolish these measures.

ARTICLE 71

Member States shall endeavour to avoid introducing within the Community any new exchange restrictions on the movement of capital and current payments connected with such movements, and shall endeavour not to make existing rules more restrictive.

They declare their readiness to go beyond the degree of liberalisation of capital movements provided for in the preceding Articles in so far as their economic situation, in particular the situation of their balance of payments, so permits.

The Commission may, after consulting the Monetary Committee, make recommendations to Member States on this subject.

ARTICLE 72

Member States shall keep the Commission informed of any movements of capital to and from third countries which come to their knowledge. The Commission may deliver to Member States any opinions which it considers appropriate on this subject.

ARTICLE 73

1. If movement of capital lead to disturbances in the functioning of the capital market in any Member State, the Commission shall, after consulting the Monetary Committee, authorise that State to take protective measures in the field of capital movements, the conditions and details of which the Commission shall determine.

The Council may, acting by a qualified majority, revoke this authorisation or amend the conditions or details thereof.

2. A Member State which is in difficulties may, however, on grounds of secrecy or urgency, take the measures mentioned above, where this proves necessary, on its own initiative. The Commission and the other Member States shall be informed of such measures by the date of their entry into force at the latest. In this event the Commission may, after consulting the Monetary Committee, decide that the State concerned shall amend or abolish the measures.

TITLE IV

Transport

ARTICLE 74

The objectives of this Treaty shall, in matters governed by this Title, be pursued by Member States within the framework of a common transport policy.

ARTICLE 75

1. For the purpose of implementing Article 74, and taking into account

the distinctive features of transport, the Council shall, acting unanimously until the end of the second stage and by a qualified majority hereafter, lay-down, on a proposal from the Commission and after consulting the Economic and Social Committee and the Assembly:

(a) common rules applicable to international transport to or from the territory of a Member State or passing across the territory of one or more Member States;

(b) the conditions under which non-resident carriers may operate transport services within a Member State;

(c) any other appropriate provisions.

2. The provisions referred to in (a) and (b) of paragraph 1 shall be laid down during the transitional period.

3. By way of derogation from the procedure provided for in paragraph 1, where the application of provisions concerning the principles of the regulatory system for transport would be liable to have a serious effect on the standard of living and on employment in certain areas and on the operation of transport facilities, they shall be laid down by the Council acting unanimously. In so doing, the Council shall take into account the need for adaptation to the economic development which will result from establishing the common market.

ARTICLE 76

Until the provisions referred to in Article 75(1) have been laid down, no Member State may, without the unanimous approval of the Council, make the various provisions governing the subject when this Treaty enters into force less favourable in their direct or indirect effect on carriers of other Member States as compared with carriers who are nationals of that State.

ARTICLE 77

Aids shall be compatible with this Treaty if they meet the needs of coordination of transport or if they represent reimbursement for the discharge of certain obligations inherent in the concept of a public service.

ARTICLE 78

Any measures taken within the framework of this Treaty in respect of transport rates and conditions shall take account of the economic circumstances of carriers.

ARTICLE 79

1. In the case of transport within the Community, discrimination which takes the form of carriers charging different rates and imposing different conditions for the carriage of the same goods over the same transport links on grounds of the country of origin or of destination of the goods in question, shall be abolished, at the latest, before the end of the second stage.

2. Paragraph 1 shall not prevent the Council from adopting other measures in pursuance of Article 75(1).

3. Within two years of the entry into force of this Treaty, the Council shall, acting by a qualified majority on a proposal from the Commission and after consulting the Economic and Social Committee, lay down rules for implementing the provisions of paragraph 1.

The Council may in particular lay down the provisions needed to enable the institutions of the Community to secure compliance with the rule laid down in paragraph 1 and to ensure that users benfit from it to the full.

4. The Commission shall, acting on its own initiative or on application by a Member State, investigate any cases of discrimination falling within paragraph 1 and, after consulting any Member State concerned, shall take the necessary decisions within the framework of the rules laid down in accordance with the provisions of paragraph 3.

ARTICLE 80

1. The imposition by a Member State, in respect of transport operations carried out with the Community, of rates and conditions involving any element of support or protection in the interest of one or more particular undertakings or industries shall be prohibited as from the beginning of the second stage, unless authorised by the Commission.

2. The Commission shall, acting on its own initiative or on application by a Member State, examine the rates and conditions referred to in paragraph 1, taking account in particular of the requirements of an appropriate regional economic policy, the needs of underdeveloped areas and the problems of areas seriously affected by political circumstances on the one hand, and of the effects of such rates and conditions on competition between the different modes of transport on the other.

After consulting each Member State concerned, the Commission shall take the necessary decisions.

3. The prohibition provided for in paragraph 1 shall not apply to tariffs fixed to meet competition.

ARTICLE 81

Charges or dues in respect of the crossing of frontiers which are charged by a carrier in addition to the transport rates shall not exceed a reasonable level after taking the cost actually incurred thereby into account.

Member States shall endeavor to reduce these costs progressively.

The Commission may make recommendations to Member States for the application of this Article.

ARTICLE 82

The provisions of this Title shall not form an obstacle to the application of measures taken in the Federal Republic of Germany to the extent that such measures are required in order to compensate for the economic disadvantages caused by the division of Germany to the economy of certain areas of the Federal Republic affected by that division.

ARTICLE 83

An Advisory Comittee consisting of experts designated by the Governments of Member States, shall be attached to the Commission. The Commission, whenever it considers it desirable, shall consult the Committee on transport matters without prejudice to the powers of the transport section of the Economic and Social Committee.

ARTICLE 84

1. The provisions of this Title shall apply to transport by rail, road and inland waterway.

2. The Council may, acting unanimously, decide whether, to what extent and by what procedure appropriate provisions may be laid down for sea and air transport.

PART THREE

Policy of the Community

TITLE I

Common Rules

CHAPTER 1

Rules on Competition

Section 1

Rules applying to undertakings

ARTICLE 85

1. The following shall be prohibited as incompatible with the common market: all agreements between undertakings, decisions by associations of undertakings and concerted practices which may affect trade between Member States and which have as their object or effect the prevention, restriction or distortion of competition within the common market, and in particular those which:

(a) directly or indirectly fix purchase or selling prices or any other trading conditions;

(b) limit or control production, markets, technical development, or investment;

(c) share markets or sources of supply;

(d) apply dissimilar conditions to equivalent transactions with other trading parties, thereby placing them at a competitive disadvantage;

(e) make the conclusion of contracts subject to acceptance by the other parties of supplementary obligations which, by their nature or according to commercial usage, have no connection with the subject of such contracts.

2. Any agreements or decisions prohibited pursuant to this Article shall be automatically void.

3. The provisions of paragraph 1 may, however, be declared inapplicable in the case of:

— any agreement or category of agreements between undertakings;

— any decision or category of decisions by associations of undertakings;

— any concerted practice or category of concerted practices;

which contributes to improving the production or distribution of goods or to promoting technical or economic progress, while allowing consumers a fair share of the resulting benefit, and which does not:

(a) impose on the undertakings concerned restrictions which are not indispensable to the attainment of these objectives;

(b) afford such undertakings the possibility of eliminating competition in respect of a substantial part of the products in question.

ARTICLE 86

Any abuse by one or more undertakings of a dominant position within the common market or in a substantial part of it shall be prohibited as incompatible with the common market is so far as it may affect trade between Member States.

Such abuse may, in particular, consist in:

(a) directly or indirectly imposing unfair purchase or selling prices or other unfair trading conditions;

(b) limiting production, markets or technical development to the prejudice of consumers;

(c) applying dissimilar conditions to equivalent transactions with other trading parties, thereby placing them at a competitive disadvantage;

(d) making the conclusion of contracts subject to acceptance by the other parties of supplementary obligations which, by their nature or according to commercial usage, have no connection with the subject of such contracts.

ARTICLE 87

1. Within three years of the entry into force of this Treaty the Council shall,

acting unanimously on a proposal from the Commission and after consulting the Assembly, adopt any appropriate regulations or directives to give effect to the principles set out in Articles 85 and 86.

If such provisions have not been adopted within the period mentioned, they shall be laid down by the Council, acting by a qualified majority on a proposal from the Commission and after consulting the Assembly.

2. The regulations or directives referred to in paragraph 1 shall be designed in particular:

(a) to ensure compliance with the prohibitions laid down in Article 85(1) and in Article 86 by making provision for fines and periodic penalty payments;

(b) to lay down detailed rules for the application of Article 85(3), taking into account the need to ensure effective supervision on the one hand, and to simplify administration to the greatest possible extent on the other;

(c) to define, if need be, in the various branches of the economy, the scope of the provisions of Articles 85 and 86;

(d) to define the respective functions of the Commission and of the Court of Justice in applying the provisions laid down in this paragraph;

(e) to determine the relationship between national laws and the provisions contained in this Section or adopted pursuant to this Article.

ARTICLE 88

Until the entry into force of the provisions adopted in pursuance of Article 87, the authorities in Member States shall rule on the admissibility of agreements, decisions and concerted practices and on abuse of a dominant position in the common market in accordance with the law of their country and with the provisions of Article 85, in particular paragraph 3, and of Article 86.

ARTICLE 89

1. Without prejudice to Article 88, the Commission shall, as soon as it takes up its duties, ensure the application of the principles laid down in Articles 85 and 86. On application by a Member State or on its own initiative, and in cooperation with the competent authorities in the Member States, who shall give it their assistance, the Commission shall investigate cases of

suspected infringement of these principles. If it finds that there has been an infringement, it shall propose appropriate measures to bring it to an end.

2. If the infringement is not brought to an end, the Commission shall record such infringement of the principles in a reasoned decision. The Commission may publish its decision and authorise Member States to take the measures, the conditions and details of which it shall determine, needed to remedy the situation.

ARTICLE 90

1. In the case of public undertakings and undertakings to which Member States grant special or exclusive rights, Member States shall neither enact nor maintain in force any measure contrary to the rules contained in this Treaty, in particular to those rules provided for in Article 7 and Articles 85 to 94.

2. Undertakings entrusted with the operation of services of general economic interest or having the character of a revenue-producing monopoly shall be subject to the rules contained in this Treaty, in particular to the rules on competition, in so far as the application of such rules does not obstruct the performance, in law or in fact, of the particular tasks assigned to them. The development of trade must not be affected to such an extent as would be contrary to the interests of the Community.

3. The Commission shall ensure the application of the provisions of this Article and shall, where necessary, address appropriate directives or decisions to Member States.

Section 2

Dumping

ARTICLE 91

1. If, during the transitional period, the Commission, on application by a Member State or by any other interested party, finds that dumping is being practised within the common market, it shall address recommendations to the person or persons with whom such practices originate for the purpose of putting an end to them.

Should the practices continue, the Commission shall authorise the injured Member State to take protective measures, the conditions and details of which the Commission shall determine.

2. As soon as this Treaty enters into force, products which originate in or are in free circulation in one Member State and which have been exported to another Member State shall, on reimportation, be admitted into the territory of the first-mentioned State free of all customs duties, quantitative restrictions or measures having equivalent effect. The Commission shall lay down appropriate rules for the application of this paragraph.

Section 3

Aids granted by States

ARTICLE 92

1. Save as otherwise provided in this Treaty, any aid granted by a Member State or through State resources in any form whatsoever which distorts or threatens to distort competition by favouring certain undertakings or the production of certain goods shall, in so far as it affects trade between Member States, be incompatible with the common market.

2. The following shall be compatible with the common market:

(a) aid having a social character, granted to individual consumers, provided that such aid is granted without discrimination related to the origin of the products concerned;

(b) aid to make good the damage caused by natural disasters or exceptional occurrences;

(c) aid granted to the economy of certain areas of the Federal Republic of Germany affected by the division of Germany, in so far as such aid is required in order to compensate for the economic disadvantages caused by that division.

3. The following may be considered to be compatible with the common market:

(a) aid to promote the economic development of areas where the standard of living is abnormally low or where there is serious underemployment;

(b) aid to promote the execution of an important project of common European interest or to remedy a serious disturbance in the economy of a Member State;

(c) aid to facilitate the development of certain economic activities or of certain economic areas, where such aid does not adversely affect trading conditions to an extent contrary to the common interest. However, the aids granted to shipbuilding as of 1 January 1957 shall, in so far as they serve only to compensate for the absence of customs protection, be progressively reduced under the same conditions as apply to the elimination of customs duties, subject to the provisions of this Treaty concerning common commercial policy towards third countries;

(d) such other categories of aid as may be specified by decision of the Council acting by a qualified majority on a proposal from the Commission.

ARTICLE 93

1. The Commission shall, in cooperation with Member States, keep under constant review all systems of aid existing in those States. It shall propose to the latter any appropriate measures required by the progressive development or by the functioning of the common market.

2. If, after giving notice to the parties concerned to submit their comments, the Commission finds that aid granted by a State or through State resources is not compatible with the common market having regard to Article 92, or that such aid is being misused, it shall decide that the State concerned shall abolish or alter such aid within a period of time to be determined by the Commission.

If the State concerned does not comply with this decision within the prescribed time, the Commission or any other interested State may, in derogation from the provisions of Article 169 and 170, refer the matter to the Court of Justice direct.

On application by a Member State, the Council, may, acting unanimously, decide that aid which that State is granting or intends to grant shall be considered to be compatible with the common market, in derogation from the provisions of Article 92 or from the regulations provided for in Article 94, if such a decision is justified by exceptional circumstances. If, as regards the aid in question, the Commission has already initiated the procedure provided for in the first subparagraph of this paragraph, the fact that the State concerned has made its application to the Council shall have the effect of suspending that procedure until the Council has made its attitude known.

If, however, the Council has not made its attitude known within three months of the said application being made, the Commission shall give its decision on the case.

3. The Commission shall be informed, in sufficient time to enable it to submit its comments, of any plans to grant or alter aid. If it considers that

any such plan is not compatible with the common market having regard to Article 92, it shall without delay initiate the procedure provided for in paragraph 2. The Member State concerned shall not put its proposed measures into effect until this procedure has resulted in a final decision.

ARTICLE 94

The Council may, acting by a qualified majority on a proposal from the Commission, make any appropriate regulations for the application of Articles 92 and 93 and may in particular determine the conditions in which Article 93(3) shall apply and the categories of aid exempted from this procedure.

CHAPTER 2

Tax Provisions

ARTICLE 95

No Member State shall impose, directly or indirectly, on the products of other Member States any internal taxation of any kind in excess of that imposed directly or indirectly on similar domestic products.

Furthermore, no Member State shall impose on the products of other Member States any internal taxation of such a nature as to afford indirect protection to other products.

Member States shall, not later than at the beginning of the second stage, repeal or amend any provisions existing when this Treaty enters into force which conflict with the preceding rules.

ARTICLE 96

Where products are exported to the territory of any Member State, any repayment of internal taxation shall not exceed the internal taxation imposed on them whether directly or indirectly.

ARTICLE 97

Member States which levy a turnover tax calculated on a cumulative multi-stage tax system may, in the case of internal taxation imposed by them on imported products or of repayments allowed by them on exported products, establish average rates for products or groups of products, provided that there is no infringement of the principles laid down in Articles 95 and 96.

Where the average rates established by a Member State do not conform to these principles, the Commission shall address appropriate directives or decisions to the State concerned.

ARTICLE 98

In the case of charges other than turnover taxes, excise duties and other forms of indirect taxation, remissions and repayments in respect of exports to other Member States may not be granted [and] countervailing charges in respect of imports from Member States may not be imposed unless the measures contemplated have been previously approved for a limited period by the Council acting by a qualified majority on a proposal from the Commission.

ARTICLE 99

The Commission shall consider how the legislation of the various Member States concerning turnover taxes, excise duties and other forms of indirect taxation, including countervailing measures applicable to trade between Member States, can be harmonised in the interest of the common market.

The Commission shall submit proposals to the Council, which shall act unanimously without prejudice to the provisions of Articles 100 and 101.

CHAPTER 3

Approximation of Laws

ARTICLE 100

The Council shall, acting unanimously on a proposal from the Commission, issue directives for the approximation of such provisions laid down by law, regulation or administrative action in Member States as directly affect the establishment or functioning of the common market.

The Assembly and the Economic and Social Committee shall be consulted in the case of directives whose implementation would, in one or more Member States, involve the amendment of legislation.

ARTICLE 101

Where the Commission finds that a difference between the provisions laid down by law, regulation or administrative action in Member States is distorting the conditions of competition in the common market and that the resultant distortion needs to be eliminated, it shall consult the Member States concerned.

If such consultation does not result in an agreement eliminating the distortion in question, the Council shall, on a proposal from the Commission, acting unanimously during the first stage and by a qualified majority thereafter, issue the necessary directives. The Commission and the Council may take any other appropriate measures provided for in this Treaty.

ARTICLE 102

1. Where there is reason to fear that the adoption or amendment of a provision laid down by law, regulation or administrative action may cause distortion within the meaning of Article 101, a Member State desiring to proceed therewith shall consult the Commission. After consulting the Member States, the Commission shall recommend to the States concerned such measures as may be appropriate to avoid the distortion in question.

2. If a State desiring to introduce or amend its own provisions does not comply with the recommendation addressed to it by the Commission, other Member States shall not be required, in pursuance of Article 101, to amend their own provisions in order to eliminate such distortion. If the Member State which has ignored the recommendation of the Commission causes distortion detrimental only to itself, the provisions of Article 101 shall not apply.

TITLE II

Economic Policy

CHAPTER 1

Conjunctural Policy

ARTICLE 103

1. Member States shall regard their conjunctural policies as a matter of common concern. They shall consult each other and the Commission on the measures to be taken in the light of the prevailing circumstances.

2. Without prejudice to any other procedures provided for in this Treaty, the Council may, acting unanimously on a proposal from the Commission, decide upon the measures appropriate to the situation.

3. Acting by a qualified majority on a proposal from the Commission, the Council shall, where required, issue any directives needed to give effect to the measures decided upon under paragraph 2.

4. The procedures provided for in this Article shall also apply if any difficulty should arise in the supply of certain products.

CHAPTER 2

Balance of Payments

ARTICLE 104

Each Member State shall pursue the economic policy needed to ensure the equilibrium of its overall balance of payments and to maintain confidence in its currency, while taking care to ensure a high level of employment and a stable level of prices.

ARTICLE 105

1. In order to facilitate attainment of the objectives set out in Article 104, Member States shall coordinate their economic policies. They shall for this purpose provide for cooperation between their appropriate administrative departments and between their central banks.

The Commission shall submit to the Council recommendations on how to achieve such cooperation.

2. In order to promote coordination of the policies of Member States in the monetary field to the full extent needed for the functioning of the common market, a Monetary Committee with advisory status is hereby set up. It shall have the following tasks:

— to keep under review the monetary and financial situation of the Member States and of the Community and the general payments system of the Member States and to report regularly thereon to the Council and to the Commission;

— to deliver opinions at the request of the Council or of the Commission or on its own initiative, for submission to these institutions.

The Member States and the Commission shall each appoint two members of the Monetary Committee.

ARTICLE 106

1. Each Member State undertakes to authorise, in the currency of the Member State in which the creditor or the beneficiary resides, any payments connected with the movement of goods, services or capital, and any transfers of capital and earnings, to the extent that the movement of goods, services, capital and persons between Member States has been liberalised pursuant to this Treaty.

The Member States declare their readiness to undertake the liberalisation of payments beyond the extent provided in the preceding subparagraph, in so far as their economic situation in general and the state of their balance of payments in particular so permit.

2. In so far as movements of goods, services, and capital are limited only by restrictions on payments connected therewith, these restrictions shall be progressively abolished by applying, *mutatis mutandis,* the provisions of the Chapters relating to the abolition of quantitative restrictions, to the liberalisation of services and to the free movement of capital.

3. Member States undertake not to introduce between themselves any new restrictions on transfers connected with the invisible transactions listed in Annex III to this Treaty.

The progressive abolition of existing restrictions shall be effected in accordance with the provisions of Articles 63 to 65, in so far as such abolition is not governed by the provisions contained in paragraphs 1 and 2 or by the Chapter relating to the free movement of capital.

4. If need be, Member States shall consult each other on the measures to be taken to enable the payments and transfers mentioned in this Article to be effected; such measures shall not prejudice the attainment of the objectives set out in this Chapter.

ARTICLE 107

1. Each Member State shall treat its policy with regard to rates of exchange as a matter of common concern.

2. If a Member State makes an alteration in its rate of exchange which is inconsistent with the objectives set out in Article 104 and which seriously dis-

torts conditions of competition, the Commission may, after consulting the Monetary Committee, authorise other Member States to take for a strictly limited period the necessary measures, the conditions and details of which it shall determine, in order to counter the consequences of such alteration.

ARTICLE 108

1. Where a Member State is in difficulties or is seriously threatened with difficulties as regards its balance of payments either as a result of an overall disequilibrium in its balance of payments, or as a result of the type of currency at its disposal, and where such difficulties are liable in particular to jeopardise the functioning of the common market or the progressive implementation of the common commercial policy, the Commission shall immediately investigate the position of the State in question and the action which, making use of all the means at its disposal, that State has taken or may take in accordance with the provisions of Article 104. The Commission shall state what measures it recommends the State concerned to take.

If the action taken by a Member State and the measures suggested by the Commission do not prove sufficient to overcome the difficulties which have arisen or which threaten, the Commission shall, after consulting the Monetary Committee, recommend to the Council the granting of mutual assistance and appropriate methods therefor.

The Commission shall keep the Council regularly informed of the situation and of how it is developing.

2. The Council, acting by a qualified majority, shall grant such mutual assistance; it shall adopt directives or decisions laying down the conditions and details of such assistance, which may take such forms as:

(a) a concerted approach to or within any other international organisations to which Member States may have recourse;

(b) measures needed to avoid deflection of trade where the State which is in difficulties maintains or reintroduces quantitative restrictions against third countries;

(c) the granting of limited credits by other Member States, subject to their agreement.

During the transitional period, mutual assistance may also take the form of special reductions in customs duties or enlargements of quotas in order to facilitate an increase in imports from the State which is in difficulties, subject to the agreement of the States by which such measures would have to be taken.

3. If the mutual assistance recommended by the Commission is not granted by the Council or if the mutual assistance granted and the measures taken are insufficient, the Commission shall authorise the State which is in difficulties to take protective measures, the conditions and details of which the Commission shall determine.

Such authorisation may be revoked and such conditions and details may be changed by the Council acting by a qualified majority.

Article 109

1. Where a sudden crisis in the balance of payments occurs and a decision within the meaning of Article 108(2) is not immediately taken, the Member State concerned may, as a precaution, take the necessary protective measures. Such measures must cause the least possible disturbance in the functioning of the common market and must not be wider in scope than is strictly necessary to remedy the sudden difficulties which have arisen.

2. The Commission and the other Member States shall be informed of such protective measures not later than when they enter into force. The Commission may recommend to the Council the granting of mutual assistance under Article 108.

3. After the Commission has delivered an opinion and the Monetary Committee has been consulted, the Council may, acting by a qualified majority, decide that the State concerned shall amend, suspend or abolish the protective measures referred to above.

Chapter 3

Commercial Policy

Article 110

By establishing a customs union between themselves Member States aim to contribute, in the common interest, to the harmonious development of world trade, the progressive abolition of restrictions on international trade and the lowering of customs barriers.

The common commercial policy shall take into account the favourable effect which the abolition of customs duties between Member States may have on the increase in the competitive strength of undertakings in those States.

ARTICLE 111

The following provisions shall, without prejudice to Articles 115 and 116, apply during the transitional period:

1. Member States shall coordinate their trade relations with third countries so as to bring about, by the end of the transitional period, the conditions needed for implementing a common policy in the field of external trade.

The Commission shall submit to the Council proposals regarding the procedure for common action to be followed during the transitional period and regarding the achievement of uniformity in their commercial policies.

2. The Commission shall submit to the Council recommendations for tariff negotiations with third countries in respect of the common customs tariff.

The Council shall authorise the Commission to open such negotiations.

The Commission shall conduct these negotiations in consultation with a special committee appointed by the Council to assist the Commission in this task and within the framework of such directives as the Council may issue to it.

3. In exercising the power conferred upon it by this Article, the Council shall act unanimously during the first two stages and by a qualified majority thereafter.

4. Member States shall, in consultation with the Commission, take all necessary measures, particularly those designed to bring about an adjustment of tariff agreements in force with third countries, in order that the entry into force of the common customs tariff shall not be delayed.

5. Member States shall aim at securing as high a level of uniformity as possible between themselves as regards their liberalisation lists in relation to third countries or groups of third countries. To this end, the Commission shall make all appropriate recommendations to Member States.

If Member States abolish or reduce quantitative restrictions in relation to third countries, they shall inform the Commission beforehand and shall accord the same treatment to other Member States.

ARTICLE 112

1. Without prejudice to obligations undertaken by them within the framework of other international organisations, Member States shall, before the end of the transitional period, progressively harmonise the system whereby they grant aid for exports to third countries, to the extent necessary to ensure that competition between undertakings of the Community is not distorted.

On a proposal from the Commission, the Council, shall, acting unanimously until the end of the second stage and by a qualified majority thereafter, issue any directives needed for this purpose.

2. The preceding provisions shall not apply to such drawback of customs duties or charges having equivalent effect nor to such repayment of indirect taxation including turnover taxes, excise duties and other indirect taxes as is allowed when goods are exported from a Member State to a third country, in so far as such drawback or repayment does not exceed the amount imposed, directly or indirectly, on the products exported.

ARTICLE 113

1. After the transitional period has ended, the common commercial policy shall be based on uniform principles, particularly in regard to changes in tariff rates, the conclusion of tariff and trade agreements, the achievement of uniformity in measures of liberalisation, export policy and measures to protect trade such as those to be taken in case of dumping or subsidies.

2. The Commission shall submit proposals to the Council for implementing the common commercial policy.

3. Where agreements with third countries need to be negotiated, the Commission shall make recommendations to the Council, which shall authorise the Commission to open the necessary negotiations.

The Commission shall conduct these negotiations in consultation with a special committee appointed by the Council to assist the Commission in this task and within the framework of such directives as the Council may issue to it.

4. In exercising the powers conferred upon it by this Article, the Council shall act by a qualified majority.

ARTICLE 114

The agreement referred to in Article 111 (2) and in Article 113 shall be concluded by the Council on behalf of the Community, acting unanimously during the first two stages and by a qualified majority thereafter.

ARTICLE 115

In order to ensure that the execution of measures of commercial policy taken in accordance with this Treaty by any Member State is not obstructed by deflection of trade, or where differences between such measures lead to economic difficulties in one or more of the Member States, the Commission shall recommend the methods for the requisite cooperation between Member States. Failing this, the Commission shall authorise Member States to take the necessary protective measures, the conditions and details of which it shall determine.

In case of urgency during the transitional period, Member States may themselves take the necessary measures and shall notify them to the other Member States and to the Commission, which may decide that the States concerned shall amend or abolish such measures.

In the selection of such measures, priority shall be given to those which cause the least disturbance to the functioning of the common market and which take into account the need to expedite, as far as possible, the introduction of the common customs tariff.

ARTICLE 116

From the end of the transitional period onwards, Member States shall, in respect of all matters of particular interest to the common market, proceed within the framework of international organisations of an economic character only by common action. To this end, the Commission shall submit to the Council, which shall act by a qualified majority, proposals concerning the scope and implementation of such common action.

During the transitional period, Member States shall consult each other for the purpose of concerting the action they take and adopting as far as possible a uniform attitude.

TITLE III

Social Policy

CHAPTER 1

Social Provisions

ARTICLE 117

Member States agree upon the need to promote improved working conditions and and an improved standard of living for workers, so as to make possible their harmonisation while the improvement is being maintained.

They believe that such a development will ensue not only from the functioning of the common market, which will favour the harmonisation of social systems, but also from the procedures provided for in this Treaty and from the approximation of provisions laid down by law, regulation or administrative action.

ARTICLE 118

Without prejudice to the other provisions of this Treaty and in conformity with its general objectives, the Commission shall have the task of promoting close cooperation between Member States in the social field, particularly in matters relating to:

— employment;

— labour law and working conditions;

— basic and advanced vocational training;

— social security;

— prevention of occupational accidents and diseases;

— occupational hygiene;

— the right of association, and collective bargaining between employers and workers.

To this end, the Commission shall act in close contact with Member States by making studies, delivering opinions and arranging consultations both on problems arising at national level and on those of concern to international organisations.

Before delivering the opinions provided for in this Article, the Commission shall consult the Economic and Social Committee.

ARTICLE 119

Each Member State shall during the first stage ensure and subsequently maintain the application of the principle that men and women should receive equal pay for equal work.

For the purpose of this Article, "pay" means the ordinary basic or minimum wage or salary and any other consideration, whether in cash or in kind, which the worker receives, directly or indirectly, in respect of his employment from his employer.

Equal pay without discrimination based on sex means:

(a) that pay for the same work at piece rates shall be calculated on the basis of the same unit of measurement;

(b) that pay for work at time rates shall be the same for the same job.

ARTICLE 120

Member States shall endeavour to maintain the existing equivalence between paid holiday schemes.

ARTICLE 121

The Council may, acting unanimously and after consulting the Economic and Social Committee, assign to the Commission tasks in connection with the implementation of common measures, particularly as regards social security for the migrant workers referred to in Article 48 to 51.

ARTICLE 122

The Commission shall include a separate chapter on social developments within the Community in its annual report to the Assembly.

The Assembly may invite the Commission to draw up reports on any particular problems concerning social conditions.

CHAPTER 2

The European Social Fund

ARTICLE 123

In order to improve employment opportunities for workers in the common market and to contribute thereby to raising the standard of living, a European Social Fund is hereby established in accordance with the provisions set out below; it shall have the task of rendering the employment of workers easier and of increasing their geographical and occupational mobility within the Community.

ARTICLE 124

The Fund shall be administered by the Commission.

The Commission shall be assisted in this task by a Committee presided over by a member of the Commission and composed of representatives of Governments, trade unions and employers' organisations.

ARTICLE 125

1. On application by a Member State the Fund shall, within the framework of the rules provided for in Article 127, meet 50% of the expenditure incurred after the entry into force of this Treaty by that State or by a body governed by public law for the purposes of:

(a) ensuring productive re-employment of workers by means of:

— vocational retraining;

— resettlement allowances;

(b) granting aid for the benefit of workers whose employment is reduced or temporarily suspended, in whole or in part, as a result of the conversion of an undertaking to other production, in order that they may retain the same wage level pending their full reemployment.

2. Assistance granted by the Fund towards the cost of vocational retraining shall be granted only if the unemployed workers could not be found employment except in a new occupation and only if they have been in productive employment for at least six months in the occupation for which they have been retrained.

Assistance towards resettlement allowances shall be granted only if the unemployed workers have been caused to change their home within the Community and have been in productive employment for at least six months in their new place of residence.

Assistance for workers in the case of the conversion of an undertaking shall be granted only if:

(a) the workers concerned have again been fully employed in that undertaking for at least six months;

(b) the Government concerned has submitted a plan beforehand, drawn up by the undertaking in question, for that particular conversion and for financing it;

(c) the Commission has given its prior approval to the conversion plan.

ARTICLE 126

When the transitional period has ended, the Council, after receiving the opinion of the Commission and after consulting the Economic and Social Committee and the Assembly, may:

(a) rule, by a qualified majority, that all or part of the assistance referred to in Article 125 shall no longer be granted; or

(b) unanimously determine what new tasks may be entrusted to the Fund within the framework of its terms of reference as laid down in Article 123.

ARTICLE 127

The Council shall, acting by a qualified majority on a proposal from the Commission and after consulting the Economic and Social Committee and the Assembly, lay down the provisions required to implement Articles 124 to 126; in particular it shall determine in detail the conditions under which assistance shall be granted by the Fund in accordance with Article 125 and the classes of undertakings whose workers shall benefit from the assistance provided for in Article 125(1)(b).

ARTICLE 128

The Council shall, acting on a proposal from the Commission and after consulting the Economic and Social Committee, lay down general principles for implementing a common vocational training policy capable of contributing to the harmonious development both of the national economies and of the common market.

TITLE IV

The European Investment Bank

ARTICLE 129

A European Investment Bank is hereby established; it shall have legal personality.

The members of the European Investment Bank shall be the Member States.

The Statute of the European Investment Bank is laid down in a Protocol annexed to this Treaty.

ARTICLE 130

The task of the European Investment Bank shall be to contribute, by having recourse to the capital market and utilising its own resources, to the balanced and steady development of the common market in the interest of the Community. For this purpose the Bank shall, operating on a non-profit-making basis, grant loans and give guarantees which facilitate the financing of the following projects in all sectors of the economy:

(a) projects for developing less developed regions;

(b) projects for modernising or converting undertakings or for developing fresh activities called for by the progressive establishment of the common market, where these projects are of such a size or nature that they cannot be entirely financed by the various means available in the individual Member States;

(c) projects of common interest to several Member States which are of such a size or nature that they cannot be entirely financed by the various means available in the individual Member States.

PART FOUR

Association of the Overseas Countries and Territories

ARTICLE 131

The Member States agree to associate with the Community the non-European countries and territories which have special relations with Belgium, France, Italy, the Netherlands and the United Kingdom.* These countries and territories (hereinafter called the "countries and territories") are listed in Annex IV to this Treaty.

The purpose of association shall be to promote the economic and social development of the countries and territories and to establish close economic relations between them and the Community as a whole.

In accordance with the principles set out in the Preamble to this Treaty, association shall serve primarily to further the interests and prosperity of the inhabitants of these countries and territories in order to lead them to the economic, social and cultural development to which they aspire.

ARTICLE 132

Association shall have the following objectives:

1. Member States shall apply to their trade with the countries and territories the same treatment as they accord each other pursuant to this Treaty.

2. Each country or territory shall apply to its trade with Member States and with the other countries and territories the same treatment as that which it applies to the European State with which it has special relations.

3. The Member States shall contribute to the investments required for the progressive development of these countries and territories.

4. For investments financed by the Community, participation in tenders and supplies shall be open on equal terms to all natural and legal persons who are nationals of a Member State or of one of the countries and territories.

5. In relations between Member States and the countries and territories the right of establishment of nationals and companies or firms shall be regulated in accordance with the provisions and procedures laid down in the Chapter relating to the right of establishment and on a non-discriminatory basis, subject to any special provisions laid down pursuant to Article 136.

ARTICLE 133

1. Customs duties on imports into the Member States of goods originating in the countries and territories shall be completely abolished in conformity

---

* First sentence as amended by Article 24(1) of the Act of Accession, modified by Article 13 of the Adaptation Decision.

with the progressive abolition of customs duties between Member States in accordance with the provisions of this Treaty.

2. Customs duties on imports into each country or territory from Member States or from the other countries or territories shall be progressively abolished in accordance with the provisions of Articles 12, 13, 14, 15 and 17.

3. The countries and territories may, however, levy customs duties which meet the needs of their development and industrialisation or produce revenue for their budgets.

The duties referred to in the preceding subparagraph shall nevertheless be progressively reduced to the level of those imposed on imports of products from the Member State with which each country or territory has special relations. The percentages and the timetable of the reductions provided for under this Treaty shall apply to the difference between the duty imposed on a product coming from the Member State which has special relations with the country or territory concerned and the duty imposed on the same product coming from within the Community on entry into the importing country or territory.

4. Paragraph 2 shall not apply to countries and territories which, by reason of the particular international obligations by which they are bound, already apply a non-discriminatory customs tariff when this Treaty enters into force.

5. The introduction of or any change in customs duties imposed on goods imported into the countries and territories shall not, either in law or in fact, give rise to any direct or indirect discrimination between imports from the various Member States.

ARTICLE 134

If the level of the duties applicable to goods from a third country on entry into a country or territory is liable, when the provisions of Article 133(1) have been applied, to cause deflections of trade to the detriment of any Member State, the latter may request the Commission to propose to the other Member States the measures needed to remedy the situation.

ARTICLE 135

Subject to the provisions relating to public health, public security or public policy, freedom of movement within Member States for workers from the countries and territories, and within the countries and territories for workers from Member States, shall be governed by agreements to be concluded subsequently with the unanimous approval of Member States.

ARTICLE 136

For an initial period of five years after the entry into force of this Treaty, the details of and procedure for the association of the countries and territories with the Community shall be determined by an Implementing Convention annexed to this Treaty.

Before the Convention referred to in the preceding paragraph expires, the Council shall, acting unanimously, lay down provisions for a further period, on the basis of the experience acquired and of the principles set out in this Treaty.

PART FIVE

Institutions of the Community

TITLE I

Provisions Governing the Institutions

CHAPTER 1

The Institutions

Section 1

The Assembly

ARTICLE 137

The Assembly, which shall consist of representatives of the peoples of the States brought together in the Community, shall exercise the advisory and supervisory powers which are conferred upon it by this Treaty.

ARTICLE 138

1. The Assembly shall consist of delegates who shall be designated by the respective Parliaments from among their members in accordance with the procedure laid down by each Member State.

2. The number of these delegates shall be as follows:

Belgium	14
Denmark	10
Germany	36
France	36
Ireland	10
Italy	36
Luxembourg	6
Netherlands	14
United Kingdom	36.*

3. The Assembly shall draw up proposals for elections by direct universal suffrage in accordance with a uniform procedure in all Member States.

The Council shall, acting unanimously, lay down the appropriate provisions, which it shall recommend to Member States for adoption in accordance with their respective constitutional requirements.

ARTICLE 139

The Assembly shall hold an annual session. It shall meet, without requiring to be convened, on the second Tuesday in March.**

The Assembly may meet in extraordinary session at the request of a majority of its members or at the request of the Council or of the Commission.

ARTICLE 140

The Assembly shall elect its President and its officers from among its members.

Members of the Commission may attend all meetings and shall, at their request, be heard on behalf of the Commission.

The Commission shall reply orally or in writing to questions put to it by the Assembly or by its members.

The Council shall be heard by the Assembly in accordance with the conditions laid down by the Council in its rules of procedure.

---

* Paragraph 2 as amended by Article 10 of the Act of Accession, modified by Article 4 of the Adaptation Decision.

**First paragraph as amended by Article 27(1) of the Merger Treaty.

ARTICLE 141

Save as otherwise provided in this Treaty, the Assembly shall act by an absolute majority of the votes cast.

The rules of procedure shall determine the quorum.

ARTICLE 142

The Assembly shall adopt its rules of procedure, acting by a majority of its members.

The proceedings of the Assembly shall be published in the manner laid down in its rules of procedure.

ARTICLE 143

The Assembly shall discuss in open session the annual general report submitted to it by the Commission.

ARTICLE 144

If a motion of censure on the activities of the Commission is tabled before it, the Assembly shall not vote thereon until at least three days after the motion has been tabled and only by open vote.

If the motion of censure is carried by a two-thirds majority of the votes cast, representing a majority of the members of the Assembly, the members of the Commission shall resign as a body. They shall continue to deal with current business until they are replaced in accordance with Article 158.*

Section 2

The Council

ARTICLE 145

To ensure that the objectives set out in this Treaty are attained, the Council shall, in accordance with the provisions of this Treaty:

— ensure coordination of the general economic policies of the Member States;

— have power to take decisions.

* Article 158 is repealed by Article 19 of the Merger Treaty; *see* Merger Treaty, Article 11.

ARTICLE 146*

ARTICLE 147**

ARTICLE 148

1. Save as otherwise provided in this Treaty, the Council shall act by a majority of its members.

2. *** Where the Council is required to act by a qualified majority, the votes of its members shall be weighted as follows:

Belgium	5
Denmark	3
Germany	10
France	10
Ireland	3
Italy	10
Luxembourg	2
Netherlands	5
United Kingdom	10.

For their adoption, acts of the Council shall require at least:

— forty-one votes in favour where this Treaty requires them to be adopted on a proposal from the Commission.

— forty-one votes in favour, cast by at least six members, in other cases.

3. Abstentions by members present in person or represented shall not prevent the adoption by the Council of acts which require unanimity.

ARTICLE 149

Where, in pursuance of this Treaty, the Council acts on a proposal from the Commission, unanimity shall be required for an act constituting an amendment to that proposal.

As long as the Council has not acted, the Commission may alter its original proposal, in particular where the Assembly has been consulted on that proposal.

---

* Repealed by Art. 7 of the Merger Treaty; *see* Merger Treaty, Art. 2.

** Repealed by Art. 7 of the Merger Treaty; *see* Merger Treaty, Art. 3.

*** Paragraph (2) as amended by Article 14 of the Act of Accession, modified by Article 8 of the Adaptation Decision.

ARTICLE 150

Where a vote is taken, any member of the Council may also act on behalf of not more than one other member.

ARTICLE 151*

ARTICLE 152

The Council may request the Commission to undertake any studies which the Council considers desirable for the attainment of the common objectives, and to submit to it any appropriate proposals.

ARTICLE 153

The Council shall, after receiving an opinion from the Commission, determine the rules governing the committees provided for in this Treaty.

ARTICLE 54**

Section 3

The Commission

ARTICLE 155

In order to ensure the proper functioning and development of the common market, the Commission shall:

— ensure that the provisions of this Treaty and the measures taken by the institutions pursuant thereto are applied;

— formulate recommendations or deliver opinions on matters dealt with in this Treaty, if it expressly so provides or if the Commission considers it necessary;

— have its own power of decision and participate in the shaping of measures taken by the Council and by the Assembly in the manner provided for in this Treaty.

---

* Repealed by Art. 7 of the Merger Treaty; see Merger Treaty, Arts. 4 and 5.

** Repealed by Art. 7 of the Merger Treaty; see Merger Treaty, Art. 6.

— exercise the powers conferred on it by the Council for the implementation of the rules laid down by the latter.

ARTICLES 156 TO 163*

Section 4

The Court of Justice

ARTICLE 164

The Court of Justice shall ensure that in the interpretation and application of this Treaty the law is observed.

ARTICLE 165

The Court of Justice shall consist of nine Judges.**

The Court of Justice shall sit in plenary session. It may, however, form chambers, each consisting of three or five Judges, either to undertake certain preparatory inquiries or to adjudicate on particular categories of cases in accordance with rules laid down for these purposes.

Whenever the Court of Justice hears cases brought before it by a Member State or by one of the institutions of the Community or, to the extent that the chambers of the Court do not have the requisite jurisdiction under the Rules of Proceedings as to give preliminary rulings on questions submitted to it pursuant to Article 177, it shall sit in plenary session.***

Should the Court of Justice so request, the Council may, acting unanimously, increase the number of Judges and make the necessary adjustments to the second and third paragraphs of this Article and to the second paragraph of Article 167.

---

* Repealed by Art. 19 of the Merger Treaty; *see* Merger Treaty, Arts. 10 to 18.

** First paragraph as amended by Art. 17 of the Act of Accession, modified by Art. 9 of the Adaptation Decision.

*** Third paragraph as amended by Art. 1 of the Council Decision of 26 November 1974 (Official Journal of the European Communities, No. L 318, 28 November 1974, p. 22).

ARTICLE 166

The Court of Justice shall be assisted by four Advocates-General.*

It shall be the duty of the Advocate-General, acting with complete impartiality and independence, to make, in open court, reasoned submissions on cases brought before the Court of Justice, in order to assist the Court in the performance of the task assigned to it in Article 164.

Should the Court of Justice so request, the Council may, acting unanimously, increase the number of Advocates-General and make the necessary adjustments to the third paragraph of Article 167.

ARTICLE 167

The Judges and Advocates-General shall be chosen from persons whose independence is beyond doubt and who possess the qualifications required for appointment to the highest judicial offices in their respective countries or who are jurisconsults of recognised competence; they shall be appointed by common accord of the Governments of the Member States for a term of six years.

Every three years there shall be a partial replacement of the Judges. Five and four Judges shall be replaced alternately.**

Every three years there shall be a partial replacement of the Advocates-General. Two Advocates-General shall be replaced on each occasion.***

Retiring Judges and Advocates-General shall be eligible for reappointment.

The Judges shall elect the President of the Court of Justice from among their number for a term of three years. He may be reelected.

ARTICLE 168

The Court of Justice shall appoint its Registrar and lay down the rules governing his service.

---

* First paragraph as amended by Article 1 of the Council Decision of 1 January 1973 increasing the number of Advocates-General (Official Journal of the European Communities, No. L 2, 1 January 1973, p. 29).

** Second paragraph as amended by Art. 19 of the Act of Accession, modified by Art. 10 of the Adaptation Decision.

*** Third paragraph as amended by Article 2 of the Council Decision of 1 January 1973 increasing the number of Advocates-General (Official Journal of the European Communities No. L 2, 1 January 1973, p. 29).

ARTICLE 169

If the Commission considers that a Member State has failed to fulfil an obligation under this Treaty, it shall deliver a reasoned opinion on the matter after giving the State concerned the opportunity to submit its observations

If the State concerned does not comply with the opinion within the period laid down by the Commission, the latter may bring the matter before the Court of Justice.

ARTICLE 170

A Member State which considers that another Member State has failed to fufil an obligation under this Treaty may bring the matter before the Court of Justice.

Before a Member State brings an action against another Member State for an alleged infringement of an obligation under this Treaty, it shall bring the matter before the Commission.

The Commission shall deliver a reasoned opinion after each of the States concerned has been given the opportunity to submit its own case and its observations on the other party's case both orally and in writing.

If the Commission has not delivered an opinion within three months of the date on which the matter was brought before it, the absence of such opinion shall not prevent the matter from being brought before the Court of Justice.

ARTICLE 171

If the Court of Justice finds that a Member State has failed to fulfil an obligation under this Treaty, the State shall be required to take the necessary measures to comply with the judgment of the Court of Justice.

ARTICLE 172

Regulations made by the Council pursuant to the provisions of this Treaty may give the Court of Justice unlimited jurisdiction in regard to the penalties provided for in such regulations.

ARTICLE 172

Regulations made by the Council pursuant to the provisions of this Treaty may give the Court of Justice unlimited jurisdiction in regard to the penalties provided for in such regulations.

ARTICLE 173

The Court of Justice shall review the legality of acts of the Council and the Commission other than recommendations or opinions. It shall for this purpose have jurisdiction in actions brought by a Member State, the Council or the Commission on grounds of lack of competence, infringement of an essential procedural requirement, infringement of this Treaty or of any rule of law relating to its application, or misuse of powers.

Any natural or legal person may, under the same conditions, institute proceedings against a decision addressed to that person or against a decision which, although in the form of a regulation or a decision addressed to another person, is of direct and individual concern to the former.

The proceedings provided for in this Article shall be instituted within two months of the publication of the measure, or of its notification to the plaintiff, or, in the absence thereof, of the day on which it came to the knowledge of the latter, as the case may be.

ARTICLE 174

If the action is well founded, the Court of Justice shall declare the act concerned to be void.

In the case of a regulation, however, the Court of Justice shall, if it considers this necessary, state which of the effects of the regulation which it has declared void shall be considered as definitive.

ARTICLE 175

Should the Council or the Commission, in infringement of this Treaty, fail to act, the Member States and the other institutions of the Community may bring an action before the Court of Justice to have the infringement established.

The action shall be admissible only if the institution concerned has first been called upon to act. If, within two months of being so called upon, the institution concerned has not defined its position, the action may be brought within a further period of two months.

Any natural or legal person may, under the conditions laid down in the preceding paragraphs, complain to the Court of Justice that an institution of the Community has failed to address to that person any act other than a recommendation or an opinion.

ARTICLE 176

The institution whose act has been declared void or whose failure to act has been declared contrary to this Treaty shall be required to take the necessary measures to comply with the judgment of the Court of Justice.

This obligation shall not affect any obligation which may result from the application of the second paragraph of Article 215.

ARTICLE 177

The Court of Justice shall have jurisdiction to give preliminary rulings concerning:

(a) the interpretation of this Treaty;

(b) the validity and interpretation of acts of the institutions of the Community;

(c) the interpretation of the statutes of bodies established by an act of the Council, where those statutes so provide.

Where such a question is raised before any court or tribunal of a Member State, that court or tribunal may, if it considers that a decision on the question is necessary to enable it to give judgment, request the Court of Justice to give a ruling thereon.

Where any such question is raised in a case pending before a court or tribunal of a Member State, against whose decisions there is no judicial remedy under national law, that court or tribunal shall bring the matter before the Court of Justice.

ARTICLE 178

The Court of Justice shall have jurisdiction in disputes relating to compensation for damage provided for in the second paragraph of Article 215.

ARTICLE 179

The Court of Justice shall have jurisdiction in any dispute between the Community and its servants within the limits and under the conditions laid down in the Staff Regulations or the Conditions of Employment.

ARTICLE 180

The Court of Justice shall, within the limits hereinafter laid down, have jurisdiction in disputes concerning:

(a) the fulfilment by Member States of obligations under the Statute of the European Investment Bank. In this connection, the Board of Directors of the Bank shall enjoy the powers conferred upon the Commission by Article 169;

(b) measures adopted by the Board of Governors of the Bank. In this connection, any Member State, the Commission or the Board of Directors of the Bank may institute proceedings under the conditions laid down in Article 173;

(c) measures adopted by the Board of Directors of the Bank. Proceedings against such measures may be instituted only by Member States or by the Commission, under the conditions laid down in Article 173, and solely on the grounds of non-compliance with the procedure provided for in Article 21(2), (5), (6) and (7) of the Statute of the Bank.

ARTICLE 181

The Court of Justice shall have jurisdiction to give judgment pursuant to any arbitration clause contained in a contract concluded by or on behalf of the Community, whether that contract be governed by public or private law.

ARTICLE 182

The Court of Justice shall have jurisdiction in any dispute between Member States which relates to the subject matter of this Treaty if the dispute is submitted to it under a special agreement between the parties.

ARTICLE 183

Save where jurisdiction is conferred on the Court of Justice by this Treaty, disputes to which the Community is a party shall not on that ground be excluded from the jurisdiction of the courts or tribunals of the Member States.

ARTICLE 184

Notwithstanding the expiry of the period laid down in the third paragraph of Article 173, any party may, in proceedings in which a regulation of the Council or of the Commission is in issue, plead the grounds specified in the first paragraph of Article 173, in order to invoke before the Court of Justice the inapplicability of that regulation.

ARTICLE 185

Actions brought before the Court of Justice shall not have suspensory effect. The Court of Justice may, however, if it considers that circumstances so require, order that application of the contested act be suspended.

ARTICLE 186

The Court of Justice may in any cases before it prescribe any necessary interim measures.

ARTICLE 187

The judgments of the Court of Justice shall be enforceable under the conditions laid down in Article 192.

ARTICLE 188

The Statute of the Court of Justice is laid down in a separate Protocol.

The Court of Justice shall adopt its rules of procedure. These shall require the unanimous approval of the Council.

CHAPTER 2

Provisions Common to Several Institutions

ARTICLE 189

In order to carry out their task the Council and the Commission shall, in accordance with the provisions of this Treaty, make regulations, issue directives, take decisions, make recommendations or deliver opinions.

A regulation shall have general application. It shall be binding in its entirety and directly applicable in all Member States.

A directive shall be binding, as to the result to be achieved, upon each

Member State to which it is addressed, but shall leave to the national authorities the choice of form and methods.

A decision shall be binding in its entirety upon those to whom it is addressed.

Recommendations and opinions shall have no binding force.

ARTICLE 190

Regulations, directives and decisions of the Council and of the Commission shall state the reasons on which they are based and shall refer to any proposals or opinions which were required to be obtained pursuant to this Treaty.

ARTICLE 191

Regulations shall be published in the Official Journal of the Community. They shall enter into force on the date specified in them or, in the absence thereof, on the twentieth day following their publication.

Directives and decisions shall be notified to those to whom they are addressed and shall take effect upon such notification.

ARTICLE 192

Decisions of the Council or of the Commission which impose a pecuniary obligation on persons other than States shall be enforceable.

Enforcement shall be governed by the rules of civil procedure in force in the State in the territory of which it is carried out. The order for its enforcement shall be appended to the decision, without other formality than verification of the authenticity of the decision, by the national authority which the Government of each Member State shall designate for this purpose and shall make known to the Commission and to the Court of Justice.

When these formalities have been completed on application by the party concerned, the latter may proceed to enforcement in accordance with the national law, by bringing the matter directly before the competent authority.

Enforcement may be suspended only by a decision of the Court of Justice. However, the courts of the country concerned shall have jurisdiction over complaints that enforcement is being carried out in an irregular manner.

CHAPTER 3

The Economic and Social Committee

ARTICLE 193

An Economic and Social Committee is hereby established. It shall have advisory status.

The Committee shall consist of representatives of the various categories of economic and social activity, in particular, representatives of producers, farmers, carriers, workers, dealers, craftsmen, professional occupations and representatives of the general public.

ARTICLE 194

The number of members of the Committee shall be as follows:

Belgium	12
Denmark	9
Germany	24
France	24
Ireland	9
Italy	24
Luxembourg	6
Netherlands	12
United Kingdom	24*

The members of the Committee shall be appointed by the Council, acting unanimously, for four years. Their appointments shall be renewable.

The members of the Committee shall be appointed in their personal capacity and may not be bound by any mandatory instructions.

ARTICLE 195

1. For the appointment of the members of the Committee, each Member State shall provide the Council with a list containing twice as many candidates as there are seats allotted to its nationals.

The composition of the Committee shall take account of the need to en-

---

* First paragraph as amended by Art. 21 of the Act of Accession, modified by Art. 11 of the Adaptation Decision.

sure adequate representation of the various categories of economic and social activity.

2. The Council shall consult the Commission. It may obtain the opinion of European bodies which are representative of the various economic and social sectors to which the activities of the Community are of concern.

ARTICLE 196

The Committee shall elect its chairman and officers from among its members for a term of two years.

It shall adopt its rules of procedure and shall submit them to the Council for its approval, which must be unanimous.

The Committee shall be convened by its chairman at the request of the Council or of the Commission.

ARTICLE 197

The Committee shall include specialised sections for the principal fields covered by this Treaty.

In particular, it shall contain an agricultural section and a transport section, which are the subject of special provisions in the Titles relating to agriculture and transport.

These specialised sections shall operate within the general terms of reference of the Committee. They may not be consulted independently of the Committee.

Sub-committees may also be established within the Committee to prepare, on specific questions or in specific fields, draft opinions to be submitted to the Committee for its consideration.

The rules of procedure shall lay down the methods of composition and the terms of reference of the specialised sections and of the subcommittees.

ARTICLE 198

The Committee must be consulted by the Council or by the Commission where this Treaty so provides. The Committee may be consulted by these institutions in all cases in which they consider it appropriate.

The Council or the Commission shall, if it considers it necessary, set the Committee, for the submission of its opinion, a time limit which may not be less than ten days from the date which the chairman receives notification to this effect. Upon expiry of the time limit, the absence of an opinion shall not prevent further action.

The opinion of the Committee and that of the specialised section, together with a record of the proceedings, shall be forwarded to the Council and to the Commission.

TITLE II

Financial Provisions

ARTICLE 199

All items of revenue and expenditure of the Community, including those relating to the European Social Fund, shall be included in estimates to be drawn up for each financial year and shall be shown in the budget.

The revenue and expenditure shown in the budget shall be in balance.

ARTICLE 200

1. The budget revenue shall include, irrespective of any other revenue, financial contributions of Member States on the following scale:

Belgium	7.9
Germany	28
France	28
Italy	28
Luxembourg	0.2
Netherlands	7.9

2. The financial contributions of Member States to cover the expenditure of the European Social Fund, however shall be determined on the following scale:

Belgium	8.8
Germany	32
France	32
Italy	20
Luxembourg	0.2
Netherlands	7

3. The scales may be modified by the Council, acting unanimously.

ARTICLE 201

The Commission shall examine the conditions under which the financial contributions of Member States provided for in Article 200 could be replaced by the Community's own resources, in particular by revenue accruing from the common customs tariff when it has been finally introduced.

To this end, the Commission shall submit proposals to the Council.

After consulting the Assembly on these proposals the Council may, acting unanimously, lay down the appropriate provisions, which it shall recommend to the Member States for adoption in accordance with their respective constitutional requirements.

ARTICLE 202

The expenditure shown in the budget shall be authorised for one financial year, unless the regulations made pursuant to Article 209 provide otherwise.

In accordance with conditions to be laid down pursuant to Article 209, any appropriations, other than those relating to staff expenditure, that are unexpended at the end of the financial year may be carried forward to the next financial year only.

Appropriations shall be classified under different chapters grouping items of expenditure according to their nature or purpose and subdivided, as far as may be necessary, in accordance with the regulations made pursuant to Article 209.

The expenditure of the Assembly, the Council, the Commission and the Court of Justice shall be set out in separate parts of the budget, without prejudice to special arrangements for certain common items of expenditure.

ARTICLE 203*

1. The financial year shall run from 1 January to 31 December.

2. Each institution of the Community shall, before 1 July, draw up estimates of its expenditure. The Commission shall consolidate these estimates in a preliminary draft budget. It shall attach thereto an opinion which may contain different estimates.

---

*Text as amended by Art. 4 of the Treaty amending Certain Budgetary Provisions.

The preliminary draft budget shall contain an estimate of revenue and an estimate of expenditure.

3. The Commission shall place the preliminary draft budget before the Council not later than 1 September of the year preceding that in which the budget is to be implemented.

The Council shall consult the Commission and, where appropriate, the other institutions concerned whenever it intends to depart from the preliminary draft budget.

The Council shall, acting by a qualified majority, establish the draft budget and forward it to the Assembly.

4. The draft budget shall be placed before the Assembly not later than 5 October of the year preceding that in which the budget is to be implemented.

The Assembly shall have the right to amend the draft budget, acting by a majority of its members, and to propose to the Council, acting by an absolute majority of the votes cast, modifications to the draft budget relating to expenditure necessarily resulting from this Treaty or from acts adopted in accordance therewith.

If, within forty-five days of the draft budget being placed before it, the Assembly has given its approval, the budget shall stand as finally adopted. If within this period the Assembly has not amended the draft budget nor proposed any modifications thereto, the budget shall be deemed to be finally adopted.

If within this period the Assembly has adopted amendments or proposed modifications, the draft budget together with the amendments or proposed modifications shall be forwarded to the Council.

5. After discussing the draft budget with the Commission, and where appropriate, with the other institutions concerned, the Council may, acting by a qualified majority, modify any of the amendments adopted by the Assembly and shall pronounce, also by a qualified majority, on the modifications proposed by the latter. The draft budget shall be modified on the basis of the proposed modifications accepted by the Council.

If, within fifteen days of the draft budget being placed before it, the Council has not modified any of the amendments adopted by the Assembly and has accepted the modifications proposed by the latter, the budget shall be deemed to be finally adopted. The Council shall inform the Assembly that it has not modified any of the amendments and has accepted the proposed modifications.

If within this period the Council has modified one or more of the amendments adopted by the Assembly or has not accepted the modifications proposed by the latter, the draft budget shall again be forwarded to the Assembly. The Council shall inform the Assembly of the results of its deliberations.

6. Within fifteen days of the draft budget being placed before it, the Assembly, which shall have been notified of the action taken on its proposed modifications, shall act, by a majority of its members and three fifths of the votes cast, on the modifications to its amendments made by the Council, and shall adopt the budget accordingly. If within this period the Assembly has not acted, the budget shall be deemed to be finally adopted.

7. When the procedure provided for in this Article has been completed, the President of the Assembly shall declare that the budget has been finally adopted.

8. A maximum rate of increase in relation to the expenditure of the same type to be incurred during the current year shall be fixed annually for the total expenditure other than that necessarily resulting from this Treaty or from acts adopted in accordance therewith.

The Commission shall, after consulting the Conjunctural Policy Committee and the Budgetary Policy Committee, declare what this maximum rate is as it results from:

— the trend, in terms of volume, of the gross national product within the Community;

— the average variation in the budgets of the Member States; and

— the trend of the cost of living during the preceding financial year.

The maximum rate shall be communicated, before 1 May, to all the institutions of the Community. The latter shall be required to conform to this during the budgetary procedure, subject to the provisions of the fourth and fifth subparagraph of this paragraph.

If, in respect of expenditure other than that necessarily resulting from this Treaty or from acts adopted in accordance therewith, the actual rate of increase in the draft budget established by the Council is over half the maximum rate, the Assembly may, exercising its right of amendment, further increase the total amount of that expenditure to a limit not exceeding half the maximum rate.

Where, in exceptional cases, the Assembly, the Council or the Commission

considers that the activities of the Communities require that the rate determined according to the procedure laid down in this paragraph should be
exceeded, another rate may be fixed by agreement between the Council, acting by a qualified majority, and the Assembly, acting by a majority of its
members and three fifths of the votes cast.

9. Each institution shall exercise the powers conferred upon it by this
Article, with due regard for the provisions of this Treaty and for acts adopted
in accordance therewith, in particular those relating to the Communities' own
resources and to the balance between revenue and expenditure.

ARTICLE 203a*

By way of derogation from the provisions of Article 203, the following
provisions shall apply to budgets for financial years preceding the financial
year 1975:

1. The financial year shall run from 1 January to 31 December.

2. Each institution of the Community shall, before 1 July, draw up estimates of its expenditure. The Commission shall consolidate these estimates
in a preliminary draft budget. It shall attach thereto an opinion which may
contain different estimates.

The preliminary draft budget shall contain an estimate of revenue and an
estimate of expenditure.

3. The Commission shall place the preliminary draft budget before the
Council not later than 1 September of the year preceding that in which the
budget is to be implemented.

The Council shall consult the Commission and, where appropriate, the
other institutions concerned whenever it intends to depart from the preliminary
draft budget.

The Council shall, acting by a qualified majority, establish the draft budget
and forward it to the Assembly.

4. The draft budget shall be placed before the Assembly not later than 5
October of the year preceding that in which the budget is to be implemented.

---

* Article added by Art. 5 of the Treaty amending Certain Budgetary Provisions.

The Assembly shall have the right to propose to the Council modifications to the draft budget.

If, within forty-five days of the draft budget being placed before it, the Assembly has given its approval or has not proposed any modifications to the draft budget, the budget shall be deemed to be finally adopted.

If within this period the Assembly has proposed modifications, the draft budget together with the proposed modifications shall be forwarded to the Council.

5. The Council shall, after discussing the draft budget with the Commission and, where appropriate, with the other institutions concerned, adopt the budget, within thirty days of the draft budget placed before it, under the following conditions.

Where a modification proposed by the Assembly does not have the effect of increasing the total amount of the expenditure of an institution, owing in particular to the fact that the increase in expenditure which it would involve would be expressly compensated by one or more proposed modifications correspondingly reducing expenditure, the Council may, acting by a qualified majority, reject the proposed modification. In the absence of a decision to reject it, the proposed modification shall stand as accepted.

Where a modification proposed by the Assembly has the effect of increasing the total amount of the expenditure of an institution, the Council must act by a qualified majority in accepting the proposed modification.

Where, in pursuance of the second or third subparagraph of this paragraph, the Council has rejected or has not accepted a proposed modification, it may, acting by a qualified majority, either retain the amount shown in the draft budget or fix another amount.

6. When the procedure provided for in this Article has been completed, the President of the Council shall declare that the budget has been finally adopted.

7. Each institution shall exercise the powers conferred upon it by this Article, with due regard for the provisions of this Treaty and for acts adopted in accordance therewith, in particular those relating to the Communities' own resources and to the balance between revenue and expenditure.

ARTICLE 204

If, at the beginning of a financial year, the budget has not yet been voted, a sum equivalent to not more than one twelfth of the budget appropriations for the preceding financial year may be spent each month in respect of any chapter or other subdivision of the budget in accordance with the provisions of the regulations made pursuant to Article 209; this arrangement shall not, however, have the effect of placing at the disposal of the Commission appropriations in excess of one twelfth of those provided for in the draft budget in course of preparation.

The Council may, acting by a qualified majority, provided that the other conditions laid down in the first paragraph are observed, authorise expenditure in excess of one twelfth.

Member States shall pay every month, on a provisional basis and in accordance with the scales laid down for the preceding financial year, the amounts necessary to ensure application of this Article.

ARTICLE 205

The Commission shall implement the budget, in accordance with the provisions of the regulations made pursuant to Article 209, on its own responsibility and within the limits of the appropriations.

The regulations shall lay down detailed rules for each institution concerning its part in effecting its own expenditure.

Within the budget, the Commission may, subject to the limits and conditions laid down in the regulations made pursuant to Article 209, transfer appropriations from one chapter to another or from one sub-division to another.

ARTICLE 206

The accounts of all revenue and expenditure shown in the budget shall be examined by an Audit Board consisting of auditors whose independence is beyond doubt, one of whom shall be chairman. The Council shall, acting unanimously, determine the number of the auditors. The auditors and the chairman of the Audit Board shall be appointed by the Council, acting unanimously, for a period of five years. Their remuneration shall be determined by the Council, acting by a qualified majority.

The purpose of the audit, which shall be based on records and, if necessary, performed on the spot, shall be to establish that all revenue has been received and all expenditure incurred in a lawful and regular manner and that the financial management has been sound. After the close of each financial year, the Audit Board shall draw up a report, which shall be adopted by a majority of its members.

The Commission shall submit annually to the Council and to the Assembly the accounts of the preceding financial year relating to the implementation of the budget, together with the report of the Audit Board. The Commission shall also forward to them a financial statement of the assets and liabilities of the Community.

The Council and the Assembly shall give a discharge to the Commission in respect of the implementation of the budget. To this end, the report of the Audit Board shall be examined in turn by the Council, which shall act by a qualified majority, and by the Assembly. The Commission shall stand discharged only after the Council and the Assembly have acted.*

ARTICLE 207

The budget shall be drawn up in the unit of account determined in accordance with the provisions of the regulations made pursuant to Article 209.

The financial contributions provided for in Article 200(1) shall be placed at the disposal of the Community by the Member States in their national currencies.

The available balances of these contributions shall be deposited with the Treasuries of Member States or with bodies designated by them. While on deposit, such funds shall retain the value corresponding to the parity, at the date of deposit, in relation to the unit of account referred to in the first paragraph.

The balances may be invested on terms to be agreed between the Commission and the Member State concerned.

The regulations made pursuant to Article 209 shall lay down the technical conditions under which financial operations relating to the European Social Fund shall be carried out.

ARTICLE 208

The Commission may, provided it notifies the competent authorities of the

---

* Fourth paragraph as amended by Art. 6 of the Treaty amending Certain Budgetary Provisions.

Member States concerned, transfer into the currency of one of the Member States its holdings in the currency of another Member State, to the extent necessary to enable them to be used for purposes which come within the scope of this Treaty. The Commission shall as far as possible avoid making such transfers if it possesses cash or liquid assets in the currencies which it needs.

The Commission shall deal with each Member State through the authority designated by the State concerned. In carrying out financial operations the Commission shall employ the services of the bank of issue of the Member State concerned or of any other financial institution approved by that State.

ARTICLE 209

The Council shall, acting unanimously on a proposal from the Commission:

(a) make financial regulations specifying in particular the procedure to be adopted for establishing and implementing the budget and for presenting and auditing accounts;

(b) determine the methods and procedure whereby the contributions of Member States shall be made available to the Commission;

(c) lay down rules concerning the responsibility of authorising officers and accounting officers and concerning appropriate arrangements for inspection.

PART SIX

General and Final Provisions

ARTICLE 210

The Community shall have legal personality.

ARTICLE 211

In each of the Member States, the Community shall enjoy the most extensive legal capacity accorded to legal persons under their laws; it may, in particular, acquire or dispose of movable and immovable property and may be a party to legal proceedings. To this end, the Community shall be represented by the Commission.

ARTICLE 212*

ARTICLE 213

The Commission may, within the limits and under the conditions laid down by the Council in accordance with the provisions of this Treaty, collect any information and carry out any checks required for the performance of the tasks entrusted to it.

ARTICLE 214

The members of the institutions of the Community, the members of committees, and the officials and other servants of the Community shall be required, even after their duties have ceased, not to disclose information of the kind covered by the obligation of professional secrecy, in particular information about undertakings, their business relations or their cost components.

ARTICLE 215

The contractual liability of the Community shall be governed by the law applicable to the contract in question.

In the case of non-contractual liability, the Community shall, in accordance with the general principles common to the laws of the Member States, make good any damage caused by its institutions or by its servants in the performance of their duties.

The personal liability of its servants towards the Community shall be governed by the provisions laid down in their Staff Regulations or in the Conditions of Employment applicable to them.

ARTICLE 216

The seat of the institutions of the Community shall be determined by common accord of the Governments of the Member States.

ARTICLE 217

The rules governing the languages of the institutions of the Community

---

* Repealed by Art. 24(2) of the Merger Treaty; see Merger Treaty, Art. 24(1), second subparagraph.

shall, without prejudice to the provisions contained in the rules of procedure of the Court of Justice, be determined by the Council, acting unanimously.

ARTICLE 218*

ARTICLE 219

Member States undertake not to submit a dispute concerning the interpretation or application of this Treaty to any method of settlement other than those provided for therein.

ARTICLE 220

Member States shall, so far as is necessary, enter into negotiations with each other with a view to securing for the benefit of their nationals:

— the protection of persons and the enjoyment and protection of rights under the same conditions as those accorded by each State to its own nationals;

— the abolition of double taxation within the Community;

— the mutual recognition of companies or firms within the meaning of the second paragraph of Article 58, the retention of legal personality in the event of transfer of their seat from one country to another, and the possibility of mergers between companies or firms governed by the laws of different countries;

— the simplification of formalities governing the reciprocal recognition and enforcement of judgments of courts or tribunals and of arbitration awards.

ARTICLE 221

Within three years of the entry into force of this Treaty, Member States shall accord nationals of the other Member States the same treatment as their own nationals as regards participation in the capital of companies or firms within the meaning of Article 58, without prejudice to the application of the other provisions of this Treaty.

---

* Repealed by the second paragraph of Art. 28 of the Merger Treaty; see Merger Treaty, first paragraph of Art. 28.

ARTICLE 222

This Treaty shall in no way prejudice the rules in Member States governing the system of property ownership.

ARTICLE 223

1. The provisions of this Treaty shall not preclude the application of the following rules:

(a) No Member State shall be obliged to supply information the disclosure of which it considers contrary to the essential interests of its security;

(b) Any Member State may take such measures as it considers necessary for the protection of the essential interests of its security which are connected with the production of or trade in arms, munitions and war material; such measures shall not adversely affect the conditions of competition in the common market regarding products which are not intended for specifically military purposes.

2. During the first year after the entry into force of this Treaty, the Council shall, acting unanimously, draw up a list of products to which the provisions of paragraph 1(b) shall apply.

3. The Council may, acting unanimously on a proposal from the Commission, make changes in this list.

ARTICLE 224

Member States shall consult each other with a view to taking together the steps needed to prevent the functioning of the common market being affected by measures which a Member State may be called upon to take in the event of serious internal disturbances affecting the maintenance of law and order, in the event of war or serious international tension constituting a threat of war, or in order to carry out obligations it has accepted for the purpose of maintaining peace and international security.

ARTICLE 225

If measures taken in the circumstances referred to in Articles 223 and 224 have the effect of distorting the conditions of competition in the common market, the Commission shall, together with the State concerned, examine how these measures can be adjusted to the rules laid down in this Treaty.

By way of derogation from the procedure laid down in Articles 169 and 170, the Commission or any Member State may bring the matter directly before the Court of Justice if it considers that another Member State is making improper use of the powers provided for in Articles 223 and 224. The Court of Justice shall give its ruling *in camera*.

ARTICLE 226

1. If, during the transitional period, difficulties arise which are serious and liable to persist in any sector of the economy or which could bring about serious deterioration in the economic situation of a given area, a Member State may apply for authorisation to take protective measures in order to rectify the situation and adjust the sector concerned to the economy of the common market.

2. On application by the State concerned, the Commission shall, by emergency procedure, determine without delay the protective measures which it considers necessary, specifying the circumstances and the manner in which they are to be put into effect.

3. The measures authorised under paragraph 2 may involve derogations from the rules of this Treaty, to such an extent and for such periods as are strictly necessary in order to attain the objectives referred to in paragraph 1. Priority shall be given to such measures as will least disturb the functioning of the common market.

ARTICLE 227

1. This Treaty shall apply to the Kingdom of Belgium, the Kingdom of Denmark, the Federal Republic of Germany, the French Republic, Ireland, the Italian Republic, the Grand Duchy of Luxembourg, the Kingdom of the Netherlands and the United Kingdom of Great Britain and Northern Ireland.*

2. With regard to Algeria and the French overseas departments, the general and particular provisions of this Treaty relating to:

— the free movement of goods;

— agriculture, save for Article 40(4);

— the liberalisation of services;

---

* Paragraph (1) as amended by Art. 26(1) of the Act of Accession, modified by Art. 15(1) of the Adaptation Decision.

— the rules on competition;

— the protective measures provided for in Articles 108, 109 and 226;

— the institutions,

shall apply as soon as this Treaty enters into force.

The conditions under which the other provisions of this Treaty are to apply shall be determined, within two years of the entry into force of this Treaty, by decisions of the Council, acting unanimously on a proposal from the Commission.

The institutions of the Community will, within the framework of the procedures provided for in this Treaty, in particular Article 226, take care that the economic and social development of these areas is made possible.

3. The special arrangements for association set out in Part Four of this Treaty shall apply to the overseas countries and territories listed in Annex IV to this Treaty.

This Treaty shall not apply to those overseas countries and territories having special relations with the United Kingdom of Great Britain and Northern Ireland which are not included in the aforementioned list.*

4. The provisions of this Treaty shall apply to the European territories for whose external relations a Member State is responsible.

5. **Notwithstanding the preceding paragraphs:

(a) This Treaty shall not apply to the Faroe Islands. The Government of the Kingdom of Denmark may, however, give notice, by a declaration deposited by 31 December 1975 at the latest with the Government of the Italian Republic, which shall transmit a certified copy thereof to each of the Governments of the other Member States, that this Treaty shall apply to those Islands. In that event, this Treaty shall apply to those Islands from the first day of the second month following the deposit of the declaration.

(b) This Treaty shall not apply to the Sovereign Base Areas of the United Kingdom of Great Britain and Northern Ireland in Cyprus.

---

* Second subparagraph added by Art. 26(2) of the Act of Accession.

** Paragraph 5 added by Art. 26(3) of the Act of Accession, modified by Art. 15(2) of the Adaptation Decision.

(c) This Treaty shall apply to the Channel Islands and the Isle of Man only to the extent necessary to ensure the implementation of the arrangements for those islands set out in the Treaty concerning the accession of new Member States to the European Economic Community and to the European Atomic Energy Community signed on 22 January 1972.

ARTICLE 228

1. Where this Treaty provides for the conclusion of agreements between the Community and one or more States or an international organisation, such agreements shall be negotiated by the Commission. Subject to the powers vested in the Commission in this field, such agreements shall be concluded by the Council, after consulting the Assembly where required by this Treaty.

The Council, the Commission or a Member State may obtain beforehand the opinion of the Court of Justice as to whether an agreement envisaged is compatible with the provisions of this Treaty. Where the opinion of the Court of Justice is adverse, the agreement may enter into force only in accordance with the procedure laid down in Article 236.

2. Agreements concluded under these conditions shall be binding on the institutions of the Community and on Member States.

ARTICLE 229

It shall be for the Commission to ensure the maintenance of all appropriate relations with the organs of the United Nations, of its specialised agencies and of the General Agreement on Tariffs and Trade.

The Commission shall also maintain such relations as are appropriate with all international organisations.

ARTICLE 230

The Community shall establish all appropriate forms of cooperation with the Council of Europe.

ARTICLE 231

The Community shall establish close cooperation with the Organisation for European Economic Cooperation, the details to be determined by common accord.

ARTICLE 232

1. The provisions of this Treaty shall not affect the provisions of the Treaty establishing the European Coal and Steel Community, in particular as regards the rights and obligations of Member States, the powers of the institutions of that Community and the rules laid down by that Treaty for the functioning of the common market in coal and steel.

2. The provisions of this Treaty shall not derogate from those of the Treaty establishing the European Atomic Energy Community.

ARTICLE 233

The provisions of this Treaty shall not preclude the existence or completion of regional unions between Belgium and Luxembourg, or between Belgium, Luxembourg and the Netherlands, to the extent that the objectives of these regional unions are not attained by application of this Treaty.

ARTICLE 234

The rights and obligations arising from agreements concluded before the entry into force of this Treaty between one or more Member States on the one hand, and one or more third countries on the other, shall not be affected by the provisions of this Treaty.

To the extent that such agreements are not compatible with this Treaty, the Member State or States concerned shall take all appropriate steps to eliminate the incompatibilities established. Member States shall, where necessary, assist each other to this end and shall, where appropriate, adopt a common attitude.

In applying the agreements referred to in the first paragraph, Member States shall take into account the fact that the advantages accorded under this Treaty by each Member State form an integral part of the establishment of the Community and are thereby inseparably linked with the creation of common institutions, the conferring of powers upon them and the granting of the same advantages by all the other Member States.

ARTICLE 235

If action by the Community should prove necessary to attain, in the course of the operation of the common market, one of the objectives of the Community and this Treaty has not provided the necessary powers, the Council shall, acting unanimously on a proposal from the Commission and after consulting the Assembly, take the appropriate measures.

ARTICLE 236

The Government of any Member State or the Commission may submit to the Council proposals for the amendment of this Treaty.

If the Council, after consulting the Assembly and, where appropriate, the Commission, delivers an opinion in favour of calling a conference of representatives of the Governments of the Member States, the conference shall be convened by the President of the Council for the purpose of determining by common accord the amendments to be made to this Treaty.

The amendments shall enter into force after being ratified by all the Member States in accordance with their respective constitutional requirements.

ARTICLE 237

Any European State may apply to become a member of the Community. It shall address its application to the Council, which shall act unanimously after obtaining the opinion of the Commission.

The conditions of admission and the adjustments to this Treaty necessitated thereby shall be the subject of an agreement between the Member States and the applicant State. This agreement shall be submitted for ratification by all the Contracting States in accordance with their respective constitutional requirements.

ARTICLE 238

The Community may conclude with a third State, a union of States or an international organisation agreements establishing an association involving reciprocal rights and obligations, common action and special procedures.

These agreements shall be concluded by the Council, acting unanimously after consulting the Assembly.

Where such agreements call for amendments to this Treaty, these amendments shall first be adopted in accordance with the procedure laid down in Article 236.

ARTICLE 239

The Protocols annexed to this Treaty by common accord of the Member States shall form an integral part thereof.

ARTICLE 240

This Treaty is concluded for an unlimited period.

Setting Up of the Institutions

ARTICLE 241

The Council shall meet within one month of the entry into force of this Treaty.

ARTICLE 242

The Council shall, within three months of its first meeting, take all appropriate measures to constitute the Economic and Social Committee.

ARTICLE 243

The Assembly shall meet within two months of the first meeting of the Council, having been convened by the President of the Council, in order to elect its officers and draw up its rules of procedure. Pending the election of its officers, the oldest member shall take the chair.

ARTICLE 244

The Court of Justice shall take up its duties as soon as its members have been appointed. Its first President shall be appointed for three years in the same manner as its members.

The Court of Justice shall adopt its rules of procedure within three months of taking up its duties.

No matter may be brought before the Court of Justice until its rules of procedure have been published. The time within which an action must be brought shall run only from the date of this publication.

Upon his appointment, the President of the Court of Justice shall exercise the powers conferred upon him by this Treaty.

ARTICLE 245

The Commission shall take up its duties and assume the responsibilities conferred upon it by this Treaty as soon as its members have been appointed.

Upon taking up its duties, the Commission shall undertake the studies and arrange the contacts needed for making an overall survey of the economic situation of the Community.

ARTICLE 246

1. The first financial year shall run from the date on which this Treaty enters into force until 31 December following. Should this Treaty, however, enter into force during the second half of the year, the first financial year shall run until 31 December of the following year.

2. Until the budget for the first financial year has been established, Member States shall make the Community interest-free advances which shall be deducted from their financial contributions to the implementation of the budget.

3. Until the Staff Regulations of officials and the Conditions of Employment of other servants of the Community provided for in Article 212 have been laid down, each institution shall recruit the Staff it needs and to this end conclude contracts of limited duration.

Each institution shall examine together with the Council any question concerning the number, remuneration and distribution of posts.

Final Provisions

ARTICLE 247

This Treaty shall be ratified by the High Contracting Parties in accordance with their respective constitutional requirements. The instruments of ratification shall be deposited with the Government of the Italian Republic.

This Treaty shall enter into force on the first day of the month following the deposit of the instrument of ratification by the last signatory State to take this step. If, however, such deposit is made less than fifteen days before the beginning of the following month, this Treaty shall not enter into force until the first day of the second month after the date of such deposit.

ARTICLE 248

This Treaty, drawn up in a single original in the Dutch. French German and Italian languages, all four texts being equally authentic, shall be deposited in the archives of the Government of the Italian Republic, which shall transmit a certified copy to each of the Governments of the other signatory States.

IN WITNESS WHEREOF, the undersigned Plenipotentiaries have signed this Treaty.

Done at Rome this twenty-fifth day of March in the year one thousand nine hundred and fifty-seven.

III. JAPANESE STATUTORY MATERIALS

1. Law Concerning Foreign Investment (1950)

(Excerpts)

CHAPTER I. GENERAL PROVISIONS

(Purpose)

Article 1. The purpose of this Law is to create a sound basis for foreign investments in Japan, by limiting the induction of foreign capital to that which will contribute to the self-support and sound development of the Japanese economy as well as to the improvement of the international balance of payments, by securing remittances arising from foreign investments, and by providing for adequate protection of such investments.

(Basic Principle)

Article 2. Foreign investments in Japan shall be permitted as freely as possible, and the system of validation pursuant to the provisions of this Law shall be relaxed and eliminated gradually as the necessity for such system diminishes.

Article 7. The Minister of Finance and the Minister of International Trade and Industry shall, in accordance with the Ministry of Finance ordinance and the Ministry of International Trade and Industry ordinance, make public a list of the kinds of desired technological assistance from foreign investors.

2 The Minister of Finance and the Minister of International Trade and Industry may revise from time to time the list made public in accordance with the provisions of the preceding paragraph.

(Standards of Validation and Designation)

Article 8. The competent Minister shall apply the following standards in validating contracts prescribed in this Law, and the priority shall be given to those which will most effectively contribute to an improvement of the international balance of payments:

(1) Directly or indirectly contributing to the development of important industries or public enterprises;

(2) Directly or indirectly contributing to improvement of the international balance of payments;

(3) Necessary for continuation, alteration and renewal of the existing technological assistance contracts in the important industries or public enterprises.

2 The competent Minister shall not validate those contracts prescribed in this Law which fall under any one of the following items:

(1) Contracts whose provisions are not fair, or are in violation of laws and regulations;

(2) Contracts whose conclusions, alterations or renewals are deemed to have been made in a manner not free of fraud, duress or undue influence;

(3) Contracts which are deemed to have an adverse effect upon recovery of the Japanese economy;

. . . . .

2. Foreign Exchange and Foreign Trade Control Law of 1949 (as amended through 1982) (excerpts)

CHAPTER I   GENERAL PROVISIONS

(Objective)

Article 1 The objective of this Law shall be, on the basis of the freedom of foreign exchange, foreign trade, and other external transactions, with necessary but minimum control or adjustment, to enable proper expansion of our external transactions, and thereby to facilitate the equilibrium of our balance of international payments and the stability of our currency, as well as to contribute towards the sound development of our national economy.

(Scope of Application)

Article 5 This Law shall also be applicable to any act performed outside Japan by any representative, agent, employee, or other operator of any juridical person having its main office in Japan in regard to the property or business of such a juridical person. It shall similarly be applicable to any act performed outside Japan by any natural person having his place of domicile in Japan, or his agent, employee, or other operator in regard to the property or business of such a natural person.

CHAPTER V   DIRECT DOMESTIC INVESTMENTS, ETC.
(Notice, etc., of direct domestic investments, etc.)

Article 26 A "foreign investor" shall mean any one of those mentioned below, which performs any one of the direct domestic investments, etc., mentioned in each Item of the next Paragraph:—

(1) A natural person who is a non-resident;

(2) A juridical person or other organization established under foreign legislation, or a juridical person or other organization having its main office in a foreign country;

(3) A company of which the number of stock or the amount of capital subscription directly owned by one or more of those mentioned in Item (1) and/or the preceding Item, and/or the number of stock or the amount of capital subscription designated by a Cabinet Order as being indirectly owned by the above-mentioned through another company or other companies, equal(s) or exceed(s) in the aggregate one-half (½) of that company's total stock issue or total subscribed capital; or

(4) Other than those mentioned in the preceding two Items, a juridical person

or other organization of which a majority number of board members (which mean directors and other similar posts, which shall apply in this Item) or board members having representing power is occupied by persons mentioned in Item (1).

2. A "direct domestic investment, etc." shall mean an act which falls under any Item below:-

(1) Acquisition of any company's stock or share (except for the acquisition by transfer from any one mentioned in each Item of the preceding Paragraph, and the acquisition of the stock of companies which is listed on the stock exchange defined by Article 2, Paragraph 11 of the Securities and Exchange Law, or the stock of companies which is designated by a Cabinet Order as being similar to the afore-mentioned listed one—collectively referred to as "listed companies, etc." in the next Item and Item (3) ——);

(2) Transfer of stock or share(s) of any company other than the listed companies, etc., which was/were acquired by the transferer prior to his acquisition of non-resident status and has/have been continuously held by him up till the time of the transfer (limited to only such transfer as made by a non-resident natural person to any one mentioned in each Item of the preceding Paragraph);

(3) Acquisition of stock of any one of the listed companies; etc. (limited to only such instances whereunder either the ratio of the number of stock of a given company acquired by a given transaction against that company's total stock issue, or the aggregate ratio of the total number of stock of a given company which becomes to be possessed by an acquirer after a given act of acquisition plus the number of stock of the same company possessed by the juridical person or other organization designated by a Cabinet Order as having a special relationship with the acquirer through stock or share holding or other similar ways against that company's total stock issue equals or exceeds a ratio determined by a Cabinet Order which shall be not less than ten-hundredth (10/100));

(4) Consent given to a substantial alteration of the objective of a company's business (limited to only such consent as given by one or more stockholder(s) or shareholder(s) who own(s) in total one-third (⅓) or more of that company's total stock issue or total subscribed capital);

(5) Establishment of a branch, etc., in Japan, or substantial alteration of the type or the business objective of a branch, etc., existing in Japan (limited to only such establishment and alteration as designated by a Cabinet Order, which is to be made by any one of those mentioned in Item (1) or (2) of the preceding Paragraph);

(6) Money lending to a juridical person having its main office in Japan in excess of an amount determined by a Cabinet Order (except for those lendings made as a business by a bank or other financial institution designated by a Cabinet Order, and lendings in our currency made by any one of those mentioned in

Item (3) or (4) of the preceding Paragraph), of which the term exceeds one year; or

(7) Any other act designated by a Cabinet Order as being similar to any one of those mentioned in each of the preceding Items.

3. Any foreign investor who wants to make a direct domestic investment, etc., mentioned in any Item of the preceding Paragraph (except for those cases determined by a Cabinet Order, in consideration of such instances as inheritance, legacy, amalgamation of juridical persons, etc.) shall give a prior notice, as a Cabinet Order provides for, to the Minister of Finance and the Minister(s) in charge of the industry involved of those matters as designated by the Cabinet Order such as the objective of the business, amount, time of execution, and others concerning that direct domestic investment, etc.

4. Any foreign investor who has given a notice under the provisions of the the the preceding Paragraph concerning the direct domestic investment, etc., mentioned in Paragraph 2 (hereinafter referred to as "direct domestic investment, etc.,") shall not execute that direct domestic investment, etc., until a period of thirty (30) days has elapsed, counting from the day of receipt of the notice by the Minister of Finance and the Minister(s) in charge of the industry involved. However, the Ministers may shorten this period when they deem it not specifically harmful, judging from the objective of the business, etc., of the direct domestic investment, etc., under notice.

5. Any person other than a foreign investor (including a juridical person or other organization, which shall also apply to Paragraph 1 of the next Article) who performs any transaction or act tantamount to a direct domestic investment, etc., on behalf of a foreign investor but not in the latter's name shall be deemed as a foreign investor, and the provisions of the preceding two Paragraphs shall apply to such a person.

(Screening of the conditions of direct domestic investments, etc., and recommendation of alteration thereof, etc.)

Article 27 When a notice is given to the Minister of Finance and the Minister(s) in charge of the industry involved under the provisions of Paragraph 3 of the preceding Article (including a notice given by a person other than a foreign investor who is deemed as a foreign investor under the provisions of Paragraph 5 of the same Article, which shall also apply to the next Paragraph and Paragraph 8), and the Ministers deem it necessary to make an inquiry in order to determine whether the direct domestic investment, etc., under notice, if executed, would cause apprehensions as to the occurrence of any of the consequences mentioned in Item (1) or (2), or whether the direct domestic investment, etc., under notice falls under Item (3) or (4), the Ministers may extend the period during which the execution of that direct domestic investment, etc., is prohibited up to four (4) months, counting from the day of their receipt of the notice:—

(1) It might imperil the national security, disturb the maintenance of public order, or hamper the protection of the safety of the general public;

(2) It might adversely and seriously affect activities of our business enterprises engaging in a line of business similar or related to the one to which the direct domestic investment, etc., is to be made, or the smooth performance of our national economy;

(3) Because it is made by a foreign investor with whose country no treaties or other international agreements are concluded by our country in regard to the direct domestic investments, etc., its particulars are required to be altered, or its execution is required to be suspended, so as to make conditions substantially equal to those allowed to our national's direct investment activities (which mean those tantamount to direct domestic investment, etc., mentioned in each Item of Paragraph 2 of the preceding Article) in that country; or

(4) When seen from its purpose of the use of funds and others, it falls under, in whole or in part, the capital transactions upon which an obligation to obtain a license is imposed under the provisions of Article 21, Paragraph 2, and therefore its particulars are required to be altered, or its execution is required to be suspended.

2. When a notice is given to the Minister of Finance and the Minister(s) in charge of the industry involved under the provisions of Paragraph 3 of the preceding Article, and the Ministers deem that, if the direct domestic investment, etc., under notice were executed, it would cause apprehensions as to the occurrence of any one of the consequences mentioned in Item (1) or (2) of the preceding Paragraph, or that the direct domestic investment, etc., under notice falls under Item (3) or (4) of the same Paragraph, they may, upon hearing the opinion of the Committee on Foreign Exchange and Other Transactions mentioned in Article 55-2, recommend the party which gave that notice, as a Cabinet Order provides for, either to alter the particulars of that direct domestic investment, etc., or to suspend the execution thereof, provided that such a recommendation is given within the period mentioned in the same Paragraph, or within the extended period provided in the next Paragraph, counting from the day of their receipt of the notice.

3. When the Committee on Foreign Exchange and Other Transactions mentioned in Article 55-2 is asked for its opinion for the inquiry provided in Paragraph 1, and tenders its intimation that to form its opinion within the period of four (4) months as provided in the same Paragraph is difficult due to the nature of the subject matter, the period provided in the same Paragraph during which the execution of the direct domestic investment, etc. is prohibited shall become five (5) months, irrespective of the provisions of the same Paragraph.

4. The party who is given recommendation under the provisions of Paragraph 2 shall inform the Minister of Finance and the Minister(s) in charge of the industry involved whether it accedes to the recommendation or not within a period of ten (10) days, counting from the day of its receipt of the recommendation.

5. The party which has informed its accession to the recommendation under the provisions of the preceding Paragraph shall execute the direct domestic investment, etc., concerning the recommendation in accordance therewith.

6. The party which has informed its accession to the recommendation under the provisions of Paragraph 4 may execute the direct domestic investment, etc., concerning the recommendation, before a period of four (4) months (or five (5) months when the period is extended under the provisions of Paragraph 3) has elapsed, counting from the day when he gave the notice thereof, irrespective of the provisions of Paragraph 1 or Paragraph 3.

7. When the party which has been given recommendation under the provisions of Paragraph 2 either fails to inform or informs its non-accession thereto under the provisions of Paragraph 4, the Minister of Finance and the Minister(s) in charge of the industry involved may direct it to alter the particulars of the relevant direct domestic investment, etc., or to suspend the execution thereof, provided that such a directive is served within the period provided in Paragraph 1 or the extended period provided in Paragraph 3, counting from the day of their receipt of the notice thereof.

8. When the Minister of Finance and the Minister(s) in charge of the industry involved deem that, due to the change of economic situations or any other reason, apprehensions as to the occurrence of the consequences mentioned in Item (1) or (2) of Paragraph 1 cease to exist even if the direct domestic investment, etc., notified under the provisions of Paragraph 3 of the preceding Article were executed, or that the direct domestic investment, etc., under notice ceases to be considered as falling under Item (3) or (4) of the same Paragraph, they may withdraw, in whole or in part, their recommendation to alter the particulars of the said direct domestic investment, etc., given to the party who has informed its accession thereto under the provisions of Paragraph 4, or their directive to alter such particulars served under the provisions of the preceding Paragraph.

9. In addition to those provided in each of the preceding Paragraphs, a Cabinet Order shall provide for the procedures of the recommendation to alter the particulars of the direct domestic investment, etc., or to suspend the execution thereof, and other necessary matters concerning the recommendation.

(Transfer of pre-emptive rights)

Article 28 Any one of those mentioned in Article 26, Paragraph 1, Item (1) or (2), which is a stockholder of a company and acquires a pre-emptive right accruing from its stockholding may transfer such a right to another party.

2. Unless option warrants are issued, any one which makes the transfer mentioned in the preceding Paragraph cannot contest against the company or other third party without the company's written consent thereto.

(Notice, etc., of conclusion, etc., of agreements for importation of technology)

Article 29 Any non-resident (including any branch, etc., in Japan of a non-resident, which shall apply to this Paragraph and Paragraph 3) and resident who are to conclude an agreement for transfer of the former's industrial property rights or other rights concerning technology, or for establishment of a right to the use of the same, or for rendering technical guidance in managerial know-how by the former, including renewal or amendment of such an agreement (hereinafter referred to as "conclusion, etc., of agreement for importation of technology") shall give a prior notice, as a Cabinet Order provides for, to the Minister of Finance and the Minister(s) in charge of the industry involved of those matters as designated by the Cabinet Order such as the particulars of that conclusion, etc., of agreement for importation of technology and others.

2. The provisions of the preceding Paragraph shall not apply to the conclusion, etc., of agreement for transfer of the technology which is developed independently by a branch, etc., in Japan of a non-resident, or to other cases determined by a Cabinet Order.

3. Any non-resident and resident who have given a notice under the provisions of Paragraph 1 concerning the conclusion, etc., of agreement for importation of technology mentioned in the same Paragraph shall not execute the conclusion, etc., of agreement for importation of technology under notice until a period of thirty (30) days has elapsed, counting from the day of receipt of the notice by the Minister of Finance and the Minister(s) in charge of the industry involved. However, the Ministers may shorten this period when they deem it not specifically harmful, judging from the type of the technology and other condition(s) of the conclusion, etc., of agreement for importation of technology under notice.

(Recommendation of alteration, etc., of conclusion, etc., of agreement for importation of technology)

Article 30 When a notice is given to the Minister of Finance and the Minister(s) in charge of the industry involved under the provisions of Paragraph 1 of the preceding Article, and the Ministers deem it necessary to make an inquiry in order to determine whether the conclusion, etc., of agreement for importation of technology under notice, if executed, would cause apprehensions as to the occurrence of any one of the below-mentioned consequences, they may extend the period during which the execution of the conclusion, etc., of agreement for importation of technology is prohibited up to four (4) months, counting from the day of their receipt of the notice:-

(1) It might imperil the national security, disturb the maintenance of public order, or hamper the protection of the safety of the general public; or

(2) It might adversely and seriously affect activities of our business enterprises engaging in a line of business similar or related to the one for which the technology is to be imported, or the smooth performance of our national economy.

2. When a notice is given to the Minister of Finance and the Minister(s) in charge of the industry involved under the provisions of Paragraph 1 of the preceding Arti-

cle, and the Ministers deem that, if the conclusion, etc., of agreement for importation of technology under notice were executed, it would cause apprehensions as to the occurrence of any consequences mentioned in each Item of the preceding Paragraph, the Ministers may, upon hearing the opinion of the Committee on Foreign Exchange and Other Transactions mentioned in Article 55-2, recommend the persons who gave the notice, as a cabinet Order provides for, either to alter the particulars of the conclusion, etc., of agreement for importation of technology, in whole or in part, or to suspend the execution thereof, provided that such recommendation is given within the period mentioned in the same Paragraph, or within the extended period provided by the next Paragraph, counting from the day of their receipt of the notice.

3. When the Committee on Foreign Exchange and Other Transactions mentioned in Article 55-2 is asked for its opinion for the inquiry mentioned in Paragraph 1, and tenders its intimation that to form its opinion within the period of four (4) months as provided by the same Paragraph is difficult due to the nature of the subject matter, the period provided in the same Paragraph during which the conclusion, etc., of agreement for importation of technology is prohibited shall become five (5) months, irrespective of the provisions of the same Paragraph.

4. When recommendation is given under the provisions of Paragraph 2, the provisions of Article 27, Paragraph 4 through Paragraph 9 shall be applicable thereto mutatis mutandis, and a Cabinet Order shall provide for the technicalities of such mutatis mutandis application.

CHAPTER VI   FOREIGN TRADE

(Principle for export)

Article 47 Export of goods shall be permitted with a minimum of restrictions, insofar as it is consistent with the objective of this Law.

(Approval for export)

Article 48 A person who is to export goods of a certain type, or to a certain destination, or under a certain way of transaction or settlement might be obligated, as a Cabinet Order provides for, to obtain approval from the Minister of International Trade and Industry.

2. No restrictions imposed by a Cabinet Order under the provisions of the preceding Paragraph shall exceed the limit necessary for the maintenance of equilibrium of balance of international payments, or for the sound development of international trade and national economy.

(Attestation for settlement of export proceeds)

Article 49 The Minister of International Trade and Industry may demand, as an Order provides for, any person who is to export goods to produce sufficient attestation that the proceeds thereof are to be settled by a method designated by a Cabinet Order.

(Embargo in case of emergency)

Article 51 When the Minister of International Trade and Industry deems it urgently necessary, he may, as an Order provides for, place an embargo by specifying the type or destination of goods for a period not exceeding one (1) month.

(Approval for import)

Article 52 For the purpose of sound development of foreign trade and the national economy, a person who is to import goods might be obligated, as a Cabinet Order provides for, to obtain approval therefor.

(Sanction)

Article 53 The minister of International Trade and Industry may prohibit any person who has contravened this Law, any Order enacted thereunder, or any disposition made thereunder in regard to exporting or importing goods from carrying out export or import transactions for a period not exceeding one (1) year.

(Supervision over the superintendents of customhouses)

Article 54 The Minister of International Trade and Industry shall, as a Cabinet Order provides for, control and supervise the superintendents of customhouses in regard to the export and import of those goods which fall under his jurisdiction.

2. The Minister of International Trade and Industry may, as a Cabinet Order provides for, delegate to the superintendents of customhouses a part of his power conferred by this Law.

(Warranty for execution of import transactions)

Article 55 A person who is to import goods might be obligated, as a Cabinet Order provides for, to submit a warranty in the form of cash, securities, etc., for the execution of his importation.

2. If a person who has obtained approval for import fails to carry out the importation, the warranty submitted by him under the preceding Paragraph may be foreclosed and devolved on the national treasury, as a Cabinet Order provides for.

CHAPTER IX PENAL PROVISIONS

Article 70 Any person who comes under any one of the following Items shall be liable to penal servitude not exceeding three (3) years, or a fine not exceeding one million (1,000,000) yen, or both. However, when three-times the amount of the subject matter of contravention exceeds one million (1,000,000) yen, a fine up to that three-times amount shall be applicable:

(21) A person who carried out any direct domestic investment, etc., by giving no

notice or a false notice in contravention of Article 26, Paragraph 3 (including a person who is deemed as a foreign investor under Paragraph 5 thereof);

(22) A person who carried out any direct domestic investment, etc., in contravention of, and during the period provided by, Article 26, Paragraph 4 (including the extended period in the event the period is extended under Article 27, Paragraph 1 or 3), (including a person who is deemed as a foreign investor under Article 26, Paragraph 5);

(23) A person who carried out any direct domestic investment, etc., in contravention of Article 27, paragraph 5 (including a person who is deemed as a foreign investor under Article 26, paragraph 5);

(24) A person who carried out any direct domestic investment, etc., in contravention of a directive of alteration or suspension served under Article 27, Paragraph 7 (including a person who is deemed as a foreign investor under Article 26, Paragraph 5);

(25) A person who carried out any conclusion, etc., of agreement for importation of technology by giving no notice or a false notice in contraventioned of Article 29, Paragraph 1;

(26) A person who carried out any conclusion, etc., of agreement for importation of technology in contravention of, and during the period provided by, Article 29, Paragraph 3 (including the extended period in the event the period is extended under Article 30, Paragraph 1 or 3);

(27) A person who carried out any conclusion, etc., of agreement for importation of technology in contravention of Article 27, Paragraph 5, of which mutatis mutandis application is provided by Article 30, Paragraph 4;

(28) A person who carried out any conclusion, etc., of agreement for importation of technology in contravention of a directive of alteration or suspension served under Article 27, Paragraph 7, of which mutatis mutandis application is provided by Article 30, Paragraph 4;

(29) A person who carried out any exportation of goods without obtaining approval as required by an Order provided by Article 48, Paragraph 1;

(30) A person who made any shipment of goods in contravention of an Order provided by Article 51;

(31) A person made any importation of goods without obtaining approval as required by an Order provided by Article 52; and

(32) A person who made any exportation or importation of goods in contravention of the prohibition imposed under Article 53.

IV. UNITED STATES STATUTORY MATERIALS

1. Trade Agreements Act of 1934

AN ACT
To amend the Tariff Act of 1930.

"PART III—PROMOTION OF FOREIGN TRADE

"SEC. 350. (a) For the purpose of expanding foreign markets for the products of the United States (as a means of assisting in the present emergency in restoring the American standard of living, in overcoming domestic unemployment and the present economic depression, in increasing the purchasing power of the American public, and in establishing and maintaining a better relationship among various branches of American agriculture, industry, mining, and commerce) by regulating the admission of foreign goods into the United States in accordance with the characteristics and needs of various branches of American production so that foreign markets will be made available to those branches of American production which require and are capable of developing such outlets by affording corresponding market opportunities for foreign products in the United States, the President, whenever he finds as a fact that any existing duties or other import restrictions of the United States or any foreign country are unduly burdening and restricting the foreign trade of the United States and that the purpose above declared will be promoted by the means hereinafter specified, is authorized from time to time—

"(1) To enter into foreign trade agreements with foreign governments or instrumentalities thereof; and

"(2) To proclaim such modifications of existing duties and other import restrictions, or such additional import restrictions, or such continuance, and for such minimum periods, of existing customs or excise treatment of any article covered by foreign trade agreements, as are required or appropriate to carry out any foreign trade agreement that the President has entered into hereunder. No proclamation shall be made increasing or decreasing by more than 50 per centum any existing rate of duty or transferring any article between the dutiable and free lists. The proclaimed duties and other import restrictions shall apply to articles the growth, produce, or manufacture of all foreign countries, whether imported directly, or indirectly: *Provided,* That the President may suspend the application to articles the growth, produce, or manufacture of any country because of its discriminatory treatment of American commerce or because of other acts or policies which in his opinion tend to defeat the purposes set forth in this section; and the proclaimed duties and other import restrictions shall be in effect from and after such time as is specified in the proclamation. The President may at any time terminate any such proclamation in whole or in part.

"(b) Nothing in this section shall be construed to prevent the application, with respect to rates of duty established under this section pursuant to agreements with countries other than Cuba, of the provisions of the treaty of commercial reciprocity concluded between the United States and the Republic of Cuba on December 11, 1902, or to preclude giving effect to an exclusive agreement with Cuba concluded under this section, modifying the existing preferential customs treatment of any article the growth, produce, or manufacture of Cuba: *Provided,* That the duties payable on such an article shall in no case be increased or decreased by more than 50 per centum of the duties now payable thereon.

"(c) As used in this section, the term 'duties and other import restrictions' includes (1) rate and form of import duties and classification of articles, and (2) limitations, prohibitions, charges, and exactions other than duties, imposed on importation or imposed for the regulation of imports."

SEC. 2. (a) Subparagraph (d) of paragraph 369, the last sentence of paragraph 1402, and the provisos to paragraphs 371, 401, 1650, 1687, and 1803 (1) of the Tariff Act of 1930 are repealed. The provisions of sections 336 and 516(b) of the Tariff Act of 1930 shall not apply to any article with respect to the importation of which into the United States a foreign trade agreement has been concluded pursuant to this Act, or to any provision of any such agreement. The third paragraph of section 311 of the Tariff Act of 1930 shall apply to any agreement concluded pursuant to this Act to the extent only that such agreement assures to the United States a rate of duty on wheat flour produced in the United States which is preferential in respect to the lowest rate of duty imposed by the country with which such agreement has been concluded on like flour produced in any other country; and upon the withdrawal of wheat flour from bonded manufacturing warehouses for exportation to the country with which such agreement has been concluded, there shall be levied, collected, and paid on the imported wheat used, a duty equal to the amount of such assured preference.

(b) Every foreign trade agreement concluded pursuant to this Act shall be subject to termination, upon due notice to the foreign government concerned, at the end of not more than three years from the date on which the agreement comes into force, and, if not then terminated, shall be subject to termination thereafter upon not more than six months' notice.

(c) The authority of the President to enter into foreign trade agreements under section 1 of this Act shall terminate on the expiration of three years from the date of the enactment of this Act.

SEC. 3. Nothing in this Act shall be construed to give any authority to cancel or reduce, in any manner, any of the indebtedness of any foreign country to the United States.

SEC. 4. Before any foreign trade agreement is concluded with any foreign government or instrumentality thereof under the provisions of this Act, reasonable public notice of the intention to negotiate an agreement with such government or instrumentality shall be given in order that any interested person may have an opportunity to present his views to the President, or to such agency as the President may designate, under such rules and regulations as the President may prescribe; and before concluding such agreement the President shall seek information and advice with respect thereto from the United States Tariff Commission, the Departments of State, Agriculture, and Commerce and from such other sources as he may deem appropriate.

Approved, June 12, 1934, 9.15 p.m.

2. Trade Agreements Extension Act of 1951, as amended through 1958 (excerpts)

AN ACT

To extend the authority of the President to enter into trade agreements under section 350 of the Tariff Act of 1930, as amended, and for other purposes.

Sec. 3. (a) Before entering into negotiations concerning any proposed foreign trade agreement under section 350 of the Tariff Act of 1930, as amended, the President shall furnish the United States Tariff Commission (hereinafter in this Act referred to as the "Commission") with a list of all articles imported into the United States to be considered for possible modification of duties and other import restrictions, imposition of additional import restrictions, or continuance of existing customs or exercise treatment. Upon receipt of such list the Commission shall make an investigation and report to the President the findings of the Commission with respect to each such article as to (1) the limit to which such modification, imposition, or continuance may be extended in order to carry out the purpose of such section 350 without causing or threatening serious injury to the domestic industry producing like or directly competitive articles; and (2) if increases in duties or additional import restrictions are required to avoid serious injury to the domestic industry producing like or directly competitive articles the minimum increases in duties or additional import restrictions required. Such report shall be made by the Commission to the President not later than six months after the receipt of such list by the Commission. No such foreign trade agreement shall be entered into until the Commission has made its report to the President or until the expiration of the six-month period.

(b) (1) In the course of any investigation pursuant to this section the Commission shall hold hearings and give reasonable public notice thereof, and shall afford reasonable opportunity for parties interested to be present, to produce evidence, and to be heard at such hearings. If in the course of any such investigation the Commission shall find with respect to any article on the list upon which a tariff concession has been granted that an increase in duty or additional import restriction is required to avoid serious injury to the domestic industry producing like or directly competitive articles, the Commission shall promptly institute an investigation with respect to that article pursuant to section 7 of this Act.

(2) In each such investigation the Commission shall, to the extent practicable and without excluding other factors, ascertain for the last calendar year preceding the investigation the average invoice price on a country-of-origin basis (converted into currency of the United States in accordance with the provisions of section 522 of the Tariff Act of 1930, as amended) at which the foreign article was sold for export to the United States, and the average prices at which the like or directly competitive domestic articles were sold at wholesale in the principal markets of the United States. The Commission shall also, to the extent practicable, estimate for each article on the list the maximum increase in annual imports which may occur without causing serious injury to the domestic industry producing like or directly competitive articles. The Commission shall request the executive departments and agencies for information in their possession concerning prices and other economic data from the principal supplier foreign country of each such article.

Sec. 4. (a) Within thirty days after any trade agreement under section 350 of the Tariff Act of 1930, as amended, has been entered into which, when effective, will (1) require or make appropriate any modification of duties or other import restrictions, the imposition of additional import restrictions, or the continuance of existing customs or excise treatment, which modification, inposition, or continuance will exceed the limit to which such modification, imposition, or continuance may be extended without causing or threatening serious injury to the domestic industry producing like or directly competitive articles as found and reported by the Tariff Commission under section 3, or (2) fail to require or make appropriate the minimum increase in duty or additional import restrictions required to avoid such injury, the President shall transmit to Congress a copy of such agreement together with a message accurately identifying the article with respect to which such limits or minimum requirements are not complied with, and stating his reasons for the action taken with respect to such article. If either the Senate or the House of Representatives, or both, are not in session at the time of such transmission, such agreement and message shall be filed with the Secretary of the Senate or the Clerk of the House of Representatives, or both, as the case may be.

(b) Promptly after the President has transmitted such foreign trade agreement to Congress the Commission shall deposit with the Committee on Ways and Means of the House of Representatives, and the Committee on Finance of the Senate, a copy of the portions of its report to the President dealing with the articles with respect to which such limits or minimum requirements are not complied with.

Sec. 5. As soon as practicable, the President shall take such action as is necessary to suspend, withdraw or prevent the application of any reduction in any rate of duty, or binding of any existing customs or exercise treatment, or other concession contained in any trade agreement entered into under the authority of section 350 of the Tariff Act of 1930, as amended and extended, to imports from the Union of Soviet Socialist Republics and to imports from any nation or area dominated or controlled by the foreign government or foreign organization controlling the world Communist movement.

Sec. 6. (a) No reduction in any rate of duty, or binding of any existing customs or excise treatment, or other concession hereafter proclaimed under section 350 of the Tariff Act of 1930, as amended, shall be permitted to continue in effect when the product on which the concession has been granted is, as a result, in whole or in part, of the duty or other customs treatment reflecting such concession, being imported into the United States in such increased quantities, either actual or relative, as to cause or threaten serious injury to the domestic industry producing like or directly competitive products.

(b) The President, as soon as practicable, shall take such action as may be necessary to bring trade agreements heretofore entered into under section 350 of the Tariff Act of 1930, as amended, into conformity with the policy established in subsection (a) of this section.

Sec. 7. (a) Upon the request of the President, upon resolution of either House of Congress, upon resolution of either the Committee on Finance of the Senate or the Committee on Ways and Means of the House of Representatives, upon its own motion, or upon application of any interested party (including any organization or group of employees), the United States Tariff Commission shall promptly make an investigation and make a report thereon not later than six months after the application is made to determine whether any product upon which a concession has been granted under a trade agreement is, as result, in whole or in part, of the duty or other customs treatment reflecting such concession, being imported into the United States in such increased quantities, either actual or relative, as to cause or threaten serious injury to the domestic industry producing like or directly competitive products.

In the course of any such investigation, whenever it finds evidence of serious injury or threat of serious injury or whenever so directed by resolution of either the Committee on Finance of the Senate or the Committee on Ways and Means of the House of Representatives, the Tariff Commission shall hold hearings giving reasonable public notice thereof and shall afford reasonable opportunity for interested parties to be present, to produce evidence, and to be heard at such hearings.

Should the Tariff Commission find, as the result of its investigation and hearings, that a product on which a concession has been granted is, as a result, in whole or in part, of the duty or other customs treatment reflecting such concession, being imported in such increased quantities, either actual or relative, as to cause or threaten serious injury to the domestic industry producing like or directly competitive products, it shall recommend to the President the withdrawal or modification of the concession, its suspension in whole or in part, or the establishment of import quotas, to the extent and for the time necessary to prevent or remedy such injury. The Tariff Commission shall immediately make public its findings and recommendations to the President, including any dissenting or separate findings and recommendations, and shall cause a summary thereof to be published in the Federal Register.

(b) In arriving at a determination in the foregoing procedure the Tariff Commission, without excluding other factors, shall take into consideration a downward trend of production, employment, prices, profits, or wages in the domestic industry concerned, or a decline in sales, an increase in imports, either actual or relative to domestic production, a higher or growing inventory, or a decline in the proportion of the domestic market supplied by domestic producers.

Increased imports, either actual or relative, shall be considered as the cause or threat of serious injury to the domestic industry producing like or directly competitive products when the Commission finds that such increased imports have contributed substantially towards causing or threatening serious injury to such industry.

(c) (1) Upon receipt of the Tariff Commission's report of its investigation and hearings, the President may make such adjustments in the rates of duty, impose such quotas, or make such other modifications as are found and reported by the Commission to be necessary to prevent or remedy serious injury to the respective domestic industry. If the President does not take such action within sixty days he shall immediately submit a report to the Committee on Ways and Means of the House and to the Committee on Finance of the Senate stating why he has not made such adjustments or modifications, or imposed such quotas.

(2) The action so found and reported by the Commission to be necessary shall take effect (as provided in the first sentence of paragraph (1) or in paragraph (3), as the case may be)—

(A) if approved by the President, or

(B) if disapproved by the President in whole or in part, upon the adoption by both Houses of the Congress (within the 60-day period following the date on which the report referred to in the second sentence of paragraph (1) is submitted to such committee), by the yeas and nays by a two-thirds vote of each House, of a concurrent resolution stating in effect that the Senate and House of Representatives approve the action so found and reported by the Commission to be necessary.

For the purposes of subparagraph (B), in the computation of the 60-day period there shall be excluded the days on which either House is not in session because of an adjournment of more than 3 days to a day certain or an adjournment of the Congress sine die.

(3) In any case in which the contingency set forth in paragraph (2) (B) occurs, the President shall (within 15 days after the adoption of such resolution) take such action as may be necessary to make the adjustments, impose the quotas, or make such other modifications as were found and reported by the Commission to be necessary.

(d) When in the judgment of the Tariff Commission no sufficient reason exists for a recommendation to the President that a concession should be withdrawn or modified or a quota established, it shall make and publish a report stating its findings and conclusions.

(e) As used in this Act, the terms "domestic industry producing like or directly competitive products" and "domestic industry producing like or directly competitive articles" mean that portion or subdivision of the producing organizations manufacturing, assembling, processing, extracting, growing, or otherwise producing like or directly competitive products or articles in commercial quantities. In applying the preceding sentence, the Commission shall (so far as practicable) distinguish or separate the operations of the producing organizations involving the like or directly competitive products or articles referred to in such sentence from the operations of such organizations involving other products or articles.

(f) In carrying out the provisions of this section the President may, notwithstanding section 350(a) (2) of the Tariff Act of 1930, as amended, impose a duty not in excess of 50 per centum ad valorem on any article not otherwise subject to duty.

Section 8. (a) In any case where the Secretary of Agriculture determines and reports to the President and to the Tariff Commission with regard to any agricultural commodity that due to the perishability of the commodity a condition exists requiring emergency treatment, the Tariff Commission shall make an immediate investigation * * * under the provisions of section 7 of this Act to determine the facts and make recommendations to the President for such relief under those provisions as may be appropriate. The President may take immediate action however, without awaiting the recommendations of the Tariff Commission if in his judgment the emergency requires such action. In any case the report and findings of the Tariff Commission and the decision of the President shall be made at the earliest possible date and in any event not more than 25 calendar days after the submission of the case to the Tariff Commission.

. . . .

Sec. 10. The enactment of this Act shall not be construed to determine or indicate the approval or disapproval by the Congress of the Executive Agreement known as the General Agreement on Tariffs and Trade.

Sec. 11. The President shall, as soon as practicable, take such measures as may be necessary to prevent the importation of ermine, fox, kolinsky, marten, mink, muskrat, and weasel furs and skins, dressed or undressed, which are the product of the Union of Soviet Socialist Republics or of Communist China.

Rules Governing Congressional Consideration of Concurrent Resolutions to Override Presidential Disapprovals of Tariff Commission Escape-Clause Recommendations

Sec. 7. (a) [of Trade Agreements Extension Act of 1958] The following subsections of this section are enacted by the Congress:

(1) As an exercise of the rulemaking power of the Senate and the House of Representatives, respectively, and as such they shall be considered as part of the rules of each House, respectively, but applicable only with respect to the procedure to be followed in such House in the case of resolutions (as

defined in subsection (b)); and such rules shall supersede other rules only to the extent that they are inconsistent therewith; and

(2) With full recognition of the constitutional right of either House to change such rules (so far as relating to the procedure in such House) at any time, in the same manner and to the same extent as in the case of any other rule of such House.

(b) As used in this section, the term "resolution" means only a concurrent resolution of the two Houses of Congress, the matter after the resolving clause of which is as follows: "That the Senate and House of Representatives approve the action—

"(1) found and reported by the United States Tariff Commission to be necessary to prevent or remedy serious injury to the respective domestic industry, in its report to the President dated   , 19 , on its escape-clause investigation numbered under the provisions of section 7 of the Trade Agreements Extension Act of 1951, as amended (19 U.S.C., sec. 1364), and

"(2) disapproved by the President in whole or in part in his report (dated   , 19) pursuant to the second sentence of paragraph (1) of section 7 (c) of such Act.",

the blank spaces therein being appropriately filled; and does not include a concurrent resolution which specifies more than one such investigation.

(c) A resolution with respect to an investigation shall be referred to the Committee on Finance of the Senate or to the Committee on Ways and Means of the House of Representatives by the President of the Senate or the Speaker of the House of Representatives, as the case may be.

(d) (1) If the committee to which has been referred a resolution with respect to an investigation has not reported it before the expiration of ten calendar days after its introduction (or, in the case of a resolution received from the other House, ten calendar days after its receipt), it shall then (but not before) be in order to move either to discharge the committee from further consideration of such resolution, or to discharge the committee from further consideration of any other resolution with respect to such investigation which has been referred to the committee.

(2) Such motion may be made only by a person favoring the resolution, shall be highly privileged (except that it may not be made after the committee has reported a resolution with respect to the same investigation), and debate thereon shall be limited to not to exceed one hour, to be equally

divided between those favoring and those opposing the resolution. No amendment to such motion shall be in order, and it shall not be in order to move to reconsider the vote by which such motion is agreed to or disagreed to.

(3) If the motion to discharge is agreed to or disagreed to, such motion may not be renewed, nor may another motion to discharge the committee be made with respect to any other resolution with respect to the same investigation.

(e) (1) When the committee has reported, or has been discharged from further consideration of, a resolution with respect to an investigation it shall at any time thereafter be in order (even though a previous motion to the same effect has been disagreed to) to move to proceed to the consideration of such resolution. Such motion shall be highly privileged and shall not be debatable. No amendment to such motion shall be in order and it shall not be in order to move to reconsider the vote by which such motion is agreed to or disagreed to.

(2) Debate on the resolution shall be limited to not to exceed ten hours, which shall be equally divided between those favoring and those opposing the resolution. A motion further to limit debate shall not be debatable. No amendment to, or motion to recommit, the resolution shall be in order, and it shall not be in order to move to reconsider the vote by which the resolution is agreed to or disagreed to.

(f) (1) All motions to postpone, made with respect to the discharge from committee, or the consideration of, a resolution with respect to an investigation, and all motions to proceed to the consideration of other business, shall be decided without debate.

3. Trade Expansion Act of 1962

TITLE I—SHORT TITLE AND PURPOSES

Section 101. *Short Title*

This Act may be cited as the "Trade Expansion Act of 1962".

Section 102. *Statement of Purposes*

The purposes of this Act are, through trade agreements affording mutual trade benefits—

(1) to stimulate the economic growth of the United States and maintain and enlarge foreign markets for the products of United States agriculture, industry, mining, and commerce;

(2) to strengthen economic relations with foreign countries through the development of open and nondiscriminatory trading in the free world; and

(3) to prevent Communist economic penetration.

TITLE II—TRADE AGREEMENTS

CHAPTER 1—GENERAL AUTHORITY

Section 201. *Basic Authority for Trade Agreements*

(a) Whenever the President determines that any existing duties or other import restrictions of any foreign country or the United States are unduly burdening and restricting the foreign trade of the United States and that any of the purposes stated in section 102 will be promoted thereby, the President may—

(1) after June 30, 1962, and before July 1, 1967, enter into trade agreements with foreign countries or instrumentalities thereof; and

(2) proclaim such modification or continuance of any existing duty or other import restriction, such continuance of existing duty-free or excise treatment, or such additional import restrictions, as he determines to be required or appropriate to carry out any such trade agreement.

(b) Except as otherwise provided in this title, no proclamation pursuant to subsection (a) shall be made—

(1) decreasing any rate of duty to a rate below 50 percent of the rate existing on July 1, 1962; or

(2) increasing any rate of duty to (or imposing) a rate more than 50 percent above the rate existing on July 1, 1934.

Section 202. *Low-Rate Articles*

Section 201(b)(1) shall not apply in the case of any article for which the rate of duty existing on July 1, 1962, is not more than 5 percent ad valorem (or ad valorem equivalent). In the case of an article subject to more than one rate of duty, the preceding sentence shall be applied by taking into account the aggregate of such rates.

CHAPTER 2—SPECIAL PROVISIONS CONCERNING EUROPEAN ECONOMIC COMMUNITY

Section 211. *In General*

(a) In the case of any trade agreement with the European Economic Community, section 201(b)(1) shall not apply to articles in any category if, before entering into such trade agreement, the President determines with respect to such category that the United States and all countries of the European Economic Community together accounted for 80 percent or more of the aggregated world export value of all the articles in such category.

(b) For purposes of subsection (a)—

(1) As soon as practicable after the date of the enactment of this Act, the President shall—

(A) after taking into account the availability of trade statistics, select a system of comprehensive classification of articles by category, and

(B) make public his selection of such system.

(2) As soon as practicable after the President has selected a system pursuant to paragraph (1), the Tariff Commission shall—

(A) determine the articles falling within each category of such system, and

(B) make public its determinations.

The determination of the Tariff Commission as to the articles included in any category may be modified only by the Tariff Commission. Such modification by the Tariff Commission may be made only for the purpose of correction, and may be made only before the date on which the first list of articles specifying this section is furnished by the President to the Tariff Commission pursuant to section 221.

(c) For the purpose of making a determination under subsection (a) with respect to any category—

(1) The determination of the countries of the European Economic Community shall be made as of the date of the request under subsection (d).

(2) The President shall determine "aggregated world export value" with respect to any category of articles—

(A) on the basis of a period which he determines to be representative for such category, which period shall be included in the most recent 5-year period before the date of the request under subsection (d) for which statistics are available and shall contain at least 2 one-year periods,

(B) on the basis of the dollar value of exports as shown by trade statistics in use by the Department of Commerce, and

(C) by excluding exports—

(i) from any country of the European Economic Community to another such country, and

(ii) to or from any country or area which, at any time during the representative period, was denied trade agreement benefits under section 231, or under section 5 of the Trade Agreements Extension Act of 1951, or under section 401(a) of the Tariff Classification Act of 1962.

(d) Before the President makes a determination under subsection (a) with respect to any category, the Tariff Commission shall (upon request of the President) make findings as to—

(1) the representative period for such category,

(2) the aggregated world export value of the articles falling within such category, and

(3) the percentage of the aggregated world export value of such articles accounted for by the United States and the countries of the European Economic Community,

and shall advise the President of such findings.

(e) The exception to section 201(b)(1) provided by subsection (a) shall not apply to any article referred to in Agricultural Handbook No. 143, United States Department of Agriculture, as issued in September 1959.

Section 212. *Agricultural Commodities*

In the case of any trade agreement with the European Economic Community, section 201(b)(1) shall not apply to any article referred to in Agricultural Handbook No. 143, United States Department of Agriculture, as issued in September 1959, if before entering into such agreement the President determines that such agreement will tend to assure the maintenance or expansion of United States exports of the like article.

Section 213. *Tropical Agricultural and Forestry Commodities*

(a) Section 201(b)(1) shall not apply to any article if, before entering into the trade agreement covering such article, the President determines that—

(1) such article is a tropical agricultural or forestry commodity;

(2) the like article is not produced in significant quantities in the United States; and

(3) the European Economic Community has made a commitment with respect to duties or other import restrictions which is likely to assure access for such article to the markets of the European Economic Community which—

(A) is comparable to the access which such article will have to the markets of the United States, and

(B) will be afforded substantially without differential treatment as among free world countries of origin.

(b) For purposes of subsection (a), a "tropical agricultural or forestry commodity" is an agricultural or forestry commodity with respect to which the President determines that more than one-half of the world production is in the area of the world between 20 degrees north latitude and 20 degrees south latitude.

(c) Before the President makes a determination under subsection (a) with respect to any article, the Tariff Commission shall (upon request of the President) make findings as to—

(1) whether or not such article is an agricultural or forestry commodity more than one-half of the world production of which is in the area of the world between 20 degrees north latitude and 20 degrees south latitude, and

(2) whether or not the like article is produced in significant quantities in the United States,

and shall advise the President of such findings.

CHAPTER 3—REQUIREMENTS CONCERNING NEGOTIATIONS

Section 221. *Tariff Commission Advice*

(a) In connection with any proposed trade agreement under this title, the President shall from time to time publish and furnish the Tariff Commission with lists of articles which may be considered for modification or continuance of United States duties or other import restrictions, or continuance of United States duty-free or exise treatment. In the case of any article with respect to which consideration may be given to reducing the rate of duty below the 50 percent limitation contained in section 201(b)(1), the list shall specify the section or sections of this title pursuant to which such consideration may be given.

(b) Within 6 months after receipt of such a list, the Tariff Commission shall advise the President with respect to each article of its judgment as to the probable economic effect of modifications of duties or other import restrictions on industries producing like or directly competitive articles, so as to assist the President in making an informed judgment as to the impact that might be caused by such modifications on United States industry, agriculture, and labor.

(c) In preparing its advice to the President, the Tariff Commission shall, to the extent practicable—

(1) investigate conditions, causes, and effects relating to competition between the foreign industries producing the articles in question and the domestic industries producing the like or directly competitive articles;

(2) analyze the production, trade, and consumption of each like or directly competitive article, taking into consideration employment, profit levels, and use of productive facilities with respect to the domestic industries concerned, and such other economic factors in such industries as it considers relevant, including prices, wages, sales, inventories, patterns of demand, capital investment, obsolescence of equipment, and diversification of production;

(3) describe the probable nature and extent of any significant change in employment, profit levels, use of productive facilities and such other conditions as it deems relevant in the domestic industries concerned which it believes such modifications would cause; and

(4) make special studies (including studies of real wages paid in foreign supplying countries), whenever deemed to be warranted, of particular proposed modifications affecting United States industry,

agriculture, and labor, utilizing to the fullest extent practicable the facilities of United States attachés abroad and other appropriate personnel of the United States.

(d) In preparing its advice to the President, the Tariff Commission shall, after reasonable notice, hold public hearings.

Section 222. *Advice from Departments*

Before any trade agreement is entered into under this title, the President shall seek information and advice with respect to such agreement from the Departments of Agriculture, Commerce, Defense, Interior, Labor, State, and Treasury, and from such other sources as he may deem appropriate.

Section 223. *Public Hearings*

In connection with any proposed trade agreement under this title, the President shall afford an opportunity for any interested person to present his views concerning any article on a list published pursuant to section 221, any article which should be so listed, any concession which should be sought by the United States, or any other matter relevant to such proposed trade agreement. For this purpose, the President shall designate an agency or an interagency committee which shall, after reasonable notice, hold public hearings, shall prescribe regulations governing the conduct of such hearings, and shall furnish the President with a summary of such hearings.

Section 224. *Prerequisite for Offers*

The President may make an offer for the modification or continuance of any duty or other import restriction, or continuance of duty-free or excise treatment, with respect to any article only after he has received advice concerning such article from the Tariff Commission under section 221(b), or after the expiration of the relevant 6-month period provided for in that section, whichever first occurs, and only after the President has received a summary of the hearings at which an opportunity to be heard with respect to such article has been afforded under section 223.

Section 225. *Reservation of Articles from Negotiations*

(a) While there is in effect with respect to any article any action taken under—

(1) section 232, 351, or 352,

(2) section 2(b) of the Act entitled "An Act to extend the authority of the President to enter into trade agreements under section 350 of the

Tariff Act of 1930, as amended," approved July 1, 1954 (19 U.S.C., sec. 1352a), or

(3) section 7 of the Trade Agreements Extension Act of 1951 (19 U.S.C., sec. 1364),

the President shall reserve such article from negotiations under this title for the reduction of any duty or other import restriction or the elimination of any duty.

(b) During the 5-year period which begins on the date of the enactment of this Act, the President shall reserve an article (other than an article which, on the date of the enactment of this Act, was described in subsection (a)(3)) from negotiation under this title for the reduction of any duty or other import restriction or the elimination of any duty where—

(1) pursuant to section 7 of the Trade Agreements Extension Act of 1951 (or pursuant to a comparable Executive Order), the Tariff Commission found by a majority of the Commissioners voting that such article was being imported in such increased quantities as to cause or threaten serious injury to an industry,

(2) such article is included in a list furnished to the Tariff Commission pursuant to section 221 (and has not been included in a prior list so furnished), and

(3) upon request on behalf of the industry, made not later than 60 days after the date of the publication of such list, the Tariff Commission finds and advises the President that economic conditions in such industry have not substantially improved since the date of the report of the finding referred to in paragraph (1).

(c) In addition to the articles described by subsections (a) and (b), the President shall also so reserve any other article which he determines to be appropriate, taking into consideration the advice of the Tariff Commission under section 221(b), any advice furnished to him under section 222, and the summary furnished to him under section 223.

Section 226. *Transmission of Agreements to Congress*

The President shall transmit promptly to each House of Congress a copy of each trade agreement entered into under this title, together with a statement, in the light of the advice of the Tariff Commission under section 221(b) and of other relevant considerations, of his reasons for entering into the agreement.

CHAPTER 4—NATIONAL SECURITY

Section 231. *Products of Communist Countries or Areas*

(a) The President shall, as soon as practicable, suspend, withdraw, or prevent the application of the reduction, elimination, or continuance of any existing duty or other import restriction, or the continuance of any existing duty-free or excise treatment, proclaimed in carrying out any trade agreement under this title or under section 350 of the Tariff Act of 1930, to products, whether imported directly or indirectly, of any country or area dominated or controlled by Communism.

(b) The President may extend the benefits of trade agreement concessions made by the United States to products, whether imported directly or indirectly, of a country or area within the purview of subsection (a) of this section which, on December 16, 1963, was receiving trade concessions, when he determines that such treatment would be important to the national interest and would promote the independence of such country or area from domination or control by international communism, and reports this determination and the reasons therefor to the Congress.

Section 232. *Safeguarding National Security*

(a) No action shall be taken pursuant to section 201(a) or pursuant to section 350 of the Tariff Act of 1930 to decrease or eliminate the duty or other import restrictions of any article if the President determines that such reduction or elimination would threaten to impair the national security.

(b) Upon request of the head of any department or agency, upon application of an interested party, or upon his own motion, the Director of the Office of Emergency Planning (hereinafter in this section referred to as the "Director") shall immediately make an appropriate investigation, in the course of which he shall seek information and advice from other appropriate departments and agencies, to determine the effects on the national security of imports of the article which is the subject of such request, application, or motion. If, as a result of such investigation, the Director is of the opinion that the said article is being imported into the United States in such quantities or under such circumstances as to threaten to impair the national security, he shall promptly so advise the President, and, unless the President determines that the article is not being imported into the United States in such quantities or under such circumstances as to threaten to impair the national security as set forth in this section, he shall take such action, and for such time, as he deems necessary to adjust the imports of such article and its derivatives so that such imports will not so threaten to impair the national security.

(c) For the purposes of this section, the Director and the President shall, in the light of the requirements of national security and without excluding other relevant factors, give consideration to domestic production needed for projected national defense requirements, the capacity of domestic industries to meet such requirements, existing and anticipated availabilities of the human resources, products, raw materials, and other supplies and services essential to the national defense, the requirements of growth of such industries and such supplies and services including the investment, exploration, and development necessary to assure such growth, and the importation of goods in terms of their quantities, availabilities, character, and use as those affect such industries and the capacity of the United States to meet national security requirements. In the administration of this section, the Director and the President shall further recognize the close relation of the economic welfare of the Nation to our national security, and shall take into consideration the impact of foreign competition on the economic welfare of individual domestic industries; and any substantial unemployment, decrease in revenues of government, loss of skills or investment, or other serious effects resulting from the displacement of any domestic products by excessive imports shall be considered, without excluding other factors, in determining whether such weakening of our internal economy may impair the national security.

(d) A report shall be made and published upon the disposition of each request, application, or motion under subsection (b). The Director shall publish procedural regulations to give effect to the authority conferred on him by subsection (b).

CHAPTER 5—ADMINISTRATIVE PROVISIONS

Section 241. *Special Representative for Trade Negotiations*

(a) The President shall appoint, by and with the advice and consent of the Senate, a Special Representative for Trade Negotiations, who shall be the chief representative of the United States for each negotiation under this title and for such other negotiations as in the President's judgment require that the Special Representative be the chief representative of the United States, and who shall be the chairman of the organization established pursuant to section 242(a). The Special Representative for Trade Negotiations shall hold office at the pleasure of the President, shall be entitled to receive the same compensation and allowances as a chief of mission, and shall have the rank of ambassador extraordinary and plenipotentiary.

(b) The Special Representative for Trade Negotiations shall, in the performance of his functions under subsection (a), seek information and advice with respect to each negotiation from representatives of industry, agriculture, and labor, and from such agencies as he deems appropriate.

Section 242. *Interagency Trade Organization*

(a) The President shall establish an interagency organization to assist him in carrying out the functions vested in him by this title and sections 351 and 352. Such organization shall, in addition to the Special Representative for Trade Negotiations, be composed of the heads of such departments and of such other officers as the President shall designate. It shall meet at such times and with respect to such matters as the President or the chairman of the organization shall direct. The organization may invite the participation in its activities of any agency not represented in the organization when matters of interest to such agency are under consideration.

(b) In assisting the President, the organization shall—

(1) make recommendations to the President on basic policy issues arising in the administration of the trade agreements program,

(2) make recommendations to the President as to what action, if any, he should take on reports with respect to tariff adjustment submitted to him by the Tariff Commission under section 301(e).

(3) advise the President of the results of hearings concerning foreign import restrictions held pursuant to section 252(d), and recommend appropriate action with respect thereto, and

(4) perform such other functions with respect to the trade agreements program as the President may from time to time designate.

(c) The organization shall, to the maximum extent practicable, draw upon the resources of the agencies represented in the organization, as well as such other agencies as it may determine, including the Tariff Commission. In addition, the President may establish by regulation such procedures and committees as he may determine to be necessary to enable the organization to provide for the conduct of hearings pursuant to section 252(d), and for the carrying out of other functions assigned to the organization pursuant to this section.

Section 243. *Congressional Delegates to Negotiations*

Before each negotiation under this title, the President shall, upon the recommendation of the Speaker of the House of Representatives, select two members (not of the same political party) of the Committee on Ways and Means, and shall, upon the recommendation of the President of the Senate, select two members (not of the same political party) of the Committee on Finance, who shall be accredited as members of the United States delegation to such negotiation.

CHAPTER 6—GENERAL PROVISIONS

Section 251. *Most-Favored-Nation Principle*

Except as otherwise provided in this title, in section 350(b) of the Tariff Act of 1930, or in section 401(a) of the Tariff Classification Act of 1962, any duty or other import restriction or duty-free treatment proclaimed in carrying out any trade agreement under this title or section 350 of the Tariff Act of 1930 shall apply to products of all foreign countries, whether imported directly or indirectly.

Section 252. *Foreign Import Restrictions*

(a) Whenever unjustifiable foreign import restrictions impair the value of tariff commitments made to the United States, oppress the commerce of the United States, or prevent the expansion of trade on a mutually advantageous basis, the President shall—

(1) take all appropriate and feasible steps within his power to eliminate such restrictions,

(2) refrain from negotiating the reduction or elimination of any United States import restriction under section 201(a) in order to obtain the reduction or elimination of any such restrictions, and

(3) notwithstanding any provision of any trade agreement under this Act and to the extent he deems necessary and appropriate, impose duties or other import restrictions on the products of any foreign country or instrumentality establishing or maintaining such foreign import restrictions against United States agricultural products, when he deems such duties and other import restrictions necessary and appropriate to prevent the establishment or obtain the removal of such foreign import restrictions and to provide access for United States agricultural products to the markets of such country or instrumentality on an equitable basis.

(b) Whenever a foreign country or instrumentality the products of which receive benefits of trade agreement concessions made by the United States—

(1) maintains nontariff trade restrictions, including variable import fees, which substantially burden United States commerce in a manner inconsistent with provisions of trade agreements, or

(2) engages in discriminatory or other acts (including tolerance of international cartels) or policies unjustifiably restricting United States commerce,

the President shall, to the extent that such action is consistent with the purposes of section 102—

(A) suspend, withdraw, or prevent the application of benefits of trade agreement concessions to products of such country or instrumentality, or

(B) refrain from proclaiming benefits of trade agreement concessions to carry out a trade agreement with such country or instrumentality.

(c) Whenever a foreign country or instrumentality, the products of which receive benefits of trade agreement concessions made by the United States, maintains unreasonable import restrictions which either directly or indirectly substantially burden United States commerce, the President may, to the extent that such action is consistent with the purposes of section 102, and having due regard for the international obligations of the United States—

(1) suspend, withdraw, or prevent the application of benefits of trade agreements concessions to products of such country or instrumentality, or

(2) refrain from proclaiming benefits of trade agreement concessions to carry out a trade agreement with such country or instrumentality.

(d) The President shall provide an opportunity for the presentation of views concerning foreign import restrictions which are referred to in subsections (a), (b), and (c) and are maintained against United States commerce. Upon request by any interested person, the President shall, through the organization established pursuant to section 242(a), provide for appropriate public hearings with respect to such restrictions after reasonable notice and provide for the issuance of regulations concerning the conduct of such hearings.

Section 253. *Staging Requirements*

(a) Except as otherwise provided in this section and in section 254, the aggregate reduction in the rate of duty on any article which is in effect on any day pursuant to a trade agreement under this title shall not exceed the aggregate reduction which would have been in effect on such day if—

(1) one-fifth of the total reduction under such agreement for such article had taken effect on the date of the first proclamation pursuant to section 201(a) to carry out such trade agreement, and

(2) the remaining four-fifths of such total reduction had taken effect

in four equal installments at 1-year intervals after the date referred to in paragraph (1).

(b) Subsection (a) shall not apply to any article with respect to which the President has made a determination under section 213(a).

(c) In the case of an article the rate of duty on which has been or is to be reduced pursuant to a prior trade agreement, no reduction shall take effect pursuant to a trade agreement entered into under section 201(a) before the expiration of 1 year after the taking effect of the final reduction pursuant to such prior agreement.

(d) If any part of a reduction takes effect, then any time thereafter during which such part of the reduction is not in effect by reason of legislation of the United States or action thereunder shall be excluded in determining—

(1) the 1-year intervals referred to in subsection (a)(2), and

(2) the expiration of the 1 year referred to in subsection (c).

Section 254. *Rounding Authority*

If the President determines that such action will simplify the computation of the amount of duty imposed with respect to an article, he may exceed the limitation provided by section 201(b)(1) or 253 by not more than whichever of the following is lesser:

(1) the difference between the limitation and the next lower whole number, or

(2) one-half of 1 percent ad valorem or an amount the ad valorem equivalent of which is one-half of 1 percent.

Section 255. *Termination*

(a) Every trade agreement entered into under this title shall be subject to termination or withdrawal, upon due notice, at the end of a period specified in the agreement. Such period shall not be more than 3 years from the date on which the agreement becomes effective. If the agreement is not terminated or withdrawn from at the end of the period so specified, it shall be subject to termination or withdrawal thereafter upon not more than 6 months' notice.

(b) The President may at any time terminate, in whole or in part, any proclamation made under this title.

Section 256. *Definitions*

For purposes of this title—

(1) The term "European Economic Community" means the instrumentality known by such name or any successor thereto.

(2) The countries of the European Economic Community as of any date shall be those countries which on such date are agreed to achieve a common external tariff through the European Economic Community.

(3) The term "agreement with the European Economic Community" means an agreement to which the United States and all countries of the European Economic Community (determined as of the date such agreement is entered into) are parties. For purposes of the preceding sentence, each country for which the European Economic Community signs an agreement shall be treated as a party to such agreement.

(4) The term "existing on July 1, 1962", as applied to a rate of duty, refers to the lowest nonpreferential rate of duty (however established, and even though temporarily suspended by Act of Congress or otherwise) existing on such date or (if lower) the lowest nonpreferential rate to which the United States is committed on such date and which may be proclaimed under section 350 of the Tariff Act of 1930.

(5) The term "existing on July 1, 1934", as applied to a rate of duty, refers to the rate of duty (however established, and even though temporarily suspended by Act of Congress or otherwise) existing on such date.

(6) The term "existing" without the specification of any date, when used with respect to any matter relating to entering into, or any proclamation to carry out, a trade agreement, means existing on the day on which such trade agreement is entered into, and, when referring to a rate of duty, refers to the rate of duty (however established, and even though temporarily suspended by Act of Congress or otherwise) existing on such day.

(7) The term "ad valorem equivalent" means the ad valorem equivalent of a specific rate or, in the case of a combination of rates including a specific rate, the sum of the ad valorem equivalent of the specific rate and of the ad valorem rate. The ad valorem equivalent shall be determined by the President on the basis of the value of imports of the article concerned during a period determined by him to be representative. In determining the value of imports, the President shall utilize, to the maximum extent practicable, the standards of valuation contained in section 402 or 402a of the Tariff Act of 1930 (19 U.S.C., sec. 1401a

or 1402) applicable to the article concerned during such representative period.

Section 257. *Relation to Other Laws*

(a) The first sentence of subsection (b) of section 350 of the Tariff Act of 1930 is amended by striking out "this section" each place it appears and inserting in lieu thereof "this section or the Trade Expansion Act of 1962". The second sentence of such subsection (b) is amended by striking out "this Act" and inserting in lieu thereof "this Act or the Trade Expansion Act of 1962". The third sentence of such subsection (b) is amended by striking out "1955," in paragraph (2) and inserting in lieu thereof "1955, and before July 1, 1962," and by adding at the end thereof the following new paragraph:

"(3) In order to carry out a foreign trade agreement entered into after June 30, 1962, and before July 1, 1967, below the lowest rate permissible by applying title II of the Trade Expansion Act of 1962 to the rate of duty (however established, and even though temporarily suspended by Act of Congress or otherwise) existing on July 1, 1962, with respect to such product."

(b) Subsections (a)(5) and (e) of section 350 of the Tariff Act of 1930 are repealed.

(c) For purposes only of entering into trade agreements pursuant to the notices of intention to negotiate published in the Federal Register of May 28, 1960, and the Federal Register of November 23, 1960, the period during which the President is authorized to enter into foreign trade agreements under section 350 of the Tariff Act of 1930 is hereby extended from the close of June 30, 1962, until the close of December 31, 1962.

(d) The second and third sentences of section 2(a) of the Act entitled "An Act to amend the Tariff Act of 1930", approved June 12, 1934, as amended (19 U.S.C., sec. 1352(a)), are each amended by striking out "this Act" and inserting in lieu thereof "this Act or the Trade Expansion Act of 1962".

(e)(1) Section 5, 6, 7, and 8(a) of the Trade Agreements Extension Act of 1951 are repealed.

(2) Action taken by the President under section 5 of such Act and in effect on the date of the enactment of this Act shall be considered as having been taken by the President under section 231.

(3) Any investigation by the Tariff Commission under section 7 of such Act which is in progress on the date of the enactment of this Act shall be

continued under section 301 as if the application by the interested party were a petition under such section for tariff adjustment under section 351. For purposes of section 301(f), such petition shall be treated as having been filed on the date of the enactment of this Act.

(f) Section 2 of the Act entitled "An Act to extend the authority of the President to enter into trade agreements under section 350 of the Tariff Act of 1930, as amended", approved July 1, 1954, is repealed. Any action (including any investigation begun) under such section 2 before the date of the enactment of this Act shall be considered as having been taken or begun under section 232.

(g)(1) Section 102(1) of the Tariff Classification Act of 1962 is amended by striking out "of schedules 1 to 7, inclusive,".

(2) Section 203 of the Tariff Classification Act of 1962 is amended to read as follows:

"SEC. 203. For purposes of applying sections 323 and 350 of the Tariff Act of 1930, as amended, and the Trade Expansion Act of 1962 with respect to the Tariff Schedules of the United States—

"(1) The rate of duty in rate column numbered 2 for each item in schedules 1 to 7, inclusive, of the Tariff Schedules of the United States shall be treated as the rate of duty existing on July 1, 1934.

"(2) The lowest preferential or nonpreferential rate of duty in rate column numbered 1 for each item in schedules 1 to 7, inclusive, of the Tariff Schedules of the United States on the effective date provided in section 501(a) of this Act shall be treated as the lowest preferential or nonpreferential rate of duty, respectively, existing on July 1, 1962; except that in the case of any such item included in a supplemental report made pursuant to section 101(c) of this Act to reflect a change proclaimed by the President after July 1, 1962 (other than a change to which the United States was committed on July 1, 1962), the rate treated as the lowest nonpreferential rate of duty existing on July 1, 1962, shall be the rate which the Commission specifically declares in such supplemental report to be the rate which, in its judgment, conforms to the fullest extent practicable to the rate regarded as existing on July 1, 1962, under section 256(4) of the Trade Expansion Act of 1962.

"(3) Legislation entering into force after the effective date provided for in section 501(a) of this Act which results in the permanent reclassification of any article without specifying the rate of duty applicable thereto, and proclamations under section 202(c) of this Act, shall be considered as having been in effect since June 30, 1962."

(h) Nothing contained in this Act shall be construed to affect in any way the provisions of section 22 of the Agricultural Adjustment Act, or to apply to any import restriction heretofore or hereafter imposed under such section.

(i) Part I of title III of the Tariff Act of 1930 is amended by adding at the end thereof the following new section:

"SEC. 323. CONSERVATION OF FISHERY RESOURCES

"Upon the convocation of a conference on the use or conservation of international fishery resources, the President shall, by all appropriate means at his disposal, seek to persuade countries whose domestic fishing practices or policies affect such resources, to engage in negotiations in good faith relating to the use or conservation of such resources. If, after such efforts by the President and by other countries which have agreed to engage in such negotiations, any other country whose conservation practices or policies affect the interests of the United States and such other countries, has, in the judgment of the President, failed or refused to engage in such negotiations in good faith, the President may, if he is satisfied that such action is likely to be effective in inducing such country to engage in such negotiations in good faith, increase the rate of duty on any fish (in any form) which is the product of such country, for such time as he deems necessary, to a rate not more than 50 percent above the rate existing on July 1, 1934."

Section 258. *References*

All provisions of law (other than this Act and the Trade Agreements Extension Act of 1951) in effect after June 30, 1962, referring to section 350 of the Tariff Act of 1930, to that section as amended, to the Act entitled "An Act to amend the Tariff Act of 1930", approved June 12, 1934, to that Act as amended, or to agreements entered into, or proclamations issued, under any of such provisions, shall be construed, unless clearly precluded by the context, to refer also to this Act, or to agreements entered into or proclamations issued, pursuant to this Act.

TITLE III—TARIFF ADJUSTMENT AND OTHER ADJUSTMENT ASSISTANCE

CHAPTER 1—ELIGIBILITY FOR ASSISTANCE

Section 301. *Tariff Commission Investigations and Reports*

(a)(1) A petition for tariff adjustment under section 351 may be filed with the Tariff Commission by a trade association, firm, certified or recognized union, or other representative of an industry.

(2) A petition for a determination of eligibility to apply for adjustment assistance under chapter 2 may be filed with the Tariff Commission by a firm or its representative, and a petition for a determination of eligibility to apply for adjustment assistance under chapter 3 may be filed with the Tariff Commission by a group of workers or by their certified or recognized union or other duly authorized representative.

(3) Whenever a petition is filed under this subsection, the Tariff Commission shall transmit a copy thereof to the Secretary of Commerce.

(b)(1) Upon the request of the President upon resolution of either the Committee on Finance of the Senate or the Committee on Ways and Means of the House of Representatives, upon its own motion, or upon the filing of a petition under subsection (a)(1), the Tariff Commission shall promptly make an investigation to determine whether, as a result in major part of concessions granted under trade agreements, an article is being imported into the United States in such increased quantities as to cause, or threaten to cause, serious injury to the domestic industry producing an article which is like or directly competitive with the imported article.

(2) In making its determination under paragraph (1), the Tariff Commission shall take into account all economic factors which it considers relevant, including idling of productive facilities, inability to operate at a level of reasonable profit, and unemployment or underemployment.

(3) For purposes of paragraph (1), increased imports shall be considered to cause, or threaten to cause, serious injury to the domestic industry concerned when the Tariff Commission finds that such increased imports have been the major factor in causing, or threatening to cause, such injury.

(4) No investigation for the purpose of paragraph (1) shall be made, upon petition filed under subsection (a)(1), with respect to the same subject matter as a previous investigation under paragraph (1), unless one year has elapsed since the Tariff Commission made its report to the President of the result of such previous investigation.

(c)(1) In the case of a petition by a firm for a determination of eligibility to apply for adjustment assistance under chapter 2, the Tariff Commission shall promptly make an investigation to determine whether, as a result in major part of concessions granted under trade agreements, an article like or directly competitive with an article produced by the firm is being imported into the United States in such increased quantities as to cause, or threaten to cause, serious injury to such firm. In making its determination under this paragraph, the Tariff Commission shall take into account all economic factors which it considers relevant, including idling of productive facilities of the firm, inability of the firm to operate at a level of reasonable profit, and unemployment or underemployment in the firm.

(2) In the case of a petition by a group of workers for a determination of eligibility to apply for adjustment assistance under chapter 3, the Tariff Commission shall promptly make an investigation to determine whether, as a result in a major part of concessions granted under trade agreements, an article like or directly competitive with an article produced by such workers' firm, or an appropriate subdivision thereof, is being imported into the United States in such increased quantities as to cause, or threaten to cause, unemployment or underemployment of a significant number or proportion of the workers of such firm or subdivision.

(3) For purposes of paragraphs (1) and (2), increased imports shall be considered to cause, or threaten to cause, serious injury to a firm or unemployment or underemployment, as the case may be, when the Tariff Commission finds that such increased imports have been the major factor in causing, or threatening to cause, such injury or unemployment or underemployment.

(d)(1) In the course of any investigation under subsection (b)(1), the Tariff Commission shall, after reasonable notice, hold public hearings and shall afford interested parties opportunity to be present, to produce evidence, and to be heard at such hearings.

(2) In the course of any investigation under subsection (c)(1) or (c)(2), thte Tariff Commission shall, after reasonable notice, hold public hearings if requested by the petitioner, or if, within 10 days after notice of the filing of the petition, a hearing is requested by any other party showing a proper interest in the subject matter of the investigation, and shall afford interested parties an opportunity to be present, to produce evidence, and to be heard at such hearings.

(e) Should the Tariff Commission find with respect to any article, as the result of its investigation, the serious injury or threat thereof described in subsection (b), it shall find the amount of the increase in, or imposition of, any duty or other import restriction on such article which is necessary to prevent or remedy such injury and shall include such finding in its report to the President.

(f)(1) The Tariff Commission shall report to the President the results of each investigation under this section and include in each report any dissenting or separate views. The Tariff Commission shall furnish to the President a transcript of the hearings and any briefs which may have been submitted in connection with each investigation.

(2) The report of the Tariff Commission of its determination under subsection (b) shall be made at the earliest practicable time, but not later than 6 months after the date on which the petition is filed (or the date on which the request or resolution is received or the motion is adopted, as the case may be). Upon making such report to the President, the Tariff Commission shall promptly make public such report, and shall cause a summary thereof to be published in the Federal Register.

(3) The report of the Tariff Commission of its determination under subsection (c)(1) or (c)(2) with respect to any firm or group of workers shall be made at the earliest practicable time, but not later than 60 days, after the date on which the petition is filed.

(g) Except as provided in section 257(e)(3), no petition shall be filed under subsection (a), and no request, resolution, or motion shall be made under subsection (b), prior to the close of the 60th day after the date of the enactment of this Act.

Section 302. *Presidential Action After Tariff Commission Determination*

(a) After receiving a report from the Tariff Commission containing an affirmative finding under section 301(b) with respect to any industry, the President may—

(1) provide tariff adjustment for such industry pursuant to section 351 or 352,

(2) provide, with respect to such industry, that its firms may request the Secretary of Commerce for certifications of eligibility to apply for adjustment assistance under chapter 2,

(3) provide, with respect to such industry, that its workers may request the Secretary of Labor for certifications of eligibility to apply for adjustment assistance under chapter 3, or

(4) take any combination of such actions.

(b)(1) The Secretary of Commerce shall certify, as eligible to apply for adjustment assistance under chapter 2, any firm in an industry with respect to which the President has acted under subsection (a)(2), upon a showing by such firm to the satisfaction of the Secretary of Commerce that the increased imports (which the Tariff Commission has determined to result from concessions granted under trade agreements) have caused serious injury or threat thereof to such firm.

(2) The Secretary of Labor shall certify, as eligible to apply for adjust-

ment assistance under chapter 3, any group of workers in an industry with respect to which the President has acted under subsection (a)(3), upon a showing by such group of workers to the satisfaction of the Secretary of Labor that the increased imports (which the Tariff Commission has determined to result from concessions granted under trade agreements) have caused or threatened to cause unemployment or underemployment of a significant number or proportion of workers of such workers' firm or subdivision thereof.

(c) After receiving a report from the Tariff Commission containing an affirmative finding under section 301(c) with respect to any firm or group of workers, the President may certify that such firm or group of workers is eligible to apply for adjustment assistance.

(d) Any certification under subsection (b) or (c) that a group of workers is eligible to apply for adjustment assistance shall specify the date on which the unemployment or underemployment began or threatens to begin.

(e) Whenever the President determines, with respect to any certification of the eligibility of a group of workers, that separations from the firm or subdivision thereof are no longer attributable to the conditions specified in section 301(c)(2) or in subsection (b)(2) of this section, he shall terminate the effect of such certification. Such termination shall apply only with respect to separations occurring after the termination date specified by the President.

CHAPTER 2—ASSISTANCE TO FIRMS

Section 311. *Certification of Adjustment Proposals*

(a) A firm certified under section 302 as eligible to apply for adjustment assistance may, at any time within 2 years after the date of such certification, file an application with the Secretary of Commerce for adjustment assistance under this chapter. Within a reasonable time after filing its application, the firm shall present a proposal for its economic adjustment.

(b) Adjustment assistance under this chapter consists of technical assistance, financial assistance, and tax assistance, which may be furnished singly or in combination. Except as provided in subsection (c), no adjustment assistance shall be provided to a firm under this chapter until its adjustment proposal shall have been certified by the Secretary of Commerce—

(1) to be reasonably calculated materially to contribute to the economic adjustment of the firm,

(2) to give adequate consideration to the interests of the workers of

such firm adversely affected by actions taken in carrying out trade agreements, and

(3) to demonstrate that the firm will make all reasonable efforts to use its own resources for economic development.

(c) In order to assist a firm which has applied for adjustment assistance under this chapter in preparing a sound adjustment proposal, the Secretary of Commerce may furnish technical assistance to such firm prior to certification of its adjustment proposal.

(d) Any certification made pursuant to this section shall remain in force only for such period as the Secretary of Commerce may prescribe.

Section 312. *Use of Existing Agencies*

(a) The Secretary of Commerce shall refer each certified adjustment proposal to such agency or agencies as he determines to be appropriate to furnish the technical and finacnial assistance necessary to carry out such proposal.

(b) Upon receipt of a certified adjustment proposal, each agency concerned shall promptly—

(1) examine the aspects of the proposal relevant to its functions, and

(2) notify the Secretary of Commerce of its determination as to the technical and financial assistance it is prepared to furnish to carry out the proposal.

(c) Whenever and to the extent that any agency to which an adjustment proposal has been referred to notifies the Secretary of Commerce of its determination not to furnish technical or financial assistance, and if the Secretary of Commerce determines that such assistance is necessary to carry out the adjustment proposal, he may furnish adjustment assistance under sections 313 and 314 to the firm concerned.

(d) There are hereby authorized to be appropriated to the Secretary of Commerce such sums as may be necessary from time to time to carry out his functions under this chapter in connection with furnishing adjustment assistance to firms, which sums are authorized to be appropriated to remain available until expended.

Section 313. *Technical Assistance*

(a) Upon compliance with section 312(c), the Secretary of Commerce may provide to a firm, on such terms and conditions as he determines to be appropriate, such technical assistance as in his judgment will materially contribute to the economic adjustment of the firm.

(b) To the maximum extent practicable, the Secretary of Commerce shall furnish technical assistance under this section and section 311(c) through existing agencies, and otherwise through private individuals, firms, or institutions.

(c) The Secretary of Commerce shall require a firm receiving technical assistance under this section or section 311(c) to share the cost thereof to the extent he determines to be appropriate.

Section 314. *Financial Assistance*

(a) Upon compliance with section 312(c), the Secretary of Commerce may provide to a firm, on such terms and conditions as he determines to be appropriate, such financial assistance in the form of guarantees of loans, agreements for deferred participations in loans, or loans, as in his judgment will materially contribute to the economic adjustment of the firm. The assumption of an outstanding indebtedness of the firm, with or without recourse, shall be considered to be the making of a loan for purposes of this section.

(b) Guarantees, agreements for deferred participations, or loans shall be made under this section only for the purpose of making funds available to the firm—

(1) for acquisition, construction, installation, modernization, development, conversion, or expansion of land, plant, buildings, equipment, facilities, or machinery, or

(2) in cases determined by the Secretary of Commerce to be exceptional, to supply working capital.

(c) To the maximum extent practicable, the Secretary of Commerce shall furnish financial assistance under this section through agencies furnishing financial assistance under other law.

Section 315. *Conditions for Financial Assistance*

(a) No loan shall be guaranteed and no agreement for deferred participation in a loan shall be made by the Secretary of Commerce in an amount which exceeds 90 percent of that portion of the loan made for purposes specified in section 314(b).

(b)(1) Any loan made or deferred participation taken up by the Secretary of Commerce shall bear interest at a rate not less than the greater of—

(A) 4 percent per annum, or

(B) a rate determined by the Secretary of the Treasury for the year in which the loan is made or the agreement for such deferred participation is entered into.

(2) The Secretary of the Treasury shall determine annually the rate referred to in paragraph (1)(B), taking into consideration the current average market yields on outstanding interest-bearing marketable public debt obligations of the United States of maturities comparable to those of the loans outstanding under section 314.

(c) Guarantees or agreements for deferred participation shall be made by the Secretary of Commerce only with respect to loans bearing interest at a rate which he determines to be reasonable. In no event shall the guaranteed portion of any loan, or the portion covered by an agreement for deferred participation, bear interest at a rate more than 1 percent per annum above the rate prescribed by subsection (b) (determined when the guarantee is made or the agreement is entered into), unless the Secretary of Commerce shall determine that special circumstances justify a higher rate, in which case such portion of the loan shall bear interest at a rate not more than 2 percent per annum above such prescribed rate.

(d) The Secretary of Commerce shall make no loan or guarantee having a maturity in excess of 25 years, including renewals and extensions, and shall make no agreement for deferred participation in a loan which has a maturity in excess of 25 years, including renewals and extensions. Such limitation on maturities shall not, however, apply to—

(1) securities or obligations received by the Secretary of Commerce as claimant in bankruptcy or equitable reorganization, or as creditor in other proceedings attendant upon insolvency of the obligor, or

(2) an extension or renewal for an additional period not exceeding 10 years, if the Secretary of Commerce determines that such extension or renewal is reasonably necessary for the orderly liquidation of the loan.

(e) No financial assistance shall be provided under section 314 unless the Secretary of Commerce determines that such assistance is not otherwise available to the firm, from sources other than the United States, on reasonable terms, and that there is reasonable assurance of repayment by the borrower.

(f) The Secretary of Commerce shall maintain operating reserves with respect to anticipated claims under guarantees and under agreements for deferred participation made under section 314. Such reserves shall be considered to constitute obligations for purposes of section 1311 of the Supplemental Appropriation Act, 1955 (31 U.S.C., sec. 200).

Section 316. *Administration of Financial Assistance*

(a) In making and administering guarantees, agreements for deferred participation, and loans under section 314, the Secretary of Commerce may—

(1) require security for any such guarantee, agreement, or loan, and enforce, waiver, or subordinate such security;

(2) assign or sell at public or private sale, or otherwise dispose of, upon such terms and conditions and for such consideration as he shall determine to be reasonable, any evidence of debt, contract, claim, personal property, or security assigned to or held by him in connection with such guarantees, agreements, or loans, and collect, compromise, and obtain deficiency judgments with respect to all obligations assigned to or held by him in connection with such guarantees, agreements, or loans until such time as such obligations may be referred to the Attorney General for suit or collection;

(3) renovate, improve, modernize, complete, insure, rent, sell, or otherwise deal with, upon such terms and conditions and for such consideration as he shall determine to be reasonable, any real or personal property conveyed to or otherwise acquired by him in connection with such guarantees, agreements, or loans;

(4) acquire, hold, transfer, release, or convey any real or personal property or any interest therein whenever deemed necessary or appropriate, and execute all legal documents for such purposes; and

(5) exercise all such other powers and take all such other acts as may be necessary or incidental to the carrying out of functions pursuant to section 314.

(b) Any mortgage acquired as security under subsection (a) shall be recorded under applicable State law.

Section 317. *Tax Assistance*

(a) If—

(1) to carry out an adjustment proposal of a firm certified pursuant to section 311, such firm applies for tax assistance under this section within 24 months after the close of a taxable year and alleges in such application that it has sustained a net operating loss for such taxable year,

(2) the Secretary of Commerce determines that any such alleged loss for such taxable year arose predominantly out of the carrying on

of a trade or business which was seriously injured, during such year, by the increased imports which the Tariff Commission has determined to result from concessions granted under trade agreements, and

(3) the Secretary of Commerce determines that tax assistance under this section will materially contribute to the economic adjustments of the firm,

then the Secretary of Commerce shall certify such determinations with respect to such firm for such taxable year. No determination or certification under this subsection shall constitute a determination of the existence or amount of any net operating loss for purposes of section 172 of the Internal Revenue Code of 1954.

(b) Effective with respect to net operating losses for taxable years ending after December 31, 1955, subsection (b) of section 172 of the Internal Revenue Code of 1954 (relating to net operating loss carrybacks and carryovers) is amended to read as follows:

"(b) NET OPERATING LOSS CARRYBACKS AND CARRYOVERS.—

"(1) YEARS TO WHICH LOSS MAY BE CARRIED.—

"(A)(i) Except as provided in clause (ii), a net operating loss for any taxable year ending after December 31, 1957, shall be a net operating loss carryback to each of the 3 taxable years preceding the taxable year of such loss.

"(ii) In the case of a taxpayer with respect to a taxable year ending on or after December 31, 1962, for which a certification has been issued under section 317 of the Trade Expansion Act of 1962, a net operating loss for such taxable year shall be a net operating loss carryback to each of the 5 taxable years preceding the taxable year of such loss.

"(B) Except as provided in subparagraph (C), a net operating loss for any taxable year ending after December 31, 1955, shall be a net operating loss carryover to each of the 5 taxable years following the taxable year of such loss.

"(C) In the case of a taxpayer which is a regulated transportation corporation (as defined in subsection (j)(1)), a net operating loss for any taxable year ending after December 31, 1955, shall (except as provided in subsection (j)) be a net operating loss carryover to each of the 7 taxable years following the taxable year of such loss.

"(2) AMOUNT OF CARRYBACKS AND CARRYOVERS.—Except as provided in subsections (i) and (j), the entire amount of the net operating loss for any taxable year (hereinafter in this section referred to as the 'loss year') shall be carried to the earliest of the taxable years to which (by reason of paragraph (1)) such loss may be carried. The portion of such loss which shall be carried to each of the other taxable years shall be the excess, if any,of the amount of such loss over the sum of the taxable income for each of the prior taxable years to which sum loss may be carried. For purposes of the preceding sentence, the taxable income for any such prior taxable year shall be computed—

"(A) with the modifications specified in subsection (d) other than paragraphs (1), (4), and (6) thereof; and

"(B) by determining the amount of the net operating loss deduction without regard to the net operating loss for the loss year or for any taxable year thereafter,

and the taxable income so computed shall not be considered to be less than zero.

"(3) SPECIAL RULES.—

"(A) Paragraph (1)(A)(ii) shall apply only if—

"(i) there has been filed, at such time and in such manner as may be prescribed by the Secretary or his delegate, a notice of filing of the application under section 317 of the Trade Expansion Act of 1962 for tax assistance, and, after its issuance, a copy of the certification under such section, and

"(ii) the taxpayer consents in writing to the assessment, within such period as may be agreed upon with the Secretary or his delegate, of any deficiency for any year to the extent attributable to the disallowance of a deduction previously allowed with respect to such net operating loss, even though at the time of filing such consent the assessment of such deficiency would otherwise be prevented by the operation of any law or rule of law.

"(B) In the case of—

"(i) a partnership and its partners, or

"(ii) an electing small business corporation under subchapter S and its shareholders, paragraph (1)(A)(ii) shall apply as determined under regulations prescribed by the Secretary or his delegate. Such paragraph shall apply to a net operating loss of a partner or such a shareholder only if it arose predominantly from losses in respect of which certifications under section 317 of the Trade Expansion Act of 1962 were filed under this section."

(c) Subsection (h) of section 6501 of the Internal Revenue Code of 1954 (relating to limitations on assessment and collection in the case of net operating loss carrybacks) is amended by inserting before the period: ", or within 18 months after the date on which the taxpayer files in accordance with section 172(b)(3) a copy of the certification (with respect to such taxable year) issued under section 317 of the Trade Expansion Act of 1962, whichever is later".

(d) Section 6511(d)(2)(A) of the Internal Revenue Code of 1954 (relating to special period of limitation on credit or refund with respect to net operating loss carrybacks) is amended to read as follows:

"(A) PERIOD OF LIMITATION.—If the claim for credit or refund relates to an overpayment attributable to a net operating loss carryback, in lieu of the 3-year period of limitation prescribed in subsection (a), the period shall be that period which ends with the expiration of the 15th day of the 40th month (or the 39th month, in the case of a corporation) following the end of the taxable year of the net operating loss which results in such carryback, or the period prescribed in subsection (c) in respect of such taxable year, whichever expires later; except that—

"(i) with respect to an overpayment attributable to a net operating loss carryback to any year on account of a certification issued to the taxpayer under section 317 of the Trade Expansion Act of 1962, the period shall not expire before the expiration of the sixth month following the month in which such certification is issued to the taxpayer, and

"(ii) with respect to an overpayment attributable to the creation of, or an increase in, a net operating loss carryback as a result of the elimination of excessive profits by a renegotiation (as defined in section 1481(a)(1)(A)), the period shall not expire before September 1, 1959, or the expiration of the twelfth month following the month in which the agreement or order for the elimination of such excessive profits becomes final, whichever is the later.

In the case of such a claim, the amount of the credit or refund may exceed the portion of the tax paid within the period provided in subsection (b)(2) or (c), whichever is applicable, to the extent of the amount of the overpayment attributable to such carryback."

Section 318. *Protective Provisions.*

(a) Each recipient of adjustment assistance under section 313, 314, or 317 shall keep records which fully disclose the amount and disposition by such recipient of the proceeds, if any, of such adjustment assistance, and which will facilitate an effective audit. The recipient shall also keep such other records as the Secretary of Commerce may prescribe.

(b) The Secretary of Commerce and the Comptroller General of the United States shall have access for the purpose of audit and examination to any books, documents, papers, and records of the recipient pertaining to adjustment assistance under sections 313, 314, and 317.

(c) No adjustment assistance shall be extended under section 313, 314, or 317 to any firm unless the owners, partners, or officers certify to the Secretary of Commerce—

(1) the names of any attorneys, agents, and other persons engaged by or on behalf of the firm for the purpose of expediting applications for such adjustment assistance, and

(2) the fees paid or to be paid to any such person.

(d) No financial assistance shall be provided to any firm under section 314 unless the owners, partners, or officers shall execute an agreement binding them and the firm for a period of 2 years after such financial assistance is provided, to refrain from employing, tendering any office or employment to, or retaining for professional services any person who, on the date such assistance or any part thereof was provided, or within one year prior thereto, shall have served as an officer, attorney, agent, or employee occupying a position or engaging in activities which the Secretary of Commerce shall have determined involve discretion with respect to the provision of such financial assistance.

Section 319. *Penalties*

Whoever makes a false statement of a material fact knowing it to be false, or knowingly fails to disclose a material fact, or whoever willfully overvalues any security, for the purpose of influencing in any way the action of the Secretary of Commerce under this chapter, or for the purpose of obtaining money, property, or anything of value under this chapter, shall be fined not more than $5,000 or imprisoned for not more than two years, or both.

Section 320. *Suits*

In providing technical and financial assistance under sections 313 and 314, the Secretary of Commerce may sue and be sued in any court of record of a State having general jurisdiction or in any United States district court, and jurisdiction is conferred upon such district court to determine such controversies without regard to the amount in controversy; but no attachment, injunction, garnishment, or other similar process, mesne or final, shall be issued against him or his property. Nothing in this section shall be construed to except the activities pursuant to sections 313 and 314 from the application of sections 507(b) and 2679 of title 28 of the United States Code, and of section 367 of the Revised Statutes (5 U.S.C., sec. 316).

CHAPTER 3—ASSISTANCE TO WORKERS

Section 321. *Authority*

The Secretary of Labor shall determine whether applicants are entitled to receive assistance under this chapter and shall pay or provide such assistance to applicants who are so entitled.

SUBCHAPTER A—TRADE READJUSTMENT ALLOWANCES

Section 322. *Qualifying Requirements*

(a) Payment of a trade readjustment allowance shall be made to an adversely affected worker who applies for such allowance for any week of unemployment which begins after the 30th day after the date of the enactment of this Act and after the date determined under section 302(d), subject to the requirements of subsections (b) and (c).

(b) Total or partial separation shall have occurred—

(1) after the date of the enactment of this Act, and after the date determined under section 302(d), and

(2) before the expiration of the 2-year period beginning on the day on which the most recent determination under section 302(d) was made, and before the termination date (if any) specified under section 302(e).

(c) Such worker shall have had—

(1) in the 156 weeks immediately preceding such total or partial separation, at least 78 weeks of employment at wages of $15 or more a week, and

(2) in the 52 weeks immediately preceding such total or partial separation, at least 26 weeks of employment at wages of $15 or more a week in a firm or firms with respect to which a determination of unemployment or underemployment under section 302 has been made, or

if data with respect to weeks of employment are not available, equivalent amounts of employment computed under regulations prescribed by the Secretary of Labor.

Section 323. *Weekly Amounts*

(a) Subject to the other provisions of this section, the trade readjustment allowance payable to an adversely affected worker for a week of unemployment shall be an amount equal to 65 percent of his average weekly wage or to 65 percent of the average weekly manufacturing wage, whichever is less, reduced by 50 percent of the amount of his remuneration for services performed during such week.

(b) Any adversely affected worker who is entitled to trade readjustment allowances and who is undergoing training approved by the Secretary of Labor, including on-the-job training, shall receive for each week in which he is undergoing any such training, a trade readjustment allowance in an amount (computed for such week) equal to the amount computed under subsection (a) or (if greater) the amount of any weekly allowance for such training to which he would be entitled under any other Federal law for the training of workers, if he applied for such allowance. Such trade readjustment allowance shall be paid in lieu of any training allowance to which the worker would be entitled under such other Federal law.

(c) The amount of trade readjustment allowance payable to an adversely affected worker under subsection (a) or (b) for any week shall be reduced by any amount of unemployment insurance which he has received or is seeking with respect to such week; but, if the appropriate State or Federal agency finally determines that the worker was not entitled to unemployment insurance with respect to such week, the reduction shall not apply with respect to such week.

(d) If unemployment insurance, or a training allowance under the Manpower Development and Training Act of 1962 or the Area Redevelopment Act, is paid to an adversely affected worker for any week of unemployment with respect to which he would be entitled (determined without regard to subsection (c) or (e) or to any disqualification under section 327) to a trade readjustment allowance if he applied for such allowance, each such week shall be deducted from the total number of weeks of trade readjustment allowance otherwise payable to him under section 324(a) when he applies for a trade readjustment allowance and is determined to be entitled to such allowance. If the unemployment insurance or the training allowance paid to such worker for any week of unemployment is less than the amount of the trade readjustment allowance to which he would be entitled if he applied for such allowance, he shall receive, when he applies for a trade readjustment allowance and is determined to be entitled to such allowance, a trade readjustment allowance for such week equal to such difference.

(e) Whenever, with respect to any week of unemployment, the total amount payable to an adversely affected worker as remuneration for services performed during such week, as unemployment·insurance, as a training allowance referred to in subsection (d), and as a trade readjustment allowance would exceed 75 percent of his average weekly wage, his trade readjustment allowance for such week shall be reduced by the amount of such excess.

(f) The amount of any weekly payment to be made under this section which is not a whole dollar amount shall be rounded upward to the next higher whole dollar amount.

(g)(1) If unemployment insurance is paid under a State law to an adversely affected worker for a week for which—

(A) he receives a trade readjustment allowance, or

(B) he makes application for a trade readjustment allowance and would be entitled (determined without regard to subsection (c) or (e)) to receive such allowance,

the State agency making such payment shall, unless it has been reimbursed for such payment under other Federal law, be reimbursed from funds appropriated pursuant to section 337, to the extent such payment does not exceed the amount of the trade readjustment allowance which such worker would have received, or would have been entitled to receive, as the case may be, if he had not received the State payment. The amount of such reimbursement shall be determined by the Secretary of Labor on the basis of reports furnished to him by the State agency.

(2) In any case in which a State agency is reimbursed under paragraph (1) for payments of unemployment insurance made to an adversely affected worker, such payments, and the period of unemployment of such worker for which such payments were made, may be disregarded under the State law (and for purposes of applying section 3303 of the Internal Revenue Code of 1954) in determining whether or not an employer is entitled to a reduced rate of contribution permitted by the State law.

Section 324. *Time Limitations on Trade Readjustment Allowances*

(a) Payment of trade readjustment allowances shall not be made to an adversely affected worker for more than 52 weeks, except that, in accordance with regulations prescribed by the Secretary of Labor—

(1) such payments may be made for not more than 26 additional weeks to an adversely affected worker to assist him to complete training approved by the Secretary of Labor, or

(2) such payments shall be made for not more than 13 additional weeks to an adversely affected worker who had reached his 60th birthday on or before the date of total or partial separation.

(b) Except for a payment made for an additional week specified in subsection (a), a trade readjustment allowance shall not be paid for a week of unemployment beginning more than 2 years after the beginning of the appropriate week. A trade readjustment allowance shall not be paid for any additional week specified in subsection (a) if such week begins more than 3 years after the beginning of the appropriate week. The appropriate week for a totally separated worker is the week of his most recent total separation. The appropriate week for a partially separated worker is the week in respect of which he first receives a trade readjustment allowance following his most recent partial separation.

Section 325. *Application of State Laws*

Except where inconsistent with the provisions of this chapter and subject to such regulations as the Secretary of Labor may prescribe, the availability and disqualification provisions of the State law—

(1) under which an adversely affected worker is entitled to unemployment insurance (whether or not he has filed a claim for such insurance), or

(2) if he is not so entitled to unemployment insurance, of the State in which he was totally or partially separated,

shall apply to any such worker who files a claim for trade readjustment allowances. The State law so determined with respect to a separation of a worker shall remain applicable, for purposes of the preceding sentence, with respect to such separation until such worker becomes entitled to unemployment insurance under another State law (whether or not he has filed a claim for such insurance).

SUBCHAPTER B—TRAINING

Section 326. *In General*

(a) To assure that the readjustment of adversely affected workers shall occur as quickly and effectively as possible, with minimum reliance upon trade readjustment allowances under this chapter, every effort shall be made to prepare each such worker for full employment in accordance with his capabilities and prospective employment opportunities. To this end, and subject to this chapter, adversely affected workers shall be afforded, where appropriate, the testing, counseling, training, and placement services provided for under any Federal law. Such workers may also be afforded supplemental assistance necessary to defray transportation and subsistence expenses for separate maintenance when such training is provided in facilities which are not within commuting distance of their regular place of residence. The Secretary of Labor in defraying such subsistence expenses shall not afford any individual an allowance exceeding $5 a day; nor shall the Secretary authorize any transportation expense exceeding the rate of 10 cents per mile.

(b) To the extent practicable, before adversely affected workers are referred to training, the Secretary of Labor shall consult with such workers' firm and their certified or recognized union or other duly authorized representative and develop a worker retraining plan which provides for training such workers to meet the manpower needs of such firm, in order to preserve or restore the employment relationship between the workers and the firm.

Section 327. *Disqualification for Refusal of Training, etc.*

Any adversely affected worker who, without good cause, refuses to accept or continue, or fails to make satisfactory progress in, suitable training to which he has been referred by the Secretary of Labor shall not thereafter be entitled to trade readjustment allowances until he enters or resumes training to which he has been so referred.

SUBCHAPTER C—RELOCATION ALLOWANCES

Section 328. *Relocation Allowances Afforded*

Any adversely affected worker who is the head of a family as defined in regulations prescribed by the Secretary of Labor and who has been totally separated may file an application for a relocation allowance, subject to the terms and conditions of this subchapter.

Section 329. *Qualifying Requirements*

(a) A relocation allowance may be granted only to assist an adversely affected worker in relocating within the United States and only if the Secretary of Labor determines that such worker cannot reasonably be expected to secure suitable employment in the commuting area in which he resides and that such worker—

(1) has obtained suitable employment affording a reasonable ex-

pectation of long-term duration in the area in which he wishes to relocate, or

(2) has obtained a bona fide offer of such employment.

(b) A relocation allowance shall not be granted to such worker unless—

(1) for the week in which the application for such allowance is filed, he is entitled (determined without regard to section 323 (c) and (e)) to a trade readjustment allowance or would be so entitled (determined without regard to whether he filed application therefor) but for the fact that he has obtained the employment referred to in subsection (a)(1), and

(2) such relocation occurs within a reasonable period after the filing of such application or (in the case of a worker who has been referred to training by the Secretary of Labor) within a reasonable period after the conclusion of such training.

Section 330. *Relocation Allowance Defined*

For purposes of this subchapter, the term "relocation allowance" means—

1) the reasonable and necessary expenses, as specified in regulations prescribed by the Secretary of Labor, incurred in transporting a worker and his family and their household effects, and

(2) a lump sum equivalent to two and one-half times the average weekly manufacturing wage.

SUBCHAPTER D—GENERAL PROVISIONS

Section 331. *Agreements With States*

(a) The Secretary of Labor is authorized on behalf of the United States to enter into an agreement with any State, or with any State agency. Under such an agreement, the State agency (1) as agent of the United States, will receive applications for, and will provide, assistance on the basis provided in this chapter, (2) where appropriate, will afford adversely affected workers who apply for assistance under this chapter testing, counseling, referral to training, and placement services, and (3) otherwise cooperate with the Secretary of Labor and with other State and Federal agencies in providing assistance under this chapter.

(b) Each agreement under this subchapter shall provide the terms and conditions upon which the agreement may be amended, suspended, or terminated.

(c) Each agreement under this subchapter shall provide that unemployment insurance otherwise payable to any adversely affected worker will not be denied or reduced for any week by reason of any right to allowances under this chapter.

Section 332. *Payments to States*

(a) The Secretary of Labor shall from time to time certify to the Secretary of the Treasury for payment to each State which has entered into an agreement under section 331(1) the sums necessary to enable such State as agent of the United States to make payments of allowances provided for by this chapter, and (2) the sums reimbursable to a State pursuant to section 323(g). The Secretary of the Treasury, prior to audit or settlement by the General Accounting Office, shall make payment to the State in accordance with such certification, from the funds for carrying out the purposes of this chapter. Sums reimbursable to a State pursuant to section 323(g) shall be credited to the account of such State in the Unemployment Trust Fund and shall be used only for the payment of cash benefits to individuals with respect to their unemployment, exclusive of expenses of administration.

(b) All money paid a State under this section shall be used solely for the purposes for which it is paid; and any money so paid which is not used for such purposes shall be returned, at the time specified in the agreement under this subchapter, to the Treasury and credited to current applicable appropriations, funds, or accounts from which payments to States under this section may be made.

(c) Any agreement under this subchapter may require any officer or employee of the State certifying payments or disbursing funds under the agreement, or otherwise participating in the performance of the agreement, to give a surety bond to the United States in such amount as the Secretary of Labor may deem necessary, and may provide for the payment of the cost of such bond from funds for carrying out the purposes of this chapter.

Section 333. *Liabilities of Certifying and Disbursing Officers*

(a) No person designated by the Secretary of Labor, or designated pursuant to an agreement under this subchapter, as a certifying officer, shall, in the absence of gross negligence or intent to defraud the United States, be liable with respect to the payment of any allowance certified by him under this chapter.

(b) No disbursing officer shall, in the absence of gross negligence or intent to defraud the United States, be liable with respect to any payment by him under this chapter if it was based upon a voucher signed by a certifying officer designated as provided in subsection (a).

Section 334. *Recovery of Overpayments*

(a) If a State agency or the Secretary of Labor, or a court of competent jurisdiction finds that any person—

(1) has made, or has caused to be made by another, a false statement or representation of a material fact knowing it to be false, or has knowingly failed or caused another to fail to disclose a material fact; and

(2) as a result of such action has received any payment of allowances under this chapter to which he was not entitled,

such person shall be liable to repay such amount to the State agency or the Secretary of Labor, as the case may be, or either may recover such amount by deductions from any allowance payable to such person under this chapter. Any such finding by a State agency or the Secretary of Labor may be made only after an opportunity for a fair hearing.

(b) Any amount repaid to a State agency under this section shall be deposited into the fund from which payment was made. Any amount repaid to the Secretary of Labor under this section shall be returned to the Treasury and credited to the current applicable appropriation, fund, or account from which payment was made.

Section 335. *Penalties*

Whoever makes a false statement of a material fact knowing it to be false, or knowingly fails to disclose a material fact, for the purpose of obtaining or increasing for himself or for any other person any payment or assistance authorized to be furnished under this chapter or pursuant to an agreement under section 331 shall be fined not more than $1,000 or imprisoned for not more than one year, or both.

Section 336. *Review*

Except as may be provided in regulations prescribed by the Secretary of Labor to carry out his functions under this chapter, determinations under this chapter as to the entitlement of individuals for adjustment assistance shall be final and conclusive for all purposes and not subject to review by any court or any other officer. To the maximum extent practicable and consistent with the purposes of this chapter, such regulations shall provide that such determinations by a State agency will be subject to review in the same manner and to the same extent as determinations under the State law.

Section 337. *Authorization of Appropriations*

There are hereby authorized to be appropriated to the Secretary of Labor such sums as may be necessary from time to time to carry out his functions under this chapter in connection with furnishing adjustment assistance to workers, which sums are authorized to be appropriated to remain available until expended.

Section 338. *Definitions*

For purposes of this chapter—

(1) The term "adversely affected employment" means employment in a firm or appropriate subdivision of a firm, if workers of such firm or subdivision are eligible to apply for adjustment assistance under this chapter.

(2) The term "adversely affected worker" means an individual who, because of lack of work in an adversely affected employment—

(A) has been totally or partially separated from such employment, or

(B) has been totally separated from employment with the firm in a subdivision of which such adversely affected employment exists.

(3) The term "average weekly manufacturing wage" means the national gross average weekly earnings of production workers in manufacturing industries for the latest calendar year (as officially published annually by the Bureau of Labor Statistics of the Department of Labor) most recently published before the period for which the assistance under this chapter is furnished.

(4) The term "average weekly wage" means one-13th of the total wages paid to an individual in the high quarter. For purposes of this computation, the high quarter shall be that quarter in which the individual's total wages were highest among the first 4 of the last 5 completed calendar quarters immediately before the quarter in which occurs the week with respect to which the computation is made. Such week shall be the week in which total separation occurred, or, in cases where partial separation is claimed, an appropriate week, as defined in regulations prescribed by the Secretary of Labor.

(5) The term "average weekly hours" means the average hours worked by the individual (excluding overtime) in the employment from which he has been or claims to have been separated in the 52 weeks (excluding weeks during which the individual was sick or on vacation) preceding the week specified in the last sentence of paragraph (4).

(6) The term "partial separation" means, with respect to an individual who has not been totally separated, that he has had his hours of

work reduced to 80 percent or less of his average weekly hours in adversely affected employment and his wages reduced to 75 percent or less of his average weekly wage in such adversely affected employment.

(7) The term "remuneration" means wages and net earnings derived from services performed as a self-employed individual.

(8) The term "State" includes the District of Columbia and the Commonwealth of Puerto Rico; and the term "United States" when used in the geographical sense includes such Commonwealth.

(9) The term "State agency" means the agency of the State which administers the State law.

(10) The term "State law" means the unemployment insurance law of the State approved by the Secretary of Labor under section 3304 of the Internal Revenue Code of 1954.

(11) The term "total separation" means the layoff or severance of an individual from employment with a firm in which, or in a subdivision of which, adversely affected employment exists.

(12) The term "unemployment insurance" means the unemployment insurance payable to an individual under any State law or Federal unemployment insurance law, including title XV of the Social Security Act, the Railroad Unemployment Insurance Act, and the Temporary Extended Unemployment Compensation Act of 1961.

(13) The term "week" means a week as defined in the applicable State law.

(14) The term "week of unemployment" means with respect to an individual any week for which his remuneration for services performed during such week is less than 75 percent of his average weekly wage and which, because of lack of work—

(A) if he has been totally separated, he worked less than the full-time week (excluding overtime) in his current occupation, or

(B) if he has been partially separated, he worked 80 percent or less of his average weekly hours.

CHAPTER 4—TARIFF ADJUSTMENT

Section 351. *Authority*

(a)(1) After receiving an affirmative finding of the Tariff Commission under section 301(b) with respect to an industry, the President may proclaim such increase in, or imposition of, any duty or other import restriction on the article causing or threatening to cause serious injury to such industry as he determines to be necessary to prevent or remedy serious injury to such industry.

(2) If the President does not, within 60 days after the date on which he receives such affirmative finding, proclaim the increase in, or imposition of, any duty or other import restriction on such article found and reported by the Tariff Commission pursuant to section 301(e)—

(A) he shall immediately submit a report to the House of Representatives and to the Senate stating why he has not proclaimed such increase or imposition, and

(B) such increase or imposition shall take effect (as provided in paragraph (3)) upon the adoption by both Houses of the Congress (within the 60-day period following the date on which the report referred to in subparagraph (A) is submitted to the House of Representatives and the Senate), by the yeas and nays by the affirmative vote of a majority of the authorized membership of each House, of a concurrent resolution stating in effect that the Senate and House of Representatives approve the increase in, or imposition of, any duty or other import restriction on the article found and reported by the Tariff Commission.

For purposes of subparagraph (B), in the computation of the 60-day period there shall be excluded the days on which either House is not in session because of adjournment of more than 3 days to a day certain or an adjournment of the Congress sine die. The report referred to in subparagraph (A) shall be delivered to both Houses of the Congress on the same day and shall be delivered to the Clerk of the House of Representatives if the House of Representatives is not in session and to the Secretary of the Senate if the Senate is not in session.

(3) In any case in which the contingency set forth in paragraph (2)(B) occurs, the President shall (within 15 days after the adoption of such resolution) proclaim the increase in, or imposition of, any duty or other import restriction on the article which was found and reported by the Tariff Commission pursuant to section 301(e).

(4) The President may, within 60 days after the date on which he receives an affirmative finding of the Tariff Commission under section 301(b) with respect to an industry, request additional information from the Tariff Commission. The Tariff Commission shall, as soon as practicable but in no event more than 120 days after the date on which it receives the

President's request, furnish additional information with respect to such industry in a supplemental report. For purposes of paragraph (2), the date on which the President receives such supplemental report shall be treated as the date on which the President received the affirmative finding of the Tariff Commission with respect to such industry.

(b) No proclamation pursuant to subsection (a) shall be made—

(1) increasing any rate of duty to a rate more than 50 percent above the rate existing on July 1, 1934, or, if the article is dutiable but no rate existed on July 1, 1934, the rate existing at the time of the proclamation,

(2) in the case of an article not subject to duty, imposing a duty in excess of 50 percent ad valorem.

For purposes of paragraph (1), the term "existing on July 1, 1934" has the meaning assigned to such term by paragraph (5) of section 256.

(c)(1) Any increase in, or imposition of, any duty or other import restriction proclaimed pursuant to this section or section 7 of the Trade Agreements Extension Act of 1951—

(A) may be reduced or terminated by the President when he determines, after taking into account the advice received from the Tariff Commission under subsection (d)(2) and after seeking advice of the Secretary of Commerce and the Secretary of Labor, that such reduction or termination is in the national interest, and

(B) unless extended under paragraph (2), shall terminate not later than the close of the date which is 4 years (or, in the case of any such increase or imposition proclaimed pursuant to such section 7, 5 years) after the effective date of the initial proclamation or the date of the enactment of this Act, whichever date is the later.

(2) Any increase in, or imposition of, any duty or other import restriction proclaimed pursuant to this section or pursuant to section 7 of the Trade Agreements Extension Act of 1951 may be extended in whole or in part by the President for such periods (not in excess of 4 years at any one time) as he may designate if he determines, after taking into account the advice received from the Tariff Commission under subsection (d)(3) and after seeking advice of the Secretary of Commerce and the Secretary of Labor, that such extension is in the national interest.

(d)(1) So long as any increase in, or imposition of, any duty or other import restriction pursuant to this section or pursuant to section 7 of the

Trade Agreements Extension Act of 1951 remains in effect, the Tariff Commission shall keep under review developments with respect to the industry concerned, and shall make annual reports to the President concerning such developments.

(2) Upon request of the President or upon its own motion, the Tariff Commission shall advise the President of its judgment as to the probable economic effect on the industry concerned of the reduction or termination of the increase in, or imposition of, any duty or other import restriction pursuant to this section or section 7 of the Trade Agreements Extension Act of 1951.

(3) Upon petition on behalf of the industry concerned, filed with the Tariff Commission not earlier than the date which is 9 months, and not later than the date which is 6 months, before the date any increase or imposition referred to in paragraph (1) or (2) of subsection (c) is to terminate by reason of the expiration of the applicable period prescribed in paragraph (1) or an extension thereof under paragraph (2), the Tariff Commission shall advise the President of its judgment as to the probable economic effect on such industry of such termination.

(4) In advising the President under this subsection as to the probable economic effect on the industry concerned, the Tariff Commission shall take into account all economic factors which it considers relevant including idling of productive facilities, inability to operate at a level of reasonable profit, and unemployment or underemployment.

(5) Advice by the Tariff Commission under this subsection shall be given on the basis of an investigation during the course of which the Tariff Commission shall hold a hearing at which interested persons shall be given a reasonable opportunity to be present, to produce evidence, and to be heard.

(e) The President, as soon as practicable, shall take such action as he determines to be necessary to bring trade agreements entered into under section 350 of the Tariff Act of 1930 into conformity with the provisions of this section. No trade agreement shall be entered into under section 201(a) unless such agreement permits action in conformity with the provisions of this section.

Section 352. *Orderly Marketing Agreements*

(a) After receiving an affirmative finding of the Tariff Commission under section 301(b) with respect to an industry, the President may, in lieu of exercising the authority contained in section 351(a)(1) but subject to the provisions of section 351(a) (2), (3), and (4), negotiate international agreements with foreign countries limiting the export from such countries and the import into the United States of the article causing or threatening to cause serious injury to such industry, whenever he determines that such action would be more appropriate to prevent or remedy serious injury to such industry than action under section 351(a)(1).

(b) In order to carry out an agreement concluded under subsection (a), the President is authorized to issue regulations governing the entry or withdrawal from warehouse of the article covered by such agreement. In addition, in order to carry out a multilateral agreement concluded under subsection (a) among countries accounting for a significant part of world trade in the article covered by such agreement, the President is also authorized to issue regulations governing the entry or withdrawal from warehouse of the like article which is the product of countries not parties to such agreement.

CHAPTER 5—ADVISORY BOARD

Section 361. *Adjustment Assistance Advisory Board*

(a) There is hereby created the Adjustment Assistance Advisory Board, which shall consist of the Secretary of Commerce, as Chairman, and the Secretaries of the Treasury, Agriculture, Labor, Interior, and Health, Education, and Welfare, the Administrator of the Small Business Administration, and such other officers as the President deems appropriate. Each member of the Board may designate an officer of his agency to act for him as a member of the Board. The Chairman may from time to time invite the participation of officers of other agencies of the executive branch.

(b) At the request of the President, the Board shall advise him and the agencies furnishing adjustment assistance pursuant to chapters 2 and 3 on the development of coordinated programs for such assistance, giving full consideration to ways of preserving and restoring the employment relationship of firms and workers where possible, consistent with sound economic adjustment.

(c) The Chairman may appoint for any industry an industry committee composed of members representing employers, workers, and the public, for the purpose of advising the Board. Members of any such committee shall, while attending meetings, be entitled to receive compensation and reimbursement as provided in section 401(3). The provisions of section 1003 of the National Defense Education Act of 1958 (20 U.S.C. 583) shall apply to members of such committee.

TITLE IV—GENERAL PROVISIONS

Section 401. *Authorities*

The head of any agency performing functions under this Act may—

(1) authorize the head of any other agency to perform any of such functions;

(2) prescribe such rules and regulations as may be necessary to perform such functions; and

(3) to the extent necessary to perform such functions, procure the temporary (not in excess of one year) or intermittent services of experts or consultants or organizations thereof, including stenographic reporting services, by contract or appointment, and in such cases such services shall be without regard to the civil service and classification laws, and, except in the case of stenographic reporting services by organizations, without regard to section 3709 of the Revised Statutes (41 U.S.C. 5). Any individual so employed may be compensated at a rate not in excess of $75 per diem, and, while such individual is away from his home or regular place of business, he may be allowed transportation and not to exceed $16 per diem in lieu of subsistence and other expenses.

Section 402. *Reports*

(a) The President shall submit to the Congress an annual report on the trade agreements program and on tariff adjustment and other adjustment assistance under this Act. Such report shall include information regarding new negotiations, changes made in duties and other import restrictions of the United States, reciprocal concessions obtained, changes in trade agreements in order to effectuate more fully the purposes of the trade agreement program (including the incorporation therein of escape clauses), the results of action taken to obtain removal of foreign trade restrictions (including discriminatory restrictions) against United States exports, remaining restrictions, and the measures available to seek their removal in accordance with the purposes of this Act, and other information relating to the trade agreements program and to the agreements entered into thereunder.

(b) The Tariff Commission shall submit to the Congress, at least once a year, a factual report on the operation of the trade agreements program.

Section 403. *Tariff Commission*

(a) In order to expedite the performance of its functions under this Act, the Tariff Commission may conduct preliminary investigations, determine the scope and manner of its proceedings, and consolidate proceedings before it.

(b) In performing its functions under this Act, the Tariff Commission may exercise any authority granted to it under any other Act.

(c) The Tariff Commission shall at all times keep informed concerning the operation and effect of provisions relating to duties or other import restrictions of the United States contained in trade agreements entered into under the trade agreements program.

Section 404. *Separability*

If any provision of this Act or the application of any provision to any circumstances or persons shall be held invalid, the validity of the remainder of this Act, and of the application of such provision to other circumstances or persons, shall not be affected thereby.

Section 405. *Definitions*

For the purposes of this Act—

(1) The term "agency" includes any agency, department, board, wholly or partly owned corporation, instrumentality, commission, or establishment of the United States.

(2) The term "duty or other import restriction" includes (A) the rate and form of an import duty, and (B) a limitation, prohibition, charge, and exaction other than duty, imposed on importation or imposed for the regulation of imports.

(3) The term "firm" includes an individual proprietorship, partnership, joint venture, association, corporation (including a development corporation), business trust, cooperative, trustees in bankruptcy, and receivers under decree of any court. A firm, together with any predecessor, successor, or affiliated firm controlled or substantially beneficially owned by substantially the same persons, may be considered a single firm where necessary to prevent unjustifiable benefits.

(4) An imported article is "directly competitive with" a domestic article at an earlier or later stage of processing, and a domestic article is "directly competitive with" an imported article at an earlier or later stage of processing, if the importation of the imported article has an economic effect on producers of the domestic article comparable to the effect of importation of articles in the same stage of processing as the domestic article. For purposes of this paragraph, the unprocessed article is at an earlier stage of processing.

(5) A product of a country or area is an article which is the growth, produce, or manufacture of such country or area.

(6) The term "modification", as applied to any duty or other import restriction, includes the elimination of any duty.

4. Trade Act of 1974

AN ACT To promote the development of an open, nondiscriminatory, and fair world economic system, to stimulate fair and free competition between the United States and foreign nations, to foster the economic growth of, and full employment in, the United States, and for other purposes.

Be it enacted by the Senate and House of Representatives of the United States of America in Congress assembled, That this Act, with the following table of contents, may be cited as the "Trade Act of 1974".

Section 2. *Statement of Purposes*

The purposes of this Act are, through trade agreements affording mutual benefits—

(1) to foster the economic growth of and full employment in the United States and to strengthen economic relations between the United States and foreign countries through open and nondiscriminatory world trade;

(2) to harmonize, reduce, and eliminate barriers to trade on a basis which assures substantially equivalent competitive opportunities for the commerce of the United States;

(3) to establish fairness and equity in international trading relations, including reform of the General Agreement on Tariffs and Trade;

(4) to provide adequate procedures to safeguard American industry and labor against unfair or injurious import competition, and to assist industries, firm workers, and communities to adjust to changes in international trade flows;

(5) to open up market opportunities for United States commerce in nonmarket economies; and

6) to provide fair and reasonable access to products of less developed countries in the United States market.

TITLE I—NEGOTIATING AND OTHER AUTHORITY

Chapter 1—Rates of Duty and Other Trade Barriers

Section 101. *Basic Authority for Trade Agreements*

(a) Whenever the President determines that any existing duties or other import restrictions of any foreign country or the United States are unduly burdening and restricting the foreign trade of the United States and that the purposes of this Act will be promoted thereby, the President—

(1) during the 5-year period beginning on the date of the enactment of this Act, may enter into trade agreements with foreign countries or instrumentalities thereof; and

(2) may proclaim such modification or continuance of any existing duty, such continuance of existing duty-free or excise treatment, or such additional duties, as he determines to be required or appropriate to carry out any such trade agreement.

(b)(1) Except as provided in paragraph (2), no proclamation pursuant to subsection (a)(2) shall be made decreasing a rate of duty to a rate below 40 percent of the rate existing on January 1, 1975.

(2) Paragraph (1) shall not apply in the case of any article for which the rate of duty existing on January 1, 1975, is not more than 5 percent ad valorem.

(c) No proclamation shall be made pursuant to subsection (a)(2) increasing any rate of duty to, or imposing a rate above, the higher of the following:

(1) the rate which is 50 percent above the rate set forth in rate column numbered 2 of the Tariff Schedules of the United States as in effect on January 1, 1975, or

(2) the rate which is 20 percent ad valorem above the rate existing on January 1, 1975.

Section 102. *Nontariff Barriers to and Other Distortions of Trade*

(a) The Congress finds that barriers to (and other distortions of) international trade are reducing the growth of foreign markets for the products of United States agriculture, industry, mining, and commerce, diminishing the intended mutual benefits of reciprocal trade concessions, adversely affecting the United States economy, preventing fair and equitable access to supplies, and preventing the development of open and nondiscriminatory trade among nations. The President is urged to take all appropriate and feasible steps within his power (including the full exercise of the rights of the United States under international agreements) to harmonize, reduce, or eliminate such barriers to (and other distortions of) international trade. The President is further urged to utilize the authority granted by subsection (b) to negotiate trade agreements with other countries and instrumentalities providing on a basis of mutuality for the harmonization, reduction, or elimination of such barriers to (and other distortions of) international trade. Nothing in this subsection shall be construed as prior approval of any legislation which may be necessary to implement an agreement concerning barriers to (or other distortions of) international trade.

(b) Whenever the President determines that any barriers to (or other distortions of) international trade of any foreign country or the United States unduly burden and restrict the foreign trade of the United States or adversely affect the United States economy, or that the imposition of such barriers is likely to result in such a burden, restriction, or effect, and that the purposes of this Act will be promoted thereby, the President, during the 5-year period beginning on the date of the enactment of this Act, may enter into trade agreements with foreign countries or instrumentalities providing for the harmonization, reduction, or elimination of such barriers (or other distortions) or providing for the prohibition of or limitations on the imposition of such barriers (or other distortions).

(c) Before the President enters into any trade agreement under this section providing for the harmonization, reduction, or elimination of a barrier to (or other distortion of) international trade, he shall consult with the Committee on Ways and Means of the House of Representatives, the Committee on Finance of the Senate, and with each committee of the House and the Senate and each joint committee of the Congress which has jurisdiction over legislation involving subject matters which would be affected by such trade agreement. Such consultation shall include all matters relating to the implementation of such trade agreement as provided in subsections (d) and (e). If it is proposed to implement such trade agreement, together with one or more other trade agreements entered into under this section, in a single implementing bill, such consultation shall include the desirability and feasibility of such proposed implementation.

(d) Whenever the President enters into a trade agreement under this section providing for the harmonization, reduction, or elimination of a barrier to (or other distortion of) international trade, he shall submit such agreement, together with a draft of an implementing bill (described in section 151(b)) and a statement of any administrative action proposed to implement such agreement, to the Congress as provided in subsection (e), and such agreement shall enter into force with respect to the United States only if the provisions of subsection (e) are complied with and the implementing bill submitted by the President is enacted into law.

(e) Each trade agreement submitted to the Congress under this subsection shall enter into force with respect to the United States if (and only if)—

(1) the President, not less than 90 days before the day on which he enters into such trade agreement, notifies the House of Representatives and the Senate of his intention to enter into such an agreement, and promptly thereafter publishes notice of such intention in the Federal Register;

(2) after entering into the agreement, the President transmits a document to the House of Representatives and to the Senate containing a copy of such agreement together with—

(A) a draft of an implementing bill and a statement of any administrative action proposed to implement such agreement, and an explanation as to how the implementing bill and proposed administrative action change or affect existing law, and

(B) a statement of his reasons as to how the agreement serves the interest of United States commerce and as to why the implementing bill and proposed administrative action is required or appropriate to carry out the agreement; and

(3) the implementing bill is enacted into law.

(f) To insure that a foreign country or instrumentality which receives benefits under a trade agreement entered into under this section is subject to the obligations imposed by such agreement, the President may recommend to Congress in the implementing bill and statement of administrative action submitted with respect to such agreement that the benefits and obligations of such agreement apply solely to the parties to such agreement, if such application is consistent with the terms of such agreement. The President may also recommend with respect to any such agreement that the benefits and obligations of such agreement not apply uniformly to all parties to such agreement, if such application is consistent with the terms of such agreement.

(g) For purposes of this section—

(1) the term "barrier" includes the American selling price basis of customs evaluation as defined in section 402 or 402a of the Tariff Act of 1930,[2] as appropriate;

---

[2] 19 U.S.C. 1401a, 1402.

(2) the term "distortion" includes a subsidy; and

(3) the term "international trade" includes trade in both goods and services.

Section 103. *Overall Negotiating Objective*

The overall United States negotiating objective under sections 101 and 102 shall be to obtain more open and equitable market access and the harmonization, reduction, or elimination of devices which distort trade or commerce. To the maximum extent feasible, the harmonization, reduction, or elimination of agricultural trade barriers and distortions shall be undertaken in conjunction with the harmonization, reduction, or elimination of industrial trade barriers and distortions.

Section 104. *Sector Negotiating Objective*

(a) A principal United States negotiating objective under sections 101 and 102 shall be to obtain, to the maximum extent feasible, with respect to appropriate product sectors of manufacturing, and with respect to the agricultural sector, competitive opportunities for United States exports to the developed countries of the world equivalent to the competitive opportunities afforded in United States markets to the importation of like or similar products, taking into account all barriers (including tariffs) to and other distortions of international trade affecting that sector.

(b) As a means of achieving the negotiating objective set forth in subsection (a), to the extent consistent with the objective of maximizing overall economic benefit to the United States (through maintaining and enlarging foreign markets for products of United States agriculture, industry, mining, and commerce, through the development of fair and equitable market opportunities, and through open and nondiscriminatory world trade), negotiations shall, to the extent feasible be conducted on the basis of appropriate product sectors of manufacturing.

(c) For the purposes of this section and section 135, the Special Representative for Trade Negotiations together with the Secretary of Commerce, Agriculture, or Labor, as appropriate, shall, after consultation with the Advisory Committee for Trade Negotiations established under section 135 and after consultation with interested private organizations, identify appropriate product sectors of manufacturing.

(d) If the President determines that competitive opportunities in one or more product sectors will be significantly affected by a trade agreement concluded under section 101 or 102, he shall submit to the Congress with each such agreement an analysis of the extent to which the negotiating objective set forth in subsection (a) is achieved by such agreement in each product sector or product sectors.

Section 105. *Bilateral Trade Agreements*

If the President determines that bilateral trade agreements will more effectively promote the economic growth of, and full employment in, the United States, then, in such cases, a negotiating objective under section 101 and 102 shall be to enter into bilateral trade agreements. Each such trade agreement shall provide for mutually advantageous economic benefits.

Section 106. *Agreements With Developing Countries*

A United States negotiating objective under sections 101 and 102 shall be to enter into trade agreements which promote the economic growth of both developing countries and the United States and the mutual expansion of market opportunities.

Section 107. *International Safeguard Procedures*

(a) A principal United States negotiating objective under section 102 shall be to obtain internationally agreed upon rules and procedures, in the context of the harmonization, reduction, or elimination of barriers to, and other distortions of, international trade, which permit the use of temporary measures to ease adjustment to changes occurring in competitive conditions in the domestic markets of the parties to an agreement resulting from such negotiations due to the expansion of international trade.

(b) Any agreement entered into under section 102 may include provisions establishing procedures for—

(1) notification of affected exporting countries,

(2) international consultations,

(3) international review of changes in trade flows,

(4) making adjustments in trade flows as the result of such changes, and

(5) international mediation.

Such agreements may also include provisions which—

(A) exclude, under specified conditions, the parties thereto from compensation obligations and retaliation, and

(B) permit domestic public procedures through which interested parties have the right to participate.

Section 108. *Access Supplies*

(a) A principal United States negotiating objective under section 102 shall be to enter into trade agreements with foreign countries and instrumentalities to assure the United States of fair and equitable access at reasonable prices to supplies of articles of commerce which are important to the economic requirements of the United States and for which the United States does not have, or cannot easily develop, the necessary domestic productive capacity to supply its own requirements.

(b) Any agreement entered into under section 102 may include provisions which—

(1) assure to the United States the continued availability of important articles at reasonable prices, and

(2) provide reciprocal concessions or comparable trade obligations, or both, by the United States.

Section 109. *Staging Requirements and Rounding Authority*

(a) Except as otherwise provided in this section, the aggregate reduction in the rate of duty on any article which is in effect on any day pursuant to a trade agreement under section 101 shall not exceed the aggregate reduction which would have been in effect on such day if—

(1) a reduction of 3 percent ad valorem or a reduction of one-tenth of the total reduction, whichever is greater, had taken effect on the effective date of the first reduction proclaimed pursuant to section 101 (a)(2) to carry out such agreement with respect to such article, and

(2) a reduction equal to the amount applicable under paragraph (1) had taken effect at 1-year intervals after the effective date of such first reduction.

This subsection shall not apply in any case where the total reduction in the rate of duty does not exceed 10 percent of the rate before the reduction.

(b) If the President determines that such action will simplify the computation of the amount of duty imposed with respect to an article, he may exceed the limitation provided by section 101(b) or subsection (a) of this section by not more than whichever of the following is lesser:

(1) the difference between the limitation and the next lower whole number, or

(2) one-half of 1 percent ad valorem.

(c)(1) No reduction in the rate of duty on any article pursuant to a trade agreement under section 101 shall take effect more than 10 years after the effective date of the first reduction proclaimed to carry out such trade agreement with respect to such article.

(2) If any part of a reduction takes effect, then any time thereafter during which such part of the reduction is not in effect by reason of legislation of the United States or action thereunder, the effect of which is to maintain or increase the rate of duty on an article, shall be excluded in determining—

(A) the 1-year intervals referred to in subsection (a)(2), and

(B) the expiration of the 10-year period referred to in paragraph (1) of this subsection.

CHAPTER 2—OTHER AUTHORITY

Section 121. *Steps To Be Taken Toward* GATT *Revision; Authorization of Appropriations for* GATT

(a) The President shall, as soon as practicable, take such action as may be necessary to bring trade agreements heretofore entered into, and the application thereof, into conformity with principles promoting the development of an open, nondiscriminatory, and fair world economic system. The action and principles referred to in the preceding sentence include, but are not limited to, the following—

(1) the revision of decisionmaking procedures in the General Agreement on Tariffs and Trade (hereinafter in this subsection referred to as "GATT") to more nearly reflect the balance of economic interests,

(2) the revision of article XIX of the GATT into a truly international safeguard procedure which takes into account all forms of import restraints countries use in response to injurious competition or threat of such competition,

(3) the extension of GATT articles to conditions of trade not presently covered in order to move toward more fair trade practices,

(4) the adoption of international fair labor standards and of public petition and confrontation procedures in the GATT,

(5) the revision of GATT articles with respect to the treatment of border adjustments for internal taxes to redress the disadvantage to countries relying primarily on direct rather than indirect taxes for revenue needs,

(6) the revision of the balance-of-payments provision in the GATT articles so as to recognize import surcharges as the preferred means by which industrial countries may handle balance-of-payments deficits insofar as import restraint measures are required,

(7) the improvement and strengthening of the provisions of GATT and other international agreements governing access to supplies of food, raw materials, and maunfactured or semi-manufactured products, including rules and procedures governing the imposition of export controls, the denial of fair and equitable access to such supplies, and effective consultative procedures on problems of supply shortages,

(8) the extension of the provisions of GATT or other international agreements to authorize multilateral procedures by contracting parties with respect to member or nonmember countries which deny fair and equitable access to supplies of food, raw materials, and manufactured or semi-manufactured products, and thereby substantially injure the international community,

(9) any revisions necessary to establish procedures for regular consultation among countries and instrumentalities with respect to international trade and procedures to adjudicate commercial disputes among such countries or instrumentalities,

(10) any revisions necessary to apply the principles of reciprocity and nondiscrimination, including the elimination of special preferences and reverse preferences, to all aspects of international trade,

(11) any revisions necessary to define the forms of subsidy to industries producing products for export and the forms of subsidy to attract foreign investment which are consistent with an open, nondiscriminatory, and fair system of international trade, and

(12) consistent with the provisions of section 107, any revisions necessary to establish within the GATT an international agreement on articles (including footwear), including the creation of regular and institutionalized mechanisms for the settlement of disputes, and of a surveillance body to monitor all international shipments in such articles.

(b) The President shall, to the extent feasible, enter into agreements with foreign countries or instrumentalities to establish the principles described in subsection (a) with respect to international trade between the United States and such countries or instrumentalities.

(c) If the President enters into a trade agreement which establishes rules or procedures, including those set forth in subsection (a), promoting the development of an open, nondiscriminatory, and fair world economic system and if the implementation of such agreement will change any provision of Federal law (including a material change in an administrative rule), such agreement shall take effect with respect to the United States only if the appropriate implementing legislation is enacted by the Congress unless implementation of such agreement is effected pursuant to authority delegated by Congress. Such trade agreement may be submitted to the Congress for approval in accordance with the procedures of section 151. Nothing in this section shall be construed as prior approval of any legislation necessary to implement a trade agreement entered into under this section.

(d) There are authorized to be appropriated annually such sums as may be necessary for the payment by the United States of its share of the expenses of the Contracting Parties to the General Agreement on Tariffs and Trade. This authorization does not imply approval or disapproval by the Congress of all articles of the General Agreement on Tariffs and Trade.

Section 122. *Balance-of-Payments Authority*

(a) Whenever fundamental international payments problems require special import measures to restrict imports—

(1) to deal with large and serious United States balance-of-payments deficits,

(2) to prevent an imminent and significant depreciation of the dollar in foreign exchange markets, or

(3) to cooperate with other countries in correcting an international balance-of-payments disequilibrium,

the President shall proclaim, for a period not exceeding 150 days (unless such period is extended by Act of Congress)—

(A) a temporary import surcharge, not to exceed 15 percent ad valorem, in the form of duties (in addition to those already imposed, if any) on articles imported into the United States;

(B) temporary limitations through the use of quotas on the importation of articles into the United States; or

(C) both a temporary import surcharge described in subparagraph (A) and temporary limitations described in subparagraph (B).

The authority delegated under subparagraph (B) (and so much of subparagraph (C) as relates to subparagraph (B)) may be exercised (i) only if international trade or monetary agreements to which the United States is a party permit the imposition of quotas as a balance-of-payments measure, and (ii) only to the extent that the fundamental imbalance cannot be dealt with effectively by a surcharge proclaimed pursuant to subparagraph (A) or (C). Any temporary import surcharge proclaimed pursuant to subparagraph (A) or (C) shall be treated as a regular customs duty.

(b) If the President determines that the imposition of import restrictions under subsection (a) will be contrary to the national interest of the United States, then he may refrain from proclaiming such restrictions and he shall—

(1) immediately inform Congress of his determination, and

(2) immediately convene the group of congressional official advisers designated under section 161(a) and consult with them as to the reasons for such determination.

(c) Whenever the President determines that fundamental international payments problems require special import measures to increase imports—

(1) to deal with large and persistent United States balance-of-trade surpluses, as determined on the basis of the cost-insurance-freight value of imports as reported by the Bureau of the Census, or

(2) to prevent significant appreciation of the dollar in foreign exchange markets.

the President is authorized to proclaim, for a period of 150 days (unless such period is extended by Act of Congress)—

(A) a temporary reduction (of not more than 5 percent ad valorem) in the rate of duty on any article; and

(B) a temporary increase in the value or quantity of articles which may be imported under any import restriction, or a temporary suspension of any import restriction.

Import liberalizing actions proclaimed pursuant to this subsection shall be of broad and uniform application with respect to product coverage except that the President shall not proclaim measures under this subsection with respect to those articles where in his judgment such action will cause or contribute to material injury to firms or workers in any domestic industry, including agriculture, mining, fishing, or commerce, or to impairment of the national security, or will otherwise be contrary to the national interest.

(d)(1) Import restricting actions proclaimed pursuant to subsection (a) shall be applied consistently with the principle of nondiscriminatory treatment. In addition, any quota proclaimed pursuant to subparagraph (B) of subsection (a) shall be applied on a basis which aims at a distribution of trade with the United States approaching as closely as possible that which various foreign countries might have expected to obtain in the absence of such restrictions.

(2) Notwithstanding paragraph (1), if the President determines that the purposes of this section will best be served by action against one or more countries having large or persistent balance-of-payments surpluses, he may exempt all other countries from such action.

(3) After such time when there enters into force for the United States new rules regarding the application of surcharges as part of a reform of internationally agreed balance-of-payments adjustments procedures, the exemption authority contained in paragraph (2) shall be applied consistently with such new international rules.

(4) It is the sense of Congress that the President seek modifications in international agreements aimed at allowing the use of surcharges in place of quantitative restrictions (and providing rules to govern the use of such surcharges) as a balance-of-payments adjustment measure within the context of arrangements for an equitable sharing of balance-of-payments adjustment responsibility among deficit and surplus countries.

(e) Import restricting actions proclaimed pursuant to subsection (a) shall be of broad and uniform application with respect to product coverage except where the President determines, consistently with the purposes of this section, that certain articles should not be subject to import restricting actions because of the needs of the United States economy. Such exceptions shall be limited to the unavailability of domestic supply at reasonable prices, the necessary importation of raw materials, avoiding serious dislocations in the supply of imported goods, and other similar factors. In addition, uniform exceptions may be made where import restricting actions will be unnecessary or ineffective in carrying out the purposes of this section, such as with respect to articles already subject to import restrictions, goods in transit, or goods under binding contract. Neither the authorization of import restricting actions nor the determination of exceptions with respect to product coverage shall be made for the purpose of protecting individual domestic industries from import competition.

(f) Any quantitative limitation proclaimed pursuant to subparagraph (B) or (C) of subsection (a) on the quantity or value, or both, of an article—

(1) shall permit the importation of a quantity or value which is not less than the quantity or value of such article imported into the United States from the foreign countries to which such limitation applies during the most recent period which the President determines is representative of imports of such article, and

(2) shall take into account any increase since the end of such representative period in domestic consumption of such article and like or similar articles of domestic manufacture or production.

(g) The President may at any time, consistent with the provisions of this section, suspend, modify, or terminate, in whole or in part, any proclamation under this section either during the initial 150-day period of effectiveness or as extended by subsequent Act of Congress.

(h) No provision of law authorizing the termination of tariff concessions shall be used to impose a surcharge on imports into the United States.

Section 123. *Compensation Authority*

(a) Whenever any action has been taken under section 203 to increase or impose any duty or other import restriction, the President—

(1) may enter into trade agreements with foreign countries or instrumentalities for the purpose of granting new concessions as compensation in order to maintain the general level of reciprocal and mutually advantageous concessions; and

(2) may proclaim such modification or continuance of any existing duty, or such continuance of existing duty-free or excise treatment, as he determines to be required or appropriate to carry out any such agreement.

(b)(1) No proclamation shall be made pursuant to subsection (a) decreasing any rate of duty to a rate which is less than 70 percent of the existing rate of duty.

(2) Where the rate of duty in effect at any time is an intermediate stage under section 109, the proclamation made pursuant to subsection (a) may provide for the reduction of each rate of duty at each such stage proclaimed under section 101 by not more than 30 percent of such rate of duty, and may provide for a final rate of duty which is not less than 70 percent of the rate of duty proclaimed as the final stage under section 101.

(3) If the President determines that such action will simplify the computation of the amount of duty imposed with a respect to an article he may exceed the limitations provided by paragraphs (1) and (2) of this subsection by not more than the lesser of—

(A) the difference between such limitation and the next lower whole number, or

(B) one-half of 1 percent ad valorem.

(4) Any concessions granted under subsection (a)(1) shall be reduced and terminated according to substantially the same time schedule for reduction applicable to the relevant import relief under section 203(h).

(c) Before entering into any trade agreement under this section with any foreign country or instrumentality, the President shall consider whether such country or instrumentality has violated trade concessions of benefit to the United States and such violation has not been adequately offset by the action of the United States or by such country or instrumentality.

(d) Notwithstanding the provisions of subsection (a), the authority delegated under section 101 shall be used for the purpose of granting new concessions as compensation within the meaning of this section until such authority terminates.

Section 124. *Two-Year Residual Authority to Negotiate Duties*

(a) Whenever the President determines that any existing duties or other import restrictions of any foreign country or the United States are unduly burdening and restricting the foreign trade of the United States and that the purposes of this Act will be promoted thereby, the President—

(1) may enter into trade agreements with foreign countries or instrumentalities thereof, and

(2) may proclaim such r .odification or continuance of any existing duty, such continuance of existing duty-free or excise treatment, or such additional duties, as he determines to be required or appropriate to carry out any such trade agreement.

(b) Agreements entered into under this section in any 1-year period shall not provide for the reduction of duties, or the continuance of duty-free or excise treatment, for articles which account for more than 2 percent of the value of the United States imports for the most recent 12-month period for which import statistics are available.

(c)(1) No proclamation shall be made pursuant to subsection (a) decreasing any rate of duty to a rate which is less than 80 percent of the existing rate of duty.

(2) No proclamation shall be made pursuant to subsection (a) decreasing or increasing any rate of duty to a rate which is lower or higher than the corresponding rate which would have resulted if the maximum authority granted by section 101 with respect to such article had been exercised.

(3) Where the rate of duty in effect at any time is an intermediate stage under section 109, the proclamation made pursuant to subsection (a) may provide for the reduction of each rate of duty at each such stage proclaimed under section 101 by not more than 20 percent of such rate of duty, and, subject to the limitation in paragraph (2), may provide for a final rate of duty which is not less than 80 percent of the rate of duty proclaimed as the final stage under section 101.

(4) If the President determines that such action will simplify the computation of the amount of duty imposed with respect to an article, he may exceed the limitations provided by paragraphs (1) and (2) of this subsection by not more than the lesser of—

(A) the difference between such limitation and the next lower whole number, or

(B) one-half of 1 percent ad valorem.

(d) Agreements may be entered into under this section only during the 2-year period which immediately follows the close of the period during which agreements may be entered into under section 101.

Section 125. *Termination and Withdrawal Authority*

(a) Every trade agreement entered into under this Act shall be subject to termination, in whole or in part, or withdrawal, upon due notice, at the end of a period specified in the agreement. Such period shall be not more than 3 years from the date on which the agreement becomes effective. If the agreement is not terminated or withdrawn from at the end of the period so specified, it shall be subject to termination or withdrawal thereafter upon not more than 6 months' notice.

(b) The President may at any time terminate in whole or in part, any proclamation made under this Act.

(c) Whenever the United States, acting in pursuance of any of its rights or obligations under any trade agreement entered into pursuant to this Act, section 201 of the Trade Expansion Act of 1962 or section 350 of the Tariff Act of 1930, withdraws, suspends, or modifies any obligation with respect to the trade of any foreign country or instrumentality thereof, the President is authorized to proclaim increased duties or other import restrictions, to the extent, at such times, and for such periods as he deems necessary or appropriate, in order to exercise the rights or fulfill the obligations of the United States. No proclamation shall be made under this subsection increasing any existing duty to a rate more than 50 percent above the rate set forth in rate column numbered 2 of the Tariff Schedules of the United States, as in effect on January 1, 1975, or 20 percent ad valorem above the rate existing on January 1, 1975, whichever is higher.

(d) Whenever any foreign country or instrumentality withdraws, suspends, or modifies the application of trade agreement obligations of benefit to the United States without granting adequate compensation therefor, the President, in pursuance of rights granted to the United States under any trade agreement and to the extent necessary to protect United States economic interests (including United States balance of payments), may—

(1) withdraw, suspend, or modify the application of substantially equivalent trade agreement obligations of benefit to such foreign country or instrumentality, and

(2) proclaim under subsection (c) such increased duties or other import restrictions as are appropriate to effect adequate compensation from such foreign country or instrumentality.

(e) Duties or other import restrictions required or appropriate to carry out any trade agreement entered into pursuant to this Act, section 201 of the Trade Expansion Act of 1962, or section 350 of the Tariff Act of 1930 shall not be affected by any termination, in whole or in part, of such agreement or by the withdrawal of the United States for such agreement and shall remain in effect after the date of such termination or withdrawal for 1 year, unless the President by proclamation provides that such rates shall be restored to the level at which they would be but for the agreement. Within 60 days after the date of any such termination or withdrawal, the President shall transmit to the Congress his recommendations as to the appropriate rates of duty for all articles which were affected by the termination or withdrawal or would have been so affected but for the preceding sentence.

(f) Before taking any action pursuant to subsection (b), (c), or (d), the President shall provide for a public hearing during the course of which interested persons shall be given a reasonable opportunity to be present, to produce evidence, and to be heard, unless he determines that such prior hearings will be contrary to the national interest because of the need for expeditious action, in which case he shall provide for a public hearing promptly after such action.

Section 126. *Reciprocal Nondiscriminatory Treatment*

(a) Except as otherwise provided in this Act or in any other provision of law, any duty or other import restriction or duty-free treatment proclaimed in carrying out trade agreement under this title shall apply to products of all foreign countries, whether imported directly or indirectly.

(b) The President shall determine, after the conclusion of all negotiations entered into under this Act or at the end of the 5-year period beginning on the date of enactment of this Act, whichever is earlier, whether any major industrial country has failed to make concessions under trade agreements entered into under this Act which provide competitive opportunities for the commerce of the United States in such country substantially equivalent to the competitive opportunities, provided by concessions made by the United States under trade agreements entered into under this Act, for the commerce of such country in the United States.

(c) If the President determines under subsection (b) that a major industrial country has not made concessions under trade agreements entered into under this Act which provide substantially equivalent competitive opportunities for the commerce of the United States, he shall, either generally with respect to such country or by article produced by such country, in order to restore equivalence of competitive opportunities, recommended to the Congress—

(1) legislation providing for the termination or denial of the benefits of concessions of trade agreements entered into under this Act made with respect to rates of duty or other import restrictions by the United States; and

(2) that any legislation necessary to carry out any trade agreement under section 102 shall not apply to such country.

(d) For purposes of this section, "major industrial country" means Canada, the European Economic Community, the individual member countries of such Community, Japan, and any other foreign country designated by the President for purposes of this subsection.

Section 127. *Reservation of Articles for National Security or Other Reasons*

(a) No proclamation shall be made pursuant to the provisions of this Act reducing or eliminating the duty or other import restriction on any article if the President determines that such reduction or elimination would threaten to impair the national security.

(b) While there is in effect with respect to any article any action taken under section 203 of this Act, or section 232 or 351 of the Trade Expansion Act of 1962 (19 U.S.C. 1862 or 1981), the President shall reserve such article from negotiations under this title (and from any action under section 122(c)) contemplating reduction or elimination of—

(A) any duty on such article,

(B) any import restriction imposed under such section, or

(C) any other import restriction, the removal of which will be likely to undermine the effect of the import restrictions referred to in subparagraph (B).

In addition, the President shall also so reserve any other article which he determines to be appropriate, taking into consideration information and advice available pursuant to and with respect to the matters covered by sections 131, 132, and 133, where applicable.

(c) The President shall submit to the Congress an annual report on section 232 of the Trade Expansion Act of 1962. Within 60 days after he takes any action under such section 232, the President shall report to the Congress the action taken and the reasons therefor.

(d) Section 232 of the Trade Expansion Act of 1962 is amended—

(1) by striking out "Director of the Office of Emergency Planning (hereinafter in this section referred to as the 'Director')" in the first sentence of subsection (b) and inserting in lieu thereof "Secretary of the Treasury (hereinafter referred to as the 'Secretary')";

(2) by striking out "advice from other appropriate departments and agencies" in the first sentence of subsection (b) and inserting in lieu thereof "advice from, and shall consult with, the Secretary of Defense, the Secretary of Commerce, and other appropriate officers of the United States";

(3) by striking out the last sentence of subsection (b) and inserting in lieu thereof the following: "The Secretary shall, if it is appropriate and after reasonable notice, hold public hearings or otherwise afford interested parties an opportunity to present information and advice relevant to such investigation. The Secretary shall report the findings of his investigation under this subsection with respect to the effect of the importation of such article in such quantities or under such circumstances upon the national security and, based on such findings, his recommendation for action or inaction under this section to the President

within one year after receiving an application from an interested party or otherwise beginning an investigation under this subsection. If the Secretary finds that such article is being imported into the United States in such quantities or under such circumstances as to threaten to impair the national security, he shall so advise the President and the President shall take such action, and for such time, as he deems necessary to adjust the imports of such article and its derivatives so that such imports will not threaten to impair the national security, unless the President determines that the article is not being imported into the United States in such quantities or under such circumstances as to threaten to impair the national security."; and

(4) by striking out "Director" each place it appears in subsections (c) and (d) and inserting in lieu thereof "Secretary".

CHAPTER 3—HEARINGS AND ADVICE CONCERNING NEGOTIATIONS

Section 131. *International Trade Commission Advice*

(a) In connection with any proposed trade agreement under chapter 1 or section 123 or 124, the President shall from time to time publish and furnish the International Trade Commission (hereafter in this section referred to as the "Commission") with lists of articles which may be considered for modification or continuance of United States duties, continuance of United States duty-free or excise treatment, or additional duties. In the case of any article with respect to which consideration may be given to reducing or increasing the rate of duty, the list shall specify the provision of this title pursuant to which such consideration may be given.

(b) Within 6 months after receipt of such a list or, in the case of a list submitted in connection with a trade agreement authorized under section 123, within 90 days after receipt of such list, the Commission shall advise the President with respect to each article of its judgment as to the probable economic effect of modifications of duties on industries producing like or directly competitive articles and on consumers, so as to assist the President in making an informed judgment as to the impact which might be caused by such modifications on United States manufacturing, agriculture, mining, fishing, labor, and consumers. Such advice may include in the case of any article the advice of the Commission as to whether any reduction in the rate of duty should take place over a longer period than the minimum periods provided by section 109(a).

(c) In addition, in order to assist the President in his determination of whether to enter into any agreement under section 102, the Commission shall make such investigations and reports as may be requested by the President, including, where feasible, advice as to the probable economic effects of modifications of any barrier to (or other distortion of) international trade on domestic industries and purchasers and on prices and quantities of articles in the United States.

(d) In preparing its advice to the President under this section, the Commission shall, to the extent practicable—

(1) investigate conditions, causes, and effects relating to competition between the foreign industries producing the articles in question and the domestic industries producing the like or directly competitive articles;

(2) analyze the production, trade, and consumption of each like or directly competitive article, taking into consideration employment, profit levels, and use of productive facilities with respect to the domestic industries concerned, and such other economic factors in such industries as it considers relevant, including prices, wages, sales, inventories, patterns of demand, capital investment, obsolescence of equipment, and diversification of production;

(3) describe the probable nature and extent of any significant change in employment, profit levels, and use of productive facilities, and such other conditions as it deems relevant in the domestic industries concerned which it believes such modifications would cause; and

(4) make special studies (including studies of real wages paid in foreign supplying countries), whenever deemed to be warranted, of particular proposed modifications affecting United States manufacturing, agriculture, mining, fishing, labor, and consumers, utilizing to the fullest extent practicable United States Government facilities abroad and appropriate personnel of the United States.

(e) In preparing its advice to the President under this section, the Commission shall, after reasonable notice, hold public hearings.

Section 132. *Advice from Departments and Other Sources*

Before any trade agreement is entered into under chapter 1 or section 123 or 124, the President shall seek information and advice with respect to such agreement from the Departments of Agriculture, Commerce, Defense, Interior, Labor, State and the Treasury, from the Special Representative for Trade Negotiations, and from such other sources as he may deem appropriate.

Section 133. *Public Hearings*

(a) In connection with any proposed trade agreement under chapter 1 or section 123 or 124, the President shall afford an opportunity for any interested person to present his views concerning any article on a list published pursuant to section 131, any article which should be so listed, any concession which should be sought by the United States, or any other matter relevant to such proposed trade agreement. For this purpose, the President shall designate an agency or an interagency committee which shall, after reasonable notice, hold public hearings and prescribe regulations governing the conduct of such hearings.

(b) The organization holding such hearings shall furnish the President with a summary thereof.

Section 134. *Prerequisites for Offers*

In any negotiations seeking an agreement under chapter 1 or section 123 or 124, the President may make an offer for the modification or continuance of any United States duty, import restrictions, or barriers to (or other distortions of) international trade, the continuance of United States duty-free or excise treatment, or the imposition of additional duties, import restriction, or other barrier to (or other distortion of) international trade, with respect to any article only after he has received a summary of the hearings at which an opportunity to be heard with respect to such article has been afforded under section 133. In addition, the President may make an offer for the modification or continuance of any United States duty, the continuance of United States duty-free or excise treatment, or the imposition of additional duties, with respect to any article included in a list published and furnished under section 131(a), only after he has received advice concerning such article from the International Trade Commission under section 131(b), or after the expiration of the 6-month or 90-day period provided for in that section, as appropriate, whichever first occurs.

Section 135. *Advice from Private Sector*

(a) The President, in accordance with the provisions of this section, shall seek information and advice from representative elements of the private sector with respect to negotiating objectives and bargaining positions before entering into a trade agreement referred to in section 101 or 102.

(b)(1) The President shall establish an Advisory Committee for Trade Negotiations to provide overall policy advice on any trade agreement referred to in section 101 or 102. The Committee shall be composed of not more than 45 individuals, and shall include representatives of government, labor, industry, agriculture, small business, service industries, retailers, consumer interests, and the general public.

(2) The Committee shall meet at the call of the Special Representative for Trade Negotiations, who shall be the Chairman. The Committee shall ter-

minate upon submission of its report required under subsection (e)(2). Members of the Committee shall be appointed by the President for a period of 2 years and may be reappointed for one or more additional periods.

(3) The Special Representative for Trade Negotiations shall make available to the Committee such staff, information, personnel, and administrative services and assistance as it may reasonably require to carry out its activities.

(c)(1) The President may, on his own initiative or at the request of organizations representing industry, labor, or agriculture, establish general policy advisory committees for industry, labor, and agriculture, respectively, to provide general policy advice on any trade agreement referred to in section 101 or 102. Such committees shall, insofar as practicable, be representative of all industry, labor, or agricultural interests (including small business interests), respectively, and shall be organized by the President acting through the Special Representative for Trade Negotiations and the Secretaries of Commerce, Labor, and Agriculture, as appropriate.

(2) The President shall, on his own initiative or at the request of organizations in a particular sector, establish such industry, labor, or agricultural sector advisory committees as he determines to be necessary for any trade negotiations referred to in section 101 or 102. Such committees shall, so far as practicable, be representative of all industry, labor, or agricultural interests including small business interests in the sector concerned. In organizing such committees the President, acting through the Special Representative for Trade Negotiations and the Secretary of Commerce, Labor, or Agriculture, as appropriate, (A) shall consult with interested private organizations, and (B) shall take into account such factors as patterns of actual and potential competition between United States industry and agriculture and foreign enterprise in international trade, the character of the nontariff barriers and other distortions affecting such competition, the necessity for reasonable limits on the number of such product sector advisory committees, the necessity that each committee be reasonably limited in size, and that the product lines covered by each committee be reasonably related.

(d) Committees established pursuant to subsection (c) shall meet at the call of the Special Representative for Trade Negotiations, before and during any trade negotiations, to provide the following:

(1) policy advice on negotiations;

(2) technical advice and information on negotiations on particular products both domestic and foreign; and

(3) advice on other factors relevant to positions of the United States in trade negotiations.

(e)(1) The Advisory Committee for Trade Negotiations, each appropriate policy advisory committee, and each sector advisory committee, if the sector which such committee represents is affected, shall meet at the conclusion of negotiations for each trade agreement entered into under this Act, to provide to the President, to Congress, and to the Special Representative for Trade Negotiations a report on such agreement. The report of the Advisory Committee for Trade Negotiations and each appropriate policy advisory committee shall include an advisory opinion as to whether and to what extent the agreement promotes the economic interests of the United States and the report of the appropriate sector committee shall include an advisory opinion as to whether the agreement provides for equity and reciprocity within the sector.

(2) The Advisory Committee for Trade Negotiations, each policy advisory committee, and each sector advisory committee shall issue a report to the Congress as soon as is practical after the end of the period which ends 5 years after the date of enactment of this Act. The report of the Advisory Committee for Trade Negotiations and each policy advisory committee shall include an advisory opinion as to whether and to what extent trade agreements entered into under this Act, taken as a whole, serve the economic interests of the United States. The report of each sector advisory committee shall include an advisory opinion on the degree to which trade agreements entered into under this Act which affect the sector represented by each such committee, taken as a whole, provide for equity and reciprocity within that sector.

(f) The provisions of the Federal Advisory Committee Act (Public Law 92–463) shall apply—

(1) to the Advisory Committee for Trade Negotiations established pursuant to subsection (b); and

(2) to all other advisory committees which may be established pursuant to subsection (c); except that the meetings of advisory groups established under subsection (c) shall be exempt from the requirements of subsections (a) and (b) of section 10 and section 11 of the Federal Advisory Committee Act (relating to open meetings, public notice, public participation, and public availability of documents), whenever and to the extent it is determined by the President or his designee that such meetings will be concerned with matters the disclosure of which would seriously compromise the Government's negotiating objectives or bargaining positions on the negotiation of any trade agreement.

(g)(1)(A) Trade secrets and commercial or financial information which is privileged or confidential, submitted in confidence by the private sector to

officers or employees of the United States in connection with trade negotiations, shall not be disclosed to any person other than to—

(i) officers and employees of the United States designated by the
Special Representative for Trade Negotiations, and

(ii) members of the Committee on Ways and Means of the House
of Representatives and the Committee on Finance of the Senate who are
accredited as official advisers under section 161(a) or are designated by
the chairman of either such committee under section 161(b)(2), and
members of the staff of either such committee designated by the chairman
under section 161(b)(2),

for use in connection with negotiation of a trade agreement referred to in section 101 or 102.

(B) Information, other than that described in paragraph (A), and advice submitted in confidence by the private sector to officers or employees of
the United States, to the Advisory Committee for Trade Negotiations or to
any advisory committee established under subsection (c), in connection with
trade negotiations, shall not be disclosed to any person other than—

(i) the individuals described in subparagraph (A), and

(ii) the appropriate advisory committees established under this section.

(2) Information submitted in confidence by officers or employees of the
United States to the Advisory Committee for Trade Negotiations, or to any
advisory committee established under subsection (c), shall not be disclosed
other than in accordance with rules issued by the Special Representative for
Trade Negotiations and the Secretary of Commerce, Labor or Agriculture,
as appropriate, after consultation with the relevant advisory committees
established under subsection (c). Such rules shall define the categories of
information which require restricted or confidential handling by such committee considering the extent to which public disclosure of such information can reasonably be expected to prejudice United States negotiating objectives. Such rules shall, to the maximum extent feasible, permit meaningful
consultations by advisory committee members with persons affected by proposed trade agreements.

(h) The Special Representative for Trade Negotiations, and the Secretary
of Commerce, Labor, or Agriculture, as appropriate, shall provide such staff,
information, personnel, and administrative services and assistance to advisory
committees established pursuant to subsection (c) as such committees may
reasonably require to carry out their activities.

(i) It shall be the responsibility of the Special Representative for Trade Negotiations, in conjunction with the Secretary of Commerce, Labor, or Agriculture, as appropriate, to adopt procedures for consultation with and obtaining information and advice from the advisory committees established pursuant to subsection (c) on a continuing and timely basis, both preparation for negotiations and actual negotiations. Such consultations shall include the provisions of information to each advisory committee as to (1) significant issues and developments arising in preparation for or in the course of such negotiations, and (2) overall negotiating objectives and positions of the United States and other parties to the negotiations. The Special Representative for Trade Negotiations shall not be bound by the advice or recommendations of such advisory committees but the Special Representative for Trade Negotiations shall inform the advisory committees of failures to accept such advice or recommendations, and the President shall include in his statement to the Congress, required by section 163, a report by the Special Representative for Trade Negotiations on consultation with such committees, issues involved in such consultation, and the reasons for not accepting advice or recommendations.

(j) In addition to any advisory committee established pursuant to this section, the President shall provide adequate, timely and continuing opportunity for the submission on an informal and, if such information is submitted under the provisions of subsection (g), confidential basis by private organizations or groups, representing labor interests, and others, of statistics, data, and other trade information, as well as policy recommendations, pertinent to the negotiation of any trade agreement referred to in section 101 or 102.

(k) Nothing contained in this section shall be construed to authorize or permit any individual to participate directly in any negotiation of any trade agreement referred to in section 101 or 102.

Chapter 4—Office of the Special Representative for Trade Negotiations

Section 141. *Office of the Special Representative for Trade Negotiations*

(a) There is established within the Executive Office of the President the Office of the Special Representative for Trade Negotiations (hereinafter in this section referred to as the "Office").

(b)(1) The Office shall be headed by the Special Representative for Trade Negotiations who shall be appointed by the President, by and with the advice and consent of the Senate. As an exercise of the rulemaking power of the Senate, any nomination of the Special Representative for Trade Negotiations submitted to the Senate for confirmation, and referred to a committee, shall be referred to the Committee on Finance. The Special Representative for Trade Negotiations shall hold office at the pleasure of the President, shall be entitled to receive the same allowances as a chief of mission, and shall have the rank of Ambassador Extraordinary and Plenipotentiary.

(2) There shall be in the Office two Deputy Special Representatives for Trade Negotiations who shall be appointed by the President, by and with the advice and consent of the Senate. As an exercise of the rulemaking power of the Senate, any nomination of a Deputy Special Representative submitted to the Senate for confirmation, and referred to a committee, shall be referred to the Committee on Finance. Each Deputy Special Representative for Trade Negotiations shall hold office at the pleasure of the President and shall have the rank of Ambassador.

(3)(A) Section 5312 of title 5, United States Code, is amended by adding at the end thereof the following new paragraph:

"(13) Special Representative for Trade Negotiations."

(B) Section 5314 of such title is amended by adding at the end thereof the following new paragraph:

"(60) Deputy Special Representatives for Trade Negotiations (2)."

(c)(1) The Special Representative for Trade Negotiations shall—

(A) be the chief representative of the United States for each trade negotiation under this title or section 301;

(B) report directly to the President and the Congress, and be responsible to the President and the Congress for the administration of trade agreements programs under this Act, the Trade Expansion Act of 1962, and section 350 of the Tariff Act of 1930;

(C) advise the President and Congress with respect to nontariff barriers to international trade, international commodity agreements, and other matters which are related to the trade agreements programs;

(D) be responsible for making reports to Congress with respect to the matter set forth in subparagraphs (A) and (B);

(E) be chairman to the interagency trade organization established pursuant to section 242(a) of the Trade Expansion Act of 1962; and

(F) be responsible for such other functions as the President may direct.

(2) Each Deputy Special Representative for Trade Negotiation shall have as his principal function the conduct of trade negotiations under this Act and shall have such other functions as the Special Representative for Trade Negotiations may direct.

(d) The Special Representative for Trade Negotiations may, for the purpose of carrying out his functions under this section—

(1) subject to the civil service and classification laws, select, appoint, employ, and fix the compensation of such officers and employees as are necessary and prescribe their authority and duties;

(2) employ experts and consultants in accordance with section 3109 of title 5, United States Code, and compensate individuals so employed for each day (including traveltime) at rates not in excess of the maximum rate of pay for grade GS–18 as provided in section 5332 of title 5, United States Code, and while such experts and consultants are so serving away from their homes or regular place of business, to pay such employees travel expenses and per diem in lieu of subsistence at rates authorized by section 5703 of title 5, United States Code, for persons in Government service employed intermittently;

(3) promulgate such rules and regulations as may be necessary to carry out the functions vested in him;

(4) utilize, with their consent, the services, personnel, and facilities of other Federal agencies;

(5) enter into and perform such contracts, leases, cooperative agreements, or other transactions as may be necessary in the conduct of the work of the Office and on such terms as the Special Representative for Trade Negotiations may deem appropriate, with any agency or instrumentality of the United States, or with any public or private person, firm, association, corporation, or institution;

(6) accept voluntary and uncompensated services, notwithstanding the provisions of section 3679(b) of the Revised Statutes (31 U.S.C. 665(b)); and

(7) adopt an official seal, which shall be judicially noticed.

(e) The Special Representative for Trade Negotiations shall, to the extent he deems it necessary for the proper administration and execution of the trade agreements programs of the United States, draw upon the resources of, and consult with, Federal agencies in connection with the performance of his functions.

(f) There are authorized to be appropriated to the Office of Special Representative for Trade Negotiations such amounts as may be necessary for the purpose of carrying out its functions for fiscal year 1976 and each fiscal year thereafter any part of which is within the 5-year period beginning on the date of the enactment of this Act.

(g)(1) The Office of Special Representative for Trade Negotiations established under Executive Order No. 11075 of January 15, 1963, as amended, is abolished.

(2) The assets, liabilities, contracts, property, and records and unexpended balances of appropriations, authorizations, allocations, and other funds employed, held, used, arising from, or available to such Office are transferred to the Office of Special Representative for Trade Negotiations established under subsection (a) of this section.

(h)(1) Any individual who holds the position of Special Representative for Trade Negotiations or a position as Deputy Special Representative for Trade Negotiations on the day before the date of enactment of this Act and who has been appointed by and with the advice and consent of the Senate may continue to hold such position without regard to the first sentence of paragraph (1) of subsection (b), or the first sentence of paragraph (2) of subsection (b), as the case may be.

(2) All personnel who on the day before the date of the enactment of this Act are employed by the Office of the Special Representative for Trade Negotiations established by Executive Order No. 11075 of January 15, 1963, as amended, are hereby transferred to the Office.

CHAPTER 5—CONGRESSIONAL PROCEDURES WITH RESPECT TO
PRESIDENTIAL ACTIONS

Section 151. *Bills Implementing Trade Agreements of Nontariff Barriers and Resolutions Approving Commercial Agreements With Communist Countries*

(a) RULES OF HOUSE OF REPRESENTATIVES AND SENATE.—This section and sections 152 and 153 are enacted by the Congress—

(1) as an exercise of the rulemaking power of the House of Representatives and the Senate, respectively, and as such they are deemed a part of the rules of each House, respectively, but applicable only with

respect to the procedure to be followed in that House in the case of implementing bills described in subsection (b)(1), implementing revenue bills described in subsection (b)(2), approval resolutions described in subsection (b)(3), and resolutions described in subsections 152(a) and 153(a); and they supersede other rules only to the extent that they are inconsistent therewith; and

(2) with rull recognition of the constitutional right of either House to change the rules (so far as relating to the procedure of that House) at any time, in the same manner and to the same extent as in the case of any other rule of that House.

(b) DEFINITIONS.—For purposes of this section—

(1) The term "implementing bill" means only a bill of either House of Congress which is introduced as provided in subsection (c) with respect to one or more trade agreements submitted to the House of Representatives and the Senate under section 102 and which contains—

(A) a provision approving such trade agreement or agreements,

(B) a provision approving the statement of administrative action (if any) proposed to implement such trade agreement or agreements, and

(C) if changes in existing laws or new statutory authority is required to implement such trade agreement or agreements, provisions, necessary or appropriate to implement such trade agreement or agreements, either repealing or amending existing laws or providing new statutory authority.

(2) The term "implementing revenue bill" means an implementing bill which contains one or more revenue measures by reason of which it must originate in the House of Representatives.

(3) The term "approval resolution" means only a concurrent resolution of the two Houses of the Congress, the matter after the resolving clause of which is as follows: "That the Congress approves the extension of nondiscriminatory treatment with respect to the products of . . . . transmitted by the President to the Congress on . . . . ", the first blank space being filled with the name of the country involved and the second blank space being filled with the appropriate date.

(c) INTRODUCTION AND REFERRAL.—

(1) On the day on which a trade agreement is submitted to the House

of Representatives and the Senate under section 102, the implementing bill submitted by the President with respect to such trade agreement shall be introduced (by request) in the House by the majority leader of the House, for himself and the minority leader of the House, or by Members of the House designated by the majority leader and minority leader of the House; and shall be introduced (by request) in the Senate by the majority leader of the Senate, for himself and the minority leader of the Senate, or by Members of the Senate designated by the majority leader and minority leader of the Senate. If either House is not in session on the day on which such a trade agreement is submitted, the implementing bill shall be introduced in that House, as provided in the preceding sentence, on the first day thereafter on which that House is in session. Such bills shall be referred by the Presiding Officers of the respective Houses to the appropriate committee, or, in the case of a bill containing provisions within the jurisdiction of two or more committees, jointly to such committees for consideration of those provisions within their respective jurisdictions.

(2) On the day on which a bilateral commercial agreement, entered into under title IV of this Act after the date of the enactment of this Act, is transmitted to the House of Representatives and the Senate, an approval resolution with respect to such agreement shall be introduced (by request) in the House by the majority leader of the House, for himself and the minority leader of the House, or by Members of the House designated by the majority leader and minority leader of the House; and shall be introduced (by request) in the Senate by the majority leader of the Senate, for himself and the minority leader of the Senate, or by Members of the Senate designated by the majority leader and minority leader of the Senate. If either House is not in session on the day on which such an agreement is transmitted, the approval resolution with respect to such agreement shall be introduced in that House, as provided in the preceding sentence, on the first day thereafter on which that House is in session. The approval resolution introduced in the House shall be referred to the Committee on Ways and Means and the approval resolution introduced in the Senate shall be referred to the Committee on Finance.

(d) AMENDMENTS PROHIBITED.—No amendment to an implementing bill or approval resolution shall be in order in either the House of Representatives or the Senate; and no motion to suspend the application of this subsection shall be in order in either House, nor shall it be in order in either House for the Presiding Officer to entertain a request to suspend the application of this subsection by unanimous consent.

(e) PERIOD FOR COMMITTEE AND FLOOR CONSIDERATION.—

(1) Except as provided in paragraph (2), if the committee or com-

mittees of either House to which an implementing bill or approval resolution has been referred have not reported it at the close of the 45th day after its introduction, such committee or committees shall be automatically discharged from further consideration of the bill or resolution and it shall be placed on the appropriate calendar. A vote on final passage of the bill or resolution shall be taken in each House on or before the close of the 15th day after the bill or resolution is reported by the committee or committees of that House to which it was referred, or after such committee or committees have been discharged from further consideration of the bill or resolution. If prior to the passage by one House of an implementing bill or approval resolution of that House, that House receives the same implementing bill or approval resolution from the other House, then—

(A) the procedure in that House shall be the same as if no implementing bill or approval resolution had been received from the other House; but

(B) the vote on final passage shall be on the implementing bill or approval resolution of the other House.

(2) The provisions of paragraph (1) shall not apply in the Senate to an implementing revenue bill. An implementing revenue bill received from the House shall be referred to the appropriate committee or committees of the Senate. If such committee or committees have not reported such bill at the close of the 15th day after its receipt by the Senate (or, if later, before the close of the 45th day after the corresponding implementing revenue bill was introduced in the Senate), such committee or committees shall be automatically discharged from further consideration of such bill and it shall be placed on the calendar. A vote on final passage of such bill shall be taken in the Senate on or before the close of the 15th day after such bill is reported by the committee or committees of the Senate to which it was referred, or after such committee or committees have been discharged from further consideration of such bill.

(3) For purposes of paragraphs (1) and (2), in computing a number of days in either House, there shall be excluded any day on which that House is not in session.

(f) FLOOR CONSIDERATION IN THE HOUSE.—

(1) A motion in the House of Representatives to proceed to the consideration of an implementing bill or approval resolution shall be highly privileged and not debatable. An amendment to the motion shall not be in order, nor shall it be in order to move to reconsider the vote by which the motion is agreed to or disagreed to.

(2) Debate in the House of Representatives on an implementing bill or approval resolution shall be limited to not more than 20 hours, which shall be divided equally between those favoring and those opposing the bill or resolution. A motion further to limit debate shall not be debatable. It shall not be in order to move to recommit an implementing bill or approval resolution or to move to reconsider the vote by which an implementing bill or approval resolution is agreed to or disagreed to.

(3) Motions to postpone, made in the House of Representatives with respect to the consideration of an implementing bill or approval resolution, and motions to proceed to the consideration of other business, shall be decided without debate.

(4) All appeals from the decisions of the Chair relating to the application of the Rules of the House of Representatives to the procedure relating to an implementing bill or approval resolution shall be decided without debate.

(5) Except to the extent specifically provided in the preceding provisions of this subsection, consideration of an implementing bill or approval resolution shall be governed by the Rules of the House of Representatives applicable to other bills and resolutions in similar circumstances.

(g) FLOOR CONSIDERATION IN THE SENATE.—

(1) A motion in the Senate to proceed to the consideration of an implementing bill or approval resolution shall be privileged and not debatable. An amendment to the motion shall not be in order, nor shall it be in order to move to reconsider the vote by which the motion is agreed to or disagreed to.

(2) Debate in the Senate on an implementing bill or approval resolution, and all debatable motions and appeals in connection therewith, shall be limited to not more than 20 hours. The time shall be equally divided between, and controlled by, the majority leader and the minority leader or their designees.

(3) Debate in the Senate on any debatable motion or appeal in connection with an implementing bill or approval resolution shall be limited to not more than 1 hour, to be equally divided between, and controlled by, the mover and the manager of the bill or resolution, except that in the event the manager of the bill or resolution is in favor of any such motion or appeal, the time in opposition thereto, shall be controlled by the minority leader or his designee. Such leaders, or either of them, may, from time under their control on the passage of an implementing bill or

approval resolution, allot additional time to any Senator during the consideration of any debatable motion or appeal.

(4) A motion in the Senate to further limit debate is not debatable. A motion to recommit an implementing bill or approval resolution is not in order.

Section 152. *Resolutions Disapproving Certain Actions*

(a) CONTENTS OF RESOLUTIONS.—

(1) For purposes of this section, the term "resolution" means only—

(A) a concurrent resolution of the two Houses of the Congress, the matter after the resolving clause of which is as follows: "That the Congress does not approve . . . . transmitted to the Congress on . . . .", the first blank space being filled in accordance with paragraph (2) and the second blank space being filled with the appropriate date; and

(B) a resolution of either House of the Congress, the matter after the resolving clause of which is as follows: "That the . . . . does not approve . . . . transmitted to the Congress on . . . .", with the first blank space being filled with the name of the resolving House, the second blank space being filled in accordance with paragraph (3), and the third blank space being filled with the appropriate date.

(2) The first blank space referred to in paragraph (1)(A) shall be filled as follows:

(A) in the case of a resolution referred to in section 203(c), with the phrase "the action taken by, or the determination of, the President under section 203 of the Trade Act of 1974"; and

(B) in the case of a resolution referred to in section 302(b), with the phrase "the action taken by the President under section 301 of the Trade Act of 1974".

(3) The second blank space referred to in paragraph (1)(B) shall be filled as follows:

(A) in the case of a resolution referred to in section 303(e) of the Tariff Act of 1930, with the phrase "the determination of the

Secretary of the Treasury under section 303(d) of the Tariff Act of 1930";

(B) in the case of a resolution referred to in section 407(c)(2), with the phrase "the extension of nondiscriminatory treatment with respect to the products of ...." (with this blank space being filled with the name of the country involved); and

(C) in the case of a resolution referred to in section 407(c)(3), with the phrase "the report of the President submitted under section .... of the Trade Act of 1974 with respect to ...." (with the first blank space being filled with "402(b)" or "409(b)", as appropriate, and the second blank space being filled with the name of the country involved).

(b) REFERENCES TO COMMITTEES.—All resolutions introduced in the House of Representatives shall be referred to the Committee on Ways and Means and all resolutions introduced in the Senate shall be referred to the Committee on Finance.

(c) DISCHARGE OF COMMITTEES.—

(1) If the committee of either House to which a resolution has been referred has not reported it at the end of 30 days after its introduction, not counting any day which is excluded under section 153(b), it is in order to move either to discharge the committee from further consideration of the resolution or to discharge the committee from further consideration of any other resolution introduced with respect to the same matter, except no motion to discharge shall be in order after the committee has reported a resolution with respect to the same matter.

(2) A motion to discharge under paragraph (1) may be made only by an individual favoring the resolution, and is highly privileged in the House and privileged in the Senate; and debate thereon shall be limited to not more than 1 hour, the time to be divided in the House equally between those favoring and those opposing the resolution, and to be divided in the Senate equally between, and controlled by, the majority leader and the minority leader or their designees. An amendment to the motion is not in order, and it is not in order to move to reconsider the vote by which the motion is agreed to or disagreed to.

(d) FLOOR CONSIDERATION IN THE HOUSE.—

(1) A motion in the House of Representatives to proceed to the consideration of a resolution shall be highly privileged and not debatable. An amendment to the motion shall not be in order, nor shall

it be in order to move to reconsider the vote by which the motion is agreed to or disagreed to.

(2) Debate in the House of Representatives on a resolution shall be limited to not more than 20 hours, which shall be divided equally between those favoring and those opposing the resolution. A motion further to limit debate shall not be debatable. No amendment to, or motion to recommit, the resolution shall be in order. It shall not be in order to move to reconsider the vote by which a resolution is agreed to or disagreed to.

(3) Motions to postpone, made in the House of Representatives with respect to the consideration of a resolution, and motions to proceed to the consideration of other business, shall be decided without debate.

(4) All appeals from the decisions of the Chair relating to the application of the Rules of the House of Representatives to the procedure relating to a resolution shall be decided without debate.

(5) Except to the extent specifically provided in the preceding provisions of this subsection, consideration of a resolution in the House of Representatives shall be governed by the Rules of the House of Representatives applicable to other resolutions in similar circumstances.

(e) FLOOR CONSIDERATION IN THE SENATE.—

(1) A motion in the Senate to proceed to the consideration of a resolution shall be privileged. An amendment to the motion shall not be in order, nor shall it be in order to move to reconsider the vote by which the motion is agreed to or disagreed to.

(2) Debate in the Senate on a resolution, and all debatable motions and appeals in connection therewith, shall be limited to not more than 20 hours, to be equally divided between, and controlled by, the majority leader and the minority leader or their designees.

(3) Debate in the Senate on any debatable motion or appeal in connection with a resolution shall be limited to not more than 1 hour, to be equally divided between, and controlled by, the mover and the manager of the resolution, except that in the event the manager of the resolution is in favor of any such motion or appeal, the time in opposition thereto, shall be controlled by the minority leader or his designee. Such leaders, or either of them, may, from time under their control on the passage of a resolution, allot additional time to any Senator during the consideration of any debatable motion or appeal.

(4) A motion in the Senate to further limit debate on a resolution, debatable motion, or appeal is not debatable. No amendment to, or motion to recommend a resolution is in order in the Senate.

(f) SPECIAL RULE FOR CONCURRENT RESOLUTIONS.—In the case of a resolution described in subsection (a)(1), if prior to the passage by one House of a resolution of that House, that House receives a resolution with respect to the same matter from the other House, then—

(1) the procedure in that House shall be the same as if no resolution had been received from the other House; but

(2) the vote on final passage shall be on the resolution of the other House.

Section 153. *Resolutions Relating to Extension of Waiver Authority Under Section 402*

(a) CONTENTS OF RESOLUTIONS.—For purposes of this section, the term "resolution" means only—

(1) a concurrent resolution of the two Houses of the Congress, the matter after the resolving clause of which is as follows: "That the Congress approves the extension of the authority contained in section 402 (c)(1) of the Trade Act of 1974 recommended by the President to the Congress on ...., except with respect to ....", with the first blank space being filled with the appropriate date and the second blank space being filled with the names of those countries, if any, with respect to which such extension of authority is not approved, and with the except clause being omitted if there is no such country; and

(2) a resolution of either House of the Congress, the matter after the resolving clause of which is as follows: "That the .... does not approve the extension of the authority contained in section 402(c) of the Trade Act of 1974 recommended by the President to the Congress on .... with respect to ....", with the first blank space being filled with the name of the resolving House, the second blank space being filled with the appropriate date, and the third blank space being filled with the names of those countries, if any, with respect to which such extension of authority is not approved, and with the with-respect-to clause being omitted if the extension of the authority is not approved with respect to any country.

(b) APPLICATION OF RULES OF SECTION 152; EXCEPTIONS.—

(1) Except as provided in this section, the provisions of section 152 shall apply to resolutions described in subsection (a).

(2) In applying section 152(c)(1), all calendar days shall be counted, and, in the case of a resolution related to section 402(d)(4), 20 calendar days shall be substituted for 30 days.

(3) That part of section 152(d)(2) which provides that no amendment is in order shall not apply to any amendment to a resolution which is limited to striking out or inserting the names of one or more countries or to striking out or inserting an except clause, in the case of a resolution described in subsection (a)(1), or a with-respect-to-clause, in the case of a resolution described in subsection (a)(2). Debate in the House of Representatives on any amendment to a resolution shall be limited to not more than 1 hour which shall be equally divided between those favoring and those opposing the amendment. A motion in the House to further limit debate on an amendment to a resolution is not debatable.

(4) That part of section 152(e)(4) which provides that no amendment is in order shall not apply to any amendment to a resolution which is limited to striking out or inserting the names of one or more countries or to striking out or inserting an except clause, in the case of a resolution described in subsection (a)(1), or a with-respect-to clause, in the case of a resolution described in subsection (a)(2). The time limit on a debate on a resolution in the Senate under section 152(e)(2) shall include all amendments to a resolution. Debate in the Senate on any amendment to a resolution shall be limited to not more than 1 hour, to be equally divided between, and controlled by, the mover and the manager of the resolution, except that in the event the manager of the resolution is in favor of any such amendment, the time in opposition thereto shall be controlled by the minority leader or his designee. The majority leader and minority leader may, from time under their control on the passage of a resolution, allot additional time to any Senator during the consideration of any amendment. A motion in the Senate to further limit debate on an amendment to a resolution is not debatable.

(c) CONSIDERATION OF SECOND RESOLUTION NOT IN ORDER.—It shall not be in order in either the House of Representatives or the Senate to consider a resolution with respect to a recommendation of the President under section 402(d) (other than a resolution described in subsection (a)(1) received from the other House), if that House has adopted a resolution with respect to the same recommendation.

Section 154. *Special Rules Relating to Congressional Procedures*

(a) Whenever, pursuant to section 102(e), 203(b), 302(a), 402(d), or 407(a) or (b), section 303(e) of the Tariff Act of 1930, a document is required to be transmitted to the Congress, copies of such document shall be delivered to both Houses of Congress on the same day and shall be delivered to the Clerk of the House of Representatives if the House is not in session and to the Secretary of the Senate if the Senate is not in session.

(b) For purposes of sections 203(c), 302(b), 407(c)(2), and 407(c)(3), the 90-day period referred to in such sections shall be computed by excluding—

(1) the days on which either House is not in session because of an adjournment of more than 3 days to a day certain or an adjournment of the Congress sine die, and

(2) any Saturday and Sunday, not excluded under paragraph (1), when either House is not in session.

CHAPTER 6—CONGRESSIONAL LIAISON AND REPORTS

Section 161. *Congressional Delegates to Negotiations*

(a) At the beginning of each regular session of Congress, the Speaker of the House of Representatives, upon the recommendation of the chairman of the Committee on Ways and Means, shall select five members (not more than three of whom are members of the same political party) of such committee, and the President pro tempore of the Senate, upon the recommendation of the chairman of the Committee on Finance, shall select five members (not more than three of whom are members of the same political party) of such committee, who shall be accredited by the President as official advisers to the United States delegations to international conferences, meetings, and negotiation sessions relating to trade agreements.

(b)(1) The Special Representative for Trade Negotiation shall keep each official adviser currently informed on United States negotiating objectives, the status of negotiations in progress, and the nature of any changes in domestic law or the administration thereof which may be recommended to Congress to carry out any trade agreement.

(2) The chairmen of the Committee on Ways and Means and the Committee on Finance may designate members (in addition to the official advisors under subsection (a)) and staff members of their respective committees who shall have access to the information provided to official advisers under paragraph (1).

Section 162. *Transmission of Agreements to Congress*

(a) As soon as practicable after a trade agreement entered into under chapter 1 or section 123 or 124 has entered into force with respect to the United States, the President shall, if he has not previously done so, transmit a copy of such trade agreement to each House of the Congress together with a statement, in the light of the advice of the International Trade Commission under section 131(b), if any, and of other relevant considerations, of his reasons for entering into the agreement.

(b) The President shall submit to each Member of Congress a summary of the information required to be transmitted to each House under subsection (a). For purposes of this subsection, the term "Member" includes any Delegate or Resident Commissioner.

Section 163. *Reports*

(a) The President shall submit to the Congress an annual report on the trade agreements program and on import relief and adjustment assistance for workers, firms, and communities under this Act. Such report shall include information regarding new negotiations; changes made in duties and non-tariff barriers and other distortions of trade of the United States; reciprocal concessions obtained; changes in trade agreements (including the incorporation therein of actions taken for import relief and compensation provided therefor); extension or withdrawal of nondiscriminatory treatment by the United States with respect to the products of a foreign country; extension, modification, withdrawal, suspension, or limitation of preferential treatment to exports of developing countries; the results of action taken to obtain removal of foreign trade restrictions (including discriminatory restrictions) against United States exports and the removal of foreign practices which discriminate against United States service industries (including transportation and tourism) and investment; and the measures being taken to seek the removal of other significant foreign import restrictions; and other information relating to the trade agreements program and to the agreements entered into thereunder. Such report shall also include information regarding the number of applications filed for adjustment assistance for workers, firms, and communities, the number of such applications which were approved, and the extent to which adjustment assistance has been provided under such approved applications.

(b) The International Trade Commission shall submit to the Congress, at least once a year, a factual report on the operation of the trade agreements program.

CHAPTER 7—UNITED STATES INTERNATIONAL TRADE COMMISSION

Section 171. *Change of Name of Tariff Commission*

(a) The United States Tariff Commission (established by section 330 of the Tariff Act of 1930) is renamed as the United States International Trade Commission.

(b) Any reference in any law of the United States, or in any order, rule, regulation, or other document, to the United States Tariff Commission (or the Tariff Commission) shall be considered to refer to the United States International Trade Commission.

Section 172. *Organization of the Commission*

(a) Subsections (a) and (b) of section 330 of the Tariff Act of 1930 (19 U.S.C. 1330) are amended to read as follows:

"(a) MEMBERSHIP.—The United States International Trade Commission (referred to in this title as the "Commission") shall be composed of six commissioners who shall be appointed by the President, by and with the advice and consent of the Senate. No person shall be eligible for appointment as a commissioner unless he is a citizen of the United States, and, in the judgment of the President, is possessed of qualifications requisite for developing expert knowledge of international trade problems and efficiency in administering the duties and functions of the Commission. A person who has served as a commissioner for more than 5 years (excluding service as a commissioner before the date of the enactment of the Trade Act of 1974) shall not be eligible for reappointment as a commissioner. Not more than three of the commissioners shall be members of the same political party, and in making appointments members of different political parties shall be appointed alternately as nearly as may be practicable.

"(b) TERMS OF OFFICE.—The terms of office of the commissioners holding office on the date of the enactment of the Trade Act of 1974 which (but for this sentence) would expire on June 16, 1975, June 16, 1976, June 16, 1977, June 16, 1978, June 16, 1979, and June 16, 1980, shall expire on December 16, 1976, June 16, 1978, December 16, 1979, June 16, 1981, December 16, 1982, and June 16, 1984, respectively. The term of office of each commissioner appointed after such date shall expire 9 years from the date of the expiration of the term for which his predecessor was appointed, except that any commissioner appointed to fill a vacancy occurring prior to the expiration of the term for which his predecessor was appointed shall be appointed for the remainder of such term."

(b) Subsection (c) of such section is amended—

(1) by striking out "The" in the first sentence and inserting in lieu thereof "(1) Except as provided in paragraph (2), the"; and

(2) by adding at the end thereof the following new paragraph:

"(2) Effective on and after June 17, 1975, the commissioner whose term is first to expire and who has at least 18 months remaining in his term shall serve as chairman during the last 18 months of his term (or, in the case of a commissioner appointed to fill a vacancy occurring during such 18-month period, during the remainder of his term), and the commissioner whose term is second to expire and who has at least 36 months remaining in his term shall serve as vice chairman during the same 18-month period (or, in the case of a commissioner appointed to fill a vacancy occurring during such 18-month period, during the remainder of such 18-month period)."

(c)(1) Section 5314 of title 5, United States Code, is amended by adding at the end thereof the following new paragraph:

"(61) Chairman, United States International Trade Commission."

(2) Section 5315 of such title is amended by striking out paragraph (24) and inserting in lieu thereof the following:

"(24) Members, United States International Trade Commission."

(3) Section 5316 of such title is amended by striking out paragraph (93).

Section 173. *Voting Record of Commissioners*

Section 332(g) of the Tariff Act of 1930 (19 U.S.C. 1332(g)) is amended—

(1) by striking out "and" before "a summary", and

(2) by inserting before the period at the end ", and a list of all votes taken by the commission during the year, showing those commissioners voting in the affirmative and the negative on each vote and those commissioners not voting on each vote and the reasons for not voting".

Section 174. *Representation in Court Proceedings*

Section 333(c) of the Tariff Act of 1930 (19 U.S.C. 1333(c)) is amended—

(1) by striking out "Upon application of the Attorney General of the United States, at" in subsection (c) and inserting in lieu thereof "At", and

(2) by adding at the end thereof the following new subsection:

"(g) REPRESENTATION IN COURT PROCEEDINGS.—The Commission shall be represented in all judicial proceedings by attorneys who are employees of the commission or, at the request of the commission, by the Attorney General of the United States."

Section 175. *Independent Budget and Authorization of Appropriations*

(a)(1) Effective with respect to the fiscal year beginning October 1, 1976, for purposes of the Budget and Accounting Act, 1921 (31 U.S.C. 1 et seq.), estimated expenditures and proposed appropriations for the United States International Trade Commission shall be transmitted to the President on or before October 15 of the year preceding the beginning of each fiscal year and shall be included by him in the Budget without revision, and the Commission shall not be considered to be a department or establishment for purposes of such Act.

(2) Section 3679 of the Revised Statutes (31 U.S.C. 665) is amended by inserting "the United States International Trade Commission," before ", or the District of Columbia" each place it appears in subsections (d) and (g).

(b) Section 330 of the Tariff Act of 1930 (19 U.S.C. 1330) is amended by adding at the end thereof the following new subsection:

"(e) AUTHORIZATION OF APPROPRIATIONS.—For the fiscal year beginning October 1, 1976, and each fiscal year thereafter, there are authorized to be appropriated to the Commission only such sums as may hereafter be provided by law."

(c)(1) Paragraph (2) is enacted as an exercise of the rulemaking power of the Senate and with full recognition of the constitutional right of the Senate to change its rules at any time.

(2) Paragraph 6(a) of rule XVI of the Standing Rules of the Senate is amended by adding at the end of the table contained therein the following:

"Committee on Finance ....For the International Trade Commission."

TITLE II—RELIEF FROM INJURY CAUSED BY IMPORT COMPETITION

CHAPTER 1—IMPORT RELIEF

Section 201. *Investigation by International Trade Commission*

(a)(1) A petition for eligibility for import relief for the purpose of facilitating orderly adjustment to import competition may be filed with the International Trade Commission (hereinafter in this chapter referred to as the "Commission") by an entity, including a trade association, firm, certified or recognized union, or group of workers, which is representative of an industry. The petition shall include a statement describing the specific purposes for which import relief is being sought, which may include such objectives as facilitating the orderly transfer of resources to alternative uses and other means of adjustment to new conditions of competition.

(2) Whenever a petition is filed under this subsection, the Commission shall transmit a copy thereof to the Special Representative for Trade Negotiations and the agencies directly concerned.

(b)(1) Upon the request of the President or the Special Representative for Trade Negotiations, upon resolution of either the Committee on Ways and Means of the House of Representatives or the Committee on Finance of the Senate, upon its own motion, or upon the filing of a petition under subsection (a)(1), the Commission shall promptly make an investigation to determine whether an article is being imported into the United States in such increased quantities as to be a substantial cause of serious injury, or the threat thereof, to the domestic industry producing an article like or directly con.petitive with the imported article.

(2) In making its determinations under paragraph (1), the Commission shall take into account all economic factors which it considers relevant, including (but not limited to)—

(A) with respect to serious injury, the significant idling of productive facilities in the industry, the inability of a significant number of firms to operate at a reasonable level of profit, and significant unemployment or underemployment within the industry;

(B) with respect to threat of serious injury, a decline in sales, a higher and growing inventory, and a downward trend in production, profits, wages, or employment (or increasing underemployment) in the domestic industry concerned; and

(C) with respect to substantial cause, an increase in imports (either actual or relative to domestic production) and a decline in the proportion of the domestic market supplied by domestic producers.

(3) For purposes of paragraph (1), in determining the domestic industry producing an article like or directly competitive with an imported article, the Commission—

(A) may, in the case of a domestic producer which also imports, treat as part of such domestic industry only its domestic production,

(B) may, in the case of a domestic producer which produces more than one article, treat as part of such domestic industry only that portion or subdivision of the producer which produces the like or directly competitive article, and

(C) may, in the case of one or more domestic producers, who produce a like or directly competitive article in a major geographic area of the United States and whose production facilities in such area for such article constitute a substantial portion of the domestic industry in the United States and primarily serve the market in such area, and where the imports are concentrated in such area, treat as such domestic industry only that segment of the production located in such area.

(4) For purposes of this section, the term "substantial cause" means a cause which is important and not less than any other cause.

(5) In the course of any proceeding under this subsection, the Commission shall, for the purpose of assisting the President in making his determinations under sections 202 and 203, investigate and report on efforts made by firms and workers in the industry to compete more effectively with imports.

(6) In the course of any proceeding under this subsection, the Commission shall investigate any factors which in its judgment may be contributing to increased imports of the article under investigation; and, whenever in the course of its investigation the Commission has reason to believe that the increased imports are attributable in part to circumstances which come within the purview of the Antidumping Act, 1921, section 303 or 337 of the Tariff Act of 1930, or other remedial provisions of law, the Commission shall promptly notify the appropriate agency so that such action may be taken as is otherwise authorized by such provisions of law.

(c) In the course of any proceeding under subsection (b), the Commission shall, after reasonable notice, hold public hearings and shall afford interested parties an opportunity to be present, to present evidence, and to be heard at such hearings.

(d)(1) The Commission shall report to the President its findings under subsection (b), and the basis therefor and shall include in each report any dissenting or separate views. If the Commission finds with respect to any article, as a result of its investigation, the serious injury or threat thereof described in subsection (b), it shall—

(A) find the amount of the increase in, or imposition of, any duty or import restriction on such article which is necessary to prevent or remedy such injury, or

(B) if it determines that adjustment assistance under chapters 2, 3, and 4 can effectively remedy such injury, recommend the provision of such assistance.

and shall include such findings or recommendation in its report to the President. The Commission shall furnish to the President a transcript of the hearings and any briefs which were submitted in connection with each investigation.

(2) The report of the Commission of its determination under subsection (b) shall be made at the earliest practicable time, but not later than 6 months after the date on which the petition is filed (or the date on which the request or resolution is received or the motion is adopted, as the case may be). Upon making such report to the President, the Commission shall also promptly make public such report (with the exception of information which the Commission determines to be confidential) and shall cause a summary thereof to be published in the Federal Register.

(e) Except for good cause determined by the Commission to exist, no investigation for the purposes of this section shall be made with respect to the same subject matter as a previous investigation under this section, unless 1 year has elapsed since the Commission made its report to the President of the results of such previous investigation.

(f)(1) Any investigation by the Commission under section 301(b) of the Trade Expansion Act of 1962 (as in effect before the date of the enactment of this Act) which is in progress immediately before such date of enactment shall be continued under this section in the same manner as if the investigation had been instituted originally under the provisions of this section. For purposes of subsection (d)(2), the petition for any investigation to which the preceding sentence applies shall be treated as having been filed, or the request or resolution as having been received or the motion having been adopted, as the case may be, on the date of the enactment of this Act.

(2) If, on the date of the enactment of this Act, the President has not

taken any action with respect to any report of the Commission containing an affirmative determination resulting from an investigation under section 301(b) of the Trade Expansion Act of 1962 (as in effect before the date of the enactment of this Act), such report shall be treated by the President as a report received by him under this section on the date of the enactment of this Act.

Section 202. *Presidential Action After Investigations*

(a) After receiving a report from the Commission containing an affirmative finding under section 201(b) that increased imports have been a substantial cause of serious injury or the threat thereof with respect to an industry, the President—

(1)(A) shall provide import relief for such industry pursuant to section 203, unless he determines that provision of such relief is not in the national economic interest of the United States, and

(B) shall evaluate the extent to which adjustment assistance has been made available (or can be made available) under chapters 2, 3, and 4 of this title to the workers and firms in such industry and to the communities in which such workers and firms are located, and, after such evaluation, may direct the Secretary of Labor and the Secretary of Commerce that expeditious consideration be given to the petitions for adjustment assistance; or

(2) if the Commission, under section 201(d), recommends the provision of adjustment assistance, shall direct the Secretaries of Labor and Commerce as described in paragraph (1)(B).

(b) Within 60 days (30 days in the case of a supplemental report under subsection (d)) after receiving a report from the Commission containing an affirmative finding under section 201(b) (or a finding under section 201 (b) which he considers to be an affirmative finding, by reason of section 330(d) of the Tariff Act of 1930, within such 60-day (or 30-day) period), the President shall—

(1) determine what method and amount of import relief he will provide, or determine that the provision of such relief is not in the national economic interest of the United States, and whether he will direct expeditious consideration of adjustment assistance petitions, and publish in the Federal Register that he has made such determination; or

(2) if such report recommends the provision of adjustment assistance, publish in the Federal Register his order to the Secretary of Labor and Secretary of Commerce for expeditious consideration of petitions.

(c) In determining whether to provide import relief and what method and amount of import relief he will provide pursuant to section 203, the President shall take into account, in addition to such other considerations as he may deem relevant—

(1) information and advice from the Secretary of Labor on the extent to which firms in the industry have applied for, are receiving, or are likely to receive adjustment assistance under chapter 2 or benefits from other manpower programs;

(2) information and advice from the Secretary of Commerce on the extent to which firms in the industry have applied for, are receiving, or are likely to receive adjustment assistance under chapters 3 and 4;

(3) the probable effectiveness of import relief as a means to promote adjustment, the efforts being made or to be implemented by the industry concerned to adjust to import competition, and other considerations relative to the position of the industry in the Nation's economy;

(4) the effect of import relief on consumers (including the price and availability of the imported article and the like or directly competitive article produced in the United States) and on competition in the domestic markets for such articles;

(5) the effect of import relief on the international economic interests of the United States;

(6) the impact on United States industries and firms as a consequence of any possible modification of duties or other import restrictions which may result from international obligations with respect to compensation;

(7) the geographic concentration of imported products marketed in the United States;

(8) the extent to which the United States market is the focal point for exports of such article by reason of restraints on exports of such article to, or on imports of such article into, third country markets; and

(9) the economic and social costs which would be incurred by taxpayers, communities, and workers, if import relief were or were not provided.

(d) The President may, within 15 days after the date on which he receives an affirmative finding of the Commission under section 201(b) with respect to an industry, request additional information from the Commission. The Commission shall, as soon as practicable but in no event more than 30 days after the date on which it receives the President's request, furnish additional information with respect to such industry in a supplemental report.

Section 203. *Import Relief*

(a) If the President determines to provide import relief under section 202(a)(1), he shall, to the extent that and for such time (not to exceed 5 years) as he determines necessary taking into account the considerations specified in section 202(c) to prevent or remedy serious injury or the threat thereof to the industry in question and to facilitate the orderly adjustment to new competitive conditions by the industry in question—

(1) proclaim an increase in, or imposition of, any duty on the article causing or threatening to cause serious injury to such industry;

(2) proclaim a tariff-rate quota on such article;

(3) proclaim a modification of, or imposition of, any quantitative restriction on the import into the United States of such article;

(4) negotiate orderly marketing agreements with foreign countries limiting the export from foreign countries and the import into the United States of such articles; or

(5) take any combination of such actions.

(b)(1) On the day on which the President proclaims import relief under this section or announces his intention to negotiate one or more orderly marketing agreements, the President shall transmit to Congress a document setting forth the action he is taking under this section. If the action taken by the President differs from the action recommended to him by the Commission under section 201(b)(1)(A), he shall state the reason for such difference.

(2) On the day on which the President determines that the provision of import relief is not in the national economic interest of the United States, the President shall transmit to Congress a document setting forth such determination and the reasons why, in terms of the national economic interest, he is not providing import relief and also what other steps he is taking, beyond adjustment assistance programs immediately available to help the industry to overcome serious injury and the workers to find productive employment.

(c)(1) If the President reports under subsection (b) that he is taking action which differs from the action recommended by the Commission under section 201(b)(1)(A), or that he will not provide import relief, the action recommended by the Commission shall take effect (as provided in paragraph (2)) upon the adoption by both Houses of Congress (within the 90-day period following the date on which the document referred to in subsection (b) is transmitted to the Congress), by an affirmative vote of a majority of the Members of each House present and voting, of a concurrent resolution disapproving the action taken by the President or his determination not to provide import relief under section 202(a)(1)(A).

(2) If the contingency set forth in paragraph (1) occurs, the President shall (within 30 days after the adoption of such resolution) proclaim the increase in, or imposition of, any duty or other import restriction on the article which was recommended by the Commission under section 201(b).

(d)(1) No proclamation pursuant to subsection (a) or (c) shall be made increasing a rate of duty to (or imposing) a rate which is more than 50 percent ad valorem above the rate (if any) existing at the time of the proclamation.

(2) Any quantitative restriction proclaimed pursuant to subsection (a) or (c) and any orderly marketing agreement negotiated pursuant to subsection (a) shall permit the importation of a quantity or value of the article which is not less than the quantity or value of such article imported into the United States during the most recent period which the President determines is representative of imports of such article.

(e)(1) Import relief under this section shall be proclaimed and take effect within 15 days after the import relief determination date unless the President announces on such date his intention to negotiate one or more orderly marketing agreements under subsection (a)(4) or (5) in which case import relief shall be proclaimed and take effect within 90 days after the import relief determination date.

(2) If the President provides import relief under subsection (a)(1), (2), (3), or (5), he may, after such relief takes effect, negotiate orderly marketing agreements with foreign countries, and may, after such agreements take effect, suspend or terminate, in whole or in part, such import relief.

(3) If the President negotiates an orderly marketing agreement under subsection (a)(4) or (5) and such agreement does not continue to be effective, he may, consistent with the limitations contained in subsection (h), provide import relief under subsection (a)(1), (2), (3), or (5).

(4) For purposes of this subsection, the term "import relief determination date" means the date of the President's determination under section 202(b).

(f)(1) For purposes of subsections (a) and (c), the suspension of item 806.30 or 807.00 of the Tariff Schedules of the United States with respect to an article shall be treated as an increase in duty.

(2) For purposes of subsections (a) and (c), the suspension of the designation of any article as an eligible article for purposes of title V shall be treated as an increase in duty.

(3) No proclamation providing for a suspension referred to in paragraph (1) with respect to any article shall be made under subsection (a) or (c) unless the Commission, in addition to making an affirmative determination with respect to such article under section 201(b), determines in the course of its investigation under section 201(b) that the serious injury (or threat thereof) substantially caused by imports to the domestic industry producing a like or directly competitive article results from the application of item 806.30 or item 807.00.

(4) No proclamation which provides solely for a suspension referred to in paragraph (2) with respect to any article shall be made under subsection (a) or (c) unless the Commission, in addition to making an affirmative determination with respect to such article under section 201(b), determines in the course of its investigation under section 201(b) that the serious injury (or threat thereof) substantially caused by imports to the domestic industry producing a like or directly competitive article results from the designation of the article as an eligible article for the purposes of title V.

(g)(1) The President shall by regulations provide for the efficient and fair administration of any quantitative restriction proclaimed pursuant to subsection (a)(3) or (c).

(2) In order to carry out an agreement concluded under subsection (a) (4), (a)(5), or (e)(2), the President is authorized to prescribe regulations governing the entry or withdrawal from warehouse of articles covered by such agreement. In addition, in order to carry out any agreement concluded under subsection (a)(4), (a)(5), or (e)(2) with one or more countries accounting for a major part of United States imports of the article covered by such agreements, including imports into a major geographic area of the United States, the President is authorized to issue regulations governing the entry or withdrawal from warehouse of like articles which are the product of countries not parties to such agreement.

(3) Regulations prescribed under this subsection shall, to the extent prac-

ticable and consistent with efficient and fair administration, insure against inequitable sharing of imports by a relatively small number of the larger importers.

(h)(1) Any import relief provided pursuant to this section shall, unless renewed pursuant to paragraph (3), terminate no later than the close of the day which is 5 years after the day on which import relief with respect to the article in question first took effect pursuant to this section.

(2) To the extent feasible, any import relief provided pursuant to this section for a period of more than 3 years shall be phased down during the period of such relief, with the first reduction of relief taking effect no later than the close of the day which is 3 years after the day on which such relief first took effect.

(3) Any import relief provided pursuant to this section or section 351 or 352 of the Trade Expansion Act of 1962 may be extended by the President, at a level of relief no greater than the level in effect immediately before such extension, for one 3 year period if the President determines, after taking into account the advice received from the Commission under subsection (i)(2) and after taking into account the considerations described in section 202(c), that such extension is in the national interest.

(4) Any import relief provided pursuant to this section may be reduced or terminated by the President when he determines, after taking into account the advice received from the Commission under subsection (i)(2) and after seeking advice of the Secretary of Commerce and the Secretary of Labor, that such reduction or termination is in the national interest.

(5) For purposes of this subsection and subsection (i), the import relief provided in the case of an orderly marketing agreement shall be the level of relief contemplated by such agreement.

(i)(1) So long as any import relief provided pursuant to this section or section 351 or 352 of the Trade Expansion Act of 1962 remains in effect, the Commission shall keep under review developments with respect to the industry concerned (including the progress and specific efforts made by the firms in the industry concerned to adjust to import competition) and upon request of the President shall make reports to the President concerning such developments.

(2) Upon request of the President or upon its own motion, the Commission shall advise the President of its judgment as to the probable economic effect on the industry concerned of the extension, reduction, or termination of the import relief provided pursuant to this section.

(3) Upon petition on behalf of the industry concerned, filed with the Commission not earlier than the date which is 9 months, and not later than the date which is 6 months, before the date any import relief provided pursuant to this section or section 351 or 352 of the Trade Expansion Act of 1962 is to terminate by reason of the expiration of the initial period therefor, the Commission shall advise the President of its judgment as to the probable economic effect on such industry of such termination.

(4) In advising the President under paragraph (2) or (3) as to the probable economic effect on the industry concerned, the Commission shall take into account all economic factors which it considers relevant, including the considerations set forth in section 202(c) and the progress and specific efforts made by the industry concerned to adjust to import competition.

(5) Advice by the Commission under paragraph (2) or (3) shall be given on the basis of an investigation during the course of which the Commission shall hold a hearing at which interested persons shall be given a reasonable opportunity to be present, to produce evidence, and to be heard.

(j) No investigation for the purposes of section 201 shall be made with respect to an article which has received import relief under this section unless 2 years have elapsed since the last day on which import relief was provided with respect to such article pursuant to this section.

(k)(1) Actions by the President pursuant to this section may be taken without regard to the provisions of section 126(a) of this Act but only after consideration of the relation of such actions to the international obligations of the United States.

(2) If the Commission treats as the domestic industry production located in a major geographic area of the United States under section 201(b)(3)(C), then the President shall take into account the geographic concentration of domestic production and of imports in that area in providing import relief, if any, which may include actions authorized under paragraph (1).

CHAPTER 2—ADJUSTMENT ASSISTANCE FOR WORKERS

SUBCHAPTER A—PETITIONS AND DETERMINATIONS

Section 221. *Petitions*

(a) A petition for a certification of eligibility to apply for adjustment assistance under this chapter may be filed with the Secretary of Labor (hereinafter in this chapter referred to as the "Secretary") by a group of workers or by their certified or recognized union or other duly authorized representative. Upon receipt of the petition, the Secretary shall promptly publish notice in the Federal Register that he has received the petition and initiated an investigation.

(b) If the petitioner, or any other person found by the Secretary to have a substantial interest in the proceedings, submits not later than 10 days after the date of the Secretary's publication under subsection (a) a request for a hearing, the Secretary shall provide for a public hearing and afford such interested persons an opportunity to be present, to produce evidence, and to be heard.

Section 222. *Group Eligibility Requirements*

The Secretary shall certify a group of workers as eligible to apply for adjustment assistance under this chapter if he determines—

(1) that a significant number or proportion of the workers in such workers' firm or an appropriate subdivision of the firm have become totally or partially separated, or are threatened to become totally or partially separated,

(2) that sales or production, or both, of such firm or subdivision have decreased absolutely, and

(3) that increases of imports of articles like or directly competitive with articles produced by such workers' firm or an appropriate subdivision thereof contributed importantly to such total or partial separation, or threat thereof, and to such decline in sales or production.

For purposes of paragraph (3), the term "contributed importantly" means a cause which is important but not necessarily more important than any other cause.

Section 223. *Determinations by Secretary of Labor*

(a) As soon as possible after the date on which a petition is filed under section 221, but in any event not later than 60 days after that date, the Secretary shall determine whether the petitioning group meets the requirements of section 222 and shall issue a certification of eligibility to apply for assistance under this chapter covering workers in any group which meets such requirements. Each certification shall specify the date on which the total or partial separation began or threatened to begin.

(b) A certification under this section shall not apply to any worker whose last total or partial separation from the firm or appropriate subdivision of the firm before his application under section 231 occurred—

(1) more than one year before the date of the petition on which such certification was granted, or

(2) more than 6 months before the effective date of this chapter.

(c) Upon reaching his determination on a petition, the Secretary shall promptly publish a summary of the determination in the Federal Register together with his reasons for making such determination.

(d) Whenever the Secretary determines, with respect to any certification of eligibility of the workers of a firm or subdivision of the firm, that total or partial separations from such firm or subdivision are no longer attributable to the conditions specified in section 222, he shall terminate such certification and promptly have notice of such termination published in the Federal Register together with his reasons for making such determination. Such termination shall apply only with respect to total or partial separations occurring after the termination date specified by the Secretary.

Section 224. *Study by Secretary of Labor when International Trade Commission begins Investigation; action where there is affirmative finding*

(a) Whenever the International Trade Commission (hereafter referred to in this chapter as the "Commission") begins an investigation under section 201 with respect to an industry, the Commission shall immediately notify the Secretary of such investigation, and the Secretary shall immediately begin a study of—

(1) the number of workers in the domestic industry producing the like or directly competitive article who have been or are likely to be certified as eligible for adjustment assistance, and

(2) the extent to which the adjustment of such workers to the import competition may be facilitated through the use of existing programs.

(b) The report of the Secretary of the study under subsection (a) shall be made to the President not later than 15 days after the day on which the Commission makes its report under section 201. Upon making his report to the President, the Secretary shall also promptly make it public (with the exception of information which the Secretary determines to be confidential) and shall have a summary of it published in the Federal Register.

(c) Whenever the Commission makes an affirmative finding under section

201(b) that increased imports are a substantial cause of serious injury or threat thereof with respect to an industry, the Secretary shall make available, to the extent feasible, full information to the workers in such industry about programs which may facilitate the adjustment to import competition of such workers, and he shall provide assistance in the preparation and processing of petitions and applications of such workers for program benefits.

SUBCHAPTER B—PROGRAM BENEFITS

PART I—TRADE READJUSTMENT ALLOWANCES

Section 231. *Qualifying Requirements for Workers*

Payment of a trade readjustment allowance shall be made to an adversely affected worker covered by a certification under subchapter A who files an application for such allowance for any week of unemployment which begins after the date specified in such certification pursuant to section 223(a), if the following conditions are met:

(1) Such worker's last total or partial separation before his application under this chapter, occurred—

(A) on or after the date, as specified in the certification under which he is covered, on which total or partial separation began or threatened to begin in the adversely affected employment, and

(B) before the expiration of the 2-year period beginning on the date on which the determination under section 223 was made, and

(C) before the termination date (if any) determined pursuant to section 223(d); and

(2) Such worker had, in the 52 weeks immediately preceding such total or partial separation, at least 26 weeks of employment at wages of $30 or more a week in adversely affected employment with a single firm or subdivision of a firm, or, if data with respect to weeks of employment are not available, equivalent amounts of employment computed under regulations prescribed by the Secretary.

Section 232. *Weekly Amounts*

(a) Subject to the other provisions of this section, the trade readjustment allowance payable to an adversely affected worker for a week of unemployment shall be—

(1) 70 percent of his average weekly wage (but not in excess of the average weekly manufacturing wage), reduced by

(2) 50 percent of the amount of the remuneration for services performed during such week.

(b) Any adversely affected worker who is entitled to trade readjustment allowances and who is undergoing training approved by the Secretary, including on-the-job training, shall receive for each week in which he is undergoing any such training, a trade readjustment allowance in an amount (computed for such week) equal to the amount computed under subsection (a) or (if greater) the amount of any weekly allowance for such training to which he would be entitled under any other Federal law for the training of workers, if he applied for such allowance. Such trade readjustment allowance shall be paid in lieu of any training allowance to which the worker would be entitled under such other Federal law.

(c) The amount of trade readjustment allowance payable to an adversely affected worker under subsection (a) for any week shall be reduced by any amount of unemployment insurance which he receives, or which he would receive if he applied for such insurance, with respect to such week; but, if the appropriate State or Federal agency finally determines that the worker was not entitled to unemployment insurance with respect to such week, the reduction shall not apply with respect to such week.

(d) If unemployment insurance, or a training allowance under any Federal law, is paid to an adversely affected worker for any week of unemployment with respect to which he would be entitled (determined without regard to subsection (c) or (e) or to any disqualification under section 236(c)) to a trade readjustment allowance if he applied for such allowance, each such week shall be deducted from the total number of weeks of trade readjustment allowance otherwise payable to him under section 233(a) when he applies for a trade readjustment allowance and is determined to be entitled to such allowance. If the unemployment insurance or the training allowance paid to such worker for any week of unemployment is less than the amount of the trade readjustment allowance to which he would be entitled if he applied for such allowance, he shall receive, when he applies for a trade readjustment allowance and is determined to be entitled to such allowance, a trade readjustment allowance for such week equal to such difference.

(e) Whenever, with respect to any week of unemployment, the total amount payable to an adversely affected worker as remuneration for services performed during such week, as unemployment insurance, as a training allowance referred to in subsection (d), and as a trade readjustment allowance exceeds 80 percent of his average weekly wage (or, if lesser, 130 percent of the average weekly manufacturing wage), then his trade readjustment allowance for such week shall be reduced by the amount of such excess.

(f) The amount of any weekly payment to be made under this section which is not a whole dollar amount shall be rounded upward to the next higher whole dollar amount.

Section 233. *Time Limitations on Trade Readjustment Allowances*

(a) Payment of trade readjustment allowances shall not be made to an adversely affected worker for more than 52 weeks, except that, in accordance with regulations prescribed by the Secretary—

(1) such payments may be made for not more than 26 additional weeks to an adversely affected worker to assist him to complete training approved by the Secretary, or

(2) such payments shall be made for not more than 26 additional weeks to an adversely affected worker who had reached his 60th birthday on or before the date of total or partial separation.

In no case may an adversely affected worker be paid trade readjustment allowances for more than 78 weeks.

(b)(1) Except for a payment made for an additional week under subsection (a)(1) or (a)(2), a trade readjustment allowance may not be paid for a week of unemployment beginning more than 2 years after the beginning of the appropriate week.

(2) A trade readjustment allowance may not be paid for an additional week specified in subsection (a)(1) if the adversely affected worker who would receive such allowance did not make a bona fide application to a training program approved by the Secretary within 180 days after the end of the appropriate week or the date of his first certification of eligibility to apply for adjustment assistance issued by the Secretary, whichever is later.

(3) A trade readjustment allowance may not be paid for an additional week specified in subsection (a) if such additional week begins more than 3 years after the beginning of the appropriate week.

(4) For purposes of this subsection, the appropriate week—

(A) for a totally separated worker is the week of his most recent total separation, and

(B) for a partially separated worker is the first week for which he receives a trade readjustment allowance following his most recent partial separation.

Section 234. *Application of State Laws*

Except where inconsistent with the provisions of this chapter and subject to such regulations as the Secretary may prescribe, the availability and disqualification provisions of the State law—

(1) under which an adversely affected worker is entitled to unemployment insurance (whether or not he has filed a claim for such insurance), or

(2) if he is not so entitled to unemployment insurance, of the State in which he was totally or partially separated,

shall apply to any such worker who files a claim for trade readjustment allowances. The State law so determined with respect to a separation of a worker shall remain applicable, for purposes of the preceding sentence, with respect to such separation until such worker becomes entitled to unemployment insurance under another State law (whether or not he has filed a claim for such insurance).

PART II—TRAINING AND RELATED SERVICES

Section 235. *Employment Services*

The Secretary shall make every reasonable effort to secure for adversely affected workers covered by a certification under subchapter A of this chapter counseling, testing, and placement services, and supportive and other services, provided for under any other Federal law. The Secretary shall, whenever appropriate, procure such services through agreements with cooperating State agencies.

Section 236. *Training*

(a) If the Secretary determines that there is no suitable employment available for an adversely affected worker covered by a certification under subchapter A of this chapter, but that suitable employment (which may include technical and professional employment) would be available if the worker received appropriate training, he may approve such training. Insofar as possible, the Secretary shall provide or assure the provision of such training on the job.

(b) The Secretary may, where appropriate, authorize supplemental assistance necessary to defray transportation and subsistence expenses for separate maintenance when training is provided in facilities which are not within commuting distance of a worker's regular place of residence. The Secretary shall not authorize payments for subsistence exceeding $15 per day; nor shall he authorize payments for transportation expenses exceeding 12 cents per mile.

(c) Any adversely affected worker who, without good cause, refuses to accept or continue, or fails to make satisfactory progress in, suitable training to which he has been referred by the Secretary shall not thereafter be entitled to payments under this chapter until he enters or resumes the training to which he has been so referred.

PART III—JOB SEARCH AND RELOCATION ALLOWANCES

Section 237. *Job Search Allowances*

(a) Any adversely affected worker covered by a certification under subchapter A of this chapter who has been totally separated may file an application with the Secretary for a job search allowance. Such allowance, if granted, shall provide reimbursement to the worker of 80 percent of the cost of his necessary job search expenses as prescribed by regulations of the Secretary, except that such reimbursement may not exceed $500 for any worker.

(b) A job search allowance may be granted only—

(1) to assist an adversely affected worker in securing a job within the United States;

(2) where the Secretary determines that such worker cannot reasonably be expected to secure suitable employment in the commuting area in which he resides; and

(3) where the worker has filed an application for such allowance with the Secretary no later than 1 year after the date of his last total separation before his application under this chapter or (in the case of a worker who has been referred to training by the Secretary) within a reasonable period of time after the conclusion of such training period.

Section 238. *Relocation Allowances*

(a) Any adversely affected worker covered by a certification under subchapter A of this chapter who has been totally separated may file an application with the Secretary for a relocation allowance, subject to the terms and conditions of this section.

(b) A relocation allowance may be granted only to assist an adversely affected worker in relocating within the United States and only if the Secretary determines that such worker cannot reasonably be expected to secure suitable employment in the commuting area in which he resides and that such worker—

(1) has obtained suitable employment affording a reasonable expectation of long-term duration in the area in which he wishes to relocate, or

(2) has obtained a bona fide offer of such employment.

(c) A relocation allowance shall not be granted to such worker unless—

(1) for the week in which the application for such allowance is filed, he is entitled to a trade readjustment allowance (determined without regard to section 232 (c) and (e)) or would be so entitled (determined without regard to whether he filed application therefor) but for the fact that he has obtained the employment referred to in subsection (b)(1), and

(2) such relocation occurs within a reasonable period after the filing of such application or (in the case of a worker who has been referred to training by the Secretary) within a reasonable period after the conclusion of such training.

Under regulations prescribed by the Secretary, a relocation allowance shall not be granted to more than one member of the family with respect to the same relocation.

(d) For the purposes of this section, the term "relocation allowance" means—

(1) 80 percent of the reasonable and necessary expenses, as specified in regulations prescribed by the Secretary, incurred in transporting a worker and his family, if any, and household effects, and

(2) a lump sum equivalent to three times the worker's average weekly wage, up to a maximum payment of $500.

SUBCHAPTER C—GENERAL PROVISIONS

Section 239. *Agreements with States*

(a) The Secretary is authorized on behalf of the United States to enter into an agreement with any State, or with any State agency (referred to in this subchapter as "cooperating States" and "cooperating States agencies" respectively). Under such an agreement, the cooperating State agency (1) as agent of the United States, will receive applications for, and will provide, payments on the basis provided in this chapter, (2) where appropriate, will afford adversely affected workers who apply for payments under this chapter testing, counseling, referral to training, and placement services, and (3) will otherwise cooperate with the Secretary and with other State and Federal agencies in providing payments and services under this chapter.

(b) Each agreement under this subchapter shall provide the terms and conditions upon which the agreement may be amended, suspended, or terminated.

(c) Each agreement under this subchapter shall provide that unemployment insurance otherwise payable to any adversely affected worker will not be denied or reduced for any week by reason of any right to payments under this chapter.

(d) A determination by a cooperating State agency with respect to entitlement to program benefits under an agreement is subject to review in the same manner and to the same extent as determinations under the applicable State law and only in that manner and to that extent.

(e) Section 3302(c) of the Internal Revenue Code of 1954 (relating to credits against Federal unemployment tax) is amended by inserting after paragraph (3) the following new paragraph:

"(4) If the Secretary of Labor determines that a State, or State agency, has not—

"(A) entered into the agreement described in section 239 of the Trade Act of 1974, with the Secretary of Labor before July 1, 1975, or

"(B) fulfilled its commitments under an agreement with the Secretary of Labor as described in section 239 of the Trade Act of 1974,

then, in the case of a taxpayer subject to the unemployment compensation law of such State, the total credits (after applying subsections (a) and (b) and paragraphs (1), (2), and (3) of this section) otherwise allowable under this section for a year during which such State or agency does not enter into or fulfill such an agreement shall be reduced by 15 percent of the tax imposed with respect to wages paid by such taxpayer during such year which are attributable to such State.".

Section 240. *Administration Absent State Agreement*

(a) In any State where there is no agreement in force between a State or its agency under section 239, the Secretary shall arrange under regulations prescribed by him for performance of all necessary functions under subchapter B of this chapter, including provision for a fair hearing for any worker whose application for payments is denied.

(b) A final determination under subsection (a) with respect to entitlement to program benefits under subchapter B of this chapter is subject to review by the courts in the same manner and to the same extent as is provided by section 205(g) of the Social Security Act (42 U.S.C. sec. 405(g)).

Section 241. *Payments to States*

(a) The Secretary shall from time to time certify to the Secretary of the Treasury for payment to each cooperating State the sums necessary to enable such State as agent of the United States to make payments provided for by this chapter. The Secretary of the Treasury, prior to audit or settlement by the General Accounting Office, shall make payment to the State from the Adjustment Assistance Trust Fund established in section 245 in accordance with such certification.

(b) All money paid a State under this section shall be used solely for the purposes for which it is paid; and money so paid which is not used for such purposes shall be returned, at the time specified in the agreement under this subchapter, to the Secretary of the Treasury and credited to Adjustment Assistance Trust Fund.

(c) Any agreement under this subchapter may require any officer or employee of the State certifying payments or disbursing funds under the agreement or otherwise participating in the performance of the agreement, to give a surety bond to the United States in such amount as the Secretary may deem necessary, and may provide for the payment of the cost of such bond from funds for carrying out the purposes of this chapter.

Section 242. *Liabilities of Certifying and Disbursing Officers*

(a) No person designated by the Secretary, or designated pursuant to an agreement under this subchapter, as a certifying officer, shall, in the absence of gross negligence or intent to defraud the United States, be liable with respect to any payment certified by him under this chapter.

(b) No disbursing officer shall, in the absence of gross negligence or intent to defraud the United States, be liable with respect to any payment by him under this chapter if it was based upon a voucher signed by a certifying officer designated as provided in subsection (a).

Section 243. *Recovery of Overpayments*

(a) If a cooperating State agency or the Secretary, or a court of competent jurisdiction finds that any person—

(1) has made or has caused to be made by another, a false statement or representation of a material fact knowing it to be false, or has knowingly failed or caused another to fail to disclose a material fact; and

(2) as a result of such action has received any payment under this chapter to which he was not entitled,

such person shall be liable to repay such amount to the State agency or the Secretary as the case may be, or either may recover such amount by deductions from any sums payable to such person under this chapter. Any such finding by a State agency or the Secretary may be made only after an opportunity for a fair hearing.

(b) Any amount repaid to a State agency under this section shall be deposited into the fund from which payment was made. Any amount repaid to the Secretary under this section shall be returned to the Secretary of the Treasury and credited to the Adjustment Assistance Trust Fund.

Section 244. *Penalties*

Whoever makes a false statement of a material fact knowing it to be false, or knowingly fails to disclose a material fact, for the purpose of obtaining or increasing for himself or for any other person any payment authorized to be furnished under this chapter or pursuant to an agreement under section 239 shall be fined not more than $1,000 or imprisoned for not more than one year, or both.

Section 245. *Creation of Trust Fund; Authorization of Appropriations out of Customs Receipts*

(a) There is hereby established on the books of the Treasury of the United States a trust fund to be known as the "Adjustment Assistance Trust Fund" (referred to in this section as the "Trust Fund"). The Trust Fund shall consist of such amounts as may be deposited in it pursuant to the authorization contained in subsection (b). Amounts in the Trust Fund may be used only to carry out the provisions of this chapter (including administrative costs). The Secretary of the Treasury shall be the trustee of the Trust Fund and shall report to the Congress not later than March 1 of each year on the operation and status of the Trust Fund during the preceding fiscal year.

(b)(1) There are hereby authorized to be appropriated to the Trust Fund, out of amounts in the general fund of the Treasury attributable to the collections of customs duties not otherwise appropriated, for each fiscal year ending after the date of the enactment of this Act, such sums as may be necessary to carry out the provisions of this chapter (including administrative costs).

(2) There are authorized to be appropriated to the Trust Fund, for purposes of training (including administrative costs) under section 236 such sums as may be necessary.

Section 246. *Transitional Provisions*

(a) Where a group of workers has been certified as eligible to apply for adjustment assistance under section 302(b)(2) or (c) of the Trade Expansion Act of 1962, any worker who has not had an application for trade readjustment allowances under section 322 of that Act denied before the effective date of this chapter may apply under section 231 of this Act as if the group certification under which he claims coverage had been made under subchapter A of this chapter.

(b) In any case where a group of workers or their certified or recognized union or other duly authorized representative has filed a petition under section 301(a)(2) of the Trade Expansion Act of 1962, more than 4 months before the effective date of this chapter and

(1) the Commission has not rejected such petition before the effective date of this chapter, and

(2) the President or his delegate has not issued a certification under section 302(c) of that Act to the petitioning group before the effective date of this chapter,

such group or representative thereof may file a new petition under section 221 of this Act, not later than 90 days after the effective date of this chapter. For purposes of section 223(b)(1), the date on which such group or representative filed the petition under the Trade Expansion Act of 1962 shall apply. Section 223(b)(2) shall not apply to workers covered by a certification issued pursuant to a petition meeting the requirements of this subsection.

(c) A group of workers may file a petition under section 221 covering weeks of unemployment (as defined in the Trade Expansion Act of 1962) beginning before the effective date of this chapter, or covering such weeks and also weeks of unemployment beginning on or after the effective date of this chapter.

(d) Any worker receiving payments pursuant to this section shall be entitled—

(1) for weeks of unemployment (as defined in the Trade Expansion Act of 1962) beginning before the effective date of this chapter, to the rights and privileges provided in chapter 3 of title III of such Act, and

(2) for weeks of unemployment beginning on or after the effective date of this chapter, to the rights and privileges provided in this chapter, except that the total number of weeks of unemployment, as defined in the Trade Expansion Act of 1962, for which trade readjustment allowances were payable under that Act shall be deducted from the total number of weeks of unemployment for which an adversely affected worker is eligible for trade readjustment allowances under this chapter.

(e) The Commission shall make available to the Secretary on request data it has acquired in investigations under section 301 of the Trade Expansion Act of 1962 concluded within the 2-year period ending on the effective date of this chapter which did not result in Presidential action under section 302 (a)(3) or 302(c) of that Act.

Section 247. *Definitions*

For purposes of this chapter—

(1) The term "adversely affected employment" means employment in a firm or appropriate subdivision of a firm, if workers of such firm or subdivision are eligible to apply for adjustment assistance under this chapter.

(2) The term "adversely affected worker" means an individual who, because of lack of work in adversely affected employment—

(A) has been totally or partially separated from such employment, or

(B) has been totally separated from employment with the firm in a subdivision of which such adversely affected employment exists.

(3) The term "average weekly manufacturing wage" means the na-

tional gross average weekly earnings of production workers in manu-facturing industries for the latest calendar year (as officially published annually by the Bureau of Labor Statistics of the Department of Labor) most recently published before the period for which the assistance under this chapter is furnished.

(4) The term "average weekly wage" means one-thirteenth of the total wages paid to an individual in the high quarter. For purposes of this computation, the high quarter shall be that quarter in which the indi-vidual's total wages were highest among the first 4 of the last 5 completed calendar quarters immediately before the quarter in which occurs the week with respect to which the computation is made. Such week shall be the week in which total separation occurred, or, in cases where partial separation is claimed, an appropriate week, as defined in regulations prescribed by the Secretary.

(5) The term "average weekly hours" means the average hours worked by the individual (excluding overtime) in the employment from which he has been or claims to have been separated in the 52 weeks (excluding weeks during which the individual was sick or on vacation) preceding the week specified in the last sentence of paragraph (4).

(6) The term "partial separation" means, with respect to an indi-vidual who has not been totally separated, that he has had—

(A) his hours of work reduced to 80 percent or less of his average weekly hours in adversely affected employment, and

(B) his wages reduced to 80 percent or less of his average weekly wage in such adversely affected employment.

(7) The term "remuneration" means wages and net earnings derived from services performed as a self-employed individual.

(8) The term "State" includes the District of Columbia and the Commonwealth of Puerto Rico; and the term "United States" when used in the geographical sense includes such Commonwealth.

(9) The term "State agency" means the agency of the State which administers the State law.

(10) The term "State law" means the unemployment insurance law of the State approved by the Secretary of Labor under section 3304 of the Internal Revenue Code of 1954.

(11) The term "total separation" means the layoff or severance of

an individual from employment with a firm in which, or in a subdivision of which, adversely affected employment exists.

(12) The term "unemployment insurance" means the unemployment insurance payable to an individual under any State law or Federal unemployment insurance law, including chapter 85 of title 5, United States Code, and the Railroad Unemployment Insurance Act.

(13) The term "week" means a week as defined in the applicable State law.

(14) The term "week of unemployment" means with respect to an individual any week for which his remuneration for services performed during such week is less than 80 percent of his average weekly wage and in which, because of lack of work—

(A) if he has been totally separated, he worked less than the full-time week (excluding overtime) in his current occupation, or

(B) if he has been partially separated, he worked 80 percent or less of his average weekly hours.

Section 248. *Regulations*

The Secretary shall prescribe such regulations as may be necessary to carry out the provisions of this chapter.

Section 249. *Subpena Power*

(a) The Secretary may require by subpena the attendance of witnesses and the production of evidence necessary for him to make a determination under the provisions of this chapter.

(b) If a person refuses to obey a subpena issued under subsection (a), a United States district court within the jurisdiction of which the relevant proceeding under this chapter is conducted may, upon petition by the Secretary, issue an order requiring compliance with such subpoena.

Section 250. *Judicial Review*

(a) A worker, group of workers, certified or recognized union, or an authorized representative of such worker or group, aggrieved by a final determination by the Secretary under the provisions of section 223 may, within 60 days after notice of such determination, file a petition for review of such determination with the United States court of appeals for the circuit in which such worker or group is located or in the United States Court of Appeals for the District of Columbia Circuit. The clerk of such court shall send a copy of such petition to the Secretary. Upon receiving such petition, the Secretary shall promptly certify and file in such court the record on which he based such determination.

(b) The findings of fact by the Secretary, if supported by substantial evidence, shall be conclusive; but the court, for good cause shown, may remand the case to the Secretary to take further evidence, and the Secretary may thereupon make new or modified findings of fact and may modify his previous action, and shall certify to the court the record of the further proceedings. Such new or modified findings of fact shall likewise be conclusive if supported by substantial evidence.

(c) The court shall have jurisdiction to affirm the action of the Secretary or to set it aside, in whole or in part. The judgment of the court shall be subject to review by the Supreme Court of the United States upon certiorari or certification as provided in section 1254 of title 28, United States Code.

CHAPTER 3—ADJUSTMENT ASSISTANCE FOR FIRMS

Section 251. *Petitions and Determinations*

(a) A petition for a certification of eligibility to apply for adjustment assistance under this chapter may be filed with the Secretary of Commerce (hereinafter in this chapter referred to as the "Secretary") by a firm or its representative. Upon receipt of the petition, the Secretary shall promptly publish notice in the Federal Register that he has received the petition and initiated an investigation.

(b) If the petitioner, or any other person, organization, or group found by the Secretary to have a substantial interest in the proceedings, submits not later than 10 days after the date of the Secretary's publication under subsection (a) a request for a hearing, the Secretary shall provide for a public hearing and afford such interested persons an opportunity to be present, to produce evidence, and to be heard.

(c) The Secretary shall certify a firm as eligible to apply for adjustment assistance under this chapter if he determines—

(1) that a significant number or proportion of the workers in such firm have become totally or partially separated, or are threatened to become totally or partially separated,

(2) that sales or production, or both, of such firm have decreased absolutely, and

(3) that increases of imports of articles like or directly competitive with articles produced by such firm contributed importantly to such total or partial separation, or threat thereof, and to such decline in sales or production.

For purposes of paragraph (3), the term "contributed importantly" means a cause which is important but not necessarily more important than any other cause.

(d) A determination shall be made by the Secretary as soon as possible after the date on which the petition is filed under this section, but in any event not later than 60 days after that date.

Section 252. *Approval of Adjustment Proposals*

(a) A firm certified under section 251 as eligible to apply for adjustment assistance may, at any time within 2 years after the date of such certification, file an application with the Secretary for adjustment assistance under this chapter. Such application shall include a proposal for the economic adjustment of such firm.

(b)(1) Adjustment assistance under this chapter consists of technical assistance and financial assistance, which may be furnished singly or in combination. The Secretary shall approve a firm's application for adjustment assistance only if he determines—

(A) that the firm has no reasonable access to financing through the private capital market, and

(B) that the firm's adjustment proposal—

(i) is reasonably calculated materially to contribute to the economic adjustment of the firm,

(ii) gives adequate consideration to the interests of the workers of such firm, and

(iii) demonstrates that the firm will make all reasonable efforts to use its own resources for economic development.

(2) The Secretary shall make a determination as soon as possible after the date on which an application is filed under this section, but in no event later than 60 days after such date.

(c) In order to assist a firm which has been certified as eligible to apply for adjustment assistance under this chapter in preparing a viable adjustment proposal, the Secretary may furnish technical assistance to such firm.

(d) Whenever the Secretary determines that any firm no longer requires assistance under this chapter, he shall terminate the certification of eligibility of such firm and promptly have notice of such termination published in the Federal Register. Such termination shall take effect on the termination date specified by the Secretary.

Section 253. *Technical Assistance*

(a) The technical assistance furnished under this chapter shall consist of—

(1) assistance to the firm in developing a proposal for its economic adjustment,

(2) assistance in the implementation of such a proposal, or

(3) both.

(b) The Secretary may provide to a firm certified under section 251, on such terms and conditions as he determines to be appropriate, such technical assistance as in his judgment will carry out the purposes of this chapter with respect to such firm.

(c) The Secretary shall furnish technical assistance under this chapter through existing agencies and through private individuals, firms, and institutions. In the case of assistance furnished through private individuals, firms, and institutions (including private consulting services), the Secretary may share the cost thereof (but not more than 75 percent of such cost may be borne by the United States).

Section 254. *Financial Assistance*

(a) The Secretary may provide to a firm, on such terms and conditions as he determines to be appropriate, such financial assistance in the form of direct loans or guarantees of loans as in his judgment will materially contribute to the economic adjustment of the firm. The assumption of an outstanding indebtedness of the firm, with or without recourse, shall be considered to be the making of a loan for purposes of this section.

(b) Loans or guarantees of loans shall be made under this chapter only for the purpose of making funds available to the firm—

(1) for acquisition, construction, installation, modernization, development, conversion, or expansion of land, plant, buildings, equipment, facilities, or machinery, or

(2) to supply such working capital as may be necessary to enable the firm to implement its adjustment proposal.

(c) To the extent that loan funds can be obtained from private sources (with or without a guarantee) at the rate provided in the first sentence of section 255(b), no direct loan shall be provided to a firm under this chapter.

Section 255. *Conditions for Financial Assistance*

(a) No financial assistance shall be provided under this chapter unless the Secretary determines—

(1) that the funds required are not available from the firm's own resources; and

(2) that there is reasonable assurance of repayment of the loan.

(b) The rate of interest on loans which are guaranteed under this chapter shall be no higher than the maximum interest per annum that a participating financial institution may establish on guaranteed loans made pursuant to section 7(a) of the Small Business Act (15 U.S.C. 636(a)). The rate of interest on direct loans made under this chapter shall be (i) a rate determined by the Secretary of the Treasury taking into consideration the current average market yield on outstanding marketable obligations of the United States with remaining periods to maturity that are comparable to the average maturities of such loans, adjusted to the nearest one-eighth of 1 percent, plus (ii) an amount adequate in the judgment of the Secretary to cover administrative costs and probable losses under the program.

(c) The Secretary shall make no loan or guarantee of a loan having a maturity in excess of 25 years, including renewals and extensions. Such limitation on maturities shall not, however, apply—

(1) to securities or obligations received by the Secretary as claimant in bankruptcy or equitable reorganization, or as creditor in other proceedings attendant upon insolvency of the obligor, or

(2) to an extension or renewal for an additional period not exceeding 10 years, if the Secretary determines that such extension or renewal is reasonably necessary for the orderly liquidation of the loan.

(d) In making guarantees of loans, and in making direct loans, the Secretary shall give priority to firms which are small within the meaning of the Small Business Act (and regulations promulgated thereunder).

(e) No loan shall be guaranteed by the Secretary in an amount which exceeds 90 percent of the balance of the loan outstanding.

(f) The Secretary shall maintain operating reserves with respect to anticipated claims under guarantees made under this chapter. Such reserves shall be considered to constitute obligations for purposes of section 1311 of the Supplemental Appropriation Act, 1955 (31 U.S.C. 200).

(g) The Secretary may charge a fee to a lender which makes a loan guaranteed under this chapter in such amount as is necessary to cover the cost of administration of such guarantee.

(h)(1) The aggregate amount of loans made to any firm which are guaranteed under this chapter and which are outstanding at any time shall not exceed $3,000,000.

(2) The aggregate amount of direct loans made to any firm under this chapter which are outstanding at any time shall not exceed $1,000,000.

Section 256. *Delegation of Functions to Small Business Administration; Authorization of Appropriations*

(a) In the case of any firm which is small (within the meaning of the Small Business Act and regulations promulgated thereunder), the Secretary may delegate all of his functions under this chapter (other than the functions under sections 251 and 252(d) with respect to the certification of eligibility and section 264) to the Administrator of the Small Business Administration.

(b) There are hereby authorized to be appropriated to the Secretary such sums as may be necessary from time to time to carry out his functions under this chapter in connection with furnishing adjustment assistance to firms, which sums are authorized to be appropriated to remain available until expended.

(c) The unexpended balances of appropriations authorized by section 312(d) of the Trade Expansion Act of 1962 are transferred to the Secretary to carry out his functions under this chapter.

Section 257. *Administration of Financial Assistance*

(a) In making and administering guarantees and loans under section 254, the Secretary may—

(1) require security for any such guarantee or loan, and enforce, waive, or subordinate such security;

(2) assign or sell at public or private sale, or otherwise dispose of, upon such terms and conditions and for such consideration as he shall determine to be reasonable, any evidence of debt, contract, claim, personal property, or security assigned to or held by him in connection with such guarantees or loans, and collect, compromise, and obtain deficiency judgments with respect to all obligations assigned to or held by him in connection with such guarantees or loans until such time as such obligations may be referred to the Attorney General for suit or collection;

(3) renovate, improve, modernize, complete, insure, rent, sell, or otherwise deal with, upon such terms and conditions and for such consideration as he shall determine to be reasonable, any real or personal property conveyed to or otherwise acquired by him in connection with such guarantees or loans;

(4) acquire, hold, transfer, release, or convey any real or personal property or any interest therein whenever deemed necessary or appropriate, and execute all legal documents for such purposes; and

(5) exercise all such other powers and take all such other acts as may be necessary or incidental to the carrying out of functions pursuant to section 254.

(b) Any mortgage acquired as security under subsection (a) shall be recorded under applicable State law.

(c) All repayments of loans, payments of interest, and other receipts arising out of transactions entered into by the Secretary pursuant to this chapter, shall be available for financing functions performed under this chapter, including administrative expenses in connection with such functions.

Section 258. *Protective Provisions*

(a) Each recipient of adjustment assistance under this chapter shall keep records which fully disclose the amount and disposition by such recipient of the proceeds, if any, of such adjustment assistance, and which will facilitate an effective audit. The recipient shall also keep such other records as the Secretary may prescribe.

(b) The Secretary and the Comptroller General of the United States shall have access for the purpose of audit and examination to any books, documents, papers, and records of the recipient pertaining to adjustment assistance under this chapter.

(c) No adjustment assistance under this chapter shall be extended to any firm unless the owners, partners, or officers certify to the Secretary—

(1) the names of any attorneys, agents, and other persons engaged by or on behalf of the firm for the purpose of expediting applications for such adjustment assistance; and

(2) the fees paid or to be paid to any such person.

(d) No financial assistance shall be provided to any firm under this chapter unless the owners, partners, or officers shall execute an agreement binding them and the firm for a period of 2 years after such financial assistance is provided, to refrain from employing, tendering any office or employment to, or retaining for professional services any person who, on the date such assistance or any part thereof was provided, or within 1 year prior thereto, shall have served as an officer, attorney, agent, or employee occupying a position or engaging in activities which the Secretary shall have determined involve discretion with respect to the provision of such financial assistance.

Section 259. *Penalties*

Whoever makes a false statement of a material fact knowing it to be false, or knowingly fails to disclose a material fact, or whoever willfully overvalues any security, for the purpose of influencing in any way a determination under this chapter, or for the purpose of obtaining money, property, or anything of value under this chapter, shall be fined not more than $5,000 or imprisoned for not more than 2 years, or both.

Section 260. *Suits*

In providing technical and financial assistance under this chapter the Secretary may sue and be sued in any court of record of a State having general jurisdiction or in any United States district court, and jurisdiction is conferred upon such district court to determine such controversies without regard to the amount in controversy; but no attachment, injunction, garnishment, or other similar process, mesne or final, shall be issued against him or his property. Nothing in this section shall be construed to except the activities pursuant to sections 253 and 254 from the application of sections 516, 547, and 2679 of title 28 of the United States Code.

Section 261. *Definitions*

For purposes of this chapter, the term "firm" includes an individual proprietorship, partnership, joint venture, association, corporation (including a development corporation), business trust, cooperative, trustee in bankruptcy, and receiver under decree of any court. A firm, together with any predecessor or successor firm, or any affiliated firm controlled or substantially beneficially owned by substantially the same persons, may be considered a single firm where necessary to prevent unjustifiable benefits.

Section 262. *Regulations*

The Secretary shall prescribe such regulations as may be necessary to carry out the provisions of this chapter.

Section 263. *Transitional Provisions*

(a) In any case where a firm or its representative has filed a petition with the International Trade Commission (hereafter in this chapter referred to as the "Commission") under section 301(a)(2) of the Trade Expansion Act of 1962, and the Commission has not made its determination under section 301(c) of that Act before the effective date of this chapter, such firm may reapply under the provisions of section 251 of this Act. In order to assist the Secretary in making his determination under such section 251 with respect to such firm, the Commission shall make available to the Secretary, on request, data it has acquired with respect to its investigation.

(b) If, on the effective date of this chapter, the President (or his delegate) has not taken action under section 302(c) of the Trade Expansion Act of 1962 with respect to a report of the Commission containing an affirmative finding under section 301(c) of that Act or a report with respect to which an equal number of Commissioners are evenly divided, the Secretary may treat such report as a certification of eligibility made under section 251 of this Act on the effective date of this chapter.

(c) Any certification of eligibility of a firm under section 302(c) of the Trade Expansion Act of 1962 made before the effective date of this chapter shall be treated as a certification of eligibility made under section 251 of this Act on the date of the enactment of this Act; except that any firm whose adjustment proposal was certified under section 311 of the Trade Expansion Act of 1962 before the effective date of this chapter may receive adjustment assistance at the level set forth in such certified proposal.

Section 264. *Study by Secretary of Commerce when International Trade Commission Begins Investigation; Action Where There is Affirmative Finding*

(a) Whenever the Commission begins an investigation under section 201 with respect to an industry, the Commission shall immediately notify the Secretary of such investigation, and the Secretary shall immediately begin a study of—

(1) the number of firms in the domestic industry producing the like or directly competitive article which have been or are likely to be certified as eligible for adjustment assistance, and

(2) the extent to which the orderly adjustment of such firms to the import competition may be facilitated through the use of existing programs.

(b) The report of the Secretary of the study under subsection (a) shall be made to the President not later than 15 days after the day on which the Commission makes its report under section 201. Upon making its report to the President, the Secretary shall also promptly make it public (with the exception of information which the Secretary determines to be confidential) and shall have a summary of it published in the Federal Register.

(c) Whenever the Commission makes an affirmative finding under section 201(b) that increased imports are a substantial cause of serious injury or threat thereof with respect to an industry, the Secretary shall make available, to the extent feasible, full information to the firms in such industry about programs which may facilitate the orderly adjustment to import competition of such firms, and he shall provide assistance in the preparation and processing of petitions and applications of such firms for program benefits.

CHAPTER 4—ADJUSTMENT ASSISTANCE FOR COMMUNITIES

Section 271. *Petitions and Determinations*

(a) A petition for certification of eligibility for adjustment assistance under this chapter may be filed with the Secretary of Commerce (hereinafter in this chapter referred to as the "Secretary") by a political subdivision of a State (hereinafter in this chapter referred to as a "community") by a group of such communities, or by the Governor of a State on behalf of such communities. Upon receipt of the petition, the Secretary shall promptly publish notice in the Federal Register that he has received the petition and initiated an investigation.

(b) If the petitioner, or any other person found by the Secretary to have a substantial interest in the proceedings, submits not later than 10 days after the Secretary's publication of notice under subsection (a) a request for a hearing the Secretary shall provide for a public hearing and afford such interested persons an opportunity to be present, to produce evidence, and to be heard.

(c) The Secretary shall certify a community as eligible for adjustment assistance under this chapter if he determines—

(1) that a significant number or proportion of the workers in the trade impacted area in which such community is located have become

totally or partially separated, or are threatened to become totally or partially separated,

(2) that sales or production, or both, of firms, or subdivisions of firms, located in the trade impacted area specified in paragraph (1) have decreased absolutely, and

(3) that increases of imports of articles like or directly competitive with articles produced by firms, or subdivisions of firms, located in the trade impacted area specified in paragraph (1) or that the transfer of firms or subdivisions of firms located in such area to foreign countries have contributed importantly to the total or partial separations, or threats thereof, described in paragraph (1) and to the decline in sales or production described in paragraph (2).

For purposes of paragraph (3), the term "contributed importantly" means a cause which is important but not necessarily more important than any other cause.

(d) As soon as possible after the date on which a petition is filed under this section, but in any event not later than 60 days after that date, the Secretary shall determine whether the petitioning community, or group of communities, meets the requirements of subsection (c) and shall issue a certification of eligibility for assistance under this chapter covering any community located in the same trade impacted area in which the petitioner is located which meets such requirements.

(e) The Secretary, after consulting the Secretary of Labor, shall establish the size and boundaries of each trade impacted area, considering the criteria in subsection (c) and, to the extent they are relevant, the factors specified as criteria for redevelopment areas under section 401 of the Public Works and Economic Development Act of 1965.

(f) If the Secretary determines that a community requires no additional assistance under this chapter, he shall terminate the certification of eligibility of such community and promptly have notice of such termination published in the Federal Register. Such termination shall take effect on the termination date specified by the Secretary.

Section 272. *Trade Impacted Area Councils*

(a) Within 60 days after a community is certified under section 271, the Secretary shall send his representatives to the trade impacted area in which such community is located to inform officials of communities and other residents of such area about benefits available to them under this Act and to assist such officials and residents in establishing a Trade Impacted Area Council for Adjustment Assistance (hereinafter in this chapter referred to as the "Council") for such area.

(b)(1) The Secretary shall establish, subject to the last sentence of this paragraph, a Council for each trade impacted area in which one or more communities are certified under section 271. Such Council shall—

(A) develop a proposal for an adjustment assistance plan for the economic rejuvenation of certified communities in its trade impacted area, and

(B) coordinate community action under the adjustment assistance plan, as approved by the Secretary.

If an appropriate entity for purposes of performing the functions specified in subparagraphs (A) and (B) already exists in such area, then the Secretary may designate such entity as the Council for such area.

(2) Such Council shall include representatives of certified communities, industry, labor, and the general public located in the trade impacted area covered by the Council.

(c) Upon application by a Council established under subsection (b), the Secretary is authorized to make grants to such Council for maintaining an appropriate professional and clerical staff. No grant shall be made to a Council to maintain staff after the period which ends 2 years after the date on which such Council is established or designated.

(d) A Council established under this section may file an application with the Secretary for adjustment assistance under this chapter. Such application shall include the Council's proposal for an adjustment assistance plan for the communities in its trade impacted area.

Section 273. *Program Benefits*

(a) Adjustment assistance under this chapter consists of—

(1) all forms of assistance, other than loan guarantees, which are provided to a redevelopment area under the Public Works and Economic Development Act of 1965, and

(2) the loan guarantee program described in subsection (d).

(b) No adjustment assistance may be extended to any community or person in a trade impacted area under this chapter unless the Secretary approves the adjustment assistance plan submitted to him under section 272(d).

(c) For purposes of the Public Works and Economic Development Act of 1965—

(1) a trade impacted area for which an adjustment assistance plan has been approved under section 272(d) shall be treated as a redevelopment area, except that—

(A) no loan guarantees may be made to any person under such Act; and

(B) no loan or grant may be made to any recipient in such an area after September 30, 1980, and

(2) approval of an adjustment assistance plan submitted under section 272(d) shall be treated as approval of an overall economic development program under section 202(b)(10) of such Act.

(d) The Secretary is authorized to guarantee loans for—

(1) the acquisition, construction, installation, modernization, development, conversion, or expansion of land, plant, buildings, equipment, facilities, or machinery, and

(2) working capital,

made to private borrowers by private lending institutions in connection with projects in trade impacted areas subject to the same terms and conditions to which loan guarantees are subject under section 202 of the Public Works and Economic Development Act of 1965, including record and audit requirements and penalties, except that—

(1) no new loan guarantee may be made under this subsection after September 30, 1982,

(2) a loan guarantee may be made for the entire amount of the outstanding unpaid balance of such loan, and

(3) no more than 20 percent of the amount of loan guarantees made under this subsection by the United States may be made in one State.

(e) The Governor of the State, the authorized representative of the community, or the Governor of the State and the authorized representative of the community, in which an applicant for a loan guarantee under subsection (b) is located may enter into an agreement with the Secretary which provides that such State or such community, or that such State and such community, will pay not to exceed one-half of the amount of any liability which arises on a loan guarantee made under subsection (d) if the State in which the applicant for such guarantee is located has established by law a program approved by the Secretary for the purposes of this section.

(f)(1) When considering whether to guarantee a loan to a corporation which is otherwise qualified for the purposes of subsection (d), the Secretary shall give preference to a corporation which agrees with respect to such loan to fulfill the following requirements—

(A) 25 percent of the principal amount of the loan is paid by the lender to a qualified trust established under an employee stock ownership plan established and maintained by the recipient corporation, by a parent or subsidiary of such corporation, or by several corporations including the recipient corporation,

(B) the employee stock ownership plan meets the requirements of this subsection, and

(C) the agreement among the recipient corporation, the lender, and the qualified trust relating to the loan meets the requirements of this section.

(2) An employee stock ownership plan does not meet the requirements of this subsection unless the governing instrument of the plan provides that—

(A) the amount of the loan paid under paragraph (1)(A) to the qualified trust will be used to purchase qualified employer securities,

(B) the qualified trust will repay to the lender the amount of such loan, together with the interest thereon, out of amounts contributed to the trust by the recipient corporation, and

(C) from time to time, as the qualified trust repays such amount, the trust will allocate qualified employer securities among the individual accounts of participants and their beneficiaries in accordance with the provisions of paragraph (4).

(3) The agreement among the recipient corporation, the lender, and the qualified trust does not meet the requirements of this subsection unless—

(A) it is unconditionally enforceable by any party against the others, jointly and severally,

(B) it provides that the liability of the qualified trust to repay loan amounts paid to the qualified trust may not, at any time, exceed an amount equal to the amount of contributions required under paragraph (2)(B) which are actually received by such trust,

(C) it provides that amounts received by the recipient corporation from the qualified trust for qualified employer securities purchased for the purpose of this subsection will be used exclusively by the recipient corporation for those purposes for which it may use that portion of the loan paid directly to it by the lender,

(D) it provides that the recipient corporation may not reduce the amount of its equity capital during the one year period beginning on the date on which the qualified trust purchases qualified employer securities for purposes of this subsection, and

(E) it provides that the recipient corporation will make contributions to the qualified trust of not less than such amounts as are necessary for such trust to meet its obligation to make repayments of principal and interest on the amount of the loan received by the trust without regard to whether such contributions are deductible by the corporation under section 404 of the Internal Revenue Code of 1954 and without regard to any other amounts the recipient corporation is obligated under law to contribute to or under the employee stock ownership plan.

4) At the close of each plan year, an employee stock ownership plan shall allocate to the accounts of participating employees that portion of the qualified employer securities the cost of which bears substantially the same ratio to the cost of all the qualified employer securities purchased under paragraph (2)(A) of this subsection as the amount of the loan principal and interest repaid by the qualified trust during that year bears to the total amount of the loan principal and interest payable by such trust during the term of such loan. Qualified employer securities allocated to the individual account of a participant during one plan year must bear substantially the same proportion to the amount of all such securities allocated to all participants in the plan as the amount of compensation paid to such participant bears to the total amount of compensation paid to all such participants during that year.

(5) For purposes of this subsection, the term—

(A) "employee stock ownership plan" means a plan described in section 407(d)(6) of the Employee Retirement Income Security Act of 1974, section 4975(e)(7) of the Internal Revenue Code of 1954, and in section 102(5) of the Regional Rail Reorganization Act of 1973, which meets the requirements of title I of the Employee Retirement Income Security Act of 1974 and of part I of subchapter D of chapter 1 of such Code,

(B) "qualified trust" means a trust established under an employee stock ownership plan and meeting the requirements of title I of the Employee Retirement Income Security Act of 1974 and of Part I of subchapter D of chapter 1 of such Code,

(C) "qualified employer securities" means common stock issued by the recipient corporation or by a parent or subsidiary of such corporation with voting power and dividend rights no less favorable than the voting power and dividend rights on other common stock issued by the issuing corporation and with voting power being exercised by the participants in the employee stock ownership plan after it is allocated to their plan accounts, and

(D) "equity capital" means, with respect to the recipient corporation, the sum of its money and other property (in an amount equal to the adjusted basis of such property but disregarding adjustments made on account of depreciation or amortization made during the period described in paragraph (3)(D)), less the amount of its indebtedness.

(g) The United States share of loan guarantees made under subsection (d) on loans which are outstanding at any time may not exceed $500,000,000.

Section 274. *Community Adjustment Assistance Fund and Authorization of Appropriations*

(a) There is established on the books of the Treasury of the United States a revolving fund to be known as the Community Adjustment Assistance Fund. The fund shall consist of such amounts as may be deposited in it pursuant to the authorization in subsection (b) and any collections, repayments of loans, or other receipts received under the program established in section 273(a). Amounts in the fund may be used only to carry out the provisions of sections 272 and 273(b), including administrative costs. Amounts appropriated to the fund shall be available to the Secretary without fiscal year limitation. Upon liquidation of all remaining obligations, any balances remaining in the fund after September 30, 1980, shall be transferred to the general fund of the Treasury.

(b) There are authorized to be appropriated to the Community Adjustment Assistance Fund, for the purpose of carrying out the provisions of sections 272 and 273(a), $100,000,000 for the fiscal year ending June 30, 1975, and such sums as may be necessary for the succeeding 7 fiscal years.

(c) There are authorized to be appropriated to the Secretary such sums as may be necessary for carrying out the loan guarantee program under section 273(d).

CHAPTER 5—MISCELLANEOUS PROVISIONS

Section 280. *General Accounting Office Report*

(a) The Comptroller General of the United States shall conduct a study of the adjustment assistance programs established under chapters 2, 3, and 4 of this title and shall report the results of such study to the Congress no later than January 31, 1980. Such report shall include an evaluation of—

(1) the effectiveness of such programs in aiding workers, firms, and communities to adjust to changed economic conditions resulting from changes in the patterns of international trade; and

(2) the coordination of the administration of such programs and other Government programs which provide unemployment compensation and relief to depressed areas.

(b) In carrying out his responsibilities under this section, the Comptroller General shall, to the extent practical, avail himself of the assistance of the Departments of Labor and Commerce. The Secretaries of Labor and Commerce shall make available to the Comptroller General any assistance necessary for an effective evaluation of the adjustment assistance programs established under this title.

Section 281. *Coordination*

There is established the Adjustment Assistance Coordinating Committee to consist of a Deputy Special Trade Representative as Chairman, and the officials charged with adjustment assistance responsibilities of the Departments of Labor and Commerce and the Small Business Administration. It shall be the function of the Committee to coordinate the adjustment assistance policies, studies, and programs of the various agencies involved and to promote the efficient and effective delivery of adjustment assistance benefits.

Section 282. *Trade Monitoring System*

The Secretary of Commerce and the Secretary of Labor shall establish and maintain a program to monitor imports of articles into the United States which will reflect changes in the volume of such imports, the relation of such imports to changes in domestic production, changes in employment within domestic industries producing articles like or directly competitive with such imports, and the extent to which such changes in production and employment are concentrated in specific geographic regions of the United States. A summary of the information gathered under this section shall be published regularly and provided to the Adjustment Assistance Coordinating Committee, the International Trade Commission, and to the Congress.

Section 283. *Firms Relocating in Foreign Countries*

Before moving productive facilities from the United States to a foreign country, every firm should—

(1) provide notice of the move to its employees who are likely to be totally or partially separated as a result of the move at least 60 days before the date of such move, and

(2) provide notice of the move to the Secretary of Labor and the Secretary of Commerce on the same day it notifies employees under paragraph (1).

(b) It is the sense of the Congress that every such firm should—

(1) apply for and use all adjustment assistance for which it is eligible under this title,

(2) offer employment opportunities in the United States, if any exist, to its employees who are totally or partially separated workers as a result of the move, and

(3) assist in relocating employees to other locations in the United States where employment opportunities exist.

Section 284. *Effective Date*

Chapters 2, 3, and 4 of this title shall become effective on the 90th day following the date of enactment of this Act and shall terminate on September 30, 1982.

TITLE III—RELIEF FROM UNFAIR TRADE PRACTICES

CHAPTER 1—FOREIGN IMPORT RESTRICTIONS AND EXPORT SUBSIDIES

Section 301. *Responses to Certain Trade Practices of Foreign Governments*

(a) Whenever the President determines that a foreign country or instrumentality—

(1) maintains unjustifiable or unreasonable tariff or other import restrictions which impair the value of trade commitments made to the United States or which burden, restrict, or discriminate against United States commerce,

(2) engages in discriminatory or other acts or policies which are unjustifiable or unreasonable and which burden or restrict United States Commerce,

(3) provides subsidies (or other incentives having the effect of subsidies) on its exports of one or more products to the United States or to other foreign markets which have the effect of substantially reducing sales of the competitive United States product or products in the United States or in those other foreign markets, or

(4) imposes unjustifiable or unreasonable restrictions on access to supplies of food, raw materials, or manufactured or semimanufactured products which burden or restrict United States commerce,

the President shall take all appropriate and feasible steps within his power to obtain the elimination of such restrictions or subsidies, and he—

(A) may suspend, withdraw, or prevent the application of, or may refrain from proclaiming, benefits of trade agreement concessions to carry out a trade agreement with such country or instrumentality; and

(B) may impose duties or other import restrictions on the products of such foreign country or instrumentality, and may impose fees or restrictions on the services of such foreign country or instrumentality, for such time as he deems appropriate.

For purposes of this subsection, the term "commerce" includes services associated with the international trade.

(b) In determining what action to take under subsection (a), the President shall consider the relationship of such action to the purposes of this Act. Action shall be taken under subsection (a) against the foreign country or instrumentality involved, except that, subject to the provisions of section 302, any such action may be taken on a nondiscriminatory treatment basis.

(c) The President in making a determination under this section, may take action under subsection (a)(3) with respect to the exports of a product to the United States by a foreign country or instrumentality if—

(1) the Secretary of the Treasury has found that such country or instrumentality provides subsidies (or other incentives having the effect of subsidies) on such exports;

(2) the International Trade Commission has found that such exports to the United States have the effect of substantially reducing sales of

the competitive United States product or products in the United States; and

(3) the President finds that the Antidumping Act, 1921, and section 303 of the Tariff Act of 1930 are inadequate to deter such practices.

(d)(1) The President shall provide an opportunity for the presentation of views concerning the restrictions, acts, policies, or practices referred to in paragraphs (1), (2), (3), and (4) of subsection (a).

(2) Upon complaint filed by any interested party with the Special Representative for Trade Negotiations alleging any such restriction, act, policy, or practice, the Special Representative shall conduct a review of the alleged restriction, act, policy, or practice, and, at the request of the complainant, shall conduct public hearings thereon. The Special Representative shall have a copy of each complaint filed under this paragraph published in the Federal Register. The Special Representative shall issue regulations concerning the filing of complaints and the conduct of reviews and hearings under this paragraph and shall submit a report to the House of Representatives and the Senate semi-annually summarizing the reviews and hearings conducted by it under this paragraph during the preceding 6-month period.

(e) Before the President takes any action under subsection (a) with respect to the import treatment of any product or the treatment of any service—

(1) he shall provide an opportunity for the presentation of views concerning the taking of action with respect to such product or service,

(2) upon request by any interested person, he shall provide for appropriate public hearings with respect to the taking of action with respect to such product or service, and

(3) he may request the International Trade Commission for its views as to the probable impact on the economy of the United States of the taking of action with respect to such product or service.

If the President determines that, because of the need for expeditious action under subsection (a), compliance with paragraphs (1) and (2) would be contrary to the national interest, then such paragraphs shall not apply with respect to such action, but he shall thereafter promptly provide an opportunity for the presentation of views concerning the action taken and, upon request by any interested person, shall provide for appropriate public hearings with respect to the action taken. The President shall provide for the issuance of regulations concerning the filing of requests for, and the conduct of, hearings under this subsection.

Section 302. *Procedure for Congressional Disapproval of Certain Actions Taken Under Section 301*

(a) Whenever the President takes any action under subparagraph (A) or (B) of section 301(a) with respect to any country or instrumentality other than the country or instrumentality whose restriction, act, policy, or practice was the cause for taking such action, he shall promptly transmit to the House of Representatives and to the Senate a document setting forth the action which he has so taken, together with his reasons therefor.

(b) If, before the close of the 90-day period beginning on the day on which the document referred to in subsection (a) is delivered to the House of Representatives and to the Senate, the two Houses adopt, by an affirmative vote of a majority of those present and voting in each House, a concurrent resolution of disapproval under the procedures set forth in section 152, then such action under section 301(a) shall have no force and effect beginning with the day after the date of the adoption of such concurrent resolution of disapproval, except with respect to the country or instrumentality whose restriction, act, policy, or practice was the cause for taking such action.

CHAPTER 2—ANTIDUMPING DUTIES

Section 321. [Subsections (a), (b), (c), (d), (e), and (g) (1) and (2) amend the Antidumping Act of 1921, as amended.]*

*   *   *   *   *

(f)(1) Section 516 of the Tariff Act of 1930 (19 U.S.C. 1516) is amended by redesignating subsections (d), (e), (f), and (g) as subsections (e), (f), (g), and (h), respectively, and by inserting after subsection (c) the following new subsection:

"(d) Within 30 days after a determination by the Secretary—

"(1) under section 201 of the Antidumping Act, 1921 (19 U.S.C. 160), that a class or kind of foreign merchandise is not being, nor likely to be, sold in the United States at less than its fair value, or

(2) under section 303 of this Act that a bounty or grant is not being paid or bestowed,

---

* See Document No. 7, p. DS-441 *infra.*

an American manufacturer, producer, or wholesaler of merchandise of the same class or kind as that described in such determination may file with the Secretary a written notice of a desire to contest such determination. Upon receipt of such notice the Secretary shall cause publication to be made thereof and of such manufacturer's, producer's, or wholesaler's desire to contest the determination. Within 30 days after such publication, such manufacturer, producer, or wholesaler may commence an action in the United States Customs Court contesting such determination.".

(2) Section 2631(b) of title 28, United States Code, is amended by inserting before the period at the end thereof ", or, in the case of an action under section 516(d) of such Act, after the date of publication of a notice under such section".

(3) Section 2632 of title 28, United States Code, is amended—

(A) by striking out the first sentence of subsection (a) and inserting in lieu thereof the following: "A party may contest (1) denial of a protest under section 515 of the Tariff Act of 1930, as amended; (2) a decision of the Secretary of the Treasury made under section 516 of the Tariff Act of 1930, as amended; or (3) a determination by the Secretary of the Treasury under section 201 of the Antidumping Act, 1921, as amended, that a class or kind of merchandise is not being, nor likely to be, sold in the United States at less than its fair value, or under section 303 of the Tariff Act of 1930 that a bounty or grant is not being paid or bestowed; by bringing a civil action in the Customs Court.";

(B) by inserting after "designee" in subsection (f) "in any action brought under subsection (a)(1) or (a)(2)"; and

(C) by adding at the end thereof the following new subsection:

"(g) Upon service of the summons on the Secretary of the Treasury or his designee in an action contesting the Secretary's determination under section 201 of the Antidumping Act, 1921, as amended, that a class or kind of foreign merchandise is not being, nor likely to be, sold in the United States at less than its fair value, the Secretary or his designee shall forthwith transmit to the United States Customs Court, as the official record of the civil action, a certified copy of the transcript of any hearing held by the Secretary in the particular antidumping proceeding pursuant to section 201(d)(1) of the Antidumping Act, 1921, as amended, and certified copies of all notices, determinations, or other matters which the Secretary has caused to be published in the Federal Register in connection with the particular Antidumping proceeding. Upon service of the summons on the Secretary of the Treasury or his designee in an action contesting the Secretary's determination under section 303 of the Tariff Act of 1930 that a bounty or grant is not being paid or bestowed, the Secretary or his designee shall forthwith transmit to the United States Customs Court, as the official record of the civil action, a certified copy of the transcript of all hearings held by the Secretary in the proceeding which resulted in such determination and certified copies of all notices, determinations, or other matters which the Secretary has caused to be published in the Federal Register in connection with such proceeding.".

* * * * *

(g) * * *

(3) The amendments made by subsection (f) shall apply with respect to determinations under section 201 of the Antidumping Act, 1921, resulting from questions of dumping raised or presented on or after the date of the enactment of this Act.

CHAPTER 3—COUNTERVAILING DUTIES

Section 331. *Amendments to Sections 303 and 516 of the Tariff Act of 1930*

(a) Section 303 of the Tariff Act of 1930 (19 U.S.C. sec. 1303) is amended to read as follows:

. . . .*

(b) So much of section 516 of the Tariff Act of 1930 (19 U.S.C. 1516) as precedes subsection (d) is amended to read as follows:

. . . .**

(c) Section 515(d) of the Tariff Act of 1930 (19 U.S.C. 1315(d)) is amended by inserting before the period at the end thereof "or the imposition of countervailing duties under section 303".

(d)(1) The amendments made by this section shall take effect on the date of the enactment of this Act.

(2) For purposes of applying the provisions of section 303(a)(4) of the Tariff Act of 1930 (as amended by subsection (a)) with respect to any investigation which was initiated before the date of the enactment of this Act under section 303 of such Act (as in effect before such date), such

---

* See Document No. 8(b), p. DS-440 *infra.*

** See Document No. 8(b), p. DS-450 *infra.*

investigation shall be treated as having been initiated on the day after such date of enactment under section 303(a)(3)(B) of such Act.

(3) Any article which is entered or withdrawn from warehouse free of duty as a result of action taken under title V of this Act shall be considered a nondutiable article for purposes of section 303 of the Tariff Act of 1930, as amended (19 U.S.C. sec. 1303).

CHAPTER 4—UNFAIR IMPORT PRACTICES

Section 341. *Amendment to Section 337 of the Tariff Act of 1930*

(a) Section 337 of the Tariff Act of 1930 (19 U.S.C. 1337) is amended to read as follows:

"Section 337. *Unfair Practices in Import Trade*

"(a) UNFAIR METHODS OF COMPETITION DECLARED UNLAWFUL.—Unfair methods of competition and unfair acts in the importation of articles into the United States, or in their sale by the owner, importer consignee, or agent of either, the effect or tendency of which is to destroy or substantially injure an industry, efficiently and economically operated, in the United States, or to prevent the establishment of such an industry, or to restrain or monopolize trade and commerce in the United States, are declared unlawful, and when found by the Commission to exist shall be dealt with, in addition to any other provisions of law, as provided in this section.

"(b) INVESTIGATION OF VIOLATIONS BY COMMISSION; TIME LIMITS.—(1) The Commission shall investigate any alleged violation of this section on complaint under oath or upon its initiative. Upon commencing any such investigation, the Commission shall publish notice thereof in the Federal Register. The Commission shall conclude any such investigation, and make its determination under this section, at the earliest practicable time, but not later than one year (18 months in more complicated cases) after the date of publication of notice of such investigation. The Commission shall publish in the Federal Register its reasons for designating any investigation as a more complicated investigation. For purposes of the one-year and 18-month periods prescribed by this subsection, there shall be excluded any period of time during which such investigation is suspended because of proceedings in a court or agency of the United States involving similar questions concerning the subject matter of such investigation.

mission shall consult with, and seek advice and information from, the
"(2) During the course of each investigation under this section, the Commission shall consult with, and seek advice and information from, the Department of Health, Education, and Welfare, the Department of Justice,

the Federal Trade Commission, and such other departments and agencies as it considers appropriate.

"(3) Whenever, in the course of an investigation under this section, the Commission has reason to believe, based on information before it, that the matter may come within the purview of section 303 or of the Antidumping Act, 1921, it shall promptly notify the Secretary of the Treasury so that such action may be taken as is otherwise authorized by such section and such Act.

"(c) DETERMINATIONS; REVIEW.—The Commission shall determine, with respect to each investigation conducted by it under this section, whether or not there is a violation of this section. Each determination under subsection (d) or (e) shall be made on the record after notice and opportunity for a hearing in conformity with the provisions of subchapter II of chapter 5 of title 5, United States Code. All legal and equitable defenses may be presented in all cases. Any person adversely affected by a final determination of the Commission under subsection (d) or (e) may appeal such determination to the United States Court of Customs and Patent Appeals. Such court shall have jurisdiction to review such determination in the same manner and subject to the same limitations and conditions as in the case of appeals from decisions of the United States Customs Court.

"(d) EXCLUSION OF ARTICLES FROM ENTRY.—If the Commission determines, as a result of an investigation under this section, that there is violation of this section, it shall direct that the articles concerned, imported by any person violating the provision of this section, be excluded from entry into the United States, unless, after considering the effect of such exclusion upon the public health and welfare, competitive conditions in the United States economy, the production of like or directly competitive articles in the United States, and United States consumers, it finds that such articles should not be excluded from entry. The Commission shall notify the Secretary of the Treasury of its action under this subsection directing such exclusion from entry, and upon receipt of such notice, the Secretary shall, through the proper officers, refuse such entry.

"(e) EXCLUSION OF ARTICLES FROM ENTRY DURING INVESTIGATION EXCEPT UNDER BOND.—If, during the course of an investigation under this section, the Commission determines that there is reason to believe that there is a violation of this section, it may direct that the articles concerned, imported by any person with respect to whom there is reason to believe that such person is violating this section, be excluded from entry into the United States, unless after considering the effect of such exclusion upon the public health and welfare, competitive conditions in the United States economy, the production of like or directly competitive articles in the United States, and United States consumers, it finds that such articles should not be excluded from entry. The Commission shall notify the Secretary of the Treasury of its action under this subsection directing such exclusion from entry, and upon receipt of such notice, the Secretary shall, through the proper officers, refuse such entry, except that such articles shall be entitled to entry under bond determined by the Commission and prescribed by the Secretary.

"(f) CEASE AND DESIST ORDERS.—In lieu of taking action under subsection (d) or (e), the Commission may issue and cause to be served on any person violating this section, or believed to be violating this section, as the case may be, an order directing such person to cease and desist from engaging in the unfair methods or acts involved, unless after considering the effect of such order upon the public health and welfare, competitive conditions in the United States economy, the production of like or directly competitive articles in the United States, and United States consumers, it finds that such order should not be issued. The Commission may at any time, upon such notice and in such manner as it deems proper, modify or revoke any such order, and, in the case of a revocation, may take action under subsection (d) or (e), as the case may be.

"(g) REFERRAL TO THE PRESIDENT.—(1) If the Commission determines that there is a violation of this section, or that, for purposes of subsection (e), there is reason to believe that there is such a violation, it shall—

"(A) publish such determination in the Federal Register, and

"(B) transmit to the President a copy of such determination and the action taken under subsection (d), (e), or (f), with respect thereto, together with the record upon which such determination is based.

"(2) If, before the close of the 60-day period beginning on the day after the day on which he receives a copy of such determination, the President, for policy reasons, disapproves such determination and notifies the Commission of his disapproval, then, effective on the date of such notice, such determination and the action taken under subsection (d), (e), or (f) with respect thereto shall have no force or effect.

"(3) Subject to the provisions of paragraph (2), such determination shall, except for purposes of subsection (c), be effective upon publication thereof in the Federal Register, and the action taken under subsection (d), (e), or (f) with respect thereto shall be effective as provided in such subsections, except that articles directed to be excluded from entry under subsection (d) or subject to a cease and desist order under subsection (f) shall be entitled to entry under bond determined by the Commission and prescribed by the Secretary until such determination becomes final.

"(4) If the President does not disapprove such determination within such 60-day period, or if he notifies the Commission before the close of such period that he approves such determination, then, for purposes of paragraph (3) and subsection (c) such determination shall become final on the day after the close of such period or the day on which the President notifies the Commission of his approval, as the case may be.

"(h) PERIOD OF EFFECTIVENESS.—Except as provided in subsections (f) and (g), any exclusion from entry or order under this section shall continue in effect until the Commission finds, and in the case of exclusion from entry notifies the Secretary of the Treasury, that the conditions which led to such exclusion from entry or order no longer exist.

"(i) IMPORTATION BY OR FOR THE UNITED STATES.—Any exclusion from entry or order under subsection (d), (e), or (f), in cases based on claims of United States letters patent, shall not apply to any articles imported by and for the use of the United States, or imported for, and to be used for, the United States with the authorization or consent of the Government. Whenever any article would have been excluded from entry or would not have been entered pursuant to the provisions of such subsections but for the operation of this subsection, a patent owner adversely affected shall be entitled to reasonable and entire compensation in an action before the Court of Claims pursuant to the procedures of section 1498 of title 28, United States Code.

"(j) DEFINITION OF UNITED STATES.—For purposes of this section and sections 338 and 340, the term 'United States' means the customs territory of the United States as defined in general headnote 2 of the Tariff Schedules of the United States."

(b) Section 332(g) of the Tariff Act of 1930 (19 U.S.C. 1332(g)) is amended by adding at the end thereof the following new sentence: "Each such annual report shall include a list of all complaints filed under section 337 during the year for which such report is being made, the date on which each such complaint was filed, and the action taken thereon, and the status of all investigations conducted by the commission under such section during such year and the date on which each such investigation was commenced."

(c) The amendments made by this section shall take effect on the 90th day after the date of the enactment of this Act, except that, for purposes of issuing regulations under section 337 of the Tariff Act of 1930, such amendments shall take effect on the date of the enactment of this Act. For purposes of applying section 337(b) of the Tariff Act of 1930 (as amended by subsection (a)) with respect to investigations being conducted by the International Trade Commission under section 337 of the Tariff Act on the day prior to the 90th day after the date of the enactment of this Act, such investigations shall be considered as having been commenced on such 90th day.

TITLE IV—TRADE RELATIONS WITH COUNTRIES NOT CURRENTLY RECEIVING NONDISCRIMINATORY TREATMENT

Section 401. *Exception of the Products of Certain Countries or Areas*

Except as otherwise provided in this title, the President shall continue to deny nondiscriminatory treatment to the products of any country, the products of which were not eligible for the rates set forth in rate column numbered 1 of the Tariff Schedules of the United States on the date of the enactment of this Act.

Section 402. *Freedom of Emigration in East-West Trade*

(a) To assure the continued dedication of the United States to fundamental human rights, and notwithstanding any other provision of law, on or after the date of the enactment of this Act products from any nonmarket economy country shall not be eligible to receive nondiscriminatory treatment (most-favored-nation treatment), such country shall not participate in any program of the Government of the United States which extends credits or credit guarantees or investment guarantees, directly or indirectly, and the President of the United States shall not conclude any commercial agreement with any such country, during the period beginning with the date on which the President determines that such country—

(1) denies its citizens the right or opportunity to emigrate;

(2) imposes more than a nominal tax on emigration or on the visas or other documents required for emigration, for any purpose or cause whatsoever; or

(3) imposes more than a nominal tax, levy, fine, fee, or other charge on any citizen as a consequence of the desire of such citizen to emigrate to the country of his choice,

and ending on the date on which the President determines that such country is no longer in violation of paragraph (1), (2), or (3).

(b) After the date of the enactment of this Act, (A) products of a non-market economy country may be eligible to receive nondiscriminatory treatment (most-favored-nation treatment), (B) such country may participate in any program of the Government of the United States which extends credits or credits or credit guarantees or investment guarantees, and (C) the President may conclude a commercial agreement with such country, only after the President has submitted to the Congress a report indicating that such country is not in violation of paragraph (1), (2), or (3) of subsection (a). Such report with respect to such country shall include information as to the nature and implementation of emigration laws and policies and restrictions or discrimination applied to or against persons wishing to emigrate. The report required by this subsection shall be submitted initially as provided herein and, with current information, on or before each June 30 and December 31 thereafter so long as such treatment is received, such credits or guarantees are extended, or such agreement is in effect.

(c)(1) During the 18-month period beginning on the date of the enactment of this Act, the President is authorized to waive by Executive order the application of subsection (a) and (b) with respect to any country, if he reports to the Congress that—

(A) he has determined that such waiver will substantially promote the objectives of this section; and

(B) he has received assurances that the emigration practices of that country will henceforth lead substantially to the achievement of the objectives of this section.

(2) During any period subsequent to the 18-month period referred to in paragraph (1), the President is authorized to waive by Executive order the application of subsections (a) and (b) with respect to any country, if the waiver authority granted by this subsection continues to apply to such country pursuant to subsection (d), and if he reports to the Congress that—

(A) he has determined that such waiver will substantially promote the objectives of this section; and

(B) he has received assurances that the emigration practices of that country will henceforth lead substantially to the achievement of the objectives of this section.

(3) A waiver with respect to any country shall terminate on the day after the waiver authority granted by this subsection ceases to be effective with respect to such country pursuant to subsection (d). The President may, at any time, terminate by Executive order any waiver granted under this subsection.

(d)(1) If the President determines that the extension of the waiver authority granted by subsection (c)(1) will substantially promote the objectives of this section, he may recommend to the Congress that such authority be extended for a period of 12 months. Any such recommendation shall—

(A) be made not later than 30 days before the expiration of such authority;

(B) be made in a document transmitted to the House of Representatives and the Senate setting forth his reasons for recommending the extension of such authority; and

(C) include, for each country with respect to which a waiver granted under subsection (c)(1) is in effect, a determination that continuation of the waiver applicable to that country will substantially promote the objectives of this section, and a statement setting forth his reasons for such determination.

(2) If the President recommends under paragraph (1) the extension of the waiver authority granted by subsection (c)(1), such authority shall continue in effect with respect to any country for a period of 12 months following the end of the 18-month period, referred to in subsection (c)(1), if, before the end of such 18-month period, the House of Representatives and the Senate adopt, by an affirmative vote of a majority of the Members present and voting in each House and under the procedures set forth in section 153, a concurrent resolution approving the extension of such authority, and such resolution does not name such country as being excluded from such authority. Such authority shall cease to be effective with respect to any country named in such concurrent resolution on the date of the adoption of such concurrent resolution. If before the end of such 18-month period, a concurrent resolution approving the extension of such authority is not adopted by the House and the Senate, but both the House and Senate vote on the question of final passage of such a concurrent resolution and—

(A) both the House and the Senate fail to pass such a concurrent resolution, the authority granted by subsection (c)(1) shall cease to be effective with respect to all countries at the end of such 18-month period;

(B) both the House and the Senate pass such a concurrent resolution which names such country as being excluded from such authority, such authority shall cease to be effective with respect to such country at the end of such 18-month period; or

(C) one House fails to pass such a concurrent resolution and the other House passes such a concurrent resolution which names such country as being excluded from such authority, such authority shall cease to be effective with respect to such country at the end of such 18-month period.

(3) If the President recommends under paragraph (1) the extension of the waiver authority granted by subsection (c)(1), and at the end of the

18-month period referred to in subsection (c)(1) the House of Representatives and the Senate have not adopted a concurrent resolution approving the extension of such authority and subparagraph (A) of paragraph (2) does not apply, such authority shall continue in effect for a period of 60 days following the end of such 18-month period with respect to any country (except for any country with respect to which such authority was not extended by reason of the application of subparagraph (B) or (C) of paragraph (2)), and shall continue in effect for a period of 12 months following the end of such 18-month period with respect to any such country if, before the end of such 60-day period, the House of Representatives and the Senate adopt, by an affirmative vote of a majority of the Members present and voting in each House and under the procedures set forth in section 153, a concurrent resolution approving the extension of such authority, and such resolution does not name such country as being excluded from such authority. Such authority shall cease to be effective with respect to any country named in such concurrent resolution on the date of the adoption of such concurrent resolution. If before the end of such 60-day period, a concurrent resolution approving the extension of such authority is not adopted by the House and Senate, but both the House and Senate vote on the question of final passage of such a concurrent resolution and—

(A) both the House and the Senate fail to pass such a concurrent resolution, the authority granted by subsection (c)(1) shall cease to be effective with respect to all countries on the date of the vote on the question of final passage by the House which votes last;

(B) both the House and the Senate pass such a concurrent resolution which names such country as being excluded from such authority, such authority shall cease to be effective with respect to such country at the end of such 60-day period; or

(C) one House fails to pass such a concurrent resolution and the other House passes such a concurrent resolution which names such country as being excluded from such authority, such authority shall cease to be effective with respect to such country at the end of such 60-day period.

(4) If the President recommends under paragraph (1) the extension of the waiver authority granted by subsection (c)(1), and at the end of the 60-day period referred to in paragraph (3) the House of Representatives and the Senate have not adopted a concurrent resolution approving the extension of such authority and subparagraph (A) of paragraph (3) does not apply, such authority shall continue in effect until the end of the 12-month period following the end of the 18-month period referred to in subsection (c)(1) with respect to any country (except for any country with respect to which such authority was not extended by reason of the application of sub-

paragraph (B) or (C) of paragraph (2) or subparagraph (B) or (C) of paragraph (3)), unless before the end of the 45-day period following such 60-day period either the House of Representatives or the Senate adopts, by an affirmative vote of a majority of the Members present and voting in that House and under the procedures set forth in section 153, a resolution disapproving the extension of such authority generally or with respect to such country specifically. Such authority shall cease to be effective with respect to all countries on the date of the adoption by either House before the end of such 45-day period of a resolution disapproving the extension of such authority, and shall cease to be effective with respect to any country on the date of the adoption by either House before the end of such 45-day period of a resolution disapproving the extension of such authority with respect to such country.

(5) If the waiver authority granted by subsection (c) has been extended under paragraph (3) or (4) for any country for the 12-month period referred to in such paragraphs, and the President determines that the further extension of such authority will substantially promote the objectives of this section, he may recommend further extensions of such authority for successive 12-month periods. Any such recommendations shall—

(A) be made not later than 30 days before the expiration of such authority;

(B) be made in a document transmitted to the House of Representatives and the Senate setting forth his reasons for recommending the extension of such authority; and

(C) include, for each country with respect to which a waiver granted under subsection (c) is in effect, a determination that continuation of the waiver applicable to that country will substantially promote the objectives of this section, and a statement setting forth his reasons for such determination.

If the President recommends the further extension of such authority, such authority shall continue in effect until the end of the 12-month period following the end of the previous 12-month extension with respect to any country (except for any country with respect to which such authority has not been extended under this subsection), unless before the end of the 60-day period following such previous 12-month extension, either the House of Representatives or the Senate adopts, by an affirmative vote of a majority of the Members present and voting in that House and under the proceedures set forth in section 153, a resolution disapproving the extension of such authority generally or with respect to such country specifically. Such authority shall cease to be effective with respect to all countries on the date of the adoption by either House before the end of such 60-day period of a resolution disapproving the extension of such authority, and shall cease to be effective with respect to any country on the date of the adoption by either House before the end of such 60-day period of a resolution disapproving the extension of such authority with respect to such country.

(e) This section shall not apply to any country the products of which are eligible for the rates set forth in rate column numbered 1 of the Tariff Schedules of the United States on the date of the enactment of this Act.

Section 403. *United States Personnel Missing in Action in Southeast Asia*

(a) Notwithstanding any other provision of law, if the President determines that a nonmarket economy country is not cooperating with the United States—

(1) to achieve a complete accounting of all United States military and civilian personnel who are missing in action in Southeast Asia,

(2) to repatriate such personnel who are alive, and

(3) to return the remains of such personnel who are dead to the United States,

then, during the period beginning with the date of such determination and ending on the date on which the President determines such country is cooperating with the United States, he may provide that—

(A) the products of such country may not receive nondiscriminatory treatment,

(B) such country may not participate, directly or indirectly, in any program under which the United States extends credit, credit guarantees, or investment guarantees, and

(C) no commercial agreement entered into under this title between such country and the United States will take effect.

(b) This section shall not apply to any country the products of which are eligible for the rates set forth in rate column numbered 1 of the Tariff Schedules of the United States on the date of the enactment of this Act.

Section 404. *Extension of Nondiscriminatory Treatment*

(a) Subject to the provisions of section 405(c), the President may by proclamation extend nondiscriminatory treatment to the products of a foreign country which has entered into a bilateral commercial agreement referred to in section 405.

(b) The application of nondiscriminatory treatment shall be limited to the period of effectiveness of the obligations of the United States to such country under such bilateral commercial agreement. In addition, in the case of any foreign country receiving nondiscriminatory treatment pursuant to this title which has entered into an agreement with the United States regarding the settlement of lend-lease reciprocal aid and claims, the application of such nondiscriminatory treatment shall be limited to periods during which such country is not in arrears on its obligations under such agreement.

(c) The President may at any time suspend or withdraw any extension of nondiscriminatory treatment to any country pursuant to subsection (a), and thereby cause all products of such country to be dutiable at the rates set forth in rate column numbered 2 of the Tariff Schedules for the United States.

Section 405. *Authority to Enter Into Commercial Agreements*

(a) Subject to the provisions of subsections (b) and (c) of this section, the President may authorize the entry into force of bilateral commercial agreements providing nondiscriminatory treatment to the products of countries heretofore denied such treatment whenever he determines that such agreements with such countries will promote the purposes of this Act and are in the national interest.

(b) Any such bilateral commercial agreement shall—

(1) be limited to an initial period specified in the agreement which shall be no more than 3 years from the date the agreement enters into force; except that it may be renewable for additional periods, each not to exceed 3 years; if—

(A) a satisfactory balance of concessions in trade and services has been maintained during the life of such agreement, and

(B) the President determines that actual or foreseeable reductions in United States tariffs and nontariff barriers to trade resulting from multilateral negotiations are satisfactorily reciprocated by the other party to the bilateral agreement;

(2) provide that it is subject to suspension or termination at any time for national security reasons, or that the other provisions of such agreement shall not limit the rights of any party to take any action for the protection of its security interests;

(3) include safeguard arrangements (A) providing for prompt consultations whenever either actual or prospective imports cause or threaten

to cause, or significantly contribute to, market disruption and (B) authorizing the imposition of such import restrictions as may be appropriate to prevent such market disruption;

(4) if the other party to the bilateral agreement is not a party to the Paris Convention for the Protection of Industrial Property, provide rights for United States nationals with respect to patents and trademarks in such country not less than the rights specified in such convention;

(5) if the other party to the bilateral agreement is not a party to the Universal Copyright Convention, provide rights for United States nationals with respect to copyrights in such country not less than the rights specified in such convention;

(6) in the case of an agreement entered into or renewed after the date of the enactment of this Act, provide arrangements for the protection of industrial rights and processes;

(7) provide arrangements for the settlement of commercial differences and disputes;

(8) in the case of an agreement entered into or renewed after the date of the enactment of this Act, provide arrangements for the promotion of trade, which may include those for the establishment or expansion of trade and tourist promotion offices, for facilitation of activities of governmental commercial officers, participation in trade fairs and exhibits, and the sending of trade missions, and for facilitation of entry, establishment, and travel of commercial representatives;

(9) provide for consultations for the purpose of reviewing the operation of the agreement and relevant aspects of relations between the United States and the other party; and

(10) provide such other arrangements of a commercial nature as will promote the purposes of this Act.

(c) An agreement referred to in subsection (a), and a proclamation referred to in section 404(a) implementing such agreement, shall take effect only if (1) approved by the Congress by the adoption of a concurrent resolution referred to in section 151, or (2) in the case of an agreement entered into before the date of the enactment of this Act and a proclamation implementing such agreement, a resolution of disapproval referred to in section 152 is not adopted during the 90-day period specified by section 407(c)(2).

Section 406. *Market Disruption*

(a)(1) Upon the filing of a petition by an entity described in section 201(a)(1), upon request of the President or the Special Representative for Trade Negotiations, upon resolution of either the Committee on Ways and Means of the House of Representatives or the Committee on Finance of the Senate, or on its own motion, the International Trade Commission (hereafter in this section referred to as the "Commission") shall promptly make an investigation to determine, with respect to imports of an article which is the product of a Communist country, whether market disruption exists with respect to an article produced by a domestic industry.

(2) The provisions of subsections (a)(2), (b)(3), and (c) of section 201 shall apply with respect to investigations by the Commission under paragraph (1).

(3) The Commission shall report to the President its determination with respect to each investigation under paragraph (1) and the basis therefor and shall include in each report any dissenting or separate views. If the Commission finds, as a result of its investigation, that market disruption exists with respect to an article produced by a domestic industry, it shall find the amount of the increase in, or imposition of, any duty or other import restriction on such article which is necessary to prevent or remedy such market disruption and shall include such finding in its report to the President. The Commission shall furnish to the President a transcript of the hearings and any briefs which may have been submitted in connection with each investigation.

(4) The report of the Commission of its determination with respect to an investigation under paragraph (1) shall be made at the earliest practicable time, but not later than 3 months after the date on which the petition is filed (or the date on which the request or resolution is received or the motion is adopted, as the case may be). Upon making such report to the President, the Commission shall also promptly make public such report (with the exception of information which the Commission determines to be confidential) and shall cause a summary thereof to be published in the Federal Register.

(b) For purposes of sections 202 and 203, an affirmative determination of the Commission under subsection (a) shall be treated as an affirmative determination under section 201(b), except that—

(1) the President may take action under sections 202 and 203 only with respect to imports from the country or countries involved of the article with respect to which the affirmative determination was made, and

(2) if such action consists of, or includes, an orderly marketing agreement, such agreement shall be entered into within 60 days after the import relief determination date.

(c) If, at any time, the President finds that there are reasonable grounds to believe, with respect to imports of an article which is the product of a Communist country, that market disruption exists with respect to an article produced by a domestic industry, he shall request the Commission to initiate an investigation under subsection (a). If the President further finds that emergency action is necessary, he may take action under sections 202 and 203 as if an affirmative determination of the Commission had been made under subsection (a). Any action taken by the President under the preceding sentence shall cease to apply (1) if a negative determination is made by the Commission under subsection (a) with respect to imports of such article, on the day on which the Commission's report of such determination is submitted to the President, or (2) if an affirmative determination is made by the Commission under subsection (a) with respect to imports of such article, on the day on which the action taken by the President pursuant to such determination becomes effective.

(d)(1) A petition may be filed with the President by an entity described in section 201(a)(1) requesting the President to initiate consultations provided for by the safeguard arrangements of any agreement entered into under section 405 with respect to imports of an article which is the product of the country which is the other party to such agreement.

(2) If the President determines that there are reasonable grounds to believe, with respect to imports of such article, that market disruption exists with respect to an article produced by a domestic industry, he shall initiate consultations with such country with respect to such imports.

(e) For purposes of this section—

(1) The term "Communist country" means any country dominated or controlled by communism.

(2) Market disruption exists within a domestic industry whenever imports of an article, like or directly competitive with an article produced by such domestic industry, are increasing rapidly, either absolutely or relatively, so as to be a significant cause of material injury, or threat thereof, to such domestic industry.

Section 407. *Procedure for Congressional Approval or Disapproval of Extension of Nondiscriminatory Treatment and Presidential Reports*

(a) Whenever the President issues a proclamation under section 404 extending nondiscriminatory treatment to the products of any foreign country, he shall promptly transmit to the House of Representatives and to the Senate a document setting forth the proclamation and the agreement the proclamation proposes to implement, together with his reasons therefor.

(b) The President shall transmit to the House of Representatives and the Senate a document containing the initial report submitted by him under section 402(b) or 409(b) with respect to a nonmarket economy country. On or before December 31 of each year, the President shall transmit to the House of Representatives and the Senate, a document containing the report required by section 402(b) or 409(b) as the case may be, to be submitted on or before such December 31.

(c)(1) In the case of a document referred to in subsection (a) (other than a document to which paragraph (2) applies), the proclamation set forth therein may become effective and the agreement set forth therein may enter into force and effect only if the House of Representatives and the Senate adopt, by an affirmative vote of a majority of those present and voting in each House, a concurrent resolution of approval (under the procedures set forth in section 151) of the extension of nondiscriminatory treatment to the products of the country concerned.

(2) In the case of a document referred to in subsection (a) which sets forth an agreement entered into before the date of the enactment of this Act and a proclamation implementing such agreement, such proclamation may become effective and such agreement may enter into force and effect after the close of the 90-day period beginning on the day on which such document is delivered to the House of Representatives and to the Senate, unless during such 90-day period either the House of Representatives or the Senate adopts, by an affirmative vote of a majority of those present and voting in that House, a resolution of disapproval (under the procedures set forth in section 152) of the extension of nondiscriminatory treatment to the products of the country concerned.

(3) In the case of a document referred to in subsection (b) which contains a report submitted by the President under section 402(b) or 409(b) with respect to a nonmarket economy country, if, before the close of the 90-day period beginning on the day on which such document is delivered to the House of Representatives and to the Senate, either the House of Repre-

sentatives or the Senate adopts, by affirmative vote of a majority of those present and voting in that House, a resolution of disapproval (under the procedures set forth in section 152) of the report submitted by the President with respect to such country, then, beginning with the day after the date of the adoption of such resolution of disapproval, (A) nondiscriminatory treatment shall not be in force with respect to the products of such country, and the products of such country shall be dutiable at the rates set forth in rate column numbered 2 of the Tariff Schedules of the United States, (B) such country may not participate in any program of the Government of the United States which extends credit or credit guarantees or investment guarantees, and (C) no commercial agreement may thereafter be concluded with such country under this title.

Section 408. *Payment by Czechoslovakia of Amounts Owed United States Citizens and Nationals*

(a) The arrangement initiated on July 5, 1974 with respect to the settlement of the claims of citizens and nationals of the United States against the Government of Czechoslovakia shall be renegotiated and shall be submitted to the Congress as part of any agreement entered into under this title with Czechoslovakia.

(b) The United States shall not release any gold belonging to Czechoslovakia and controlled directly or indirectly by the United States pursuant to the provisions of the Paris Reparations Agreement of January 24, 1946, or otherwise, until such agreement has been approved by the Congress.

Section 409. *Freedom to Emigrate to Join a Very Close Relative in the United States*

(a) To assure the continued dedication of the United States to the fundamental human rights and welfare of its own citizens, and notwithstanding any other provision of law, on or after the date of the enactment of this Act, no nonmarket economy country shall participate in any program of the Government of the United States which extends credits or credit guarantees or investment guarantees, directly or indirectly, and the President of the United States shall not conclude any commercial agreement with any such country, during the period beginning with the date on which the President determines that such country—

(1) denies its citizens the right or opportunity to join permanently through emigration, a very close relative in the United States, such as a spouse, parent, child, brother, or sister;

(2) imposes more than a nominal tax on the visas or other documents required for emigration described in paragraph (1); or

(3) imposes more than a nominal tax, levy, fine, fee, or other charge on any citizen as a consequence of the desire of such citizen to emigrate as described in paragraph (1),

and ending on the date on which the President determines that such country is no longer in violation of paragraph (1), (2), or (3).

(b) After the date of the enactment of this Act, (A) a nonmarket economy country may participate in any program of the Government of the United States which extends credits or credit guarantees or investment guarantees, and (B) the President may conclude a commercial agreement with such country, only after the President has submitted to the Congress a report indicating that such country is not in violation of paragraph (1), (2), or (3) of subsection (a). Such report with respect to such country shall include information as to the nature and implementation of its laws and policies and restrictions or discrimination applied to or against persons wishing to emigrate to the United States to join close relatives. The report required by this subsection shall be submitted initially as provided herein and, with current information, on or before each June 30 and December 31 thereafter, so long as such credits or guarantees are extended or such agreement is in effect.

(c) This section shall not apply to any country the products of which are eligible for the rates set forth in rate column numbered 1 of the Tariff Schedules of the United States on the date of enactment of this Act.

(d) During any period that a waiver is in effect with respect to any nonmarket economy country under section 402(c), the provisions of subsections (a) and (b) shall not apply with respect to such country.

Section 410. *East-West Trade Statistics Monitoring System*

The International Trade Commission shall establish and maintain a program to monitor imports of articles into the United States from nonmarket economy countries and exports of articles from the United States to nonmarket economy countries. To the extent feasible, the Commission shall coordinate such program with any relevant data gathering programs presently conducted by the Secretary of Commerce. The Secretary of Commerce shall provide the Commission with an information which, in the determination of the Commission, is necessary to carry out this section. The Commission shall publish a detailed summary of the data collected under the East-West Trade Statistics Monitoring System not less frequently than once each calendar quarter and shall transmit such publication to the East-West Foreign Trade Board and to Congress. Such publication shall include data on the effect of such imports, if any, on the production of like, or directly competitive, articles in the United States and on employment within the industry which produces like, or directly competitive, articles in the United States.

Section 411. *East-West Foreign Trade Board*

(a) The President shall establish an East-West Foreign Trade Board (hereinafter referred to as the "Board") to monitor trade between persons and agencies of the United States Government and nonmarket economy countries or instrumentalities of such countries to insure that such trade will be in the national interest of the United States.

(b)(1) Any person who exports technology vital to the national interest of the United States to a nonmarket economy country or an instrumentality of such country, and any agency of the United States which provides credits, guarantees or insurance to such country or such instrumentality in an amount in excess of $5,000,000 during any calendar year, shall file a report with the Board in such form and manner as the Board requires which describes the nature and terms of such export or such provision.

(2) For purposes of paragraph (1), if the total amount of credits, guarantees and insurance which an agency of the United States provides to all nonmarket economy countries and the instrumentalities of such countries exceeds $5,000,000 during a calendar year, then all subsequent provisions of credits, guarantees or insurance in any amount, during such year shall be reported to the Board under the provisions of paragraph (1).

(c) The Board shall submit to Congress a quarterly report on trade between the United States and nonmarket economy countries and instrumentalities of such countries. Such report shall include a review of the status of negotiations of bilateral trade agreements between the United States and such countries under this title, the activities of joint trade commissions created pursuant to such agreements, the resolution of commercial disputes between the United States and such countries, any exports from such countries which have caused disruption of United States markets, and recommendations for the promotion of east-west trade in the national interest of the United States.

TITLE V—GENERALIZED SYSTEM OF PREFERENCES

Section 501. *Authority to Extend Preferences*

The President may provide duty-free treatment for any eligible article from any beneficiary developing country in accordance with the provisions of this title. In taking any such action, the President shall have due regard for—

(1) the effect such action will have on furthering the economic development of developing countries;

(2) the extent to which other major developed countries are undertaking a comparable effort to assist developing countries by granting generalized preferences with respect to imports of products of such countries; and

(3) the anticipated impact of such action on United States producers of like or directly competitive products.

Section 502. *Beneficiary Developing Country*

(a)(1) For purposes of this title, the term "beneficiary developing country" means any country with respect to which there is in effect an Executive order by the President of the United States designating such country as a beneficiary developing country for purposes of this title. Before the President designates any country as a beneficiary developing country for purposes of this title, he shall notify the House of Representatives and the Senate of his intention to make such designation, together with the considerations entering into such decision.

(2) If the President has designated any country as a beneficiary developing country for purposes of this title, he shall not terminate such designation (either by issuing an Executive order for that purpose or by issuing an Executive order which has the effect of terminating such designation) unless, at least 60 days before such termination, he has notified the House of Representatives and the Senate and has notified such country of his intention to terminate such designation, together with the considerations entering into such decision.

(3) For purposes of this title, the term "country" means any foreign country, any overseas dependent territory or possession of a foreign country, or the Trust Territory of the Pacific Islands. In the case of an association of countries which is a free trade area or customs union, the President may by Executive order provide that all members of such association other than members which are barred from designation under subsection (b) shall be treated as one country for purposes of this title.

(b) No designation shall be made under this section with respect to any of the following:

Australia

Austria

Canada

Czechoslovakia

European Economic Community member states

Finland

Germany (East)

Hungary

Iceland

Japan

Monaco

New Zealand

Norway

Poland

Republic of South Africa

Sweden

Switzerland

Union of Soviet Socialist Republics

In addition, the President shall not designate any country a beneficiary developing country under this section—

(1) if such country is a Communist country, unless (A) the products of such country receive nondiscriminatory treatment, (B) such country is a contracting party to the General Agreement on Tariffs and Trade and a member of the International Monetary Fund, and (C) such country is not dominated or controlled by international communism;

(2) if such country is a member of the Organization of Petroleum Exporting Countries, or a party to any other arrangement of foreign countries, and such country participates in any action pursuant to such arrangement the effect of which is to withhold supplies of vital commodity resources from international trade or to raise the price of such commodities to an unreasonable level and to cause serious disruption of the world economy; withhold supplies of vital commodity resources from international trade or to raise the price of such commodities to an unreasonable level which causes serious disruptions of the world economy;

(3) if such country affords preferential treatment to the products of a developed country, other than the United States, which has, or is likely to have, a significant adverse effect on United States commerce, unless the President has received assurances satisfactory to him that such preferential treatment will be eliminated before January 1, 1976, or that action will be taken before January 1, 1976, to assure that there will be no such significant adverse effect, and he reports those assurances to the Congress;

(4) if such country—

(A) has nationalized, expropriated, or otherwise seized ownership or control of property owned by a United States citizen or by a corporation, partnership, or association which is 50 percent or more beneficially owned by United States citizens,

(B) has taken steps to repudiate or nullify an existing contract or agreement with a United States citizen or a corporation, partnership, or association which is 50 percent or more beneficially owned by United States citizens, the effect of which is to nationalize, expropriate, or otherwise seize ownership or control of property so owned, or

(C) has imposed or enforced taxes or other exactions, restrictive maintenance or operational conditions, or other measures with respect to property so owned, the effect of which is to nationalize, expropriate, or otherwise seize ownership or control of such property,

unless—

(D) the President determines that—

(i) prompt, adequate, and effective compensation has been or is being made to such citizen, corporation, partnership, or association,

(ii) good faith negotiations to provide prompt, adequate, and effective compensation under the applicable provisions of international law are in progress, or such country is otherwise taking steps to discharge its obligations under international law with respect to such citizen, corporation, partnership, or association, or

(iii) a dispute involving such citizen, corporation, partnership, or association over compensation for such a seizure has been submitted to arbitration under the provisions of the Convention for the Settlement of Investment Disputes, or in another mutually agreed upon forum, and

promptly furnishes a copy of such determination to the Senate and House of Representatives;

(5) if such country does not take adequate steps to cooperate with the United States to prevent narcotic drugs and other controlled substances (as listed in the schedules in section 202 of the Comprehensive Drug Abuse Prevention and Control Act of 1970 (21 U.S.C. 812)) produced, processed, or transported in such country from entering the United States unlawfully; and

(6) if such country fails to act in good faith in recognizing as binding or in enforcing arbitral awards in favor of United States citizens or a corporation, partnership or association which is 50 percent or more beneficially owned by United States citizens, which have been made by

arbitrators appointed for each case or by permanent arbitral bodies to which the parties involved have submitted their dispute.

Paragraphs (4), (5), and (6) shall not prevent the designation of any country as a beneficiary developing country under this section if the President determines that such designation will be in the national economic interest of the United States and reports such determination to the Congress with his reasons therefor.

(c) In determining whether to designate any country a beneficiary developing country under this section, the President shall take into account—

(1) an expression by such country of its desire to be so designated;

(2) the level of economic development of such country, including its per capita gross national product, the living standards of its inhabitants, and any other economic factors which he deems appropriate;

(3) whether or not the other major developed countries are extending generalized preferential tariff treatment to such country; and

(4) the extent to which such country has assured the United States it will provide equitable and reasonable access to the markets and basic commodity resources of such country.

(d) General headnote 3(a) to the Tariff Schedules of the United States (19 U.S.C. 1202) (relating to products of insular possessions) is amended by adding at the end thereof the following new paragraph:

"(iii) Subject to the limitations imposed under sections 503(b) and 504(c) of the Trade Act of 1974, articles designated eligible articles under section 503 of such Act which are imported from an insular possession of the United States shall receive duty treatment no less favorable than the treatment afforded such articles imported from a beneficiary developing country under title V of such Act."

(e) The President may exempt from the application of paragraph (2) of subsection (b) any country during the period during which such country (A) is a party to a bilateral or multilateral trade agreement to which the United States is also a party if such agreement fulfills the negotiating objectives set forth in section 108 of assuring the United States fair and equitable access at reasonable prices to supplies of articles of commerce important to the economic requirements of the United States and (B) is not in violation of such agreement by action denying the United States such fair and equitable access.

Section 503. *Eligible Articles*

(a) The President shall, from time to time, publish and furnish the International Trade Commission with lists of articles which may be considered for designation as eligible articles for purposes of this title. Before any such list is furnished to the Commission, there shall be in effect an Executive order under section 502 designating beneficiary developing countries. The provisions of sections 131, 132, 133, and 134 of this Act shall be complied with as though action under section 501 were action under section 101 of this Act to carry out a trade agreement entered into under section 101. After receiving the advice of the Commission with respect to the listed articles, the President shall designate those articles he considers appropriate to be eligible articles for purposes of this title by Executive order.

(b) The duty-free treatment provided under section 501 with respect to any eligible article shall apply only—

(1) to an article which is imported directly from a beneficiary developing country into the customs territory of the United States; and

(2)(A) if the sum of (i) the cost or value of the materials produced in the beneficiary developing country plus (ii) the direct costs of processing operations performed in such beneficiary developing country is not less than 35 percent of the appraised value of such article at the time of its entry into the customs territory of the United States; or

(B) if the sum of (i) the cost or value of the materials produced in 2 or more countries which are members of the same association of countries which is treated as one country under section 502(a)(3), plus (ii) the direct costs of processing operations performed in such countries is not less than 50 percent of the appraised value of such article at the time of its entry into the customs territory of the United States.

For purposes of paragraph (2)(A), the term "country" does not include an association of countries which is treated as one country under section 502 (a)(3) but does include a country which is a member of any such association. The Secretary of the Treasury shall prescribe such regulations as may be necessary to carry out this subsection.

(c)(1) The President may not designate any article as an eligible article under subsection (a) if such article is within one of the following categories of import-sensitive articles—

(A) textile and apparel articles which are subject to textile agreements,

(B) watches,

(C) import-sensitive electronic articles,

(D) import-sensitive steel articles,

(E) footwear articles specified in items 700.05 through 700.27, 700.29 through 700.53, 700.55.23 through 700.55.75, and 700.60 through 700.80 of the Tariff Schedules of the United States,

(F) import-sensitive semimanufactured and manufactured glass products, and

(G) any other articles which the President determines to be import-sensitive in the context of the Generalized System of Preferences.

(2) No article shall be an eligible article for purposes of this title for any period during which such article is the subject of any action proclaimed pursuant to section 203 of this Act or section 232 or 351 of the Trade Expansion Act of 1962.

Section 504. *Limitations on Preferential Treatment*

(a) The President may withdraw, suspend, or limit the application of the duty-free treatment accorded under section 501 with respect to any article or with respect to any country; except that no rate of duty may be established in respect of any article pursuant to this section other than the rate which would apply but for this title. In taking any action under this subsection, the President shall consider the factors set forth in sections 501 and 502(c).

(b) The President shall, after complying with the requirements of section 502(a)(2), withdraw or suspend the designation of any country as a beneficiary developing country if, after such designation, he determines that as the result of changed circumstances such country would be barred from designation as a beneficiary developing country under section 502(b). Such country shall cease to be a beneficiary developing country on the day on which the President issues an Executive order revoking his designation of such country under section 502.

(c)(1) Whenever the President determines that any country—

(A) has exported (directly or indirectly) to the United States during a calendar year a quantity of an eligible article having an appraised value in excess of an amount which bears the same ratio to $25,000,000 as the gross national product of the United States for the preceding calendar year, as determined by the Department of Commerce, bears to the gross national product of the United States for calendar year 1974, or

(B) except as provided in subsection (d), has exported (either directly or indirectly) to the United States a quantity of any eligible article equal to or exceeding 50 percent of the appraised value of the total imports of such article into the United States during any calendar year,

then, not later than 60 days after the close of such calendar year, such country shall not be treated as a beneficiary developing country with respect to such article, except that, if before such 60th day, the President determines and publishes in the Federal Register that, with respect to such country—

(i) there has been an historical preferential trade relationship between the United States and such country,

(ii) there is a treaty or trade agreement in force covering economic relations between such country and the United States, and

(iii) such country does not discriminate against, or impose unjustifiable or unreasonable barriers to, United States commerce,

then he may designate, or continue the designation of, such country as a beneficiary developing country with respect to such article.

(2) A country which is no longer treated as a beneficiary developing country with respect to an eligible article by reason of this subsection may be redesignated, subject to the provisions of section 502, a beneficiary developing country with respect to such article if imports of such article from such country did not exceed the limitations in paragraph (1) of this subsection during the preceding calendar year.

(d) Subsection (c)(1)(B) does not apply with respect to any eligible article if a like or directly competitive article is not produced on the date of enactment of this Act in the United States.

(e) No action pursuant to section 501 may affect any tariff duty imposed by the Legislature of Puerto Rico pursuant to section 319 of the Tariff Act of 1930 (19 U.S.C. sec. 1319) on coffee imported into Puerto Rico.

Section 505. *Time Limit on Title; Comprehensive Review*

(a) No duty-free treatment under this title shall remain in effect after the date which is 10 years after the date of the enactment of this Act.

(b) On or before the date which is 5 years after the date of the enactment of this Act, the President shall submit to the Congress a full and complete report of the operation of this title.

TITLE VI—GENERAL PROVISIONS

Section 601. *Definitions*

For purposes of this Act—

(1) The term "duty" includes the rate and form of any import duty, including but not limited to tariff-rate quotas.

(2) The term "other import restriction" includes a limitation, prohibition, charge, and exaction other than duty, imposed on importation or imposed for the regulation of importation. The term does not include any orderly marketing agreement.

(3) The term "ad valorem" includes ad valorem equivalent. Whenever any limitation on the amount by which or to which any rate of duty may be decreased or increased pursuant to a trade agreement is expressed in terms of an ad valorem percentage, the ad valorem amount taken into account for purposes of such limitation shall be determined by the President on the basis of the value of imports of the articles concerned during the most recent representative period.

(4) The term "ad valorem equivalent" means the ad valorem equivalent of a specific rate or, in the case of a combination of rates including a specific rate, the sum of the ad valorem equivalent of the specific rate and of the ad valorem rate. The ad valorem equivalent shall be determined by the President on the basis of the value of imports of the article concerned during the most recent representative period. In determining the value of imports, the President shall utilize, to the maximum extent practicable, the standards of valuation contained in section 402 or 402a of the Tariff Act of 1930 (19 U.S.C. sec. 1401a or 1402) applicable to the article concerned during such representative period.

(5) An imported article is "directly competitive with" a domestic article at an earlier or later stage of processing, and a domestic article is "directly competitive with" an imported article at an earlier or later stage of processing, if the importation of the article has an economic effect on producers of the domestic article comparable to the effect of importation of articles in the same stage of processing as the domestic article. For

purposes of this paragraph, the unprocessed article is at an earlier stage of processing.

(6) The term "modification", as applied to any duty or other import restriction, includes the elimination of any duty or other import restriction.

(7) The term "existing" means (A) when used, without the specification of any date, with respect to any matter relating to entering into or carrying out a trade agreement or other action authorized by this Act, existing on the day on which such trade agreement is entered into or such other action is taken; and (B) when used with respect to a rate of duty, the nonpreferential rate of duty (however established, and even though temporarily suspended by Act of Congress or otherwise) set forth in rate column numbered 1 of schedules 1 through 7 of the Tariff Schedules of the United States on the date specified or (if no date is specified) on the day referred to in clause (A).

(8) A product of a country or area is an article which is the growth, produce, or manufacture of such country or area.

(9) The term "nondiscriminatory treatment" means most-favored-nation treatment.

(10) The term "commerce" includes services associated with international trade.

Section 602. *Relation to Other Laws*

(a) The second and third sentences of section 2(a) of the Act entitled "An Act to amend the Tariff Act of 1930," approved June 12, 1934, as amended (19 U.S.C. sec. 1352(a)), are each amended by striking out "this Act or the Trade Expansion Act of 1962" and inserting in lieu thereof "this Act or the Trade Expansion Act of 1962 or the Trade Act of 1974".

(b) Section 242 of the Trade Expansion Act of 1962 is amended as follows:

(1) by striking out "351 and 352" in subsection (a) and inserting in lieu thereof "201, 202, and 203 of the Trade Act of 1974";

(2) by striking out "with respect to tariff adjustment" in subsection (b)(2);

(3) by striking out "301(e)" in subsection (b)(2) and inserting in lieu thereof "201(d) of the Trade Act of 1974";

(4) by striking out "concerning foreign import restrictions" in subsection (b)(3); and

(5) by striking out "section 252(d)" each place it appears and inseting in lieu thereof "subsections (c) and (d) of section 301 of the Trade Act of 1974".

(c) Section 351(c)(1)(B) of the Trade Expansion Act of 1962 is amended by striking out "unless extended under paragraph (2)," and inserting in lieu thereof the following: "unless extended under section 203 of the Trade Act of 1974,".

(d) Sections 202, 211, 212, 213, 221, 222, 223, 224, 225, 226, 231, 241, 243, 252, 253, 254, 255(a), 256, so much of 301 and 302 as is not repealed by subsection (e), 351(c)(2) and (d)(3), 361, 401, 402, 403, 404, and 405(1), (3), (4), and (5) of the Trade Expansion Act of 1962 are repealed.

(e) Sections 301(a)(2) and (3), (c), (d)(2), (f)(1) and (3), 302(b) (1) and (2), (c), (d), and (e), 311 through 315, 317(a), 321 through 338 of the Trade Expansion Act of 1962 are repealed on the 90th day following the date of the enactment of this Act.

(f) All provisions of law (other than this Act, the Trade Expansion Act of 1962, and the Trade Agreements Extension Act of 1951) in effect after the date of enactment of this Act, referring to section 350 of the Tariff Act of 1930, to that section as amended, to the Act entitled "An Act to amend the Tariff Act of 1930," approved June 12, 1934, to that Act as amended or to the Trade Expansion Act of 1962, or to agreements entered into, or proclamations issued, or actions taken under any of such provisions, shall be construed, unless clearly precluded by the context, to refer also to this Act, or to agreements entered into or proclamations or orders issued, pursuant to this Act.

Section 603. *International Trade Commission*

(a) In order to expedite the performance of its functions under this Act, the International Trade Commission may conduct preliminary investigations, determine the scope and manner of its proceedings, and consolidate proceedings before it.

(b) In performing its functions under this Act, the Commission may exercise any authority granted to it under any other Act.

(c) The Commission shall at all times keep informed concerning the operation and effect of provisions relating to duties or other import restrictions of the United States contained in trade agreements entered into under the trade agreements program.

Section 604. *Consequential Changes in the Tariff Schedules*

The President shall from time to time, as appropriate, embody in the Tariff Schedules of the United States the substance of the relevant provisions of this Act, and of other Acts affecting import treatment, and actions thereunder, including modification, continuance, or imposition of any rate of duty or other import restriction.

Section 605. *Separability*

If any provision of this Act or the application of any provision to any circumstances or persons shall be held invalid, the validity of the remainder of this Act, and of the application of such provision to other circumstances or persons, shall not be affected thereby.

Section 606. *International Drug Control*

The President shall submit a report to Congress at least once each calendar year listing those foreign countries in which narcotic drugs and other controlled substances (as listed under section 202 of the Comprehensive Drug Abuse Prevention and Control Act of 1970 (21 U.S.C. 812)) are produced, processed, or transported for unlawful entry into the United States. Such report shall include a description of the measures such countries are taking to prevent such production, processing, or transport.

Section 607. *Voluntary Limitations on Exports of Steel to the United States*

No person shall be liable for damages, penalties, or other sanctions under the Federal Trade Commission Act (15 U.S.C. 41–77) or the Antitrust Acts (as defined in section 4 of the Federal Trade Commission Act (15 U.S.C. 44)), or under any similar State law, on account of his negotiating, entering into, participating in, or implementing an arrangement providing for the voluntary limitation on exports of steel and steel products to the United States, or any modification or renewal of such an arrangement, if such arrangement or such modification or renewal—

(1) was undertaken prior to the date of the enactment of this Act at the request of the Secretary of State or his delegate, and

(2) ceases to be effective not later than January 1, 1975.

Section 608. *Uniform Statistical Data on Imports, Exports, and Production*

(a) Section 484(e) of the Tariff Act of 1930 (19 U.S.C. 1484(e)) is amended to read as follows:

"(e) STATISTICAL ENUMERATION.—The Secretary of the Treasury, the Secretary of Commerce, and the United States International Trade Commission are authorized and directed to establish from time to time for statistical purposes an enumeration of articles in such detail as in their judgment may be necessary, comprehending all merchandise imported into the United States and exported from the United States, and shall seek, in conjunction with statistical programs for domestic production, to establish the comparability thereof with such enumeration of articles. All import entries and export declarations shall include or have attached thereto an accurate statement specifying, in terms of such detailed enumeration, the kinds and quantities of all merchandise imported and exported and the value of the total quantity of each kind of article."

(b) In carrying out the responsibilities under section 484(e), Tariff Act of 1930 and other pertinent statutes, the Secretary of Commerce and the United States International Trade Commission shall conduct jointly a study of existing commodity classification systems with a view to identifying the appropriate principles and concepts which should guide the organization and development of an enumeration of articles which would result in comparability of United States import, production, and export data. The Secretary and the United States International Trade Commission shall submit a report to both Houses of Congress and to the President with respect to such study no later than August 1, 1975.

(c) In further connection with its responsibilities pursuant to subsections (a) and (b), the United States International Trade Commission shall undertake an investigation under section 332(g) of the Tariff Act of 1930 which would provide the basis for—

(1) a report on the appropriate concepts and principles which should underlie the formulation of an international commodity code adaptable for modernized tariff nomenclature purposes and for recording, handling, and reporting of transactions in national and international trade, taking into account how such a code could meet the needs of sound customs and trade reporting practices reflecting the interests of United States and other countries, such report to be submitted to both Houses of Congress and to the President as soon as feasible, but in any event, no later than June 1, 1975; and

(2) full and immediate participation by the United States Interna-

tional Trade Commission in the United States contribution to technical work of the Harmonized Systems Committee under the Customs Co-operation Council to assure the recognition of the needs of the United States business community in the development of a Harmonized Code reflecting sound principles of commodity identification and specification and modern producing methods and trading practices,

and, in carrying out such responsibilities, the Commission shall report to both Houses of Congress and to the President, as it deems appropriate.

(d) The President is requested to direct the appropriate agencies to co-operate fully with the Secretary of Commerce and the United States International Trade Commission in carrying out their responsibilities under subsections (a), (b), and (c).

(e) The amendment made by subsection (a) insofar as it relates to export declarations shall take effect on January 1, 1976.

Section 609. *Submission of Statistical Data on Imports and Exports*

(a) Section 301 of title 13, United States Code, is amended—

(1) by inserting "(a)" before "The Secretary"; and

(2) by adding at the end thereof the following new subsections:

"(b) The Secretary shall submit to the Committee on Ways and Means of the House of Representatives and the Committee on Finance of the Senate, on quarterly and cumulative bases, statistics on United States imports for consumption and United States exports by country and by product. Statistics on United States imports shall be submitted in accordance with the Tariff Schedules of the United States Annotated and general statistical headnote 1 thereof, in detail as follows:

"(1) net quantity;

"(2) United States customs value;

"(3) purchase price or its equivalent;

"(4) equivalent of arm's length value;

"(5) aggregate cost from port of exportation to United States port of entry;

"(6) a United States port of entry value comprised of (5) plus (4), if applicable, or, if not applicable, (5) plus (3); and

"(7) for transactions where (3) and (4) are equal, the total value of such transactions.

The data for paragraphs (1), (2), (3), (5), and (6) shall be reported separately for nonrelated and related party transactions, and shall also be reported as a total of all transactions.

"(c) In submitting any information under subsection (b) with respect to exports, the Secretary shall state separately from the total value of all exports—

"(1)(A) the value of agricultural commodities exported under the Agricultural Trade Development and Assistance Act of 1954, as amended; and

"(B) the total amount of all export subsidies paid to exporters by the United States under such Act for the exportation of such commodities; and

"(2) the value of goods exported under the Foreign Assistance Act of 1961.

"(d) To assist the Secretary to carry out the provisions of subsections (b) and (c)—

"(1) the Secretary of Agriculture shall furnish information to the Secretary concerning the value of agricultural commodities exported under provisions of the Agricultural Trade Development and Assistance Act of 1954, as amended, and the total amounts of all export subsidies paid to exporters by the United States under such Act for the exportation of such commodities; and

"(2) the Secretary of State shall furnish information to the Secretary concerning the value of goods exported under the provisions of the Foreign Assistance Act of 1961, as amended."

(b) The amendments made by subsection (a) shall take effect on January 1, 1975.

Section 610. *Gifts Sent from Insular Possessions*

(a) Section 321(a)(2)(A) of the Tariff Act of 1930 (19 U.S.C. 1321 (a)(2)(A)) is amended by inserting after "United States" the following:

"($20, in the case of articles sent as bona fide gifts from persons in the Virgin Islands, Guam, and American Samoa)".

(b) The amendment made by subsection (a) shall apply with respect to articles entered, or withdrawn from warehouse, for consumption after the date of the enactment of this Act.

Section 611. *Review of Protests in Import Surcharge Cases*

Notwithstanding the provisions of section 515(a) of the Tariff Act of 1930 (19 U.S.C. 1515(a)), in the case of any protest under section 514 of such Act involving the imposition of an import surcharge in the form of a supplemental duty pursuant to Presidential Proclamation 4074, dated August 17, 1971, the time for review and allowing or denying the protest shall not expire until five years from the date the protest was filed in accordance with such section 514.

Section 612. *Trade Relations With Canada*

It is the sense of the Congress that the United States should enter into a trade agreement with Canada which will guarantee continued stability to the economies of the United States and Canada. In order to promote such economic stability, the President may initiate negotiations for a trade agreement with Canada to establish a free trade area covering the United States and Canada. Nothing in this section shall be construed as prior approval of any legislation which may be necessary to implement such a trade agreement.

Section 613. *Limitation on Credit to Russia*

After the date of enactment of the Trade Act of 1974, no agency of the Government of the United States, other than the Commodity Credit Corporation, shall approve any loans, guarantees, insurance, or any combination thereof, in connection with exports to the Union of Soviet Socialist Republics in an aggregate amount in excess of $300,000,000 without prior congressional approval as provided by law.

5. Antidumping Act of 1921 (as Amended Through 1970)

DUMPING INVESTIGATION

SEC. 201. (a) Whenever the Secretary of the Treasury (hereinafter called the "Secretary") determines that a class or kind of foreign merchandise is being, or is likely to be, sold in the United States or elsewhere at less than its fair value, he shall so advise the United States Tariff Commission, and the said Commission shall determine within three months thereafter whether an industry in the United States is being or is likely to be injured, or is prevented from being established, by reason of the importation of such merchandise into the United States. The said Commission, after such investigation as it deems necessary, shall notify the Secretary of its determination, and, if that determination is in the affirmative, the Secretary shall make public a notice (hereinafter in this Act called a "finding") of his determination and the determination of the said Commission. For the purposes of this subsection, the said Commission shall be deemed to have made an affirmative determination if the Commissioners of the said Commission voting are evenly divided as to whether its determination should be in the affirmative or in the negative. The Secretary's finding shall include a description of the class or kind of merchandise to which it applies in such detail as he shall deem necessary for the guidance of customs officers.

(b) Whenever, in the case of any imported merchandise of a class or kind as to which the Secretary has not so made public a finding, the Secretary has reason to believe or suspect, from the invoice or other papers or from information presented to him or to any person to whom authority under this section has been delegated, that the purchase price is less, or that the exporter's sales price is less or likely to be less, than the foreign market value (or, in the absence of such value, than the constructed value), he shall forthwith publish notice of that fact in the Federal Register and shall authorize, under such regulations as he may prescribe, the withholding of appraisement reports as to such merchandise entered, or withdrawn from warehouse, for consumption, not more than one hundred and twenty days before the question of dumping has been raised by or presented to him or any person to whom authority under this section has been delegated, until the further order of the Secretary, or until the Secretary has made public a finding as provided for in subdivision (a) in regard to such merchandise.

(c) The Secretary, upon determining whether foreign merchandise is being, or is likely to be, sold in the United States at less than its fair value, and the United States Tariff Commission, upon making its determination under subsection (a) of this section, shall each publish such determination in the Federal Register, with a statement of the reasons therefor, whether such determination is in the affirmative or in the negative.

SPECIAL DUMPING DUTY

SEC. 202. (a) In the case of all imported merchandise, whether dutiable or free of duty, of a class or kind as to which the Secretary of the Treasury has made public a finding as provided for in section 201, entered, or withdrawn from the warehouse, for consumption, not more than one hundred and twenty days before the question of dumping was raised by or presented to the Secretary or any person to whom authority under section 201 has been delegated, and as to which no appraisement has been made before such finding has been so made public, if the purchase price or the exporter's sales price is less than the foreign market value (or, in the absence of such value, than the constructed value) there shall be levied, collected, and paid, in addition to any other duties imposed thereon by law, a special dumping duty in an amount equal to such difference.

(b) In determining the foreign market value for the purposes of subsection (a), if it is established to the satisfaction of the Secretary or his delegate that the amount of any difference between the purchase price and the foreign market value (or that the fact that the purchase price is the same as the foreign market value) is wholly or partly due to—

(1) the fact that the wholesale quantities, in which such or similar merchandise is sold or, in the absence of sales, offered for sale for exportation to the United States in the ordinary course of trade, are less or are greater than the wholesale quantities in which such or similar merchandise is sold or, in the absence of sales, offered for sale in the principal markets of the country of exportation in the ordinary course of trade for home consumption (or, if not so sold or offered for sale for home consumption, then for exportation to countries other than the United States),

(2) other differences in circumstances of sale, or

(3) the fact that merchandise described in subdivision (C), (D), (E), or (F) of section 212(3) is used in determining foreign market value,

then due allowance shall be made therefor.

(c) In determining the foreign market value for the purposes of subsection (a), if it is established to the satisfaction of the Secretary or his delegate that the amount of any difference between the exporter's sales price and the foreign market value (or that the fact that the exporter's sales price is the same as the foreign market value) is wholly or partly due to—

(1) the fact that the wholesale quantities in which such or similar merchandise is sold or, in the absence of sales, offered for sale in the principal markets of the United States in the ordinary course of trade, are less or are greater than the wholesale quantities in which such or

similar merchandise is sold or, in the absence of sales, offered for sale in the principal markets of the country of exportation in the ordinary course of trade for home consumption (or, if not so sold or offered for s؟'ٮ for home consumption, then for exportation to countries other than the United States),

(2) other differences in circumstances of sale, or

(3) the fact that merchandise described in subdivision (C), (D), (E), or (F) of section 212(3) is used in determining foreign market value,

then due allowance shall be made therefor.

PURCHASE PRICE

SEC. 203. That for the purposes of this title, the purchase price of imported merchandise shall be the price at which such merchandise has been purchased or agreed to be purchased, prior to the time of exportation, by the person by whom or for whose account the merchandise is imported, plus, when not included in such price, the cost of all containers and coverings and all other costs, charges, and expenses incident to placing the merchandise in condition, packed ready for shipment to the United States, less the amount, if any, included in such price, attributable to any additional costs, charges, and expenses, and United States import duties, incident to bringing the merchandise from the place of shipment in the country of exportation to the place of delivery in the United States; and plus the amount, if not included in such price, of any export tax imposed by the country of exportation on the exportation of the merchandise to the United States; and plus the amount of any import duties imposed by the country of exportation which have been rebated, or which have not been collected, by reason of the exportation of the merchandise to the United States; and plus the amount of any taxes imposed in the country of exportation upon the manufacturer, producer, or seller, in respect to the manufacture, production or sale of the merchandise, which have been rebated, or which have not been collected, by reason of the exportation of the merchandise to the United States.

EXPORTER'S SALES PRICE

SEC. 204. That for the purpose of this title the exporter's sales price of imported merchandise shall be the price at which such merchandise is sold or agreed to be sold in the United States, before or after the time of importation, by or for the account of the exporter, plus, when not included in such price, the cost of all containers and coverings and all other costs, charges, and expenses incident to placing the merchandise in condition, packed ready for shipment to the United States, less (1) the amount, if any, included in such price, attributable to any additional costs, charges, and expenses, and United States import duties, incident to bringing the merchandise from the place of shipment in the country of exportation to the place of delivery in the United States, (2) the amount of the commissions, if any, for selling in the United States the particular merchandise under consideration, (3) an amount equal to the expenses, if any, generally incurred by or for the account of the exporter in the United States in selling identical or substantially identical merchandise, and (4) the amount of any export tax imposed by the country of exportation on the exportation of the merchandise to the United States; and plus the amount of any import duties imposed by the country of exportation which have been rebated, or which have not been collected, by reason of the exportation of the merchandise to the United States; and plus the amount of any taxes imposed in the country of exportation upon the manufacturer, producer, or seller in respect to the manufacture, production, or sale of the merchandise, which have been rebated, or which have not been collected, by reason of the exportation of the merchandise to the United States.

FOREIGN MARKET VALUE

SEC. 205. For the purposes of this title, the foreign market value of imported merchandise shall be the price, at the time of exportation of such merchandise to the United States, at which such or similar merchandise is sold or, in the absence of sales, offered for sale in the principal markets of the country from which exported, in the usual wholesale quantities and in the ordinary course of trade for home consumption (or, if not so sold or offered for sale for home consumption, or if the Secretary determines that the quantity sold for home consumption is so small in relation to the quantity sold for exportation to countries other than the United States as to form an inadequate basis for comparison, then the price at which so sold or offered for sale for exportation to countries other than the United States), plus, when not included in such price, the cost of all containers and coverings and all other costs, charges, and expenses incident to placing the merchandise in condition packed ready for shipment to the United States, except that in the case of merchandise purchased or agreed to be purchased by the person by whom or for whose account the merchandise is imported, prior to the time of exportation, the foreign market value shall be ascertained as of the date of such purchase or agreement to purchase. In the ascertainment of foreign market value for the purposes of this title no pretended sale or offer for sale, and no sale or offer for sale intended to establish a fictitious market, shall be taken into account. If such or similar merchandise is sold or, in the absence of sales, offered for sale through a sales agency or other organization related to the seller in any of the respects described in section 207, the prices at which such or similar merchandise is sold or, in the absence of sales, offered for sale by such sales agency or other organization may be used in determining the foreign market value.

CONSTRUCTED VALUE

SEC. 206. (a) For the purposes of this title, the constructed value of imported merchandise shall be the sum of—

(1) the cost of materials (exclusive of any internal tax applicable in the country of exportation directly to such materials or their disposition, but remitted or refunded upon the exportation of the article in the production of which such materials are used) and of fabrication or other processing of any kind employed in producing such or similar merchandise, at a time preceding the date of exportation of the merchandise under consideration which would ordinarily permit the production of that particular merchandise in the ordinary course of business;

(2) an amount for general expenses and profit equal to that usually reflected in sales of merchandise of the same general class or kind as the merchandise under consideration which are made by producers in the country of exportation, in the usual wholesale quantities and in the ordinary course of trade, except that (A) the amount for general expenses shall not be less than 10 per centum of the cost as defined in paragraph (1), and (B) the amount for profit shall not be less than 8 per centum of the sum of such general expenses and cost; and

(3) the cost of all containers and coverings of whatever nature, and all other expenses incidental to placing the merchandise under consideration in condition, packed ready for shipment to the United States.

(b) For the purposes of this section, a transaction directly or indirectly between persons specified in any one of the paragraphs in subsection (c) of this section may be disregarded if, in the case of any element of value required to be considered, the amount representing that element does not fairly reflect the amount usually reflected in the market under consideration of merchandise of the same general class or kind as the merchandise under consideration. If a transaction is disregarded under the preceding sentence and there are no other transactions available for consideration, then the determination of the amount required to be considered shall be based on the best evidence available as to what the amount would have been if the transaction had occurred between persons not specified in any one of the paragraphs in subsection (c).

(c) The persons referred to in subsection (b) are:

(1) Members of a family, including brothers and sisters (whether by the whole or half blood), spouse, ancestors, and lineal descendants;

(2) Any officer or director of an organization and such organization;

(3) Partners;

(4) Employer and employee;

(5) Any person directly or indirectly owning, controlling, or holding with power to vote, 5 per centum or more of the outstanding voting stock or shares of any organization and such organization; and

(6) Two or more persons directly or indirectly controlling, controlled by, or under common control with, any person.

EXPORTER

SEC. 207. That for the purposes of this title the exporter of imported merchandise shall be the person by whom or for whose account the merchandise is imported into the United States:

(1) If such person is the agent or principal of the exporter, manufacturer, or producer; or

(2) If such person owns or controls, directly or indirectly, through stock ownership or control or otherwise, any interest in the business of the exporter, manufacturer, or producer; or

(3) If the exporter, manufacturer, or producer owns or controls, directly or indirectly, through stock ownership or control or otherwise, any interest in any business conducted by such person; or

(4) If any person or persons, jointly or severally, directly or indirectly, through stock ownership or control or otherwise, own or control in the aggregate 20 per centum or more of the voting power or control in the business carried on by the person by whom or for whose account the merchandise is imported into the United States, and also 20 per centum or more of such power or control in the business of the exporter, manufacturer, or producer.

OATHS AND BONDS ON ENTRY

SEC. 208. That in the case of all imported merchandise, whether dutiable or free of duty, of a class or kind as to which the Secretary has made public a finding as provided in section 201, and delivery of which has not been made by the appropriate customs officer before such finding has been so made public, unless the person by whom or for whose account such merchandise is imported makes oath before such customs officer, under regulations prescribed by the Secretary, that he is not an exporter, or unless such person declares under oath at the time of entry, under regulations prescribed by the Secretary, the exporter's sales price of such merchandise, it shall be unlawful for such customs officer to deliver the merchandise until such person has made oath before such customs officer under regulations prescribed by the Secretary, that the merchandise has not been sold or agreed to be sold by such person, and has given bond to such customs officer, under regulations prescribed by the Secretary, with sureties approved by such customs officer, in an amount equal to the estimated value of the merchandise, conditioned: (1) that he will report to such customs officer the exporter's sales price of the merchandise within 30 days after such merchandise has been sold or agreed to be sold in the United States, (2) that he will pay on demand from such customs officer the amount of special dumping duty, if any, imposed by this title upon such merchandise, and (3) that he will furnish to such customs officer such information as may be in his possession and as may be necessary for the ascertainment of such duty, and will keep such records as to the sale of such merchandise as the Secretary may by regulation prescribe.

DUTIES OF APPRAISERS

SEC. 209. That in the case of all imported merchandise, whether dutiable or free of duty, of a class or kind as to which the Secretary has made public a finding as provided in section 201, and as to which the appropriate customs officer has made no appraisement before such finding has been so made public, it shall be the duty of such customs officer, by all reasonable ways and means to ascertain, estimate, and appraise (any invoice or affidavit thereto or statement of constructed value to the contrary notwithstanding) the foreign market value or the constructed value, as the case may be, the purchase price, and the exporter's sales price, and any other facts which the Secretary may deem necessary for the purposes of this title.

APPEALS AND PROTESTS

SEC. 210. That for the purposes of this title the determination of the appropriate customs officer as to the foreign market value or the constructed value, as the case may be, the purchase price, and the exporter's sales price, and the action of such customs officer in assessing special dumping duty, shall have the same force and effect and be subject to the same right of protest, under the same conditions and subject to the same limitations; and the general appraisers, the Board of General Appraisers, and the Court of Customs Appeals shall have the same jurisdiction, powers, and duties in connection with such protests as in the case of appeals and protests relating to customs duties under existing law.

DRAWBACKS

SEC. 211. That the special dumping duty imposed by this title shall be treated in all respects as regular customs duties within the meaning of all laws relating to the drawback of customs duties.

DEFINITIONS

SEC. 212. For the purposes of this title—

(1) The term "sold or, in the absence of sales, offered for sale" means sold or, in the absence of sales, offered—

(A) to all purchasers at wholesale, or

(B) in the ordinary course of trade to one or more selected purchasers at wholesale at a price which fairly reflects the market value of the merchandise,

without regard to restrictions as to the disposition or use of the merchandise by the purchaser except that, where such restrictions are found to affect the market value of the merchandise, adjustment shall be made therefor in calculating the price at which the merchandise is sold or offered for sale.

(2) The term "ordinary course of trade" means the conditions and practices which, for a reasonable time prior to the exportation of the merchandise under consideration, have been normal in the trade under consideration with respect to merchandise of the same class or kind as the merchandise under consideration.

(3) The term "such or similar merchandise" means merchandise in the first of the following categories in respect of which a determination for the purposes of this title can be satisfactorily made:

(A) The merchandise under consideration and other merchandise which is identical in physical characteristics with, and was produced in the same country by the same person as, the merchandise under consideration.

(B) Merchandise which is identical in physical characteristics with, and was produced by another person in the same country, as the merchandise under consideration.

(C) Merchandise (i) produced in the same country and by the

same person as the merchandise under consideration, (ii) like the merchandise under consideration in component material or materials and in the purposes for which used, and (iii) approximately equal in commercial value to the merchandise under consideration.

(D) Merchandise which satisfies all the requirements of subdivision (C) except that it was produced by another person.

(E) Merchandise (i) produced in the same country and by the same person and of the same general class or kind as the merchandise under consideration, (ii) like the merchandise under consideration in the purposes for which used, and (iii) which the Secretary or his delegate determines may reasonably be compared for the purposes of this title with the merchandise under consideration.

(F) Merchandise which satisfies all the requirements of subdivision (E) except that it was produced by another person.

(4) The term "usual wholesale quantities", in any case in which the merchandise in respect of which value is being determined is sold in the market under consideration at different prices for different quantities, means the quantities in which such merchandise is there sold at the price or prices for one quantity in an aggregate volume which is greater than the aggregate volume sold at the price or prices for any other quantity.

SHORT TITLE

SEC. 213. That this title may be cited as the "Antidumping Act, 1921."

6. Congressional Response to International Antidumping Code

Title II, Pub. L. 90–634 Oct. 24, 1968

DETERMINATIONS UNDER THE ANTIDUMPING ACT, 1921

SEC. 201. (a) Nothing contained in the International Antidumping Code, signed at Geneva on June 30, 1967, shall be construed to restrict the discretion of the United States Tariff Commission in performing its duties and functions under the Antidumping Act, 1921, and in performing their duties and functions under such Act the Secretary of the Treasury and the Tariff Commission shall—

(1) resolve any conflict between the International Antidumping

Code and the Antidumping Act, 1921, in favor of the Act as applied by the agency administering the Act, and

(2) take into account the provisions of the International Antidumping Code only insofar as they are consistent with the Antidumping Act, 1921, as applied by the agency administering the Act.

7. Antidumping Act of 1921 (1975-1979)

DUMPING INVESTIGATION

Sec. 201. (a) Whenever the Secretary of the Treasury (hereinafter called the "Secretary") determines that a class or kind of foreign merchandise is being, or is likely to be, sold in the United States or elsewhere at less than its fair value, he shall so advise the United States International Trade Commission, and the Commission shall determine within three months thereafter whether an industry in the United States is being or is likely to be injured, or is prevented from being established, by reason of the importation of such merchandise into the United States. The Commission, after such investigation as it deems necessary, shall notify the Secretary of its determination, and, if that determination is in the affirmative, the Secretary shall make public a notice (hereinafter in this Act called a "finding") of his determination and the determination of the Commission. For the purposes of this subsection, the Commission shall be deemed to have made an affirmative determination if the Commissioners of the Commission voting are evenly divided as to whether its determination should be in the affirmative or in the negative. The Secretary's finding shall include a description of the class or kind of merchandise to which it applies in such detail as he shall deem necessary for the guidance of customs officers.

(b)(1) In the case of any imported merchandise of a class or kind as to which the Secretary has not so made public a finding, he shall, within six months after the publication under subsection (c)(1) of a notice of initiation of an investigation—

(A) determine whether there is reason to believe or suspect, from the invoice or other papers or from information presented to him or to any other person to whom authority under this section has been delegated, that the purchase price is less, or that the exporter's sales price is less or likely to be less, than the foreign market value (or, in the absence of such value, than the constructed value); and

(B) if his determination is affirmative, publish a notice of that fact in the Federal Register, and require under such regulations as he may prescribe, the withholding of appraisement as to such merchandise entered, or withdrawn from warehouse, for consumption on or after the date of publication of that notice in the Federal Register (or such earlier date, not more than one hundred and twenty days before the date of publication under subsection (c)(1) of notice of initiation of the investigation, as the Secretary may prescribe), until the further order of the Secretary, or until the Secretary has made public a finding as provided for in subsection (a) in regard to such merchandise; or

(C) if his determination is negative (or if he tentatively determines that the investigation should be discontinued), publish notice of that fact in the Federal Register.

(2) If in the course of an investigation under this subsection the Secretary concludes that the determination provided for in paragraph (1) cannot reasonably be made within six months, he shall publish notice of this in the Federal Register, together with a statement of reasons therefor, in which case the determination shall be made within nine months after the publication in the Federal Register of the notice of initiation of the investigation.

(3) Within three months after publication in the Federal Register of a determination under paragraph (1), the Secretary shall make a final determination whether the foreign merchandise in question is being or is likely to be sold in the United States at less than its fair value (or a final discontinuance of the investigation).

(c)(1) The Secretary shall, within thirty days of the receipt of information alleging that a particular class or kind of merchandise is being or is likely to be sold in the United States or elsewhere at less than its fair value and that an industry in the United States is being or is likely to be injured, or is prevented from being established, by reason of the importation of such merchandise into the United States, determine whether to initiate an investigation into the question of whether such merchandise in fact is being or is likely to be sold in the United States or elsewhere at less than its fair value. If his determination is affirmative he shall publish notice of the initiation of such an investigation in the Federal Register. If it is negative, the inquiry shall be closed.

(2) If, in the course of making a determination under paragraph (1), the Secretary concludes, from the information available to him, that there is substantial doubt whether an industry in the United States is being or is likely to be injured, or is prevented from being established, by reason of the importation of such merchandise into the United States, he shall forward to

the Commission the reasons for such substantial doubt and a preliminary indication, based upon whatever price information is available, concerning possible sales at less than fair value, including possible margins of dumping and the volume of trade. If within thirty days after receipt of such information from the Secretary, the Commission, after conducting such inquiry as it deems appropriate, determines there is no reasonable indication that an industry in the United States is being or is likely to be injured, or is prevented from being established, by reason of the importation of such merchandise into the United States, it shall advise the Secretary of its determination and any investigation under subsection (b) then in progress shall be terminated.

(d)(1) Before making any determination under subsection (a), the Secretary or the Commission, as the case may be, shall, at the request of any foreign manufacturer or exporter, or any domestic importer, of the foreign merchandise in question, or of any domestic manufacturer, producer, or wholesaler of merchandise of the same class or kind, conducts a hearing at which—

(A) any such person shall have the right to appear by counsel or in person; and

(B) any other person, firm, or corporation may make application and, upon good cause shown, may be allowed by the Secretary or the Commission, as the case may be, to intervene and appear at such hearing by counsel or in person.

(2) The Secretary, upon determining whether foreign merchandise is being, or is likely to be, sold in the United States at less than its fair value, and the Commission, upon making its determination under subsection (a), shall publish in the Federal Register such determination, whether affirmative or negative, together with a complete statement of findings and conclusions, and the reasons or bases therefor, on all the material issues of fact or law presented (consistent with confidential treatment granted by the Secretary or the Commission, as the case may be, in the course of making its determination).

(3) The hearings provided for under this section shall be exempt from sections 554, 555, 556, 557, and 702 of title 5 of the United States Code. The transcript of any hearing, together with all information developed in connection with the investigation (other than items to which confidential treatment has been granted by the Secretary or the Commission, as the case may be), shall be made available in the manner and to the extent provided in section 552(b) of such title.

SPECIAL DUMPING DUTY

SEC. 202. (a) In the case of all imported merchandise whether dutiable or free of duty, of a class or kind as to which the Secretary of the Treasury has made public a finding as provided for in section 201, entered, or withdrawn from warehouse, for consumption, not more than one hundred and twenty days before the question of dumping was raised by or presented to the Secretary or any person to whom authority under section 201 has been delegated, and as to which no appraisement has been made before such finding has been so made public, if the purchase price or the exporter's sales price is less than the foreign market value (or, in the absence of such value, than the constructed value) there shall be levied, collected, and paid, in addition to any other duties imposed thereon by law, a special dumping duty in an amount equal to such difference.

(b) In determining the foreign market value for the purposes of subsection (a), if it is established to the satisfaction of the Secretary or his delegate that the amount of any difference between the purchase price and the foreign market value (or that the fact that the purchase price is the same as the foreign market value) is wholly or partly due to—

(1) the fact that the wholesale quantities, in which such or similar merchandise is sold or, in the absence of sales, offered for sale for exportation to the United States in the ordinary course of trade, are less or are greater than the wholesale quantities in which such or similar merchandise is sold or, in the absence of sales, offered for sale in the principal markets of the country of exportation in the ordinary course of trade for home consumption (or, if not so sold or offered for sale for home consumption, then for exportation to countries other than the United States),

(2) other differences in circumstances of sale, or

(3) the fact that merchandise described in subdivision (C), (D), (E), or (F) of section 212(3) is used in determining foreign market value,

then due allowance shall be made therefor.

(c) In determining the foreign market value for the purposes of subsection (a), if it is established to the satisfaction of the Secretary or his delegate that the amount of any difference between the exporter's sales price and the foreign market value (or that the fact that the exporter's sales price is the same as the foreign market value) is wholly or partly due to—

(1) the fact that the wholesale quantities in which such or similar merchandise is sold or, in the absence of sales, offered for sale in the principal markets of the United States in the ordinary course of trade, are less or are greater than the wholesale quantities in which such or similar merchandise is sold or, in the absence of sales, offered for sale in the principal markets of the country of exportation in the ordinary course of trade for home consumption (or, if not so sold or offered for sale for home consumption, then for exportation to countries other than the United States),

(2) other differences in circumstances of sale, or

(3) the fact that merchandise described in subdivision (C), (D), (E), or (F) of section 212(3) is used in determining foreign market value,

then due allowance shall be made therefor.

PURCHASE PRICE

SEC. 203.* For the purposes of this title, the purchase price of imported merchandise shall be the price at which such merchandise has been purchased or agreed to be purchased, prior to the time of exportation, by the person by whom or for whose account the merchandise is imported, plus, when not included in such price, the cost of all containers and coverings and all other costs, charges, and expenses incident to placing the merchandise in condition, packed ready for shipment to the United States, less the amount, if any, included in such price, attributable to any additional costs, charges, and expenses, and United States import duties, incident to bringing the merchandise from the place of shipment in the country of exportation to the place of delivery in the United States; and less the amount, if included in such price, of any export tax imposed by the country of exportation on the

---

* As amended and restated by sec. 321(b) of Public Law 93–618 (88 Stat. 1978 at 2045). Subsection (g)(2) of that section provided that:

"The amendments made by subsections (b) through (e) of this section shall apply with respect to all merchandise which is not appraised on or before the date of the enactment of this Act: except that such amendments shall not apply with respect to any merchandise which—

(A) was exported from the country of exportation before such date of the enactment, and

(B) is subject to a finding under the Antidumping Act, 1921, which (i) is outstanding on such date of enactment, or (ii) was revoked on or before such date of enactment but is still applicable to such merchandise."

exportation of the merchandise to the United States; and plus the amount of any import duties imposed by the country of exportation which have been rebated, or which have not been collected, by reason of the exportation of the merchandise to the United States; and plus the amount of any taxes imposed in the country of exportation directly upon the exported merchandise or components thereof, which have been rebated, or which have not been collected, by reason of the exportation of the merchandise to the United States, but only to the extent that such taxes are added to or included in the price of such or similar merchandise when sold in the country of exportation; and plus the amount of any taxes rebated or not collected, by reason of the exportation of the merchandise to the United States, which rebate or noncollection has been determined by the Secretary to be a bounty or grant within the meaning of section 303 of the Tariff Act of 1930.

EXPORTER'S SALES PRICE

SEC. 204. For the purposes of this title, the exporter's sale price of imported merchandise shall be the price at which such merchandise is sold or agreed to be sold in the United States, before or after the time of importation, by or for the account of the exporter, plus, when not included in such price, the cost of all containers and coverings and all other costs, charges, and expenses incident to placing the merchandise in condition, packed ready for shipment to the United States, less (1) the amount, if any, included in such price, attributable to any additional costs, charges, and expenses, and United States import duties, incident to bringing the merchandise from the place of shipment in the country of exportation to the place of delivery in the United States, (2) the amount of the commissions, if any, for selling in the United States the particular merchandise under consideration, (3) an amount equal to the expenses, if any, generally incurred by or for the account of the exporter in the United States in selling identical or substantially identical merchandise, (4) the amount of any export tax imposed by the country of exportation on the exportation of the merchandise to the United States, and (5) the amount of any increased value, including additional material and labor, resulting from a process of manufacture or assembly performed on the imported merchandise after the importation of the merchandise and before its sale to a person who is not the exporter of the merchandise within the meaning of section 207; and plus the amount of any import duties imposed by the country of exportation which have been rebated, or which have not been collected, by reason of the exportation of the merchandise to the United States; and plus the amount of any taxes imposed in the country of exportation directly upon the exported merchandise or components thereof, which have been rebated, or which have not been collected, by reason of the exportation of the merchandise to the United States, but only to the extent that such taxes are added to or included in the price of such or similar merchandise when sold in the country of exportation; and plus the amount of any taxes rebated, or not collected, by reason of the exportation of the merchandise to the United States, which rebate or noncollection has been determined by the Secretary to be a bounty or grant within the meaning of section 303 of the Tariff Act of 1930.

FOREIGN MARKET VALUE

SEC. 205. (a) For the purposes of this title, the foreign market value of imported merchandise shall be the price, at the time of exportation of such merchandise to the United States, at which such or similar merchandise is sold or, in the absence of sales, offered for sale in the principal markets of the country from which exported, in the usual wholesale quantities and in the ordinary course of trade for home consumption (or, if not so sold or offered for sale for home consumption, or if the Secretary determines that the quantity sold for home consumption is so small in relation to the quantity sold for exportation to countries other than the United States as to form an inadequate basis for comparison, then the price at which so sold or offered for sale for exportation to countries other than the United States), plus, when not included in such price, the cost of all containers and coverings and all other costs, charges, and expenses incident to placing the merchandise in condition packed ready for shipment to the United States, except that in the case of merchandise purchased or agreed to be purchased by the person by whom or for whose account the merchandise is imported, prior to the time of exportation, the foreign market value shall be ascertained as of the date of such purchase or agreement to purchase. In the ascertainment of foreign market value for the purposes of this title no pretended sale or offer for sale, and no sale or offer for sale intended to establish a fictitious market, shall be taken into account. If such or similar merchandise is sold or, in the absence of sales, offered for sale through a sales agency or other organization related to the seller in any of the respects described in section 207, the prices at which such or similar merchandise is sold or, in the absence of sales, offered for sale by such sales agency or other organization may be used in determining the foreign market value.

(b) Whenever the Secretary has reasonable grounds to believe or suspect that sales in the home market of the country of exportation, or, as appropriate, to countries other than the United States, have been made at prices which represent less than the cost of producing the merchandise in question, he shall determine whether, in fact, such sales were made at less than the cost of producing the merchandise. If the Secretary determines that sales made at less than cost of production (1) have been made over an extended period of time and in substantial quantities, and (2) are not at prices which permit recovery of all costs within a reasonable period of time in the normal course of trade, such sales shall be disregarded in the determination of foreign market value. Whenever sales are disregarded by virtue of having been made at less than the cost of production and the remaining sales, made at not less than cost of production, are determined to be inadequate as a basis for the determination of foreign market value, the Secretary shall determine that no foreign market value exists and employ the constructed value of the merchandise in question.

(c) If available information indicates to the Secretary that the economy of extent that sales or offers of sales of such or similar merchandise in that country or to countries other than the United States do not permit a determination of foreign market value under subsection (a), the Secretary shall determine the foreign market value of the merchandise on the basis of the normal costs, expenses, and profits as reflected by either—

(1) the prices, determined in accordance with subsection (a) and section 202, at which such or similar merchandise of a non-state-controlled-economy country or countries is sold either (A) for consumption in the home market of that country or countries, or (B) to other countries, including the United States; or

(2) the constructed value of such or similar merchandise in a non-state-controlled-economy country or countries as determined under section 206.

(d) Whenever, in the course of an investigation under this Act, the Secretary determines that—

(1) merchandise exported to the United States is being produced in facilities which are owned or controlled, directly or indirectly, by a person, firm, or corporation which also owns or controls, directly or indirectly, other facilities for the production of such or similar merchandise which are located in another country or countries;

(2) the sales of such or similar merchandise by the company concerned in the home market of the exporting country are non-existing or inadequate as a basis for comparison with the sales of the merchandise to the United States; and

(3) the foreign market value of such or similar merchandise produced in one or more of the facilities outside the country of exportation is higher than the foreign market value, or if there is no foreign market value, the constructed value, of such or similar merchandise produced in the facilities located in the country of exportation,

he shall determine the foreign market value of such merchandise by reference to the foreign market value at which such or similar merchandise is sold in substantial quantities by one or more facilities outside the country of exportation. The Secretary in making any determination under this paragraph, shall make adjustments for the difference between the costs of production (including taxes, labor, materials, and overhead) of such or similar merchandise produced in facilities outside the country of exportation and costs of production of such or similar merchandise produced in the facilities in the country of exportation, if such differences are demonstrated to his satisfaction. For the purpose of this subsection, in determining foreign market value of such or similar merchandise produced in a country outside of the country of exportation, the Secretary shall determine its price at the time of exportation from the country of exportation and shall make any adjustments required by section 205(a) for the cost of all containers and coverings and all other costs, charges, and expenses incident to placing the merchandise in condition packed ready for shipment to the United States by reference to such costs in the country of exportation.

CONSTRUCTED VALUE

SEC. 206. (a) For the purposes of this title, the constructed value of imported merchandise shall be the sum of—

(1) the cost of materials (exclusive of any internal tax applicable in the country of exportation directly to such materials or their disposition, but remitted or refunded upon the exportation of the article in the production of which such materials are used) and of fabrication or other processing of any kind employed in producing such or similar merchandise, at a time preceding the date of exportation of the merchandise under consideration which would ordinarily permit the production of that particular merchandise in the ordinary course of business;

(2) an amount for general expenses and profit equal to that usually reflected in sales of merchandise of the same general class or kind as the merchandise under consideration which are made by producers in the country of exportation, in the usual wholesale quantities and in the ordinary course of trade, except that (A) the amount for general expenses shall not be less than 10 per centum of the cost as defined in paragraph (1), and (B) the amount for profit shall not be less than 8 per centum of the sum of such general expenses and cost; and

(3) the cost of all containers and coverings of whatever nature, and all other expenses incidental to placing the merchandise under consideration in condition, packed ready for shipment to the United States.

(b) For the purposes of this section, a transaction directly or indirectly between persons specified in any one of the paragraphs in subsection (c) of this section may be disregarded if, in the case of any element of value required to be considered, the amount representing that element does not fairly reflect the amount usually reflected in the market under consideration of merchandise of the same general class or kind as the merchandise under consideration. If a transaction is disregarded under the preceding sentence and there are no other transactions available for consideration, then the determination of the amount required to be considered shall be based on the best evidence available as to what the amount would have been if the transaction had occurred between persons not specified in any one of the paragraphs in subsection (c).

(c) The persons referred to in subsection (b) are:

(1) Members of a family, including brothers and sisters (whether by the whole or half blood), spouse, ancestors, and lineal descendants;

(2) Any officer or director of an organization and such organization;

(3) Partners;

(4) Employer and employee;

(5) Any person directly or indirectly owning, controlling, or holding with power to vote, 5 per centum or more of the outstanding voting stock or shares of any organization and such organization; and

(6) Two or more persons directly or indirectly controlling, controlled by, or under common control with, any person.

EXPORTER

SEC. 207. That for the purposes of this title the exporter of imported merchandise shall be the person by whom or for whose account the merchandise is imported into the United States:

(1) If such person is the agent or principal of the exporter, manufacturer, or producer; or

(2) If such person owns or controls, directly or indirectly, through stock ownership or control or otherwise, any interest in the business of the exporter, manufacturer, or producer; or

(3) If the exporter, manufacturer, or producer owns or controls, directly or indirectly, through stock ownership or control or otherwise, any interest in any business conducted by such person; or

(4) If any person or persons, jointly or severally, directly or indirectly, through stock ownership or control or otherwise, own or control in the aggregate 20 per centum or more of the voting power or control in the business carried on by the person by whom or for whose account the merchandise is imported into the United States, and also 20 per centum or more of such power or control in the business of the exporter, manufacturer, or producer.

OATHS AND BONDS ON ENTRY

SEC. 208. That in the case of all imported merchandise, whether dutiable or free of duty, of a class or kind as to which the Secretary has made public a finding as provided in section 201, and delivery of which has not been made by the appropriate customs officer before such finding has been so made public, unless the person by whom or for whose account such merchandise is imported makes oath before such customs officer, under regulations prescribed by the Secretary, that he is not an exporter, or unless such person declares under oath at the time of entry, under regulations prescribed by the Secretary, the exporter's sales price of such merchandise, it shall be unlawful for such customs officer to deliver the merchandise until such person has made oath before such customs officer under regulations prescribed by the Secretary, that the merchandise has not been sold or agreed to be sold by such person, and has given bond to such customs officer, under regulations prescribed by the Secretary, with sureties approved by such customs officer, in an amount equal to the estimated value of the merchandise, conditioned: (1) that he will report to such customs officer the exporter's sales price of the merchandise within 30 days after such merchandise has been sold or agreed to be sold in the United States, (2) that he will pay on demand from such customs officer the amount of special dumping duty, if any, imposed by this title upon such merchandise, and (3) that he will furnish to such customs officer such information as may be in his possession and as may be necessary for the ascertainment of such duty, and will keep such records as to the sale of such merchandise as the Secretary may by regulation prescribe.

DUTIES OF APPRAISERS

SEC. 209. That in the case of all imported merchandise, whether dutiable or free of duty, of a class or kind as to which the Secretary has made public a finding as provided in section 201, and as to which the appropriate customs officer has made no appraisement before such finding has been so made public, it shall be the duty of such customs officer, by all reasonable ways and means to ascertain, estimate, and appraise (any invoice or affidavit thereto or statement of constructed value to the contrary notwithstanding) the foreign market value or the constructed value, as the case may be, the purchase price, and the exporter's sales price, and any other facts which the Secretary may deem necessary for the purposes of this title.

APPEALS AND PROTESTS

SEC. 210. That for the purposes of this title the determination of the appropriate customs officer as to the foreign market value or the constructed value, as the case may be, the purchase price, and the exporter's sales price, and the action of such customs officer in assessing special dumping duty, shall have the same force and effect and be subject to the same right of protest, under the same conditions and subject to the same limitations; and the general appraisers, the Board of General Appraisers, and the Court of Customs Appeals shall have the same jurisdiction, powers, and duties in connection with such protests as in the case of appeals and protests relating to customs duties under existing law.

DRAWBACKS

SEC. 211. That the special dumping duty imposed by this title shall be treated in all respects as regular customs duties within the meaning of all laws relating to the drawback of customs duties.

DEFINITIONS

SEC. 212. For the purposes of this title—

(1) The term "sold or, in the absence of sales, offered for sale" means sold or, in the absence of sales, offered—

(A) to all purchasers at wholesale, or

(B) in the ordinary course of trade to one or more selected purchasers at wholesale at a price which fairly reflects the market value of the merchandise,

without regard to restrictions as to the disposition or use of the merchandise by the purchaser except that, where such restrictions are found to affect the market value of the merchandise, adjustment shall be made therefor in calculating the price at which the merchandise is sold or offered for sale.

(2) The term "ordinary course of trade" means the conditions and practices which, for a reasonable time prior to the exportation of the merchandise under consideration, have been normal in the trade under consideration with respect to merchandise of the same class or kind as the merchandise under consideration.

(3) The term "such or similar merchandise" means merchandise in the

first of the following categories in respect of which a determination for the purposes of this title can be satisfactorily made:

(A) The merchandise under consideration and other merchandise which is identical in physical characteristics with, and was produced in the same country by the same person as, the merchandise under consideration.

(B) Merchandise (i) produced in the same country and by the same person as the merchandise under consideration, (ii) like the merchandise under consideration in component material or materials and in the purposes for which used, and (iii) approximately equal in commercial value to the merchandise under consideration.

(C) Merchandise (i) produced in the same country and by the same person and of the same general class or kind as the merchandise under consideration, (ii) like the merchandise under consideration in the purposes for which used, and (iii) which the Secretary or his delegate determines may reasonably be compared for the purposes of this title with the merchandise under consideration.

(4) The term "usual wholesale quantities", in any case in which the merchandise in respect of which value is being determined is sold in the market under consideration at different prices for different quantities, means the quantities in which such merchandise is there sold at the price or prices for one quantity in an aggregate volume which is greater than the aggregate volume sold at the price or prices for any other quantity.

SHORT TITLE

SEC. 213. That this title may be cited as the "Antidumping Act, 1921."

8. U.S. Countervailing Duties Statute*

(a) (1930 Version)

Section 303. *Countervailing Duties*

Whenever any country, dependency, colony, province, or other political subdivision of government, person, partnership, association, cartel, or corporation shall pay or bestow, directly or indirectly, any bounty or grant upon the manufacture or production or export of any article or merchandise manufactured or produced in such country, dependency, colony, province, or other

---

* Tariff Act of 1930, 19 U.S.C. § 1303.

political subdivision of government, and such article or merchandise is dutiable under the provisions of this Act, then upon the importation of any such article or merchandise into the United States, whether the same shall be imported directly from the country of production or otherwise, and whether such article or merchandise is imported in the same condition as when exported from the country of production or has been changed in condition by remanufacture or otherwise, there shall be levied and paid, in all such cases, in addition to the duties otherwise imposed by this Act, an additional duty equal to the net amount of such bounty or grant, however the same be paid or bestowed. The Secretary of the Treasury shall from time to time ascertain and determine, or estimate, the net amount of each such bounty or grant, and shall declare the net amount so determined or estimated. The Secretary of the Treasury shall make all regulations he may deem necessary for the identification of such articles and merchandise and for the assessment and collection of such additional duties.

(b) (1975-1979)

"Section 303. *Countervailing Duties*

(a) LEVY OF COUNTERVAILING DUTIES.—(1) Whenever any country, dependency, colony, province, or other political subdivision of government, person, partnership, association, cartel, or corporation, shall pay or bestow, directly or indirectly, any bounty or grant upon the manufacture or production or export of any article or merchandise manufactured or produced in such country, dependency, colony, province, or other political subdivision of government, then upon the importation of such article or merchandise into the United States, whether the same shall be imported directly from the country of production or otherwise, and whether such article or merchandise is imported in the same condition as when exported from the country of production or has been changed in condition by remanufacture or otherwise, there shall be levied and paid, in all such cases, in addition to any duties otherwise imposed, a duty equal to the net amount of such bounty or grant, however the same be paid or bestowed.

(2) In the case of any imported article or merchandise which is free of duty, duties may be imposed under this section only if there is an affirmative determination by the Commission under subsection (b)(1); except that such a determination shall not be required unless a determination of injury is required by the international obligations of the United States.

(3) In the case of any imported article or merchandise as to which the Secretary of the Treasury (hereafter in this section referred to as the 'Secretary') has not determined whether or not any bounty or grant is being paid or bestowed—

(A) upon the filing of a petition by any person setting forth his belief that a bounty or grant is being paid or bestowed, and the reasons therefor, or

(B) whenever the Secretary concludes, from information presented to him or to any person to whom authority under this section has been delegated, that a formal investigation is warranted into the question of whether a bounty or grant is being paid or bestowed,

the Secretary shall initiate a formal investigation to determine whether or not any bounty or grant is being paid or bestowed and shall publish in the Federal Register notice of the initiation of such investigation.

(4) Within six months from the date on which a petition is filed under paragraph (3)(A) or on which notice is published of an investigation initiated under paragraph (3)(B), the Secretary shall make a preliminary determination, and within twelve months from such date shall make a final determination, as to whether or not any bounty or grant is being paid or bestowed.

(5) The Secretary shall from time to time ascertain and determine, or estimate, the net amount of each such bounty or grant, and shall declare the net amount so determined or estimated.

(6) The Secretary shall make all regulations he deems necessary for the identification of articles and merchandise subject to duties under this section and for the assessment and collection of such duties. All determinations by the Secretary under this section, and all determinations by the Commission under subsection (b)(1), (whether affirmative or negative) shall be published in the Federal Register.

(b) INJURY DETERMINATIONS WITH RESPECT TO DUTY-FREE MERCHANDISE; SUSPENSION OF LIQUIDATION.—(1) Whenever the Secretary makes a final determination under subsection (a) that a bounty or grant is being paid or bestowed with respect to any article or merchandise which is free of duty and a determination by the Commission is required under subsection (a)(2), he shall—

A) so advise the Commission, and the Commission shall determine within three months thereafter, and after such investigation as it deems necessary, whether an industry in the United States is being or is likely to be injured, or is prevented from being established, by reason of the importation of such article or merchandise into the United States; and the Commission shall notify the Secretary of its determination; and

(B) require, under such regulations as he may prescribe, the suspension of liquidation as to such article or merchandise entered, or withdrawn from warehouse, for consumption on or after the date of the publication in the Federal Register of his final determination under subsection (a), and such suspension of liquidation shall continue until the further order of the Secretary or until he has made public an order as provided for in paragraph (3).

(2) For the purposes of this subsection, the Commission shall be deemed to have made an affirmative determination if the commissioners voting are evenly divided as to whether its determination should be in the affirmative or in the negative.

(3) If the determination of the Commission under paragraph (1)(A) is in the affirmative, the Secretary shall make public an order directing the assessment and collection of duties in the amount of such bounty or grant as is from time to time ascertained and determined, or estimated, under subsection (a).

(c) APPLICATION OF AFFIRMATIVE DETERMINATION.—An affirmative final determination by the Secretary under subsection (a) with respect to any imported article or merchandise shall apply with respect to articles entered, or withdrawn from warehouse, for consumption on or after the date of the publication in the Federal Register of such determination. In the case of any imported article or merchandise which is free of duty, so long as a finding of injury is required by the international obligations of the United States, the preceding sentence shall apply only if the Commission makes an affirmative determination of injury under subsection (b)(1).

(d) TEMPORARY PROVISION WHILE NEGOTIATIONS ARE IN PROCESS.—(1) It is the sense of the Congress that the President, to the extent practicable and consistent with United States interests, seek through negotiations the establishment of internationally agreed rules and procedures governing the use of subsidies (and other export incentives) and the application of countervailing duties.

(2) If, after seeking information and advice from such agencies as he may deem appropriate, the Secretary of the Treasury determines, at any time during the four-year period beginning on the date of the enactment of the Trade Act of 1974, that—

(A) adequate steps have been taken to reduce substantially or eliminate during such period the adverse effect of a bounty or grant which he has determined is being paid or bestowed with respect to any article or merchandise;

(B) there is a reasonable prospect that, under section 102 of the Trade Act of 1974, successful trade agreements will be entered into with foreign countries or instrumentalities providing for the reduction or elimination of barriers to or other distortions of international trade; and

(C) the imposition of the additional duty under this section with respect to such article or merchandise would be likely to seriously jeopardize the satisfactory completion of such negotiations;

the imposition of the additional duty under this section with respect to such article or merchandise shall not be required during the remainder of such four-year period. This paragraph shall not apply with respect to any case involving non-rubber footwear pending on the date of the enactment of the Trade Act of 1974 until and unless agreements which temporize imports of non-rubber footwear become effective.

(3) The determination of the Secretary under paragraph (2) may be revoked by him, in his discretion, at any time, and any determination made under such paragraph shall be revoked whenever the basis supporting such determination no longer exists. The additional duty provided under this section shall apply with respect to any affected articles or merchandise entered, or withdrawn from warehouse, for consumption on or after the date of publication of any revocation under this subsection in the Federal Register.

(e) REPORTS TO CONGRESS.—(1) Whenever the Secretary makes a determination under subsection (d)(2) with respect to any article or merchandise, he shall promptly transmit to the House of Representatives and the Senate a document setting forth the determination, together with his reasons therefor.

(2) If, at any time after the document referred to in paragraph (1) is delivered to the House of Representatives and the Senate, either the House or the Senate adopts, by an affirmative vote of a majority of those present and voting in that House, a resolution of disapproval under the procedures set forth in section 152, then such determination under subsection (d)(2) with respect to such article or merchandise shall have no force or effect beginning with the day after the date of the adoption of such resolution of disapproval, and the additional duty provided under this section with respect to such article or merchandise shall apply with respect to articles or merchandise entered, or withdrawn from warehouse, for consumption on or after such day.

9. Provisions Concerning Judicial Review of Customs Decisions*

(a) (1930 Version)

Section 514. *Protest Against Collector's Decisions*

Except as provided in subdivision (b) of section 516 of this Act (relating to protests by American manufacturers, producers, and wholesalers), all decisions of the collector, including the legality of all orders and findings entering into the same, as to the rate and amount of duties chargeable, and as to all exactions of whatever character (within the jurisdiction of the Secretary of the Treasury), and his decisions excluding any merchandise from entry or delivery, under any provision of the customs laws, and his liquidation or reliquidation of any entry, or refusal to pay any claim for drawback, or his refusal to reliquidate any entry for a clerical error discovered within one year after the date of entry, or within sixty days after liquidation or reliquidation when such liquidation or reliquidation is made more than ten months after the date of entry, shall, upon the expiration of sixty days after the date of such liquidation, reliquidation, decision, or refusal, be final and conclusive upon all persons (including the United States and any officer thereof), unless the importer, consignee, or agent of the person paying such charge or exaction, or filing such claim for drawback, or seeking such entry or delivery, shall, within sixty days after, but not before such liquidation, reliquidation, decision, or refusal, as the case may be, as well in cases of merchandise entered in bond as for consumption, file a protest in writing with the collector setting forth distinctly and specifically, and in respect to each entry, payment, claim, decision, or refusal, the reasons for the objection thereto. The reliquidation of an entry shall not open such entry so that a protest may be filed against the decision of the collector upon any question not involved in such reliquidation.

Section 515. *Same*

Upon the filing of such protest the collector shall within ninety days thereafter review his decision, and may modify the same in whole or in part and thereafter remit or refund any duties, charge, or exaction found to have been assessed or collected in excess, or pay any drawback found due, of which notice shall be given as in the case of the original liquidation, and against which protest may be filed within the same time and in the same manner and under the same conditions as against the original liquidation or decision. If the collector shall, upon such review, affirm his original decision, or if a protest shall be filed against his modification of any decision, and, in

---

* Tariff Act of 1930, 19 USC § 1514–16.

the case of merchandise entered for consumption, if all duties and charges shall be paid, then the collector shall forthwith transmit the entry and the accompanying papers, and all the exhibits connected therewith, to the United States Customs Court for due assignment and determination, as provided by law. Such determination shall be final and conclusive upon all persons, and the papers transmitted shall be returned, with the decision and judgment order thereon, to the collector, who shall take action accordingly, except in cases in which an appeal shall be filed in the United States Court of Customs and Patent Appeals within the time and in the manner provided by law.

Section 516. *Appeal or Protest by American Producers*

(a) VALUE.—Whenever an American manufacturer, producer, or wholesaler believes that the appraised value of any imported merchandise of a class or kind manufactured, produced, or sold at wholesale by him is too low, he may file with the Secretary of the Treasury a complaint setting forth the value at which he believes the merchandise should be appraised and the facts upon which he bases his belief. The Secretary shall thereupon transmit a copy of such complaint to the appraiser at each port of entry where the merchandise is usually imported. Until otherwise directed by the Secretary, the appraiser shall report each subsequent importation of the merchandise giving the entry number, the name of the importer, the appraised value, and his reasons for the appraisement. If the Secretary does not agree with the action of the appraiser, he shall instruct the collector to file an appeal for a reappraisement as provided in section 501 of this Act, and such manufacturer, producer, or wholesaler shall have the right to appear and to be heard as a party in interest under such rules as the United States Customs Court may prescribe. The Secretary shall notify such manufacturer, producer, or wholesaler of the action taken by such appraiser, giving the port of entry, the entry number, and the appraised value of such merchandise and the action he has taken thereon. If the appraiser advances the entered value of merchandise upon the information furnished by the American manufacturer, producer, or wholesaler, and an appeal is taken by the consignee, such manufacturer, producer, or wholesaler shall have the right to appear and to be heard as a party in interest, under such rules as the United States Customs Court may prescribe. If the American manufacturer, producer, or wholesaler is not satisfied with the action of the Secretary, or the action of the appraiser thereon, he may file, within thirty days after the date of the mailing of the Secretary's notice, an appeal for a reappraisement in the same manner and with the same effect as an appeal by a consignee under the provisions of section 501 of this Act.

(b) CLASSIFICATION.—The Secretary of the Treasury shall, upon written request by an American manufacturer, producer, or wholesaler, furnish the classification of and the rate of duty, if any, imposed upon designated imported merchandise of a class or kind manufactured, produced, or sold at wholesale by him. If such manufacturer, producer, or wholesaler believes that the proper rate of duty is not being assessed, he may file a complaint with the Secretary of the Treasury setting forth a description of the merchandise, the classification, and the rate or rates of duty he believes proper, and the reasons for his belief. If the Secretary decides that the classification of or rate of duty assessed upon the merchandise is not correct, he shall notify the collectors as to the proper classification and rate of duty and shall so inform such manufacturer, producer, or wholesaler, and such rate of duty shall be assessed upon all such merchandise imported or withdrawn from warehouse after thirty days after the date of such notice to the collectors. If the Secretary decides that the classification and rate of duty are correct, he shall so inform such manufacturer, producer, or wholesaler, and shall, under such regulations as he may prescribe, cause publication to be made of his decision, together with notice that the classification of and the rate of duty, on all such merchandise imported or withdrawn from warehouse after the expiration of thirty days after such publication will be subject to the decision of the United States Customs Court in the event that a protest is filed under the provisions of this subdivision. If dissatisfied with the decision of the Secretary, such manufacturer, producer, or wholesaler may file with him a notice that he desires to protest the classification or the rate of duty imposed upon the merchandise, and upon receipt of such notice the Secretary shall furnish him with such information as to the entries and consignees of such merchandise, entered after the expiration of thirty days after the publication of the decision of the Secretary, at the port of entry designated by the manufacturer, producer, or wholesaler in his notice of desire to protest, as will enable him to protest the classification of or the rate of duty imposed upon such merchandise when liquidated at such port. The Secretary shall direct the collector at such port to notify such manufacturer, producer, or wholesaler immediately upon the liquidation of the first of such entries to be liquidated. Such manufacturer, producer, or wholesaler, may file, within thirty days after the date of such liquidation, with the collector of such port a protest in writing setting forth a description of the merchandise and the classification and the rate of duty he believes proper. Upon the filing of any such protest the collector shall notify the Secretary of the Treasury who shall order the suspension, pending the decision of the United States Customs Court upon such protest, of the liquidation, at all ports, of all unliquidated entries of such merchandise imported or withdrawn from warehouse after the expiration of thirty days after the publication of the Secretary's decision. All entries of such merchandise so imported or withdrawn shall be liquidated, or if already liquidated, shall, if necessary, be reliquidated, in conformity with such decision of the United States Customs Court. If, upon appeal to the Court of Customs and Patent Appeals, the decision of the United States Customs Court is reversed, the classification of the merchandise and the rate of duty imposed thereon shall be in accordance with the decision of the Court of Customs and Patent Appeals, and any necessary reliquidation shall be made. The provisions of this subdivision shall apply only in the case of complaints filed after the effective date of this Act.

(c) HEARING AND DETERMINATION.—A copy of every appeal and every protest filed by an American manufacturer, producer, or wholesaler under the provisions of this section shall be mailed by the collector to the consignee or his agent within five days after the filing thereof, and such consignee or his agent shall have the right to appear and to be heard as a party in interest before the United States Customs Court. The collector shall transmit the entry and all papers and exhibits accompanying or connected therewith to the United States Customs Court for due assignment and determination of the proper value or of the proper classification and rate of duty. The decision of the United States Customs Court upon any such appeal or protest shall be final and conclusive upon all parties unless an appeal is taken by either party to the Court of Customs and Patent Appeals, as provided in sections 501 and 515 of this Act.

(d) INSPECTION OF DOCUMENTS.—In proceedings instituted under the provisions of this section an American manufacturer, producer, or wholesaler shall not have the right to inspect any documents or papers of the consignee or importer disclosing any information which the United States Customs Court or any judge or division thereof shall deem unnecessary or improper to be disclosed to him.

9. (b) Provisions Concerning Judicial Review of Customs Decisions*

(b) (1975-1979)

Section 514. *Finality of Decisions; Protests.*—

(a) FINALITY OF DECISIONS.—Except as provided in section 501 (relating to voluntary reliquidations), section 516 (relating to petitions by American manufacturers, producers, and wholesalers), section 520 (relating to refunds and errors), and section 521 (relating to reliquidations on account of fraud) of this Act, decisions of the appropriate customs officer, including the legality of all orders and findings entering into the same, as to—

(1) the appraised value of merchandise;

---

* Tariff Act of 1930 as amended through 1978. 19 USC §§ 1514–16 (1976). The version here reproduced represents a consolidation of amendments adopted in the Customs Courts Act of 1970, Pub. L. 91–271, and the Trade Act of 1975.

(2) the classification and rate and amount of duties chargeable;

(3) all charges or exactions of whatever character within the jurisdiction of the Secretary of the Treasury;

(4) the exclusion of merchandise from entry or delivery under any provision of the customs laws;

(5) the liquidation or reliquidation of an entry, or any modification thereof;

(6) the refusal to pay a claim for drawback; and

(7) the refusal to reliquidate an entry under section 520(c) of this Act,

shall be final and conclusive upon all persons (including the United States and any officer thereof) unless a protest is filed in accordance with this section, or unless a civil action contesting the denial of a protest, in whole or in part, is commenced in the United States Customs Court in accordance with section 2632 of title 28 of the United States Code within the time prescribed by section 2631 of that title. When a judgment or order of the United States Customs Court has become final, the papers transmitted shall be returned, together with a copy of the judgment or order to the appropriate customs officer, who shall take action accordingly.

(b) PROTESTS.—

(1) IN GENERAL.—A protest of a decision under subsection (a) shall be filed in writing with the appropriate customs officer designated in regulations prescribed by the Secretary, setting forth distinctly and specifically each decision described in subsection (a) as to which protest is made; each category of merchandise affected by each such decision as to which protest is made; and the nature of each objection and reasons therefor. Only one protest may be filed for each entry of merchandise, except that where the entry covers merchandise of different categories, a separate protest may be filed for each category. In addition, separate protests filed by different authorized persons with respect to any one category of merchandise that is the subject of a protest are deemed to be part of a single protest. A protest may be amended, under regulations prescribed by the Secretary, to set forth objections as to a decision or decisions described in subsection (a) which were not the subject of the original protest, in the form and manner prescribed for a protest, any time prior to the expiration of the time in which such protest could have been filed under this section. New grounds in support of objections raised by a valid protest or amendment thereto may be presented for

consideration in connection with the review of such protest pursuant to section 515 of this Act at any time prior to the disposition of the protest in accordance with that section. Except as otherwise provided in section 557(b) of this Act, protests may be filed by the importer, consignee, or any authorized agent of the person paying any charge or exaction, or filing any claim for drawback, or seeking entry or delivery, with respect to merchandise which is the subject of a decision in subsection (a).

(2) TIME FOR FILING.—A protest of a decision, order, or finding described in subsection (a) shall be filed with such customs officer within ninety days after but not before—

(A) notice of liquidation or reliquidation, or

(B) in circumstances where subparagraph (A) is inapplicable, the date of the decision as to which protest is made.

(c) LIMITATION ON PROTEST OF RELIQUIDATIONS.—The reliquidation of an entry shall not open such entry so that a protest may be filed against the decision of the customs officer upon any question not involved in such reliquidation.

Section 515. *Review of Protests.*—

(a) ADMINISTRATIVE REVIEW AND MODIFICATION OF DECISIONS.—Unless a request for an accelerated disposition of a protest is filed in accordance with subsection (b) of this section the appropriate customs officer, within two years from the date a protest was filed in accordance with section 514 of this Act, shall review the protest and shall allow or deny such protest in whole or in part. Thereafter, any duties, charge, or exaction found to have been assessed or collected in excess shall be remitted or refunded and any drawback found due shall be paid. Upon the request of the protesting party, filed within the time allowed for the filing of a protest under section 514 of this Act, a protest may be subject to further review by another appropriate customs officer, under the circumstances and in the form and manner that may be prescribed by the Secretary in regulations, but subject to the two-year limitation prescribed in the first sentence of this subsection. Notice of the denial of any protest shall be mailed in the form and manner prescribed by the Secretary.

(b) REQUEST FOR ACCELERATED DISPOSITION OF PROTEST.—A request for accelerated disposition of a protest filed in accordance with section 514 of this Act may be mailed by certified or registered mail to the appropriate customs officer any time after ninety days following the filing of such protest. For purposes of section 1582 of title 28 of the United States Code, a protest which has not been allowed or denied in whole or in part within thirty days following the date of mailing by certified or registered mail of a request for accelerated disposition shall be deemed denied on the thirtieth day following mailing of such request.

Section 516. *Petitions by American Manufacturers, Producers, or Wholesalers*

(a) The Secretary shall, upon written request by an American manufacturer, producer, or wholesaler, furnish the classification, the rate of duty, the additional duty described in section 303 of this Act (hereinafter in this section referred to as 'countervailing duties'), if any, and the special duty described in section 202 of the Antidumping Act, 1921 (hereinafter in this section referred to as 'antidumping duties'), if any, imposed upon designated imported merchandise of a class or kind manufactured, produced, or sold at wholesale by him. If such manufacturer, producer, or wholesaler believes that the appraised value is too low, that the classification is not correct, that the proper rate of duty is not being assessed, or that countervailing duties or antidumping duties should be assessed, he may file a petition with the Secretary setting forth (1) a description of the merchandise, (2) the appraised value, the classification, or the rate or rates of duty that he believes proper, and (3) the reasons for his belief including, in appropriate instances, the reasons for his belief that countervailing duties or antidumping duties should be assessed.

(b) If, after receipt and consideration of a petition filed by an American manufacturer, producer, or wholesaler, the Secretary decides that the appraised value of the merchandise is too low, that the classification of the article or rate of duty assessed thereon is not correct, or that countervailing duties or antidumping duties should be assessed, he shall determine the proper appraised value or classification, rate of duty, or countervailing duties, or antidumping duties and shall notify the petitioner of his determination. Except for countervailing duty and antidumping duty purposes, all such merchandise entered for consumption or withdrawn from warehouse for consumption more than thirty days after the date such notice to the petitioner is published in the weekly Customs Bulletin shall be appraised or classified or assessed as to rate of duty in accordance with the Secretary's determination. For countervailing duty purposes, the procedures set forth in section 303 shall apply. For antidumping duty purposes, the procedures set forth in section 201 of the Antidumping Act, 1921, shall apply.

(c) If the Secretary decides that the appraised value or classification of the articles or the rate of duty with respect to which a petition was filed pursuant to subsection (a) is correct, or that countervailing duties or antidumping duties should not be assessed, he shall so inform the petitioner. If dissatisfied with the decision of the Secretary, the petitioner may file with the

Secretary, not later than thirty days after the date of the decision, notice that he desires to contest the appraised value or classification of, or rate of duty assessed upon or the failure to assess countervailing duties or antidumping duties upon, the merchandise. Upon receipt of notice from the petitioner, the Secretary shall cause publication to be made of his decision as to the proper appraised value or classification or rate of duty or that countervailing duties or antidumping duties should not be assessed and of the petitioner's desire to contest, and shall thereafter furnish the petitioner with such information as to the entries and consignees of such merchandise, entered after the publication of the decision of the Secretary at such ports of entry designated by the petitioner in his notice of desire to contest, as will enable the petitioner to contest the appraised value or classification of, or rate of duty imposed upon or failure to assess countervailing duties or antidumping duties upon, such merchandise in the liquidation of one such entry at such port. The Secretary shall direct the appropriate Customs officer at such ports to notify the petitioner by mail immediately when the first of such entries is liquidated.

(d) Within 30 days after a determination by the Secretary—

(1) under section 201 of the Antidumping Act, 1921 (19 U.S.C. 160), that a class or kind of foreign merchandise is not being, nor likely to be, sold in the United States at less than its fair value, or

(2) under section 303 of this Act that a bounty or grant is not being paid or bestowed,

an American manufacturer, producer, or wholesaler of merchandise of the same class or kind as that described in such determination may file with the Secretary a written notice of a desire to contest such determination. Upon receipt of such notice the Secretary shall cause publication to be made thereof and of such manufacturer's, producer's, or wholesaler's desire to contest the determination. Within 30 days after such publication, such manufacturer, producer, or wholesaler may commence an action in the United States Customs Court contesting such determination.

(e) Notwithstanding the filing of an action pursuant to section 2632 of title 28 of the United States Code, merchandise of the character covered by the published decision of the Secretary (when entered for consumption or withdrawn from warehouse for consumption on or before the date of publication of a decision of the United States Customs Court or of the United States Court of Customs and Patent Appeals, not in harmony with the published decision of the Secretary) shall be appraised or classified, or both, and the entries liquidated, in accordance with the decision of the Secretary and, except as otherwise provided in this chapter, the final liquidations of these entries shall be conclusive upon all parties.

(f) The consignee or his agent shall have the right to appear and to be heard as a party in interest before the United States Customs Court.

(g) If the cause of action is sustained in whole or in part by a decision of the United States Customs Court or of the United States Court of Customs and Patent Appeals, merchandise of the character covered by the published decision of the Secretary, which is entered for consumption or withdrawn from warehouse for consumption after the date of publication of the court decision, shall be subject to appraisement, classification, and assessment of duty in accordance with the final judicial decision in the action, and the liquidation of entries covering the merchandise so entered or withdrawn shall be suspended until final disposition is made of the action, whereupon the entries shall be liquidated, or if necessary, reliquidated in accordance with the final decision.

(h) Regulations shall be prescribed by the Secretary to implement the procedures required under this section.

(c) As Amended Through 1982

Section 1514. *Protest Against Decision of Appropriate Customs Officer*

Finality of decisions; return of papers

(a) Except as provided in subsection (b) of this section, section 1501 of this title (relating to voluntary reliquidations), section 1516 of this title (relating to petitions by domestic interested parties as defined in section 1677(9)(C), (D), and (E) of this title), section 1520 of this title (relating to refunds and errors), and section 1521 of this title (relating to reliquidations on account of fraud), decisions of the appropriate customs officer, including the legality of all orders and findings entering into the same, as to—

(1) the appraised value of merchandise;

(2) the classification and rate and amount of duties chargeable;

(3) all charges or exactions of whatever character within the jurisdiction of the Secretary of the Treasury;

(4) the exclusion of merchandise from entry or delivery or a demand for redelivery to customs custody under any provision of the customs laws, except a determination appealable under section 1337 of this title;

(5) the liquidation or reliquidation of an entry, or any modification thereof;

(6) the refusal to pay a claim for drawback; and

(7) the refusal to reliquidate an entry under section 1520(c) of this title,

shall be final and conclusive upon all persons (including the United States and any officer thereof) unless a protest is filed in accordance with this section, or unless a civil action contesting the denial of a protest, in whole or in part, is commenced in the United States Court of International Trade in accordance with chapter 169 of Title 28 within the time prescribed by section 2636 of that title. When a judgment or order of the United States Court of International Trade has become final, the papers transmitted shall be returned, together with a copy of the judgment or order to the appropriate customs officer, who shall take action accordingly.

Finality and conclusiveness of customs officers' determinations

(b) With respect to determinations made under section 1303 of this title or subtitle IV of this chapter which are reviewable under section 1516a of this title, determinations of the appropriate customs officer are final and conclusive upon all persons (including the United States and any officer thereof) unless a civil action contesting a determination listed in section 1516a of this title is commenced in the United States Court of International Trade.

Form, number, and amendment of protest; filing of protest

(c)(1) A protest of a decision under subsection (a) of this section shall be filed in writing with the appropriate customs officer designated in regulations prescribed by the Secretary, setting forth distinctly and specifically each decision described in subsection (a) of this section as to which protest is made; each category of merchandise affected by each such decision as to which protest is made; and the nature of each objection and reasons therefor. Only one protest may be filed for each entry of merchandise, except that where the entry covers merchandise of different categories, a separate protest may be filed for each category. In addition, separate protests filed by different authorized persons with respect to any one category of merchandise that is the subject of a protest are deemed to be part of a single protest. A protest may be amended, under regulations prescribed by the Secretary, to set forth objections as to a decision or decisions described in subsection (a) of this section which were not the subject of the original protest, in the form and manner prescribed for a protest, any time prior to the expiration of the time in which such protest could have been filed under this section. New grounds in support of objections raised by a valid protest or amendment thereto may be presented for consideration in connection with the review of such protest pursuant to section 1515 of this title at any time prior to the disposition of the protest in accordance with that section. Except as provided in sections 1485(d) and 1557(b) of this title, protests may be filed with respect to merchandise which is the subject of a decision specified in subsection (a) of this section by—

(A) the importers or consignees shown on the entry papers, or their sureties;

(B) any person paying any charge or exaction;

(C) any person seeking entry or delivery;

(D) any person filing a claim for drawback; or

(E) any authorized agent of any of the persons described in clauses (A) through (D).

(2) A protest of a decision, order, or finding described in subsection (a) of this section shall be filed with such customs officer within ninety days after but not before—

(A) notice of liquidation or reliquidation, or

(B) in circumstances where subparagraph (A) is inapplicable, the date of the decision as to which protest is made.

A protest by a surety which has an unsatisfied legal claim under its bond may be filed within 90 days from the date of mailing of notice of demand for payment against its bond. If another party has not filed a timely protest, the surety's protest shall certify that it is not being filed collusively to extend another authorized person's time to protest as specified in this subsection.

Limitation on protest of reliquidation

(d) The reliquidation of an entry shall not open such entry so that a protest may be filed against the decision of the customs officer upon any question not involved in such reliquidation.

Section 1515. *Review of Protests; Administrative Review and Modification of Decisions; Request for Accelerated Disposition of Protest*

(a) Unless a request for an accelerated disposition of a protest is filed in accordance with subsection (b) of this section the appropriate customs officer, within two years from the date a protest was filed in accordance with section 1514 of this title, shall review the protest and shall allow or deny such protest in whole or in part. Thereafter, any duties, charge, or exaction found to have been assessed or collected in excess shall be remitted or refunded and any drawback found due shall be paid. Upon the request of the protesting party, filed within the time allowed for the filing of a protest under section 1514 of this title, a protest may be subject to further review by another appropriate customs officer, under the circumstances and in the form and manner that may be prescribed by the Secretary in regulations, but subject to the two-year limitation prescribed in the first sentence of this subsection. Notice of the denial of any protest shall be mailed in the form and manner prescribed by the Secretary. Such notice shall include a statement of the reasons for the denial, as well as a statement informing the protesting party of his right to file a civil action contesting the denial of a protest under section 1514 of this title.

(b) A request for accelerated disposition of a protest filed in accordance with section 1514 of this title may be mailed by certified or registered mail to the appropriate customs officer any time after ninety days following the filing of such protest. For purposes of section 1581 of Title 28, a protest which has not been allowed or denied in whole or in part within thirty days following the date of mailing by certified or registered mail of a request for accelerated disposition shall be deemed denied on the thirtieth day following mailing of such request.

Section 1516. *Petitions by Domestic Interested Parties*

Request for classification and rate of duty; petition;
definition of interested party

(a)(1) The Secretary shall, upon written request by an interested party furnish the classification and the rate of duty imposed upon designated imported merchandise of a class or kind manufactured, produced, or sold at wholesale by such interested party. If the interested party believes that the appraised value, the classification, or rate of duty is not correct, it may file a petition with the Secretary setting forth—

(A) a description of the merchandise,

(B) the appraised value, the classification, or the rate of duty that it believes proper, and

(C) the reasons for its belief.

(2) As used in this section, the term "interested party" means a person who is—

(A) a manufacturer, producer, or wholesaler in the United States;

(B) a certified union or recognized union or group of workers which is representative of an industry engaged in the manufacture, production, or wholesale in the United States; or

(C) a trade or business association a majority of whose members are manufacturers, producers, or wholesalers in the United States, of goods of the same class or kind as the designated imported merchandise.

Determination on petition

(b) If, after receipt and consideration of a petition filed by such an interested party, the Secretary determines that the appraised value, the classification, or rate of duty is not correct, he shall determine the proper appraised value, classification, or rate of duty and shall notify the petitioner of his determination. All such merchandise entered for consumption or withdrawn from warehouse for consumption more than thirty days after the date such notice to the petitioner is published in the weekly Customs Bulletin shall be appraised, classified, or assessed as to the rate of duty in accordance with the Secretary's determination.

Contest by petitioner of appraised value, classification, or rate of duty

(c) If the Secretary determines that the appraised value, classification, or rate of duty with respect to which a petition was filed pursuant to subsection (a) of this section is correct, he shall notify the petitioner. If dissatisfied with the determination of the Secretary, the petitioner may file with the Secretary, not later than thirty days after the date of the notification, notice that it desires to contest the appraised value, classification, or rate of duty. Upon receipt of notice from the petitioner, the Secretary shall cause publication to be made of his determination as to the proper appraised value, classification, or rate of duty and of the petitioner's desire to contest, and shall thereafter furnish the petitioner with such information as to the entries and consignees of such merchandise, entered after the publication of the determination of the Secretary, at such ports of entry designated by the petitioner in his notice of desire to contest, as will enable the petitioner to contest the appraised value, classification, or rate of duty imposed upon such merchandise in the liquidation of one such entry at such port. The Secretary shall direct the appropriate customs officer at such ports to immediately notify the petitioner by mail when the first of such entries is liquidated.

Appraisal, classification, and liquidation of entries of merchandise covered
by published decisions of Secretary

(d) Notwithstanding the filing of an action pursuant to chapter 169 of Title 28, merchandise of the character covered by the published decision of the Secretary (when entered for consumption or withdrawn from warehouse for consumption on or before the date of publication of a decision of the United States Court of International Trade or of the United States Court of Customs and Patent Appeals, not in harmony with the published decision of the Secretary) shall be appraised or classified, or both, and the entries liquidated, in accordance with the decision of the Secretary and, except as otherwise provided in this chapter, the final liquidations of these entries shall be conclusive upon all parties.

Consignee or his agent as party in interest before Court of International Trade

(e) The consignee or his agent shall have the right to appear and to be heard as a party in interest before the United States Court of International Trade.

Appraisement, classification, and assessment of duty of merchandise covered by
published decison of Secretary in accordance with final judicial decision of
Court of International Trade or Court of Cusoms and Patent Appeals
sustaining cause of action in whole or in part; suspension of
liquidation of entries; publication

(f) If the cause of action is sustained in whole or in part by a decision of the United States Court of International Trade or of the United States Court of Customs and Patent Appeals, merchandise of the character covered by the published decision of the Secretary, which is entered for consumption or withdrawn from warehouse for consumption after the date of publication in the Federal Register by the Secretary or the administering authority of a notice of the court decision, shall be subject to appraisement, classification, and assessment of duty in accordance with the final judicial decision in the action, and the liquidation of entries covering the merchandise so entered or withdrawn shall be suspended until final disposition is made of the action, whereupon the entries shall be liquidated, or if necessary, reliquidated in accordance with the final decision. Such notice of the court decision shall be published within ten days from the date of the issuance of the court decision.

Regulations implementing required procedures

(g) Regulations shall be prescribed by the Secretary to implement the procedures required under this section.

Section 1516a. *Judicial Review in Countervailing Duty and Antidumping Duty Proceedings*

(a) Review of determination.—

(1) Review of certain determinations.—

(A) Thirty-day review.—Within 30 days after the date of publication in the Federal Register of notice of—

(i) a determination by the Secretary or the administering authority, under section 1303(a)(3), 1673a(c), or 1671a(c) of this title, not to initiate an investigation,

(ii) a determination by the administering authority or the Commission, under section 1675(b) of this title, not to review an agreement or a determination based upon changed circumstances, or

(iii) a negative determination by the Commission, under section 1671b(a) or 1673b(a) of this title, as to whether there is reasonable indication of material injury, threat of material injury or material retardation,

an interested party who is a party to the proceeding in connection with which the matter arises may commence an action in the United States Court of International Trade by filing concurrently a summons and complaint, each with the content and in the form, manner, and style prescribed by the rules of that court, contesting any factual findings or legal conclusions upon which the determination is based.

(B) Ten-day review.—Within 10 days after the date of publication in the Federal Register of notice of—

(i) a determination by the administering authority, under section 1671b(c) or 1673b(c) of this title, that a case is extraordinarily complicated, or

(ii) a negative determination by the administering authority under section 1671b(b) or 1673b(b) of this title,

an interested party who is a party to the proceeding in connection with which the matter arises may commence an action in the United States Court of International Trade by filing concurrently a summons and complaint, each with the content and in the form, manner, and style prescribed by the rules of that court, contesting any factual findings or legal conclusions upon which the determination is based.

(2) Review of determinations on record.—

(A) In general.—Within thirty days after the date of publication in the Federal Register of—

(i) notice of any determination described in clause (ii), (iii), (iv), or (v) of subparagraph (B), or

(ii) an antidumping or countervailing duty order based upon any determination described in clause (i) of subparagraph (B),

an interested party who is a party to the proceeding in connection with which the matter arises may commence an action in the United States Court of International Trade by filing a summons, and within thirty days thereafter a complaint, each with the content and in the form, manner, and style prescribed by the rules of that court, contesting any factual findings or legal conclusions upon which the determination is based.

(B) Reviewable determinations.—The determinations which may be contested under subparagraph (A) are as follows:

(i) Final affirmative determinations by the Secretary and by the Commission under section 1303 of this title, or by the administering authority and by the Commission under section 1671d or 1673d of this title.

(ii) A final negative determination by the Secretary, the administering authority, or the Commission under section 1303, 1671d, or 1673d of this title.

(iii) A determination, other than a determination reviewable under paragraph (1), by the Secretary, the administering authority, or the Commission under section 1675 of this title.

(iv) A determination by the administering authority, under section 1671c or 1673c of this title, to suspend an antidumping duty or a countervailing duty investigation.

(v) An injurious effect determination by the Commission under section 1671c(h) or 1673c(h) of this title.

(3) Procedures and fees.—The procedures and fees set forth in chapter 169 of Title 28 apply to an action under this section.

(b) Standards of review.—

(1) Remedy.—The court shall hold unlawful any determination, finding, or conclusion found—

(A) in an action brought under paragraph (1) of subsection (a) of this section, to be arbitrary, capricious, an abuse of discretion, or otherwise not in accordance with law, or

(B) in an action brought under paragraph (2) of subsection (a) of this section, to be unsupported by substantial evidence on the record, or otherwise not in accordance with law.

(2) Record for review.—

(A) In general.—For the purposes of this subsection, the record, unless otherwise stipulated by the parties, shall consist of—

(i) a copy of all information presented to or obtained by the Secretary, the administering authority, or the Commission during the course of the administrative proceeding, including all governmental memoranda pertaining to the case and the record of ex parte meetings required to be kept by section 1677f(a)(3) of this title; and

(ii) a copy of the determination, all transcripts or records of conferences or hearings, and all notices published in the Federal Register.

(B) Confidential or privileged material.—The confidential or privileged status accorded to any documents, comments, or information shall be preserved in any action under this section. Notwithstanding the preceding sentence, the court may examine, in camera, the confidential or privileged material, and may disclose such material under such terms and conditions as it may order.

(c) Liquidation of entries.—

(1) Liquidation in accordance with determination.—Unless such liquidation is enjoined by the court under paragraph (2) of this subsection, entries of merchandise of the character covered by a determination of the Secretary, the administering authority, or the Commission contested under subsection (a) of this section shall be liquidated in accordance with the determination of the Secretary, the administering authority, or the Commission, if they are entered, or withdrawn from warehouse, for consumption on or before the date of publication in the Federal Register by the Secretary or the administering authority of a notice of a decision of the United States Court of International Trade, or of the United States Court of Customs and Patent Appeals, not in harmony with that determination. Such notice of a decision shall be published within ten days from the date of the issuance of the court decision.

(2) Injunctive relief.—In the case of a determination described in paragraph (2) of subsection (a) of this section by the Secretary, the administering authority, or the Commission, the United States Court of International Trade may enjoin the liquidation of some or all entries of merchandise covered by a determination of the Secretary, the administering authority, or the Commission, upon a request by an interested party for such relief and a proper showing that the requested relief should be granted under the circumstances.

(3) Remand for final disposition.—If the final disposition of an action brought under this section is not in harmony with the published determination of the Secretary, the administering authority, or the Commission, the matter shall be remanded to the Secretary, the administering authority, or the Commission, as appropriate, for disposition consistent with the final disposition of the court.

(d) Standing.—Any interested party who was a party to the proceeding under section 1303 of this title or subtitle IV of this chapter shall have the right to appear and be heard as a party in interest before the United States Court of International Trade. The party filing the action shall notify all such interested parties of the filing of an action under this section, in the form, manner, style, and within the time prescribed by rules of the court.

(e) Liquidation in accordance with final decision.—If the cause of action is sustained in whole or in part by a decision of the United States Court of International Trade or of the United States Court of Customs and Patent Appeals—

(1) entries of merchandise of the character covered by the published determina-

tion of the Secretary, the administering authority, or the Commission, which is entered, or withdrawn from warehouse, for consumption after the date of publication in the Federal Register by the Secretary or the administering authority of a notice of the court decision, and

(2) entries, the liquidation of which was enjoined under subsection (c)(2) of this section,

shall be liquidated in accordance with the final court decision in the action. Such notice of the court decision shall be published within ten days from the date of the issuance of the court decision.

(f) Definitions.—For purposes of this section—

(1) Administering authority.—The term "administering authority" means the administering authority described in section 1677(1) of this title.

(2) Commission.—The term "Commission" means the United States International Trade Commission.

(3) Interested party.—The term "interested party" means any person described in section 1677(9) of this title.

(4) Secretary.—The term "Secretary" means the Secretary of the Treasury.

10. TRADE AGREEMENTS ACT OF 1979*

(a) A Brief Summary**

Approval of Trade Agreements

Approved the MTN codes and the statements of administrative action summarizing changes in U.S. law that were submitted with the legislation.

Provided that the trade agreements would have legal standing in the United States primarily as they were implemented in the trade bill, and that no provision of any agreement would take precedence over domestic laws in the event of a conflict.

The agreements would not become effective until Europe, Japan, and Canada also completed their domestic implementing procedures. Under an exception to this rule, the President could accept a particular agreement if only one industrial country had not accepted the agreement and acceptance by that country was not considered essential.

Provided that if any future change in U.S. law was necessary to conform to a code requirement, the President must consult with congressional committees at least a month before submitting a draft bill. Any legislation would be considered under the fast-track procedures of the 1974 Trade Act.

Title 1—Countervailing and Antidumping Duties

Allowed countervailing duties to offset export business subsidies if the administering agency (currently the Department of Commerce) determined that an import was either directly or indirectly subsidized, and the International Trade Commission (ITC) determined that a domestic industry had been materially injured or threatened with injury.

Defined material injury as "a harm which is not inconsequential, immaterial, or unimportant."

Allowed investigations to be initiated by the agency itself or by a domestic manufacturer, labor union, or trade association.

Set new procedures to shorten investigations, which currently take about one year, to about seven months. Importers would be forced to deposit a bond or cash in less than three months (compared to a year or more under current law) if a preliminary investigation found the imports were subsidized.

---

* Pub. L. 96–39, 93 Stat. 189, (July 16, 1979).

** Source: Office of the United States Trade Representative, A Preface to Trade, pp. 13–17 (1982)

Allowed the agency to drop the investigation if the foreign government or exporters agreed to eliminate the subsidy or cease exports within six months, or if the foreign government agreed to negotiate an agreement that would offset the effect of the subsidy or reduce the volume of exports.

Required the agency to verify the accuracy of any information submitted to it before making a final determination. If it was unable to verify the information, it must rely on the best information available, which could include the information submitted by the domestic industry.

Allowed confidential information to be made available to lawyers for other parties in the investigation under an administrative or court order; if a party failed to provide information, determinations would be made on the basis of the best available evidence.

Provided for an antidumping duty if the U.S. administering agency (currently the Department of Commerce) found that merchandise was being or was likely to be sold in the United States at less than fair value, and if the ITC determined that a domestic industry was materially injured or threatened with material injury. The duty would be the amount by which the home market price exceeded the U.S. price for the merchandise. (Dumping is the practice of selling exports below the price charged in the domestic market; antidumping duties are intended to make up the difference between the home market price and the export price.)

Established new procedures that shortened normal cases to about nine months. (Under current law cases normally take from nine to 15 months, but some cases have taken many years.)

Allowed the Customs Service six months to determine the amount of dumping and assess the duty (delays in assessments have averaged three years). During the assessment period importers of dumped products would have to pay estimated antidumping duties.

Provided that investigations may be initiated by the agency or upon petition by a manufacturer, union, or trade association.

Allowed the agency to drop an investigation if exporters stopped shipping the merchandise within six months or agreed to stop dumping the merchandise by increasing the price to about the home market value.

Title II—Customs Valuation

Established five methods of determining the value of imports to simplify the process of assessing duties (replacing the nine methods under current laws).

Established as the primary method the transaction value, defined as "the price actually paid or payable for the merchandise when sold for exportation to the United States," with additions for extra costs such as packing costs, selling commissions, and "assists" (certain free or reduced cost products and services—such as materials, tools, or design and development work—supplied by the buyer for the production or sale of the merchandise).

Listed four alternative methods to transaction value in order of preference: (1) transaction value of identical merchandise; (2) transaction value of similar merchandise; (3) deductive value, which takes the price of similar merchandise and subtracts additional costs for insurance, transportation, taxes and commissions; and (4) computer value, which is the sum of production and materials costs, profit and general expenses, packing costs, and assists.

Allowed "reasonable adjustments" to be made to one of the previous methods to arrive at a value if none of these methods could be used.

Repealed the American Selling Price (ASP) system of valuation, which based duties for some chemicals and rubber footwear on the price of comparable domestic products.

Converted ASP rates of duty into tariffs estimated to provide the same protection currently provided under ASP.

Title III—Government Procurement

Gave the President the authority, beginning January 1, 1981, to waive the application of discriminatory government procurement laws such as the Buy American Act for purchases covered by the agreement. (Current law gives domestic bidders on government contracts a 6 percent price preference over foreign bidders, 12 percent for small business or labor surplus areas, and 50 percent for Defense Department procurement.)

Excluded from the waiver provision several U.S. agencies, including the Departments of Transportation and Energy, the Tennessee Valley Authority, and the Army Corps of Engineers. Also excluded were purchases under $190,000, state and local government purchases, current preferences for small and minority businesses, strategic goods, and purchases for farm support or human feeding programs such as the U.S. school lunch program.

Directed the President to designate major industrial countries as eligible for non-discriminatory bidding under the agreement only if they had signed the Geneva procurement code. Nonindustrial countries could be given a waiver if they allow reciprocal government procurement opportunities for U.S. products; the least-developed countries would be eligible without providing reciprocity.

Authorized the President to bar purchases from ineligible countries, but allowed him to give nonindustrial countries two years to provide reciprocal opportunities before invoking the prohibition.

Directed the President to seek new opportunities for U.S. exports in future negotiations. If negotiations with specific countries did not result in expanded procurement opportunites, the President could recommend legislation to prohibit purchases from those countries by federal agencies not currently covered by the Agreement.

Directed the President to submit a report to Congress before January 1, 1981, that assessed the effect of the procurement provisions in areas of high unemployment.

Title IV—Product Standards

Recognized that federal and state agencies have a legitimate need to develop new product standards if they do not create unnecessary obstacles to foreign trade and if the purpose of the standard is to achieve a "legitimate domestic objective" such as the protection of health or safety, essential security, environmental or consumer interests.

Directed federal agencies to use standards in a way that treats imported products "no less favorably" than similar domestic products, including the use of tests and any fees charged for tests, and to adopt international standards unless factors such as national security requirements or the prevention of deceptive practices made adoption of the international standard inappropriate.

Expressed the sense of Congress that no state agency or private organization should use standards that create obstacles to foreign trade.

Gave the Office of the United States Trade Representative (USTR) responsibility for coordinating international trade policy issues connected with the standards code and for monitoring foreign implementation of the agreement, established offices in the Commerce and Agriculture Departments to gather and publish information on standards.

Allowed other nations that have signed the code or observed its provisions to file a complaint with USTR alleging that specific domestic practices violate U.S. obligations under the standards code. USTR is directed to resolve the complaint "on a mutually satisfactory basis" through consultations or submit the complaint for international arbitration if both parties consent.

Title V—Tariff Negotiations

Implemented tariff concessions that exceeded the authority granted the President in the 1974 Trade Act and made other technical changes in U.S. tariff schedules.

Allowed the President the give the least-developed countries full tariff reductions (instead of phased reductions stretching over eight years) on products that are not import-sensitive.

Title VI—Civil Aircraft Agreement

Eliminated all duties on civil aircraft, engines, and parts intended for use in civil aircraft.

Title VII—Agricultural Agreements

Implemented bilateral agreements on cheese, other dairy products, and meat.

Allowed the President to proclaim import quotas, up to an annual level of 111,000 metric tons, on about 85 percent of cheeses now imported. Provided a "fast-track" complaint procedure to protect domestic producers against subsidies on foreign cheeses, and directed the President to impose fees or quantitative restrictions if foreign governments did not eliminate subsidies.

Set a minimum annual level of meat imports at 1.2 billion pounds.

Title VIII—Liquor Duties

Repealed the wine gallon method of assessing duties on imported liquor, under which liquor was taxed on the basis of quantity rather than alcoholic content. Provided that liquor would be taxed solely on the basis of alcohol content, with the tax based on the finished product after it has been diluted and bottled.

Allowed a 15-day deferral period for payment on spirits bottled in the United States (phased in over a three-year period).

Title IX—Enforcement

Authorized the President to take action against unreasonable foreign trade practices under the current agreements.

Introduced specific time limits for investigating and taking action on complaints.

Allowed any interested person to file a petition alleging unfair trade practices with the Trade Representative's office, which has 45 days to determine if an investigation is necessary.

Directed USTR to request consultation with the foreign country involved in the dispute as part of its investigation. If the dispute could not be resolved through consultations, then the Trade Representative could request proceedings under the international dispute settlement procedures of the agreement.

Directed the Trade Representative to make recommendations to the President within seven to 12 months after initiating an investigation.

Title X—Judicial Review

Provided increased opportunities for judicial review of some provisional and all final rulings by the Treasury Department and ITC in antidumping and countervailing duty cases.

Expanded opportunities for judicial review of determinations by the Customs Service concerning the appraised value or rate of duty of imported goods.

Allowed any interested party involved in the proceeding to take legal action and allowed any party to challenge the amount of a countervailing or dumping duty, as well as the failure to assess a duty.

Provided expedited review procedures for antidumping and countervailing duty cases, including a requirement that any party could challenge a court decision within

30 days after the decision, and that these cases would be given priority in Customs Court.

Title XI—Miscellaneous Provisions

Extended for an additional eight years the President's authority to negotiate trade agreements with foreign countries to reduce or eliminate nontariff barriers. Trade agreements submitted to Congress would be handled under the expedited procedures of the 1974 Trade Act.

Clarified existing law by authorizing President to sell import licenses at public auction. (Under existing programs import licenses were allocated by the U.S. government on a first-come, first-served basis.)

Continued the private sector advisory committee structure established in the 1974 Trade Act, with a broadened mandate to include advice on the implementation of the trade agreements.

Authorized the President to study the desirability of negotiating trade agreements with North American countries.

Required monthly statistics on imports and the balance-of-trade to include the cost of freight charges, insurance charges, and other expenses of bringing goods from the port of exportation to the U.S. port of entry, commonly known as the cost-insurance-freight (C.I.F.) value.

Required the President to submit a trade reorganization proposal to Congress.

Prohibited the President from giving a developing country duty-free treatment for certain products provided under the Generalized System of Preferences (GSP) if that country is a member of the Organization of Petroleum Exporting Countries (OPEC) and "interrupts or terminates" petroleum deliveries to the United States.

Communist Nations

Authorized the President to extend most-favored-nation (MFN) status to nonmarket (communist) countries, but bared MFN treatment and trade credits for communist countries that did not permit free emigration of their citizens.

Permitted the President to waive this restriction for 18 months if he received assurances from a country that its policies would henceforth lead to substantially free emigration, and if he so informed Congress. After 18 months the continuation of MFN granted under a waiver would be subject to congressional approval.

Provided that MFN treatment would last only as long as a bilateral trade agreement was in effect; the agreement would have a lifespan of up to three years, would be renewable, and would have a number of conditions to protect U.S. trade.

Authorized the President to deny MFN and government credits and guarantees if the foreign nation did not cooperate in accounting for and returning missing U.S. personnel in Southeast Asia.

Required the resolution of dispute involving gold owed to U.S. citizens before Czechoslovakia would be eligible for MFN or a bilateral trade treaty.

Established a 12-member East-West Foreign Trade Board to monitor trade with Communist countries; transactions involving more than $500 million would be subject to congressional veto.

Limited U.S. loans, guarantees, credits, and insurance to Communist countries to an aggregate total of $300 million without prior congressional approval, with the exemption of the Commodity Credit Corporation.

(b) Trade Agreements Act of 1979

Table of Contents

SECTION 1. SHORT TITLE; TABLE OF CONTENTS; PURPOSES.

(a) Short Title—This Act may be cited as the "Trade Agreements Act of 1979".

(b) Table of Contents—

Sec. 1. Short title; table of contents; purposes.

Sec. 2. Approval of trade agreements.

Sec. 3. Relationship of trade agreements to United States law.

TITLE I—COUNTERVAILING AND ANTIDUMPING DUTIES

Sec. 101. Addition of new countervailing and antidumping duties title to Tariff Act of 1930.

Sec. 102. Pending investigations; purposes.

Sec. 103. Amendment of section 303 of the Tariff Act of 1930.

Sec. 104. Transition rules for countervailing duty orders.

Sec. 105. Continuation of certain waivers.

Sec. 106. Conforming changes.

Sec. 107. Effective date.

TITLE II—CUSTOMS VALUATION*

Subtitle A—Valuation Standards Amendments

Sec. 201. Valuation of imported merchandise.

---

* Not reproduced.

Sec. 202. Conforming amendments.

Sec. 203. Presidential report on operation of the Agreement.

Sec. 204. Transition to valuation standards under this title.

Subtitle B—Final List and American Selling Price Rate Conversions

Sec. 221. Amendment of tariff schedules.

Sec. 222. Final list rate conversions.

Sec. 223. American selling price rate conversion.

Sec. 224. Treatment of converted rates as existing rates for purposes of trade agreement authority.

Sec. 225. Modification of tariff treatment of certain chemicals and chemical products.

TITLE III—GOVERNMENT PROCUREMENT*

Sec. 301. General authority to modify discriminatory purchasing requirements.

Sec. 302. Authority to encourage reciprocal competitive procurement practices.

Sec. 303. Waiver of discriminatory purchasing requirements with respect to purchases of civil aircraft.

Sec. 304. Expansion of the coverage of the Agreement.

Sec. 305. Monitoring and enforcement.

Sec. 306. Labor surplus area studies.

Sec. 307. Availability of information to Congressional advisers.

Sec. 308. Definitions.

Sec. 309. Effective dates.

TITLE IV—TECHNICAL BARRIERS TO TRADE (STANDARDS)*

Subtitle A—Obligations of the United States

Sec. 401. Certain standards-related activities.

Sec. 402. Federal standards-related activities.

Sec. 403. State and private standards-related activities.

Subtitle B—Functions of Federal Agencies

Sec. 411. Functions of Special Representative.

Sec. 412. Establishment and operation of technical offices.

---

* Not reproduced.

Sec. 413. Representation of United States interests before international standards organizations.

Sec. 414. Standards information center.

Sec. 415. Contracts and grants.

Sec. 416. Technical assistance.

Sec. 417. Consultations with representatives of domestic interests.

Subtitle C—Administrative and Judicial Proceedings Regarding Standards Related Activites

CHAPTER 1—REPRESENTATIONS ALLEGING UNITED STATES VIOLATIONS OF OBLIGATIONS

Sec. 421. Right of action under this chapter.

Sec. 422. Representations.

Sec. 423. Action after receipt of representations.

Sec. 424. Procedure after finding by international forum.

CHAPTER 2—OTHER PROCEEDINGS REGARDING CERTAIN STANDARDS-RELATED ACTIVITIES

Sec. 441. Finding of reciprocity required in administrative proceedings.

Sec. 442. Not cause for stay in certain circumstances.

Subtitle D—Definitions and Miscellaneous Provisions

Sec. 451. Definitions

Sec. 452. Exemptions under title.

Sec. 453. Reports to Congress on operation of Agreement.

Sec. 454. Effective date.

TITLE V—IMPLEMENTATION OF CERTAIN TARIFF NEGOTIATIONS*

Sec. 501. Amendment of tariff schedules.

Sec. 502. Effective dates of certain tariff reductions.

Sec. 503. Staging of certain tariff reduction.

---

* Not reproduced.

Sec. 504. Snapback of textile tariff reductions.

Sec. 505. Goat and sheep (except lamb) meat.

Sec. 506. Certain fresh, chilled, or frozen beef.

Sec. 507. Yellow Dent corn.

Sec. 508. Carrots.

Sec. 509. Dinnerware.

Sec. 510. Tariff treatment of watches.

Sec. 511. Brooms.

Sec. 512. Agricultural and horticultural machinery, equipment, implements, and parts.

Sec. 513. Wool.

Sec. 514. Conversion to ad valorem equivalents of certain column 2 tariff rates.

TITLE VI—CIVIL AIRCRAFT AGREEMENT*

Sec. 601. Civil aircraft and parts.

TITLE VII—CERTAIN AGRICULTURAL MEASURES*

Sec. 701. Limitation on cheese imports.

Sec. 702. Enforcement.

Sec. 703. Limitation on imports of chocolate crumb.

Sec. 704. Amendments to meat import law.

TITLE VIII—TREATMENT OF DISTILLED SPIRITS*

Subtitle A—Tax Treatment

Sec. 801. Short title; amendment of 1954 Code.

Sec. 802. Repeal of wine-gallon method of taxing distilled spirits.

Sec. 803. Repeal of recification taxes on distilled spirits.

Sec. 804. Determination and payment of tax.

Sec. 805. All-in-bond method of determining excise tax on distilled spirits.

Sec. 806. Removal of requirement of on-site inspection.

---

* Not reproduced.

Sec. 807. Technical, conforming, and clerical amendments.

Sec. 808. Transitional rules relating to determination and payment of tax.

Sec. 809. Transitional rules relating to all-in-bond method.

Sec. 810. Effective date.

Subtitle B—Tariff Treatment

Sec. 851. Repeal of provision that each wine gallon is to be counted as at least one proof gallon.

Sec. 852. Changes in rates of duty.

Sec. 853. Effective date for sections 851 and 852.

Sec. 854. Review of international trade in alcoholic beverages.

Sec. 855. Authority to proclaim existing rates for certain items.

Sec. 856. Application of section 311 of the Tariff Act of 1930.

TITLE IX—ENFORCEMENT OF UNITED STATES RIGHTS

Sec. 901. Enforcement of United States rights under trade agreements and response to certain foreign practices.

Sec. 902. Conforming amendments.

Sec. 903. Effective date.

TITLE X—JUDICIAL REVIEW**

Sec. 1001. Judicial review.

Sec. 1002. Effective date and transitional rules.

TITLE XI—MISCELLANEOUS PROVISIONS

Sec. 1101. Extension of nontariff barrier negotiating authority.

Sec. 1102. Auction of import licenses.

Sec. 1103. Advice from private sector.

Sec. 1104. Study of possible agreements with North American countries.

Sec. 1105. Amendments to section 337 of the Tariff Act of 1930.

Sec. 1106. Technical amendments to the Trade Act of 1974.

Sec. 1107. Technical amendments to the Tariff Schedules of the United States.

** See Document 9(c).

Sec. 1108. Reporting of statistics on a cost-insurance-freight basis.

Sec. 1109. Reorganizing and restructuring of international trade functions of the United States Government.

Sec. 1110. Study of export trade policy.

Sec. 1111. Generalized system of preferences.

Sec. 1112. Concession-related revenue losses to United States possessions.

Sec. 1113. No budget authority for any fiscal year before fiscal year 1981.

Sec. 1114. Effective date.

(C) INTRODUCTORY SECTIONS

Sec. 1.

(c) PURPOSES—The purposes of this Act are—

(1) to approve and implement the trade agreements negotiated under the Trade Act of 1974;

(2) to foster the growth and maintenance of an open world trading system;

(3) to expand opportunities for the commerce of the United States in international trade; and

(4) to improve the rules of international trade and to provide for the enforcement of such rules, and for other purposes.

Sec. 2. *Approval of Trade Agreements.*

(a) Approval of Agreements and Statements of Administrative Action—In accordance with the provisions of sections 102 and 151 of the Trade Act of 1974 (19 U.S.C. 2112 and 2191), the Congress approves the trade agreements described in subsection (c) submitted to the Congress on June 19, 1979, and the statements of administrative action proposed to implement such trade agreements submitted to the Congress on that date.

(b) Acceptance of Agreements by the President—

(1) In General.—The President may accept for the United States the final legal instruments or texts embodying each of the trade agreements approved by the Congress under subsection (a). The President shall submit a copy of each final instrument or text to the Congress on the date such text or instrument is available, together with a notification of any changes in the instruments or texts, including their annexes, if any, as accepted and the texts of such agreements as submitted to the Congress under subsection (a). Such final legal instruments or texts shall be deemed to be the agreements submitted to and approved by the Congress under subsection (a) if such changes are —

(A) only rectifications of a formal character or minor technical or clerical changes which do not affect the substance or meaning of the texts as submitted to the Congress on June 19, 1979, or

(B) changes in annexes to such agreements, and the President determines that the balance of United States rights and obligations under such agreements is maintained.

(2) Application of Agreement Between the United States and Other Countries— No agreement accepted by the President under paragraph (l) shall apply between the United States, and any other country unless the President determines that such country—

(A) has accepted the obligations of the agreement with respect to the United States, and

(B) should not otherwise be denied the benefits of the agreement with respect to the United States because such country has not accorded adequate benefits, including substantially equal competitive opportunities for the commerce of the United States to the extent required under section 126(c) of the Trade Act of 1974 (19 U.S.C. 2136(c)), to the United States.

(3) Limitations on Acceptance Concerning Major Industrial Countries.—The President may not accept an agreement described in paragraph (l), (2), (3), (4), (5), (6), (7), (9), (10), or (11) of subsection (c), unless he determines that each major industrial country (as defined in section 126(d) of the Trade Act of 1974 (19 U.S.C. 2136(d)) is also accepting the agreement. Notwithstanding the preceding sentence, the President may accept such an agreement, if he determines that only one major industrial country is not accepting that agreement and the acceptance of that agreement by that country is not essential to the effective operation of the agreement, and if—

(A) that country is not a major factor in trade in the products covered by that agreement,

(B) the President has authority to deny the benefits of the agreement to that country and has taken steps to deny the benefits of the agreement to that country, or

(C) a significant portion of United States trade would benefit from the agreement, notwithstanding such nonacceptance, and the President determines and reports to the Congress that it is in the national interest of the United States to accept the agreement.

For purposes of this paragraph, the acceptance of an agreement by the European Communities on behalf of its member countries shall also be treated as acceptance of that agreement by each member country, and acceptance of an agreement by all the member countries of the European Communities shall also be treated as acceptance of that agreement by the European Communities.

(c) Trade Agreements to Which This Act Applies—The trade agreements to which subsection (a) applies are the following:

(l) The Agreement on Implementation of Article VII of the General Agreement on Tariffs and Trade (relating to customs valuation).

(2) The Agreement on Government Procurement.

(3) The Agreement on Import Licensing Procedures.

(4) The Agreement on Technical Barriers to Trade (relating to product standards).

(5) The Agreement on Interpretation and Application of Articles VI, XVI, and XXIII of the General Agreement on Tariffs and Trade (relating to subsidies and countervailing measures).

(6) The Agreement on Implementation of Article VI of the General Agreement on Tariffs and Trade (relating to antidumping measures).

(7) The International Dairy Arrangement.

(8) Certain bilateral agreements on cheese, other dairy products, and meat.

(9) The Arrangement Regarding Bovine Meat.

(10) The Agreement on Trade in Civil Aircraft.

(11) Texts Concerning a Framework for the Conduct of World Trade.

(12) Certain Bilateral Agreements to Eliminate the Wine-Gallon Method of Tax and Duty Assessment.

(13) Certain other agreements to be reflected in Schedule XX of the United States to the General Agreement on Tariffs and Trade, including Agreements—

(A) to Modify United States Watch Marking Requirements, and to Modify United States Tariff Nomenclatures and Rates of Duty for Watches,

(B) to Provide Duty-Free Treatment for Agricultural and Horticultural Machinery, Equipment, Implements, and Parts Thereof, and

(C) to Modify United States Tariff Nomenclature and Rates of Duty for Ceramic Tableware.

(14) The Agreement with the Hungarian People's Republic.

Sec. 3. *Relationship of Trade Agreements to United States Law.*

(a) United States Statutes to Prevail in Conflict—No provision of any trade agreement approved by the Congress under section 2(a), nor the application of any such provision to any person or circumstance, which is in conflict with any statute of the United States shall be given effect under the laws of the United States.

(b) Implementing Regulations—Regulations necessary or appropriate to carry out actions proposed in any statement or proposed administrative action submitted to the Congress under section 102 of the Trade Act of 1974 to implement each agreement approved under section 2(a) shall be issued within 1 year after the date of entry into force of such agreement with respect to the United States.

(c) Changes in Statutes to Implement a Requirement Amendment or Recommendation.—

(1) Presidential Determination—Whenever the President determines that it is necessary or appropriate to amend, repeal, or enact a statute of the United States in order to implement any requirement of, amendment to, or recommendation under such an agreement, he shall submit to the Congress a draft of a bill to accomplish the amendment, repeal, or enactment and a statement of any administrative action proposed to implement the requirement, amendment, or recommendation. Not less than 30 days before submitting such a bill, the President shall consult with the Committee on Ways and Means of the House of Representatives, the Committee on Finance of the Senate, and each committee of the House or Senate which has jurisdiction over legislation involving subject matters which would be affected by such amendment, repeal, or enactment. The consultation shall treat all matters relating to the implementation of such requirement, amendment, or recommendation, as provided in paragraphs (2) and (3).

(2) Conditions for Taking Effect under United States Law.—No such amendment shall enter into force with respect to the United States, and no such requirement, amendment, or recommendation shall be implemented under United States law, unless—

(A) The President, after consultation with the Congress under paragraph (1), notifies the House of Representatives and the Senate of his determination and publishes notice of that determination in the Federal Register,

(B) The President transmits a document to the House of Representatives and to the Senate containing a copy of the text of such requirement, amendment, or recommendation, together with—

(i) a draft of a bill to amend or repeal provisions of existing statutes or to create statutory authority and an explanation as to how the bill and any proposed administrative action affect existing law, and

(ii) a statement of how the requirement, amendment, or recommendation serves the interests of United States commerce and why the legislative and administrative action is necessary or appropriate to carry out the requirement, amendment, or recommendation, and

(C) the bill submitted by the President is enacted into law.

(3) Recommendations as to Application—The President may make the same type of recommendations, in the same manner and subject to the same conditions, to the Congress with respect to the application of any such requirement, amendment, or recommendation as he may make, under section 102(f) of the Trade Act of 1974, with respect to a trade agreement.

(4) Congressional Procedures Applicable—The bill submitted by the President shall be introduced in accordance with the provisions of subsection (c)(1) of section 151 of the Trade Act of 1974, and the provisions of subsections (d), (e), (f), and (g) of such section shall apply to the consideration of the bill. For the purpose of applying section 151 of such Act to such bill—

(A) the term "trade agreement" shall be treated as a reference to the requirement, amendment, or recommendation, and

(B) the term "implementing bill" or "implementing revenue bill", whichever is appropriate, shall be treated as a reference to the bill submitted by the President.

(e) Congressional Liason—Paragraph (1) of section 161(b) of the Trade Act of 1974 (19 U.S.C. 2211(b)) is amended by inserting "or any requirement of, amendment to, or recommendation under, such agreement" immediately after "trade agreement".

(f) Unspecified Private Remedies Not Created.—Neither the entry into force with respect to the United States of any agreement approved under section 2(a), nor the enactment of this Act, shall be construed as creating any private right of action or remedy for which provision is not explicitly made under this Act or under the laws of the United States.

(d) TITLE I—COUNTERVAILING AND ANTIDUMPING DUTIES

SEC. 101. *Addition of New Countervailing and Antidumping Duties Title to Tariff Act of 1930.*

The Tariff Act of 1930 is amended by adding at the end thereof the followig new title:

"TITLE VII—COUNTERVAILING AND ANTIDUMPING DUTIES

"Subtitle A—Imposition of Countervailing Duties

"Sec. 701. Countervailing duties imposed.

"Sec. 702. Procedures for initiating a countervailing duty investigation.

"Sec. 703. Preliminary determinations.

"Sec. 704. Termination or suspension of investigation.

"Sec. 705. Final determinations.

"Sec. 706. Assessment of duty.

"Sec. 707. Treatment of difference between deposit of estimated countervailing duty and final assessed duty under countervailing duty order.

"Subtitle B—Imposition of Antidumping Duties

"Sec. 731. Antidumping duties imposed.

"Sec. 732. Procedures for initiating an antidumping duty investigation.

"Sec. 733. Preliminary determinations.

"Sec. 734. Termination or suspension of investigation.

"Sec. 735. Final determinations.

"Sec. 736. Assessment of duty.

"Sec. 737. Treatment of difference between deposit of estimated antidumping duty and final assessed duty under antidumping duty order.

"Sec. 738. Conditional payment of antidumping duty.

"Sec. 739. Duties of customs officers.

"Sec. 740. Antidumping duty treated as regular duty for drawback purposes.

"Subtitle C—Review of Determinations

"Sec. 751. Administrative Review of Determinations

"Subtitle D—General Provisions

"Sec. 771. Definitions; special rules.

"Sec. 772. United States price.

"Sec. 773. Foreign market value.

"Sec. 774. Hearings.

Sec. 775. Subsidy practices discovered during an investigation.

"Sec. 776. Verification of information.

"Sec. 777. Access to information.

"Sec. 778. Interest on certain overpayments and underpayments.

"Subtitle A—Imposition of Countervailing Duties

"Section 701. *Countervailing Duties Imposed*

"(a) General Rule.—If—

"(l) the administering authority determines that—

"(A) a country under the Agreement, or

"(B) a person who is a citizen or national of such a country, or a corporation, association, or other organization organized in such a country,

is providing, directly or indirectly, a subsidy with respect to the manufacture, production, or exportation of a class or kind of merchandise imported into the United States, and

"(2) the Commission determines that—

"(A) an industry in the United States—

"(i) is materially injured, or

"(ii) is threatened with material injury, or

"(B) the establishment of an industry in the United States is materially retarded, by reason of imports of that merchandise,

then there shall be imposed upon such merchandise a countervailing duty, in addition to any other duty imposed, equal to the amount of the net subsidy.

"(b) Country under the Agreement.—For purposes of this subtitle, the term 'country under the Agreement' means a country—

"(1) between the United States and which the Agreement on Subsidies and Countervailing Measures applies, as determined under section 2(b) of the Trade Agreements Act of 1979,

"(2) which has assumed obligations with respect to the United States which are substantially equivalent to obligations under the Agreement, as determined by the President, or

"(3) with respect to which the President determines that—

"(A) there is an agreement in effect between the United States and that country which—

"(i) was in force on June 19, 1979, and

"(ii) requires unconditional most-favored-nation treatment with respect to articles imported into the United States,

"(B) the General Agreement on Tariffs and Trade does not apply between the United States and that country, and

"(C) the agreement described in subparagraph (A) does not expressly permit—

"(i) actions required or permitted by the General Agreement on Tariffs and Trade, or required by the Congress, or

"(ii) nondiscriminatory prohibitions or restrictions on importation which are designed to prevent deceptive or unfair practices.

"(c) Cross Reference—

"For provisions of law applicable in the case of merchandise which is the product of a country other than a country under the Agreement, see section 303 of this Act.

"Section 702. *Procedures for Initiating a Countervailing Duty Investigation.*

"(a) Initiation by Administering Authority—A countervailing duty investigation shall be commenced whenever the administering authority determines, from information available to it, that a formal investigation is warranted into the question of whether the elements necessary for the imposition of a duty under section 701(a) exist.

"(b) Initiation by Petition—

"(1) Petition Requirements—A countervailing duty proceeding shall be commenced whenever an interested party described in subparagraph (C), (D), or (E) of section 771(9) files a petition with the administering authority, on behalf of an industry, which alleges the elements necessary for the imposition of the duty imposed by section 701(a), and which is accompanied by information reasonably available to the petitioner supporting those allegations. The petition may be amended at such time, and upon such conditions, as the administering authority and the Commission may permit.

"(2) Simultaneous Filing with Commission.—The petitioner shall file a copy of the petition with the Commission on the same day as it is filed with the administering authority.

"(c) Petition Determination—Within 20 days after the date on which a petition is filed under subsection (b), the administering authority shall—

"(1) determine whether the petition alleges the elements necessary for the imposition of a duty under section 701(a) and contains information reasonably available to the petitioner supporting the allegations,

"(2) if the determination is affirmative, commence an investigation to determine whether a subsidy is being provided with respect to the class or kind of merchandise described in the petition, and provide for the publication of notice of the determination to commence an investigation in the Federal Register, and

"(3) if the determination is negative, dismiss the petition, terminate the proceeding, notify the petitioner in writing of the reasons for the determination, and provide the publication of notice of the determination in the Federal Register.

"(d) Notification to Commission of Determination.—The administering authority shall—

"(1) notify the Commission immediately of any determination it makes under subsection (a) or (c), and

"(2) if the determination is affirmative, make available to the Commission such information as it may have relating to the matter under investigation, under such procedures as the administering authority and the Commission may establish to prevent disclosure, other than the consent of the party providing it or under protective order, of any information to which confidential treatment has been given by the administering authority.

"Sec. 703. *Preliminary Determinations.*

"(a) Determination by Commission of Reasonable Indication of Injury.—Except in the case of a petition dismissed by the administering authority under section 702(c)(3), the Commission, within 45 days after the date on which a petition is filed under section 702(b) or on which it receives notice from the administering authority of an investigation commenced under section 702(a), shall make a determination, based upon the best information available to it at the time of the determination, of whether there is a reasonable indication that—

"(1) an industry in the United States—

"(A) is materially injured, or

"(B) is threatened with material injury, or

"(2) the establishment of an industry in the United States is materially retarded,

by reason of imports of the merchandise which is the subject of the investigation by the administering authority. If that determination is negative, the investigation is terminated.

"(b) Preliminary Determination by Administering Authority—Within 85 days after the date on which a petition is filed under section 702(b), or an investigation is commenced under section 702(a), but not before an affirmative determination by the Commission under subsection (a) of this section, the administering authority shall make a determination, based upon the best information available to it at the time of the determination, of whether there is a reasonable basis to believe or suspect that a subsidy is being provided with respect to the merchandise which is the subject of the investigation. If the determination of the administering authority under this subsection is affirmative, the determination shall include an estimate of the net subsidy.

"(c) Extension of Period in Extraordinarily Complicated Cases.

"(1) In General.—If—

"(A) the petitioner makes a timely request for an extension of the period within which the determination must be made under subsection (b), or

"(B) the administering authority concludes that the parties concerned are cooperating and determines that-

"(i) the case is extraordinarily complicated by reason of—

"(I) the number and complexity of the alleged subsidy practices;

"(II) the novelty of the issues presented;

"(III) the need to determine the extent to which particular subsidies are used by individual manufacturers, producers, and exporters; or

"(IV) the number of firms whose activities must be investigated; and

"(ii) additional time is necessary to make the preliminary determination,

then the administering authority may postpone making the preliminary determination under subsection (b) until not later than the 150th day after the date on which a petition is filed under section 702(b), or an investigation is commenced under section 702(a).

"(2) Notice of Postponement.—The administering authority shall notify the parties to the investigation, not later than 20 days before the date on which the preliminary determination would otherwise be required under subsection (b), if it intends to postpone making the preliminary determination under paragraph (1). The notification shall include an explanation of the reasons for the postponement. Notice of the postponement shall be published in the Federal Register.

"(d) Effect of Determination by the Administering Authority.—If the preliminary determination of the administering authority under subsection (b) is affirmative, the administering authority—

"(1) shall order the suspension of liquidation of all entries of merchandise subject to the determination which are entered, or withdrawn from warehouse, for consumption on or after the date of publication of the notice of the determination in the Federal Register,

"(2) shall order the posting of a cash deposit, bond, or other security, as it deems appropriate, for each entry of the merchandise concerned equal to the estimated amount of the net subsidy, and

"(3) shall make available to the Commission all information upon which its determination was based and which the Commission considers relevant to its injury determination, under such procedures as the administering authority and the Commission may establish to prevent disclosure, other than with the consent of the party providing it or under protective order, of any information to which confidential treatment has been given by the administering authority.

"(e) Critical Circumstances Determinations—

"(1) In General.—If a petitioner alleges critical circumstances in its original petitioner, or by amendment at any time more than 20 days before the date of a final determination by the administering authority, then the administering authority shall promptly determine, on the basis of the best information available to it at that time, whether there is a reasonable basis to believe or suspect that—

"(A) the alleged subsidy is inconsistent with the Agreement, and

"(B) there have been massive imports of the class or kind of merchandise which is the subject of the investigation over a relatively short period.

"(2) Suspension of Liquidation.—If the determination of the administering authority under paragraph (1) is affirmative, then any suspension of liquidation ordered under subsection (d)(1) shall apply, or, if notice of such suspension of liquidation is already published, be amended to apply, to unliquidated entries of merchandise entered, or withdrawn from warehouse, for consumption on or after the date which is 90 days before the date on which suspension of liquidation was first ordered.

"(f) Notice of Determinations.—Whenever the Commission or the administering authority makes a determination under this section, it shall notify the petitioner, other parties to the investigation, and the other agency of its determination and of the facts and conclusions of law upon which the determination is based, and it shall publish notice of its determination in the Federal Register.

Sec. 704. *Termination or Suspension of Investigation.*

"(a) Termination of Investigation on Withdrawal of Petition.—An investigation under this subtitle may be terminated by either the administering authority or the Commission after notice to all parties to the investigation, upon withdrawal of the petition by the petitioner. The Commission may not terminate an investigation under the preceding sentence before a preliminary determination is made by the administering authority under section 703(b).

"(b) Agreements to Eliminate or Offset Completely a Subsidy or To Cease Exports of Subsidized Merchandise.—The administering authority may suspend an investigation if the government of the country in which the subsidy practice is alleged to occur agrees, or exporters who account for substantially all of the imports of the merchandise which is the subject of the investigation agree—

"(1) to eliminate the subsidy completely or to offset completely the amount of the net subsidy, with respect to that merchandise exported directly or indirectly to the United States, within 6 months after the date on which the investigation is suspended, or

"(2) to cease exports of that merchandise to the United States within 6 months after the date on which the investigation is suspended.

"(c) Agreements Eliminating Injurious Effect.—

"(1) General Rule.—If the administering authority determines that extraordinary circumstances are present in a case, it may suspend an investigation upon the acceptance of an agreement from a government described in subsection (b) , or from exporters described in subsection (b) , if the agreement will eliminate completely the injurious effect of exports to the United States of the merchandise which is the subject of the investigation.

"(2) Certain Additional Requirements.—Except in the case of an agreement by a foreign government to restrict the volume of imports of the merchandise which is the subject of the investigation into the United States, the administering authority may not accept an agreement under this subsection unless—

"(A) the suppression or undercutting of price levels of domestic products by imports of that merchandise will be prevented, and

"(B) at least 85 percent of the net subsidy will be offset.

"(3) Quantitative Restrictions Agreements.—The administering authority may accept an agreement with a foreign government under this subsection to restrict the volume of imports of merchandise which is the subject of an investigation into the United States, but it may not accept such an agreement with exporters.

"(4) Definition of Extraordinary Circumstances.—

"(A) Extraordinary Circumstances.—For purposes of this subsection, the term 'extraordinary circumstances' means circumstances in which—

"(i) suspension of an investigation will be more beneficial to the domestic industry than continuation of the investigation, and

"(i) the investigation is complex.

"(B) Complex.—For purposes of this paragraph, the term 'complex' means—

"(i) there are a large number of alleged subsidy practices and the practices are complicated, "(ii) the issues raised are novel, or

"(iii) the numbers of exporters involved is large.

"(d) Additional Rules and Conditions—

"(1) Public Interest; Monitoring.—The administrating authority shall not accept an agreement under subsection (b) or

(c) unless—

"(A) it is satisfied that suspension of the investigation is in the public interest, and

"(B) effective monitoring of the agreement by the United States is practicable.

"(2) Exports of Merchandise to the United States Not to Increase During Interim Period.—The administering authority may not accept any agreement under subsection (b) unless that agreement provides a means of ensuring that the quantity of the merchandise covered by that agreement exported to the United States during the period provided for elimination or offset of the subsidy or cessation of exports does not exceed the quantity of such merchandise exported to the United States during the most recent representative period determined by the administering authority.

"(3) Regulations Governing Entry or Withdrawals.—In order to carry out an agreement concluded under subsection (b) or (c), the administering authority is authorized to prescribe regulations governing the entry, or withdrawal from warehouse, for consumption of merchandise covered by such agreement.

"(e) Suspension of Investigation Procedure.—Before an investigation may be suspended under subsection (b) or (c) the administering authority shall—

"(1) notify the petitioner of, and consult with the petitioner concerning, its intention to suspend the investigation, and notify other parties to the investigation and the Commission not less than 30 days before the date on which it suspends the investigation,

"(2) provide a copy of the proposed agreement to the petitioner at the time of the notification, together with an explanation of how the agreement will be carried out and enforced (including any action required of foreign governments), and of how the agreement will meet the requirements of subsections (b) and (d) or (c) and (d), and

"(3) permit all parties to the investigation to submit comments and information for the record before the date on which notice of suspension of the investigation is published under subsection (f)(1)(A).

"(f) Effects of Suspension of Investigation—

"(1) In General.—If the administering authority determines to suspend an investigation upon acceptance of an agreement described in subsection (b) or (c), then—

"(A) it shall suspend the investigation, publish notice of suspension of the investigation, and issue an affirmative preliminary determination under section 703(b) with respect to the merchandise which is the subject of the investigation, unless it has previously issued such a determination in the same investigation,

"(B) the Commission shall suspend any investigation it is conducting with respect to that merchandise, and

"(C) the suspension of investigation shall take effect on the day on which such notice is published.

"(2) Liquidation of Entries—

"(A) Cessation of Exports; Complete Elimination of Net Subsidy.—If the agreement accepted by the administering authority is an agreement described in subsection (b), then—

"(i) notwithstanding the affirmative preliminary determination required under paragraph (1)(A), the liquidation of entries of merchandise which is the subject of the investigation shall not be suspended under section 703(d)(1),

"(ii) if the liquidation of entries of such merchandise was suspended pursuant to a previous affirmative preliminary determination in the same case with respect to such merchandise, that suspension of liquidation shall terminate, and

"(iii) the administering authority shall refund any cash deposit and release any bond or other security deposited under section 703(d)(1).

"(B) Other Agreements.—If the agreement accepted by the administering authority is an agreement described in subsection (c), then the liquidation of entries of the merchandise which is the subject of the investigation shall be suspended under section 703(d)(1), or, if the liquidation of entries of such merchandise was suspended pursuant to a previous affirmative preliminary determination in the same case, that suspension of liquidation shall continue in effect, subject to subsection (h)(3), but the security required under section 703(d)(2) may be adjusted to reflect the effect of the agreement.

"(3) Where Investigation is Continued.—If, pursuant to subsection (g), the administering authority and the Commission continue an investigation in which an agreement has been accepted under subsection (b) or (c), then—

"(A) if the final determination by the administering authority or the Commission under section 705 is negative, the agreement shall have no force or effect and the investigation shall be terminated, or86

"(B) if the final determinations by the administering authority and the Commission under such section are affirmative, the agreement shall remain in force, but the administering authority shall not issue a countervailing duty order in the case so long as—

"(i) the agreement remains in force,

"(ii) the agreement continues to meet the requirements of subsections (b) and (d) or (c) and (d), and

"(iii) the parties to the agreement carry out their obligations under the agreement in accordance with its terms.

"(g) Investigation to be Continued Upon Request—If the administering authority, within 20 days after the date of publication of the notice of suspension of an investigation, receives a request for the continuation of the investigation from—

"(1) the government of the country in which the subsidy practice is alleged to occur, or

"(2) an interested party described in subparagraph (C), (D), or (E) of section 771(9) which is a party to the investigation, then the administering authority and the Commission shall continue the investigation.

"(h) Review of Suspension.—

"(1) In General.—Within 20 days after the suspension of an investigation under subsection (c), an interested party which is a party to the investigation and which is described in subparagraph (C), (D), or (E) of section 771(9) may, by petition filed with the Commission and with notice to the administering authority, ask for a review of the suspension.

"(2) Commission Investigation.—Upon receipt of a review petition under paragraph (1), the Commission shall, within 75 days after the date on which the petition is filed with it, determine whether the injurious effect of imports of the merchandise which is the subject of the investigation is eliminated completely by the agreement. If the Commission's determination under this subsection is negative, the investigation shall be resumed on the date of publication of notice of such determination as if the affirmative preliminary determination under section 703(b) had been made on that date.

"(3) Suspension of Liquidation to Continue During Review Period.—The suspension of liquidation of entries of the merchandise which is the subject of the investigation shall terminate at the close of the 20-day period beginning on the day after the date on which notice of suspension of the investigation is published in the Federal Register, or, if a review petition is filed under paragraph (1) with respect to the suspension of the investigation, in the case of an affirmative determination by the Commission under paragraph (2), the date on which notice of the affirmative determination by the Commission is published. If the determination of the Commission under paragraph (2) is affirmative, then the administering authority shall—

"(A) terminate the suspension of liquidation under section 703(d)(1), and

"(B) release any bond or other security, and refund any cash deposit, required under section 703(d)(2).

"(i) Violation of Agreement.—

"(1) In General.—If the administering authority determines that an agreement accepted under subsection (b) or (c) is being, or has been, violated, or no longer meets the requirements of such subsection (other than the requirement, under subsection (c)(1), of elimination of injury) and subsection (d), then, on the date of publication of its determination, it shall—

"(A) suspend liquidation under section 703(d)(1) of unliquidated entries of the merchandise made on or after the later of—

"(i) the date which is 90 days before the date of publication of the notice of suspension of liquidation, or

"(ii) the date on which the merchandise, the sale or export to the United States of which was in violation of the agreement, or under an agreement which no longer meets the requirements of subsections (b) and (d) or (c) and (d), was first entered, or withdrawn from warehouse, for consumption,

"(B) if the investigation was not completed, resume the investigation as if its affirmative preliminary determination under section 703(b) were made on the date of its determination under this paragraph,

"(C) if the investigation was completed under subsection (g), issue a countervailing duty order under section 706(a) effective with respect to entries of merchandise the liquidation of which was suspended, and

"(D) notify the petitioner, interested parties who are or were parties to the investigation, and the Commission of its action under this paragraph.

"(2) Intentional Violation to be Punished by Civil Penalty.—Any person who intentionally violates an agreement accepted by the administering authority under subsection (b) or (c) shall be subject to a civil penalty assessed in the same amount, in the same manner, and under the same procedure, as the penalty imposed for a fraudulent violation of section 592(a) of this Act.

"(j) Determination Not to Take Agreement into Account.—In making a final determination under section 705, or in conducting a review under section 751, in a case in which the administering authority has terminated a suspension of investigation under subsection (i)(1), or continued an investigation under subsection (g), the Commission and the administering authority shall consider all of the merchandise which is the subject of the investigation, without regard to the effect of any agreement under subsection (b) or (c).

"Section 705. *Final Determinations.*

"(a) Final Determination by Administering Authority.—

"(1) In General.—Within 75 days after the date of its preliminary determination under section 703(b), the administering authority shall make a final determination of whether or not a subsidy is being provided with respect to the merchandise.

"(2) Critical Circumstances Determinations.—If the final determination of the administering authority is affirmative, then that determination, in any investigation in which the presence of critical circumstances has been alleged under section 703(e), shall also contain a finding as to whether—

"(A) the subsidy is inconsistent with the Agreement, and

"(B) there have been massive imports of the class or kind of merchandise involved over a relatively short period.

"(b) Final Determination by Commission.—

"(1) In General.—The Commission shall make a final determination of whether—

"(A) an industry in the United States—

"(i) is materially injured, or

"(ii) is threatened with material injury, or

"(B) the establishment of an industry in the United States is materially retarded,

by reason of imports of the merchandise with respect to which the administering authority has made an affirmative determination under subsection (a).

"(2) Period for Injury Determination Following Affirmative Preliminary Determination by Administering Authority.—If the preliminary determination by the administering authority under section 703(b) is affirmative, then the Commission shall make the determination required by paragraph (1) before the later of—

"(A) the 120th day after the day on which the administering authority makes its affirmative preliminary determination under section 703(b), or

"(B) the 45th day after the day on which the administering authority makes its affirmative final determination under subsection (a).

"(3) Period for Injury Determination Following Negative Preliminary Determination by Administering Authority.—If the preliminary determination by the administering authority under section 703(b) is negative, and its final determination under subsection (a) is affirmative, then the final determination by the Commission under this subsection shall be made within 75 days after the date of that affirmative final determination.

"(4) Certain Additional Findings.—

"(A) If the finding of the administering authority under subsection (a)(2) is affirmative, then the final determination of the Commission shall include findings as to whether—

"(i) there is material injury which will be difficult to repair, and

"(ii) the material injury was by reason of such massive imports of the subsidized merchandise over a relatively short period.

"(B) If the final determination of the Commission is that there is no material injury but that there is threat of material injury, then its determination shall also include a finding as to whether material injury by reason of imports of the merchandise with respect to which the administering authority has made an affirmative determination under subsection (a) would have been found but for any suspension of liquidation of entries of that merchandise.

"(c) Effect of Final Determinations.—

"(1) Effect of Affirmative Determination by the Administering Authority.—If the determination of the administering authority under subsection (a) is affirmative, then—

"(A) the administering authority shall make available to the Commission all information upon which such determination was based and which the Commission considers relevant to its determination, under such procedures as the administering authority and the Commission may establish to prevent disclosure, other than with the consent of the party providing it or under protective order, of any information to which confidential treatment has been given by the administering authority, and

"(B) in cases where the preliminary determination by the administering authority under section 703(b) was negative, the administering authority shall order under paragraphs (1) and (2) of section 703(d) the suspension of liquidation and the posting of a cash deposit, bond, or other security.

"(2) Issuance of Order; Effect of Negative Determination.—If the determinations of the administering authority and the Commission under subsections (a)(1) and (b)(1) are affirmative, then the administering authority shall issue a countervailing duty order under section 706(a). If either of such determinations is negative, the investigation shall be terminated upon the publication of notice of that negative determination and the administering authority shall—

"(A) terminate the suspension of liquidation under section 703(d)(1), and

"(B) release any bond or other security and refund any cash deposit required under section 703(d)(2).

"(3) Effect of Negative Determinations Under Subsections (a)(2) and (b)(4)(A).—If the determination of the administering authority or the Commission under subsection (a)(2) and (b)(4)(A), respectively, is negative, then the administering authority shall—

"(A) terminate any retroactive suspension of liquidation required under section 703(e)(2), and

"(B) release any bond or other security, and refund any cash deposit required, under section 703(d)(2) with respect to entries of the merchandise the liquidation of which was suspended retroactively under section 703(e)(2).

"(d) Publication of Notice of Determinations.—Whenever the administering authority or the Commission makes a determination under this section, it shall notify the petitioner, other parties to the investigation, and the other agency of its determination and of the facts and conclusions of law upon which the determination is based, and it shall publish notice of its determination in the Federal Register.

Section 706. *Assessment of Duty.*

"(a) Publication of Countervailing Duty Order.—Within 7 days after being notified by the Commission of an affirmative determination under section 705(b), the administering authority shall publish a countervailing duty order which—

"(1) directs customs officers to assess a countervailing duty equal to the amount of the net subsidy determined or estimated to exist, within 6 months after the date on which the administering authority receives satisfactory information upon which the assessment may be based, but in no event later than 12 months after the end of the annual accounting period of the manufacturer or exporter within which the merchandise is entered, or withdrawn from warehouse, for consumption,

"(3) requires the deposit of estimated countervailing duties pending liquidation of entries of merchandise at the same time as estimated normal customs duties on that merchandise are deposited.

"(b) Imposition of Duties.—

"(1) General Rule.—If the Commission, in its final determination under section 705(b), finds material injury or threat of material injury which, but for the suspension of liquidation under section 703(d)(1), would have led to a finding of material injury, then entries of the merchandise subject to the countervailing duty order, the liquidation of which has been suspended under section 703(d)(1), shall be subject to the imposition of countervailing duties under section 701(a).

"(2) Special Rule.—If the Commission, in its final determination under section 705(b), finds threat of material injury, other than threat of material injury described in paragraph (1), or material retardation of the establishment of an industry in the United States, then merchandise subject to a countervailing duty order which is entered, or withdrawn from warehouse, for consumption on or after the date of publication of notice of an affirmative determination of the Commission under section 705(b) shall be subject to the imposition of countervailing duties under section 701(a), and the administering authority shall release any bond or other security, and refund any cash deposit made, to secure the payment of countervailing duties with respect to entries of the merchandise entered, or withdrawn from warehouse, for consumption before that date.

Section 707. *Treatment of Difference between Deposit of Estimated Countervailing Duty and Final Assessed Duty under Countervailing Duty Order.*

"(a) Deposit of Estimated Countervailing Duty Under Section 703(d)(2).—If the amount of a cash deposit, or the amount of any bond or other security, required as security for an estimated countervailing duty under section 703(d)(2) is different from the amount of the countervailing duty determined under a countervailing duty order issued under section 706, then the difference for entries of merchandise entered, or withdrawn from warehouse, for consumption before notice of the affirmative determination of the Commission under section 705(b) is published shall be—

"(1) disregarded, to the extent that the cash deposit, bond, or other security is lower than the duty under the order, or

"(2) refunded or released, to the extent that the cash deposit, bond, or other security is higher than the duty under the order.

"(b) Deposit of Estimated Countervailing Duty Under Section 706(a)(3).—If the amount of an estimated countervailing duty deposited under section 706(a)(3) is different from the amount of the countervailing duty determined under a countervailing duty order issued under section 706, then the difference for entries of merchandise entered, or withdrawn from warehouse, for consumption after notice of the affirmative determination of the Commission under section 705(b) is published shall be—

"(1) collected, to the extent that the deposit under section 706(a)(3) is lower than the duty determined under the order, or

"(2) refunded, to the extent that the deposit under section 706(a)(3) is higher than the duty determined under the order, together with interest as provided by section 778.

"Subtitle B—Imposition of Antidumping Duties

Section 731. *Antidumping Duties Imposed.*

"If—

"(1) the administering authority determines that a class or kind of foreign merchandise is being, or is likely to be, sold in the United States at less than its fair value, and

"(2) the Commission determines that—

"(A) an industry in the United States—

"(i) is materially injured, or

"(ii) is threatened with material injury, or

"(B) the establishment of an industry in the United States is materially retarded,

by reason of imports of that merchandise,

then there shall be imposed upon such merchandise an antidumping duty, in addition to any other duty imposed, in an amount equal to the amount by which the foreign market value exceeds the United States price for the merchandise.

Section 732. *Procedures for Initiating an Antidumping Duty Investigation.*

"(a) Initiation by Administering Authority.—An antidumping duty investigation shall be commenced whenever the administering authority determines, from information available to it, that a formal investigation is warranted into the question of whether the elements necessary for the imposition of a duty under section 731 exist.

"(b) Initiation by Petition.—

"(1) Petition Requirements.—An antidumping proceeding shall be commenced whenever an interested party described in subparagraph (C), (D), or (E) of section 771(9) files a petition with the administering authority, on behalf of an industry, which alleges the elements necessary for the imposition of the duty imposed by section 731, and which is accompanied by information reasonably available to the petitioner supporting those allegations. The petition may be amended at such time, and upon such conditions, as the administering authority and the Commission may permit.

"(2) Simultaneous Filing with Commission.—The petitioner shall file a copy of the petition with the Commission on the same day as it is filed with the administering authority.

"(c) Petition Determination.—Within 20 days after the date on which a petition is filed under subsection (b), the administering authority shall—

"(1) determine whether the petition alleges the elements necessary for the imposition of a duty under section 731 and contains information reasonably available to the petitioner supporting the allegations,

"(2) if the determination is affirmative, commence an investigation to determine whether the class or kind of merchandise described in the petition is being, or is likely to be, sold in the United States at less than its fair value, and provide for the publication of notice of the determination in the Federal Register, and

"(3) if the determination is negative, dismiss the petition, terminate the proceeding, notify the petitioner in writing of the reasons for the determination, and provide for the publication of notice of the determination in the Federal Register.

"(d) Notification to Commission of Determination.—The administering authority shall—

"(1) notify the Commission immediately of any determination it makes under subsection (a) or (c), and

"(2) if the determination is affirmative, make available to the Commission such information as it may have relating to the matter under investigation, under such procedures as the administering authority and the Commission may establish to prevent disclosure, other than with the consent of the party providing it or under protective order, of any information to which confidential treatment has been given by the administering authority.

Section 733. *Preliminary Determinations.*

"(a) Determination by Commission of Reasonable Indication of Injury.—Except in the case of a petition dismissed by the administering authority under section 732(c)(3), the Commission, within 45 days after the date on which a petition is filed under section 732(b) or on which it receives notice from the administering authority of an investigation commenced under section 732(a), shall make a determination, based upon the best information available to it at the time of the determination, of whether there is a reasonable indication that—

"(1) an industry in the United States—

"(A) is materially injured, or

"(B) is threatened with material injury, or

"(2) the establishment of an industry in the United States is materially retarded,

by reason of imports of the merchandise which is the subject of the investigation by the administering authority. If that determination is negative, the investigation shall be terminated.

"(b) Preliminary Determination by Administering Authority.—

"(1) Period of Antidumping Duty Investigation.—Within 160 days after the date on which a petition is filed under section 732(b), or an investigation is commenced under section 732(a), but not before an affirmative determination by the Commission under subsection (a) of this section, the administering authority shall make a determination, based upon the best information available to it at the time of the determination, of whether there is a reasonable basis to believe or suspect that the merchandise is being sold, or is likely to be sold at less than fair value. If the determination of the administering authority under this subsection is affirmative, the determination shall include the estimated average amount by which the foreign market value exceeds the United States price.

"(2) Preliminary Determination Under Waiver of Verification.—Within 75 days after the initiation of an investigation, the administering authority shall cause an official designated for such purpose to review the information concerning the case received during the first 60 days of the investigation, and, if there appears to be sufficient information available upon which the preliminary determination can reasonably be based, to disclose to the petitioner and any interested party, then a party to the proceedings that requests such disclosure, all available nonconfidential information and all other information which is disclosed pursuant to section 777. Within 3 days (not counting Saturdays, Sundays, or legal public holidays) after such disclosure, the petitioner and each party which is an interested party described in subparagraph (C), (D), or (E) of section 771(9) to whom such disclosure was made may furnish to the administering authority an irrevocable written waiver of verification of the information received by the authority, and an agreement that it is willing to have a preliminary determination made on the basis of the record then available to the authority. If a timely waiver and agreement have been received from the petitioner and each party which is an interested party described in subparagraph (C), (D), or (E) of section 771(9) to whom the disclosure was made, and the authority finds that sufficient information is then available upon which the preliminary determination can reasonably be based, a preliminary determination shall be made within 90 days after the commencement of the investigation on the basis of the record established during the first 60 days after the investigation was commenced.

"(c) Extension of Period in Extraordinarily Complicated Cases.—

"(1) In general.—If—

"(A) The petitioner makes a timely request for an extension of the period within which the determination must be made under subsection (b)(1), or

"(B) the administering authority concludes that the parties concerned are cooperating and determines that—

"(i) the case is extraordinarily complicated by reason of—

"(I) the number and complexity of the transactions to be investigated or adjustments to be considered,

"(II) the novelty of the issues presented, or

"(III) the number of firms whose activities must be investigated, and

"(ii) additional time is necessary to make the preliminary determination, then the administering authority may postpone making the preliminary determination under subsection (b)(1)until not later than the 210th day after the date on which a petition is filed under section 732(b), or an investigation is commenced under section 732(a).

"(2) Notice of Postponement.—The administering authority shall notify the parties to the investigation, not later than 20 days before the date on which the preliminary determination would otherwise be required under subsection (b)(1), if it intends to postpone making the preliminary determination under paragraph (1). The notification shall include an explanation of the reasons for the postponement, and notice of the postponement shall be published in the Federal Register.

"(d) Effect of Determination by the Administering Authority.—If the preliminary determination of the administering authority under subsection (b) is affirmative, the administering authority—

"(1) shall order the suspension of liquidation of all entries of merchandise subject to the determination which are entered, or withdrawn from warehouse, for consumption on or after the date of publication of the notice of the determination in the Federal Register,

"(2) shall order the posting of a cash deposit, bond, or other security, as it deems appropriate, for each entry of the merchandise concerned equal to the estimated average amount by which the foreign market value exceeds the United States price, and

"(3) shall make available to the Commission all information upon which such determination was based and which the Commission considers relevant to its injury determination, under such procedures as the administering authority and the Commission may establish to prevent disclosure, other than with the consent of the party providing it or under protective order, of any information to which confidential treatment has been given by the administering authority.

"(e) Critical Circumstances Determinations.—

"(1) In General.—If a petitioner alleges critical circumstances in its original petition, or by amendment at any time more than 20 days before the date of a final determination by the administering authority, then the administering authority shall promptly determine, on the basis of the best information available to it at that time, whether there is a reasonable basis to believe or suspect that—

"(A)(i) there is a history of dumping in the United States or elsewhere of the class or kind of the merchandise which is the subject of the investigation, or

"(ii) the person by whom, or for whose account, the merchandise was imported knew or should have known that the exporter was selling the merchandise which is the subject of the investigation at less than its fair value, and

"(B) there have been massive imports of the class or kind of merchandise which is the subject of the investigation over a relatively short period.

"(2) Suspension of Liquidation.—If the determination of the administering authority under paragraph (1) is affirmative, then any suspension of liquidation ordered under subsection (d)(1) shall apply, or, if notice of such suspension of liquidation is already published, be amended to apply, to unliquidated entries of merchandise entered, or withdrawn from warehouse, for consumption on or after the date which is 90 days before the date on which suspension of liquidation was first ordered.

"(f) Notice of Determinations.—Whenever the Commission or the administering authority makes a determination under this section, it shall notify the petitioner, other parties to the investigation, and the other agency of its determination and of the facts and conclusions of law upon which the determination is based, and it shall publish notice of its determination in the Federal Register.

Section 734. *Termination or Suspension of Investigation.*

"(a) Termination of Investigation on Withdrawal of Petition.—An investigation under this subtitle may be terminated by either the administering authority or the Commission after notice to all parties to the investigation, upon withdrawal of the petition by the petitioner. The Commission may not terminate an investigation under the preceding sentence before a preliminary determination is made by the administering authority under section 733(b).

"(b) Agreements to Eliminate Completely Sales at Less Than Fair Value or To Cease Exports of Merchandise.—The administering authority may suspend an investigation if the exporters of the merchandise which is the subject of the investigation who account for substantially all of the imports of that merchandise agree—

"(1) to cease exports of the merchandise to the United States within 6 months after the date on which the investigation is suspended, or

"(2) to revise their prices to eliminate completely any amount by which the foreign market value of the merchandise which is the subject of the agreement exceeds the United States price of that merchandise.

"(c) Agreements Eliminating Injurious Effect.—

"(1) General Rule.—If the administering authority determines that extraordinary circumstances are present in a case, it may suspend an investigation upon the acceptance of an agreement to revise prices from exporters of the merchandise which is the subject of the investigation who account for substantially all of the imports of that merchandise into the United States, if the agreement will eliminate completely the injurious effect of export to the United States of that merchandise and if—

"(A) the suppression or undercutting of price levels of domestic products by imports of that merchandise will be prevented, and

"(B) for each entry of each exporter the amount by which the estimated foreign market value exceeds the United States price will not exceed 15 percent of the weighted average amount by which the estimated foreign market value exceeded the United States price for all less-than-fair-value entries of the exporter examined during the course of the investigation.

"(2) Definition of Extraordinary Circumstances.—

"(A) Extraordinary circumstances.—For purposes of this subsection, the term 'extraordinary circumstances' means circumstances in which—

"(i) suspension of an investigation will be more beneficial to the domestic industry than continuation of the investigation, and

"(ii) the investigation is complex.

"(B) Complex.—For purposes of this paragraph, the term 'complex' means—

"(i) there are a large number of transactions to be investigated or adjustments to be considered,

"(ii) the issues raised are novel, or

"(iii) the number of firms involved is large.

"(d) Additional Rules and Conditions.—

"(1) Public Interest; Monitoring.—The administering authority shall not accept an agreement under subsection (b) or (c) unless—

"(A) it is satisfied that suspension of the investigation is in the public interest, and

"(B) effective monitoring of the agreement by the United States is practicable.

"(2) Exports of Merchandise to United States Not to Increase During Interim Period.—The administering authority may not accept any agreement under subsection (b)(1) unless that agreement provides a means of ensuring that the quantity of the merchandise covered by the agreement exported to the United States during the period provided for cessation of exports does not exceed the quantity of such merchandise exported to the United States during the most recent representative period determined by the administering authority.

"(e) Suspension of Investigation Procedure.—Before an investigation may be suspended under subsection (b) or (c) the administering authority shall—

"(1) notify the petitioner of, and consult with the petitioner concerning, its intention to suspend the investigation, and notify other parties to the investigation and the Commission not less than 30 days before the date on which it suspends the investigation,

"(2) provide a copy of the proposed agreement to the petitioner at the time of the notification, together with an explanation of how the agreement will be carried out and enforced, and of how the agreement will meet the requirements of subsections (b) and (d) or (c) and (d), and

"(3) permit all parties to the investigation to submit comments and information for the record before the date on which notice of suspension of the investigation is published under subsection (f)(1)(A).

"(f) Effects of Suspension of Investigation.—

"(1) In General.—If the administering authority determines to suspend an investigation upon acceptance of an agreement described in subsection (b) or (c), then—

"(A) it shall suspend the investigation, publish notice of suspension of the investigation, and issue an affirmative preliminary determination under section 733(b) with respect to the merchandise which is the subject of the investigation, unless it has previously issued such a determination in the same investigation,

"(B) the Commission shall suspend any investigation it is conducting with respect to that merchandise, and

"(C) the suspension of investigation shall take effect on the day on which such notice is published.

"(2) Liquidation of Entries.—

"(A) Cessation of Exports; Complete Elimination of Dumping Margin.—If the agreement accepted by the administering authority is an agreement described in subsection (b), then—

"(i) notwithstanding the affirmative preliminary determination required under paragraph (1)(A), the liquidation of entries of merchandise which is the subject of the investigation shall not be suspended under section 733(d)(1),

"(ii) if the liquidation of entries of such merchandise was suspended pursuant to a previous affirmative preliminary determination in the same case with respect to such merchandise, that suspension of liquidation shall terminate, and

"(iii) the administering authority shall refund any cash deposit and release any bond or other security deposited under section 733(d)(2).

"(B) Other Agreements.—If the agreement accepted by the administering authority is an agreement described in subsection (c), the liquidation of entries of the merchandise subject to the investigation shall be suspended under section 733(d)(1), or, if the liquidation of entries of such merchandise was suspended pursuant to a previous affirmative preliminary determination in the same case, that suspension of liquidation shall continue in effect, subject to subsection (h)(3), but the security required under section 733(d)(2) may be adjusted to reflect the effect of the agreement.

"(3) Where Investigation Is Continued.—If, pursuant to subsection (g), the administering authority and the Commission continue an investigation in which an agreement has been accepted under subsection (b) or (c), then—

"(A) if the final determination by the administering authority or the Commission under section 735 is negative, the agreement shall have no force or effect and the investigation shall be terminated, or

"(B) if the final determinations by the administering authority and the Commission under such section are affirmative, the agreement shall remain in force, but the administering authority shall not issue an antidumping duty order in the case so long as—

"(i) the agreement remains in force,

"(ii) the agreement continues to meet the requirements of subsections (b) and (d), or (c) and (d), and

"(iii) the parties to the agreement carry out their obligations under the agreement in accordance with its terms.

"(g) Investigation To Be Continued Upon Request.—If the administering authority, within 20 days after the date of publication of the notice of suspension of an investigation, receives a request for the continuation of the investigation from—

"(1) an exporter or exporters accounting for a significant proportion of exports to the United States of the merchandise which is the subject of the investigation, or

"(2) an interested party described in subparagraph (C), (D), or (E) of section 771(9) which is a party to the investigation, then the administering authority and the Commission shall continue the investigation.

"(h) Review of Suspension.—

"(1) In General.—Within 20 days after the suspension of an investigation under subsection (c), an interested party which is a party to the investigation and which is described in subparagraph (C), (D,) or (E) of section 771(9) may, by petition filed with the Commission and with notice to the administering authority, ask for a review of the suspension.

"(2) Commission Investigation.—Upon receipt of a review petition under paragraph (1), the Commission shall, within 75 days after the date on which the petition is filed with it, determine whether the injurious effect of imports of the merchandise which is the subject of the investigation is eliminated completely by the agreement. If the Commission's determination under this subsection is negative, the investigation shall be resumed on the date of publication of notice of such determination as if the affirmative preliminary determination under section 733(b) had been made on that date.

"(3) Suspension of Liquidation to Continue During Review Period.—The suspension of liquidation of entries of the merchandise which is the subject of the investigation shall terminate at the close of the 20-day period beginning on the day after the date on which notice of suspension of the investigation is published in the Federal Register, or, if a review petition is filed under paragraph (1) with respect to the suspension of the investigation, in the case of an affirmative determination by the Commission under paragraph (2), the date on which notice of an affirmative determination by the Commission is published. If the determination of the Commission under paragraph (2) is affirmative, then the administering authority shall—

"(A) terminate the suspension of liquidation under section 733(d)(1), and

"(B) release any bond or other security, and refund any cash deposit, required under section 733(d)(2).

"(i) Violation of Agreement.—

"(1) In General.—If the administering authority determines that an agreement accepted under subsection (b) or (c) is being, or has been, violated, or no longer meets the requirements of such subsection (other than the requirement, under subsection (c)(1) of elimination of injury) and subsection (d), then, on the date of publication of its determination, it shall—

"(A) suspend liquidation under section 733(d)(1) of unliquidated entries of the merchandise made on the later of—

"(i) the date which is 90 days before the date of publication of the notice of suspension of liquidation, or

"(ii) the date on which the merchandise, the sale or export to the United States of which was in violation of the agreement, or under an agreement which no longer meets the requirements of subsections (b) and (d), or (c) and (d), was first entered, or withdrawn from warehouse, for consumption,

"(B) if the investigation was not completed, resume the investigation as if its affirmative preliminary determination were made on the date of its determination under this paragraph,

"(C) if the investigation was completed under subsection (g), issue an antidumping duty order under section 736(a) effective with respect to entries of merchandise liquidation of which was suspended, and

"(D) notify the petitioner, interested parties who are or were parties to the investigation, and the Commission of its action under this paragraph.

"(2) Intentional Violation to be Punished by Civil Penalty—Any person who intentionally violates an agreement accepted by the administering authority under subsection (b) or (c) shall be subject to a civil penalty assessed in the same amount, in the same manner, and under the same procedures, as the penalty imposed for a fraudulent violation of section 592(a) of this Act.

"(j) Determination Not To Take Agreement Into Account.—In making a final determination under section 735, or in conducting a review under section 751, in a case in which the administering authority has terminated a suspension of investigation under subsection (i)(1), or continued an investigation under subsection (g), the Commission and the administering authority shall consider all of the merchandise which is the subject of the investigation without regard to the effect of any agreement under subsection (b) or (c).

Section 735. *Final Determinations.*

"(a) Final Determination by Administering Authority.—

"(1) General rule.—Within 75 days after the date of its preliminary determination under section 733(b), the administering authority shall make a final determination of whether the merchandise which was the subject of the investigation is being or is likely to be, sold in the United States at less than its fair value.

"(2) Extention of period for determination.—The administering authority may postpone making the final determination under paragraph (1) until not later than the 135th day after the date on which it published notice of its preliminary determination under section 733(b) if a request in writing for such a postponement is made by—

"(A) exporters who account for a significant proportion of exports of the merchandise which is the subject of the investigation, in a proceeding in which the preliminary determination by the administering authority under section 733(b) was affirmative, or

"(B) the petitioner, in a proceeding in which the preliminary determination by the administering authority under section 733(b) was negative.

"(3) Critical circumstances determinations.—If the final determination of the administering authority is affirmative, then that determination, in any investigation in which the presence of critical circumstances has been alleged under section 733(e), shall also contain a finding of whether—

"(A)(i) there is a history of dumping in the United States or elsewhere of the class or kind of merchandise which is the subject of the investigation, or

"(ii) the person by whom, or for whose account, the merchandise was imported knew or should have known that the exporter was selling the merchandise which is the subject of the investigation at less than its fair value, and

"(B) there have been massive imports of the merchandise which is the subject of the investigation over a relatively short period.

"(b) Final Determination by Commission.—

"(1) In general.—The Commission shall make a final determination of whether—

"(A) an industry in the United States—

"(i) is materially injured, or

"(ii) is threatened with material injury, or

"(B) the establishment of an industry in the United States is materially retarded,

by reason of imports of the merchandise with respect to which the administering authority has made an affirmative determination under subsection (a)(1).

"(2) Period for injury determination following affirmative preliminary determination by administering authority.—If the preliminary determination by the administering authority under section 733(b) is affirmative, then the Commission shall make the determination required by paragraph (1) before the later of—

"(A) the 120th day after the day on which the administering authority makes its affirmative preliminary determination under section 733(b), or

"(B) the 45th day after the day on which the administering authority makes its affirmative final determination under subsection (a).

"(3) Period for injury determination following negative preliminary determination by administering authority.—If the preliminary determination by the administering authority under section 733(b) is negative, and its final determination under subsection (a) is affirmative, then the final determination by the Commission under this subsection shall be made within 75 days after the date of that affirmative final determination.

"(4) Certain additional findings.—

"(A) If the finding of the administering authority under subsection (a)(2) is affirmative, then the final determination of the Commission shall include a finding as to whether the material injury is by reason of massive imports described in subsection (a)(3) to an extent that, in order to prevent such material injury from recurring, it is necessary to impose the duty imposed by section 731 retroactively on those imports.

"(B) If the final determination of the Commission is that there is no material injury but that there is threat of material injury, then its determination shall also include a finding as to whether material injury by reason of the imports of the merchandise with respect to which the administering authority has made an affirmative determination under subsection (a) would have been found but for any suspension of liquidation of entries of the merchandise.

"(c) Effect of Final Determinations.—

"(1) Effect of affirmative determination by the administering authority.—If the determination of the administering authority under subsection (a) is affirmative, then—

"(A) the administering authority shall make available to the Commission all information upon which such determination was based and which the Commission considers relevant to its determination, under such procedures as the administering authority and the Commission may establish to prevent disclosure, other than with the consent of the party providing it or under protective order, of any information as to which confidential treatment has been given by the administering authority, and

"(B) in cases where the preliminary determination by the administering authority under section 733(b) was negative, the administering authority shall order under paragraphs (1) and (2) of section 733(d) the suspension of liquidation and the posting of a cash deposit, bond, or other security.

"(2) Issuance of order; effect of negative determination.—If the determinations of the administering authority and the Commission under subsections (a)(1) and (b)(1) are affirmative, then the administering authority shall issue an antidumping duty order under section 736(a). If either of such determinations is negative, the investigation shall be terminated upon the publication of notice of that negative determination and the administering authority shall—

"(A) terminate the suspension of liquidation under section 703(d)(1), and

"(B) release any bond or other security, and refund any cash deposit, required under section 733(d)(2).

"(3) Effect of negative determinations under subsections (a)(3) and (b)(4)(A).— If the determination of the administering authority or the Commission under subsection (a)(3) or (b)(4)(A), respectively, is negative, then the administering authority shall—

"(A) terminate any retroactive suspension of liquidation required under section 733(e)(2, and

"(B) release any bond or other security, and refund any cash deposit required, under section 733(d)(2) with respect to entries of the merchandise the liquidation of which was suspended retroactively under section 733(e)(2).

"(d) Publication of Notice of Determinations.—Whenever the administering authority or the Commission makes a determination under this section, it shall notify the petitioner, other parties to the investigation, and the other agency of its determination and of the facts and conclusions of law upon which the determination is based, and it shall publish notice of its determination in the Federal Register.

Section 736. *Assessment of Duty.*

"(a) Publication of Antidumping Duty Order.—Within 7 days after being notified by the Commission of an affirmative determination under section 735(b), the administering authority shall publish an antidumping duty order which—

"(1) directs customs officers to assess an antidumping duty equal to the amount by which the foreign market value of the merchandise exceeds the United States price of the merchandise, within 6 months after the date on which the administering authority receives satisfactory information upon which the assessment may be based, but in no event later than—

"(A) 12 months after the end of the annual accounting period of the manufacturer or exporter within which the merchandise is entered, or withdrawn from warehouse, for consumption, or

"(B) in the case of merchandise not sold prior to its importation into the United States, 12 months after the end of the annual accounting period of the manufacturer or exporter within which it is sold in the United States to a person who is not the exporter of that merchandise,

"(2) includes a description of the class or kind of merchandise to which it applies, in such detail as the administering authority deems necessary, and

"(3) requires the deposit of estimated antidumping duties pending liquidation of entries of merchandise at the same time as estimated normal customs duties on that merchandise are deposited.

"(b) Imposition of Duty.—

"(1) General rule.—If the Commission, in its final determination under section 735(b), finds material injury or threat of material injury which, but for the suspension of liquidation under section 733(d)(1) would have led to a finding of material injury, then entries of the merchandise subject to the antidumping duty order, the liquidation of which has been suspended under section 733(d)(1), shall be subject to the imposition of antidumping duties under section 731.

"(2) Special rule.—If the Commission, in its final determination under section 735(b), finds threat of material injury, other than threat of material injury described in paragraph (1), or material retardation of the establishment of an industry in the United States, then merchandise subject to an antidumping duty order which is entered, or withdrawn from warehouse, for consumption on or after the date of publication of notice of an affirmative determination of the Commission under section 735(b) shall be subject to the assessment of antidumping duties under section 731, and the administering authority shall release any bond or other security, and refund any cash deposit made, to secure the payment of antidumping duties with respect to entries of the merchandise entered, or withdrawn from warehouse, for consumption before that date.

"(c) Security in Lieu of Estimated Duty Pending Early Determination of Duty.—

"(1) Conditions for waiver of deposit of estimated duties.—The administering authority may permit, for not more than 90 days after the date of publication of an order under subsection (a), the posting of a bond or other security in lieu of the deposit of estimated antidumping duties required under subsection (a)(3) if, on the basis of information presented to it by any manufacturer, producer, or exporter in such form and within such time as it may require, it is satisfied that it will be able to determine, within 90 days after the date of publication of an order under subsection (a), the foreign market value and the United States price for all merchandise of such manufacturer, producer, or exporter described in that order which was entered, or withdrawn from warehouse, for consumption on or after the date of publication of—

"(A) an affirmative preliminary determination by the administering authority under section 733(b), or

"(B) if its determination under section 733(b) was negative, an affirmative final determination by the administering authority under section 735(a),

and before the date of publication of the affirmative final determination by the Commission under section 735(b).

"(2) Notice; hearing.—If the administering authority permits the posting of a bond or other security in lieu of the deposit of estimated antidumping duties under paragraph (1), it shall—

"(A) publish notice of its action in the Federal Register, and

"(B) upon the request of any interested party, hold a hearing in accordance with section 774 before determining the foreign market value and the United States price of the merchandise.

"(3) Determinations to be basis of antidumping duty.—The administering authority shall publish notice in the Federal Register of the results of its determination of foreign market value and United States price, and that determination shall be the basis for the assessment of antidumping duties on entries of merchandise to which the notice under this subsection applies and also shall be the basis for the deposit of estimated antidumping duties on future entries of merchandise of manufacturers, producers, or exporters described in paragraph (1) to which the order issued under subsection (a) applies.

Section 737. *Treatment of Difference between Deposit of Estimated Antidumping Duty and Final Assessed Duty Under Antidumping Duty Order.*

"(a) Deposit of Estimated Antidumping Duty Under Section 733(d)(2).—If the amount of a cash deposit collected as security for an estimated antidumping duty under section 733(d)(2) is different from the amount of the antidumping duty determined under an antidumping duty order published under section 736, then the difference for entries of merchandise entered, or withdrawn from warehouse, for consumption before notice of the affirmative determination of the Commission under section 735(b) is published shall be—

"(1) disregarded, to the extent the cash deposit collected is lower than the duty under the order, or

"(2) refunded, to the extent the cash deposit is higher than the duty under the order.

"(b) Deposit of Estimated Antidumping Duty Under Section 736(a)(3).—If the amount of an estimated antidumping duty deposited under section 736(a)(3) is different from the amount of the antidumping duty determined under an antidumping duty order published under section 736, then the difference for entries of merchandise entered, or withdrawn from warehouse, for consumption after notice of the affirmative determination of the Commission under section 735 (b) is published shall be—

"(1) collected, to the extent that the deposit under section 736(a)(3) is lower than the duty determined under the order, or

"(2) refunded, to the extent that the deposit under section 736(a)(3) is higher than the duty determined under the order, together with interest as provided by section 778.

Section 738. *Conditional Payment of Antidumping Duty.*

"(a) General Rule.—For all entries, or withdrawals from warehouse, for consumption of merchandise subject to an antidumping duty order on or after the date of publication of such order, no customs officer may deliver merchandise of that class or kind to the person by whom or for whose account it was imported unless that person complies with the requirements of subsection (b) and deposits with the appropriate customs officer an estimated antidumping duty in an amount determined by the administering authority.

"(b) Importer Requirements.—In order to meet the requirements of this subsection, a person shall—

"(1) furnish, or arrange to have furnished, to the appropriate customs officer such information as the administering authority deems necessary for determining the United States price of the merchandise imported by or for the account of that person, and such other information as the administering authority deems necessary for ascertaining any antidumping duty to be imposed under this title;

"(2) maintain and furnish to the customs officer such records concerning the sale of the merchandise as the administering authority, by regulation, requires;

"(3) state under oath before the customs officer that he is not an exporter, or if he is an exporter, declare under oath at the time of entry the exporter's sales price of the merchandise to the customs officer if it is then known, or, if not, so declare within 30 days after the merchandise has been sold, or has been made the subject of an agreement to be sold, in the United States; and

"(4) pay, or agree to pay on demand, to the customs officer the amount of antidumping duty imposed under section 731 on that merchandise.

Section 739. *Duties of Customs Officers.*

"In the case of all imported merchandise or a class or kind as to which the administering authority has published an antidumping duty order under section 736 under which entries have not been liquidated, the appropriate customs officer shall, by all reasonable ways and means and consistently with the provisions of this title, ascertain and determine, or estimate, the foreign market value, the United States price, and any other information which the administering authority deems necessary for the purposes of administering this title.

Section 740. *Antidumping Duty Treated as Regular Duty for Draw-Back Purposes.*

"The antidumping duty imposed by section 731 shall be treated in all respects as a normal customs duty for the purpose of any law relating to the drawback of customs duties.

"Subtitle C—Review of Determinations

Section 751. *Administrative Review of Determinations.*

"(a) Periodic Review of Amount of Duty.—

"(1) In General.—At least once during each 12-month period beginning on the anniversary of the date of publication of a countervailing duty order under this title or under section 303 of this Act, an antidumping duty order under this title or a finding under the Antidumping Act, 1921, or a notice of the suspension of an investigation, the administering authority, after publication of notice of such review in the Federal Register, shall—

"(A) review and determine the amount of any net subsidy,

"(B) review, and determine (in accordance with paragraph (2)), the amount of any antidumping duty, and

"(C) review the current status of, and compliance with, any agreement by reason of which an investigation was suspended, and review the amount of any net subsidy or margin of sales at less than fair value involved in the agreement,

and shall publish the results of such review, together with notice of any duty to be assessed, estimated duty to be deposited, or investigation to be resumed in the Federal Register.

"(2) Determination of Antidumping Duties.—For the purpose of paragraph (1)(B), the administering authority shall determine—

"(A) the foreign market value and United States price of each entry of merchandise subject to the antidumping duty order and included within that determination, and

"(B) the amount, if any, by which the foreign market value of each such entry exceeds the United States price of the entry.

The administering authority, without revealing confidential information, shall publish notice of the results of the determination of antidumping duties in the Federal Register, and that determination shall be the basis for the assessment of antidumping duties on entries of the merchandise included within the determination and for deposits of estimated duties.

"(b) Reviews Upon Information or Request.—

"(1) In General.—Whenever the administering authority or the Commission receives information concerning, or a request for the review of, an agreement accepted under section 704 or 734 or an affirmative determination made under section 704(h)(2), 705(a), 705(b), 734(h)(2), 735(a), or 735(b), which shows changed circumstances sufficient to warrant a review of such determination, it shall conduct such a review after publishing notice of the review in the Federal Register. In reviewing its determination under section 704(h)(2) or 734(h)(2), the Commission shall consider whether, in the light of changed circumstances, an agreement accepted under section 704(c) or 734(c) continues to eliminate completely the injurious effects of imports of the merchandise.

"(2) Limitation on period for review.—In the absence of good cause shown—

"(A) the Commission may not review a determination under section 705(b) or 735(b), and

"(B) the administering authority may not review a determination under section 705(a) or 735(a), or the suspension of an investigation suspended under section 704 or 734,

less than 24 months after the date of publication of notice of that determination or suspension.

"(c) Revocation of Countervailing Duty Order or Antidumping Duty Order.— The administering authority may revoke, in whole or in part, a countervailing duty order or an antidumping duty order, or terminate a suspended investigation, after review under this section. Any such revocation or termination shall apply with respect to unliquidated entries of merchandise entered, or withdrawn from warehouse, for consumption on and after a date determined by the administering authority.

"(d) Hearings.—Whenever the administering authority or the Commission conducts a review under this section it shall, upon the request of any interested party, hold a hearing in accordance with section 774(b) in connection with that review.

"(e) Determination That Basis for Suspension No Longer Exists.—If the determination of the Commission under the last sentence of subsection (b)(1) is negative, the agreement shall be treated as not accepted, beginning on the date of the publication of the Commission's determination, and the administering authority and the Commission shall proceed, under section 704(i) or 734(i), as if the agreement had been violated on that date, except that no duty under any order subsequently issued shall be assessed on merchandise entered, or withdrawn from warehouse, for consumption before that date.

"Subtitle D—General Provisions

"Section 771. *Definitions; Special Rules.*

"For purposes of this title—

"(1) Administering Authority.—The term 'administering authority' means the Secretary of the Treasury, or any other officer of the United States to whom the responsibility for carrying out the duties of the administering authority under this title are transferred by law.

"(2) Commission.—The term 'Commission' means the United States International Trade Commission.

"(3) Country.—The term 'country' means a foreign country, a political subdivision, dependent territory, or possession of a foreign country, and, except for the purpose of antidumping proceedings, may include an association of 2 or more foreign countries, political subdivisions, dependent territories, or possessions of countries into a customs union outside the United States.

"(4) Industry.—

"(A) In general.—The term 'industry' means the domestic producers as a whole of a like product, or those producers whose collective output of the like product constitutes a major proportion of the total domestic production of that product.

"(B) Related parties.—When some producers are related to the exporters or importers, or are themselves importers of the allegedly subsidized or dumped merchandise, the term 'industry' may be applied in appropriate circumstances by excluding such producers from those included in that industry.

"(C) Regional industries.—In appropriate circumstances, the United States, for a particular product market, may be divided into 2 or more markets and the producers within each market may be treated as if they were a separate industry if—

"(i) the producers within such market sell all or almost all of their production of the like product in question in that market, and

"(ii) the demand in that market is not supplied, to any substantial degree, by producers of the product in question located elsewhere in the United States.

In such appropriate circumstances, material injury, the threat of material injury, or material retardation of the establishment of an industry may be found to exist with respect to an industry even if the domestic industry as a whole, or those producers whose collective output of a like product constitutes a major proportion of the total domestic production of that product, is not injured, if there is a concentration of subsidized or dumped imports into such an isolated market and if the producers of all, or almost all, of the production within that market are being materially injured or threatened by material injury, or if the establishment of an industry is being materially retarded, by reason of the subsidized or dumped imports.

"(D) Product lines.—The effect of subsidized or dumped imports shall be assessed in relation to the United States production of a like product if available data permit the separate identification of production in terms of such criteria as the production process or the producer's profits. If the domestic production of the like product has no separate identity in terms of such criteria, then the effect of the subsidized or dumped imports shall be assessed by the examination of the production of the narrowest group or range of products, which includes a like product, for which the necessary information can be provided.

"(5) Subsidy.—The term 'subsidy' has the same meaning as the term 'bounty or grant' as that term is used in section 303 of this Act, and includes, but is not limited to, the following:

"(A) Any export subsidy described in Annex A to the Agreement (relating to illustrative list of export subsidies).

"(B) The following domestic subsidies, if provided or required by government action to a specific enterprise or industry, or group of enterprises or industries, whether publicly or privately owned, and whether paid or bestowed directly or indirectly on the manufacture, production, or export of any class or kind of merchandise:

"(i) The provision of capital, loans, or loan guarantees on terms inconsistent with commercial considerations.

"(ii) The provision of goods or services at preferential rates.

"(iii) The grant of funds or forgiveness of debt to cover operating losses sustained by a specific industry.

"(iv) The assumption of any costs or expenses of manufacture, production, or distribution.

"(6) Net subsidy.—For the purpose of determining the net subsidy, the administering authority may subtract from the gross subsidy the amount of—

"(A) any application fee, deposit, or similar payment paid in order to qualify for, or to receive, the benefit of the subsidy,

"(B) any loss in the value of the subsidy resulting from its deferred receipt, if the deferral is mandated by Government order, and

"(C) export taxes, duties, or other charges levied on the export of merchandise to the United States specifically intended to offset the subsidy received.

"(7) Material injury.—

"(A) In general.—The term 'material injury' means harm which is not inconsequential, immaterial, or unimportant.

"(B) Volume and consequent impact.—In making its determinations under sections 703(a), 705(b), 733(a), and 735(b), the Commission shall consider, among other factors—

"(i) the volume of imports of the merchandise which is the subject of the investigation,

"(ii) the effect of imports of that merchandise on prices in the United States for like products, and

"(iii) the impact of imports of such merchandise on domestic producers of like products.

"(C) Evaluation of volume and of price effects.—For purposes of subparagraph (B)—

"(i) Volume.—In evaluating the volume of imports of merchandise, the Commission shall consider whether the volume of imports of the merchandise, or any increase in that volume, either in absolute terms or relative to production or consumption in the United States, is significant.

"(ii) Price.—In evaluating the effect of imports of such merchandise on prices, the Commission shall consider whether—

"(I) there has been significant price undercutting by the imported merchandise as compared with the price of like products of the United States, and

"(II) the effect of imports of such merchandise otherwise depresses prices to a significant degree or prevents price increases, which otherwise would have occurred, to a significant degree.

"(iii) Impact on affected industry.—In examining the impact on the affected industry, the Commission shall evaluate all relevant economic factors which have a bearing on the state of the industry, including, but not limited to—

"(I) actual and potential decline in output, sales, market share, profits, productivity, return on investments, and utilization of capacity,

"(II) factors affecting domestic prices, and

"(III) actual and potential negative effects on cash flow, inventories, employment, wages, growth, ability to raise capital, and investment.

"(D) Special rules for agricultural products.—

"(i) The Commission shall not determine that there is no material injury or threat of material injury to United States producers of an agricultural commodity merely because the prevailing market price is at or above the minimum support price.

"(ii) In the case of agricultural products, the Commission shall consider any increased burden on government income or price support programs.

"(E) Special rules.—For purposes of this paragraph—

"(i) Nature of subsidy.—In determining whether there is a threat of material injury, the Commission shall consider such information as may be presented to it by the administering authority as to the nature of the subsidy (particularly as to whether the subsidy is an export subsidy inconsistent with the Agreement) provided by a foreign country and the effects likely to be caused by the subsidy.

"(ii) Standard for determination.—The presence or absence of any factor which the Commission is required to evaluate under subparagraph (C) or (D) shall not necessarily give decisive guidance with respect to the determination by the Commission of material injury.

"(8) Agreement on subsidies and countervailing measures; agreement.—The terms 'Agreement on Subsidies and Countervailing Measures' and 'Agreement' mean the Agreement on Interpretation and Application of Articles VI, XVI, and XXIII of the General Agreement on Tariffs and Trade (relating to subsidies and countervailing measures) approved under section 2(a) of the Trade Agreements Act of 1979.

"(9) Interested party.—The term 'interested party' means—

"(A) a foreign manufacturer, producer, or exporter, or the United States importer, of merchandise which is the subject of an investigation under this title or a trade or business association a majority of the members of which are importers of such merchandise,

"(B) the government of a country in which such merchandise is produced or manufactured,

"(C) a manufacturer, producer, or wholesaler in the United States of a like product,

"(D) a certified union or recognized union or group of workers which is representative of an industry engaged in the manufacture, production, or wholesale in the United States of a like product, and

"(E) a trade or business association a majority of whose members manufacture, produce, or wholesale a like product in the United States.

"(10) Like product.—The term 'like product' means a product which is like, or in the absence of like, most similar in characteristics and uses with, the article subject to an investigation under this title.

"(11) Affirmative determinations by divided commission.—If the Commissioners voting on a determination by the Commission are evenly divided as to whether the determination should be affirmative or negative, the Commission shall be deemed to have made an affirmative determination. For the purpose of applying this paragraph when the issue before the Commission is to determine whether there is—

"(A) material injury to an industry in the United States,

"(B) threat of material injury to such an industry, or

"(C) material retardation of the establishment of an industry in the United States,

by reason of imports of the merchandise, an affirmative vote on any of the issues shall be treated as a vote that the determination should be affirmative.

"(12) Attribution of Merchandise to Country of Manufacture or Production.—For purposes of subtitle A, merchandise shall be treated as the product of the country in which it was manufactured or produced without regard to whether it is imported directly from that country and without regard to whether it is imported in the same condition as when exported from that country or in a changed condition by reason of remanufacture or otherwise.

"(13) Exporter.—For the purpose of determining United States price, the term 'exporter' includes the person by whom or for whose account the merchandise is imported into the United States if—

"(A) such person is the agent or principal of the exporter, manufacturer, or producer;

"(B) such person owns or controls, directly or indirectly, through stock ownership or control or otherwise, any interest in the business of the exporter, manufacturer, or producer;

"(C) the exporter, manufacturer, or producer owns or controls, directly or indirectly, through stock ownership or control or otherwise, any interest in any business conducted by such person; or

"(D) any person or persons, jointly or severally, directly or indirectly, through stock ownership or control or otherwise, own or control in the aggregate 20 percent or more of the voting power or control in the business carried on by the person by whom or for whose account the merchandise is imported into the United States, and also 20 percent or more of such power or control in the business of the exporter, manufacturer, or producer.

"(14) Sold or, in the Absence of Sales, Offered for Sale.—The term 'sold or, in the absence of sales, offered for sale' means sold or, in the absence of sales, offered—

"(A) to all purchasers at wholesale, or

"(B) in the ordinary course of trade to one or more selected purchasers at wholesale at a price which fairly reflects the market value of the merchandise,

without regard to restrictions as to the disposition or use of the merchandise by the purchaser except that, where such restrictions are found to affect the market value of the merchandise, adjustment shall be made therefor in calculating the price at which the merchandise is sold or offered for sale.

"(15) Ordinary Course of Trade.—The term 'ordinary course of trade' means the conditions and practices which, for a reasonable time prior to the exportation of the merchandise which is the subject of an investigation, have been normal in the trade under consideration with respect to merchandise of the same class or kind.

"(16) Such or Similar Merchandise.—The term 'such or similar merchandise' means merchandise in the first of the following categories in respect of which a determination for the purposes of subtitle B of this title can be satisfactorily made:

"(A) The merchandise which is the subject of an investigation and other merchandise which is identical in physical characteristics with, and was produced in the same country by the same person as, that merchandise.

"(B) Merchandise—

"(i) produced in the same country and by the same person as the merchandise which is the subject of the investigation,

"(ii) like that merchandise in component material or materials and in the purposes for which used, and

"(iii) approximately equal in commercial value to that merchandise.

"(C) Merchandise—

"(i) produced in the same country and by the same person and of the same general class or kind as the merchandise which is the subject of the investigation,

"(ii) like that merchandise in the purposes for which used, and

"(iii) which the administering authority determines may reasonably be compared with that merchandise.

"(17) Usual Wholesale Quantities.—The term 'usual wholesale quantities', in any case in which the merchandise which is the subject of the investigation is sold in the market under consideration at different prices for different quantities, means the quantities in which such merchandise is there sold at the price or prices for one quantity in an aggregate volume which is greater than the aggregate volume sold at the price or prices for any other quantity.

"Section 772. *United States Price.*

"(a) United States Price.—For purposes of this title, the term 'United States price' means the purchase price, or the exporter's sales price, of the merchandise, whichever is appropriate.

"(b) Purchase Price.—For purposes of this section, the term 'purchase price' means the price at which merchandise is purchased, or agreed to be purchased, prior to the date of importation, from the manufacturer or producer of the merchandise for exportation to the United States. Appropriate adjustments for costs and expenses under subsection (d) shall be made if they are not reflected in the price paid by the person by whom, or for whose account, the merchandise is imported.

"(c) Exporter's Sales Price.—For purposes of this section, the term 'exporter's sales price' means the price at which merchandise is sold or agreed to be sold in the United States, before or after the time of importation, by or for the account of the exporter, as adjusted under subsections (d) and (e).

"(d) Adjustments to Purchase Price and Exporter's Sales Price.—The purchase price and the exporter's sales price shall be adjusted by being—

"(1) increased by —

"(A) when not included in such price, the cost of all containers and coverings and all other costs, charges, and expenses incident to placing the merchandise in condition, packed ready for shipment to the United States,

"(B) the amount of any import duties imposed by the country of exportation which have been rebated, or which have not been collected, by reason of the exportation of the merchandise to the United States;

"(C) the amount of any taxes imposed in the country of exportation directly upon the exported merchandise or components thereof, which have been rebated, or which have not been collected, by reason of the exportation of the merchandise to the United States, but only to the extent that such taxes are added to or included in the price of such or similar merchandise when sold in the country of exportation; and

"(D) the amount of any countervailing duty imposed on the merchandise under subtitle A of this title or section 303 of this Act to offset an export subsidy, and

"(2) reduced by—

"(A) except as provided in paragraph (1)(D), the amount, if any, included in such price, attributable to any additional costs, charges, and expenses, and United States import duties, incident to bringing the merchandise from the place of shipment in the country of exportation to the place of delivery in the United States; and

"(B) the amount, if included in such price, of any export tax, duty, or other charge imposed by the country of exportation on the exportation of the merchandise to the United States other than an export tax, duty, or other charge described in section 771(6)(C).

"(e) Additional Adjustments to Exporter's Sales Price.—For purposes of this section, the exporter's sales price shall also be adjusted by being reduced by the amount, if any, of—

"(1) commissions for selling in the United States the particular merchandise under consideration,

"(2) expenses generally incurred by or for the account of the exporter in the United States in selling identical or substantially identical merchandise, and

"(3) any increased value, including additional material and labor, resulting from a process of manufacture or assembly performed on the imported merchandise after the importation of the merchandise and before its sale to a person who is not the exporter of the merchandise.

Section 773. *Foreign Market Value.*

"(a) Determination; Fictitious Market; Sales Agencies.—For purposes of this title—

"(1) In General.—The foreign market value of imported merchandise shall be the price, at the time of exportation of such merchandise to the United States—

"(A) at which such or similar merchandise is sold or, in the absence of sales, offered for sale in the principal markets of the country from which exported, in the usual wholesale quantities in the ordinary course of trade for home consumption, or

"(B) if not sold or offered for sale for home consumption or if the administering authority determines that the quantity sold for home consumption is so small in relation to the quantity sold for exportation to countries other than the United States as to form an inadequate basis for comparison, then the price at which so sold or offered for sale for exportation to countries other than the United States,

increased by, when not included in such price, the cost of all containers and coverings and all other costs, charges, and expenses incident to placing the merchandise in condition packed ready for shipment to the United States, except that in the case of merchandise purchased or agreed to be purchased by the person by whom or for whose account the merchandise is imported, prior to the time of importation, the foreign market value shall be ascertained as of the date of such purchase or agreemtn to purchase. In the ascertainment of foreign market value for the purposes of this title no pretended sale or offer for sale, and no sale or offer for sale intended to establish a fictitious market, shall be taken into account.

"(2) Use of Constructed Value.—If the administering authority determines that the foreign market value of imported merchandise cannot be determined under paragraph (1)(A), then, notwithstanding paragraph (1)(B), the foreign market value of the merchandise may be the constructed value of that merchandise, as determined under subsection (e).

"(3) Indirect Sales and Offers for Sale.—If such or similar merchandise is sold or, in the absence of sales, offered for sale through a sales agency or other organization related to the seller in any of the respects described in section 771(13), the prices at which such or similar merchandise is sold or, in the absence of sales, offered for sale by such sales agency or other organization may be used in determining the foreign market value.

"(4) Other Adjustments.—In determining foreign market value, if it is established to the satisfaction of the administering authority that the amount of any difference between the United States price and the foreign market value (or that the fact that the United States price is the same as the foreign market value) is wholly or partly due to—

"(A) the fact that the wholesale quantities, in which such or similar merchandise is sold or, in the absence of sales, offered for sale, for exportation to, or in the principal markets of, the United States, as appropriate, in the ordinary course of trade, are less or are greater than the wholesale quantities in which such or similar merchandise is sold or, in the absence of sales, offered for sale, in the principal markets of the country of exportation in the ordinary course of trade for home consumption (or, if not so sold for home consumption, then for exportation to countries other than the United States);

"(B) other differences in circumstances of sale; or

"(C) the fact that merchandise described in paragraph (B) or (C) of section 771(16) is used in determining foreign market value,

then due allowance shall be made therefor.

"(b) Sales at Less than Cost of Production.—Whenever the administering authority has reasonable grounds to believe or suspect that sales in the home market of the country of exportation, or, as appropriate, to countries other than the United States, have been made at prices which represent less than the cost of producing the merchandise in question, it shall determine whether, in fact, such sales were made at less than the cost of producing the merchandise. If the administering authority determines that sales made at less than the cost of production—

"(1) have been made over an extended period of time and in substantial quantities, and

"(2) are not at prices which permit recovery of all costs within a reasonable period of time in the normal course of trade,

such sales shall be disregarded in the determination of foreign market value. Whenever sales are disregarded by virtue of having been made at less than the cost of production and the remaining sales, made at not less than cost of production, are determined to be inadequate as a basis for the determination of foreign market value under subsection (a), the administering authority shall employ the constructed value of the merchandise to determine its foreign market value.

"(c) State-Controlled Economies.—If available information indicates to the administering authority that the economy of the country from which the merchandise is exported is State-controlled to an extent that sales or offers of sales of such or similar merchandise in that country or to countries other than the United States do not permit a determination of foreign market value under subsection (a) of this section, the administering authority shall determine the foreign market value of the merchandise on the basis of the normal costs, expenses, and profits as reflected by either—

"(1) the prices, determined in accordance with subsection (a) of this section, at which such or similar merchandise of a non-State-controlled-economy country or countries is sold either—

"(A) for consumption in the home market of that country or countries, or

"(B) to other countries, including the United States; or

"(2) the constructed value of such or similar merchandise in a non-State-controlled-economy country or countries as determined under subsection (e).

"(d) Special Rule for Certain Multinational Corporations.—Whenever, in the course of an investigation under this title, the administering authority determines that—

"(1) merchandise exported to the United States is being produced in facilities which are owned or controlled, directly or indirectly, by a person, firm or corporation which also owns or controls, directly or indirectly, other facilities for the production of such or similar merchandise which are located in another country or countries;

"(2) the sales of such or similar merchandise by the company concerned in the home market of the exporting country are nonexistent or inadequate as a basis for comparison with the sales of the merchandise to the United States; and

"(3) the foreign market value of such or similar merchandise produced in one or more of the facilities outside the country of exportation is higher than the foreign market value of such or similar merchandise produced in the facilities located in the country of exportation,

it shall determine the foreign market value of such merchandise by reference to the foreign market value at which such or similar merchandise is sold in substantial quantities by one or more facilities outside the country of exportation. The administering authority, in making any determination under this paragraph, shall make adjustments for the difference between the costs of production (including taxes, labor, materials, and overhead) of such or similar merchandise produced in facilities outside the country of exportation and costs of production of such or similar merchandise produced in the facilities in the country of exportation, if such differences are demonstrated to its satisfaction. For the purposes of this subsection, in determining foreign market value of such or similar merchandise produced in a country outside the country of exportation, the administering authority shall determine its price at the time of exportation from the country of exportation and shall make any adjustments required by subsection (a) of this section for the cost of all containers and coverings and all other costs, charges, and expenses incident to placing the merchandise in condition packed ready for shipment to the United States by reference to such costs in the country of exportation.

"(e) Constructed Value.—

"(1) Determination.—For the purposes of this title, the constructed value of imported merchandise shall be the sum of—

"(A) the cost of materials (exclusive of any internal tax applicable in the country of exportation directly to such materials or their disposition, but remitted or refunded upon the exportation of the article in the production of which such materials are used) and of fabrication or other processing of any kind employed in producing such or similar merchandise, at a time preceding the date of exportation of the merchandise under consideration which would ordinarily permit the production of that particular merchandise in the ordinary course of business;

"(B) an amount for general expenses and profit equal to that usually reflected in sales of merchandise of the same general class or kind as the merchandise under consideration which are made by producers in the country of exportation, in the usual wholesale quantities and in the ordinary course of trade, except that—

"(i) the amount for general expenses shall not be less than 10 percent of the cost as defined in subparagraph (A), and "(ii) the amount for profit shall not be less than 8 percent of the sum of such general expenses and cost; and

"(C) the cost of all containers and coverings of whatever nature, and all other expenses incidental to placing the merchandise under consideration in condition, packed ready for shipment to the United States.

"(2) Transactions Disregarded; Best Evidence.—For the purposes of this subsection, a transaction directly or indirectly between persons specified in any one of the subparagraphs in paragraph (3) of this subsection may be disregarded if, in the case of any element of value required to be considered, the amount representing that element does not fairly reflect the amount usually reflected in sales in the market under consideration of merchandise under consideration. If a transaction is disregarded under the preceding sentence and there are no other transactions available for consideration, then the determination of the amount required to be considered shall be based on the best evidence available as to what the amount would have been if the transaction had occurred between persons not specified in any one of the subparagraphs in paragraph (3) of this section.

"(3) Related parties.—The persons referred to in paragraph (2) of this subsection are:

"(A) Members of a family, including brothers and sisters (whether by the whole or half blood), spouse, ancestors, and lineal descendants.

"(B) Any officer or director of an organization and such organization.

"(C) Partners.

"(D) Employer and employee.

"(E) Any person directly or indirectly owning, controlling, or holding with power to vote, 5 percent or more of the outstanding voting stock or shares of any organization and such organization.

"(F) Two or more persons directly or indirectly controlling, controlled by, or under common control with, any person.

"(f) Authority to Use Sampling Techniques and to Disregard Insignificant Adjustments.—For the purpose of determining foreign market value under this section, the administering authority may—

"(1) use averaging or generally recognized sampling techniques whenever a significant volume of sales is involved or a significant number of adjustments to prices is required, and

"(2) decline to take into account adjustments which are insignificant in relation to the price or value of the merchandise.

"Section 774. *Hearings.*

"(a) Investigation Hearings.—The administering authority and the Commission shall each hold a hearing in the course of an investigation upon the request of any party to the investigation before making a final determination under section 705 or 735.

"(b) Procedures.—Any hearing required or permitted under this title shall be conducted after notice published in the Federal Register, and a transcript of the hearing shall be prepared and made available to the public. The hearing shall not be subject to the provisions of subchapter II of chapter 5 of title 5, United States Code, or to section 702 of such title.

"Section 775. *Subsidy Practices Discovered During an Investigation.*

"If, in the course of an investigation under this title, the administering authority discovers a practice which appears to be a subsidy, but was not included in the matters alleged in a countervailing duty petition, then the administering authority—

"(1) shall include the practice in the investigation if it appears to be a subsidy with respect to the merchandise which is the subject of the investigation, or

"(2) shall transfer the information concerning the practice (other than confidential information) to the library maintained under section 777(a)(1), if the practice appears to be a subsidy with respect to any other merchandise.

"Section 776. *Verification of Information.*

"(a) General Rule.—Except with respect to information the verification of which is waived under section 733(b)(2), the administering authority shall verify all information relied upon in making a final determination in an investigation. In publishing such a determination, the administering authority shall report the methods and procedures used to verify such information. If the administering authority is unable to verify the accuracy of the information submitted, it shall use the best information available to it as the basis for its determination, which may include the information submitted in support of the petition.

"(b) Determinations to be Made on Best Information Available.—In making their determinations under this title, the administering authority and the Commission shall, whenever a party or any other person refuses or is unable to produce information requested in a timely manner and in the form required, or otherwise significantly impedes an investigation, use the best information otherwise available.

"Section 777. *Access to Information.*

"(a) Information Generally Made Available.—

"(1) Public Information Function.—There shall be established a library of information relating to foreign subsidy practices and countervailing measures. Copies of material in the library shall be made available to the public upon payment of the costs of preparing such copies.

"(2) Progress of Investigation Reports.—The administering authority and the Commission shall, from time to time upon request, inform the parties to an investigation of the progress of that investigation.

"(3) Ex Parte Meetings.—The administering authority and the Commission shall maintain a record of ex parte meetings between—

"(A) interested parties or other persons providing factual information in connection with an investigation, and

"(B) the person charged with making the determination, and any person charged with making a final recommendation to that person, in connection with that investigation.

The record of the ex parte meeting shall include the identity of the persons present at the meeting, the date, time, and place of the meeting, and a summary of the matters discussed or submitted. The record of the ex parte meeting shall be included in the record of the proceeding.

"(4) Summaries; nonconfidential submissions.—The administering authority and the Commission may disclose—

"(A) any confidential information received in the course of a proceeding if it is disclosed in a form which cannot be associated with, or otherwise be used to identify, operations of a particular person, and

"(B) any information submitted in connection with a proceeding which is not designated as confidential by the person submitting it.

"(b) Confidential Information.—

"(1) Confidentiality maintained.—Except as provided in subsection (a)(4)(A) and subsection (c), information submitted to the administering authority or the Commission which is designated as confidential by the person submitting it shall not be disclosed to any person (other than an officer or employee of the administering authority or the Commission who is directly concerned with carrying out the investigation in connection with which the information is submitted) without the consent of the person submitting it. The administering authority and the Commission may require that information for which confidential treatment is requested be accompanied by a non-confidential summary in sufficient detail to permit a reasonable understanding of the substnace of the infromation submitted in confidence, or a statement that the information is not susceptible to summary, accompanied by a statement of the reasons in support of the contention.

"(2) Unwarranted designation.—If the administering authority or the Commission determines, on the basis of the nature and extent of the information or its availability from public sources, that designation of any information as confidential is unwarranted, then it shall notify the person who submitted it and ask for an explanation of the reasons for the designation. Unless that person persuades the administering authority or the Commission that the designation is warranted, or withdraws the designation, the administering authority or the Commission, as the case may be, shall return it to the party submitting it.

"(c) Limited Disclosure of Certain Confidential Information Under Protective Order.—

"(1) Disclosure by Administering Authority or Commission.—

"(A) In General.—Upon receipt of an application, which describes with particularity the information requested and sets forth the reasons for the request, the administering authority and the Commission may make confidential information submitted by any other party to the investigation available under a protective order described in subparagraph (B).

"(B) Protective Order.—The protective order under which information is made available shall contain such requirements as the administering authority or the Commission may determine by regulation to be appropriate. The administering authority and the Commission shall provide by regulation for such sanctions as the administering authority and the Commission determine to be appropriate, including disbarment from practice before the agency.

"(2) Disclosure Under Court Order.—If the administering authority denies a request for information under paragraph (1), or the Commission denies a request for confidential information submitted by the petitioner or an interested party in support of the petitioner concerning the domestic price or cost of production of the like product, then application may be made to the United States Customs Court for an order directing the administering authority or the Commission to make the information available. After notification of all parties to the investigation and after an opportunity for a hearing on the record, the court may issue an order, under such conditions as the court deems appropriate, which shall not have the effect of stopping or suspending the investigation, directing the administering authority or the Commission to make all or a portion of the requested information described in the preceding sentence available under a protective order and setting forth sanctions for violation of such order if the court finds that, under the standards applicable in proceedings of the court, such an order is warranted, and that—

"(A) the administering authority or the Commission has denied access to the information under subsection (b)(1),

"(B) the person on whose behalf the information is requested is an interest party who is a party to the investigation in connection with which the information was obtained or developed, and

"(C) the party which submitted the information to which the request relates has been notified, in advance of the hearing, of the request made under this section and of its right to appear and be heard.

Section 778. *Interest on Certain Overpayments and Underpayments.*

"(a) General Rule.—Interest shall be payable on overpayments and underpayments of amounts deposited on merchandise entered, or withdrawn from warehouse, for consumption on and after the date on which notice of an affirmative determination by the Commission under section 705(b) or 735(b) with respect to such merchandise is published.

''(b) Rate.—The rate at which such interest is payable shall be 8 percent per annum, or, if higher, the rate in effect under section 6621 of the Internal Revenue Code of 1954 on the date on which the rate or amount of the duty is finally determined.''.

Section 102. *Pending Investigations.*

(a) Pending Investigations of Bounties or Grants.—If, on the effective date of the application of title VII of the Tariff Act of 1930 to imports from a country, there is an investigation in progress under section 303 of that Act as to whether a bounty or grant is being paid or bestowed on imports from such country, then:

(1) If the Secretary of the Treasury has not yet made a preliminary determination under section 303 of that Act as to whether a bounty or grant is being paid or bestowed, he shall terminate the investigation under section 303 and the mater previously under investigation shall be subject to this title as if the affirmative determination called for in section 702 of that Act were made with respect to that matter on the effective date of the application of title VII of that Act to such country.

(2) If the Secretary has made a preliminary determination under section 303, but not a final determination, as to whether a bounty or grant is being paid or bestowed, he shall terminate the investigation under such section 303 and the matter previously under investigation shall be subject to the provisions of title VII of that Act as if the preliminary determinations under section 303 were a preliminary determination under section 703 of that title made on the effective date of the application of that title to such country.

(b) Pending Investigations of Less-Than-Fair-Value Sales.—If, on the effective date of title VII of the Tariff Act of 1930, there is an investigation in progress under the Antidumping Act, 1921, as to whether imports from a country are being, or are likely to be, sold in the United States or elsewhere at less than fair value, then:

(1) If the Secretary has not yet made a preliminary determination under the Antidumping Act, 1921, as to the question of less-than-fair-value sales, he shall terminate the investigation and the United States International Trade Commission shall terminate any investigation under section 201(c)(2) of the Antidumping Act, 1921, and the matter previously under investigation shall be subject to the provisions of title VII of the Tariff Act of 1930 as if the affirmative determination called for in section 732 were made with respect to such matter on the effective date of title VII of the Tariff Act of 1930.

(2) If the Secretary has made under the Antidumping Act, 1921, a preliminary determination, but not a final determination, that imports from such country are

being or are likely to be sold in the United States or elsewhere at less than fair value, the investigation shall be terminated and the matter previously under investigation shall be subject to the provisions of title VII of the Tariff Act of 1930 as if the preliminary detemination under the Antidumping Act, 1921, were a preliminary determination under section 733 of that title made on the effective date of title VII of the Tariff Act of 1930.

(c) Pending Investigations of Injury.—If, on the effective date of the application of title VII of the Tariff Act of 1930 to imports from a country, the United States International Trade Commission is conducting an investigation under section 303 of the Tariff Act of 1930 or section 201(a) of the Antidumping Act, 1921, as to whether an industry in the United States is being, or is likely to be injured, or is prevented from being established, it shall terminate any such investigation and initiate an investigation, under subtitle A or B of title VII of the Tariff Act of 1930, which shall be completed within 75 days, and—

   (1) treat any final determination of the Secretary of the Treasury under section 303 as a final determination under section 705(a) of the Tariff Act of 1930 and consider the net amount of the bounty or grant estimated or determined under section 303 as the net subsidy amount under subtitle A of that title; and

   (2) treat any final determination of the Secretary of the Treasury under the Antidumping Act, 1921, as a final determination under section 735(a) of the Tariff Act of 1930.

Section 103. *Amendment of Section 303 of the Tariff Act of 1930.*

(a) Application of Section 303.—Paragraph (1) of section 303(a) of the Tariff Act of 1930 (19 U.S.C. 1303(a)) is amended by striking out "Whenever" and inserting in lieu thereof the following: "Except in the case of an article or merchandise which is the product of a country under the Agreement (within the meaning of section 701(b) of this Act), whenever".

(b) Certain Provisions of New Law to Apply.—Section 303 of such Act (19 U.S.C. 1303) is amended—

   (1) by striking out paragraphs (3) through (6) of subsection (a),
   (2) by striking out subsections (b) and (c) and inserting in lieu thereof the following new subsection:

"(b) The duty imposed under subsection (a) shall be imposed, under regulations prescribed by the administering authority (as defined in section 771(1)), in accordance with title VII of this Act (relating to the imposition of countervailing duties) except that, in the case of any imported article or merchandise which is not free of duty—

   "(1) no determination by the United States International Trade Commission under section 703(a), 704, or 705(b) shall be required,

   "(2) an investigation may not be suspended under section 704(c),

   "(3) no determination as to the presence of critical circumstances shall be made under section 703(e) or 705(a)(2) or (b)(4)(A), and

"(4) any reference to determinations by the Commission, or to the suspension of an investigation under section 704(c) which are not permitted or required by this subsection shall be disregarded.'', and

(3) by adding at the end thereof the following new subsection:

"(f) Cross Reference.—

"For provisions of law applicable in the case of articles and merchandise which are the product of countries under the agreement within the meaning of section 701(b) of this Act, see title VII of this Act.''.

(c) Conforming Amendment.—Paragraph 2 of section 303(a) of such Act (19 U.S.C. 1303(a)) is amended—

(1) by striking out "is an affirmative determination" and inserting in lieu thereof "are affirmative determinations", and

(2) by striking out "subsection (b)(1)" and inserting in lieu thereof "title VII".

Section 104. *Transition Rules for Countervailing Duty Orders.*

(a) Waived Countervailing Duty Orders.—

(1) Notification of Commission.—The administering authority shall notify the United States International Trade Commission by January 7, 1980, of any countervailing duty order in effect on January 1, 1980—

(A)(i) for which the Secretary of the Treasury has waived the imposition of countervailing duties under section 303(d) of the Tariff Act of 1930 (19 U.S.C. 1303(d)), and

(ii) which applies to merchandise other than quota cheese (as defined in section 701(c)(1) of this Act), which is a product of a country under the Agreement,

(B) published on or after the date of the enactment of this Act, and before January 1, 1980, with respect to products of a country under the Agreement (as defined in section 701(b) of the Tariff Act of 1930), or

(C) applicable to frozen, boneless beef from European Communities under Treasury Decision 76-109,

and shall furnish to the Commission the most current information it has with respect to the net subsidy benefitting the merchandise subject to the countervailing duty order.

(2) Determination by the commission.—Within 180 days after the date on which it receives the information from the administering authority under paragraph (1), the Commission shall make a determination of whether—

(A) an industry in the United States—

(i) is materially injured, or

(ii) is threatened with material injury, or

(B) the establishment of an industry in the United States is materially retarded, by reason of imports of the merchandise subject to the order.

    (3) Effect of Determination.—

        (A) Affirmative Determination.—Upon being notified by the Commission of an affirmative determination under paragraph (2), the administering authority shall terminate the waiver of imposition of countervailing duties for merchandise subject to the order, if any. The countervailing duty order under section 303 of the Tariff Act of 1930 which applies to that merchandise shall remain in effect until revoked, in whole or in part, under section 751(d) of such Act.

        (B) Negative Determination.—Upon being notified by the Commission of a negative determination under paragraph (2), the administering authority shall revoke the countervailing duty order, and publish notice in the Federal Register of the revocation.

(b) Other Countervailing Duty Orders.—

    (1) Review by Commission Upon Request.—In the case of a countervailing duty order issued under section 303 of the Tariff Act of 1930 (19 U.S.C. 1303)—

        (A) which is not a countervailing duty order to which subsection (a) applies,

        (B) which applies to merchandise which is the product of a country under the Agreement, and

        (C) which is in effect on January 1, 1980, or which is issued pursuant to court order in an action brought under section 516(d) of that Act before that date,

the Commission, upon the request of the government of such a country or of exporters accounting for a significant proportion of exports to the United States of merchandise which is covered by the order, submitted within 3 years after the effective date of title VII of the Tariff Act of 1930 shall make a determination under paragraph (2) of this subsection.

    (2) Determination by the Commission.—In a case described in paragraph (1) with respect to which it has received a request for review, the Commission shall commence an investigation to determine whether—

        (A) an industry in the United States—

            (i) would be materially injured, or

            (ii) would be threatened with material injury, or

        (B) the establishment of an industry in the United States would be materially retarded,

by reason of imports of the merchandise covered by the countervailing duty order if the order were to be revoked.

    (3) Suspension of Liquidation; Investigation Time Limits.—Whenever the Commission receives a request under paragraph (1), it shall promptly notify the administering authority and the administering authority shall suspend liquidation of entries of the affected merchandise made on or after the date of receipt of the Commission's notification, or in the case of butter from Australia, entries of mer-

chandise subject to the assessment of countervailing duties under Tresury Decision 42937, as amended, and collect estimated countervailing duties pending the determination of the Commission. The Commission shall issue its determination in any investigation under this subsection not later than 3 years after the date of commencement of such investigation.

(4) Effect of Determination.—

(A) Affirmative Determination.—Upon being notified of an affirmative determination under paragraph (2) by the Commission, the administering authority shall liquidate entries of merchandise the liquidation of which was suspended under paragraph (3) of this subsection and impose countervailing duties in the amount of the estimated duties required to be deposited. The countervailing duty order shall remain in effect until revoked, in whole or in part, under section 751(c) of the Tariff Act of 1930.

(B) Negative Determination.—Upon being notified of a negative determination under paragraph (2) by the Commission, the administering authority shall revoke the countervailing duty order then in effect, publish notice thereof in the Federal Register, and refund, without payment of interest, any estimated countervailing duties collected during the period of suspension of liquidation.

(c) All Outstanding Countervailing Duty Orders.—Subject to the provisions of subsections (a) and (b), any countervailing duty order issued under section 303 of the Tariff Act of 1930 which is—

(1) in effect on the effective date of title VII of the Tariff Act of 1930 (as added by section 101 of this Act), or

(2) issued pursuant to court order in a proceeding brought before that date under section 516(d) of the Tariff Act of 1930, shall remain in effect after that date and shall be subject to review under section 751 of the Tariff Act of 1930.

(d) Publication of Notice of Determinations.—Whenever the Commission makes a determination under subsection (a) or (b), it shall publish notice of that determination in the Federal Register and notify the administering authority of its determination.

(e) Definitions.—Whenever any term which is defined in section 771 of the Tariff Act of 1930 is used in this section, it has the same meaning as when it is used in title VII of that Act.

Section 105. *Continuation of Certain Waivers.*

(a) Waivers.—Subparagraph (B) of section 303(d)(4) of the Tariff Act of 1930 (19 U.S.C. 1303(d)(4)) is amended to read as follows:

"(B) Any determination made by the Secretary under this subsection with respect to merchandise of a country which, if title VII of the Tariff Act of 1930 were in effect, would, as determined by the President, be a country under the Agreement (within the meaning of section 701(b) of such Act), which is in effect on September 29, 1979, or on the day before the date of the enactment of the Trade Agreements Act of 1979 (whichever of such dates first occurs), shall remain in effect until whichever of the following dates first occurs:

"(i) The date on which the United States International Trade Commission makes a determination under section 104 of the Trade Agreements Act of 1979.

"(ii) The date such determination is revoked under paragraph (3).

"(iii) The date of adoption of a resolution of disapproval of such determination under subsection (e)(2)."

(b) Effective Date.—The amendment made by subsection (a) shall take effect on the date of enactment of this Act.

Section 106. *Conforming Changes.*

(a) Repeal of Old Law.—The Antidumping Act, 1921 (19 U.S.C. 160 et. seq.) is hereby repealed but findings in effect on the effective date of this Act, or issued pursuant to court order in an action brought before that date, shall remain in effect, subject to review under section 751 of the Tariff Act of 1930.

(b) Conforming Amendments.—

(1) Section 337(b)(3) of the Tariff Act of 1930 (19 U.S.C. 1337(b)(3)) is amended by striking out "the Antidumping Act, 1921" and inserting in lieu thereof "subtitle B of title VII of the Tariff Act of 1930".

(2) Section 503 of the Automotive Products Trade Act of 1965 (19 U.S.C. 2033) is amended by striking out "the Anti-Dumping Act, 1921 (19 U.S.C. 160–173)" and inserting in lieu thereof "subtitle B of title VII of the Tariff Act of 1930,".

(3) Section 201(b)(6) of the Trade Act of 1974 (19 U.S.C. 2251(b)(6)) is amended by striking out "the Antidumping Act, 1921, section 303 or 337" and inserting in lieu thereof "subtitles A and B of title VII or section 337".

Section 107. *Effective Date.*

Except as otherwise provided in this title, this title and the amendments made by it shall take effect on January 1, 1980, if—

(1) the Agreement on Interpretation and Application of Aritcles VI, XVI, XXIII of the General Agreement on Tariffs and Trade (relating to subsidies and countervailing measures), and

(2) the Agreement on Implementation of Article VI of the General Agreement on Tariffs and Trade (relating to antidumping measures),

approved by the Congress under section 2(a) of this Act have entered into force with respect to the United States as of that date.

(c) TITLE IX—ENFORCEMENT OF UNITED STATES RIGHTS

Section 901. *Enforcement of United States Rights under Trade Agreements and Response to Certain Foreign Practices.*

Chapter I of title III of the Trade Act of 1974 (19 U.S.C. 2411) is amended to read as follows:

"CHAPTER 1—ENFORCEMENT OF UNITED STATES RIGHTS UNDER TRADE AGREEMENTS AND RESPONSE TO CERTAIN FOREIGN TRADE PRACTICES

"Section 301. *Determinations and Action by President.*

"(a) Determinations Requiring Action.—If the President determines that action by the United States is appropriate—

"(1) to enforce the rights of the United States under any trade agreement; or

"(2) to respond to any act, policy, or practice of a foreign country or instrumentality that—

"(A) is inconsistent with the provisions of, or otherwise denies benefits to the United States under, any trade agreement, or

"(B) is unjustifiable, unreasonable, or discriminatory and burdens or restricts United States commerce;

the President shall take all appropriate and feasible action within his power to enforce such rights or to obtain the elimination of such act, policy, or practice. Action under this section may be taken on a nondiscriminatory basis or solely against the products or services of the foreign country or instrumentality involved.

"(b) Other Action.—Upon making a determination described in subsection (a), the President, in addition to taking action referred to in such subsection, may—

"(1) suspend, withdraw, or prevent the application of, or refrain from proclaiming, benefits of trade agreement concessions to carry out a trade agreement with the foreign country or instrumentality involved; and

"(2) impose duties or other import restrictions on the products of, and fees or restrictions on the services of, such foreign country or instrumentality for such time as he determines appropriate.

"(c) Presidential Procedures.—

"(1) Action on Own Motion.—If the President decides to take action under this section and no petition requesting action on the matter involved has been filed under section 302, the President shall publish notice of his determination, including the reasons for the determination in the Federal Register. Unless he determines that expeditious action is required, the President shall provide an opportunity for the presentation of views concerning the taking of such action.

"(2) Action Requested by Petition.—Not later than 21 days after the date on which he receives the recommendation of the Special Representative under section 304 with respect to a petiton, the President shall determine what action, if any, he will take under this section, and shall publish notice of his determination, including the reasons for the detetermination, in the Federal Register.

"(d) Special Provisions.—

"(1) Definition of Commerce.—For purposes of this section, the term 'commerce' includes, but is not limited to, services associated with international trade, whether or not such services are related to specific products.

"(2) Vessel Construction Subsidies.—An act, policy, or practice of a foreign country or instrumentality that burdens or restricts United States commerce may include the provision, directly or indirectly, by that foreign country or instrumentality of subsidies for the construction of vessels used in the commercial transportation by water of goods between foreign countries and the United States.

"Section 302. *Petitions for Presidential Action.*

"(a) Filing of Petition with Special Representative.—Any interested person may file a petition with the Special Representative for Trade Negotiations (hereinafter in this chapter referred to as the 'Special Representative') requesting the President to take action under section 301 and setting forth the allegations in support of the request. The Special Representative shall review the allegations in the petition and, not later than 45 days after the date on which he received the petition, shall determine whether to initiate an investigation.

"(b) Determinations Regarding Petitions.—

"(1) Negative Determination.—If the Special Representative determines not to initiate an investigation with respect to a petition, he shall inform the petitioner of his reasons therefor and shall publish notice of the determination, together with a summary of such reasons, in the Federal Register.

"(2) Affirmative Determination.—If the Special Representative determines to initiate an investigation with respect to a petition, he shall initiate an investigation regarding the issues raised. The Special Representative shall publish the text of the petition in the Federal Register and shall, as soon as possible, provide opportunity for the presentation of views concerning the issues, including a public hearing—

"(A) within the 30-day period after the date of the determination (or on a date after such period if agreed to by the petitioner), if a public hearing within such period is requested in the petition; or

"(B) at such other time if a timely request therefor is made by the petitioner.

"Section 303. *Consultation Upon Initiation of Investigation.*

"On the date an affirmative determination is made under section 302(b) with respect to a petition, the Special Representative, on behalf of the United States, shall request consultations with the foreign country or instrumentality concerned regarding issues raised in the petition. If the case involves a trade agreement and a mutually acceptable resolution is not reached during the consultation period, if any, specified in the trade agreement, the Special Representative shall promptly request proceedings on the matter under the formal dispute settlement procedures provided under such agreement. The Special Representative shall seek information and advice from the petitioner and the appropriate private sector representatives provided for under section 135 in preparing United States presentations for consultations and dispute settlement proceedings.

"Section 304. *Recommendations by the Special Representative.*

"(a) Recommendations.—

"(1) In General.—On the basis of the investigation under section 302, and the consultations (and the proceedings, if applicable) under section 303, and subject to subsection (b), the Special Representative shall recommend to the President what action, if any, he should take under section 301 with respect to the issues raised in the petition. The Special Representative shall make that recommendation not later than—

"(A) 7 months after the date of the initiation of the investigation under section 302(b)(2) if the petition alleges only an export subsidy covered by the Agreement on Interpretation and Application of Articles VI, XVI, and XXIII of the General Agreement on Tariffs and Trade (relating to subsidies and countervailing measure and hereinafter referred to in this section as the 'Subsidies Agreement');

"(B) 8 months after the date of the investigation initiation if the petition alleges any matter covered by the Subsidies Agreement other than only an export subsidy;

"(C) in the case of a petition involving a trade agreement approved under section 2(a) of the Trade Agreements Act of 1979 (other than the Subsidies Agreement), 30 days after the dispute settlement procedure is concluded; or

"(D) 12 months after the date of the investigation initiation in any case not described in subparagraph (A), (B), or (C).

"(2) Special Rule.—In the case of any petition—

"(A) an investigation with respect to which is initiated on or after the date of the enactment of the Trade Agreements Act of 1979 (including any petition treated under section 903 of that Act as initiated on such date); and

"(B) to which the 12-month time limitation set forth in subparagraph (D) of paragraph (1) would but for this paragraph apply;

if a trade agreement approved under section 2(a) of such Act of 1979 that relates to any allegation made in the petition applies between the United States and a foreign country or instrumentality before the 12-month period referred to in subparagraph (B) expires, the Special Representative shall make the recommendation required under paragraph (1) with respect to the petition not later than the close of the period specified in subparagraph (A), (B), or (C), as appropriate, of such paragraph, and for purposes of such subparagraph (A) or (B), the date of the application of such trade agreement between the United States and the foreign country or instrumentality concerned shall be treated as the date on which the investigation with respect to such petition was initiated; except that consultations and proceedings under section 303 need not be undertaken within the period specified in such subparagraph (A), (B), or (C), as the case may be, to the extent that the requirements under such section were complied with before such period begins.

"(3) Report if Settlement Delayed.—In any case in which a dispute is not resolved before the close of the minimum dispute settlement period provided for in a trade agreement referred to in paragraph (1)(C) (other than the Subsidies Agreement), the Special Representative, within 15 days after the close of such period, shall submit a report to Congress setting forth the reasons why the dispute was not resolved within the minimum period, the status of the case at the close of the period, and the prospects for resolution. For purposes of this paragraph, the minimum dispute settlement period provided for under any such trade agreement is the total period of time that results if all stages of the formal dispute settlement procedures are carried out within the time limitations specified in the agreement, but computed without regard to any extension authorized under the agreement of any stage.

"(b) Consultation Before Recommendation.—Before recommending that the President take action under section 301 with respect to the treatment of any product or service of a foreign country or instrumentality which is the subject of a petition filed under section 302, the Special Representative, unless he determines that expeditious action is required—

"(1) shall provide opportunity for the presentation of views, including a public hearing if requested by any interested person;

"(2) shall obtain advice from the appropriate private sector advisory representatives provided for under section 135; and

"(3) may request the views of the International Trade Commission regarding the probable impact on the economy of the United States of the taking of action with respect to such product or service.

If the Special Representative does not comply with paragraphs (1) and (2) because expeditious action is required, he shall, after making the recommendation concerned to the President, comply with such paragraphs.

"Section. 305. *Requests for Information.*

"(a) In General.—Upon receipt of written request therefor from any person, the Special Representative shall make available to that person information (other than that to which confidentiality applies) concerning—

"(1) the nature and extent of a specific trade policy or practice of a foreign government or instumentality with respect to particular merchandise, to the extent that such information is available to the Special Representative or other Federal agencies;

"(2) United States rights under any trade agreement and the remedies which may be available under that agreement and under the laws of the United States; and

"(3) past and present domestic and international proceedings or actions with respect to the policy or practice concerned.

"(b) If Information Not Available.—If information that is requested by an interested party under subsection (a) is not available to the Special Representative or other Federal agencies, the Special Representative shall, within 30 days after recept of the request—

"(1) request the information from the foreign government; or

"(2) decline to request the information and inform the person in writing of the reasons for the refusal.

"Section 306. *Administration.*

"The Special Representative shall—

"(1) issue regulations concerning the filing of petitions and the conduct of investigations and hearings under this chapter;

"(2) keep the petitioner regularly informed of all determinations and developments regarding his case under this section, including the reasons for any undue delays; and

"(3) submit a report to the House of Representatives and the Senate semi-annually describing the petitions filed and the determinations made (and reasons therefor) under section 302, developments in and current status of each such proceeding, and the actions taken, or the reasons for no action, by the President under section 301.".

Section 902. *Conforming Amendments.*

(a) Elimination of Congressional Procedures.—Chapter 5 of title I of the Trade Act of 1974 is amended as follows:

(1) Section 152(a) is amended—

(A) by amending paragraph (1)(A) to read as follows:

"(A) a concurrent resolution of the two Houses of the Congress, the matter after the resolving clause of which is as follows: 'That the Congress does not approve the action taken by, or the determination of, the President under section 203 of the Trade Act of 1974 transmitted to the Congress on   ,', the blank space being filled with the appropriate date; and'':

(B) by striking out "paragraph (3)," in paragraph (1)(B) and inserting in lieu thereof "paragraph (2),";

(C) by striking out paragraph (2); and

(D) by redesignating paragraph (3) as paragraph (2)

(2) Section 154 is amended by striking out "302(a)," in subsection (a); and by striking out "302(b)," in subsection (b).

(b) Table of Contents.—The table of contents of the Trade Act of 1974 is amended by striking out

"CHAPTER 1—FOREIGN IMPORT RESTRICTIONS AND EXPORT SUBSIDIES

"Sec. 301. Responses to certain trade practices of foreign governments.

"Sec. 302. Procedure of or congressional disapproval of certain actions taken under section 301.";

and inserting in lieu thereof the following:

"CHAPTER 1—ENFORCEMENT OF UNITED STATES RIGHTS UNDER TRADE AGREEMENTS AND RESPONSE TO CERTAIN FOREIGN TRADE PRACTICES

"Sec. 301. Determinations and action by President.

"Sec. 302. Petitions for Presidential action.

"Sec. 303. Consultation upon initiation of investigation.

"Sec. 304. Recommendations by the Special Representative.

"Sec. 305. Requests for information.

"Sec. 306. Administration."

(c) Trade Expansion Act of 1962.—Section 242 of the Trade Expansion Act of 1962 (19 U.S.C. 1982) is amended by striking out "subsections (c) and (d)" each place it appears and inserting in lieu thereof "section 302(b)(2)".

Section 903. *Effective Date.*

The amendments made by sections 901 and 902 shall take effect on the date of the enactment of this Act. Any petition for review filed with the Special Representative for Trade Negotiations under section 301 of the Trade Act of 1974 (as in effect on the day before such date of enactment) and pending on such date of enactment shall be treated as an investigation initiated on such date of enactment under section 302(b)(2) of the Trade Act of 1974 (as added by section 901 of this Act) and any information developed by, or submitted to, the Special Representative before such date of enactment under the review shall be treated as part of the information developed during such investigation.

. . .

(f) TITLE XI—MISCELLANEOUS PROVISIONS

Section 1101. Extension of Nontariff Barrier Negotiating Authority.

Section 102(b) of the Trade Act of 1974 (19 U.S.C. 2112) is amended by striking out "5-year period" and inserting in lieu thereof "13-year period".

Section 1102. *Auction of Import Licenses.*

(a) In General.—Notwithstanding any other provision of law, the President may sell import licenses at public auction under such terms and conditions as he deems appropriate. Regulations prescribed under this subsection shall, to the extent practicable and consistent with efficient and fair administration, insure against inequitable sharing of imports by a relatively small number of the larger importers.

(b) Definition of Import License.—For purposes of this section, the term "import license" means any documentation used to administer a quantitative restriction imposed or modified after the date of enactment of this Act under—

(1) section 125, 203, 301, or 406 of the Trade Act of 1974 (19 U.S.C. 2135, 2253, 2411, or 2436),

(2) the International Emergency Economic Powers Act (50 U.S.C. App. 1701–1706),

(3) authority under the headnotes of the Tariff Schedules of the United Staes, but not including any quantitative restriction imposed under section 22 of the Agricultural Adjustment Act of 1934 (7 U.S.C. 624),

(4) the Trading with the Enemy Act (50 U.S.C. App. 1–44),

(5) section 204 of the Agricultural Act of 1956 (7 U.S.C. 1854) other than for meat or meat products, or

(6) any Act enacted explicitly for the purpose of implementing an international agreement to which the United States is a party, including such agreements relating to commodities, but not including any agreement relating to cheese or dairy products.

Section 1103. *Advice from Private Sector.*

Section 135 of the Trade Act of 1974 (19 U.S.C. 2155) is amended—

(1) by striking out,"in accordance with the provisions of this section," in subsection (a),

(2) by inserting before the period in subsection (a) a comma and the following: "with respect to the operation of any trade agreement once entered into, and wih respect to other matters arising in connection with the administration of the trade policy of the United States",

(3) by striking out "any trade agreement referred to in section 101 or 102" in subsection (b)(1) and inserting in lieu thereof the following: "matters referred to in subsection (a)",

(4) by striking out subsection (b)(2) and inserting in lieu thereof the following:

"(2) The Committee shall meet at the call of the Special Representative for Trade Negotiaions. The Chairman of the Committee shall be elected by the Committee from among its members. Members of the Committee shall be appointed by the President for a period of 2 years and may be reappointed for one or more additional periods.",

(5) by striking out so much of subsection (c) as precedes paragraphs (2) and inserting in lieu thereof the following:

"(c)(1) The President may, on his own initiative, or at the request of organizations representing industry, labor, agriculture, or services, estblish general policy advisory committees for industry, labor, agriculture, or services, respectively, to provide general policy advice on maters reffered to in subsection (a). Such committees shall, insofar as is practicable, be representative of all industry, labor, agricultural, and service interests, respectively, including small business interests, and shall be organized by the Special Representative for Trade Negotiations and the Secretary of Commerce, Labor, or Agriculture, as appropriate.'',

(6) by striking out the first two sentences of subsection (c)(2) and inserting in lieu thereof the following: ''The President shall establish such sectoral or functional advisory committees as may be appropriate. Such committees shall, insofar as is practicable, be representative of all industry, labor, agricultural, or service interests (including small business interests) in the sector or functional areas concerned.'',

(7) by striking out ''the President, acting through the Special Representative for Trade Negotiations and'' in the third sentence of subsection (c)(2) and inserting in lieu thereof the following: ''the Special Representative for Trade Negotiations and'',

(8) by striking out ''product sector'' in the last sentence of subsection (c)(2),

(9) by inserting, ''in the case of each sectoral committee,'' in the last sentence of subsection (c)(2) immediately before ''the product lines'',

(10) by striking out subsection (d) and inserting in lieu thereof the following:

''(d) Committees established under subsection (c) shall meet at the call of the Special Representative for Trade Negotiations and the Secretary of Agriculture, Commerce, or Labor, as appropriate, to provide policy advice, technical advice and information, and advice on other factors relevant to the matters referred to in subsection (a).'',

(11) by striking out ''and each sector advisory committee, if the sector,'' in the first sentence of subsection (e)(1) and inserting in lieu thereof the following: ''and each sector or functional advisory committee, if the sector or area'',

(12) by inserting ''or functional area'' immediately after ''appropriate sector'' in the second sentence of subsection (e)(1),

(13) by inserting ''or within the functional area'' immediately before the period at the end of subsection (e)(1),

(14) by striking out subsection (e)(2) and redesignating subsection (e)(1) as subsection (e),

(15) by—

    (A) striking out ''groups'' in subsection (f)(2) and inserting in lieu thereof ''committees'', and

    (B) striking out ''on the negotiation of any trade agreement'' in such subsection and inserting in lieu thereof ''with respect to matters referred to in subsection (a)'',

(16) by striking out "a trade agreement referred to in section 101 or 102" in subsection (g)(1)(A) and inserting in lieu thereof the following: "matters referred to in subsection (a)",

(17) by—

(A) striking out "trade negotiations" in subsection (g)(1)(B) and inserting in lieu thereof "matters referred to in subsection (a)", and

(B) striking out "proposed trade agreements" in subsection (g)(2) and inserting in lieu thereof "matters reffered to in subsection (a)",

(18) by—

(A) striking out ", both during preparation for negotiations and actual negotiations" in the first sentence of subsection (i),

(B) striking out "arising in preparation for on in the course of such negotiations" in the second sentence of such subsection, and

(C) striking out "to the negotiations" in the second sentence of such subsection and inserting in lieu thereof the following: "with respect to matters referred to in subsection (a)",

(19) by striking out "trade agreement referred to in section 101 or 102" in subsections (j) and (k) and inserting in lieu thereof "matters referred to in subsection (a)",

(20) by adding at the end of subsection (k) the following new sentence: "To the maximum extent practicable, the members of the committees established under subsections (b) and (c), and other appropriate parties, shall be informed and consulted before and during any such negotiations and may be permitted to participate in international meetings to the extent the head of the United States delegation deems appropriate, but may not speak or negotiate for the United States.", and

(21) by adding at the end thereof the following new subsection:

"(1) The provisions of title XVIII of the Food and Agriculture Act of 1977 shall not apply to an advisory committee established under subsection (c)."

Section 1104. Study of Possible Agreements with North American Countries.

(a) In General.—Section 612 of the Trade Act of 1974 (19 U.S.C. 2486) is amended by inserting "(a)" before "It" and by adding at the end thereof the following:

(b) The President shall study the desirability of entering into trade agreements with countries in the northern portion of the western hemisphere to promote the economic growth of the United States and such countries and the mutual expansion of market opportunities and report to the Committee on Ways and Means of the House of Representatives and the Committee on Finance of the Senate his findings and conclusions within 2 years after the date of enactment of this Act. The study shall include an examination of competitive opportunities and conditions of competition between such countries and the United States in the agricultural, energy, and other appropriate sectors.

(b) Clerical Amendments.—

(1) The caption of section 612 of such Act is amended to read as follows:

"Section 612. Trade Relations with North American Countries.".

(2) The table of contents of such Act is amended by striking out the item relating to section 612 and inserting in lieu thereof the following new item;

"Section 612. Trade relations with North American countries.".

Section 1105. Amendments to Section 337 of the Tariff Act of 1930.

(a) Relationship to Countervailing and Antidumping Duty Investigations.— Paragraph (3) of section 337(b) of the Tariff Act of 1930 (19 U.S.C. 1337) is amended—

(1) by striking out "the matter" and inserting in lieu thereof "a matter, in whole or in part,", and

(2) by adding at the end thereof the following: "If the Commission has reason to believe the matter before it is based solely on alleged acts and effects which are within the purview of section 303, 701, or 731 of this Act, it shall terminate, or not institute, any investigation into the matter. If the Commission has reason to believe the matter before it is based in part on alleged acts and effects which are within the purview of section 303, 701, or 731 of this Act, and in part on alleged acts and effects which may, independently from or in conjunction with those within the purview of such section, establish a basis for relief under this section, then it may institute or continue an investigation into the matter. If the Commission notifies the Secretary or the administering authority (as defined in section 771(1) of this Act) with respect to a matter under this paragraph, the Commission may suspend its investigation during the time the matter is before the Secretary or administering authority for final decision. For purposes of computing the 1-year or 18-month periods prescribed by this subsection, there shall be excluded such period of suspension. Any final decision of the Secretary under section 303 of this Act or by the administering authority under section 701 or 731 of this Act with respect to the matter within such section 303, 701, or 731 of which the Commission has notified the Secretary or administering authority shall be conclusive upon the Commission with respect to the issue of less-than-fair-value sales or subsidization and the matters necessary for such decision.".

(b) Civil Penalty for Violation of Order.—Subsection (f) of section 337 of such

Act (19 U.S.C. 1337(f)) is amended by inserting "(1)" before "In lieu of", and by adding at the end thereof the following new paragraph:

"(2) Any person who violates an order issued by the Commission under paragraph (1) after it has become final shall forfeit and pay to the United States a civil penalty for each day on which an importation of articles, or their sale, occurs in violation of the order of not more than the greater of $10,000 or the domestic value of the articles entered or sold on such day in violation of the order. Such penalty shall accrue to the United States and may be recovered for the United States in a civil action brought by the Commission in the Federal District Court for the District of Columbia or for the district in which the violation occurs. In such actions, the United States district courts may issue mandatory injunctions incorporating the relief sought by the Commission as they deem appropriate in the enforcement of such final orders of the Commission.".

(c) Conforming Amendment.—The fourth sentence of section 337(c) of such Act (19 U.S.C. 1337(c)) is amended by striking out "(d) or (e)" and inserting in lieu thereof "(d), (e), or (f)".

Section 1106. Technical Amendments to the Trade Act of 1974.

(a) Amendment of Trade Act of 1974.—Except as otherwise specifically provided in this section, any reference in this section by way of amendment, repeal, or other change to a provision of law is a reference to the specified provision of the Trade Act of 1974.

(b) Table of Contents.—In the table of contents the item relating to section 261 is amended to read as follows:

"Sec. 261. Definition of firm.".

(c) Title I.—

(1) Section 102(e)(2) is amended by striking out "copy of such agreement" and inserting in lieu thereof "copy of the final legal text of such agreement". The amendment made by the preceding sentence shall apply with respect to trade agreements submitted to the Congress under section 102 of the Trade Act of 1974 after the date of the enactment of this Act.

(2) The next to last sentence of section 121(c) is amended to read as follows: "Such trade agreement may be entered into under section 102.".

(3) Paragraph (2) of section 109(c) is amended by striking out "such" and inserting in lieu thereof "any".

(4) Section 5315(24) of title 5, United States Code, is amended by inserting immediately after "Commission" the following: "(5)".

(5) Paragraph (1) of section 152(c) is amended by striking out "153(b)" and inserting in lieu thereof "154(b)".

(d) Title II.—

(1) Section 203(a)(4) is amended by inserting, "conclude, and carry out" immediately after "negotiate".

(2) Section 203(b) is amended by—

(A) striking out "On the day on which the President proclaims import relief under this section or announces his intention to negotiate one or more orderly marketing agreements," in paragraph (1) and inserting in lieu thereof "On the day the President determines under section 202 to provide import relief, including announcement of his intention to negotiate an orderly marketing agreement,",

(B) striking out "201(b)(1)(A)" in paragraph (1) and inserting in lieu thereof "201(d)(1)(A)", and

(C) adding at the end thereof the following new paragraph:

"(3) On the day on which the President proclaims any import relief under this section not reported pursuant to paragraph (1), he shall transmit to Congress a document setting forth the action he is taking and the reasons therefor.

(3) Section 203(c)(1) is amended by—

(A) striking out "201(b)(1)(A) and inserting in lieu thereof "201(d)(1)(A)", and

(B) by inserting "under the procedures set forth in section 152" immediately after "voting".

(4) Section 203(e)(3) is amended by striking out "(1), (2), (3) or (5)".

(5) Section 203(g)(1) is amended by—

(A) striking out "quantitative"; and

(B) striking out "pursuant to this subsection (a)(3) or (c)" and inserting in lieu thereof "pursuant to this section".

(6) Section 203(g)(2) is amended by striking out "or (e)(2)" each place it appears and inserting in lieu thereof "(e)(2), or (e)(3)".

(7) Subsection (h) of section 203 is amended by—

(A) inserting "or (i)(3)" after "(i)(2)" in paragraphs (3) and (4), and

(B) by striking out "one 3-year period" in paragraph (3) and inserting in lieu thereof "one period of not more than 3 years".

(8) The caption of section 261 is amended to read as follows:

Section 261. Definition of Firm.''.

(e) Title III.—Section 331(c) is amended by striking out "515(d)" and inserting in lieu thereof "315(d)".

(f) Title IV.—

(1) Section 402(c)(1) is amended by striking out "subsection (a)" and inserting in lieu thereof "subsections (a)".

(2) Section 404(c) is amended by striking out the comma.

(3) Section 405(b)(8) is amended by striking out "those" and inserting in lieu thereof "arrangements".

(g) Title V.—

(1) Section 502(b)(2) is amended by striking out "withhold supplies of vital commodity resources from international trade or to raise the price of such commodities to an unreasonable level which causes serious disruption of the world economy;".

(2) Section 502(b)(6) is amended by inserting a comma after "partnership".

(3) Section 504(c)(1) is amended—

(A) by striking out "60 days" and inserting in lieu thereof "90 days", and

(B) by striking out "60th day," and inserting in lieu thereof "90th day,".

(h) Title VI.—

(1) Section 601(2) is amended by striking out "and" and inserting in lieu thereof "or".

(2) Section 602(a) is amended by striking out, "as amended".

(3) Section 602(f) is amended by striking out the last comma.

Section 1107. Technical Amendments to the Tariff Schedules of the United States.

(a) General Headnote Changes.—The general headnotes for the Tariff Schedules of the United States (19 U.S.C. 1202) are amended—

(1) by inserting "and" after "subpart E" in headnote 3(a)(i), and

(2) by striking out "Germany (the Soviet zone and the Soviet sector of Berlin)" in headnote 3(e) and inserting in lieu thereof "German Democratic Republic and East Berlin."

(b) Tobacco.—Schedule 1, part 13 of such Schedules is amended by redesignating headnotes 5 and 6 as 3 and 4, respectively.

(c) Fluoranthene.—Schedule 4, part 1, subpart A, item 401.36 of such Schedules is amended to read "Fluoranthene."

(d) Structures.—Schedule 6, part 3, subpart F of such Schedules is amended by striking out items 652.97 and 652.99 and the superior heading thereto and by inserting in lieu thereof the following:

652.97	Offshore oil and natural gas drilling and production	9.5% ad val.	45% ad val.
653.00	Other	9.5% ad val.	45% ad val.
653.01	Other	9.5% ad val.	45% ad val.

(e) Measuring, Testing, and Controlling Instruments.—Schedule 7, part 2, subpart D of such Schedules is amended—

(1) by striking out "711.00" in headnote 1 and headnote 2(a) and inserting "711.04" in lieu thereof; and

(2) by striking out "712.00 to 712.99" in headnote 2 and inserting "712.05 to 712.51" in lieu thereof.

(f) Photographic Products.—The article description in item 722.10 of such Schedules is amended to read as follows: "Having a photographic lens valued over 50 percent of the value of the article.".

(g) Buttons.—Schedule 7, part 7, subpart A of such Schedules is amended—

(1) by striking out "745.22," in headnote 2(a); and

(2) by redesignating headnote 4 as headnote 3.

(h) Pressure-Sensitive Articles.—Schedule 7, part 13, subpart A, headnote 1(ii) of such Schedules is amended by striking "13B" and inserting "13C" in lieu thereof.

Section 1108. Reporting of Statistics on a Cost-Insurance-Freight Basis.

(a) In General.—Section 301 of title 13, United States Code, is amended by adding at the end thereof the following new subsections:

"(e) There shall be reported, on monthly and cumulative bases, for each item in the Tariff Schedules of the United States Annotated, the United States port of entry value (as determined under subsection (b)(6)). There shall be reported, on monthly and cumulative bases, the balance of international trade for the United States reflecting (1) the aggregate value of all United States imports as reported in accordance with the first sentence of this subsection, and (2) the aggregate value of all United States exports. The values and balance of trade required to be reported by this subsection shall be released no later than 48 hours before the release of any other government statistics concerning values of United States imports or United States balance of trade, or statistics from which such values or balance may be derived.

"(f) On or before January 1, 1981, and as often thereafter as may be necessary to reflect significant changes in rates, there shall be reported for each item of the Tariff Schedules of the United States Annotated, the ad valorem or ad valorem equivalent rate of duty which would have been required to be imposed on dutiable imports under that item, if the United States customs values of such imports were based on the United States port of entry value (as reported in accordance with the first sentence of subsection (e)) in order to collect the same amount of duties on imports under that item as are currently collected.''.

(b) Effective Date.—The amendment made by subsection (a) shall apply to reports made after December 31, 1979.

Section 1109. Reorganizing and Restructuring of International Trade Functions of the United States Government.

(a) In General.—The President shall submit to the Congress, not later than July 10, 1979, a proposal to restructure the international trade functions of the Executive Branch of the United States Government. In developing his proposal, the President shall consider, among other possibilities, strengthening the coordination and functional responsibilities of the Office of the Special Representative for Trade Negotiations to include, among other things, representation of the United States in all matters before the General Agreement on Tariffs and Trade, the establishment of a board of trade with a coordinating mechanism in the Executive Office of the President, and the establishment of a Department of International Trade and Investment. The recommendations of the President, as embodied in such proposal, shoud include a monitoring and enforcement structure which would insure protection of United States rights under agreements negotiated pursuant to the Tokyo Round of the Multilateral Trade Negotiations and all other elements of multilateral and bilateral international trade agreements. The proposal should result in an upgrading of commercial programs and commercial attaches overseas to assure that United States trading partners are meeting their trade agreement obligations, particularly those entered into under such agreements, including the tendering procedures of the Agreement on Government Procurement.

(b) Congressional Action.—In order to ensure that the 96th Congress takes final action on a comprehensive reorganization of trade functions as soon as possible, the appropriate committee of each House of the Congress shall give the proposal by the President immediate consideration and shall make its best efforts to take final committee action to reoganize and restructure the international trade functions of the United States Government by November 10, 1979.

Section 1110. Study of Export Trade Policy.

(a) Review of Export Promotion and Disincentives.—The President shall review all export promotion functions of the executive branch and potential programmatic and regulatory disincentives to exports, and shall submit to the Congress a report of that review not later than July 15, 1980. The report should make particular reference to those activities which enhance the role of small and medium-sized businesses in export trade.

(b) Conditions of Competition Study.—Not later than July 15, 1980, the President shall submit to the Congress a study of the factors bearing on the competitive posture of United States producers and the policies and programs required to strengthen the relative competitive position of the United States in world markets.

Section 1111. Generalized System of Preferences.

(a) In General.—Title V of the Trade Act of 1974 (19 U.S.C. 2461 et seq.) is amended as follows:

(1) Section 502(a)(3) is amended by inserting "or which is contributing to comprehensive regional economic integration among its members through appropriate means, including, but not limited to, the reduction of duties," immediately before "the President".

(2) Section 502(e) is amended by—

(A) inserting "(1)" immediately after "(e)"; and

(B) adding at the end thereof the following new paragraph:

"(2) The President may exempt from the application of paragraph (2) of subsection (b) any country that enters into a bilateral product-specific trade agreement with the United States under section 101 or 102 of the Trade Act of 1974 before January 3, 1980. The President shall terminate the exemption granted to any country under the preceding sentence if that country interrupts or terminates the delivery of supplies of petroleum and petroleum products to the Unitesd States.".

(3) Section 503(b) is amended—

(A) by amending paragraph (2) to read as follows:

"(2) If the sum of (A) the cost or value of the materials produced in the beneficiary developing country or any 2 or more countries which are members of the same association of countries which is treated as one country under section 502(a)(3), plus (B) the direct costs of processing operations performed in such beneficiary developing country or such member countries is not less than 35 percent of the appraised value of such article at the time of its entry into the customs territory of the United States."; and

(B) by striking out the penultimate sentence.

(4) Section 504 is amended—

(A) by adding at the end of subsection (c) the following new paragraph:

"(3) For purposes of this subsection, the term 'country' does not include an association of countries which is treated as one country under section 502(a)(3), but does include a country which is a member of any such association."; and

(B) by inserting at the end of subsection (d) the following new sentence: "The President may disregard subsection (c)(1)(B) with respect to any eligible article if the appraised value of the total imports of such article into the United States during the preceding calendar year is not in excess of an amount which bears the same ratio to $1,000,000 as the gross national product of the United States for that calendar year, as determined by the Department of Commerce, bears to the gross national product of the United States for calendar year 1979.".

(b) Effective Date.—The amendments made by paragraph (4) of subsection (a) shall take effect on April 1, 1980.

Section 1112. Concession-Related Revenue Losses to United States Possessions.

(a) Determinations by Secretary of Commerce.—

(1) Impact of Concessions.—Upon the request of the government of a possession of the United States, the Secretary of Commerce shall determine before January 1, 1980—

(A) whether a concession was granted by the United States in the Tokyo Round of the Multilateral Trade Negotiations on an article produced in that possession on which excise taxes are levied by the United States, and

(B) whether the sum of the amounts transferred and paid over to that possession attributable to such taxes for calendar year 1978 were equal to, or greater than, an amount equal to 10 percent of the tax revenues (not including revenues associated with petroleum or petroleum products) of that possession for 1978.

(2) Annual Determination.—If the determinations of the Secretary under subparagraphs (A) and (B) of paragraph (1) are affirmative, then he shall determine, within 3 months after the close of each of the fiscal years 1980 through 1984, whether that concession contributed importantly to a reduction in the sum of the amount transferred and paid over to that possession on account of such excise taxes for the most recently closed fiscal year. In making his determination, the Secretary shall take into account the extent to which other factors may have contributed to the reduction. The Secretary shall determine the amount of the reduction by subtracting the amount so transferred and paid over for the fiscal year from the amount which would have been transferred and paid over for the fiscal year if the products of the possession with respect to which the excise tax is imposed had maintained a share of the United States market for that product which was the share of the United States market for the product for fiscal year 1979.

(b) Inclusion of Compensatory Amount in Budget of the United States.—If the Secretary determines an amount under subsection (a)(2), he shall advise the President of that amount and the President may include, in the first Budget or Supplemental Budget submitted under the Budget and Accounting Act, 1921, after receiving such advice, an amount, equal to the amount so determined by the Secretary, for payment to the government of that possession to offset the amount of the reduction. If the President includes an amount different from the amount determined by the Secretary or no amount, the President shall promptly submit a report to the Congress setting forth his reasons for submitting such a different amount. Upon appropriation, such sums shall be paid promptly to the government of such possession. There are authorized to be appropriated such sums as may be necessary for the purposes of this section for fiscal years 1981 through 1985.

(c) Report to the Congress.—On January 31, 1984, the President shall report to the Congress on the operation of this section, the reductions in revenues determined under this section, and any reductions which are likely to occur in fiscal years beginning after September 30, 1984. If he determines that such action is warranted, he shall recommend to the Congress in such report an extension of the application of this section to such fiscal years.

Sec. 1113. No Budget Authority For Any Fiscal Year Before Fiscal Year 1981.

Nothing in this Act shall be construed as authorizing the enactment of new budget authority for any fiscal year beginning before October 1, 1980.

Sec. 1114. Effective Date.

Except as otherwise provided in this title, this title shall take effect on the date of enactment of this Act.

Approved July 26, 1979.

11. REORGANIZATION OF U.S. TRADE FUNCTIONS

CONSOLIDATION OF FEDERAL TRADE FUNCTIONS

(a) President Carter's Message to Congress
(September 25, 1979).

To the Congress of the United States:

I transmit herewith Reorganization Plan No. 3 of 1979, to consolidate trade functions of the United States Government. I am acting under the authority vested in me by the Reorganization Act of 1977, chapter 9 of title 5 of the United States Code, and pursuant to section 1109 of the Trade Agreements Act of 1979, which directs that I transmit to the Congress a proposal to restructure the international trade functions of the Executive branch.

The goal of this reorganization is to improve the capacity of the Government to strengthen the export performance of the United States industry and to assure fair international trade practices, taking into account the interests of all elements of our economy.

Recent developments, which have raised concern about the vitality of our international trade performance, have focused much attention on the way our trade machinery is organized. These developments include our negative trade balance, increasing dependence upon foreign oil, and international pressures on the dollar. New challenges, such as implementation of the Multilateral Trade Negotiation (MTN) agreements and trade with non-market economies, will further test our Government trade organization.

We must be prepared to apply domestically the MTN codes on procurement, subsidies, standards, and customs valuation. We also must monitor major implementation measures abroad, reporting back to American business on important developments and, where necessary, raising questions internationally about foreign implementation. MTN will work—will open new markets for U.S. labor, farmers, and business—only if we have adequate procedures for aggressively monitoring and enforcing it. We intend to meet our obligations, and we expect others to do the same.

The trade machinery we now have cannot do this job effectively. Although the Special Trade Representative (STR) takes the lead role in administering the trade agreements program, many issues are handled elsewhere and no agency has across-the-board leadership in trade. Aside from the Trade Representative and the Export-Import Bank, trade is not the primary concern of any Executive branch agency where trade functions are located. The current arrangements lack a central authority capable of planning a coherent trade strategy and assuring its vigorous implementation.

This reorganization is designed to correct such deficiencies and to prepare us for strong enforcement of the MTN codes. It aims to improve our export promotion activities so that United States exporters can take full advantage of trade opportunities in foreign markets. It provides for the timely and efficient administration of our unfair trade laws. It also establishes an efficient mechanism for shaping an effective, comprehensive United States trade policy.

To achieve these objectives, I propose to place policy coordination and negotiation—those international trade functions that most require comprehensiveness, influence, and Government-wide perspective—in the Executive Office of the President. I propose to place operational and implementation responsibilities, which are staff-intensive, in line departments that have the requisite resources and knowledge of the major sectors of our economy to handle them. I have concluded that building our trade structure on STR and Commerce, respectively, best satisfies these considerations.

I propose to enhance STR, to be renamed the Office of the United States Trade Representative, by centralizing in it international trade policy development, coordination and negotiation functions. The Commerce Department will become the focus of non-agricultural operational trade responsibilities by adding to its existing duties those for commercial representation abroad, antidumping and countervailing duty cases, the non-agricultural aspects of MTN implementation, national security investigations, and embargoes.

THE UNITED STATES TRADE REPRESENTATIVE

The Trade Representative, with the advice of the Trade Policy Committee, will be responsible for developing and coordinating our international trade and direct investment policy, including the following areas:

Import remedies.—The Trade Representative will exercise policy oversight of the application of import remedies, analyze long-term trends in import remedy cases and recommend any necessary legislative changes. For antidumping and countervailing duty matters, such coordination, to the extent legally permissible, will be directed toward the establishment of new precedents, negotiation of assurances, and coordination with other trade matters, rather than case-by-case fact finding and determinations.

East-West trade policy.—The Trade Representative will have lead responsibility for East-West trade negotiations and will coordinate East-West trade policy. The Trade Policy Committee will assume the responsibilities of the East-West Foreign Trade Board.

International investment policy.—The Trade Representative will have the policy lead regarding issues of direct foreign investment in the United States, direct investment by Americans abroad, operations of mutinational enterprises, and mutilateral agreements on international investment, insofar as such issues relate to international trade.

International commodity policy.—The Trade Representative will assume responsibility for commodity negotiations and also will coordinate commodity policy.

Energy Trade.—While the Departments of Energy and State will continue to share responsibility for international energy issues, the Trade Representative will coordinate energy trade matters. The Department of Energy will become a member of the TPC.

Export-expansion policy.—To ensure a vigorous and coordinated Government-vide export expansion effort, policy oversight of our export expansion activities will be the responsibility of the Trade Representative.

The Trade Representative will have the lead role in bilateral and multilateral trade, commodity, and direct investment negotiations. The Trade Representative will represent the United States in General Agreement on Tariffs and Trade (GATT) matters. Since the GATT will be the principal international forum for implementing and interpreting the MTN agreements and since GATT meetings, including committee and working group meetings, occur almost continuously, the Trade Representative will have a limited number of permanent staff in Geneva. In some cases, it may be necessary to assign a small number of USTR staff abroad to assist in oversight of MTN enforcement. In this event, appropriate positions will be authorized. In recognition of the responsibility of the Secretary of State regarding our foreign policy, the activities of overseas personnel of the Trade Representative and the Commerce Department will be fully coordinated with other elements of our diplomatic missions.

In addition to his role with regard to GATT matters, the Trade Representative will have the lead responsibility for trade and commodity matters considered in the Organization for Economic Cooperation and Development (OECD) and the United Nations Conference on Trade and Development (UNCTAD) when such matters are the primary issues under negotiation. Because of the Secretary of State's foreign policy responsibilities, and the responsibilities of the Director of the International Development Cooperation Agency as the President's principal advisor on development, the Trade Representative will exercise his OECD and UNCTAD responsibilities in close cooperation with these officials.

To ensure that all trade negotiations are handled consistently and that our negotiating leverage is employed to the maximum, the Trade Representative will manage the negotiation of particular issues. Where appropriate, the Trade Representative may delegate responsibility for negotiations to other agencies with expertise on the issues under consideration. He will coordinate the operational aspects of negotiations through a Trade Negotiating Committee, chaired by the Trade Representative and including the Departments of Commerce, State, Treasury, Agriculture and Labor.

The Trade Representative will be concerned not only with ongoing negotiations and coordination of specific, immediate issues, but also—very importantly—with the development of long-term United States trade strategies and policies. He will oversee implementation of the MTN agreements, and will advise the President on the effects of other Government policies (e.g., antitrust, taxation) on U.S. trade. In order to participate more fully in oversight of international investment and export financing activities, the Trade Representative will become a member of the National Advisory Council on International Monetary and Financial Policies and the Boards of the Export-Import Bank and the Overseas Private Investment Corporation.

In performing these functions, the Trade Representative will act as the principal trade spokesman of the President. To assure that our trade policies take into account the broadest range of perspectives, the Trade Representative will consult with the Trade Policy Committee, whose mandate and membership will be expanded. The Trade Representative will, as appropriate, invite agencies such as the Export-Import Bank and the Overseas Private Investment Corporation to participate in TPC meetings in addition to the permanent TPC members. When different departmental views on trade matters exist within the TPC as will be the case from time to time in this complex policy area, I will expect the Trade Representative to resolve policy disagreements in his best judgment, subject to appeal to the President.

THE DEPARTMENT OF COMMERCE

The Department of Commerce, under this proposal, will become the focal point of operational responsibilities in the non-agricultural trade area. My reorganization plan will transfer to the Commerce Department important responsibilities for administration of countervailing and antidumping matters, foreign commercial representation, and MTN implementation support. Consolidating these trade functions in the Department of Commerce builds upon an agency with extensive trade experience. The Department will retain its operational responsibilities in such areas as export controls, East-West trade, trade adjustment assistance to firms and communities, trade policy analysis, and monitoring foreign compliance with trade agreements. The Department will be substantially reorganized to consolidate and reshape its trade functions under an Under Secretary for International Trade.

With this reorganization, trade functions will be strengthened within the Department of Commerce, and such related effects in the Department as improvement of industrial innovation and productivity, encouraging local and regional economic development, and sectoral analysis, will be closely linked to an aggressive trade program. Fostering the international competitiveness of American industry will become the principal mission of the Department of Commerce.

Import remedies.

I propose to transfer to the Department of Comerce responsibility for administration of the countervailing duty and antidumping statutes. This function will be performed efficiently and effectively in an organizational setting where trade is the primary mission. This activity will be directed by a new Assistant Secretary for Trade Administration, subject to Senate confirmation. Although the plan permits its provisions to take effect as late as October 1, 1980, I intend to make this transfer effective by January 1, 1980, so that it will occur as the new MTN codes take effect. Commerce will continue its supportive role in the staffing of other unfair trade practice issues, such as cases arising under section 301 of the Trade Act of 1974.

Commercial representation

This reorganization plan will transfer to the Department of Commerce responsibility for commercial representation abroad. This transfer would place both domestic and overseas export promotion activities under a single organization, directed by an Assistant Secretary for Export Development, charged with aggressively expanding U.S. export opportunities. Placing this Foreign Commercial Service in the Commerce Department will allow commercial officers to concentrate on the promotion of U.S. exports as their principal activity.

Initially, the transfer of commercial representation from State to Commerce will involve all full-time overseas trade promotion and commercial positions (approximately 162), responsibility for this function in the countries (approximately 60) to which these individuals are assigned, and the associated foreign national employees in those countries. Over time, the Department of Commerce undoubtedly will review the deployment of commercial officers in light of changing trade circumstances and propose extensions or alterations of coverage of the Foreign Commercial Service.

MTN implementation

I am dedicated to the aggressive implementation of the Multilateral Trade Agreements. The United States must seize the opportunities and enforce the obligations created by these agreements. Under this proposal, the Department of Commerce will assign high priority to this task. The Department of Commerce will be responsible for the day-to-day implementation of non-agricultural aspects of the MTN agreements. Management of this function will be a principal assignment of an Assistant Secretary for Trade Policy and Programs. Implementation activities will include:

monitoring agreements and targeting problems for consultation and negotiation;

operating a Trade Complaint Center where the private sector can receive advice as to the recourse and remedies available;

aiding in the settlement of disputes, including staffing of formal complaint cases;

identifying problem areas for consideration by the Trade Representative and the Trade Policy Committee;

educational and promotion programs regarding the provisions of the agreements and the processes for dealing with problems that arise;

providing American business with basic information on foreign laws, regulations and procedures;

consultations with private sector advisory committees; and general analytical support.

These responsibilities will be handled by a unit built around the staff from Commerce that provided essential analytical support to STR throughout the MTN negotiation process. Building implementation of MTN around this core group will assure that the government's institutional memory and expertise on MTN is most effectively devoted to the challenge ahead. When American business needs information or encounters problems in the MTN area, it can turn to the Department of Commerce for knowledgeable assistance.

Matching the increased importance of trade in the Department's mission will be a much strengthened trade organization within the Department. By creating a number of new senior level positions in the Department, we will ensure that trade policy implementation receives the kind of day-to-day top management attention that it both demands and requires.

With its new responsibilities and resources, the Department of Commerce will become a key participant in the formulation of our trade policies. Much of the analysis in support of trade policy formulation will be conducted by the Department of Commerce, which will be close to the operational aspects of the problems that raise policy issues.

To succeed in global competition, we must have a better understanding of the problems and prospects of U.S. industry, particularly in relation to the growing strength of industries abroad. This is the key reason why we will upgrade sectoral analysis capabilities throughout the Department of Commerce, including the creation of a new Bureau of Industrial analysis. Commerce, with its ability to link trade to policies affecting industry, is uniquely suited to serve as the principal technical expert within the Government on special industry sector problems requiring international consultation, as well as to provide industry-specific information on how tax, regulatory and other Government policies affect the international competitiveness of the U.S. industries.

Commerce will also expand its traditional trade policy focus on industrial issues to deal with the international trade and investment problems of our growing services sector. Under the proposal, there will be comprehensive service industry representation in our industry advisory process, as well as a continuing effort to bring services under international discipline. I expect the Commerce Department to play a major role in developing new service sector initiatives for consideration within the Government.

After an investigation lasting over a year, I have found that this reorganization is necessary to carry out the policy set forth in section 901(a) of title 5 of the United States Code. As described above, this reorganization will increase significantly our ability to implement the MTN agreements efficiently and effectively and will improve greatly the services of the government with regard to export development. These improvements will be achieved with no increse in personnel or expenditures, except for an annual expense of about $300,000 for the salaries and clerical support of the three additional senior Commerce Department officials and a non-recurring expense of approximately $600,000 in connection with the transfers of functions provided in the plan. I find that the reorganization made by this plan makes necessary the provisions for the appointment and pay of a Deputy Secretary, an Under Secretary for International Trade, and two additional Assistant Secretaries of the Department of Commerce, and additional members of the Boards of Directors of the Export-Import Bank and the Overseas Private Investment Corporation.

It is indeed appropriate that this proposal follows so soon after the overwhelming approval by the Congress of the Trade Agreements Act of 1979, for it will sharpen and unify trade policy direction, improve the efficiency of trade law enforcement, and enable us to negotiate abroad from a position of strength. The extensive discussions between Administration officials and the Congress on this plan have been a model of the kind of cooperation that can exist between two branches. I look forward to our further cooperation in successfully implementing both this reorganization proposal and the MTN agreements.

(b) Reorganization Plan No. 3 of 1979

Reorganization of Functions Relating to
International Trade

Section 1. Office of the United States Trade Representative

(a) The Office of the Special Representative for Trade Negotiations is redesignated the Office of the United States Trade Representative.

(b)(1) The Special Representative for Trade Negotiations is redesignated the United States Trade Representative (hereinafter referred to as the "Trade Representative"). The Trade Representative shall have primary responsibility, with the advice of the interagency organization established under section 242 of the Trade Expansion Act of 1962 (19 U.S.C. 1872)(hereinafter referred to as the "Committee"), for developing, and for coordinating the implementation of, United States international trade policy, including commodity matters and, to the extent they are related to international trade policy, direct investment matters. The Trade Representative shall serve as the principal advisor to the President on international trade policy and shall advise the President on the impact of other policies of the United States Government on international trade.

(2) The Trade Representative shall have lead responsibility for the conduct of international trade negotiations, including commodity and direct investment negotiations in which the United States partcipates.

(3) To the extent necessary to assure the coordination of international trade policy, and consistent with any other law, the Trade Representative, with the advice of the Committee, shall issue policy guidance to departments and agencies on basic issues of policy and interpretation arising in the exercise of the following international trade

functions. Such guidance shall determine the policy of the United States with respect to international trade issues arising in the exercise of such functions:

(A) matters concerning the General Agreement on Tariffs and Trade, including implementation of the trade agreements set forth in section 2(c) of the Trade Agreements Act of 1979; United States Government positions on trade and commodity matters dealt with by the Organization for Economic Cooperation and Development, the United Nations Conference on Trade and Development, and other multilateral organizations; and the assertion and protection of the rights of the United States under bilateral and multilateral international trade and commodity agreements;

(B) expansion of exports from the United States;

(C) policy research on international trade, commodity, and direct investment matters;

(D) to the extent permitted by law, overall United States policy with regard to unfair trade practices, including enforcement of countervailing duties and antidumping functions under section 303 and title VII of the Tariff Act of 1930;

(E) bilateral trade and commodity issues, including East-West trade matters; and

(F) international trade issues involving energy.

(4) All functions of the Trade Representative shall be conducted under the direction of the President.

(c) The Deputy Special Representatives for Trade Negotiations are redesignated Deputy United States Trade Representatives.

Section 2. Department of Commerce

(a) The Secretary of Commerce (hereinafter referred to as the "Secretary") shall have, in addition to any other functions assigned by law, general operational responsibility for major nonagricultural international trade functions of the United States Government, including export development, commercial representation abroad, the administration of the antidumping and countervailing duty laws, export controls, trade adjustment assistance to firms and communities, research and analysis, and monitoring compliance with international trade agreements to which the United States is a party.

(b)(1) There shall be in the Department of Commerce (hereinafter referred to as the "Department") a Deputy Secretary appointed by the President, by and with the advice and consent of the Senate. The Deputy Secretary shall receive compensation at the rate payable for Level II of the Executive Schedule, and shall perform such duties and exercise such powers as the Secretary may from time to time prescribe.

(2) The position of Under Secretary of Commerce established under section 1 of the Act of June 5, 1939 (ch. 180, 53 Stat. 808; 15 U.S.C. 1502) is abolished.

(c) There shall be in the Department an Under Secretary for International Trade appointed by the President, by and with the advice and consent of the Senate. The Under Secretary for International Trade shall receive compensation at the rate payable for Level III of the Executive Schedule, and shall perform such duties and exercise such powers as the Secretary may from time to time prescribe.

(d) There shall be in the Department two additional Assistant Secretaries appointed by the President, by and with the advice and consent of the Senate. Each such Assistant Secretary shall receive compensation at the rate payable for Level IV of the Executive Schedule, and shall perform such duties and exercise such powers as the Secretary may from time to time prescribe.

Section 3. Export-Import Bank of the United States

The Trade Representative and the Secretary shall serve, ex officio and without vote, as additional members of the Board of Directors of the Export-Import Bank of the United States.

Section 4. Overseas Private Investment Corporation

(a) The Trade Representative shall serve, ex officio, as an additional voting member of the Board of Directors of the Overseas Private Investment Corporation. The Trade Representative shall be the Vice Chair of such Board.

(b) There shall be an additional member of the Board of Directors of the Overseas Private Investment Corporation who shall be appointed by the President of the United States, by and with the advice and consent of the Senate, and who shall not be an official or employee of the Government of the United States. Such Director shall be appointed for a term of no more than three years.

Section 5. Transfer of Functions

(a)(1) There are transferred to the Secretary all functions of the Secretary of the Treasury, the General Counsel of the Department of the Treasury, or the Department of the Treasury pursuant to the following:

(A) section 305(b) of the Trade Agreements Act of 1979 (19 U.S.C. 2515(b)), to be exercised in consultation with the Secretary of the Treasury;

(B) section 232 of the Trade Expansion Act of 1962 (19 U.S.C. 1862);

(C) section 303 and title VII (including section 771(1)) of the Tariff Act of 1930 (19 U.S.C. 1303, 1671 et seq.), except that the Customs Service of the Department of the Treasury shall accept such deposits, bonds, or other security as deemed appropriate by the Secretary, shall assess and collect such duties as may be directed by the Secretary, and shall furnish such of its important records or copies thereof as may be requested by the Secretary incident to the functions transferred by this subparagraph;

(D) sections 514, 515, and 516 of the Tariff Act of 1930 (19 U.S.C. 1514, 1515, and 1516) insofar as they relate to any protest, petition, or notice of desire to contest described in section 1002(b)(1) of the Trade Agreements Act of 1979;

(E) with respect to the functions transferred by subparagraph (C) of this paragraph, section 318 of the Tariff Act of 1930 (19 U.S.C. 1318), to be exercised in consultation with the Secretary of the Treasury;

(F) with respect to the functions transferred by subparagraph (C) of this paragraph, section 502(b) of the Tariff Act of 1930 (19 U.S.C. 1502(b)), and, insofar as it provides authority to issue regulations and disseminate information, to be exercised in consultation with the Secretary of the Treasury to the extent that the Secretary of the Treasury has responsibility under subparagraph (C), section 502(a) of such Act (19 U.S.C. 1502(a));

(G) with respect to the functions transferred by subparagraph (C) of this paragraph, section 617 of the Tariff Act of 1930 (19 U.S.C. 1617); and

(H) section 2632(e) of title 28 of the United States Code, insofar as it relates to actions taken by the Secretary reviewable under section 516A of the Tariff Act of 1930 (19 U.S.C. 1516(a)).

(2) The Secretary shall consult with the Trade Representative regularly in exercising the functions transferred by subparagraph (C) of paragraph (1) of this subsection, and shall consult with the Trade Representative regarding any substantive regulation proposed to be issued to enforce such functions.

(b)(1) There are transferred to the Secretary all trade promotion and commercial functions of the Secretary of State or the Department of State that are—

(A) performed in full-time overseas trade promotion and commercial positions; or

(B) performed in such countries as the President may from time to time prescribe.

(2) To carry out the functions transferred by paragraph (1) of this subsection, the President, to the extent he deems it necessary, may authorize the Secretary to utilize Foreign Service personnel authorities and to exercise the functions vested in the Secretary of State by the Foreign Service Act of 1946 (22 U.S.C. 801 et seq.) and by any other laws with respect to personnel performing such functions.

(c) There are transferred to the President all functions of the East-West Foreign Trade Board under section 411(c) of the Trade Act of 1974 (19 U.S.C. 2441(c)).

(d) Appropriations available to the Department of State for Fiscal Year 1980 for representation of the United States concerning matters arising under the General Agreement on Tariffs and Trade and trade and commodity matters dealt with under the auspices of the United Nations Conference on Trade and Development are transferred to the Trade Representative.

(e) There are transferred to the interagency organization established under section 242 of the Trade Expansion Act of 1962 (19 U.S.C. 1872) all functions of the East-West Foreign Trade Board under section 411(a) and (b) of the Trade Act of 1974 (19 U.S.C. 2441(a) and (b)).

Section 6. Abolition

The East-West Foreign Trade Board established under section 411 of the Trade Act of 1974 (19 U.S.C. 2441) is abolished.

Section 7. Responsibility of the Secretary of State

Nothing in this reorganization plan is intended to derogate from the responsibility of the Secretary of State for advising the President on foreign policy matters, including the foreign policy aspects of international trade and trade-related matters.

Section 8. Incidental transfers; interim officers

(a) So much of the personnel, property, records, and unexpended balances of appropriations, allocations, and other funds employed, used, held, available, or to be made available in connection with the functions transferred under this reorganization plan as the Director of the Office of Management and Budget shall determine shall be transferred to ther appropriate agency, organization, or component at such time or times as such Director shall provide, except that no such unexpended balances transferred shall be used for purposes other than those for which the appropriation originally was made. The Director of the Office of Management and Budget shall provide for terminating the affairs of any agency abolished herein and for such further measures and dispositions as such Director deems necessary to effectuate the purposes of the reorganization plan.

(b) Pending the assumption of office by the initial officers provided for in section 2 of this reorganization plan, the functions of each such office may be performed, for up to a total of 60 days, by such individuals as the President may designate. Any individual so designated shall be compensated at the rate provided herein for such position.

Section 9. Effective date

The provisions of this reorganization plan shall take effect October 1, 1980, or at such earlier time or times as the President shall specify, but not sooner than the earliest time allowable under section 906 of title 5 of the United States Code.

V. MISCELLANEOUS DOCUMENTS

1. GATT: Waiver Granted in Connection with the European Coal and Steel Community

Decision of 10 November 1952

Considering that the Kingdom of Belgium, the French Republic, the Federal Republic of Germany, the Republic of Italy, the Grand Duchy of Luxemburg and the Kingdom of the Netherlands (hereinafter referred to as "the member States") have concluded on 18 April 1951 a Treaty constituting the European Coal and Steel Community (hereinafter referred to as "the Treaty") and an Annexed Convention containing the Transitional Provisions referred to in Article 85 of the Treaty (hereinafter referred to as "the Convention");

that the member States have specifically undertaken to eliminate and prohibit within the Community import and export duties, or charges with an equivalent effect, and quantitative restrictions on coal and steel products, and to prevent any restrictive or discriminatory practices impeding normal competition so far as they relate to coal and steel products;

that the stated objective of the member States in removing the barriers to the free movement of coal and steel products among their territories is not only to develop closer integration of the economies of those States and to contribute to the maintenance of good understanding among them, but also to contribute to the economic expansion, the development of employment and the improvement of the standard of living in the member States;

that the realisation of these aims, if accompanied by appropriate trade policies on the part of the Community, could benefit other contracting parties to the General Agreement by increasing supplies of coal and steel products, and by providing increased markets for commodities used by the coal and steel industry and for other products and thereby would contribute to the objectives of the General Agreement as defined in the preamble;

that the Community has undertaken to take account of the interests of third countries both as consumers and as suppliers of coal and steel products, to further the development of international trade, and to ensure that equitable prices are charged by its producers in markets outside the Community;

that the member States propose to harmonize their customs duties and other trade regulations applicable to coal and steel products originating in the territories of the other contracting parties to the General Agreement, upon a basis which shall be lower and less restrictive than the general incidence of the duties and regulations of commerce now applicable; and

that, in order to fulfil the undertakings referred to above, it will also be necessary for the Community to avoid placing unreasonable barriers upon exports to third countries, including, specifically, unreasonable duties and unreasonable quantitative restrictions;

Taking Note of the undertakings made by the High Authority on this date that, in the exercise of the powers which the Treaty confers upon it and to the extent that such powers permit, it will act in accordance with the obligations which would apply if the Community were a single contracting party consisting of the European territories of the member States, and, further, that within the limits of these same powers, upon invitation of any of the member States issued at the request of any other contracting party or the CONTRACTING PARTIES, it will participate together with the member State or States concerned in all consultations undertaken in accordance with the provisions of the General Agreement;

of the undertakings of the member States that if, in accordance with the provisions of the General Agreement, a consultation is to take place with one or more member States of the Community with respect to a question on which the High Authority possesses any powers, and if any other contracting party or the CONTRACTING PARTIES so request, the High Authority will be invited to be represented at such consultation; and

of the representations of the member States (*a*) that Article 71 of the Treaty prevents any of the institutions of the Community from requiring such member States to take actions which are inconsistent with their obligations under the General Agreement as modified by this waiver, and (*b*) that, whenever a question arises as to the consistency of any action of the Community or of the member States, taken or proposed to be taken, with the obligations of the member States to other contracting parties under the General Agreement, any recommendation, finding or decision by the CONTRACTING PARTIES with respect to such action or proposed action of the Community or the member States shall have the same force and effect as it would have if the recommendation, finding or decision were made in respect of such action or proposed action on the part of any other contracting party under the General Agreement;

The CONTRACTING PARTIES

Decide, in accordance with paragraph 5(*a*) of Article XXV of the General Agreement and with the principle that the Governments of the member States should be enabled to act for the purposes of the General Agreement, insofar as this may be shown to be necessary to the accomplishment of the objectives of the Treaty and the Convention and of the tasks of the Community and its institutions under those instruments, as if the European territories of those States constituted the territory of a single contracting party insofar as coal and steel products are concerned, as follows:

I.

1. The Governments of the member States, notwithstanding the provisions of paragraph 1 of Article I of the General Agreement, will be free to eliminate, or, as regards imports of coke and steel products into the territory of the Italian Republic, to reduce by stages and ultimately to eliminate, customs duties and other charges imposed on or in connection with the importation or exportation of coal and steel products from or to the territories of any other of the member States, without being required to extend the same treatment to the like products imported from or exported to the territories of any other contracting party.

2. The French Government, notwithstanding the provisions of paragraph 1 of Article I of the General Agreement, will be free to extend to coal and steel products originating in the metropolitan territories of the other member States, when imported into the territories of the French Union listed in Annex B to the General Agreement, such preferences as are extended, in accordance with paragraphs 2 and 4 of Article I of the General Agreement, to coal and steel products originating in that part of metropolitan France which is in Europe or when imported into Algeria, the same treatment as that extended to coal and steel products originating elsewhere in metropolitan France in accordance with the status of Algeria as a part of metropolitan France.

3. The Governments of the member States, notwithstanding the provisions of paragraphs 1 and 2 of Article XIII of the General Agreement, will be free to refrain from imposing any prohibitions or restrictions on the importation or exportation of coal and steel products from or to the territories of any other member State, although instituting or maintaining such prohibitions or restrictions upon the importation or exportation of coal and steel products from or to the territories of other contracting parties; *provided* that the prohibitions or restrictions so instituted or maintained are in all other respects consistent with the General Agreement.

4. The Belgian, Luxemburg and Netherlands Governments will be free to modify the concessions contained in Schedule II annexed to the General Agreement to the extent necessary to establish and maintain, for a period which shall expire not later than five years after the date of the creation of the common coal market, tariff quotas for items *ex* 697 (carburised ferro-

manganese), 703*a*, 704*c* and 705*a*, by raising the duties on such imports of products specified under these items as exceed the said quotas; *provided* that such duties shall not be higher than

12 per cent   for item *ex* 697

 8 per cent   for iron or steel coils for re-rolling included under item *ex* 703 *a*

11 per cent   for universal plates of iron or steel included under item *ex* 703 *a*

18 per cent   for sheets and plates of iron or steel, flat, hot-rolled, not pickled (unworked sheets), of a thickness of not less than 2 millimeters and of a strength of less than 56 kg. per square millimeter, included under item *ex* 703 *a*

20 per cent   for sheets and plates of iron or steel, flat, hot-rolled, not-pickled (unworked sheets), of a thickness of not less than 2 millimeters and of a strength of not less than 56 kg. per square millimeter, included under item *ex* 703 *a*

22 per cent   for other sheets and plates of iron steel, flat, hot-rolled, not pickled (unworked sheets), included under item *ex* 703 *a*

18 per cent   for item 704 *c*

22 per cent   for item 705 *a*.

and that these quotas shall be sufficient to satisfy the domestic demand for these products. These Governments will also be free, for the purposes specified in Section 15, paragraph 7, of the Convention, and under the circumstances specified in that paragraph, to raise by not more than 2 per cent *ad valorem* the duties contained in Schedule II annexed to the General Agreement for Tariff items *ex* 697, 703*a*, 704*c* and 705*a*, as soon as the system of tariff quotas is abandoned.

5. The Belgian Government, notwithstanding the provisions of paragraph 1 of Article XI, will be free to maintain or institute quantitative restrictions, otherwise consistent with the General Agreement, on the import of coal products, to the extent necessary to avoid sudden and harmful shifts in production during the transition period as defined in Section 1, paragraph 4, of the Convention; *provided* that such restrictions shall be eliminated not later than seven years from the date on which the common market for coal products is created.

6. Insofar as the General Agreement permits contracting parties to take certain measures pursuant to Articles VI and XIX to protect their domestic production or pursuant to Article XI to prevent or relieve critical shortages of products essential to them, or requires contracting parties when acting pursuant to Articles XVII and XX to observe the rules of non-discrimination or of equitable treatment, the Governments of the members States, acting singly or as a Community, shall exercise those rights or fulfil those obligations as

if the European territories of those States constituted the territories of a single contracting party insofar as coal and steel products are concerned.

II.

7. From the date of the creation of the common market for coal products and until the end of the transitional period as defined in Section I, paragraph 4, of the Convention, the Governments of the member States will submit an annual report to the CONTRACTING PARTIES on the measures taken by them towards the full application of the Treaty.

III.

For the purposes of this Decision:

8. The territories of the member States shall be the European territories of those States; subject to the provisions of paragraph 2 of the Section I above, this Decision shall not apply to the other territories of those States, even if those territories are part of the customs territory of the metropolitan country for the purposes of the General Agreement.

9. The phrase "coal and steel products" shall mean the products listed in the Annex to this Decision.

10. The waivers set forth in this Decision shall apply to each coal and steel product from the date on which the common market is established with respect to such product.

IV.

11. The CONTRACTING PARTIES, in considering any question relat'ng to this Decision, will pay full regard to the considerations and the undertakings set out in the preamble and to the principle set out in the paragraph immediately preceding Section I of this Decision.

ANNEX

COAL AND STEEL PRODUCTS

Combustibles:
Pit-coal.
Briquettes of pit-coal.
Coke, except coke for electrodes and petroleum coke:
Semi-coke of pit-coal.
Lignite briquettes.
Lignite:
Semi-coke of lignite.

Steel:

Raw materials for the production of pig-iron and steel:

Iron ore (except pyrites).

Scrap iron.

Manganese ore.

Pig-iron and ferro-alloys:

Pig-iron for the manufacture of steel.

Foundry pig-iron and other raw pig-irons.

Spiegeleisen and carburetted ferro-managanese.

Raw and semi-finished products of iron, ordinary steel or special steel, including re-used and reclaimed products:

Liquid steel poured or not poured in ingots, including ingots destined for iron-works.

Semi-finished products; blooms, billets, brames, slabs, wide hot-rolled coils (other than coils considered finished products).

Hot finished products of iron, ordinary steel or special steel:

Rails, sleepers, tie plates and splice bars, beams, heavy sections and bars of 80 mm. or more, and sheet pilings.

Bars and sections of less than 80 mm. and plates of less than 150 mm.

Wide rod.

Rounds and squares for tubes.

Strips and hot rolled strips (including strips for tubes).

Hot rolled sheets less than 3 mm. (not covered and covered).

Plates and sheets 3 mm. thick or more, wide plates of 150 mm. or more.

Finished products of iron, of ordinary steel or of special steel:

Tinplate, lead sheets, black iron, galvanized sheets, other covered sheets.

Cold rolled sheets less than 3 mm.

Magnetic sheets.

Strips for making tinplate.

2. Steel Import Quota Bill (1967)

90TH CONGRESS
1ST SESSION

S. 2537

IN THE SENATE OF THE UNITED STATES

OCTOBER 16, 1967

Mr. HARTKE (for himself, Mr. DIRKSEN, Mr. ALLOTT, Mr. BAYH, Mr. BENNETT, Mr.BIBLE, Mr. BOGGS, Mr. BREWSTER, Mr. BYRD of West Virginia, Mr. CARLSON, Mr. CLARK, Mr. COTTON, Mr. CURTIS, Mr. DOMINICK, Mr. EASTLAND, Mr. FANNIN, Mr. HANSEN, Mr. HILL, Mr. HOLLINGS, Mr. HRUSKA, Mr. JORDAN of Idaho, Mr. LAUSCHE, Mr. MILLER, Mr. MONTOYA, Mr. MUNDT, Mr. MURPHY, Mr. PROUTY, Mr. RANDOLPH, Mr. RIBICOFF, Mr. SCOTT, Mrs. SMITH, Mr. SPARKMAN, Mr. THURMOND, Mr. TOWER, Mr. YOUNG of North Dakota, and Mr. YOUNG of Ohio) introduced the following bill; which was read twice and referred to the Committee on Finance

A BILL

To provide for orderly trade in iron and steel mill products.

Be it enacted by the Senate and House of Representatives of the United States of America in Congress assembled, That this Act may be cited as the "Iron and Steel Orderly Trade Act of 1967"

SEC. 2. The Congress finds that increased imports of pig iron and steel mill products have adversely affected the United States balance of payments, contributed substantially to reduced employment opportunities for United States workers in the domestic iron and steel industry, and captured such an increasing share of the market for pig iron and steel mill products in the United States as to threaten the soundness of the domestic iron and steel industry and therefore the national security.

It is, therefore, declared to be the policy of the Congress that access to the United States market for foreign-produced pig iron and steel mill products should be on an equitable basis to insure orderly trade in pig iron and steel mill products, alleviate United States balance-of-payments problems, provide an opportunity for a strong and expanding United States iron and steel industry, and prevent further disruption of United States markets and unemployment of United States iron and steel workers.

SEC. 3. As used in this Act—

(1) The term "category" means a seven-digit item number which appears in the Tariff Schedules of the United States Annotated (1965) published by the United States Tariff Commission as in effect on the date of enactment of this Act and which is—

(A) within the range beginning with item 608.1500 and ending with item 610.5260 (except that an item within such range which is specified in section 7 shall be included in the term "category" only as provided in such section 7); or

(B) one of the following item numbers:

607.1500	642.9700
607.1800	646.2500
642.0200	646.2620
642.3500	646.2640
642.9000	690.2500
642.9100	690.3000
642.9600	

(2) The term "imports" refers to United States imports in any category or categories within the meaning of paragraph (1).

(3) The term "consumption" means, with respect to any category or with respect to all categories, the sum of United States mill shipments plus imports minus United States exports.

(4) The term "year" means calendar year.

SEC. 4. The President may, after consultation with all nations having an interest in supplying pig iron and steel mill products to the United States, negotiate multilateral or bilateral agreements establishing, for periods beginning on or after the date of the enactment of this Act, annual quantitative limitations on United States imports of such products subject to the following provisions:

(1) Total imports for each year shall not exceed an amount determined by applying to the average annual consumption during the three years immediately preceding the year in which the limitation is to be effective a percentage equal to the percentage of average annual consumption represented by imports during the years 1964 through 1966, inclusive.

(2) The percentage of total imports in any year represented by imports in a particular category shall not exceed the percentage of total imports during the years 1964 through 1965, inclusive, represented by imports in that category.

(3) The percentage of total imports in any year represented by imports from a particular nation shall not exceed the percentage of total

imports during the years 1964 through 1966, inclusive, represented by imports from that nation.

SEC. 5. For periods after the one hundred and eightieth day after the date of the enactment of this Act, the President shall, within the overall limits set forth in paragraph (2) of section 4, by proclamation restrict annual imports from each nation which is at any time on or. after such one hundred and eightieth day not a party to an agreement then limiting current imports negotiated pursuant to section 4 to an amount determined by applying the percentage of consumption represented by imports from that nation during the years 1959 through 1966, inclusive, to the average annual consumption during the three years immediately preceding the year in which the restriction is to apply.

SEC. 6. Within the overall limitations imposed under section 4, the President may adjust the share of United States imports in any category which may be supplied by any nation. In making this adjustment the President shall be guided principally by historical import patterns, but may modify such patterns to accommodate interests of developing nations or other changing conditions of international trade.

SEC. 7. If imports in any year in any of the following item numbers appearing in the Tariff Schedules of the United States Annotated (1965) published by the United States Tariff Commission as in effect on the date of the enactment of this Act reach 120 percent of imports in that items number during the year immediately prior to the year in which this Act is enacted, then such item number shall be considered a category under paragraph (1) of section 3, and this Act shall take effect with respect to such category on the 1st day of January following the year in which the 120 percent level was reached:

608.1000	610.8020	642.9300	652.9400
608.2500	610.8040	646.2000	652.9500
608.2700	642.0800	646.2700	652.9600
609.1200	642.1020	646.2800	653.0200
609.1300	642.1040	646.3000	653.0300
609.1500	642.1200	646.4000	680.4000
609.8400	642.1400	646.5400	688.3000
609.8600	642.1620	646.5600	688.3500
609.8800	642.1800	652.9000	688.4000
609.9000	642.8000	652.9200	

SEC. 8. (1) The amount of imports in any category in either half of any year shall not exceed 60 percent of the total permissible amount of import in that category for that year.

(2) Should any limitation imposed under this Act take effect on any day other than January 1 of a year, such limitation shall apply pro rata during the remaining portion of such year.

SEC. 9. (1) Import limitations established under this Act shall be administered by the Secretary of Commerce. The Secretary may issue such regulations as may be necessary or appropriate to carry out the purposes of this Act.

(2) Whenever the Secretary of Commerce determines it to be necessary to avoid disruption of regional markets, he shall provide by regulation that the proportionate share of total imports and imports in any category from any nation entering through any port of entry in or near such regional markets shall not exceed the proportionate share of such imports entering through such port during the applicable based period. The Secretary shall conduct the review required to make such a determination at least annually.

(3) Upon the expiration of five years after the date of the enactment of this Act, the Secretary of Commerce shall submit a report to the Congress as to the effects of the import limitations established under this Act on (1) the economic soundness of the iron and steel industry and employment opportunities in such industry, (2) the general economy, (3) the United States balance of payments, and (4) the national security, together with his recommendations as to whether such import limitations should be continued, modified, or revoked. Before making such report, the Secretary shall conduct a hearing at which all interested parties shall have an opportunity to be heard.

3. Voluntary Restraint Agreements of 1972

THE WHITE HOUSE

TEXTS OF LETTERS TO THE SECRETARY OF STATE FROM
THE ASSOCIATIONS OF THE STEEL PRODUCERS OF THE
EUROPEAN COAL AND STEEL COMMUNITY (ECSC) AND
THE ASSOCIATION OF STEEL PRODUCERS OF
THE UNITED KINGDOM; JAPAN IRON AND
STEEL EXPORTERS' ASSOCIATION

(a) *The European Producers*

May 2, 1972

Dear Mr. Secretary:

The Associations of the Steel Producers of the European Coal and Steel Community (ECSC) and the Association of Steel Producers of the United Kingdom, declare their intention to limit through December 31, 1974, exports of steel mill products to the United States. The following are the terms under which these exports will be regulated:

1. *Total Exports and Growth Rate*

The total quantity of steel mill products to be shipped to the United States by the above-mentioned producer associations will not exceed 7,270,000 metric tons (8,013,794 net tons) during calendar year 1972. The growth rate of exports of steel mill products will not exceed one percent (1%) in calendar year 1973 over the calendar year 1972 limit of shipments and the growth rate of exports of steel mill products will not exceed two and one-half percent (2.5%) in 1974 over the calendar year 1973 limit of shipments.

In accordance with this growth rate, such shipments will not exceed 7,342,000 metric tons (8,093,573 net tons) in calendar year 1973 and 7,525,550 metric tons (8,295,910 net tons) in calendar year 1974.

The above-mentioned producers associations will endeavor to ensure that shipments in either calendar semester of a given year will be held to no more than sixty percent (60%) of the total annual quantitative limit.

2. *Product Mix*

Within the foregoing limitations, the above-mentioned producer associations will limit their shipments of stainless, alloy and high speed steel mill products which are covered by the ECSC Treaty to total quantities not to exceed the following (metric tons);

Stainless Steel Mill Products

1972	16,873
1973	15,871
1974	16,268

Alloy Steel Mill Products

1972	77,927
1973	68,351
1974	70,059

High Speed Steel Mill Products

1972	120
1973	99
1974	101

Within these total quantities the above-mentioned producer associations will not depart significantly from the product mix in each calendar year as compared with the pattern of such shipments to the United States over recent years.

Concerning high speed steel mill products and stainless and alloy steel mill products which are not covered by the ECSC treaty, the above-mentioned producer associations will use their best efforts, consistent with legal requirements, to induce producers who are not members of the above-mentioned producer associations to limit their shipments to the following quantities (metric tons):

High Speed Steel Mill Products

1972	360
1973	370
1974	379

Stainless Steel Mill Products

1972	7,211
1973	6,633
1974	6,800

Alloy Steel Mill Products

1972	34,993
1973	35,034
1974	35,910

Exports of the aforementioned products will be regulated by reference to the classifications of the Brussels Tariff Nomenclature (BTN). A concordance of the BTN with the relevant classifications contained in tariff schedules of the United States Annotated (TSUSA) is appended.

With respect to other categories of steel mill products, the above-mentioned producer associations will generally maintain the product mix in each calendar year in accordance with the average shipments for the period 1969, 1970, 1971.

With reference to exports of cold finished steel bars, special efforts will be made, consistent with legal requirements, to confine shipments during calendar year 1972 to a level of not more than two and one-half percent (2.5%)

greater than during calendar year 1970 and to maintain a growth rate of two and one-half percent (2.5%) of the preceding year's limit during each of calendar years 1973 and 1974.

3. *Fabricated structural steels*

Such products are not considered steel mill products and are not within the limitations set forth in paragraph 1 above. However, with reference to shipments of fabricated structural steel products according to the definitions of the BTN, special efforts will be made, consistent with legal requirements, to confine the shipments by the aforementioned producer associations during calendar year 1972 to a level not more than two and one-half percent greater than during calendar year 1970, outside the quantitative limit as described in paragraph one above, and to maintain a growth rate of two and one-half percent (2.5%) of the preceding year's limit during each of calendar years 1973 and 1974.

4. *Geographic Mix*

During calendar years 1972, 1973 and 1974, the above-mentioned producer associations will endeavor to the fullest extent possible to avoid growth in shipments of steel mill products to any particular customs region of the United States (Atlantic Coast, Gulf Coast/Mexican Border, Pacific Coast, Great Lakes/Canadian Border, and off-shore regions) in excess of the approximate proportions of calendar years 1969, 1970 and 1971.

5. *Consultations*

The above-mentioned producer associations, through their authorized representatives, hold themselves ready to consult with representatives of the United States Government on any problem or question that may arise with respect to this voluntary restraint undertaking. They expect that, similarly, the United States Government would be prepared to consult with their representatives on any problem or question that may arise with respect to this voluntary restraint undertaking. They reserve the right to request consultation in the event that they consider they have been placed in a disadvantageous position with respect to other exporters of steel to the United States by developments in the international steel market taking place subsequent to entering this undertaking, or if developments in the international steel market should take place which could substantially impair the carrying out of this undertaking. Similarly, they recognize that the United States Government may request consultation if it considers that developments in the international steel market have taken place during the term of this undertaking which substantially affect any of the provisions of this arrangement.

The above-mentioned producer associations reserve the right to request consultation with respect to the exclusion in particular situations from the export limitation quantity in paragraph 1 above of shipments of large-diameter line pipe.

6. This voluntary restraint undertaking is based on the following assumptions:

a. The provisions of paragraphs 1, 2, 3, 4 and 5 of this letter shall not have disadvantageous effects for the above-mentioned producer associations as compared with the undertakings made or to be made by producers of other countries concerning their exports to the United States market.

b. The United States Government will take no unilateral actions to restrict the quantity of steel mill products to be imported by the United States from Belgium, France, the German Federal Republic, Italy, Luxemburg, the Netherlands, and the United Kingdom, or to raise the tariffs thereon, including the new imposition of a surcharge, or to impose any other measure of similar effect.

c. This undertaking is made with the understanding that it is not in violation of any law of the United States or international rule, especially the provisions of the treaty establishing the European Coal and Steel Community or decisions of the European Economic Commission.

Sincerely yours,

This letter is signed on behalf of the under-mentioned associations by:

Comite de la Siderurgie Belge,
KSJ Baron Van Der Rest, President

Wirtschaftsvereinigung Eisen und Stahl Industrie
Hans-Jorg Sendler

Chambre Syndicale de la Siderurgie Francaise,
M. Jacques Ferry, President

British Steel Corporation,
Mark Littman
Deputy Chairman on behalf of
Lord Melchett, Chairman

British Independent Steel Producers Association
Sir Douglas Bruce-Gardner, Chairman

Associazione Industrie Siderurgiche Italiane "Assider"
Dott Mario D'onofrio, Delegato Della Presidenza

Groupement de l'Industrie Siderurgique Luxembourgeoise,
M. Rene Schmit, President

Vereniging de Nederlandsche Ijzer en Staalproducerende Industrie,
M. Everet Van Veelan, Chairman.

*   *   *   *   *

(b) *The Japanese Producers*   May 4, 1972

Dear Mr. Secretary:

In order to assist in the maintenance of an orderly market for steel in the United States, the Japan Iron and Steel Exporters' Association (hereinafter referred to as the Association) declares its intention, with the cooperation of associations for steel mill products not covered by the Association, to extend through December 31, 1974, its limitations on steel mill product exports to the United States, as initiated by its memorandum of December 23, 1968. The following are the terms under which these exports will be regulated:

1. Total exports and growth rate. The total quantity of Japanese steel mill products to be shipped to the United States during calendar year 1972 will not exceed 5,895,000 metric tons.

The growth rate of exports of the aforementioned products will not exceed 2½ percent per annum in each of the years 1973 and 1974 over the preceding year's limit of shipments. In accordance with this growth rate, such shipments will not exceed 6,042,000 metric tons during calendar year 1973 and 6,193,000 metric tons during calendar year 1974.

Shipments in either semester (6-month period) of a given year will be held to no more than sixty (60) percent of the total annual quantitative limit.

2. Product mix. Within the foregoing overall limitations, shipments of specialty steel mill products will be confined to total quantities not to exceed the following (in metric tons):

	1972	1973	1974
Stainless Steel	72,463	68,840	70,561
Tool Steel	893	915	938
Other special Steel	155,935	141,901	145,448

With respect to the aforementioned specialty steel mill products, the Association will not depart significantly from the product mix in each calendar year as compared with the pattern of such shipments to the United States over recent years.

Since exports will be regulated by reference to Japanese customs clearance statistics, which are based upon the Brussels Nomenclature, Japanese classifications of the above grades of steel will be used, provided that in the case of tool steel a separate consideration will be given to the shipments in accordance with the definitions of the Tariff Schedules of the United States Annotated.

With respect to other categories of steel mill products, the Association will generally maintain the product mix in each calendar year in accordance with the average shipments for the period 1969, 1970 and 1971.

With special reference to exports of cold finished carbon steel bars, shipments will be confined during calendar year 1972 to a level of not more than 2½ percent greater than during 1970. A growth rate of 2½ percent of the preceding year's limit will not be exceeded during calendar years 1973 and 1974.

3. Fabricated structural steels. Such products are not considered steel mill products and are not within the limitations set forth in paragraph 1 above. However, with reference to shipments of fabricated structural steel products, as defined below, according to the definitions of the Japanese customs tariff—namely: electric poles (towers) and parts thereof, of iron or steel: steel towers and parts thereof, of iron or steel, n. e. s.: bridges and parts thereof, of iron or steel: flood gates and parts thereof, of iron or steel, n. e. s.: structures and parts thereof, or iron or steel, n. e. s.: bars, rods, plates, sheets, tubes, pipes and other materials, worked for structural use, of iron or steel—special efforts will be made to confine the shipments by Japanese steel producers during calendar year 1972 to a level of not more than 2½ percent greater than during 1970, outside the quantitative limit as described in paragraph 1 above. A growth rate of 2½ percent of the preceding year's limit will not be exceeded during calendar years 1973 and 1974. It is understood that problems relating to the shipments of fabricated structural steels may be reviewed at the end of 1972 in accordance with paragraph 5.

4. Geographic mix. During calendar years 1972, 1973 and 1974, the Association will endeavor to the fullest extent possible to avoid growth in shipments of steel mill products to any particular customs region of the United States (Atlantic Coast, Gulf Coast-Mexican Border, Pacific Coast, Great Lakes-Canadian Border, and off shore regions) in excess of the approximate proportions of calendar years 1969, 1970 and 1971. With specific reference to the Pacific Coast customs region, shipments will be confined to a level not exceeding one-third of total shipments of steel mill products to the United States.

5. Consultations. The Association through its authorized representatives, holds itself ready to consult with representatives of the United States Government on any problem or question that may arise with respect to this voluntary restraint undertaking. The Association expects that, similarly, the United States Government would be prepared to consult with the representa-

tives of the Association on any problem or question that may arise with respect to this voluntary restraint undertaking.

The Association reserves the right to request consultation with respect to the exclusion from the export limitation quantity in paragraph 1 above of shipments of large-diameter line pipe (48 inch diameter or wider) when such pipe cannot be supplied from domestic production in the United States.

6. This voluntary restraint undertaking is based upon the following assumptions:

A. That, in consideration of the voluntary restraint undertaking in the existing memorandum of December 23, 1968, the terms of the undertaking of paragraphs 1, 2, 3, 4, and 5 above as well as the Association's share of total United States imports of steel mill products, will not be disadvantageous to the Association as compared with the undertakings made or to be made by the members of the European Coal and Steel Community.

B. That the United States Government will take no unilateral actions to restrict the quantity of United States imports of steel mill products, or to raise the tariffs thereon, including any new imposition of supplemental duties: and

C. That this undertaking is made with the understanding that it is not in violation of United States law or international laws.

Yours sincerely,

/s/

Yoshihiro Inayama
Chairman
Japan Iron and Steel
Exporters Association

4. **Orderly Marketing Agreement concerning Specialty Steel Imports between Japan and the United States (June 11, 1976)**

(Excerpts)

The Special Representative for Trade Negotiations to the Japanese Ambassador

JUNE 11, 1976

EXCELLENCY,

I have the honour to refer to the recent discussions held under Article XIX of the General Agreement on Tariffs and Trade between the representatives of the Government of the United States of America and of the Government of Japan during which the Government of the United States of America informed the Government of Japan of import relief measures for specialty steel to be taken by the Government of the United States of America in accordance with sec. 203(a) of the Trade Act of 1974. I have further the honour to confirm that the Government of the United States of America will implement its obligations under the following provisions:

1. (a) The Government of the United States of America will limit imports from Japan of the categories of specialty steel as set forth in Annex A (hereinafter referred to as "the categories") for the period of three years beginning June 14, 1976. In the event that restraint levels as defined in Annex D(b) are reached in any category or categories prior to the end of a restraint period as set forth in Annex B, the Government of the United States of America, unless otherwise mutually agreed, will delay further importation in the categories affected until after the end of that restraint period.

(b) Imports will be counted against restraint levels on the basis of date of entry, or withdrawal from warehouse, for consumption.

(c) The Government of the United States of America will not limit imports from Japan of the categories below the restraint levels therefor.

(d) Imports from Japan of each category during the first half of a restraint period will not exceed 60 percent of the base limit as defined in Annex D(a), or the base limit as adjusted during the first half of the restraint period pursuant to paragraph 3, unless otherwise mutually agreed.

2. (a) If imports from Japan of any category appear likely to exceed the restraint level, or 60 percent thereof in the first half of a restraint period, the Government of the United States of America will endeavor to notify the Government of Japan to that effect.

(b) Should it become necessary for the Government of the United States of America to delay importation in any category due to filling of the restraint level, as much prior notification as possible will be given to the Government of Japan.

3. (a) Any base limit as defined in Annex D(a) may be exceeded in a restraint period by no more than the percentage of that base limit as set forth in Annex C, provided that there is an equal tonnage reduction in the base limit for one or more other categories in the same period.

(b) Following notification by the Government of Japan at the earliest possible date of its intention concerning subparagraph (a) above, the Government of the United States of America will make an appropriate adjustment of the applicable base limits, consistent with Annex C.

4. (a) For each category having a shortfall, carryover will be permitted by up to 4 percent of the base limit for the restraint period in which the shortfall occurs, but not in excess of the actual shortfall. Shortfalls in one category may not be applied to any other category. Such carryover will be permitted only during the first thirty days of the restraint period following the one in which the shortfall occurs.

(b) For the purpose of this paragraph, a shortfall occurs when imports of any category from Japan during any restraint period are below the base limit for that category.

(c) If, in accordance with the provisions of paragraph 3, all or part of a base limit of any category has been reallocated to the base limit of one or more other categories, such amounts will not be considered a shortfall and hence not available for carryover.

5. If the Government of Japan considers that as a result of the application of the provisions of this Note, Japan is placed in an inequitable position vis-a-vis third countries in respect of specialty steel imports into the United States, the Government of Japan may request consultations with the Government of the United States of America.

6. (a) Mutually satisfactory administrative arrangements or adjustments may be made to resolve minor problems arising out of the implementation of the provisions of this Note, including differences in procedure or operation.

(b) The two Governments may amend the provisions of this Note, if such amendments are mutually agreeable.

7. (a) No provision of this Note will be construed as affecting the respective positions of the two Governments with respect to paragraphs 3(c) and 3(d) of the Declaration of Ministers approved at Tokyo on 14 September, 1973.

(b) No provision of this Note will be construed as applying to prices or production of specialty steel, or allocation of shipments among firms selling or buying specialty steel.

8. (a) Either Government may request consultations on any matters arising from the provisions of this Note. Such consultations will take place at a mutually convenient time not later than thirty days from the date on which such request is made, unless otherwise mutually agreed.

(b) If, in the view of either Government, the economic conditions prevailing at the time of the recent discussions mentioned above have changed substantially, that Government may initiate consultations for the purpose of discussing the possibility of liberalizing or terminating the import relief measures referred to in the provisions of this Note prior to the expiration of the period of three years.

(c) Either Government may terminate the provisions of this Note in their entirety by giving sixty-days' written notice to the other Government.

9. The reciprocal rights and obligations of the two Governments under the General Agreement on Tariffs and Trade will be reserved while the provisions of this Note remain in effect. For the purpose of the time limitation as set forth in Article XIX(3)(a) of the General Agreement on Tariffs and Trade, the period of ninety days will be considered to begin on the date of termination of the provisions of this Note in their entirety and continue so long as import relief measures by the Government of the United States of America on all or part of the categories remain in force.

10. (a) The Government of Japan will provide promptly to the Government of the United States of America monthly data on exports of the categories to the United States.

(b) The Government of the United States of America will provide promptly to the Government of Japan monthly data on imports of the categories from Japan.

I have further the honour to request you to confirm on behalf of the Government of Japan that it will implement its obligations under the above provisions and to propose that this Note and Your Excellency's Note in reply will constitute an agreement between the two Governments as characterized in the above provisions.

Accept, Excellency, the renewed assurances of my highest consideration.

FREDERICK B. DENT

Frederick B. Dent
*Special Representative for
Trade Negotiations*

His Excellency
FUMIHIKO TOGO
*Ambassador Extraordinary and
Plenipotentiary of Japan*

Annex A

The following items from the Tariff Schedules of the United States An-

notated (as revised May 1, 1976) are covered by the provisions of the Note
and are included in the five basic categories used for setting base limits:

Category	Description and TSUSA Items
I	Stainless Steel Sheet and Strip
	608.85 40
	608.88 40
	609.06 30
	609.07 20
	609.08 20
II	Stainless Steel Plate
	608.85 10
	608.89 10
III	Stainless Steel Bar
	608.52 10
	608.52 50
IV	Stainless Steel Rod
	608.76 20
	608.78 20
V	Alloy Tool Steel

	608.52 20	608.78 60
	608.52 30	608.85 06
	608.52 60	608.88 06
	608.52 70	609.06 65
	608.76 40	609.07 65
	608.76 60	609.08 65
	608.78 40	

Annex B

The base limits for the five categories will apply for the restraint periods
as follows:

Thousands of Short Tons

Restraint Period	Stainless Steel				Alloy Tool Steel	Total Specialty Steel
	Sheet and Strip	Plate	Bar	Rod		
June 14, 1976 to June 13, 1977	38.6	5.6	13.0	5.7	3.5	66.4
June 14, 1977 to June 13, 1978	38.9	5.9	14.0	5.9	3.7	68.4
June 14, 1978 to June 13, 1979	39.8	6.3	14.5	6.0	3.8	70.4

Annex C

Maximum percentage increases in base limits of receiving categories, as referred to in paragraph 3 of the Note, are as follows:

Restraint Period	Stainless Steel				Alloy Tool Steel
	Sheet and Strip	Plate	Bar	Rod	
June 14, 1976– June 13, 1977	10	1	1	1	1
June 14, 1977– June 13, 1978	10	1	3	3	3
June 14, 1978– June 13, 1979	10	1	3	3	3

Annex D

For the purposes of the provisions of the Note:

(a) The term "base limit" means the amount of imports of a category of specialty steel from Japan into the United States in short tons as set forth in Annex B that may be entered, or withdrawn from warehouse, for consumption in any restraint period, prior to any adjustment allowed under paragraph 3 of the Note.

(b) The term "restraint level" means a base limit referred to in (a) above with adjustment, if any, pursuant to the provisions of paragraph 3 of the Note.

(c) The term "imports" refers to United States imports classified under the items listed in Annex A entered for consumption (encompassing trans-shipments through third countries and shipments diverted to the United States market while in transit; informal entries (valued at less than $250); temporary imports under bond; re-imports of items exported for processing (TSUSA806.30); and United States Government imports).

(d) The term "restraint period" means a twelve-month period running from June 14 of one year through June 13 of the subsequent year.

The Japanese Ambassador to the Special Representative for Trade Negotiations

EMBASSY OF JAPAN
WASHINGTON

June 11, 1976

Excellency:

I have the honour to acknowledge the receipt of Your Excellency's Note of today's date which reads as follows:

[. . . . .]

I have further the honour to confirm on behalf of the Government of Japan that it will implement its obligations under the above provisions and to agree that Your Excellency's Note and this Note will constitute an agreement between the two Governments as characterized in the above provisions.

Accept, Excellency, the renewed assurances of my highest consideration.

Ambassador Extraordinary and
Plenipotentiary of Japan

His Excellency

Frederick B. Dent
The Special Representative
for Trade Negotiations

[RELATED NOTE]

EMBASSY OF JAPAN
WASHINGTON
June 11, 1976

Excellency:

On behalf of the Government of Japan, I have the honor to inform you of the intention of the Government of Japan that the rights under Article XIX (3) (a) of the General Agreement on Tariffs and Trade, if invoked by the Government of Japan after the termination of the effectiveness of the Notes exchanged, will not be exercised with respect to the import relief measures for specialty steel taken by the Government of the United States of America before such termination.

(signature)
Ambassador Extraordinary and
Plenipotentiary of Japan

His Excellency
Frederick B. Dent
The Special Representative
for Trade Negotiations

Agreed Minutes

The representatives of the Government of Japan and of the Government of the United States of America wish to record the following understanding concerning the Notes exchanged on June 11, 1976.

1. It is understood that the content of the Notes exchanged does not prejudice the respective positions of the two Governments with respect to Article XIX(1) of the General Agreement on Tariffs and Trade.

2. Imports entering under the carryover provisions of paragraph 4 of the Notes exchanged will be counted as if entered in the restraint period in which the shortfall occurred.

3. It is intended that consultations under paragraph 8(b) of the Notes exchanged will be held in any case before the end of the 2nd restraint period.

4. Consultations under paragraph 8(a) of the Notes exchanged may cover the problem of spacing and possible amendments to the percentages for the 2nd and 3rd restraint periods provided for in Annex C to the Notes exchanged.

5. Consultations between the Government of Japan and the Government of the United States of America will be initiated by written notice to the Ministry of Foreign Affairs in the case of Japan and the Office of the Special Representative for Trade Negotiations in the case of the United States.

6. Japan will be allocated 45.2 percent of total specialty steel imports permitted from all sources into the United States in each restraint period. Any resulting increase in the amount of total specialty steel imports permitted from Japan by applying this share will be added to the base limits for the stainless steel sheet and strip referred to in Annex B to the Notes exchanged.

7. It is understood that if there are any exclusions made from Annex A to the Notes exchanged, there will be appropriate corresponding reductions in the base limits in Annex B to the Notes exchanged, in an amount to be mutually agreed.

For the Government of
Japan

For the Government of the
United States of America

. . . .

. . . .

(signature)

(signature)

Washington, D. C., June 11, 1976

5. Implementation of Trigger Price Mechanism by U.S. Treasury (January 9, 1978)

DEPARTMENT OF THE TREASURY

Office of the Secretary

"TRIGGER PRICES" FOR IMPORTED STEEL MILL PRODUCTS

On December 28, 1977, the Treasury Department announced proposed rule-making procedures with respect to regulations applicable to the information required to be filed at the time of importation of certain articles of steel (42 FR 65214). As was there indicated, the Secretary intends to implement a "trigger price mechanism" as recommended to, and approved by, the President. For that purpose, "trigger prices" for steel mill products are to be published as the basis upon which imported steel products will be monitored for the purpose of determining whether investigations under the Antidumping Act of 1921, as amended, 19 U.S.C. § 160 et seq., would be appropriate.

I am hereby announcing the base prices to be used in the trigger price mechanism (TPM) for certain imported steel mill products. These prices are based upon evidence made available to the Treasury Department by the Japanese Ministry of International Trade and Industry (MITI) concerning the current cost of producing steel in Japan, recognized as the most efficient exporting country today, as well as other information available to the Department. The data supplied by MITI were compiled by the six major, integrated steel companies in Japan, as well as by a number of smaller, electric-furnace steel makers.

The methodology employed in arriving at a cost of production estimate is similar to that utilized in the Council on Wage and Price Stability (CWPS) Report to the President on Prices and Costs in the United States Steel Industry, released in October 1977, but the product coverage is different.

The individual components of the cost of producing raw steel are totaled and then divided by the appropriate yield factor to obtain the cost of finished steel products. To that figure, appropriate coefficients, expressing the average experience of the Japanese firms in producing individual types of steel mill products, are used to derive the costs of those products. The conclusions published in the CWPS Report concerning costs of producing steel in Japan were based on average data for the Japanese steel industry as a whole, as reflected in published sources. The figures for the estimated costs of production being published today are for items produced principally by the large, integrated companies and, therefore, are based on information from these firms. As a result, they differ from the estimates published in the CWPS Report. The data being submitted by the smaller, nonintegrated companies through MITI will be utilized to construct the costs of production for such items as alloy products, wire, and small structural shapes. These cost estimates will be published shortly.

The total Japanese costs of production for the major firms are found to be:

TABLE 1.—*Estimated Japanese cost of production*

(Per net ton of finished produce)

Raw materials	$165.19
Labor	68.56
Other expenses	19.39
Depreciation	16.79
Interest plus profit	33.83
Less scrap credit	−5.96
Total	297.80

1. *The construction of "trigger prices" for "steel mill products."* "Steel mill products" include a wide variety of commodities, produced in a multitude of grades and sizes. For each major steel mill product (excluding stainless steel) imported into the U.S. in significant quantities, a set of "base prices" is being or will be announced, based upon the estimated Japanese costs of production of all steel products. Most of these base prices are being announced with this notice; others—including alloy products, wire, tubular and the remaining bar products—will be announced shortly, as soon as the necessary information is obtained and analyzed. Some products which are not imported in significant quantities, or for which cost data are difficult to obtain, may not be assigned a base trigger price. The Treasury Department will continually review the coverage of the trigger price mechanism at a later date to determine the appropriateness of the coverage of product categories.

Most imported steel mill products are sold to specifications for width, thickness, chemistry, or surface preparation that differ from the base product. To establish "trigger prices" for most of these combinations, "extra" charges must be added to the base price. A complete set of charges for extras is being supplied by MITI as a reflection of the Japanese Differentials between the various combinations. In many cases, these "extras" charges are similar to those charged for extras by the U.S. industry; in others they diverge. The Treasury Department will publish the extras charges it will use for the trigger price mechanism as soon as possible.

2. *Cost of production for basic carbon steel products.* The estimated cost of production for the base products comprising the most significant imports, as produced by the six integrated Japanese firms, are listed in table 2. The Treasury estimates are based on an addition of raw material inputs, labor expenses, overhead, and a profit margin, as well as all other capital charges for all steel, multiplied by an appropriate coefficient based on the experience of the reporting firms.

3. *Importation charges.* To the estimated cost of production for each steel mill product consisting of its base price and "extras," there must be added importation costs (excluding duty) from Japan. The resulting total constitutes the Treasury trigger price. The importation costs include Japanese inland

freight, loading, ocean freight, insurance, interest, and wharfage charges. These have been calculated for each broad product category on the basis of existing data on average freight rates and wharfage charges for each of four regions of the country—East, West, Gulf, and Great Lakes. Insurance and interest costs have been estimated, based on reported transactions. The resulting importation costs for each major product category appear in table 3. Importers' sales commissions are excluded, since the "trigger price" is based upon the cost to the importer, assuming the importer is dealing on an arms' length basis. To the extent the importer is related to the producer exporting the steel mill product and the transfer price does not reflect an arms' length transaction, the first resale price by the related importer to an unrelated U.S. buyer will be used as the comparison with the trigger price.

TABLE 2

ESTIMATED COST OF PRODUCTION INCLUDING ALL CAPITAL CHARGES—BASE ITEMS (F.O.B., JAPAN)

Category Number	Products	Specification	Dimension	Cost of Production ($/Net Ton)
II	Wire Rods			
	Commercial Quality	AISI 1008	5.5m/m	240
	Welding Quality	JIS G3503 SRWYLL equivalent	5.5m/m	241
	High Carbon	AISI 1065 (specific)	5.5m/m	280
	Cold Heading Quality	AISI 1038 (specific)	12.7m/m	289
III	Wide Flange Beams	ASTM A36	12" x 12"	235
IV	Sheet Piling	ASTM A-372	ARCH WEB PDA-27	265
V	Steel plates	ASTM A36	1/2" x 80" x 240"	241
X	Hot-rolled Carbon Bars	AISI 1045	40 mm round x 4 me	308
XXII	Black Plate	ASTM A-625-76	0.0083" x 34" x Coil	338
XXIII	Electrolytic Tin Plate	SR-25/25	75L x 34" x C	433
XXV and XXIX	Hot-Rolled Steel Sheets in Coil	ASTM A569	0.121" x 48" x C	210
XXVI and XXX	Cold-Rolled Steel Sheets in Coil	ASTM A366	1.0m/m x 48" x C	269
XXVI	Electrical Steel Sheets			
	Grain-Oriented	M-4	0.012" x 33" x C	907
	Non-Oriented	M-45	0.018" x 36" x C	488

XXVII	Electro-Galvanized Iron Sheets in Coil	EGC-10g/M²	1.0m/m x 48″ x C	311
XXVII	Galvanized Iron Sheets in Coil	ASTM A525G90	0.8m/m x 48″ x C	313
XXXII	Tin Free Steel Sheets in Coil	SR	75L x 34″ x C	375

TABLE 3

IMPORTATION CHARGES ON JAPANESE STEEL PRODUCTS
($/net ton)

Product	Freight	Insurance	Interest	Handling	Total
II Wire Rods					
Commercial Quality					
East	28.13	2.69	6.73	3.63	41.18
Lakes	40.83	2.82	8.66	3.63	55.94
Gulf	23.59	2.65	6.62	4.54	37.40
Pacific	22.69	2.64	5.10	2.72	33.15
High Carbon					
East	28.13	3.13	7.87	3.63	42.76
Lakes	40.83	3.25	10.06	3.63	57.77
Gulf	23.59	3.08	7.76	4.54	38.97
Pacific	22.69	3.07	5.98	2.72	34.46
III Wide Flange Beams					
East	30.85	2.66	6.57	3.63	43.71
Lakes	42.65	2.78	8.44	3.63	57.50
Gulf	27.22	2.62	6.48	4.54	40.86
Pacific	24.50	2.60	4.97	2.72	34.79
IV Sheet Piling					
East	30.85	2.96	7.31	3.63	44.75
Lakes	42.65	3.08	9.35	3.63	58.71
Gulf	27.22	2.92	6.56	4.54	41.24
Pacific	24.50	2.90	5.53	2.72	35.65
V Plates					
East	28.13	2.69	7.04	3.63	41.49
Lakes	36.30	2.77	8.91	3.63	51.61
Gulf	22.69	2.64	6.91	4.54	36.78
Pacific	22.69	2.64	5.35	2.72	33.40
X Hot Rolled Carbon Bars					
East	28.13	3.36	8.77	3.63	43.89
Lakes	40.83	3.49	11.18	3.63	59.13
Gulf	23.59	3.32	8.66	4.54	40.11
Pacific	22.69	3.31	6.68	2.72	35.40
XXII Black Plate					
East	24.50	3.62	9.55	3.63	41.30
Lakes	31.76	3.70	11.97	3.63	51.06
Gulf	20.87	3.59	9.46	4.54	38.46
Pacific	20.87	3.59	7.32	2.72	34.50

TABLE 3

(continued)

	Product	Freight	Insurance	Interest	Handling	Total
XXIII	Electrolytic Tin Plate					
	East	30.85	4.64	11.77	3.63	50.89
	Lakes	33.58	4.67	14.57	3.63	56.45
	Gulf	24.50	4.58	11.62	4.54	45.24
	Pacific	23.59	4.57	8.97	2.72	39.85
XXXII	Tin Free Steel					
	East	30.85	4.06	10.83	3.63	49.37
	Lakes	33.58	4.09	13.40	3.63	54.70
	Gulf	24.50	4.00	10.67	4.54	43.71
	Pacific	23.59	3.99	8.24	2.72	38.54
XXV						
XXIX	Hot Rolled Sheets					
	East	24.50	2.34	6.14	3.63	36.61
	Lakes	31.76	2.42	7.77	3.63	45.58
	Gulf	20.87	2.31	6.05	4.54	33.77
	Pacific	20.87	2.31	4.68	2.72	30.58
XXVI						
XXX	Cold Rolled Sheets					
	East	24.50	2.94	7.73	3.63	38.80
	Lakes	31.76	3.01	9.73	3.63	48.13
	Gulf	20.87	2.90	7.64	4.54	35.95
	Pacific	20.87	2.90	5.91	2.72	32.40
XXVII	Galvanized Sheets and Electro Galvanized					
	East	24.50	3.36	8.91	3.63	40.40
	Lakes	32.67	3.45	11.21	3.63	50.96
	Gulf	20.87	3.33	8.82	4.54	37.56
	Pacific	21.78	3.34	6.84	2.72	34.68
XXII	Electrical Sheets					
	East	29.95	7.27	19.55	3.63	60.40
	Lakes	33.58	7.31	24.16	3.63	68.68
	Gulf	24.50	7.22	19.41	4.54	55.67
	Pacific	23.59	7.21	15.00	2.72	48.52

4. *Assumptions utilized in estimating Japanese cost of production.*—(a) *Exchange rate.* All calculations have been based upon an exchange rate of 240 yen to the U.S. dollar applied to the most recent data made available on raw material, labor, capital, and other costs incurred by the Japanese steel industry.

(b) *Capacity utilization.* All calculations have been based upon a "standard" utilization ratio of 85 percent of capacity. While the Japanese industry is currently operating at only 70 percent of capacity, it has averaged more than 85 percent utilization through its business cycles since 1956. Therefore, a standard volume, equal to 85 percent of capacity, is considered the appropriate basis for calculating Japanese production costs.

(c) *Labor productivity.* All calculations have been derived from an estimated labor usage of 7 man-hours per metric ton of raw steel produced. At present, the entire Japanese steel industry is utilizing nearly 10 man-hours per metric ton of raw steel, but this includes the labor-intensive specialty steel firms. Moreover, the Japanese industry has reduced its employment levels by less than 1.5 percent since 1973, while it has reduced output by more than 10 percent. During this period, the industry has made continued technological progress. Therefore, it can expand output to 85 percent of capacity with little or no additional employment. At this higher level of utilization, the average man-hours per metric ton of crude steel for the entire industry would be approximately 8.2. Excluding specialty steel production and eliminating labor not applied to steelmaking operations, the average man-hours required at an 85 percent capacity utilization in integrated carbon steel production has been determined to be about 7 man-hours per metric ton.

(d) *Yield.* The Japanese steel industry yield from raw steel to finished products is placed at 80 percent in calculating production cost. In the CWPS Report, the Japanese yield was estimated to be 77.8 percent in 1976 on a U.S. product-mix basis. The evidence obtained from the MITI and other sources indicates that this estimate was too low.

A study to be released next year by the International Iron and Steel Institute, based in Brussels, demonstrates that the Japanese steel industry obtains a yield of more than 93 percent from raw steel to such semifinished products as billets, blooms, and slabs. By contrast, the IISI study shows that the U.S. industry obtains only an 86 percent yield from raw steel to these semifinished products. This difference of more than 7 percent is attributable to more continuous casting in Japan and Japanese experience in both continuous casting and the rolling of ingots.

From the semifinished stage to the final product, the Japanese industry as a whole also enjoys a considerable advantage because of computer control of rolling mills, more precise control over the thickness of the final product, cold scarfing tetchniques, longer runs, and larger coils. The U.S. industry realizes an 83 percent yield from semifinished to finished products. A conservative estimate of Japanese yields from semifinished products, is 86 percent. Therefore, the Japanese yield to finished products has been calculated as: $0.86 \times 0.93 = 0.80$. This 80 percent yield factor is used in the cost calculation in table 1.

(e) *Capital costs.* Total depreciation charges per net ton of finished products are approximately $17 for the six largest firms. Net interest expenses and a profit margin add another $34 per net finished ton. The total before-tax payments to capital are therefore $50.62 per net ton, or more than 13 percent of total assets related to steel production. This compares most favorably with the better years for the U.S. industry in the past decade. In the boom year of 1974, U.S. producers realized 20 percent on assets before taxes, but this was the only year in the past decade in which these gross returns were greater than 15 percent. In calculating total charges against capital, interest charges were adjusted to avoid double counting for the highly leveraged Japanese steel firms. Total interest payments, depreciation and other fixed charges represent overhead expenses of considerably more than 10 percent of direct costs.

(f) *Scrap netback.* In calculating production costs based upon Japanese raw materials and labor costs, it is necessary to credit the Japanese firms for scrap or secondary product generated. Yield factors reported by the Japanese industry were not used in the calculation of trigger prices in the belief that some of the products considered "finished" would be regarded by U.S. standards as low quality, perhaps not much above scrap. However, this low quality product must receive a cost credit based, at the minimum, on the current market price of high quality scrap. So doing yields a value of $5.96 per net ton of finished steel.

5. *Implementation of the trigger price mechanism.*—(a) *Publication.* The trigger prices hereby established and to be published for additional products in the near future will be applicable to all shipments loaded for export through the second calendar quarter of 1978. Cost of production data will be collected and reviewed on a continuous basis and trigger prices will be revised on a quarterly basis to reflect changes in costs and in exchange rates. It is the present intention of the Treasury Department to announce trigger prices 60 to 90 days before they become applicable. Therefore, trigger prices applicable to shipments loaded during the third calendar quarter in 1978 will be published during April 1978. Revised trigger prices will be established within 5 percent above or below any revised cost of production data where necessary to minimize fluctuations.

(b) *Imports below trigger prices.* Following the date as of which the special steel summary invoice (SSSI) is to be used for steel imports, currently estimated to be February 15, 1978, all imports of steel mill products loaded for export to the United States after the publication of the relevant trigger prices will be examined by the Customs Service. Forms reflecting substantial or repeated imports at prices below applicable trigger prices will be investigated by the Special Customs Steel Task Force. If the accompanying documentation demonstrates to the satisfaction of the Secretary that the prices for any particular shipment were fixed before the publication of the applicable trigger price and could not be varied in accordance with the terms of the parties' contract, no immediate formal investigation will be initiated in the absence of other information indicating that such shipments are at less than fair value, as defined in the Antidumping Act. In all other cases in which a shipment is found to be at prices below applicable trigger prices, the Customs

Service may initiate immediate, informal inquiries of the importer to determine whether such sale is less than fair value within the meaning of the Antidumping Act. Unless the Secretary is satisfied within the time to be allotted therefor, that no reasonable possibility of sales at less than fair value may be found, an antidumping proceeding notice will promptly be published with respect to that shipment and other shipments of such or similar merchandise from the same exporter or from the same country of exportation as he deems appropriate.

(c) *Rights of interested parties preserved.* Implementation of the trigger price mechanism is not intended to deny to any party interested in the importation of steel mill products any rights it may have under the Antidumping Act or other applicable law. It is intended and will be used solely to enable the Secretary to determine on an expedited basis whether or not to initiate antidumping proceedings pursuant to section 153.30(a) of the Customs regulations and to reach the stage of making a tentative determination with respect to sales at less than fair value within a period substantially shorter than the six months provided in section 153.32 of the Customs regulations.

6. *Public comment.* Comments from the public should be addressed to:

Peter D. Ehrenhaft, Deputy Assistant Secretary and Special Counsel (Tariff Affairs), Room 3424, Main Treasury, Washington, D.C. 20220.

Dated: December 30, 1977.

ANTHONY M. SOLOMON,
Acting Secretary of the Treasury

6. U.S. Treasury Revisions of Trigger Price Mechanism*

(July 1978)

DEPARTMENT OF THE TREASURY

Office of the Secretary

REVISIONS BY TREASURY STEEL TRIGGER
PRICE TASK FORCE

I. INTRODUCTION AND SUMMARY

Most of the trigger prices announced to date by the Treasury have been based on aggregate average cost data compiled by the six largest Japanese integrated steel companies, as submitted to the U.S. Governemnt by the Japanese Government (Ministry of International Trade and Commerce) in December 1977. The Steel Trigger Price Task Force was formed in March 1978 to review the data thus submitted and the methodology used, as well as to perform additional analysis and research on Japanese steel production costs. Based on the review, possible adjustments to the average cost as well as individual product cost relationships and "gaps" and "anomalies" in product coverage were considered.

The nine-person task force consisted of two steel engineers, two economists, two accountants with knowledge of Japanese accounting practices, and three representatives of the Treasury Department and Customs Service. The task force visited several U.S. plants and conducted extended discussions with U.S. steel company representatives, focusing on the methodology for calculating steel production costs. The task force also reviewed dozens of written submissions by interested parties that either raised questions about cost-related aspects of the trigger price mechanism or pointed out gaps or anomalies in the system as originally structured.

In Japan, the task force conducted numerous discussions with Japanese MITI officials and steel industry representatives. In these discussions, the task force probed the cost information submitted by MITI in December 1977 and made numerous requests for additional data. The task force also visited eight Japanese steel mills, five of which the task force itself had selected. These visits consisted of (1) a tour of plant facilities selected by the task force and other facilities chosen by the plant management; and (2) discussions with plant managers and mill supervisors concerning specific aspects of production practice, performance data, and production costs.

The result of the task force's analysis is an upward revision of the average

---

* 43 Fed. Reg. 32710, July 27, 1978.

costs of the six largest integrated Japanese steel producers from $297.80 to $300.76 per net ton of finished product. The principal changes are:

Operating rate: The task force has revised Japanese production costs using a 5-year average operating rate. *The change increases the cost of production by about $18 per net ton over the original calculations* (which used an 85 percent operating rate—the average experienced by the Japanese steel industry over the past 20 years).

Yield: The task force has revised the yield percentage from 80 percent to 82.7 percent, which reduces Japanese production costs by about $12. In addition, part of the output treated as yield loss—and formerly valued as scrap—has been revalued as secondary quality material, resulting in a $9 yield credit (which is $3 more than the previous scrap credit). In total, *the yield adjustments result in a downward revision of costs by $15 per net ton.*

Other: The above changes necessitated some adjustments in "other expenses" and capital charges, including profit. Profit is charged at 8 percent of all noncapital costs.

Details of these changes are explained below.

II. REVISIONS IN AVERAGE PRODUCTION COSTS

The task force has made revisions in various components of cost that comprise the average cost per ton of finished product. To explain these revisions, two adjustments of prime importance are first explained because they permeate all of the identified cost components. These adjustments are in (i) the capacity utilization used to calculate fixed costs per unit, and (ii) the yield of finished steel mill products from raw steel. Based on these adjustments, specific changes in the identified cost components—raw materials, labor, other expenses, and capital charges—are calculated.

A. CAPACITY UTILIZATION

The allocation of fixed costs of production to units produced is based upon an average operating rate over a period of time. Such a calculation cannot be based upon the current operating rate because it would be unrealistic to treat costs at either the high end or low end of an operating cycle as representative for determining "average" costs. For the purposes of establishing a threshold for Treasury investigations under the Antidumping Act, such an average cost figure appears most appropriate. The concept of allocating fixed costs over some "reasonable period of time" is found in section 205(b) of the Act concerning the determination of sales at less than the cost of producing merchandise and has been interpreted by Treasury to require consideration of operating rates over the most recent business cycle of the industry concerned.

In the January 3 trigger price calculations, costs were based on an 85 percent-operating rate, reflecting the average rate of utilization for the Japanese steel industry over the past 20 years. Moreover, MITI assumed that all labor, capital, and "other" expenses do not vary with the rate of capacity utilization.

Period of measurement. After a careful examination of the issue, the task force recommended and the Secretary has determined that the minimum period for measuring capacity utilization in the construction of trigger prices should be 5 years. Since steelmaking assets are long-lived, and the demand for steel is sensitive to fluctuations in general economic conditions, it is necessary to calculate costs at some normal or average utilization rate over the business cycle. This requires a 5-year period—1973 to 1977—to reflect approximately the shortest reasonable business cycle in the steel industry.

Thus, whereas the January cost calculations were based on a 20-year average capacity utilization in the Japanese steel industry, the task force's revisions are based on a 5-year average.

Percentage of capacity utilization. Capacity utilization can be measured as a percentage of either (1) theoretical (or "rated") capacity; or (2) actual (or "effective") capacity.[1]

The Japanese steel industry has begun to calculate capacity utilization in terms of effective capacity, taking October of 1973—a month of peak output —as 100-percent utilization.[2] Measured by that standard, the Japanese steel industry has been operating at an average of 83.2 percent over the past 5 years. That figure is equivalent to a 73.2-percent operating rate under the theoretical method of defining capacity utilization.

In any event, regardless of which definition is used, the salient factor for cost calculations is not the absolute percentage of capacity utilization, but the relationship between current utilization and average (or "standard') utilization.

Japanese costs of production for the six largest integrated producers in the first 6 months of fiscal year 1977 were provided by MITI assuming 95 percent effective utilization (termed "standard volume"). The task force re-

---

[1] Rated capacity is an engineering assessment of the theoretical maximum output of one piece of equipment (e.g., a steel furnace). It takes no account of other production constraints, such as coordination with other equipment. Effective capacity attempts to take account of all production constraints that affect actual output and is thus smaller than rated capacity.

[2] Effective capacity can be measured in different ways. MITI calculated effective capacity at 88 percent of rated capacity. Another method would be to base effective capacity on peak-to-peak output over a period of years. The two approaches will give slightly different results, but are reconcilable. In any event, it is not the absolute number, but the relation between the average capacity utilization and current capacity utilization that is relevant for cost calculations.

calculated these MITI costs on a current effective capacity utilization basis of 66.6 percent (58.6 percent rated) in the first 6 months of fiscal year 1977. These latter costs were then adjusted to represent 83.29 percent effective (73.2 percent rated) capacity utilization, incorporating the following assumptions:

1. All raw material costs were assumed to be 100 percent variable (i.e., cost per ton of output is not affected by changes in capacity utilization);

2. Labor costs were assumed to be 50 percent variable and 50 percent fixed (i.e., 50 percent not affected by capacity utilization, 50 percent varying inversely with capacity utilization);

3. Other expenses: 50 percent variable, 50 percent fixed;

4. Depreciation: 10 percent variable, 90 percent fixed;

5. Interest: 25 percent variable, 75 percent fixed.

The treatment of costs as fixed or variable is based upon a large number of factors considered by the task force. For example, it is appropriate to treat labor as being 50 percent affected by capacity utilization even though the original MITI calculations assumed labor to be unaffected by changes in capacity utilization because of certain unique features of Japanese corporate employment practices. The variability of labor is supported by a number of factors: Labor hours have dropped rather sharply with steel output in the past 3 years; in many cases, attrition of the workforce has occurred through retirement; finally, some workers are now being loaned out to other enterprises.

Since reductions in the rate of capacity utilization lead to lower rates of consumption of capital facilities which are banked, 10 percent of depreciation is assumed to be variable. Similarly, the working capital required to support raw materials, work in process, and final materials is reduced when production declines. Therefore, 25 percent of interest expense is assumed to be variable.

Based on these assumptions and a rated capacity utilization of 73.2 percent, the average Japanese production costs are approximately $18 higher than the original cost calculations. The effect of reducing the average rate of capacity utilization upon which trigger prices are calculated is not as large as might otherwise be expected because the change influences only capital costs and other expenses. As explained below, labor costs have already been adjusted to reconcile the original MITI submission with published statistics. That prior adjustment thus mitigated the effect of the capacity utilization adjustment now made by the task force, and no change was now made to the labor component.

B. YIELD

The task force examined Japanese production practices carefully in order to obtain a measure of the yield from crude steel (the first solid state) to finished products. In addition, official industry and government publications were analyzed in order to reconcile the estimated flows of crude, intermediate, and finished products. Based on these studies, the Japanese yield—having been lowered from the 86.5 percent claimed by the Japanese to 80 percent for the Japanese cost calculations—has been raised to 82.7 percent for a number of reasons.

The technology used by the Japanese integrated producers is of a very recent vintage. They utilize process computers far more extensively than U.S. companies. Their rolling mills allow the production of finished products with minimal yield losses and crown. Continuous casting is far more extensively used than in the United States. Finally, Japanese plants are much newer, allowing them to roll larger coils from longer slabs than is generally the U.S. practice. Specifically:

1. *Continuous casting.* The Japanese producers utilize continuous casting for 35.1 percent of their raw steel production, as compared with 10.5 percent in the United States in 1977. By itself, this increases yield by 3.23 percent, but it also increases, the yield from ingots to slabs because the number of killed, hot-top ingots is reduced. In total, the effect of greater continuous casting in Japan is to increase the integrated producers' yield to 5.9 percent over their U.S. counterparts.

2. *Computer process control.* The use of computers to control the production processes from primary production to product finishing provides a substantial increase in yield for the Japanese integrated producers. The computers increase yield through improvements in the "provisioning" of ingots and slabs (i.e., the more precise matching of ingot and slab size to final product to minimize yield loss), the improved scheduling and loading of production, improved quality, and better order and inventory control. The effect of these process controls is to increase yield by an estimated 3.2 percent over U.S. experience.

3. *Design of plant and equipment.* The newer facilities in Japan allow their producers to roll larger, high quality products because of:

Large continuous caster cross sections.
Long slab capacity in reheat furnaces.
In-process scales for weighing products.
Large rolls on rolling mills.
Great distance between rolling-mill stands.
Roll bending.

Large coilers.
Long run-out tables.
Large cooling tables.

The effect of all of these plant characteristics is to improve yield by an estimated 1.8 percent.

4. *Product mix*. The Japanese integrated firms produce a smaller proportion of coated products than U.S. firms, more large structural shapes, more wire rods, and slightly less uncoated flat-rolled products. Given Japanese yields on each product, this product mix increases their yield by 0.5 percent.

The combined effect of the above influences upon yield is to give the Japanese producers at least an 11.4 percentage point advantage over U.S. producers who reported a 71.3 percent yield in 1976. Therefore, the revised base trigger prices incorporate an 82.7 percent average yield from crude to finished steel.

Since the Japanese integrated producers reported an 86.5 percent yield in their original data submission through MITI, the difference (3.8 percent in finished steel production between that figure and the 82.7 percent figure now adopted by the task force must be given a value. The task force has decided to apply a credit representing the value of this production, treating it as neither prime quality product nor scrap, but as secondary quality material. Accordingly, the January scrap credit—relabeled a yield credit—has been raised from $5.96 to $8.90 per net ton of finished product.

C. RAW MATERIALS COMPONENT

Basic raw materials include iron ore, coal, purchased scrap, fuel oil, and electricity. Other raw materials include ferroalloys, lubricants, water, rolls, alloying materials, and limestone. Other raw materials also include fees paid for services performed by subsidiaries. The principal item of this type is, for some firms, a coke processing fee (i.e., some Japanese steel plants buy coal and send it to a subsidiary for coking, paying a fee for such processing).

The task force has reviewed both the basic raw materials and other raw material costs provided by MITI and published in the January 3 release, and has examined extensively the practice of having the coking operation done by a subsidiary. It also examined the coal and coke usage ratios based on all available information.

The task force has found no reason to correct or adjust the cost for raw materials published on January 3. Thus, the only revision that has been made to the Japanese data submission on raw materials is an exchange rate adjustment on other raw materials from 242.5 yen = $1 to 240 yen = $1 — the applicable yen/dollar rate at the time the raw materials costs were first calculated.

D. LABOR COSTS

In the January 3 release, labor costs were shown as $54.85 per net ton of crude steel at standard volume. In deriving this figure, Treasury raised the original man-hours estimate provided by MITI to 7 man-hours per metric ton to correspond more closely with other available statistics.

After careful examination of the factors observed and data gathered in Japan, the task force believes the January man-hours adjustment accurately reflects the labor requirement at the new average capacity utilization. Accordingly, the January calculation of total labor costs has not been changed.

The $8.64 hourly labor costs reported by MITI for 1977 includes all costs associated with labor—whether for direct employees or subcontracted or loaned-out workers. Similarly, the January 3 estimate of 7 man-hours per metric ton of crude steel (6.35 per net ton) embraces all workers, including head office employees, plant employees, and subcontract workers (37.8 percent of the total).

The figure of 7 man-hours per metric ton was derived from two sources: (1) A MITI submission; and (2) process-by-process man-hours per ton data acquired by the task force in Japan. Data from both sources were adjusted to the standard volume man-hours per ton, applying the assumption that 50 percent of labor varies with capacity utilization, and 50 percent is fixed. The process-by-process data were compared with U.S. estimates, and their validity was also assessed by onsite inspection of work practices in Japanese plants.

Both the MITI submission and process-by-process man-hour data gave similar total man-hour per ton results. Further, both aggregate and process-by-process labor utilization in Japan are in line with those in the more efficient U.S. plants. However, the 7 figure shown for Japan excludes work performed in those operations where a complete service was paid for on a fee basis by a Japanese steel producer. For example, as noted earlier, in some Japanese firms, coke production services were paid for on a fee basis, so coke production workers were excluded from the firm's man-hour data. In that circumstance, the task force assured itself that the fee for coke production services was included in that firm's costs for other raw materials.

E. OTHER EXPENSES

Because of its residual nature, the category other expenses is difficult to measure and verify. The representatives of MITI and the major producers have indicated this category embraces the following items:

i. Repairs.
ii. Maintenance.
iii. Utilities (excluding electricity).
iv. Water.
v. Oxygen.
vi. Travel.
vii. Design fees.
viii. Enterprise taxes.
ix. Advertising.
x. Postage.
xi. Entertainment.
xii. Professional dues.
xiii. Standards inspection.
xiv. Books.
xv. Printing.
xvi. Donations.
xvii. Office and factory supplies.
xviii. Rents.

No one of these items accounts for as much as $3 per net ton of finished product.

In the January 3 release, these other expenses were shown as totaling $19.39 per net finished ton. Since MITI treated these as fixed expenses, this estimate is consistent with $24.74 at actual 1977 volume. In their financial statements for fiscal year 1977, the six major integrated Japanese steel companies reported total materials and other expenses of $182.62 at an exchange rate of 240 yen per dollar. The total of raw materials and other expenses at actual volume per the January 3 announcement may be calculated at $178.10, or only slightly below the calculation based upon the public financial statements. The task force used the MITI report of other expenses and adjusted for the revised standard volume and a finished product yield of 82.7 percent. The final calculation, therefore, is $24.03 per net finished ton for the other expenses component of costs.

F. CAPITAL CHANGES

The necessary costs of capital—interest, depreciation, and profit—have been calculated on the basis of the revised capacity estimate for standard volume. Depreciation is assumed to be 90 percent fixed, while interest charges are assumed to be 75 percent fixed—the remaining 25 representing interest charges on working capital which varies with production levels.

Depreciation, adjusted to actual volume in 1977, may be calculated from the original MITI submission to be $21.42 per net ton of finished product.

This estimate is very close to the amount reported for fiscal year 1977 by the six largest producers in their annual public financial statements. Adjusting for standard volume at the assumed ratio (90 percent fixed, 10 percent variable) reduces this figure to $18.64 per net ton. Adjusting to a yield for finished products of 82.7 percent raises the figure to $19.50.

Interest is calculated to be $20.77 per net ton at actual volume, somewhat above the $19.10 per ton for fiscal year 1977 shown in the published financial statements. Since interest charges vary directly with several factors—work in progress, the level of raw materials inventories, and the level of finished product inventories—total interest expenses should be related to the volume of production. An analysis of the assets of the six major companies suggests that approximately 25 percent of interest charges are for this working capital and the remaining 75 percent are fixed. At the revised standard volume, therefore, interest per net finished ton is $18.47 based upon the initial MITI submission. Finally, adjusting to an 82.7 percent yield from raw steel to finished product produces the calculation of $19.32 per finished ton reported above.

Returns to capital were expressed in the January 3 announcement by using the 8 percent of all costs principle found in section 206 of the Antidumping Act for calculating "constructed value." This was the equivalent of a 13.1-percent before-tax return on total steelmaking assets, a reasonable return based upon the risk level of the industry. In the current revision, profit is again charged at 8 percent of all noncapital costs—$250.79 per net ton. Therefore, profit is calculated to be $20.06 per net ton. This raises total capital charges from $50.62 in the January 3 calculation to $58.88 per net ton of finished product.

G. SUMMARY OF COST REVISIONS

Overall, the most significant revisions made by the task force derive from (1) the lowering of the Japanese capacity utilization rate (which increased costs by about $18 per net ton) and (2) the raising of the Japanese yield ratio and the creation of a secondary quality material credit (which together reduced costs by about $15).

In terms of each cost component, the revised figures and the original January 3 estimates are as follows:

*Cost of production per net finished ton for 6
integrated Japanese producers*

[Assumptions: 83.2 pct of effective capacity (73.2
pct rated) and 82.7 pct yield]

	Jan. 3 estimate*	Revised estimate
Basic raw materials (per raw ton)	$84.90	$84.90
Other raw materials (per raw ton)	47.26	47.76
Labor (per raw ton)	54.85*	54.87
Total labor and materials (per raw ton)	187.01	187.53

[Assumptions: 83.2 pct of effective capacity (73.2
pct rated) and 82.7 pct yield]

	Jan. 3 estimate*	Revised estimate
Total labor and materials per finished net ton (yield factor)	233.76	226.76
Other expenses	19.39	24.03
Depreciation	16.79	19.50
Interest ⎱	33.82	⎰ 19.32
Profit ⎰		⎱ 20.06
Yield credit	−5.96	−8.90
Total costs:		
Per net ton	297.80	300.76
Per metric ton	328.26	321.53

* The Jan. 3 costs assumed 85 pct effective (74.8 pct rated) capacity utilization and 80 pct yield. Accordingly, the column of January figures reflects those assumptions.

Both totals reflect costs prior to any adjustments announced for the third and fourth quarters.

III. CHANGES IN SELECTED FLAT ROLLED
BASE TRIGGER PRICES

As part of its work, the Steel Task Force conducted a comprehensive review of the structure of, and relationships between, the trigger prices for flat-rolled products. Data on costs of producing individual products were collected from a number of producers in different countries. The Japanese producers also supplied some detail on the structure of their costs. Finally, the Task Force constructed a detailed input-output model of flat-rolled production processes.

As a result of its investigation, the task force has recommended that minor adjustments be made in the trigger prices for hot rolled and galvanized coils. Larger revisions have been recommended for several tin-mill products, particularly double-reduced tin plate. All changes in base trigger prices described below include the effect of the increase in the estimated average cost of production of all products calculated by the task force.

Hot rolled sheet.—The base trigger price on hot rolled sheet is being increased 3.3 percent to reflect the more realistic assessment of finishing costs, including tempering and side trimming. An extra is being developed for theoretical billing of hot rolled sheet, and a trigger price has been set for hot rolled band, as reported in accompanying Treasury releases.

Galvanized iron sheets in coil.—The price of galvanized iron sheet in coil is being increased by 3.9 percent in order to reflect more accurately the yield loss in producing galvanized sheet from cold-rolled sheet. The original galvanized sheet coefficient submitted by MITI was found to contain an excessive yield gain for the galvanizing process.

Tin mill products.—Data received from numerous other producers, including North American firms, suggests that the markup of single-reduced tin plate over cold-rolled sheet is excessive. Therefore, the base price for single-reduced tin plate is being reduced 1.6 percent.

With respect to double-reduced tin plate, the original MITI submission assumed costs on par with single-reduced tin plate. A reasonable differential between single- and double-reduced tin plate, given cost estimates submitted by other sources, requires a 9.5 percent increase in the extra for 55# basebox weight with a 0.25 percent coating. Other extras will be adjusted accordingly.

Finally, the base trigger prices for tin-free steel and black plate are being reduced by 2.4 and 6.8 percent, respectively, as a result of cost differential data obtained from a number of sources.

The combined effect of these changes is to raise trigger prices by approximately 0.6 percent for the entire imported product mix. The specific dollar effects of these revisions are shown below:

Revisions of base trigger prices for certain products

[In dollars per net ton]

Product	Original base trigger prices	Revised base trigger prices	
		Task force[1]	Task force*
Hot rolled sheet	210	217	239
Galvanized sheet	311	323	356
Tin-free steel	375	366	403
Black plate	338	315	347
Single-reduced tin plate	433	426	470
Double-reduced tin plate[2]	431	472	520

[1] Including effect of increase in average cost of production.

[2] 55# base-box weight; 0.25# coating.

* In metric tons.

Again, these revisions reflect costs for these products prior to any exchange rate, labor, and materials adjustments announced for the third and fourth quarters of 1978.

IV. EFFECTIVE DATE OF TASK FORCE REVISIONS

The average cost derived in Part II above and the base trigger prices for the named products derived in Part III will be effective October 1. In each instance, quarterly revisions must be applied to calculate the actual base trigger prices applicable on that date to a particular product. Until October 1, applicable trigger prices for the products affected by task force revisions will be those announced in previous publications.

Trigger prices used by the Customs Service are expressed in terms of metric tons (rather than the net tons used in calculations described above). Hence, revised trigger prices will similarly be expressed in terms of metric tons for use in monitoring imports.

Dated: July 19, 1978.

W. MICHAEL BLUMENTHAL,
Secretary of the Treasury.

IMPORTED STEEL MILL PRODUCTS TRIGGER PRICE MECHANISM*

Fourth Quarter Revision of Trigger Prices

The Treasury Department hereby revises trigger prices for imported steel mill products for the Fourth Quarter of 1978. Each quarter, revisions are made to reflect changes in, e.g., the dollar-yen exchange rate, raw materials costs, and labor usage rates. In the current instance, the Fourth Quarter revisions build upon the revised average costs ($300.76 per net ton) as recommended by the Steel Task Force.

Adjustments for the Fourth Quarter (effective for all shipments exported on or after October 1, 1978) reflect a yen exchange rate of 215 yen per dollar (the average for May 15 through July 14). This results in an upward revision of 3.36 percent for products produced by the major integrated producers. Beyond the yen rate change, for electric furnace producers a 3.03 percent increase in wage rates is applied, resulting in an overall increase of 4.6 percent for products produced by these producers.

The adjustment methodology may be summarized as follows: for the integrated steel producers, the new cost per average ton of finished steel products (as reconstituted by the Task Force and published today) is revised to reflect the Third Quarter adjustment (announced May 5, 1978) and then to reflect the applicable yen exchange rate of 215 for the Fourth Quarter. For the integrated producers, there are no raw materials adjustments (because major raw materials supply contracts are unchanged from prior quarters) and no labor cost adjustment (because the fiscal year 1978 wage increase was reflected in the adjustments previously made for the Third Quarter).

The resulting new average base price for the products made by the integrated producers is $329.42 per net ton ($363 per metric ton). This base price will be effective October 1, 1978.

. . . . .

A. INTEGRATED PRODUCERS

The fourth quarter adjustment is interrelated with the basic revision in average costs undertaken by the Department's Steel Task Force, which has reviewed the trigger costs announced January 3, 1978. The review has established a new original base trigger cost of $300.76 per net ton of finished

---

* Excerpts only. The complete announcement appears in 43 Fed. Reg. 32713, July 27, 1978.

product (formerly $297.80). This base change, plus the task force's restructuring of cost components, affect the quarterly revision calculations.

. . . . .

Table I below show *revised* costs per ton of finished product (as per task force revisions) and the appropriate increase to reflect the fourth quarter of 1978. These are expressed in metric tons, consistent with the prices published by the Customs Service, and a conversion to net tons is shown for comparative purposes.

TABLE I.—*Revised estimates of Japanese costs of
production: Integrated producers*

[U.S. dollars per metric ton of finished products]

	Jan. 9, 1978[1]	Third quarter*	Fourth quarter adjustment
Basic raw materials	$113.17	$116.20	$116.20
Other raw materials	63.66	67.60	71.06
Labor	73.14	80.86	85.02
Other expenses	26.48	28.12	29.56
Depreciation	21.49	22.82	23.99
Interest	21.30	22.62	23.78
Profit	22.11	23.42	24.14
Yield credit	−9.81	−10.31	−10.57
Total dollars per metric ton	331.54	351.33	363.12
Total dollars per net ton	300.76	318.73	329.42

[1] Revised average cost in metric tons.

* See the proviso on the previous page concerning the limited purpose for which third quarter numbers are recalculated.

NOTE:—This revised fourth quarter base price of $363.12 per metric ton will be used to calculate base prices for the fourth quarter for each product produced by the integrated producers.

7. U.S. Treasury Determination of Sales at Less than Fair Value Carbon Steel Plate from Japan (January 9, 1978)

DEPARTMENT OF THE TREASURY
OFFICE OF THE SECRETARY

CARBON STEEL PLATE FROM JAPAN

DETERMINATION OF SALES AT LESS THAN FAIR VALUE

AGENCY: U.S. Treasury Department
ACTION: Determination of Sales at Less Than Fair Value
SUMMARY:

This notice is to advise the public that an antidumping investigation has resulted in a determination that carbon steel plate from Japan is being sold at less than fair value. (Sales at less than fair value generally occur when the price of merchandise sold for exportation to the United States is less than the price of such or similar merchandise sold in the home market or to third countries or the constructed value of the merchandise). This case is being referred to the United States International Trade Commission for a determination concerning possible injury to an industry in the United States.

FINAL DETERMINATION OF SALES AT LESS THAN FAIR VALUE

On the basis of the information developed in the Customs Service investigation and for the reasons noted below, carbon steel plate from Japan, is being or is likely to be sold at less than fair value within the meaning of section 201(a) of the Act (19 U.S.C. 160(a)).

STATEMENT OF REASONS ON WHICH THIS DETERMINATION IS BASED

The reasons and bases for the above determination are as follows:

a. *Scope of the Investigation.* It appears that during the period of investigation covering October 1, 1976 to March 31, 1977, over 70 percent of the imports of the subject merchandise from Japan were manufactured by Nippon Steel Corporation (Nippon Steel), Nippon Kokan K.K. (NKK), Sumitomo Metal Industries, Ltd. (Sumitomo), Kawasaki Steel Corporation (Kawasaki), and Kobe Steel, Ltd. (Kobe). Therefore, the investigation was limited to these five manufacturers.

b. *Basis of Comparison.* For the purpose of considering whether the merchandise in question is being, or is likely to be, sold at less than fair value, within the meaning of the Act, the proper basis of comparison appears to be between purchase price and home market price of such or similar merchandise on all sales by Nippon Steel, NKK, and Kobe, and on most sales by Sumitomo and Kawasaki. Purchase price, as defined in section 203 of the Act (19 U.S.C. 162), was used for most sales since those export sales were made to unrelated Japanese trading companies. On the remaining sales by Sumitomo and Kawasaki, the proper basis of comparison appears to be between exporter's sales price, as defined in section 204 of the Act (19 U.S.C. 163), and home market price, since those sales in the United States are made by importers who are related to those manufacturers. Home market price, as defined in section 153.2, Customs Regulations (19 CFR 153.2), was used since such or similar merchandise was sold in the home market in sufficient quantities at not less than the cost of production to provide a basis of comparison for fair value purposes.

In accordance with section 153.31(b), Customs Regulations (19 CFR 153.31(b)), home market pricing information was obtained for the period October 1, 1976, through March 31, 1977. Since the question of sales prices below cost was raised, cost information was requested with respect particularly to the period April 1, 1976, through March 31, 1977.

c. *Purchase Price*. For the purpose of this tentative determination of sales at less than fair value, purchase price has been calculated on the basis of the f.o.b. or f.a.s. price to the unrelated trading company for export to the United States. A deduction has been made for inland transportation costs included in the price.

d. *Exporter's Sales Price*. For the purpose of this tentative determination of sales at less than fair value, exporter's sales price has been calculated on the basis of the price to the first unrelated purchaser in the United States. Deductions have been made for ocean freight and insurance, brokerage charges, import duties, and for expenses incurred in selling the merchandise in the United States.

e. *Home Market Price*. For the purpose of this determination of sales at less than fair value, the home market price has been calculated on the basis of the delivered, net, packed price. Adjustments have been made for interest costs, freight, reimbursements to customers for defective merchandise, and packing cost differentials, as appropriate, in accordance with section 153.10, Customs Regulations (19 CFR 153.10). Adjustments for interest costs relate to extended payment terms granted to customers in the home market.

Additional adjustments were claimed by counsel for differences in circumstances of sale in accordance with section 153.10, Customs Regulations (19 CFR 153.10), for warehousing costs for inventory purposes, salemen's salaries and office expenses, higher computer costs involved in following orders in the home market, bad debts, and technical services. These expenses do not bear a direct relationship to the sales under consideration and no adjustment has been allowed for these expenses.

Where exporter's sales price was used as the basis of comparison, selling expenses incurred in the home market were deducted from the home market price, up to the amount incurred in the United States, in accordance with section 153.10, Customs Regulations (19 CFR 153.10).

Counsel for petitioner has claimed that sales of this merchandise for home consumption or to third countries have been made in substantial quantities over an extended period of time at prices which are less than the cost of production within the meaning of section 205(b) of the Act and which do not permit recovery of all costs within a reasonable period of time in the normal course of trade. Because some evidence was received indicating that such claims may have been well founded, it was determined that an investigation of respondents' costs of production was warranted.

Respondents sought a hearing to contest the substantiality of the petitioner's claims and to raise alleged conflicts between section 205(b) of the Act and the General Agreement on Tariffs and Trade and the International Anti-Dumping Code. No hearing was deemed necessary, however, since (1) the evidence of possible sales below cost of production was considered sufficiently reliable to warrant a further inquiry which would permit the respondents to provide such facts—as they were by far in the best position to do—to demonstrate their actual costs of production, and (2) the mere inquiry into whether sales in the home market or to third countries fell within the provisions of section 205(b) of the Act gave rise to no conflict with applicable provisions of the GATT or the International Anti-Dumping Code. There is no question that responding to requests for information concerning costs of production may be time-consuming and costly and that its delivery creates a possible risk of its release to competitors or other parties. However, neither of these factors can be an acceptable basis to the Secretary for declining to investigate allegations based upon a *prima facie* showing as made by the complainant in this case. In that connection, it is imperative to underscore, first, that the mere investigation of the facts does not in any way suggest that the outcome of the inquiry has been predetermined; on the contrary, an effort is made to obtain the most complete factual picture necessary to reach the required decisions within the time constraints of the law. Second, the respondents are generally best able to provide the type of information requested. However, their refusal to provide it cannot prevent the Secretary from applying the Act on the basis of whatever evidence he has available, including that furnished solely by the complainant. And, third, serious effort is made by the Department to assure to all parties submitting information that may properly be considered confidential that its confidentiality is preserved.

The respondents in this case nevertheless declined to provide any information concerning their costs of production prior to the publication of the Tentative Determination. Under those circumstances, relying on section 153.31(a) of the Customs Regulations, the best evidence of costs of production was utilized in an effort to determine whether § 205(b) of the Act was applicable. Using the information described in that Determination, including the financial statements filed by the respondents with the Japanese Ministry of Finance, it was tentatively determined that virtually all sales in the home market during the period of investigation were below what appeared to be the cost of producing carbon steel plate. Accordingly, those sales were disregarded in establishing "fair value." No evidence of third country sales having been submitted, weighted average margins of 32 percent were then found between the constructed value of the merchandise and the applicable purchase or exporter's sale prices of the five respondents.

Following publication of the Tentative Determination, the respondents decided that they would furnish some information regarding their costs of production. Claiming the effort would be complex and time-consuming, they requested an extension of the date by which a Final Determination in this case would be made. The suggestion was made that, analogizing to § 201 (b)(2) of the Act, dealing with investigations *preceding* the publication of a Tentative Determination, a three-month extension should also be possible in the making of the Final Determination. However, the applicable section 201(b)(3) is mandatory in fixing three months as the maximum time within which a Final Determination must be made following publication of a Tentative Determination. Accordingly, the request for an extension was denied.

The information furnished by the respondents concerning their costs of production was not identical in each case. Some have provided some data concerning costs of raw materials, labor and similar elements of costs of production, claimed to be drawn from the books and records of the companies that are maintained in the ordinary course of their business. However, due to the shortness of time between the submission of this data and the date by which a Final Determination was due, it has not been possible for Customs Service personnel to "verify" that data pursuant to standards and procedures normally followed and developed over many years of experience both under the Antidumping Act and other customs laws. Such verification normally includes a comparison of the submissions made to the Customs Service with the actual books and records of the companies, a comparison of such books and records with underlying source documents (such as suppliers' invoices, payroll checks and delivery receipts), and a review of the accounting practices used to keep the company books for conformity with generally accepted accounting principles. However, it has not been the past practice of the Customs Service—nor, indeed, would it be possible in view of the time restrictions imposed by the law and the resources available for investigating antidumping complaints—to conduct what an accountant would regard as an "audit" of respondents' operations. And the Antidumping Act imposes no such obligation on the Treasury Department in implementing the law. However, it was not possible to follow even the normal procedures for verification in this case.

The complainant has urged that because of their belated submission and the lack of opportunity for normal verification, all of the respondents' submissions be totally disregarded. As the Treasury Department has no authority to require respondents to furnish information and to submit to verification, the Secretary has generally declined to consider incomplete or unverified information, since to do otherwise may discourage cooperation in the submission and verification of data considered essential in administering the law. However, it would be patently self-denying to disregard information not verified by the methods normally used by the Customs Service if other relevant evidence available to the Secretary tends to corroborate a respondent's submission. There are, in fact, instances in which the best "verification" of cost information may be available from sources external to the books and records of a particular respondent. Therefore, the complainant's suggestion has not been followed.

A further problem is presented by other data submitted which was even further removed from the facts, based on the books and records of the companies, normally used to calculate cost of production. This data was derived by using as a starting point a company's published financial statements, apparently audited by independent certified public accountants and submitted under local law to the Japanese Ministry of Finance, and applying a series of allocations to the aggregate cost data there reflected to arrive at a cost of production of the merchandise relevant to these proceedings. The use of this technique can, of course, lend itself to manipulation and abuse. Most fundamentally, if a company, as a whole, is profitable as a result of the sale of all products and services, and cost allocations are based solely on sales revenues, then no single product will be shown as having been sold at a loss. A company deriving significant income from wholly unrelated activities, for example, the sale of securities held in portfolios, could thereby purport to demonstrate that no losses were experienced in steel plate operations even if more traditional cost accounting practices would clearly demonstrate a contrary result.

Nevertheless, as with "unverified" cost data submitted, the Secretary is not required to disregard information submitted in this form, if it can be corroborated from other sources. And, indeed, it would be anomolous to disregard it entirely and, at the same time, use the same financial statements submitted to the Ministry of Finance as the "best available evidence" of costs—as was done at the time of the Tentative Determination.

The present case is unique in that at the very time it has been under consideration, the Treasury Department has been establishing a "trigger price mechanism" (TPM) to monitor the prices of imported steel mill products. As reflected in *Federal Register* notices published on December 30, 1977 (42 Fed. Reg. 65214) and January 9, 1978 (43 Fed. Reg. 1464), this mechanism is based upon determinations of the costs of producing steel in Japan, including the carbon plate that is the subject of these proceedings. The cost of production has been calculated on the basis of submissions made by the six largest steel companies in Japan, including the five respondents in this case, to the Japanese Ministry of International Trade and Industry and transmitted, in aggregate form, to the U.S. Treasury Department. These cost figures were analyzed and corroborated by the staff of the Council on Wage and Price Stability.

It has been concluded that the information developed in the context of establishing the "trigger prices" for the TPM, appropriately adjusted for the time period under investigation in this case, constitutes the "best available evidence" of the cost of producing the subject merchandise by respondents. Information submitted by respondents has been examined and has also been taken into consideration to the extent it is not inconsistent with the information from which the "trigger prices" were calculated. The company data was used primarily in determining the appropriate relationship between the cost of producing finished steel products and the cost of producing the merchandise subject to this investigation by all the firms in the aggregate.

The cost of production thus established has been compared with the home market prices of each of the five companies under investigation. Any sale made at a price less than such cost of production has been disregarded and the remaining sales, made at not less than the cost of production, have been utilized in determining the appropriate home market price for each company. In each instance, the remaining, above-cost sales representing at least 10% of all sales during the period, were deemed adequate for the purpose of establishing a foreign market value for that respondent.

Counsel for petitioner has claimed that possible additional dumping margins may have been created by sales below the cost of acquisition by trading companies which export carbon steel plate from Japan and also sell this merchandise to ultimate users and other home market purchasers. Information relevant to this claim was collected from trading companies accounting for more than 60 percent of the subject merchandise exported to the United States by the respondent manufacturers. Examination of this information indicated that in virtually all instances sales to unrelated United States buyers were made at prices equal to or greater than the cost of acquisition plus the relevant selling, shipping and other related expenses. It has therefore been determined that no basis exists to deviate from the normal practice of examining pricing behavior at the primary level of trade. Therefore for purposes of this determination, prices of the five respondent manufacturers in the home market and for export to the U.S. have been utilized for fair value comparison purposes.

f. *Result of Fair Value Comparisons.* Using the above criteria, purchase price of exporter's sales price was found to be lower than the home market price of such merchandise. Comparisons were made on a significant portion of the subject merchandise sold to the United States during the investigative period. Weighted average margins over the total sales compared for each firm were approximately 9.1 percent for Nippon Steel, 7.3 percent for NKK, 18.5 percent for Sumitomo, 5.4 percent for Kawasaki, and 13.9 percent for Kobe.

The Secretary has provided an opportunity to known interested persons to present written and oral views pursuant to section 153.40, Customs Regulations (19 CFR 153.40).

The U.S. International Trade Commission is being advised of this determination.

This determination is being published pursuant to section 201(d) of the Act (19 U.S.C. 160(d)).

Robert S. Mundheim
General Counsel of the
Treasury

8. Joint Statement by Minister Ushiba and Ambassador Strauss (January 13, 1978)

1. On January 12 and 13, 1978 the Governments of Japan and the United States of America, through their representatives, Minister of State for External Economic Affairs, Mr. Nobuhiko Ushiba, and the President's Special Representative for Trade Negotiations, Ambassador Robert S. Strauss, consulted upon a series of policies and measures designed to contribute to global economic expansion and to strengthen their economic relations. The objective of the consultations was to develop common policies which would facilitate constructive adjustment to changing world economic conditions and the economic relationship between Japan and the United States.

2. In particular, Minister Ushiba and Ambassador Strauss agreed that a new course of action, building on the steps outlined below, was necessary to avert increasing unemployment and a worldwide reversion to protectionism.

Increased Economic Growth

3. Both sides agreed to take major steps to achieve high levels of non-inflationary, economic growth. The Government of Japan reiterated its recently adopted real growth target of seven percent for Japan Fiscal Year (JFY) 1978, and stated its intention to take all reasonable and appropriate measures, including those previously announced with respect to public expenditures, in order to achieve this target.

The Government of the United States confirmed its intention to pursue policies aimed at the maintenance of substantial, non-inflationary economic growth, as will soon be detailed by President Carter.

4. Both sides agreed that in the present international economic situation, the accumulation of a large current account surplus was not appropriate.

Accordingly, Japan has undertaken steps aimed at achieving a marked diminution of its current account surplus. The Minister added that in JFY 1978 Japan's current account surplus would be considerably reduced through the expansion of domestic demand, the effect of yen appreciation in recent months, and a series of new measures for improving the access of foreign goods to the Japanese market. In JFY 1979, and thereafter, under present international economic conditions, all reasonable efforts would be continued with a view to further reducing Japan's current account surplus, aiming at equilibrium, with deficit accepted if it should occur.

The United States stated its intention to improve its balance of payments position by such measures as reducing its dependence on imported oil and increasing its exports, thereby improving the underlying conditions upon which the value of the dollar fundamentally depends. The Ambassador expressed confidence that in the next ninety days an effective energy program would be enacted by the Congress.

Trade Objectives

5. To preserve and strengthen the open world trading system, both sides fully support the acceleration and early conclusion of the Tokyo Round of the Multilateral Trade Negotiations (MTN), each making substantial contributions in full cooperation with other participants to reduce or eliminate tariff and non-tariff barriers to trade.

6. Both governments agreed that their joint objective in these negotiations is to achieve basic equity in their trading relations by affording to major trading countries substantially equivalent competitive opportunities on a reciprocal basis.

To achieve parity in their trading relations and equivalent openness of their markets, deeper than formula tariff reductions would be utilized.

In this connection, both sides expressed their intent in the course of the MTN to consider favorably taking deeper than formula tariff reductions on items of interest to each other with the aim of seeking to achieve comparable average levels of bond tariffs, taking into account non-tariff measures at the end of the MTN, taking fully into account the interests of third countries.

7. The Government of Japan intends to take all appropriate steps to increase imports of manufactures. The Goverment anticipated that the total volume of imports of manufactures, as well as the share of these imports in total Japanese imports, would continue to increase steadily. Both sides agreed to review progress in these matters in the Joint Trade Facilitation Committee or other appropriate forums and to take whatever corrective actions might be necessary.

Trade Measures

8. The Minister stated that Japan is taking the following significant actions to increase imports:

—Advance tariff reductions on $2 billion of imports effective April 1.

—Removal of quota controls on twelve products.

—As regards high quality beef, we shall make mutual efforts to exploit demand so that within the hotel and general quotas there will be an increase in importation by 10,000 tons on a global basis beginning in JFY 1978.

—A three-fold increase in orange imports to 45,000 tons.

—A four-fold increase to 4,000 tons in the quota for citrus juice.

—Conducting a sweeping review of its foreign exchange control system and planning a new system based on the principle that all transactions should be free unless specifically prohibited. As a forerunner of the new system, certain immediate measures of liberalization are to be announced soon.

—Formation of an inter-industry citrus group to study the present state and future developments in the citrus situation including juice blending and seasonal quota, and to report to their Governments by November 1, 1978.

—Dispatch of a forest products study group to the U.S. Northwest with the objective of expanding and upgrading this trade.

—Dispatch to the United States of a mission to explore the possibility of purchasing electric power plant machinery and equipment, including nuclear plant components and equipment.

—Dispatch to the United States of a government-industry buying mission sponsored by the Joint Trade Facilitation Committee.

—A Japanese Cabinet decision to secure for foreign suppliers substantially increased opportunities under government procurement systems.

—Simplification of inspection requirements on imports.

—Expansion of credit for imports into Japan.

—Relaxation of rules for the standard method of settlement.

—Cooperation in international efforts to curb excessive competition in export credits.

Economic Cooperation

9. Referring to official development assistance (ODA), the Minister reaffirmed the intention of the Government of Japan to more than double its aid in five years and noted that, as part of such efforts, proposed ODA for

JFY 1978 had substantially increased, and that the quality of ODA had improved through an increase of grant aid. He added that the Government of Japan would pursue its basic policy of general untying of its financial assistance.

Ambassador Strauss welcomed these developments and noted that the President would seek legislation to increase substantially U.S. bilateral and multilateral aid to developing countries.

Review Procedures

10. In addition, both sides agreed:

—to coordinate closely with each other and their trading partners including the European Communities in multilateral and bilateral forums.

—to improve access to Japanese markets, by making every effort to assure the success of the Joint Trade Facilitation Committee in its work to increase imports of manufactures, and resolve concrete problems encountered in trade with Japan including the aim of overcoming non-tariff barriers by applying a liberal approach.

—to continue regular technical exchanges on growth problems and prospects through the Joint Economic Projections Study Group.

—to review global and bilateral economic policy this spring in Washington at the next meeting of the Sub-Cabinet Group.

—to review progress made in all these areas at a meeting between Minister Ushiba and Ambassador Strauss next October.

9. Decision of The OECD Council Establishing A Steel Committee

(October 1978)

The Council,

Having regard to the Convention on the Organisation for Economic Co-operation and Development of 14th December, 1960 (hereinafter referred to as the "Convention") and, in particular, Articles 5(a), 6, 12, 13 and 20 thereof;

Having regard to the Rules of Procedure of the Organization;

Having regard to the Financial Regulations of the Organisation and, in particular, Articles 5 and 14(b) thereof;

Having regard to the Communiqué approved by the Council meeting at Ministerial Level on 15th June, 1978 and, in particular, Annex II thereof (PRESS/A(78)23);

Considering that the Ad Hoc Working Group on the Steel Industry has reached the conclusion that a Steel Committee should be established within the framework of the Organisation under Part II of the Budget and that a number of Member countries as well as the European Communities have expressed their intention to participate therein;

Noting that the Member countries participating in the proposed Committee and the European Communities agree as initial commitment to the multilateral guidelines set out in Paragraph 6 of the Annex hereto;

DECIDES:

ARTICLE 1

In order to seek solutions to the problems experienced by the Steel Industry and achieve the objectives set out in the Annex, a Steel Committee (hereinafter referred to as the "Committee") is established within the framework of OECD and shall have the functions and the initial work programme set out in the Annex.

ARTICLE 2

(a) Participants in the Committee shall be:

   (i) Australia, Austria, Belgium, Canada, Denmark, Finland, France, Germany, Greece, Ireland, Italy, Japan, Luxembourg, the Netherlands, Norway, Spain, Sweden, Switzerland, the United Kingdom, the United States and the European Communities,

(ii) Any other Member country of the Organisation which decides to participate in the Committee at a later stage, and

(iii) Any non-Member country which becomes a participant in the Committee in conformity with the provisions of paragraph (b).

(b) The Committee shall, if the OECD Member countries participating therein so decide, propose to the Council that a non-Member country with substantial steel interests should be invited to become a participant in the Committee. In making such a proposal the Committee must be satisfied that the non-Member country has agreed and is able to undertake the same commitments, as appropriate, with regard to the Committee's work as the OECD Member countries which participate therein and that its participation in the Committee would contribute to achieving the objectives of the Committee. Such proposal shall specify the relevant provisions in respect of the non-Member country's participation in the Committee's work.

ARTICLE 3

Expenditure required for the functioning of the Committee shall be defrayed from the appropriations authorised for that purpose under Part II of the Budget of the Organisation. The Committee shall prepare each year a Programme of Work and this with the corresponding budgetary proposals shall be submitted by the Secretary-General to the Council.

ARTICLE 4

The Committee may make proposals to the Council on any matter within its terms of reference and, at the request of the Council or on its own initiative, the Committee may submit other communications to the Council. The Committee shall also make an annual report to the Council on its activities.

ARTICLE 5

(a) The provisions of the Rules of Procedure of the Organisation shall apply to the Committee to the extent that this Decision does not derogate therefrom.

(b) The Committee may make recommendations to participants within the scope of its terms of reference.

(c) The Annex to the Rules of Procedure is amended by the insertion of a new paragraph as follows:

"26. Steel Committee. Its terms of reference are defined in the Decision of the Council establishing a Steel Committee."

ARTICLE 6

This Decision and the Annex shall take effect on 26th October, 1978.

ANNEX

PROBLEMS

1. The world's steel industry is experiencing serious difficulties of both a cyclical and structural nature. These difficulties are widespread and are characterised by:

—persistent excess capacity;

—an exceptionally low level of demand;

—unjustifiably low prices on world markets;

—marked changes in traditional trade patterns;

—major dislocations of labour, frequently in areas already experiencing high unemployment;

—depressed financial performance among producers, which holds down investments needed for modernisation and rationalisation of plants;

—increasing governmental intervention in steel supply and demand, especially with foreign trade.

2. In virtually all major steel-producing nations, steel occupies a central place in the national economy. In a number of major areas, the magnitude of structural problems confronting the steel sector and resultant social and economic implications of the necessary structural adjustments are substantial.

3. The interrelationship of developments in the steel sectors from country to country and the potential that unilateral actions and policies can aggravate the problems of other have become clear. The convergence of cyclical problems among many nations serves to intensify the problems faced by each. There is general recognition that there may well be recurring cyclical difficulties.

OBJECTIVES

4. In view of these difficulties, governments need to work closely together in order to:

—ensure that trade in steel will remain as unrestricted and free of distortion as possible. Restrictive actions should be avoided and, where necessary, strictly limited in scope and time, and in conformity with GATT rules[1];

---

[1] It is noted that references to GATT rules and provisions in this Annex do

—encourage reduction of barriers to trade;

—enable governments to act promptly to cope with crisis situations in close consultation with interested trading partners and in conformity with agreed principles;

—facilitate needed structural adaptations that will diminish pressures for trade actions and promote rational allocation of productive resources with the aim of achieving fully competitive enterprises;

—ensure that measures affecting the steel industry are consistent to the extent possible with general economic policies and take into account implications for related industries, including steel-consuming industries;

—avoid encouraging economically unjustified investments while recognising legitimate development needs;

—facilitate multilateral co-operation consistent with the need to maintain competition, to anticipate and, to the extent possible, prevent problems.

COMMITTEE FUNCTIONS

5. The Steel Committee will meet regularly and additionally as required to:

(1) continuously follow national, regional and world supply and demand conditions in steel and closely related industries, including steel-consuming industries, with a view to identifying potential problems and implications and making assessments and forecasts available to all interested parties;

(2) continuously follow the evolution of national, regional and world steel industries with regard to employment, profits, investments, capacity, input costs, productivity, and other aspects of viability and competitiveness;

(3) develop common perspectives regarding emerging problems or concerns in the steel sector and establish, where appropriate, multilateral objectives or guidelines for government policies;

(4) regularly review and assess government policies and actions in the steel sector in the light of the current situation, agreed multilateral objectives and guidelines and the GATT and other relevant international agreements;

(5) identify deficiencies and gaps in existing data needed by the Committee with a view to improving national inputs to the Committee and cross-national comparability of data.

---

not alter the rights and obligations under the GATT of individual participants which are contracting parties to the GATT nor confer by implication equivalent rights or obligations on participants which are not contracting parties to the GATT.

INITIAL COMMITMENTS

6. Participants in the Steel Committee agree to the following multilateral guidelines:

A. With respect to steel crisis trade actions:

1. No actions should be inconsistent with GATT provisions.

2. When actions are necessary they should be as limited and temporary as practicable and appropriate to the causes which led to their introduction.

3. All actions[2] taken by participants should be reported promptly to the Steel Committee, and in conformity with GATT rules, to the GATT. The status and rationale for maintaining such actions should be reported periodically to the Steel Committee. Participants agree to consult on any trade action of interest to another participant.

4. When taking action under domestic law and procedures to deal with serious difficulties of its industry, a participant shall take into account the concerns of trading partners that traditional trade flows established under normal conditions of competition not be severely disrupted.

5. Price guidelines should be in conformity with the international Anti-Dumping Code and are appropriate only during crisis periods of substantial excess capacity in exporting countries, widespread price cutting by many exporters over many products in the importing market or on world markets, and depressed domestic industry conditions such as low capacity utilisation, profits, sales, investments and employment. Such actions should be expeditiously removed or liberalised as conditions improve.

6. Such price guidelines should neither exceed the lowest normal prices in the supplying country or countries where normal conditions of competition are prevailing, nor exceed the sums of the full costs of production (including overheads) and profit, as determined over a reasonable period of recent time, in the supplying country or countries; delivery costs to the importing market and import duties may be included in the event that price guidelines are established on a delivered basis.

B. Participants in the Steel Committee recall their determination to abstain from destructive competition in official support of export credit; they agree that their policies in the field of export credits for steel plant and equipment will be fully consistent with the Arrangement on Guidelines for Officially Sup-

---

[2] It is understood that these include all safeguard measures subject to the reporting requirements under the GATT.

ported Export Credits and contribute to the avoidance of competitive subsidisation of such exports.

C. Participants, recalling the general orientations for adjustment policies adopted as part of the Communiqué of the June 1978 Meeting of the Council at Ministerial level, agree that domestic policies to sustain steel firms during crisis periods should not shift the burden of adjustment to other countries and thus increase the likelihood of restrictive trade actions by other countries (e.g. by artificially stimulating exports or by artificially displacing imports). Further, as a general rule, domestic measures should not prevent marginal facilities from closing in those instances where the facilities cannot become commercially viable within a reasonable period of time.

D. Participants in the Steel Committee agree to make every effort to provide effective programmes for steel worker readaptation away from facilities affected by structural adjustments into alternative employment. To this end, they will periodically exchange information on the effectiveness of policies and programmes to assist steel workers and communities.

E. Any actions to restrict trade in steelmaking materials should be reported promptly to the Steel Committee and be subject to consultation with affected parties.

INITIAL WORK PROGRAMME

7. With respect to the commitments agreed in this resolution the Steel Committee should promptly undertake an examination of government policies affecting the steel sector in the following areas:

   (1) evolution of trade flows and the impact on them of government measures;

   (2) guidelines for steel trade actions;

   (3) adaptation of production structure through modernisation, closures and reconversions;

   (4) re-adaptation of labour;

   (5) domestic policies to sustain steel production and stimulate steel demand in times of crisis;

   (6) domestic pricing and supply;

   (7) government export credits for steel plant and equipment.

The Committee will continue the work initiated in the Ad Hoc Steel Group and may undertake examinations in other areas as deemed appropriate by the participants.

10. Japan: Measures of Restraint on Automobile Exports (May, 1981)

1. The Government of Japan acknowledges that the United States Government, with the intention of coping with the difficulties the automobile industry is experiencing at the present time, has formulated policies for the revitalization of that industry, and that some of the measures including those to ease regulations have already been implemented. We also fully recognize that both management and labor of the auto industry, as evidenced by their recent statements, are making sincere efforts toward its revitalization. The Government of Japan, predicated upon the above types of efforts being made in the U.S., taking the board view of maintaining the free trade system and further developing U.S.-Japan economic relations, has decided to implement, as a temporary and exceptional measure, those measures detailed in item # 3 below with regard to passenger car exports to the United States.

2. Regarding the U.S.-Japan automobile question, Japan has cooperated with the United States in the so-called 'automobile package' of May 1980 which included an abolition in principle of all customs duties on automobile parts, measures to promote investment in the United States, etc., and this appears to be proceeding satisfactorily. Also, Japanese automobile manufacturers for some time have been actively engaging in joint capital ventures and other forms of cooperation with the Big Three U.S. automobile manufacturers, and these types of cooperative relationships have also been advancing at a good pace with the agreement between Mitsubishi and Chrysler for new measures of cooperation, and on-going negotiations between Toyota and Ford on joint automobile production. Furthermore, with regard to automobile exports to the United States, since last fall we have taken in cognizance of the difficulties facing the U.S. automobile industry, such measures as the public announcements on projections of passenger car exports reflecting prudent export policies of the Japanese automobile industry on their exports to the United States.

As a continuation of these measures, based upon the conditions in # 1 above, the new measures Japan is preparing to take are going to be implemented with the understanding that equity will not be lost between our new measures and the United States' imports from a third country.

3. With the understanding that the key steps toward the revitalization of the U.S. automobile industry should be taken within the first 3 years, the following measures will be implemented over a 3-year period ending March 1984:

(1) For a three- year period until the end of March 1984, a new oversight system on passenger car exports to the United States will be implemented based upon the authority of the Foreign Exchange and the Foreign Trade Control Law, wherein each automobile manufacturing company will be required to submit monthly reports concerning their exports of passenger cars (as categorized by the Japan Automobile Manufacturers Association statistics, hereafter so defined) to the United States (the 50 states and the District of Columbia, hereafter so defined).

(2) During the first year (April 1981 thru March 1982) the Ministry of International Trade and Industry will control the export of passenger cars to the United States by issuing individual directives to each manufacturer as administrative measures, so that exports will be within 1,680,000 automobiles.

(3) During the second year (April 1982 thru March 1983) application of the same types of measures will be used to control exports of passenger cars to the United States. The level for this year will be determined by multiplying the amount of the expansion of the market by 16.5% to determine the amount of increase in the level of exports and this figure will be added to the figure for the first year.

(4) In order to insure that the measures in (2) and (3) above are carried out, based upon the provisions in the Foreign Exchange and the Foreign Trade Control Law, the export approval system would be promptly applied to passenger car exports to the United States in the unlikely event that it would be necessary.

(5) During the third year (April 1983 thru March 1984) the exports of passenger cars to the United States will be watched closely under the oversight system as detailed in (1) above. In addition, it will be discussed at the end of the second year whether or not to contine the restrictions on the number of exported units taking into consideration trends in the U.S. passenger car market and so forth.

(6) The aforementioned measures will expire, in any event, after March 1984.

Regarding the export of passenger cars to Puerto Rico and regarding the export of vans (which the Japan Automobile Manufacturers Association statistics regard as commercial vehicles, but which the U.S. classifies as passenger vehicles) to both the United States and Puerto Rico, separate measures will be taken.

4. The Government of Japan expects that responsible persons in the United States will evaluate these measures and take appropriate actions regarding any domestic protectionist trends. Also, we understand that the opinion of the U.S. anti-trust authorities has been clearly given that these measures pose no problem with the U.S. anti-trust laws.

Japan has the heart-felt desire that the United States will revitalize the U.S. automobile industry through its own efforts so that an active U.S. economy will be reborn.

11. Proposed Domestic Content Legislation*

H.R. 5133

Be it enacted by the Senate and House of Representatives of the United States of America in Congress assembled.

Section 1. *Short Title.*

This Act may be cited as the "Fair Practices in Automotive Products Act".

Section 2. *Purpose.*

The purpose of this Act is to encourage the production of automotive products in the United States.

Section 3. *Definitions.*

(a) In General.—As used in this Act—

(1) The term "automotive products" means motor vehicles and parts for use in the production of new motor vehicles.

(2) The term "added domestic value", when used with respect to a vehicle manufacturer for any model year, means the aggregate of—

(A) the production costs of all automotive products sold by the vehicle manufacturer in the United States, other than for export, during that model year, and

(B) the export value of all automotive products that were either—

(i) manufactured by the vehicle manufacturer in the United States and exported from the United States by, or on behalf of, such manufacturer during that model year, or

(ii) manufactured in the United States by any other person and purchased by the vehicle manufacturer and exported from the United States by, or on behalf of, such manufacturer during that model year, but only to the extent that the export value of such automotive products is not included in automotive products to which clause (i) applies; reduced by the aggregate appraised value, as determined for purposes of the customs laws, of all automotive products that were entered by, or on behalf of, the vehicle manufacturer during that model year.

---

* As considered by full House of Representatives, Dec. 1982 prior to introduction of floor amendments.

(3) The term "domestic content ratio" means, with respect to a vehicle manufacturer for any model year, the percentage determined by multiplying by one hundred the factor obtained by dividing—

(A) the added domestic value determined for that manufacturer for that model year under paragraph (2); by

(B) the production costs determined, for purposes of paragraph (2)(A), for that manufacturer for that model year.

(4) The term "entered" means entered, or withdrawn from warehouse for consumption, within the customs territory of the United States.

(5) The term "model year" means a vehicle manufacturer's annual production period (as determined by the Secretary) which includes January 1 of a calendar year, or if a vehicle manufacturer does not have an annual production period, the calendar year. A model year shall be designated by the year in which January 1 occurs.

(6) The term "motor vehicle" means any three-wheeled or four-wheeled vehicle propelled by fuel which is manufactured primarily for use on the public streets, roads, and highways (except any vehicle operated exclusively on a rail or rails), and which is rated at ten thousand pounds gross vehicle weight or less. Such term does not include (A) any motorcycle, or (B) any vehicle determined by the Secretary to be an automobile capable of off-highway operation within the meaning of section 501(3) of the Motor Vehicle Information and Cost Savings Act.

(7) The term "production cost" means, with respect to an automotive product, the wholesale price to dealers in the United States for that product as set forth in the vehicle manufacturer's official dealer price list that is in effect at the time the product is sold at wholesale.

(8) The term "Secretary" means the Secretary of Transportation.

(9) The term "vehicle manufacturer" means any person engaged in the business of producing motor vehicles for ultimate retail sale in the United States and includes as one entity all persons who control, are controlled by, or are in common control with, such person. Such term also includes any predecessor or successor of such a vehicle manufacturer.

(b) DETERMINATION OF ADDED DOMESTIC VALUE.—For purposes of applying paragraph (2) of subsection (a)—

(1) Two or more vehicle manufacturers may not include, for purposes of determining their respective added domestic values, the value of the same automotive product; but such manufacturers may, under rules prescribed under section 4(b), apportion the value of that automotive product among them.

(2) The term "export value" means, with respect to an automotive product—

(A) the free-on-board price for which the vehicle manufacturer sells the product for exportation from the United States; or

(B) if the vehicle manufacturer sells the product for such exportation to a buyer that controls, is controlled by, or is under common control with, such manufacturer, the price at which such or similar products are freely offered for free-on-board sale to all purchasers in the principal markets of the United States in the usual wholesale quantities and in the ordinary course of trade for such exportation.

(3) Any automotive product that is entered by a person other than a vehicle manufacturer shall, if such product is purchased or otherwise acquired by the manufacturer (and whether or not used in the fabrication of another automotive product which is acquired by that manufacturer), be treated as having been entered by that manufacturer.

Section 4. *Content Ratios for Model Year 1984 and Thereafter*

(a) RATIOS.—For each model year beginning after January 1, 1983, the minimum domestic content ratio for a vehicle manufacturer shall not be less than the higher of—

(1) the domestic content ratio achieved by the vehicle manufacturer in model year 1983 reduced by 10 per centum; or

(2) the applicable minimum content ratio specified in the following table:

Number of motor vehicles produced by the manufacturer and sold in the United States during such year:	Minimum domestic content ratio:
Model Year 1984	
Not over 100,000	0 percent.
Over 100,000 but not over 900,000....	The number, expressed as a percentage, determined by dividing the number of vehicles sold by 30,000.
Over 900,000......................	30 percent.
Model Year 1985	
Not over 100,000	0 percent.
Over 100,000 but not over 900,000 ...	The number, expressed as a percentage, determined by dividing the number of vehicles sold by 15,000.
Over 900,000......................	60 percent.

Each Model Year After Model Year 1985

Not over 100,000 .... 0 percent.

Over 100,000 but not over 900,000 ... The number, expressed as a percentage, determined by dividing the number of vehicles sold by 10,000.

Over 900,000 .... 90 percent.

(b) Allocation of Automotive Products Among Manufacturers.—In order to carry out the purpose of this Act, the Secretary shall prescribe rules for allocating automotive products among vehicle manufacturers in appropriate cases such as where—

(1) a vehicle manufacturer sells automotive products manufactured by it in the United States to another vehicle manufacturer;

(2) two or more vehicle manufacturers in joint venture product automotive products in the United States; and

(3) a vehicle manufacturer produces motor vehicles for ultimate retail sale in the United States, some of which will be sold by that manufacturer and some by another vehicle manufacturer.

Section. 5. *Information and Reports.*

(a) Vehicle Manufacturers Records and Information.—Each vehicle manufacturer that produces more than one hundred thousand motor vehicles for sale in the United States during any model year after model year 1982 must establish and maintain such records, and provide such information, regarding the production and sale of automotive products by it as the Secretary by rule shall require for purposes of carrying out section 4(a) and the enforcement provisions of section 6.

(b) Authority To Obtain Information.—

(1) The authority granted to the Secretary under subsection (b)(1) of section 505 of the Motor Vehicle Information and Cost Saving Act (as in effect on the date of the enactment of this Act) to obtain information and data, and access thereto, that is deemed advisable by him for purposes of carrying out part V of that Act may be used by the Secretary for purposes of obtaining the information and data, and access thereto, that is necessary or appropriate to carry out section 4(a) and section 6.

(2) The authority granted to the district courts of the United States under subsection (b)(2) of such section 505 to enforce compliance with action taken by the Secretary under subsection (b)(1) of such section may be used by such courts to enforce actions taken by the Secretary pursuant to paragraph (1) for purposes of carrying out this Act.

(3) The Secretary shall disclose any information and data obtained under this subsection and subsection (a) to the public only in accordance with section 552 of title 5, United States code; and any matter described in subsection (b)(4) of such

section shall not be disclosed to the public, except that where such matter may be relevant to any administrative or judicial proceeding to enforce this Act, such matter may be disclosed in such proceeding only in a manner which would not result in competitive damage or disadvantage, as determined by the Secretary or a court, because of such disclosure.

(c) Annual Reports.—As soon as practicable after the close of each model year after January 1, 1983, the Secretary shall prepare and make available to the public a report setting forth the domestic content ratio achieved by each vehicle manufacturer during such model year.

Section. 6. Enforcement

(a) FAILURE TO MEET CONTENT RATIOS.—(1) It is unlawful for a vehicle manufacturer to fail to meet for any model year the applicable minimum domestic content ratio required under section 4(a).

(2) If the Secretary finds, after notice and an opportunity for a hearing in accordance with section 554 of title 5, United States Code, that a vehicle manufacturer has violated paragraph (1), the Secretary shall issue an order prohibiting the vehicle manufacturer from entering, or having entered on its behalf, during the twelve-month period beginning on the date on which the finding becomes final—

(A) a quantity of motor vehicles that exceeds the total quantity of motor vehicles that was entered by, or on behalf of, that manufacturer during the model year in which such violation occurred reduced by the number of motor vehicles that bears to such total quantity the same percentage by which the vehicle manufacturer failed to meet the domestic content ratio for that model year; and

(B) parts for motor vehicles in an aggregate value (as appraised for purposes of the customs laws) that exceeds the total aggregate appraised value of parts for motor vehicles that were entered by, or on behalf of, that manufacturer during the model year in which such violation occurred reduced by parts of an aggregate value the same percentage by which the vehicle manufacturer failed to meet the domestic content ratio for that model year.

(3) An order issued pursuant to paragraph (2) shall specify the total number of motor vehicles and the aggregate appraised value of parts for motor vehicles that may be entered during the applicable twelve-month period by, or on behalf of, the vehicle manufacturer. The Commissioner of Customs shall take such action as may be necessary to ensure that the entries made by, or on behalf of, the vehicle manufacturer during such twelve-month period do not exceed the limits specified in the order.

(4) Any person against whom an order is issued under paragraph (2) may, within sixty calendar days after the date of the order, institute an action in the United States court of appeals for the appropriate judicial circuit for judicial review of such order in accordance with chapter 7 of title 5, United States Code. The court shall have jurisdiction to enter a judgment affirming, modifying, or setting aside in whole or

in part, the order of the Secretary, or the court may remand the proceeding to the Secretary for such further action as the court may direct.

(b) OTHER VIOLATIONS.—(1) Any person who knowingly violates any provision of this Act (other than failure to meet the applicable domestic content ratio for any model year) or any rule or regulation issued under this Act shall be liable to the United States for a civil penalty of not more than $10,000. Each day of a continuing violation under this subsection shall constitute a separate offense.

(2)(A) Before issuing an order assessing a civil penalty against any person for violation of paragraph (1), the Secretary shall provide to such person written notice of the proposed penalty.

(B) The Secretary shall promptly assess such penalty, by order, after the date of the receipt of the notice under subparagraph (A) of the proposed penalty.

(C) If the penalty has not been paid within sixty calendar days after the assessment order has been made under subparagraph (B), the Secretary shall institute an action in the appropriate district court of the United States for an order affirming the assessment of the civil penalty. The court shall have authority to review de novo the law and the facts involved, and shall have jurisdiction to enter a judgment enforcing, modifying, and enforcing as so modified, or setting aside in whole or in part, such assessment.

(D) If any person fails to pay an assessment of a civil penalty after the appropriate district court has entered final judgment in favor of the Secretary under subparagraph (C), the Secretary shall institute an action to recover the amount of such penalty in any appropriate district court of the United States. In such action, the validity and appropriateness of such final assessment order or judgment shall not be subject to review.

(3) The Secretary may compromise, modify, or remit, with or without conditions, any penalty that is subject to imposition or that has been imposed under this subsection.

Section 7. *Study of Discriminatory Practices Affecting Domestic Production of Motor Vehicle Parts.*

Within one year after the date of the enactment of this Act, the Secretary and the Federal Trade Commission shall jointly undertake an investigation, and submit to Congress a written report, regarding those policies and practices of vehicle manufacturers that are used to persuade United States motor vehicle dealers, in chosing replacement parts for motor vehicles, to favor foreign-made parts rather than domestically produced parts. Such report shall include, but not be limited to, recommended administrative or legislative action that the Secretary and the Federal Trade Commission consider appropriate to assure that domestic producers of replacement parts are accorded fair access to the United States market for such parts.

8. *GAO Report*

Not later than one year after the date of the enactment of this Act and each year thereafter, the Comptroller General of the United States shall transmit to the Congress a report on the impact of this Act on the automotive and related industries in the United States. Each report shall contain an analysis of the impact of this Act during the period for which the report is submitted—

(1) on the prices of new, domestic and foreign motor vehicles;

(2) on the employment within the United States in motor vehicle manufacturing and in related industries and on employment in the United States in export industries;

(3) on the productivity and profits of vehicle manufacturers who have sales of their motor vehicle in the United States;

(4) on the productivity and profits of foreign vehicle manufacturers who have production facilities in the United States; and

(5) on the development of motor vehicles suitable for use in more than one country. Each report shall also contain recommendations for such legislation as the Comptroller General determines is appropriate.

12. U.S.-ECSC STEEL ARRANGEMENTS 1982

Arrangements Concerning Trade in Certain Steel Products and Steel Pipes and Tubes between The European Communities and the United States of America

(a) ARRANGEMENT

concerning trade in certain steel products between the European Coal and Steel Community (hereinafter called "the ECSC") and the United States (hereinafter called "the US").

1. Basis of the Arrangement

Recognizing the policy of the ECSC of restructuring its steel industry including the progressive elimination of state aids pursuant to the ECSC State Aids Code; recognizing also the proceess of modernization and structural change in the United States of America (herin after called the "USA"); recognizing the importance as concluded by the OECD of restoring the competitiveness of OECD steel industries; and recognizing, therefore, the importance of stability in trade in certain steel products between the European Community (hereinafter called "the Community") and the USA;

The objective of this Arrangement is to give time to permit restructuring and therefore to create a period of trade stability. To this effect the ECSC* shall restrain exports to or destined for consumption in the USA of products described in Article 3 a) originating in the Community (such exports hereinafter called "the Arrangement products") for the period 1st November 1982 to 31st December 1985.

The ECSC shall ensure that in regard to exports effected between 1st August and 31st October 1982, aberrations from seasonal trade patterns of Arrangement products will be accommodated in the ensuing licensing period.

2. Condition - Withdrawal of Petitions; New Petitions

a) The entry into effect of this Arrangement is conditional upon:

(1) the withdrawal of the petitions and termination of all investigations concerning all countervailing duty and antidumping duty petitions listed in Appendix A at the latest by 21st October 1982; and

(2) receipt by the US at the same time of an undertaking from all such petitioners not to file any petitions seeking import relief under US law, including countervailing duty, antidumping duty, section 301 of the Trade Act of 1974 (other

---

* To the extent that the Arrangement products are subject to the Treaty establishing the European Economic Community (the EEC), the term "ECSC" should be substituted by "the EEC".

than section 301 petitions relating to third country sales by US exporters) or Section 337 of the Tariff Act of 1930, on the Arrangement products during the period in which this Arrangement is in effect.

b) If during the period in which this Arrangement is in effect any such investigations* or investigations under Section 201 of the Trade Act of 1974, Section 232 of the Trade Expansion Act of 1962, or Section 301 of the Trade Act of 1974 (other than Section 301 petitions relating to third country sales by US exporters) are initiated or petitions filed or litigation (including anti-trust litigation) instituted with respect to the Arrangement products, and the petitioner or litigant is one of those referred to in Article 2 a), the ECSC shall be entitled to terminate the Arrangement with respect to some or all of the Arrangement products after consultations with the US, at the earliest 15 days after such consultation.

If such petitions are filed or litigation commenced by petitioners or litigants other than those referred to in the previous paragraph, or investigations initiated, on any of the Arrangement products, the ECSC will be entitled to terminate the Arrangement with respect to Arrangement product which is the subject of the petition, litigation or investigation, after consultation with the US at the earliest 15 days after such consultation. In addition, if during these consultations it is determined that the petition, litigation or investigation threatens to impair the attainment of the objectives of the Arrangement, then the ECSC shall be entitled to terminate the Arrangement with respect to some or all Arrangement products at the earliest 15 days after such consultations.

These consultations will take into accont the nature of the petitions or ltigation, the identity of the petitioner or litigant, the amount of trade involved, the scope of relief sought and other relevant factors.

c) If, during the term of this Arrangement, any of the above mentioned proceedings or litigation is instituted in the USA against certain steel products as defined in Article 3 b) imported from the Community which are not subject to this Arrangement and which substantially threaten its objective, then the ECSC and the US, before taking any other measure, shall consult to consider appropriate remedial measures.

3. Product Description

a) The products are:

Hot-rolled sheet and strip

Cold-rolled sheet

Plate

Structurals

---

* With respect to any Section 337 investigation, the parties shall consult to determine the basis for the investigation.

Wire rods

Hot-rolled bars

Coated sheet

Tin plate

Rails

Sheet piling

as described and classified in Appendix B by reference to corresponding Tariff Schedules of the United States Annotated (TSUSA) item numbers and EC NIMEXE classification numbers.

b) For purposes of this Arrangement, the term "certain steel products" refers to the products described in Appendix E.

4. Export Limits

a) For the period 1st November 1982 to 31st December 1983 (hereinafter called "the Initial Period") and thereafter for each of the years 1984 and 1985 export licences shall be required for the Arangement products. Such licences shall be issued to Community exporters for each product in quantities no greater than the following percentages of the projected US Apparent Consumption (hereinafter called "export ceilings") for the relevant period:

Product	Percentage
Hot-rolled sheet and strip	6.81
Cold-rolled sheet	5.11
Plate	5.36
Structurals	9.91
Wire rods	4.29
Hot-rolled bars	2.38
Coated sheet	3.27
Tin plate	2.20
Rails	8.90
Sheet piling	21.85

For the purposes of this Arrangement, "US Apparent Consumption" shall mean shipments (deliveries) minus exports plus imports, as described in Appendix D.

b) Where Arrangement products imported into the USA are subsequently reexported therefrom, without having been subject to substantial transformation, the export ceiling for such products for the period corresponding to the time of such reexport shall be increased by the same amount.

c) For the purposes of this Arrangement the USA shall comprise both the US

Customs Territory and US Foreign Trade Zones. In consequence the entry into the US Customs Territory of Arrangement products which have already entered into a Foreign Trade Zone shall not then be again taken into account as imports of Arrangement products.

5. Calculation and Revision of US Apparent Consumption Forecast and of Export Limits.

The US, in agreement with ECSC, will select an independent forecaster which will provide the estimate of U.S. Apparent Consumption for the purposes of this Arrangement.

For the Initial Period, a first projection of the U.S. Apparent Consumption by product will be established as early as possible and in any event before 20th October 1982. A provisional export ceiling for each product will then be calculated for that period by multiplying the U.S. Apparent Consumption of each product by the percentage indicated in Article 4 for that product. These figures for projected consumption will be revised in December 1982, February, May, August and October of 1983, by the said independent forecasters, and appropriate adjustments will be made to the export ceilings for each product taking into account licences already issued under Article 4.

The same procedure will be followed to calculate and revise the US Apparent Consumption and export ceilings for 1984 and for 1985, the first projection being established by the independent forecasters by 1st October of 1983 and 1984 respectively.

In February of each year as from 1984, adjustments to that year's export ceiling for each product will be made for differences between the forecasted U.S. Apparent Consumption and actual U.S. apparent consumption of that product in the previous year or (in February 1984) in the Initial Period.

6. Export Licences

a) By Decisions and Regulations to be published in the Official Journal of the European Communities the ECSC will require an export licence for all Arrangement products. Such export licences will be issued in a manner that will avoid abnormal concentration in exports of Arrangement products to the USA taking into account seasonal trade patterns. The ECSC shall take such action, including the imposition of penalties, as may be necessary to make effective the obligations resulting from the export licences. The ECSC will inform the U.S. of any violations concerning the export licences which come to its attention and the action taken with respect thereto.

Export licences will provide that shipment must be made within a period of three months.

Export licences will be issued against the export ceiling for the Initial Period or a specific calendar year as the case may be. Export licences may be used as early as 1st December of the previous year within a limit of eight (8) per cent of the ceiling for the given year. Export licences may not be used after 31st December of the year for which they are issued except that licences not so used may be used during the first two months of the following year with a limit of eight (8) percent of the export ceiling of the previous year or of eight (8) percent of eighty-six (86) percent of the export ceiling of the Initial Period, as the case may be.

b) The ECSC will require that the Arrangement products shall be accompanied by a certificate, substantially in the form set out on Appendix C, endorsed in relation to such a licence. The U.S. shall require presentation of such cetificate as a condition for entry into the USA of the Arrangement products. The U.S. shall prohibit entry of such products not accompanied by such a certificate.

7. Technical Adjustments

a) The specific product export ceilings provided for in Article 4 may be adjusted by the ECSC with notice to the U.S. Adjustments to increase the volume of one product must be offset by an equivalent volume reduction for another product for the same period. Notwithstanding the preceding sentences, no adjustment may be made under this paragraph which results in an increase or a decrease in a specific product limitation under Article 4 by more than five (5) percent by volume for the relevant period.

The ECSC and the U.S. may agree to increase the above percentage limit.

b) Normally, only one change in a specific product export ceiling in a given year or the Initial Period may be made by an adjustment under the preceding paragraph or use of licences in December or January/February under Article 6(a). Accordingly, changes in a given year or the Initial Period by use of more than one of those three provisions may be made only upon aggrement between the ECSC and the U.S..

8. Short Supply

On the occasion of each quarterly consultation provided for in Article 10 the U.S. and the ECSC will examine the supply and demand situation in the USA for each of the products listed in Appendix B. If the U.S. in consultation with the ECSC determines that because of abnormal supply or demand factors, the US steel industry will be unable to meet demand in the USA for a particular product (including substantial objective evidence such as allocation, extended delivery periods or other relevant factors) an additional tonnage shall be allowed for such product or products by a special issue of licences limited to 10 pecent of the ECSC's unadjusted export ceiling for that product or products. In extraordinary circumstances as determined by the U.S. in consulatation with the ECSC the U.S. will increase the allowable level of special licences.

Each authorized special issue export licence and certificate derived therefrom shall be so marked. Each such licence must be used within 180 days after the start of the quarter when that special issue began.

9. Monitoring

The ECSC will within one month of each quarter and for the first time by 31st January 1983 supply the U.S. with such non-confidential information on all export licences issued for Arrangement products as is required for the proper functioning of this Arrangement.

the U.S. will collect and transmit quarterly to the ECSC all non-confidential information relating to certificates received during the preceding quarter in respect of the Arrangement products, and relating to actions taken in respect of Arrangement products for violations of customs laws.

10. General

Quarterly consultations shall take place between the ECSC and the U.S. on any matter arising out of the operation of the Arrangement. Consultations shall be held at any other time at the request of either the ECSC or the U.S. to discuss any matters including trends in the importation of certain steel products which impair or threaten to impair the attainment of the objectives of this Arrangement.

In particular, if imports from the ECSC of certain steel products other than Arrangement products or of alloy Arrangement products show a significant increase indicating the possibility of diversion of trade from Arrangement products to certain steel products other than Arrangement products or from carbon to alloy within the same Arrangement product, consultations will be held between the U.S. and the ECSC with the objective of preventing such diversion, taking into account the ECSC 1981 US market share levels.

Should these consultations demonstrate that there has indeed been a diversion of trade which is such as to impair the attainment of the objectives of the Arrangement, then within 60 days of the request for consultations both sides will take the necessary measures for the products concerned in order to prevent such a diversion. For alloy Arrangement products, such measures will include the creation of separate products for purposes of Articles 3 and 4 at the ECSC 1981 U.S. market share levels. For certain steel products other than Arrangement products, such measures may include the creation of products for purposes of Articles 3 and 4.

Consultations will also be held if there are indications that imports from third countries are replacing imports from the ECSC.

11. Scope of the Arrangement

This Arrangement shall apply to the U.S. Customs Territory (except as otherwise provided in Article 4(c)) and to the territories to which the Treaty establishing the ECSC as presently constituted applies on the conditions laid down in that Treaty.

12. Notices

For all purposes hereunder the U.S. and the ECSC shall be represented by and all communications and notices shall be given and addressed to:

for the ECSC

The Commission of the European Communities

(Directorates General for External Relations (I) and for

Internal Market and Industrial Affairs (III))

rue de la Loi, 200

1049 Brussels, BELGIUM

Tel: 235.11.11

Telex: 21877 COMEU B

for the U.S.

U.S. Department of Commerce

Deputy Assistant Secretary for Import Administration

International Trade Administration

Washington, D.C. 20230

Tel: 202/377-17-80

Telex: 892536 USDOC WSH DAS/IA/ITA

APPENDIX A

List of countervailing duty (CVD) and antidumping duty (AD) petitions* to be withdrawn:

CVD petitions, filed on January 11, 1982, by (1) United States Steel Corporation, (2) Bethlehem Steel Corporation, and (3) Republic Steel Corporation, Inland Steel Company, Jones and Laughlin Steel, Inc., National Steel Corporation, and Cyclops Corporation concerning certain steel products from Belgium, France, the Federal Republic of Germany, Italy, Luxembourg, the Netherlands, the United Kingdom, and the European Communities.

AD petitions, filed on January 11, 1982, by (1) United States Steel Corporation, and (2) Bethlehem Steel Corporation concerning certain steel products from Belgium, France, the Federal Republic of Germany, Italy, Luxembourg, the Netherlands, and the United Kingdom.

CVD petitions, filed on February 8, 1982, by Atlantic Steel Corporation, Georgetown Steel Corporation, Georgetown Texas Steel Corporation, Keystone Consolidated, Inc., Korf Industries, Inc., Penn Dixie Steel Corporation and Raritan River Steel Company concerning carbon steel wire rod from Belgium and France.

CVD petitions, filed on May 7, 1982, by United States Steel Corporation concerning carbon steel welded pipe from France, the Federal Republic of Germany and Italy.

CVD petition, filed on September 3, 1982, by CF and I Steel Corporation concerning steel rails from the European Communities.

---

* For purposes of this Arrangement, the term "petitions" covers all matters included in the petitions filed on the dates listed whether or not the DOC initiated investigations on the products or countries concerned.

AD petitions, filed on September 3, 1982, by CF and I Steel Corporation concerning steel rails from France, the Federal Republic of Germany and the United Kingdom.

(b) AGREED MINUTE
October 21, 1982

This Minute records the understanding between the USG and EC Commission with respect to the fourth paragraph of Article 1 of the Arrangement.

The EC estimates that exports of Arrangement products during the period August, September and October 1982 will not exceed 968,000 metric tons. This level of exports would not be an aberration within the meaning of Article 1. This conclusion is based on the assumption that definitive export statistics will not be at variance with this estimate. If exports are not in line with this estimate, then the EC will adjust the export ceilings for the Initial Period to reflect excess exports.

Brussels, October 21, 1982

(c) EXCHANGE OF LETTERS—DAVIGNON-BALDRIDGE

The Honorable Malcolm Baldrige
Secretary
Department of Commerce
Washington D.C. 20230
U.S.A.

Dear Mr. Secretary,
As we have discussed, the European Coal and Steel Community and the European Economic Community (EC) are prepared to restrain certain steel exports to the United States.

It is our understanding that, in conjunction with such action by the EC, the United States Government is prepared to undertake certain other actions vis-a-vis trade in these products.

The elements of our program and a description of the complementary U.S. actions are set forth in the enclosed text (the "Arrangement").

In entering into this Arrangement, the EC does not admit to having bestowed subsidies on the manufacture, production or exportation of the products that are the subject of the countervailing duty petitions to be withdrawn or that any such subsidies have caused any material injury in the U.S.A. Neither does it admit that its enterprises have engaged in dumping practices which are the subject of the anti-

NOTE: Appendices B-E, containing various definitions of products and sample forms, are omitted.

dumping duty petitions to be withdrawn or that any such practices have caused any material injury in the U.S.A.

This Arrangement is entered into without prejudice to the rights of the U.S. Government and of the EC under the GATT.

We understand that the US Government recognizes the implications of this Arrangement vis-a-vis trade in certain steel products as defined in the Arrangement with the EC for international competitiveness, national economic and security interests, and trade in capital goods, and will be fully cognizant of these implications in exercising its discretionary authority under section 337 of the Tariff Act of 1930, section 201 and 301 of the Trade Act of 1974, section 232 of the Trade Expansion Act of 1962, and section 103 of the Revenue Act of 1971 with regard to such products and shall do so only after consultations with the EC.

The independent forecaster for the purposes of Article 5 of the Arrangement shall be Data Resources, Inc.

Consultations between the EC and the US will be held in 1985 to review the desirability of extending and possibly modifying the Arrangement.

I look forward to hearing from you at your early convenience.

Yours faithfully,

E. DAVIGNON
Vice President

*   *   *

October 21, 1982

Vicomte Etienne Davignon

Vice-President of the European Communities

Rue de la Loi 200

049 Brussels

Belgium

Dear Mr. Vice-President:

I have received your letter of October 21, 1982, worded as follows:

[. . .]

I have the honor to confirm the agreement of the U.S. Government with the contents of your letter.

Very truly yours,

Secretary of Commerce

(d) EXCHANGE OF LETTERS—DAVIGNON-BALDRIGE
ON PIPES AND TUBES

Brussels, 21 October 1982

The Honorable Malcolm Baldrige
Secretary
Department of Commerce
Washington, D.C. 20230
U.S.A.

Dear Mr. Secretary,

In our conversations we agreed to have an exchange of letters concerning pipes and tubes establishing the following.

A. It has been agreed during negotiations on trade in steel mill products between the European Communities (EC) and the United States (US) that for the duration of the Arrangement negotiated for those products diversions of trade from steel products decribed in Appendix B of the steel Arrangement towards pipes and tubes should be avoided. The US Government wishes trade in the tube sector to be examined at this stage. The Communities are of the opinion that such a diversion will not take place insofar as annual exports of pipes and tubes to the US do not exceed the 1979–1981 average share of annual US apparent consumption. In the light of its market forecasts, the European Economic Community believes that exports of pipes and tubes to the US will not exceed this average. The EC expects that in these circumstances US steel producers will withdraw all pending countervailing duty petitions involving EC exports of pipe and tube to the US and will undertake not to file any petitions seeking import relief under US law including countervailing duty, antidumping duty, section 301 of the Trade Act of 1974 (other than section 301 petitions relating to third country sales by US exporters) or section 337 of the Tariff Act of 1930 on these products.

B. The Community will establish measures with respect to exports of pipes and tubes from the Community to the US. Such measures will include communication to the US Department of Commerce of orders for exports to the US as shown in the order books of the European industry as of 1 October 1982. The measures will also provide for the Community to communicate to the Department of Commerce each month through 1985 the ex-mill shipments destined for export to the US.

C. Consultations may be requested at any time by the EC or US in the light of the market developments or in the event of any particular problem in trade between the EC and the US in pipes and tubes. In the context of consultations all statistical evidence that is available will be presented.

D. If estimates based on the above information and projections of US apparent consumption of pipes and tubes show that the 1979–1981 average described in paragraph A might be exceeded or that a distortion of the pattern of US–EC trade is occurring within the pipe and tube sector, consultations between the EC and the US will take place in order to find an appropriate solution. If after 60 days no solution has been found each party will take within its legislative and regulatory framework, measures which it considers necessary. In doing so both parties will act in a complementary fashion in order to prevent diversion.

E. If in any consultations held pursuant to paragraph D above it appears (based on substantial objective evidence such as allocation, extended delivery periods or other relevant factors) that the exceeding of the average described in paragraph A is due to supply or demand factors and that the US steel industry will be unable to meet demand in the US for a particular product then diversion shall not be considered to exist.

F. If during the period in which the arrangement provided for in this exchange of letters is in effect, any petition seeking import relief under US law, including CVD, AD, Section 337 of the Tariff Act of 1930, Section 201 of the Trade Act of 1974, Section 301 of the Trade Act of 1974, or Section 232 of the Trade Expansion Act of 1962, are filed or investigations initiated or litigation (including antitrust litigation) instituted with respect to pipe and tube products, and the petitioner or litigant is one of those referred to in paragraph A of the present exchange of letters or in Article 2 a) of the Arrangement concerning certain steel products, the EC shall be entitled to terminate the present exchange of letters after consultation with the US, at the earliest 15 days after such consultations.

If such petitions are filed or litigation commenced by petitioners or litigants other than those referred to in the previous paragraph, or investigations initiated on pipe and tube products, the EC will be entitled to terminate this exchange of letters if during consultation with the US it is determined that the petition, litigation or investigation threatens to impair the attainment of the objective of this exchange of letters.

These consultations will take into account the nature of the petitions, or litigation, the identity of the petitioner or litigant, the amount of trade involved, the scope of relief sought, and other relevant factors.

I should be grateful if you would confirm the agreement of your Government with the foregoing.

Yours faithfully,
On behalf of the Council of the
European Communities
E. DAVIGNON
Vice-President of the
Commission of the European Communities

October 21, 1982

Vicomte Etienne Davignon
Vice-President of the European Communities
Rue de la Loi 200
1049 Brussels
Belgium

Dear Mr. Vice-President:

I am writing you this letter to record the agreement of the U.S. government to your letter of October 21, 1982, which reads as follows:

[. . .]

Sincerely,
Secretary of Commerce

   (e) LETTER SENT TO CHIEF EXECUTIVE OFFICERS OF
             PETITIONING STEEL COMPANIES

October 21, 1982

Dear CEOs:

This letter is in response to questions you have raised with respect to the steel trade Arrangements reached between the United States and the European Communities (EC).

Entry into effect of the Arrangements are conditional upon, inter alia, U.S. Government receipt of an undertaking from all petitioners listed in appendix A of the Arrangement not to file certain petitions seeking import relief. Such an undertaking does not, of course, waive your statutory rights to file such petitions. It is a statement of your commitment not to file such petitions on Arrangement products or pipe and tube imports from the EC while the Arrangements are in effect.

If a petition is filed on an Arrangement product, Article 2 b) would apply. Because Arrangement products are defined in Article 1 as "exports to or destined for consumption in the U.S. of products described in Article 3 a) originating in the Community," Article 2 b) does not apply to petitions or litigation that will not affect U.S. imports of those products from the EC.

With respect to Article 7 a) of the Arrangement on certain steel products, the U.S. Government will not agree to increase the percentage limit beyond ten percent.

With respect to Article 8 of the Arrangement on certain steel products and Paragraph E of the Arrangement on pipe and tube, the determination would be made by the U.S. following a review of relevant information, including that obtained from U.S. producers and consumers.

With respect to Article 10, the U.S. Government will request consultations anytime that imports from Europe of certain steel products other than an Arrangement product exceed the EC 1981 market share of U.S. apparent consumption and any of your companies asks us to request such consultations.

Forecasts of U.S. market demand for certain steel products and for pipe and tube will be secured from Data Resources, Incorporated, and will be used in connection with both the Arrangement on certain steel products and the Arrangement on pipe and tube.

The historical data on pipe and tube and the 1982 change in the U.S. tariff schedule preclude precise identification of product categories at this time. We will consult with the EC upon entry into force of the Arrangements to identify relevant product categories for the purposes of the pipe and tube Arrangement. The consultation would follow a review by the U.S. of relevant information, including that obtained from U.S. producers and consumers. I have enclosed a list of the TSUSA items included in the pipe and tube Arrangement.

To restate what I have told you personally several times, this Administration is committed to effectively enforce these Arrangements.
Sincerely,
Secretary of Commerce

*   *   *

(f) LETTER—BALDRIGE—DAVIGNON ON SPECIAL EXPORT CERTIFICATE

October 21, 1982

Vicomte Etienne Davignon
Vice-President of the European Communities
Rue de la Loi 200
1049 Brussels
Belgium

Dear Mr. Vice-President:

This letter is in further response to your letter of October 21, 1982, and concerns Article 6 b) of the document entitled "Arrangement" enclosed therewith.

Public Law 97–276, signed into law on October 2, 1982, provides the United States Government authority to fulfill its responsibilities under Article 6 b) of the Arrangement. Section 153 of that law amended Title IV of the Tariff Act of 1930 by adding a new section 626. The text of this new section is enclosed.

Sincerely,
Secretary of Commerce

*   *   *

Enacted as Section 153 of P.L. 97–276, October 2, 1982

(85)SEC. 153. Title IV of the Tariff Act of 1930 (19 U.S.C. 1401 et seq.) is amended by adding after section 625 the following new section:

"SEC. 626. (a) In order to monitor and enforce export measures required by a foreign government or customs union, pursuant to an international arrangement with the United States, the Secretary of the Treasury may, upon receipt of a request by the President of the United States and by a foreign government or customs union, require the presentation of a valid export license or other documents issued by such foreign government or customs union as a condition for entry into the United States of steel mill products specified in the request. The Secretary may provide by regulation for the terms and conditions under which such merchandise attempted to be entered without an accompanying valid export license or other documents may be denied entry into the United States.

"(b) This section applies only to requests received by the Secretary of the Treasury prior to January 1, 1983, and for the duration of the arrangements.".

l3. GATT Ministerial Declaration (Nov. 29, 1982)

1. The Contracting Parties to the General Agreement on Tariffs and Trade have met at Ministerial level on 24–29 November 1982. They recognize that the multilateral trading system, of which the General Agreement is the legal foundation, is seriously endangered. In the current crisis of the world economy, to which the lack of convergence in national economic policies has contributed, protectionist pressures on governments have multiplied, disregard of GATT disciplines has increased and certain shortcomings in the functioning of the GATT system have been accentuated. Conscious of the role of the GATT system in furthering economic well-being and an unprecedented expansion of world trade, and convinced of the lasting validity of the basic principles and objectives of the General Agreement in a world of increasing economic interdependence, the Contracting Parties are resolved to overcome these threats to the system.

2. The deep and prolonged crisis of the world economy has severely depressed levels of production and trade. In many countries growth rates are low or negative; there is growing unemployment and a climate of uncertainty, exacerbated by persistent inflation, high rates of interest and volatile exchange rates, which seriously inhibit investment and structural adjustment and intensify protectionist pressures. Many countries, and particularly developing countries, now face critical difficulties created by the combination of uncertain and limited access to export markets, declining external demand, a sharp fall in commodity prices and the high cost of borrowing. The import capacity of developing countries, which is essential to their economic growth and development, is being impaired and is no longer serving as a dynamic factor sustaining the exports of the developed world. Acute problems of debt servicing threaten the stability of the financial system.

3. In the field of trade, the responses of governments to the challenges of the crisis have too often been inadequate and inward-looking. Import restrictions have increased and a growing proportion of them have for various reasons been applied outside GATT disciplines, thus undermining the multilateral trading system. Trade patterns have also been adversely affected by certain forms of economic assistance for production and exports and by some restrictive trade measures applied for non-economic purposes. In the depressed economic circumstances these measures, together with continuing pressures for further protective action, have contributed to further delays in necessary structural adjustment, increased economic uncertainty and discouraged productive investment.

4. The results of the Tokyo Round, including in particular the implementation on schedule of the tariff reductions, have provided some impetus to the functioning of the trading system. However, despite the strength and resilience which it has shown, the stresses on the system, which are reflected in the growing number and intensity of disputes between contracting parties, many of which remain unresolved, have made more pronounced certain shortcomings in its functioning. Existing strains have been aggravated by differences of perception regarding the balance of

rights and obligations under the GATT, the way in which these rights and obligations have been implemented and the extent to which the interests of different contracting parties have been met by the GATT. There are also concerns over the manner in which rights are being pursued as well as the manner in which obligations are being fulfilled. Disagreements persist over the interpretation of some important provisions and over their application. Disciplines governing the restriction of trade through safeguard measures are inadequate; there is widespread dissatisfaction with the application of GATT rules and the degree of liberalization in relation to agricultural trade, even though such trade has continued to expand; trade in textiles and clothing continues to be treated under an Arrangement which is a major derogation from the General Agreement—a matter of critical importance to developing countries in particular. Such differences and imbalances are particularly detrimental to the stability of the international trading system when they concern access to the markets of major trading countries or when, through the use of export subsidies, competition among major suppliers is distorted.

5. The Contracting Parties recognize that the interdependence of national economies means that no country can solve its trade problems in isolation and also that solutions would be greatly facilitated by parallel efforts in the financial and monetary fields. In this light, they commit themselves to reduce trade frictions, overcome protectionist pressures, avoid using export subsidies inconsistent with Article XVI of the GATT and promote the liberalization and expansion of trade. They are therefore determined to create, through concerted action, a renewed consensus in support of the GATT system, so as to restore and reinforce confidence in its capacity to provide a stable and predictable trading environment and respond to new challenges.

6. The Contracting Parties have accordingly decided:

to reaffirm their commitment to abide by their GATT obligations and to support and improve the GATT trading system, so that it may contribute vigorously to the further liberalization and expansion of trade based on mutual commitment, mutual advantage and overall reciprocity, and the most-favoured-nation clause;

to preserve, in the operation and functioning of GATT instruments, the unity and consistency of the GATT system; and

to ensure that GATT provides a continuing forum for negotiation and consultation, in which an appropriate balance of rights and obligations can be assured for all contracting parties and the rules and procedures of the system are effectively and fairly applied, on the basis of agreed interpretations, for the economic development and benefit of all.

7. In drawing up the work programme and priorities for the 1980's, the contracting parties undertake, individually and jointly:

(i) to make determined efforts to ensure that trade policies and measures are consistent with GATT principles and rules and to resist protectionist pressures in the formulation and implementation of national trade policy and in proposing legislation; and also to refrain from taking or maintaining any measures inconsistent with GATT and to make determined efforts to avoid measures which would limit or distort international trade;

(ii) to give fullest consideration, in the application of measures falling within the GATT framework, and in the general exercise of their GATT rights, to the trading interests of other contracting parties and the shared objective of trade liberalization and expansion;

(iii) to abstain from taking restrictive trade measures, for reasons of a non-economic character, not consistent with the General Agreement;

(iv)(a) to ensure the effective implementation of GATT rules and provisions and specifically those concerning the developing countries, thereby furthering the dynamic role of developing countries in international trade;

(b) to ensure special treatment for the least-developed countries, in the context of differential and more favourable treatment for developing countries, in order to ameliorate the grave economic situation of these countries;

(v) to bring agriculture more fully into the multilateral trading system by improving the effectiveness of GATT rules, provisions and disciplines and through their common interpretation; to seek to improve terms of access to markets; and to bring export competition under greater discipline. To this end a major two-year work programme shall be undertaken.

(vi) to bring into effect expeditiously a comprehensive understanding on safeguards to be based on the principles of the General Agreement;

(vii) to ensure increased transparency of trade measures and the effective resolution of disputes through improvements in the operation of the pertinent procedures, supported by a determination to comply with rulings and respect recommendations;

(viii) to examine ways and means of, and to pursue measures aimed at, liberalizing trade in textiles and clothing, including the eventual application of the General Agreement, after the expiry of the 1981 Protocol extending the Arrangement Regarding International Trade in Textiles, it being understood that in the interim the parties to the Arrangement shall adhere strictly to its rules;

(ix) to give continuing consideration to changes in the trading environment so as to ensure that the GATT is responsive to these changes.

SAFEGUARDS

The Contracting Parties decide:

1. That, having regard to the objectives and disciplines of the General Agreement, there is need for an improved and more efficient safeguard system which pro-

vides for greater predictability and clarity and also greater security and equity for both importing and exporting countries, so as to preserve the results of trade liberalization and avoid the proliferation of restrictive measures; and

2. That to this end, effect should be given to a comprehensive understanding to be based on the principles of the General Agreement which would contain, *inter alia*, the following elements:

(i) Transparency;

(ii) Coverage;

(iii) Objective criteria for action including the concept of serious injury or threat thereof;

(iv) Temporary nature, degressivity and structural adjustment;

(v) Compensation and retaliation; and

(vi) Notification, consultation, multilateral surveillance and dispute settlement with particular reference to the role and functions of the Safeguards Committee.

3. That such an understanding should be drawn up by the Council for adoption by the Contracting Parties not later than their 1983 Session.

GATT RULES AND ACTIVITIES RELATING TO DEVELOPING COUNTRIES

The Contracting Parties:

1. Instruct the Committee on Trade and Development bearing in mind particularly the special responsibility of the developed contracting parties in this regard, to consult on a regular basis with contracting parties individually or collectively, as appropriate to examine how individual contracting parties have responded to the requirements of Part IV.

2. Urge contracting parties to implement more effectively Part IV and the Decision of 28 November 1979 regarding "differential and more favourable treatment, reciprocity and fuller participation of developing countries";

3. Urge contracting parties to work towards further improvement of GSP or MFN treatment for products of particular export interest to least-developed countries, and the elimination or reduction of non-tariff measures affecting such products;

4. Agree to strengthen the technical co-operation programme of GATT;

5. Instruct the Committee on Trade and Development to carry out an examination of the prospects for increasing trade between developed and developing countries and the possibilities in GATT for facilitating this objective;

To this effect, the Contracting Parties are also taking the decisions annexed and decide to review the action taken in these areas at their 1984 Session.

DISPUTE SETTLEMENT PROCEDURES

The Contracting Parties:

Agree that the Understanding on Notification, Consultation, Surveillance and Dispute Settlement negotiated during the Tokyo Round (hereinafter referred to as the "Understanding") provides the essential framework of procedures for the settlement of disputes among contracting parties and that no major change is required in this framework, but that there is scope for more effective use of the existing mechanism and for specific improvements in procedures to this end;

And agree further that:

(i) With reference to paragraph 8 of the Understanding, if a dispute is not resolved through consultations, any party to a dispute may, with the agreement of the other party, seek the good offices of the Director-General or of an individual or group of persons nominated by the Director-General. This conciliatory process would be carried out expeditiously, and the Director-General would inform the Council of the outcome of the conciliatory process. Conciliation proceedings, and in particular positions taken by the parties to the dispute during conciliation, shall be confidential, and without prejudice to the rights of either party in any further proceedings under Article XXIII:2. It would remain open at any time during any conciliatory process for either party to the dispute to refer the matter to the Contracting Parties.

(ii) In order to ensure more effective compliance with the provisions of paragraphs 11 and 12 of the Understanding, the Director-General shall inform the Council of any case in which it has not been found possible to meet the time limits for the establishment of a panel.

(iii) With reference to paragraph 13 of the Understanding, contracting parties will co-operate effectively with the Director-General in making suitably qualified experts available to serve on panels. Where experts are not drawn from Geneva, any expenses, including travel and subsistence allowance, shall be met from the GATT budget.

(iv) The secretariat of GATT has the responsibility of assisting the panel, especially on the legal, historical and procedural aspects of the matters dealt with.

(v) The terms of reference of a panel should be formulated so as to permit a clear finding with respect to any contravention of GATT provisions and/or on the question of nullification and impairment of benefits. In terms of paragraph 16 of the Understanding, and after reviewing the facts of the case, the applicability of GATT provisions and the arguments advanced, the panel should come to such a finding. Where a finding establishing a contravention of GATT provisions or nullification and impairment is made, the panel should make such suggestions as appropriate for dealing with the matter as would assist the Contracting Parties in making recommendations to the contracting parties which they consider to be concerned, or give a ruling on the matter, as appropriate.

(vi) Panels would aim to deliver their findings without undue delay, as provided in paragraph 20 of the Understanding. If a complete report cannot be made within the period foreseen in that paragraph, panels would be expected to so advise the Council and the report should be submitted as soon as possible thereafter.

(vii) Reports of panels should be given prompt consideration by the Contracting Parties. Where a decision on the findings contained in a report calls for a ruling or recommendation by the Council, the Council may allow the contracting party concerned a reasonable specified time to indicate what action it proposes to take with a view to a satisfactory settlement of the matter, before making any recommendation or ruling on the basis of the report.

(viii) The recommendation or ruling made by the Contracting Parties shall be aimed at achieving a satisfactory settlement of the matter in accordance with GATT obligations. In furtherance of the provisions of paragraph 22 of the Understanding the Council shall periodically review the action taken pursuant to such recommendations. The contracting party to which such a recommendation has been addressed, shall report within a reasonable specified period on action taken or on its reasons for not implementing the recommendation or ruling by the Contracting Parties. The contracting party bringing the case may also ask the Contracting Parties to make suitable efforts with a view to finding an appropriate solution as provided in paragraph 22 of the Understanding.

(ix) The further action taken by the Contracting Parties in the above circumstances might include a recommendation for compensatory adjustment with respect to other products or authorization for the suspension of such concessions or other obligations as foreseen in Article XXIII:2, as the Contracting Parties may determine to be appropriate in the circumstances.

(x) The Parties to a dispute would fully participate in the consideration of the matter by the Contracting Parties under paragraph (vii) above, including the consideration of any rulings or recommendations the Contracting Parties might make pursuant to Article XXIII:2 of the General Agreement, and their views would be fully recorded. They would likewise participate and have their views recorded in the considerations of the further actions provided for under paragraphs (viii) and (ix) above. The Contracting Parties reaffirmed that consensus will continue to be the traditional method of resolving disputes; however, they agreed that obstruction in the process of dispute settlement shall be avoided.[1] It is understood that decisions in this process cannot add to or diminish the rights and obligations provided in the General Agreement.

---

[1] This does not prejudice the provisions on decision making in the General Agreement.

TRADE IN AGRICULTURE

With the purpose of accelerating the achievement of the objectives of the General Agreement, including Part IV, and recognizing that there is an urgent need to find lasting solutions to the problems of trade in agricultural products, the Contracting Parties decide:

1. That the following matters be examined, in the light of the objectives, principles and relevant provisions of the General Agreement and also taking into account the effects of national agricultural policies, with the purpose of making appropriate recommendations. The examination shall cover all measures affecting trade, market access and competition and supply in agricultural products, including subsidies and other forms of assistance.

(i) Trade measures affecting market access and supplies, with a view to achieving greater liberalization in the trade of agricultural products, with respect to tariffs and non-tariff measures, on a basis of overall reciprocity and mutual advantage under the General Agreement.

(ii) The operation of the General Agreement as regards subsidies affecting agriculture, especially export subsidies, with a view to examining its effectiveness, in the light of actual experience, in promoting the objectives of the General Agreement and avoiding subsidization seriously prejudicial to the trade or interests of contracting parties. Other forms of export assistance will be included in this examination.

(iii) Trade measures affecting agriculture maintained under exceptions or derogations without prejudice to the rights of contracting parties under the General Agreement.

2. That in carrying out the tasks enumerated above, full account shall be taken of the need for a balance rights and obligations under the GATT, and of the special needs of developing countries in the light of the GATT provisions providing for differential and more favourable treatment for such contracting parties. Full account shall also be taken of specific characteristics and problems in agriculture, of the scope for improving the operation of GATT rules, provisions and disciplines and agreed interpretations of its provisions.

3. That for the purpose of carrying out this work, an improved and unified system of notifications shall be introduced so as to ensure full transparency.

4. That a Committee on Trade in Agriculture shall be established, open to all contracting parties, for the purpose of carrying out the tasks enumerated above and of making recommendations with a view to achieving greater liberalization in the trade of agricultural products. The Committee will report periodically on the results achieved and make appropriate recommendations to the Council and the Contracting Parties for consideration not later than their 1984 Session.

TROPICAL PRODUCTS

The Contracting Parties decide to carry out, on the basis of the work programme pursued by the Committee on Trade and Development, consultations and appropriate negotiations aimed at further liberalization of trade in tropical products, including in their processed and semi-processed forms, and to review the progress achieved in eliminating or reducting existing obstacles to trade in tropical products at their 1984 Session.

QUANTITATIVE RESTRICTIONS AND OTHER NON-TARIFF MEASURES

The Contracting Parties decide:

1. To review, in a group created for the purpose, existing quantitative restrictions and other non-tariff measures, the grounds on which these are maintained, and their conformity with the provisions of the General Agreement, so as to achieve the elimination of quantitative restrictions which are not in conformity with the General Agreement or their being brought into conformity with the General Agreement, and also to achieve progress in liberalizing other quantitative restrictions and non-tariff measures, adequate attention being given to the need for action on quantitative restrictions and other measures affecting products of particular export interest to developing countries; and

2. That the group should make progress reports to the Council and that its complete report containing its findings and conclusions should be available for consideration by the Contracting Parties at their 1984 Session.

TARIFFS

The Contracting Parties decide:

1. That prompt attention should be given to the problem of escalation of tariffs on products with increased processing with a view to effective action towards the elimination or reduction of such escalation where it inhibits international trade, taking into account the concerns relating to exports of developing countries; and agree

2. That wide acceptance of a common system for classifying products for tariff and statistical purposes would facilitate world trade and therefore recommend prompt action towards the introduction of such a system. They take note of the ongoing work to this end in the Customs Co-operation Council. They further agree that, if such a system is introduced, the general level of benefits provided by GATT concessions must be maintained, that existing concessions should normally remain unchanged and that any negotiations that may prove necessary should be initiated promptly so as to avoid any undue delay in the implementation of a system. They also agree that technical support shall be provided by the GATT secretariat to developing Contracting Parties in order to fully assist their participation in such a process.

MTN AGREEMENTS AND ARRANGEMENTS

The Contracting Parties decide to review the operation of the MTN Agreements and Arrangements, taking into account reports from the Committees or Councils concerned, with a view to determining what action if any is called for, in terms of their decision of November 1979. The Contracting Parties further agree that, for this purpose, the review should focus on the adequacy and effectiveness of these Agreements and Arrangements and the obstacles to the acceptance of these Agreements and Arrangements by interested parties.

STRUCTURAL ADJUSTMENT AND TRADE POLICY

The Contracting Parties decide to continue the work on structural adjustment and trade policy in order to focus on the interaction between structural adjustment and the fulfillment of the objectives of the General Agreement, and to review the results of this work at their 1983 Session.

TRADE IN COUNTERFEIT GOODS

The Contracting Parties instruct the Council to examine the question of counterfeit goods with a view to determining the appropriateness of joint action in the GATT framework on the trade aspects of commercial counterfeiting and, if such joint action is found to be appropriate, the modalities for such action, having full regard to the competence of other international organizations. For the purposes of such examination, the Contracting Parties request the Director-General to hold consultations with the Director-General of WIPO in order to clarify the legal and institutional aspects involved.

EXPORT OF DOMESTICALLY PROHIBITED GOODS

The Contracting Parties decide that contracting parties shall, to the maximum extent feasible, notify GATT of any goods produced and exported by them but banned by their national authorities for sale on their domestic markets on grounds of human health and safety. At their 1984 Session, the Contracting Parties will consider in the light of experience gained with this notification procedure, the need for study of problems relevant to the GATT in relation to exports of domestically prohibited goods and of any action that may be appropriate to deal with such problems.

EXPORT CREDITS FOR CAPITAL GOODS

The Contracting Parties:

1. Are aware that official export credit provisions on capital goods which apply to developing countries may pose problems for the expansion of imports into these countries consistent with their trade and development needs;

2. Therefore recommend that contracting parties, members of those international arrangements concerning official export credit matters, when reviewing or revising their various international undertakings, give special attention to relevant credit provisions, including specific terms and conditions, in order to facilitate the expansion of developing countries' imports of capital goods consistent with their trade and development needs; and

3. Request the Director-General of the GATT to consult with the contracting parties concerned and report to the 39th Session.

TEXTILES AND CLOTHING

The Contracting Parties decide:

1. To carry out on a priority basis a study of:

(i) the importance of textiles and clothing in world trade and particularly for the trade prospects of developing countries;

(ii) the impact on economic activity and prospects of countries participating in textiles trade, of the existing systems of restraints and restrictions relating to textiles and clothing, principally the MFA;

(iii) consequences for economic and trade prospects in these countries of a phasing out on the basis of the provisions of the General Agreement, or of the continued maintenance, of the restraints and restrictions applied under the existing textile and clothing regimes, principally the MFA; and

2. To examine expeditiously, taking into account the results of such a study, modalities of further trade liberalization in textiles and clothing including the possibilities for bringing about the full application of GATT provisions to this sector of trade.

3. This work should be completed for consideration by the Contracting Parties at their 1984 Session.

PROBLEMS OF TRADE IN CERTAIN NATURAL RESOURCE PRODUCTS

The Contracting Parties decide:

1. That problems relating to trade in the following natural resource products including in their semi-processed and processed forms, falling under the competence of the General Agreement relating to tariffs, non-tariff measures and other factors affecting trade, should be examined with a view to recommending possible solutions:

(a) Non-ferrous metals and minerals

(b) Forestry products

(c) Fish and fisheries products

2. That for this purpose the Council should decide, for each of these three items, the terms of reference, time frame and procedures.

EXCHANGE RATE FLUCTUATIONS AND THEIR EFFECT ON TRADE

The Contracting Parties decide:

To request the Director-General to consult the Managing Director of the International Monetary Fund on the possibility of a study of the effects of erratic fluctuations in exchange rates on international trade, to report to the Council on the results of these consultations and to forward any such study to the Council so that it may consider any implications for the General Agreement.

DUAL PRICING AND RULES OF ORIGIN

The Contracting Parties decide:

To request the Council to make arrangements for studies of dual-pricing practices and rules of origin; and

To consider what further action may be necessary with regard to these matters when the results of these studies are available.

SERVICES

The Contracting Parties decide:

1. To recommend to each contracting party with an interest in services of different types to undertake, as far as it is able, national examination of the issues in this sector.

2. To invite contracting parties to exchange information on such matters among themselves, inter alia through international organizations such as GATT. The complication and distribution of such information should be based on as uniform a format as possible.

3. To review the results of these examinations, along with the information and comments provided by relevant international organizations, at their 1984 Session and to consider whether any multilateral action in these matters is appropriate and desirable.

ANNEX

GATT RULES AND ACTIVITIES RELATING TO DEVELOPING COUNTRIES

The Contracting Parties:

1. Decide, in order to improve the review and surveillance procedures in regard to the implementation of Part IV, that:

(a) the Committee on Trade and Development, bearing in mind particularly the special responsibility of the developed contracting parties in this regard, shall adopt a programme of consultations with contracting parties individually or collectively, as appropriate, to examine how individual contracting parties have responded to the requirements of Part IV;

(b) each such consultation shall be based on information supplied by the contracting party or parties in question and additional factual material prepared by the secretariat;

(c) the Committee on Trade and Development shall also examine other aspects of existing procedures for reviewing the implementation of Part IV and for dealing with problems relating to the application of its provisions, and prepare guidelines for their improvement.

2. Invite the Committee on Trade and Development to review the operation of the Enabling Clause as provided for in its paragraph 9, with a view to its more effective implementation, *inter alia*, with respect to objectivity and transparency of modifications to GSP schemes and the operation of consultative provision relating to differential and more favourable treatment for developing countries;

3. Invite contracting parties to pursue action as follows towards facilitating trade of least-developed countries and reducing tariff and non-tariff obstacles to their exports:

(a) further improve GSP or m.f.n. treatment for products of particular export interest to least-developed countries, with the objective of providing fullest possible duty-free access to such products;

(b) use, upon request and where feasible, of more flexible requirements for rules of origin for products of particular export interest to least-developed countries;

(c) eliminate or reduce non-tariff measures affecting products of particular export interest to least-developed countries;

(d) facilitate the participation of least-developed countries in MTN Agreements and Arrangements;

(e) strengthen the technical assistance facilities of the GATT secretariat targeted to the special requirements of least-developed countries;

(f) strengthen trade promotion activities, through the ITC and other initiatives, such as by encouraging the establishment of import promotion offices in importing countries;

(g) give more emphasis to the discussion and examination of policy issues of interest to least-developed countries in the context of further efforts to liberalize trade.

4. Decide to strengthen the Technical Co-operation programme of the GATT with a view to facilitating the more effective participation of developing countries in the GATT trading system:

(a) by responding to increasing requests for seminars and other technical assistance activities;

(b) by permitting increased participation in the GATT Commercial Policy Courses, and the inclusion in the training programme of a regular course in the Spanish language;

(c) by encouraging, in the context of this programme, appropriate contributions from individual contracting parties.

5. Invite contracting parties individually to grant new voluntary contributions or provide other forms of assistance to the ITC.

VI. SELECTED DOCUMENTS OF THE MULTILATERAL TRADE NEGOTIATIONS

1. The Tokyo Declaration (Sept. 14, 1973)

1. The ministers, having considered the report of the Preparatory Committee for the Trade Negotiations and having noted that a number of governments have decided to enter into comprehensive mutilateral trade negotiations in the framework of GATT and that other governments have indicated their intention make a decision as soon as possible, declare the negotiations officially open. Those governments which have decided to negotiate have notified the Director-General of GATT to this effect, and the Ministers agree that it will be open to any other government, through a notification to the Director-General, to participate in the negotiations. The Ministers hope that the negotiations will involve the active participation of as many countries as possible. They expect the negotiations to be engaged effectively as rapidly as possible, and that, to that end, the governments concerned will have such authority as may be required.

2. The negotiations shall aim to:

— achieve the expansion and ever-greater liberalization of world trade and improvement in the standard of living and welfare of the people of the world, objectives which can be achieved, *inter alia,* through the progressive dismantling of obstacles to trade and the improvement of the international framework for the conduct of world trade.

— secure additional benefits for the international trade of developing countries so as to achieve a substantial increase in their foreign exchange earnings, the diversification of their exports, the acceleration of the rate of growth of their trade, taking into account their development needs, an improvement in the possibilities for these countries to participate in the expansion of world trade and a better balance as between developed and developing countries in the sharing of the advantages resulting from this expansion, through in the largest possible measure, a substantial improvement in the conditions of access for the products of interest to the developing countries and, wherever appropriate, measures designed to attain stable, equitable and remunerative prices for primary products.

To this end, co-ordinated efforts shall be made to solve in an equitable way the trade problems of all participating countries, taking into account the specific trade problems of the developing countries.

3. To this end, the negotiations should aim, *inter alia,* to:

(a) conduct negotiations on tariffs by employment of appropriate formulae of as general application as possible;

(b) reduce or eliminate non-tariff measures or, where this is not appropriate, to reduce or eliminate their trade restricting or distorting effects, and to bring such measures under more effective international discipline;

(c) include an examination of the possibilities for the co-ordinated reduction or elimination of all barriers to trade in selected sectors as a complementary technique;

(d) include an examination of the adequacy of the multilateral safeguard system, considering particularly the modalities of application of Article XIX, with a view to furthering trade liberalization and preserving its results;

(e) include, as regards agriculture, an approach to negotiations which, while in line with the general objectives of the negotiations, should take account of the special characteristics and problems in this sector;

(f) treat tropical products as a special and priority sector.

4. The negotiations shall cover tariffs, non-tariff barriers and other measures which impede or distort international trade in both industrial and agricultural products, including tropical products and raw materials, whether in primary form or at any state of processing including in particular products of export interest to developing countries and measures affecting their exports.

5. The negotiations shall be conducted on the basis of the principles of mutual advantage, mutual commitment and overall reciprocity, while observing the most-favored-nation clause, and consistently with the provisions of the General Agreement relating to such negotiations. Participants shall jointly endeavour in the negotiations to achieve, by appropriate methods, an overall balance of advantage at the highest possible level. The developed countries do not expect reciprocity for commitments made by them in the negotiations to reduce or remove tariff and other barriers to the trade of developing countries, i.e., the developed countries do not expect the developing countries, in the course of the trade negotiations, to make contributions which are inconsistent with their individual development, financial and trade needs. The Ministers recognize the need for special measures to be taken in the negotiations to assist the developing countries in their efforts to increase their export earnings and promote their economic development and, where appropriate, for priority attention to be given to products or areas of interest to developing countries. They also recognize the importance of maintaining and improving the Generalized System of Preferences. They further recognize the importance of the application of differential measures to developing countries

in ways which will provide special and more favourable treatment for them in areas of the negotiation where this is feasible and appropriate.

6. The Ministers recognize that the particular situation and problems of the least developed among the developing countries shall be given special attention, and stress the need to ensure that these countries receive special treatment in the context of any general or specific measures taken in favour of the developing countries during the negotiations.

7. The policy of liberalizing world trade cannot be carried out successfully in the absence of parallel efforts to set up a monetary system which shields the world economy from the shocks and imbalances which have previously occurred. The Ministers will not lose sight of the fact that the effforts which are to be made in the trade field imply continuing efforts to maintain orderly conditions and to establish a durable and equitable monetary system.

The Ministers recognize equally that the new phase in the liberalization of trade which it is their intention to undertake should facilitate the orderly functioning the monetary system.

The Ministers recognize that they should bear these considerations in mind both at the opening of and throughout the negotiations. Efforts in these two fields will thus be able to contribute effectively to an improvement of international economic relations, taking into account the special characteristics of the economies of the developing countries and their problems.

8. The negotiations shall be considered as one undertaking, the various elements of which shall move forward together.

9. Support is reaffirmed for the principles, rules and disciplines provided for under the General Agreement.[1] Consideration shall be given to improvements in the international framework for the conduct of world trade which might be desirable in the light of progress in the negotiations and, in this endeavour, care shall be taken to ensure that any measures introduced as a result are consistent with the overall objectives and principles of the trade negotiations and particularly of trade liberalization.

10. A Trade Negotiations Committee is established, with authority, taking into account the present Declaration, *inter alia:*

(a) to elaborate and put into effect detailed trade negotiating plans and to

---

[1] This does not necessarily represent the views of representatives of countries not now parties to the General Agreement. [Footnotes in original.]

establish appropriate negotiating procedures, including special procedures for the negotiations between developed and developing countries;

(b) to supervise the progress of the negotiations.

The Trade Negotiations Committee shall be open to participating governments.[2] The Trade Negotiations Committee shall hold its opening meeting not later than 1 November 1973.

11. The Ministers intend that the trade negotiations be concluded in 1975.

2. Agreement on Subsidies and Countervailing Duties

Agreement on Interpretation and Application of
Articles VI, XVI and XXIII of the General Agreement
*on Tariffs and Trade**

The signatories[1] to this Agreement,

Noting that Ministers on 12–14 September 1973 agreed that the Tokyo Round of Multilateral Trade Negotiations should, *inter alia,* reduce or eliminate the trade restricting or distorting effects of non-tariff measures, and bring such measures under more effective international discipline;

Recognizing that subsidies are used by governments to promote important objectives of national policy;

Recognizing also that subsidies may have harmful effects on trade and production;

Recognizing that the emphasis of this Agreement should be on the effects of subsidies and that these effects are to be assessed in giving due account to the internal economic situation of the signatories concerned as well as to the state of international economic and monetary relations;

Desiring to ensure that the use of subsidies does not adversely affect or prejudice the interests of any signatory to this Agreement, and that countervailing measures do not unjustifiably impede international trade, and that re-

---

[2] Including the European Communities.

* This Agreement has been prepared and advanced by the delegations of Austria, Brazil, Bulgaria, Canada, European Communities, Finland, Hungary, India, Japan, Mexico, Norway, Poland, Sweden, Switzerland and the United States. [All footnotes appear in the original, but have been renumbered to run consecutively.]

[1] The term "signatories" is hereinafter used to mean parties to this Agreement.

lief is made available to producers adversely affected by the use of subsidie within an agreed international framework of rights and obligations;

Taking into account the particular trade, development and financial needs of developing countries;

Desiring to apply fully and to interpret the provisions of Articles VI, XVI and XXIII of the General Agreement on Tariffs and Trade[2] (hereinafter referred to as "the General Agreement" or "GATT") only with respect to subsidies and countervailing measures and to elaborate rules for their application in order to provide greater uniformity and certainty in their implementation;

Desiring to provide for the speedy, effective and equitable resolution of disputes arising under this Agreement,

Have agreed as follows:

PART I

Article 1—*Application of Article VI of the General Agreement*[3]

Signatories shall take all necessary steps to ensure that the imposition of a countervailing duty[4] on any product of the territory of any signatory imported into the territory of another signatory is in accordance with the provisions of Article VI of the General Agreement and the terms of this Agreement.

Article 2—*Domestic procedures and related matters*

1. Countervailing duties may only be imposed pursuant to investigations initiated[5] and conducted in accordance with the provisions of this Article. An investigation to determine the existence, degree and effect of any alleged

---

[2] Wherever in this Agreement there is reference to "the terms of this Agreement" or the "articles" or "provisions of this Agreement" it shall be taken to mean, as the context requires, the provisions of the General Agreement as interpreted and applied by this Agreement.

[3] The provisions of both Part I and Part II of this Agreement may be invoked in parallel: however, with regard to the effects of a particular subsidy in the domestic market of the importing country, only one form of relief (either a countervailing duty or an authorized countermeasure) shall be available.

[4] The term "countervailing duty" shall be understood to mean a special duty levied for the purpose of off-setting any bounty or subsidy bestowed directly or indirectly upon the manufacture, production or export of any merchandise, as provided for in Article VI:3 of the General Agreement.

[5] The term "initiated" as used hereinafter means procedural action by which signatory formally commences an investigation as provided in paragraph 3 of this Article.

subsidy shall normally be initiated upon a written request by or on behalf of the industry affected. The request shall include sufficient evidence of the existence of (a) a subsidy and, if possible, its amount; (b) injury within the meaning of Article VI as interpreted by this Agreement[6] and (c) a causal link between the subsidized imports and the alleged injury. If in special circumstances the authorities concerned decide to initiate an investigation without having received such a request, they shall proceed only if they have sufficient evidence on all points under (a) to (c) above.

(2) Each signatory shall notify the Committee of Signatories[7] (a) which of its authorities are competent to initiate and conduct investigations referred to in this Article and (b) its domestic procedures governing the initiation and conduct of such investigations.

3. When such authorities are satisfied that there is sufficient evidence to justify initiating an investigation, the signatory or signatories, the products of which are subject to such investigation and the exporters and importers known to the investigating authorities to have an interest therein and the complainants shall be notified and a public notice shall be given. In determining whether to initiate an investigation, the investigating authority should take into account the position adopted by the affiliates of a complainant party[8] which are resident in the territory of another signatory.

4. Upon initiation of an investigation and thereafter, the evidence of both a subsidy and injury caused thereby should be considered simultaneously. In any event the evidence of both the existence of subsidy and injury shall be considered simultaneously (a) in the decision whether or not to initiate an investigation and (b) thereafter during the course of the investigation, starting on a date not later than the earliest date on which in accordance with the provisions of this Agreement provisional measures may be applied.

5. The public notice referred to in paragraph 3 above shall describe the subsidy practice or practices to be investigated. Each signatory shall ensure that its authorities afford all interested signatories and all interested parties[9]

---

[6] Under this Agreement the term "injury" shall, unless otherwise specified, be taken to mean material injury to a domestic industry, threat of material injury to a domestic industry or material retardation of the establishment of such an industry and shall be interpreted in accordance with the provisions of Article 6.

[7] As established in Part V of this Agreement and hereinafter referred to as the Committee.

[8] For the purpose of this Agreement "party" means any natural or juridical person resident in the territory of any signatory.

[9] Any "interested signatory" or "interested party" shall refer to a signatory or a party economically affected by the subsidy in question.

a reasonable opportunity, upon request, to see all relevant information that is not confidential (as indicated in paragraphs 6 and 7 below) and that is used by the authorities in the investigation, and to present in writing, and upon justification orally, their views to the investigating authorities.

6. Any information which is by nature confidential or which is provided on a confidential basis by parties to an investigation shall, upon cause shown, be treated as such by the investigating authorities. Such information shall not be disclosed without specific permission of the party submitting it.[10] Parties providing confidential information may be requested to furnish nonconfidential summaries thereof. In the event such parties indicate that such information is not susceptible of summary, a statement of reasons why summarization is not possible must be provided.

7. However, if the investigating authorities find that a request for confidentiality is not warranted and if the party requesting confidentiality is unwilling to disclose the information, such authorities may disregard such information unless it can otherwise be demonstrated to their satisfaction that the information is correct.[11]

8. The investigating authorities may carry out investigations in the territory of other signatories as required, provided they have notified in good time the signatory in question and unless the latter objects to the investigation. Further, the investigating authorities may carry out investigations on the premises of a firm and may examine the records of a firm if (i) the firm so agrees and (ii) the signatory in question is notified and does not object.

9. In cases in which any interested party or signatory refuses access to, or otherwise does not provide, necessary information within a reasonable period or significantly impedes the investigation, preliminary and final findings,[12] affirmative or negative, may be made on the basis of the facts available.

10. The procedures set out above are not intended to prevent the authorities of a signatory from proceeding expeditiously with regard to initiating an investigation, reaching preliminary or final findings, whether affirmative or negative, or from applying provisional or final measures, in accordance with relevant provisions of this Agreement.

---

[10] Signatories are aware that in the territory of certain signatories disclosure pursuant to a narrowly-drawn protective order may be required.

[11] Signatories agree that requests for confidentiality should not be arbitrarily rejected.

[12] Because of different terms used under different systems in various countries the term "finding" is hereinafter used to mean a formal decision or determination.

11. In cases where products are not imported directly from the country of origin but are exported to the country of importation from an intermediate country, the provisions of this Agreement shall be fully applicable and the transaction or transactions shall, for the purposes of this Agreement, be regarded as having taken place between the country of origin and the country of importation.

12. An investigation shall be terminated when the investigating authorities are satisfied either that no subsidy exists or that the effect of the alleged subsidy on the industry is not such as to cause injury.

13. An investigation shall not hinder the procedures of customs clearance.

14. Investigations shall, except in special circumstances, be concluded within one year after their initiation.

15. Public notice shall be given of any preliminary or final finding whether positive or negative and of the revocation of a finding. In the case of a positive finding each such notice shall set forth the findings and conclusions reached on all issues of fact and law considered material by the investigating authorities, and the reasons and basis therefor. In the case of a negative finding each notice shall set forth at least the basic conclusions and a summary of the reasons therefor. All notices of finding shall be forwarded to the signatory or signatories the products of which are subject to such finding and to the exporters known to have an interest therein.

16. Signatories shall report without delay to the Committee all preliminary or final actions taken with respect to countervailing duties. Such reports will be available in the GATT secretariat for inspection by government representatives. The signatories shall also submit, on a semi-annual basis, reports on any countervailing duty actions taken within the preceding six months.

Article 3—*Consultations*

1. As soon as possible after a request for initiation of an investigation is accepted, and in any event before the initiation of any investigation, signatories the products of which may be subject to such investigations shall be afforded a reasonable opportunity for consultations with the aim of clarifying the situation as to the matters referred to in Article 2, paragraph 1 above and arriving at a mutually agreed solution.

2. Furthermore, throughout the period of investigation, signatories the products of which are the subject of the investigation shall be afforded a

reasonable opportunity to continue consultations, with a view to clarifying the factual situation and to arriving at a mutually agreed solution.[13]

3. Without prejudice to the obligation to afford reasonable opportunity for consultation, these provisions regarding consultations are not intended to prevent the investigating authorities, in accordance with the provisions of this Agreement, from proceeding expeditiously with regard to initiating the investigation, reaching a preliminary or final finding, affirmative or negative, or applying a provisional or final measure.

4. The signatory which intends to initiate any investigation or is conducting such an investigation shall permit, on request, the signatory or signatories the products of which are subject to such investigation access to non-confidential evidence including the non-confidential summary of confidential data being used for initiating or conducting the investigation.

Article 4—*Imposition of countervailing duties*

1. The decision whether or not to impose a countervailing duty in cases where all requirements for the imposition have been fulfilled and the decision whether the amount of the countervailing duty to be imposed shall be the full amount of the subsidy or less are decisions to be made by the authorities of the importing signatory. It is desirable that the imposition be permissive in the territory of all signatories and that the duty be less than the total amount of the subsidy if such lesser duty would be adequate to remove the injury to the domestic industry.

2. No countervailing duty shall be levied[14] on any imported product in excess of the amount of the subsidy found to exist, calculated in terms of subsidization per unit of the subsidized and exported product.[15]

3. When a countervailing duty is imposed in respect of any product, such countervailing duty shall be levied, in the appropriate amounts, on a nondis-

---

[13] It is particularly important, in accordance with the provisions of this paragraph, that no affirmative finding whether preliminary or final be made without reasonable opportunity for consultations having been given. Such consultations may establish the basis for proceeding under the provisions of Part VI of this Agreement.

[14] As used in this Agreement "levy" shall mean the definitive or final legal assessment or collection of a duty or tax.

[15] An understanding among signatories should be developed setting out the criteria for the calculation of the amount of the subsidy.

criminatory basis on imports of such product from all sources found to be subsidized and to be causing injury, except as to imports from those sources which have renounced any subsidies in question or from which undertakings under the terms of this Agreement have been accepted.

4. If, after reasonable efforts have been made to complete consultations, a signatory makes a final determination of the existence and amount of the subsidy and that, through the effects of the subsidy, the subsidized imports are causing injury, it may impose a countervailing duty in accordance with the provisions of this section unless the subsidy is withdrawn.

5. (a) Proceedings may[16] be suspended or terminated without the imposition of provisional measures or countervailing duties, if undertakings are accepted under which:

(1) the government of the exporting country agrees to eliminate or limit the subsidy or take other measures concerning its effects; or

(2) the exporter agrees to revise its prices so that the investigating authorities are satisfied that the injurious effect of the subsidy is eliminated. Price increases under undertakings shall not be higher than necessary to eliminate the amount of the subsidy. Price undertakings shall not be sought or accepted from exporters unless the importing signatory has first (a) initiated an investigation in accordance with the provisions of Article 2 of this Agreement and (b) obtained the consent of the exporting signatory. Undertakings offered need not be accepted if the authorities of the importing signatory consider their acceptance impractical, for example if the number of actual or potential exporters is too great, or for other reasons.

(b) If the undertakings are accepted, the investigation of injury shall nevertheless be completed if the exporting signatory so desires or the importing signatory so decides. In such a case, if a determination of no injury or threat thereof is made, the undertaking shall automatically lapse, except in cases where a determination of no threat of injury is due in large part to the existence of an undertaking; in such cases the authorities concerned may require that an undertaking be maintained for a reasonable period consistent with the provisions of this Agreement.

(c) Price undertakings may be suggested by the authorities in the importing country, but no exporter shall be forced to enter into such an under-

---

[16] The word "may" shall not be interpreted to allow the simultaneous continuation of proceedings with the implementation of price undertakings, except as provided in paragraph 5(b) of this Article.

taking. The fact that governments or exporters do not offer such under-takings or do not accept an invitation to do so, shall in no way prejudice the consideration of the case. However, the authorities are free to deter-mine that a threat of injury is more likely to be realized if the subsidized imports continue.

6. Authorities in an importing country may require any government or exporter from whom undertakings have been accepted to provide periodically information relevant to the fulfilment of such undertakings, and to permit verification of pertinent data. In case of violation of undertakings, the author-ities of the importing country may take expeditious actions under this Agree-ment in conformity with its provisions which may constitute immediate application of provisional measures using the best information available. In such cases definitive duties may be levied in accordance with this Agreement on goods entered for consumption not more than ninety days before the application of such provisional measures, except that any such retroactive assessment shall not apply to imports entered before the violation of the undertaking.

7. Undertakings shall not remain in force any longer than countervailing duties could remain in force under the Agreement. The authorities of an importing country shall review the need for the continuation of any under-taking, where warranted, on their own initiative, or if interested exporters or importers of the product in question so request and submit positive informa-tion substantiating the need for such review.

8. Whenever a countervailing duty investigation is suspended or terminated pursuant to the provisions of paragraph 5 above and whenever an undertaking is terminated, this fact shall be officially notified and must be published. Such notices shall set forth at least the basic conclusions and a summary of the reasons therefor.

9. A countervailing duty shall remain in force only as long as, and to the extent necessary to counteract the subsidization which is causing injury. The investigating authorities shall review the need for continued imposition of the duty, where warranted, on their own initiative or if any interested party so requests and submits positive information substantiating the need for re-view.

Article 5—*Provisional measures and retroactivity*

1. Provisional measures may be taken only after a preliminary positive finding has been made that a subsidy exists and that there is sufficient evi-dence of injury as provided for in Article 2, paragraph 1(a) to (c). Pro-

visional measures shall not be applied unless the authorities concerned judge that they are necessary to prevent injury being caused during the period of investigation.

2. Provisional measures may take the form of provisional countervailing duties guaranteed by cash deposits or bonds equal to the amount of the provisionally calculated amount of subsidization.

3. The imposition of provisional measures shall be limited to as short a period as possible, not exceeding four months.

4. Relevant provisions of Article 4 shall be followed in the imposition of provisional measures.

5. Where a final finding of injury (but not of a threat thereof or of a material retardation of the establishment of an industry) is made or in the case of a final finding of threat of injury where the effect of the subsidized imports would, in the absence of the provisional measures, have led to a finding of injury, countervailing duties may be levied retroactively for the period for which provisional measures, if any, have been applied.

6. If the definitive countervailing duty is higher than the amount guaranteed by the cash deposit or bond, the difference shall not be collected. If the definitive duty is less than the amount guaranteed by the cash deposit or bond, the excess amount shall be reimbursed or the bond released in an expeditious manner.

7. Except as provided in paragraph 5 above, where a finding of threat of injury or material retardation is made (but no injury has yet occurred) a definitive countervailing duty may be imposed only from the date of the finding of threat of injury or material retardation and any cash deposit made during the period of the application of provisional measures shall be refunded and any bonds released in an expeditious manner.

8. Where a final finding is negative any cash deposit made during the period of the application of provisional measures shall be refunded and any bonds released in an expeditious manner.

9. In critical circumstances where for the subsidized product in question the authorities find that injury which is difficult to repair is caused by massive imports in a relatively short period of a product benefiting from export subsidies paid or bestowed inconsistently with the provisions of the General Agreement and of this Agreement and where it is deemed necessary, in order to preclude the recurrence of such injury, to assess countervailing duties retroactively on those imports, the definitive countervailing duties may be assessed

on imports which were entered for consumption not more than ninety days prior to the date of application of provisional measures.

Article 6—*Determination of injury*

1. A determination of injury[17] for purposes of Article VI of the General Agreement shall involve an objective examination of both (a) the volume of subsidized imports and their effect on prices in the domestic market for like products[18] and (b) the consequent impact of these imports on domestic producers of such products.

2. With regard to volume of subsidized imports the investigating authorities shall consider whether there has been a significant increase in subsidized imports, either in absolute terms or relative to production or consumption in the importing country. With regard to the effect of the subsidized imports on prices, the investigating authorities shall consider whether there has been a significant price undercutting by the subsidized imports as compared with the price of a like product of the importing country, or whether the effect of such imports is otherwise to depress prices to a significant degree or prevent price increases, which otherwise would have occurred, to a significant degree. No one or several of these factors can necessarily give decisive guidance.

3. The examination of the impact on the industry concerned shall include an evaluation of all relevant economic factors and indices having a bearing on the state of the industry such as actual and potential decline in output, sales, market share, profits, productivity, return on investments, or utilization of capacity; factors affecting domestic prices; actual and potential negative effects on cash flow, inventories, employment, wages, growth, ability to raise capital or investment and, in the case of agriculture, whether there has been an increased burden on government support programmes. This list is not exhaustive, nor can one or several of these factors necessarily give decisive guidance.

4. It must be demonstrated that the subsidized imports are, through the

---

[17] Determinations of injury under the criteria set forth in this Article shall be based on positive evidence. In determining threat of injury the investigating authorities, in examining the factors listed in this Article, may take into account the evidence on the nature of the subsidy in question and the trade effects likely to arise therefrom.

[18] Throughout this Agreement the term "like product" ("produit similaire") shall be interpreted to mean a product which is identical, i.e. alike in all respects to the product under consideration or in the absence of such a product, another product which, although not alike in all respects, has characteristics closely resembling those of the product under consideration.

effects[19] of the subsidy, causing injury within the meaning of this Agreement. There may be other factors[20] which at the same time are injuring the industry, and the injuries caused by other factors must not be attributed to the subsidized imports.

5. In determining injury, the term "domestic industry" shall, except as provided in paragraph 7 below, be interpreted as referring to the domestic producers as a whole of the like products or to those of them whose collective output of the products constitutes a major proportion of the total domestic production of those products, except that when producers are related[21] to the exporters or importers or are themselves importers of the allegedly subsidized product the industry may be interpreted as referring to the rest of the producers.

6. The effect of the subsidized imports shall be assessed in relation to the domestic production of the like product when available data permit the separate identification of production in terms of such criteria as: the production process, the producers' realization, profits. When the domestic production of the like product has no separate identity in these terms the effects of subsidized imports shall be assessed by the examination of the production of the narrowest group or range of products, which includes the like product, for which the necessary information can be provided.

7. In exceptional circumstances the territory of a signatory may, for the production in question, be divided into two or more competitive markets and the producers within each market may be regarded as a separate industry if (a) the producers within such market sell all or almost all of their production of the product in question in that market, and (b) the demand in that market is not to any substantial degree supplied by producers of the product in question located elsewhere in the territory. In such circumstances, injury may be found to exist even where a major portion of the total domestic industry is not injured provided there is a concentration of subsidized imports into such an isolated market and provided further that the subsidized imports are causing injury to the producers of all or almost all of the production within such market.

---

[19] As set forth in paragraphs 2 and 3 of this Article.

[20] Such factors can include *inter alia,* the volume and prices of nonsubsidized imports of the product in question, contraction in demand or changes in the pattern of consumption, trade restrictive practices of and competition between the foreign and domestic producers, developments in technology and the export performance and productivity of the domestic industry.

[21] The Committee should develop a definition of the word "related" as used in this paragraph.

8. When the industry has been interpreted as referring to the producers in a certain area, as defined in paragraph 7 above, countervailing duties shall be levied only on the products in question consigned for final consumption to that area. When the constitutional law of the importing country does not permit the levying of countervailing duties on such a basis, the importing signatory ᵤᵧ levy the countervailing duties without limitation, only if (1) the exporters shall have been given an opportunity to cease exporting at subsidized prices to the area concerned or otherwise give assurances pursuant to Article 4, paragraph 5, of this Agreement, and adequate assurances in this regard have not been promptly given, and (2) such duties cannot be levied only on products of specific producers which supply the area in question.

9. Where two or more countries have reached under the provisions of Article XXIV:8(a) of the General Agreement such a level of integration that they have the characteristics of a single, unified market the industry in the entire area of integration shall be taken to be the industry referred to in paragraphs 5 to 7 above.

PART II

Article 7—*Notification of subsidies*[22]

1. Having regard to the provisions of Article XVI:1 of the General Agreement, any signatory may make a written request for information on the nature and extent of any subsidy granted or maintained by another signatory (including any form of income or price support) which operates directly or indirectly to increase exports of any product from or reduce imports of any product into its territory.

2. Signatories so requested shall provide such information as quickly as possible and in a comprehensive manner, and shall be ready upon request to provide additional information to the requesting signatory. Any signatory which considers that such information has not been provided may bring the matter to the attention of the Committee.

3. Any interested signatory which considers that any practice of another signatory having the effects of a subsidy has not been notified in accordance with the provisions of Article XVI:1 of the General Agreement may bring

---

[22] In this Agreement, the term "subsidies" shall be deemed to include subsidies granted by any government or any public body within the territory of a signatory. However, it is recognized that for signatories with different federal systems of government, there are different divisions of powers. Such signatories accept nonetheless the international consequences that may arise under this Agreement as a result of the granting of subsidies within their territories.

the matter to the attention of such other signatory. If the subsidy practice is not thereafter notified promptly, such signatory may itself bring the subsidy practice in question to the notice of the Committee.

Article 8—*Subsidies—General Provisions*

1. Signatories recognize that subsidies are used by governments to promote important objectives of social and economic policy. Signatories also recognize that subsidies may cause adverse effects to the interests of other signatories.

2. Signatories agree not to use export subsidies in a manner inconsistent with the provisions of this Agreement.

3. Signatories further agree that they shall seek to avoid causing, through the use of any subsidy:

(a) injury to the domestic industry of another signatory;[23]

(b) nullification or impairment of the benefits accruing directly or indirectly to another signatory under the General Agreement;[24] or

(c) serious prejudice to the interests of another signatory.[25]

4. The adverse effects to the interests of another signatory required to demonstrate nullification or impairment[26] or serious prejudice may arise through:

(a) the effects of the subsidized imports in the domestic market of the importing signatory;

---

[23] The term injury to domestic industry is used here in the same sense as it is used in Part I of this Agreement.

[24] Benefits accruing directly or indirectly under the General Agreement include the benefits of tariff concessions bound under Article II of the General Agreement.

[25] Serious prejudice to the interests of another signatory is used in this Agreement in the same sense as it is used in Article XVI:1 of the General Agreement and includes threat of serious prejudice.

[26] Signatories recognize that nullification or impairment of benefits may also arise through the failure of a signatory to carry out its obligations under the General Agreement or this Agreement. Where such failure concerning export subsidies is determined by the Committee to exist. adverse effects may, without prejudice to paragraph 9 of Article 18 below, be presumed to exist. The other signatory will be accorded a reasonable opportunity to rebut this presumption.

(b) the effects of the subsidy in displacing or impeding the imports of like products into the market of the subsidizing country; or

(c) the effects of the subsidized exports in displacing[27] the exports of like products of another signatory from a third country market.[28]

Article 9—*Export subsidies on products other than certain primary products*[29]

1. Signatories shall not grant export subsidies on products other than certain primary products.

2. The practices listed in points (a) to (l) in the Annex are illustrative of export subsidies.

Article 10—*Export subsidies on certain primary products*[30]

1. In accordance with the provisions of Article XVI:3 of the General Agreement, signatories agree not to grant directly or indirectly any export subsidy on certain primary products in a manner which results in the signatory granting such subsidy having more than an equitable share of world export trade in such product, account being taken of the shares of the signatories in trade in the product concerned during a previous representative period, and any special factors which may have affected or may be affecting trade in such product.

2. For purposes of Article XVI:3 of the General Agreement and paragraph 1 above:

(a) "more than an equitable share of world export trade" shall include any case in which the effect of an export subsidy granted by a signatory is to displace the exports of another signatory bearing in mind the developments on world markets;

---

[27] The term "displacing" shall be interpreted in a manner which takes into account the trade and development needs of developing countries and in this connection is not intended to fix traditional market shares.

[28] The problem of third country markets so far as certain primary products are concerned are dealt with exclusively under Article 10 below.

[29] For definition of "certain primary products" see footnote to Article 10 below.

[30] For purposes of this Agreement "certain primary products" means the products enumerated in Note Ad Article XVI of the General Agreement, Section B, paragraph 2, with the deletion of the words "or any mineral."

(b) with regard to new markets traditional patterns of supply of the product concerned to the world market, region or country, in which the new market is situated shall be taken into account in determining "equitable share of world export trade";

(c) "a previous representative period" shall normally be the three most recent calendar years in which normal market conditions existed.

3. Signatories further agree not to grant export subsidies on exports of certain primary products to a particular market in a manner which results in prices materially below those of other suppliers to the same market.

Article 11—*Subsidies other than export subsidies*

1. Signatories recognize that subsidies other than export subsidies are widely used as important instruments for the promotion of social and economic policy objectives and do not intend to restrict the right of signatories to use such subsidies to achieve these and other important policy objectives which they consider desirable. Signatories note that among such objectives are:

—the elimination of industrial, economic and social disadvantages of specific regions;

—to facilitate the restructuring, under socially acceptable conditions, of certain sectors, especially where this has become necessary by reason of changes in trade and economic policies, including international agreements resulting in lower barriers to trade;

—generally to sustain employment and to encourage re-training and change in employment;

—to encourage research and development programmes, especially in the field of high-technology industries;

—the implementation of economic programmes and policies to promote the economic and social development of developing countries;

—redeployment of industry in order to avoid congestion and environmental problems.

2. Signatories recognize, however, that subsidies other than export subsidies, certain objectives and possible forms of which are described respectively, in paragraphs 1 and 3 of this Article, may cause or threaten to cause injury to a domestic industry of another signatory or serious prejudice to the

interests of another signatory or may nullify or impair benefits accruing to another signatory under the General Agreement, in particular where such subsidies would adversely affect the conditions of normal competition. Signatories shall therefore seek to avoid causing such effects through the use of subsidies. In particular, signatories, when drawing up their policies and practices in this field, in addition to evaluating the essential internal objectives to be achieved, shall also weigh, as far as practicable, taking account of the nature of the particular case, possible adverse effects on trade. They shall also consider the conditions of world trade, production (e.g., price, capacity utilization etc.) and supply in the product concerned.

3. Signatories recognize that the objectives mentioned in paragraph 1 above may be achieved, *inter alia,* by means of subsidies granted with the aim of giving an advantage to certain enterprises. Examples of possible forms of such subsidies are: government financing of commercial enterprises, including grants, loans or guarantees; government provision or government financed provision of utility, supply distribution and other operational or support services or facilities; government financing of research and development programmes; fiscal incentives; and government subscription to, or provision of, equity capital.

The signatories note that the above forms of subsidy are normally granted either regionally or by sector. The enumeration of forms of subsidy set out above is illustrative and non-exhaustive, and reflects these currently granted by a number of signatories to this Agreement.

Signatories recognize, nevertheless, that the enumeration of forms of subsidy set out above should be reviewed periodically and that this should be done, through consultations, in conformity with the spirit of Article XVI:5 of the General Agreement.

4. The signatories recognize further that, without prejudice to their rights under this Agreement, nothing in paragraphs 1-3 above and in particular the enumeration of forms of subsidy creates, in itself, any basis for action under the General Agreement, as interpreted by this Agreement.

Article 12—*Consultations*

1. Whenever a signatory has reason to believe that an export subsidy is being granted or maintained by another signatory in a manner inconsistent with the provisions of this Agreement, such signatory may request consultations with such other signatory.

2. A request for consultations under paragraph 1 above shall include a

statement of available evidence with regard to the existence and nature of the subsidy in question.

3. Whenever a signatory has reason to believe that any subsidy is being granted or maintained by another signatory and that such subsidy either causes injury to its domestic industry, nullification or impairment of benefits accruing to it under the General Agreement, or serious prejudice to its interests, such signatory may request consultations with such other signatory.

4. A request for consultations under paragraph 3 above shall include a statement of available evidence with regard to (a) the existence and nature of the subsidy in question and (b) the injury to the domestic industry caused or, in the case of nullification or impairment, or serious prejudice, the adverse effects caused to the interests of the signatory requesting consultations.

5. Upon request for consultations under paragraph 1 or paragraph 2 above, the signatory believed to be granting or maintaining the subsidy practice in question shall enter into such consultations as quickly as possible. The purpose of the consultations shall be to clarify the facts of the situation and to arrive at a mutually acceptable solution.

Article 13—*Conciliation, dispute settlement and authorized countermeasures*

1. If, in the case of consultations under paragraph 1 of Article 12, a mutually acceptable solution has not been reached within thirty days[31] of the request for consultations, any signatory party to such consultations may refer the matter to the Committee for conciliation in accordance with the provisions of Part VI.

2. If, in the case of consultations under paragraph 3 of Article 12, a mutually acceptable solution has not been reached within sixty days of the request for consultations, any signatory party to such consultations may refer the matter to the Committee for conciliation in accordance with the provisions of Part VI.

3. If any dispute arising under this Agreement is not resolved as a result of consultations or conciliations, the Committee shall, upon request, review the matter in accordance with the dispute settlement procedures of Part VI.

4. If, as a result of its review, the Committee concludes that an export subsidy is being granted in a manner inconsistent with the provisions of this

---

[31] Any time periods mentioned in this Article and in Article 18 may be extended by mutual agreement.

Agreement or that a subsidy is being granted or maintained in such a manner as to cause injury, nullification or impairment, or serious prejudice, it shall make such recommendations[32] to the parties as may be appropriate to resolve the issue and, in the event the recommendations are not followed, it may authorize such countermeasures as may be appropriate, taking into account the degree and nature of the adverse effects found to exist.

PART III

Article 14—Developing countries

1. Signatories recognize that subsidies are an integral part of economic development programmes of developing countries.

2. Accordingly, this Agreement shall not prevent developing country signatories from adopting measures and policies to assist their industries, including those in the export sector. In particular the commitment of Article 9 shall not apply to developing country signatories, subject to the provisions of paragraphs 5 through 8 below.

3. Developing country signatories agree that export subsidies on their industrial products shall not be used in a manner which causes serious prejudice to the trade or production of another signatory.

4. There shall be no presumption that export subsidies granted by developing country signatories result in adverse effects, as defined in this Agreement, to the trade or production of another signatory. Such adverse effects shall be demonstrated by positive evidence, through an economic examination of the impact on trade or production of another signatory.

5. A developing country signatory should endeavour to enter into a commitment[33] to reduce or eliminate export subsidies when the use of such export subsidies is inconsistent with its competitive and development needs.

6. When a developing country has entered into a commitment to reduce or eliminate export subsidies, as provided in paragraph 5 above, countermeasures pursuant to the provisions of Parts II and VI of this Agreement against any export subsidies of such developing country shall not be authorized for other signatories of this Agreement, provided that the export subsidies in question

---

[32] In making such recommendations, the Committee shall take into account the trade, development and financial needs of developing country signatories.

[33] It is understood that after this Agreement has entered into force, any such proposed commitment shall be notified to the Committee in good time.

are in accordance with the terms of the commitment referred to in paragraph 5 above.

7. With respect to any subsidy, other than an export subsidy, granted by a developing country signatory, action may not be authorized or taken under Parts II and VI of this Agreement, unless nullification or impairment of tariff concessions or other GATT obligations is found to exist as a result of such subsidy, in such a way as to displace or impede imports of like products into the market of the subsidizing country, or unless injury to domestic industry in the importing market occurs in terms of Article VI of the General Agreement, as interpreted and applied by this Agreement. Signatories recognize that in developing countries, governments may play a large rôle in promoting economic growth and development. Intervention by government in the economy, for example through the practices enumerated in paragraph 3 of Article 11, shall not, *per se,* be considered subsidies.

8. "The Committee shall, upon request by an interested signatory, undertake a review of a specific export subsidy practice of a developing country signatory to examine the extent to which the practice is in conformity with the objectives of this Agreement. If a developing country has entered into a commitment pursuant to paragraph 5 of this Article, it shall not be subject to such review for the period of that commitment."

9. The Committee shall, upon request by an interested signatory, also undertake similar reviews of measures maintained or taken by developed country signatories under the provisions of this Agreement which affect interests of a developing country signatory.

10. Signatories recognize that the obligations of this Agreement with respect to export subsidies for certain primary products apply to all signatories.

PART IV

Article 15—*Special situations*

In cases of alleged injury caused by imports from a country described in the notes and supplementary provisions to the General Agreement (Annex I, Article VI, paragraph 1, point 2) the importing signatory may base its procedures and measures either

(a) on this Agreement, or, alternatively

(b) on the Anti-dumping Code,

it being understood that in both cases the calculation of the margin of dumping or of the amount of the estimated subsidy can be made by comparison of the export price with:

(a) the price at which a like product of a country other than the importing signatory or those mentioned above is sold, or

(b) the constructed value[34] of a like product in a country other than the importing signatory or those mentioned above.

If neither prices nor constructed value as established under (a) or (b) above provide an adequate basis for determination of dumping or subsidization then the price in the importing signatory, if necessary duly adjusted to reflect reasonable profits, may be used.

All calculations shall be based on prices or costs ruling at the same level of trade, normally at the ex factory level, and in respect of operations made as nearly as possible at the same time. Due allowance shall be made in each case, on its merits, for the difference in conditions and terms of sale or in taxation and for the other differences affecting price comparability, so that the method of comparison applied is appropriate and not unreasonable.

PART V

Article 16—*Committee of Signatories*

1. There shall be established under this Agreement a Committee of Signatories composed of representatives from each of the signatories to this Agreement. The Committee shall elect its own Chairman and shall meet not less than twice a year and otherwise as envisaged by relevant provisions of this Agreement at the request of any signatory. The Committee shall carry out responsibilities as assigned to it under this Agreement or by the signatories and it shall afford signatories the opportunity of consulting on any matters relating to the operation of the Agreement or the furtherance of its objectives. The GATT secretariat shall act as the secretariat to the Committee.

2. The Committee may set up subsidiary bodies as appropriate.

3. In carrying out their functions, the Committee and any subsidiary bodies may consult with and seek information from any source they deem appropriate. However, before the Committee or a subsidiary body seeks such information from a source within the jurisdiction of a signatory, it shall inform the signatory involved.

---

[34] Constructed value means cost of production plus a reasonable amount for administration, selling and any other costs and for profits.

PART VI

Article 17—*Conciliation*

1. In cases where matters are referred to the Committee for conciliation failing a mutually agreed solution in consultations under any provision of this Agreement, the Committee shall immediately review the facts involved and, through its good offices, shall encourage the signatories involved to develop a mutually acceptable solution.[35]

2. Signatories shall make their best efforts to reach a mutually satisfactory solution throughout the period of conciliation.

3. Should the matter remain unresolved, notwithstanding efforts at conciliation made under paragraph 2 above, any signatory involved may, thirty days after the request for conciliation, request that a panel be established by the Committee in accordance with the provisions of Article 18 below.

Article 18—*Dispute settlement*

1. The Committee shall establish a panel upon request pursuant to paragraph 3 of Article 17.[36] A panel so established shall review the facts of the matter and, in light of such facts, shall present to the Committee its findings concerning the rights and obligations of the signatories party to the dispute under the relevant provisions of the General Agreement as interpreted and applied by this Agreement.

2. A panel should be established within thirty days of a request therefor[37] and a panel so established should deliver its findings to the Committee within sixty days after its establishment.

3. When a panel is to be established, the Chairman of the Committee, after securing the agreement of the signatories concerned, should propose the composition of the panel. Panels shall be composed of three or five members, preferably governmental, and the composition of panels should not give rise to delays in their establishment. It is understood that citizens of countries

---

[35] In this connection, the Committee may draw signatories' attention to those cases in which, in its view, there is no reasonable basis supporting the allegations made.

[36] This does not preclude, however, the more rapid establishment of a panel when the Committee so decides, taking into account the urgency of the situation.

[37] The parties to the dispute would respond within a short period of time, i.e., seven working days, to nominations of panel members by the Chairman of the Committee and would not oppose nominations except for compelling reasons.

whose governments[38] are parties to the dispute would not be members of the panel concerned with that dispute.

4. In order to facilitate the constitution of panels, the Chairman of the Committee should maintain an informal indicative list of governmental and non-governmental persons qualified in the fields of trade relations, economic development, and other matters covered by the General Agreement and this Agreement, who could be available for serving on panels. For this purpose, each signatory would be invited to indicate at the beginning of every year to the Chairman of the Committee the name of one or two persons who would be available for such work.

5. Panel members would serve in their individual capacities and not as government representatives, nor as representatives of any organization. Governments would therefore not give them instructions with regard to matters before a panel. Panel members should be selected with a view to ensuring the independence of the members, a sufficiently diverse background and a wide spectrum of experience.

6. To encourage development of mutually satisfactory solutions between the parties to a dispute and with a view to obtaining their comments, each panel should first submit the descriptive part of its report to the parties concerned, and should subsequenly submit to the parties to the dispute its conclusions, or an outline thereof, a reasonable period of time before they are circulated to the Committee.

7. If a mutually satisfactory solution is developed by the parties to a dispute before a panel, any signatory with an interest in the matter has a right to enquire about and be given appropriate information about that solution and a notice outlining the solution that has been reached shall be presented by the panel to the Committee.

8. In cases where the parties to a dispute have failed to come to a satisfactory solution, the panels shall submit a written report to the Committee which should set forth the findings of the panel as to the questions of fact and the application of the relevant provisions of the General Agreement as interpreted and applied by this Agreement and the reasons and bases therefor.

9. The Committee shall consider the panel report as soon as possible and, taking into account the findings contained therein, may make recommendations to the parties with a view to resolving the dispute. If the Committee's recommendations are not followed within a reasonable period, the Committee

---

[38] The term "governments" is understood to mean governments of all member countries in cases of customs unions.

may authorize appropriate countermeasures (including withdrawal of GATT concessions or obligations) taking into account the nature and degree of the adverse effect found to exist. Committee recommendations should be presented to the parties within thirty days of the receipt of the panel report.

PART VII

Article 19—*Final provisions*

1. No specific action against a subsidy of another signatory can be taken except in accordance with the provisions of the General Agreement, as interpreted by this Agreement.[39]

Acceptance and accession

2. (a) This Agreement shall be open for acceptance by signature or otherwise, by governments contracting parties to the GATT and by the European Economic Community.

(b) This Agreement shall be open to accession by any other government on terms, related to the effective application of rights and obligations under this Agreement, to be agreed between that government and the signatories, by the deposit with the Director-General to the CONTRACTING PARTIES to the GATT of an instrument of accession which states the terms so agreed.

(c) CONTRACTING PARTIES may accept this Agreement in respect of those territories for which they have international responsibility, provided that the GATT is being applied in respect of such territories in accordance with the provisions of Article XXVI:5(a) or (b) of the General Agreement; and in terms of such acceptance, each such territory shall be treated as though it were a signatory.

Reservations

3. Reservations may not be entered in respect of any of the provisions of this Agreement without the consent of the other signatories.

Entry into force

4. This Agreement shall enter into force on 1 January 1980 for the govern-

---

[39] This paragraph is not intended to preclude action under other relevant provisions of the General Agreement, where appropriate.

ments[40] which have accepted or acceded to it by that date. For each other government it shall enter into force on the thirtieth day following the date of its acceptance or accession to this Agreement.

National legislation

5. (a) Each government accepting or acceding to this Agreement shall take all necessary steps, of a general or particular character, to ensure, not later than the date of entry into force of this Agreement for it, the conformity of its laws, regulations and administrative procedures with the provisions of this Agreement as they may apply to the signatory in question.

(b) Each signatory shall inform the Committee of any changes in its laws and regulations relevant to this Agreement and in the administration of such laws and regulations.

Review

6. The Committee shall review annually the implementation and operation of this Agreement taking into account the objectives thereof. The Committee shall annually inform the CONTRACTING PARTIES to the GATT of developments during the period covered by such reviews.[41]

Amendments

7. The signatories may amend this Agreement having regard, *inter alia,* to the experience gained in its implementation. Such an amendment, once the signatories have concurred in accordance with procedures established by the Committee, shall not come into force for any signatory until it has been accepted by such signatory.

Withdrawal

8. Any signatory may withdraw from this Agreement. The withdrawal shall take effect upon the expiration of sixty days from the day on which written

---

[40] The term "governments" is deemed to include the competent authorities of the European Economic Community.

[41] At the first such review, the Committee shall, in addition to its general review of the operation of the Agreement, offer all interested signatories an opportunity to raise questions and discuss issues concerning specific subsidy practices and the impact on trade, if any, of certain direct tax practices.

notice of withdrawal is received by the Director-General to the CONTRACT-
ING PARTIES to the GATT. Any signatory may upon such notification request
an immediate meeting of the Committee.

Non-application of this Agreement between particular signatories

9. This Agreement shall not apply as between any two signatories if either
of the signatories, at the time either accepts or accedes to this Agreement,
does not consent to such application.

Annex

10. The annex to this Agreement constitutes an integral part thereof.

Secretariat

11. This Agreement shall be serviced by the GATT secretariat.

Deposit

12. This Agreement shall be deposited with the Director-General to the
CONTRACTING PARTIES to the GATT, who shall promptly furnish to each
signatory and each contracting party to the GATT a certified copy thereof
and of each amendment thereto pursuant to paragraph 7, and a notification
of each acceptance thereof or accession thereto pursuant to paragraph 2,
or each withdrawal therefrom pursuant to paragraph 8 above.

Registration

13. This Agreement shall be registered in accordance with the provisions
of Article 102 of the Charter of the United Nations.

Done at Geneva this . . . . day of . . . . nineteen
hundred and seventy-nine in a single copy, in the English, French and Spanish
languages, each text being authentic.

ANNEX

Illustrative List of Export Subsidies

(a) The provision by governments of direct subsidies to a firm or any industry contingent upon export performance.

(b) Currency retention schemes or any similar practices which involve a bonus on exports.

(c) Internal transport and freight charges on export shipments, provided or mandated by governments, on terms more favourable than for domestic shipments.

(d) The delivery by governments or their agencies of imported or domestic products or services for use in the production of exported goods, on terms or conditions more favourable than for delivery of like or directly competitive products or services for use on the production of goods for domestic consumption, if (in the case of products) such terms or conditions are more favourable than those commercially available on world markets to its exporters.

(e) The full or partial exemption, remission, or deferral specifically related to exports, of direct taxes[1] or social welfare charges paid or payable by industrial or commercial enterprises.[2]

(f) The allowance of special deductions directly related to exports or export performance, over and above those granted in respect to production for domestic consumption, in the calculation of the base on which direct taxes are charged.

(g) The exemption or remission in respect of the production and distribution of exported products, of indirect taxes[1] in excess of those levied in respect of the production and distribution of like products when sold for domestic consumption.

(h) The exemption, remission or deferral of prior stage cumulative indirect taxes[1] on goods or services used in the production of exported products in excess of the exemption, remission or deferral of like prior stage cumulative indirect taxes on goods or services used in the production of like products when sold for domestic consumption; provided, however, that prior stage cumulative indirect taxes may be exempted, remitted or deferred on exported products even when not exempted, remitted or deferred on like products when sold for domestic consumption, if the prior stage cumulative indirect taxes are levied on goods that are physically incorporated (making normal allowance for waste) in the exported product.[3]

(i) The remission or drawback of import charges[1] in excess of those levied on imported goods that are physically incorporated (making normal allowances for waste) in the exported product; provided, however, that in particular cases a firm may use a quantity of home market goods equal to, and having the same quality and characteristics as, the imported goods as a substitute for them in order to benefit from this provision if the import and the corresponding export operations both occur within a reasonable time period, normally not to exceed two years.

(j) The provision by governments (or special institutions controlled by governments) of export credit guarantee or insurance programmes, of insurance or guarantee programmes against increases in the costs of exported products[4] or of exchange risk programmes, at premium rates, which are manifestly inadequate to cover the long-term operating costs and losses of the programmes.[5]

(k) The grant by governments (or special institutions controlled by and/or acting under the authority of governments) of export credits at rates below those which they actually have to pay for the funds so employed (or would have to pay if they borrowed on international capital markets in order to obtain funds of the same maturity and denominated in the same currency as the export credit), or the payment by them of all or part of the costs incurred by exporters or financial institutions in obtaining credits, in so far as they are used to secure a material advantage in the field of export credit terms.

Provided, however, that if a signatory is a party to an international undertaking on official export credits to which at least twelve original signatories[6] to this Agreement are parties as of 1 January 1979 (or a successor undertaking which has been adopted by those original signatories), or if in practice a signatory applies the interest rates provisions of the relevant undertaking, an export credit practice which is in conformity with those provisions shall not be considered an export subsidy prohibited by this Agreement.

(l) Any other charge on the public account constituting an export subsidy in the sense of Article XVI of the General Agreement.

NOTES

[1] For the purpose of this Agreement:

The term "direct taxes" shall mean taxes on wages, profits, interest, rents, royalties, and all other forms of income, and taxes on the ownership of real property.

The term "import charges" shall mean tariffs, duties, and other fiscal charges not elsewhere enumerated in this note that are levied on imports.

The term "indirect taxes" shall mean sales, excise, turnover, value added, franchise, stamp, transfer, inventory and equipment taxes, border taxes and all taxes other than direct taxes and import charges.

"Prior stage" indirect taxes are those levied on goods or services used directly or indirectly in making the product.

"Cumulative" indirect taxes are multi-staged taxes levied where there is no mechanism for subsequent crediting of the tax if the goods or services subject to tax at one stage of production are used in a succeeding stage of production.

"Remission" of taxes includes the refund or rebate of taxes.

[2] The signatories recognize that deferral need not amount to an export subsidy where, for example, appropriate interest charges are collected. The signatories further recognize that nothing in this text prejudges the disposition by the CONTRACTING PARTIES of the specific issues raised in GATT document L/4422.

The signatories reaffirm the principle that prices for goods in transactions between exporting enterprises and foreign buyers under their or under the same control should for tax purposes be the prices which would be charged between independent enterprises acting at arm's length. Any signatory may draw the attention of another signatory to administrative or other practices which may contravene this principle and which result in a significant saving of direct taxes in export transactions. In such circumstances the signatories shall normally attempt to resolve their differences using the facilities of existing bilateral tax treaties or other specific international mechanisms, without prejudice to the rights and obligations of signatories under the General Agreement, including the right of consultation created in the preceding sentence.

Paragraph (e) is not intended to limit a signatory from taking measures to avoid the double taxation of foreign source income earned by its enterprises or the enterprises of another signatory.

Where measures incompatible with the provisions of paragraph (e) exist, and where major practical difficulties stand in the way of the signatory concerned bringing such measures promptly into conformity with the Agreement, the signatory concerned shall, without prejudice to the rights of other signatories under the General Agreement or this Agreement, examine methods of bringing these measures into conformity within a reasonable period of time.

In this connection the European Economic Community has declared that Ireland intends to withdraw by 1 January 1981 its system of preferential tax measures related to exports, provided for under the Corporation Tax Act of 1976, whilst continuing nevertheless to honour legally binding commitments entered into during the lifetime of this system.

[3] Paragraph (h) does not apply to value-added tax systems, and border-tax adjustment in lieu thereof and the problem of the excessive remission of value-added taxes is exclusively covered by paragraph (g).

[4] The signatories agree that nothing in this paragraph shall prejudge or influence the deliberations of the panel established by the GATT Council on 6 June 1978 (C/M/126).

[5] In evaluating the long-term adequacy of premium rates, costs and losses of insurance programmes, in principle only such contracts shall be taken into account that were concluded after the date of entry into force of this Agreement.

[6] An original signatory to this Agreement shall mean any signatory which adheres ad referendum to the Agreement on or before 30 June 1979.

3. Draft Agreement on Safeguards

Outline of an Arrangement

The following text represents a substantive basis for a likely agreement in this area:

(It was agreed that the draft preamble would need to be reviewed in the light of the provisions of this Agreement).

Draft Preamble for Safeguard Agreement

Parties to this Agreement,

Considering that Ministers agreed in a declaration at Tokyo on 14 September 1973 that comprehensive multilateral negotiations in the framework of the GATT should aim, *inter alia,* to include an examination of the adequacy of the multilateral safeguard system, considering particularly the modalities of application of Article XIX, with a view to furthering trade liberalization and preserving its results;

Having concluded as a result of their examination that the application of multilaterally agreed rules to safeguard measures could be improved and their mechanisms more clearly defined;

Recognizing that procedures needed to deal with emergency situations in which any products are imported in such increased quantities and under such conditions as to cause or threaten serious injury to domestic producers are provided for in Article XIX of the General Agreement;

Recognizing, however, that recourse to safeguard measures can have harmful effects on the interests of other countries and desiring to ensure that such measures are not more restrictive nor longer than necessary to prevent or remedy the serious injury or the threat thereof;

Recognizing that safeguard measures should not be used as a substitute for structural adjustment to [changed conditions of fair competition]; [shifts in comparative advantage];

Recalling the provisions of Article XXXVII of the General Agreement;

Desiring that safeguard measures should not constitute an unjustifiable impediment to world trade;

Desiring to ensure that all recourse to safeguard measures be appropriately brought within the framework of an improved international discipline;

Desiring, therefore, to elaborate supplementary rules and procedures regarding the application of Article XIX of the General Agreement, in order to provide greater uniformity and certainty in the implementation of its provisions,

Hereby agree as follows;

GENERAL PROVISIONS

1. The parties to this Agreement agree that safeguard measures may be taken only under the circumstances provided for in Article XIX. In all such cases the parties undertake to observe the requirements set out below which, together with those of Article XIX itself, shall govern the implementation of that Article among the parties to this Agreement.[1]

2. The provisions of paragraph 1 shall be without prejudice to the rights and obligations of GATT contracting parties regarding restrictive measures permitted for specified purposes under the terms of other GATT provisions, protocols, and agreements or arrangements negotiated under GATT auspices.[2]

Chapter 1—Serious Injury and Causality

1. In the implementation of paragraph 1 of Article XIX, parties to this Agreement agree that safeguard action may only follow a determination by the domestic authorities concerned that imports of a particular product[3] are causing or threatening to cause serious injury to [a major part of all] domestic producers of like or directly competitive products. The determination in all cases shall be made on the basis of positive findings of fact and not on mere conjecture, or remote or hypothetical possibility. In the case of serious

---

[1] The applicability of this Agreement to non-adhering contracting parties is being discussed.

[2] It is understood that the term "agreements or arrangements negotiated under GATT auspices" refers to instruments resulting from mutilateral negotiations convened or sponsored by the CONTRACTING PARTIES (e.g. the Multi-Fiber Arrangement, and non-tariff measure and commodity codes negotiated in the Tokyo Round or other GATT "rounds"), where such instruments expressly permit the taking of restrictive measures in specified circumstances.

[3] A representative of several contracting parties understands that this language refers to imports of a particular product into the territory of a contracting party.

injury such a determination shall be made only when imports have increased in such quantities, [or in such quantities relative to domestic production] and under such conditions demonstrably as to [account for the principal] cause [of] serious injury sustained by domestic producers. In the case of threat of serious injury, such a determination shall be made only when imports have increased in such quantities [or in such quantities relative to domestic production] and under such conditions that serious injury, although not yet existing, is clearly imminent.

2. Determination of the existence of serious injury or threat thereof shall be based on examination of objective factors having a bearing on the state of the domestic producers, such as: [development and prospects with regard to] output, turnover, inventories, market share, profits, domestic prices, exports, domestic employment and wages, utilization of productive capacity, productivity, and investment [, as well as the size of the market]. [No positive determination of the existence of serious injury or threat thereof shall be made where these indicators are not adverse.] The list is not exhaustive, nor can any one or several of the factors necessarily give decisive guidance.

3. It must be demonstrated that imports are the [principal] cause of the serious injury or threat thereof. Injury caused or threatened by other factors must not be attributed to imports. Therefore, the determination of [principal] cause shall be based on an examination of the effect of imports on one hand and on the other hand, all other relevant factors which, individually or in combination, may be adversely affecting the domestic producers [, for example: competition among domestic producers, contraction in demand due to substitution by other products or to changes in consumer tastes, decline in domestic consumption or production, shifts in technology, structural deficiencies or loss of competitive advantage].

4. [(a) The term "domestic producers" shall be interpreted as referring to the domestic producers as a whole of the like products or the directly competitive products or to those of them whose collective output of the products constitutes a major proportion of the total domestic production of those products.][4]

(b) Where two or more countries have reached such a level of integration that they have characteristics of a single, unified market, the producers in the entire area of integration shall be taken to be the producers referred to [in subparagraph (a)].

---

[4] This paragraph is an alternative to the bracketed language beginning on the fifth line of paragraph 1. It would be for consideration whether language along the lines of Article 4(a)(ii) of the Anti-Dumping Code should be included.

Chapter 2—Domestic Procedures[5]

1. No safeguard action may be implemented by a party to this Agreement, unless previously designated governmental authorities, pursuant to domestic procedures previously established and made public, have examined the case in question and determined that the requirements of Chapter 1 have been met. Investigations shall normally be initiated upon a request on behalf of the producers affected [, supported by evidence on serious injury. If in special circumstances the previously designated governmental authorities of a signatory decide to initiate an examination or an investigation without having received such a request, they shall proceed only if they have evidence on serious injury].

2. In examining the case(s), the authorities shall, subsequent to [reasonable public notice] [such notice as may be necessary], afford interested parties an opportunity to present their views and relevant evidence by way of public hearings [or] [and] otherwise, in order to facilitate the development of the fullest possible information upon which the authorities may judge the need for safeguard action. All information provided on a confidential basis shall be treated as strictly confidential by the authorities.

3. If the authorities determine, with respect to the case in question, as a result of their examination, that the requirements of Chapter 1 have been met, they shall communicate to the exporting parties to this Agreement concerned, [other interested parties to this Agreement, where deemed appropriate,] and to directly interested [domestic] private parties the fact of such determination, indicating factors considered, criteria applied and rationale used in arriving at their determination. Such determination shall be made [[public and shall be] available in written form to any interested party to this Agreement and to any interested [domestic] [private] party [upon request], [unless there exist special reasons against doing so]].

[4. Except for good cause determined by the authorities to exist, no investigation for the purpose of safeguard action shall be made with respect to the same subject matter as a previous investigation unless [one year has] [two years have] elapsed since the examination under this Chapter was concluded.]

Chapter 3—Conditions

Safeguard measures should be proportionate[6] to the injury caused or threatened to be caused. Therefore:

---

[5] Some delegations have expressed doubts as to whether this Chapter is necessary and have reserved their position.

[6] The suggestion was made that tariff increases should take preference over quantitative import restrictions or similar measures.

(a) Product coverage of a safeguard measure shall be limited to imports of the particular product or products causing or threatening serious injury, although appropriate allowance may be made for dealing with the possibility of circumvention through, for example, minor design or processing changes or incomplete assembly of component parts.

(b) A safeguard measure shall remain in force only so long as may be necessary to prevent or remedy serious injury to domestic producers. At the time it takes a safeguard measure, the importing signatory shall stipulate the period of validity of such measure [which initially shall not exceed . . . . months]. If the serious injury or threat thereof continues to exist, the safeguard measure may be extended beyond such initial period after notification [and consultation] in accordance with Chapter 5 below.[7] [The extension shall be on terms [no more] [less] restrictive than those obtaining immediately prior to the extension.] [In no case shall the safeguard measure and its extension(s) total more than [3] [8] years.]

(c) [No safeguard measure shall be implemented [by developed countries] with respect to any product which was subject to a safeguard measure within the preceding two years.]

(d)[8] Safeguard measures shall [to the extent feasible] be progressively liberalized during the period of their application to encourage the adjustment of domestic producers to import competition.

(e) Safeguard measures shall not [normally] reduce the level of imports below the level in [a] [the most] recent representative period [(i.e. a twelve-month period terminating (. . . .) months preceding the month in which domestic procedures provided for in Chapter 7 are initialled)].

[Chapter 4—Nature of Safeguard Action.* This is the most controversial part of the safeguards code. The present Article XIX requires a country taking safeguard action to restrict imports of the product concerned from all sources—that is, to take action on a most-favored-nation (MFN) basis. Some countries want the MFN requirement retained. Others insist that a country should have the right to restrict imports from the source (or a few

---

[7] A number of delegations consider that the extension of any safeguard measure should be subject to prior approval by the Committee.

[8] Some delegations have proposed the following addition:

Developed parties shall take appropriate policy measures to encourage their domestic producers to adjust out of product sectors in which comparative advantage has shifted in favour of less-developed contracting parties.

* Note by U.S. Delegation.

sources) if it can be shown that imports from that source (or those sources) are the cause of serious injury.

The specific conditions on selective action and the role of the surveillance body is still unsettled in the code.]

[*Chapter 4 bis—Use of Export Restraints.* One of the ways in which countries protect domestic producers from injurious import competition without making use of Article XIX is by inducing the exporting country to curtail its exports of the product concerned. Another way is arranging for the formation of an international cartel. This issue is closely related to the selectivity issue. The extent to which such arrangements participated in or encouraged by governments are covered by the conditions and criteria of the code for other safeguard actions has not yet been determined. Language on this issue is still under discussion and has not been included in the latest formal document.]

Chapter 5—Notification, Consultation

1. A party to this Agreement shall, in accordance with paragraph 2 of Article XIX, notify the CONTRACTING PARTIES[9] in writing that it is considering the implementation of a safeguard measure under this Agreement. The notification shall be made as far in advance as may be practicable, [but in any case not less than [20] days prior to the implementation of the measure]. It shall contain all available relevant particulars and details including a precise description of the product in respect of which the measure is to be implemented, the type of measure envisaged, the date of implementation, the expected duration of the measure and the justification for the measure in terms of the requirements set out in Chapter 1 above.

2. A party considering the implementation of a safeguard measure shall be prepared to consult, before the measure is implemented:

(a) with those parties to this Agreement that have a substantial interest as exporters of the product concerned [or whose trade interests are likely to be substantially affected]; and

(b) in the Committee upon the request of a party to this Agreement in accordance with the provisions of Chapter 6 paragraph 5 below.

---

* Note by U.S. Delegation.

[9] Among parties to this Agreement, notifications to "the CONTRACTING PARTIES" would be referred to the Committee; consultations with "the CONTRACTING PARTIES" would be conducted in the Committee.

Consultations requested shall begin as soon as possible and no later than thirty days from the receipt of the request.

[3. In the "critical circumstances" referred to in Article XIX, a safeguard measure may be introduced immediately following notification. In this case the measure taken will be on a provisional basis [with a maximum validity of [sixty] days] and the party taking the measure shall be prepared to consult immediately as provided in paragraph 2 of Article XIX].

[3. In critical circumstances, where delay would cause damage which it would be difficult to repair, a safeguard measure may be taken provisionally without prior consultation, on the condition that consultations shall be effected immediately after such measure].[10]

4. When a party implements a safeguard measure it shall promptly file a supplementary notification giving full details concerning the action being taken. It shall promptly notify the CONTRACTING PARTIES[11] if the measure is modified or discontinued.

5. A party considering the extension of a safeguard measure shall notify the CONTRACTING PARTIES[11] [—] days before its scheduled expiration and shall be prepared to consult as prescribed in paragraph 2(a) and (b) above [, before the measure is extended]. The notification shall provide justification for the extension in terms of the requirements of Chapters 1 and 2 above.

6. Parties to this Agreement shall accord sympathetic consideration to and shall afford adequate opportunity for prompt consultation regarding such representations as may be made by another party with respect to any matter affecting the operation of this Agreement.

7.[12] In conducting consultations provided for in the preceding paragraphs,

---

[10] This alternative is exactly analogous to the third sentence of Article XIX:2 and should be read in context with the rest of Article XIX:2 which refers to prior notification.

[11] Among parties to this Agreement, notifications to "the CONTRACTING PARTIES" would be referred to the Committee; consultations with "the CONTRACTING PARTIES" would be conducted in the Committee.

[12] It would be for consideration whether this paragraph should be included as an annex to this Agreement. Several delegations consider that, while the provision of adequate data for consultations is important, this question should be approached in a flexible manner and might be left for further elaboration in the Committee on Safeguard Measures.

a party considering the implementation of, or [extension of] [extending][13] a safeguard measure shall present, to the extent not already provided in accordance with paragraph 1 above, all relevant particulars and details in writing as far in advance as may be practicable, but in any case not later than [twenty days prior to] the beginning of the consultations. These particulars shall include data relating to:

(a) demonstration of the existence of serious injury or threat thereof as well as causality in accordance with the provisions of Chapter 1 above;

(b) demonstration of compliance with the conditions provided for in Chapter 2 above;

(c) in cases where paragraph 3 above has been invoked, demonstration of the existence of critical circumstances, in addition to the data listed in (a) and (b) above; and

(d) in cases of extension of an action, the period of extension, the justification for the extension, progress made towards the removal of the safeguard measure and, where relevant, towards adjustment of the domestic producers to import competition.

Chapter 6—Surveillance and Dispute Settlement[14]

Committee on Safeguard Measures

1. There is established within the framework of GATT[15] a Committee on Safeguard Measures (referred to herein as "the Committee") composed of representatives from each of the parties to this Agreement. The Committee shall elect its own Chairman and shall meet as provided for in this Agreement. The Committee shall carry out the responsibilities assigned to it under this Agreement. The GATT secretariat shall act as the secretariat to the Committee.

---

[13] It remains for consideration whether these provisions of this paragraph apply to short extensions of safeguard measures of short durations.

[14] One delegation has made it clear that it is unable to accept the establishment of a Committee, and of more specific procedures for surveillance and dispute settlement in this Agreement, except in the context of an Agreement which contains satisfactory and workable provisions for the selective application of safeguard measures.

[15] It remains to be considered whether the Committee on Safeguard Measures should report to the CONTRACTING PARTIES.

2. The Committee may set up subsidiary bodies.

3. In carrying out their functions, the Committee and any subsidiary body may consult with and seek appropriate information, consistently with domestic laws, from any source[16] they deem appropriate.

Surveillance[17]

4. The Committee shall meet at least once a year to review the operation of this Agreement.

5. Any party may request the Committee, by written communication to the Chairman, to examine a safeguard measure, which has been notified or which is in force, if the measure is affecting, or is likely to affect, its trade interests [as an exporter]. The Committee shall, on receipt of such a request by the Chairman, meet promptly[18] to conduct the examination requested.

6. Any party maintaining a safeguard measure in force shall once a year, on a date set by the Committee, submit a written report to the Committee with factual data to explain why the measure is still necessary and what progress is being made towards its removal and, where relevant, towards adjustment of the domestic producers to import competition. The Committee shall, on the basis of these reports and other information available to it, review annually all safeguard measures in force.

7. Any party may request the Committee, by written communication to the Chairman, to examine any situation affecting, or likely to affect, its trade interests where it appears another party is not meeting its obligations under the Agreement. The Committee shall, on receipt of such a request by the Chairman, meet promptly to conduct the examination requested.

8. The Committee shall be responsible for resolution of specific questions of interpretation of the Agreement.

---

[16] It is for consideration whether in practice the Committee and its subsidiary bodies would need to consult or seek information from sources other than the governments of parties to the Agreement.

[17] One delegation was of the view that the Committee should be a compact body like the Committee on Balance of Payments and that its mandate should include making findings and recommendations including disapproving measures found to be inconsistent with the provisions of the Code in the course of the normal periodic review of safeguard measures and not only in the context of specific initiatives or complaints from affected parties.

[18] Except for holiday periods, the word "promptly" in this Chapter means within thirty days, or sooner if possible.

Dispute Settlement[19]

9. Any party that considers that a benefit accruing to it directly or indirectly under this Agreement is being nullified or impaired, or that the achievement of any objective of this Agreement is being impeded by another party or parties, may request, by written communication to the Chairman, that the Committee meet to examine the situation. It is understood that the Committee's examination may cover any safeguard measure which is in force and which affects or is likely to affect the trade interests of another party; or any situation where it appears that a party is not carrying out its obligations under this Agreement. The Committee shall promptly investigate any matter so referred to it and shall make appropriate recommendations to the parties which it considers to be concerned [or give a ruling on the matter, as appropriate].

10. The Committee may disapprove of any suspension of concessions or other obligations, referred to in Chapter 3 [, which it determines to be more than "substantially equivalent"]. Any party with respect to which another party proposes to suspend concessions or other obligations pursuant to Chapter 3 may, by written communication to the Chairman, request the Committee to disapprove of such suspension [if that party considers it to be more than "substantially equivalent"]. The Committee shall promptly investigate the matter and decide whether so to disapprove of the suspension.

Note: It is understood that the substance of the provisions contained in the dispute settlement section of an "Understanding Regarding Notification, Consultation, Dispute Settlement and Surveillance" being negotiated elsewhere will be included in this section of the Safeguard Agreement. Appropriate modifications would need to be made to adapt the provisions to the requirements of the Safeguard Agreement, e.g. to take account of the role of the Committee on Safeguard Measures.

Note: It is understood that if a dispute arose regarding the Agreement and between parties to it that the provisions of this Chapter would be used in trying to resolve that dispute. It may be necessary to specify in what way Article XXIII of the GATT might be resorted to [when parties to this Agreement have exhausted the possibilities for dispute settlement under it].

(*Note:* A number of delegations reserve their position on this Chapter as a whole and consider that it requires further examination in the light of other aspects of the draft Code.)

---

[19] It is understood that the first stage in the dispute settlement process would be bilateral consultations between the parties concerned.

Chapter 7—Response To Safeguard Measures

1. Parties confirm that the right of a contracting party to the General Agreement to suspend substantially equivalent concessions or other obligations under Article XIX:3(a) is maintained. If, however, following the consultations described in Chapter 5, a party affected as an exporter of the product concerned to the territory of the party taking the safeguard action agrees that the requirements of this Agreement have been met by the latter party, the affected exporting party [shall] [should normally] [may] refrain from exercising its rights under Article XIX:3(a) of the General Agreement with respect to the suspension of substantially equivalent concessions or other obligations so long as the safeguard action continues to comply fully with the requirements of this Agreement.

[2. Notwithstanding the provisions of paragraph 1, and the ninety-day limitation prescribed in Article XIX:3(a), if the affected exporting party subsequently has reason to consider that, although the safeguard action in question may have met the requirements of this Agreement, that action has nevertheless had a serious adverse effect on its trade interests, then it would be open to that party, during the period the safeguard measure is in force, to pursue its rights under Article XIX:3(a) with respect to the suspension of substantially equivalent concessions or other obligations. [In such a case, however, consideration of "substantially equivalent concessions" would be related to the effect of the measure which has been used by the importing party rather than to the amount of the trade covered by the safeguard measure.]]

[3. The party taking safeguard action shall provide substantially equivalent compensation to [developing] parties affected as exporters of the product concerned. In that event, the [developing] parties concerned shall refrain from exercising their rights under Article XIX:3(a).]

[*Chapter 8—Developing Countries.* This chapter is now under discussion and may include a provision that may provide special benefits for developing countries. Signatories would agree to make an effort to avoid safeguard actions on products of special interest to developing countries and, if action is taken, to limit, if feasible, its extent and duration. When safeguard actions are taken, signatories might permit imports from developing countries which are small suppliers or new market-entrants to continue to have market access with moderate growth on favorable terms. Developed signatories, however, are reserving the right to withdraw this favorable treatment from individual developing countries when such countries, or relevant sectors

* Note by U.S. Delegation.

within those countries, achieve higher levels of development or become competitive. It is likely that provisions containing some or all of these elements will be included in a final package.]

Chapter 9—Final Provisions[20]

[1. All safeguard measures in force notified under Article XIX of the General Agreement by a party and in force the date of entry into force of the Agreement for it, shall be terminated no more than [. . . . . year(s)] from that date unless extended in accordance with the provisions of this Agreement.]

[2. All other pre-existing restrictive measures [subject to] [which would be required to be notified under] this Agreement and maintained by a party at the time the Agreement enters into force shall be notified to the Committee no later than the date of entry into force of the Agreement for that party. Any such measures not so notified shall be terminated forthwith. Measures which are notified shall be terminated no later than [. . . . . . year(s)] following the date indicated above unless extended in accordance with the provisions of this Agreement.]

3. The Committee shall examine measures which were maintained before entry into force of this Agreement and which a party proposes to extend under paragraphs 1 or 2 above, in order to determine whether the measures are in conformity with the provisions of this Agreement.

4. Each party to this Agreement shall, promptly following the date the Agreement enters into force for it, notify the Committee of its legislation, regulations and administrative procedures to be used in the implementation of this Agreement. Thereafter, each party shall notify promptly the Committee of any change in such legislation, regulations and procedures. These legislations, regulations and administrative procedures of each party shall be open to examination by the Committee pursuant to Chapter 6 above.

Note: Consideration is being given to provisions governing the use of automatic licensing and similar surveillance measures for safeguard-related purposes.

Note: Additional provisions remain to be developed.

---

[20] One delegation emphasizes that existing discriminatory bilateral safeguard arrangements should be abolished under a new safeguard system, and that existing discriminatory quantitative restrictions should be eliminated immediately.

4. Agreements Relating to the Framework for the Conduct of International Trade

DIFFERENTIAL AND MORE FAVOURABLE TREATMENT RECIPROCITY AND FULLER PARTICIPATION OF DEVELOPING COUNTRIES

Decision of 28 November 1979

Following negotiations within the framework of the Multilateral Trade Negotiations, the CONTRACTING PARTIES *decide* as follows:

1. Notwithstanding the provisions of Article I of the General Agreement, contracting parties may accord differential and more favourable treatment to developing countries[1], without according such treatment to other contracting parties.

2. The provisions of paragraph 1 apply to the following[2]:

    (*a*) preferential tariff treatment accorded by developed contracting parties to products originating in developing countries in accordance with the Generalized System of Preferences[3];

    (*b*) differential and more favourable treatment with respect to the provisions of the General Agreement concerning non-tariff measures governed by the provisions of instruments multilaterally negotiated under the auspices of the GATT;

    (*c*) regional or global arrangements entered into amongst less-developed contracting parties for the mutual reduction or elimination of tariffs and, in accordance with criteria or conditions which may be prescribed by the CONTRACTING PARTIES, for the mutual reduction or elimination of non-tariff measures, on products imported from one another;

    (*d*) special treatment on the least developed among the developing countries in the context of any general or specific measures in favour of developing countries.

3. Any differential and more favourable treatment provided under this clause:

    (*a*) shall be designed to facilitate and promote the trade of developing countries and not to raise barriers to or create undue difficulties for the trade of any other contracting parties;

---

[1] The words "developing countries" as used in this text are to be understood to refer also to developing territories.

[2] It would remain open for the CONTRACTING PARTIES to consider on an *ad hoc* basis under the GATT provisions for joint action any proposals for differential and more favourable treatment not falling within the scope of this paragraph.

[3] As described in the Decision of the CONTRACTING PARTIES of 25 June 1971, relating to the establishment of "generalized, non-reciprocal and non-discriminatory preferences beneficial to the developing countries".

(b) shall not constitute an impediment to the reduction or elimination of tariffs and other restrictions to trade on a most-favoured-nation basis;

(c) shall in the case of such treatment accorded by developed contracting parties to developing countries be designed and, if necessary, modified, to respond positively to the development, financial and trade needs of developing countries.

4. Any contracting party taking action[1] to introduce an arrangement pursuant to paragraphs 1, 2 and 3 above or subsequently taking action to introduce modification or withdrawal of the differential and more favourable treatment so provided shall:

(a) notify the CONTRACTING PARTIES and furnish them with all the information they may deem appropriate relating to such action;

(b) afford adequate opportunity for prompt consultations at the request of any interested contracting party with respect to any difficulty or matter that may arise. The CONTRACTING PARTIES shall, if requested to do so by such contracting party, consult with all contracting parties concerned with respect to the matter with a view to reaching solutions satisfactory to all such contracting parties.

5. The developed countries do not expect reciprocity for commitments made by them in trade negotiations to reduce or remove tariffs and other barriers to the trade of developing countries, i.e., the developed countries do not expect the developing countries, in the course of trade negotiations, to make contributions which are inconsistent with their individual development, financial and trade needs. Developed contracting parties shall therefore not seek, neither shall less-developed contracting parties be required to make, concessions that are inconsistent with the latter's development, financial and trade needs.

6. Having regard to the special economic difficulties and the particular development, financial and trade needs of the least-developed countries, the developed countries shall exercise the utmost restraint in seeking any concessions or contributions for commitments made by them to reduce or remove tariffs and other barriers to the trade of such countries, and the least-developed countries shall not be expected to make concessions or contributions that are inconsistent with the recognition of their particular situation and problems.

7. The concessions and contributions made and the obligations assumed by developed and less-developed contracting parties under the provisions of the General Agreement should promote the basic objectives of the Agreement, including those embodied in the Preamble and in Article XXXVI. Less-developed contracting

---

[1] Nothing in these provisions shall affect the rights of contracting parties under the General Agreement.

parties expect that their capacity to make contributions or negotiated concessions or take other mutually agreed action under the provisions and procedures of the General Agreement would improve with the progressive development of their economies and improvement in their trade situation and they would accordingly expect to participate more fully in the framework of rights and obligations under the General Agreement.

8. Particular account shall be taken of the serious difficulty of the least-developed countries in making concessions and contributions in view of their special economic situation and their development, financial and trade needs.

9. The contracting parties will collaborate in arrangements for review of the operation of these provisions, bearing in mind the need for individual and joint efforts by contracting parties to meet the development needs of developing countries and the objectives of the General Agreement.

DECLARATION ON TRADE MEASURES TAKEN FOR BALANCE-OF-PAYMENTS PURPOSES

Adopted on 28 November 1979

The *CONTRACTING PARTIES*,

Having regard to the provisions of Articles XII and XVIII:B of the General Agreement;

Recalling the procedures for consultations on balance-of-payments restrictions approved by the Council on 28 April 1970 (BISD, Eighteenth Supplement, pages 48–53) and the procedures for regular consultations on balance-of-payments restrictions with developing countries approved by the Council on 19 December 1972 (BISD, Twentieth Supplement, pages 47–49);

Convinced that restrictive trade measures are in general an inefficient means to maintain or restore balance-of-payments equilibrium;

Noting that restrictive import measures other than quantitative restrictions have been used for balance-of-payments purposes;

Reaffirming that restrictive import measures taken for balance-of-payments purposes should not be taken for the purpose of protecting a particular industry or sector;

Convinced that the contracting parties should endeavour to avoid that restrictive import measures taken for balance-of-payments purposes stimulate new investments that would not be economically viable in the absence of the measures;

Recognizing that the less-developed contracting parties must take into account their individual development, financial and trade situation when implementing restrictive import measures taken for balance-of-payments purposes;

Recognizing that the impact of trade measures taken by developed countries on the economies of developing countries can be serious;

Recognizing that deveoped contracting parties should avoid the imposition of restrictive trade measures for balance-of-payments purposes to the maximum extent possible,

Agree as follows:

1. The procedures for examination stipulated in Articles XII and XVIII shall apply to all restrictive import measures taken for balance-of-payments purposes. The application of restrictive import measures taken for balance-of-payments purposes shall be subject to the following conditions in addition to those provided for in Articles XII, XIII, XV and XVIII without prejudice to other provisions of the General Agreement:

   (*a*) in applying restrictive import measures contracting parties shall abide by the disciplines provided for in the GATT and give preference to the measure which has the least disruptive effect on trade[1];

   (*b*) the simultaneous application of more than one type of trade measure for this purpose should be avoided;

   (*c*) whenever practicable, contracting parties shall publicly announce a time schedule for the removal of the measures.

The provisions of this paragraph are not intended to modify the substantive provisions of the General Agreement.

2. If, notwithstanding the principles of this Declaration, a developed contracting party is compelled to apply restrictive import measures for balance-of-payments purposes, it shall, in determining the incidence of its measures, take into account the export interests of the less-developed contracting parties and may exempt from its measures products of export interest to those contracting parties.

3. Contracting parties shall promptly notify to the GATT the introduction or intensification of all restrictive import measures taken for balance-of-payments purposes. Contracting parties which have reason to believe that a restrictive import measure applied by another contracting party was taken for balance-of-payments purposes may notify the measure to the GATT or may request the GATT secretariat to seek information on the measure and make it available to all contracting parties if appropriate.

4. All restrictive import measures taken for balance-of-payments purposes shall be subject to consultation in the GATT Committee on Balance-of-Payments Restrictions (hereafter referred to as "Committee").

5. The membership of the Committee is open to all contracting parties indicating their wish to serve on it. Efforts shall be made to ensure that the composition of

---

[1] It is understood that the less-developed contracting parties must take into account their individual development, financial and trade situation when selecting the particular measure to be applied.

the Committee reflects as far as possible the characteristics of the contracting parties in general in terms of their geographical location, external financial position and stage of economic development.

6. The Committee shall follow the procedures for consultations on balance-of-payments restrictions approved by the Council on 28 April 1970 and set out in BISD, Eighteenth Supplement, pages 48–53, (hereinafter referred to as "full consultation procedures") or the procedures for regular consultations on balance-of-payments restrictions with developing countries approved by the Council on 19 December 1972 and set out in BISD, Twentieth Supplement, pages 47–49, (hereinafter referred to as "simplified consultation procedures") subject to the provisions set out below.

7. The GATT secretariat, drawing on all appropriate sources of information, including the consulting contracting party, shall with a view to facilitating the consultations in the Committee prepare a factual background paper describing the trade aspects of the measures taken, including aspects of particular interest to less-developed contracting parties. The paper shall also cover such other matters as the Committee may determine. The GATT secretariat shall give the consulting contracting party the opportunity to comment on the paper before it is submitted to the Committee.

8. In the case of consultations under Article XVIII:12(b) the Committee shall base its decision on the type of procedure on such factors as the following:

   (a) the time elapsed since the last full consultations;

   (b) the steps the consulting contracting party has taken in the light of conclusions reached on the occasion of previous consultations;

   (c) the changes in the overall level or nature of the trade measures taken for balance-of-payments purposes;

   (d) the changes in the balance-of-payments situation or prospects;

   (e) whether the balance-of-payments problems are structural or temporary in nature.

9. A less-developed contracting party may at any time request full consultations.

10. The technical assistance services of the GATT secretariat shall, at the request of a less-developed consulting contracting party, assist it in preparing the documentation for the consultations.

11. The Committee shall report on its consultations to the Council. The reports on full consultations shall indicate:

   (a) the Committee's conclusions as well as the facts and reasons on which they are based;

(b) the steps the consulting contracting party has taken in the light of conclusions reached on the occasion of previous consultations;

(c) in the case of less developed contracting parties, the facts and reasons on which the Committee based its decision on the procedure followed; and

(d) in the case of developed contracting parties, whether alternative economic policy measures are available.

If the Committee finds that the consulting contracting party's measures

(a) are in important respects related to restrictive trade measures maintained by another contracting party[1] or
(b) have a significant adverse impact on the export interests of a less-developed contracting party,

it shall so report to the Council which shall take such further action as it may consider appropriate.

12. In the course of full consultations with a less-developed contracting party the Committee shall, if the consulting contracting party so desires, give particular attention to the possibilties for alleviating and correcting the balance-of-payments problem through measures that contracting parties might take to facilitate an expansion of the export earnings of the consulting contracting party, as provided for in paragraph 3 of the full consultation procedures.

13. If the Committee finds that a restrictive import measure taken by the consulting contracting party for balance-of-payments purposes is inconsistent with the provisions of Articles XII, XVIII:B or this Declaration, it shall, in its report to the Council, make such findings as will assist the Council in making appropriate recommendations designed to promote the implementation of Articles XII and XVIII:B and this Declaration. The Council shall keep under surveillance any matter on which it has made recommendations.

SAFEGUARD ACTION FOR DEVELOPMENT PURPOSES

Decision of 28 November 1979

1. The CONTRACTING PARTIES recognize that the implementation by less-developed contracting parties of programmes and policies of economic development aimed at raising the standard of living of the people may involve in addition to the establish-

---

[1] It is noted that such a finding is more likely to be made in the case of recent measures than of measures in effect for some considerable time.

ment of particular industries[1] the development of new or the modification or extension of existing production structures with a view to achieving fuller and more efficient use of resources in accordance with the priorities of their economic development. Accordingly, they agree that a less-developed contracting party may, to achieve these objectives, modify or withdraw concessions included in the appropriate schedules annexed to the General Agreement as provided for in Section A of Article XVIII or, where no measure consistent with the other provisions of the General Agreement is practicable to achieve these objectives, have recourse to Section C of Article XVIII, with the additional flexibility provided for below. In taking such action the less-developed contracting party concerned shall give due regard to the objectives of the General Agreement and to the need to avoid unnecessary damage to the trade of other contracting parties.

2. The CONTRACTING PARTIES recognize further that there may be unusual circumstances where delay in the application of measures which a less-developed contracting party wishes to introduce under Section A or Section C of Article XVIII may give rise to difficulties in the application of its programmes and policies of economic development for the aforesaid purposes. They agree, therefore, that in such circumstances, the less-developed contracting party concerned may deviate from the provisions of Section A and paragraphs 14, 15, 17 and 18 of Section C to the extent necessary for introducing the measures contemplated on a provisional basis immediately after notification.

3. It is understood that all other requirements of the preambular part of Article XVIII and of Sections A and C of that Article, as well as the Notes and Supplementary Provisions set out in Annex I under these Sections will continue to apply to the measures to which this Decision relates.

4. The CONTRACTING PARTIES shall review this decision in the light of experience with its operation, with a view to determining whether it should be extended, modified or discontinued.

UNDERSTANDING REGARDING NOTIFICATION, CONSULTATION, DISPUTE SETTLEMENT AND SURVEILLANCE

Adopted on 28 November 1979

1. The CONTRACTING PARTIES reaffirm their adherence to the basic GATT mechanism for the management of disputes based on Articles XXII and XXIII.[1]

---

[1] As referred to in paragraphs 2, 3, 7, 13 and 22 of Article XVIII and in the Note to these paragraphs.

[1] It is noted that Article XXV may, as recognized by the CONTRACTING PARTIES, *inter alia*, when they adopted the report of the Working Party on particular difficulties connected with trade in primary products (L/930), also afford an appropriate avenue for consultation and dispute settlement in certain circumstances.

With a view to improving and refining the GATT mechanism, the CONTRACTING PARTIES agree as follows:

Notification

2. Contracting parties reaffirm their commitment to existing obligations under the General Agreement regarding publication and notification.[2]

3. Contracting parties moreover undertake, to the maximum extent possible, to notify the CONTRACTING PARTIES of their adoption of trade measures affecting the operation of the General Agreement, it being understood that such notification would of itself be without prejudice to views on the consistency of measures with or their relevance to rights and obligations under the General Agreement. Contracting parties should endeavour to notify such measures in advance of implementation. In other cases, where prior notification has not been possible, such measures should be notified promptly ex post facto. Contracting parties which have reason to believe that such trade measures have been adopted by another contracting party may seek information on such measures bilaterally, from the contracting party concerned.

Consultations

4. Contracting parties reaffirm their resolve to strengthen and improve the effectiveness of consultative procedures employed by contracting parties. In that connexion, they undertake to respond to requests for consultations promptly and to attempt to conclude consultations expeditiously, with a view to reaching mutually satisfactory conclusions. Any requests for consultations should include the reasons therefor.

5. During consultations, contracting parties should give special attention to the particular problems and interests of less-developed contracting parties.

6. Contracting parties should attempt to obtain satisfactory adjustment of the matter in accordance with the provisions of Article XXIII:1 before resorting to Article XXIII:2.

Dispute settlement

7. The CONTRACTING PARTIES agree that the customary practice of the GATT in the field of dispute settlement, described in the Annex, should be continued in the future, with the improvements set out below. They recognize that the efficient functioning of the system depends on their will to abide by the present understanding. The CONTRACTING PARTIES reaffirm that the customary practice includes the procedures for the settlement of disputes between developed and less-developed countries adopted by the CONTRACTING PARTIES in 1966 (BISD, fourteenth supplement,

---

[2] See secretariat note, Notifications required from contracting parties (MTN/FR/W/17, dated 1 August 1978).

page 18) and that these remain available to less-developed contracting parties wishing to use them.

8. If a dispute is not resolved through consultations the contracting parties concerned may request an appropriate body or individual to use their good offices with a view to the conciliation of the outstanding differences between the parties. If the unresolved dispute is one in which a less-developed contracting party has brought a complaint against a developed contracting party, the less-developed contracting party may request the good offices of the Director-General who, in carrying out his tasks, may consult with the Chairman of the CONTRACTING PARTIES and the Chairman of the Council.

9. It is understood that requests for conciliation and the use of the dispute settlement procedures of Article XXIII:2 should not be intended or considered as contentious acts and that, if disputes arise, all contracting parties will engage in these procedures in good faith in an effort to resolve the disputes. It is also understood that complaints and counter-complaints in regard to distinct matters should not be linked.

10. It is agreed that if a contracting party invoking Article XXIII:2 requests the establishment of a panel to assist these CONTRACTING PARTIES to deal with the matter, the CONTRACTING PARTIES would decide on its establishment in accordance with standing practice. It is also agreed that the CONTRACTING PARTIES would similarly decide to establish a working party if this were requested by a contracting party invoking the Article. It is further agreed that such requests would be granted only after the contracting party concerned had had an opportunity to study the complaint and respond to it before the CONTRACTING PARTIES.

11. When a panel is set up, the Director-General, after securing the agreement of the contracting parties concerned, should propose the composition of the panel, of three or five members depending on the case, to the CONTRACTING PARTIES for approval. The members of a panel would preferably be governmental. It is understood that citizens of countries whose governments[1] are parties to the dispute would not be members of the panel concerned with that dispute. The panel should be constituted as promptly as possible and normally not later than thirty days from the decision by the CONTRACTING PARTIES.

12. The parties to the dispute would respond within a short period of time, i.e., seven working days, to nominations of panel members by the Director-General and would not oppose nominations except for compelling reasons.

---

[1] In the case customs unions or common markets are parties to a dispute, this provision applies to citizens of all member countries of the customs unions or common markets.

13. In order to facilitate the constitution of panels, the Director-General should maintain an informal indicative list of governmental and nongovernmental persons qualified in the fields of trade relations, economic development, and other matters covered by the General Agreement, and who could be available for serving on panels. For this purpose, each contracting party would be invited to indicate at the beginning of every year to the Director-General the name of one or two persons who would be available for such work.[2]

14. Panel members would serve in their individual capacities and not as government representatives, nor as representatives of any organization. Governments would therefore not give them instructions nor seek to influence them as individuals with regard to matters before a panel. Panel members should be selected with a view to ensuring the independence of the members, a sufficiently diverse background and a wide spectrum of experience.[3]

15. Any contracting party having a substantial interest in the matter before a panel, and having notified this to the Council, should have an opportunity to be heard by the panel. Each panel should have the right to seek information and technical advice from any individual or body which it deems appropriate. However, before a panel seeks such information or advice from an individual or body within the jurisdiction of a State it shall inform the government of that State. Any contracting party should respond promptly and fully to any request by a panel for such information as the panel considers necessary and appropriate. Confidential information which is provided should not be revealed without formal authorization from the contracting party providing the information.

16. The function of panels is to assist the CONTRACTING PARTIES in discharging their responsibilities under Article XXIII:2. Accordingly, a panel should make an objective assessment of the matter before it, including an objective assessment of the facts of the case and the applicability of and conformity with the General Agreement and, if so requested by the CONTRACTING PARTIES, make such other findings as will assist the CONTRACTING PARTIES in making the recommendations or in giving the rulings provided for in Article XXIII:2. In this connexion, panels should consult regularly with the parties to the dispute and give them adequate opportunity to develop a mutually satisfactory solution.

17. Where the parties have failed to develop a mutually satisfactory solution, the panel should submit its findings in a written form. The report of a panel should normally set out the rationale behind any findings and recommendations that it makes. Where a bilateral settlement of the matter has been found, the report of the panel

---

[2] The coverage of travel expenses should be considered within the limits of budgetary possibilities.

[3] A statement is included in the Annex describing the current practice with respect to inclusion on panels of persons from developing countries.

may be confined to a brief description of the case and to reporting that a solution has been reached.

18. To encourage development of mutually satisfactory solutions between the parties and with a view to obtaining their comments, each panel should first submit the descriptive part of its report to the parties concerned, and should subsequently submit to the parties to the dispute its conclusions, or an outline thereof, a reasonable period of time before they are circulated to the CONTRACTING PARTIES.

19. If a mutually satisfactory solution is developed by the parties to a dispute before a panel, any contracting party with an interest in the matter has a right to enquire about and be given appropriate information about that solution in so far as it relates to trade matters.

20. The time required by panels will vary with the particular case.[1] However, panels should aim to deliver their findings without undue delay, taking into account the obligation of the CONTRACTING PARTIES to ensure prompt settlement. In cases of urgency the panel would be called upon to deliver its findings within a period normally of three months from the time the panel was established.

21. Reports of panels and working parties should be given prompt consideration by the CONTRACTING PARTIES. The CONTRACTING PARTIES should take appropriate action on reports of panels and working parties within a reasonable period of time. If the case is one brought by a less-developed contracting party, such action should be taken in a specially convened meeting, if necessary. In such cases, in considering what appropriate action might be taken the CONTRACTING PARTIES shall take into account not only the trade coverage of measures complained of, but also their impact on the economy of less-developed contracting parties concerned.

22. The CONTRACTING PARTIES shall keep under surveillance any matter on which they have made recommendations or given rulings. If the CONTRACTING PARTIES' recommendations are not implemented within a reasonable period of time, the contracting party bringing the case may ask the CONTRACTING PARTIES to make suitable efforts with a view to finding an appropriate solution.

23. If the matter is one which has been raised by a less-developed contracting party, the CONTRACTING PARTIES shall consider what further action they might take which would be appropriate to the circumstances.

Surveillance

24. The CONTRACTING PARTIES agree to conduct a regular and systematic review of developments in the trading system. Particular attention would be paid to

---

[1] An explanation is included in the Annex that "in most cases the proceedings of the panels have been completed within a reasonable period of time, extending from three to nine months".

developments which affect rights and obligations under the GATT, to matters affecting the interests of less-developed contracting parties, to trade measures notified
in accordance with this understanding and to measures which have been subject to
consultation, conciliation or dispute settlement procedures laid down in this
understanding.

Technical assistance

25. The technical assistance services of the GATT secretariat shall, at the request
of a less-developed contracting party, assist it in connexion with matters dealt with
in this understanding.

ANNEX

Agreed Description of the Customary Practice of the GATT in the Field of Dispute Settlement (Article XXIII:2)

1. Any dispute which hs not been settled bilaterally under the relevant provisions
of the General Agreement may be referred to the CONTRACTING PARTIES[1] which
are obliged, pursuant to Article XXIII:2, to investigate matters submitted to them
and make appropriate recommendations or give a ruling on the matter as appropriate.
Article XXIII:2 does not indicate whether disputes should be handled by a working
party or by a panel.[2]

2. The CONTRACTING PARTIES adopted in 1966 a decision establishing the procedure
to be followed for Article XXIII consultations between developed and less-developed
contracting parties (BISD, 14th Supplement, page 18). This procedure provides,
inter alia, for the Director-General to employ his good offices with a view to
facilitating a solution, for setting up a panel with the task of examining the problem in order to recommend appropriate solutions, and for time-limits for the execution of the different parts of this procedure.

3. The function of a panel has normally been to review the facts of a case and the
applicability of GATT provisions and to arrive at an objective assessment of these
matters. In this connexion, panels have consulted regularly with the parties to the
dispute and have given them adequate opportunity to develop a mutually satisfactory solution. Panels have taken appropriate account of the particular interests of
developing countries. In cases of failure of the parties to reach a mutually satisfac-

---

[1] The Council is empowered to act for the CONTRACTING PARTIES, in accordance with normal GATT practice.

[2] At the Review Session (1955) the proposal to institutionalize the procedures of panels
was not adopted by CONTRACTING PARTIES mainly because they preferred to preserve the
existing situation and not to establish judicial procedures which might put excessive strain
on the GATT.

tory settlement, panels have normally given assistance to the CONTRACTING PARTIES in making recommendations or in giving rulings as envisaged in Article XXIII:2.

4. Before bringing a case, contracting parties have exercised their judgment as to whether action under Article XXIII:2 would be fruitful. Those cases which have come before the CONTRACTING PARTIES under this provision have, with few exceptions, been brought to a satisfactory conclusion. The aim of the CONTRACTING PARTIES has always been to secure a positive solution to a dispute. A solution mutually acceptable to the parties to a dispute is clearly to be preferred. In the absence of a mutually agreed solution, the first objective of the CONTRACTING PARTIES is usually to secure the withdrawal of the measures concerned if these are found to be inconsistent with the General Agreement. The provision of compensation should be resorted to only if the immediate withdrawal of the measure is impracticable and as a temporary measure pending the withdrawal of the measures which are inconsistent with the General Agreement. The last resort which Article XXIII provides to the country invoking this procedure is the possibility of suspending the application of concessions or other obligations on a discriminatory basis vis-a-vis the other contracting party, subject to authorization by the CONTRACTING PARTIES of such measures. Such action has only rarely been contemplated and cases taken under Article XXIII:2 have led to such action in only one case.

5. In practice, contracting parties have had recourse to Article XXIII only when in their view a benefit accruing to them under the General Agreement was being nullified or impaired. In cases where there is an infringement of the obligations assumed under the General Agreement, the action is considered *prima facie* to constitute a case of nullification or impairment. A *prima facie* case of nullification or impairment would *ipso facto* require consideration of whether the circumstances are serious enough to justify the authorization of suspension of concessions or obligations, if the contracting party bringing the complaint so requests. This means that there is normally a presumption that a breach of the rules has an adverse impact on other contracting parties, and in such cases, it is up to the contracting parties against whom the complaint has been brought to rebut the charge. Paragraph 1(b) permits recourse to Article XXIII if nullification or impairment results from measures taken by other contracting parties whether or not these conflict with the provisions of the General Agreement, and paragraph 1(c) if any other situation exists. If a contracting party bringing an Article XXIII case claims that measures which do not conflict with the provisions of the General Agreement have nullified or impaired benefits accruing to it under the General Agreement, it would be called upon to provide a detailed justification.

6. Concerning the customary elements of the procedures regarding working parties and panels, the following elements have to be noted:

(i) working parties are instituted by the Council upon the request of one or several contracting parties. The terms of reference of working parties are generally ''to examine the matter in the light of the relevant provisions of the General Agreement and to report to the Council''. Working parties set up their own working procedures. The practice for working parties has been to hold one or two meetings to examine the matter and a final meeting to discuss conclusions. Working parties are open to participation of any contracting party which has an interest in the matter. Generally working parties consist of a number of delegations varying from about five to twenty according to the importance of the question and the interests involved. The countries who are parties to the dispute are always members of the Working Party and have the same status as other delegations. The report of the Working Party represents the views of all of its members and therefore records different views if necessary. Since the tendency is to strive for consensus, there is generally some measure of negotiation and compromise in the formulation of the Working Party's report. The Council adopts the report. The reports of working parties are advisory opinions on the basis of which the CONTRACTING PARTIES may take a final decision.

(ii) In the case of disputes, the CONTRACTING PARTIES have established panels (which have been called by different names) or working parties in order to assist them in examining questions raised under Article XXIII:2. Since 1952, panels have become the usual procedure. However, the Council has taken such decisions only after the party concerned has had an occasion to study the complaint and prepare its response before the Council. The terms of reference are discussed and approved by the Council. Normally, these terms of reference are ''to examine the matter and to make such findings as will assist the CONTRACTING PARTIES in making the recommendations or rulings provided for in paragraph 2 of Article XXIII''. When a contracting party having recourse to Article XXIII:2 raised questions relating to the suspension of concessions or other obligations, the terms of reference were to examine the matter in accordance with the provisions of Article XXIII:2. Members of the panel are usually selected from permanent delegations or, less frequently, from the national administrations in the capitals amongst delegates who participate in GATT activities on a regular basis. The practice has been to appoint a member or members from developing countries when a dispute is between a developing and a developed country.

(iii) Members of the panels are expected to act impartially without instructions from their governments. In a few cases, in view of the nature and complexity of the matter, the parties concerned have agreed to designate non-government experts. Nominations are proposed to the parties concerned by the GATT secretariat. The composition of panels (three or five members depending on the case) has been agreed upon by the parties concerned and approved by the GATT Council. It is recognized that a broad spectrum of opinion has been beneficial in difficult cases, but that the number of panel members has sometimes delayed the composition of panels, and therefore the process of dispute settlement.

(iv) Panels set up their own working procedures. The practice for the panels has been to hold two or three formal meetings with the parties concerned. The panel invited the parties to present their views either in writing and/or orally in the presence of each other. The panel can question both parties on any matter which it considers relevant to a dispute. Panels have also heard the views of any contracting party having a substantial interest in the matter, which is not directly party to the dispute, but which has expressed in the Council a desire to present its views. Written memoranda submitted to the panel have been considered confidential, but are made available to the parties to the dispute. Panels often consult with and seek information from any relevant source they deem appropriate and they sometimes consult experts to obtain their technical opinion on certain aspects of the matter. Panels may seek advice or assistance from the secretariat in its capacity as guardian of the General Agreement, especially on historical or procedural aspects. The secretariat provides the secretary and technical services for panels.

(v) Where the parties have failed to develop a mutually satisfactory solution, the panel has submitted its findings in a written form. Panel reports have normally set out findings of fact, the applicability of relevant provisions, and the basic rationale behind any findings and recommendations that it has made. Where a bilateral settlement of the matter has been found, the report of the panel has been confined to a brief description of the case and to reporting that a solution has been reached.

(vi) The reports of panels have been drafted in the absence of the parties in the light of the information and the statements made.

(vii) To encourage development of mutually satisfactory solutions between the parties and with a view to obtaining their comments, each panel has normally first submitted the descriptive part of its report to the parties concerned, and also their conclusions, or an outline thereof, a reasonable period of time before they have been circulated to the Contracting Parties.

(viii) In accordance with their terms of reference established by the CONTRACTING PARTIES panels have expressed their views on whether an infringement of certain rules of the General Agreement arises out of the measure examined. Panels have also, if so requested by the CONTRACTING PARTIES, formulated draft recommendations addressed to the parties. In yet other cases panels were invited to give a technical opinion on some precise aspect of the matter (e.g. on the modalities of a withdrawal or suspension in regard to the volume of trade involved). The opinions expressed by the panel members on the matter are anonymous and the panel deliberations are secret.

(ix) Although the CONTRACTING PARTIES have never established precise deadlines for the different phases of the procedure, probably because the matters submitted to panels differ as to their complexity and their urgency, in most cases the proceedings of the panels have been completed within a reasonable period of time, extending from three to nine months.

The 1966 decision by the CONTRACTING PARTIES referred to in paragraph 2 above lays down in its paragraph 7 that the Panel shall report within a period of sixty days from the date the matter was referred to it.

5. Agreement on Technical Barriers to Trade (Standards) (excerpts)

* * * * *

1. *General provisions*

1.1 General terms for standardization and certification shall normally have the meaning given to them by definitions adopted within the United Nations System and by international standards organizations taking into account their context and in light of the object and purpose of this Agreement.

1.2 However, for the purposes of this Agreement the meaning of the terms given in Annex 1 applies.

1.3 All products, including industrial [and agricultural] products, shall be subject to the provisions of this Agreement.

1.4 Purchasing specifications prepared by governmental bodies for production or consumption requirements of governmental bodies are not subject to the provisions of this Agreement but are addressed in the Agreement on Government Procurement, according to its coverage.

1.5 Adherents shall not take measures which have the effect of directly or indirectly, requiring or encouraging bodies other than central government bodies, to act in a manner inconsistent with provisions of this Code which apply to their central government bodies.

1.6 All references in the Code to technical regulations, standards, methods for assuring conformity with technical regulations or standards and certification systems shall be construed to include any amendments thereto and any additions to the rules or the product coverage thereof, except amendments and additions of an insignificant nature.

Technical regulations and standards

2. *Preparation, adoption and application of technical regulations and standards by central government bodies*

With respect to their central government bodies:

2.1 Parties shall ensure that technical regulations and standards are not prepared, adopted or applied with a view to creating obstacles to international trade. Furthermore, products imported from the territory of any Party shall be accorded treatment no less favourable than that accorded to like products of national origin and to like products originating in any other country in relation to such technical regulations or standards. They shall likewise ensure that neither technical regulations nor standards themselves nor their application have the effect of creating unnecessary obstacles to international trade.

* * * * *

Certification systems

7. *Certification systems operated by central government bodies*

With respect to their central government bodies:

7.1 Parties shall ensure that certification systems are not formulated or applied with a view to creating obstacles to international trade. They shall likewise ensure that neither such certification systems themselves nor their application have the effect of creating unnecessary obstacles to international trade.

7.2 Parties shall ensure that certification systems are formulated and applied so as to grant access for suppliers of like products originating in the territories of other Parties under conditions no less favourable than those accorded to suppliers of like products of national origin or originating in any other country, including the determination that such suppliers are able and willing to fulfil the requirements of the system. Access for suppliers is obtaining certification from the importing adherent under the rules of the system. Access for suppliers also includes receiving the mark of the system, if any, under conditions no less favourable than those to suppliers of like products of national origin or originating in any other country.

* * * * *

Institutions, consultation and dispute settlement

13. *The Committee on Technical Barriers to Trade*

There shall be established under this Agreement:

13.1 A Committee on Technical Barriers to Trade composed of representatives from each of the Parties to this Agreement (hereafter referred to as "the Committee"). The Committee shall elect its own Chairman and shall meet as necessary but no less than once a year for the purpose of affording Parties to this Agreement the opportunity of consulting on any matters relating to the operation of this Agreement or the furtherance of its objectives and shall carry out responsibilities as assigned to it under this Agreement or by the Parties.

13.2 Working parties, panels or other bodies as may be appropriate, which shall carry out such responsibilities as may be assigned to them by the Committee in accordance with the relevant provisions of this Agreement.

14. *Consultation and dispute settlement*

Consultation

14.1 Each Party shall afford sympathetic considerations to and adequate opportunity for prompt consultation regarding representations made by other Parties with respect to any matter affecting the operation of this Agreement.

14.2 If any Party considers that any benefit accruing to it, directly or indirectly, under this Agreement is being nullified or impaired, or that the attainment of any objective of this Agreement is being impeded, by another Party or Parties, the Party may make written representations or proposals to the other Parties which it considers to be concerned. Any Party or Parties shall give sympathetic consideration to the representations or proposals made to it, with a view to reaching a satisfactory resolution of the matter.

Resolution of disputes

14.3 It is the first intention of Parties that all disputes under this Agreement shall be promptly and expeditiously resolved, particularly in the case of perishable products.

14.4 If no solution has been reached after consultations under Article 14.1 and 14.2, the Committee shall meet at the request of any Party to the dispute within thirty days of receipt of such a request, to investigate the matter with a view to facilitating a mutually satisfactory solution.

14.5 In investigating the matter and in selecting subject, *inter alia,* to the provisions of Articles 14.9 and 14.4, the appropriate procedures the Committee shall take into account whether the issues in dispute relate to commercial policy considerations and/or to questions of a technical nature requiring detailed consideration by experts.

14.6 In the case of perishable products the Committee shall, in keeping with Article 14.3, consider the matter in the most expeditious manner possible with a view to facilitating a mutually satisfactory solution within three months of the request for the Committee investigation.

14.7 It is understood that where disputes arise affecting products with a definite crop cycle of twelve months, every effort would be made by the Committee to deal with these disputes within a period of twelve months.

14.8 During any phase of a dispute settlement procedure including the earliest phase, competent bodies and experts in matters under consideration may be consulted and invited to attend the meetings of the Committee; appropriate information and assistance may be requested from such bodies and experts.

Technical issues

14.9 If no mutually satisfactory solution has been reached under the procedures of Article 14.4 within three months of the request for the Committee investigation, upon the request of any Party to the dispute who considers the issues to relate to questions of a technical nature the Committee shall establish a technical expert group and direct it to:

examine the matter;

consult with the parties to the dispute and give full opportunity for them to develop a mutually satisfactory solution;

make statement concerning the facts of the matter; and

make such findings as will assist the Committee in making recommendations or giving rulings on the matter, including *inter alia,* and if appropriate, findings concerning the detailed scientific judgments involved, whether the measure was necessary for the protection of human, animal or plant life or health, and whether a legitimate scientific judgment is involved.

14.10 Technical expert groups shall be governed by the procedures of Annex 2.

14.11 The time required by the technical expert group considering questions of a technical nature will vary with the particular case. The technical expert group should aim to deliver its findings to the Committee within six months from the date the technical issue was referred to it, unless extended by mutual agreement between the parties to the dispute.

14.12 Reports should set out the rationale behind any findings that they make.

14.13 If no mutually satisfactory solution has been reached after completion of the procedures in this Article, and any Party to the dispute requests a panel, the Committee shall establish a panel which shall operate under the provisions of Article 14.15 to 14.18 below.

Panel proceedings

14.14 If no mutually satisfactory solution has been reached under the procedures of Article 14.4 within three months of the request for the Committee investigation and the procedures of Article 14.9 to 14.13 have not been invoked, the Committee shall, upon request of any Party to the dispute, establish a panel.

14.15 When a panel is established, the Committee shall direct it to:

examine the matter;

consult with parties to the dispute and give full opportunity for them to develop a mutually satisfactory solution;

make a statement concerning the facts of the matter as they relate to the application of provisions of this Code and make such findings as will assist the Committee in making recommendations or giving rulings on the matter.

14.16 Panels shall be governed by the procedures in Annex 3.

14.17 Panels shall use the report of any expert group established under Article 14.9 as the basis for its consideration of issues that involve questions of a technical nature.

14.18 The time required by panels will vary with the particular case. They should aim to deliver their findings, and where appropriate, recommendations, to the Committee without undue delay, normally within a period of four months from the date that the panel was established.

Enforcement

14.19 After the investigation is complete or after the report of a technical expert group, working group, panel, or other body is presented to the Committee, the Committee shall give the matter prompt consideration. With respect to panel reports, the Committee shall take appropriate action normally within thirty days of receipt of the report, unless extended by the Committee including:

a statement concerning the facts of the matter, or

recommendations to one or more Parties to the Agreement; or

any other ruling which it deems appropriate.

14.20 If a Party to which recommendations are addressed considers itself unable to implement them, it should promptly furnish reasons in writing to the Committee. In that event, the Committee shall consider what further action may be appropriate.

14.21 If the Committee considers that the circumstances are serious enough to justify such action, it may authorize one or more Parties to this Agreement to suspend, in respect of any other Party, the application of such obligations under this Agreement as it determines to be appropriate in the circumstances. In this respect, the Committee may, *inter alia,* authorize the suspension of the application of obligations, including those in Articles 5 to 9, in order to restore mutual economic advantage and balance of rights and obligations.

14.22 The Committee shall keep under surveillance any matter on which it has made recommendations or given rulings.

Other provisions relating to dispute settlement

Procedures

14.23 If disputes arise between Parties relating to rights and obligations of this Agreement, Parties should complete the dispute settlement procedures under this Agreement before availing themselves of any rights which they have under the GATT. Parties recognize that, in any case so referred to the CONTRACTING PARTIES, any finding, recommendation or ruling pursuant to Article 14.9 to 14.18 may be taken into account by the CONTRACTING PARTIES, to the extent they relate to matters involving equivalent rights and obligations under the General Agreement. When Parties resort to GATT Article XXIII a determination under that Article shall be based on GATT provisions only.

Levels of obligation

14.24 The dispute settlement provisions set out above can be invoked in cases where a Party considers that another Party has not achieved satisfactory results under Articles 3, 4, 6, 8 and 9 and its trade interests are significantly affected. In this respect, such results shall be equivalent to those envisaged in Articles 2, 5 and 7 as if the body in question were a Party.

Processes and production methods

14.25 The dispute settlement procedures set out above can be invoked in cases where a Party considers that obligations under this Agreement are being circumvented by the drafting of requirements in terms of processes and production methods rather than in terms of characteristics of products.

Retroactivity

14.26 To the extent that a Party considers that technical regulations, standards, methods for assuring conformity with technical regulations or standards, or certification systems which exist at the time of entry into force of this Agreement are not consistent with the provisions of this Agreement, such regulations, standards, methods and systems shall be subject to the enforcement provisions in Articles 13 and 14 of this Agreement in so far as they are applicable.

*   *   *   *   *

Annex 3

Panels

The following procedures shall apply to panels established in accordance with the provisions of Article 14.

1. In order to facilitate the constitution of panels, the Chairman of the Committee shall maintain an informal indicative list of government officials knowledgeable in the area of technical barriers to trade and experienced in the field of trade relations and economic development. This list may also include persons other than government officials. In this connexion, each adherent shall be invited to indicate at the beginning of every year to the Chairman of the Committee the name(s) of the one or two governmental experts whom the Parties to this Agreement would be willing to make available for such work. When a panel is established under Article 14.13, the Chairman, within seven days shall propose the composition of the panel consisting of three or five members, preferably government officials. The parties directly concerned shall react within seven working days to nominations of panel

members by the Chairman and shall not oppose nominations except for compelling reasons. Citizens of countries whose central governments are parties to a dispute shall not be eligible for membership of the panel concerned with that dispute. Panel members shall serve in their individual capacities and not as government representatives, nor as representatives of any organization. Governments or organizations shall therefore not give them instructions with regard to matters before a panel.

2. Each panel shall develop its own working procedures. All Parties having a substantial interest in the matter and having notified this to the Committee, shall have an opportunity to be heard. Each panel may consult and seek information and technical advice from any source it deems appropriate. Before a panel seeks such information or technical advice from a source within the jurisdiction of a Party, it shall inform the government of that Party. In case such consultation with competent bodies and experts is necessary it should be at the earliest possible stage of the dispute settlement procedure. Any Party shall respond promptly and fully to any request by a panel for such information as the panel considers necessary and appropriate. Confidential information provided to the panel shall not be revealed without formal authorization from the government or person providing the information. Where such information is requested from the panel but release of such information by the panel is not authorized, a non-confidential summary of the information, will be provided by the government or person supplying the information.

3. Where the parties to a dispute have failed to come to a satisfactory solution, the panel shall submit its findings in a written form. Panel reports should normally set out the rationale behind any findings and recommendations that it makes. Where a bilateral settlement of the matter has been found, the report of the panel may be confined to a brief description of the case and to reporting that a solution has been reached.

4. To encourage development of mutually satisfactory solutions between the parties and with a view to obtaining their comments, each panel should first submit the descriptive part of its report to the parties concerned, and should subsequently submit to the parties to the dispute its conclusions, or an outline thereof, a reasonable period of time before they are circulated to the Parties.

6. Revised Anti-Dumping Code

Agreement on Implementation of Article VI
of the General Agreement on Tariffs and Trade*

The Parties to this Agreement (hereinafter referred to as "Parties"),

Recognizing that anti-dumping practices should not constitute an unjustifiable impediment to international trade and that anti-dumping duties may be applied against dumping only if such dumping causes or threatens material injury to an established industry or materially retards the establishment of an industry;

Considering that it is desirable to provide for equitable and open procedures as the basis for a full examination of dumping cases;

Taking into account the particular trade, development and financial needs of developing countries;

Desiring to interpret the provisions of Article VI of the General Agreement on Tariffs and Trade (hereinafter referred to as "General Agreement" or "GATT") and to elaborate rules for their application in order to provide greater uniformity and certainty in their implementation; and

Desiring to provide for the speedy, effective and equitable settlement of disputes arising under this Agreement;

Hereby agree as follows:

Part I - Anti-Dumping Code

Article 1

Principles

The imposition of an anti-dumping duty is a measure to be taken only under the circumstances provided for in Article VI of the General Agreement and pursuant to investigations initiated[1] and conducted in accordance with the provisions of this Code. The following provisions govern the application of Article VI of the General Agreement in so far as action is taken under anti-dumping legislation or regulations.

Article 2.

Determination of Dumping

1. For the purpose of this Code a product is to be considered as being dumped,

---

* TIAS 1700; 61 Stat., pts. 5 and 6. [Footnote added by the Department of State.]

[1] The term "initiated" as used hereinafter means the procedural action by which a Party formally commences an investigation as provided in paragraph 6 of Article 6.

i.e. introduced into the commerce of another country at less than its normal value, if the export price of the product exported from one country to another, is less than the comparable price, in the ordinary course of trade, for the like product when destined for consumption in the exporting country.

2. Throughout this Code the term "like product" ("produit similaire") shall be interpreted to mean a product which is identical, i.e. alike in all respects to the product under consideration, or in the absence of such a product, another product which, although not alike in all respects, has characteristics closely resembling those of the product under consideration.

3. In the case where products are not imported directly from the country of origin but are exported to the country of importation from an intermediate country, the price at which the products are sold from the country of export to the country of importation shall normally be compared with the comparable price in the country of export. However, comparison may be made with the price in the country of origin, if, for example, the products are merely transshipped through the country of export, or such products are not produced in the country of export, or there is no comparable price for them in the country of export.

4. When there are no sales of the like product in the ordinary course of trade in the domestic market of the exporting country or when, because of the particular market situation, such sales do not permit a proper comparison, the margin of dumping shall be determined by comparison with a comparable price of the like product when exported to any third country which may be the highest such export price but should be a representative price, or with the cost of production in the country of origin plus a reasonable amount for administrative, selling and any other costs and for profits. As a general rule, the addition for profit shall not exceed the profit normally realized on sales of products of the same general category in the domestic market of the country of origin.

5. In cases where there is no export price or where it appears to the authorities[2] concerned that the export price is unreliable because of association or a compensatory arrangement between the exporter and the importer or a third party, the export price may be constructed on the basis of the price at which the imported products are first resold to an independent buyer, or if the products are not resold to an independent buyer, or not resold in the condition as imported, on such reasonable basis as the authorities may determine.

6. In order to effect a fair comparison between the export price and the domestic price in the exporting country (or the country of origin) or, if applicable, the price established pursuant to the provisions of Article VI:1(b) of the General Agreement, the two prices shall be compared at the same level of trade, normally at the ex-factory

---

[2] When in this Code the term "authorities" is used, it shall be interpreted as meaning authorities at an appropriate, senior level.

level, and in respect of sales made at as nearly as possible the same time. Due allowance shall be made in each case, on its merits, for the differences in conditions and terms of sale, for the differences in taxation, and for the other differences affecting price comparability. In the cases referred to in paragraph 5 of Article 2 allowance for costs, including duties and taxes, incurred between importation and resale, and for profits accruing, should also be made.

7. This Article is without prejudice to the second Supplementary Provision to paragraph 1 of Article VI in Annex I of the General Agreement.

Article 3

Determination of Injury[3]

1. A determination of injury for purposes of Article VI of the General Agreement shall be based on positive evidence and involve an objective examination of both (a) the volume of the dumped imports and their effect on prices in the domestic market for like products, and (b) the consequent impact of these imports on domestic producers of such products.

2. With regard to volume of the dumped imports the investigating authorities shall consider whether there has been a significant increase in dumped imports, either in absolute terms or relative to production or consumption in the importing country. With regard to the effect of the dumped imports on prices, the investigating authorities shall consider whether there has been a significant price undercutting by the dumped imports as compared with the price of a like product of the importing country, or whether the effect of such imports is otherwise to depress prices to a significant degree or prevent price increases, which otherwise would have occurred, to a significant degree. No one or several of these factors can necessarily give decisive guidance.

3. The examination of the impact on the industry concerned shall include an evaluation of all relevant economic factors and indices having a bearing on the state of the industry such as actual and potential decline in output, sales, market share, profits, productivity, return on investments, or utilization of capacity; factors affecting domestic prices; actual and potential negative effects on cash flow, inventories, employment, wages, growth, ability to raise capital or investments. This list is not exhaustive, nor can one or several of these factors necessarily give decisive guidance.

4. It must be demonstrated that the dumped imports are, through the effects[4] of dumping, causing injury within the meaning of this Code. There may be other

---

[3] Under this Code the term "injury" shall, unless otherwise specified, be taken to mean material injury to a domestic industry, threat of material injury to a domestic industry or material retardation of the establishment of such an industry and shall be interpreted in accordance with the provisions of this Article.

[4] As set forth in paragraphs 2 and 3 of this Article.

factors[5] which at the same time are injuring the industry, and the injuries caused by other factors must not be attributed to the dumped imports.

5. The effect of the dumped imports shall be assessed in relation to the domestic production of the like product when available data permit the separate identification of production in terms of such criteria as: the production process, the producers' realizations, profits. When the domestic production of the like product has no separate identity in these terms the effects of the dumped imports shall be assessed by the examination of the production of the narrowest group or range or products, which includes the like product, for which the necessary information can be provided.

6. A determination of threat or injury shall be based on facts and not merely on allegation, conjecture or remote possibility. The change in circumstances which would create a situation in which the dumping would cause injury must be clearly foreseen and imminent.[6]

7. With respect to cases where injury is threatened by dumped imports, the application of anti-dumping measures shall be studied and decided with special care.

Article 4

Determination of Industry

1. In determining injury the term "domestic industry" shall be interpreted as referring to the domestic producers as a whole of the like products or to those of them whose collective output of the products constitutes a major proportion of the total domestic production of those products, except that

(i) when producers are related[7] to the exporters or importers or are themselves importers of the allegedly dumped product, the industry may be interpreted as referring to the rest of the producers;

(ii) in exceptional circumstances the territory of a Party may, for the production in question, be divided into two or more competitive markets and the producers within each market may be regarded as a separate industry if (a) the producers within such market sell all or almost all of their production of the product in question in that market, and (b) the demand in that market is not to any substantial degree supplied by producers of the product in question located elsewhere in the

---

[5] Such factors include, *inter alia*, the volume and prices of imports not sold at dumping prices, contradiction in demand or changes in the patterns of consumption, trade restrictive practices of and competition between the foreign and domestic producers, developments in technology and the export performance and productivity of the domestic industry.

[6] One example, though not an exclusive one, is that there is convincing reason to believe that there will be, in the immediate future, substantially increased importations of the product at dumped prices.

[7] An understanding among Parties should be developed defining the word "related" as used in this Code.

territory. In such circumstances, injury may be found to exist even where a major portion of the total domestic industry is not injured provided there is a concentration of dumped imports into such an isolated market and provided further that the dumped imports are causing injury to the producers of all or almost all of the production within such market.

2. When the industry has been interpreted as referring to the producers in a certain area, i.e. a market as defined in paragraph 1(ii), anti-dumping duties shall be levied[8] only on the products in question consigned for final consumption to that area. When the constitutional law of the importing country does not permit the levying of anti-dumping duties on such a basis, the importing Party may levy the anti-dumping duties without limitation only if (1) the exporters shall have been given an opportunity to cease exporting at dumped prices to the area concerned or otherwise give assurances pursuant to Article 7 of this Code, and adequate assurances in this regard have not been promptly given, and (2) such duties cannot be levied on specific producers which supply the area in question.

3. Where two or more countries have reached under the provisions of Article XXIV:8(a) of the General Agreement such a level of integration that they have the characteristics of a single, unified market, the industry in the entire area of integration shall be taken to be the industry referred to in paragraph 1 above.

4. The provisions of paragraph 5 of Article 3 shall be applicable to this Article.

Article 5

Initiation and Subsequent Investigation

1. An investigation to determine the existence, degree and effect of any alleged dumping shall normally be initiated upon a written request by or on behalf of the industry[9] affected. The request shall include sufficient evidence of the existence of (a) dumping; (b) injury within the meaning of Article VI of the General Agreement as interpreted by this Code and (c) a causal link between the dumped imports and the alleged injury. If in special circumstances the authorities concerned decide to initiate an investigation without having received such a request, they shall proceed only if they have sufficient evidence on all points under (a) to (c) above.

2. Upon initiation of an investigation and thereafter, the evidence of both dumping and injury caused thereby should be considered simultaneously. In any event the evidence of both dumping and injury shall be considered simultaneously (a) in the decision whether or not to initiate an investigation, and (b) thereafter, during the course of the investigation, starting on a date not later than the earliest date on which in accordance with the provisions of this Code provisional measures may be applied, except in the cases provided for in paragraph 3 of Article 10 in which the authorities accept the request of the exporters.

---

[8] As used in this Code "levy" shall mean the definitive or final legal assessment or collection of a duty or tax.

[9] As defined in Article 4.

3. An application shall be rejected and an investigation shall be terminated promptly as soon as the authorities concerned are satisfied that there is not sufficient evidence of either dumping or of injury to justify proceeding with the case. There should be immediate termination in cases where the margin of dumping or the volume of dumped imports, actual or potential, or the injury is negligible.

4. An anti-dumping proceeding shall not hinder the procedures of customs clearance.

5. Investigations shall, except in special circumstances, be concluded within one year after their initiation.

Article 6

Evidence

1. The foreign suppliers and all other interested parties shall be given ample opportunity to present in writing all evidence that they consider useful in respect to the anti-dumping investigation in question. They shall also have the right, on justification, to present evidence orally.

2. The authorities concerned shall provide opportunities for the complainant and the importers and exporters known to be concerned and the governments of the exporting countries, to see all information that is relevant to the presentation of their cases, that is not confidential as defined in paragraph 3 below, and that is used by the authorities in an anti-dumping investigation, and to prepare presentations on the basis of this information.

3. Any information which is by nature confidential (for example, because its disclosure would be of significant competitive advantage to a competitor or because its disclosure would have a significantly adverse effect upon a person supplying the information or upon a person from whom he acquired the information) or which is provided on a confidential basis by parties to an anti-dumping investigation shall, upon cause shown, be treated as such by the investigating authorities. Such information shall not be disclosed without specific permission of the party submitting it.[10] Parties providing confidential information may be requested to furnish non-confidential summaries thereof. In the event that such parties indicate that such information is not susceptible of summary, a statement of the reasons why summarization is not possible must be provided.

4. However, if the authorities concerned find that a request for confidentiality is not warranted and if the supplier is either unwilling to make the information public or to authorize its disclosure in generalized or summary form, the authorities would be free to disregard such information unless it can be demonstrated to their satisfac-

---

[10] Parties are aware that in the territory of certain Parties disclosure pursuant to a narrowly drawn protective order may be required.

tion from appropriate sources that the information is correct.[11]

5. In order to verify information provided or to obtain further details the authorities may carry out investigations in other countries as required, provided they obtain the agreement of the firms concerned and provided they notify the representatives of the government of the country in question and unless the latter object to the investigation.

6. When the competent authorities are satisfied that there is sufficient evidence to justify initiating an anti-dumping investigation pursuant to Article 5, the Party or Parties the products of which are subject to such investigation and the exporters and importers known to the investigating authorities to have an interest therein and the complainants shall be notified and a public notice shall be given.

7. Throughout the anti-dumping investigation all parties shall have a full opportunity for the defence of their interests. To this end, the authorities concerned shall, on request, provide opportunities for all directly interest parties to meet those parties with adverse interests, so that opposing views may be presented and rebuttal arguments offered. Provision of such opportunities must take account of the need to preserve confidentiality and of the convenience to the parties. There shall be no obligation on any party to attend a meeting and failure to do so shall not be prejudicial to that party's case.

8. In cases in which any interestesd party refuses access to, or otherwise does not provide, necessary information within a reasonable period or significantly impedes the investigation, preliminary and final findings[12], affirmative or negative, may be made on the basis of the facts available.

9. The provisions of this Article are not intended to prevent the authorities of a Party from proceeding expeditiously with regard to initiating an investigation, reaching preliminary or final findings, whether affirmative or negative, or from applying provisional or final measures, in accordance with the relevant provisions of this Code.

Article 7

Price Undertakings

1. Proceedings may[13] be suspended or terminated without the imposition of provisional measures or anti-dumping duties upon receipt of satisfactory voluntary

---

[11] Parties agree that requests for confidentiality should not be arbitrarily rejected.

[12] Because of different terms used under different systems in various countries the term "finding" is hereinafter used to mean a formal decision or determination.

[13] The word "may" shall not be interpreted to allow the simultaneous continuation of proceedings with the implementation of price undertakings except as provided in paragraph 3.

undertakings from any exporter to revise its prices or to cease exports to the area in question at dumped prices so that the authorities are satisfied that the injurious effect of the dumping is eliminated. Price increases under such undertakings shall not be higher than necessary to eliminate the margin of dumping.

2. Price undertakings shall not be sought or accepted from exporters unless the authorities of the importing country have initiated an investigation in accordance with the provisions of Article 5 of this Code. Undertakings offered need not be accepted if the authorities consider their acceptance impractical, for example, if the number of actual or potential exporters is too great, or for other reasons.

3. If the undertakings are accepted, the investigation of injury shall nevertheless be completed if the exporter so desires or the authorities so decide. In such a case, if a determination of no injury or threat thereof is made, the undertaking shall authomatically lapse except in cases where a determination of no threat of injury is due in large part to the existence of a price undertaking. In such cases the authorities concerned may require that an undertaking may be maintained for a reasonable period consistent with the provisions of this Code.

4. Price undertakings may be suggested by the authorities of the importing country, but no exporter shall be forced to enter into such an undertaking. The fact that exporters do not offer such undertakings, or do not accept an invitation to do so, shall in no way prejudice the consideration of the case. However, the authorities are free to determine that a threat of injury is more likely to be realized if the dumped imports continue.

5. Authorities of an importing country may require any exporter from whom undertakings have been accepted to provide periodically information relevant to the fulfillment of such undertakings, and to permit verification of pertinent data. In case of violation of undertakings, the authorities of the importing country may take, under this Code in conformity with its provisions, expeditious actions which may constitute immediate application of provisional measures using the best information available. In such cases definitive duties may be levied in accordance with this Code on goods entered for consumption not more than ninety days before the application of such provisional measures, except that any such retroactive assessment shall not apply to imports entered before the violation of the undertaking.

6. Undertakings shall not remain in force any longer than anti-dumping duties could remain in force under this Code. The authorities of an importing country shall review the need for the continuation of any price undertaking, where warranted, on their own initiative or if interested exporters or importers of the product in question so request and submit positive information substantiating the need for such review.

7. Whenever an anti-dumping investigation is suspended or terminated pursuant to the provisions of paragraph 1 above and whenever an undertaking is terminated, this fact shall be officially notified and must be published. Such notices shall set forth at least the basic conclusions and a summary of the reasons therefor.

Article 8

Imposition and Collection of Anti-Dumping Duties

1. The decision whether or not to impose an anti-dumping duty in cases where all requirements for the imposition have been fulfilled and the decision whether the amount of the anti-dumping duty to be imposed shall be the full margin of dumping or less, are decisions to be made by the authorities of the importing country or customs territory. It is desirable that the imposition be permissive in all countries or customs territories Parties to this Agreement, and that the duty be less than the margin, if such lesser duty would be adequate to remove the injury to the domestic industry.

2. When an anti-dumping duty is imposed in respect of any product, such anti-dumping duty shall be collected in the appropriate amounts in each case, on a non-discriminatory basis on imports of such product from all sources found to be dumped and causing injury, except as to imports from those sources, from which price under-takings under the terms of this Code have been accepted. The authorities shall name the supplier or suppliers of the product concerned. If, however, several suppliers from the same country are involved, and it is impracticable to name all these sup-pliers, the authorities may name the supplying country concerned. If several sup-pliers from more than one country are involved, the authorities may name either all the suppliers involved, or, if this, is impracticable, all the supplying countries involved.

3. The amount of the anti-dumping duty must not exceed the margin of dumping as established under Article 2. Therefore, if subsequent to the application of the anti-dumping duty it is found that the duty so collected exceeds the actual dumping margin, the amount in excess of the margin shall be reimbursed as quickly as possible.

4. Within a basic price system the following rules shall apply, provided that their application is consistent with the other provisions of this Code:

If several suppliers from one or more countries are involved, anti-dumping duties may be imposed on imports of the product in question found to have been dumped and to be causing injury from the country or countries concerned, the duty being equivalent to the amount by which the export price is less than the basic price established for this purpose, not exceeding the lowest normal price in the supplying country or countries where normal conditions of competition are prevailing. It is understood that, for products which are sold below this already established basic price, a new anti-dumping investigation shall be carried out in each particular case, when so demanded by the interested parties and the demand is supported by rele-vant evidence. In cases where no dumping is found, anti-dumping duties collected shall be reimbursed as quickly as possible. Furthermore, if it can be found that the duty so collected exceeds the actual dumping margin, the amount in excess of the margin shall be reimbursed as quickly as possible.

5. Public notice shall be given of any preliminary or final finding whether affirm-

ative or negative and of the revocation of a finding. In the case of affirmative finding each such notice shall set forth the findings and conclusions reached on all issues of fact and law considered material by the investigating authorities, and the reasons and basis therefor. In the case of a negative finding, each notice shall set forth at least the basic conclusions and a summary of the reasons therefor. All notices of findings shall be forwarded to the Party or Parties the products of which are subject to such finding and to the exporters known to have an interest therein.

Article 9

Duration of Anti-Dumping Duties

1. An anti-dumping duty shall remain in force only as long as, and to the extent necessary to counteract dumping which is causing injury.

2. The investigating authorities shall review the need for the continued imposition of the dury, where warranted, on their own initiative or if any interested party so requests and submits positive information substantiating the need for review.

Article 10

Provisional Measures

1. Provisional measures may be taken only after a preliminary affirmative finding has been made that there is dumping and that there is sufficient evidence of injury, as provided for in (a) to (c) of paragraph 1 of Article 5 Provisional measures shall not be applied unless the authorities concerned judge that they are necessary to prevent injury being caused during the period of investigation.

2. Provisional measures may take the form of a provisional duty or, preferably, a security—by cash deposit or bond—equal to the amount of the anti-dumping duty provisionally estimated, being not greater than the provisionally estimated margin of dumping. Withholding of appraisement is an appropriate provisional measure, provided that the normal duty and the estimated amount of the anti-dumping duty be indicated and as long as the withholding of appraisement is subject to the same conditions as other provisional measures.

3. The imposition of provisional measures shall be limited to as short a period as possible, not exceeding four months or, on decision of the authorities concerned, upon request by exporters representing a significant percentage of the trade involved to a period not exceeding six months.

4. The relevant provisions of Article 8 shall be followed in the application of provisional measures.

Article 11

Retroactivity

1. Anti-dumping duties and provisional measures shall only be applied to

products which enter for consumption after the time when the decision taken under paragraph 1 of Article 8 and paragraph 1 of Article 10, respectively, enters into force, except that in cases:

(i) Where a final finding of injury (but not of a threat thereof or of a material retardation of the establishment of an industry) is made or, in the case of a final finding of threat of injury, where the effect of the dumped imports would, in the absence of the provisional measures, have led to a finding of injury, anti-dumping duties may be levied retroactively for the period for which provisional measures, if any, have been applied.

If the anti-dumping duty fixed in the final decision is higher than the provisionally paid duty, the difference shall not be collected. If the duty fixed in the final decision is lower than the provisionally paid duty or the amount estimated for the purpose of the security, the difference shall be reimbursed or the duty recalculated, as the case may be.

(ii) Where for the dumped product in question the authorities determine

(a) either that there is a history of dumping which caused injury or that the importer was, or should have been, aware that the exporter practices dumping and that such dumping would cause injury, and

(b) that the injury is caused by sporadic dumping (massive dumped imports of a product in a relatively short period) to such an extent that, in order to preclude it recurring, it appears necessary to levy an anti-dumping duty retroactively on those imports,

the duty may be levied on products which were entered for consumption not more than 90 days prior to the date of application of provisional measures.

2. Except as provided in paragraph 1 above where a finding of threat of injury or material retardation is made (but no injury has yet occurred) a definitive anti-dumping duty may be imposed only from the date of the finding of threat of injury or material retardation and any cash deposit made during the period of the application of provisional measures shall be refunded and any bonds released in an expeditious manner.

3. Where a final finding is negative any cash deposit made during the period of the application of provisional measures shall be refunded and any bonds released in an expeditious manner.

Article 12

Anti-Dumping Action on behalf of a Third Country

1. An application for anti-dumping action on behalf of a third country shall be made by the authorities of the third country requesting action.

2. Such an application shall be supported by price information to show that the

imports are being dumped and by detailed information to show that the alleged dumping is causing injury to the domestic industry concerned in the third country. The government of the third country shall afford all assistance to the authorities of the importing country to obtain any further information which the latter may require.

3. The authorities of the importing country in considering such an application shall consider the effects of the alleged dumping on the industry concerned as a whole in the third country; that is to say the injury shall not be assessed in relation only to the effect of the alleged dumping on the industry's exports to the importing country or even on the industry's total exports.

4. The decision whether or not to proceed with a case shall rest with the importing country. If the importing country decides that it is prepared to take action, the initiation of the approach to the CONTRACTING PARTIES seeking their approval for such action shall rest with the importing country.

Article 13

Developing Countries

It is recognized that special regard must be given by developed countries to the special situation of developing countries when considering the application of anti-dumping measures under this Code. Possibilities of constructive remedies provided for by this Code shall be explored before applying anti-dumping duties where they would affect the essential interests of developing countries.

PART II

Article 14

Committee on Anti-Dumping Practices

1. There shall be established under this Agreement a Committee on Anti-Dumping Practices (hereinafter referred to as the "Committee") composed of representatives from each of the Parties. The Committee shall elect its own Chairman and shall meet not less than twice a year and otherwise as envisaged by relevant provisions of this Agreement at the request of any Party. The Committee shall carry out responsibilities as assigned to it under this Agreement or by the Parties and it shall afford Parties the opportunity of consulting on any matters relating to the operation of the Agreement or the furtherance of its objectives. The GATT secretariat shall act as the secretariat to the Committee.

2. The Committee may set up subsidiary bodies as appropriate.

3. In carrying out their functions, the Committee and any subsidiary bodies may consult with and seek information from any source they deem appropriate. However, before the Committee or a subsidiary body seeks such information from a source within the jurisdiction of a Party, it shall inform the Party involved. It shall obtain the consent of the Party and any firm to be consulted.

4. Parties shall report without delay to the Committee all preliminary or final anti-dumping actions taken. Such reports will be available in the GATT secretariat for inspection by government representatives. The Parties shall also submit, on a semi-annual basis, reports of any anti-dumping actions taken within the preceding six months.

Article 15[14]

Consultation, Conciliation and Dispute Settlement

1. Each Party shall afford sympathetic consideration to, and shall afford adequate opportunity for consultation regarding, representations made by another Party with respect to any matter affecting the operation of this Agreement.

2. If any Party considers that any benefit accruing to it, directly or indirectly, under this Agreement is being nullified or impaired, or that the achievement of any objective of the Agreement is being impeded, by another Party or Parties, it may, with a view to reaching a mutually satisfactory resolution of the matter, request in writing consultations with the Party or Parties in question. Each Party shall afford sympathetic consideration to any request from another Party for consultation. The Parties concerned shall initiate consultation promptly.

3. If any Party considers that the consultation pursuant to paragraph 2 has failed to achieve a mutually agreed solution and final action has been taken by the administering authorities of the importing country to levy definitive anti-dumping duties or to accept price undertakings, it may refer the matter to the Committee for conciliation. When a provisional measure has a significant impact and the Party considers the measure was taken contrary to the provisions of paragraph 1 of Article 10 of this Agreement, a Party may also refer such matter to the Committee for conciliation. In cases where matters are referred to the Committee for conciliation the Committee shall meet within thirty days to review the matter, and, through its good offices, shall encourage the Parties involved to develop a mutually acceptable solution.[15]

4. Parties shall make their best efforts to reach a mutually satisfactory solution throughout the period of conciliation.

5. If no mutually agreed solution has been reached after detailed examination by the Committee under paragraph 3 within three months, the Committee shall, at the request of any party to the dispute, establish a panel to examine the matter, based upon:

(a) a written statement of the Party making the request indicating how a benefit

---

[14] If disputes arise between Parties relating to rights and obligations under this Agreement, Parties should complete the dispute settlement procedures under this Agreement before availing themselves of any rights which they have under the GATT.

[15] In this connection the Committee may draw Parties' attention to those cases in which, in its view, there are no reasonable bases supporting the allegations made.

accruing to it, directly or indirectly, under this Agreement has been nullified or impaired, or that the achieving of the objectives of the Agreement is being impeded, and

(b) the facts made available in conformity with appropriate domestic procedures to the authorities of the importing country.

6. Confidential information provided to the panel shall not be revealed without formal authorization from the person or authority providing the information. Where such information is requested from the panel but release of such information by the panel is not authorized, a non-confidential summary of the information, authorized by the authority or person providing the information, will be provided.

7. Further to paragraphs 1–6 the settlement of disputes shall *mutatis mutandis* be governed by the provisions of the Understanding regarding Notification, Consultation, Dispute Settlement and Surveillance. Panel members shall have relevant experience and be selected from Parties not parties to the dispute.

PART III

Article 16

Final Provisions

1. No specific action against dumping of exports from another Party can be taken except in accordance with the provisions of the General Agreement, as interpreted by this Agreement.[16]

Acceptance and accession

2. (a) This Agreement shall be open for acceptance by signature or otherwise, by governments contracting parties to the GATT and by the European Economic Community.

(b) This Agreement shall be open for acceptance by signature or otherwise by governments having provisionally acceded to the GATT, on terms related to the effective application of rights and obligations under this Agreement, which take into account rights and obligations in the instruments providing for their provisional accession.

(c) This Agreement shall be open to accession by any other government on terms, related to the effective application of rights and obligations under this Agreement, to be agreed between that government and the Parties, by the deposit with the Director-General to the CONTRACTING PARTIES to the GATT of an instrument of accession which states the terms so agreed.

---

[16] This is not intended to preclude action under other relevant provisions of the General Agreement, as appropriate.

(d) In regard to acceptance, the provisions of Article XXVI:5(a) and (b) of the General Agreement would be applicable.

Reservations

3. Reservations may not be entered in respect of any of the provisions of this Agreement without the consent of the other Parties.

Entry into force

4. This Agreement shall enter into force on 1 January 1980 for the governments[17] which have accepted or acceded to it by that date. For each other government it shall enter into force on the thirtieth day following the date of its acceptance or accession to this Agreement.

Denunciation of the 1967 Agreement

5. Acceptance of this Agreement shall carry denunciation of the Agreement on Implementation of Article VI of the General Agreement on Tariffs and Trade, done at Geneva on 30 June 1967,* which entered into force on 1 July 1968, for Parties to the 1967 Agreement. Such denunciation shall take effect for each Party to this Agreement on the date of entry into force of this Agreement for each such Party.

National legislation

6. (a) Each government accepting or acceding to this Agreement shall take all necessary steps, of a general or particular character, to ensure, not later than the date of entry into force of this Agreement for it, the conformity of its laws, regulations and administrative procedures with the provisions of this Agreement as they may apply for the Party in question.

(b) Each Party shall inform the Committee of any changes in its laws and regulations relevant to this Agreement and in the administration of such laws and regulations.

Review

7. The Committee shall review annually the implementation and operation of this Agreement taking into account the objectives thereof. The Committee shall annually inform the CONTRACTING PARTIES to the GATT of developments during the period covered by such reviews.

Amendments

8. The Parties may amend this Agreement having regard, *inter alia*, to the experience gained in its implementation. Such an amendment, once the Parties have

---

[17] The term "government" is deemed to include the competent authorities of the European Economic Community.

* TIAS 6431; 19 UST 4348. [Footnote added by the Department of State.]

concurred in accordance with procedures established by the Committee, shall not come into force for any Party until it has been accepted by such Party.

Withdrawal

9. Any Party may withdraw from this Agreement. The withdrawal shall take effect upon the expiration of sixty days from the day on which written notice of withdrawal is received by the Director-General to the CONTRACTING PARTIES to the GATT. Any Party may upon such notification request an immediate meeting of the Committee.

Non-application of this Agreement between particular Parties

10. This Agreement shall not apply as between any two Parties if either of the Parties, at the time either accepts or accedes to this Agreement, does not consent to such application.

Secretariat

11. This Agreement shall be serviced by the GATT secretariat.

Deposit

12. This Agreement shall be deposited with the Director-General to the CONTRACTING PARTIES to the GATT, who shall promptly furnish to each Party and each contracting party to the GATT a certified copy thereof and of each amendment thereto pursuant to paragraph 8, and a notification of each acceptance thereof or accession thereto pursuant to paragraph 2, and of each withdrawal therefrom pursuant to paragraph 9 of this Article.

Registration

13. This Agreement shall be registered in accordance with the provisions of Article 102 of the Charter of the United Nations.[*]

Done at Geneva this twelfth day of April nineteen hundred and seventy-nine in a single copy, in the English, French and Spanish languages, each text being authentic.

---

[*] TS 993; 59 Stat. 1052. [Footnote added by the Department of State.]

7. Tokyo Round Agreements: Legal Status as at 5 February 1982

COUNTRIES CONTRACTING PARTIES	Geneva 1979 Protocol	Suppl 1979 Protocol	Tech Barriers	Gov't Procur	Subsid Counter-vail	Bovine Meat	Dairy	Customs Val Agreement	Customs Val Protocol	Import Lic	Civil Aircraft	Anti-Dumping
Argentina	A		S			S	S	S*	S	S		
Australia		A	A		A*	A	A			A		A
Austria	A	A	A	A	A	A	A	A	A	A	A	A
Belgium	A	A	A	A				A*	A		A	A*
Brazil	A	A	A		A	A						A
Canada	A	A	A	A	A	A		A*	A	A	A	
Chile	A	A	A		A					A		A
Czechoslovakia	A									A	A*	
Denmark	A*	A	A*									
Dominican Republic						S	S					
Egypt	A	A	S	A	S	A	A	A	A	S	S	S
EEC	A	A	A	A	A	A	A	A	A	A	A	A
Finland	A	A	A		A					A	A	A
France	A	A	A*								A	
Germany (Fed. Rep.)	A	A	A*								A*	
Greece			S								S	
Hungary	A		A*	A		A	A	A	A	A		A
Iceland	A	A										
India		A			A			A*	A*	A		A
Indonesia		A										
Ireland	A	A	A								A	
Israel	S	A	A									
Italy	A		A								S	

Country											
Ivory Coast		A									
Jamaica	A	A									A
Japan	A*	A	A	A	A	A	A	A	A	A	A
Korea		A	A	A*	A*	A*	A	A		A
Luxembourg	A	A	A	A				A	
Malaysia	A	A								A
Netherlands	A	A	A	A			A	
New Zealand	A	A*	A*	A	A	A	A	A	A
Norway	A	A	A	A	A	A	A	A	A	A	A
Pakistan	A	A	A			A	A	A
Peru	A							
Philippines		A					A*	A*
Poland	A							
Romania	A	A	A	A	A	A	A	A	A
Rwanda		S	S					
Singapore	A	A	A	A		A	
South Africa	A	A	A	A	A	A	A
Spain	A	A	A	A	A*	A*	A	A
Sweden	A	A	A	A	A	A	A	A	A	A
Switzerland	A	A	A*	A	A	A	A	A	A	A
United Kingdom	A*	A*	A*	A*	A*	A*	A*	A*	A*	A*
United States	A	A	A	A	A	A	A	A	A	A
Uruguay	A	A	A	A				
Yugoslavia	A	S	S	S	S	S	S	S	S
Zaire	A	A						
OTHER COUNTRIES									
Bulgaria				A	A			
Tunisia**		A		A	A			

** Provisional accession to GATT - * Reservation, condition and/or declaration - A : Accepted - S : Signed (acceptance pending)

Table I-I. Shares of World Trade (Exports),[a]
by Area and Country, 1973, 1977–1981

(Percent)

Area and country	1970	1973	1977	1978	1979	1980	1981
Developed countries	72	71	64	67	66	63	63
United States	14	12	11	11	11	11	11
Canada	5	4	4	4	4	3	3
Japan	6	7	7	8	6	7	8
European Community	36	37	34	35	36	33	31
France	6	6	6	6	6	6	5
F. R. Germany	11	12	11	11	11	10	9
Italy	4	4	4	4	4	4	4
United Kingdom	6	5	5	6	6	6	6
Other developed countries	11	11	8	9	9	13	10
Developing countries	17	19	26	23	25	28	27
OPEC	5	7	13	11	13	15	14
Other	12	12	13	12	12	13	14
Eastern trading area[b]	10.5	10	10	10	9	9	10

[a] Exports valued f.o.b.

[b] Albania, Bulgaria, Czechoslovakia, German Democratic Republic, Hungary, Poland, Romania, USSR, China, Mongolia, North Korea, Viet Nam.

Source: GATT, *International Trade* (Geneva, various annual issues).

Table I-2. World trade: Exports and imports, 1965, 1970, 1975, and 1979–82.
(Billions of U.S. Dollars)

Area and Country	1965	1970	1975	1979	1980	1981	1982[1]
			Exports, f.o.b.[2]				
Developed Countries[3]	130.1	226.7	585.7	1,085.7	1,283.9	1,258.9	1,199.7
United States	27.5	43.2	108.1	182.0	220.8	233.7	212.9
Canada	8.4	16.7	34.1	58.3	67.7	72.6	71.1
Japan	8.5	19.3	55.7	102.3	130.4	151.5	140.3
European Community[4]	65.2	113.6	300.6	577.2	665.8	612.8	599.3
France	10.2	18.1	53.1	100.7	116.0	106.4	96.4
West Germany	17.9	34.2	90.2	171.8	192.9	176.1	175.7
Italy	7.2	13.2	34.8	72.2	77.7	75.3	77.3
United Kingdom	13.8	19.6	44.5	86.4	110.1	102.7	95.5
Other developed countries	20.5	33.7	87.1	165.8	199.1	188.2	176.1
Developing countries	40.2	61.7	226.5	452.8	608.8	606.1	525.9
Oil exporting countries[5]	10.5	17.5	113.6	214.3	301.2	276.4	212.8
Other	29.6	44.2	113.0	238.5	307.6	329.6	313.1
Communist countries[6]	23.2	34.9	90.5	170.4	203.1	213.2	215.6
U.S.S.R.	8.2	12.8	33.4	64.9	76.4	79.4	80.9
Eastern Europe	11.8	18.2	45.3	77.9	87.5	91.1	90.1
China	2.0	2.2	7.3	13.5	18.9	21.4	23.0
TOTAL	193.5	323.3	902.7	1,708.9	2,095.8	2,078.2	1,941.2

Imports, c.i.f.[7]

Developed countries[3]	137.5	237.8	618.1	1,182.7	1,427.1	1,358.3	1,290.4
United States	23.2	42.7	105.9	222.2	257.0	273.4	261.4
Canada	8.7	14.3	36.2	57.0	62.8	70.0	60.8
Japan	8.2	18.9	57.8	109.8	141.3	142.9	132.0
European Community[4]	70.5	118.9	306.4	611.1	729.2	644.2	628.1
France	10.4	19.1	54.0	107.0	134.9	121.0	116.6
West Germany	17.6	29.9	74.9	159.6	188.0	163.9	154.9
Italy	7.4	15.0	38.4	77.9	99.5	91.1	90.5
United Kingdom	16.1	22.0	53.3	99.6	115.8	102.0	100.1
Other developed countries	27.0	43.1	111.8	182.6	236.8	227.9	208.1
Developing countries	43.5	67.8	221.6	408.0	540.1	595.2	562.4
Oil exporting countries[5]	6.4	9.9	52.8	100.1	137.2	162.0	163.9
Other	37.2	57.9	168.9	307.8	402.9	433.2	398.5
Communist countries[6]	22.5	34.1	100.8	170.9	202.8	211.2	209.3
U.S.S.R.	8.0	11.7	37.1	58.0	68.5	73.2	80.1
Eastern Europe	11.6	18.5	51.3	83.0	93.1	97.3	89.2
China	1.8	2.2	7.4	15.7	20.9	19.6	19.1
TOTAL	203.5	339.7	940.5	1,761.6	2,170.0	2,164.7	2,062.1

[1] Preliminary estimates.
[2] Free-on-board ship value.
[3] Includes the OECD countries, South Africa, and non-OECD Europe.
[4] Includes Belgium, Luxembourg, Denmark, Greece, Ireland, and the Netherlands, not shown separately.
[5] Includes Algeria, Ecuador, Gabon, Indonesia, Iran, Iraq, Kuwait, Libya, Nigeria, Oman, Qatar, Saudi Arabia, United Arab Emirates, and Venezuela.
[6] Includes North Korea, Vietnam, Albania, Cuba, Mongolia, and Yugoslavia, not shown separately.
[7] Cost, insurance, and freight value, except Eastern Europe (except Hungary) and U.S.S.R., which are f.o.b. (free on board)

SOURCE: ECONOMIC REPORT OF THE PRESIDENT (Feb. 1983)

Table I-3. Trade Balances of Selected Areas and Countries 1965, 1970, 1975, and 1979–82.
(Billions of U.S. Dollars)

Area and Country	1965	1970	1975	1979	1980	1981	1982[1]
	World trade balance[2]						
Developed countries[3]	−7.4	−11.2	−32.5	−97.1	−143.2	−99.4	−90.7
United States	4.3	.5	2.2	−40.2	−36.2	−39.6	−48.5
Canada	−.2	2.5	−2.1	1.3	4.9	2.6	10.3
Japan	.3	.4	−2.1	−7.5	−10.9	8.6	8.3
European Community[4]	−5.3	−5.2	−5.7	−33.9	−63.3	−31.4	−28.8
France	−.2	−1.0	−.8	−6.3	−18.9	−14.5	−20.2
West Germany	.3	4.3	15.2	12.2	4.9	12.2	20.8
Italy	−.2	−1.8	−3.6	−5.7	−21.8	−15.8	−13.2
United Kingdom	−2.3	−2.4	−8.8	−13.2	−5.7	.7	−4.6
Other developed countries	−6.4	−9.4	−24.7	−16.8	−37.7	−39.7	−32.0
Developing countries	−3.3	−6.1	4.9	44.8	68.6	10.8	−36.5
Oil exporting countries[5]	4.2	7.6	60.8	114.2	164.0	114.4	48.9
Other	−7.5	−13.6	−55.9	−69.4	−95.4	−103.6	−85.4

Table I-3. Trade Balances of Selected Areas and Countries 1965, 1970, 1975, and 1979–82.
(Billions of U.S. Dollars)

Area and Country	1965	1970	1975	1979	1980	1981	1982[1]
			World trade balance[2]				
Communist countries[6]	.7	.8	−10.3	−.5	.3	2.0	6.3
U.S.S.R.	.2	1.1	−3.7	6.9	7.9	6.2	.8
Eastern Europe	.2	−.3	−6.0	−5.1	−5.6	−6.1	.8
China	.2	.0	−.1	−2.2	−2.0	1.8	3.9
TOTAL[7]	−10.0	−16.4	−37.8	−52.7	−74.2	−86.5	−120.9

[1] Preliminary estimates.

[2] Exports f.o.b. (free on board ship value) less imports c.i.f. (cost, insurance, and freight)

[3] Includes the OECD countries, South Africa, and non-OECD Europe.

[4] Include Belgium, Luxembourg, Denmark, Greece, Ireland, and the Netherlands, not shown separately.

[5] Includes Algeria, Ecuador, Gabon, Indonesia, Iran, Iraq, Kuwait, Libya, Nigeria, Oman, Qatar, Saudi Arabia, United Arab Emirates, and Venezuala.

[6] Includes North Korea, Vietnam, Albania, Cuba, Mongolia, and Yugoslavia, not shown separately.

[7] Asymmetries arise in global payments aggregations because of discrepancies in coverage, classification, timing, and valuation in the recording of transactions by the countries involved.

SOURCE: ECONOMIC REPORT OF THE PRESIDENT (Feb. 1983)

Table I-4. Changes in World Trade
(Percentage changes)

	Average 1963-72	1973	1974	1975	1976	1977	1978	1979	1980	1981	1982
World trade											
Volume	8.5	12.5	4.5	−4.0	11.0	5.0	5.5	6.5	2.0	—	2.0
Unit volume (in U.S. dollar terms)	3.0	22.5	38.5	9.5	1.5	8.5	10.0	18.5	19.5	−1.5	2.5
(in SDR terms)[5]	2.0	11.5	37.5	8.5	7.0	7.5	2.5	15.0	19.0	9.0	5.0
Volume of trade											
Exports											
Industrial countries	9.0	13.2	7.1	−4.6	10.6	5.1	6.1	6.7	4.6	2.6	2.0
Developing countries											
Oil exporting countries	9.1	14.8	−0.9	−11.5	14.3	0.6	−4.0	3.0	−12.8	−16.3	−9.0
Non-oil developing countries	6.7	8.9	−0.1	−0.5	11.6	4.7	9.5	9.4	5.6	3.9	6.5
Imports											
Industrial countries	9.0	12.1	0.7	−8.1	13.9	4.2	5.2	8.4	−1.3	−2.3	2.0
Developing countries											
Oil exporting countries	8.3	20.3	38.5	41.4	20.6	15.2	4.8	−12.3	14.9	19.8	5.0
Non-oil developing countries	6.2	11.6	7.5	−4.4	3.8	6.7	8.0	11.0	3.9	2.2	3.0

Table I–4. Changes in World Trade (Cont.)
(Percentage changes)

Unit value of trade (in SDR terms)[5]	Average 1963-72	1973	1974	1975	1976	1977	1978	1979	1980	1981	1982
Exports											
Industrial countries	2.1	9.8	23.7	10.7	5.6	6.7	5.3	12.1	11.8	6.3	6.0
Developing countries											
Oil exporting countries	2.6	25.7	202.5	4.0	11.8	8.4	−6.3	42.1	58.2	22.0	—
Non-oil developing countries	1.2	21.1	37.7	−1.9	12.6	12.9	−1.8	13.9	19.0	9.5	3.5
Imports											
Industrial countries	1.8	11.7	40.5	7.9	6.6	7.9	2.5	15.2	21.0	6.9	4.5
Developing countries											
Oil exporting countries	2.1	12.5	26.9	9.9	5.7	7.7	4.9	10.5	11.7	8.7	5.5
Non-oil developing countries	1.1	14.2	45.8	7.8	6.2	6.5	2.5	14.2	24.3	12.0	5.5

Table I-5. Growth Rate in Real Gross National Product, 1960-82.
(Percentage change)

Area and country	1960–73 annual average	1974	1975	1976	1977	1978	1979	1980	1981	1982	U.S. dollar value in 1981 (billions)
United State	4.2	−.6	−1.1	5.4	5.5	4.8	3.2	−.2	2.0	−1.8	2,926
Canada	5.4	3.6	1.2	5.5	2.1	3.7	3.5	.0	3.0	−5.0	280
Japan	10.5	−.3	1.4	6.5	5.3	5.1	5.6	4.2	2.9	2.5	1,150
European Community[3]	4.7	1.6	−1.2	5.0	2.4	3.3	3.4	1.1	−.4	.3	2,420
France	5.7	3.2	.2	5.2	3.1	3.7	3.5	1.2	.3	1.5	577
West Germany	4.8	.5	−1.8	5.2	2.8	3.6	4.5	1.8	−.3	−1.3	687
Italy	5.2	4.1	−3.6	5.9	1.9	2.7	4.9	4.0	−.2	.8	299
United Kingdom	3.2	−1.0	−.6	3.6	1.3	3.3	1.4	−1.8	−.8	.5	502

Table I-5. Growth Rate in Real Gross National Product, 1960–82. (Cont.)
(Percentage change)

Area and country	1960–73 annual average	1974	1975	1976	1977	1978	1979	1980	1981	1982	U.S. dollar value in 1981 (billions)
Communist countries[5]	4.9	4.0	3.3	3.7	4.0	4.8	2.4	2.1	1.2	1.4	2,740
U.S.S.R.	4.9	3.9	1.7	4.8	3.2	3.4	.8	1.3	1.8	.16	1,587
Eastern Europe	4.1	4.7	4.1	3.4	2.8	3.0	1.3	.4	–1.0	–.7	671
China	6.4	3.7	7.7	.6	8.6	11.6	8.5	6.2	3.0	5.0	328
Developing countries[6]	—	—	—	—	—	—	—	—	2.7	.8	1,965
Oil exporting[7]	9.0	8.0	–.3	12.3	5.9	1.9	2.3	–3.0	–.5	1.2	540
Other	5.8	5.6	4.0	5.4	4.8	5.5	4.9	4.4	3.1	.7	1,425
TOTAL	—	—	—	—	—	—	—	—	1.8	.2	11,725

Source: Economic Reports of the President, 1982, 1983.

Table II-1. International Comparisons of Economic Performance, Japan and Major Western Industrialized Countries[a]

Item	Japan	United States	West Germany	United Kingdom	France	Italy
(1) Population, 1972 (millions)	107.0	208.8	61.7	55.9	51.7	54.3
(2) Gross national product (billions of current dollars)						
1952[b]	16.3	348.2	31.9	44.3	40.4	17.1
1972[c]	299.2	1,159.3	260.2	153.0	197.7	117.6
(3) Gross national product per capita (current dollars)						
1952	188	2,181	643	870	947	359
1972	2,823	5,551	4,218	2,472	3,823	2,164
(4) Gross domestic investment as percent of gross national product						
1952[d]	27.2	17.1	22.8	10.6	18.9	19.5
1971[e]	36.3	17.4	27.5	18.1	28.0	20.4
(5) Government current expenditure as percent of gross national product						
1952[f]	10.9	20.1	16.2	19.1	15.9	12.1
1971[g]	14.4	24.7	22.0	34.2	21.1	25.1
(6) Exports and imports[h] as percent of gross national product						
1952	26.6	9.0	31.5	45.1	29.8	25.0
1971[i]	21.2	11.7	41.8	44.4	32.9	38.0
(7) Share of world trade (percent)[j]						
1952	2.2	17.1	5.2	11.0	5.4	2.5
1972[k]	6.2	12.5	10.2	6.2	6.3	4.5
(8) Percent of labor force in agriculture						
Early 1950s[l]	41.7	12.2	23.2	5.1	27.7	32.8
1972[m]	19.1	4.2	8.2	3.1	12.3	17.5
(9) Average annual rate of price change (percent)[n]						
1953–62: Wholesale price index	−0.1	0.9	0.9[o]	0.1[o]	3.4	0.2
Consumer price index	2.8	1.3	1.9	3.0	4.1	2.4

1963–72: Wholesale price index	1.3	2.6	1.6	3.7	3.2	2.7
Consumer price index	5.2	3.5	3.3	5.2	4.3	3.9
1972–73: Wholesale price index	14.8	12.2	8.0	6.7	13.1	15.4
Consumer price index	11.1	6.0	6.7	8.8	7.1	10.2
July 1973–July 1974: Wholesale price index	34.2	20.4	15.3	25.0	32.5	41.8
Consumer price index	25.2	11.8	6.9	17.1	14.4	16.8

Sources: Item (1): Organisation for Economic Co-operation and Development, *OECD Observer*, no. 68 (February 1974), Item (2): United Nations, *Yearbook of National Accounts Statistics, 1957; UN, Statistical Yearbook, 1957*, p. 494, and *1973*, table 183. Item (3): GNP data same as for item (2); population data from UN, *Statistical Yearbook, 1957*, table 1, and *1973*, table 183. Item (4): UN, *Yearbook of National Accounts Statistics, 1957 and 1972*. Item (5): ibid. Item (6): ibid. Item (7): UN, *Yearbook of International Trade Statistics, 1954*, table A, pp. 12–19, and *1972–73*, table A, pp. 14–21. Item (8): International Labour Office, *Year Book of Labour Statistics, 1957*, table 4, and *1973*, table 2. Item (9): UN, *Statistical Yearbook, 1962*, tables 161, 168, and *1973*, tables 172, 173; OECD, *Main Economic Indicators*, September 1974, pp. 144–48.

a It should be noted that not all economic indicators are internationally comparable; for example, the United States classifies as government current expenditures certain items included in gross domestic investment by other nations.

b Currencies converted into dollars at official exchange rates.

c Gross domestic product in purchasers' values.

d Ratio of gross domestic capital formation to gross national product.

e Ratio of gross domestic capital formation to gross domestic product in purchasers' values.

f Ratio of general government consumption expenditure to gross national product.

g For all countries except Japan, ratio of current disbursements of central, state, and local governments to gross domestic product; for Japan, disbursements of general government only.

h Exports and imports of goods and services.

i Ratio of exports and imports to gross domestic product.

j Share of world trade = (import + export)/(world import + world export) × 100.

k World trade in U.S. dollars: imports are $427.5 billion; exports are $412.4 billion. Excludes trade among China, Mongolia, North Korea, North Vietnam, and the two Germanys.

l Data are for 1950 for the United States and West Germany, 1951 for the United Kingdom and Italy, 1954 for France, and 1955 for Japan.

m Data are for 1966 for the United Kingdom, 1970 for Japan, 1971 for West Germany, and 1972 for the remainder.

n Compound annual rate of growth for the periods indicated.

o 1954–62.

Table II-2. European Economic Community Impact on International Trade

(Value in Billions of Dollars, F.O.B.; percentage changes from preceding years)

Year	Intra-EEC exports		EEC exports to rest of world		EEC imports from rest of world		World exports, excl. all EEC trade	
	Value	Percent change	Value	Percent change	Value	Percent change	Value	Percent change
1953*	4.6		10.1		9.9		63.6	
1958*	7.5		15.9		14.1		83.9	
1963	23.6		28.7		30.2		102.4	
1973	113.1		98.7		95.4		362.5	
1974	138.8	22.7	135.6	37.4	150.1	57.3	561.2	54.8
1975	145.9	5.1	149.9	10.5	140.6	− 6.8	578.9	3.2
1976	168.8	15.7	157.6	5.1	165.5	17.7	666.6	15.1
1977	196.0	16.1	186.0	18.0	178.6	7.9	743.0	11.5
1978	241.8	23.4	220.1	18.3	201.9	13.0	840.6	13.1
1979	315.2	30.4	262.0	19.0	270.1	33.8	1,057.5	25.8
1980	335.2	6.3	327.2	24.9	360.6	33.5	1,323.6	25.2
1981	310.2	− 7.5	302.8	− 7.5	310.8	− 13.8	1,355.0	2.4

Source: GATT, *International Trade* (Geneva, various annual issues). & figures pertain to original six EEC members.

Table II–3. Share of World Exports

(Percent)

	1970	1975	1979	1980	1981	1982
United States	15.4	13.6	12.1	12.0	13.0	12.8
France	6.4	6.7	6.7	6.3	5.9	5.8
Germany, Fed. Rep.	12.1	11.4	11.5	10.5	9.8	10.7
United Kingdom	7.0	5.6	6.1	6.3	5.8	5.9
Japan	6.9	7.1	6.8	7.1	8.4	8.4

Table II-4. Value and Share of Industrial Countries Manufactured Exports

	Value (Billions of dollars)					Share (percent)			
	1970	1975	1981	1982	—	1970	1975	1981	1982
United States	29	71	154	140		21.3	19.1	20.7	12.8
France	14	40	75	70		9.1	10.2	9.4	5.8
Germany, Fed. Rep.	31	80	151	153		19.8	20.1	18.7	10.7
United Kingdom	17	37	70.4	65		10.4	8.9	8.5	5.9
Japan	18	53	147	134		8.9	11.4	14.5	8.4

Table III-1. World Production of Crude Steel: 1870–1959 (m. tons.)

Some Figures on Steel

	United Kingdom	United States	Germany West	Germany East	France	Benelux	Italy	U.S.S.R. (Russia)	Japan	Other	Total
1870	.22	.04	.13	—	.08	—	—	.01	—	.11	.51
1880	1.29	1.25	.69	—	.38	.13	—	.29	—	.53	4.18
1890	3.58	4.28	2.10	—	.67	.32	.28	.38	—	2.28	12.28
1900	4.90	10.19	6.36	—	1.54	.81	.13	2.16	—	3.24	27.69
1910	6.37	26.09	12.89	—	3.36	2.50	.72	3.48	—	6.89	58.94
1920	9.07	42.13	8.40	—	3.00	1.80	.76	.16	.83	8.37	71.42
1925	7.39	45.39	12.00	—	7.33	4.56	1.76	1.84	1.30	14.81	89.05
1930	7.33	40.70	11.35	—	9.30	5.53	1.72	5.77	2.29	18.90	93.59
1935	9.86	34.09	14.09	—	6.18	4.78	2.17	12.32	4.63	17.09	98.03
1940	12.98	59.81	17.70	—	4.34	2.88	2.22	18.01	6.75	38.90	139.25
1945	11.82	71.16	1.52	—	1.63	1.00	.39	12.11	1.93	12.97	112.90
1950	16.29	86.46	11.93	.98	8.52	6.61	2.33	26.87	4.76	30.20	186.43
1955	19.79	104.50	21.00	2.47	12.39	9.90	5.31	44.56	9.26	48.20	264.99
1959	20.19	83.43	25.41	3.54	14.98	11.59	6.66	58.76	16.37	71.60	297.55

SOURCE: Duncan Burn, THE STEEL INDUSTRY 1939-1959: A STUDY IN COMPETITION AND PLANNING (1961) Table 105.

Table III-2. World Production of Crude Steel (1967–1981)

(Thousands net tons)	1967	1968	1969	1970	1971	1972	1973	1974	1975	1976	1977	1978	1979	1980	1981
WESTERN EUROPE															
Denmark	442	504	531	521	519	549	499	591	614	796	755	951	886	809	675
France	21,669	22,490	24,812	26,206	25,180	26,514	27,855	29,785	23,734	25,603	24,365	25,178	25,750	25,547	23,436
F. R. of Germany	33,889	45,370	49,950	49,649	44,437	48,176	49,537	58,678	44,546	46,752	42,972	45,474	50,750	48,323	45,867
Ireland	60	75	89	82	88	85	128	121	89	64	52	76	79	2	35
Italy	17,515	18,699	18,108	19,044	19,237	21,840	23,142	26,239	24,102	25,855	25,722	26,767	26,731	29,212	27,312
Belgium-Luxembourg	14,455	16,836	19,338	19,454	19,321	22,174	23,308	24,321	18,077	19,095	17,178	19,170	20,272	18,673	17,718
Netherlands	3,749	4,085	5,194	5,558	5,603	6,156	6,198	6,434	5,310	5,032	5,426	6,154	6,400	5,803	6,028
United Kingdom	26,836	29,124	29,693	30,707	26,719	27,989	29,456	24,696	21,878	24,761	22,561	22,451	23,725	12,431	17,166
Sub Total	126,420	138,428	148,592	151,692	141,280	153,344	165,510	171,539	138,127	147,959	139,031	146,221	154,593	140,800	138,232
Austria	3,332	3,822	4,328	4,496	4,365	4,485	4,771	5,180	4,485	4,934	4,777	4,779	5,420	5,096	5,132
Finland	453	803	1,078	1,288	1,130	1,605	1,780	1,825	1,781	1,817	2,539	2,572	2,716	2,765	2,658
Greece	231	231	496	496	523	744	1,198	1,054	992	1,223	1,102	1,032	1,102	1,323	993
Norway	871	908	941	959	975	1,010	1,061	1,006	982	977	879	879	982	950	935
Portugal	347	345	441	424	454	468	552	440	488	508	586	689	739	726	607
Spain	4,974	5,603	6,598	8,150	8,846	10,500	11,684	12,679	12,237	12,105	12,312	12,499	13,501	13,936	14,241
Sweden	5,256	5,676	5,866	6,059	5,810	5,795	6,242	6,601	6,185	5,665	4,374	4,767	5,217	4,670	4,156
Switzerland	491	499	551	578	586	598	644	653	492	595	723	864	977	1,024	992
Turkey	1,098	1,111	1,289	1,446	1,361	1,716	1,492	1,753	1,877	2,174	2,056	2,394	2,641	2,795	2,673
Yugoslavia	2,019	2,200	2,447	2,456	2,704	2,852	2,950	3,126	3,214	3,032	3,508	3,810	3,897	4,006	4,384
Total Western Europe	145,493	159,679	172,625	178,046	168,035	183,131	198,005	150,707	170,834	180,990	171,887	180,506	191,785	178,091	175,003

Table III-2. World Production of Crude Steel (1967-1981) (Cont.)

(Thousands net tons)	1967	1968	1969	1970	1971	1972	1973	1974	1975	1976	1977	1978	1979	1980	1981
EASTERN EUROPE															
Bulgaria	1,365	1,610	1,670	1,984	2,147	2,338	2,476	2,411	2,497	2,712	2,853	2,722	2,736	2,830	2,866
Czechoslovakia	11,026	11,635	11,907	12,654	13,303	14,030	14,504	15,035	15,798	16,196	16,594	16,859	16,333	16,452	16,755
East Germany	5,122	5,175	5,666	5,980	6,333	6,685	6,454	6,796	7,143	7,429	7,551	7,690	7,743	8,056	8,267
Hungary	3,019	3,200	3,342	3,428	3,428	3,608	3,673	3,823	4,049	4,026	4,104	4,274	4,309	4,152	3,968
Poland	11,477	12,402	12,402	12,952	13,986	14,797	15,495	16,045	16,542	17,240	19,666	21,219	21,184	21,478	17,196
Rumania	4,506	4,765	6,107	7,184	7,499	8,158	8,996	9,744	10,525	12,092	12,629	12,984	14,230	14,523	14,881
Total Eastern Europe	36,517	38,519	41,094	44,183	46,697	49,617	51,598	53,855	56,546	59,695	63,397	65,748	66,535	67,491	63,933
U.S.S.R.	112,695	117,431	121,601	127,742	132,979	138,438	144,933	150,135	155,784	159,614	161,659	166,929	164,339	163,064	164,245
NORTH AMERICA															
Canada	9,701	11,251	10,307	12,346	12,169	13,077	14,757	14,998	14,359	14,689	15,026	16,423	17,723	17,528	16,135
United States	126,921	131,098	141,070	131,329	120,212	133,104	150,423	145,496	116,783	128,213	125,333	137,031	136,341	111,835	120,828
Total North America	136,666	142,350	151,378	143,675	132,382	146,180	165,181	160,494	131,142	142,605	140,359	153,454	154,064	129,363	136,963
LATIN AMERICA															
Argentina	1,462	1,718	1,863	2,009	2,111	2,371	2,431	2,594	2,434	2,657	2,959	3,067	3,526	2,962	2801
Brazil	4,040	4,907	5,429	5,941	6,610	7,185	7,881	8,284	9,245	10,200	12,306	13,454	15,314	16,875	14,565
Chile	695	626	706	652	721	695	605	699	560	554	621	679	708	823	724
Columbia	284	285	300	342	358	411	399	343	430	407	359	430	398	443	437
Cuba	112	132	131	154	176	204	242	264	331	275	331	331	331	331	331
Mexico	3,032	3,589	3,822	4,278	4,212	4,880	5,247	5,639	5,822	5,829	6,121	7,398	7,722	7,825	8,384
Peru	88	117	214	104	197	392	530	530	475	385	418	416	481	518	397
Venezuela	760	948	926	1,022	1,018	1,172	1,147	1,147	1,172	1,032	885	948	1,660	2,006	2,238
Total Latin America	10,775	12,336	13,390	14,503	15,404	17,194	18,370	19,500	20,469	21,371	24,000	26,777	30,140	31,886	29,877

Table III-2. World Production of Crude Steel (1967–1981) (Cont.)

(Thousands net tons)	1967	1968	1969	1970	1971	1972	1973	1974	1975	1976	1977	1978	1979	1980	1981
AFRICA															
Algeria	—		—	—	—	100	215	191	244	392	—	—	—	—	—
Zimbabwe	148	165E	331	412	484	509	551	551E	551	551	551	772	816	887	762
Tunisia	51	90	110	110	100	147	154	145	143	112E	—	—	—	—	—
South Africa	4,080	4,465	5,098	5,244	5,380	5,883	6,307	6,437	7,530	7,833	8,053	8,710	9,784	9,996	9,858
Total Africa	4,279	4,721	5,539	5,766	5,963	6,638	7,228	7,324	8,468	8,889	8,604	9,482	10,600	10,883	10,620
MIDDLE EAST															
Egypt	441E	496E	496E	496E	496E	496E	579	551	551	551	661	661	882	882	992
Iran	—	—	—	—	—	—	265	625	607	661	716	1,433	1,576	1,323	1,323
Israel	66	66	66	66	72	72	72	83	66	77	79	104	118	127	126
Other	16	16	16	16	16	16E	16E	16E	16E	16E	56	201	624	624	715
Total Middle East	523	579	579	579	584	584	931	1,275	1,241	1,306	1,512	2,399	3,200	2,956	3,156

Table III-2. World Production of Crude Steel (1967–1981) (Cont.)

(Thousands net tons)	1967	1968	1969	1970	1971	1972	1973	1974	1975	1976	1977	1978	1979	1980	1981
ASIA															
China	15,432E	16,535E	17,637E	19,841E	23,148E	25,353E	28,660E	28,660E	28,660E	23,148	25,794	35,031	38,007	40,918	39,242
Hong Kong	94	99	105	110	116	121	127	132E	135E	135E	—	—	—	—	—
India	6,979	7,108	7,228	6,918	6,725	7,557	7,594	7,791	8,808	10,322	11,033	11,132	11,162	10,487	11,883
Indonesia	—	—	—	11	11	33	55	88	110	153	—	—	—	—	—
Japan	68,513	73,737	90,572	103,200	97,617	106,813	131,530	129,115	112,780	118,370	112,882	112,551	123,180	122,791	112,077
Malaysia	66	77	81	134	176	206	198	201	202	209	—	—	—	—	—
Dem. Rep. of Korea	1,598E	1,929	2,205	2,403	2,601	2,756	3,197	3,527	3,197	3,307	3,472	5,600	5,952	6,343	6,063
Philippines	94	101	130	144	175	224	280	307	343	433	331	304	438	364	386
Singapore	66	115	119	118	135	218	232	214	216	224	—	—	—	—	—
Rep. of Korea	331	410	411	530	520	646	1,275	2,146	2,198	3,875	4,677	5,477	8,389	9,433	11,853
Taiwan (ROC)	488	522	529	386	518	595	590	993	1,113	1,794	1,951	3,783	4,685	4,657	3,465
Thailand	38	130	133	192	209	312	357	359	277	310	—	—	—	—	—
Total Asia	93,699	100,763	119,151	133,658	131,954	144,836	174,462	173,534	158,037	162,279	160,140	173,878	191,813	195,043	184,969
OCEANIA															
Australia	7,016	7,270	7,551	7,539	7,444	7,442	8,487	8,612	8,674	8,591	8,084	8,373	8,950	8,365	8,416
New Zealand	72	96	112	173	159	173	209	214	204	236	240	248	252	254	244
Total Oceania	7,088	7,367	7,864	7,712	7,603	7,615	8,696	8,612	8,674	8,591	8,324	9,838	9,202	8,619	8,660

Table III-3. Steel Production, Capacity, and Capacity Utilization: Japan, ECSC, and United States
(Millions of tons)

Year	Japan			EC (6)			United States		
	Raw steel production[a] MT	Usable capacity[b] MT	Capacity utilization (%)	Raw steel production MT	Usable capacity[c] MT	Capacity utilization (%)	Raw steel production NT	Rated capacity[d] NT	Capacity utilization (%)
1956	11.1	12.4	89.5	57.0	59.1	96.4	115.22	130.91	88.0
1957	12.6	14.8	85.1	59.8	63.5	94.2	112.72	137.10	82.2
1958	12.1	17.6	68.7	57.9	67.7	85.5	85.26	144.24	59.1
1959	16.6	21.15	78.5	63.2	70.5	89.6	93.45	148.12	63.1
1960	22.1	25.15	87.9	73.1	76.5	95.6	99.28	149.00	66.6
1961	28.3	30.0	94.3	73.5	80.2	91.6	98.01	149.8	65.4
1962	27.5	34.3	80.2	73.0	83.4	87.5	98.33	150.4	65.4
1963	31.5	38.1	82.7	73.2	87.9	83.3	109.26	151.1	72.3
1964	39.8	43.2	92.1	82.9	92.1	90.0	127.08	151.9	83.7
1965	41.2	49.3	83.6	86.0	102.1	84.2	131.46	152.7	86.1

[a] Japan Iron and Steel Federation, *Monthly Report of the Iron and Steel Statistics*, various issues.

[b] Calculated by interpolating between peak monthly production points assuming constant compound growth between peaks. Calculated by Professor Donald Barnett, University of Windsor, Windsor, Ontario, Canada, and Institute for Iron and Steel Studies, *Steel Industry in Brief: Japan 1977*.

[c] EC, *Investment in the Community Coal Mining, Iron and Steel Industries*, EC includes only West Germany, France, Belgium, Netherlands, Luxembourg, and Italy.

[d] From Barry Bosworth, "Capacity Creation in Basic Materials Industries," *Brookings Papers in Economic Activity*, No. 2, 1976, table 1, p. 304.

Source: Council on Wage and Price Stability, "Prices and Costs in the United States Steel Industry," Oct. 1977, p. 145.

Table III-3 (Cont'd.)

Year	Japan			EC(6)			United States		
	Raw steel production[a] MT	Usable capacity[b] MT	Capacity utilization (%)	Raw steel production MT	Usable capacity[c] MT	Capacity utilization (%)	Raw steel production NT	Rated capacity[d] NT	Capacity utilization (%)
1966	47.8	56.6	84.4	85.1	108.3	78.6	134.10	153.5	87.4
1967	62.2	67.2	92.6	89.9	112.3	80.1	127.21	154.2	82.5
1968	66.9	77.5	86.3	98.6	115.1	85.7	131.46	155.0	84.8
1969	82.2	89.6	91.7	107.3	120.6	89.0	141.26	155.5	90.8
1970	93.3	103.65	90.0	109.2	126.6	86.2	131.51	155.5	84.6
1971	88.6	110.15	80.4	103.4	135.1	76.5	120.44	156.2	77.1
1972	96.9	118.8	81.6	113.1	138.8	81.5	133.10	154.6	86.1
1973	119.3	129.1	92.4	122.9	144.4	85.1	150.80	155.0	97.3
1974	117.1	140.15	83.6	132.6	150.4	88.2	145.72	155.57	93.7
1975	102.3	150.0	68.2	104.8	162.3	64.6	116.64	156.5	74.5
1976	107.4	151.0	71.1	110.8	169.4	65.4	127.3	159.0	80.1

Table III–4. United States Imports of Steel Mill Products, 1960–1982

(Millions of Net Tons)

Year	Total U.S. Steel Consumption	Total	Percent of Consumption	Japan	EEC	Other
1960	71.5	3.3	4.6	17.9	68.7	13.4
1961	67.3	3.2	4.8	18.8	66.9	14.3
1962	72.6	4.1	5.6	26.1	57.0	16.9
1963	78.8	5.5	7.0	33.2	47.6	19.2
1964	87.9	6.4	7.3	38.0	44.6	17.4
1965	100.6	10.4	10.3	42.5	47.3	11.2
1966	99.0	10.8	10.9	45.1	42.7	12.2
1967	93.7	11.5	12.2	39.0	49.4	11.6
1968	107.6	18.0	16.7	40.6	46.8	12.6
1969	102.7	14.0	13.7	44.6	43.4	12.0
1970	97.1	13.4	13.8	44.4	40.4	15.2
1971	102.5	18.3	17.9	37.7	46.5	15.8
1972	106.6	17.7	16.6	36.4	44.0	19.6
1973	122.5	15.1	12.4	37.2	43.0	19.8
1974	119.6	16.0	13.4	38.6	40.2	21.2
1975	89.0	12.0	13.5	48.6	34.3	17.1
1976	101.2	14.3	14.1	55.9	19.4	24.7
1977	108.4	19.3	17.8	40.5	35.3	24.3
1978	116.6	21.1	18.1	30.7	35.3	33.9
1979	115.0	17.5	15.2	36.2	30.9	32.9
1980	95.2	15.5	16.3	38.8	25.1	36.1
1981	104.0	19.9	19.1	31.3	32.6	36.1
1982	74.6	16.7	22.3	31.0	33.5	35.8

Source: AISI, *Annual Statistical Reports.*

Table III-5. Weight and Percentage of Steel in U.S.-Built New Cars 1975–1985

MATERIALS USAGE IN NEW CARS, 1975–1985

Model Year	1975		1976		1977		1978		1979		1980		1985	
Total Dry Weight (lbs) (1)	3,970		3,900		3,830		3,440		3,330		3,080		2,400	
Material Mix	%	Pounds	%	Pounds	%	Pounds	%	Pounds	%	Pounds	%	Pounds	%	Pounds
High Strength Steel	2.7	106	3.3	129	3.6	138	3.8	131	4.6	154	5.4	165	12.5	300
Plain Carbon Steel	58.3	2,315	57.6	2,247	56.7	2,173	56.2	1,932	55.1	1,833	54.2	1,669	44.0	1,056
Iron	15.8	626	15.4	599	15.2	581	14.9	513	14.7	490	14.9	458	9.0	216
Aluminum	2.2	86	2.4	92	2.8	107	3.3	114	3.9	129	4.0	124	6.5	156
Copper	0.9	37	0.9	36	0.8	32	0.8	28	0.8	28	0.8	25	1.0	24
Lead	0.7	29	0.7	28	0.7	28	0.7	24	0.7	24	0.7	22	1.0	24
Zinc	1.3	53	1.2	48	1.0	40	0.9	31	0.8	27	0.6	19	0.5	12
Glass	2.4	94	2.4	92	2.4	91	2.5	86	2.5	84	2.6	80	3.0	72
Rubber	4.0	160	4.2	165	4.2	162	4.2	144	4.3	143	4.0	124	4.5	180
Other Plastics	4.2	168	4.4	173	4.9	186	5.2	179	5.8	191	6.0	184	10.5	252
Other	7.5	297	7.5	290	7.7	295	7.5	258	6.8	227	6.8	212	7.5	180

(1) Dry Weight—The weight of the vehicle excluding fluids.
SOURCE: U.S. Department of Transportation. *The U.S. Automobile Industry*, January 1981.

Table III-6.
Total Steel Mill Products (15 categories) Subject to the U.S.-E.C. Arrangement:

[1]U.S. producers' shipments, imports for consumption.

[2]Exports of domestic merchandise, and apparent consumption, 1981-82, and by specified periods, 1981, 1982 and 1983.

Period	Producers' Shipments	Imports		Exports	Apparent Consumption	Ratio of imports to consumption	
		Total	From EC			Total	From EC
		------- Short	tons -------			------Percent------	
1981	60,851,891	10,879,553	4,172,631	1,412,249	70,319,195	15.5	5.9
1982[3]	44,546,215	9,182,789	3,616,353	707,001	53,022,003	17.3	6.8
1981:							
April-June	17,066,789	2,771,092	985,275	386,102	19,451,779	14.2	5.1
July-September	14,779,761	3,109,972	1,281,450	330,491	17,579,242	17.7	7.3
October-December	12,313,155	3,101,658	1,440,876	356,956	15,057,857	20.6	9.6
1982:							
January-March	11,973,249	2,481,673	843,499	199,659	14,255,263	17.4	5.9
April-June	11,587,556	2,366,535	957,330	182,115	13,771,976	17.2	7.0
July-September	10,548,946	2,039,232	768,152	177,327	12,410,851	16.4	6.2
October-December	9,605,864	2,295,349	1,047,373	147,900	11,753,313	19.5	8.9
1983:							
January-March	11,656,114	2,212,856	615,974	131,428	13,737,542	16.1	4.5
1982:							
April	3,889,430	421,042	137,264	61,734	4,248,738	9.9	3.2
May	3,701,221	876,421	313,140	73,234	4,504,408	19.5	7.0

Table III-6. (Cont.)

Period	Producers' Shipments	Imports		Exports	Apparent Consumption	Ratio of imports to consumption	
		Total	From EC			Total	From EC
	------	------	Short tons ------			--- Percent ---	
1982:							
June	3,998,259	1,069,073	506,926	47,147	5,020,185	21.3	10.1
July	3,422,523	543,360	236,586	58,237	3,907,646	13.9	6.1
August	3,569,432	807,602	247,105	63,776	4,313,258	18.7	5.7
September	3,585,692	688,270	284,461	55,314	4,218,648	16.3	6.7
October	3,245,143	742,010	292,311	51,858	3,935,295	18.9	7.4
November	3,076,907	819,562	374,321	49,138	3,847,331	21.3	9.7
December	3,284,189	733,777	380,741	46,904	3,971,062	18.5	9.6
1983:							
January	3,487,617	769,777	298,364	45,525	4,211,869	18.3	7.1
February	3,529,467	749,100	159,785	38,821	4,239,746	17.7	3.8
March	4,525,981	693,979	157,825	47,082	5,172,878	13.4	3.1
April	4,129,970	740,897	175,102	53,101	4,817,766	15.4	3.6
Percentage change:							
Apr. 1983/Mar. 1983	—	-8.7	6.8	10.9	12.8	-6.9	—
Apr. 1983/Apr. 1982	6.2	76.0	27.6	-14.0	13.4	—	—

[1] Arrangement Concerning Trade in Certain Steel Products effective in October 1982.

[2] Data coverage on imports does not strictly conform to products subject to the U.S.-EC Arrangement: see explanation in preface.

[3] Data on producers' shipments, apparent consumption and ratio of imports to consumption adjusted due to revision in producers' shipments.

SOURCE: Compiled from data of the American Iron & Steel Institute and official statistics of the U.S. Department of Commerce.

Table III-7. Composite prices for finished steel products and prices for selected steel products subject to the U.S.-EC Arrangement[1]

Product	1982			1983					Percentage change, May from April
	Oct.	Nov.	Dec.	Jan.	Feb.	Mar.	Apr.	May	
			Per short ton						
Composite[2]	$506	$506	$506	$506	$524	$524	$524	$524	—
Hot-rolled sheet, 0.075 inch thick	416	416	416	416	441	441	441	441	—
Cold-rolled sheet, class 1	493	493	493	493	523	523	523	523	—
Carbon grade plate	485	485	485	485	515	515	515	515	—
Standard structurals	478	478	478	478	478	478	478	478	—
Wire rod	447	447	447	447	447	447	447	447	—
Hot-rolled carbon bar (special quality)	479	479	479	479	516	516	516	516	—
Galvanized, hot-dipped sheet	543	543	543	543	560	560	560	560	—
Tin plate, single reduced electrolytic, 0.25 pound[3]	797	797	797	797	797	797	797	797	—
Standard rails, No. 1	487	487	487	487	487	487	487	487	—
Sheet piling	529	529	529	529	529	529	529	529	—

[1] Mill base list prices; transaction prices are likely to differ.

[2] Prices based on weighted index of steel bar, shapes, plate, wire, rail, black pipe, and hot- and cold-rolled sheet and strip.

[3] Tin plate prices are quoted by the base box. These prices are converted to a per ton basis assuming a base box weight of 70 pounds.

SOURCE: *Iron Age* and *American Metal Market*, various issues.

Table IV-1.
The Automobile Industry, 1970–80 (passenger cars)

	Year	Community	U.S.A.	Japan	Rest of world	Total
Passenger cars on	1970	53,770	88,209	8,041	38,180	188,000
the road (000)	1975	70,258	105,987	16,683	60,672	253,600
	1980	86,534	120,104	23,655	86,892	317,185
% change 1970-80		+60.9	+36.1	+194.1	+127.00	+68.7
Car ownership (number	1970	214	431	77	12	51
of cars per 1,000	1975	272	496	149	17	63
inhabitants)	1980	332	540	202	23	79
% change 1970-80		+55.1	+25.2	+162.3	+91.6	+54.9
Registrations	1970	6,751	8,388	2,379	4,582	22,100
(000)	1975	6,964	8,262	2,738	7,745	25,709
	1980	8,535	8,801	2,886	10,528	30,750
% change 1970-80		+26.4	+4.9	+21.3	+129.8	+39.1
Production	1970	9,424	6,550	3,179	3,547	22,700
(000)	1975	8,328	6,717	4,568	5,787	25,400
	1980	9,545	7,000	7,050	7,155	30,750
% change 1970-80		+1.3	+6.9	+121.7	+101.7	+35.4
Exports	1970	2,458	285	726	1,307	4,776
(000)	1975	2,050	640	1,827	1,808	6,325
	1980	1,898	695	3,820	2,034	8,447
% change 1970-80		−22.8	+148.2	+426.2	+55.6	+76.9
Imports	1970	149	2,007[1]	18	2,275	4,449
(000)	1975	599	2,077	42	3,414	6,132
	1980	1,362	2,830	47	4,203	8,442
% change 1970-80		+810.0	+41.0	+161.1	+84.7	89.8

SOURCE: Marketing Systems, Commission of the European Communities, *The European Automobile Industry*, EC Bull. Supplement 2/81.
[1]Including imports from Canada

Table IV-2.
Estimated hourly compensation of production workers in the motor vehicle and equipment industries, 1975-80

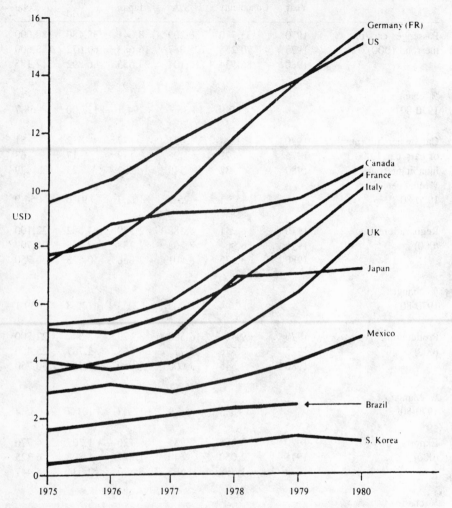

SOURCE: Commission of the European Communities, *The European Automobile Industry*, EC Bull. Supplement 2/81.

Table IV-3.
Geographical breakdown of Japanese exports of passenger cars

Destination	1970 Volume ×(000)	%	1979 Volume ×(000)	%	1980 Volume ×(000)	%
North America of which:	404.5	55.7	1,648.4	53.1	1,986.7	52.0
United States	339.5	46.8	1,587.5	51.2	1,850.0	48.4
Community (Nine) of which:	44.6	6.1	630.2	20.3	743.4	19.5
FR of Germany	0.4	0.1	175.9	5.7	211.0	5.5
France	1.5	0.2	47.6	1.5	54.8	1.4
Italy	0.4	0.1	1.6	0.1	0.3	
Netherlands	15.2	2.1	94.1	3.0	117.0	3.1
Belgium/Luxem-bourg	17.0	2.3	81.3	2.6	105.6	2.8
United Kingdom	5.0	0.7	175.7	5.7	201.1	5.3
Ireland			27.0	0.9	28.1	0.7
Denmark	5.1	0.7	27.0	0.9	25.5	0.7
Rest of Western Europe of which: Greece	56.5 3.8	7.8 0.5	179.6 15.7	5.8 0.5	217.0 10.7	5.7 0.3
Nine + Greece	48.4	6.7	645.9	20.8	754.1	19.7
Asia of which:	63.9	8.8	345.1	11.1	485.1	12.7
Middle East	7.7	1.1	149.2	4.8	209.9	5.5
Saudi Arabia	1.3	0.2	100.2	3.2	130.3	3.4
Australia & New Zealand	86.3	11.9	149.5	4.8	165.0	4.3
Africa	39.6	5.4	72.3	2.3	117.5	3.1
Latin America	29.8	4.1	72.4	2.3	104.1	2.7
Eastern Europe	0.4	0.1	4.5	0.1	2.0	0.1
World	*725.6*	*100.0*	*3,102.0*	*100.0*	*3,820.8*	*100.0*

SOURCE: *Commission of the European Communities, The European Automobile Industry,* EC Bull. Supplement 2/81.

Table IV-4.
New Passenger Automobiles:
U.S. imports for consumption, by principal sources, 1980–81.

Source	1980	1981	1982
	Quantity in units		
Japan	1,991,502	1,911,525	1,801,185
Canada	628,335	563,943	702,495
West Germany	338,710	234,052	259,385
Sweden	61,495	68,042	89,231
Italy	46,889	21,635	9,402
United Kingdom	32,519	12,728	13,023
France	47,386	42,476	50,032
Finland	1,227	—	—
All other	1,940	1,884	1,654
Total	3,150,013	2,856,285	2,926,407
	Value (1,000 dollars)		
Japan	8,228,793	9,491,229	9,608,019
Canada	3,798,290	4,268,013	5,787,377
West Germany	3,283,977	2,623,315	3,173,372
Sweden	465,615	568,917	832,011
Italy	327,813	175,834	103,227
United Kingdom	292,709	251,173	326,967
France	257,403	283,120	324,980
Finland	9,682	—	—
All other	10,874	32,994	23,555
Total	16,675,156	17,694,595	20,179,508

[1]Data include imports into Puerto Rico; data for 1981–82 do not include automobiles assembled in Foreign Trade zones.

[2]January-December 1982 and July-December 1981 data include TSUSA number 692.1005.

SOURCE: U.S. International Trade Commission, Monthly Reports on U.S. Automobile Industry.

NOTE: Because of rounding, figures may not add to the totals shown.

Table IV-5.
Sales of New Passenger Automobiles:
Domestic and Imported 1980–82 (000's)

	Domestic Automobiles[1]	Imports Automobiles[2]	Total U.S. Sales	Ratio of import sales to total
1980	6578	2394	8972	26.7
1981	6205	2321	8257	27.2
1982	5757	2215	7973	27.8

[1]Includes U.S. and Canadian Built Automobiles sold in the U.S.
[2]Does not include automobiles imported from Canada.

TABLE OF CASES

[References are to Sections]

[Principal Cases are shown in italics]

A

Algonquin SNG, Inc. v. Federal Energy Administration . . . . § 5.52 N.h
American Express Company v. United States . . . . § 4.46(c) N.g
ASG Industries v. United States . . . . § 7.62 N.i

B

Bercut-Vandervoort & Co. v. United States . . . . § 2.44(d) N.m

C

Carbon Steel Bars and Shapes from Canada . . . . § 4.43 N.w
Carbon Steel Plate from Japan . . . . § 8.24(c) N.s
Carbon Steel Plate from Mexico . . . . § 7.42(b) N.l
Certain Motor Vehicles . . . . §§ *8.13*, 8.2
Chicago & Southern Air Lines, Inc. v. Waterman
    Steamship Corp. . . . . § 5.52 N.j
City Lumber Co. v. United States . . . . § 4.43 N.o
Commission of the EEC v. Italian Republic . . . . § 4.46(d) N.k
Connors Steel Co. v. United States . . . . § 8.65(d) N.p
Consumers Union of United States, Inc. v. Committee for the
    Implementation of Textile Agreements . . . . § 5.52 N.i
Consumers Union of U.S., Inc. v. Kissinger . . . §§ *5.42, 5.52, 5.53, 5.54, 5.55*
Consumers Union of United States, Inc. v. Rogers, et al . . . . § *5.41*
Curtiss-Wright Export Co. v. United States . . . . § 5.52 N.j

D

Davis Walker Corporation v. Blumenthal et al . . . . § *6.25*
Downs v. United States . . . . § 4.45(e) N.r, § 4.47(c) N.i

E

Ellis K. Orlowitz v. United States . . . . § 4.43 N.o

F

Federal Energy Administration v. Algonquin SNG, Inc. . . . . § 5.52, N.h

[References are to Sections]

Federal Trade Commission v. Cement Institute . . . . § 4.2 at N.h

France, Merchandise from, Countervailing duty proceedings . . . .
§ 4.45 (b) at Ns. j-k

Fullilove v. Kreps . . . . § 7.43 N.h

G

G. S. Nicholas & Co. v. United States . . . . § 4.45(b) and N.f, 4.45(e), N.r

Guy W. Capps, Inc., United States v. . . . . § 5.42 (Concurrence) N.l

H

Hammond Lead Products Inc., United States v. . . . . § 4.45(e) at N.u

Holtzman v. Schlesinger . . . . § 5.52 N.e

I

International Fruit Company N.V. et al v. Produktschap voor
Groenten en Fruit. . . . . § 3.26

K

Krupp Stahl A.G. v. Comm'n of the European Communities . . . . . . § 8.64 N.g

L

Luftig v. McNamara . . . . § 5.52 N.e

M

Massachusetts v. Laird . . . . § 5.52 N.e

Michelin Tire Corp. v. United States . . . . § 7.62 N.i

Michelin Tire Subsidy Case . . . . *§ 4.46(d)*

Mitchell v. Laird . . . . § 5.52 N.e

Modine Manufacturing Company . . . . § 8.23(a) at N.f

N

National Milk Producers Federation v. Shultz. . . . . § 4.45(e) N.w

New England Conference v. Morton, Secretary of the Interior . . . . . . § 5.4 N.a

Nicholas, G.S. & Co. v. United States . . . . § 4.45(b) at N.f, 4.45(e) N.r

O

Orlando v. Laird . . . . § 5.52 N.e

[References are to Sections]

P

Panama Refining Co. v. Ryan .... § 5.52 N.j
Parker v. Brown .... § 5.41 N.e
Perchloroethylene from Belgium, France and Italy .... § 7.63 N.f
Portland Cement from Canada .... § 4.42 N.j
Portland Cement from the Dominican Republic .... § 4.42 N.m

R

Republic Steel Corp. v. United States .... § 8.53 N.n

S

Schechter Poultry Corp. v. United States .... § 5.52 N.j
Schieffelin & Co. and Beittzell & Co. v. United States .... § 2.44(d) N.m
Schleslinger v. Holtzman .... § 5.52 N.e
SCM Corp. v. United States .... § 7.62 N.d
SCM Corp. v. U.S. International Trade Commission .... § 7.62 N.d
Spain, Almonds from, Countervailing duty proceedings .... § 4.45(b) at N.h
Star Industries, Inc. v. United States .... § 3.62(e)
Star Industries, Inc., United States v. .... §§ 3.62(f), 3.63, 5.52 N.f
Steel Antidumping Cases (1980) .... § 8.52 at Ns. l–o
Steel Antidumping Cases (1982) .... §§ 8.53 at N.b, 8.65
Steel Products from Italy .... § 4.46 N.k
Steel Reinforcing Bars .... § 4.43 N.w
Steel Subsidy Cases (1982) .... §§ 8.53, 8.6
Steel Welded Wire Mesh .... § 4.46 N.k

T

Television Sets from Japan .... § 4.41 N.f
Trenton Potteries Co., United States v. .... § 7.33 N.m
Triangle Conduit & Cable Co. v. Federal Trade Commission ...... § 4.2 N.h

U

United States v. Curtiss-Wright Export Co. .... § 5.52 N.j
United States v. Hammond Lead Products Inc. .... § 4.45(e) at N.u
United States v. Star Industries, Inc. .... §§ 3.62(f), 3.63, 5.52 N.f
United States v. Guy W. Capps, Inc. .... § 5.42 (Concurrence) N.l
United States v. Trenton Potteries Co. .... § 7.33 N.m
United States v. United States Steel Corporation .... § 4.2 at Ns. d–e

[References are to Sections]

United States v. Yoshida Int'l, Inc. . . . . § 5.52 N.g
United States v. Zenith Radio Corporation . . . . § 4.47(c) at N.k
United States Steel, Application for Countervailing Duties . . . § 4.47(a), (b), (d)
United States Steel Corporation, United States v. . . . . § 4.2 at Ns. d–e

V

Velvel v. Nixon . . . . § 5.52 N.e

W

Walter Holm Company v. Hardin . . . . § 3.26(a) N.e
Wire Rod Cases . . . . §§ 4.43, 4.44

X

X-Radial Steel Belted Tires from Canada . . . . § 4.46 N.l

Y

Yoshida Int'l Inc., United States v. . . . . § 5.52 N.g
Yoshida Int'l Inc. v. United States . . . . § 5.42, N.ll
Youngstown Sheet & Tube Company v. Sawyer . . . . § 5.52 N.k

Z

Zenith Radio Corporation v. United States . . . . §§ 4.47(c), 5.52 N.i

INDEX

A

[References are to Sections]

ABSOLUTE SCARCITY..§ 1.21

ACCESSION TREATY
Great Britain, Ireland and Denmark to EEC..§ 3.15 at N.g.

AD VALOREM TARIFF..§ 2.43(a)

ADJUSTMENT ASSISTANCE
In Trade Expansion Act of 1962..§ 3.53 at Ns. w–y, § 3.65

AISI
See American Iron and Steel Institute..§ 5.57(b)

AMERICAN IRON AND STEEL INSTITUTE
ECSC-MITI Agreements..§ 5.57(b–c)
And MTN Implementing Legislation..§ 7.43 at N.n.

AMERICAN SELLING PRICE (ASP)
In Kennedy Round..§ 3.72 at Ns. m–r

AMERICAN SOCIETY OF INTERNATIONAL LAW
On Dispute Settlement..§ 7.35(a).

ANTIDUMPING
GATT Article VI..§ 2.44 (a)(z)
Theory..§ 2.44 (a)(2), § 4.41

ANTIDUMPING ACT of 1921
And International Anti-Dumping Code..§ 4.44(b)–(f)
Proposed Amendment..§ 4.43(e)
And Trigger Price Mechanism..§ 6.12 § 6.2
The Wire Rod Cases..§ 4.43
Withholding of Appraisement..§ 4.44(a)

ANTITRUST LIABILITY
And Voluntary Restraint Agreements on Steel..§§ 5.41, 5.42, 5.53
And Japanese Measures of Restraint on Automobile Exports..§ 8.42
Toyota-General Motors Joint Venture..§ 8.46(d)-(e)

ASP
See American Selling Price..§ 3.72 at Ns. m–r

ASSOCIATION AGREEMENTS
European Community..§ 3.14 at Ns. d–i
And the GATT..§ 3.14 at Ns. d–i

ATHENS TREATY
Association Agreement of EEC with Greece..§ 3.14 at Ns. e–g

[References are to Sections]

ATLANTIC COUNCIL OF THE U.S.
On Safeguards..§ 7.32 (d) N.i.

AUTOMOBILE INDUSTRY..§§ 8.1–8.4
And American Economy..§ 8.11
Consumer Demand..§ 8.23
Escape Clause Case..§ 8.13
European Automobile Industry..§ 8.47
Prices Compared—Domestic and Imported..§ 8.22 N.f.
Quality Differences Domestic and Imported..§ 8.22, 8.23
Reagan Administration and..§ 8.3
Rise of Imports..§ 8.12
And shifts in Technology..§ 8.48
U.S.-Canada Integration..§ 8.23
Voluntary Restraint Agreement..§ 8.41(a)
World Market Shares..§ 8.47(e)

B

BALDRIGE, SECRETARY MALCOLM
And Auto Import Restraints..§ 8.3 at N.1
And Steel Imports from European Community..§ 8.53 at N.g

BARCELO, PROF. JOHN
On Subsidies..§ 7.33(c)

BROCK, AMBASSADOR WILLIAM
And Auto Import Restraints..§ 8.3, § 8.41

BUY AMERICAN ACT.. ..§§ 7.12 N.d., 7.24 N.(c)

C

CALHOUN, JOHN C...§ 3.51 at N.f.

CANADA
Imports of Automobiles From and U.S. Escape Clause case..§ 8.23(b)
Integration of North American Automobile Industry..§ 8.23(a)
Trigger Price Mechanism..§ 6.46(c)

"CHICKEN WAR"..§§ 3.25, 7.35 N.a.
And GATT Article XXVIII..§ 3.62 (d)–(f)
U.S. Retaliation..§ 3.62(d)

CHRYSLER CORPORATION
Threatened with Bankruptcy..§ 8.12 at N.m.

COMMON AGRICULTURAL POLICY (EC)..§ 3.25
And British Membership Negotiations..§ 3.15 at Ns. b–c
And the Chicken War..§ 3.25 (e)
And the GATT..§ 3.14 at N.b., § 3.25 (c), § 3.26
And Rome Treaty..§ 3.25 (a)
And the U.S...§ 3.25 (d-e)

COMMON EXTERNAL TARIFF (EC)
And Association Agreements..§ 3.14 at Ns. d–i
And the GATT..§ 3.14 at Ns. a–c
in Rome Treaty..§ 3.13 at Ns. c–e, § 3.23 (d)

COMMON MARKET
See European Community..§ 3.13

COMMONWEALTH PREFERENCES
And ECSC..§ 3.12 N.g
And GATT Article I..§ 2.33 (i)
Introduced..§ 2.1 at N.q

COMPARATIVE ADVANTAGE
Economic Theory..§ 1.23, § 1.3
And the GATT..§ 2.41
And Kennedy Round..§ 3.73
Reviewed in Light of State Practice..§ 8.71

CONNALLY, GOV. JOHN B.
On Trade Policy..§ 8.76 (c)

CONTENT LEGISLATION—See Import Restraint Proposals

COUNCIL OF MINISTERS
European Community..§ 3.13 at Ns. f–j, § 3.24 (a)–(c)

COUNTERVAILING DUTIES..§§ 4.45–47, 7.22, 7.33–.34, 7.43 at Ns. m–v, 8.53
GATT Article VI..§ 2.44 (c)
And Injury to Domestic Industry..§§ 7.22, 7.33(b), 8.53 at N.n
Theory..§ 2.44(c)
U.S. Procedure..§§ 4.45(f), 7.63(d)
Waivers of U.S. Duties..§ 7.42(b)
Procedure under 1979 Act..§ 7.63 at N.m
Statutory Timetable Under 1979 Act..§ 7.63(d)

[References are to Sections]

COURT OF INTERNATIONAL TRADE
Created..§ 7.62 at Ns. l–o
Scope of Review..§ 7.62 at Ns. m–n

COURT OF JUSTICE
European Community..§§ 3.13 at N.g, 3.24(a), 3.26, 4.46 N.k, 8.64 N.g

CUSTOMS COURT
Changes in 1980..§ 7.62 at Ns. 1–0

CUSTOMS UNIONS
Economic Theory..§ 3.11, § 3.21
GATT Article XXIV..§ 2.32(6), § 2.46, § 3.11
And the GATT..§ 3.11, § 3.22
U.S. View..§ 3.11 at Ns. f–1

CUSTOMS VALUATION
In MTN..§§ 7.24(c), 7.41(d)

D

DAM, PROF. KENNETH W.
On Dumping..§ 2.44(a) N.d
On Subsidies..§ 7.33(d)

DANFORTH, SENATOR JOHN C.
Automobile Quota Bill..§ 8.3 at Ns. f,k.

DAVIGNON PLAN I..§ 6.32

DAVIGNON PLAN II..§ 6.33

DAVIGNON PLAN III..§ 8.51
And Countervailing Duties..§ 8.64

DISCRIMINATORY QUOTA PROHIBITION
GATT Article XIII..§ 2.33(4)

DISPUTE SETTLEMENT
And MTN..§§ 7.23, 7.35

DOMESTIC INTERNATIONAL SALES CORPORATION (DISC)..
§§ 3.43(d), 7.23 N.p

DUMPING
And European Controls On Steel Imports..§ 6.33 at N.k
And the GATT..§ 2.44(a), § 4.41(a)
Combined with subsidies..§ 8.65
Theory..§ 2.44(a), § 4.41(a)

[References are to Sections]

DUMPING—Cont.
And Trigger Price Mechanism. .§§ 6.12, 8.52
In U.S. Trade Agreements Legislation. .§§ 4.41–4, 7.63(d)

E

ECSC
See European Coal and Steel Community

ECSC-MITI AGREEMENTS. .§ 5.57
And the GATT. .§ 5.57(e)
And Voluntary Restraint Agreements. .§ 5.57(d)

EEC
See European Economic Community

EFTA
See European Free Trade Area

ESCAPE CLAUSE
And U.S. automobile industry. .§ 8.13
GATT Article XIX. .§ 2.33(6)
And Market Disruption. .§ 7.21
And Specialty Steel. .§ 5.56
In Trade Act of 1974. .§ 5.56(b)
In U.S. Trade Agreements Legislation. .§ 2.33(b), § 3.52 at Ns. m–p, § 3.53
  at Ns. r–v, § 4.48(a), § 5.56(b), § 8.13

EURATOM
See European Atomic Energy Community

EUROFER
See European Confederation of Iron and Steel Industries. .§ 6.43(a)

EUROPEAN ATOMIC ENERGY COMMUNITY. .§ 3.13 at Ns. a–b

EUROPEAN COAL & STEEL COMMUNITY (ECSC). .§ 3.12, § 6.3–6.4
Agreement with U.S. on Steel Export Quotas. .§ 8.53
Confrontation with U.S. over Steel Exports. .§ 8.53 at N.k
Davignon Plan
    And Bresciani. .§ 6.44
    Comparison with TPM. .§ 6.41, § 6.45
Davignon Plan I. .§ 6.32
    Guide or Reference Prices. .§ 6.32 at p–r
    Import Licenses. .§ 6.32 at Ns. t–u

[References are to Sections]

EUROPEAN COAL & STEEL COMMUNITY (ESCS)—Cont.
Davignon Plan I—Cont.
    And International Anti-Dumping Code..§ 6.32 at Ns. x–a
Davignon Plan II..§ 6.33
    Basic Prices..§ 6.33 at Ns. p–t
    EFTA Agreements with..§ 6.33 at Ns. p–t
    Agreements with Japan..§ 6.33 at Ns. t–w
Davignon Plan III..§ 8.51
ECSC-MITI Agreements..§ 5.57
Forward Programmes..§ 6.31
And the GATT..§ 3.12 at Ns. h–r
And GATT Article XXIV..§ 3.12 at Ns. j–k
Harmonization of National Policies..§ 3.12 at Ns. j–k
High Authority..§ 3.12 at Ns. i–j, § 3.24
In Kennedy Round..§ 3.72
Merger with EEC and Euratom..§ 3.24
Paris Treaty..§ 3.12 at Ns. h–r, § 3.24
Schuman Plan..§ 3.12 at Ns. e–h
Simonet Plan..§ 6.31 at Ns. f–o
Subsidies for Steel Production Analyzed..§ 8.62

EUROPEAN COMMON MARKET
See European Community..§ 3.13

EUROPEAN COMMUNITY..§§ 3.1, 3.2, 6.3–6.4, 8.5–8.6
Accession Treaty..§ 3.15 at N.g.
Association Agreements..§ 3.14 at Ns. d–i
Athens Treaty..§ 3.14
Atomic Energy Community..§ 3.13 at Ns. a–b
Coal and Steel Community..§ 3.12
Commission..§ 3.13 at Ns. f–j, § 3.24 (a)–(c)
Common Agricultural Policy..§ 3.14 at N.b, § 3.25
    And U.S. Trigger Price Mechanism..§ 6.22
Common External Tariff..§ 3.13 at Ns. c–e, § 3.23(d)
Common Market..§ 3.13
Council of Ministers..§ 3.13 at Ns. f–j, § 3.24 (a)–(c)
Court of Justice..§ 3.13 at N.g, § 3.24 (a)–(c), § 3.26
Customs Unions and the GATT..§ 3.11, § 3.13
French Vetoes of British Membership..§ 3.15 at Ns. b–f
And the GATT..§ 3.14
Great Britain, Membership Application..§ 3.15
In Kennedy Round..§ 3.7
And Manufacture of Automobiles..§ 8.47

[References are to Sections]

EUROPEAN COMMUNITY—Cont.
Merger Treaty..§ 3.24(a)
And Orderly Marketing Agreements..§ 5.56(e)
Origins of..§ 3.12
Rome Treaty..§ 3.13
Spaak Report..§ 3.13 at Ns. a–b
And Trade Expansion Act of 1962..§ 3.53 at Ns. d–o
And U.S. Trigger Price Mechanism..§ 6.21(b), § 6.22
Voluntary Restraint Agreements..§ 5.1–.32, § 5.51, § 6.11 at N.i

**EUROPEAN CONFEDERATION OF IRON AND
STEEL INDUSTRIES (EUROFER)**..§ 6.43(a)

EUROPEAN DEFENSE COMMUNITY..§ 3.13 at N.a.

EUROPEAN ECONOMIC COMMUNTIY (EEC)
See European Community

EUROPEAN FREE TRADE AREA (EFTA)..§ 3.15
And Davignon Plan..§ 6.33 at Ns. q–t

EXPORT INCOME DEDUCTION SYSTEM (JAPAN)..§ 3.33 at Ns. t–u

EXPORT SUBSIDIES..§ 2.44 (b), 7.22, 7.33–34

EXPORT SUBSIDY LIMITATION
GATT Article XVI..§ 2.32(5), 7.22, 7.41(a)

F

FEDERAL CIRCUIT, COURT OF APPEALS FOR THE
And Review of Federal Trade Decisions..§ 7.62 at Ns. v–s

FEDERAL COURTS IMPROVEMENT ACT OF 1982..§ 7.62 at N.r

FORDNEY-McCUMBER TARIFF ACT OF 1922..§ 2.1 at Ns. j–k, § 3.51
at N.b, § 3.72 at Ns. m–o.

FRANCE
Aids to Steel Industry..§ 8.63
Nationalization of Steel Industry..§ 6.33 at N.f.
Vetoes British Membership in EEC..§ 3.15 at Ns. d–f

FREE TRADE AREA
And European Coal and Steel Community ..§ 3.12 at Ns. j–k
GATT Article XXIV..§ 2.32(b)

[References are to Sections]

FRIENDSHIP, COMMERCE AND NAVIGATION TREATIES
And MFN Obligations . . § 7.63(c) at N.e.

G

GATT
See General Agreement on Tariffs and Trade

GENERAL AGREEMENT ON TARIFFS AND TRADE
Agricultural Exception . . § 2.32(2)
Article I
    Most-Favored-Nation Principle . . § 2.32(1)
Article II
    Reduction of Trade Barriers . . § 2.32(2)
Article III
    National Treatment Requirement: Health and Safety Regulations . .
  § 2.44(d)(2).
    National Treatment Requirement: Taxes . . § 2.44(d)(1)
Article VI
    Countervailing Duties . . § 2.44(c)
    Dumping Definition . . § 2.44(a)(1).
Article XI
    Agricultural Exception . . § 2.32(2)
    EC Court of Justice Opinion . . § 3.26
    Non-Tariff Barrier Prohibition . . § 2.32(4), § 2.43(c–e)
Article XII
    Balance of Payments Exception . . § 2.33(4)
Article XII
    Japan's Use of . . § 3.33 at Ns. o–p
Article XIII
    Prohibition on Discrimination in Quotas . . § 2.33(4)
Article XVI
    Export Subsidy Limitation . . §§2.32(5), 2.44(b), 3.43(b–f), 7.22, 7.33(d)
Article XIX . . § 8.21(c), (d)
    Escape Clause . . §§ 2.33(b), 7.12, 7.21, 7.31–.32, 8.21
    And MFN . . § 7.32(b)
Article XXI
    National Security Exception . . § 2.33(3)
Article XXIV
    Customs Union and Free Trade Area Provisions . . §§ 2.32(6), 2.46,
3.11, 3.21–3
    European Coal and Steel Community . . § 3.12 at Ns. j–k

[References are to Sections]

GENERAL AGREEMENT ON TARIFFS AND TRADE—Cont.

Article XXIV—Cont.
    European Community..§ 3.13 at Ns. b–j, 3.14 at Ns. a–c, 3.21–.22

Article XXVIII
    And the Chicken War..§ 3.62(d)–(f)
    Right to Withdraw Concessions..§ 2.33(5)
    U.S. Customs Court Interpretation..§ 3.62(e)
    U.S. Court of Customs and Patent Appeals Interpretation..§ 3.62 (f)

Article XXVIII bis
    Multilateral Negotiations..§ 2.32(3)

Article XXXV
    And Japan..§§ 2.33(7) at N.t, 3.33
    MFN Exception..§§ 2.33(7), 3.33

Balance of Payments Exception..§ 2.33(4)

Background..§ 2.1

And the Chicken War..§ 3.62(d)–(f)

And Common Agricultural Policy..§§ 3.14 at N.b, 3.25

And Common External Tariff..§ 3.14 at Ns. a–c

And Comparative Advantage..§ 2.41

Basic Principles..§ 2.32

Countervailing Duties..§§ 2.44(c) 7.22

Customs Unions and Free Trade Provisions..§§ 2.32(b), 2.46

Discriminatory Quotas Prohibition..§ 2.33(4)

And Dispute Settlement..§§ 7.23 N.o, 7.35(d)

Dumping..§ 2.44(a)(1)

Escape Clause..§§ 2.33(6), 7.21

And the European Coal and Steel Community..§ 3.12 at Ns. h–r

And the European Community..§§ 3.13 at Ns. b–j, 3.14

And Export Subsidies..§§ 2.32(5), 7.22

Grandfather Clause..§ 2.33(1)

Growth..§ 2.31

Havana Charter..§ 2.2 at Ns. q–x

Introduction to..§ 2

And Japan..§ 3.33
    And Article XXXV..§§ 2.33 at N.t, 3.33

Most-Favored-Nation Principle..§§ 2.32(1), 2.42

Most-Favored-Nation Principle Exception..§ 2.33(7)

Multilateral Negotiations Principle..§ 2.32(3)

National Security Exception..§ 2.33(3)

National Treatment Requirement: Health And Safety Regulations..§ 2.44(d)(2)

National Treatment Requirement: Taxes..§ 2.44(d)(1)

Non-Tariff Barrier Prohibition..§ 2.32(4)

[References are to Sections]

GENERAL AGREEMENT ON TARIFFS AND TRADE—Cont.
Origins..§ 2.2
Protocol of Provisional Application..§ 2.2 at Ns. p–q
Qualifications..§ 2.33
Reduction of Trade Barriers Principle..§ 2.32(2)
Relation to U.S. Domestic Law..§§ 2.2 at Ns. n–q, 4.45(e), 4.46 N.j.
Right to Withdraw Concessions..§ 2.33(5)
And Voluntary Restraint Agreements..§ 5.55

GRANDFATHER CLAUSE
GATT Article I..§ 2.33(1)

GREAT BRITAIN
EEC Membership Application..§ 3.15
And EFTA..§ 3.15 at Ns. a–b
And aids to British steel industry..§§ 8.51 N.b, 8.63(f) N.b

H

HAMILTON, ALEXANDER..§§ 1.3 N.c, 3.51 at N.f

HARMONIZATION OF NATIONAL POLICIES
And The European Coal And Steel Community..§ 3.12 at Ns. j–k

HAVANA CHARTER..§ 2.2 at Ns. q–x

HUDEC, PROF. ROBERT
On Dispute Settlement In GATT..§§ 7.23 N.n, 7.35(d)
On GATT as a Legal System..§ 2.45 N.p

I

IACOCCA, LEE A.
On Automobile Import Restraints..§ 8.44

IMPERIAL PREFERENCES
Post War Anglo-American Issue..§ 2.2 N.c
See also Commonwealth Preferences

IMPORT QUOTAS
Contrasted with Tariffs..§ 2.43(c–e)
GATT Article XI..§§ 2.32(4), 2.43(c)–(e)
Proposed U.S. Legislation (1967)..§ 5.11
And Specialty Steel..§ 5.56
And Steel..§ 6.11 at Ns. n–p
Theory..§§ 2.43(c)–(e), 5.21–.24

[References are to Sections]

IMPORT RESTRAINT PROPOSALS
Content Legislation. . § 8.46(a), (b)
Reciprocity Legislation. . § 8.46(a) at N.t

INJURY STANDARD
In Countervailing Duty Cases. . § 7.63(b)
In Escape Clause Cases. . §§ 8.13, 8.24(c)

INTERNATIONAL ANTI-DUMPING CODE
Kennedy Round. . § 4.44(b)–(f)
And Subsidies Code. . §§ 7.44 at N.g, 7.54

INTERNATIONAL IRON AND STEEL INSTITUTE
And "Organized" Steel Markets. . § 6.41 at N.o

INTERNATIONAL MONETARY FUND
And Japan. . § 3.33 at Ns. o–q

INTERNATIONAL TRADE ORGANIZATION (ITO). . § 2.2 at Ns. f–x

J

JACKSON, PROF. JOHN H.
On GATT Article XIX. . § 8.21(d) N.d

JAPAN. . § 3.3–3.4
And Agriculture. . § 7.24(d) N.h
Economic Growth. . §§ 3.31, 3.41, 3.44
    Government Role in. . § 3.32
ECSC-MITI Agreements. . § 5.57
Export Income Deduction System. . § 3.33 at Ns. t–u
And the GATT. . § 3.33
And GATT Article XXXV. . §§ 2.33 at N.t, 3.33
And International Monetary Fund. . § 3.33 at Ns. o–q
Japan Export Trade Organization (JETRO). . § 3.33 at Ns. s–t
In Kennedy Round. . § 3.7
Measures of Restraint On Automobile Exports. . §§ 8.3, 8.41, 8.42
    And U.S. Antitrust Laws. . § 8.42(c), (d).
Ministry of International Trade and Industry (MITI). . § 3.32
Orderly Marketing. . §§ 3.33 N.x, 3.45
Orderly Marketing Agreements For Specialty Steel. . § 5.56(d)–(e)
Protectionist Devices. . §§ 3.33 at Ns. j–v, 3.43
Trading Companies. . § 3.42
And Trigger Price Mechanism. . §§ 6.12, 6.23
And Voluntary Restraint Agreements. . §§ 5.1–.32, 5.51, 6.11 at N.h

[References are to Sections]

JUDICIAL REVIEW OF TRADE DETERMINATIONS (U.S.)
Expanded in 1979 Trade Agreements Act..§ 7.62
Scope Of Review of Anti-Dumping And Countervailing Duty Determination..
  § 7.62 at Ns. a–k

K

KENNEDY ROUND..§ 3.7
Linear Reduction..§ 3.71
Group on Antidumping Policies..§ 4.44(b)
International Anti-Dumping Code..§ 4.44(b–f)
Sectors Negotiations..§ 3.72
Results..§ 3.73
And Steel..§ 3.72 at Ns. a–l

L

LAMBSDORFF, COUNT OTTO
Criticism of Davignon Plan..§ 6.43(c)
And Agreement with Japan on automobile exports..§ 8.47(f)

LINEAR DUTY REDUCTIONS
And Kennedy Round..§ 3.71

LONG, OLIVIER
On Dangers of Protectionism..§ 7.21 at N.c
On Outcome of MTN..§ 7.44
Director General of GATT
     Replacement for..§ 7.55(d)
And Tokyo Round..§ 7.12 at N.l

M

MALMGREN, HARALD
On Quid Pro Quo for Import Relief..§ 8.74

MARKET DISRUPTION..§§ 7.21, 7.31–.32, 7.55
And Discrimination..§ 7.32

MEASURES OF RESTRAINT ON JAPANESE AUTO EXPORTS..
  ..§§ 8.3–.4
And antitrust exposure..§ 8.42
Text of communiqué..§ 8.3 at N.m

MERGER TREATY (EC)..§ 3.24(a) at N.o

MFN
See Most-Favored-Nation Principle

[References are to Sections]

MINISTRY OF INTERNATIONAL TRADE AND INDUSTRY (JAPAN) (MITI)..§ 3.32
ECSC-MITI Agreements..§ 5.57

MITI
See Ministry of International Trade And Industry

MIXED TARIFF..§ 2.43(a), N.1

MOST-FAVORED-NATIONAL TREATMENT
Conditional and Unconditional Contrasted..§ 7.63(c)

MOST-FAVORED-NATION PRINCIPLE
And Customs Unions..§ 3.11
Customs Union Exception, GATT Article XXIV..§ 2.46
Exception, GATT Article XXXV..§ 2.33(7)
GATT, Article I..§ 2.32(1)
And Duty Reduction..§ 2.41-.42
Historical Development..§§ 2.1, 2.42(a), 2.42(d)
And Market Disruption..§ 7.32
And MTN Codes..§ 7.63(c)
In U.S. Trade Policy..§ 3.62
And Safeguards..§ 7.32

MTN
See Multilateral Trade Negotiations

MULTILATERAL TRADE NEGOTIATIONS
Agenda..§ 7.12
And Agriculture..§ 7.24(d)
And Customs Valuation..§ 7.24(c)
And the Developing Countries..§§ 7.24(e), 7.44, 7.51(c)
And Dispute Settlement..§§ 7.23, 7.35-.38
"Framework for International Trade"..§ 7.23 at N.s
And Government Procurement..§ 7.24(a)
And Safeguards..§§ 7.21, 7.31-.32, 7.55
Safeguards Code..§§ 7.21, 7.31-.32, 7.41(b), 7.43 at Ns. b-e
    And Injury Standard..§ 7.64
Selectivity Issue..§§ 7.32, 7.41(b), 7.43, 7.55
Setting For..§ 7.11
Subsidies Code..§§ 7.41(a), 7.44, 7.52-.53
And Subsidies and Countervailing Duties..§§ 7.22, 7.33-.34, 7.41(a), 7.52-.53
And Tariffs..§§ 7.25, 7.41(e), 7.51
Tariff Harmonization Formula..§ 7.41(e) at N.i
Tariff-Cutting Formula..§ 7.41(e) at N.i

[References are to Sections]

MULTILATERAL TRADE NEGOTIATIONS—Cont.
And Technical Standards..§ 7.24(b)
Technical Working Groups..§ 7.12 at N.1
Tokyo Declaration..§ 7.12 at Ns. i–j
U.S. Implementing Legislation..§§ 7.42, 7.43, 7.57
And Trade Act of 1974..§ 7.12 at N.g

N

NATIONAL SECURITY EXCEPTION
GATT Article XXI..§ 2.33(3)

NATIONAL SECURITY IMPORT LIMITATION
U.S. Trade Expansion Act..§§ 3.66, 4.48(b), 5.42, N.10

NATIONAL TREATMENT REQUIREMENT
GATT Article III: Health and Safety Regulations..§ 2.44(d)(2)
GATT Article III: Taxes..§ 2.44(d)(1)

NEW INTERNATIONAL ECONOMIC ORDER..§ 2.31, N.f

O

OECD
See Organization for Economic Cooperation and Development

OEEC
See Organization for European Economic Cooperation

OMA'S
See Orderly Marketing Agreements

ORDERLY MARKETING AGREEMENTS
And GATT Article XIX..§§ 5.56(e), 7.2
Japanese Definition..§ 3.33, N.x
Japanese Development of..§ 3.45
For Specialty Steel..§ 5.56(d–e)
And Steel Industry..§ 4.48(c)
U.S. Trade Expansion Act of 1962..§ 3.53 at Ns. z–e

**ORGANIZATION FOR ECONOMIC COOPERATION AND
DEVELOPMENT**..§ 6.11 at N.b
Ad Hoc Steel Group..§ 6.11 at N.h

ORGANIZATION FOR EUROPEAN ECONOMIC COOPERATION
..§ 3.12 at Ns. a–d

[References are to Sections]

P

PARIS TREATY
And Davignon Plan..§§ 6.31, 6.32, 8.51
European Coal and Steel Community..§§ 3.12 at Ns. h–r, 3.24
Loan and Guarantee Authority..§ 8.64
"Manifest Crisis"..§§ 6.31 at N.i, 8.51 at N.a, 8.62, N.d.

PERIL-POINT PROCEDURE
In U.S. Trade Agreements Legislation..§§ 3.52 at Ns. n–p, 3.53 at Ns. p–u

PRODUCTION SUBSIDIES
Contrasted with Subsidies on Exports..§§ 2.44(b), 7.33(c), 7.41(a), 7.41, 8.63–.64

PROTOCOL OF PROVISIONAL APPLICATION (GATT)..§ 2.2 at Ns. p–q
And MTN Codes..§ 7.63(c) at N.h

Q

QUANTITATIVE RESTRICTIONS..§ 2.32(4), 2.33(2), 2.43
See Import Quotas

QUOTAS
See Import Quotas..§ 2.43(e)

R

RECIPROCAL TRADE AGREEMENTS PROGRAM (U.S.)..§§ 2.1 at Ns. s–t, 3.52
And Escape Clause..§§ 2.33(6), 3.52 at Ns. m–p
Extensions..§§ 2.2 Ns. h, s, 2.31 N.a
And Peril-Point Procedure..§ 3.52 at Ns. n–p

RECIPROCITY
In Kennedy Round..§§ 3.71, 3.72
And the Subsidies Issue..§ 7.34(a)
U.S. Trade Policy..§ 3.61

RECIPROCITY LEGISLATION
See Import Restraint Proposals

RELATIVE EFFICIENCY..§§ 1.22, 1.37(d)

REORGANIZATION OF U.S. TRADE FUNCTIONS..§ 7.61

REPORT ON MANUFACTURERS (HAMILTON)..§§ 1.3, N.c, 3.51 at N.f

[References are to Sections]

ROME TREATY
And European Community..§§ 3.13, 3.24(a)–(c)

S

SALES AT LESS THAN FAIR VALUE
In U.S. Trade Agreements Legislation..§ 4.41
And Trigger Price Mechanism..§ 6.12

SCHUMAN PLAN..§ 3.12 at Ns. e–h

SAFEGUARDS
Efforts to Establish Rules For,..§§ 7.21, 7.31, 8.75

SECTORAL NEGOTIATIONS
In Kennedy Round..§ 3.72

SELECTIVITY
See Under Multilateral Trade Negotiations.

SHERMAN ANTI-TRUST ACT
In Consumers Union Suit..§§ 5.41 at Ns. c, i, 5.42 (III), 5.53

SMOOT-HAWLEY TARIFF ACT OF 1930..§§ 2.1 at Ns. n–p, 3.51 at Ns.
d–e

SOLOMON, ANTHONY M.
See Trigger Price Mechanism..§ 6.12

SPAAK, PAUL HENRI
Report on European Integration..§ 3.13

SPECIAL REPRESENTATIVE FOR TRADE NEGOTIATIONS (STR)
Inception..§ 3.67
On ECSC-MITI Agreements..§ 5.57(f)
And MTN Implementing Legislation..§§ 7.42(b), 7.43

SPECIALIZATION AND EFFICIENCY..§§ 1.22, 1.31

SPECIALTY STEEL..§§ 5.31, N.c, 5.56

SPECIFIC TARIFF..§ 2.43(a)

STEEL..§ 4, §5, §6, §8.5–8.6
Agreement between United States and European Community (1982)..§ 8.53 at
Ns. m–v
The American Steel Industry..§§ 4.2, 4.3
    Basing Point System..§ 4.2 at Ns. g–h

[References are to Sections]

STEEL—Cont.
The American Steel Industry—Cont.
    Import Competition. . § 4.3
    1960's Crisis. . § 4.3
    1970's Crisis. . § 6.11
Antidumping Actions. . § 8.52 at Ns. h–o
Countervailing Duty Actions (1982). . § 8.53 at Ns. d–f, i
European Steel Industry. . §§ 6.3–4, 8.51
Kennedy Round Sectoral Negotiations. . § 3.72
Specialty Steel
    And Escape Clause. . § 5.56
    Orderly Marketing Agreements. . § 5.56(d)–(e)
Trigger Price Mechanism. . § 6.12
U.S. Imports
    Studies on. . § 6.11 N.c
    Senate Staff Study. . § 4.3

STR
See Special Representative for Trade Negotiations. . § 3.67

STRAUSS, AMBASSADOR ROBERT S. . . § 3.67, 7.12, 7.42(b), 7.43

SUBSIDIES
Compared to Dumping. . § 7.54
Definition in Trade Agreements Act of 1979. . § 7.63(b) at N.j
GATT Article XVI. . § 2.44(b)
Procedure in Subsidy Cases. . § 7.63(b) at Ns. d–k, 7.63(d)
Production and Export Aids Distinguished. . §§ 2.44(b), 7.33(a), (c), 8.63
And Remission of Taxes. . §§ 4.46–.47, 7.22 at Ns. j–l
Theory. . §§ 2.44(b), 3.43, 4.45
U.S. Policy. . § 4.45

SUBSIDIES CODE (MTN)
Legislative Implementation. . § 7.63(c)

SUZUKI, PRIME MINISTER ZENKO. . § 8.47(f)

T

TARIFF COMMISSION, U.S.. . § 3.51 at Ns. v–c

TARIFF HARMONIZATION
In Kennedy Round. . § 3.71
In MTN. . § 7.41(e) at N.i

[References are to Sections]

TARIFFS
Contrasted with Import Quotas..§ 2.43(c) and (d)
Ad Valorem, Specific, and Mixed..§ 2.43(a)
Surcharges..§ 2.33, N.o
U.S. Tariff Acts..§ 3.51

TECHNICAL STANDARDS..§§ 2.44(d)(2), 7.24(b)

TOKYO ROUND
See Multilateral Trade Negotiations..§ 7

TOYOTA-GENERAL MOTORS AGREEMENT..§ 8.46(d) and (e).

TRADE AGREEMENTS ACT OF 1979..§ 7.63
Acceptance of Tokyo Round Agreements..§ 7.63(a)
Changes in U.S. Trade Law..§ 7.63(b)
And Countervailing Duties..§ 7.63(b) at Ns. e–f
Procedure in Trade Cases..§ 7.63(d)

TRADE AGREEMENTS EXTENSION ACT OF 1945..§ 3.52 at Ns. i–k

TRADE EXPANSION ACT OF 1962..§ 3.53
And Adjustment Assistance..§§ 3.53 at Ns. w–y, 3.65
Escape Clause..§§ 3.53 at Ns. r–v, 4.48(a)
And European Community..§§ 3.15 at Ns. c–d, 3.53, 3.64
And MFN..§ 3.62
National Security Import Limitation..§§ 3.66, 4.48(b)
Orderly Marketing Provision..§§ 3.53 at Ns. z–e, 4.48(c)
Peril-Point Procedure..§ 3.53 at Ns. p–v
Special Representative for Trade Negotiations..§ 3.67

TRADING COMPANIES (JAPAN)..§ 3.42

TRADE ACT OF 1974
Amendments to Antidumping Act..§ 6.12
Amendments to Countervaiing Duty Statute..§ 4.47(b)
Amendments to Escape Clause..§ 5.56(b)
Delays in Passage..§ 7.12 N.k
And MTN..§ 7.12
Provisions for Implementing MTN..§ 7.42
And "Unfair Trade" Policies..§ 5.57(b–d)

TRIGGER PRICE MECHANISM..§§ 6.12, 6.2
Compared with Common Agricultural Policy..§ 6.22
Compared with Davignon Plan..§ 6.41
And U.S. Trade Policy..§ 6.27

TRIGGER PRICE MECHANISM—Cont.
Suspended (1980)..§ 8.52 at N.i
Revived (1980)..§ 8.52 at Ns. q–v
Terminated (1982)..§ 8.53 at N.j

U

UNCTAD
See United Nations Conference on Trade And Development

UNESCO
See United Nations Economic and Social Council

UNITED NATIONS CONFERENCE ON TRADE AND DEVELOPMENT
And the GATT..§§ 2.31 at N.f, 7.44 at N.e

UNITED NATIONS CONFERENCE ON TRADE AND EMPLOYMENT
Havana Conference..§ 2.2 at Ns. q–r

UNITED NATIONS ECONOMIC AND SOCIAL COUNCIL..§ 2.2 at N.j

UNITED STATES
Antidumping Laws..§ 4.41–.44
Council on Wage and Price Stability
      Steel Import Quotas..§ 6.11 at N.n
Countervailing Duty Policy..§ 4.45
Import Quotas
      For Specialty Steel..§ 5.56
Import Quota Proposals..§ 5.11
In Kennedy Round..§ 3.7
Orderly Marketing Agreements for Specialty Steel..§ 5.56(d)–(e)
Reciprocal Trade Agreements Program..§§ 2.1 at Ns. s–t, 3.52
      Extensions..§§ 2.2 Ns. h, s, 2.31 N.a
Reciprocity Policy..§ 3.61
Subsidies Policy..§ 3.61
Trade Agreements Act of 1979..§ 7.63
Trade Legislation, History..§ 3.51

UNITED STATES-CANADA AUTOMOTIVE AGREEMENT..§ 8.23(a)

UNITED STATES DEPARTMENT OF COMMERCE
And Steel Subsidy Cases..§§ 8.53, 8.63–.64
Assigned Trade Regulation Functions..§ 7.61 at Ns. k–l
And Trigger Price Mechanism..§ 8.52

UNITED STATES INTERNATIONAL TRADE COMMISSION
Automobile Escape Clauses Cases..§§ 8.13, 8.2
And Steel Subsidy Cases..§ 8.5 at Ns. i, n; n–o
And Trade Agreements Act of 1979..§ 7.62 at Ns. d–h

[References are to Sections]

And Technical Standards..§ 7.24(b)

U.S. STEEL
Organization of..§ 4.2
Subsidies Complaint..§§ 4.47, 7.43 at Ns. n–o
Unfair Trade Practices Complaint..§ 5.57

UNITED STATES SUPREME COURT
And Countervailing Duty Statute..§§ 4.45(b), 4.47(c)

UNITED STATES TARIFF COMMISSION
Dumping Injury Determination..§§ 4.41(a), 4.42, 4.43(c)
Escape Clause Injury Determination..§ 3.53 at Ns. r–v
See also U.S. International Trade Commission

UNITED STATES TRADE LEGISLATION
Adjustment Assistance
        Compared to Escape Clause..§ 3.65(d)–(e)
        Trade Expansion Act of 1962..§§ 3.53 at Ns. w–y, 3.65
American Selling Price..§ 3.72 at Ns. m–r
Antidumping Act of 1921
        Dumping Injury Determination..§§ 4.41(a), 4.42, 4.43(c)
        And International Antidumping Code..§ 4.44(b)–(f)
        Proposed Amendment..§ 4.43(e)
        Sales at Less Than Fair Value..§§ 4.41, 4.43(a)–(b), 6.12
        Trade Act of 1974 Amendment..§§ 6.12, 6.2
        The Wire Rod Cases..§ 4.43
        Withholding of Appraisement..§§ 4.44(a), 8.53 N.f
Countervailing Duty Statute..§§ 4.45–.47, 7.33(a), 7.63(d)
Escape Clause
        Compared to Adjustment Assistance..§ 3.65(d)–(e)
        In U.S. Trade Agreement Acts..§§ 2.33(b), 3.52 at Ns. m–p, 3.53 at
Ns. r–v, 4.48(a), 5.56(b)
Fordney-McCumber Tariff Act of 1922..§§ 2.1 at Ns. j–k, 3.51 at N.b, 3.72
at Ns. m–o
MFN Trade Policy..§§ 3.62, 7.63(c)
National Security Import Limitation..§ 3.66
Peril-Point Procedure..§ 3.52 at Ns. n–p, 3.53 at Ns. p–v
Proposal for a Single Import Relief Standard..§ 7.63
Smoot-Hawley Tariff Act of 1930..§§ 2.1 at Ns. n–p, 3.51 at Ns. d–e
Trade Act of 1974.. § 4.47(b), 5.56(b), 6.12, 7.12
Trade Agreements Act of 1979..§ 7.63
Trade Agreements Extension Act of 1945..§ 3.52 at Ns. i–k
Trade Expansion Act of 1962..§ 3.53
        And Adjustment Assistance..§§ 3.53 at Ns. w–y, 3.65

[References are to Sections]

UNITED STATES TRADE LEGISLATION—Cont.
Trade Expansion Act of 1962—Cont.
  Escape Clause..§§ 3.53 at Ns. r–v, 4.48(a)
  And European Community..§§ 3.15 at N.c, 3.53, 3.64
  And MFN..§ 3.62
  National Security Import Limitation..§§ 3.66, 4.48(b)
  Orderly Marketing Provision..§§ 3.53 at Ns. z–e, 4.48(c)
  Peril-Point Procedure..§ 3.53 at Ns. p–v
  Special Representative for Trade Negotiations..§ 3.67
Trade Regulation Up to 1934..§ 3.51

UNITED STATES TRADE REPRESENTATIVE
In 1980 Reorganization Plan..§ 7.61 at Ns. m–o
And Measures of Restraint concerning Auto Exports from Japan..§§ 8.3 at
  Ns. m–p; 8.41–.42

UNITED STATES AS A TRADING NATION..§§ 3.5, 3.6

UNITED STATES TREASURY DEPARTMENT
Countervailing Duty Determination..§ 4.45–6
And International Antidumping Code..§ 4.44(e)–(f)
Japanese Carbon Steel Plate Case..§ 6.11 at Ns. k–m
Sales at Less Than Fair Value Determination..§§ 4.41, 4.43(a)–(b)
And Trigger Price Mechanism..§§ 6.12, 6.2
The Wire Rod Cases..§ 4.43(a)–(b)
Zenith Radio Corporation Complaint..§ 4.47(b)–(d)

V

VALUE ADDED TAX..§ 4.47(a)

VARIABLE LEVY SYSTEM (EC)..§ 3.25(b–c)

VAT
See Value Added Tax

VOLUNTARY RESTRAINT AGREEMENTS (STEEL)..§ 5
Background..§ 5.11
Consumers Union Challenge..§ 5.4
And the GATT..§ 5.55
In Operation..§ 5.31
Renewal (1972)..§ 5.32
Automobiles From Japan to European Community..§ 8.47
Automobiles From Japan to U.S...§§ 8.3, 8.41–.42
European Motives..§ 5.51(b)
Japanese Motives..§ 5.51(b)

VRA'S
See Voluntary Restraint Agreements

Z

ZAIBATSU (JAPAN) . . § 3.42(b)